MW01221689

Pass SQL Exam 70-461 & Job Interview: Programming SQL Server 2012

Kalman Toth

Pass SQL Exam 70-461 & Job Interview:
Programming SQL Server 2012

Copyright © 2012 by Kalman Toth
All rights reserved.

ISBN-13: 978-1481858328
ISBN-10: 1481858327

Trademark Notices

Microsoft is a trademark of Microsoft Corporation.
SQL Server 2012 is a program product of Microsoft Corporation.
SQL Server 2008 is a program product of Microsoft Corporation.
SQL Server 2005 is a program product of Microsoft Corporation.
SQL Server 2000 is a program product of Microsoft Corporation.
SQL Server Management Studio (SSMS) is a program product of Microsoft Corporation.
SQL Server Data Tools (SSDT) is a program product of Microsoft Corporation.
Microsoft Help Viewer is a program product of Microsoft Corporation.
SQL Server Analysis Services (SSAS) is a program product of Microsoft Corporation.
SQL Server Integration Services (SSIS) is a program product of Microsoft Corporation.
SQL Server Reporting Services (SSRS) is a program product of Microsoft Corporation.
SQL Azure is a program product of Microsoft Corporation.
Office Visio is a program product of Microsoft Corporation.
Visual SourceSafe is a program product of Microsoft Corporation.
Exam 70-461 is an exam product of Microsoft Corporation.
ORACLE is a trademark of ORACLE Corporation.
Java is a trademark of ORACLE Corporation.
DB2 is a trademark of IBM Corporation.
SYBASE is a trademark of Sybase Corporation.
McAfee is a trademark of McAfee Corporation.
ALL PHOTOS IN THIS BOOK ARE THE COPYRIGHTED PROPERTY OF THE AUTHOR.

Warning and Disclaimer

Every effort has been made to ensure accuracy, however, no warranty of any kind or fitness implied. The information & programs are provided on an "as is" basis. Neither the author nor the publisher & resellers will be held liable for any damages caused, or alleged to be caused, either directly or indirectly by the content of this book.

Pass SQL Exam 70-461 & Job Interview:

Programming SQL Server 2012

Contents at a Glance

About the Author

Kalman Toth has been working with relational database technology since 1990 when one day his boss, at a commodity brokerage firm in Greenwich, Connecticut, had to leave early and gave his SQL Server login & password to Kalman along with a small SQL task. Kalman was a C/C++ developer fascinated by SQL, therefore, he studied a Transact-SQL manual 3 times from start to end "dry", without any server access. His boss was satisfied with the execution of SQL task and a few days later Kalman's dream came true: he got his very own SQL Server login. His relational database career since then includes database design, database development, database administration, OLAP architecture and Business Intelligence development. Applications included enterprise-level general ledger & financial accounting, bond funds auditing, international stock market feeds processing, broker-dealer firm risk management, derivative instruments analytics, consumer ecommerce database management for online dating, personal finance, physical fitness, diet and health. Currently he is Principal Trainer at www.sqlusa.com. His MSDN forum participation in the Transact-SQL and SQL Server Tools was rewarded with the Microsoft Community Contributor award. Kalman has a Master of Arts degree in Physics from Columbia University and a Master of Philosophy degree in Computing Science also from Columbia. Microsoft certifications in database administration, development and Business Intelligence. The dream SQL career took him across United States & Canada as well as South America & Europe. SQL also involved him in World History. At one time he worked for Deloitte & Touche on the 96th floor of World Trade Center North. On September 11, 2001, he was an RDBMS consultant at Citibank on 111 Wall Street. After escaping at 10:30 on that fateful Tuesday morning in the heavy dirt smoke, it took 10 days before he could return to his relational database development job just 1/2 mile from the nearly three thousand victims buried under steel. What Kalman loves about SQL is that the same friendly, yet powerful, commands can process 2 records or 2 million records or 200 million records the same easy way. His current interest is Artificial Intelligence. He is convinced that machine intelligence will not only replace human intelligence but surpass it million times in the near future. His hobby is flying gliders & vintage fighter planes. Accessibility: http://twitter.com/sqlusa, http://www.sqlusa.com/contact2005/, Transact-SQL & Database Design MSDN forums (moderator).

CONTENTS

INTRODUCTION

Developers across the world are facing database issues daily. While they are immersed in procedural languages with loops , RDBMS forces them to think in terms of sets without loops. It takes transition. It takes training. It takes experience. Developers are exposed also to Excel worksheets or spreadsheets as they were called in the not so distant past. So if you know worksheets how hard databases can be? After all worksheets look pretty much like database tables? The big difference is connections among well-designed tables. A database is a set of connected tables which represent entities in the real world. A database can be 100 connected tables or 3000. The connection is very simple: row A in table Alpha has affiliated data with row B in table Beta. But even with 200 tables and 300 connections (FOREIGN KEY references), it takes a good amount of time to familiarize to the point of acceptable working knowledge.

"The Cemetery of Computer Languages" is expanding. You can see tombstones like PL/1, Forth, Ada, Pascal, LISP, RPG, APL, SNOBOL, JOVIAL, Algol and the list goes on. For some, the future is in question: PowerBuilder, ColdFusion, FORTRAN & COBOL. SQL on the other hand running strong after 3 decades of glorious existence. What is the difference? The basic difference is that SQL can handle large datasets in a consistent manner based on mathematical foundations. You can throw together a computer language easy: assignment statements, looping, if-then conditional, 300 library functions, and voila! Here is the new language: Mars/1, named after the red planet to be fashionable with NASA's new Mars robot. But can Mars/1 JOIN a table of 1 million rows with a table of 10 million rows in a second? The success of SQL language is so compelling that other technologies are tagged onto it like XML/XQuery which deals with semi-structured information objects.

In SQL you are thinking at a high level. In C# or Java, you are dealing with details, lots of them. That is the big difference. Why is so much of the book dedicated to database design? Why not plunge into SQL coding and sooner or later the developer will get a hang of the design? Because high level thinking requires thinking at the database design level. A farmer has 6 mules, how do we model it in the database? We design the Farmer and FarmAnimal tables, then connect them with FarmerID FOREIGN KEY in FarmAnimal referencing the FarmerID PRIMARY KEY in the Farmer table. What is the big deal about it, looks so simple? In fact, how about just calling the tables Table1 & Table2 to be more generic? Ouch... meaningful naming is the very basis of good database design. Relational database design is truly simple for simple well-understood models. The challenge starts in modeling complex objects such as financial derivative instruments, airplane passenger scheduling or social network website. When you need to add 5 new tables to a 1000 tables database and hook them in (define FOREIGN KEY references) correctly, it is a huge challenge. To begin with, some of the 5 new tables may already be redundant, but you don't know that until you understand what the 1000 tables are really storing. Frequently, learning the application area is the biggest challenge for a developer when starting a new job.

The SQL language is simple to program and read even if when touching 10 tables. Complexities are abound though. The very first one: does the SQL statement touch the right data set? 999 records and 1000 or 998? T-SQL statements are turned into Transact-SQL scripts, stored procedures, user-defined functions and triggers, server-side database objects. They can be 5 statements or 1000 statements long programs. The style of Transact-SQL programming is different from the style in procedural programming languages. There are no arrays, only tables or table variables. Typically there is no looping, only set-based operations. Error control is different. Testing & debugging is relatively simple in Transact-SQL due to the interactive environment and the magic of selecting & executing a part without recompiling the whole.

WHO THIS BOOK IS FOR

Developers, programmers and systems analysts who are new to relational database technology. Also developers, designers and administrators, who know some SQL programming and database design, wish to expand their RDBMS design & development technology horizons. Familiarity with other computer language is assumed. The book has lots of queries, lots of T-SQL scripts, plenty to learn. The best way to learn it is to type in the query in your own SQL Server copy and test it, examine it, change it. Wouldn't it be easier just to copy & paste it? It would but the learning value would diminish. You need to feel the SQL language in your fingers. SQL queries must "pour" out from your fingers into the keyboard. Why is that so important? After everything can be found on the web and just copy & paste? Well not exactly. If you want to be an expert, it has to be in your head not on the web. Second, when your supervisor is looking over your shoulder, "Charlie, can you tell me what is the total revenue for March?", you have to be able to type in the query without SQL forum search and provide the results to your superior promptly.

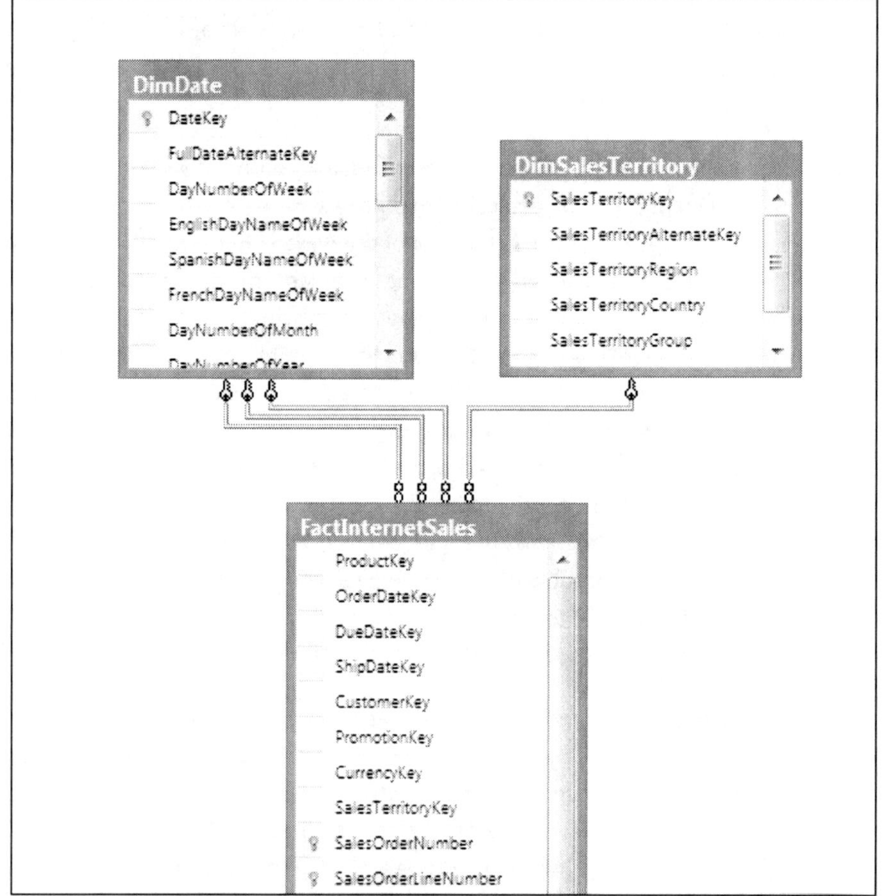

ABOUT THIS BOOK

Beginning relational database design and beginning Transact-SQL programming. It is not a reference manual, rather learn by examples: there are over 1,100 SELECT queries in the book. Instead of imaginary tables, the book uses the SQL Server sample databases for explanations and examples: pubs (PRIMARY KEYs 9, FOREIGN KEYs 10) , Northwind (PRIMARY KEYs 13, FOREIGN KEYs 13) and the AdventureWorks family. Among them: AdventureWorks, AdventureWorks2008, AdventureWorks2012 (PRIMARY KEYs 71, FOREIGN KEYs 90), & AdventureWorksDW2012 (PRIMARY KEYs 27, FOREIGN KEYs 44). The book introduces relational database design concepts, then reinforces them again and again, not to bore the reader, rather indoctrinate with relational database design principles. Light weight SQL starts at the beginning of the book, because working with database metadata (not the content of the database, rather data which describes the database) is essential for understanding database design. By the time the reader gets to T-SQL programming, already knows basic SQL programming from the database design section of the book. The book was designed to be readable in any environment, even on the beach laptop around or no laptop in sight at all. All queries are followed by results row count and /or full/partial results listing in tabular (grid) format. For full benefits though, the reader should try out the T-SQL queries and scripts as he progresses from page to page, topic to topic. Example for SQL Server 2012 T-SQL query and results presentation.

```
SELECT          V.Name                                  AS Vendor,
                FORMAT(SUM(POH.TotalDue), 'c', 'en-US') AS [Total Purchase],
                FORMAT(AVG(POH.TotalDue), 'c', 'en-US') AS [Average Purchase]
FROM AdventureWorks.Purchasing.Vendor AS V
   INNER JOIN AdventureWorks.Purchasing.PurchaseOrderHeader AS POH
        ON V.VendorID = POH.VendorID
GROUP BY V.Name  ORDER BY Vendor;
-- (79 row(s) affected) - Partial results.
```

Vendor	Total Purchase	Average Purchase
Advanced Bicycles	$28,502.09	$558.86
Allenson Cycles	$498,589.59	$9,776.27
American Bicycles and Wheels	$9,641.01	$189.04
American Bikes	$1,149,489.84	$22,539.02

CONVENTIONS USED IN THIS BOOK

The Transact-SQL queries and scripts (sequence of statements) are shaded.

The number of resulting rows is displayed as a comment line: -- (79 row(s) affected) .

The results of the queries is usually displayed in grid format.

Less frequently the results are enclosed in comment markers: /*...... */ .

When a query is a trivial variation of a previous query, no result is displayed.

While the intention of the book is database design & database development, SQL Server installation and some database administration tasks are included.

"Apparatus Intelligentia

vincet

Humanum Intelligentia"

Dedicated to

John von Neumann

The Father of the Modern Computer

This page is intentionally left blank.

CHAPTER 1: SQL Server Sample & System Databases

AdventureWorks Series of OLTP Databases

AdventureWorks sample On Line Transaction Processing (OLTP) database has been introduced with SQL Server 2005 to replace the previous sample database Northwind, a fictional gourmet food items distributor. The intent of the AdventureWorks sample database is to support the business operations of AdventureWorks Cycles, a fictitious mountain, touring and road bike manufacturer. The company sells through dealer network and online on the web. In addition to bikes, it sells frames and parts as well as accessories such as helmets, biking clothes and water bottles. The AdventureWorks2012 database image of Touring-1000 Blue, 50 bike in Production.ProductPhoto table **stored in a varbinary(max) data type column**.

T-SQL query to generate the list of tables of AdventureWorks2012 in 5 columns. The core query is simple. Presenting the results in 5 columns instead of 1 column adds a bit of complexity.

```
;WITH cteTableList AS (       SELECT CONCAT(SCHEMA_NAME(schema_id), '.', name)             AS TableName,
  (( ROW_NUMBER() OVER( ORDER BY CONCAT(SCHEMA_NAME(schema_id),'.', name)) ) % 5)       AS Remainder,
  (( ROW_NUMBER() OVER( ORDER BY CONCAT(SCHEMA_NAME(schema_id),'.', name)) - 1 )/ 5)    AS Quotient
                              FROM AdventureWorks2012.sys.tables),
CTE AS (SELECT TableName, CASE WHEN Remainder=0 THEN 5 ELSE Remainder END AS Remainder, Quotient
        FROM cteTableList)
SELECT  MAX(CASE WHEN Remainder = 1 THEN TableName END),
        MAX(CASE WHEN Remainder = 2 THEN TableName END),
        MAX(CASE WHEN Remainder = 3 THEN TableName END),
        MAX(CASE WHEN Remainder = 4 THEN TableName END),
        MAX(CASE WHEN Remainder = 5 THEN TableName END)
FROM  CTE GROUP  BY Quotient ORDER  BY Quotient;
GO
```

The query result set in grid format: tables in AdventureWorks2012

dbo.AWBuildVersion	dbo.DatabaseLog	dbo.ErrorLog	HumanResources.Department	HumanResources.Employee
HumanResources.EmployeeDepartmentHistory	HumanResources.EmployeePayHistory	HumanResources.JobCandidate	HumanResources.Shift	Person.Address
Person.AddressType	Person.BusinessEntity	Person.BusinessEntityAddress	Person.BusinessEntityContact	Person.ContactType
Person.CountryRegion	Person.EmailAddress	Person.Password	Person.Person	Person.PersonPhone
Person.PhoneNumberType	Person.StateProvince	Production.BillOfMaterials	Production.Culture	Production.Document
Production.Illustration	Production.Location	Production.Product	Production.ProductCategory	Production.ProductCostHistory
Production.ProductDescription	Production.ProductDocument	Production.ProductInventory	Production.ProductListPriceHistory	Production.ProductModel
Production.ProductModelIllustration	Production.ProductModelProductDescriptionCulture	Production.ProductPhoto	Production.ProductProductPhoto	Production.ProductReview
Production.ProductSubcategory	Production.ScrapReason	Production.TransactionHistory	Production.TransactionHistoryArchive	Production.UnitMeasure
Production.WorkOrder	Production.WorkOrderRouting	Purchasing.ProductVendor	Purchasing.PurchaseOrderDetail	Purchasing.PurchaseOrderHeader
Purchasing.ShipMethod	Purchasing.Vendor	Sales.CountryRegionCurrency	Sales.CreditCard	Sales.Currency
Sales.CurrencyRate	Sales.Customer	Sales.PersonCreditCard	Sales.SalesOrderDetail	Sales.SalesOrderHeader
Sales.SalesOrderHeaderSalesReason	Sales.SalesPerson	Sales.SalesPersonQuotaHistory	Sales.SalesReason	Sales.SalesTaxRate
Sales.SalesTerritory	Sales.SalesTerritoryHistory	Sales.ShoppingCartItem	Sales.SpecialOffer	Sales.SpecialOfferProduct
Sales.Store	NULL	NULL	NULL	NULL

Diagram of Person.Person & Related Tables

Database diagram displays the Person.Person and related tables. PRIMARY KEYs are marked with a gold (in color display) key. The "oo-------->" line is interpreted as many-to-one relationship. For example a person (one) can have one or more (many) credit cards. The "oo" side is the table with **FOREIGN KEY** referencing the gold key side table with the **PRIMARY KEY**.

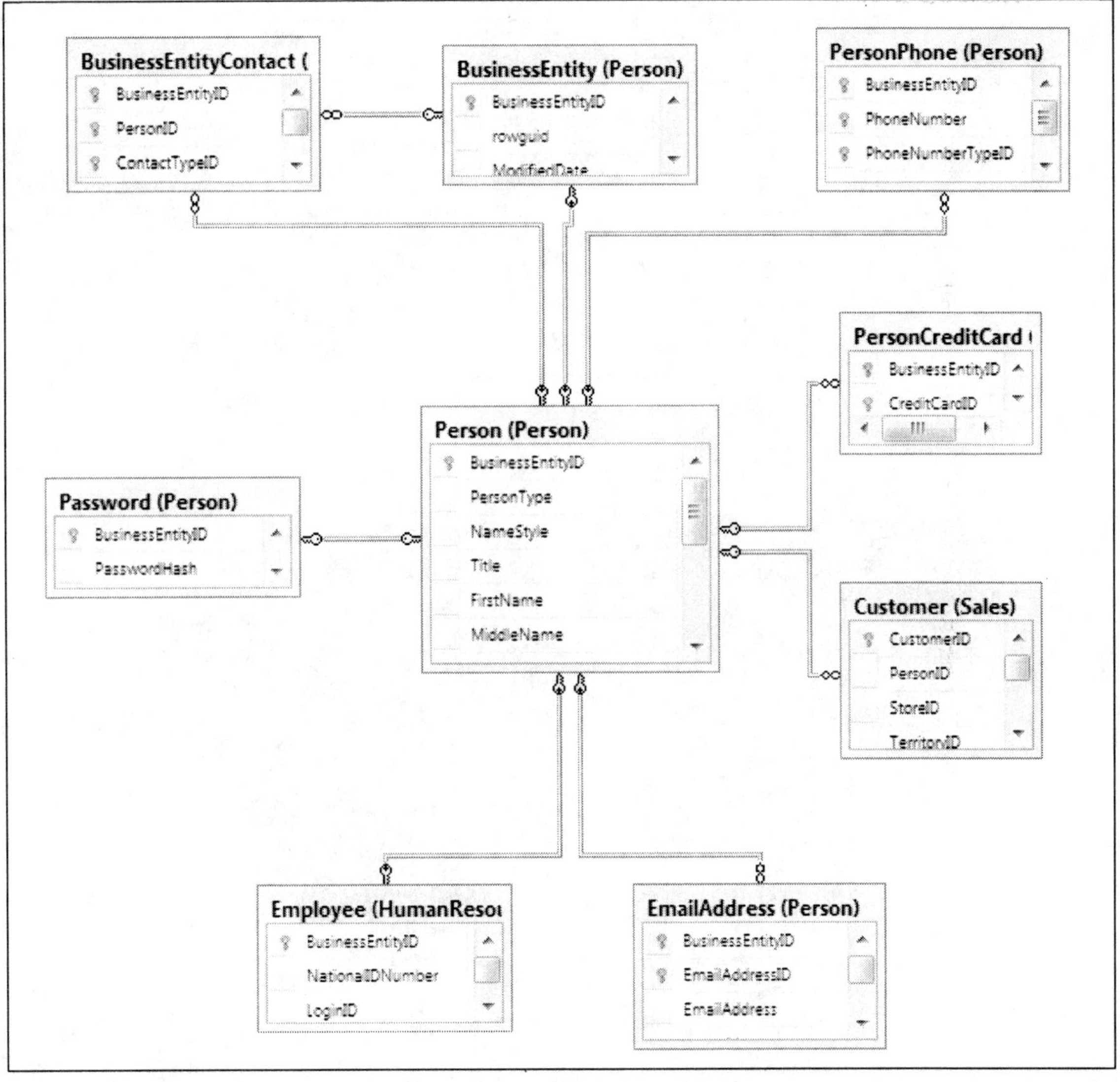

Diagram of Sales.SalesOrderHeader and Related Tables

Database diagram displays Sales.SalesOrderHeader and all tables related with **FOREIGN KEY** constraints. The SalesOrderHeader table stores the general information about each order. Line items, e.g. 5 Helmets at $30 each, are stored in the SalesOrderDetail table.

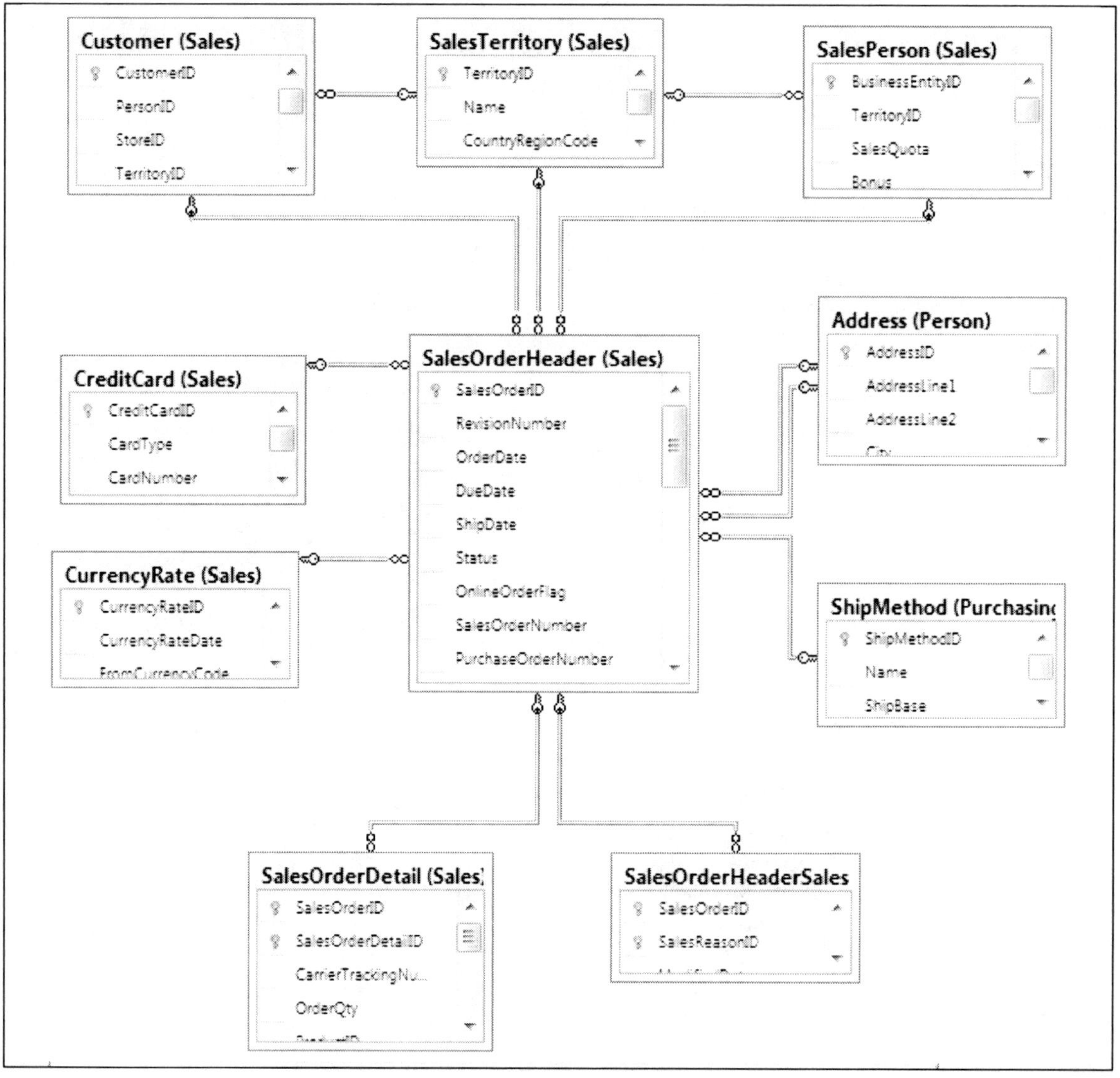

SELECT Query Basics

We have to use "light-weight" SQL (Structured Query Language) in the database design lessons. The reason is that rather difficult to discuss any database related topic without demonstration T-SQL scripts, in fact it would not make sense. **Relational database** and the **SQL language** are "married" to each other forever and ever.

The Simplest SELECT Statement

The simplest SELECT statement is "SELECT * FROM TableNameX" as demonstrated following. The "*" means wildcard inclusion of all columns in the table. Since there is no any other clause in the SELECT statement, it means also to retrieve all rows in the **table in no particular order**. Small tables which were populated in order are usually retrieved in order even though there is no ORDER BY clause. But this behaviour is purely coincidental. **Only ORDER BY clause can guarantee a sorted output.**

```
SELECT * FROM AdventureWorks2012.HumanResources.Department;
-- (16 row(s) affected)
```

DepartmentID	Name	GroupName	ModifiedDate
1	Engineering	Research and Development	2002-06-01 00:00:00.000
2	Tool Design	Research and Development	2002-06-01 00:00:00.000
3	Sales	Sales and Marketing	2002-06-01 00:00:00.000
4	Marketing	Sales and Marketing	2002-06-01 00:00:00.000
5	Purchasing	Inventory Management	2002-06-01 00:00:00.000
6	Research and Development	Research and Development	2002-06-01 00:00:00.000
7	Production	Manufacturing	2002-06-01 00:00:00.000
8	Production Control	Manufacturing	2002-06-01 00:00:00.000
9	Human Resources	Executive General and Administration	2002-06-01 00:00:00.000
10	Finance	Executive General and Administration	2002-06-01 00:00:00.000
11	Information Services	Executive General and Administration	2002-06-01 00:00:00.000
12	Document Control	Quality Assurance	2002-06-01 00:00:00.000
13	Quality Assurance	Quality Assurance	2002-06-01 00:00:00.000
14	Facilities and Maintenance	Executive General and Administration	2002-06-01 00:00:00.000
15	Shipping and Receiving	Inventory Management	2002-06-01 00:00:00.000
16	Executive	Executive General and Administration	2002-06-01 00:00:00.000

When tables are JOINed, SELECT * returns all the columns with all the data in the participant tables.

```
SELECT TOP 3 * FROM Sales.SalesOrderHeader H
        INNER JOIN Sales.SalesOrderDetail D
            ON H.SalesOrderID = D.SalesOrderID;
-- 121,317 rows in the JOIN
```

SELECT Query with WHERE Clause Predicate

Query to demonstrate how can we be selective with columns, furthermore, filter returned rows (WHERE clause) and sort them (ORDER BY clause).

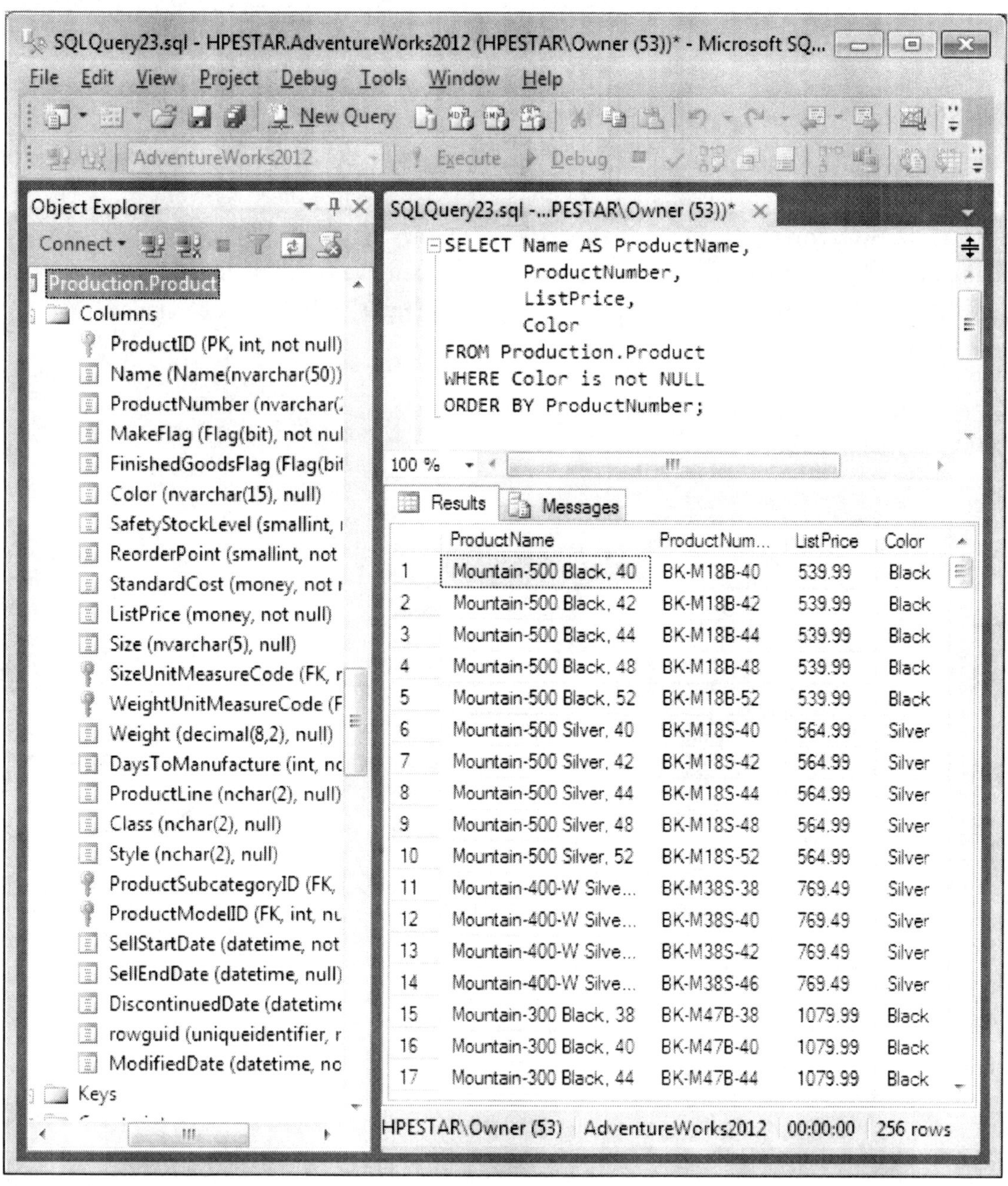

Aggregating Data with GROUP BY Query

The second basic query is GROUP BY aggregation which creates a **summary** of detail data. GROUP BY query can be used to preview, review, survey , assess, and analyze data at a high level.

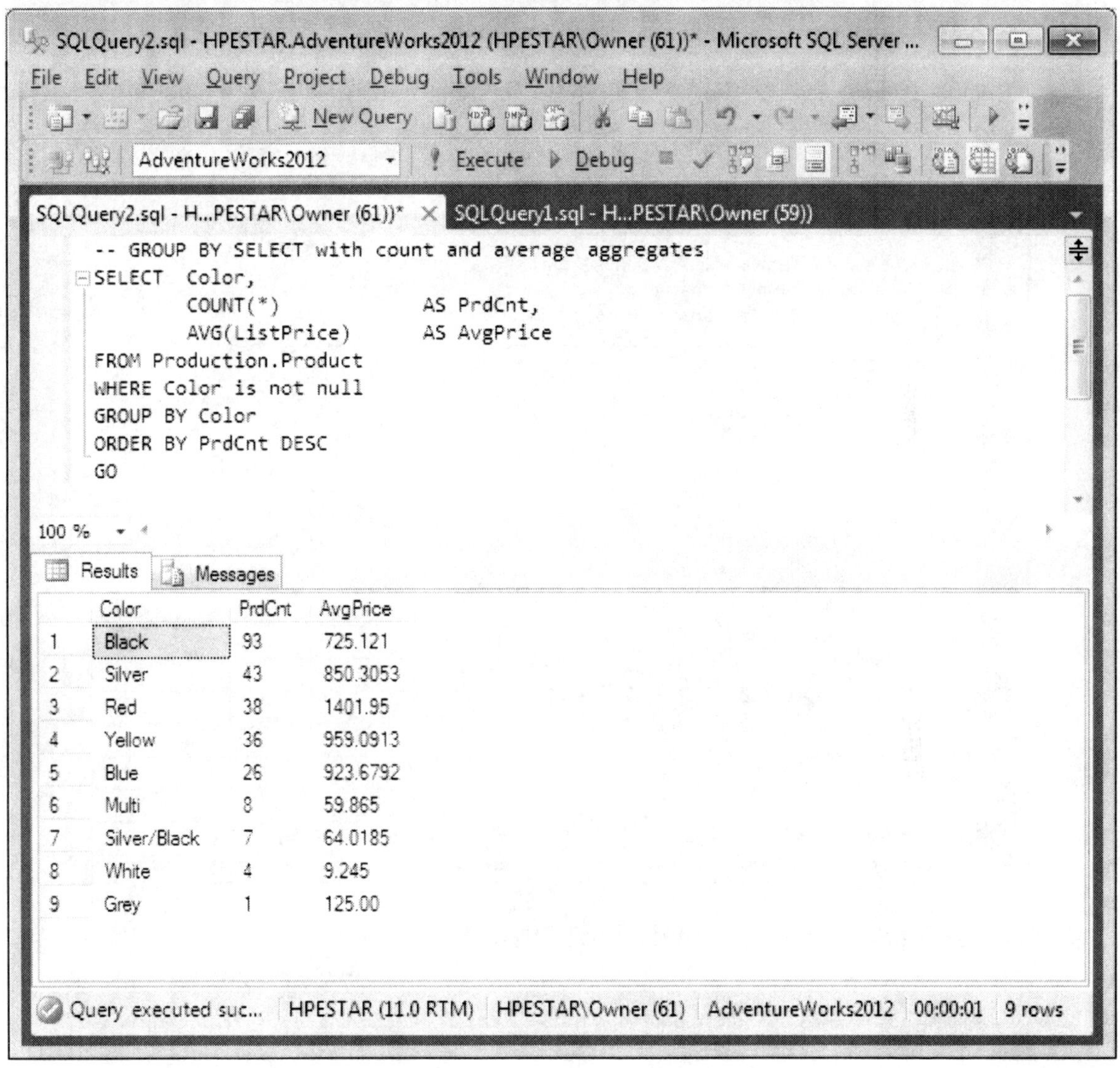

```
-- GROUP BY SELECT with count and average aggregates
SELECT  Color,
        COUNT(*)            AS PrdCnt,
        AVG(ListPrice)      AS AvgPrice
FROM Production.Product
WHERE Color is not null
GROUP BY Color
ORDER BY PrdCnt DESC
GO
```

	Color	PrdCnt	AvgPrice
1	Black	93	725.121
2	Silver	43	850.3053
3	Red	38	1401.95
4	Yellow	36	959.0913
5	Blue	26	923.6792
6	Multi	8	59.865
7	Silver/Black	7	64.0185
8	White	4	9.245
9	Grey	1	125.00

NOTE
GROUP BY aggregate queries can efficiently "fingerprint" (profile) data in tables, even millions of rows. GROUP BY aggregates form the computational base of Business Intelligence.

GROUP BY Query with 2 Tables & ORDER BY for Sorting

JOINing two tables on matching KEYs, FOREIGN KEY to PRIMARY KEY, to combine the data contents in a consistent fashion.

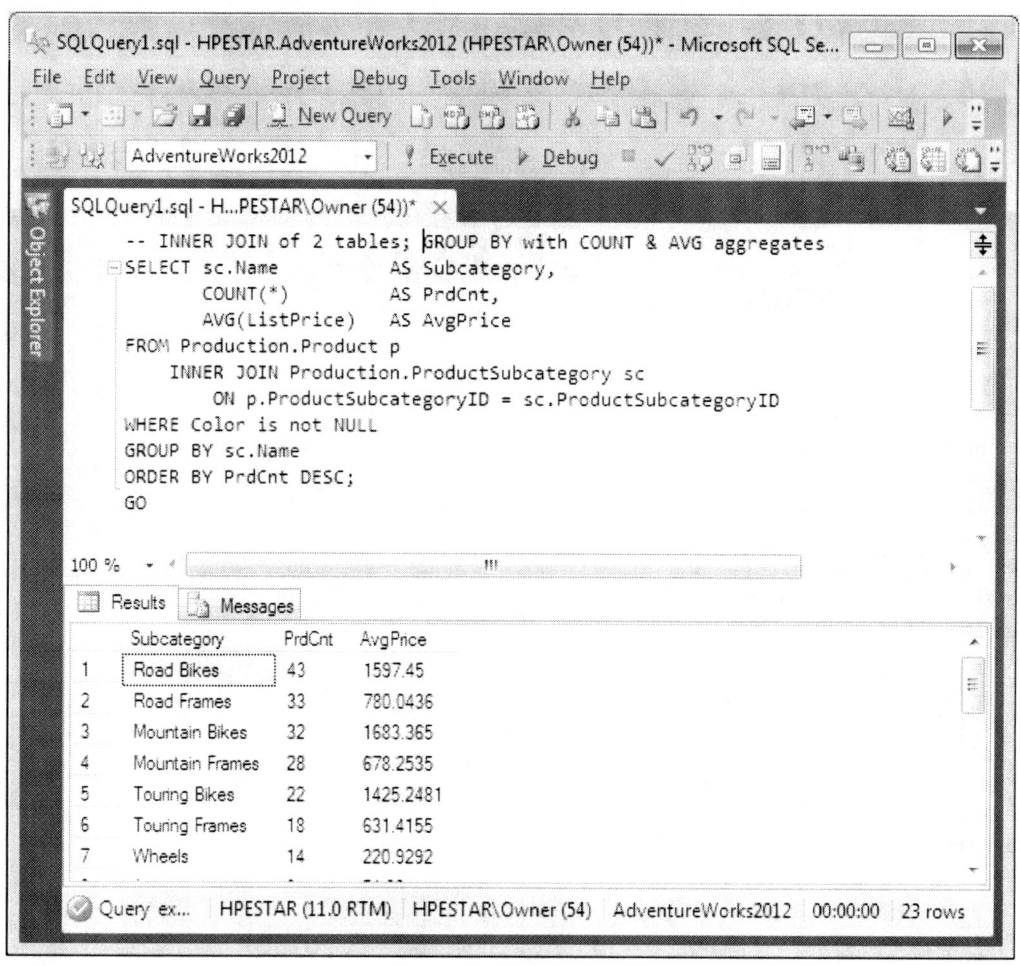

LEN(), DATALENGTH(), LTRIM() & RTRIM() Functions

The LEN() function counts characters without the trailing spaces. DATALENGTH() counts storage bytes including trailing spaces. LTRIM() trims leading spaces, RTRIM() trims trailing spaces.

```
DECLARE @W varchar(32)= CHAR(32)+'Denver'+CHAR(32);
DECLARE @UW nvarchar(32) = CHAR(32)+N'MEGŐRZÉSE'+CHAR(32);  -- UNICODE 2 bytes per character
SELECT Length=LEN(@W), DLength=DATALENGTH (@W);                                        -- 7  8
SELECT Length=LEN(@UW), DLength=DATALENGTH (@UW);                                      -- 10 22
SELECT Length=LEN(LTRIM(RTRIM(@W))), DLength=DATALENGTH (LTRIM(RTRIM(@W)));            -- 6  6
SELECT Length=LEN(LTRIM(RTRIM(@UW))), DLength=DATALENGTH (LTRIM(RTRIM(@UW)));          -- 9  18
```

Finding All Accessories in Production.Product Table

Query to list all accessories (a category) for sale.

```
USE AdventureWorks2012;
```

```
SELECT      UPPER(PC.Name) AS Category, PSC.Name              AS Subcategory,
            P.Name AS Product, FORMAT(ListPrice, 'c', 'en-US') AS ListPrice,
            FORMAT(StandardCost, 'c', 'en-US')                 AS StandardCost
FROM Production.Product AS P
   INNER JOIN Production.ProductSubcategory AS PSC
            ON PSC.ProductSubcategoryID = P.ProductSubcategoryID
   INNER JOIN Production.ProductCategory AS PC
            ON PC.ProductCategoryID = PSC.ProductCategoryID
WHERE PC.Name = 'Accessories'
ORDER BY Category, Subcategory, Product;      -- (29 row(s) affected)
```

Category	Subcategory	Product	ListPrice	StandardCost
ACCESSORIES	Bike Racks	Hitch Rack - 4-Bike	$120.00	$44.88
ACCESSORIES	Bike Stands	All-Purpose Bike Stand	$159.00	$59.47
ACCESSORIES	Bottles and Cages	Mountain Bottle Cage	$9.99	$3.74
ACCESSORIES	Bottles and Cages	Road Bottle Cage	$8.99	$3.36
ACCESSORIES	Bottles and Cages	Water Bottle - 30 oz.	$4.99	$1.87
ACCESSORIES	Cleaners	Bike Wash - Dissolver	$7.95	$2.97
ACCESSORIES	Fenders	Fender Set - Mountain	$21.98	$8.22
ACCESSORIES	Helmets	Sport-100 Helmet, Black	$34.99	$13.09
ACCESSORIES	Helmets	Sport-100 Helmet, Blue	$34.99	$13.09
ACCESSORIES	Helmets	Sport-100 Helmet, Red	$34.99	$13.09
ACCESSORIES	Hydration Packs	Hydration Pack - 70 oz.	$54.99	$20.57
ACCESSORIES	Lights	Headlights - Dual-Beam	$34.99	$14.43
ACCESSORIES	Lights	Headlights - Weatherproof	$44.99	$18.56
ACCESSORIES	Lights	Taillights - Battery-Powered	$13.99	$5.77
ACCESSORIES	Locks	Cable Lock	$25.00	$10.31
ACCESSORIES	Panniers	Touring-Panniers, Large	$125.00	$51.56
ACCESSORIES	Pumps	Minipump	$19.99	$8.25
ACCESSORIES	Pumps	Mountain Pump	$24.99	$10.31
ACCESSORIES	Tires and Tubes	HL Mountain Tire	$35.00	$13.09
ACCESSORIES	Tires and Tubes	HL Road Tire	$32.60	$12.19
ACCESSORIES	Tires and Tubes	LL Mountain Tire	$24.99	$9.35
ACCESSORIES	Tires and Tubes	LL Road Tire	$21.49	$8.04
ACCESSORIES	Tires and Tubes	ML Mountain Tire	$29.99	$11.22
ACCESSORIES	Tires and Tubes	ML Road Tire	$24.99	$9.35
ACCESSORIES	Tires and Tubes	Mountain Tire Tube	$4.99	$1.87
ACCESSORIES	Tires and Tubes	Patch Kit/8 Patches	$2.29	$0.86
ACCESSORIES	Tires and Tubes	Road Tire Tube	$3.99	$1.49
ACCESSORIES	Tires and Tubes	Touring Tire	$28.99	$10.84
ACCESSORIES	Tires and Tubes	Touring Tire Tube	$4.99	$1.87

Using Implicit or Explicit Conversion

Implicit conversion results in simpler code and may even be faster. However, if we really need a specific conversion, explicit conversion should be used. In the ShipDate datetime column example, the implicit & explicit conversions yield the same results.

```
SELECT SalesOrderID, OrderDate, ShipDate, CustomerID, SubTotal
FROM Sales.SalesOrderHeader
WHERE ShipDate = '2008-03-08';                    -- Implicit conversion to datetime

/*     WHERE Shipdate = CONVERT(DATETIME, '2008-03-08');    -- Explicit conversion
       WHERE Shipdate = CONVERT(DATE, '2008-03-08');        -- Explicit conversion */

-- (247 row(s) affected) - Partial results.
```

SalesOrderID	OrderDate	ShipDate	CustomerID	SubTotal
65089	2008-02-29 00:00:00.000	2008-03-08 00:00:00.000	30079	1466.01
65090	2008-02-29 00:00:00.000	2008-03-08 00:00:00.000	29812	98.774
65151	2008-03-01 00:00:00.000	2008-03-08 00:00:00.000	30072	76.20
65152	2008-03-01 00:00:00.000	2008-03-08 00:00:00.000	29592	11710.422
65153	2008-03-01 00:00:00.000	2008-03-08 00:00:00.000	29501	2428.476
65154	2008-03-01 00:00:00.000	2008-03-08 00:00:00.000	30113	26709.588
65155	2008-03-01 00:00:00.000	2008-03-08 00:00:00.000	29579	32798.562
65156	2008-03-01 00:00:00.000	2008-03-08 00:00:00.000	29714	30238.236
65157	2008-03-01 00:00:00.000	2008-03-08 00:00:00.000	29485	22021.782
65158	2008-03-01 00:00:00.000	2008-03-08 00:00:00.000	29736	67831.3271
65159	2008-03-01 00:00:00.000	2008-03-08 00:00:00.000	29622	13573.704
65160	2008-03-01 00:00:00.000	2008-03-08 00:00:00.000	29957	52766.5746
65161	2008-03-01 00:00:00.000	2008-03-08 00:00:00.000	29799	4386.402
65162	2008-03-01 00:00:00.000	2008-03-08 00:00:00.000	30037	4634.91
65163	2008-03-01 00:00:00.000	2008-03-08 00:00:00.000	29629	59234.838
65164	2008-03-01 00:00:00.000	2008-03-08 00:00:00.000	29950	24795.1796
65165	2008-03-01 00:00:00.000	2008-03-08 00:00:00.000	29762	4480.614
65166	2008-03-01 00:00:00.000	2008-03-08 00:00:00.000	29494	26.724
65167	2008-03-01 00:00:00.000	2008-03-08 00:00:00.000	29696	19300.926
65168	2008-03-01 00:00:00.000	2008-03-08 00:00:00.000	29496	20857.776
65169	2008-03-01 00:00:00.000	2008-03-08 00:00:00.000	29840	12.144
65170	2008-03-01 00:00:00.000	2008-03-08 00:00:00.000	29709	5438.028
65171	2008-03-01 00:00:00.000	2008-03-08 00:00:00.000	29803	4718.898
65172	2008-03-01 00:00:00.000	2008-03-08 00:00:00.000	29821	21439.446
65173	2008-03-01 00:00:00.000	2008-03-08 00:00:00.000	29639	65622.167

How Can SQL Work without Looping?

Looping is implicit in the SQL language. The commands are set oriented and carried out for each member of the set be it 5 or 500 millions in an unordered manner.

```
SELECT * FROM AdventureWorks2012.Sales.SalesOrderDetail;    (121317 row(s) affected)
```

SQL Server database engine looped through internally on all rows in SalesOrderDetail table in an unordered way. In fact the database engine may have used some ordering for efficiency, but that behaviour is a blackbox as far as programming concerned. Implicit looping makes SQL statements so simple, yet immensely powerful for information access from low level to high level.

Single-Valued SQL Queries

Single-valued SQL queries are very important because **we can use them where ever the T-SQL syntax requires a single value just by enclosing the query in parenthesis**. The next T-SQL query returns a single value, a cell from the table which is the intersection of a row and a column.

```
SELECT ListPrice FROM AdventureWorks2012.Production.Product  WHERE ProductID = 800;
-- (1 row(s) affected)
```

ListPrice
1120.49

The ">" comparison operator requires a single value on the right hand side so we plug in the single-valued query. The WHERE condition is evaluated for each row (implicit looping).

```
SELECT ProductID, Name AS ProductName, ListPrice
FROM AdventureWorks2012.Production.Product                          -- 504 rows
WHERE ListPrice > 2 *   (
                        SELECT ListPrice FROM AdventureWorks2012.Production.Product
                        WHERE ProductID = 800
                        )
ORDER BY ListPrice DESC, ProductName;     -- (35 row(s) affected) - Partial results.
```

ProductID	ProductName	ListPrice
750	Road-150 Red, 44	3578.27
751	Road-150 Red, 48	3578.27
752	Road-150 Red, 52	3578.27
753	Road-150 Red, 56	3578.27
749	Road-150 Red, 62	3578.27
771	Mountain-100 Silver, 38	3399.99

Data Dictionary Description of Tables in the Sales Schema

It is not easy to understand a database with 70 tables, even harder with 2,000 tables. Documentation is very helpful, if not essential, for any database. SQL Server provides Data Dictionary facility for documenting tables and other objects in the database. Data which describes the design & structure of a database is called **metadata**. Here is the high level documentation of tables in the Sales schema using the fn_listextendedproperty system function.

```
SELECT
    CONCAT('Sales.', objname COLLATE DATABASE_DEFAULT)    AS TableName,
    value                                                  AS [Description]
FROM fn_listextendedproperty (NULL, 'schema', 'Sales', 'table', default, NULL, NULL)
ORDER BY TableName;
```

TableName	Description
Sales.ContactCreditCard	Cross-reference table mapping customers in the Contact table to their credit card information in the CreditCard table.
Sales.CountryRegionCurrency	Cross-reference table mapping ISO currency codes to a country or region.
Sales.CreditCard	Customer credit card information.
Sales.Currency	Lookup table containing standard ISO currencies.
Sales.CurrencyRate	Currency exchange rates.
Sales.Customer	Current customer information. Also see the Individual and Store tables.
Sales.CustomerAddress	Cross-reference table mapping customers to their address(es).
Sales.Individual	Demographic data about customers that purchase Adventure Works products online.
Sales.SalesOrderDetail	Individual products associated with a specific sales order. See SalesOrderHeader.
Sales.SalesOrderHeader	General sales order information.
Sales.SalesOrderHeaderSalesReason	Cross-reference table mapping sales orders to sales reason codes.
Sales.SalesPerson	Sales representative current information.
Sales.SalesPersonQuotaHistory	Sales performance tracking.
Sales.SalesReason	Lookup table of customer purchase reasons.
Sales.SalesTaxRate	Tax rate lookup table.
Sales.SalesTerritory	Sales territory lookup table.
Sales.SalesTerritoryHistory	Sales representative transfers to other sales territories.
Sales.ShoppingCartItem	Contains online customer orders until the order is submitted or cancelled.
Sales.SpecialOffer	Sale discounts lookup table.
Sales.SpecialOfferProduct	Cross-reference table mapping products to special offer discounts.
Sales.Store	Customers (resellers) of Adventure Works products.
Sales.StoreContact	Cross-reference table mapping stores and their employees.

NULL Values in Tables & Query Results

NULL means no value. If so why do we capitalize it? We don't have to. Somehow, it became a custom in the RDBMS industry, nobody knows anymore how it started. Since the U.S. default collation for server and databases are case insensitive, we can just use "null" as well. **NULL value is different from empty string ('') or 0 (zero) which can be tested by the "=" or "!=" operators.** If a database table does not have a value in a cell for whatever reason, it is marked (flagged) as NULL by the database engine. When a value is entered, the NULL marking goes away. **NULL values can be tested by "IS NULL" or "IS NOT NULL" operators, but not the "=" or "!=" operators.**

The likelihood is high that the color attribute is not applicable to items like tire tube, that is the reason that some cell values were left unassigned (null).

```
SELECT TOP 5    Name                            AS ProductName,
                ProductNumber,
                ListPrice,
                Color
FROM AdventureWorks2012.Production.Product
WHERE Color IS NULL  ORDER BY ProductName DESC;
```

ProductName	ProductNumber	ListPrice	Color
Water Bottle - 30 oz.	WB-H098	4.99	NULL
Touring Tire Tube	TT-T092	4.99	NULL
Touring Tire	TI-T723	28.99	NULL
Touring Rim	RM-T801	0.00	NULL
Touring End Caps	EC-T209	0.00	NULL

We can do random selection as well and get a mix of products with color and null value.

```
SELECT TOP 5    Name AS ProductName,
                ProductNumber,
                ListPrice,
                Color
FROM AdventureWorks2012.Production.Product  ORDER BY NEWID();    -- Random sort
```

ProductName	ProductNumber	ListPrice	Color
Touring-1000 Yellow, 46	BK-T79Y-46	2384.07	Yellow
HL Spindle/Axle	SD-9872	0.00	NULL
ML Mountain Tire	TI-M602	29.99	NULL
Road-650 Red, 60	BK-R50R-60	782.99	Red
Pinch Bolt	PB-6109	0.00	NULL

NULL Values Generated by Queries

NULL values can be generated by queries as well. Typically, LEFT JOIN, RIGHT JOIN and some functions generate NULLs. The meaning of OUTER JOINs: include no-match rows from the left or right table in addition to the matching rows.

```
SELECT TOP 5
        PS.Name                     AS Category,
        P.Name                      AS ProductName,
        ProductNumber,
        ListPrice,
        Color
FROM AdventureWorks2012.Production.Product P
  RIGHT JOIN AdventureWorks2012.Production.ProductSubcategory PS
      ON PS.ProductSubcategoryID = P.ProductSubcategoryID
         AND ListPrice >= 3500.0
ORDER BY newid();
GO
```

Category	ProductName	ProductNumber	ListPrice	Color
Road Bikes	Road-150 Red, 62	BK-R93R-62	3578.27	Red
Road Bikes	Road-150 Red, 52	BK-R93R-52	3578.27	Red
Bib-Shorts	NULL	NULL	NULL	NULL
Socks	NULL	NULL	NULL	NULL
Cranksets	NULL	NULL	NULL	NULL

Some system functions, like the brand new TRY_CONVERT(), can generate NULL values as well. If the PostalCode cannot be converted into an integer, TRY_CONVERT() returns NULL.

```
SELECT TOP 5    ConvertedZip = TRY_CONVERT(INT, PostalCode),
                AddressLine1,
                City,
                PostalCode
FROM Person.Address  ORDER by newid();
```

ConvertedZip	AddressLine1	City	PostalCode
91945	5979 El Pueblo	Lemon Grove	91945
NULL	7859 Green Valley Road	London	W1V 5RN
3220	6004 Peabody Road	Geelong	3220
NULL	6713 Eaker Way	Burnaby	V3J 6Z3
NULL	5153 Hackamore Lane	Shawnee	V8Z 4N5

Building an FK-PK Diagram in AdventureWorks2012

The **FOREIGN KEY - PRIMARY KEY** diagram of AdventureWorks2012 database with over 70 tables can be built just by adding the tables to the diagram. The FK-PK lines are automatically drawn. An FK-PK line represents a predefined referential constraint.

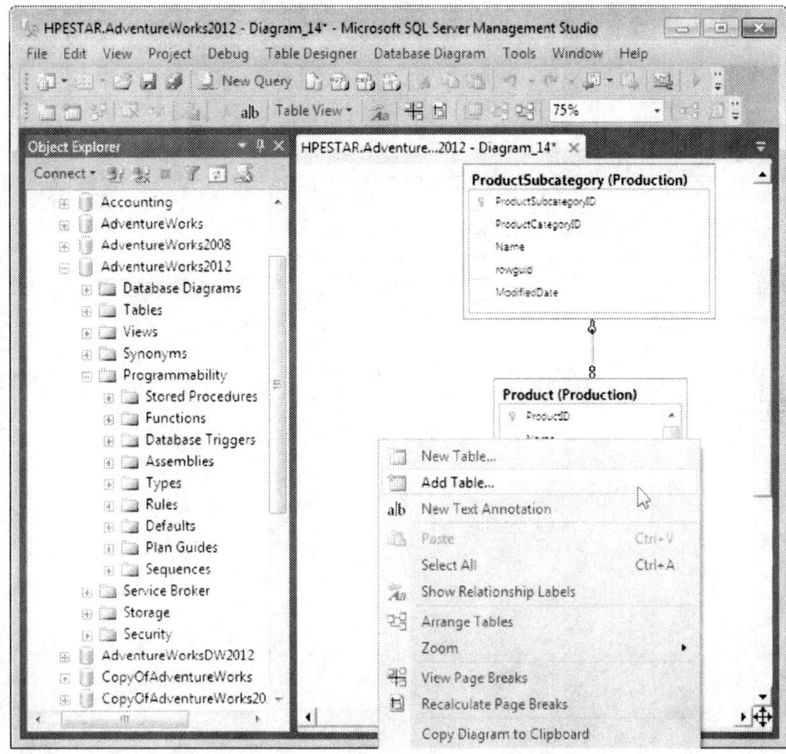

While all tables are important in a database, tables with the most connections play central roles, in a way analogous to the Sun with planets around it.

```
-- PRIMARY KEY tables with the most FOREIGN KEY references
SELECT      schema_name(schema_id)      AS SchemaName,
            o.name                      AS PKTable,
            count(*)                    AS FKCount
FROM sys.sysforeignkeys s   INNER JOIN sys.objects o     ON s.rkeyid = o.object_id
GROUP BY schema_id, o.name   HAVING count(*) >= 5   ORDER BY FKCount DESC;
```

SchemaName	PKTable	FKCount
Production	Product	14
Person	Person	7
HumanResources	Employee	6
Person	BusinessEntity	5
Sales	SalesTerritory	5

AdventureWorksDW2012 Data Warehouse Database

AdventureWorksDW series contain second hand data only since they are Data Warehouse databases. All data originates from other sources such as the AdventureWorks OLTP database & Excel worksheets. Tables in the data warehousing database are divided into two groups: dimension tables & fact tables.

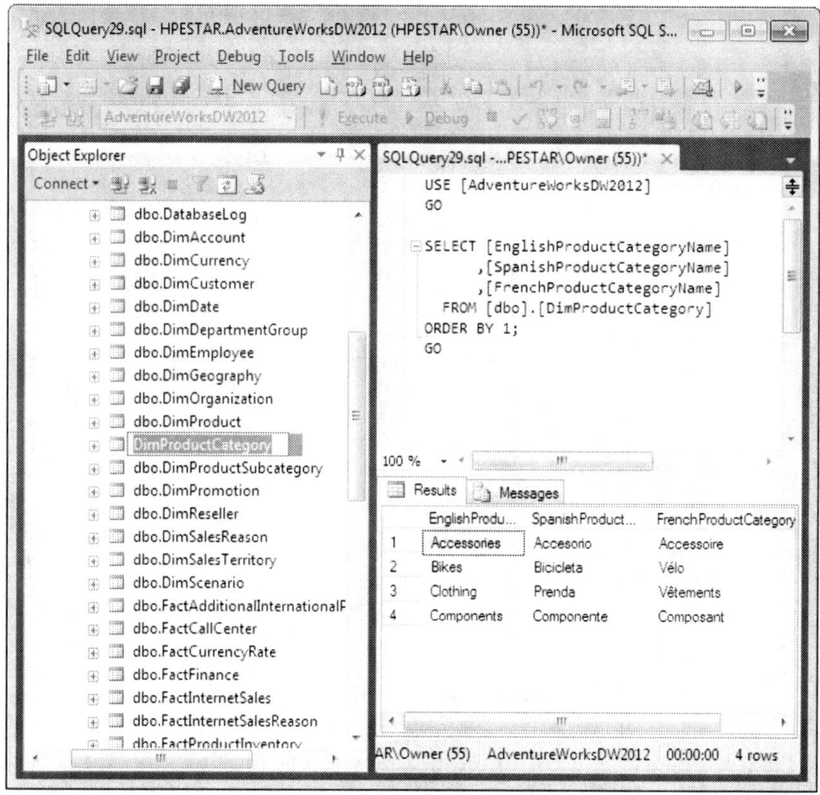

Simple data warehouse query.

```
SELECT          D.CalendarYear AS [Year], C.SalesTerritoryCountry AS [Country],
                FORMAT(SUM(S.SalesAmount),'c0','en-US') AS TotalSales
FROM FactInternetSales AS S  INNER JOIN DimDate AS D ON S.OrderDateKey = D.DateKey
        INNER JOIN DimSalesTerritory AS C ON S.SalesTerritoryKey = C.SalesTerritoryKey
GROUP BY D.CalendarYear, C.SalesTerritoryCountry  ORDER BY Year DESC, SUM(S.SalesAmount) DESC;
```

Year	Country	TotalSales
2008	United States	$3,324,031
2008	Australia	$2,563,884
2008	United Kingdom	$1,210,286
2008	Germany	$1,076,891
2008	France	$922,179

Diagram of a Star Schema in AdventureWorksDW2012

The high level star schema diagram in AdventureWorksDW2012 Data Warehouse database with FactResellerSales fact table and related dimension tables. The temporal dimension table DimDate plays a central role in Business Intelligence data analytics.

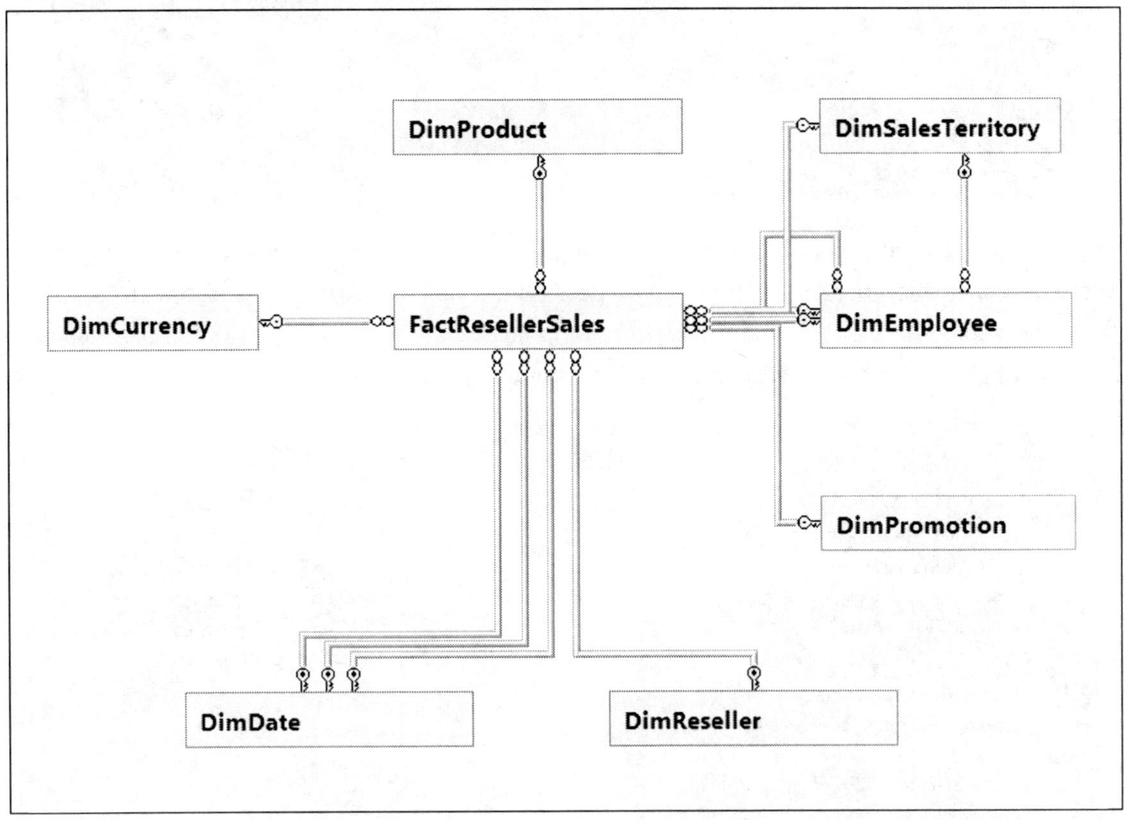

Distribution of **PRIMARY KEY - FOREIGN KEY** relationships can be generated from metadata (system views - sys.) for the entire Data Warehouse.

```
SELECT   schema_name(schema_id) AS SchemaName, o.name AS PKTable,  count(*) AS FKCount
FROM sys.sysforeignkeys s   INNER JOIN sys.objects o    ON s.rkeyid = o.object_id
GROUP BY schema_id, o.name  HAVING COUNT(*) > 2 ORDER BY FKCount DESC;
```

SchemaName	PKTable	FKCount
dbo	DimDate	12
dbo	DimCurrency	4
dbo	DimSalesTerritory	4
dbo	DimEmployee	3
dbo	DimProduct	3

AdventureWorks2008 Sample Database

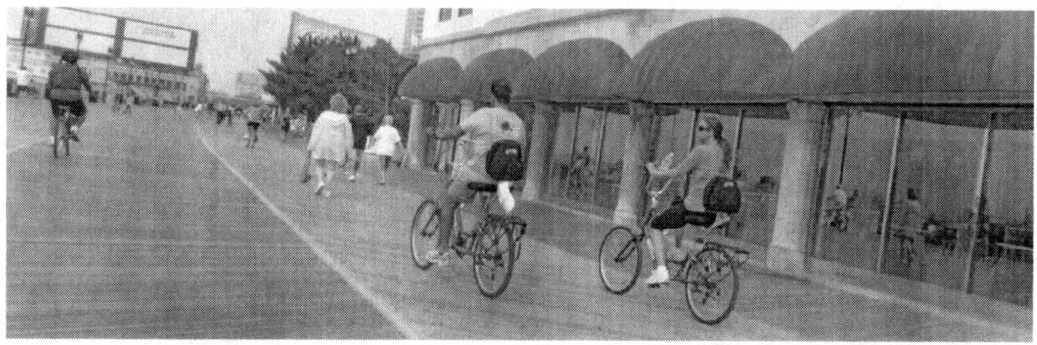

There were substantial changes made from the prior version of the sample database. Among them demonstration use of the **hierarchyid** data type which has been introduced with SS 2008 to support sophisticated tree hierarchy processing. In addition employee, customer and dealer PRIMARY KEYs are pooled together and called BusinessEntityID.

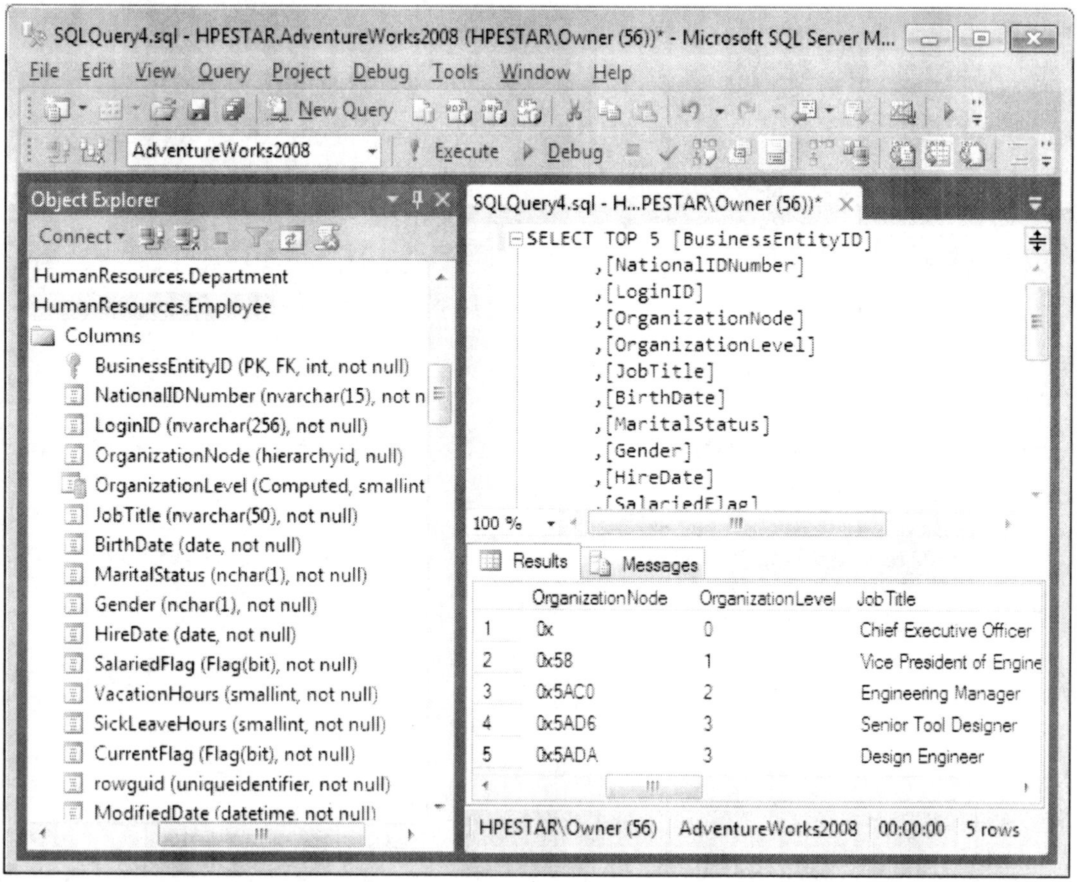

SQLQuery4.sql - HPESTAR.AdventureWorks2008 (HPESTAR\Owner (56))* - Microsoft SQL Server M...
File Edit View Query Project Debug Tools Window Help
New Query
AdventureWorks2008
Execute Debug
Object Explorer
Connect
HumanResources.Department
HumanResources.Employee
Columns
BusinessEntityID (PK, FK, int, not null)
NationalIDNumber (nvarchar(15), not n
LoginID (nvarchar(256), not null)
OrganizationNode (hierarchyid, null)
OrganizationLevel (Computed, smallint
JobTitle (nvarchar(50), not null)
BirthDate (date, not null)
MaritalStatus (nchar(1), not null)
Gender (nchar(1), not null)
HireDate (date, not null)
SalariedFlag (Flag(bit), not null)
VacationHours (smallint, not null)
SickLeaveHours (smallint, not null)
CurrentFlag (Flag(bit), not null)
rowguid (uniqueidentifier, not null)
ModifiedDate (datetime, not null)
SQLQuery4.sql - H...PESTAR\Owner (56))*
SELECT TOP 5 [BusinessEntityID]
,[NationalIDNumber]
,[LoginID]
,[OrganizationNode]
,[OrganizationLevel]
,[JobTitle]
,[BirthDate]
,[MaritalStatus]
,[Gender]
,[HireDate]
,[SalariedFlag]
100 %
Results
Messages
OrganizationNode OrganizationLevel JobTitle
1 0x 0 Chief Executive Officer
2 0x58 1 Vice President of Engine
3 0x5AC0 2 Engineering Manager
4 0x5AD6 3 Senior Tool Designer
5 0x5ADA 3 Design Engineer
HPESTAR\Owner (56) AdventureWorks2008 00:00:00 5 rows

AdventureWorks2012 Sample Database

There were no apparent design changes made from the prior version of the sample database. A significant content change: dates were advanced 4 years. An OrderDate (Sales.SalesOrderHeader table) of 2004-02-01 in previous versions is now 2008-02-01.

The OrderDate statistics in the two sample databases.

```
SELECT  [Year]              = YEAR(OrderDate),       OrderCount       = COUNT(*)
FROM AdventureWorks2008.Sales.SalesOrderHeader GROUP BY YEAR(OrderDate)
ORDER BY [Year];
```

Year	OrderCount
2001	1379
2002	3692
2003	12443
2004	13951

```
SELECT  [Year]              = YEAR(OrderDate),       OrderCount       = COUNT(*)
FROM AdventureWorks2012.Sales.SalesOrderHeader GROUP BY YEAR(OrderDate)
ORDER BY [Year];
```

Year	OrderCount
2005	1379
2006	3692
2007	12443
2008	13951

Starting with SQL Server 2012, numeric figures, among others, can be formatted with the FORMAT function.

```
SELECT  [Year]              = YEAR(OrderDate),
        OrderCount          = FORMAT(COUNT(*), '###,###')
FROM AdventureWorks2012.Sales.SalesOrderHeader
GROUP BY YEAR(OrderDate)  ORDER BY [Year];
```

Year	OrderCount
2005	1,379
2006	3,692
2007	12,443
2008	13,951

Production.Product and Related Tables

The Product table is the "center" of the database. The reason is that AdventureWorks Cycles is a product base company selling through dealers and directly to consumers through the internet. You may wonder why are we pushing **FOREIGN KEY - PRIMARY KEY** relationship so vehemently? Because there is nothing else to a database just **well-designed tables and their connections which are FK-PK constraints**.

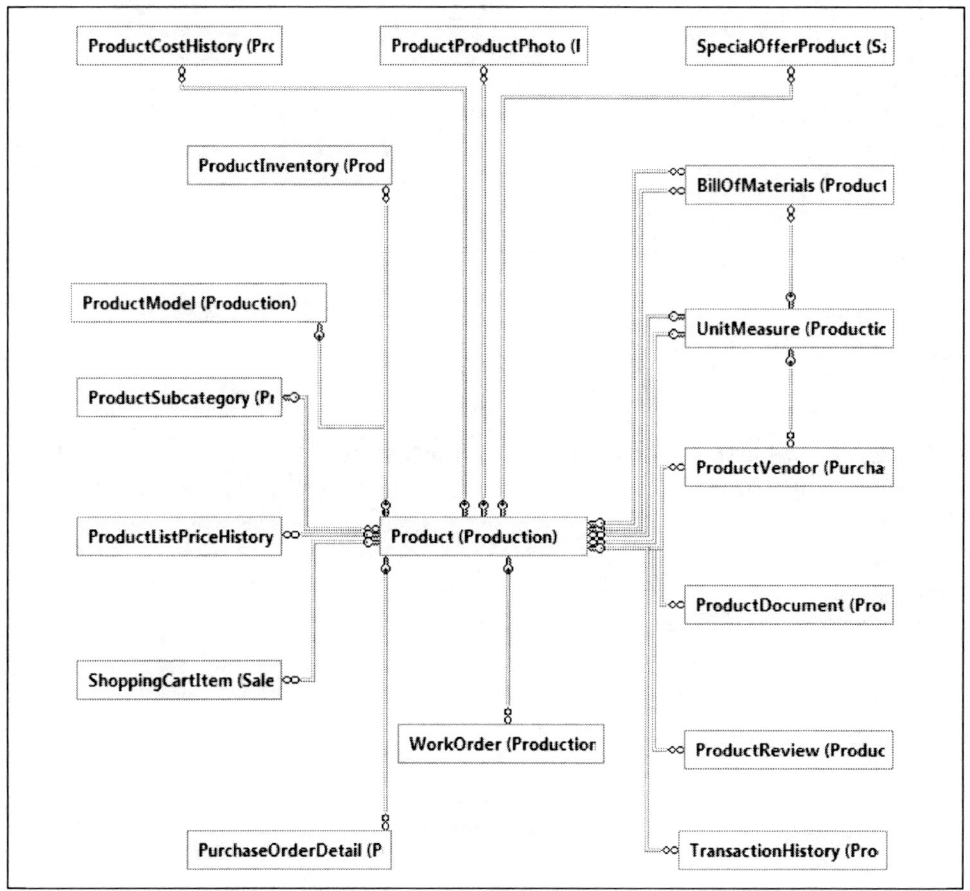

Simple OLTP query.

```
SELECT Color, WOCount=COUNT(*)  FROM Production.WorkOrder W
        INNER JOIN Production.Product P    ON W.ProductID = P.ProductID  WHERE Color != ''
GROUP BY Color ORDER BY WOCount DESC;
```

Color	WOCount
Black	18952
Silver	6620
Yellow	5231
Red	4764
Blue	2319

Descriptions of Columns in Production.Product Table

Queries to list the description of table and columns from Extended Property (data dictionary).

```
USE AdventureWorks2012;
SELECT          objname AS TableName, value   AS [Description]
FROM fn_listextendedproperty( NULL, 'schema', 'Production', 'table', 'Product', NULL, NULL);
```

TableName	Description
Product	Products sold or used in the manfacturing of sold products.

```
SELECT          'Production.Product'          AS TableName,             -- String literal
                objname                       AS ColumnName,
                value                         AS [Description]
FROM fn_listextendedproperty( NULL, 'schema', 'Production', 'table',
                              'Product', 'column', default);
```

TableName	ColumnName	Description
Production.Product	ProductID	Primary key for Product records.
Production.Product	Name	Name of the product.
Production.Product	ProductNumber	Unique product identification number.
Production.Product	MakeFlag	0 = Product is purchased, 1 = Product is manufactured in-house.
Production.Product	FinishedGoodsFlag	0 = Product is not a salable item. 1 = Product is salable.
Production.Product	Color	Product color.
Production.Product	SafetyStockLevel	Minimum inventory quantity.
Production.Product	ReorderPoint	Inventory level that triggers a purchase order or work order.
Production.Product	StandardCost	Standard cost of the product.
Production.Product	ListPrice	Selling price.
Production.Product	Size	Product size.
Production.Product	SizeUnitMeasureCode	Unit of measure for Size column.
Production.Product	WeightUnitMeasureCode	Unit of measure for Weight column.
Production.Product	Weight	Product weight.
Production.Product	DaysToManufacture	Number of days required to manufacture the product.
Production.Product	ProductLine	R = Road, M = Mountain, T = Touring, S = Standard
Production.Product	Class	H = High, M = Medium, L = Low
Production.Product	Style	W = Womens, M = Mens, U = Universal
Production.Product	ProductSubcategoryID	Product is a member of this product subcategory. Foreign key to ProductSubCategory.ProductSubCategoryID.
Production.Product	ProductModelID	Product is a member of this product model. Foreign key to ProductModel.ProductModelID.
Production.Product	SellStartDate	Date the product was available for sale.
Production.Product	SellEndDate	Date the product was no longer available for sale.
Production.Product	DiscontinuedDate	Date the product was discontinued.
Production.Product	rowguid	ROWGUIDCOL number uniquely identifying the record. Used to support a merge replication sample.
Production.Product	ModifiedDate	Date and time the record was last updated.

Mountain Bikes in Production.Product Table

Query to list all mountain bikes offered for sale by AdventureWorks Cycles with category, subcategory, list price and standard cost information.

```
USE AdventureWorks2012;
SELECT  UPPER(PC.Name) AS Category, PSC.Name AS Subcategory,
        P.Name AS Product, FORMAT(ListPrice, 'c', 'en-US') AS ListPrice,
        FORMAT(StandardCost, 'c', 'en-US') AS StandardCost
FROM Production.Product AS P
  INNER JOIN Production.ProductSubcategory AS PSC
             ON PSC.ProductSubcategoryID = P.ProductSubcategoryID
  INNER JOIN Production.ProductCategory AS PC
             ON PC.ProductCategoryID = PSC.ProductCategoryID
WHERE PSC.Name = 'Mountain Bikes'
ORDER BY Category, Subcategory, Product;
```

Category	Subcategory	Product	ListPrice	StandardCost
BIKES	Mountain Bikes	Mountain-100 Black, 38	$3,374.99	$1,898.09
BIKES	Mountain Bikes	Mountain-100 Black, 42	$3,374.99	$1,898.09
BIKES	Mountain Bikes	Mountain-100 Black, 44	$3,374.99	$1,898.09
BIKES	Mountain Bikes	Mountain-100 Black, 48	$3,374.99	$1,898.09
BIKES	Mountain Bikes	Mountain-100 Silver, 38	$3,399.99	$1,912.15
BIKES	Mountain Bikes	Mountain-100 Silver, 42	$3,399.99	$1,912.15
BIKES	Mountain Bikes	Mountain-100 Silver, 44	$3,399.99	$1,912.15
BIKES	Mountain Bikes	Mountain-100 Silver, 48	$3,399.99	$1,912.15
BIKES	Mountain Bikes	Mountain-200 Black, 38	$2,294.99	$1,251.98
BIKES	Mountain Bikes	Mountain-200 Black, 42	$2,294.99	$1,251.98
BIKES	Mountain Bikes	Mountain-200 Black, 46	$2,294.99	$1,251.98
BIKES	Mountain Bikes	Mountain-200 Silver, 38	$2,319.99	$1,265.62
BIKES	Mountain Bikes	Mountain-200 Silver, 42	$2,319.99	$1,265.62
BIKES	Mountain Bikes	Mountain-200 Silver, 46	$2,319.99	$1,265.62
BIKES	Mountain Bikes	Mountain-300 Black, 38	$1,079.99	$598.44
BIKES	Mountain Bikes	Mountain-300 Black, 40	$1,079.99	$598.44
BIKES	Mountain Bikes	Mountain-300 Black, 44	$1,079.99	$598.44
BIKES	Mountain Bikes	Mountain-300 Black, 48	$1,079.99	$598.44
BIKES	Mountain Bikes	Mountain-400-W Silver, 38	$769.49	$419.78
BIKES	Mountain Bikes	Mountain-400-W Silver, 40	$769.49	$419.78
BIKES	Mountain Bikes	Mountain-400-W Silver, 42	$769.49	$419.78
BIKES	Mountain Bikes	Mountain-400-W Silver, 46	$769.49	$419.78
BIKES	Mountain Bikes	Mountain-500 Black, 40	$539.99	$294.58
BIKES	Mountain Bikes	Mountain-500 Black, 42	$539.99	$294.58
BIKES	Mountain Bikes	Mountain-500 Black, 44	$539.99	$294.58
BIKES	Mountain Bikes	Mountain-500 Black, 48	$539.99	$294.58
BIKES	Mountain Bikes	Mountain-500 Black, 52	$539.99	$294.58
BIKES	Mountain Bikes	Mountain-500 Silver, 40	$564.99	$308.22
BIKES	Mountain Bikes	Mountain-500 Silver, 42	$564.99	$308.22
BIKES	Mountain Bikes	Mountain-500 Silver, 44	$564.99	$308.22
BIKES	Mountain Bikes	Mountain-500 Silver, 48	$564.99	$308.22
BIKES	Mountain Bikes	Mountain-500 Silver, 52	$564.99	$308.22

Prior SQL Server Sample Databases

There are two other sample databases used in the releases of SQL Server: **Northwind** and **pubs**. Northwind has been introduced with SQL Server 7.0 in 1998. That SQL Server version had very short lifetime, replaced with SQL Server 2000 in year 2000. The pubs sample database originates from the time Microsoft & Sybase worked jointly on the database server project around 1990. Despite the relative simplicity of pre-2005 sample databases, they were good enough to demonstrate basic RDBMS SQL queries.

Book sales summary GROUP BY aggregation query.

```
USE pubs;
SELECT pub_name                 AS Publisher,
    au_lname                    AS Author,
    title                       AS Title,
    SUM(qty)                    AS SoldQty
FROM   authors
    INNER JOIN titleauthor
        ON authors.au_id = titleauthor.au_id
    INNER JOIN titles
        ON titles.title_id = titleauthor.title_id
    INNER JOIN publishers
        ON publishers.pub_id = titles.pub_id
    INNER JOIN sales
        ON sales.title_id = titles.title_id
GROUP  BY       pub_name,
                au_lname,
                title
ORDER BY Publisher, Author, Title;
-- (23 row(s) affected) - Partial results.
```

Publisher	Author	Title
Algodata Infosystems	Bennet	The Busy Executive's Database Guide
Algodata Infosystems	Carson	But Is It User Friendly?
Algodata Infosystems	Dull	Secrets of Silicon Valley
Algodata Infosystems	Green	The Busy Executive's Database Guide
Algodata Infosystems	Hunter	Secrets of Silicon Valley
Algodata Infosystems	MacFeather	Cooking with Computers: Surreptitious Balance Sheets
Algodata Infosystems	O'Leary	Cooking with Computers: Surreptitious Balance Sheets
Algodata Infosystems	Straight	Straight Talk About Computers
Binnet & Hardley	Blotchet-Halls	Fifty Years in Buckingham Palace Kitchens
Binnet & Hardley	DeFrance	The Gourmet Microwave

Northwind Sample Database

The Northwind database contains well-prepared sales data for a fictitious company called Northwind Traders, which imports & exports specialty gourmet foods & drinks from wholesale suppliers around the world. The company's sales offices are located in Seattle & London. Among gourmet food item products: Carnarvon Tigers, Teatime Chocolate Biscuits, Sir Rodney's Marmalade, Sir Rodney's Scones, Gustaf's Knäckebröd, Tunnbröd & Guaraná Fantástica.

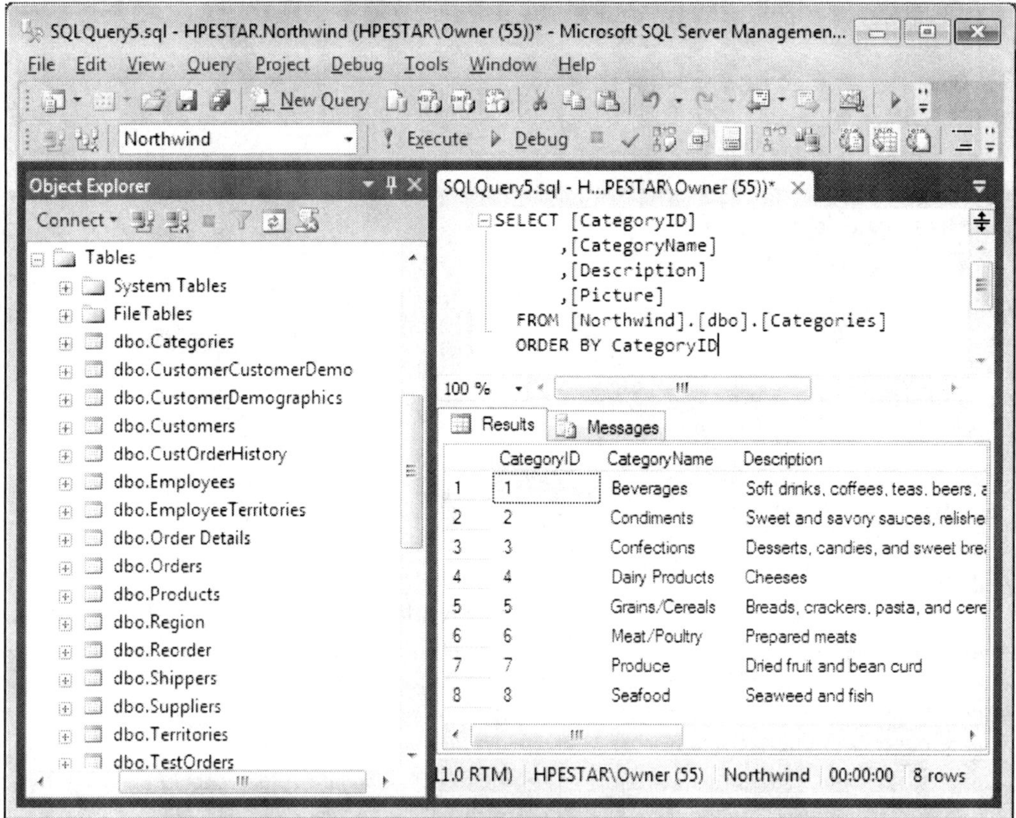

Diagram of Northwind Database

The basic diagram of Northwind database excluding a few ancillary tables. The Orders table is central since the business is wholesale distribution (reselling) of high-end food products.

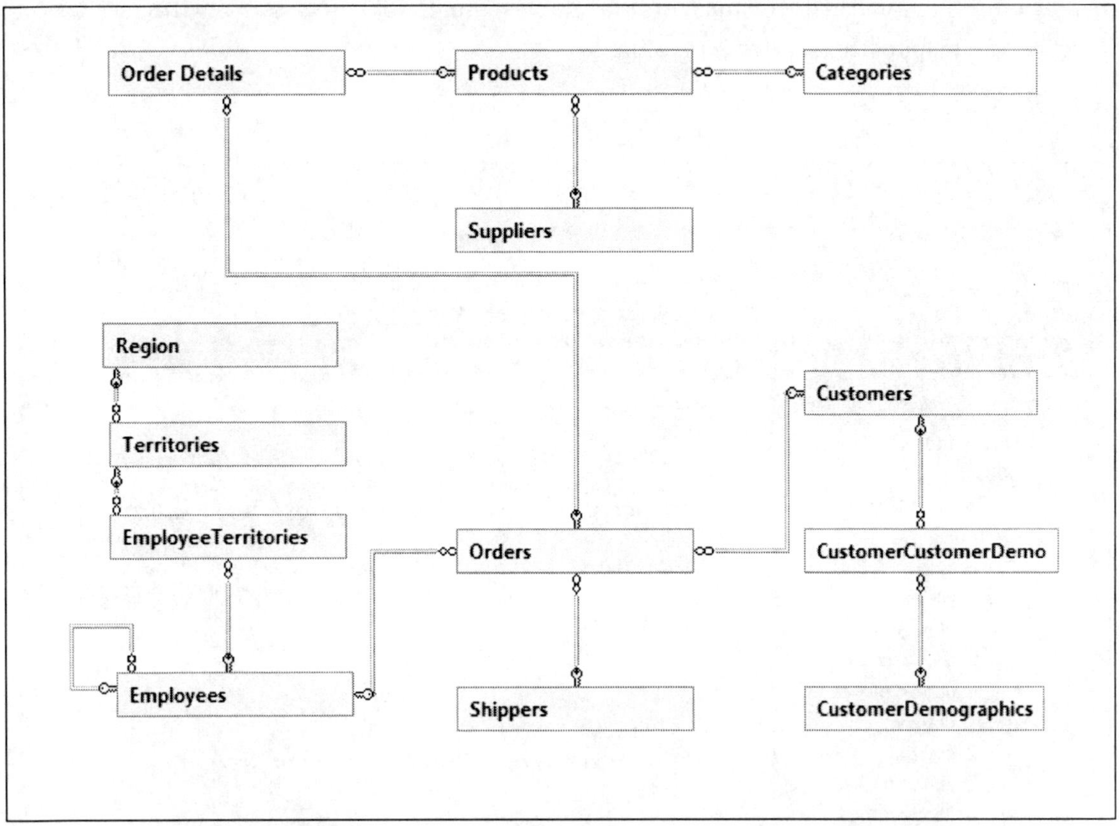

pubs Sample Database

The pubs database is a very small and simple publishing database, yet it demonstrates the main features of database design such as PRIMARY KEYs, FOREIGN KEYs, and junction table reflecting many-to-many relationship. The main entities (tables) are: (book) titles, authors, titleauthor (junction table), publishers, sales & royalties.

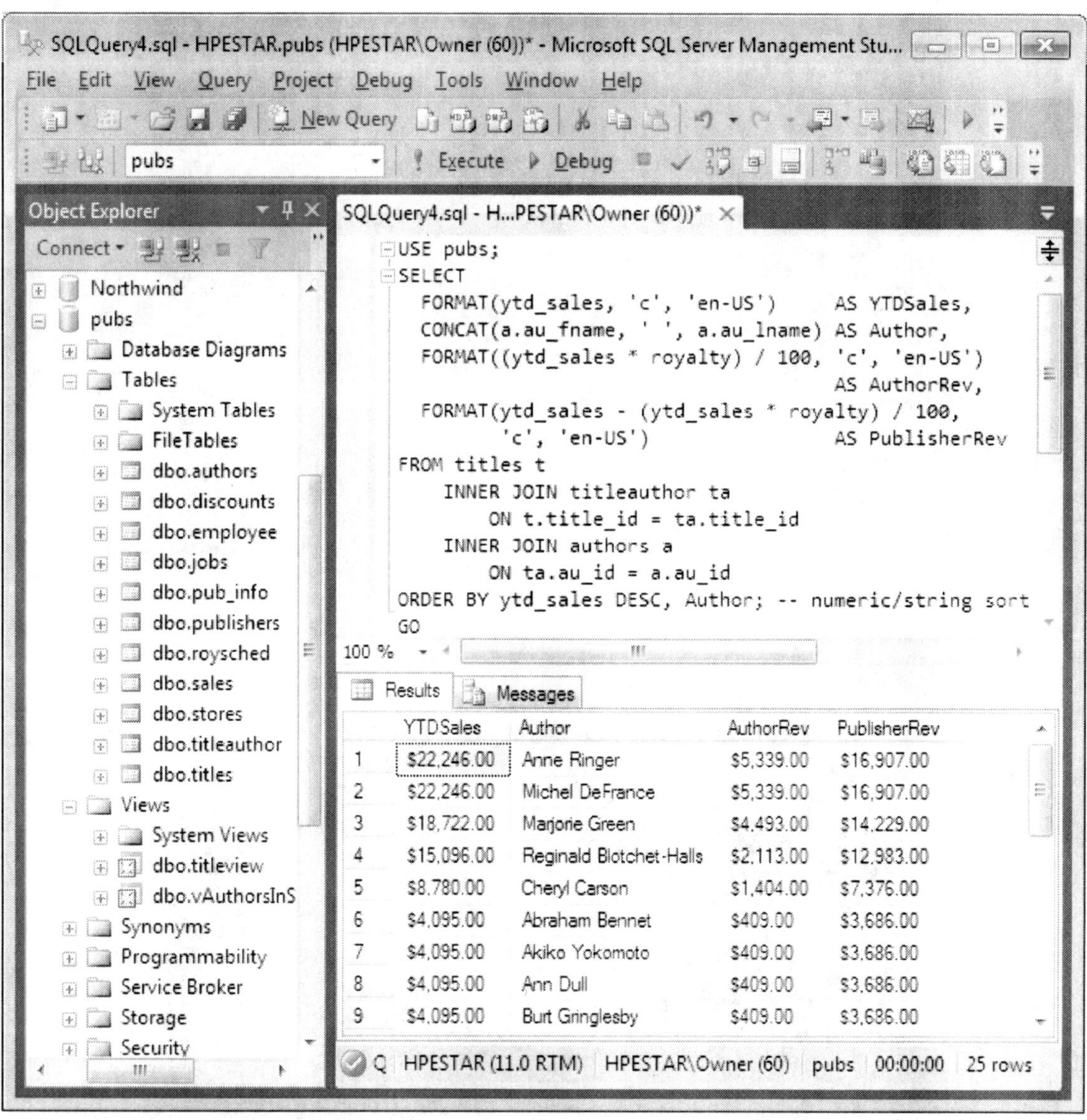

Book Titles in pubs Database

The titles table has the most interesting content in the pubs database as demonstrated by the following T-SQL query.

```
SELECT  TOP 4 title_id AS TitleID, title AS Title, type                          AS Type,
        pub_id AS PubID, FORMAT(price, 'c','en-US')                              AS Price,
        FORMAT(advance, 'c','en-US')                                             AS  Advance,
        FORMAT(royalty/100.0, 'p') AS Royalty, FORMAT(ytd_sales, 'c', 'en-US')   AS YTDSales,
        Notes
FROM pubs.dbo.titles
ORDER BY title;
```

TitleID	Title	Type	PubID	Price	Advance	Royalty	YTDSales	Notes
PC1035	But Is It User Friendly?	popular_comp	1389	$22.95	$7,000.00	16.00 %	$8,780.00	A survey of software for the naive user, focusing on the 'friendliness' of each.
PS1372	Computer Phobic AND Non-Phobic Individuals: Behavior Variations	psychology	0877	$21.59	$7,000.00	10.00 %	$375.00	A must for the specialist, this book examines the difference between those who hate and fear computers and those who don't.
BU1111	Cooking with Computers: Surreptitious Balance Sheets	business	1389	$11.95	$5,000.00	10.00 %	$3,876.00	Helpful hints on how to use your electronic resources to the best advantage.
PS7777	Emotional Security: A New Algorithm	psychology	0736	$7.99	$4,000.00	10.00 %	$3,336.00	Protecting yourself and your loved ones from undue emotional stress in the modern world. Use of computer and nutritional aids emphasized.

Diagram of pubs Database

Since pubs is a small database, the diagram conveniently fits on a page.

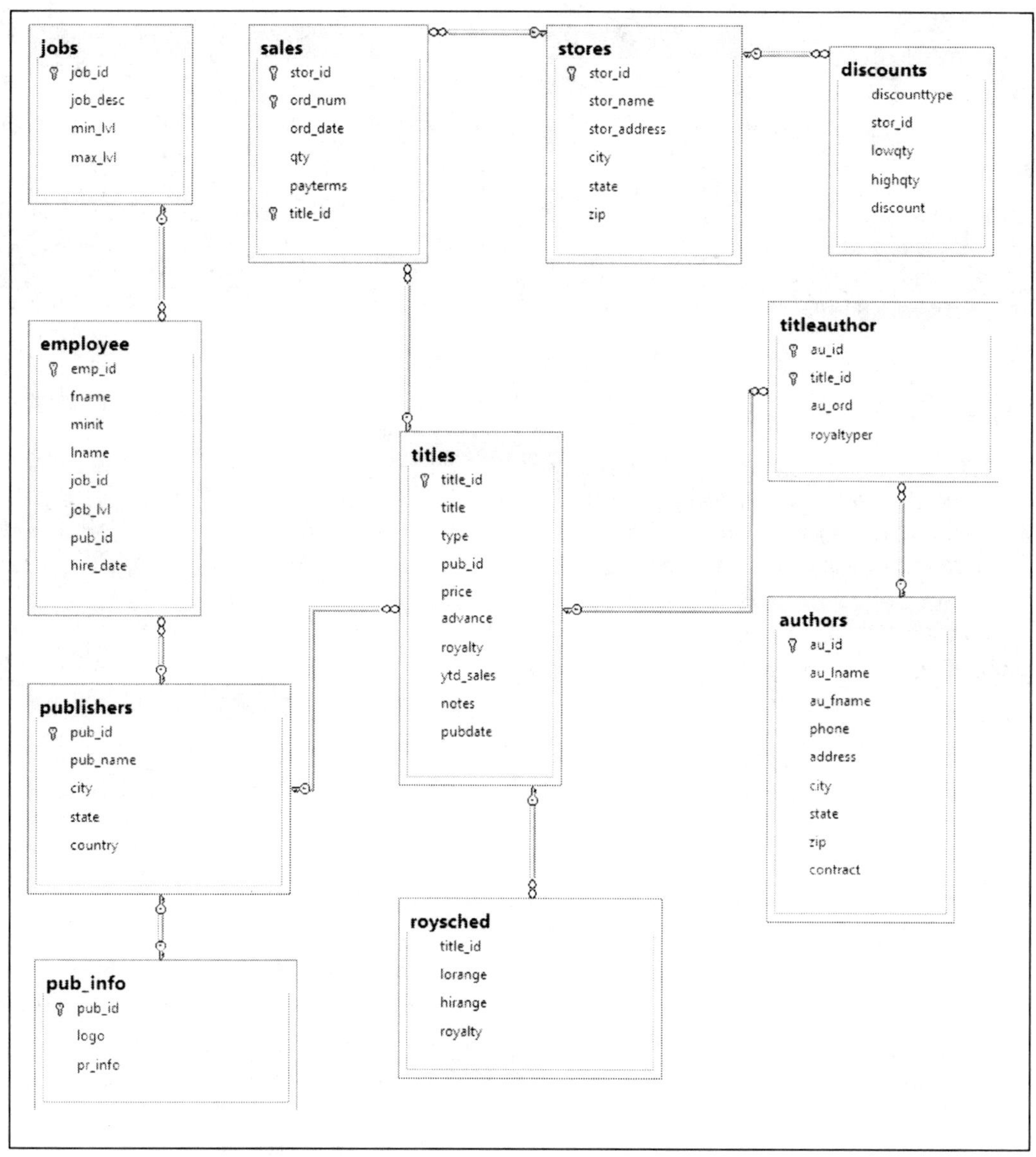

Simple JOIN on non-key columns.

```
USE pubs; SELECT p.*, a.* FROM authors AS a
INNER JOIN publishers AS p ON a.city = p.city ORDER BY p.city, a.au_lname;
```

pub_id	pub_name	city	state	country	au_id	au_lname	au_fname	phone	address	city	state	zip	contract
1389	Algodata Infosystems	Berkeley	CA	USA	409-56-7008	Bennet	Abraham	415 658-9932	6223 Bateman St.	Berkeley	CA	94705	1
1389	Algodata Infosystems	Berkeley	CA	USA	238-95-7766	Carson	Cheryl	415 548-7723	589 Darwin Ln.	Berkeley	CA	94705	1

SQL Server System Databases

The master, model, tempdb and msdb are system databases for special database server operations purposes. SSMS Object Explorer drill-down listing of system databases.

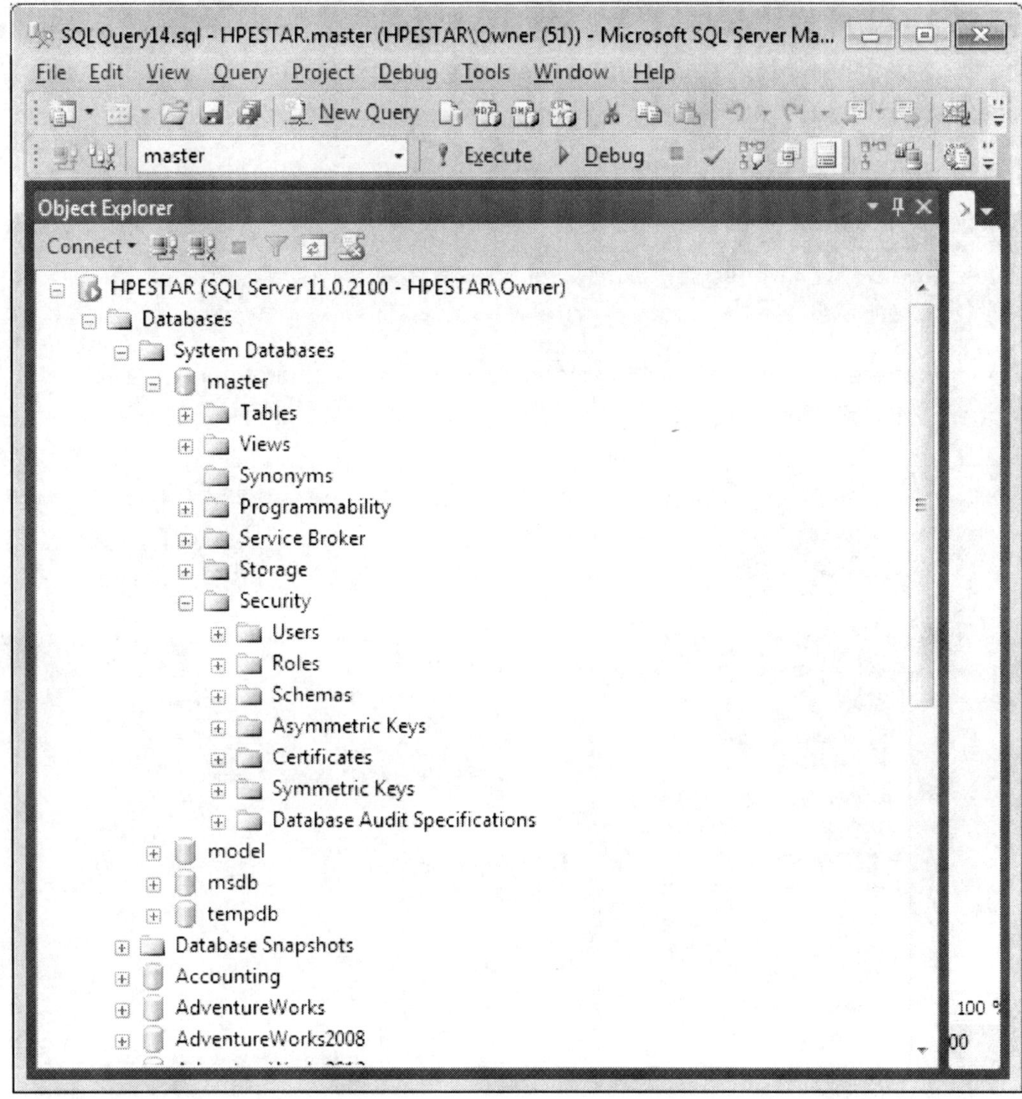

Query to create a new table in tempdb for development purposes.

```
SELECT * INTO tempdb.dbo.Product
FROM AdventureWorks2012.Production.Product
WHERE ListPrice > 0.0;
-- (304 row(s) affected)
```

The master Database

The master system database is the nerve center of SQL Server. It contains tables and db objects essential for server operations. System tables are accessible only through read-only views. System tables cannot be changed by users. A subset of the system views are called Dynamic Management Views (DMV) which return server state information for monitoring the operational aspects of a SQL Server instance, diagnosing problems, and performance tuning. Dynamic Management Functions (DMF) are applied in conjunction with DMVs.

```
SELECT TOP 5    ST.text,
                EQS.*
FROM master.sys.dm_exec_query_stats AS EQS                          -- DMV
CROSS APPLY master.sys.dm_exec_sql_text(EQS.sql_handle) as ST       -- DMF
ORDER BY last_worker_time DESC;
```

SQL Server Management Studio Object Explorer display of some objects in the master database and a query listing all databases.

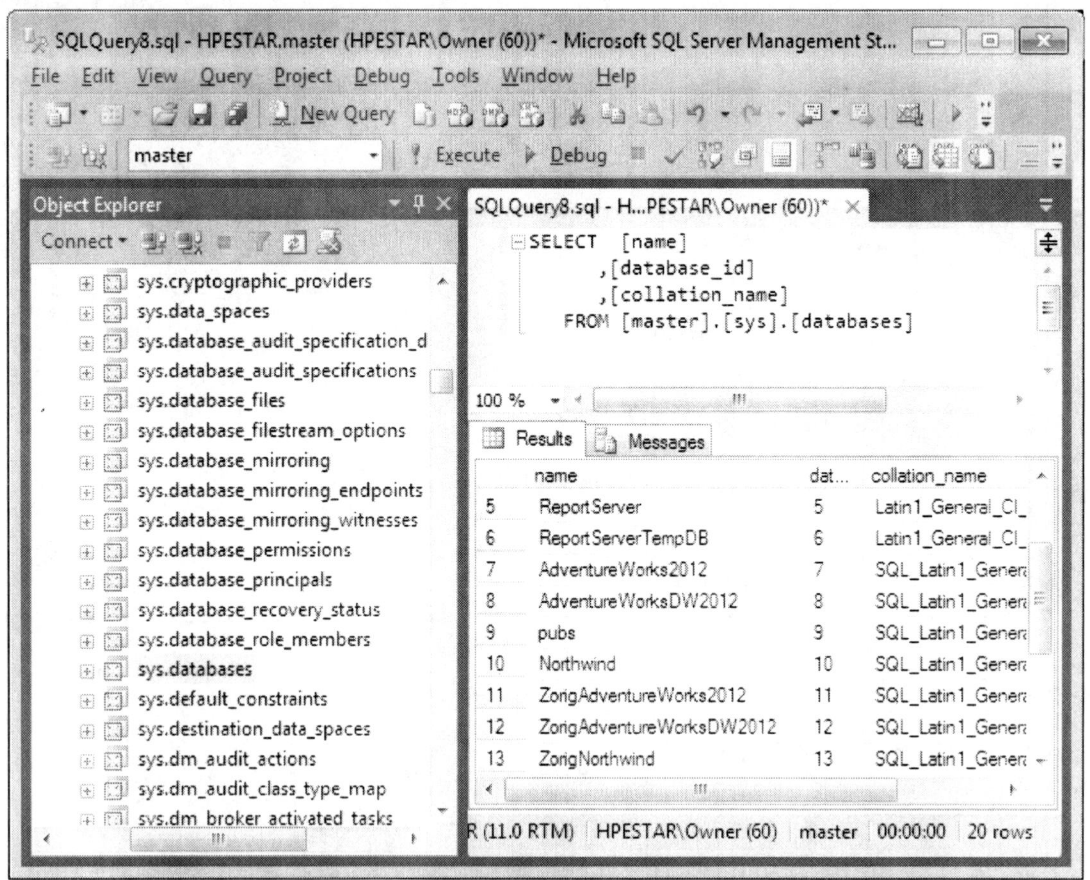

An Important System View In master Database: sys.databases

```
SELECT TOP (10) name, database_id
FROM master.sys.databases
ORDER BY database_id;
```

name	database_id
master	1
tempdb	2
model	3
msdb	4
ReportServer	5
ReportServerTempDB	6
AdventureWorks2012	7
AdventureWorksDW2012	8
pubs	9
Northwind	10

spt_values table in master database can be used for integer sequence with a range of 0 - 2047.

```
-- End of the range - BOTTOM
SELECT TOP 5 number FROM master.dbo.spt_values WHERE TYPE='P'
ORDER BY number DESC;
```

number
2047
2046
2045
2044
2043

Example for using the sequence in spt_values to generate DATE and MONTH sequences.

```
SELECT TOP 5 number,   dateadd(day, number, '20000101')        AS "Date",
                       dateadd(mm, number, '20000101')         AS "Month"
FROM master.dbo.spt_values  WHERE type = 'P'  ORDER BY number;
```

number	Date	Month
0	2000-01-01 00:00:00.000	2000-01-01 00:00:00.000
1	2000-01-02 00:00:00.000	2000-02-01 00:00:00.000
2	2000-01-03 00:00:00.000	2000-03-01 00:00:00.000
3	2000-01-04 00:00:00.000	2000-04-01 00:00:00.000
4	2000-01-05 00:00:00.000	2000-05-01 00:00:00.000

The model Database

The model database serves as prototype for a new database. The model database is also the prototype for tempdb when the SQL Server instance started. Upon server shutdown or restart everything is wiped out of tempdb, it starts with a clean slate as a copy of the model database. Therefore we should only place objects into the tempdb can be purged any time.

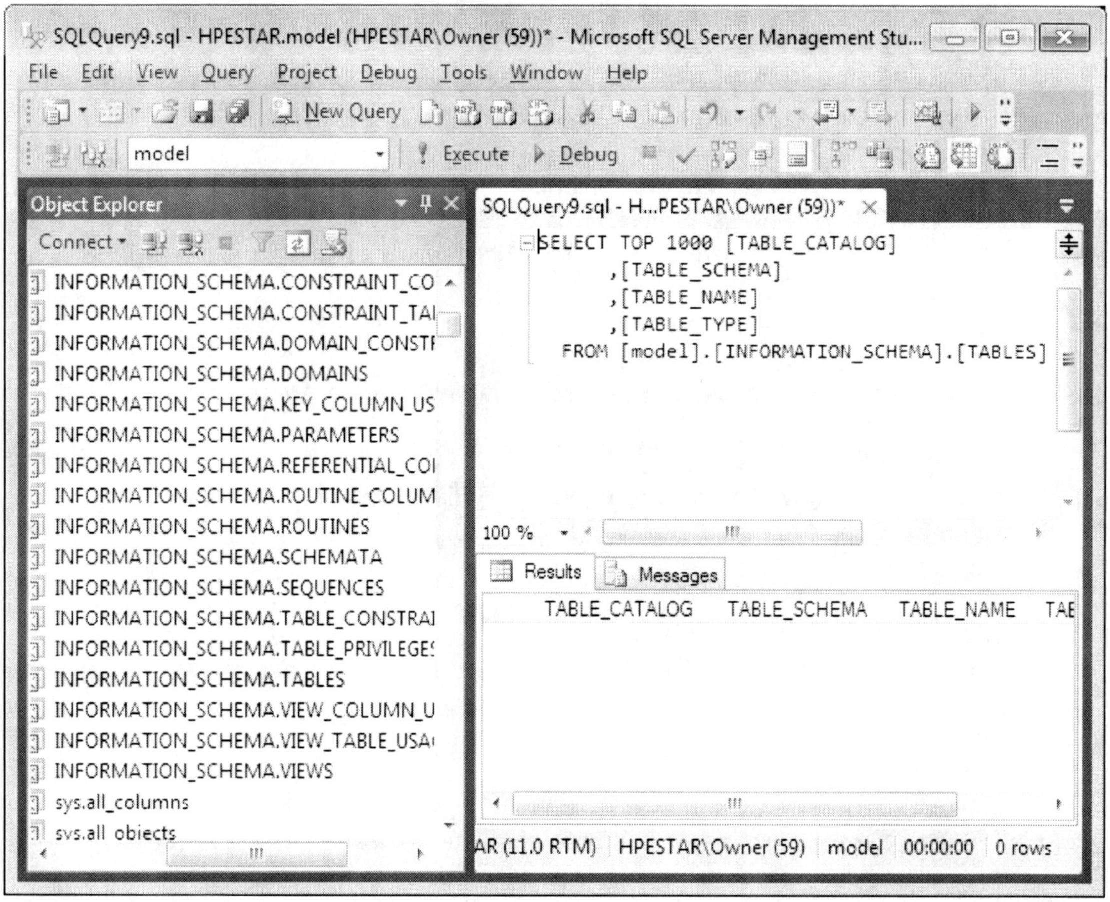

SQLQuery9.sql - HPESTAR.model (HPESTAR\Owner (59))* - Microsoft SQL Server Management Stu...

Object Explorer

INFORMATION_SCHEMA.CONSTRAINT_CO
INFORMATION_SCHEMA.CONSTRAINT_TAI
INFORMATION_SCHEMA.DOMAIN_CONSTI
INFORMATION_SCHEMA.DOMAINS
INFORMATION_SCHEMA.KEY_COLUMN_US
INFORMATION_SCHEMA.PARAMETERS
INFORMATION_SCHEMA.REFERENTIAL_COI
INFORMATION_SCHEMA.ROUTINE_COLUM
INFORMATION_SCHEMA.ROUTINES
INFORMATION_SCHEMA.SCHEMATA
INFORMATION_SCHEMA.SEQUENCES
INFORMATION_SCHEMA.TABLE_CONSTRAI
INFORMATION_SCHEMA.TABLE_PRIVILEGES
INFORMATION_SCHEMA.TABLES
INFORMATION_SCHEMA.VIEW_COLUMN_U
INFORMATION_SCHEMA.VIEW_TABLE_USA
INFORMATION_SCHEMA.VIEWS
sys.all_columns
sys.all_objects

```
SELECT TOP 1000 [TABLE_CATALOG]
      ,[TABLE_SCHEMA]
      ,[TABLE_NAME]
      ,[TABLE_TYPE]
  FROM [model].[INFORMATION_SCHEMA].[TABLES]
```

TABLE_CATALOG	TABLE_SCHEMA	TABLE_NAME	TAE

AR (11.0 RTM) | HPESTAR\Owner (59) | model | 00:00:00 | 0 rows

The msdb Database

The msdb database is used for server internal operations such as support for SQL Server Agent job scheduling facility or keeping track of database the all important backups and restores.

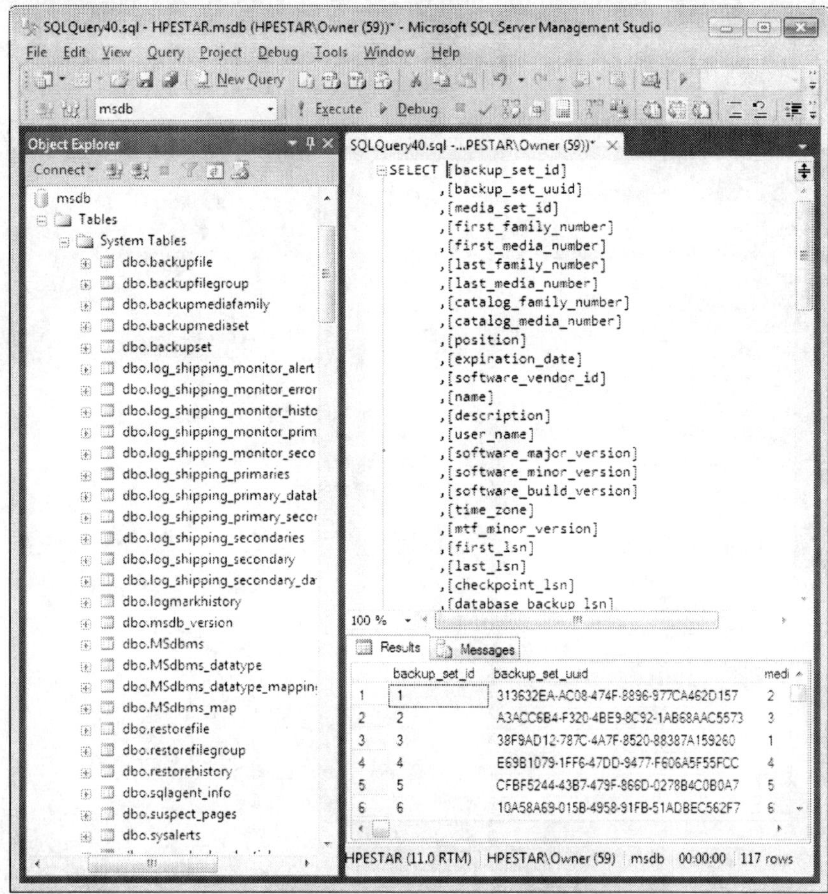

Database backup history query using table in msdb database.

```
SELECT  s.name AS Name, CONVERT(DATE,MAX(b.backup_finish_date)) AS LastGoodBackup,
        b.type AS Type
FROM master.dbo.sysdatabases AS s
LEFT OUTER JOIN msdb.dbo.backupset AS b ON s.name = b.database_name
GROUP BY s.name, b.type ORDER BY Name, Type;
```

Name	LastGoodBackup	Type
Accounting	2016-11-29	D
AdventureWorks	2016-11-29	D
AdventureWorks2008	2016-11-29	D
AdventureWorks2012	2016-11-29	D

The tempdb Database

The tempdb serves as temporary database for system operations such as sorting. Temporary tables (#temp1) and global temporary tables (##globaltemp1) are stored in the tempdb as well. "Permanent" tables can be created in tempdb with a short lifetime which lasts till shutdown or restart.

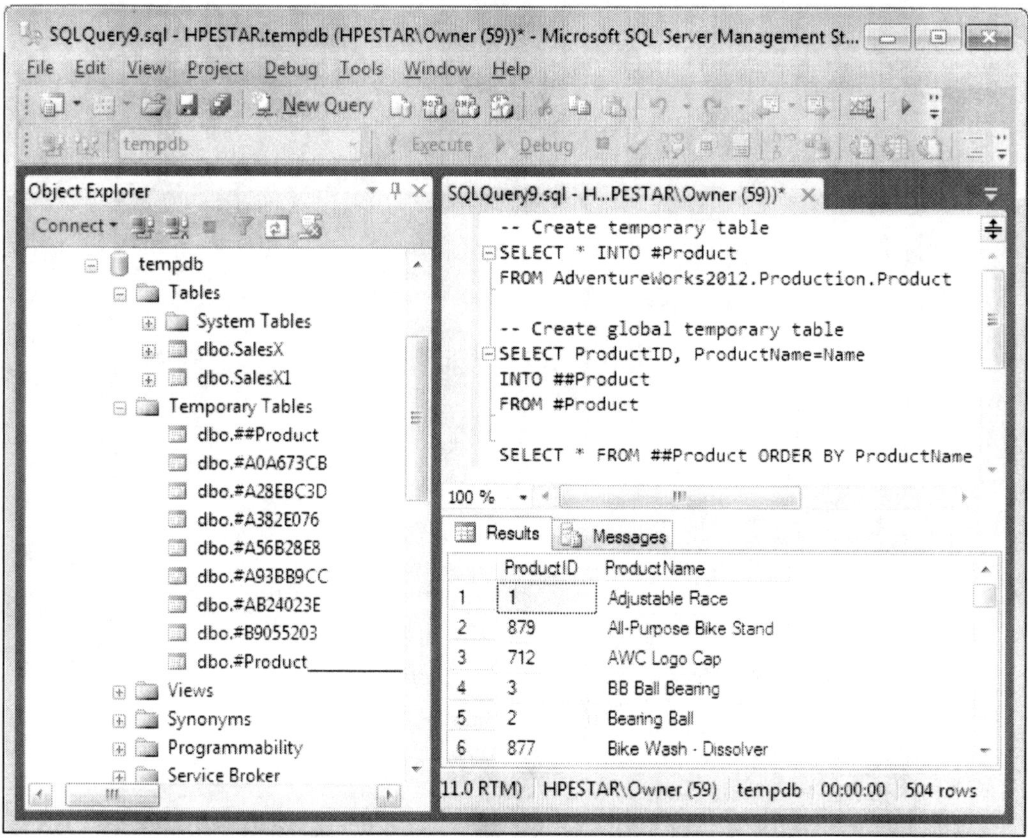

Sudden Death in tempdb When Server Restarts

Even though a temporary table and a global temporary table are created and queried in the context setting for AdventureWorks2012 database, they are placed into tempdb automatically. Same consideration when a temporary table is created from a stored procedure which is compiled in an application database. Upon server restart everything is wiped out of tempdb, rebirth follows as a copy of model db. We should not place anything into tempdb we cannot afford to lose. tempdb is also used by SQL Server engine for operations such as version control, sorting and more.

Instead of GUI & mouse use T-SQL scripts which can be saved as .sql disk files.

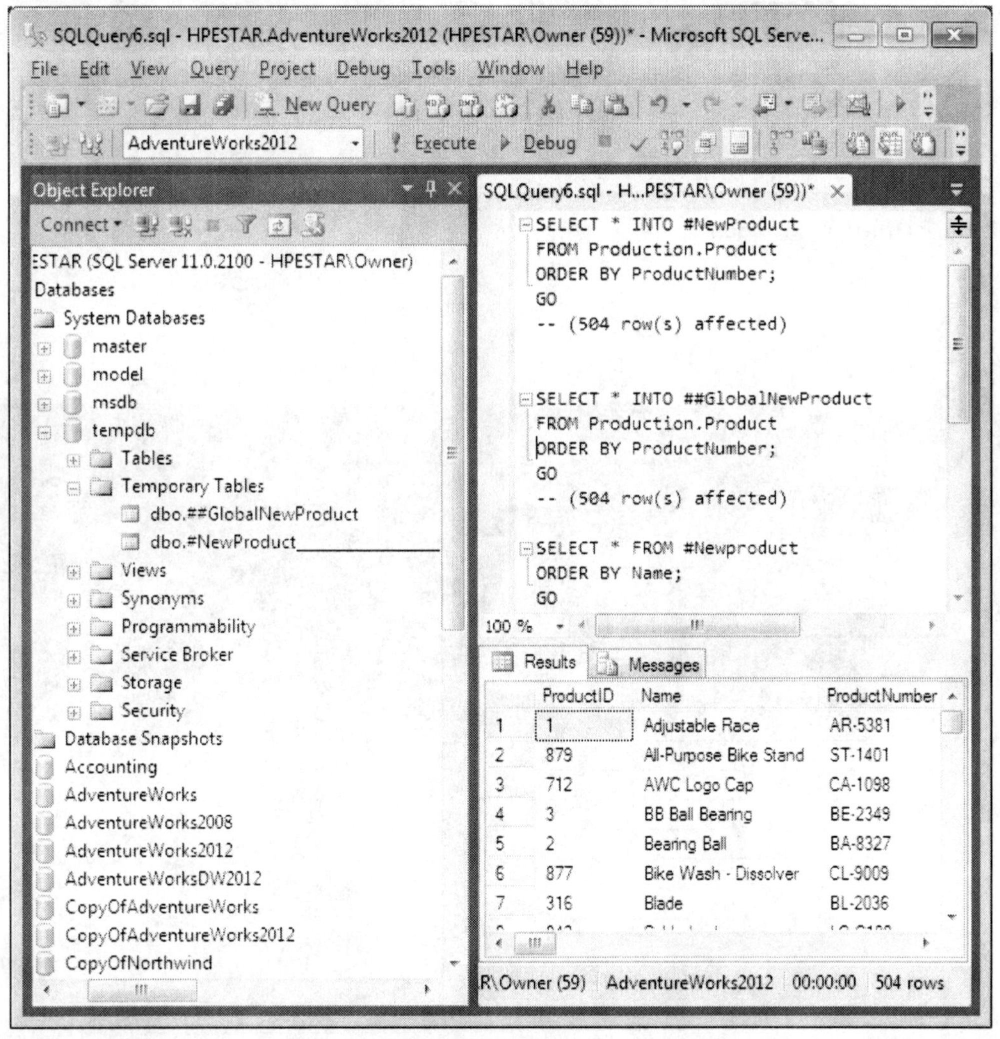

CHAPTER 2: Installing SQL Server 2012

SQL Server 2012 Express Edition Installation

The **Express Edition** is free. It can be installed from the following webpage.

http://www.microsoft.com/sqlserver/en/us/editions/2012-editions/express.aspx

Installation instructions provided.

SQL Server 2012 Evaluation Edition Installation

The **Evaluation Edition** is free for a certain time period like 6 months. It can be installed from the following webpage.

http://www.microsoft.com/en-us/download/details.aspx?id=29066

Installation instructions provided.

SQL Server 2012 Pay Edition Installation

The installation process from the distribution DVD is fairly automatic. Product key (4 x 5 alphanumeric) entry is required near the beginning of the installation.

Planning tab has the preparation steps.

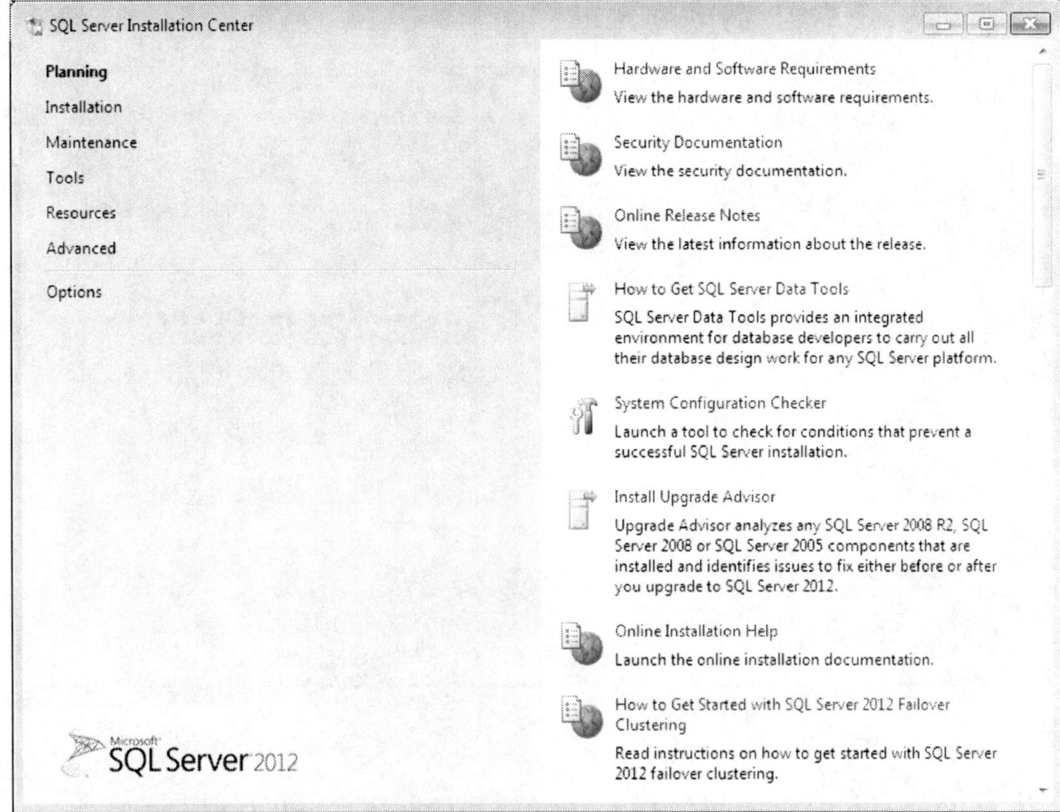

T-SQL Tidbits: MONEY Data Type

Data type	Range	Storage	Precision	Scale
MONEY	-922,337,203,685,477.5808 to 922,337,203,685,477.5807	8 bytes	19	4

MONEY is fixed precision (number of all digits) & fixed scale (number of decimals). MONEY corresponds to DECIMAL(19,4). DECIMAL (or NUMERIC) is variable precision. MONEY can be used for national currencies.

SELECT TOP(1) FORMAT(Subtotal,'c0','en-US') FROM AdventureWorks2012.Sales.SalesOrderHeader;	$20,566
SELECT TOP(1) FORMAT(Subtotal,'c2','de-DE') FROM AdventureWorks2012.Sales.SalesOrderHeader;	20.565,62 €
SELECT TOP(1) FORMAT(Subtotal,'c2','en-GB') FROM AdventureWorks2012.Sales.SalesOrderHeader;	£20,565.62

The Installation tab has the SQL Server and Client Tools (SS Management Studio is a client tool) install options.

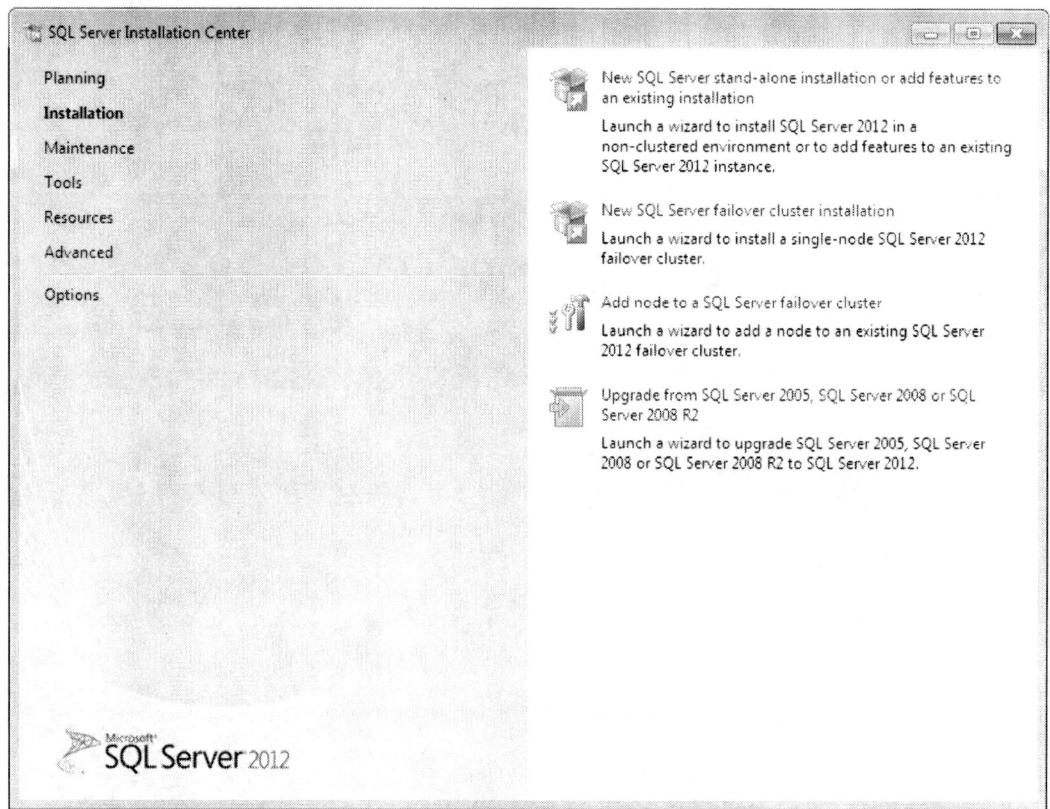

T-SQL Tidbits: Differences Between Stored Procedure & Function

- Stored procedure is READ/WRITE database. Function is READ database only.
- A function (UDF) can be called from a stored procedure but not vice versa.
- Stored procedure is called by: EXEC SprocName.
- Scalar-valued (single value) function is called by: SELECT dbo.FunctionName...
- Table-valued function is called by: SELECT ... FROM dbo.FunctionName... or CROSS APPLY.
- Function defintion T-SQL logic has more limitations than stored procedure logic.
- An inline table-valued function is defined by a single query with optional parameter.
- Result set of a stored procedure cannot be used in a JOIN (work around OPENQUERY).

Setup Support Rules page shows the results of preliminary checks for installation readiness. Failed issues require fix.

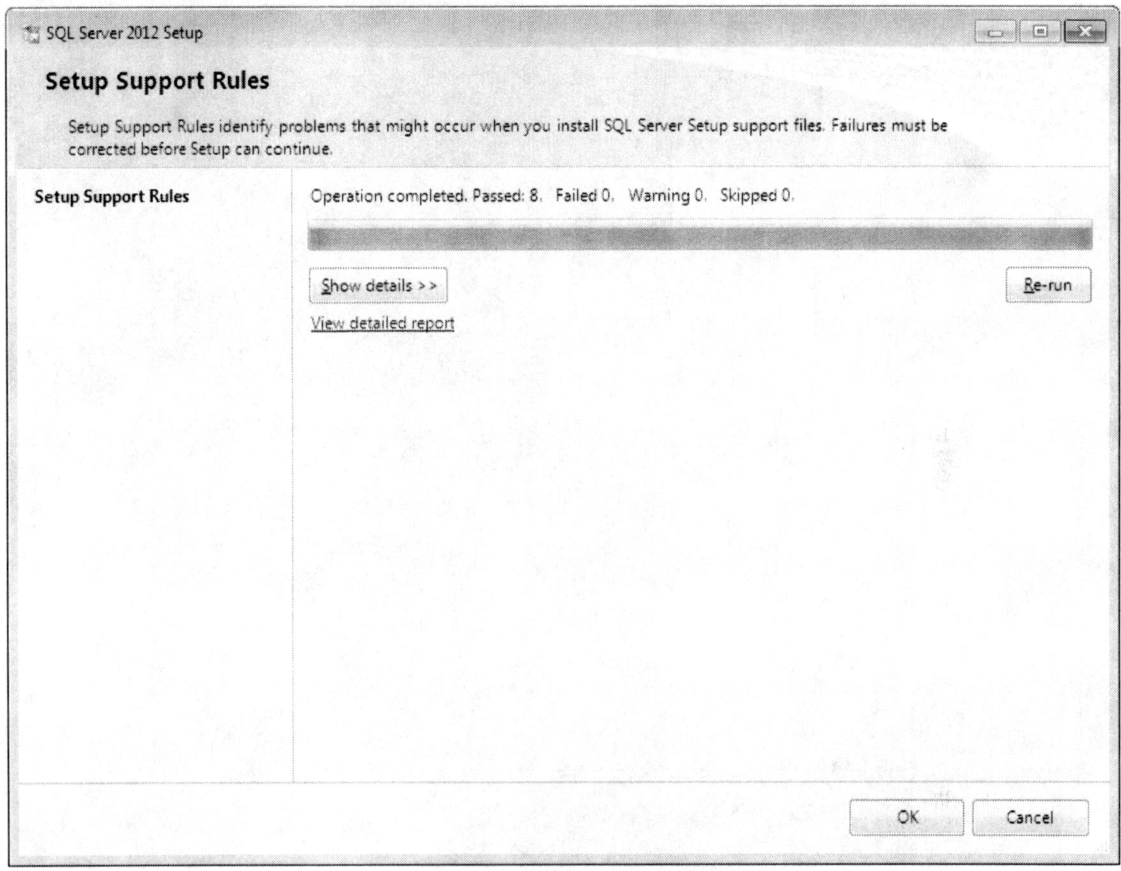

T-SQL Tidbits: Using ROLLUP & CUBE with GROUP BY

To generate automatic aggregation for grouping levels, ROLLUP or CUBE can be used.

```
SELECT [Year]=YEAR(OrderDate), [Month]=MONTH(OrderDate), Total=SUM(Subtotal)
FROM AdventureWorks2012.Sales.SalesOrderHeader
GROUP BY ROLLUP (YEAR(OrderDate), MONTH(OrderDate));
-- (42 row(s) affected)
```

```
SELECT [Year]=YEAR(OrderDate), [Month]=MONTH(OrderDate), Total=SUM(Subtotal)
FROM AdventureWorks2012.Sales.SalesOrderHeader
GROUP BY CUBE (YEAR(OrderDate), MONTH(OrderDate));
-- (54 row(s) affected)
```

Product Updates page checks the web for latest updates.

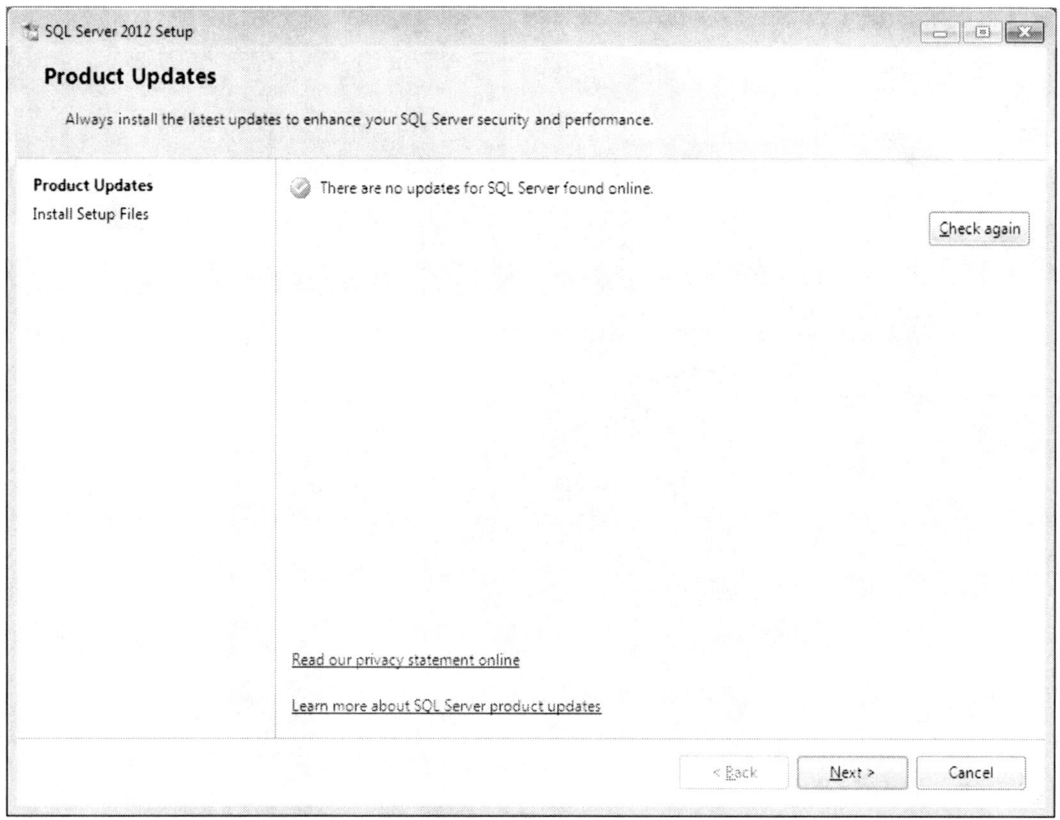

T-SQL Tidbits: Object Delimiters in T-SQL

Quoted identifiers are delimited by double quotation marks (").

```
SELECT * FROM "HumanResources"."Department";  -- ANSI
```

Bracketed identifiers are delimited by brackets ([ ]).

```
SELECT * FROM [HumanResources].[Department];
```

Spaces are allowed in identifiers, but they usually lead to confusion & loss of productivity. Ditto for double underscores (__) in identifiers.

Setup Support Rules page performs a number of internal system checks.

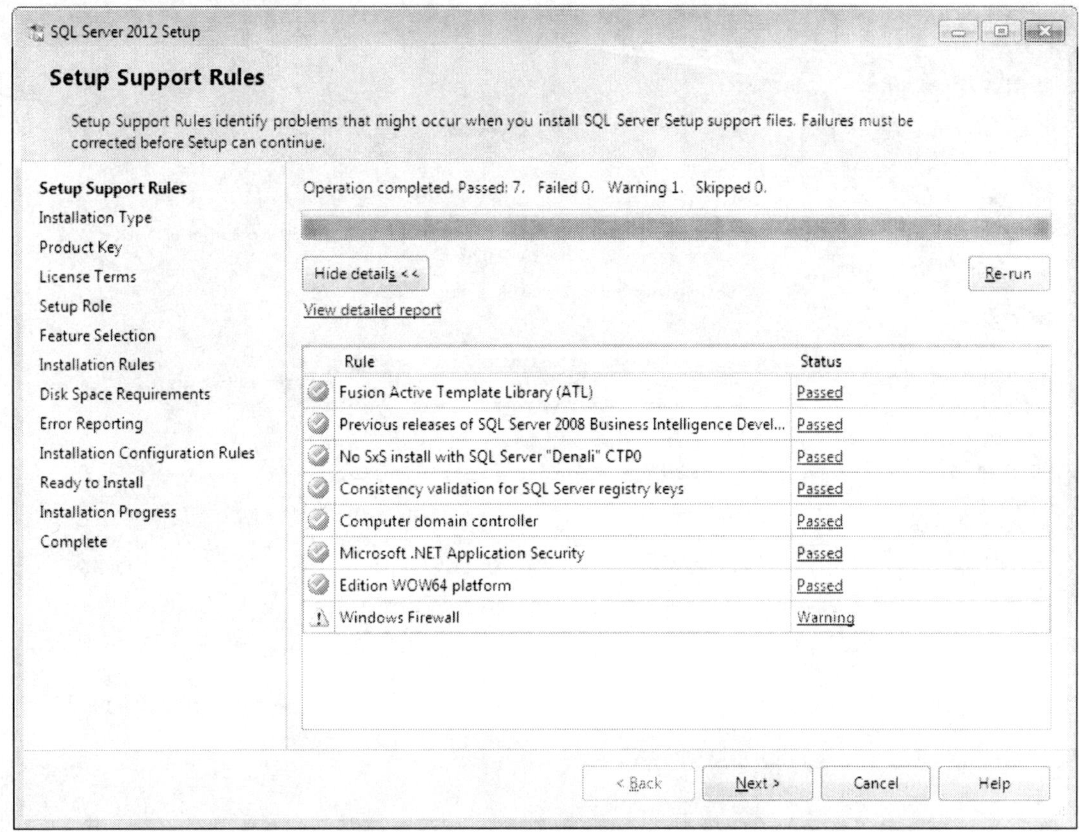

T-SQL Tidbits: Difference between View and Inline Table-Valued Function (ITVF)

Both are single statement definition & both return a table dataset, that is common. Differences:

- ITVF can accept parameter(s)
- View is database READ/WRITE (the underlying table)
- ITVF database READ only
- View can be indexed (indexed view)
- View can have instead of trigger giving it more logic & WRITE capability

Installation Type page displays currently installed SQL Server products.

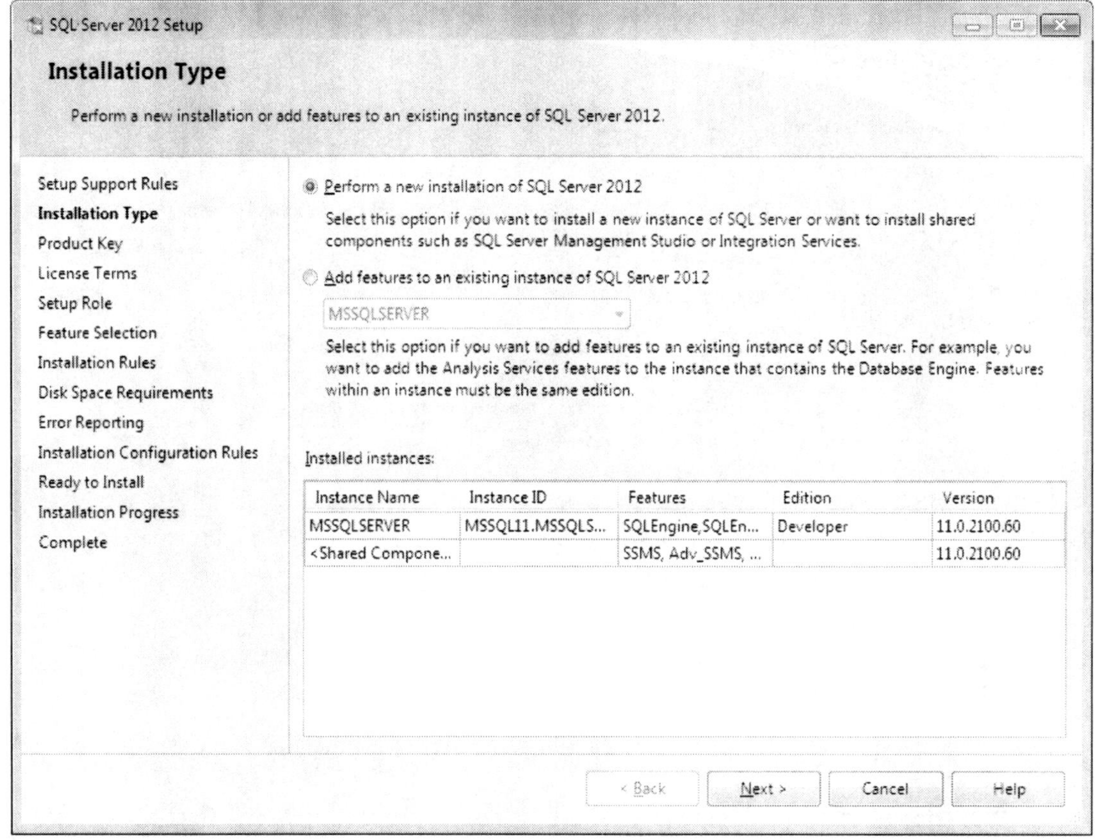

T-SQL Tidbits: View Can Be Used in a Table-Valued Function but Not Vice Versa

A view can be used READ only just like a table in a table-valued function. A TVF cannot be used in a view with parameter (it can be used with no parameter or literal value).

```
USE AdventureWorks2012;
GO
CREATE FUNCTION ufnProdColor(@Color varchar(20)) RETURNS TABLE AS
RETURN (SELECT * FROM Production.Product WHERE Color=@Color);
GO
CREATE VIEW vProdColor AS SELECT * FROM dbo.ufnProdColor( @Color );
GO
/*Msg 137, Level 15, State 2, Procedure vProdColor, Line 2 Must declare the scalar variable "@Color". */
```

Product Key page requests key entry from packaging box inside cover.

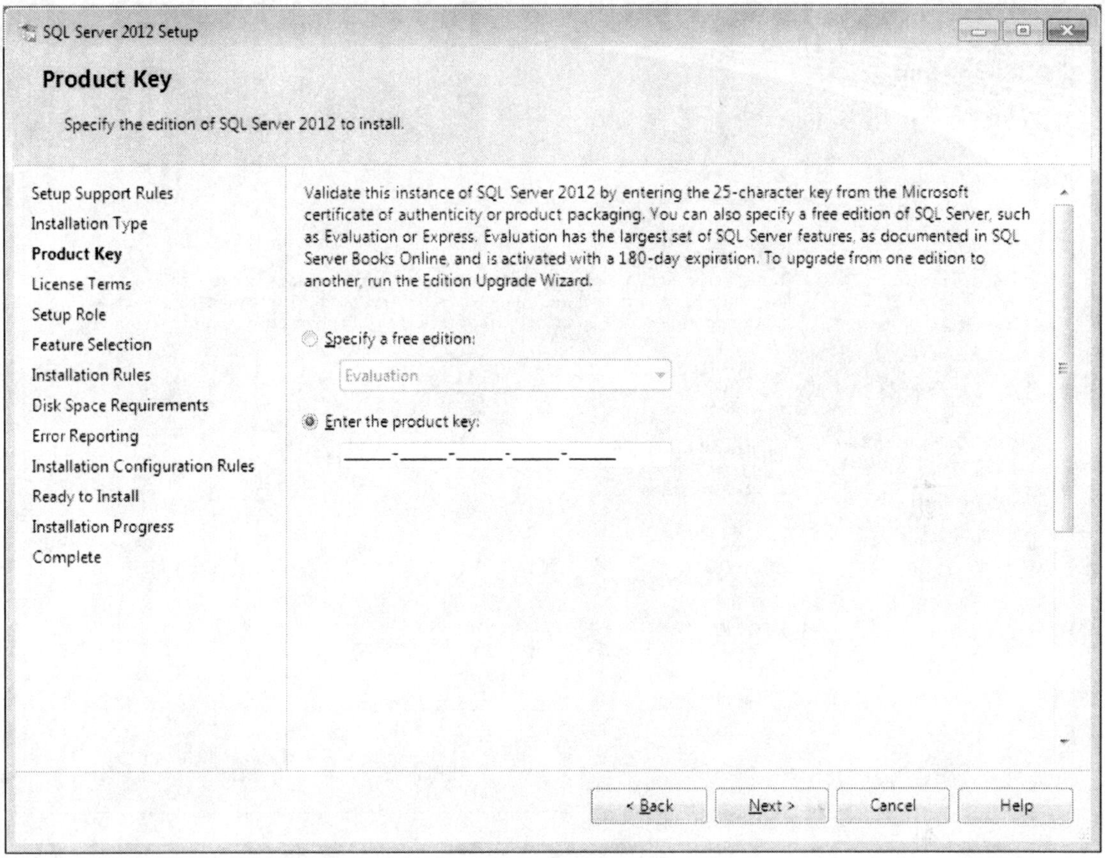

SQL Server 2012 Setup

Product Key

Specify the edition of SQL Server 2012 to install.

Setup Support Rules
Installation Type
Product Key
License Terms
Setup Role
Feature Selection
Installation Rules
Disk Space Requirements
Error Reporting
Installation Configuration Rules
Ready to Install
Installation Progress
Complete

Validate this instance of SQL Server 2012 by entering the 25-character key from the Microsoft certificate of authenticity or product packaging. You can also specify a free edition of SQL Server, such as Evaluation or Express. Evaluation has the largest set of SQL Server features, as documented in SQL Server Books Online, and is activated with a 180-day expiration. To upgrade from one edition to another, run the Edition Upgrade Wizard.

Specify a free edition:

Evaluation

Enter the product key:

< Back | Next > | Cancel | Help

T-SQL Tidbits: The SOUNDEX() Function to Check Sound Alikes

The soundex() function is very useful for testing different spelling of words such as names.

```
USE AdventureWorks2012;
SELECT DISTINCT LastName FROM Person.Person WHERE soundex(LastName)=soundex('Steel');
```

LastName
Seidel
Sotelo
Stahl
Steel
Steele

License terms page requires acceptance checkmark.

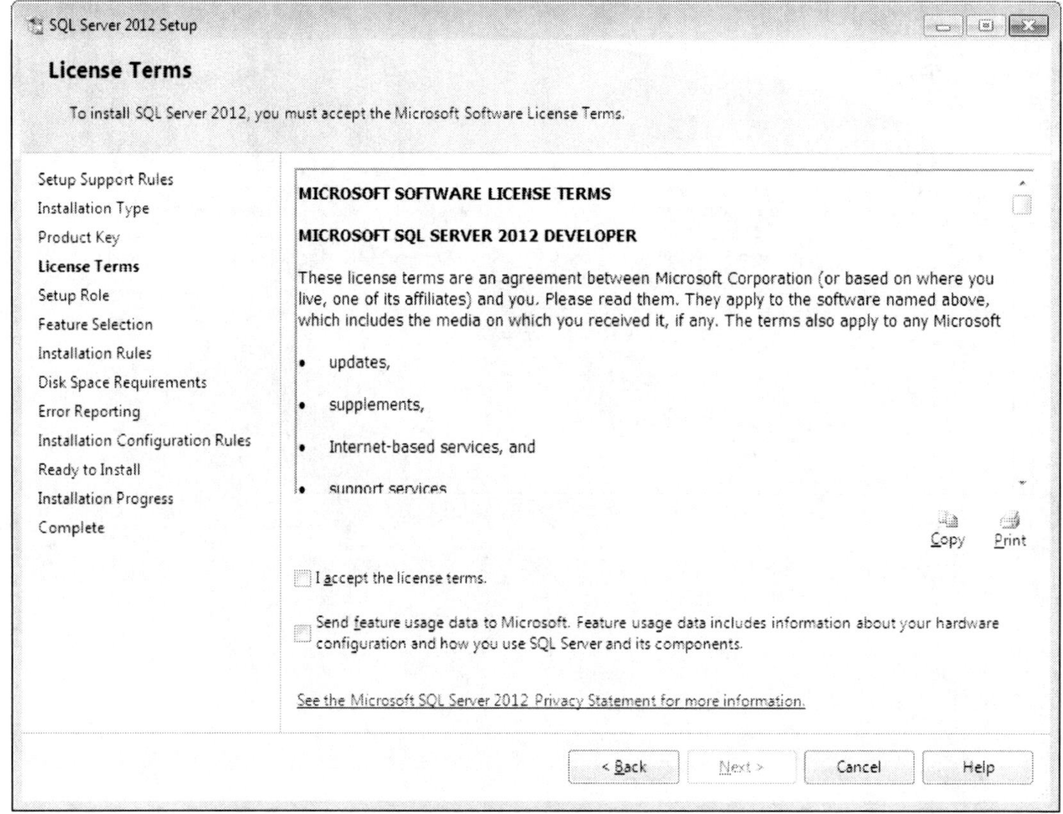

T-SQL Tidbits: SELECT Query Results in Text Mode

```
USE AdventureWorks2012; SELECT TOP 1 * FROM Sales.SalesOrderHeader H
        INNER JOIN Sales.SalesOrderDetail D  ON H.SalesOrderID = D.SalesOrderID;
```

```
SalesOrderID RevisionNumber OrderDate          DueDate          ShipDate          Status OnlineOrderFlag SalesOrderNumber
PurchaseOrderNumber    AccountNumber  CustomerID  SalesPersonID TerritoryID BillToAddressID ShipToAddressID ShipMethodID CreditCardID
CreditCardApprovalCode CurrencyRateID SubTotal          TaxAmt          Freight          TotalDue          Comment
rowguid                    ModifiedDate          SalesOrderID SalesOrderDetailID CarrierTrackingNumber    OrderQty ProductID   SpecialOfferID UnitPrice
UnitPriceDiscount    LineTotal                    rowguid                    ModifiedDate
------------ ------------- ---------------------- ---------------------- ---------------------- ------ -------------- ------------------------- ------------------------ -------------- ----------- -
------------ ----------- --------------- --------------- ------------ ------------ --------------------- ------------- --------------------- --------------------- --------------------- -----------------
---- --------------------------------------------------------------------------------------------------------------------------------- ----------------------------------- ----------------------- -------
----- ------------------ ------------------------- -------- ----------- ------------- --------------------- --------------------- ------------------------------------- -------------------------------
---- -----------------------
43659    3          2005-07-01 00:00:00.000 2005-07-13 00:00:00.000 2005-07-08 00:00:00.000 5    0          SO43659          PO522145787
10-4020-000676  29825     279     5     985     985     5     16281     105041Vi84182     NULL     20565.6206     1971.5149
616.0984          23153.2339          NULL                                                  79B65321-39CA-4115-9CBA-
8FE0903E12E6 2005-07-08 00:00:00.000 43659     1          4911-403C-98          1     776     1          2024.994          0.00
2024.994000                    B207C96D-D9E6-402B-8470-2CC176C42283 2005-07-01 00:00:00.000
```

Setup Role page lists installation options. "All Features with Defaults" is the easiest to install.

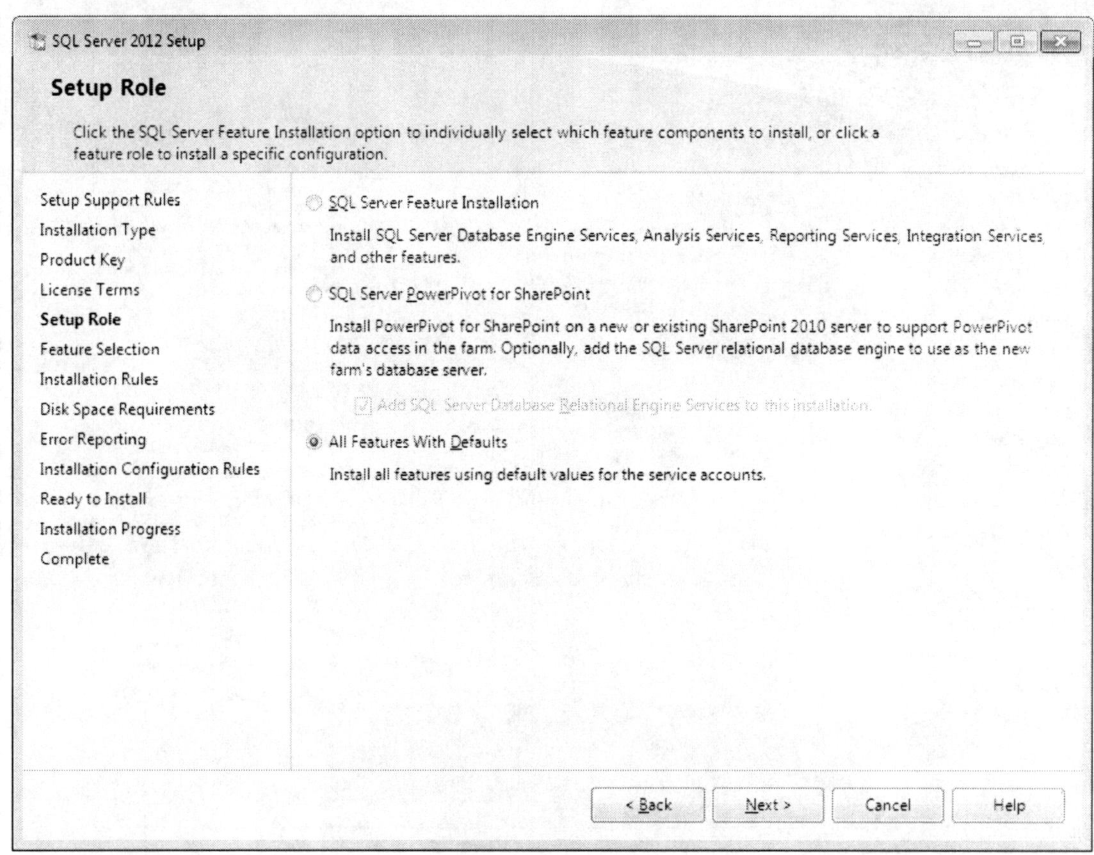

T-SQL Tidbits: ANSI Syntax Options in T-SQL

There are a few opportunities to use ANSI-SQL (same in ORACLE, SYBASE & DB2) syntax:

- CURRENT_TIMESTAMP (ANSI) instead of getdate() (T-SQL)
- COALESCE (ANSI) instead of isnull() (T-SQL)
- INFORMATION_SCHEMA views instead of some sys (system) views
- " (double quote) object delimiter (ANSI) instead of square brackets []
- SET ANSI_... options

Feature Selection page can be used to pick & choose features.

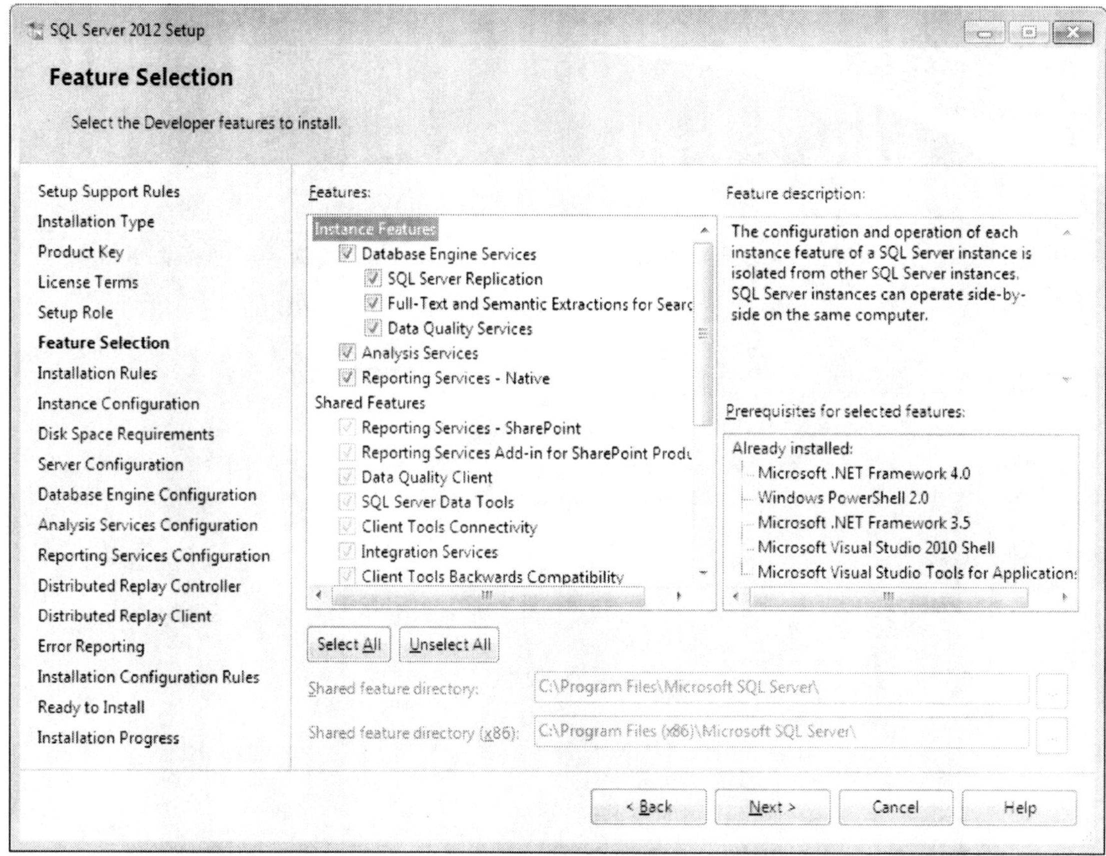

T-SQL Tidbits: ANSI JOIN vs. Ye Olde Way JOIN

Using INNER JOIN (LEFT, RIGHT) and the ON clause is called ANSI-style JOIN. The old-fashioned JOIN looks like following. The WHERE clause predicates are a mixture of JOIN conditions and WHERE filters.

```
SELECT SUM(Subtotal) AS Revenue, OrderDate, ProductID, COUNT(*) AS QtySold
FROM Sales.SalesOrderDetail AS sod, Sales.SalesOrderHeader AS soh
WHERE sod.SalesOrderID = soh.SalesOrderID
        AND YEAR(OrderDate) = 2007
GROUP BY OrderDate, ProductID;
```

Installation Rules page performs further internal system checks.

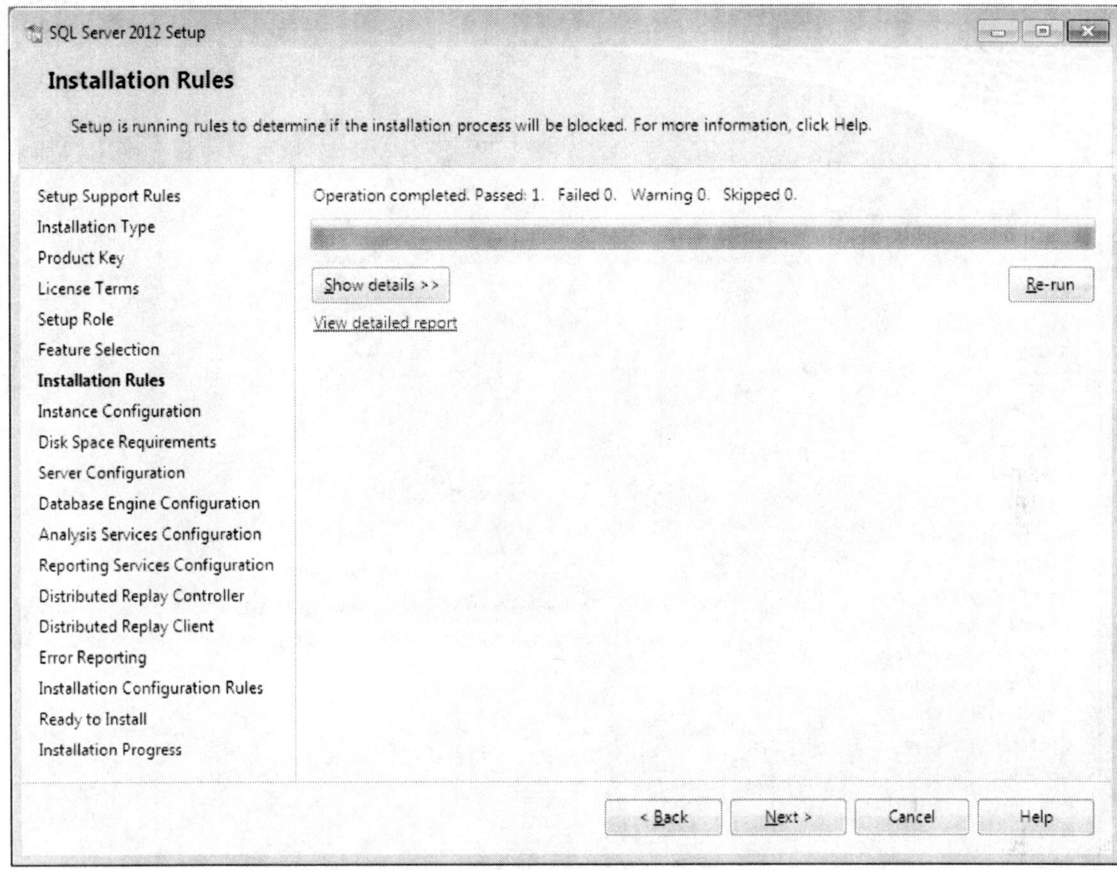

T-SQL Tidbits: How to Change a View into Indexed View

There are strict restrictions of what kind of SELECT summary query qualifies for an indexed view. It has to be schema bound, no CTE in definition and **COUNT_BIG** has to be used as examples.

```
CREATE VIEW Sales.vSalesOrder   WITH SCHEMABINDING  AS
  SELECT SUM(Subtotal) AS Revenue, OrderDate, ProductID, COUNT_BIG(*) AS QtySold
  FROM Sales.SalesOrderDetail AS sod INNER JOIN Sales.SalesOrderHeader AS soh
                ON sod.SalesOrderID = soh.SalesOrderID GROUP BY OrderDate, ProductID;
GO
CREATE UNIQUE CLUSTERED INDEX idxvOrders ON Sales.vSalesOrder (OrderDate, ProductID);
GO
```

Instance Configuration page requires name entrance for the named instance since the default instance is already installed.

The SQL Server reference is [YOURSERVER] for the default instance and [YOURSERVER\INSTANCENAME] for the named instance.

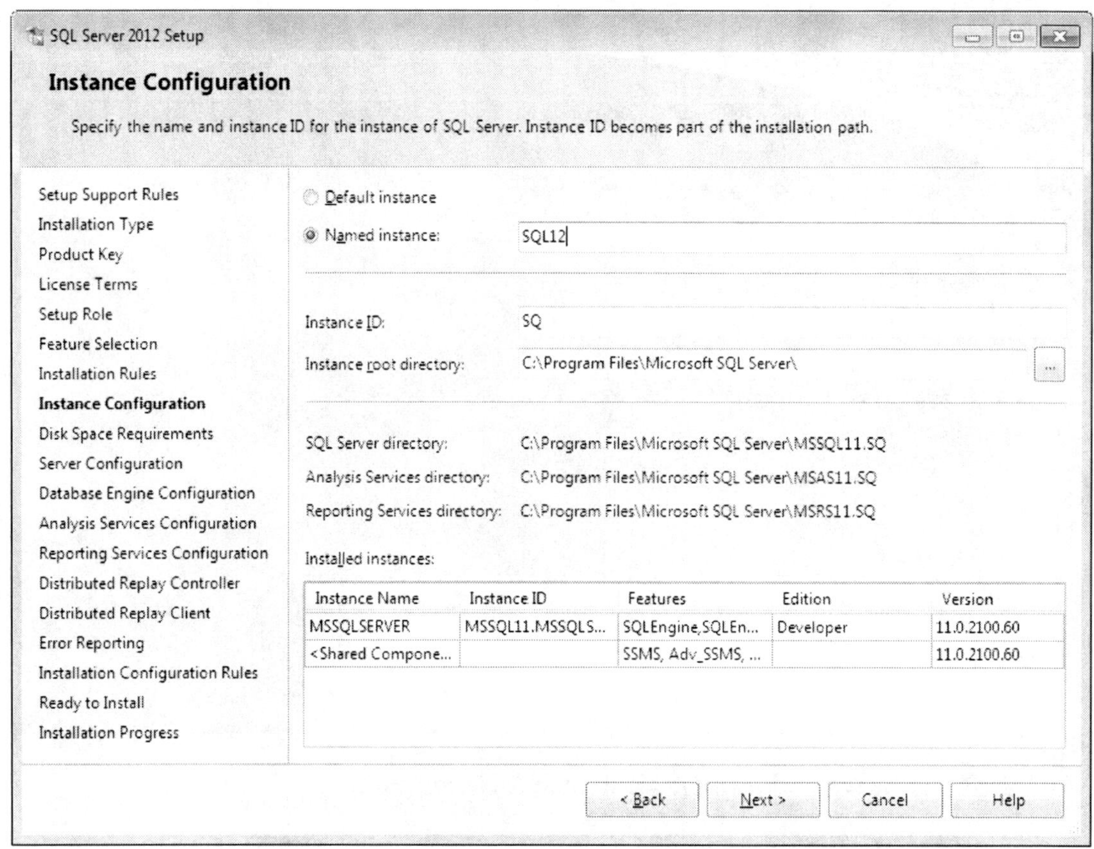

T-SQL Tidbits: The difference between T-SQL Script and Stored Procedure

A script is a client side T-SQL program stored in an editor, in an application program or disk file. Stored procedure is a compiled server-side object with a name. A T-SQL script can readily be turned into a stored procedure since there are not many rules such as no "GO"-s allowed (sproc definition is a single batch, a script can have many batches). The big advantage of the stored procedure over script is that it can be executed just by supplying the parameters by any client software since it is stored on the server and compiled.

Disk Space Requirements page checks for available disk space.

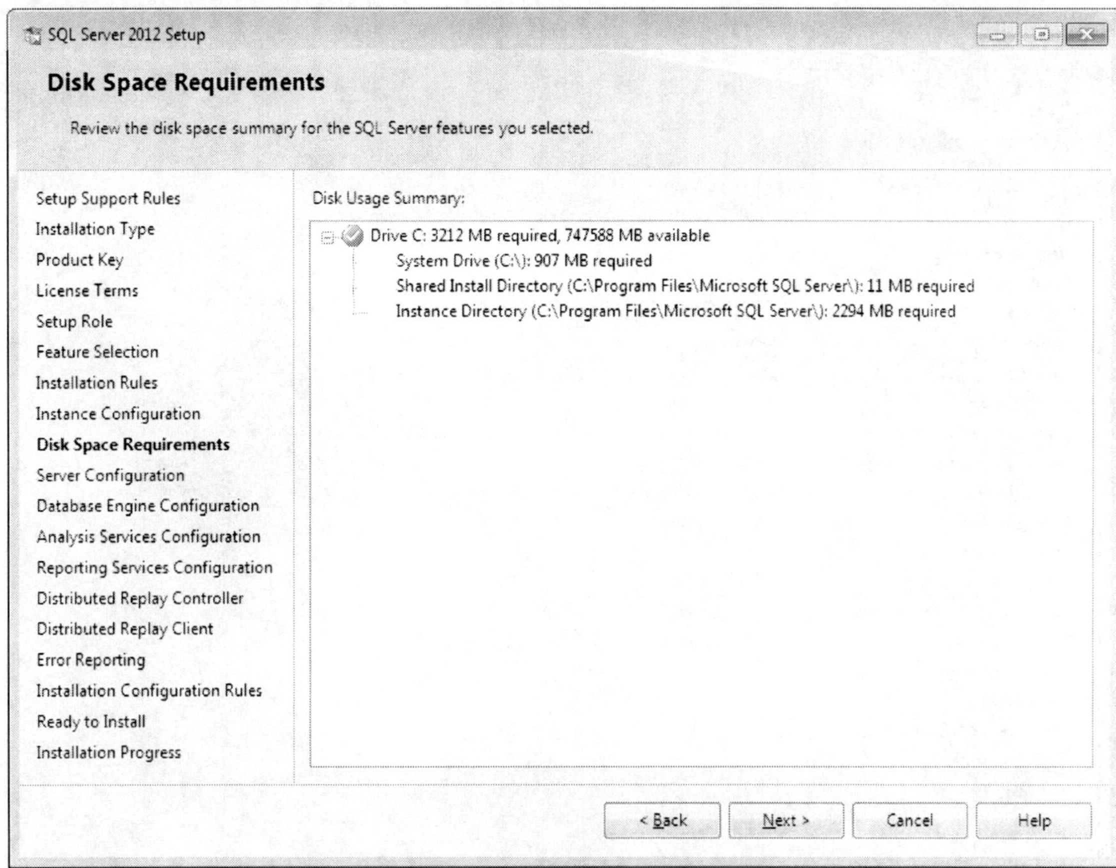

T-SQL Tidbits: Computed Column & PERSISTED Computed Column

Making a (virtual) computed column PERSISTED enables the use of features like indexing (to speed search) or constraints (like CHECK constraint: ProfitRate >= 0.25).

```
USE tempdb; SELECT ProductID, ListPrice, StandardCost INTO ProductProfit
FROM AdventureWorks2012.Production.Product WHERE ListPrice > 0.0;
ALTER TABLE ProductProfit ADD ProfitMargin AS ListPrice - StandardCost;
ALTER TABLE ProductProfit ADD ProfitRate AS (ListPrice - StandardCost) / ListPrice PERSISTED;
SELECT TOP 1 * FROM ProductProfit;
```

ProductID	ListPrice	StandardCost	ProfitMargin	ProfitRate
514	133.34	98.77	34.57	0.2592

The Server Configuration page covers accounts, startup type and collation.

For example, SQL Server Agent (job management) can be set to automatic instead of manual startup.

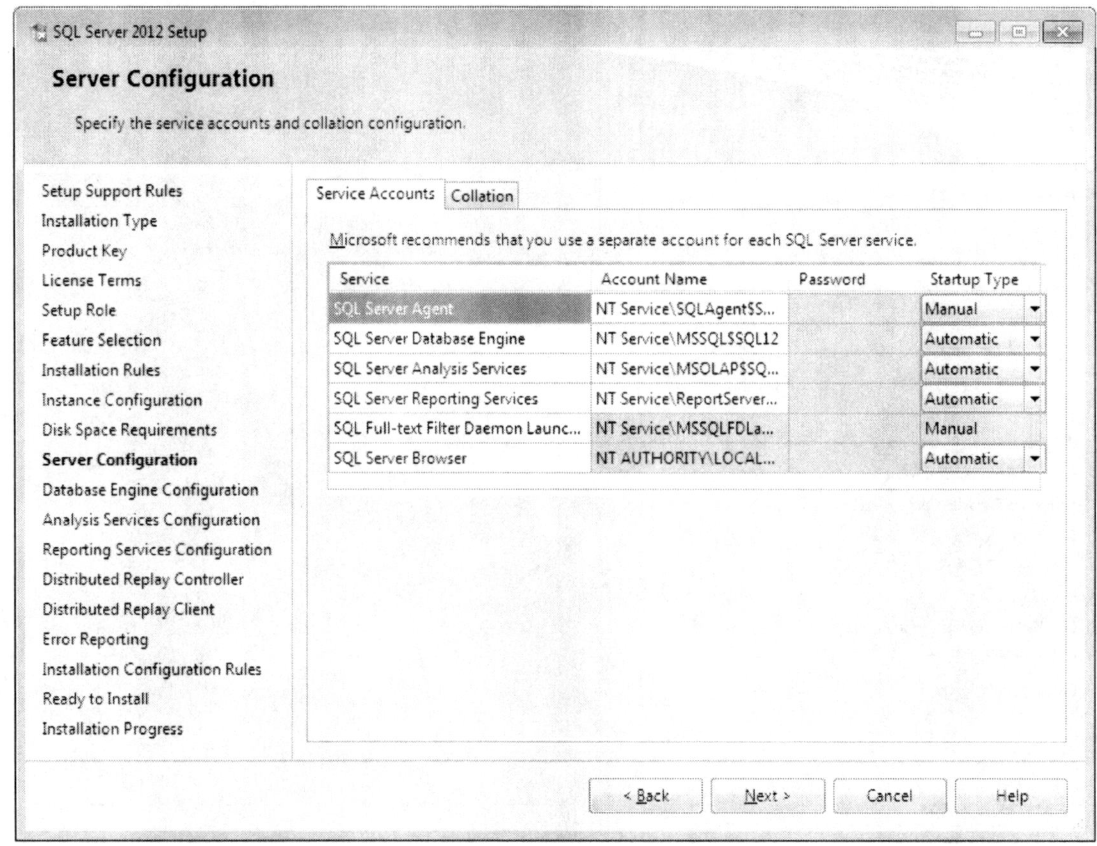

T-SQL Tidbits: What is common between computed column & view?

They are both virtual: virtual column and virtual table. That means, they are not stored in the database as data, rather SQL Server generates them dynamically when invoked.

They can be changed into persisted status with stored data values:

- Use the PERSISTED modifier for computed column
- Redefine the view with SCHEMABINDING & create a UNIQUE CLUSTERED index on it as an indexed view

The collation page offers choosing a different collation from the default. Note: selecting collation requires quite an expertise, safest choice is the default.

The "_CI_AS" suffix in the collation name means Case Insensitive, Accent Sensitive (foreign word with accent marks on E & O: PÉNZSZERZŐ).

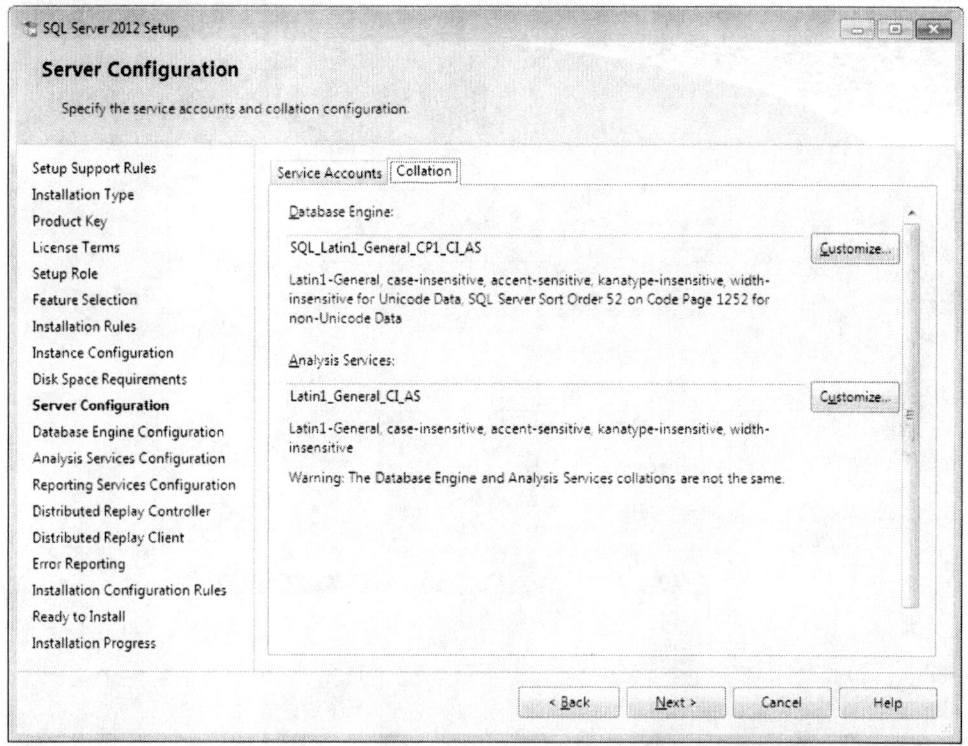


```
-- Case Insensitive, Accent Sensitive sort
DECLARE @Words TABLE ([Foreign] nvarchar(32)); INSERT @Words VALUES
(N'PÉNZSZERZŐ'),(N'Pénzszerző'), (N'PENZSZERZŐ'), (N'pÉNZSZERZŐ'), (N'PÉNZSZERZŐ'), (N'pENZSZERZŐ'),
(N'pénzszerző'), (N'péNZSZERZŐ') ;
SELECT * FROM @Words ORDER BY [Foreign];
```

Foreign
PENZSZERZŐ
pENZSZERZŐ
pénzszerző
péNZSZERZŐ
pÉNZSZERZŐ
PÉNZSZERZŐ
PÉNZSZERZŐ
Pénzszerző

The Database Engine Configuration page offers administrator accounts, data directories and FILESTREAM setup options.

FILESTREAM is required for FileTable, a new feature of SQL Server 2012.

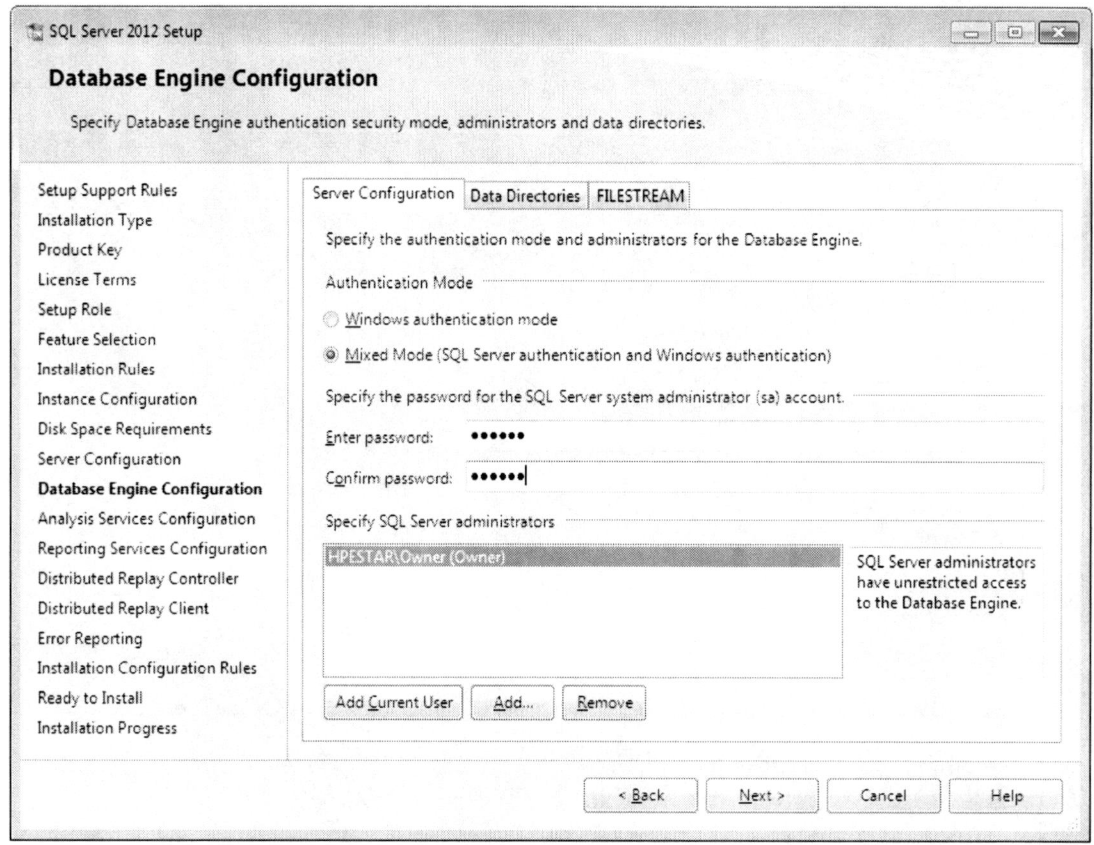

T-SQL Tidbits: Table INSERT and/or DELETE are Slow

Typical reasons for INSERT/DELETE taking 10 seconds instead of 10 msecs:

- Indexes are fragmented; Solution: REBUILD all indexes every weekend
- Too many indexes on the table; Solution: DROP non-critical indexes
- Complex trigger(s) on the table; Solution: optimize trigger(s) or find alternative solution
- For large block INSERT/DELETE: drop indexes & triggers; reapply them after data move

Error Reporting page has checkmark option to report errors automatically.

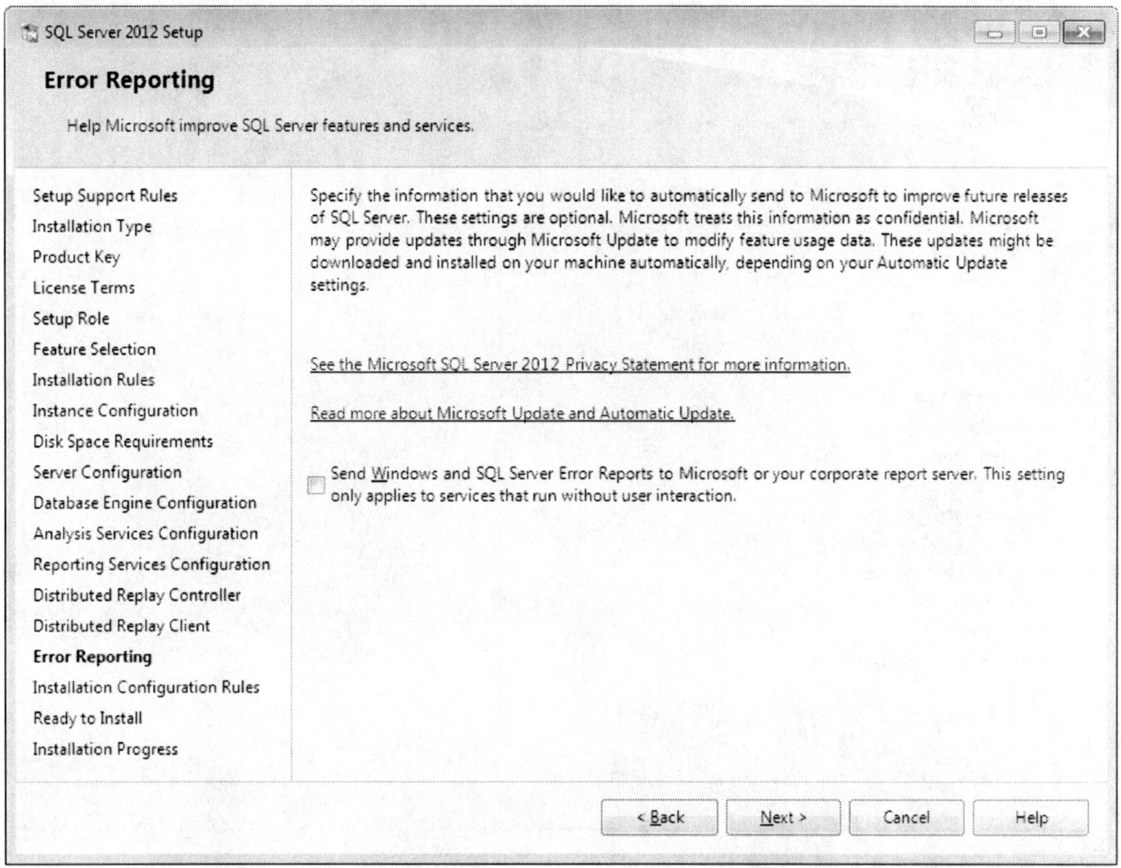

T-SQL Tidbits: Queries & Stored Procedures Fast Yesterday, Slow Today

Typical reason: STATISTICS are out of date. SQL Server optimizer uses the STATISTICS to prepare an efficient execution plan. Since lots of data may have been added yesterday to various tables & indexed views, STATISTICS are no longer valid, the database engine prepares inefficient plans.

Solution: UPDATE STATISTICS every night or turn on the SET AUTO_UPDATE_STATISTICS ON database option.

Installation Configuration Rules page performs a final check.

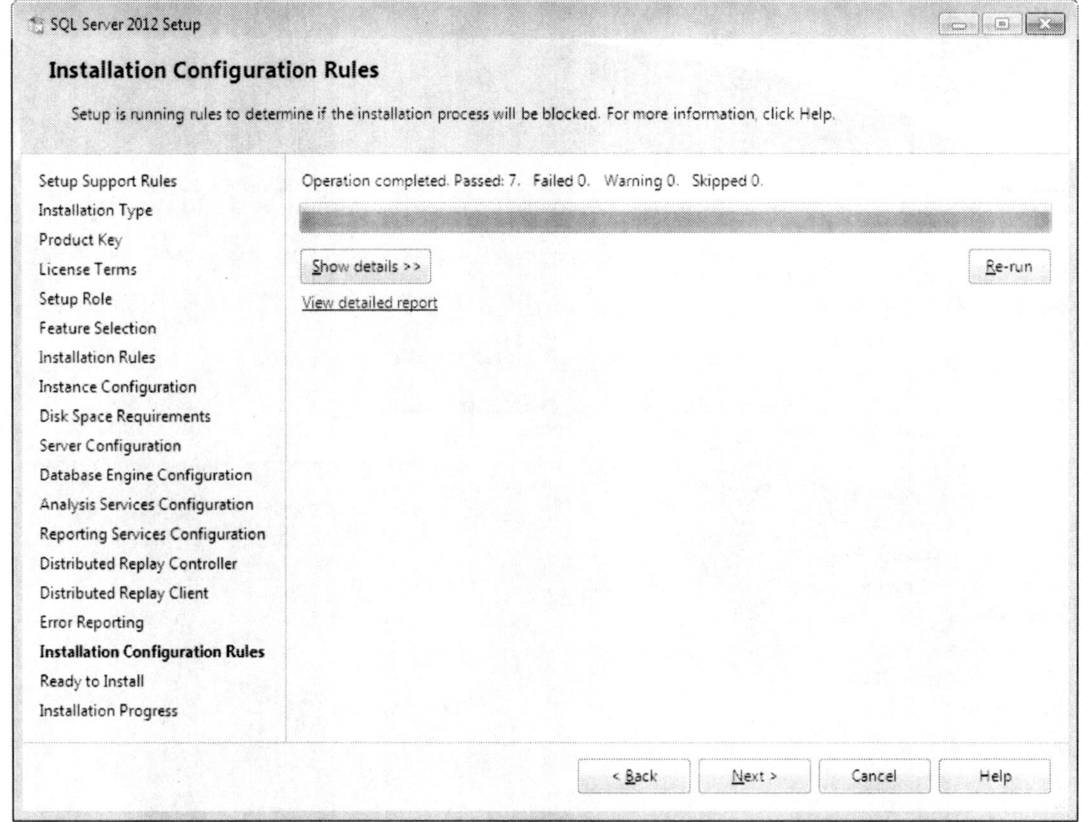

T-SQL Tidbits: Window, Windowing, Ranking, Aggregate & Analytic Functions

Window, windowing & ranking are frequently used synonymously**.** The common feature: they all work with the **OVER clause which has the PARTITION BY option** (few aggregate functions are exceptions). **A "window"** can be **all the rows** or just **one partition of rows** such as employees in a department when PARTITION BY Department is specified.

The ranking functions:

- ROW_NUMBER() sequence number generator
- RANK() ranks data with ties; skipping rank numbers
- DENSE_RANK() same as RANK() with no skipping in numbers (sequential numbering)
- NTILE() divides data in N equal size segments

Ready to Install page shows the action plan.

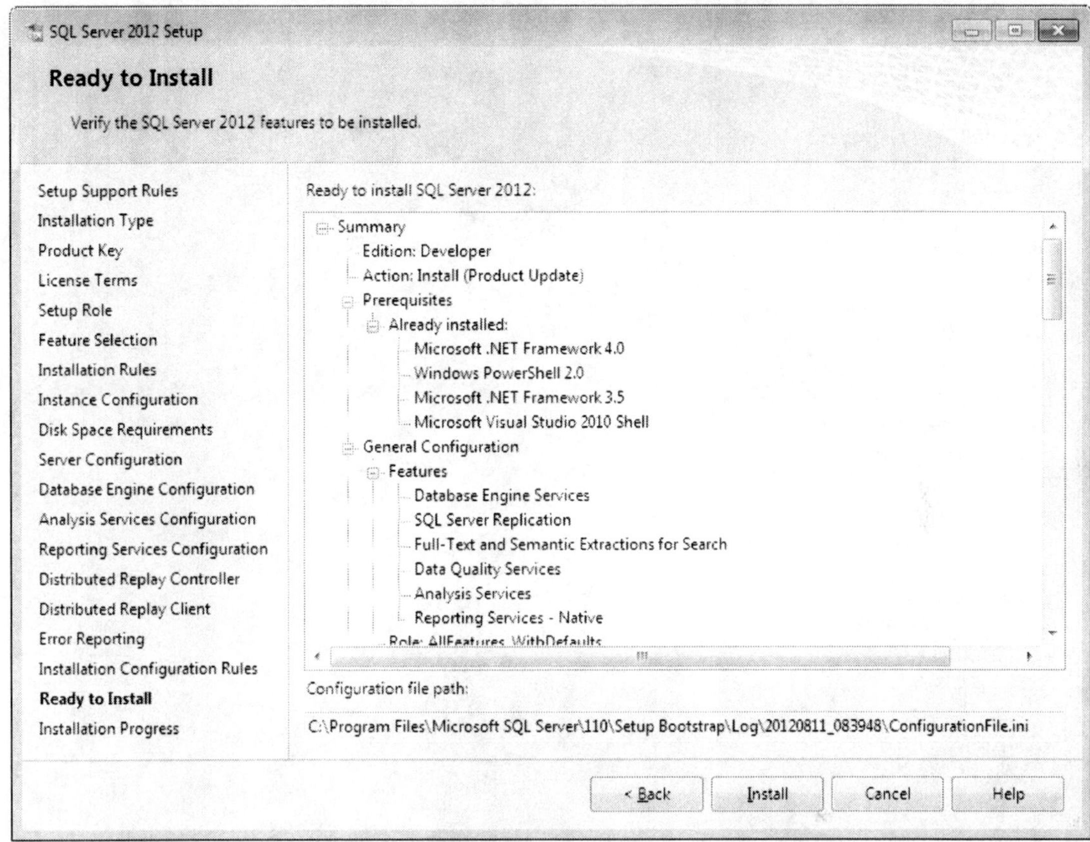

T-SQL Tidbits: FOREIGN KEY Constraint is the ONLY WAY to Connect Tables

There are different naming for table connections in a database: parent-child tables, master-detail tables, header-detail tables, or dimension-fact tables in a data warehouse database. These are all functional relationship descriptions. In database schematics there is only one kind of connection: **FOREIGN KEY** column in a table **references** a **PRIMARY KEY** column in the same (self-referencing tree structure) or other table. UNIQUE KEY or unique index column can also be referenced but rarely used. Example with object delimiters ([], square brackets).

```
ALTER TABLE [Production].[Product]  ADD  CONSTRAINT FK_PrdModel FOREIGN KEY([ProductModelID])
REFERENCES [Production].[ProductModel] ([ProductModelID]);
```

Installation Progress page displays progress messages (this part will take a few minutes).

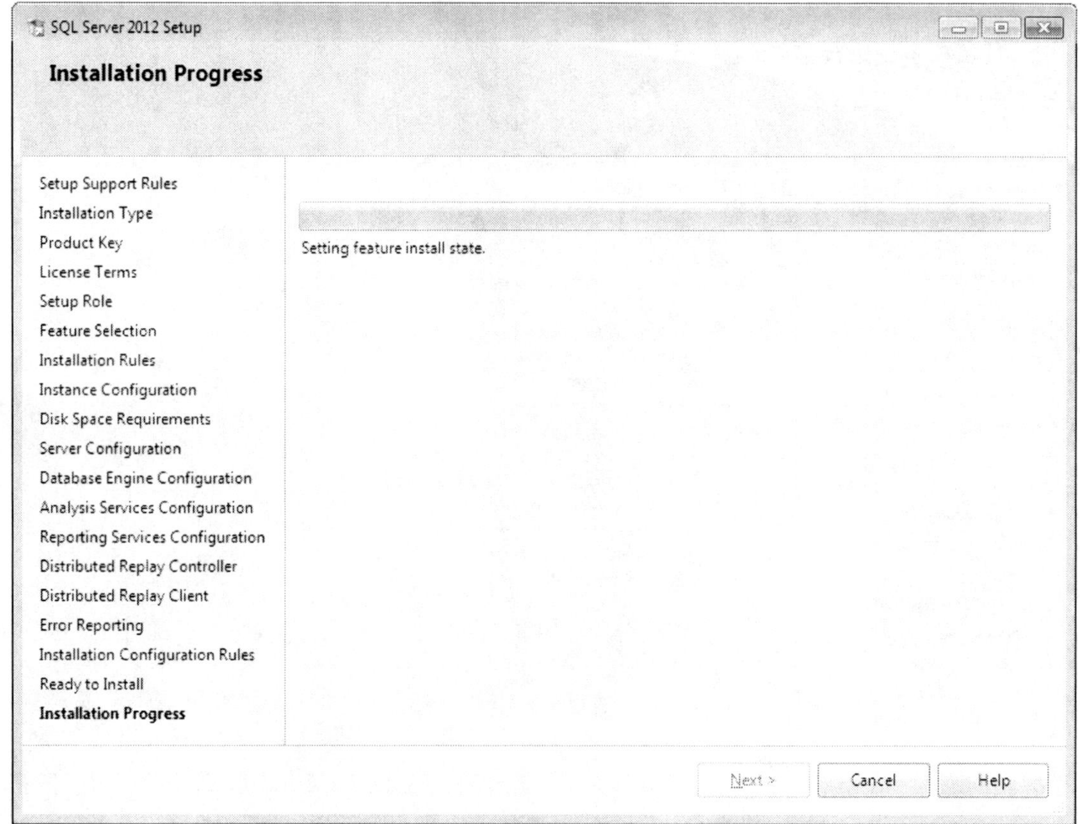

T-SQL Tidbits: Programming the Modular Way

The elements are there in T-SQL for modular programming: **scalar-valued functions, table-valued functions, views**, and **CTE**-s.

However, **T-SQL is an interpreted language** and performance rules. For example, it is usually better in performance to include some logic in a stored procedure inline rather than call a UDF, especially if the UDF is called many times. Or to create a temporary table from a view (SELECT * INTO #tempX FROM viewX) and use the temporary table in the query instead of the (virtual) view.

If there is no performance issue, modular programming is the right way to go.

The Complete page displays successful installation information or failure.

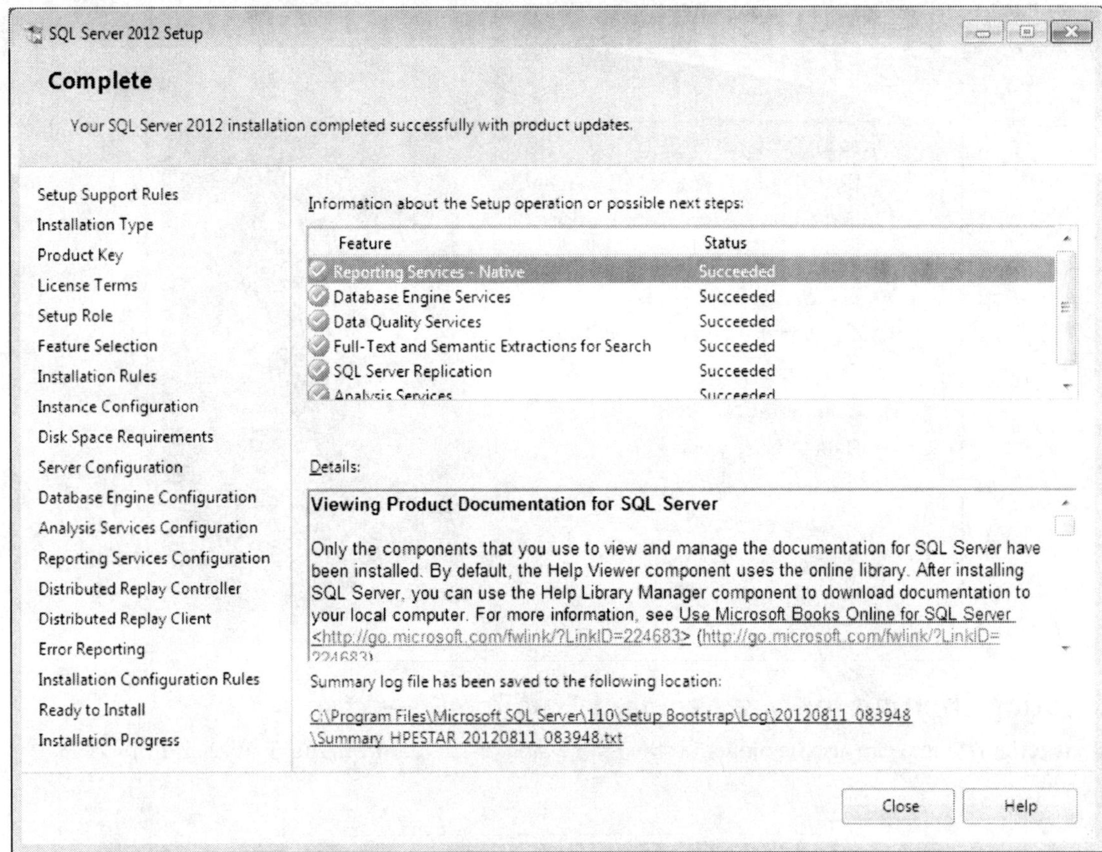

T-SQL Tidbits: Updating Inventory Table from an Application Program

It can be done four ways. Note that function cannot change database, it has only READ ONLY access to the database. A robust database solution requires that we don't do anything on the client-side which can be done on the server-side.

- **Through stored procedure: usual choice, very flexible with full programming logic. Stored procedure is a compiled server-side object**.
- Table itself: forces logic into client-side application which can be done on server-side.
- Though view: same problem as above. View cannot have logic (a workaround is instead of trigger).
- Through (after) trigger: only if stored procedure cannot be used.

Start Menu for SQL Server 2012

The Start Menu has all the components related to SQL Server including Management Studio and SQL Server Data Tools for Business Intelligence (SSAS, SSIS & SSRS) application design.

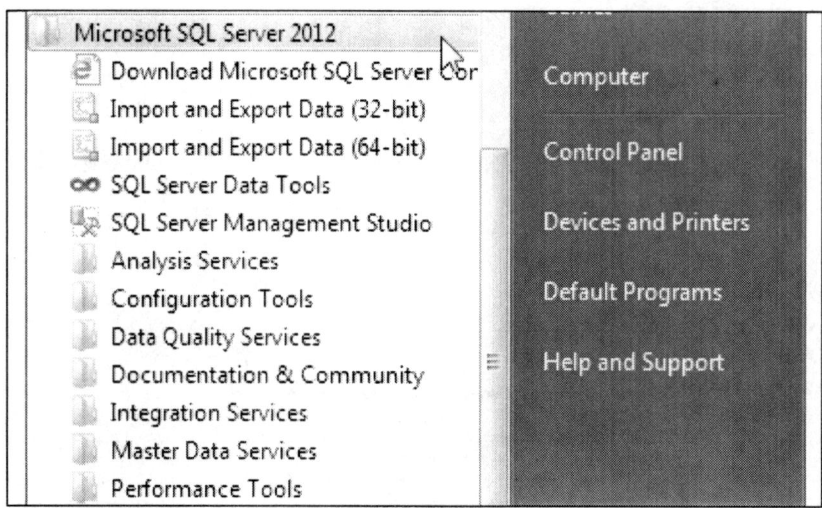

Creating Shortcut for Management Studio on Desktop

Management Studio can also be pinned to the Start Menu or Taskbar from the right-click drop-down menu.

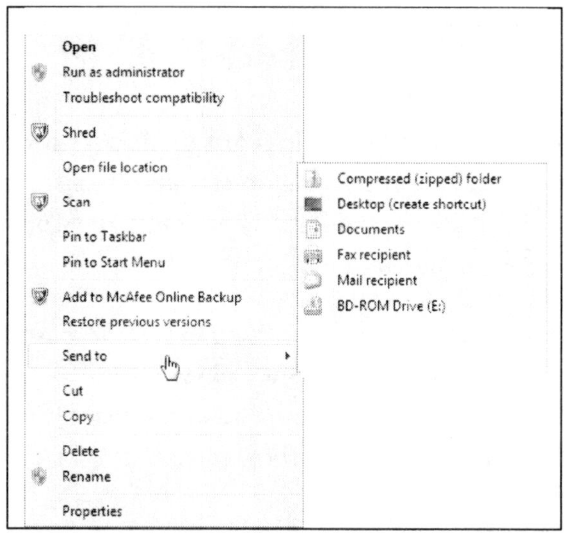

Launching SQL Server Configuration Manager

Expand (left click) the Configuration Tools tab on the Start Menu and click on SQL Server Configuration Manager.

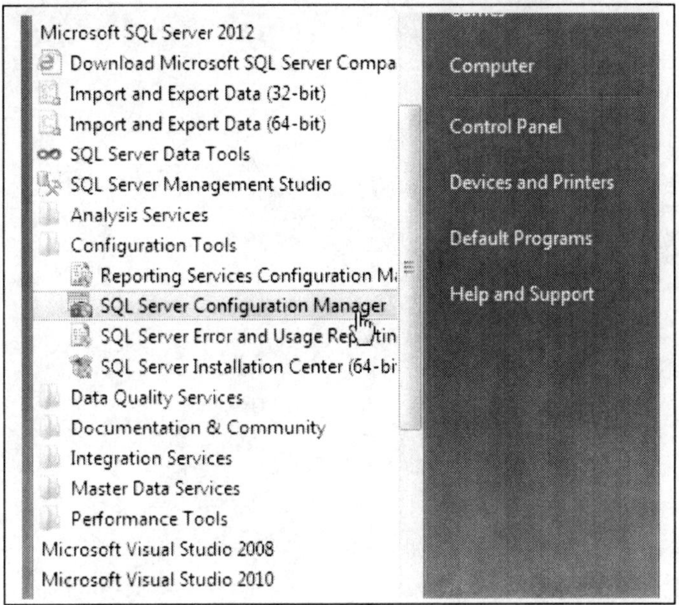

SQL Server should be running by itself after installation, if not, it can be started and/or reconfigured.

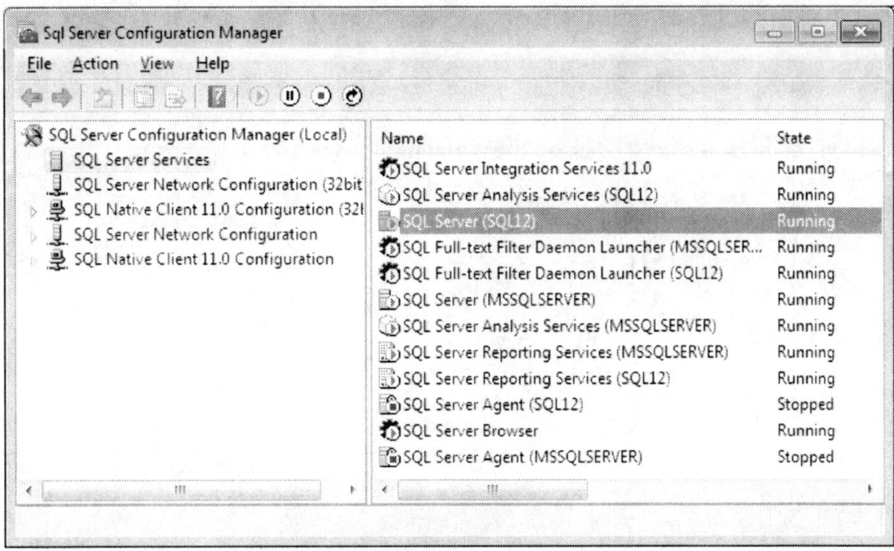

Starting, Restarting & Stopping SQL Server

Right click on the server name in Configuration Manager launches the control menu. To start the server, click on Start.

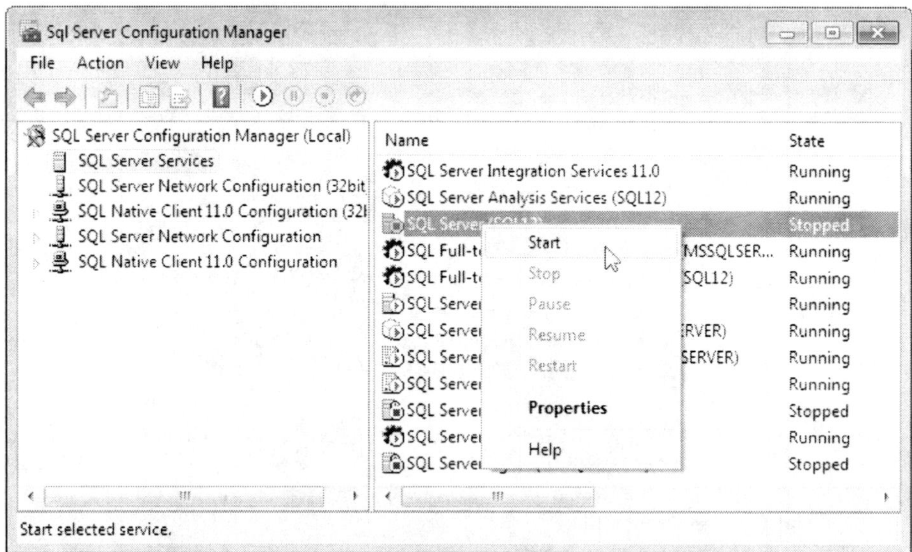

Message window pops up.

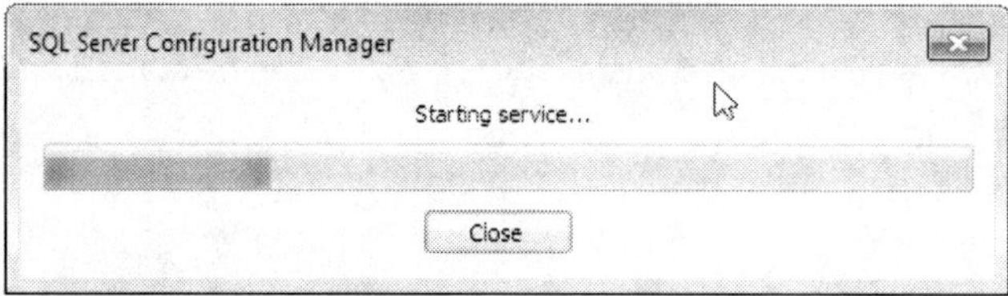

To stop a running server or restart it, click on the menu item respectively.

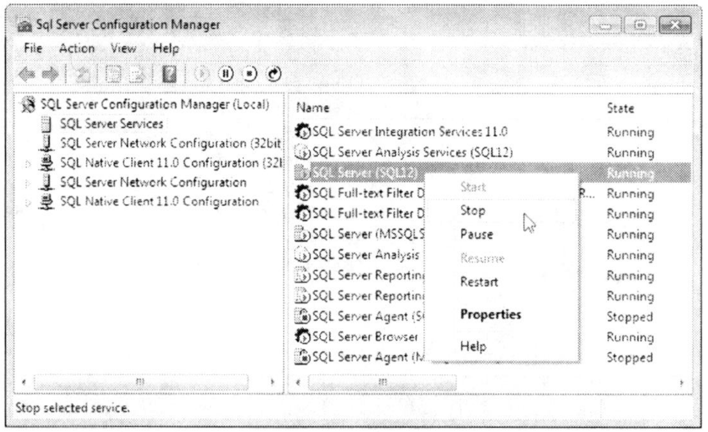

Connecting to the New Named SQL Server Instance

The newly installed SS instance is ready for use. Here is how we can connect to it from SSMS Object Explorer. NOTE: on your computer you will see YOURCOMPUTERNAME instead of "HPESTAR".

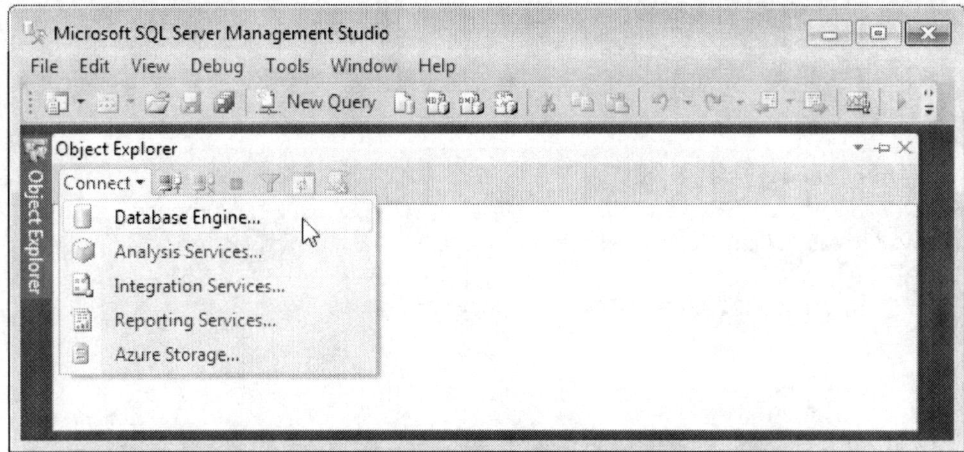

T-SQL Tidbits: Turn a Query Into a Simple Stored Procedure

```
USE AdventureWorks;
GO
CREATE PROC sprocListStores AS
	SELECT Name AS Store, AccountNumber
	FROM Sales.Store AS S   INNER JOIN Sales.Customer AS C    ON S.CustomerID = C.CustomerID
	WHERE C.CustomerType = N'S'  ORDER BY Store ;
GO
EXEC sprocListStores;
```

Investigating the New SQL Server Instance

We can start discovering the new SQL Server instance in Query Editor & Object Explorer.

```
SELECT @@version;
-- Microsoft SQL Server 2012 - 11.0.2100.60 (X64)
```

```
SELECT @@SERVERNAME;
-- YOURSERVERNAME\SQL12;
```

```
-- SS Version, Level (service pack), Edition
SELECT   CONCAT ('Microsoft SQL Server ',convert(varchar, SERVERPROPERTY('ProductVersion') ), ' -- ',
         convert(varchar, SERVERPROPERTY('ProductLevel') ), ' -- ',convert(varchar,
SERVERPROPERTY('Edition') ));
-- Microsoft SQL Server 11.0.2100.60 -- RTM -- Developer Edition (64-bit)
```

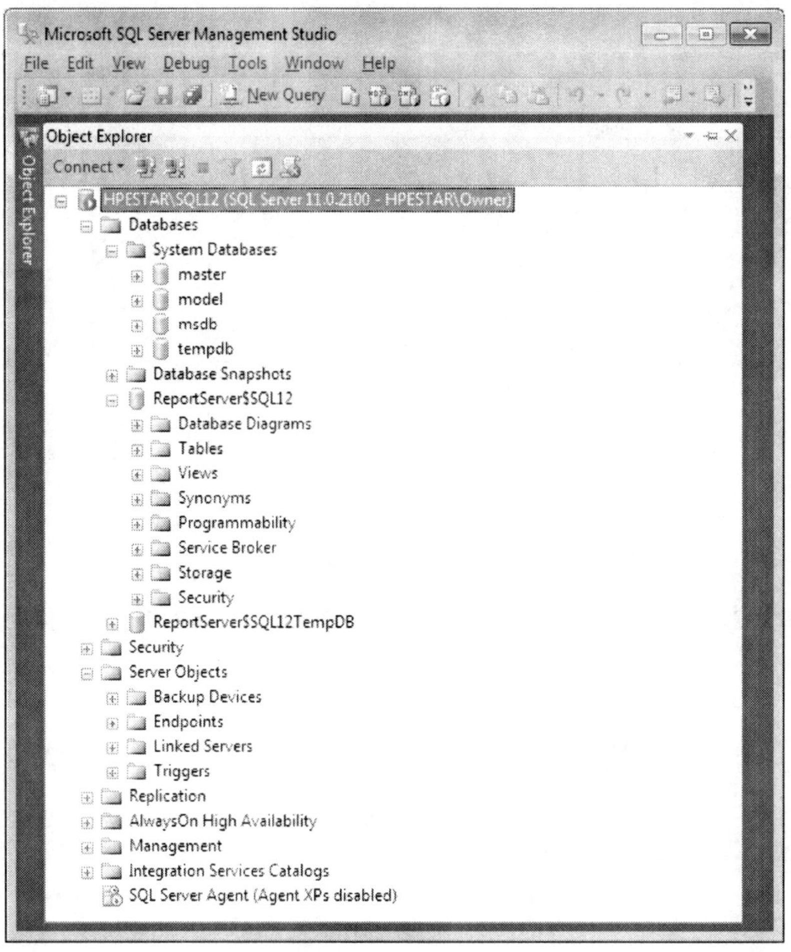

Connecting to 2 SQL Server Instances Simultaneously

SSMS Object Explorer support multiple SS instances connections. Warning: **Production, QA and Development SS instances may look similar, an opportunity to get confused and carry out actions on the wrong server**. Best prevention: **take regular database backups and connect only to one SQL Server instance at one time**.

The first connection is the named instance, the second is the default instance.

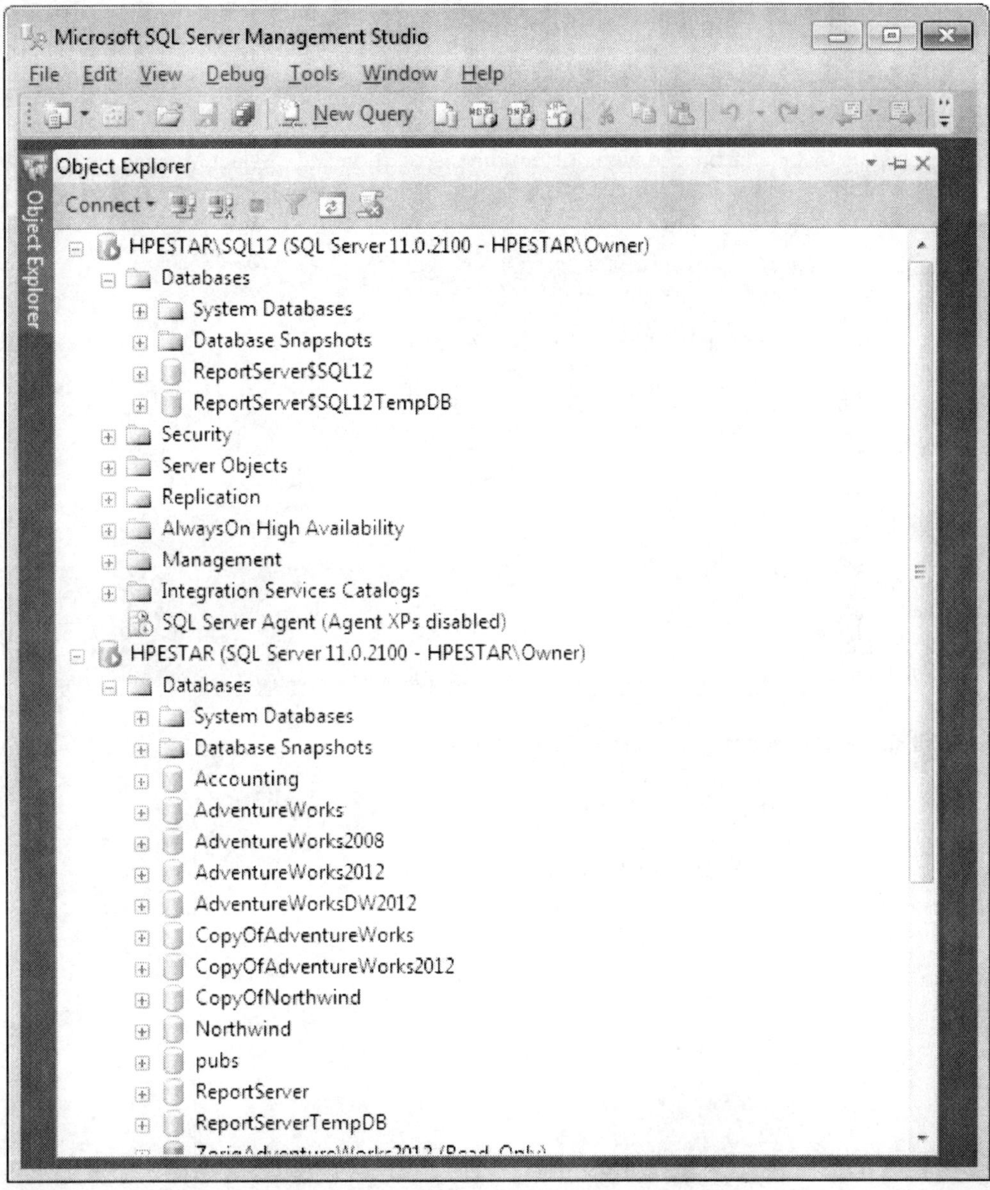

BACKUP DATABASE Command

Database backup command; the backup filename can be changed at will to reflect the backup date. The [ ] object delimiters are optional in this case (required for imbedded spaces/special characters).

```
BACKUP DATABASE [AdventureWorks2012] TO  DISK = N'F:\data\backup\AW20161023.bak';
```

```
-- Dynamic backup filename with datestamp
DECLARE @Filename nvarchar(64) = CONCAT(N'F:\data\backup\AW', CONVERT(varchar, CONVERT(DATE, getdate())),'.bak');
BACKUP DATABASE [AdventureWorks2012] TO  DISK = @Filename;
-- AW2018-08-23.bak
```

Installing Books Online - BOL

Books Online can be installed from the web or from the distribution DVD. Select Manage Help Settings from the Help menu in Management Studio.

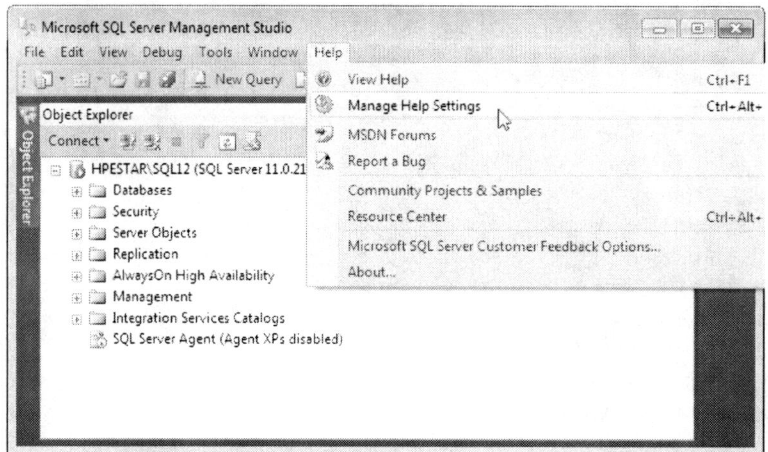

Select **Install content from online** from the pop-up panel.

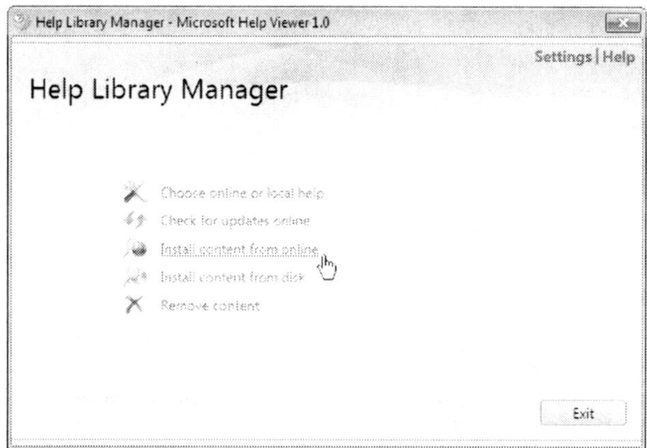

Add Books Online to the to do list on the dialog box.

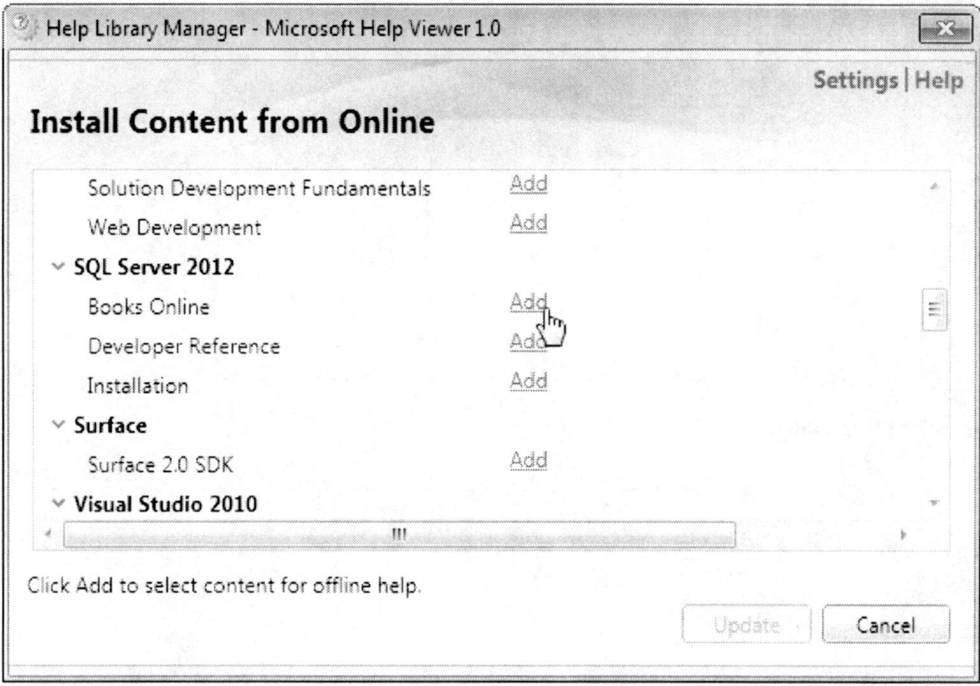

Click on UPDATE button.

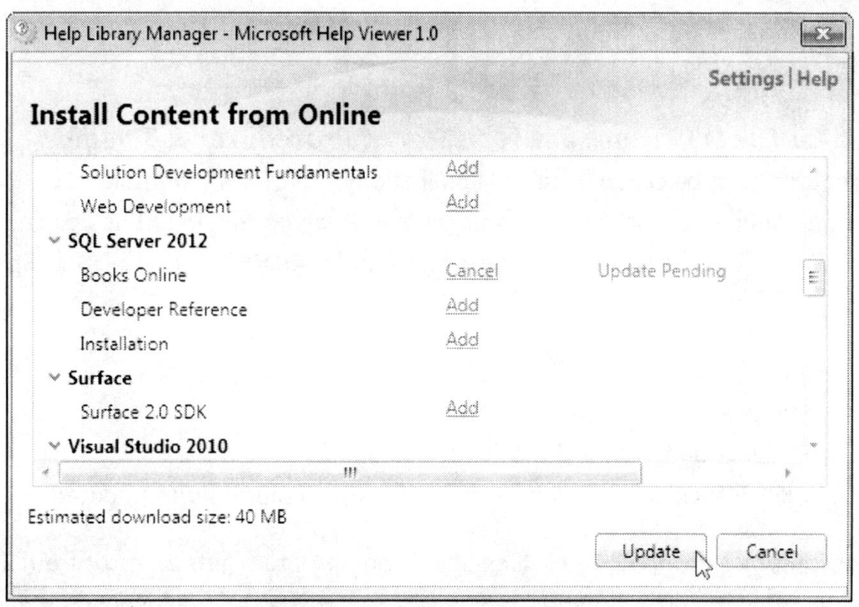

Updating will take a few minutes.

Finish panel. Click in Finish button.

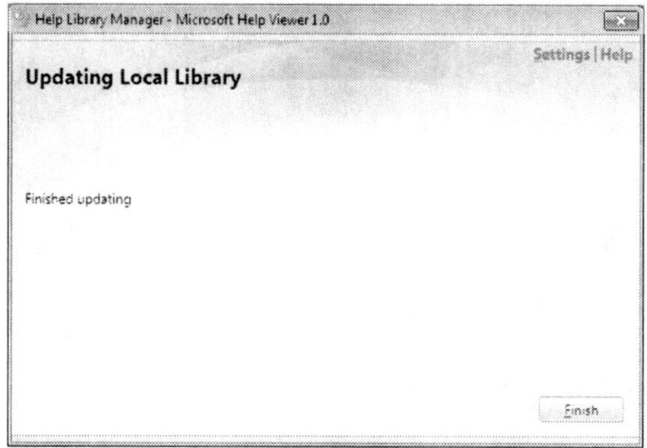

T-SQL Tidbits: The Difference between Stored Procedures & Triggers

Stored procedures must be called from the application or EXEC statement in T-SQL. Triggers fire automatically on defined events such as table update. Triggers can be defined on the following objects: table(DML), view(DML, instead of trigger), database(DDL) & server(DDL). Special to triggers:

- inserted table
- deleted table
- UPDATE() function to check if a column was updated
- COLUMNS_UPDATED() function to check if a set of columns was updated

If a stored procedure is dropped, the calling application program gets an error from SQL Server. If a trigger is dropped, no error is generated by SQL Server (stealth behaviour).

Creating Shortcut for Books Online on Desktop.

Follow the usual process for shortcut creation, start with right click on SQL Server Documentation.

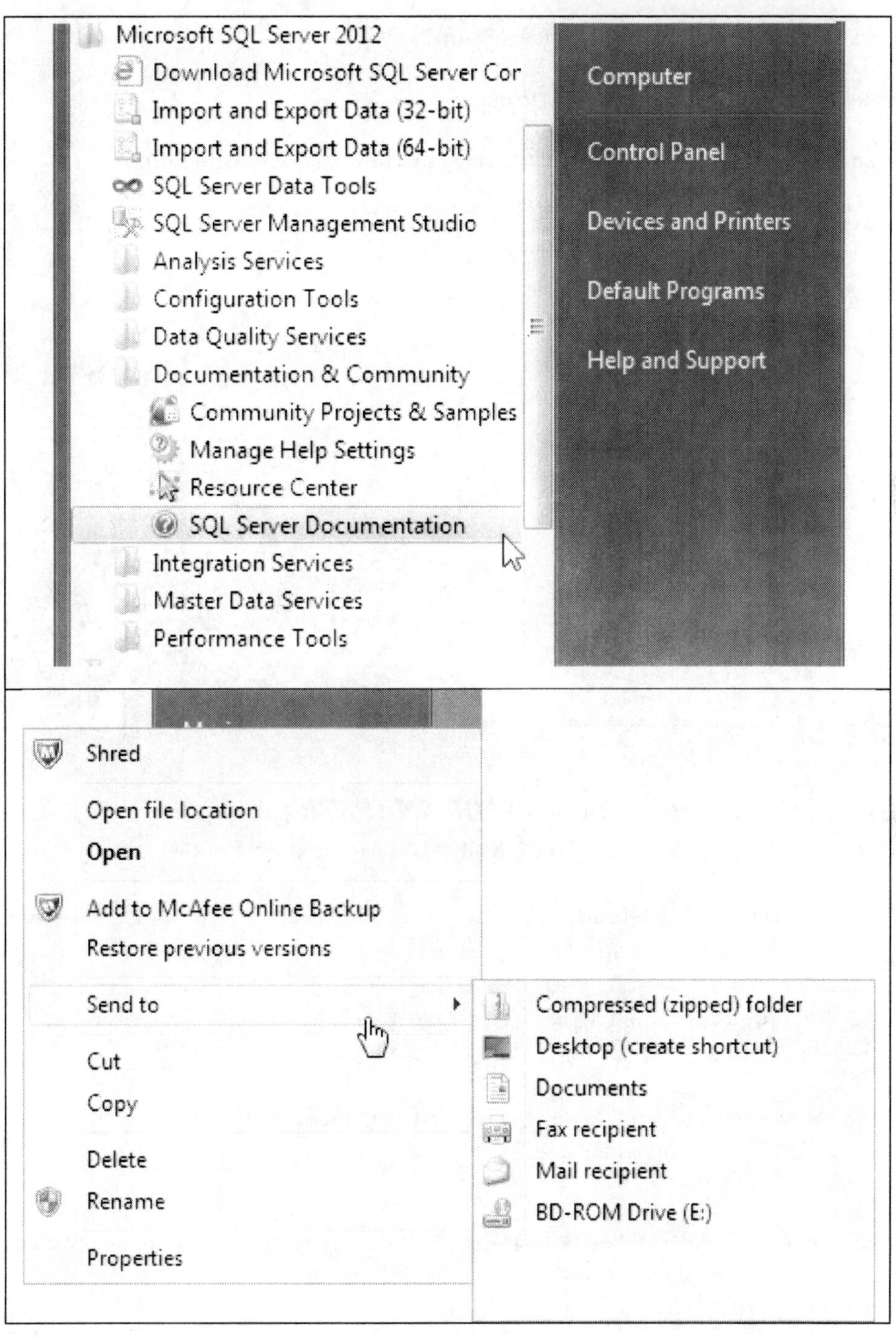

Installing Developer Reference

To install Developer Reference follow the same process as for Book Online.

Click on Update button. Update will take a few minutes.

Developer Reference will install into Books Online.

Desktop segment with SSMS, SSDT and Books Online (includes Developer Reference).

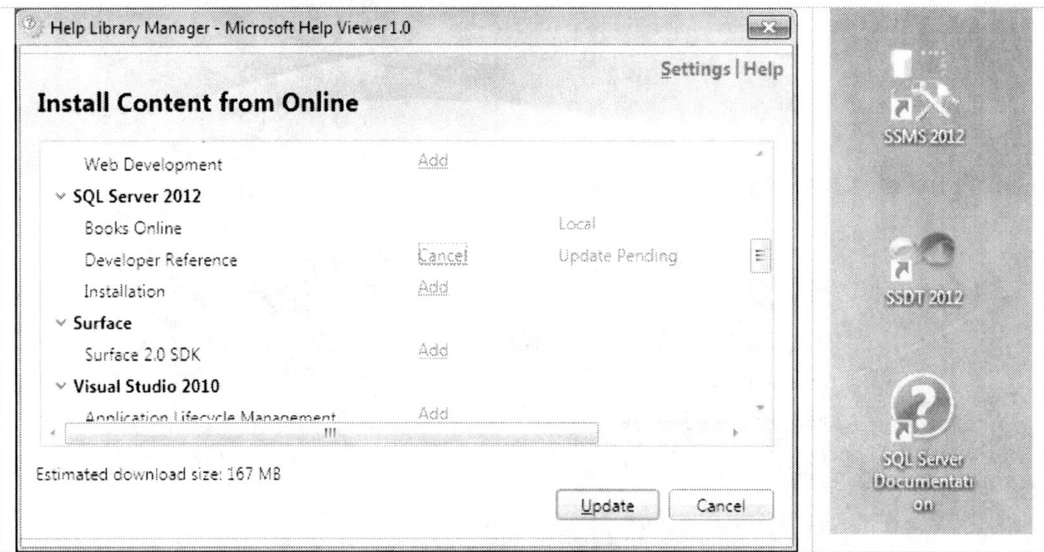

T-SQL Tidbits: XML Formatting with FOR XML PATH ('elementname')

In addition to RAW, AUTO & EXPLICIT, FOR XML PATH can be used for XML output formatting.

```
SELECT  ProductNumber AS '@ProductNumber', Color AS '@Color', Name AS '@ProductName',
                    StandardCost, ListPrice
FROM Production.Product  WHERE ListPrice > 0.0 AND Color is not NULL
ORDER BY Color, ProductNumber
FOR XML PATH ('ProductColors');      -- (245 row(s) affected) - Partial results.
```

```
<ProductColors ProductNumber="BK-M18B-40" Color="Black" ProductName="Mountain-500 Black, 40">
  <StandardCost>294.5797</StandardCost>
  <ListPrice>539.9900</ListPrice>
</ProductColors>
<ProductColors ProductNumber="BK-M18B-42" Color="Black" ProductName="Mountain-500 Black, 42">
  <StandardCost>294.5797</StandardCost>
  <ListPrice>539.9900</ListPrice>
</ProductColors>
```

Searching Books Online Contents Mode

Books Online is the complete reference tool for SQL Server. The implementation in Microsoft Help Viewer is new to SQL Server 2012. In the Contents mode, you drill-down in the left pane and read the article in the right pane.

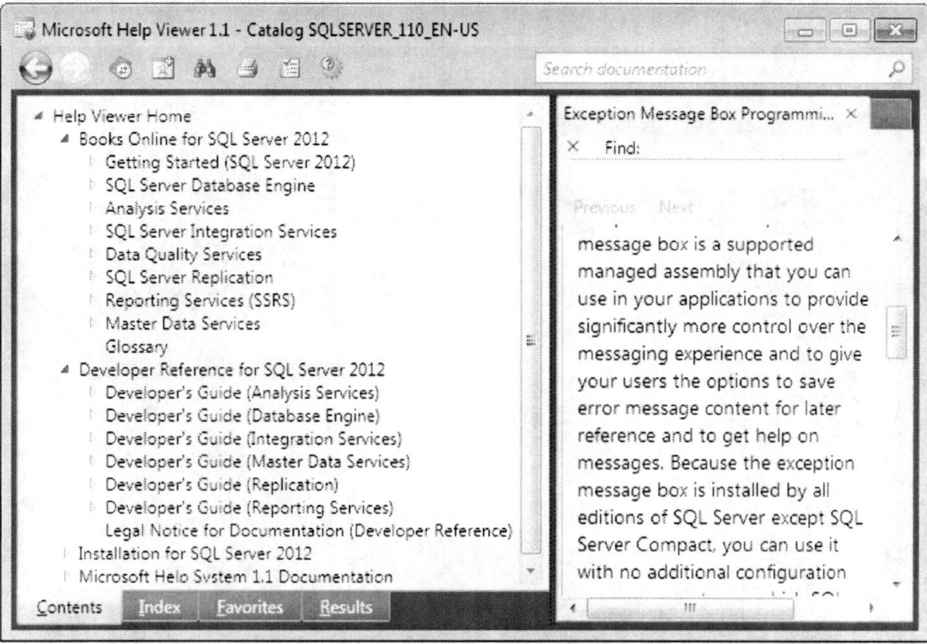

When you click on a Contents item, the corresponding article pops up in the right pane.

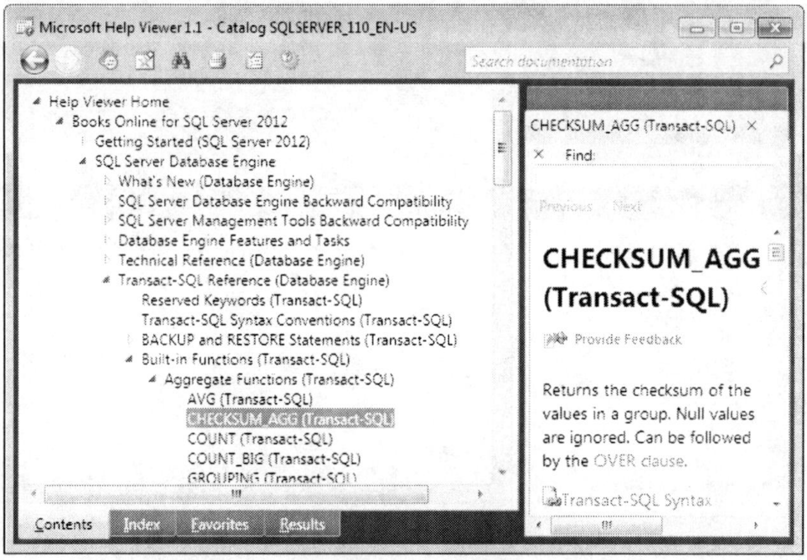

Searching Books Online Index Mode

In the Index Mode, items are listed alphabetically. When you click on an item, the corresponding article pops up in the right pane.

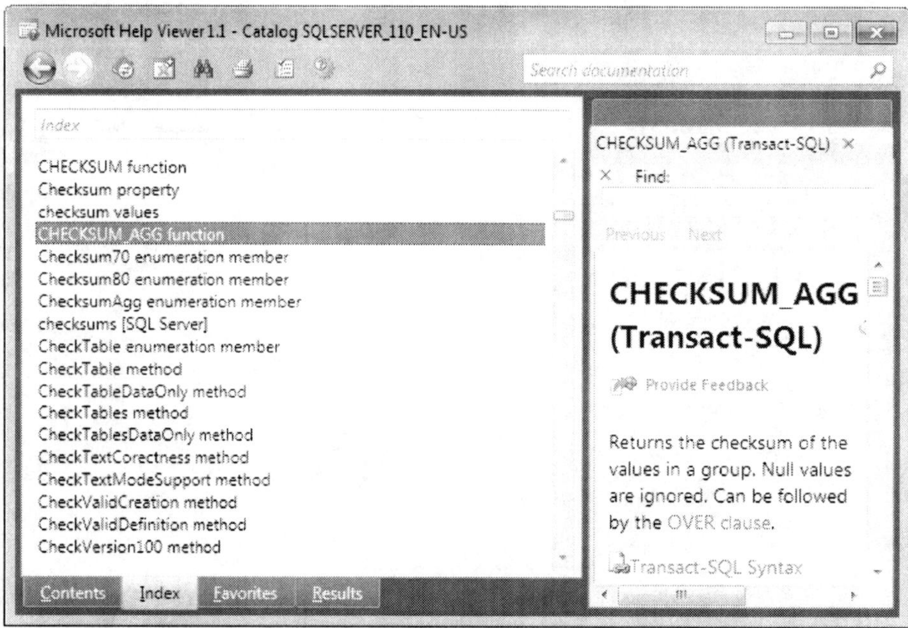

Searching the Web for SQL Server MSDN Articles

When searching the web for SS documentation use the prefix "SQL SERVER" or "T-SQL" before the keyword.

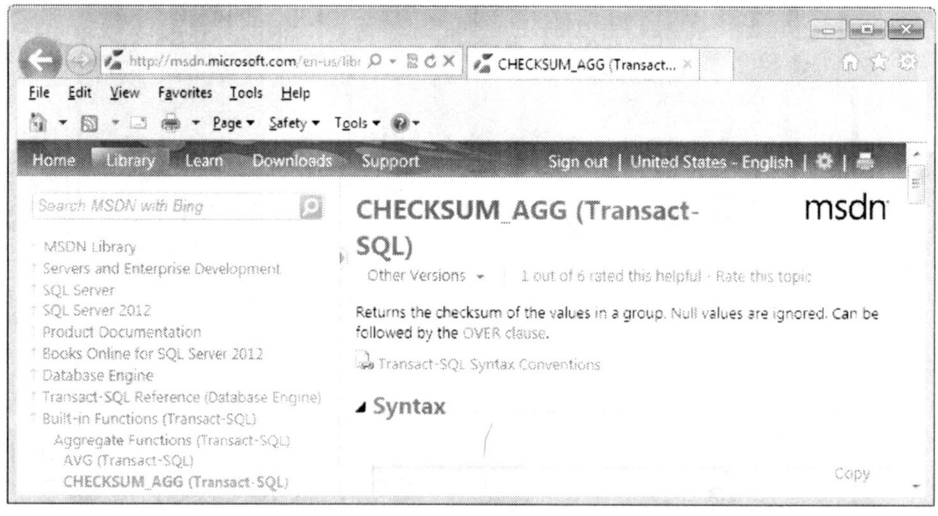

Installing AdventureWorks2012 Sample Database

AdventureWorks2012 and other related databases can be installed from the following webpage: http://msftdbprodsamples.codeplex.com/releases/view/55330

Community Projects & Samples from the Start Menu will bring up the following site: http://sqlserversamples.codeplex.com/

Installing Northwind & pubs Sample Databases

Here is the download website with instructions. http://www.microsoft.com/en-us/download/details.aspx?displaylang=en&id=23654

CHAPTER 3: Structure of the SELECT Statement

The SELECT Clause

The SELECT clause is the only required clause in a SELECT statement, all the other clauses are optional. The SELECT columns can be literals (constants), expressions, table columns and even subqueries. Lines can be commented with "--".

```
SELECT 15 * 15;                                  -- 225
```

```
SELECT Today = convert(DATE, getdate());                  -- 2016-07-27    -- getdate() T-SQL only
SELECT Today = convert(DATE, CURRENT_TIMESTAMP);          -- 2016-07-27    -- ANSI SQL
```

```
SELECT     Color,
           ProdCnt               = COUNT(*),
           AvgPrice              = FORMAT(AVG(ListPrice),'c','en-US')
FROM AdventureWorks2012.Production.Product p
WHERE Color is not null
GROUP BY Color
     HAVING count(*) > 10
ORDER BY AvgPrice DESC;
```

Color	ProdCnt	AvgPrice
Yellow	36	$959.09
Blue	26	$923.68
Silver	43	$850.31
Black	93	$725.12
Red	38	$1,401.95

```
-- Equivalent with column aliases on the right
SELECT     Color,
           COUNT(*)                              AS ProdCnt,
           FORMAT(AVG(ListPrice),'c','en-US')    AS AvgPrice
FROM AdventureWorks2012.Production.Product p  WHERE Color is not null
GROUP BY Color HAVING count(*) > 10  ORDER BY AvgPrice DESC;
GO
```

SELECT with Search Expression

SELECT statement can have complex expressions for text or numbers as demonstrated in the next T-SQL query for finding the street name in AddressLine1 column.

```
SELECT  AddressID,
        SUBSTRING(AddressLine1, CHARINDEX(' ', AddressLine1+' ', 1) +1,
        CHARINDEX(' ', AddressLine1+' ', CHARINDEX(' ', AddressLine1+' ', 1) +1) -
        CHARINDEX(' ', AddressLine1+' ', 1) -1)                         AS StreetName,
        AddressLine1,
        City
FROM AdventureWorks2012.Person.Address
WHERE ISNUMERIC (LEFT(AddressLine1,1))=1
  AND City = 'Seattle'
ORDER BY AddressLine1;
-- -- (141 row(s) affected)- Partial results.
```

AddressID	StreetName	AddressLine1	City
13079	boulevard	081, boulevard du Montparnasse	Seattle
859	Oak	1050 Oak Street	Seattle
110	Slow	1064 Slow Creek Road	Seattle
113	Ravenwood	1102 Ravenwood	Seattle
95	Bradford	1220 Bradford Way	Seattle
32510	Steven	1349 Steven Way	Seattle
118	Balboa	136 Balboa Court	Seattle
32519	Mazatlan	137 Mazatlan	Seattle
25869	Calle	1386 Calle Verde	Seattle
114	Yorba	1398 Yorba Linda	Seattle
15657	Book	151 Book Ct	Seattle
105	Stillman	1619 Stillman Court	Seattle
18002	Carmel	1635 Carmel Dr	Seattle
19813	Acardia	1787 Acardia Pl.	Seattle
16392	Orchid	1874 Orchid Ct	Seattle
18053	Green	1883 Green View Court	Seattle
13035	Mt.	1887 Mt. Diablo St	Seattle
29864	Valley	1946 Valley Crest Drive	Seattle
13580	Hill	2030 Hill Drive	Seattle
106	San	2144 San Rafael	Seattle

```
-- Search for Crest in the middle of AddessLine1
SELECT * FROM AdventureWorks2012.Person.Address
WHERE AddressLine1 LIKE '% Crest %';
-- (21 row(s) affected)
```

SELECT Statement with Subquery

Two Northwind category images, Beverages & Dairy Products, from the dbo.Categories table.

The following SELECT statement involves a subquery which is called a derived table. It also demonstrates that INNER JOIN can be performed with a GROUP BY subquery as well not only with another table or view.

```
USE Northwind;
SELECT      c.CategoryName                          AS Category,
            cnum.NoOfProducts                       AS CatProdCnt,
            p.ProductName                           AS Product,
            FORMAT(p.UnitPrice,'c', 'en-US')        AS UnitPrice
 FROM    Categories c
            INNER JOIN Products p       ON c.CategoryID = p.CategoryID
            INNER JOIN (    SELECT          c.CategoryID,
                                            NoOfProducts = count(* )
                            FROM    Categories c
                                    INNER JOIN Products p
                                    ON c.CategoryID = p.CategoryID
                            GROUP BY c.CategoryID
                        ) cnum                              -- derived table
                    ON c.CategoryID = cnum.CategoryID
ORDER BY Category, Product;        -- (77 row(s) affected) - Partial results.
```

Category	CatProdCnt	Product	UnitPrice
Dairy Products	10	Mozzarella di Giovanni	$34.80
Dairy Products	10	Queso Cabrales	$21.00
Dairy Products	10	Queso Manchego La Pastora	$38.00
Dairy Products	10	Raclette Courdavault	$55.00
Grains/Cereals	7	Filo Mix	$7.00
Grains/Cereals	7	Gnocchi di nonna Alice	$38.00
Grains/Cereals	7	Gustaf's Knäckebröd	$21.00
Grains/Cereals	7	Ravioli Angelo	$19.50
Grains/Cereals	7	Singaporean Hokkien Fried Mee	$14.00
Grains/Cereals	7	Tunnbröd	$9.00

Creating Delimited String List (CSV) with XML PATH

The XML PATH clause , the text() (extract text without xml tags) function and correlated subquery is used to create a comma delimited string within the SELECT columns. Note: it cannot be done using traditional (without XML) SQL single statement, it can be done with multiple SQL statements only. STUFF() string function is applied to replace the leading comma with an empty string. The **[text()]** is not a column alias rather a FOR XML PATH clause related xquery function.

```
USE AdventureWorks;

SELECT  Territory          = st.[Name],
        SalesYTD =  FORMAT(floor(SalesYTD), 'c', 'en-US'), -- currency format
        SalesStaffAssignmentHistory =

          STUFF((SELECT CONCAT(', ', c.FirstName, SPACE(1), c.LastName)       AS [text()]
                FROM   Person.Contact c
                 INNER JOIN Sales.SalesTerritoryHistory sth
                 ON c.ContactID = sth.SalesPersonID
                WHERE  sth.TerritoryID =   st.TerritoryID
                ORDER  BY StartDate
                FOR XML PATH ('') ), 1, 1, SPACE(0))

FROM   Sales.SalesTerritory st
ORDER  BY SalesYTD DESC;
GO
```

Territory	SalesYTD	SalesStaffAssignmentHistory
Southwest	$8,351,296.00	Shelley Dyck, Jauna Elson
Canada	$6,917,270.00	Carla Eldridge, Michael Emanuel, Gail Erickson
Northwest	$5,767,341.00	Shannon Elliott, Terry Eminhizer, Martha Espinoza
Central	$4,677,108.00	Linda Ecoffey, Maciej Dusza
France	$3,899,045.00	Mark Erickson
Northeast	$3,857,163.00	Maciej Dusza, Linda Ecoffey
United Kingdom	$3,514,865.00	Michael Emanuel
Southeast	$2,851,419.00	Carol Elliott
Germany	$2,481,039.00	Janeth Esteves
Australia	$1,977,474.00	Twanna Evans

```
-- Comma delimited list of column names
SELECT CONCAT(',', c.name)  AS [text()]
FROM  sys.columns c   WHERE c.[object_id] = OBJECT_ID('Purchasing.PurchaseOrderDetail')
ORDER BY column_id FOR XML PATH('');
```

Logical Processing Order of the SELECT Statement

The results from the previous step will be available to the next step. The logical processing order for a SELECT statement is the following. Actual processing by the database engine may be different due to performance and other considerations.

1.	**FROM**
2.	**ON**
3.	**JOIN**
4.	**WHERE**
5.	**GROUP BY**
6.	**WITH CUBE or WITH ROLLUP**
7.	**HAVING**
8.	**SELECT**
9.	**DISTINCT**
10.	**ORDER BY**
11.	**TOP**

As an example, it is logical to filter with the WHERE clause prior to applying GROUP BY. It is also logical to sort when the final result set is available.

```
SELECT Color, COUNT(*) AS ColorCount  FROM AdventureWorks2012.Production.Product
WHERE Color is not NULL  GROUP BY Color ORDER BY ColorCount DESC;
```

Color	ColorCount
Black	93
Silver	43
Red	38
Yellow	36
Blue	26
Multi	8
Silver/Black	7
White	4
Grey	1

The TOP Clause

The TOP clause filters results according the sorting specified in an ORDER BY clause, otherwise random filtering takes place.

Simple TOP usage to return 10 rows only.

```
SELECT TOP 10 SalesOrderID, OrderDate,  TotalDue
FROM AdventureWorks2012.Sales.SalesOrderHeader  ORDER BY TotalDue DESC;
```

SalesOrderID	OrderDate	TotalDue
51131	2007-07-01 00:00:00.000	187487.825
55282	2007-10-01 00:00:00.000	182018.6272
46616	2006-07-01 00:00:00.000	170512.6689
46981	2006-08-01 00:00:00.000	166537.0808
47395	2006-09-01 00:00:00.000	165028.7482
47369	2006-09-01 00:00:00.000	158056.5449
47355	2006-09-01 00:00:00.000	145741.8553
51822	2007-08-01 00:00:00.000	145454.366
44518	2005-11-01 00:00:00.000	142312.2199
51858	2007-08-01 00:00:00.000	140042.1209

TOP function usage: not known in advance how many rows will be returned due to "TIES".

```
SELECT   TOP 1 WITH TIES  coalesce(Color, 'N/A')                AS Color,
             FORMAT(ListPrice, 'c', 'en-US')                   AS ListPrice,
             Name                                              AS ProductName,
             ProductID
FROM     AdventureWorks2012.Production.Product
ORDER BY ROW_NUMBER()  OVER(PARTITION BY Color ORDER BY ListPrice DESC);
```

.

Color	ListPrice	ProductName	ProductID
N/A	$229.49	HL Fork	804
Black	$3,374.99	Mountain-100 Black, 38	775
Red	$3,578.27	Road-150 Red, 62	749
Silver	$3,399.99	Mountain-100 Silver, 38	771
Blue	$2,384.07	Touring-1000 Blue, 46	966
Grey	$125.00	Touring-Panniers, Large	842
Multi	$89.99	Men's Bib-Shorts, S	855
Silver/Black	$80.99	HL Mountain Pedal	937
White	$9.50	Mountain Bike Socks, M	709
Yellow	$2,384.07	Touring-1000 Yellow, 46	954

The DISTINCT Clause to Omit Duplicates

The DISTINCT clause returns only unique results, omitting duplicates in the result set.

```
USE AdventureWorks2012;
SELECT DISTINCT Color FROM Production.Product
WHERE Color is not NULL
ORDER BY Color;
GO
```

Color
Black
Blue
Grey
Multi
Red
Silver
Silver/Black
White
Yellow

```
SELECT DISTINCT ListPrice
FROM Production.Product
 WHERE ListPrice > 0.0
ORDER BY ListPrice DESC;
GO
-- (102 row(s) affected) - Partial results.
```

ListPrice
3578.27
3399.99
3374.99
2443.35

```
-- Using DISTINCT in COUNT - NULL is counted
SELECT      COUNT(*)                    AS TotalRows,
            COUNT(DISTINCT Color)       AS ProductColors,
            COUNT(DISTINCT Size)        AS ProductSizes
FROM AdventureWorks2012.Production.Product;
```

TotalRows	ProductColors	ProductSizes
504	9	18

The CASE Conditional Expression

The CASE conditional expression evaluates to a **single value of the same data type**, therefore **it can be used anywhere in a query where a single value is required.**

```
SELECT          CASE ProductLine
                        WHEN 'R' THEN 'Road'
                        WHEN 'M' THEN 'Mountain'
                        WHEN 'T' THEN 'Touring'
                        WHEN 'S' THEN 'Other'
                        ELSE 'Parts'
                END                             AS Category,
                Name                            AS ProductName,
                ProductNumber
FROM AdventureWorks2012.Production.Product
ORDER BY ProductName;
GO
-- (504 row(s) affected) - Partial results.
```

Category	ProductName	ProductNumber
Touring	Touring-3000 Blue, 62	BK-T18U-62
Touring	Touring-3000 Yellow, 44	BK-T18Y-44
Touring	Touring-3000 Yellow, 50	BK-T18Y-50
Touring	Touring-3000 Yellow, 54	BK-T18Y-54
Touring	Touring-3000 Yellow, 58	BK-T18Y-58
Touring	Touring-3000 Yellow, 62	BK-T18Y-62
Touring	Touring-Panniers, Large	PA-T100
Other	Water Bottle - 30 oz.	WB-H098
Mountain	Women's Mountain Shorts, L	SH-W890-L

Query to return different result sets for repeated execution due to newid().

```
SELECT  TOP 3 CompanyName,    City=CONCAT(City, ', ', Country),         PostalCode,
        [IsNumeric] =  CASE     WHEN PostalCode like '[0-9][0-9][0-9][0-9][0-9]'
                                THEN '5-Digit Numeric'     ELSE 'Other'  END
FROM    Northwind.dbo.Suppliers
ORDER BY NEWID();                               -- random sort
GO
```

CompanyName	City	PostalCode	IsNumeric
PB Knäckebröd AB	Göteborg, Sweden	S-345 67	Other
Gai pâturage	Annecy, France	74000	5-Digit Numeric
Heli Süßwaren GmbH & Co. KG	Berlin, Germany	10785	5-Digit Numeric

Same query as above expanded with ROW_NUMBER() and another CASE expression column.

```
SELECT       ROW_NUMBER() OVER (ORDER BY Name)                    AS RowNo,
             CASE ProductLine
              WHEN 'R' THEN 'Road'
              WHEN 'M' THEN 'Mountain'
              WHEN 'T' THEN 'Touring'
              WHEN 'S' THEN 'Other'
              ELSE 'Parts'
             END                                     AS Category,
             Name                                    AS ProductName,
             CASE WHEN Color is null THEN 'N/A'
                    ELSE Color END                   AS Color,
             ProductNumber
FROM Production.Product    ORDER BY ProductName;
-- (504 row(s) affected) - Partial results.
```

RowNo	Category	ProductName	Color	ProductNumber
1	Parts	Adjustable Race	N/A	AR-5381
2	Mountain	All-Purpose Bike Stand	N/A	ST-1401
3	Other	AWC Logo Cap	Multi	CA-1098
4	Parts	BB Ball Bearing	N/A	BE-2349
5	Parts	Bearing Ball	N/A	BA-8327
6	Other	Bike Wash - Dissolver	N/A	CL-9009
7	Parts	Blade	N/A	BL-2036
8	Other	Cable Lock	N/A	LO-C100
9	Parts	Chain	Silver	CH-0234
10	Parts	Chain Stays	N/A	CS-2812

Testing PostalCode with ISNUMERIC and generating a flag with CASE expression.

```
SELECT   TOP (4) AddressID,    City,    PostalCode                              AS Zip,
          CASE WHEN ISNUMERIC(PostalCode) = 1 THEN 'Y'  ELSE 'N'  END     AS IsZipNumeric
FROM     AdventureWorks2008.Person.Address  ORDER BY NEWID();
```

AddressID	City	Zip	IsZipNumeric
16704	Paris	75008	Y
26320	Grossmont	91941	Y
27705	Matraville	2036	Y
18901	Kirkby	KB9	N

The OVER Clause

The OVER clause defines the partitioning and sorting of a rowset (intermediate result set) preceding the application of an associated window function, such as ranking. Window functions are also dubbed as ranking functions.

```
USE AdventureWorks2012;
-- Query with three different OVER clauses
SELECT  ROW_NUMBER() OVER ( ORDER BY SalesOrderID, ProductID)              AS RowNum
        ,SalesOrderID, ProductID, OrderQty
        ,RANK() OVER(PARTITION BY SalesOrderID ORDER BY OrderQty DESC)     AS Ranking
        ,SUM(OrderQty) OVER(PARTITION BY SalesOrderID)                     AS TotalQty
        ,AVG(OrderQty) OVER(PARTITION BY SalesOrderID)                     AS AvgQty
        ,COUNT(OrderQty) OVER(PARTITION BY SalesOrderID)  AS "Count"  -- T-SQL keyword, use "" or []
        ,MIN(OrderQty) OVER(PARTITION BY SalesOrderID)                     AS "Min"
        ,MAX(OrderQty) OVER(PARTITION BY SalesOrderID)                     AS "Max"
FROM Sales.SalesOrderDetail
WHERE SalesOrderID BETWEEN 61190 AND 61199
ORDER BY RowNum;
-- (143 row(s) affected) - Partial results.
```

RowNum	SalesOrderID	ProductID	OrderQty	Ranking	TotalQty	AvgQty	Count	Min	Max
1	61190	707	4	13	159	3	40	1	17
2	61190	708	3	18	159	3	40	1	17
3	61190	711	5	8	159	3	40	1	17
4	61190	712	12	2	159	3	40	1	17
5	61190	714	3	18	159	3	40	1	17
6	61190	715	5	8	159	3	40	1	17
7	61190	716	5	8	159	3	40	1	17
8	61190	858	4	13	159	3	40	1	17
9	61190	859	7	6	159	3	40	1	17
10	61190	864	8	4	159	3	40	1	17
11	61190	865	3	18	159	3	40	1	17
12	61190	870	9	3	159	3	40	1	17
13	61190	876	4	13	159	3	40	1	17
14	61190	877	5	8	159	3	40	1	17
15	61190	880	1	34	159	3	40	1	17
16	61190	881	5	8	159	3	40	1	17
17	61190	883	2	26	159	3	40	1	17
18	61190	884	17	1	159	3	40	1	17
19	61190	885	3	18	159	3	40	1	17
20	61190	886	1	34	159	3	40	1	17
21	61190	889	2	26	159	3	40	1	17
22	61190	892	4	13	159	3	40	1	17
23	61190	893	3	18	159	3	40	1	17
24	61190	895	1	34	159	3	40	1	17

FROM Clause: Specifies the Data Source

The FROM clause specifies the source data sets for the query such as tables, views, derived tables and table-valued functions. Typically the tables are JOINed together. The most common JOIN is INNER JOIN which is based on equality between FOREIGN KEY and PRIMARY KEY values in the two tables.

PERFORMANCE NOTE
All FOREIGN KEYs should be indexed. PRIMARY KEYs are indexed automatically with unique index.

```
USE AdventureWorks2012;
GO
SELECT
  ROW_NUMBER() OVER(ORDER BY SalesYTD DESC)                                AS RowNo,
  ROW_NUMBER() OVER(PARTITION BY PostalCode ORDER BY SalesYTD DESC)      AS SeqNo,
              CONCAT(p.FirstName, SPACE(1), p.LastName)              AS SalesStaff,
              FORMAT(s.SalesYTD,'c','en-US')                         AS YTDSales,
              City,
              a.PostalCode                                           AS ZipCode
FROM Sales.SalesPerson AS s
   INNER JOIN Person.Person AS p
     ON s.BusinessEntityID = p.BusinessEntityID
   INNER JOIN Person.Address AS a
     ON a.AddressID = p.BusinessEntityID
WHERE TerritoryID IS NOT NULL    AND SalesYTD <> 0 ORDER BY ZipCode, SeqNo;
```

RowNo	SeqNo	SalesStaff	YTDSales	City	ZipCode
1	1	Linda Mitchell	$4,251,368.55	Issaquah	98027
3	2	Michael Blythe	$3,763,178.18	Issaquah	98027
4	3	Jillian Carson	$3,189,418.37	Issaquah	98027
8	4	Tsvi Reiter	$2,315,185.61	Issaquah	98027
12	5	Garrett Vargas	$1,453,719.47	Issaquah	98027
14	6	Pamela Ansman-Wolfe	$1,352,577.13	Issaquah	98027
2	1	Jae Pak	$4,116,871.23	Renton	98055
5	2	Ranjit Varkey Chudukatil	$3,121,616.32	Renton	98055
6	3	José Saraiva	$2,604,540.72	Renton	98055
7	4	Shu Ito	$2,458,535.62	Renton	98055
9	5	Rachel Valdez	$1,827,066.71	Renton	98055
10	6	Tete Mensa-Annan	$1,576,562.20	Renton	98055
11	7	David Campbell	$1,573,012.94	Renton	98055
13	8	Lynn Tsoflias	$1,421,810.92	Renton	98055

The WHERE Clause to Filter Records (Rows)

The WHERE clause filters the rows generated by the query. Only rows satisfying (TRUE) the WHERE clause predicates are returned.

> PERFORMANCE NOTE
> All columns in WHERE clause should be indexed.

```
USE AdventureWorks2012;
```

String equal match predicate - equal is TRUE, not equal is FALSE.

```
SELECT ProductID, Name, ListPrice, Color
FROM Production.Product  WHERE Name = 'Mountain-100 Silver, 38' ;
```

ProductID	Name	ListPrice	Color
771	Mountain-100 Silver, 38	3399.99	Silver

```
-- Function equality predicate
SELECT * FROM Sales.SalesOrderHeader WHERE YEAR(OrderDate) = 2008;
-- (13951 row(s) affected)
```

> **PERFORMANCE NOTE**
> **When a column is used as a parameter in a function (e.g. YEAR(OrderDate)), index (if any) usage is voided. Instead of random SEEK, all rows are SCANned in the table. The predicate is not SARGable.**

```
-- String wildcard match predicate
SELECT ProductID, Name, ListPrice, Color
FROM Production.Product  WHERE Name LIKE ('%touring%');
```

```
-- Integer range predicate
SELECT ProductID, Name, ListPrice, Color
FROM Production.Product  WHERE ProductID >= 997 ;
```

```
-- Double string wildcard match predicate
SELECT ProductID, Name, ListPrice, Color
FROM Production.Product  WHERE Name LIKE ('%bike%')  AND Name LIKE ('%44%');
```

```
-- String list match predicate
SELECT ProductID, Name, ListPrice, Color  FROM Production.Product
WHERE Name IN ('Mountain-100 Silver, 44', 'Mountain-100 Black, 44');
```

The GROUP BY Clause to Aggregate Results

The GROUP BY clause is applied to partition the rows and calculate aggregate values. An extremely powerful way of looking at the data from a summary point of view.

```
SELECT
            V.Name                                      AS Vendor,
            FORMAT(SUM(TotalDue), 'c', 'en-US')         AS TotalPurchase,
            A.City,
            SP.Name                                     AS State,
            CR.Name                                     AS Country
FROM Purchasing.Vendor AS V
  INNER JOIN Purchasing.VendorAddress AS VA
            ON VA.VendorID = V.VendorID
  INNER JOIN Person.Address AS A
            ON A.AddressID = VA.AddressID
  INNER JOIN Person.StateProvince AS SP
            ON SP.StateProvinceID =  A.StateProvinceID
  INNER JOIN Person.CountryRegion AS CR
            ON CR.CountryRegionCode = SP.CountryRegionCode
 INNER JOIN Purchasing.PurchaseOrderHeader POH
            ON POH.VendorID = V.VendorID
GROUP BY  V.Name, A.City, SP.Name, CR.Name
ORDER BY SUM(TotalDue) DESC,  Vendor;   -- TotalPurchase does a string sort instead of numeric
GO
-- (79 row(s) affected) - Partial results.
```

Vendor	TotalPurchase	City	State	Country
Superior Bicycles	$5,034,266.74	Lynnwood	Washington	United States
Professional Athletic Consultants	$3,379,946.32	Burbank	California	United States
Chicago City Saddles	$3,347,165.20	Daly City	California	United States
Jackson Authority	$2,821,333.52	Long Beach	California	United States
Vision Cycles, Inc.	$2,777,684.91	Glendale	California	United States
Sport Fan Co.	$2,675,889.22	Burien	Washington	United States
Proseware, Inc.	$2,593,901.31	Lebanon	Oregon	United States
Crowley Sport	$2,472,770.05	Chicago	Illinois	United States
Greenwood Athletic Company	$2,472,770.05	Lemon Grove	Arizona	United States
Mitchell Sports	$2,424,284.37	Everett	Washington	United States
First Rate Bicycles	$2,304,231.55	La Mesa	New Mexico	United States
Signature Cycles	$2,236,033.80	Coronado	California	United States
Electronic Bike Repair & Supplies	$2,154,773.37	Tacoma	Washington	United States
Vista Road Bikes	$2,090,857.52	Salem	Oregon	United States
Victory Bikes	$2,052,173.62	Issaquah	Washington	United States
Bicycle Specialists	$1,952,375.30	Lake Oswego	Oregon	United States

The HAVING Clause to Filter Aggregates

The HAVING clause is similar to the WHERE clause filtering but applies to GROUP BY aggregates.

```
USE AdventureWorks;
SELECT
        V.Name                                  AS Vendor,
        FORMAT(SUM(TotalDue), 'c', 'en-US')     AS TotalPurchase,
        A.City,
        SP.Name                                 AS State,
        CR.Name                                 AS Country
FROM Purchasing.Vendor AS V
  INNER JOIN Purchasing.VendorAddress AS VA
        ON VA.VendorID = V.VendorID
  INNER JOIN Person.Address AS A
        ON A.AddressID = VA.AddressID
  INNER JOIN Person.StateProvince AS SP
        ON SP.StateProvinceID =   A.StateProvinceID
  INNER JOIN Person.CountryRegion AS CR
        ON CR.CountryRegionCode = SP.CountryRegionCode
  INNER JOIN Purchasing.PurchaseOrderHeader POH
        ON POH.VendorID = V.VendorID
GROUP BY  V.Name, A.City, SP.Name, CR.Name
HAVING SUM(TotalDue) < $26000    -- HAVING clause predicate
ORDER BY SUM(TotalDue) DESC,  Vendor;
```

Vendor	TotalPurchase	City	State	Country
Speed Corporation	$25,732.84	Anacortes	Washington	United States
Gardner Touring Cycles	$25,633.64	Altadena	California	United States
National Bike Association	$25,513.90	Sedro Woolley	Washington	United States
Australia Bike Retailer	$25,060.04	Bellingham	Washington	United States
WestAmerica Bicycle Co.	$25,060.04	Houston	Texas	United States
Ready Rentals	$23,635.06	Kirkland	Washington	United States
Morgan Bike Accessories	$23,146.99	Albany	New York	United States
Continental Pro Cycles	$22,960.07	Long Beach	California	United States
American Bicycles and Wheels	$9,641.01	West Covina	California	United States
Litware, Inc.	$8,553.32	Santa Cruz	California	United States
Business Equipment Center	$8,497.80	Everett	Montana	United States
Bloomington Multisport	$8,243.95	West Covina	California	United States
International	$8,061.10	Salt Lake City	Utah	United States
Wide World Importers	$8,025.60	Concord	California	United States
Midwest Sport, Inc.	$7,328.72	Detroit	Michigan	United States
Wood Fitness	$6,947.58	Philadelphia	Pennsylvania	United States
Metro Sport Equipment	$6,324.53	Lebanon	Oregon	United States
Burnett Road Warriors	$5,779.99	Corvallis	Oregon	United States
Lindell	$5,412.57	Lebanon	Oregon	United States
Consumer Cycles	$3,378.17	Torrance	California	United States
Northern Bike Travel	$2,048.42	Anacortes	Washington	United States

The ORDER BY Clause to Sort Results

The ORDER BY clause sorts the result set. It guarantees ordering according to the columns or expressions listed from major to minor keys. Unique ordering requires a set of keys which generate unique data rows. The major key, YEAR(HireDate), in the first example is not sufficient for uniqueness.

```
USE AdventureWorks2012;          -- Sort on 2 keys
SELECT BusinessEntityID AS EmployeeID, JobTitle, HireDate
FROM HumanResources.Employee  ORDER BY YEAR(HireDate) DESC, EmployeeID;
-- (290 row(s) affected) - Partial results.
```

EmployeeID	JobTitle	HireDate
285	Pacific Sales Manager	2007-04-15
286	Sales Representative	2007-07-01
288	Sales Representative	2007-07-01

```
-- Sort on CASE conditional expression
SELECT   BusinessEntityID AS SalesStaffID, CONCAT(LastName, ', ', FirstName) AS FullName,
         CASE CountryRegionName WHEN 'United States' THEN TerritoryName
                  ELSE '' END AS TerritoryName, CountryRegionName
FROM Sales.vSalesPerson   WHERE TerritoryName IS NOT NULL          -- view
ORDER BY CASE WHEN CountryRegionName != 'United States' THEN  CountryRegionName
                  ELSE TerritoryName  END;
```

SalesStaffID	FullName	TerritoryName	CountryRegionName
286	Tsoflias, Lynn		Australia
278	Vargas, Garrett		Canada
282	Saraiva, José		Canada

The EXCEPT & INTERSECT Set Operators

The EXCEPT operator & the INTERSECT operator require the column lists are compatible for the comparison.

```
USE tempdb; -- Prepare two tables with 400 random(newid()) picks from the Product table
SELECT TOP (400) * INTO Prod1 FROM AdventureWorks2012.Production.Product ORDER BY NEWID();
SELECT TOP (400) * INTO Prod2 FROM AdventureWorks2012.Production.Product ORDER BY NEWID();

-- EXCEPT SET OPERATOR - no match rows
SELECT * FROM PROD1 EXCEPT SELECT * FROM PROD2;  -- (81 row(s) affected)

-- INTERSECT SET OPERATOR - matching rows
SELECT * FROM PROD1 INTERSECT SELECT * FROM PROD2;  -- (319 row(s) affected)
```

CTE - Common Table Expression

CTE helps with structured programming by the definition of named subqueries at the beginning of the query. It supports nesting and recursion.

```
USE AdventureWorks;
-- Testing CTE
WITH CTE (SalesPersonID, NumberOfOrders, MostRecentOrderDate)
    AS  (           SELECT SalesPersonID, COUNT(*), CONVERT(date, MAX(OrderDate))
                    FROM Sales.SalesOrderHeader
                    GROUP BY SalesPersonID   )
SELECT * FROM CTE;
-- (18 row(s) affected) - Partial results.
```

SalesPersonID	NumberOfOrders	MostRecentOrderDate
284	39	2004-05-01
278	234	2004-06-01
281	242	2004-06-01

```
-- Using CTE in a query
;WITH CTE (SalesPersonID, NumberOfOrders, MostRecentOrderDate)
    AS  ( SELECT SalesPersonID, COUNT(*), CONVERT(date, MAX(OrderDate))
        FROM Sales.SalesOrderHeader    GROUP BY SalesPersonID        )
-- Start of outer (main) query
 SELECT         E.EmployeeID,
                OE.NumberOfOrders                          AS EmpOrders,
                OE.MostRecentOrderDate                     AS EmpLastOrder,
                E.ManagerID,
                OM.NumberOfOrders                          AS MgrOrders,
                OM.MostRecentOrderDate                     AS MgrLastOrder
 FROM   HumanResources.Employee AS E
        INNER JOIN CTE AS OE                    ON E.EmployeeID = OE.SalesPersonID
        LEFT OUTER JOIN CTE AS OM               ON E.ManagerID = OM.SalesPersonID
ORDER BY EmployeeID;
-- (17 row(s) affected) - Partial results.
```

EmployeeID	EmpOrders	EmpLastOrder	ManagerID	MgrOrders	MgrLastOrder
268	48	2004-06-01	273	NULL	NULL
275	450	2004-06-01	268	48	2004-06-01
276	418	2004-06-01	268	48	2004-06-01
277	473	2004-06-01	268	48	2004-06-01
278	234	2004-06-01	268	48	2004-06-01

Combining Results of Multiple Queries with UNION

UNION and UNION ALL (no duplicates elimination) operators can be used to **stack result sets from two or more queries into a single result set**.

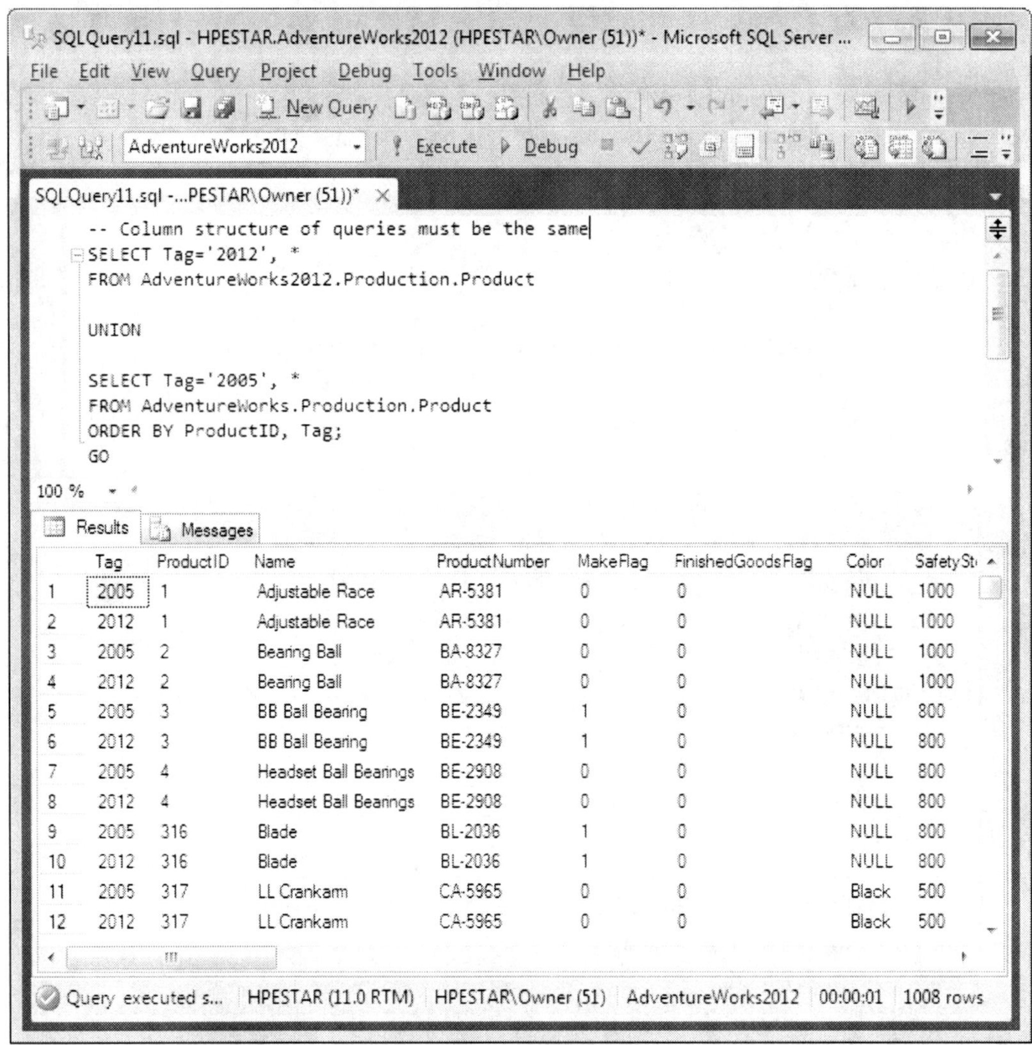

```
-- Combining data from OLTP & data warehouse databases
SELECT FirstName, LastName, 0 AS TotalChildren
FROM AdventureWorks2012.Person.Person
UNION ALL
SELECT FirstName, LastName, TotalChildren
FROM AdventureWorksDW2012..DimCustomer;
```

TOP n by Group Query with OVER PARTITION BY

OVER PARTITION BY method is very convenient for TOP n by group selection. List of top 3 orders placed by resellers (customers of AdventureWorks Cycles).

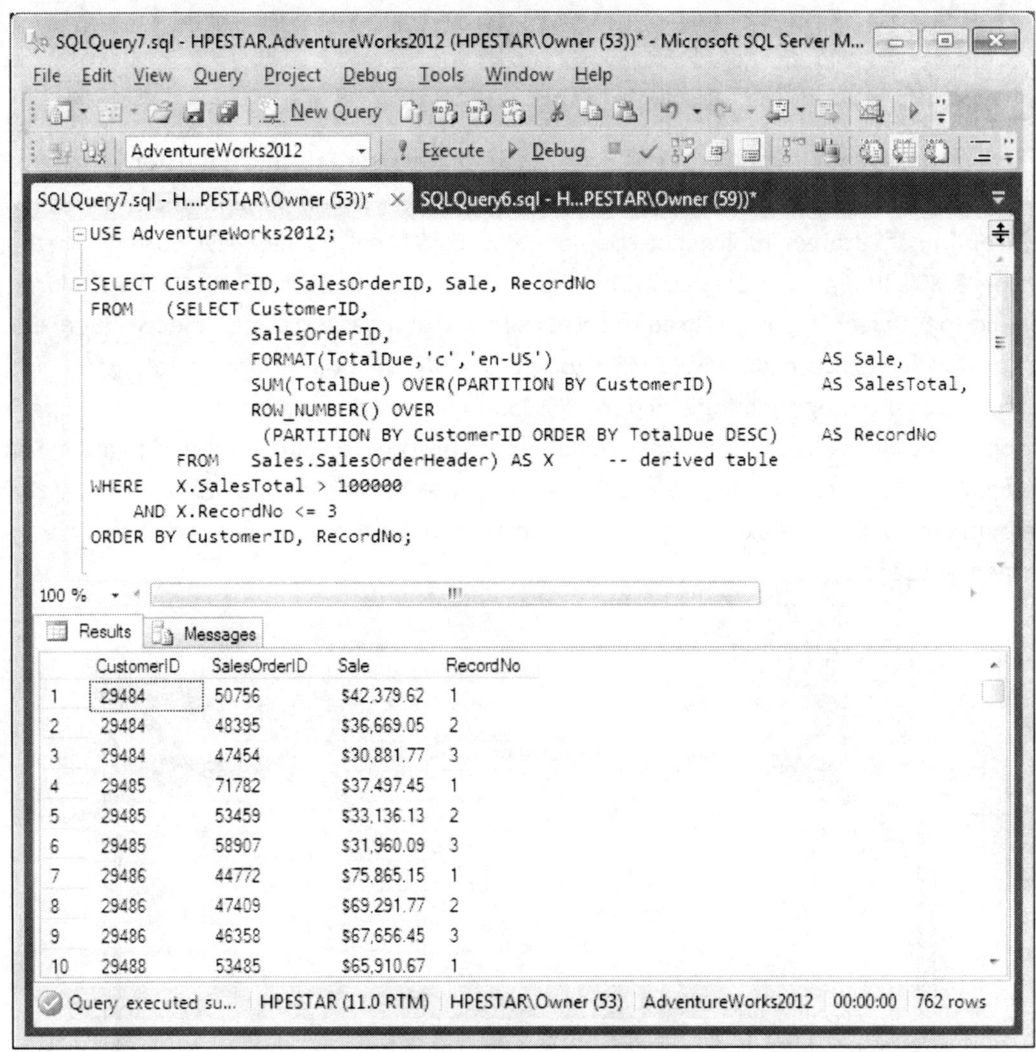

	CustomerID	SalesOrderID	Sale	RecordNo
1	29484	50756	$42,379.62	1
2	29484	48395	$36,669.05	2
3	29484	47454	$30,881.77	3
4	29485	71782	$37,497.45	1
5	29485	53459	$33,136.13	2
6	29485	58907	$31,960.09	3
7	29486	44772	$75,865.15	1
8	29486	47409	$69,291.77	2
9	29486	46358	$67,656.45	3
10	29488	53485	$65,910.67	1

```
-- Row numbering by partitioning view results
SELECT ROW_NUMBER() OVER(PARTITION BY PhoneNumberType ORDER BY SalesYTD DESC) RN,
       CONCAT(FirstName, ' ', LastName) as Name, ROUND(SalesYTD,2,1) AS YTDSales,
       PhoneNumberType
FROM AdventureWorks2012.Sales.vSalesPerson
ORDER BY PhoneNumberType, RN;
```

CHAPTER 4: SQL Server Management Studio

SQL Server Programming, Administration & Management Tool

SQL Server Management Studio (SSMS) is a GUI (Graphical User Interface) tool for accessing, configuring, managing, administering, and developing all major components of SQL Server with the exception of Business Intelligence components: SSAS (Analysis Services), SSRS (Reporting Services) & SSIS (Integration Services). The two main environments in SSMS: Object Explorer and Query Editor. Object Explorer is used to access servers, databases and db objects. Query Editor is to develop and execute queries. SSMS is used by a DBA (Data Base Administrator) for administrative and programming functions. SSMS can also be used by a database developer to develop application related db objects such as stored procedures, functions and triggers. Some developers prefer to stay in Visual Studio environment which has features to support database development albeit not as extensive as Management Studio. A typical screen display of Management Studio.

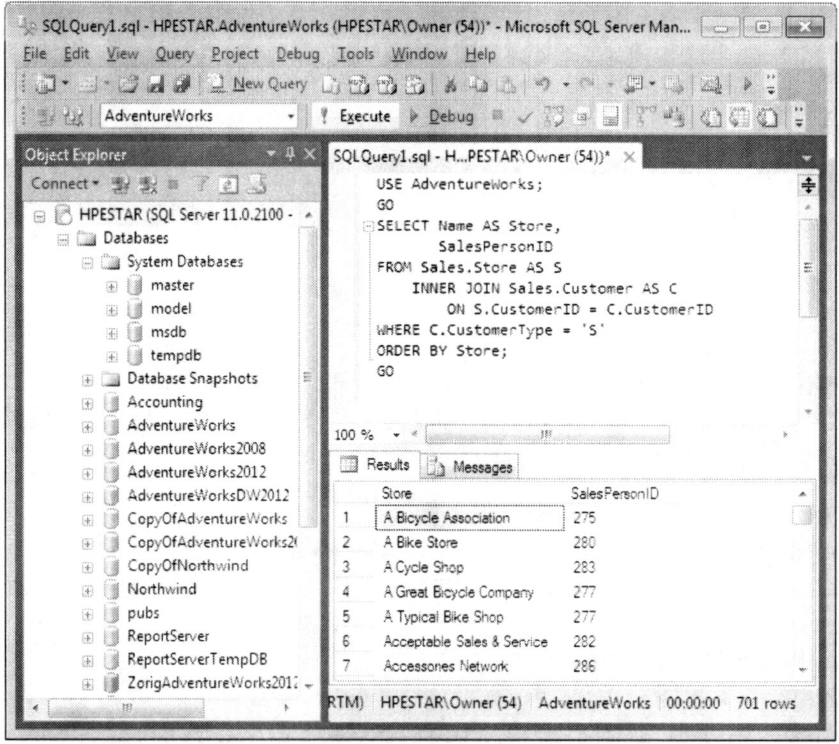

Query Editor

The Query Editor is used to type in queries, edit them and submit them for execution by the server. Queries can also be loaded from a disk file, typically with .sql extension. In addition to textual query development, a number of special tools available such as graphical query designer, debugger, execution plan display and query analysis by the Database Engine Tuning Advisor. IntelliSense provides contextual assistance with SQL syntax checking and guessing object names in a drop-down menu based on the typed prefix.

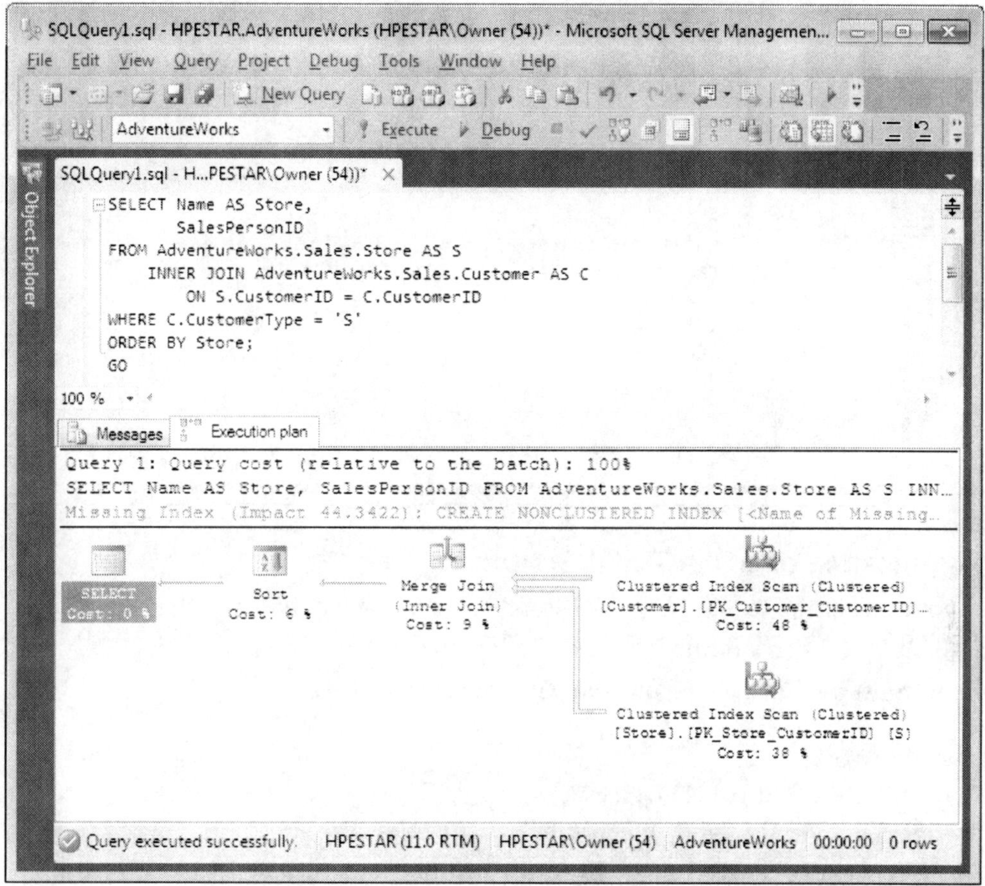

T-SQL Tidbits: Nested CONVERTs for Integer Date Conversion to Datetime/ Date

Note: string date like '20160201' converts directly to date/datetime.

```
DECLARE @intdate int = 20160201;  SELECT CONVERT(datetime, @intdate);
GO        -- Msg 8115...Arithmetic overflow error...
DECLARE @intdate int = 20160201;  SELECT CONVERT(date, @intdate);
GO        -- Msg 529,...Explicit conversion from data type int to date is not allowed.
DECLARE @intdate int = 20160201;  SELECT CONVERT(date, CONVERT(varchar,@intdate));  -- 2016-02-01
```

Execute All Batches in Query Editor

The entire content of the Query Editor is executed when we click on the Execute button. Batches typically separated by "GO" on a separate line.

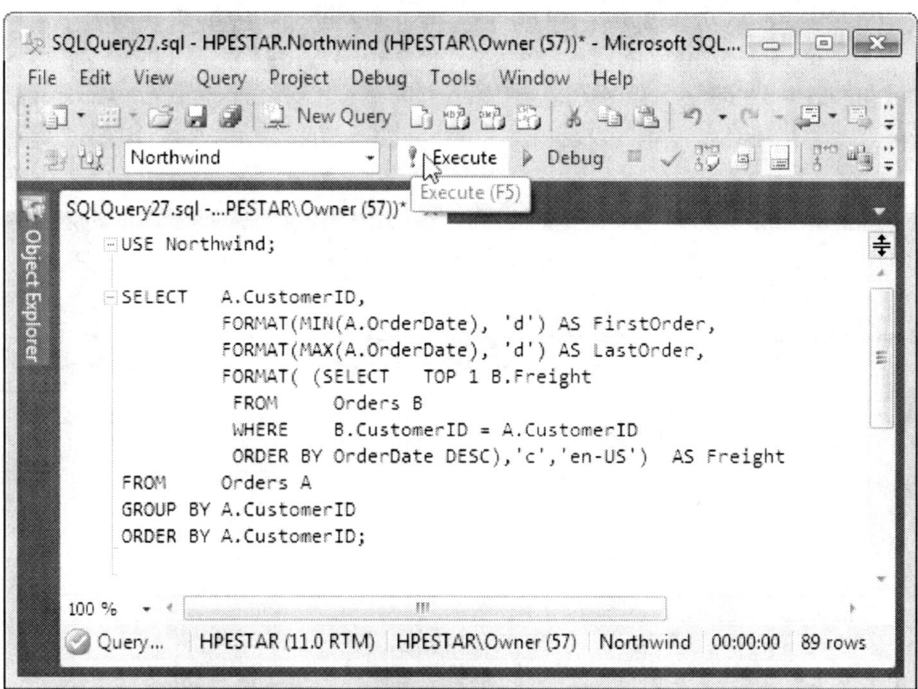

The Significance of GO in T-SQL Scripts

"GO" is not transmitted to SQL Server. "GO" indicates the end of batch to the client software such as SSMS. "GO" also indicates the end of a logical unit to the human reader. Certain statements must be the first line, or have "GO" preceding them.

```
USE AdventureWorks2012;
CREATE FUNCTION Z () RETURNS TABLE AS
RETURN  SELECT * FROM Production.ProductSubcategory;
GO     /* Msg 111, Level 15, State 1, Line 2   'CREATE FUNCTION' must be the first statement in a
query batch. */
```

```
USE AdventureWorks2012;
GO
CREATE FUNCTION Z () RETURNS TABLE AS RETURN SELECT * FROM
Production.ProductSubcategory;
GO
-- Command(s) completed successfully.
```

The Results Pane contains the result rows of the query. It is currently set to Grid format.

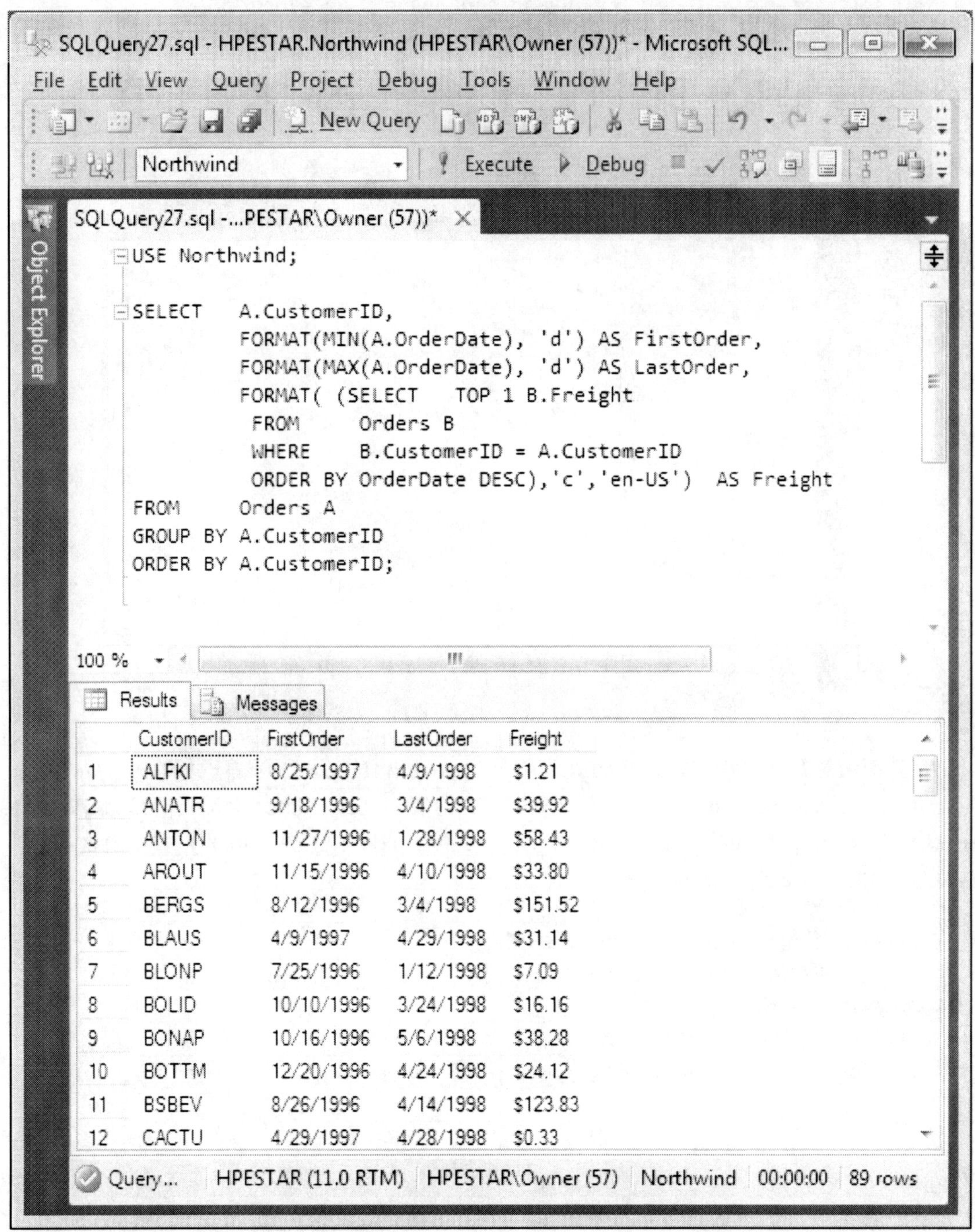

The Messages Pane gets the row count values, warning & error messages as well as the output of the PRINT & RAISERROR statements if any.

The client software also gets the same messages following query execution.

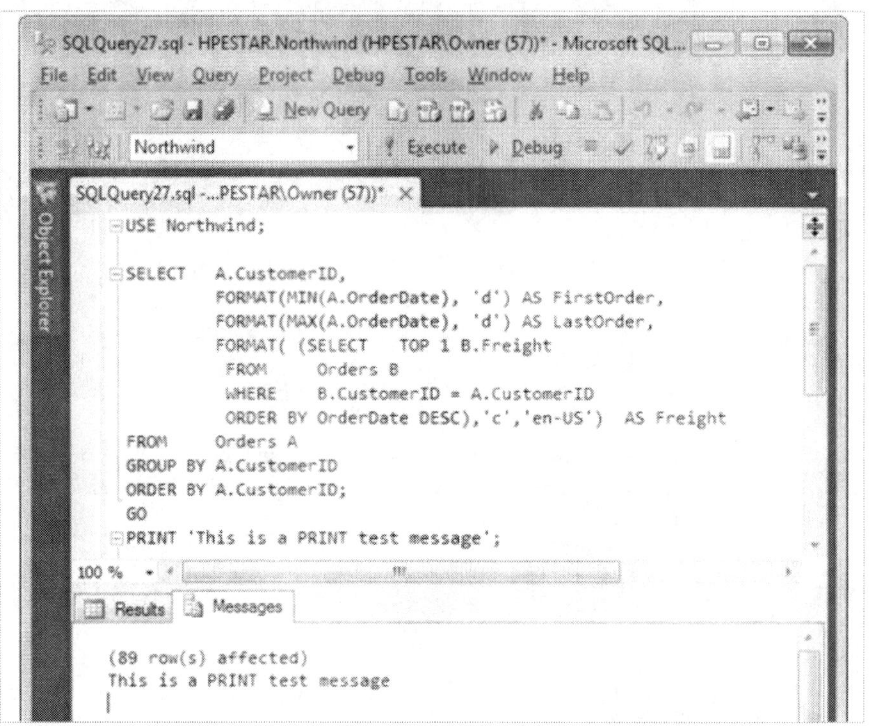

T-SQL Tidbits: Window Function RANK() Usage with GROUP BY AVG Aggregate

The difference in window functions: ROW_NUMBER() & NTILE() do not handle TIES in the data, but RANK() (skips) & DENSE_RANK() (no skip in sequence) do. DENSE_RANK(), RANK() & ROW_NUMBER() yield same results if there are no TIES.

```
SELECT  TOP (3) Color, AVG(ListPrice) AS AvgPrice,
                RANK() OVER (ORDER BY AVG(ListPrice) DESC) AS Rank
FROM Production.Product
WHERE Color is not NULL AND ListPrice > 0.0
GROUP BY Color  ORDER BY Rank;
```

Color	AvgPrice	Rank
Red	1416.3945	1
Silver	1026.4148	2
Yellow	968.8063	3

Routing Results to Grid, Text or File

Results can be routed to Grid, Text or File from the right-click menu or the Query drop-down menu.

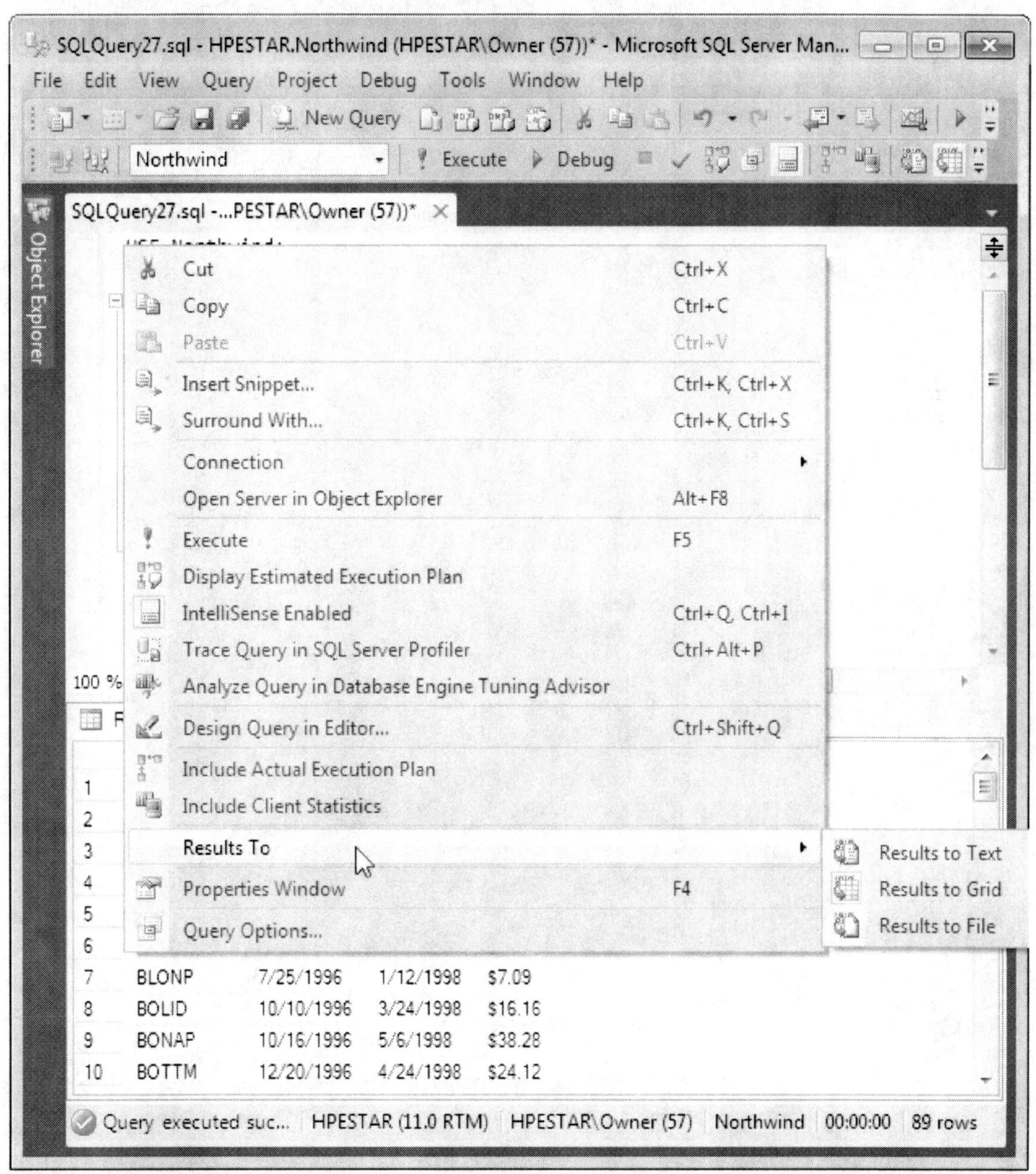

Routing Results to Text

The following screen window image displays results in text format. Messages also come to the Results window, following the results rows.

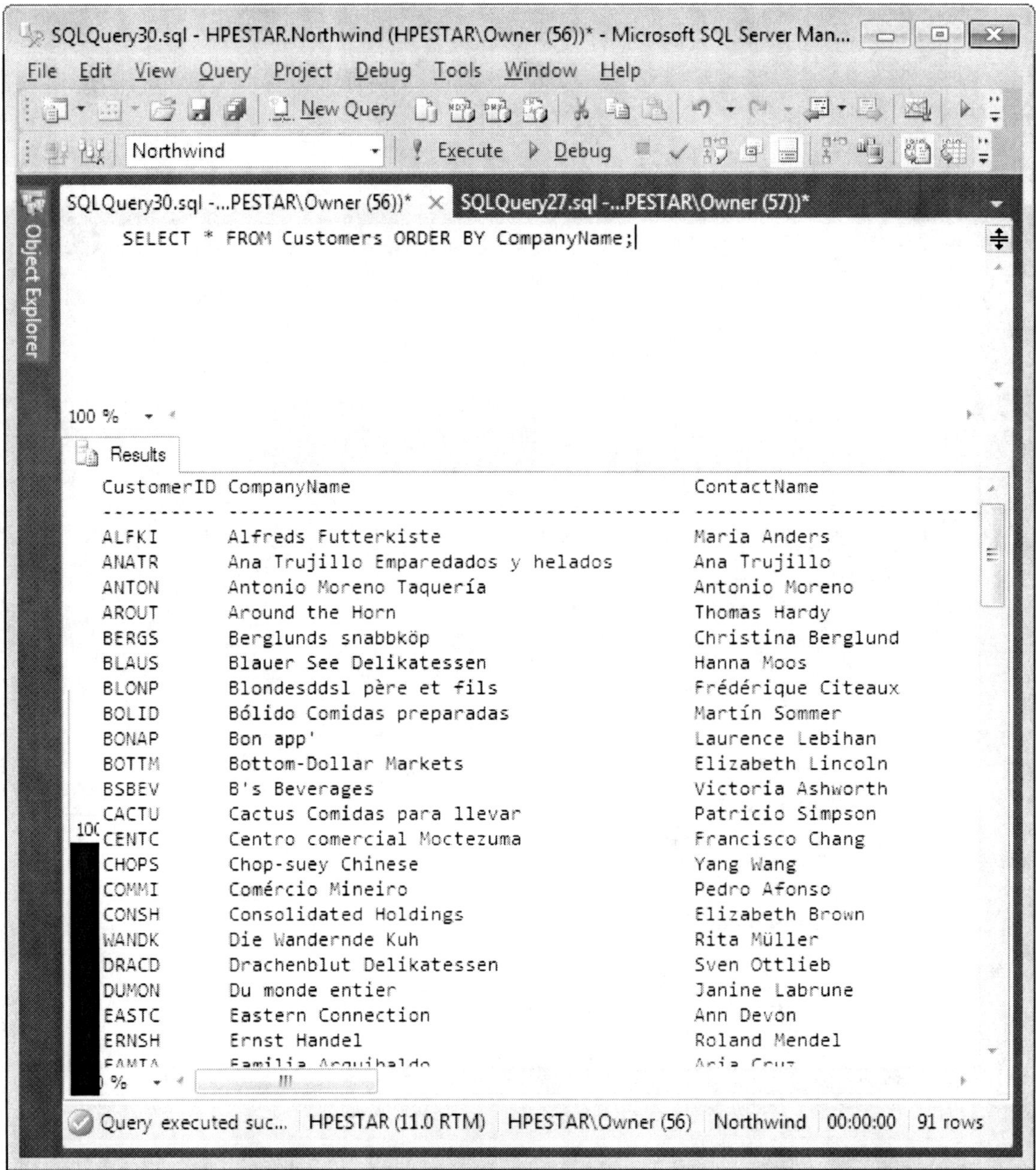

Routing Results to File

When the routing option is file, the file save window pops up upon query execution.

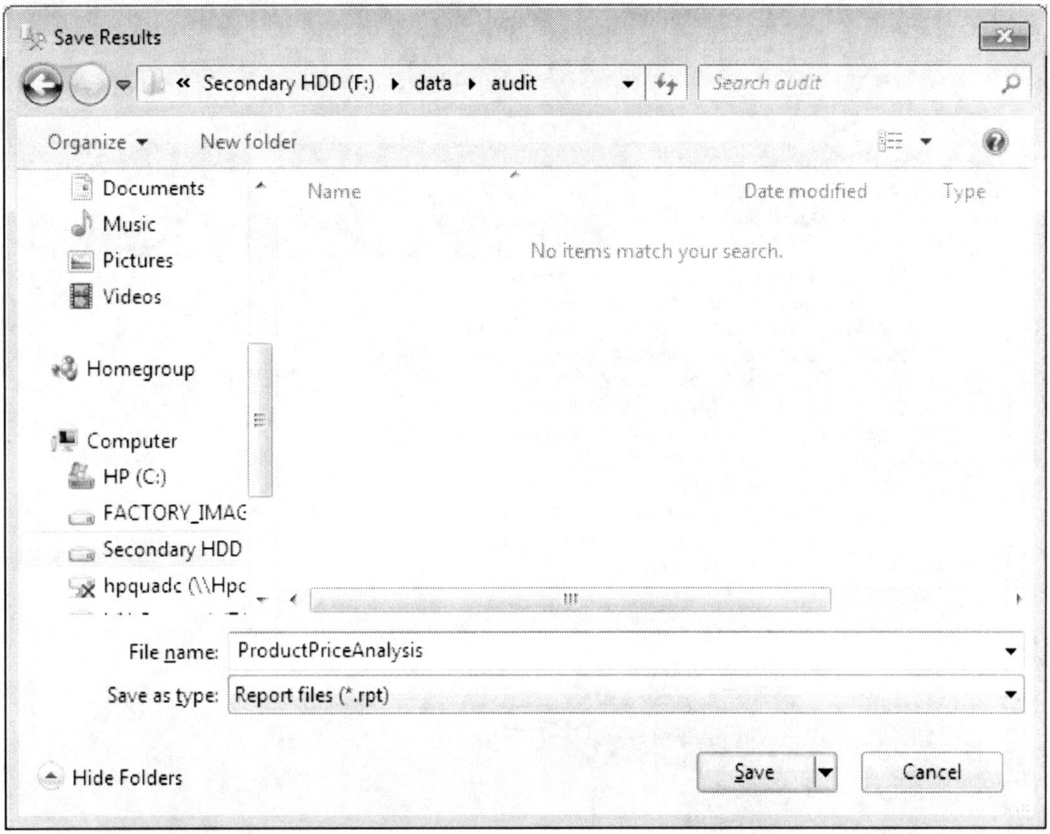

Save Results
« Secondary HDD (F:) ▸ data ▸ audit
Search audit
Organize
New folder
Documents
Music
Pictures
Videos
Homegroup
Computer
HP (C:)
FACTORY_IMAG
Secondary HDD
hpquadc (\\Hpc
Name
Date modified
Type
No items match your search.
File name: ProductPriceAnalysis
Save as type: Report files (*.rpt)
Hide Folders
Save
Cancel

Part of the file in Notepad.

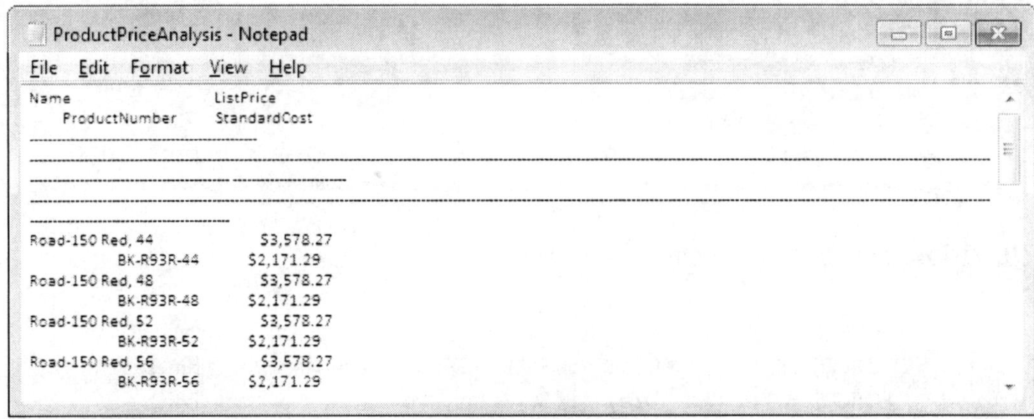

ProductPriceAnalysis - Notepad
File Edit Format View Help
Name ListPrice
ProductNumber StandardCost
Road-150 Red, 44 $3,578.27
BK-R93R-44 $2,171.29
Road-150 Red, 48 $3,578.27
BK-R93R-48 $2,171.29
Road-150 Red, 52 $3,578.27
BK-R93R-52 $2,171.29
Road-150 Red, 56 $3,578.27
BK-R93R-56 $2,171.29

Saving Results in CSV Flat File Format

Results can also be saved in CSV (comma separated values) format which can be read by Excel and other software.

T-SQL Tidbits: Optimizer "FORCE" Commands

SET FORCEPLAN ON	Process tables same order as in JOIN
FORCESEEK	Use index SEEK only on table or view (table hint)
FORCESCAN	Use index SCAN only on table or view(table hint)

The saving file dialog box is configured automatically to csv saving.

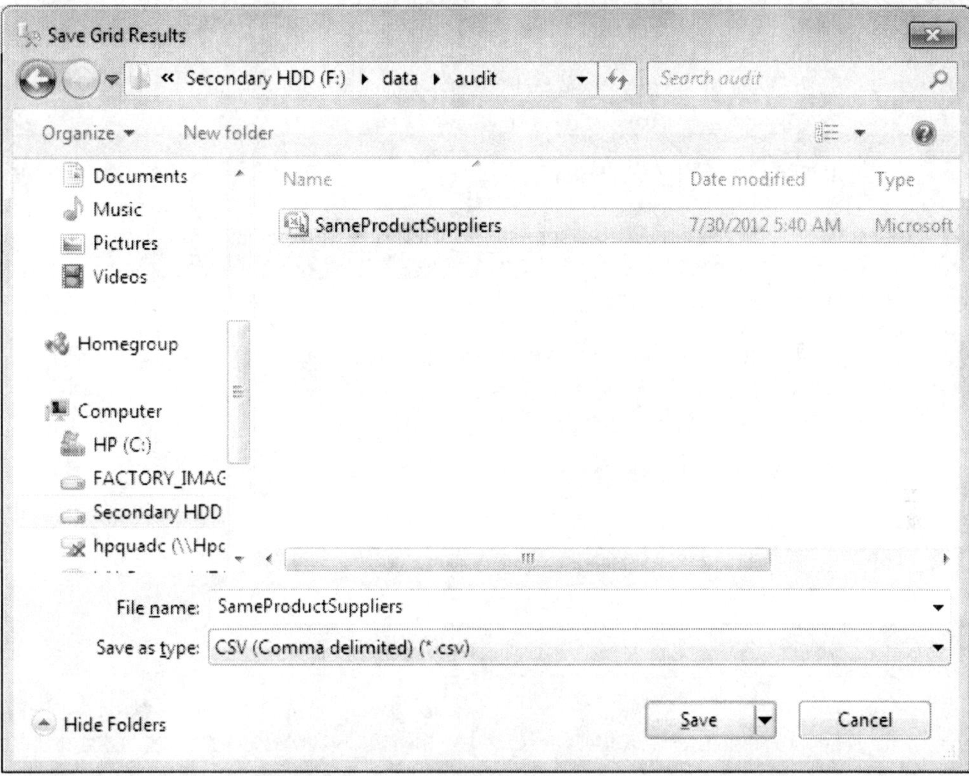

Part of the file in Notepad window.

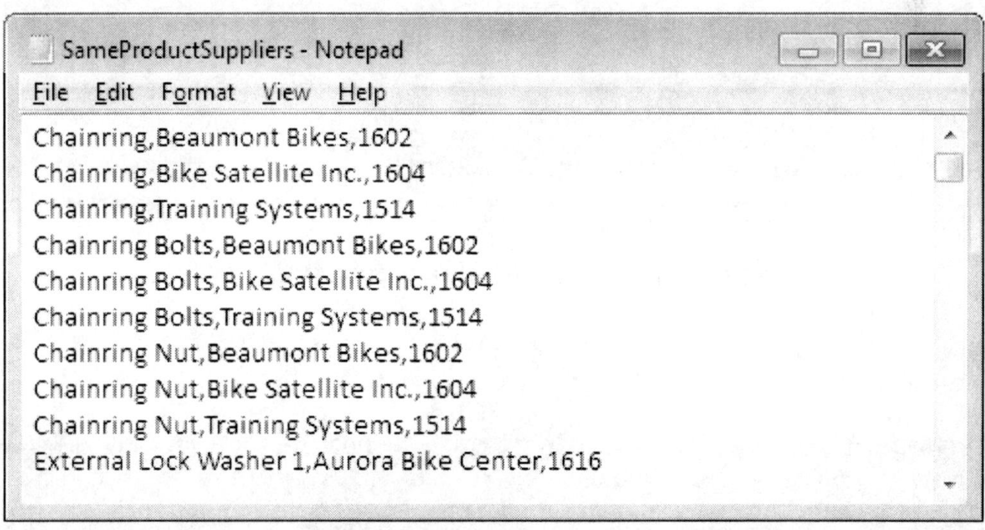

Copy & Paste Results to Excel

Using the copy / copy with headers option in SSMS result window, the query results can simply be pasted into an Excel worksheet. Excel may do implicit conversions on some columns.

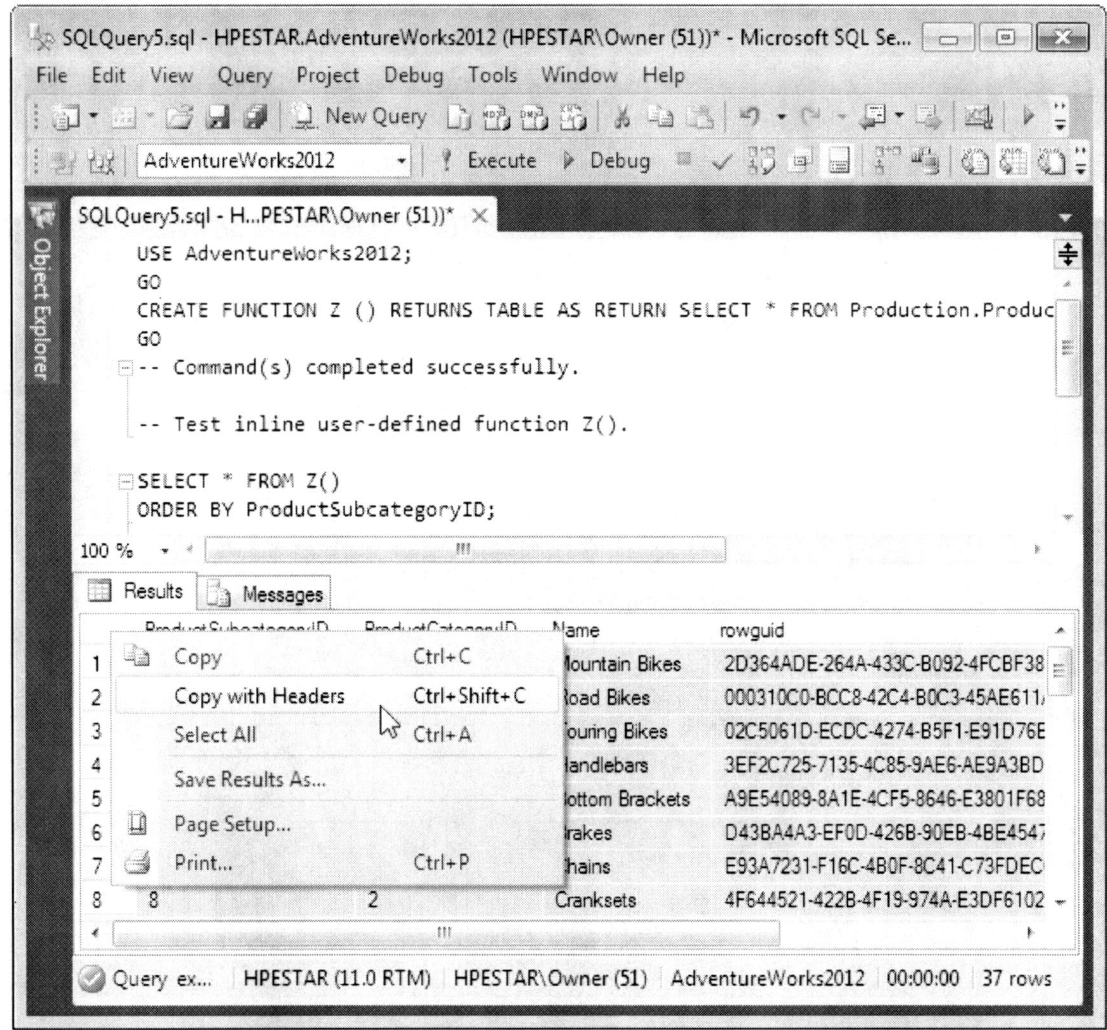

T-SQL Tidbits: Locking the Table with TABLOCK for Multiple UPDATEs

TABLOCK is a table hint.

```
USE AdventureWorks2012;
GO
UPDATE Production.Product WITH (TABLOCK)  SET ListPrice *=  1.02            -- 2% price increase
                    WHERE ProductNumber LIKE 'FR-%';
GO -- (79 row(s) affected)
```

After pasting into an Excel worksheet some formatting may be necessary such as for datetime columns.

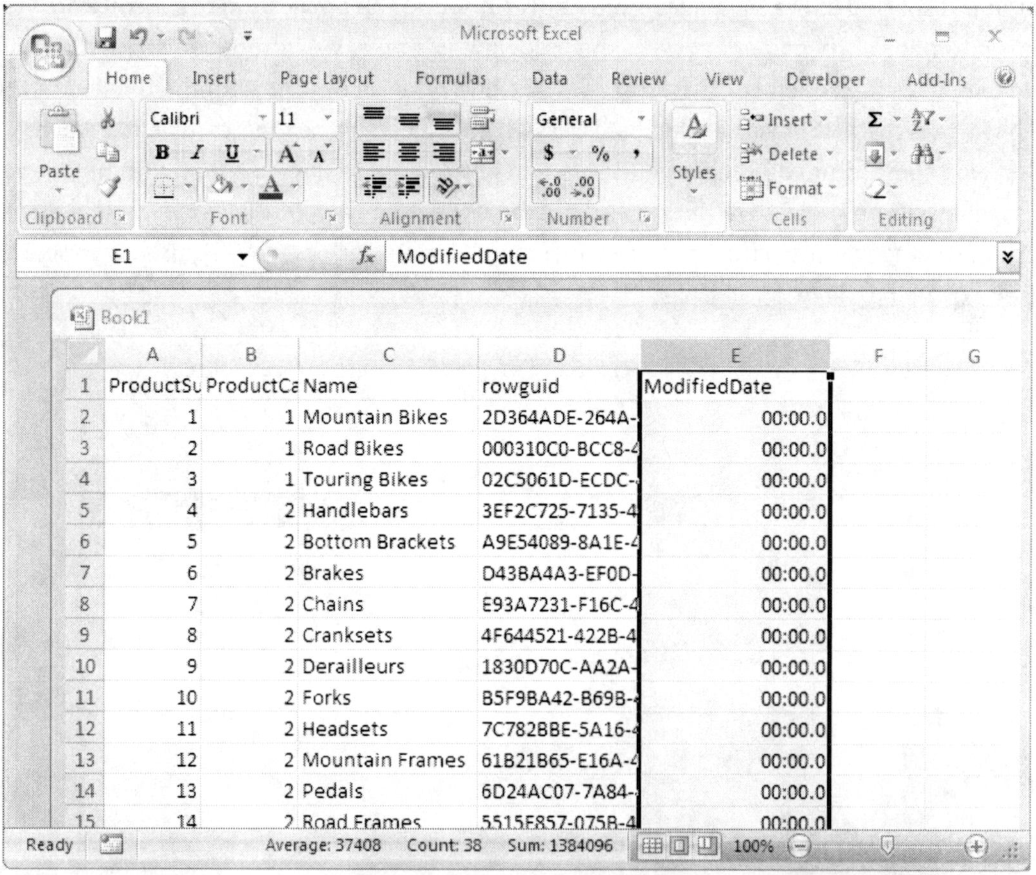

Microsoft Excel

E1 | ModifiedDate

Book1

	A	B	C	D	E
1	ProductSu	ProductCa	Name	rowguid	ModifiedDate
2	1	1	Mountain Bikes	2D364ADE-264A-	00:00.0
3	2	1	Road Bikes	000310C0-BCC8-4	00:00.0
4	3	1	Touring Bikes	02C5061D-ECDC-	00:00.0
5	4	2	Handlebars	3EF2C725-7135-4	00:00.0
6	5	2	Bottom Brackets	A9E54089-8A1E-4	00:00.0
7	6	2	Brakes	D43BA4A3-EF0D-	00:00.0
8	7	2	Chains	E93A7231-F16C-4	00:00.0
9	8	2	Cranksets	4F644521-422B-4	00:00.0
10	9	2	Derailleurs	1830D70C-AA2A-	00:00.0
11	10	2	Forks	B5F9BA42-B69B-	00:00.0
12	11	2	Headsets	7C782BBE-5A16-	00:00.0
13	12	2	Mountain Frames	61B21B65-E16A-4	00:00.0
14	13	2	Pedals	6D24AC07-7A84-	00:00.0
15	14	2	Road Frames	5515F857-075B-4	00:00.0

Ready | Average: 37408 | Count: 38 | Sum: 1384096 | 100%

Error Handling & Debugging

Error handling and debugging is a major part of database development work. When there is an error, it is displayed in the Messages area (or returned to the application client software) which automatically becomes active. In the following example, we introduced an invalid column name which resulted in error. The error message line reference starts with the top line of the batch which is the first line after the first "GO" which indicates a new batch. The red wave-underlining comes from optional IntelliSense and not related to the execution attempt error message. IntelliSense gives warning ahead of time if it detects a potential error. Simple errors can be corrected with help from the error message. Complex errors may required web search and/or examining the query in parts.

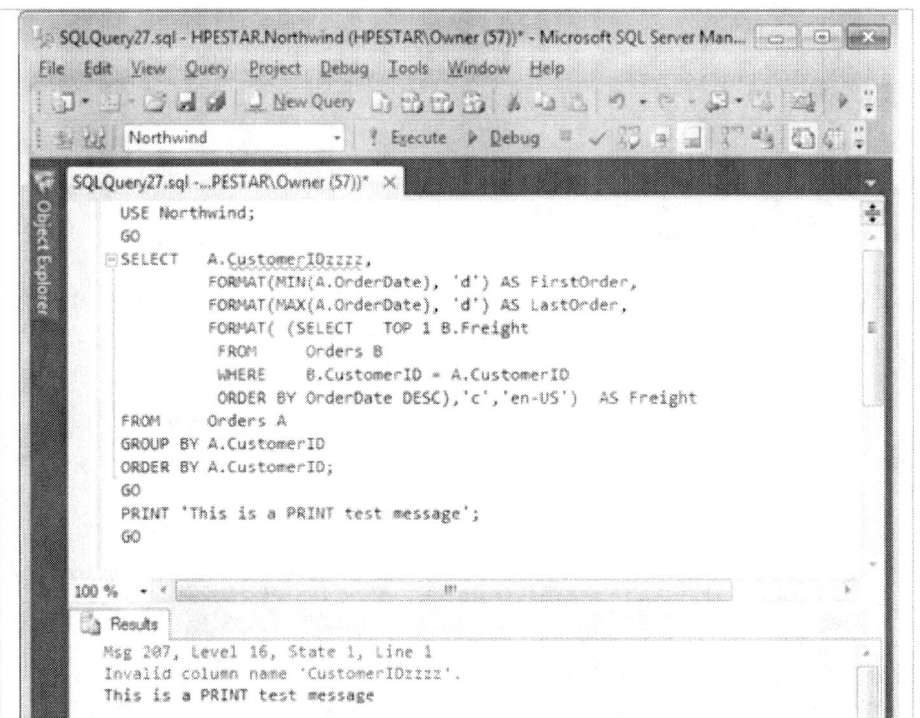

T-SQL Tidbits: Temporary Tables in Stored Procedures

Temporary tables (#table) and **table variables** (@table - typically for small datasets) can be used for passing table datasets from one query to another. Both temporary tables & table variables are multi-users enabled. Global temporary tables (##table) and regular tables in tempdb (temdb.dbo.tablename) can be used as well but they are single use only.

When SQL Server restarts, all temporary objects are gone. In UDF-s, table variables can be used.

Locating the Error Line in a Query

Position the cursor on the error and double click. The error line will be highlighted. This method does not work for all errors.

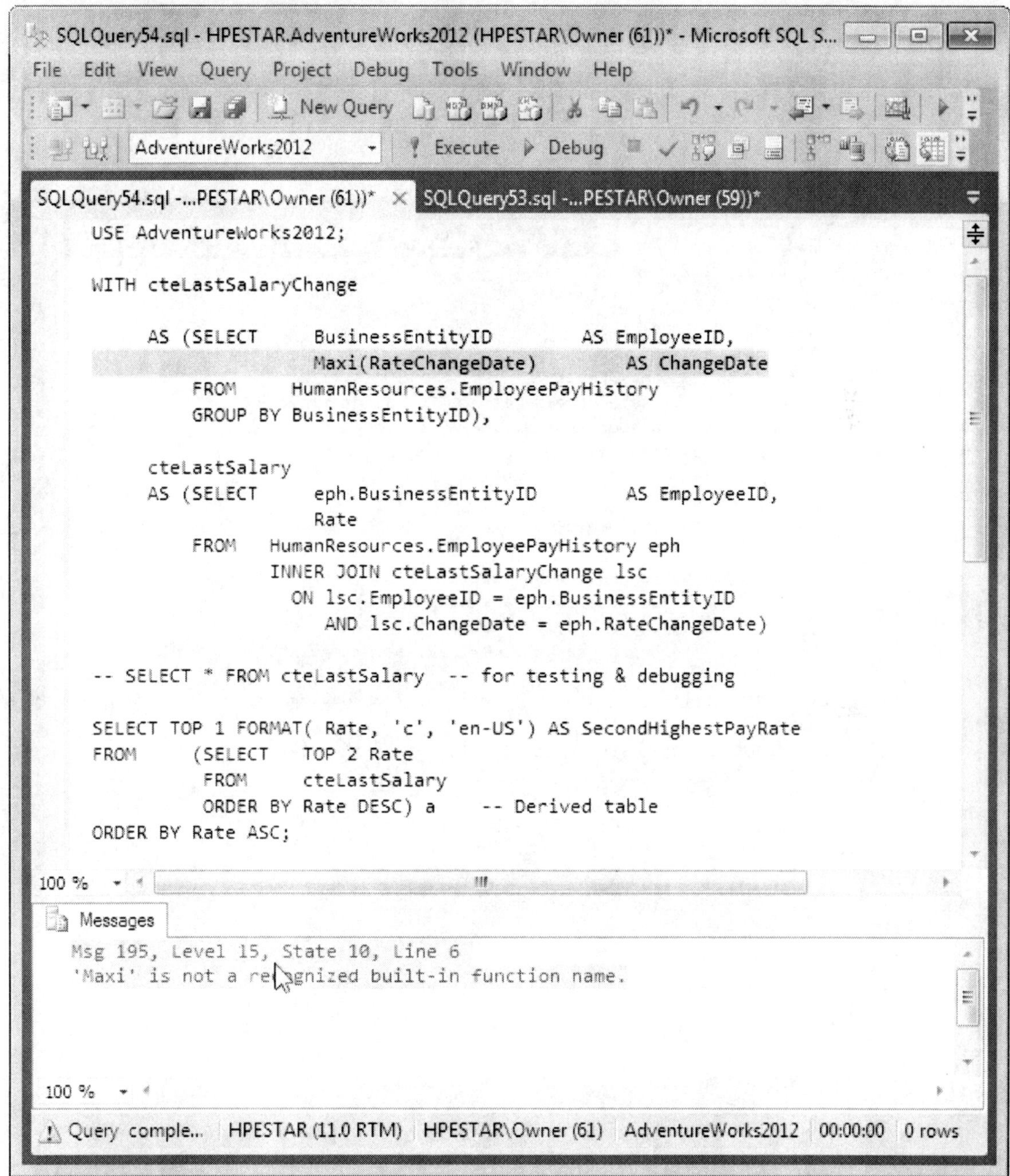

Error Message Pointing to the Wrong Line

For some errors, the first line of the query (3) is returned by the database engine not the actual error line (13). The error message is still very helpful though in this instance.

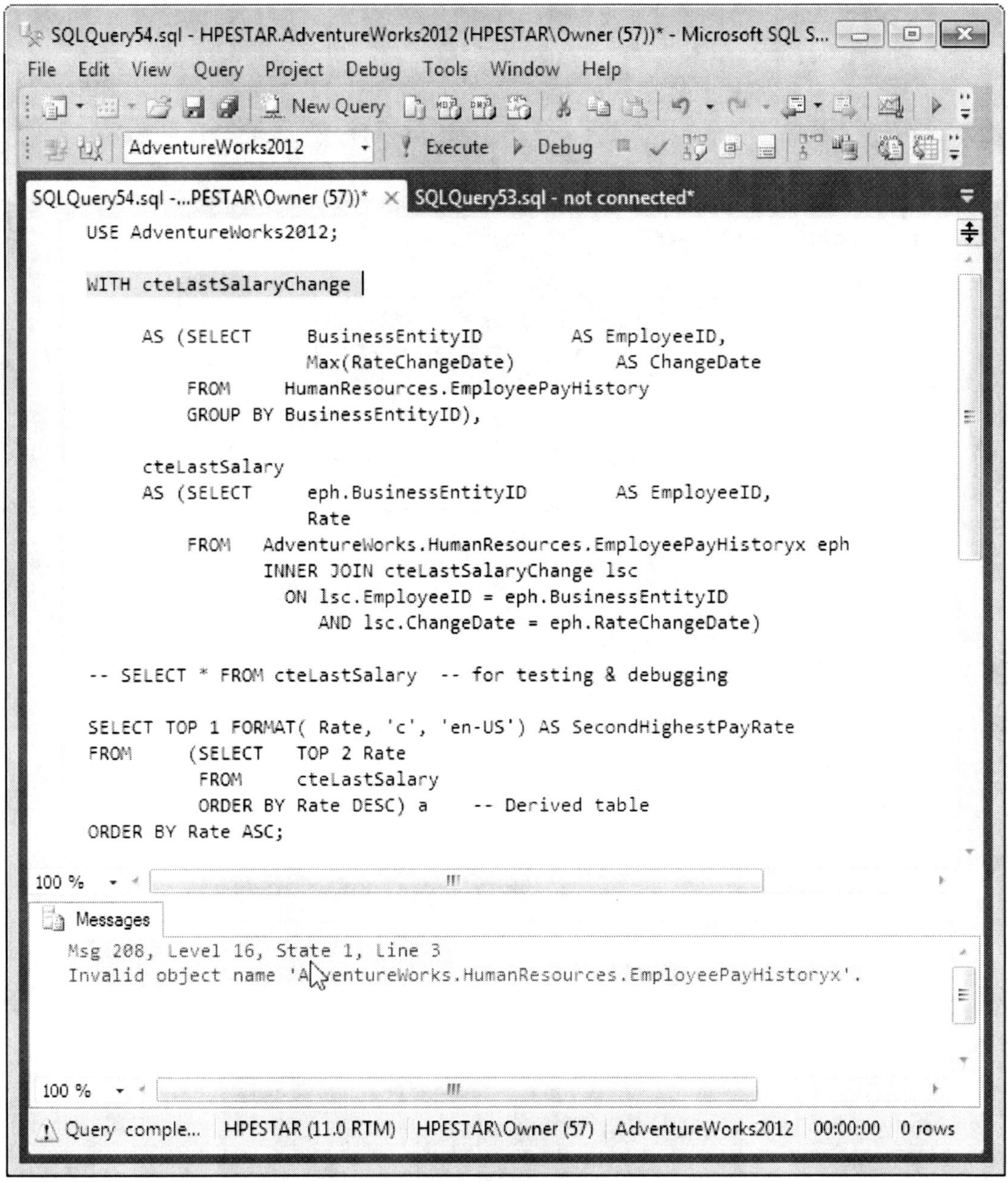

Parsing a Query for Syntax Errors

A query (or one or more batches) can be parsed for syntax errors. Parsing catches syntax errors such as using "ORDER" instead of "ORDER BY" for sorting.

Deferred Name Resolution Process

Deferred Name Resolution Process: Only syntax errors are caught when parsed, not execution (runtime) errors as shown in the following demo which has an invalid table reference (EmployeePayHistoryx). Similarly, **stored procedures can be compiled without errors with invalid table references**. A table need not exist for stored procedure compilation, only for execution.

Executing Single Batch Only

A single batch can be executed by selecting (highlighting) it and clicking on Execute.

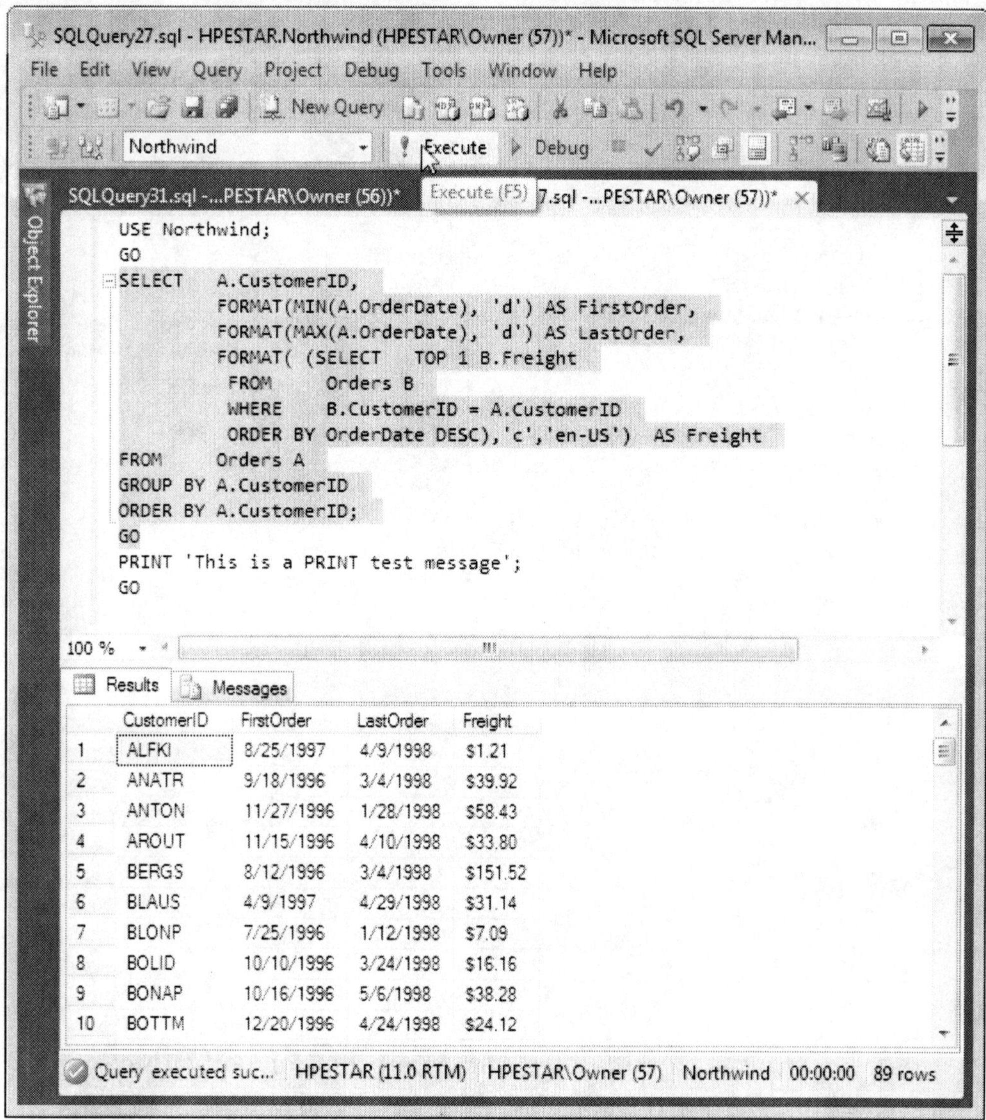

T-SQL Tidbits: CONTEXT_INFO

CONTEXT_INFO (SET option) can be used to communicate between stored procedure & trigger.

> Article: **How to use CONTEXT_INFO in SQL Server**
> http://www.sql-server-performance.com/2008/how-to-use-context-info/

Executing Part of a Query

A part of a query can be executed as long as it is a valid query, otherwise error results. The query part has to be selected (highlighted) and the Execute button has to be pushed. The selected part of the query is considered a batch which is sent to the server. In this example, we executed the subquery (inner query) in the WHERE clause predicate.

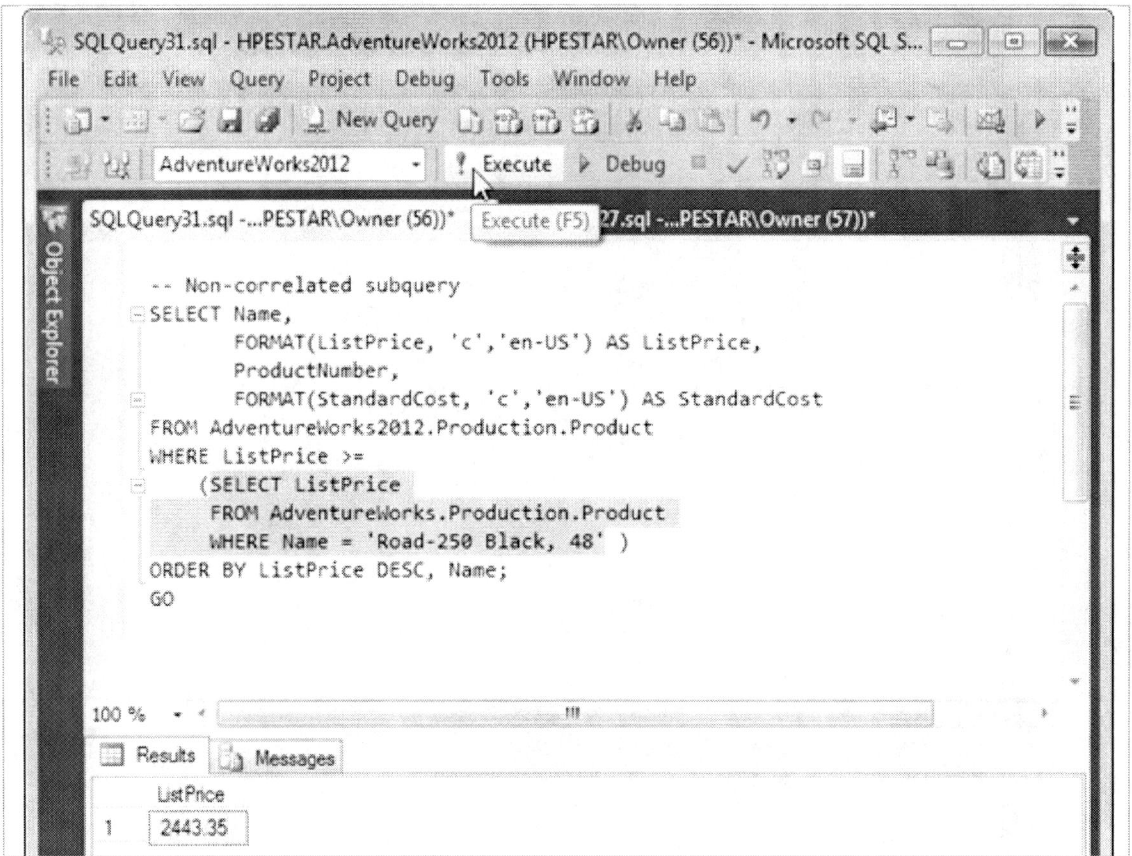

T-SQL Tidbits: Assigning One-Part Column Names in Derived Table & CTE

Column list mapping (column aliases) can optionally be specified both for derived table (X) and CTE.

```
SELECT * FROM                                                          -- Outer query
        (SELECT Color, AVG(ListPrice), MIN(ListPrice), MAX(ListPrice)  -- Subquery
        FROM Production.Product GROUP BY Color)
AS X (Color, AvgPrice, MinPrice, MaxPrice)                             -- Derived table
ORDER BY MaxPrice DESC, Color;                                         -- Outer query sort
```

Object Explorer

SSMS Object Explorer functions as:

- A tree-based directory of all database objects
- A launching base for graphical user-interface tools
- An access way to object properties

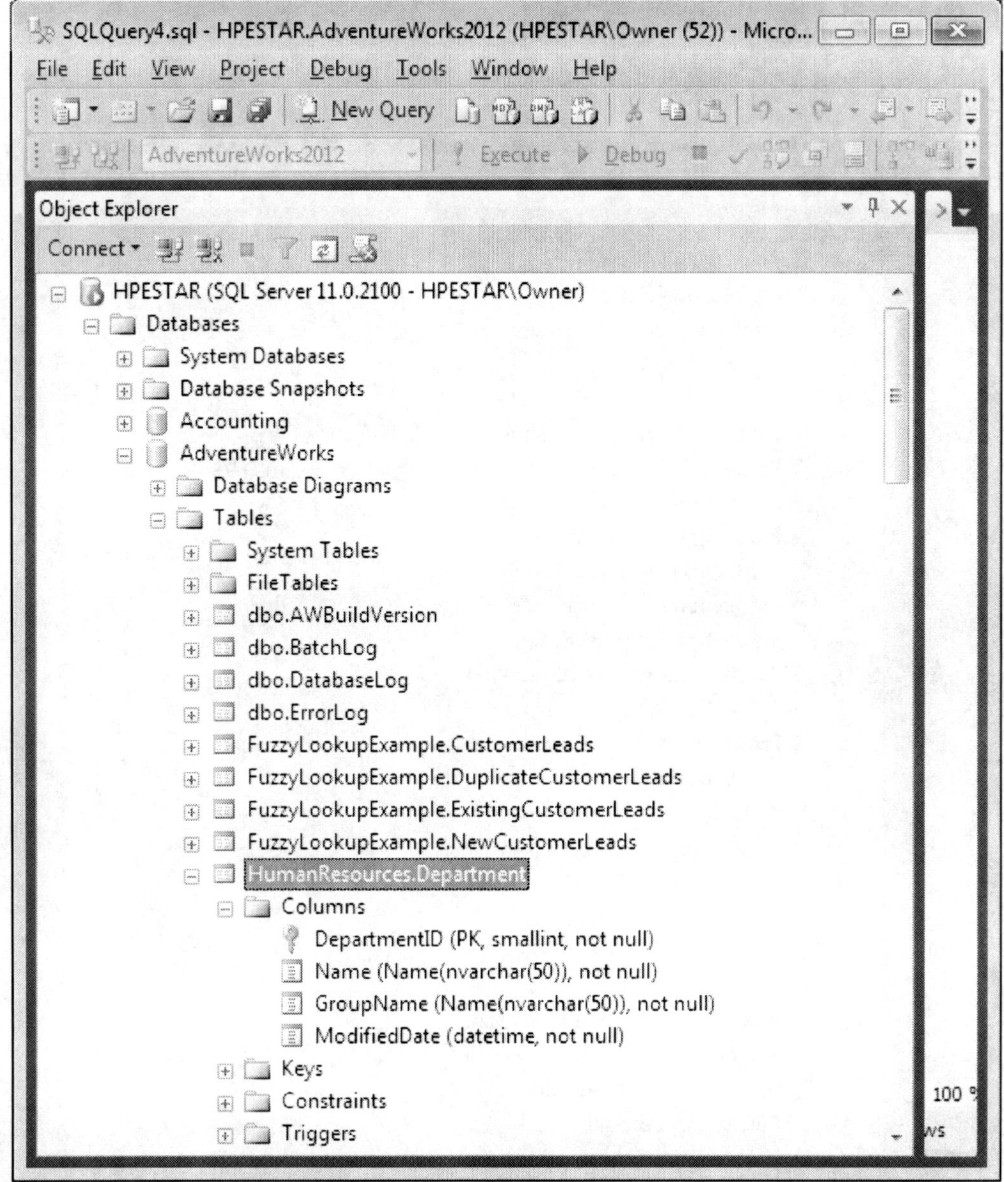

Context-Sensitive Right-Click Menu

Based on what object the cursor is on, right-click menu changes accordingly, it is context-sensitive. In the following demo the cursor is on table object when we right click on the mouse.

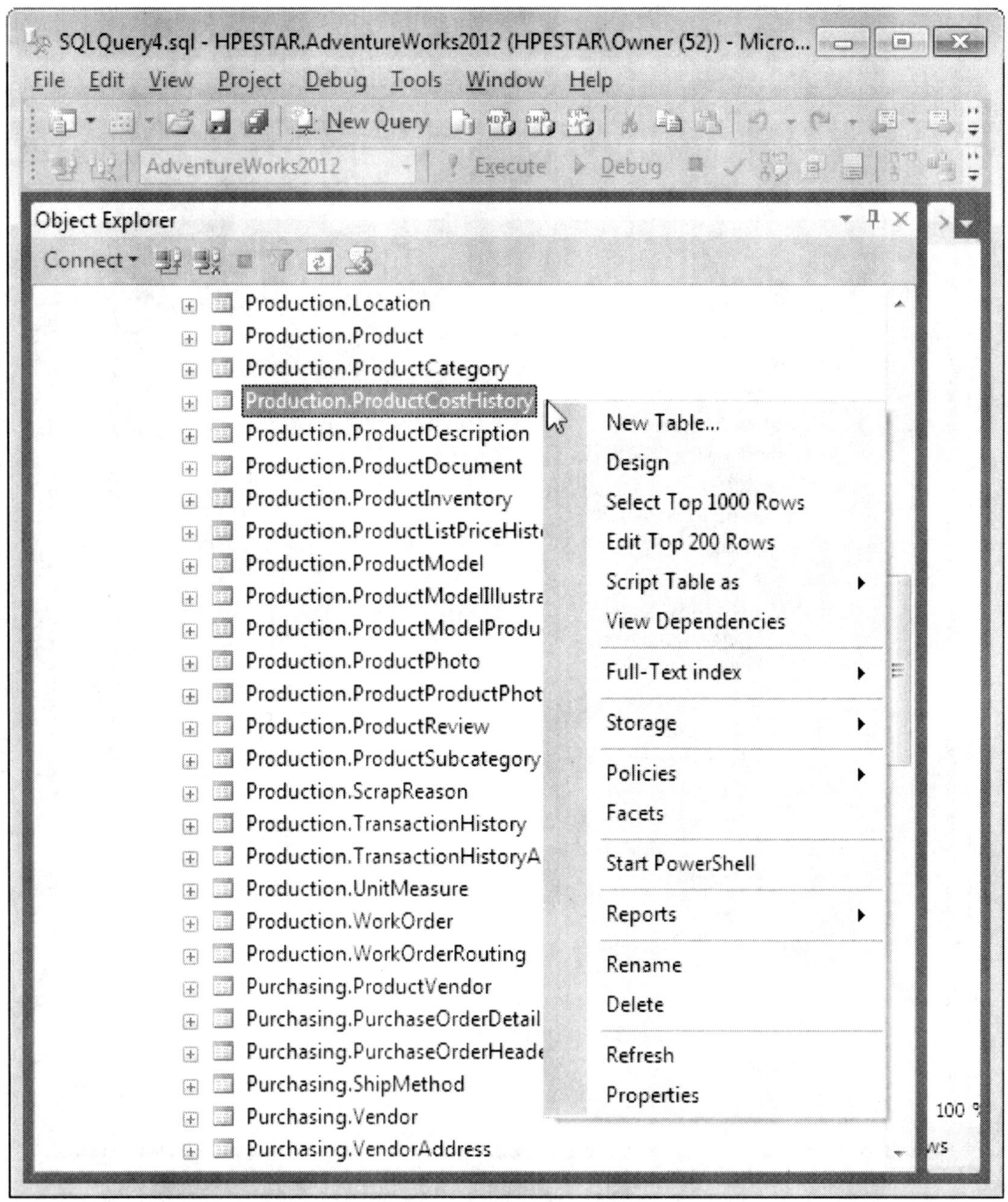

Server Administration & Management Tools

All the available SQL Server administration and management tools can be accessed from the Object Explorer. Usually the Database Administrator (DBA) uses these tools.

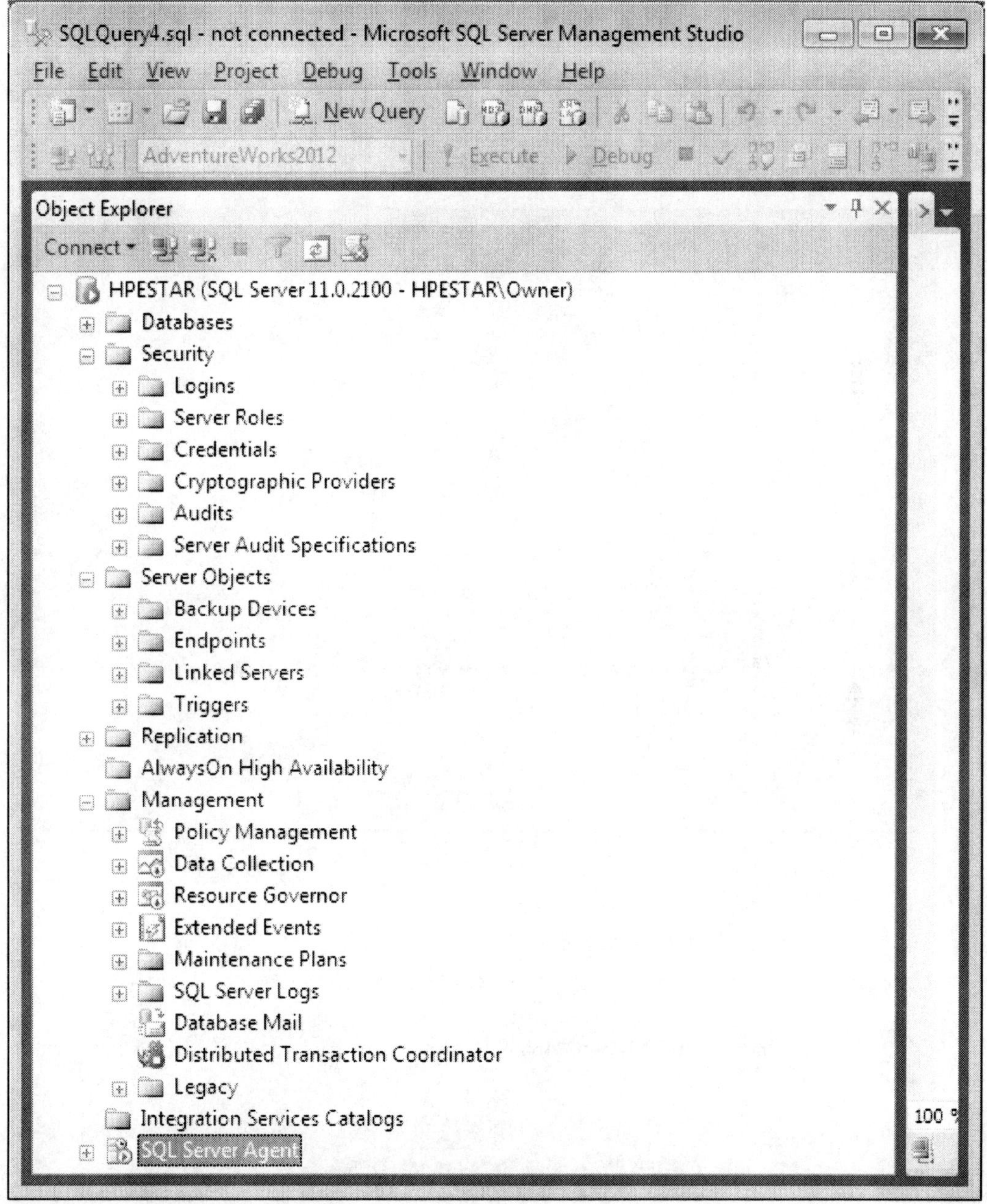

SQL Server Agent Jobs to Automate Administration Tasks

SQL Server Agent is a job creation and scheduling facility with notification features. For example, database backup job can be scheduled to execute 2:15AM every night as shown on the following dialog box. Stored procedure execution can also be setup as a job and scheduled for periodic execution.

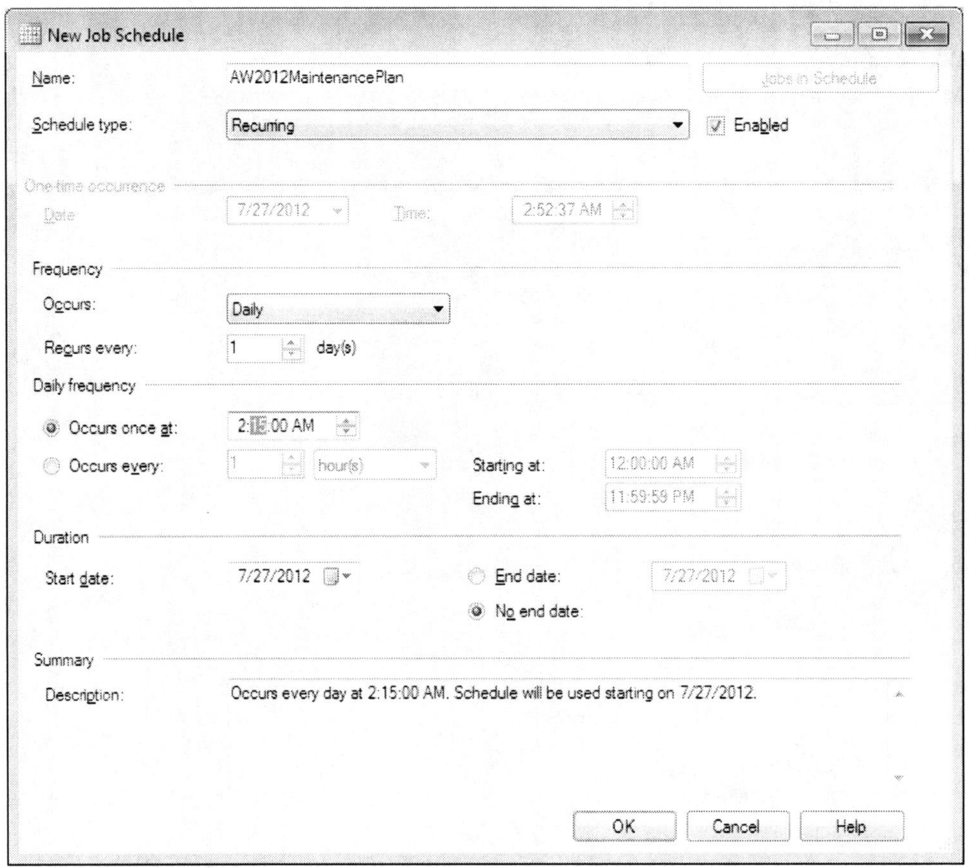

T-SQL Tidbits: Simple UNION Usage

The UNION operator eliminates duplicates, UNION ALL does not.

```
SELECT OrderDate, 'PurchaseOrder' AS OrderType, Subtotal
FROM Purchasing.PurchaseOrderHeader
UNION
SELECT OrderDate, 'SalesOrder', Subtotal
FROM Sales.SalesOrderHeader   ORDER BY OrderDate, Subtotal DESC;
```

Job properties panel can be used to create and manage jobs with multiple job steps and multiple schedules.

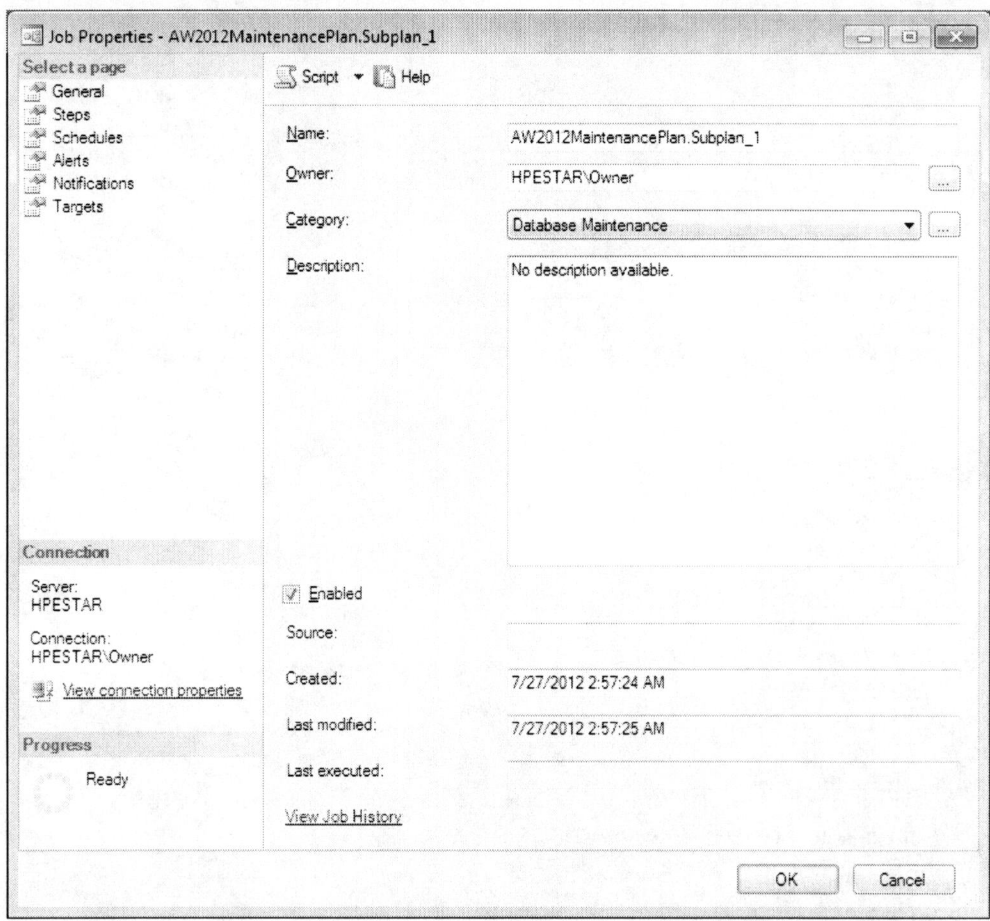

T-SQL Tidbits: The Difference Between JOIN or CROSS APPLY a TVF

JOINing a TVF is like JOINing a table. **CROSS APPLY invokes the TVF for each row of the query**.

```
SELECT   LastExec = max(last_execution_time),  Query = Text
FROM     sys.dm_exec_query_stats AS eqs CROSS JOIN
sys.dm_exec_sql_text(0x02000000F357FB0698831C6C49A6A474C29E6767F82DDD620000000000000000000000000000000000000000
000) AS SQL
WHERE    Text LIKE ('%AdventureWorks%') AND Text NOT LIKE ('%CONTAIN%')
GROUP BY Text ORDER BY Query; -- (1 row(s) affected)
```

```
SELECT   LastExec = max(last_execution_time),  Query = Text, MIN(eqs.sql_handle)
FROM     sys.dm_exec_query_stats AS eqs CROSS APPLY sys.dm_exec_sql_text(eqs.sql_handle) AS SQL
WHERE    Text LIKE ('%AdventureWorks%') AND Text NOT LIKE ('%CONTAIN%')
GROUP BY Text ORDER BY Query; -- (9 row(s) affected)
```

Graphical Query Designer

The Design Query in Editor entry on the Query drop-down menu launches the graphical Query Designer which can be used to design the query with GUI method and the T-SQL SELECT code will be generated automatically upon completion.

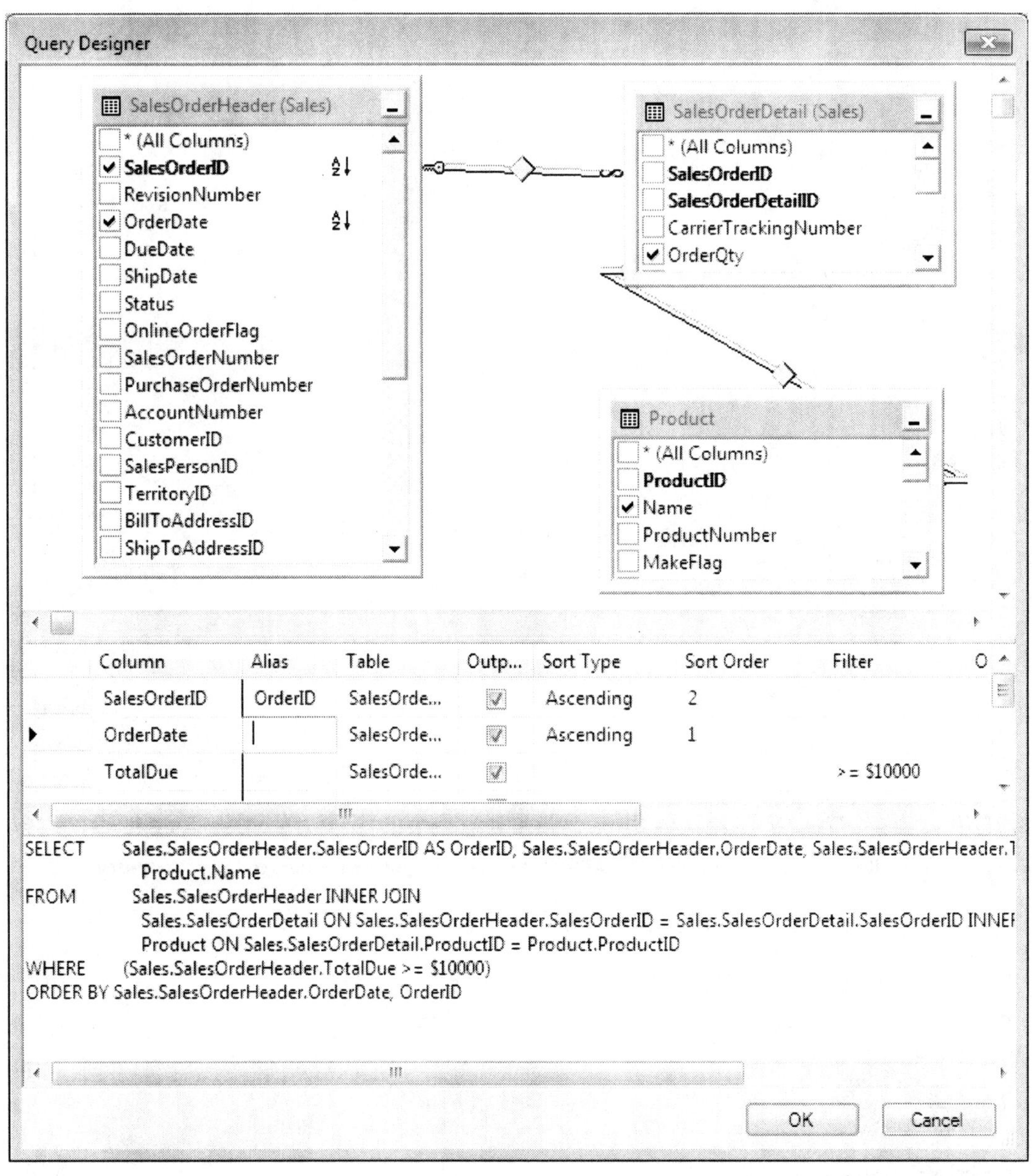

Designing a GROUP BY Query in Query Designer

Query Designer can be used to design from simple to complex queries. It can also serve as a starter query for a more complex query. It is really easy to get the tables JOINs graphically.

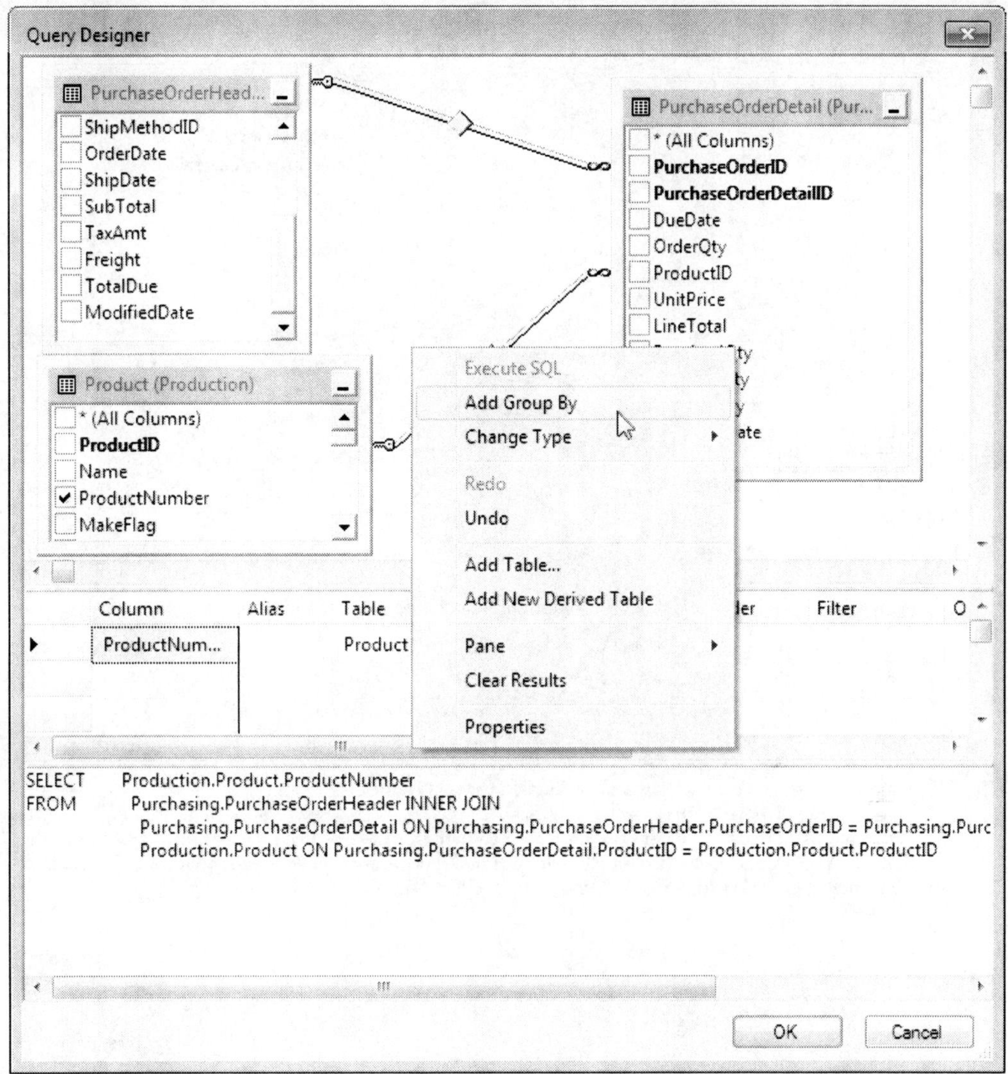

T-SQL Tidbits: Why Are INSTEAD OF Triggers Associated with Views?

Actually, INSTEAD OF triggers can be used on tables as well. INSTEAD OF triggers greatly expand the functionality of views, for example, to update underlying tables or access other tables. That is the basis of the common association. "**INSTEAD OF trigger gives wings to a view so it can soar!**"

AFTER trigger cannot be created on a view. When we don't specify in a CREATE TRIGGER the type, we create an AFTER trigger.

The Production.Product.Name column will also be configured as GROUP BY (drop-down default).

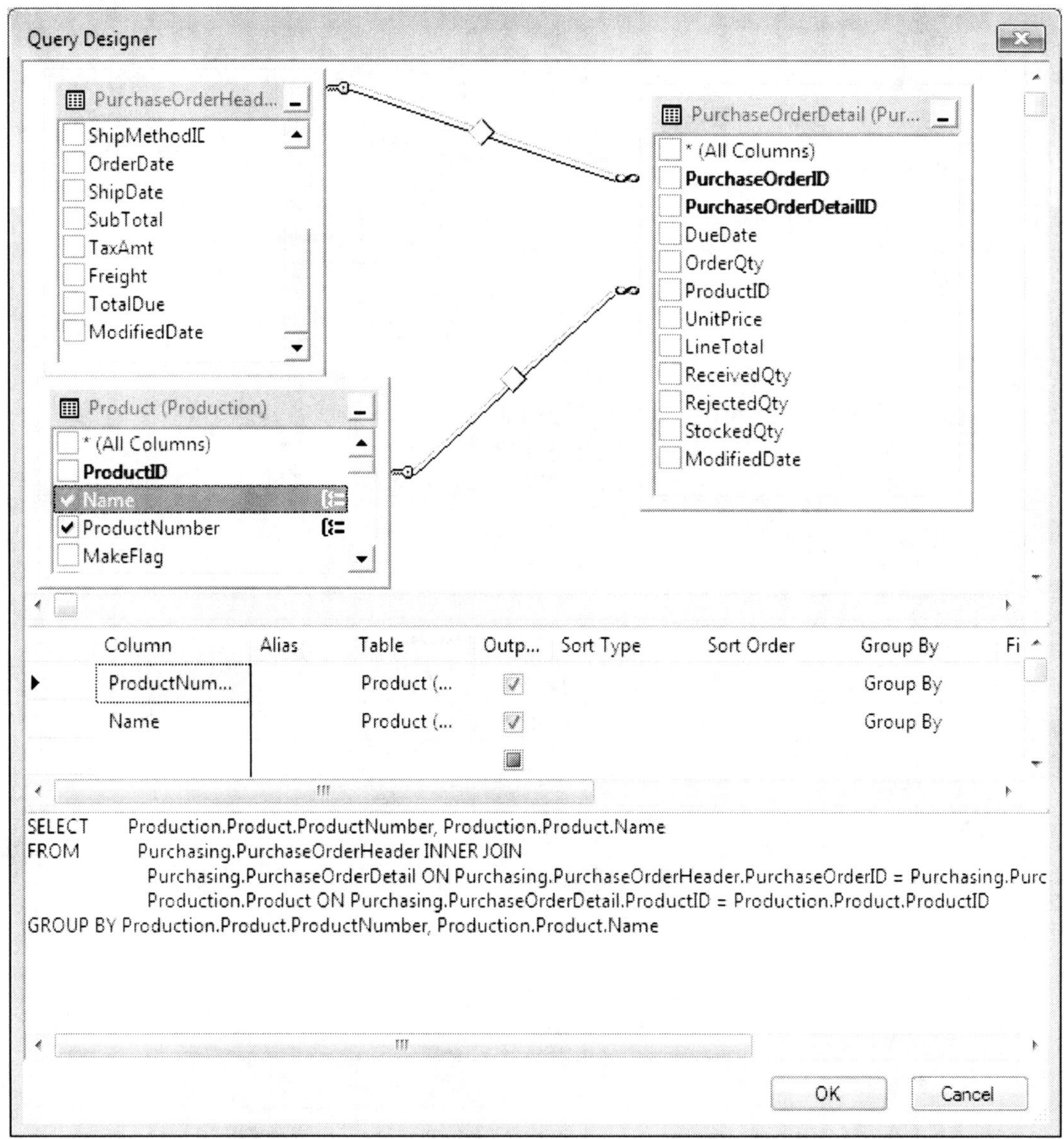

T-SQL Tidbits: Biggest Mistake Beginners Do with Triggers

Having statement like DECLARE @OrderNo INT; SELECT @OrderNo = OrderNumber FROM inserted . However, inserted may hold 1000 rows. In fact that is the best to assume when programming a trigger: inserted & deleted with 1000 rows each. Reason: trigger is called for each firing statement not for each row. In an UPDATE trigger, we can check which column changed by: IF UPDATE(Salary) AND UPDATE(Bonus) ..... Using the OUTPUT clause for auditing, we may avoid using a trigger for the task.

We add the TotalDue column and change the summary function to "SUM" from "Group by" and configure sorting on the first column.

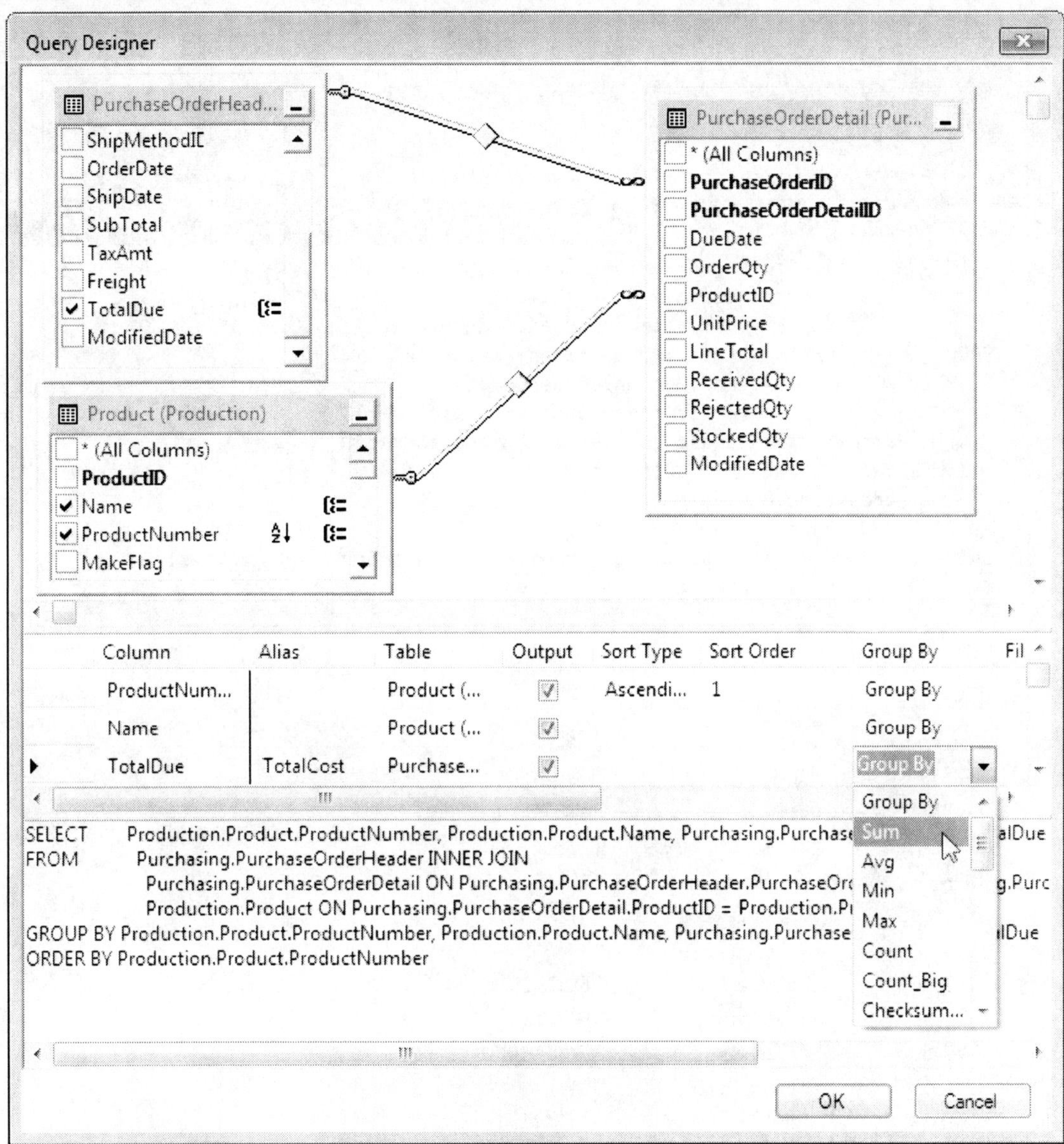

T-SQL Tidbits: CHECK Constraint vs. Trigger

CHECK constraint is the first choice, the simpler solution. CHECK constraint with UDF can carry out CHECKs involving other tables. Trigger can CHECK and also WRITE the database. Complex enterprise business rules can be implemented with triggers.

After pressing OK, the query is moved into the Query Editor window. Frequently it requires reformatting.

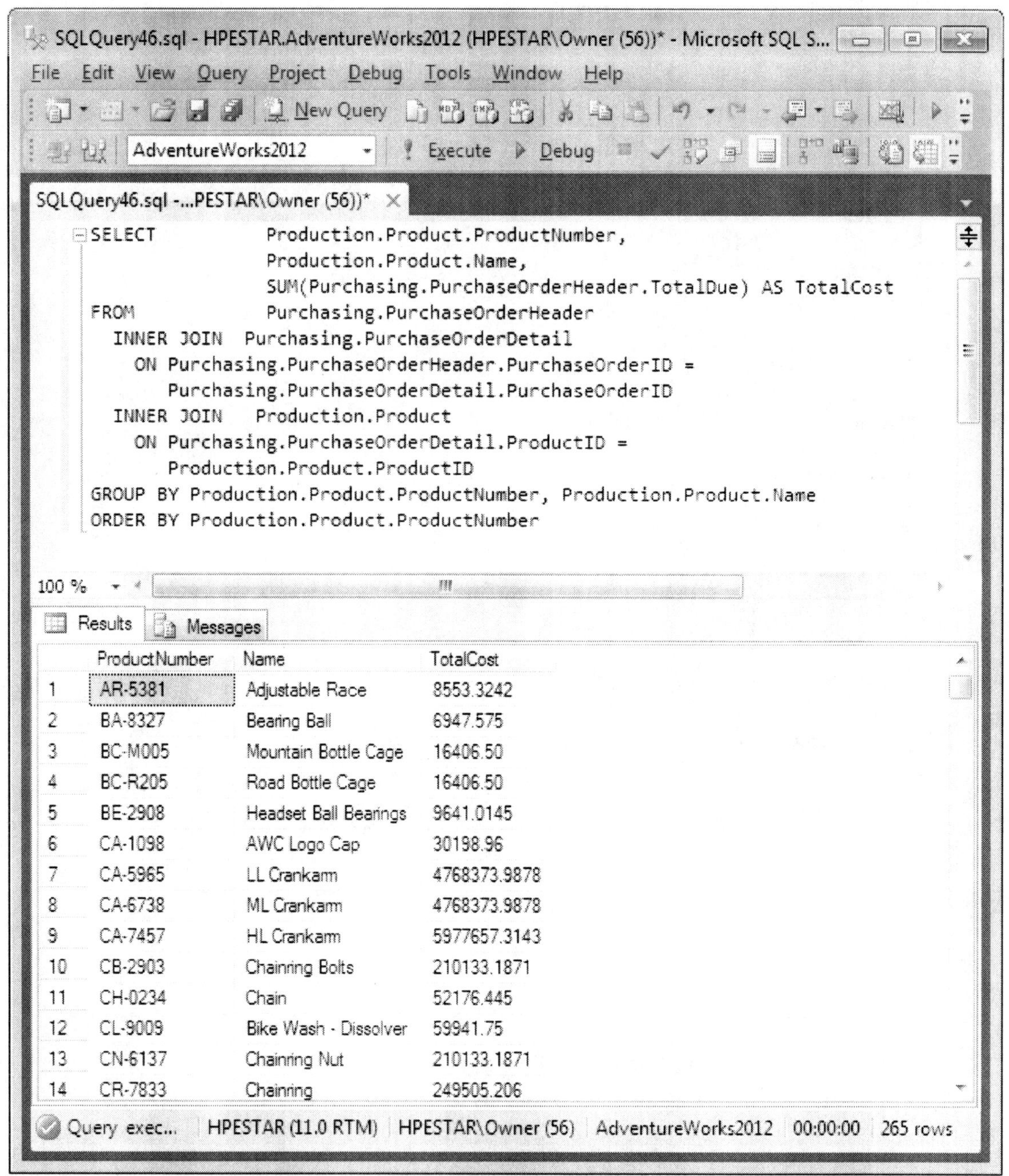

The only remaining issue with the query is the 3-part column references which is hard to read. We can change the query for readability improvement by using table aliases.

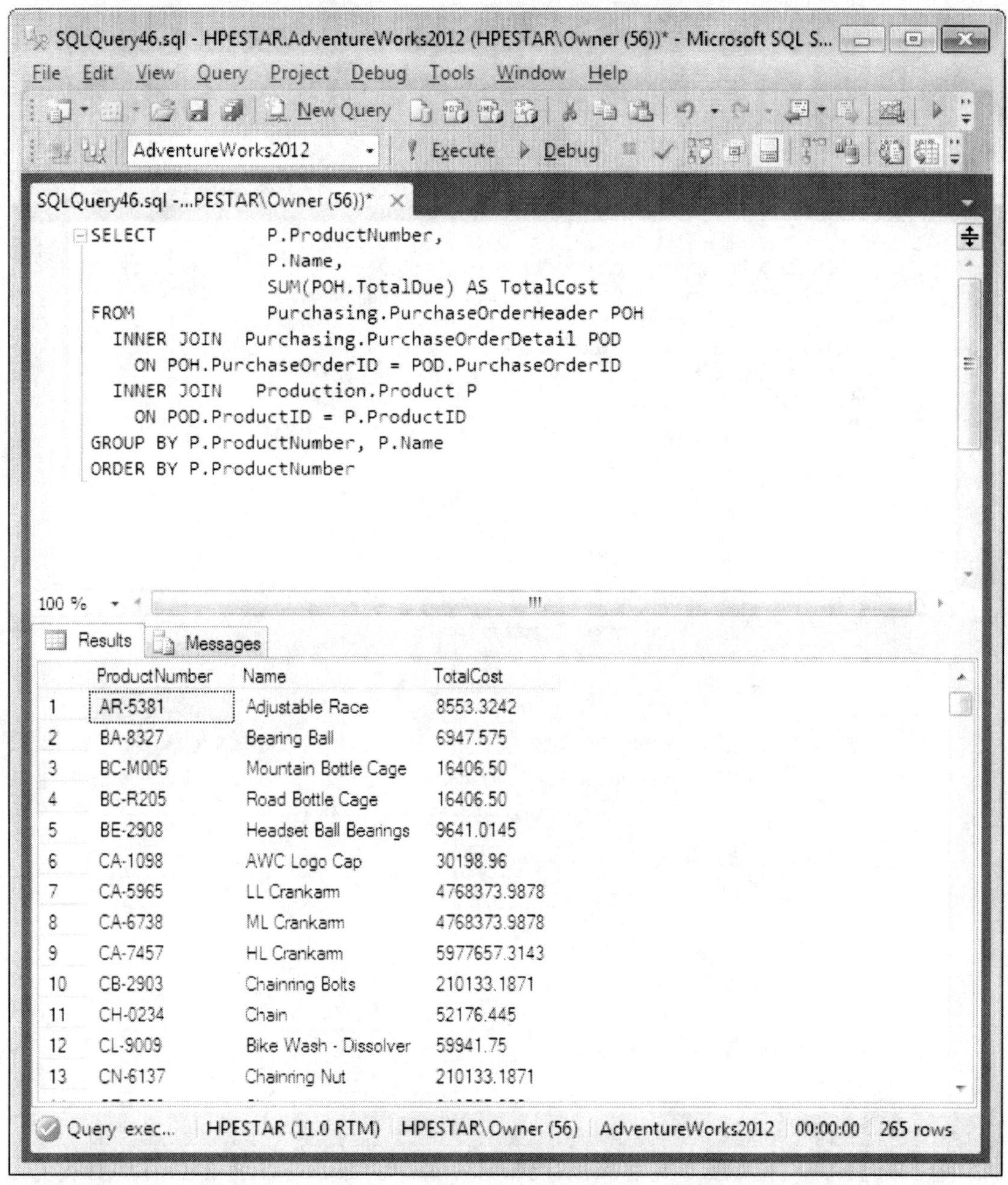

Graphically Editing of an Existing Query

An existing query, exception certain complex queries, can be uploaded into the Graphical Query Designer the following way: select (highlight) the query and right-click for the drop-down menu; click on Design Query in Editor.

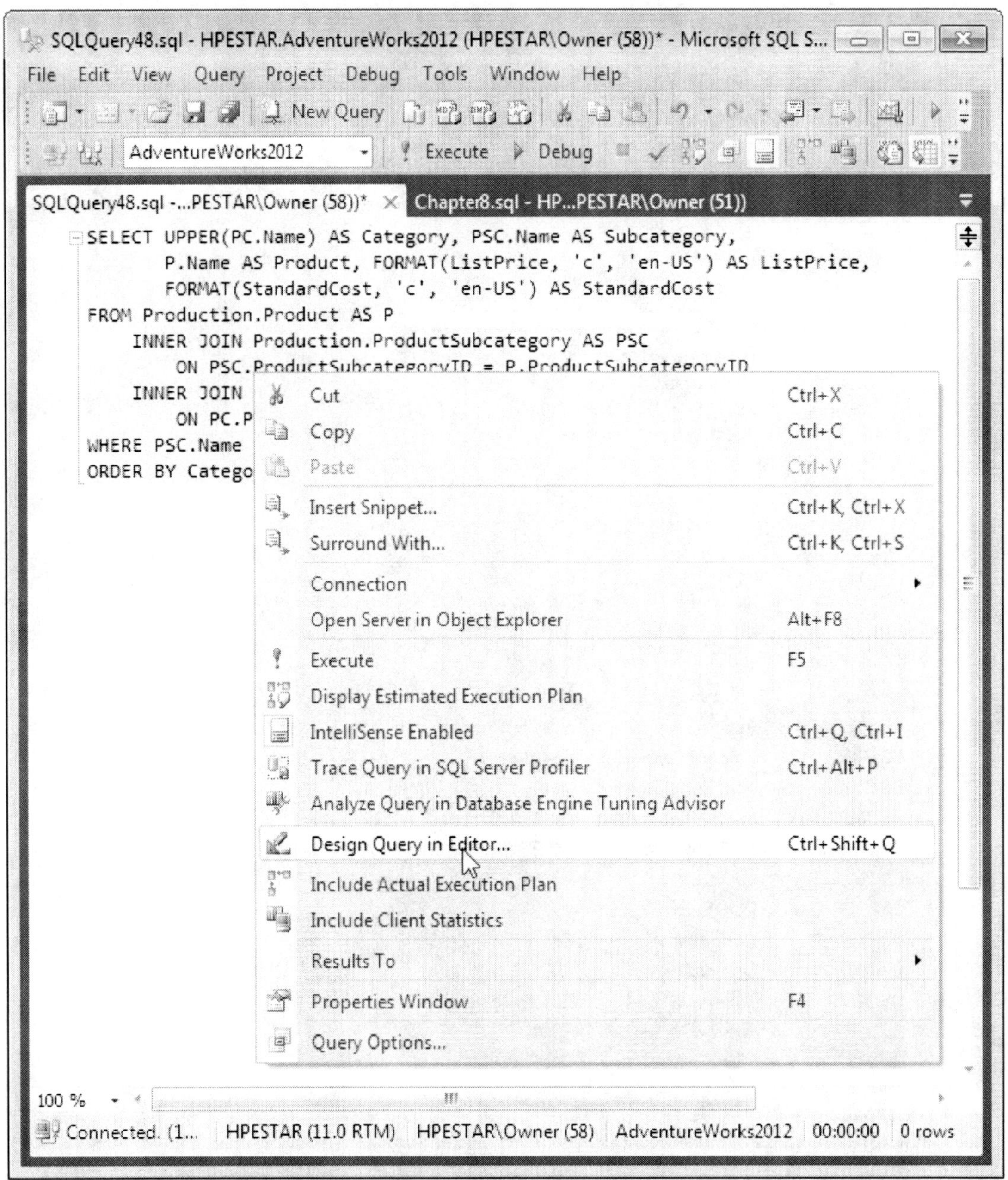

Following screen image shows the query in the Graphical Query Designer after some manual beautifying such as moving the tables for better display.

The query can be edited graphically and upon clicking on "OK", the query text is updated in the Query Editor window.

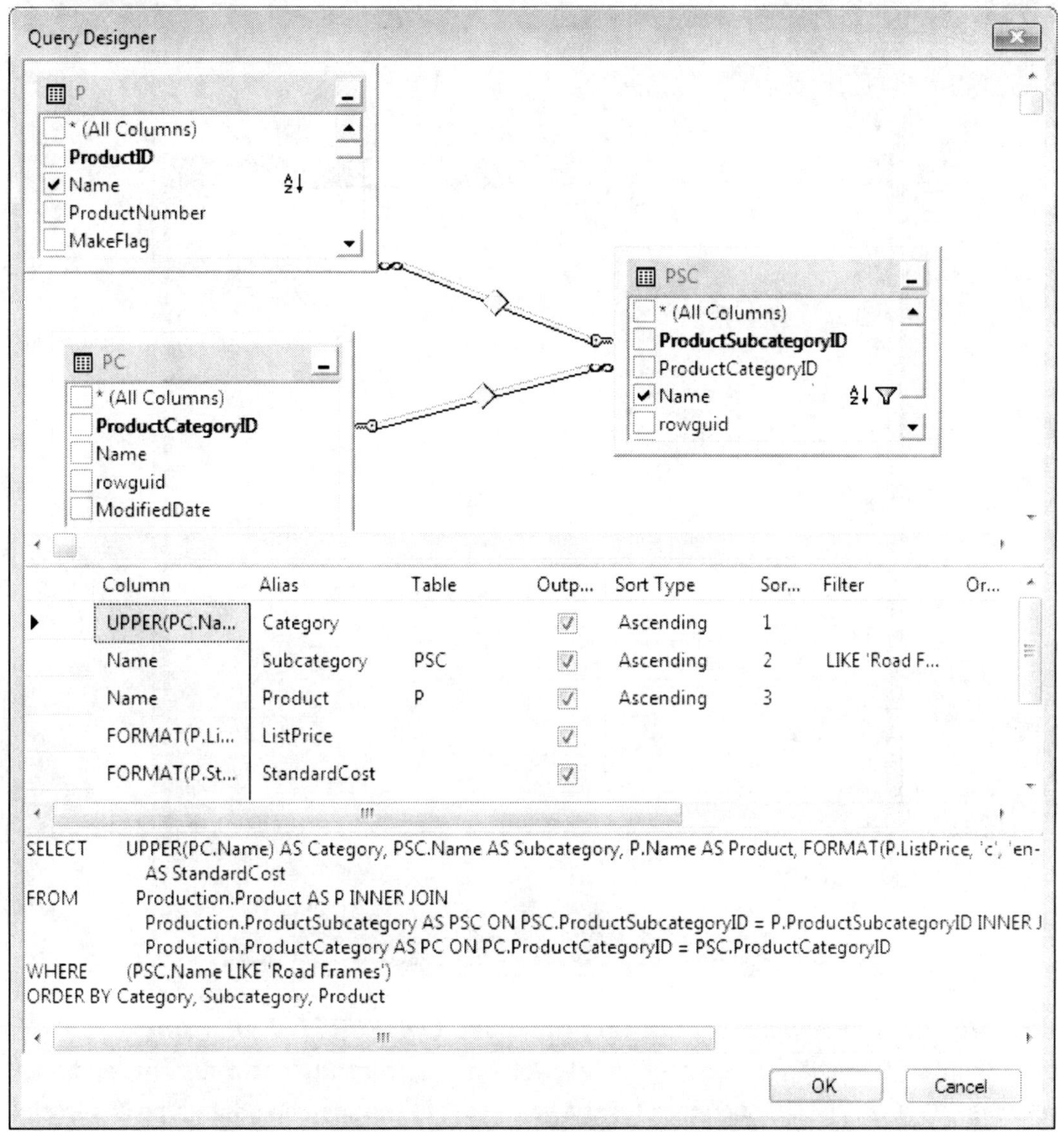

T-SQL Tidbits: ISDATE() & ISNUMERIC() Data Validity Functions

The ISDATE() function checks if a string date is valid based on dateformat setting. The ISNUMERIC() function checks if a string is valid numeric value. New to SS 2012 are TRY_PARSE() & TRY_CONVERT() which return NULL for invalid string values.

Configuring Line Numbers in Query Editor

Line numbering is an option which is off by default. Line numbers are helpful to find errors in large queries or T-SQL scripts (a sequence of T-SQL statements) when the error references a line number. Following is an example an error which includes the line number.

T-SQL Tidbits: The New TRY_PARSE() and TRY_CONVERT() Functions

The TRY_PARSE() function can be used only for converting from string to date/time and number types. The TRY_CONVERT() function returns a value cast to the specified data type if succeeds; otherwise, returns null.

```
SELECT TRY_PARSE('Oct 23, 2016' AS datetime2 USING 'en-US'); -- 2016-10-23 00:00:00.0000000
SELECT TRY_PARSE('Okt 23, 2016' AS datetime2 USING 'en-US'); -- NULL
SET DATEFORMAT dmy; SELECT TRY_CONVERT(datetime2, '12/31/2016'); -- NULL
SET DATEFORMAT mdy; SELECT TRY_CONVERT(datetime2, '12/31/2016'); -- 2016-12-31 00:00:00.0000000
```

Configuring Line Numbers in Query Editor

The Display Line Numbers option in the query editor can be activated from Options.

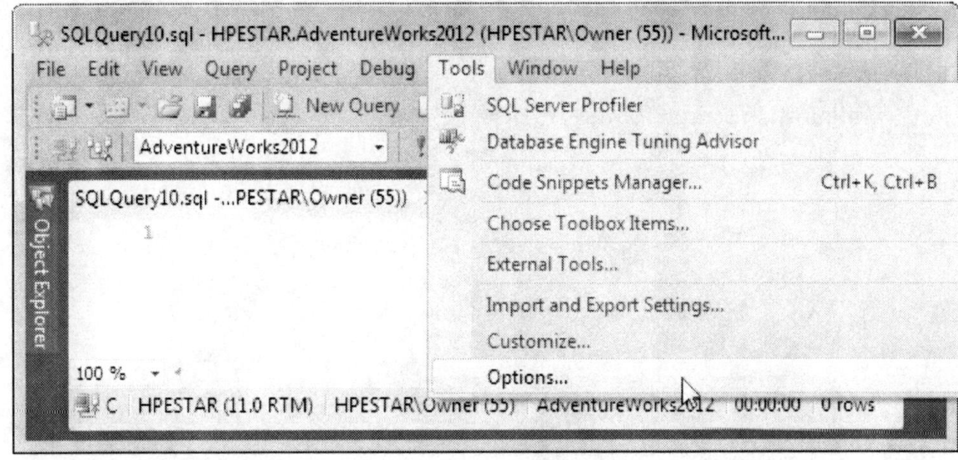

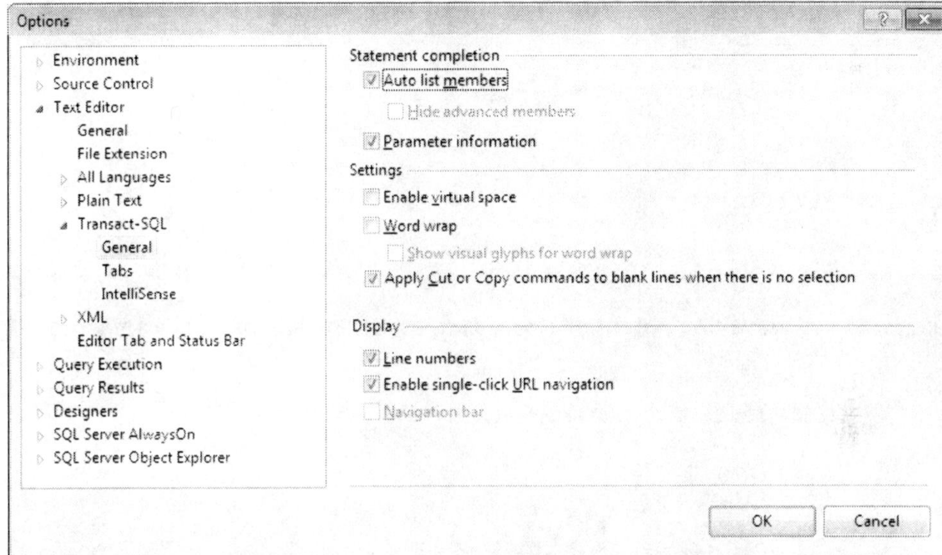

T-SQL Tidbits: FORMATting International Dates with FORMAT()

The new to SQL Server 2012 FORMAT function is quite flexible in date formatting, beyond the CONVERT function. Note: for UK, you have to use "GB".

```
SELECT FORMAT(getdate(),'','en-US');          -- 12/27/2016 3:34:31 AM
SELECT FORMAT(getdate(),'','en-GB');          -- 27/12/2016 03:35:12
SELECT FORMAT(getdate(),'','de-DE');          -- 27.12.2016 03:35:12
SELECT FORMAT(getdate(),'','hu-HU');          -- 2016.12.27. 3:35:53
```

IntelliSense - Your Smart Assistant

IntelliSense is a smart agent in Query Editor. It helps completing long object names and pointing out potential errors by red wave-lining (squiggly) them.

The Options configuration screen for IntelliSense.

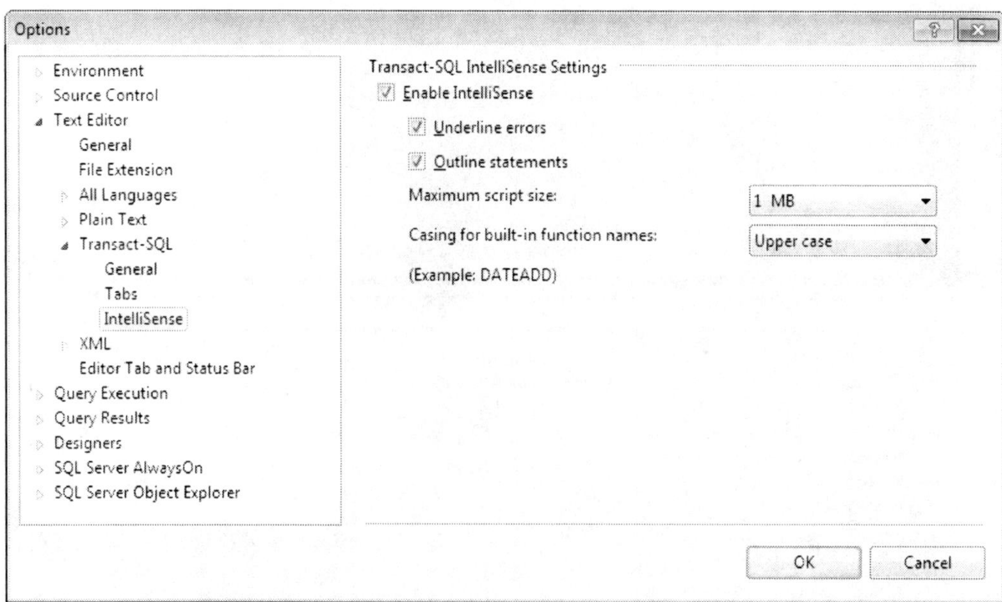

Underlining with red wave-line potential errors such as misspelling of a column name.

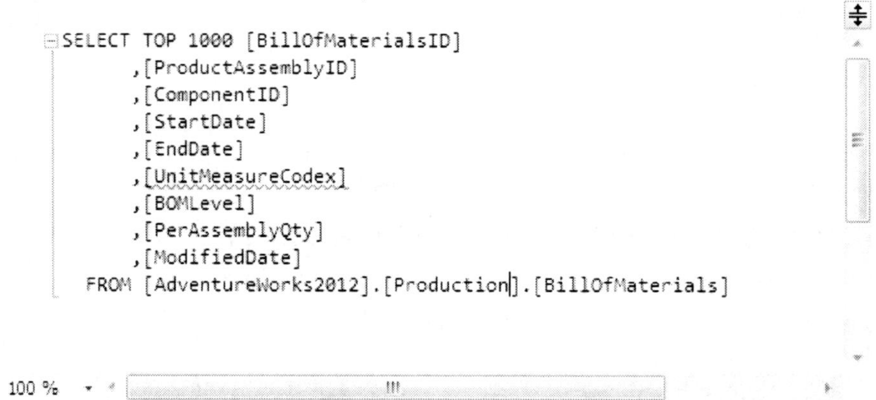

T-SQL Tidbits: CASE Expression Returns a Single Value of the Same Type

We can use a CASE expression anywhere in a query where a single value is required. We can program a CASE expression instead of IIF or ISNULL for example.

IntelliSense Guessing and Completing Object Names

Screenshots show IntelliSense in action when typing queries.

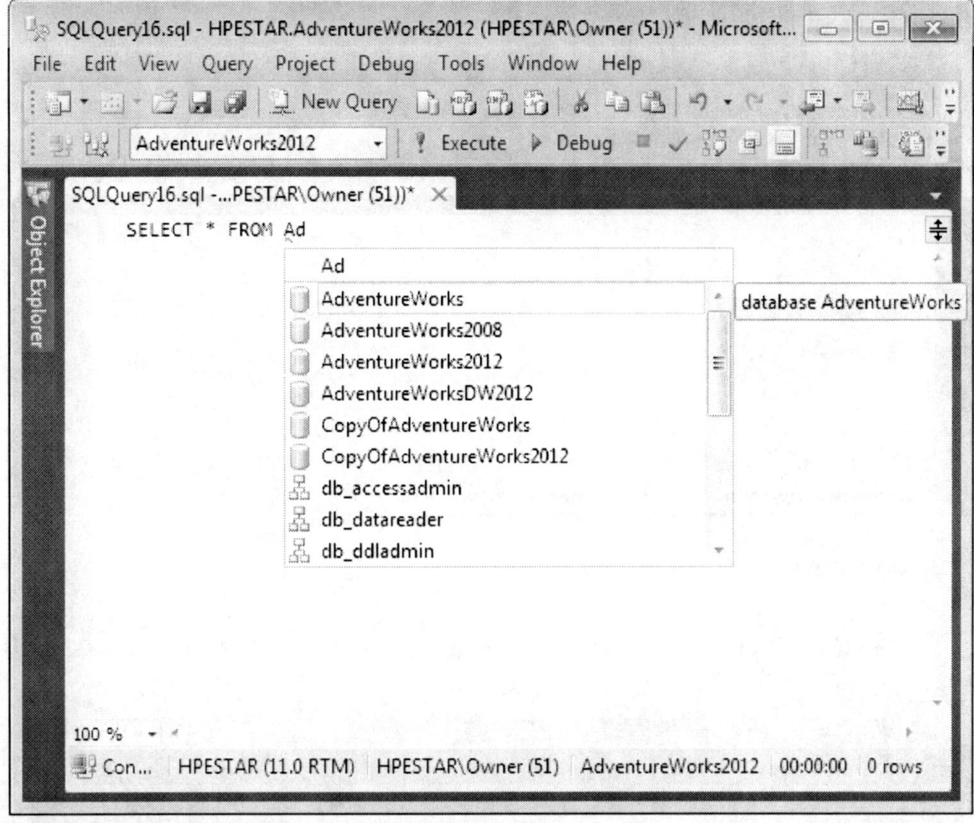

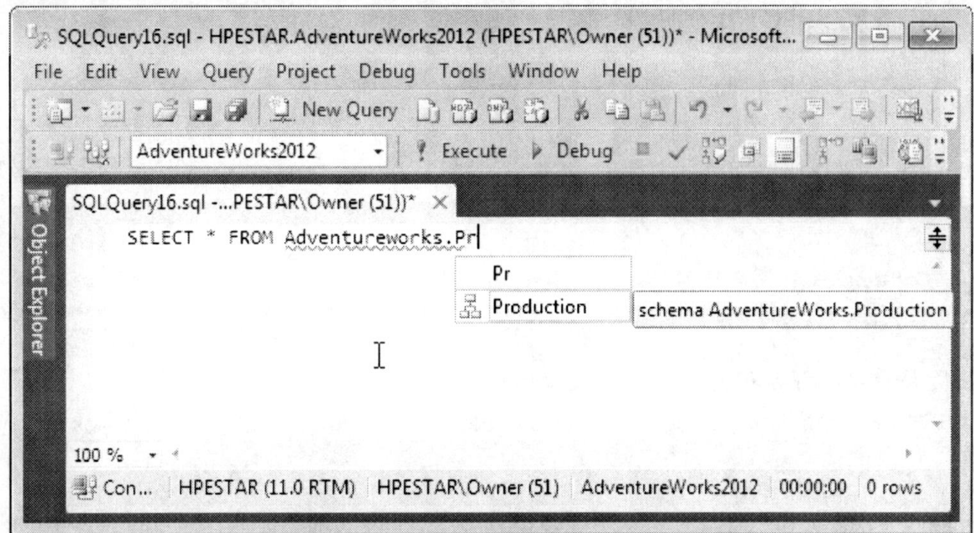

IntelliSense drop-down menu for "Prod".

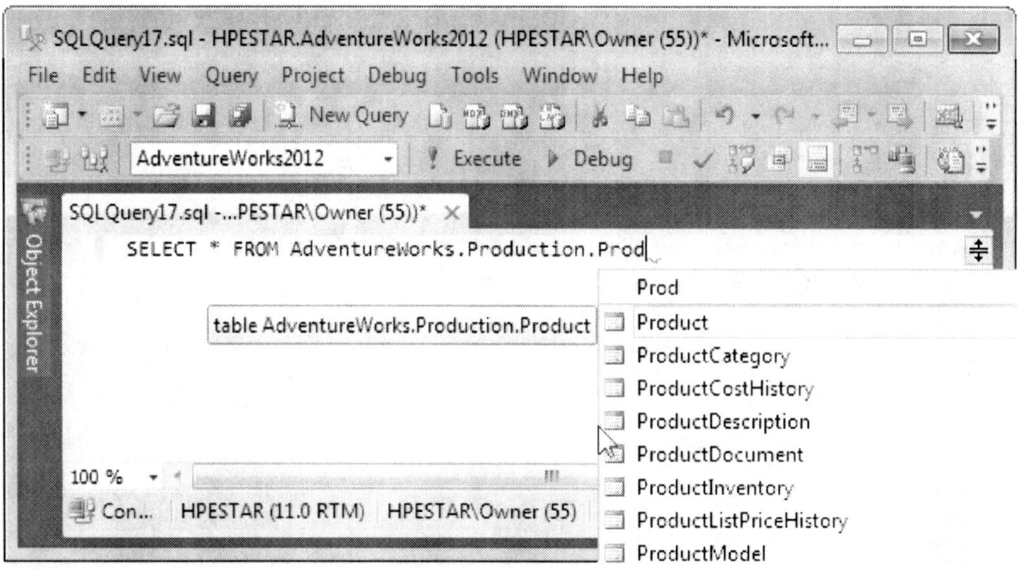

IntelliSense drop-down menu for "ProductS".

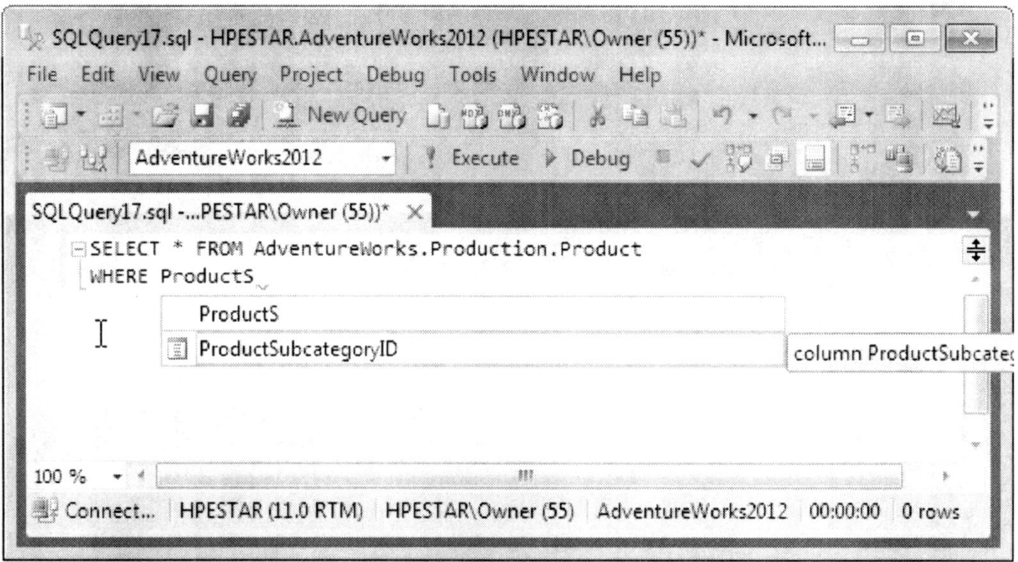

T-SQL Tidbits: Using ROWLOCK Locking Hint

Use ROWLOCK when updating a single row. The database engine may escalate it to page lock or table lock.

```
UPDATE Person.Person WITH (ROWLOCK) SET LastName='Smythe' WHERE BusinessEntityID = 1000;
```

IntelliSense completion assistance for "ProductN"

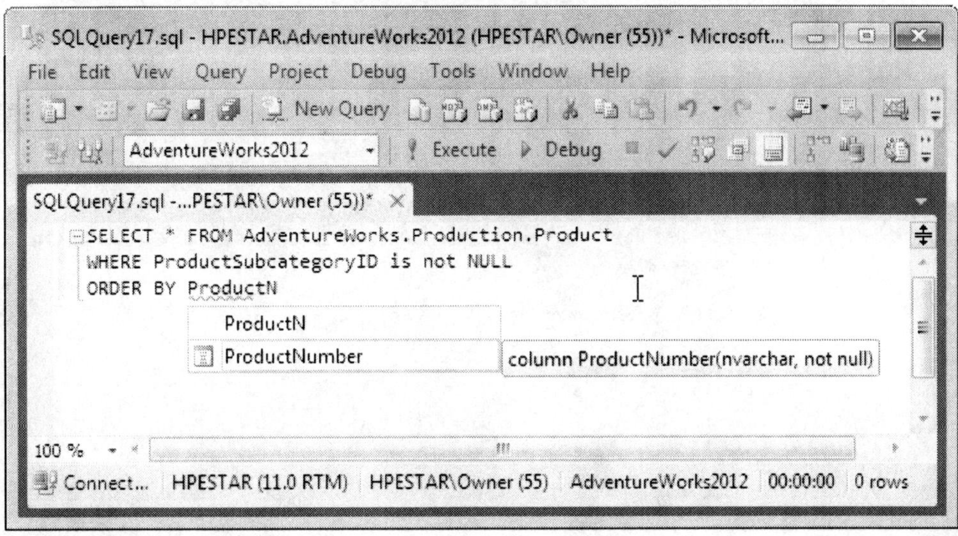

IntelliSense completion assistance for "Produ"

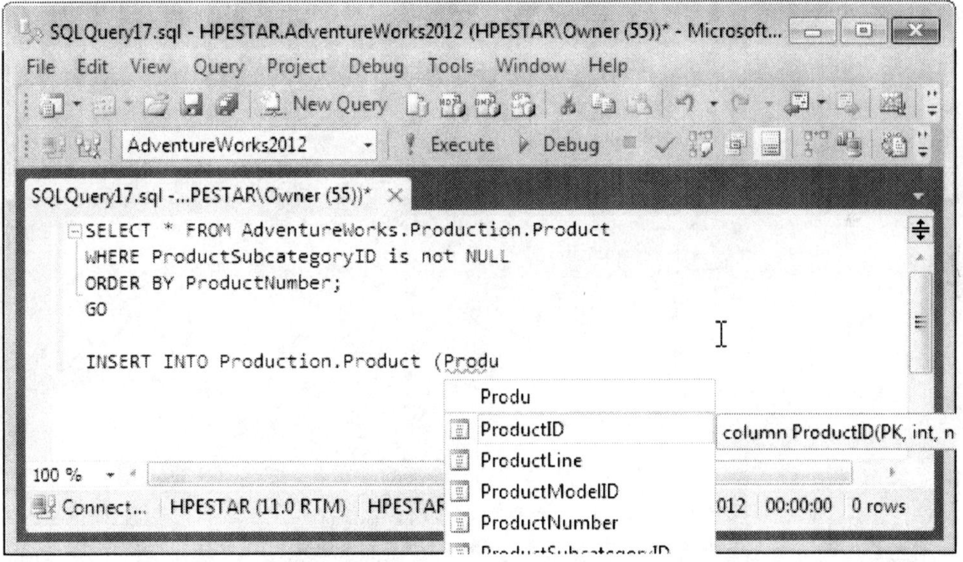

T-SQL Tidbits: Using OPTIMIZE FOR

For example, when you expect that the most frequent predicate usage is Canada, the OPTIMIZE FOR hint can be used.

```
   .... AND Country = @Country
OPTION (OPTIMIZE FOR (@Country = 'CA'))
```

IntelliSense Assisting with User-Defined Objects

IntelliSense helps out with a user-defined stored procedure execution.

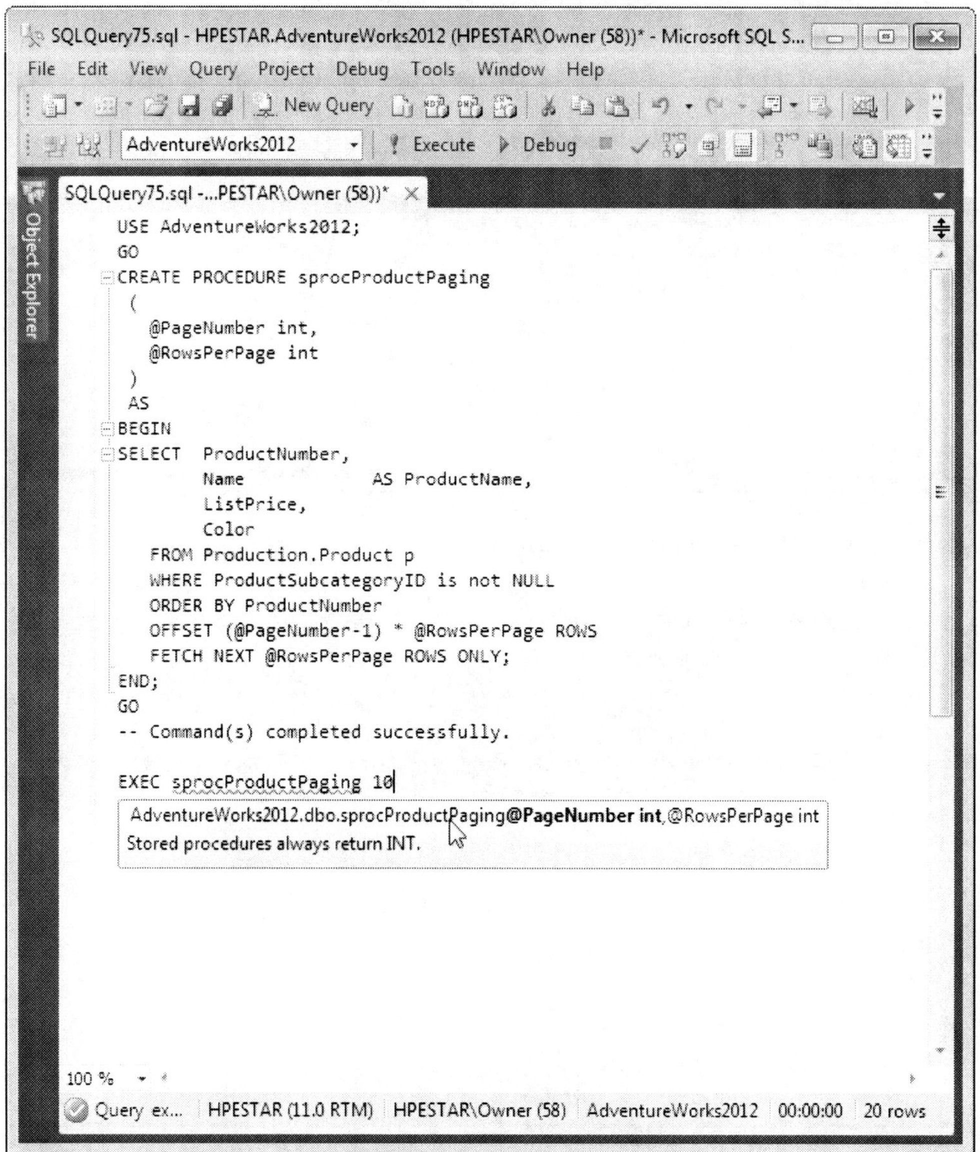

T-SQL Tidbits: Composite Indexes

Composite indexes can be used, however, if an index is wide, performance suffers. Indexes with INCLUDE (a newer variation for composite index, popular for covering a query) have the included columns at the leaf level only. Same rule applies: narrower the index with INCLUDE, better the performance.

IntelliSense Smart Guessing Partial Word in Middle of Object Names

You don't have to remember how an object name starts. You just have to remember some part of the name. Looking for the system view associated with "waits".

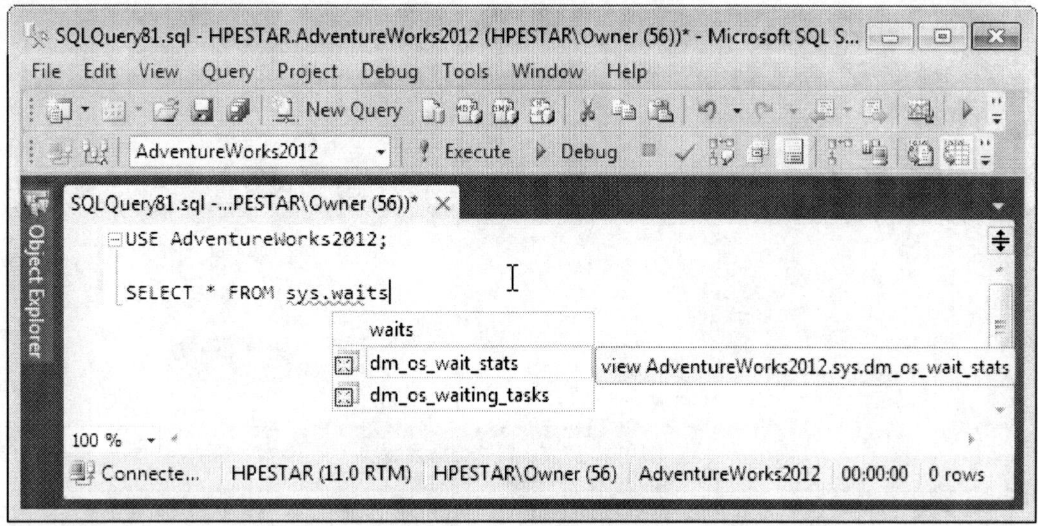

Looking for the SalesOrderHeader table but only remembering "head".

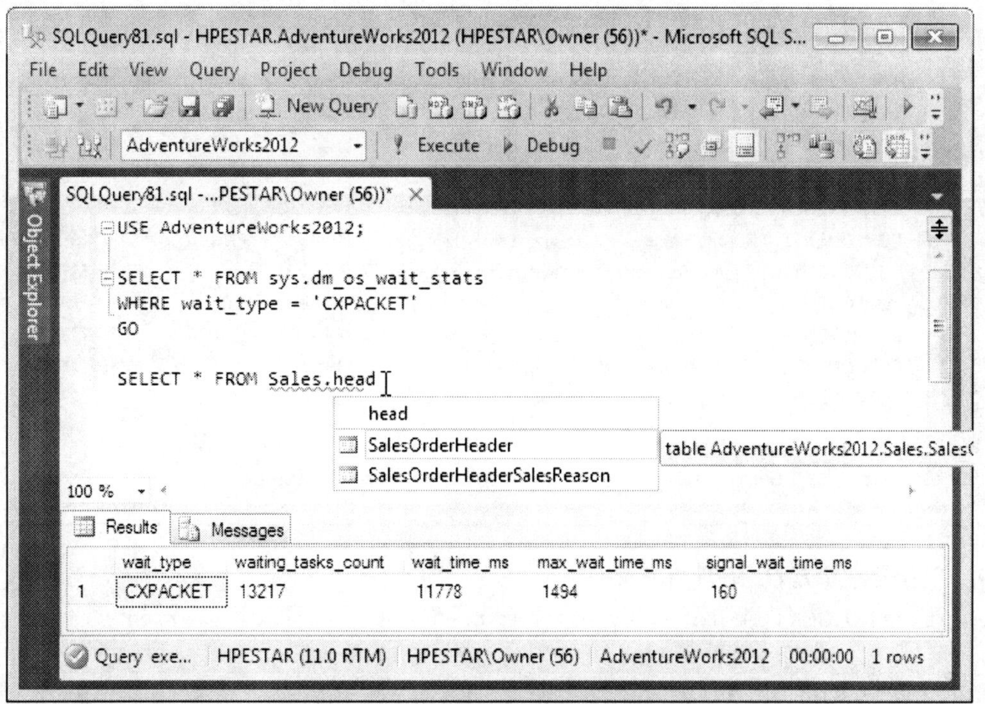

Hovering over Red Squiggly Underline Errors for Explanation

IntelliSense red wave (squiggly) underlining of errors which is caused, actually, by a single invalid table reference.

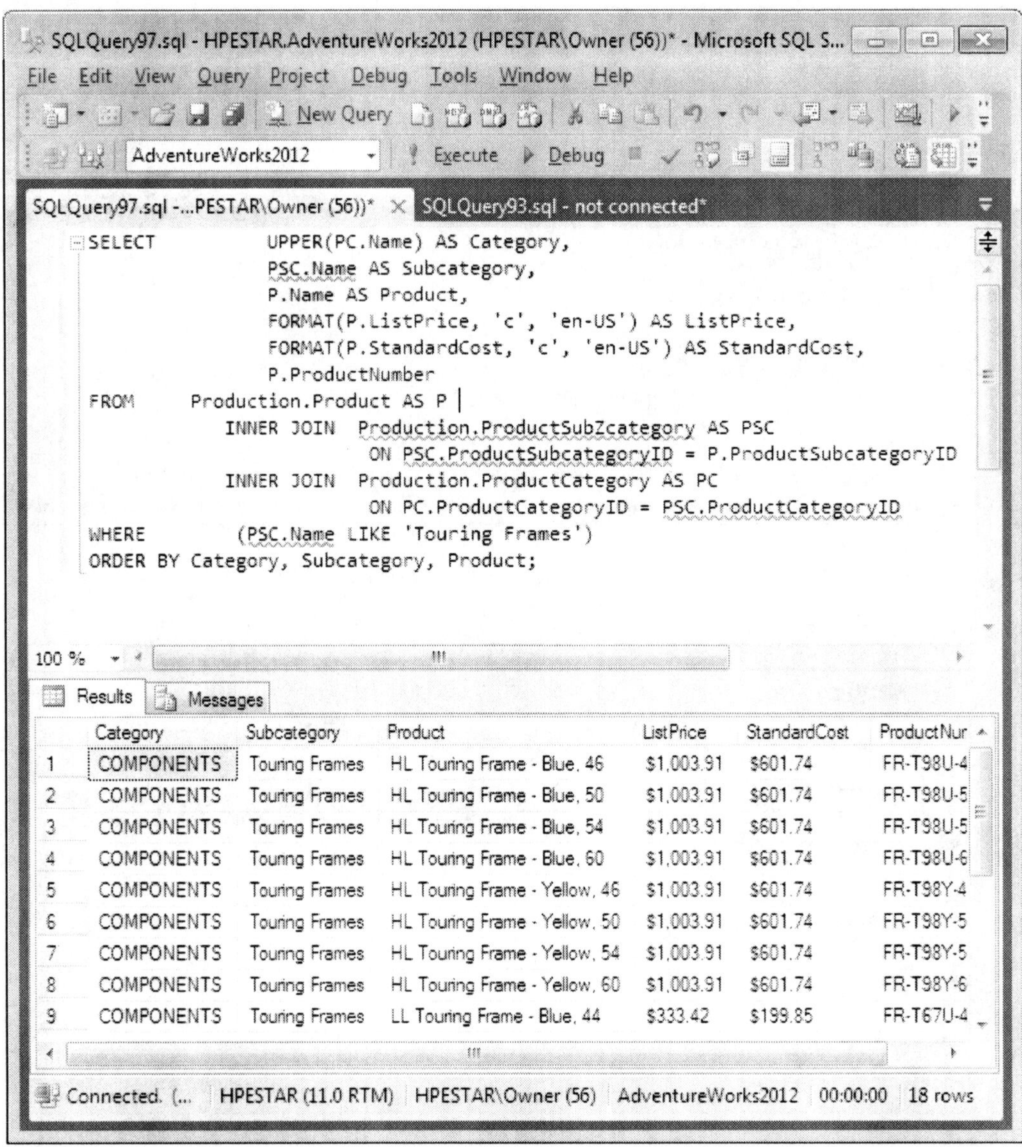

	Category	Subcategory	Product	ListPrice	StandardCost	ProductNur
1	COMPONENTS	Touring Frames	HL Touring Frame - Blue, 46	$1,003.91	$601.74	FR-T98U-4
2	COMPONENTS	Touring Frames	HL Touring Frame - Blue, 50	$1,003.91	$601.74	FR-T98U-5
3	COMPONENTS	Touring Frames	HL Touring Frame - Blue, 54	$1,003.91	$601.74	FR-T98U-5
4	COMPONENTS	Touring Frames	HL Touring Frame - Blue, 60	$1,003.91	$601.74	FR-T98U-6
5	COMPONENTS	Touring Frames	HL Touring Frame - Yellow, 46	$1,003.91	$601.74	FR-T98Y-4
6	COMPONENTS	Touring Frames	HL Touring Frame - Yellow, 50	$1,003.91	$601.74	FR-T98Y-5
7	COMPONENTS	Touring Frames	HL Touring Frame - Yellow, 54	$1,003.91	$601.74	FR-T98Y-5
8	COMPONENTS	Touring Frames	HL Touring Frame - Yellow, 60	$1,003.91	$601.74	FR-T98Y-6
9	COMPONENTS	Touring Frames	LL Touring Frame - Blue, 44	$333.42	$199.85	FR-T67U-4

T-SQL Tidbits: NOLOCK Table Hint

We can use the NOLOCK table hint if dirty reads are not an issue. It increases concurrency:

```
SELECT COUNT(*) FROM Production.TransactionHistory WITH(NOLOCK);
```

Common Error: The multi-part identifier "abc" could not be bound.

Hovering over the first error results in an explanation pop-up. This is a distant error, the kind usually the hardest to solve, because, actually, it is a secondary error caused by the primary error which is located on a different line. In this instance, there are few lines difference only, but in a large stored procedure the difference can be 200 lines as an example.

```
PSC.Name AS Subcategory,
```

The multi-part identifier "PSC.Name" could not be bound.

Hovering over the second error yields the cause of all errors: "ProductSubZcategory".

```
Production.ProductSubZcategory AS PSC
```

Invalid object name 'Production.ProductSubZcategory'.

The remaining error messages are all "multi-part..." caused by the solitary invalid table reference.

```
PSC.ProductSubcategoryID = P.ProductSubcategoryID
```

The multi-part identifier "PSC.ProductSubcategoryID" could not be bound.

After fixing the table name, all errors are gone.

```
SELECT          UPPER(PC.Name)                          AS Category,
                PSC.Name                                AS Subcategory,
                P.Name                                  AS Product,
                FORMAT(P.ListPrice, 'c', 'en-US')       AS ListPrice,
                FORMAT(P.StandardCost, 'c', 'en-US')    AS StandardCost,
                P.ProductNumber
FROM     Production.Product AS P
            INNER JOIN  Production.ProductSubcategory AS PSC
                            ON PSC.ProductSubcategoryID = P.ProductSubcategoryID
            INNER JOIN  Production.ProductCategory AS PC
                            ON PC.ProductCategoryID = PSC.ProductCategoryID
WHERE         (PSC.Name LIKE 'Touring Frames')
ORDER BY Category, Subcategory, Product;
```

Refreshing IntelliSense Cache for New DB Objects

IntelliSense cache is not updated real-time. If new objects are created in another connection (session), they will not be seen until exit SSMS/reenter or IntelliSense cache is updated. No red-wave underline for the **newly created object SOD** in the same connection.

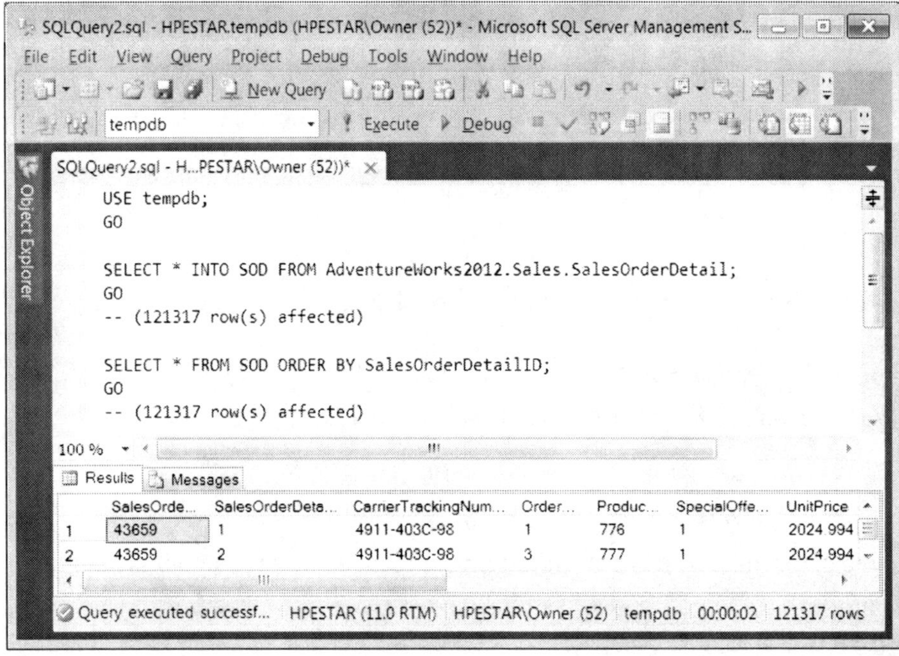

In another connection, the query works, but there are red squiggly underlining for the new table & column.

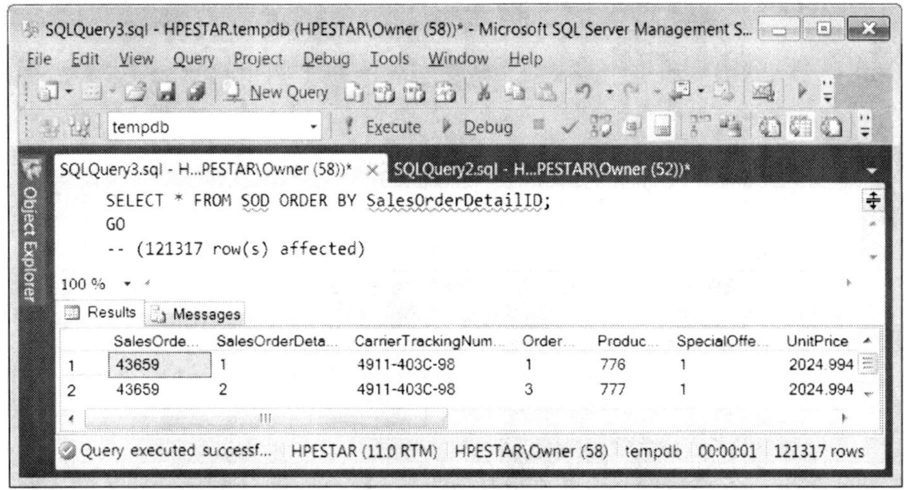

Refreshing IntelliSense Local Cache

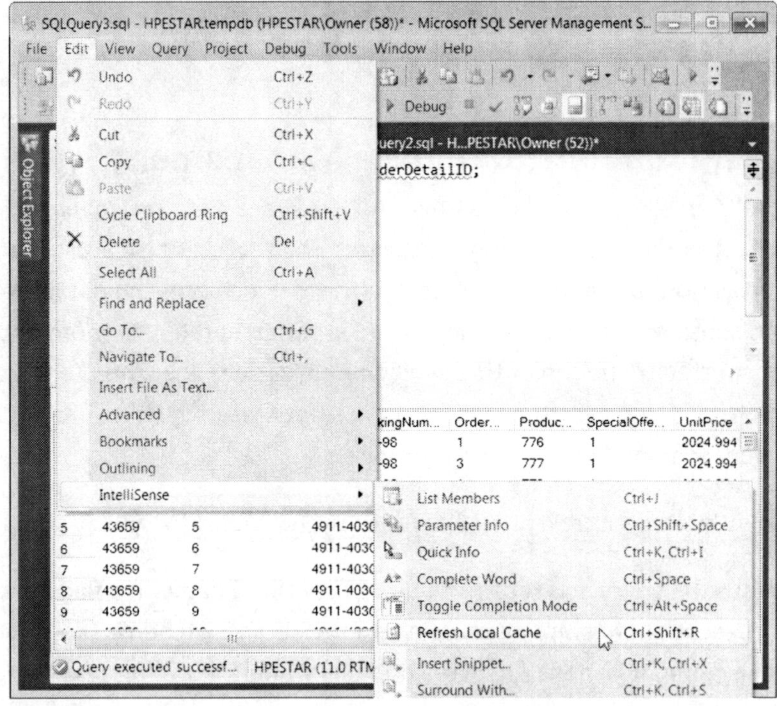

Squiggly red line goes away in all connections for the new database objects.

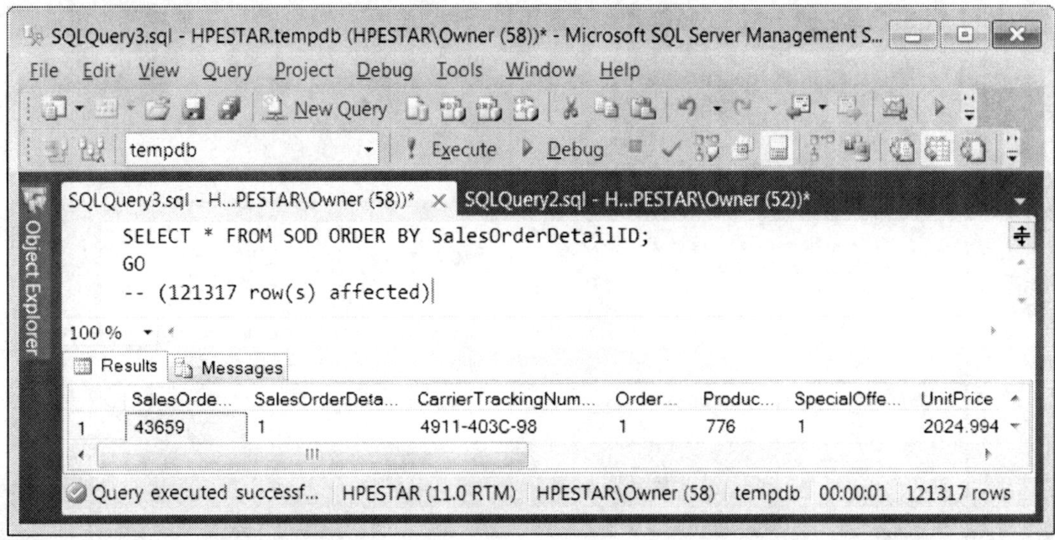

CHAPTER 5: Basic Concepts of Client-Server Computing

Client - Server Relational Database Management System

The "server" is SQL Server, operating on a powerful hardware platform, managing databases and related items. The client is application software. The real client is naturally a human user who runs the application software. Automated software which uses the database for one thing or another is also considered a "client". The client computer, in the next room or thousands of miles away, is connected to the server through communications link. The client software sends a request, a query, to SQL Server, after execution the server returns the results to the client. An example for a query sent by the client to the server:

```
SELECT ListPrice FROM AdventureWorks2012.Production.Product WHERE ProductID = 800;
```

SQL Server executes the query and returns "1120.49" to the client with a flag indicating successful query execution. A tempting analogy is a restaurant: kitchen is the server, patrons are the clients and the communications / delivery done by waiters & waitresses.

Screenshot displays SQL Server (highlighted) along with other related software such as SQL Server Agent (job scheduling facility) , SSIS (data transformation & transfer), SSRS (Reporting), SSAS (OLAP Cube) and other auxiliary software.

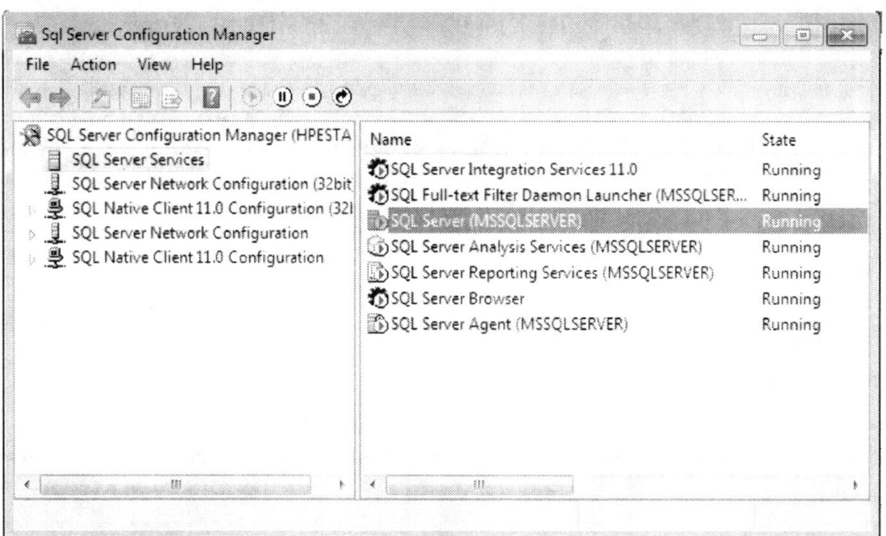

Database Objects on Server-Side

Screenshot of Object Explorer displays almost all important database objects with the exception of constraints, triggers and indexes.

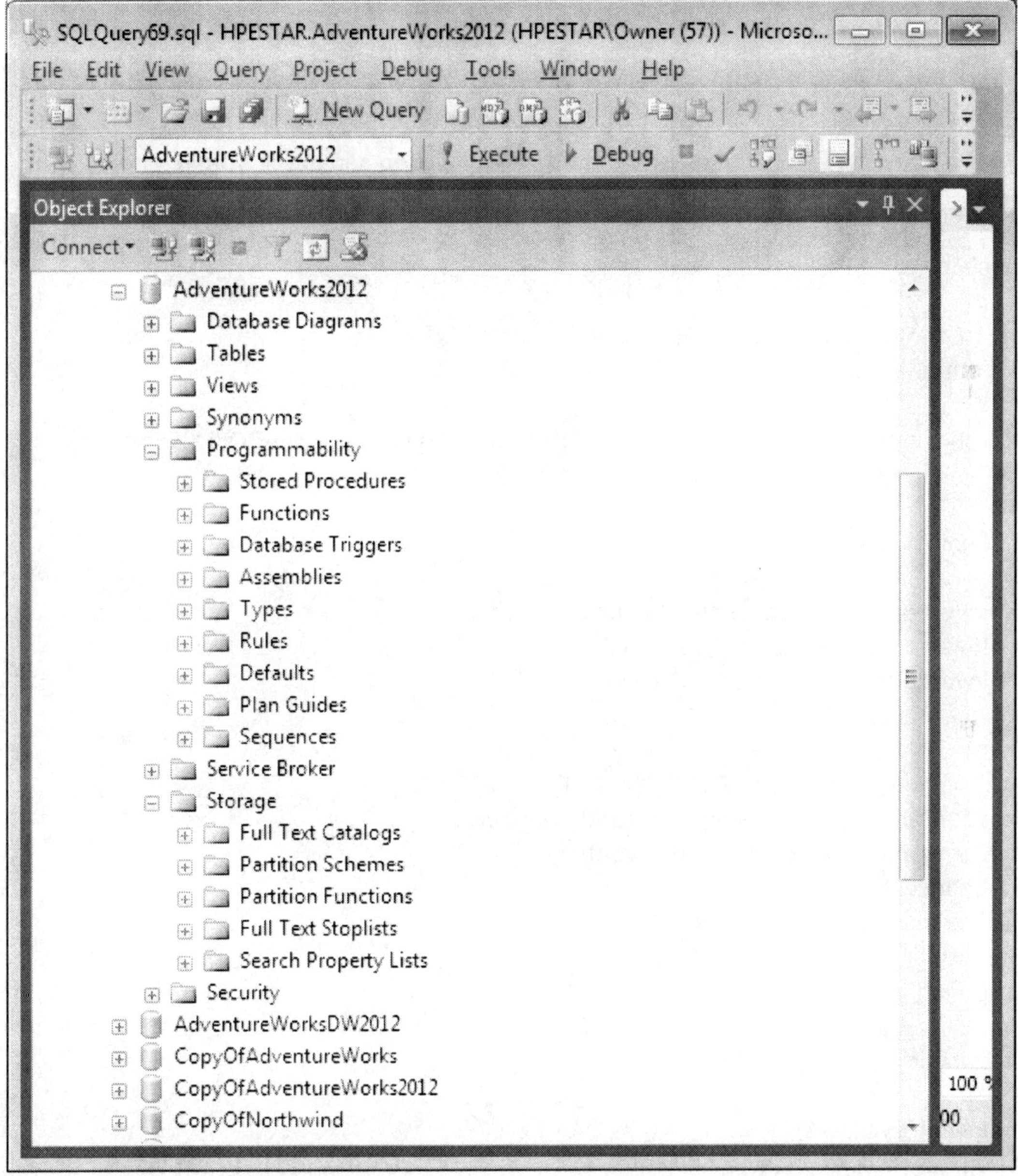

Database Related Items on Client-Side

On the client side the following items:

- SQL Server client libraries to access the server and database
- SQL queries imbedded in application programs
- Stored procedure calls imbedded in application software

Queries by themselves are not database object. To make them database objects we have to build stored procedures, functions or views around them.

The following code segment illustrates database connection and query from ASP to Inventory database. In ANSI SQL terminology catalog means database.

```
' Connect
<%
Dim StrConnInventory
Dim ConnInventory

StrConnInventory = "Provider=SQLOLEDB.1;Data Source=LONDONHEADOFFICE;Initial
Catalog=Inventory;User ID=finance;Password=fa$nAnCe#9*"

Set ConnInventory = Server.CreateObject("ADODB.Connection")

ConnInventory.ConnectionTimeout = 4000
ConnInventory.CommandTimeout = 4000
ConnInventory.Open StrConnInventory

' Query
Dim YourQuery As String = "SELECT Name, Price FROM Product"
 Dim YourCommand As New SqlCommand(YourQuery)
 YourCommand.Connection = ConnInventory
 YourConnection.Open()
 YourCommand.ExecuteNonQuery()
 Response.Write(YourCommand)
 YourCommand.Connection.Close()
%>
' Disconnect
<%
ConnInventory.Close
Set ConnInventory = Nothing
%>
```

SQL Server Profiler to Monitor Client-Server Communications

SQL Server Profiler, a tool in SSMS, has two modes of operations: interactive GUI and silent T-SQL script based operation. The simplest use of the Profiler is to check what queries are sent to the server (SQL Server) from the client and how long does processing take (duration). The client software sending the queries is SSMS. Even though SSMS appears as the "face of SQL Server", it is only a client software.

```
USE pubs;
GO
SELECT * FROM titles;
GO
```

```
USE Northwind;
GO
SELECT * FROM Products ORDER BY ProductName;
GO
```

```
USE AdventureWorks2012;
DECLARE @Date char(8) = '20080201';
SELECT * FROM Sales.SalesOrderHeader WHERE OrderDate=@Date;      -- Implicit conversion to datetime
GO
```

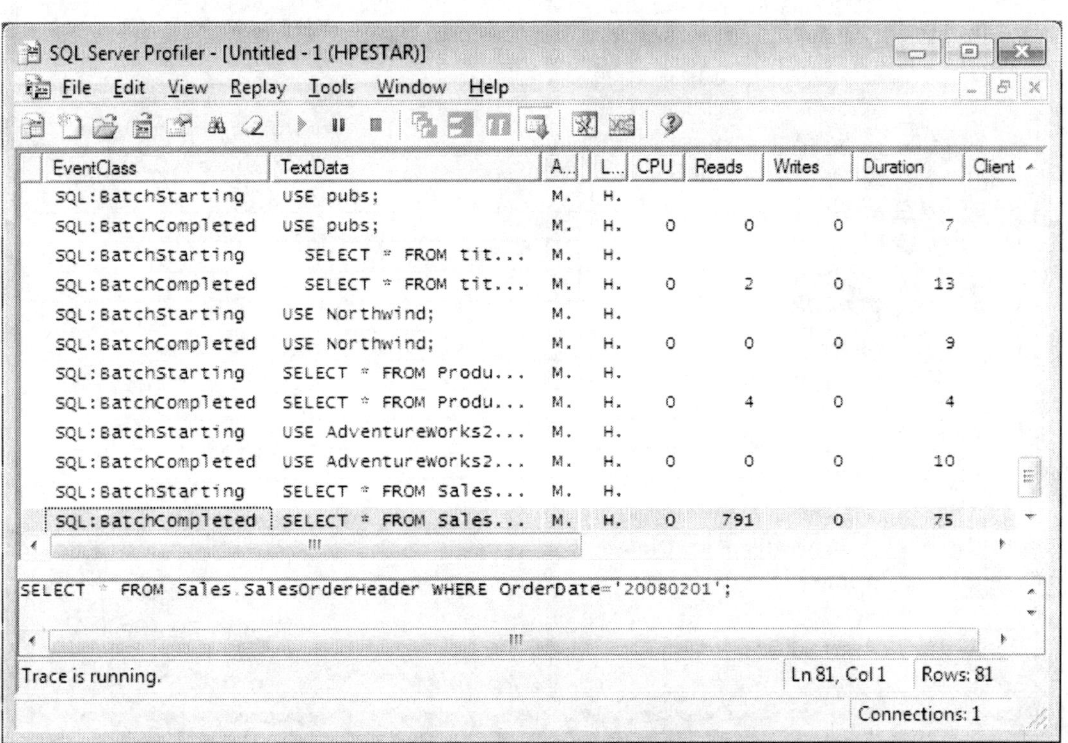

Table - Database Object

A database table holds data in tabular format by rows and columns. The main method of connecting tables is FOREIGN KEY referencing PRIMARY KEY. A set of connected tables makes up the database. Screenshot displays the structure and partial content of Northwind database Products table.

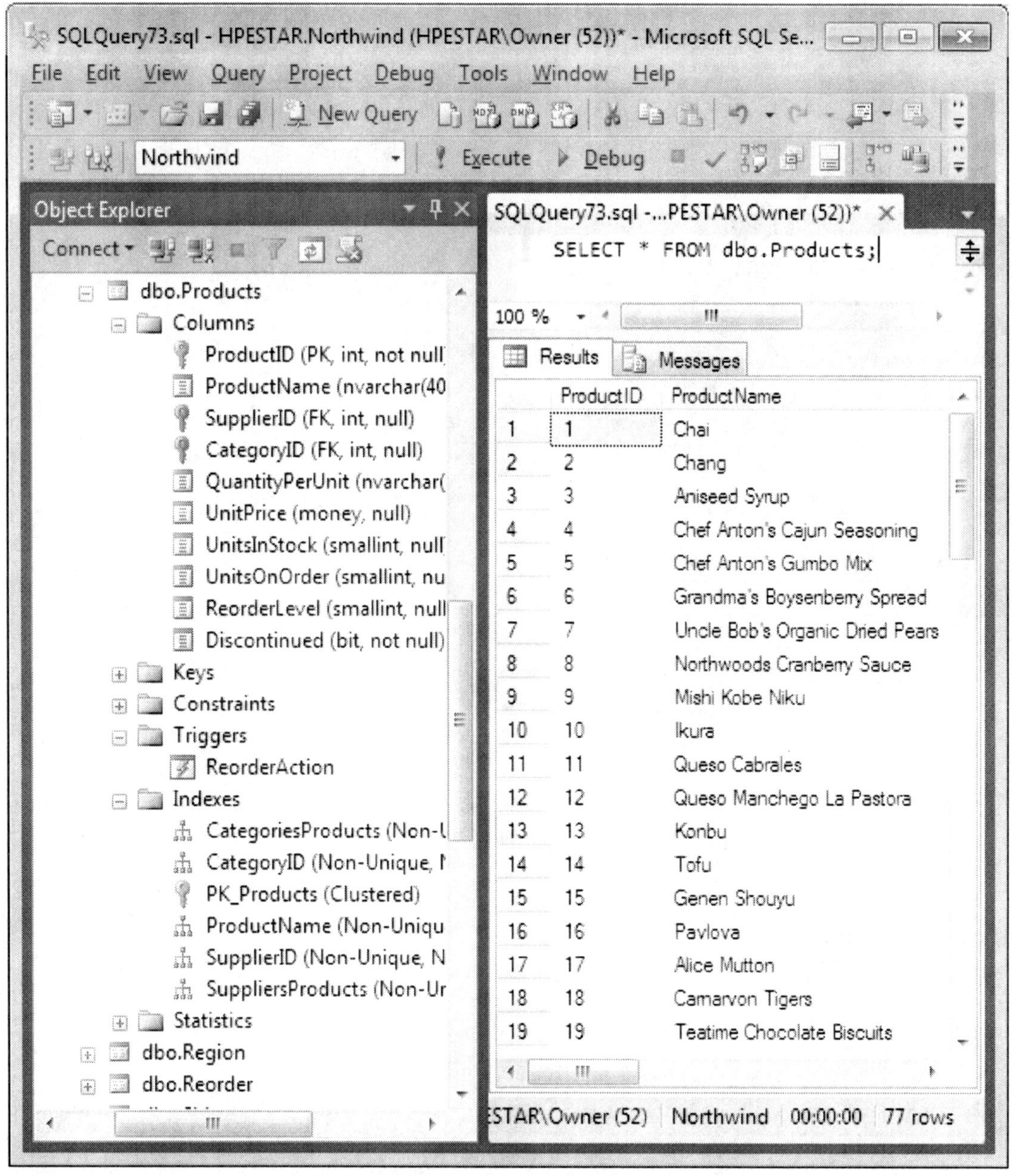

Tables in Production Schema

The listing and data dictionary description of tables in AdventureWorks2012 Production schema.

```
USE AdventureWorks2012;

SELECT  CONCAT('Production.', objname COLLATE DATABASE_DEFAULT) AS TableName,
        value                                                   AS [Description]
FROM fn_listextendedproperty (          NULL,
                            'schema', 'Production',
                            'table', default,
                             NULL, NULL)
ORDER BY TableName;
```

TableName	Description
Production.BillOfMaterials	Items required to make bicycles and bicycle subassemblies. It identifies the hierarchical relationship between a parent product and its components.
Production.Culture	Lookup table containing the languages in which some AdventureWorks data is stored.
Production.Document	Product maintenance documents.
Production.Illustration	Bicycle assembly diagrams.
Production.Location	Product inventory and manufacturing locations.
Production.Product	Products sold or used in the manfacturing of sold products.
Production.ProductCategory	High-level product categorization.
Production.ProductCostHistory	Changes in the cost of a product over time.
Production.ProductDescription	Product descriptions in several languages.
Production.ProductDocument	Cross-reference table mapping products to related product documents.
Production.ProductInventory	Product inventory information.
Production.ProductListPriceHistory	Changes in the list price of a product over time.
Production.ProductModel	Product model classification.
Production.ProductModelIllustration	Cross-reference table mapping product models and illustrations.
Production.ProductModelProductDescriptionCulture	Cross-reference table mapping product descriptions and the language the description is written in.
Production.ProductPhoto	Product images.
Production.ProductProductPhoto	Cross-reference table mapping products and product photos.
Production.ProductReview	Customer reviews of products they have purchased.
Production.ProductSubcategory	Product subcategories. See ProductCategory table.
Production.ScrapReason	Manufacturing failure reasons lookup table.
Production.TransactionHistory	Record of each purchase order, sales order, or work order transaction year to date.
Production.TransactionHistoryArchive	Transactions for previous years.
Production.UnitMeasure	Unit of measure lookup table.
Production.WorkOrder	Manufacturing work orders.
Production.WorkOrderRouting	Work order details.

Index - Database Object

An index on a table is a B-tree based structure which speeds up random searches. **Typically PRIMARY KEY (automatic), FOREIGN KEY and WHERE clause columns have indexes.** If the index is constructed on more than one column, it is called **composite index**. If all the columns in a query are in the index, it is called **covering index**. Properties dialog box displays the PRIMARY KEY composite index of the EmployeeDepartmentHistory table.

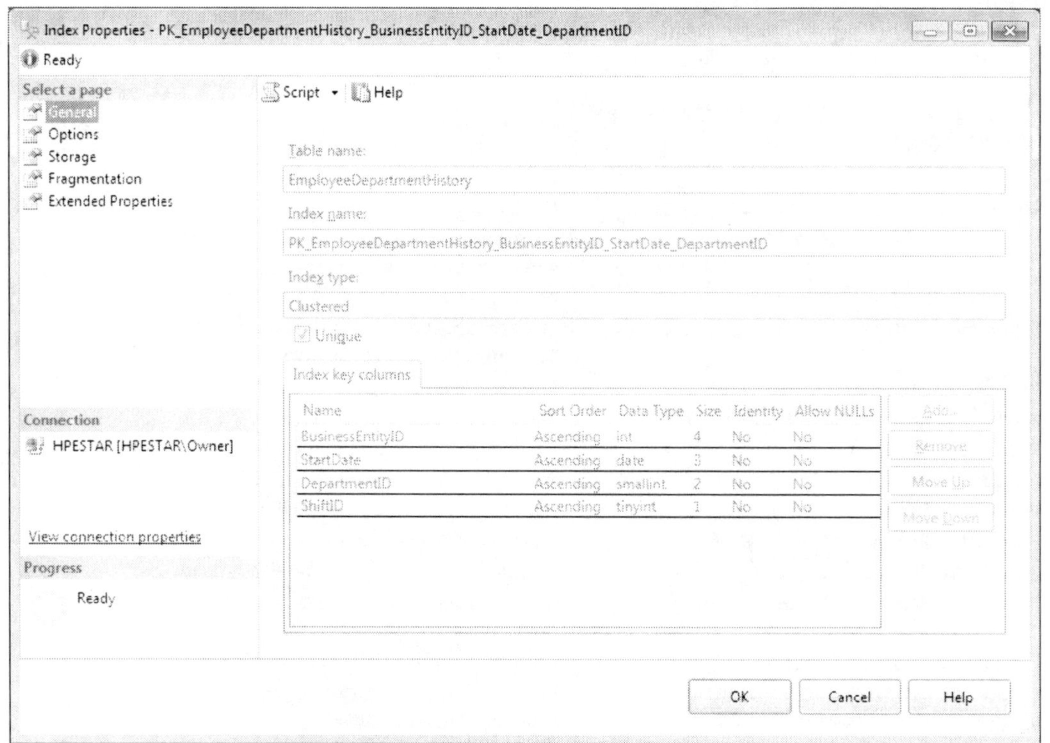

Index Description in Data Dictionary

The indexes listing for Product, SalesOrderHeader & SalesOrderDetail tables.

```
USE AdventureWorks2012;
```

```
SELECT  objtype                         AS ObjectType,
        'Sales.SalesOrderHeader'        AS TableName,
        objname                         AS ObjectName,
        value                           AS [Description]
FROM fn_listextendedproperty (NULL, 'schema', 'Sales', 'table', 'SalesOrderHeader', 'index', default)

UNION

SELECT objtype, 'Sales.SalesOrderDetail', objname, value
FROM fn_listextendedproperty (NULL, 'schema', 'Sales', 'table', 'SalesOrderDetail', 'index', default)

UNION

SELECT objtype, 'Production.Product', objname,  value
FROM fn_listextendedproperty (NULL, 'schema', 'Production', 'table', 'Product', 'index', default)
ORDER BY TableName;
GO
```

ObjectType	TableName	ObjectName	Description
INDEX	Production.Product	AK_Product_Name	Unique nonclustered index.
INDEX	Production.Product	AK_Product_ProductNumber	Unique nonclustered index.
INDEX	Production.Product	AK_Product_rowguid	Unique nonclustered index. Used to support replication samples.
INDEX	Production.Product	PK_Product_ProductID	Clustered index created by a primary key constraint.
INDEX	Sales.SalesOrderDetail	AK_SalesOrderDetail_rowguid	Unique nonclustered index. Used to support replication samples.
INDEX	Sales.SalesOrderDetail	IX_SalesOrderDetail_ProductID	Nonclustered index.
INDEX	Sales.SalesOrderDetail	PK_SalesOrderDetail_SalesOrderID_SalesOrderDetailID	Clustered index created by a primary key constraint.
INDEX	Sales.SalesOrderHeader	AK_SalesOrderHeader_rowguid	Unique nonclustered index. Used to support replication samples.
INDEX	Sales.SalesOrderHeader	AK_SalesOrderHeader_SalesOrderNumber	Unique nonclustered index.
INDEX	Sales.SalesOrderHeader	IX_SalesOrderHeader_CustomerID	Nonclustered index.
INDEX	Sales.SalesOrderHeader	IX_SalesOrderHeader_SalesPersonID	Nonclustered index.
INDEX	Sales.SalesOrderHeader	PK_SalesOrderHeader_SalesOrderID	Clustered index created by a primary key constraint.

Constraint - Database Object

The PRIMARY KEY constraint ensures that each row has a unique ID. The FOREIGN KEY constraint ensures that the FK points to (references) a valid PK. CHECK constraint enforces formulas (check clauses) defined for a column such as OrderQty > 0. If the formula evaluates to TRUE, the CHECK constraint satisfied, otherwise ERROR condition is generated by the database engine. SSMS screenshot shows a CHECK constraints listing query and results in the Northwind database.

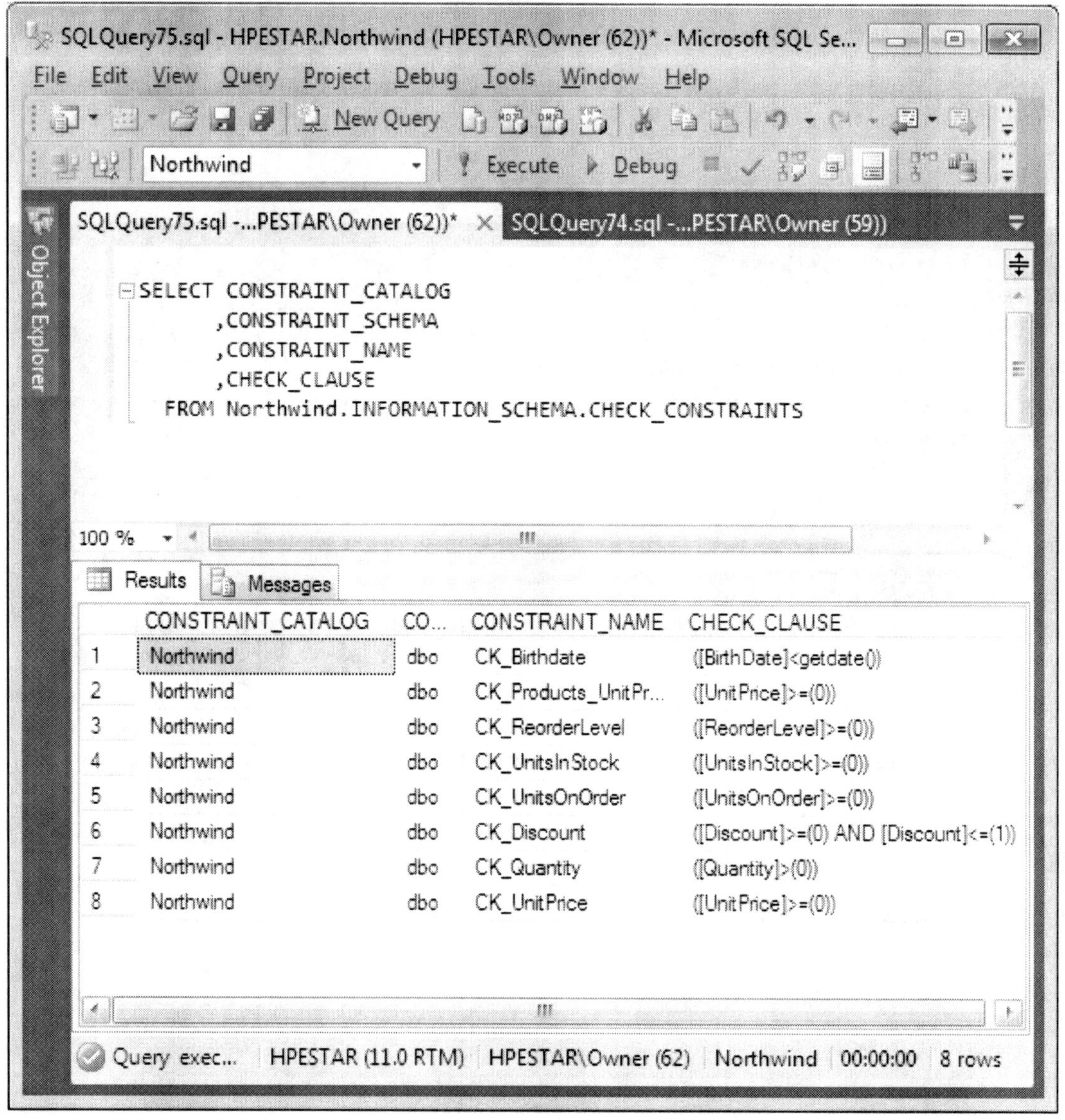

PRIMARY KEY & FOREIGN KEY Constraint Descriptions in Data Dictionary

Query to retrieve constraint descriptions (extended properties) for Product, SalesOrderHeader & SalesOrderDetail tables. Note: *description* not definition.

```
USE AdventureWorks2012;

-- UNION of 3 result sets
SELECT objtype AS ObjectType, 'Sales.SalesOrderHeader' AS TableName,
        objname as ObjectName, value AS [Description]
FROM fn_listextendedproperty (NULL, 'schema', 'Sales', 'table', 'SalesOrderHeader', 'constraint', default)
WHERE left(convert(varchar,value),7)='Foreign' or left(convert(varchar,value),7)='Primary'
UNION
SELECT objtype, 'Sales.SalesOrderDetail', objname,  value
FROM fn_listextendedproperty (NULL, 'schema', 'Sales', 'table', 'SalesOrderDetail', 'constraint', default)
WHERE left(convert(varchar,value),7)='Foreign' or left(convert(varchar,value),7)='Primary'
UNION
SELECT objtype, 'Production.Product', objname,  value
FROM fn_listextendedproperty (NULL, 'schema', 'Production', 'table', 'Product', 'constraint', default)
WHERE left(convert(varchar,value),7)='Foreign' or left(convert(varchar,value),7)='Primary'
ORDER BY        TableName,
                ObjectName DESC;
GO
```

ObjectType	TableName	ObjectName	Description
CONSTRAINT	Production.Product	PK_Product_ProductID	Primary key (clustered) constraint
CONSTRAINT	Production.Product	FK_Product_UnitMeasure_WeightUnitMeasureCode	Foreign key constraint referencing UnitMeasure.UnitMeasureCode.
CONSTRAINT	Production.Product	FK_Product_UnitMeasure_SizeUnitMeasureCode	Foreign key constraint referencing UnitMeasure.UnitMeasureCode.
CONSTRAINT	Production.Product	FK_Product_ProductSubcategory_ProductSubcategoryID	Foreign key constraint referencing ProductSubcategory.ProductSubcategoryID.
CONSTRAINT	Production.Product	FK_Product_ProductModel_ProductModelID	Foreign key constraint referencing ProductModel.ProductModelID.
CONSTRAINT	Sales.SalesOrderDetail	PK_SalesOrderDetail_SalesOrderID_SalesOrderDetailID	Primary key (clustered) constraint
CONSTRAINT	Sales.SalesOrderDetail	FK_SalesOrderDetail_SpecialOfferProduct_SpecialOfferIDProductID	Foreign key constraint referencing SpecialOfferProduct.SpecialOfferIDProductID.
CONSTRAINT	Sales.SalesOrderDetail	FK_SalesOrderDetail_SalesOrderHeader_SalesOrderID	Foreign key constraint referencing SalesOrderHeader.PurchaseOrderID.
CONSTRAINT	Sales.SalesOrderHeader	PK_SalesOrderHeader_SalesOrderID	Primary key (clustered) constraint
CONSTRAINT	Sales.SalesOrderHeader	FK_SalesOrderHeader_ShipMethod_ShipMethodID	Foreign key constraint referencing ShipMethod.ShipMethodID.
CONSTRAINT	Sales.SalesOrderHeader	FK_SalesOrderHeader_SalesTerritory_TerritoryID	Foreign key constraint referencing SalesTerritory.TerritoryID.
CONSTRAINT	Sales.SalesOrderHeader	FK_SalesOrderHeader_SalesPerson_SalesPersonID	Foreign key constraint referencing SalesPerson.SalesPersonID.
CONSTRAINT	Sales.SalesOrderHeader	FK_SalesOrderHeader_Customer_CustomerID	Foreign key constraint referencing Customer.CustomerID.
CONSTRAINT	Sales.SalesOrderHeader	FK_SalesOrderHeader_CurrencyRate_CurrencyRateID	Foreign key constraint referencing CurrencyRate.CurrencyRateID.
CONSTRAINT	Sales.SalesOrderHeader	FK_SalesOrderHeader_CreditCard_CreditCardID	Foreign key constraint referencing CreditCard.CreditCardID.
CONSTRAINT	Sales.SalesOrderHeader	FK_SalesOrderHeader_Address_ShipToAddressID	Foreign key constraint referencing Address.AddressID.
CONSTRAINT	Sales.SalesOrderHeader	FK_SalesOrderHeader_Address_BillToAddressID	Foreign key constraint referencing Address.AddressID.

View - Database Object

A SELECT query, with some restrictions, can be repackaged as view and thus become a server-side object, a coveted status, from "homeless" to "mansion". The creation of view is very simple, basically a name assignment is required as shown in the following demonstration. As soon as the CREATE VIEW statement is executed successfully the query, unknown to the SQL Server so far, becomes an "official" SQL Server database object, stored in the database. A view, a virtual table, can be used just like a table in SELECT queries. A note about the query: **the column aliases FirstAuthor and SecondAuthor cannot be used in the WHERE clause, only in the ORDER BY clause if present.**

SELECT results from views require ORDER BY if sorting is desired. There is no way around it.

```
USE pubs;
GO
```

```
CREATE VIEW vAuthorsInSameCity AS
SELECT          FirstAuthor       = CONCAT(au1.au_fname,' ', au1.au_lname),
                SecondAuthor      = CONCAT(au2.au_fname,' ', au2.au_lname),
                FirstCity         = au1.city,
                SecondCity        = au2.city
FROM    authors au1     INNER JOIN authors au2          ON au1.city = au2.city
WHERE   CONCAT(au1.au_fname,' ', au1.au_lname) < CONCAT(au2.au_fname,' ', au2.au_lname);
GO
```

```
SELECT * FROM vAuthorsInSameCity ORDER BY FirstAuthor, SecondAuthor
GO  -- (13 row(s) affected) - Partial results.
```

FirstAuthor	SecondAuthor	FirstCity	SecondCity
Abraham Bennet	Cheryl Carson	Berkeley	Berkeley
Albert Ringer	Anne Ringer	Salt Lake City	Salt Lake City

View can be changed at will with the ALTER VIEW statement & dropped with DROP VIEW.

```
ALTER VIEW vAuthorsInSameCity AS          SELECT
        FirstAuthor= CONCAT(au1.au_fname,' ', au1.au_lname),
        SecondAuthor= CONCAT(au2.au_fname,' ', au2.au_lname),
        FirstAuthorCity    = au1.city, SecondAuthorCity        = au2.city
FROM    authors au1   INNER JOIN authors au2   ON au1.city = au2.city
WHERE   CONCAT(au1.au_fname,' ', au1.au_lname) < CONCAT(au2.au_fname,' ', au2.au_lname);
GO
```

```
IF (OBJECT_ID('dbo.vAuthorsInSameCity','V') IS NOT NULL)
        DROP VIEW vAuthorsInSameCity;  -- Command(s) completed successfully.
```

View Descriptions in Data Dictionary

Query to list view descriptions in selected schemas.

```
USE AdventureWorks2012;
SELECT  CONCAT('Sales.', objname COLLATE DATABASE_DEFAULT)           AS ViewName,
        value                                                        AS [Description]
FROM fn_listextendedproperty (NULL, 'schema', 'Sales', 'view', default, NULL, NULL)
UNION
SELECT  CONCAT('Production.', objname COLLATE DATABASE_DEFAULT), value
FROM fn_listextendedproperty (NULL, 'schema', 'Production', 'view', default, NULL, NULL)
UNION
SELECT  CONCAT('HumanResources.', objname COLLATE DATABASE_DEFAULT), value
FROM fn_listextendedproperty (NULL, 'schema', 'HumanResources', 'view', default, NULL, NULL)
UNION
SELECT  CONCAT('Person.', objname COLLATE DATABASE_DEFAULT),  value
FROM fn_listextendedproperty (NULL, 'schema', 'Person', 'view', default, NULL, NULL)
ORDER BY ViewName; -- (18 row(s) affected) - Partial results.
```

ViewName	Description
HumanResources.vEmployee	Employee names and addresses.
HumanResources.vEmployeeDepartment	Returns employee name, title, and current department.
HumanResources.vEmployeeDepartmentHistory	Returns employee name and current and previous departments.
HumanResources.vJobCandidate	Job candidate names and resumes.

CREATE Indexed View for Business Critical Queries

An indexed view is stored like a table unlike a standard view which is a virtual table with a query that is evaluated upon view invocation. Performance is the main benefit of an indexed view, but it comes at a cost: it slows down INSERTs and other operations in the underlying tables.

```
IF OBJECT_ID ('Sales.vSalesByDateByProduct', 'V') IS NOT NULL DROP VIEW Sales.vSalesByDateByProduct ;
GO
CREATE VIEW Sales.vSalesByDateByProduct WITH SCHEMABINDING AS
  SELECT OrderDate, ProductNumber, SUM(LineTotal) AS TotalSales, COUNT_BIG(*) AS Items
  FROM Sales.SalesOrderDetail AS sod INNER JOIN Sales.SalesOrderHeader AS soh
    ON soh.SalesOrderID = sod.SalesOrderID  INNER JOIN Production.Product p ON sod.ProductID=p.ProductID
    GROUP BY OrderDate, ProductNumber;
GO
CREATE UNIQUE CLUSTERED INDEX idxVSalesCI ON Sales.vSalesByDateByProduct (OrderDate, ProductNumber);
GO
SELECT * FROM Sales.vSalesByDateByProduct ORDER BY OrderDate, ProductNumber;
GO -- (26878 row(s) affected) - Partial results.
```

OrderDate	ProductNumber	TotalSales	Items
2005-07-01 00:00:00.000	BK-M82B-38	44549.868000	7
2005-07-01 00:00:00.000	BK-M82B-42	32399.904000	8
2005-07-01 00:00:00.000	BK-M82B-44	46574.862000	7

Graphical View Designer

A view can be designed graphically or an existing view altered by using the Design option on the View drop-down menu in SSMS Object Explorer. First we create a view, then enter the graphical view designer to take a look.

```
USE [Northwind];
GO
CREATE VIEW [dbo].[ListOfProducts] AS
SELECT Categories.CategoryName as Category, ProductName, CompanyName AS Supplier
FROM Categories          INNER JOIN Products  ON Categories.CategoryID = Products.CategoryID
                         INNER JOIN Suppliers  ON Suppliers.SupplierID = Products.SupplierID
WHERE (((Products.Discontinued)=0));
GO
```

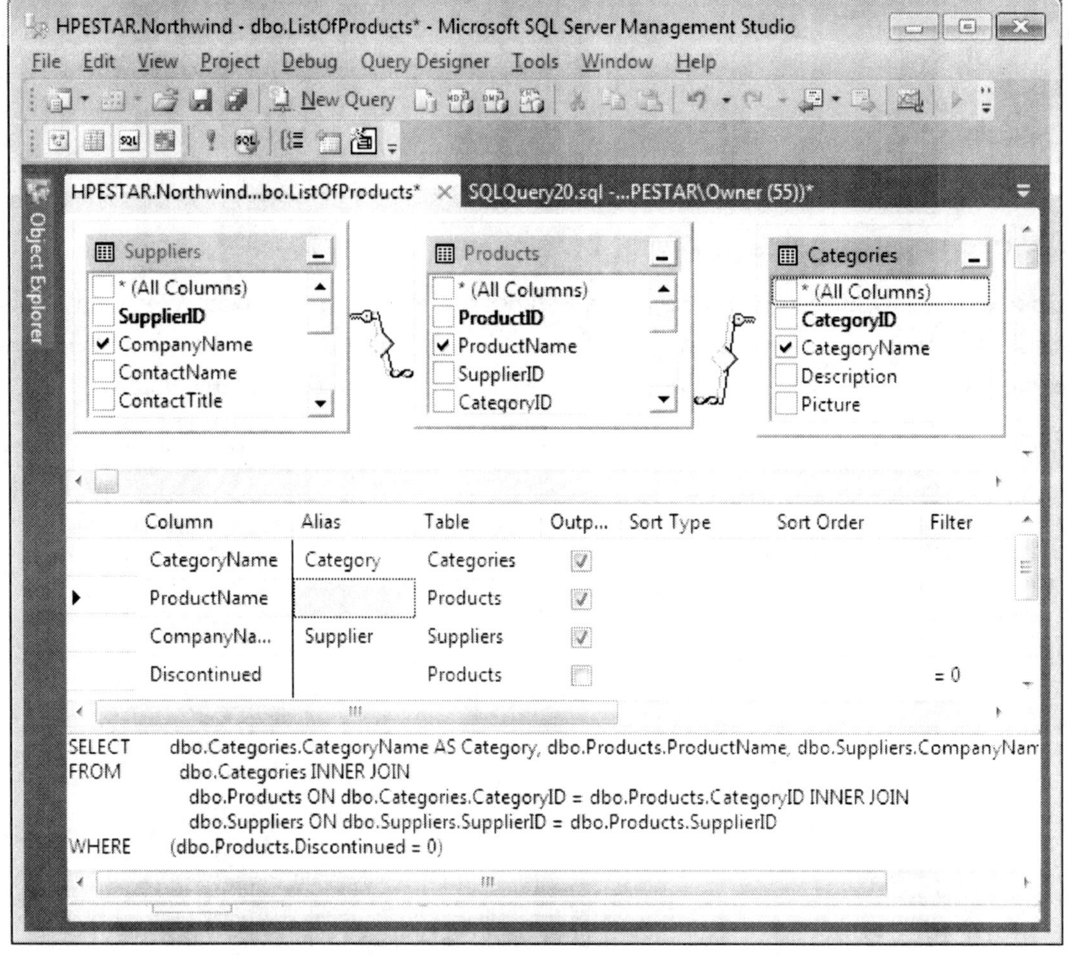

Stored Procedure: Server-Side Program

Stored procedures are T-SQL programs with optional input/output parameters. They vary from very simply to extremely complex. Following is the query which we will transform into a stored procedure, a server-side database object. Typical "read" stored procedure returns table-like results to the client application software just like a SELECT query. That is though not a requirement. For example, a stored procedure can perform table updates returning only success or failure information.

```
USE AdventureWorks2012;
GO
SELECT        P.Name                          AS Product,
              L.Name                          AS [Inventory Location],
              SUM(PI.Quantity)                AS [Qty Available]
FROM Production.Product AS P
  INNER JOIN Production.ProductInventory AS PI
              ON P.ProductID = PI.ProductID
  INNER JOIN Production.Location AS L
              ON PI.LocationID = L.LocationID
 INNER JOIN Production.ProductSubcategory SC
              ON P.ProductSubcategoryID = SC.ProductSubcategoryID
WHERE SC.Name = 'Touring Bikes' GROUP BY P.Name, L.Name  ORDER BY P.Name;
GO -- (44 row(s) affected) - Partial results.
```

Product	Inventory Location	Qty Available
Touring-1000 Blue, 46	Final Assembly	86
Touring-1000 Blue, 46	Finished Goods Storage	99
Touring-1000 Blue, 50	Final Assembly	81

Simple Stored Procedure with Encryption

WITH ENCRYPTION can be used in CREATE PROCEDURE to make the stored procedure source code unreadable on the server. Encrypted or not, stored procedure source code should be saved to a disk file or source control software such as Visual SourceSafe.

```
CREATE PROCEDURE sprocProductList WITH ENCRYPTION AS
SET NOCOUNT ON
SELECT * FROM Production.Product ORDER BY Name;
GO
```

```
EXEC sp_helptext 'dbo.sprocProductList';
-- The text for object 'dbo.sprocProductList' is encrypted.
```

Stored Procedure with Input Parameters

To make the stored procedure even more useful, we replace the literal 'Touring Bikes' with an input parameter.

```
CREATE PROC uspProductInventoryLocation @Subcategory nvarchar(50)
AS
BEGIN
SET NOCOUNT ON;  -- Turn off count messages
SELECT          P.Name                                      AS Product,
                L.Name                                      AS [Inventory Location],
                SUM(PI.Quantity)                            AS [Qty Available],
                FORMAT(MIN(P.SellStartDate), 'yyyy/MM/dd')  AS SellStartDate
FROM Production.Product AS P
   INNER JOIN Production.ProductInventory AS PI
                ON P.ProductID = PI.ProductID
   INNER JOIN Production.Location AS L
                ON PI.LocationID = L.LocationID
  INNER JOIN Production.ProductSubcategory SC
                ON P.ProductSubcategoryID = SC.ProductSubcategoryID
WHERE SC.Name = @Subcategory
GROUP BY P.Name, L.Name ORDER BY P.Name, L.Name;
END
GO
```

Permissions script follows. Usually the first line (GRANT EXECUTE) done. InventoryMgr is a user-defined database role. Each member of that role will be able to execute the stored procedure.

```
GRANT EXECUTE ON [dbo].[uspProductInventoryLocation] TO InventoryMgr;
DENY ALTER ON [dbo].[uspProductInventoryLocation] TO InventoryMgr;
DENY CONTROL ON [dbo].[uspProductInventoryLocation] TO InventoryMgr;
DENY TAKE OWNERSHIP ON [dbo].[uspProductInventoryLocation] TO InventoryMgr;
DENY VIEW DEFINITION ON [dbo].[uspProductInventoryLocation] TO InventoryMgr;
GO
```

```
-- Execute stored procedure with parameter
EXEC uspProductInventoryLocation 'Touring Bikes';          -- (44 row(s) affected)
```

```
EXEC uspProductInventoryLocation 'Mountain Bikes';         -- (64 row(s) affected) - Partial results.
```

Product	Inventory Location	Qty Available	SellStartDate
Mountain-100 Black, 38	Final Assembly	56	2005/07/01
Mountain-100 Black, 38	Finished Goods Storage	99	2005/07/01
Mountain-100 Black, 42	Final Assembly	116	2005/07/01
Mountain-100 Black, 42	Finished Goods Storage	78	2005/07/01
Mountain-100 Black, 44	Final Assembly	100	2005/07/01

Stored Procedure Descriptions in Data Dictionary

Query to list stored procedure descriptions in selected schemas.

```
USE AdventureWorks2012;
SELECT   CONCAT('dbo.', objname COLLATE DATABASE_DEFAULT)          AS SprocName,
         value                                                     AS [Description]
FROM fn_listextendedproperty (NULL, 'schema', 'dbo', 'procedure', default, NULL, NULL)
WHERE LEN(convert(nvarchar(max),value)) > 4
UNION
SELECT   CONCAT('dbo.', objname COLLATE DATABASE_DEFAULT),  value
FROM fn_listextendedproperty (NULL, 'schema', 'HumanResources', 'procedure', default, NULL, NULL)
ORDER BY SprocName;  -- (8 row(s) affected) - Partial results.
```

SprocName	Description
dbo.uspGetBillOfMaterials	Stored procedure using a recursive query to return a multi-level bill of material for the specified ProductID.
dbo.uspGetEmployeeManagers	Stored procedure using a recursive query to return the direct and indirect managers of the specified employee.
dbo.uspGetManagerEmployees	Stored procedure using a recursive query to return the direct and indirect employees of the specified manager.
dbo.uspGetWhereUsedProductID	Stored procedure using a recursive query to return all components or assemblies that directly or indirectly use the specified ProductID.
dbo.uspLogError	Logs error information in the ErrorLog table about the error that caused execution to jump to the CATCH block of a TRY...CATCH construct. Should be executed from within the scope of a CATCH block otherwise it will return without inserting error information.

Turning a Query into a Simple Stored Procedure

It is easy to change a query into a simple (no parameters, no t-sql logic) stored procedure.

```
USE AdventureWorks2012;
GO
CREATE PROCEDURE uspSalesOrderProductList  AS
        SELECT OrderDate, SOH.SalesOrderID, ProductID, OrderQty, LineTotal
        FROM Sales.SalesOrderHeader SOH
           INNER JOIN Sales.SalesOrderDetail SOD   ON SOH.SalesOrderID = SOD.SalesOrderID
        ORDER BY SOH.SalesOrderID, ProductID;
GO
```

```
EXEC uspSalesOrderProductList;  -- (121329 row(s) affected)
```

Trigger: Event Fired Server-Side Program

Trigger is like a stored procedure with four differences:

- Trigger is fired by an event such as table insert not by a call like a stored procedure.
- Trigger has the deleted (old row copy) and inserted (new row copy) tables available.
- Trigger does not have input/output parameter option.
- Trigger never returns table-like results.

Trigger to synchronize data in StateTaxFreeBondArchive table if data is inserted or updated in the StateTaxFreeBond table.

```
CREATE TRIGGER trgFillInMissingCouponRate  ON [dbo].StateTaxFreeBond
FOR INSERT, UPDATE  AS
BEGIN
    UPDATE StateTaxFreeBondArchive   SET CouponRate = isnull(i.CouponRate,m.CouponRate)
    FROM StateTaxFreeBondArchive m   INNER JOIN inserted i      ON m.MBCID = i.MBCID
END
```

Once a trigger is compiled, it is active and working silently in the background whenever insert, update or delete event fires it up. **It is important to note that there is a downside to the trigger** "stealth" operation: if a trigger is dropped , it may not be noticed as part of the day-to-day operation. This behaviour is unlike stored procedure whereby if dropped, it causes error in the calling application software which can be noticed by users.

There are 2 special update functions for triggers: UPDATE() and COLUMNS_UPDATED(). The latter returns a binary pattern of updated columns:

Column Position	1	2	3	4	5	6	7	8
Binarymask	1	2	4	8	16	32	64	128

```
IF (COLUMNS_UPDATED() & 38) = 38     -- Columns 2, 3, 6:  all were updated
```

```
IF (COLUMNS_UPDATED() & 38) > 0      -- Columns 2, 3, 6:  at least one was updated
```

The column numbers can be found in the INFORMATION_SCHEMA.COLUMNS view as ORDINAL_POSITION. The UPDATE() trigger function can be used the following way.

```
IF ( UPDATE (SalaryRate) OR UPDATE (SSNo) ) BEGIN  RAISERROR (50017, 16, 10)  END;
```

Error message 50017 is a custom error message created with sp_addmessage.

Article: **Define custom error messages in SQL Server 2005**
http://www.techrepublic.com/blog/datacenter/define-custom-error-messages-in-sql-server-2005/390

Function: Read-Only Server-Side Program

A user-defined function is also a program like a stored procedure, however, **no database change can be performed within a function, read only**. The database can be changed both in a trigger and a stored procedure. The following T-SQL script demonstrates the creation and use of a table-valued user-defined function. The other function type is scalar-valued, returns only a single value.

```
CREATE FUNCTION dbo.ufnSplitCommaDelimitedIntegerString (@NumberList nvarchar(max))
RETURNS @SplitList TABLE ( Element INT )
AS
 BEGIN
   DECLARE @Pointer    int,
        @Element nvarchar(32)
   SET @NumberList = LTRIM(RTRIM(@NumberList))
   IF ( RIGHT(@NumberList, 1) != ',' )
    SET @NumberList=@NumberList + ','
   SET @Pointer = CHARINDEX(',', @NumberList, 1)
   IF REPLACE(@NumberList, ',', '') <> ''
    BEGIN
      WHILE ( @Pointer > 0 )
       BEGIN
         SET @Element = LTRIM(RTRIM(LEFT(@NumberList, @Pointer - 1)))
         IF ( @Element <> '' )
          INSERT INTO @SplitList
          VALUES     (CONVERT(int, @Element))
         SET @NumberList = RIGHT(@NumberList,
                  LEN(@NumberList) - @Pointer  )
         SET @Pointer = CHARINDEX(',', @NumberList, 1)
       END
    END
   RETURN
 END;
GO
SELECT * FROM  dbo.ufnSplitCommaDelimitedIntegerString ('1, 2, 4, 8, 16, 32, 64, 128, 256');
```

Element
1
2
4
8
16
32
64
128
256

Simple Cursor Execution of a Simple Stored Procedure

Set-based operation are generally preferred over cursors. However, to execute a stored procedure for a data set or dynamic SQL requires cursor. That means WHILE loop.

```
USE AdventureWorks2012;
GO
CREATE PROCEDURE sprocProductDatetimestamp  @ProductID INT AS
        SET NOCOUNT ON;
        UPDATE Production.Product SET ModifiedDate = ModifiedDate /* getdate() */
        WHERE ProductID = @ProductID;
        RETURN (@@ROWCOUNT);
GO
```

```
DECLARE ProductCursor CURSOR LOCAL FAST_FORWARD FOR
        SELECT DISTINCT ProductID FROM Sales.SalesOrderDetail
        WHERE SalesOrderDetailID BETWEEN 10000 AND 10090;

DECLARE @PID INT;  OPEN ProductCursor; FETCH NEXT FROM ProductCursor INTO @PID;
```

```
WHILE (@@fetch_status = 0)  BEGIN
        EXEC sprocProductDatetimestamp @PID;    PRINT @PID;   -- for testing & debugging
        FETCH NEXT FROM ProductCursor INTO @PID;
END
```

```
CLOSE ProductCursor; DEALLOCATE ProductCursor;
```

User-Defined Function Descriptions in Data Dictionary

Query to list user-defined function descriptions in the default "dbo" schema. "dbo" stands for database owner, a database role.

```
USE AdventureWorks2012;
SELECT    CONCAT('dbo.', objname COLLATE DATABASE_DEFAULT)              AS UDFName,
          value                                                         AS [Description]
FROM fn_listextendedproperty (NULL, 'schema', 'dbo', 'function', default, NULL, NULL)
WHERE LEN(convert(nvarchar(max),value)) > 4  ORDER BY UDFName; -- (11 row(s) affected) - Partial results.
```

UDFName	Description
dbo.ufnGetAccountingEndDate	Scalar function used in the uSalesOrderHeader trigger to set the starting account date.
dbo.ufnGetAccountingStartDate	Scalar function used in the uSalesOrderHeader trigger to set the ending account date.
dbo.ufnGetContactInformation	Table value function returning the first name, last name, job title and contact type for a given contact.

Sequence - Database Object

The INT IDENTITY(1,1) function commonly used as **SURROGATE PRIMARY KEY** is limited to the host table. Sequence object, new in SQL Server 2012, can be shared by tables and programs. T-SQL script to demonstrate how two tables can share an integer sequence.

```
USE AdventureWorks2012;
GO
CREATE SEQUENCE CustomerSequence as INT  START WITH 1  INCREMENT BY 1;
GO
CREATE TABLE LONDONCustomer
 (          CustomerID          INT PRIMARY KEY,
            Name                NVARCHAR(64),
            ModifiedDate        DATE default (CURRENT_TIMESTAMP)      );
GO
```

ALTER TABLE & ALTER COLUMN demonstration.

```
ALTER TABLE LONDONCustomer ALTER COLUMN Name NVARCHAR(128) NOT NULL;
ALTER TABLE LONDONCustomer ADD UNIQUE(Name);
```

```
CREATE TABLE NYCCustomer
 (          CustomerID          INT PRIMARY KEY,
            Name                NVARCHAR(64) NOT NULL UNIQUE,
            ModifiedDate        DATE default (CURRENT_TIMESTAMP)      );
GO
INSERT NYCCustomer (CustomerID, Name)
VALUES  (NEXT VALUE FOR CustomerSequence, 'Richard Blackstone'),
        (NEXT VALUE FOR CustomerSequence, 'Anna Smithfield');
GO
SELECT * FROM NYCCustomer;
```

CustomerID	Name	ModifiedDate
1	Richard Blackstone	2016-07-18
2	Anna Smithfield	2016-07-18

```
INSERT LONDONCustomer (CustomerID, Name)
VALUES  (NEXT VALUE FOR CustomerSequence, 'Kevin Lionheart'),
        (NEXT VALUE FOR CustomerSequence, 'Linda Wakefield');
GO
SELECT * FROM LONDONCustomer;
```

CustomerID	Name	ModifiedDate
3	Kevin Lionheart	2016-07-18
4	Linda Wakefield	2016-07-18

ROW_NUMBER() and Ranking Functions

Ranking functions (window functions), introduced with SQL Server 2005, provide sequencing and ranking items in a partition or all. ROW_NUMBER() function is probably most used.

```
SELECT   CustomerID,        CONVERT(date, OrderDate)                                    AS OrderDate,
         RANK() OVER ( PARTITION BY CustomerID ORDER BY OrderDate DESC)              AS RankNo
FROM   AdventureWorks2012.Sales.SalesOrderHeader   ORDER  BY CustomerID,   RankNo;
GO   -- (31465 row(s) affected) - Partial results.
```

CustomerID	OrderDate	RankNo
11014	2007-11-01	1
11014	2007-09-24	2
11015	2007-07-22	1
11016	2007-08-13	1
11017	2008-04-16	1
11017	2007-07-05	2
11017	2005-07-15	3

Partition data by CustomerID and rank it OrderDate DESC.

```
SELECT *
FROM   (SELECT CustomerID,        CONVERT(date, OrderDate)                              AS OrderDate,
         RANK()  OVER (PARTITION BY CustomerID   ORDER BY OrderDate DESC)             AS RankNo
     FROM   AdventureWorks2012.Sales.SalesOrderHeader)  x -- derived table
WHERE  RankNo  BETWEEN 1 AND 4ORDER  BY CustomerID;     --  (29383 row(s) affected)  - Partial results.
```

CustomerID	OrderDate	RankNo
11675	2007-08-13	1
11675	2006-04-27	2
11676	2008-06-11	1
11676	2008-02-21	2

Dividing Products into Two Groups with NTILE(2)

```
SELECT ROW_NUMBER() OVER(ORDER BY ListPrice DESC, ProductNumber)          AS RN,
        ProductNumber,  ListPrice,
        NTILE(2) OVER (ORDER BY ListPrice DESC,  ProductNumber)                AS Tile
FROM AdventureWorks2012.Production.Product
WHERE ListPrice > 0 ORDER BY Tile, RN;                -- (304 row(s) affected) - Partial results.
```

RN	ProductNumber	ListPrice	Tile
151	FR-R38B-60	337.22	1
152	FR-R38B-62	337.22	1
153	FR-R38R-44	337.22	2
154	FR-R38R-48	337.22	2

Query to Compare ROW_NUMBER, RANK, DENSE_RANK & NTILE

```
USE AdventureWorks;
SELECT c.AccountNumber                                              AS CustAccount,
    FLOOR(h.SubTotal / 1000)                                        AS [SubTotal (Thousands $)],
    ROW_NUMBER() OVER(   ORDER BY FLOOR(h.SubTotal /1000) DESC)     AS RowNumber,
    RANK()  OVER(   ORDER BY FLOOR(h.SubTotal /1000) DESC)          AS Rank,
    DENSE_RANK()   OVER(ORDER BY FLOOR(h.SubTotal /1000) DESC)      AS DenseRank,
    NTILE(5)   OVER(    ORDER BY FLOOR(h.SubTotal /1000) DESC)      AS NTile
FROM   Sales.Customer c   INNER JOIN Sales.SalesOrderHeader h       ON c.CustomerID = h.CustomerID
    INNER JOIN Sales.SalesTerritory t                ON h.TerritoryID = t.TerritoryID
WHERE  t.Name = 'Germany'    AND OrderDate >= '20040101' AND OrderDate  <  DATEADD(yy, 1, '20040101' )
        AND SubTotal >= 4000.0  ORDER  BY RowNumber;
```

CustAccount	SubTotal (Thousands $)	RowNumber	Rank	DenseRank	NTile
AW00000230	100.00	1	1	1	1
AW00000230	88.00	2	2	2	1
AW00000302	77.00	3	3	3	1
AW00000320	68.00	4	4	4	1
AW00000536	68.00	5	4	4	1
AW00000536	64.00	6	6	5	1
AW00000266	58.00	7	7	6	1
AW00000302	44.00	8	8	7	2

Comparing RANK(skipping) & DENSE_RANK(no skipping)

Usually it is better to use DENSE_RANK() when there are **ties in the data** to avoid skipping in rank number.

```
SELECT [FullName],[SalesTerritory], ROUND([2008]/1000000, 0) AS SalesInMillions
        ,RANK() OVER (ORDER BY ROUND([2008]/1000000, 0) DESC) AS [Rank]
        ,DENSE_RANK() OVER (ORDER BY ROUND([2008]/1000000, 0) DESC) AS [DenseRank]
        ,ROW_NUMBER() OVER (ORDER BY ROUND([2008]/1000000, 0) DESC, FullName) AS [RN]
FROM [AdventureWorks2012].[Sales].[vSalesPersonSalesByFiscalYears] ORDER BY DenseRank, RN;
```

FullName	SalesTerritory	SalesInMillions	Rank	DenseRank	RN
Jae B Pak	United Kingdom	4.00	1	1	1
Linda C Mitchell	Southwest	4.00	1	1	2
Michael G Blythe	Northeast	4.00	1	1	3
Jillian Carson	Central	3.00	4	2	4
José Edvaldo Saraiva	Canada	3.00	4	2	5
Ranjit R Varkey Chudukatil	France	3.00	4	2	6
David R Campbell	Northwest	2.00	7	3	7
Rachel B Valdez	Germany	2.00	7	3	8
Shu K Ito	Southwest	2.00	7	3	9
Tete A Mensa-Annan	Northwest	2.00	7	3	10
Tsvi Michael Reiter	Southeast	2.00	7	3	11
Garrett R Vargas	Canada	1.00	12	4	12
Lynn N Tsoflias	Australia	1.00	12	4	13
Pamela O Ansman-Wolfe	Northwest	1.00	12	4	14

Dynamic SQL To Soar Beyond the Limits of Static SQL

Static (regular) T-SQL syntax does not accept variables at all places in a query. With dynamic SQL we can overcome the limitation. Dynamic SQL script uses table list metadata from the INFORMATION_SCHEMA.TABLES system view to build a COUNT() query for all tables. COUNT(*) returns 4 bytes integer. For large values COUNT_BIG() returns an 8 bytes integer.

```
DECLARE @SQL nvarchar(max) = '', @Schema sysname, @Table sysname;
SELECT TOP 20 @SQL = CONCAT(@SQL , 'SELECT ''',QUOTENAME(TABLE_SCHEMA),'.',
          QUOTENAME(TABLE_NAME),'''',
          '= COUNT(*) FROM ', QUOTENAME(TABLE_SCHEMA),'.',QUOTENAME(TABLE_NAME) , ';',
          CHAR(10))
FROM INFORMATION_SCHEMA.TABLES
WHERE TABLE_TYPE='BASE TABLE';
PRINT @SQL;           -- Test & debug - Partial results.
```

SELECT '[Production].[BillOfMaterials]'= COUNT(*) FROM [Production].[BillOfMaterials];
SELECT '[Production].[Culture]'= COUNT(*) FROM [Production].[Culture];

```
EXEC sp_executesql @SQL  -- Dynamic SQL query execution
-- Partial results.
```

[Production].[ScrapReason]
16

[HumanResources].[Shift]
3

Parameterized Dynamic SQL Query Execution

The dynamic SQL string has a parameterized query. It can only be executed if the parameter(s) is supplied when dynamic execution is called.

```
DECLARE @LastName varchar(30) = 'O''Brien';
DECLARE @DynamicSQL nvarchar(max)= 'SELECT BusinessEntityID, FirstName, LastName
               FROM AdventureWorks2012.Person.Person ';
SET @DynamicSQL = CONCAT(@DynamicSQL, 'WHERE LastName = @pLastName');
PRINT @DynamicSQL;  -- testing & debugging
```

```
EXEC sp_executesql  @DynamicSQL, N'@pLastName varchar(40)', @pLastName = @LastName;
```

BusinessEntityID	FirstName	LastName
1553	Tim	O'Brien

Built-in System Functions

SQL Server T-SQL language has a large collection of system functions such as date & time, string and math function. The nested REPLACE string function can be used to remove unwanted characters from a string.

```
DECLARE @text nvarchar(128) = '#1245! $99^@';
SELECT REPLACE(REPLACE(REPLACE(REPLACE(REPLACE(REPLACE(REPLACE(REPLACE(REPLACE(@text,
        '!',''),'@',''),'#',''),'$',''),'%',''),'^',''),'&',''),'*',''),' ','');     -- 124599
```

All the system function are listed in SSMS Object Explorer under the Programmability tab.

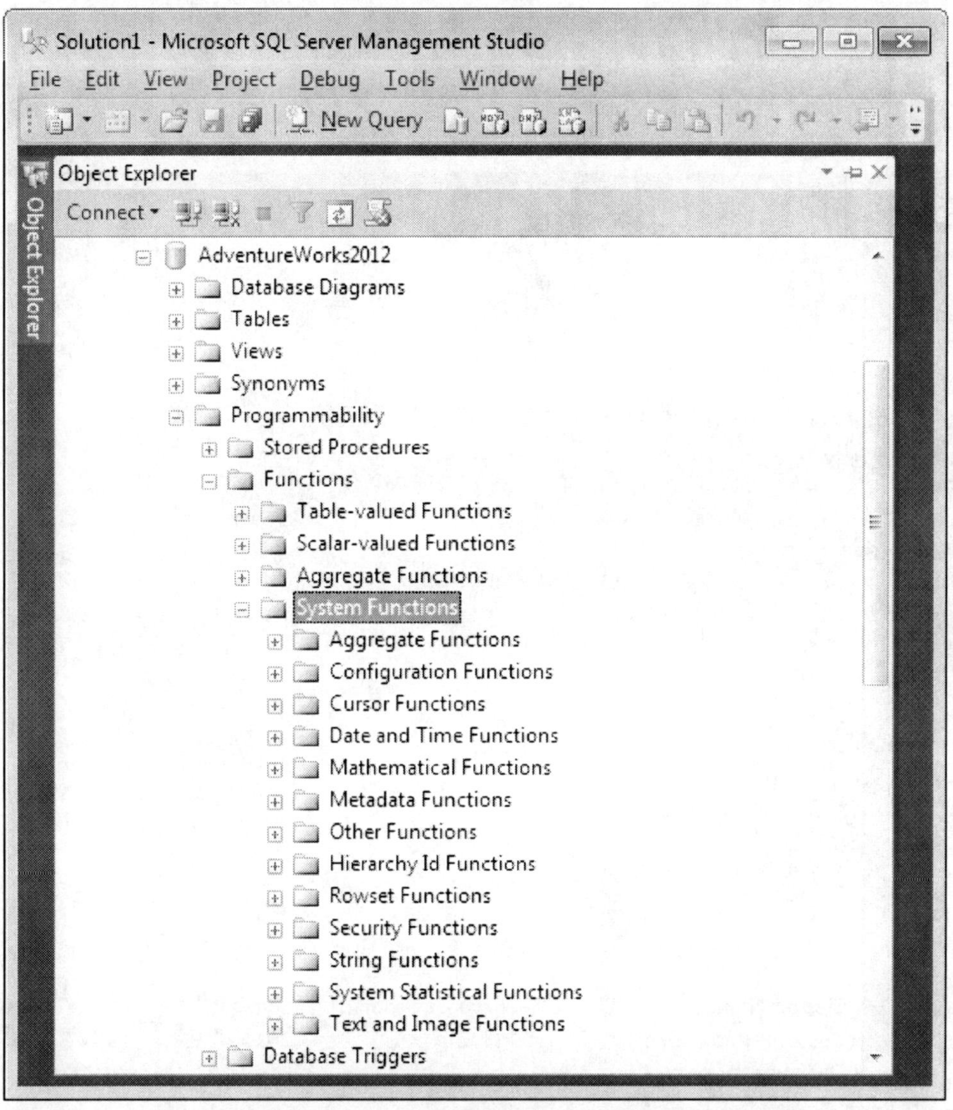

Local Variables & Table Variables in T-SQL

Local variables with different data types have scope of a batch or a stored procedure/trigger/function. Note that a "GO" in T-SQL script indicates end of batch, therefore the end of scope for local variables. Table variable is a virtual table with similar scope to local variable. Script to demonstrate local and table variables.

```
DECLARE @i INT;  SET @i = 999;

SELECT @i + @i;
-- 1998

SELECT @i = 555;  -- assignment
SELECT @i + @i;
GO
-- 1110
```

```
DECLARE @i INT = 999;                -- new in SQL Server 2008
SET @i += 1;                         -- new in SQL Server 2008

SELECT @i;
GO
-- 1000
```

```
DECLARE @OrderShipperJunction TABLE                          -- Table variable
 (
   ShipperID            SMALLINT IDENTITY ( 1, 1 ) PRIMARY KEY,
   ShipperName          NVARCHAR(64),
   PurchaseOrderID      INT,
   ShipDate             DATE DEFAULT (CURRENT_TIMESTAMP),
   FreightCost          SMALLMONEY
 ) ;
INSERT @OrderShipperJunction
    (ShipperName,
     PurchaseOrderID,
     FreightCost)
VALUES('Custom Motor Bike Distributor',      11111,      177.34)

SELECT * FROM   @OrderShipperJunction
GO
```

ShipperID	ShipperName	PurchaseOrderID	ShipDate	FreightCost
1	Custom Motor Bike Distributor	11111	2016-07-18	177.34

Metadata Visibility Through System Views

The system views provide SQL Server and database metadata which can be used just for viewing in SSMS Object Explorer or programmatically in T-SQL scripts. The system views are based on system tables which are no longer accessible since SQL Server 2005. The system view sys.objects contains all the basic info on each and every user objects in the database with the exception of indexes. Query to retrieve partial data form sys.objects system view.

```
select
   s.name                              as [Schema],
   o.name                              as [Name],
   o.type_desc                         as [Type],
   o.create_date                       as CreateDate
from    sys.objects o
           inner join sys.schemas s
              on s.schema_id = o.schema_id
where is_ms_shipped = 0
order by [Type], [Schema], [Name]
-- (722 row(s) affected)  -  Partial results.
```

Schema	Name	Type	CreateDate
HumanResources	Department	USER_TABLE	2012-03-14 13:14:19.267
HumanResources	Employee	USER_TABLE	2012-03-14 13:14:19.303
HumanResources	EmployeeDepartmentHistory	USER_TABLE	2012-03-14 13:14:19.313
HumanResources	EmployeePayHistory	USER_TABLE	2012-03-14 13:14:19.320
HumanResources	JobCandidate	USER_TABLE	2012-03-14 13:14:19.337
HumanResources	Shift	USER_TABLE	2012-03-14 13:14:19.593
Person	Address	USER_TABLE	2012-03-14 13:14:19.140
Person	AddressType	USER_TABLE	2012-03-14 13:14:19.150
Person	BusinessEntity	USER_TABLE	2012-03-14 13:14:19.183
Person	BusinessEntityAddress	USER_TABLE	2012-03-14 13:14:19.190
Person	BusinessEntityContact	USER_TABLE	2012-03-14 13:14:19.197
Person	ContactType	USER_TABLE	2012-03-14 13:14:19.207
Person	CountryRegion	USER_TABLE	2012-03-14 13:14:19.220
Person	EmailAddress	USER_TABLE	2012-03-14 13:14:19.290
Person	Password	USER_TABLE	2012-03-14 13:14:19.350
Person	Person	USER_TABLE	2012-03-14 13:14:19.357
Person	PersonPhone	USER_TABLE	2012-03-14 13:14:19.370
Person	PhoneNumberType	USER_TABLE	2012-03-14 13:14:19.377
Person	StateProvince	USER_TABLE	2012-03-14 13:14:19.623
Production	BillOfMaterials	USER_TABLE	2012-03-14 13:14:19.170
Production	Culture	USER_TABLE	2012-03-14 13:14:19.237

Constructing T-SQL Identifiers

Identifiers are the names given to SQL Server & database objects such as linked servers, tables, views or stored procedures.

Very simple rule: **do not include any special character in an identifier other than single underscore (_). Double underscore in an identifier inevitably leads to confusion, loss of database developer productivity.**

Creating good identifiers helps with productivity in database development, administration and maintenance. Using names AccountsPayable1 and AccountsPayable2 as variations for AccountsPayable is not good because the 1,2 suffixes are meaningless. On the other hand AccountsPayableLondon & AccountsPayableNYC are good, meaningful names. The list of identifiers can be enumerated from AdventureWorks2012.sys.objects.

```
SELECT name FROM AdventureWorks2012.sys.objects   ORDER BY name; -- (820 row(s) affected)
```

Selected results with comments.

Identifier(name)	**Style Comment**
Account	single word
AddressType	double words CamelCase style
BillOfMaterials	CamelCase (also known as Pascal case)
BusinessEntityContact	CamelCase
CK__ImageStore__67152DD3	double underscore separator, CK prefix for CHECK CONSTRAINT
CK_Document_Status	single underscore separator
CK_EmployeeDepartmentHistory_EndDate	mixed - CamelCase and underscore
DF__ImageStor__is_sy__75634D2A	database engine (system) generated name
sp_creatediagram	old-fashioned, sp prefix for system procedure
syscscolsegments	old-fashioned with abbreviations
ufnGetProductDealerPrice	Hungarian naming, ufn stands for user(-defined) function
vSalesPersonSalesByFiscalYears	Hungarian naming, v prefix is for view

The Use of [] - Square Brackets in Identifiers

Each identifier can be enclosed in square brackets, but not required. If the identifier is the same as a T-SQL reserved keyword, then it is required. Square brackets are also required when the identifier includes a special character such as space. Double quotes can be used also but that becomes very confusing when single quotes are present. The use of brackets is demonstrated in the following T-SQL script.

```
USE Northwind;
```

```
-- Syntax error without brackets since table name has space
SELECT * FROM Order Details;
/* ERROR
Msg 156, Level 15, State 1, Line 3
Incorrect syntax near the keyword 'Order'.
*/
```

```
-- Valid statement with brackets around table name
SELECT * FROM [Order Details];
-- (2155 row(s) affected)
```

```
-- Create and populate table with SELECT INTO
-- Error since ORDER is a reserved keyword
SELECT * INTO Order FROM Orders;
/* ERROR
Msg 156, Level 15, State 1, Line 1
Incorrect syntax near the keyword 'Order'.
*/
```

```
-- With brackets, query is valid
SELECT * INTO [Order] FROM Orders;
-- (830 row(s) affected)
```

When a database object is scripted out in SSMS Object Explore, the identifiers are surrounded with square brackets even when not needed as shown in the following demonstration.

```
CREATE TABLE [dbo].[Order Details](
	[OrderID] [int] NOT NULL,
	[ProductID] [int] NOT NULL,
	[UnitPrice] [money] NOT NULL,
	[Quantity] [smallint] NOT NULL,
	[Discount] [real] NOT NULL,
 CONSTRAINT [PK_Order_Details] PRIMARY KEY CLUSTERED
 (	[OrderID] ASC,
	[ProductID] ASC));
```

CHAPTER 6: Fundamentals of Relational Database Design

Logical Data Modeling

Logical data modeling is the first step in database design. The task can be carried out by systems analysts, subject-matter experts, database designers or lead database developers. Small budget projects usually settle for an experienced database developer in the design role. The database design team spends time with the future users (stakeholders) of the database to find out the expectations and requirements for the new database. As soon as the design team has some basic idea of functional requirements, the iterative process continues with discussing entities (corresponds to tables in the database) and their relationships with the users. For example the Order entity has many to many relationship to the Product entity. A Product occurs in many orders, and an Order may hold many products.

Physical Data Modeling

Physical Data Modeling is the process of translating the logical data model into actual database tables and related objects such as PRIMARY KEY and FOREIGN KEY constraints. If a software tool was used to design the logical data model then the forward engineering feature can be applied to generate SQL scripts to create tables and related database objects. **An important step in this process is the design of indexes to support SQL query performance**. Example for Data Warehouse dimension table implementation.

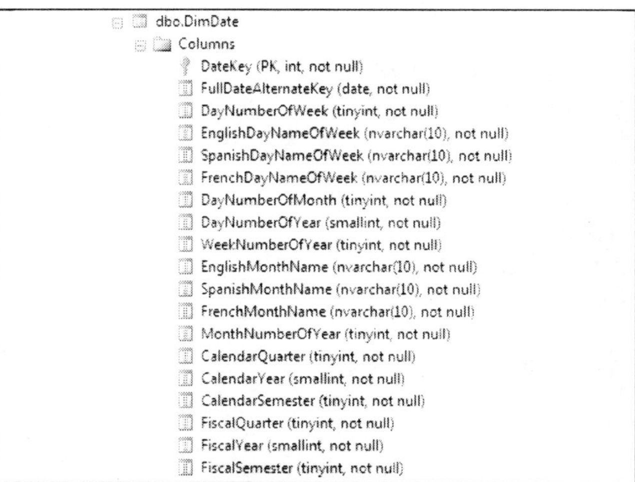

Column Definitions for the FactInternetSales Table

Table columns for a fact table in AdventureWorksDW2012 database. PK stands for PRIMARY KEY, FK for FOREGN KEY. The PRIMARY KEY is a composite of 2 columns: SalesOrderNumber and SalesOrderLineNumber.

The screen image is from SSMS Object Explorer.

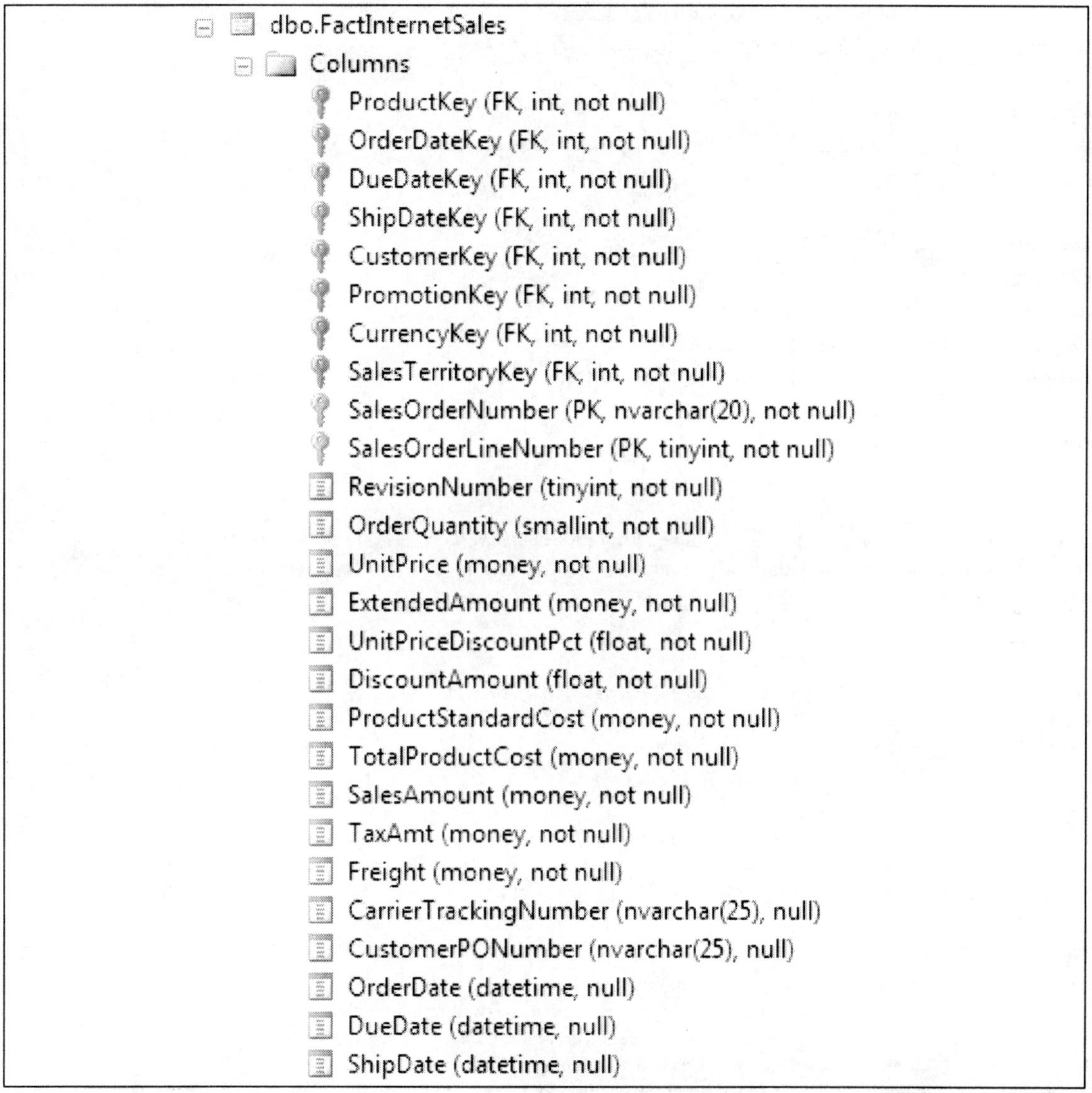

```
dbo.FactInternetSales
  Columns
    ProductKey (FK, int, not null)
    OrderDateKey (FK, int, not null)
    DueDateKey (FK, int, not null)
    ShipDateKey (FK, int, not null)
    CustomerKey (FK, int, not null)
    PromotionKey (FK, int, not null)
    CurrencyKey (FK, int, not null)
    SalesTerritoryKey (FK, int, not null)
    SalesOrderNumber (PK, nvarchar(20), not null)
    SalesOrderLineNumber (PK, tinyint, not null)
    RevisionNumber (tinyint, not null)
    OrderQuantity (smallint, not null)
    UnitPrice (money, not null)
    ExtendedAmount (money, not null)
    UnitPriceDiscountPct (float, not null)
    DiscountAmount (float, not null)
    ProductStandardCost (money, not null)
    TotalProductCost (money, not null)
    SalesAmount (money, not null)
    TaxAmt (money, not null)
    Freight (money, not null)
    CarrierTrackingNumber (nvarchar(25), null)
    CustomerPONumber (nvarchar(25), null)
    OrderDate (datetime, null)
    DueDate (datetime, null)
    ShipDate (datetime, null)
```

Table Column Data Types

Exact Numerics

bigint	8 byte signed integer -- Exact Numerics
bit	Boolean
decimal	5 - 17 bytes decimal number with variable precision
int	4 byte signed integer
money	8 byte with ten-thousandth accuracy
numeric	Same as decimal
smallint	2 byte signed integer
smallmoney	4 byte with ten-thousandth accuracy
tinyint	1 byte signed integer

Approximate Numerics

float	4 - 8 byte floating point -- Approximate Numerics
real	4 byte floating point

Date and Time

date	3 byte date only
datetime	8 byte date & time
datetime2	6 - 8 byte date & time
datetimeoffset	10 byte date & time with time zone
smalldatetime	4 byte date & time
time	5 byte time only

Character Strings

char	Fixed length ASCII character storage - 1 byte for each character -- Character String
text	Variable-length ASCII data with a maximum string length of 2^31-1 (deprecated)
varchar	Variable length ASCII character storage

Unicode Character Strings

nchar	Fixed length UNICODE character storage - 2 bytes for each character
ntext	Variable-length UNICODE data with a maximum string length of 2^30-1 (deprecated)
nvarchar	Variable length UNICODE character storage

Binary Strings

binary	Fixed-length binary data with maximum storage size of 2^31-1 bytes -- Binary String
image	Variable-length binary data with maximum storage size of 2^31-1 bytes (deprecated)
varbinary	Variable-length binary data with maximum storage size of 2^31-1 bytes

Other Data Types

cursor	Contains a reference to a cursor - not for column use
hierarchyid	Represents a position in a tree hierarchy, typically a few bytes up to 892 bytes
sql_variant	Stores values of various SQL Server data types, maximum length of 8016 bytes
table	Store a result set for processing at a later time, not for columns
timestamp	8 byte generated binary number, mechanism for version-stamping table rows
uniqueidentifier	16 byte GUID - Globally Unique Identifier
xml	Stores XML data up to 2GB in size

Date Type max_length, precision, scale & collation_name Listing

Database metadata on data types can be found in types system view.

```
SELECT          name, system_type_id, max_length, precision, scale,
                isnull(collation_name, SPACE(0)) AS collation_name
FROM AdventureWorks2012.sys.types WHERE schema_id = 4 ORDER BY name;
```

name	system_type_id	max_length	precision	scale	collation_name
bigint	127	8	19	0	
binary	173	8000	0	0	
bit	104	1	1	0	
char	175	8000	0	0	SQL_Latin1_General_CP1_CI_AS
date	40	3	10	0	
datetime	61	8	23	3	
datetime2	42	8	27	7	
datetimeoffset	43	10	34	7	
decimal	106	17	38	38	
float	62	8	53	0	
geography	240	-1	0	0	
geometry	240	-1	0	0	
hierarchyid	240	892	0	0	
image	34	16	0	0	
int	56	4	10	0	
money	60	8	19	4	
nchar	239	8000	0	0	SQL_Latin1_General_CP1_CI_AS
ntext	99	16	0	0	SQL_Latin1_General_CP1_CI_AS
numeric	108	17	38	38	
nvarchar	231	8000	0	0	SQL_Latin1_General_CP1_CI_AS
real	59	4	24	0	
smalldatetime	58	4	16	0	
smallint	52	2	5	0	
smallmoney	122	4	10	4	
sql_variant	98	8016	0	0	
sysname	231	256	0	0	SQL_Latin1_General_CP1_CI_AS
text	35	16	0	0	SQL_Latin1_General_CP1_CI_AS
time	41	5	16	7	
timestamp	189	8	0	0	
tinyint	48	1	3	0	
uniqueidentifier	36	16	0	0	
varbinary	165	8000	0	0	
varchar	167	8000	0	0	SQL_Latin1_General_CP1_CI_AS
xml	241	-1	0	0	

U.S. Default Collation SQL_Latin1_General_CP1_CI_AS

Interpretation:

- SQL collation not Windows
- Latin 1 alphabet
- Code page 1 for sorting
- Case insensitive
- Accent sensitive

SQL_Latin1_General_CP1_CI_AS is the default collation of SQL Server 2012 in the United States. Only a handful of experts around the world really understand collations. You first encounter with collation will probably be like the following error.

```
SELECT CONCAT('Production.', objname) AS TableName, value AS [Description]
FROM fn_listextendedproperty (NULL, 'schema', 'Production', 'table', default, NULL, NULL);
GO
/* Msg 468, Level 16, State 9, Line 1
Cannot resolve the collation conflict between "SQL_Latin1_General_CP1_CI_AS" and
"Latin1_General_CI_AI" in the concat operation.
*/
```

The easiest fix in most collation error cases is placing COLLATE DATABASE_DEFAULT following the right most operator.

```
SELECT CONCAT('Production.', objname COLLATE DATABASE_DEFAULT) AS TableName,
                    value AS [Description]
FROM fn_listextendedproperty (NULL, 'schema', 'Production', 'table', default, NULL, NULL);
```

There are a number of articles on the web which deal extensively with collations.

Collation is a column level property. Server and database collations are only defaults. To change the collation of a column, use ALTER TABLE.

```
-- SQL Server Change Column Collation
SELECT * INTO Product FROM AdventureWorks2012.Production.Product;
GO
ALTER TABLE Product ALTER COLUMN Name nvarchar(50) COLLATE SQL_Latin1_General_CP1_CS_AS null;
GO -- (504 row(s) affected)
```

DATE & DATETIME Temporal Data Types

DATE data type has been introduced with SQL Server 2008. DATETIME on the other hand is around since the inception of SQL Server. A good deal of programming effort goes into supporting hundreds of different string date & time formats. Each country has its own string date formats adding more to the general confusion. As an example in the United States the mdy string date format is used. In the United Kingdom, the dmy format is used. When one looks at a date like 10/11/2015, it is not apparent which date format is it. In a globalized world the data flows freely from one country to another, frequently without adequate documentation, hence the loss of database developer productivity as related to date & time data issues. List of century (CCYY or YYYY) datetime conversions styles (stylenumber >= 100).

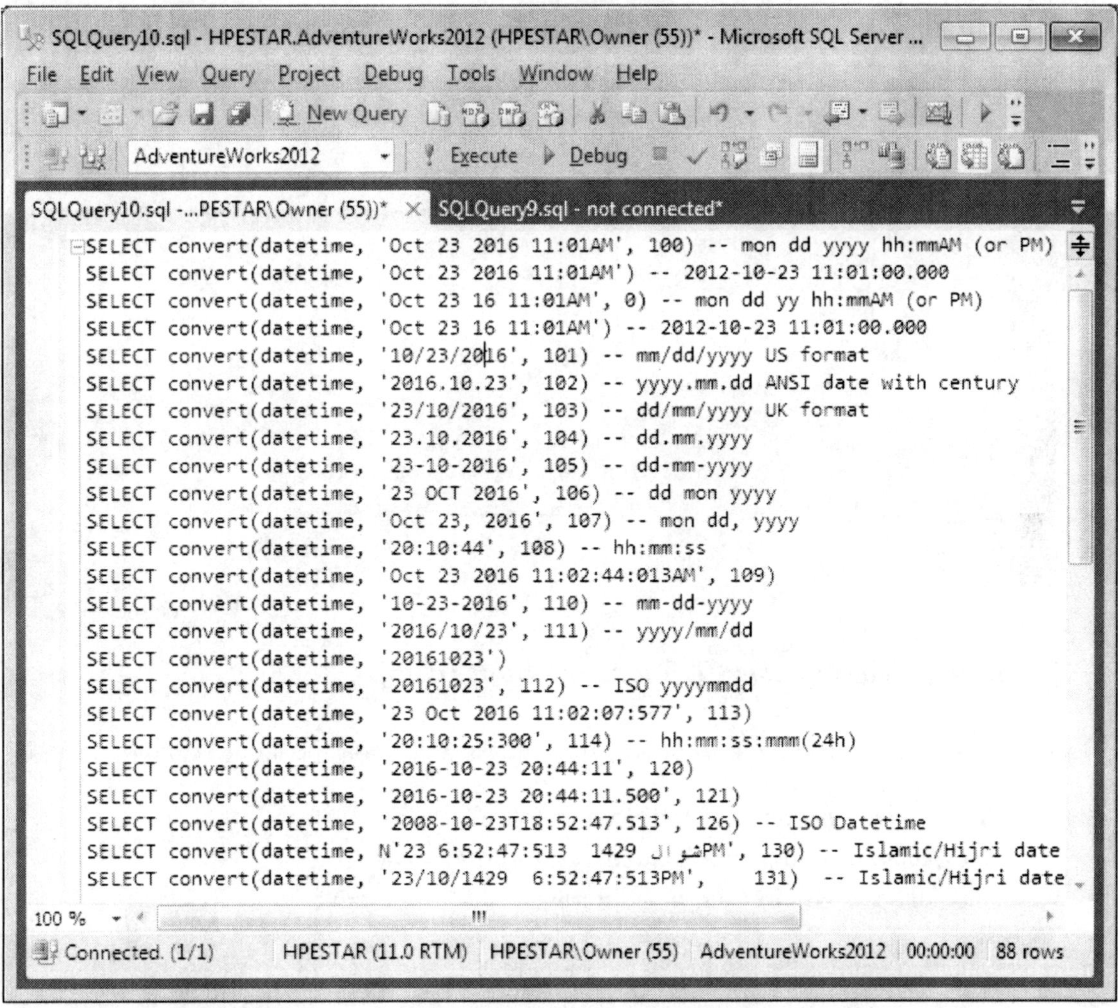

Two Ways of Commenting in T-SQL Scripts

Line comment is prefixed by "--". Multiple lines comment has to be enclosed with "/*" and "*/".

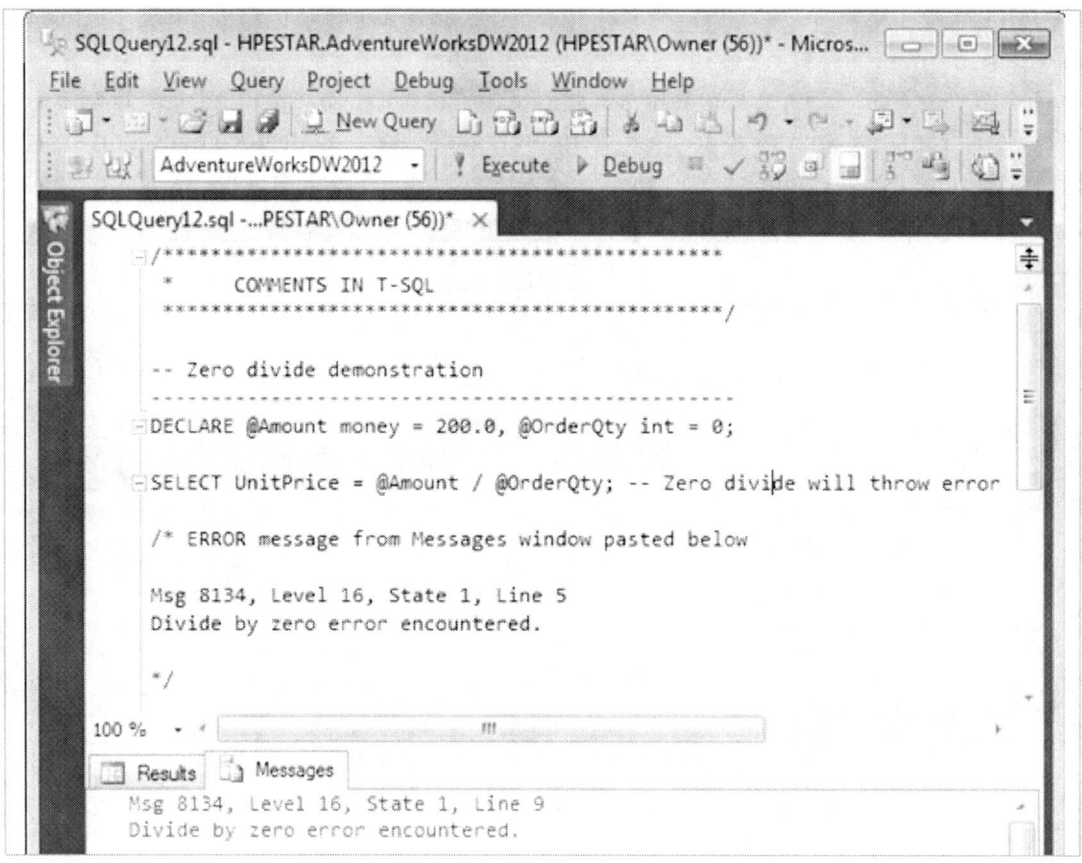

T-SQL Tidbits: Types of User-Defined Functions (UDF)

There are 3 types of user-defined functions, all database READ only, no indexing, no triggers:

- Scalar-valued function: multi-statements, returns a single-value
- Table-valued function: multi-statements, returns a table
- Inline table-valued function: single statement, returns a table

The table-valued functions (last two) can be used in JOINs and CROSS APPLYs.

Diagram of EmployeeDepartmentHistory and Related Tables

EmployeeDepartmentHistory is a simple junction table with three FOREIGN KEYs to the Employee, Shift and Department tables respectively.

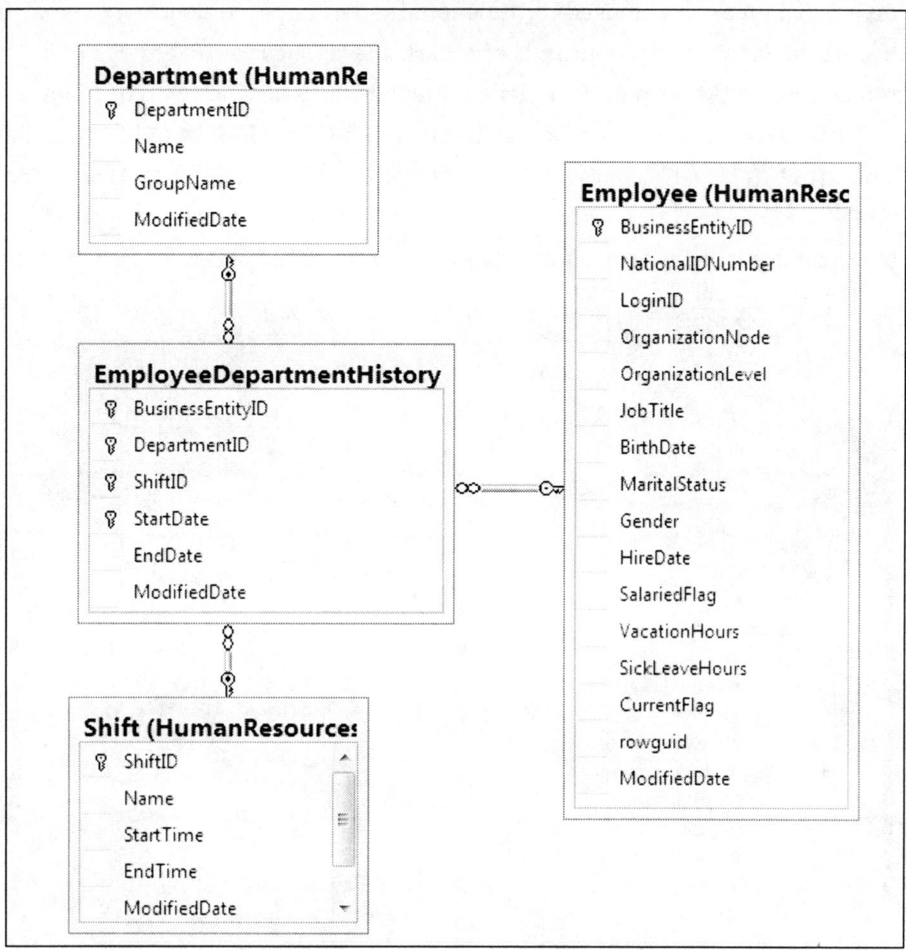

T-SQL Tidbits: ALTER Object vs. DROP/CREATE Object

ALTER object changes definition of an object **without affecting** any of the object properties such as security permissions and data dictionary (extended properties) or dependent objects. **When an object is DROPped, all properties are dropped** and they have to be recreated after the object is recreated. Dependent objects maybe affected as well. Therefore, in production normally we use ALTER object.

```
CREATE PROCEDURE sprocProdPhotoList AS SELECT * FROM Production.ProductPhoto;
GO
ALTER PROCEDURE sprocProdPhotoList AS SELECT * FROM Production.ProductPhoto ORDER BY ProductPhotoID;
```

Exploring Database Schemas

A schema - introduced in SQL Server 2005 - is a single-level container of database objects to replace database object "owner" in previous SQL Server versions. **The default schema is "dbo", database owner**. Schemas can be used for functional separation of objects which may be essential in large databases with thousands of tables. The application schemas in AdventureWorks: HumanResources, Production, Purchasing, Sales, and Person. The word "schemas" also used in database terminology to mean table definition scripts or database diagram. Screenshot to display all the schemas in AdventureWorks2012 and to demonstrate the use of the CREATE SCHEMA statement. Database object reference in SQL Server 2012 is: "dbname.schemaname.objectname" like "AdventureWorks2012.Sales.SalesOrderheader".

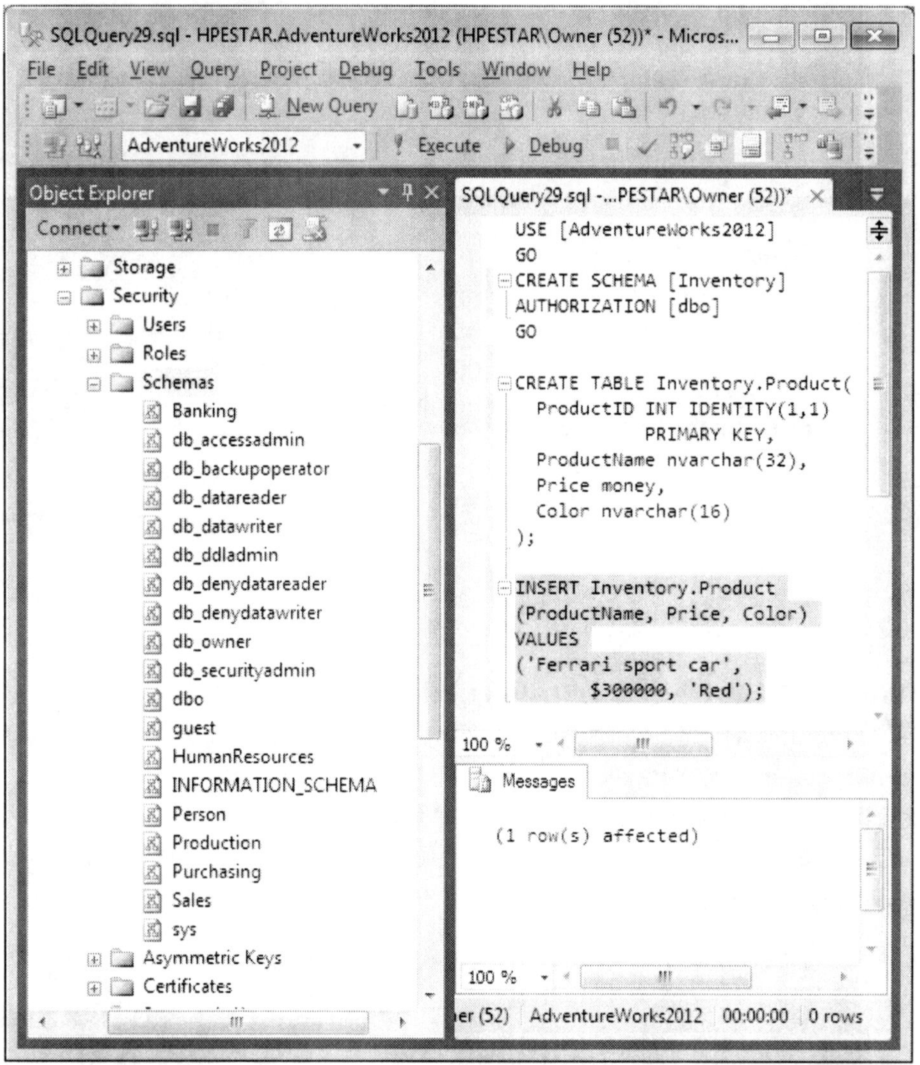

SCHEMA_NAME() Function

The SCHEMA_NAME() function can be used to obtain the name of a schema based on the schema_id parameter. Query to list all 3 database objects with the name "Product" in 3 different schemas.

```
SELECT          CONCAT(SCHEMA_NAME(schema_id),'.',name) as ObjectName,
                name, object_id, schema_id, type, type_desc
FROM sys.objects
WHERE name = 'Product' ORDER BY ObjectName;
```

ObjectName	name	object_id	schema_id	type	type_desc
dbo.Product	Product	264388011	1	U	USER_TABLE
Inventory.Product	Product	1533964541	11	U	USER_TABLE
Production.Product	Product	1973582069	7	U	USER_TABLE

T-SQL query to display all the schemas in AdventureWorks2012.

```
SELECT s.*,  p.name as PrincipalName
FROM AdventureWorks2012.sys.schemas s
  INNER JOIN AdventureWorks2012.sys.database_principals p    ON s.principal_id = p.principal_id
ORDER BY principal_id, s.name;
```

name	schema_id	principal_id	PrincipalName
Banking	10	1	dbo
dbo	1	1	dbo
HumanResources	5	1	dbo
Inventory	11	1	dbo
Person	6	1	dbo
Production	7	1	dbo
Purchasing	8	1	dbo
Sales	9	1	dbo
guest	2	2	guest
INFORMATION_SCHEMA	3	3	INFORMATION_SCHEMA
sys	4	4	sys
db_owner	16384	16384	db_owner
db_accessadmin	16385	16385	db_accessadmin
db_securityadmin	16386	16386	db_securityadmin
db_ddladmin	16387	16387	db_ddladmin
db_backupoperator	16389	16389	db_backupoperator
db_datareader	16390	16390	db_datareader
db_datawriter	16391	16391	db_datawriter
db_denydatareader	16392	16392	db_denydatareader
db_denydatawriter	16393	16393	db_denydatawriter

Tables in HumanResources, Person & Purchasing Schemas

Query to list tables in the above schemas with data dictionary description.

```
USE AdventureWorks2012;
SELECT  CONCAT('Purchasing.', objname COLLATE DATABASE_DEFAULT)      AS TableName,
        value                                                        AS [Description]
FROM fn_listextendedproperty (NULL, 'schema', 'Purchasing', 'table', default, NULL, NULL)
UNION
SELECT  CONCAT('Person.', objname COLLATE DATABASE_DEFAULT)          AS TableName,
        value                                                        AS [Description]
FROM fn_listextendedproperty (NULL, 'schema', 'Person', 'table', default, NULL, NULL)
UNION
SELECT  CONCAT('HumanResources.', objname COLLATE DATABASE_DEFAULT) AS TableName,
        value                                                        AS [Description]
FROM fn_listextendedproperty (NULL, 'schema', 'HumanResources', 'table', default, NULL, NULL)
ORDER BY TableName;
```

TableName	Description
HumanResources.Department	Lookup table containing the departments within the Adventure Works Cycles company.
HumanResources.Employee	Employee information such as salary, department, and title.
HumanResources.EmployeeDepartmentHistory	Employee department transfers.
HumanResources.EmployeePayHistory	Employee pay history.
HumanResources.JobCandidate	Résumés submitted to Human Resources by job applicants.
HumanResources.Shift	Work shift lookup table.
Person.Address	Street address information for customers, employees, and vendors.
Person.AddressType	Types of addresses stored in the Address table.
Person.BusinessEntity	Source of the ID that connects vendors, customers, and employees with address and contact information.
Person.BusinessEntityAddress	Cross-reference table mapping customers, vendors, and employees to their addresses.
Person.BusinessEntityContact	Cross-reference table mapping stores, vendors, and employees to people
Person.ContactType	Lookup table containing the types of business entity contacts.
Person.CountryRegion	Lookup table containing the ISO standard codes for countries and regions.
Person.EmailAddress	Where to send a person email.
Person.Password	One way hashed authentication information
Person.Person	Human beings involved with AdventureWorks: employees, customer contacts, and vendor contacts.
Person.PersonPhone	Telephone number and type of a person.
Person.PhoneNumberType	Type of phone number of a person.
Person.StateProvince	State and province lookup table.
Purchasing.ProductVendor	Cross-reference table mapping vendors with the products they supply.
Purchasing.PurchaseOrderDetail	Individual products associated with a specific purchase order. See PurchaseOrderHeader.
Purchasing.PurchaseOrderHeader	General purchase order information. See PurchaseOrderDetail.
Purchasing.ShipMethod	Shipping company lookup table.
Purchasing.Vendor	Companies from whom Adventure Works Cycles purchases parts or other goods.

The CREATE TABLE Statement

Creates a table based on column name, data type & size specifications. Constraint and default information can be included as well, or alternately given as a separate ALTER TABLE statement.

Branch Banking Database with ON DELETE CASCADE

T-SQL script to create basic banking application tables. Preceding the first CREATE TABLE, we execute a CREATE SCHEMA to group the tables within one schema.

```
USE AdventureWorks2012;
GO
```

```
CREATE SCHEMA Banking;
GO
```

```
CREATE TABLE Banking.Branch
 (
  BranchID     INT IDENTITY ( 1, 1 ),
  BranchName   CHAR(32) NOT NULL UNIQUE,
  BranchCity   CHAR(32) NOT NULL,
  Assets       MONEY NOT NULL,
  ModifiedDate DATETIME DEFAULT (getdate()),
  PRIMARY KEY ( BranchID ),
 );

CREATE TABLE Banking.Account
 (
  AccountID     INT IDENTITY ( 1, 1 ) UNIQUE,
  BranchID      INT NOT NULL,
  AccountNumber CHAR(20) NOT NULL UNIQUE,
  AccountType   CHAR(12) NOT NULL CONSTRAINT ATC CHECK (AccountType IN ('C', 'S')),
  Balance       MONEY NOT NULL,
  ModifiedDate  DATETIME DEFAULT (getdate()),
  PRIMARY KEY ( AccountID ),
  FOREIGN KEY ( BranchID ) REFERENCES Banking.Branch(BranchID) ON DELETE   CASCADE
 );
```

-- T-SQL script continued

```
CREATE TABLE Banking.[Transaction]
 (
  TransactionID INT IDENTITY ( 1, 1 ) PRIMARY KEY,
  AccountID    INT NOT NULL  REFERENCES Banking.Account    ON DELETE  CASCADE,  -- FK
  TranType     CHAR(1),
  Amount       MONEY,
  ModifiedDate  DATETIME DEFAULT (getdate()),
  UNIQUE ( AccountID, ModifiedDate)
 );

CREATE TABLE Banking.Customer
 (
  CustomerID   INT IDENTITY ( 1, 1 ) PRIMARY KEY,
  Name        CHAR(32) NOT NULL,
  SSNo        CHAR(9) NOT NULL UNIQUE,
  [Type]      CHAR(20) NOT NULL,
  Street      VARCHAR(32) NOT NULL,
  City        CHAR(32) NOT NULL,
  [State]     CHAR(32) NOT NULL,
  Zip         CHAR(10) NOT NULL,
  Country     CHAR(32) NOT NULL,
  ModifiedDate DATETIME DEFAULT (getdate())
 );

CREATE TABLE Banking.Loan
 (
  LoanID      INT IDENTITY ( 1, 1 ) PRIMARY KEY,
  BranchID    INT NOT NULL REFERENCES Banking.Branch    ON DELETE    CASCADE,   -- FK
  LoanNumber   CHAR(20) NOT NULL UNIQUE,
  LoanType    VARCHAR(30) NOT NULL,
  Amount      MONEY NOT NULL,
  ModifiedDate DATETIME DEFAULT (getdate())
 );
```

-- T-SQL script continued

```
CREATE TABLE Banking.Depositor
 (
   CustomerID   INT NOT NULL,
   AccountID    INT NOT NULL,
   ModifiedDate DATETIME DEFAULT (getdate()),
   PRIMARY KEY ( CustomerID, AccountID ),
   FOREIGN KEY ( AccountID ) REFERENCES Banking.Account(AccountID) ON DELETE   CASCADE,
   FOREIGN KEY ( CustomerID ) REFERENCES Banking.Customer(CustomerID)
 );

CREATE TABLE Banking.Borrower
 (
   CustomerID   INT NOT NULL,
   LoanID       INT NOT NULL,
   ModifiedDate DATETIME DEFAULT (getdate()),
   PRIMARY KEY ( CustomerID, LoanID ),
   FOREIGN KEY ( CustomerID ) REFERENCES Banking.Customer(CustomerID),
   FOREIGN KEY ( LoanID ) REFERENCES Banking.Loan(LoanID)
 );
```

Managing Table & Object Security

This security discussion is more appropriate to 2-tier server architecture (SQL Server-clients) where clients have direct access to the server. In a 3-tier architecture (server-webserver-clients), the intermediate web/application server software manages client access to SQL Server, users cannot directly access the server. A user can be permissioned with the GRANT and DENY commands. The GRANT OPTION gives this user GRANT rights to other users.

```
USE [AdventureWorks2012];
GRANT VIEW CHANGE TRACKING ON [Person].[Person] TO [KevinM] WITH GRANT OPTION;
GRANT VIEW DEFINITION ON [Person].[Person] TO [KevinM] WITH GRANT OPTION;
GRANT DELETE ON [Person].[Person] TO [KevinM];
GRANT INSERT ON [Person].[Person] TO [KevinM];
GRANT REFERENCES ON [Person].[Person] TO [KevinM];
GRANT SELECT ON [Person].[Person] TO [KevinM];
GRANT UPDATE ON [Person].[Person] TO [KevinM];
DENY ALTER ON [Person].[Person] TO [KevinM];
DENY CONTROL ON [Person].[Person] TO [KevinM];
DENY TAKE OWNERSHIP ON [Person].[Person] TO [KevinM];
```

The preferred way of implementing security is through roles: fixed or user-defined. Roles are permissioned and users become members of roles. The user-defined database role, InventoryStaff, is created with owner rights to dbo, Production, Purchasing & Sales schemas; KevinM & MaryS database users are added as members of the new role. Since SELECT is granted to InventoryStaff role on the Product table, KevinM & MaryS inherit this permission.

```
CREATE ROLE [InventoryStaff] AUTHORIZATION [dbo];
ALTER AUTHORIZATION ON SCHEMA::[Production] TO [InventoryStaff];
ALTER AUTHORIZATION ON SCHEMA::[Purchasing] TO [InventoryStaff];
ALTER AUTHORIZATION ON SCHEMA::[Sales] TO [InventoryStaff];
ALTER ROLE [InventoryStaff] ADD MEMBER [KevinM];
ALTER ROLE [InventoryStaff] ADD MEMBER [MaryS];
GRANT SELECT ON [Production].[Product] TO [InventoryStaff];
```

MSDN Article: **Permissions Hierarchy (Database Engine)** http://msdn.microsoft.com/en-us/library/ms191465.aspx
MSDN Article: **Ownership Chains** http://msdn.microsoft.com/en-us/library/ms188676%28v=sql.105%29.aspx

SQL Server 2012 supports user-defined server roles in addition to fixed server roles.

TechNet Article: **SQL Server: User-Defined Roles** http://technet.microsoft.com/en-us/magazine/hh641407.aspx

Temporary Tables: Workhorses of SQL Server

So much so that they even have their own database: tempdb. Temporary tables (example: #Product1) can be applied in queries just like permanent tables. The differences are:

- Temporary tables are created in tempdb.
- Temporary tables have limited life.

There are two versions:

- Temporary tables (#tempA) are multi-user automatically, cannot be shared among connections.
- Global temporary tables (##gtempB) is single-user, can be shared among connections.

Global temporary tables are used only for special purposes since they make stored procedures single user only.

Temporary tables can be created by CREATE TABLE or SELECT INTO methods.

```
USE AdventureWorks2012;
GO
-- Command(s) completed successfully.
```

```
-- Create temporary table with CREATE TABLE
CREATE TABLE #Product
 (
        ProductID INT,
        ProductName nvarchar(50),
        ListPrice money,
        Color varchar(16)
);
GO
-- Command(s) completed successfully.
```

```
INSERT INTO #Product
SELECT  ProductID,
        Name,
        ListPrice,
        Color
FROM Production.Product ORDER BY Name;
GO  --(504 row(s) affected)
```

Temporary Tables Are Handy When Developing Scripts Or Stored Procedures

```
SELECT TOP 10 * FROM #Product
ORDER BY ProductName;
GO
```

ProductID	ProductName	ListPrice	Color
1	Adjustable Race	0.00	NULL
879	All-Purpose Bike Stand	159.00	NULL
712	AWC Logo Cap	8.99	Multi
3	BB Ball Bearing	0.00	NULL
2	Bearing Ball	0.00	NULL
877	Bike Wash - Dissolver	7.95	NULL
316	Blade	0.00	NULL
843	Cable Lock	25.00	NULL
952	Chain	20.24	Silver
324	Chain Stays	0.00	NULL

```
DROP TABLE #Product;
GO
```

```
-- CREATE temporary table with SELECT INTO
SELECT ProductID, ProductName = Name, ListPrice, StandardCost, Color
INTO #ProductA
FROM Production.Product
ORDER BY ProductName;
GO
```

```
SELECT TOP 10 * FROM #ProductA
ORDER BY ProductName;
```

ProductID	ProductName	ListPrice	StandardCost	Color
1	Adjustable Race	0.00	0.00	NULL
879	All-Purpose Bike Stand	159.00	59.466	NULL
712	AWC Logo Cap	8.99	6.9223	Multi
3	BB Ball Bearing	0.00	0.00	NULL
2	Bearing Ball	0.00	0.00	NULL
877	Bike Wash - Dissolver	7.95	2.9733	NULL
316	Blade	0.00	0.00	NULL
843	Cable Lock	25.00	10.3125	NULL
952	Chain	20.24	8.9866	Silver
324	Chain Stays	0.00	0.00	NULL

```
DROP TABLE #ProductA;
GO
```

ALTER TABLE for Changing Table Definition

An empty table can easily be altered by ALTER TABLE. A populated table change (alter) may require additional operations such as data conversion to the new column data type. Generally increasing the size of a column is a safe change even if the table is populated. If we were to change size from 25 to 10, truncation may occur (data loss), for which we would have to plan by examining what will be lost if any. When decreasing string column size, we can use the LEFT function to truncate the string. T-SQL script to increase the size of a column from 25 to 32, then decrease it 9.

```
USE CopyOfAdventureWorks2012;
-- Sales.SalesOrderDetail columns
/*Name    Policy Health State
SalesOrderID (PK, FK, int, not null)
SalesOrderDetailID (PK, int, not null)
CarrierTrackingNumber (nvarchar(25), null) ..... */
```

```
-- Increase column size of CarrierTrackingNumber
ALTER TABLE Sales.SalesOrderDetail    ALTER COLUMN CarrierTrackingNumber nvarchar(32)  null;
```

```
/* Columns after ALTER TABLE
Name       Policy Health State
SalesOrderID (PK, FK, int, not null)
SalesOrderDetailID (PK, int, not null)
CarrierTrackingNumber (nvarchar(32), null) .....            */
```

```
SELECT TOP (1) SalesOrderID, CarrierTrackingNumber FROM  Sales.SalesOrderDetail ORDER BY SalesOrderID;
```

SalesOrderID	CarrierTrackingNumber
43659	4911-403C-98

We shall now decrease the size to 9 characters, but first truncate the extra characters. Without the UPDATE, the following error happens.

```
/* Msg 8152, Level 16, State 13, Line 1 String or binary data would be truncated. The statement has been terminated.*/
```

```
UPDATE Sales.SalesOrderDetail SET CarrierTrackingNumber = LEFT (CarrierTrackingNumber,9);
-- (121317 row(s) affected)
```

```
-- Decrease column size of CarrierTrackingNumber
ALTER TABLE Sales.SalesOrderDetail    ALTER COLUMN CarrierTrackingNumber nvarchar(9)  null;
-- Command(s) completed successfully.
```

```
SELECT TOP (1) SalesOrderID, CarrierTrackingNumber FROM  Sales.SalesOrderDetail  ORDER BY SalesOrderID;
```

SalesOrderID	CarrierTrackingNumber
43659	4911-403C

ALTER TABLE: Add New Column with DEFAULT CONSTRAINT

If we don't specify WITH VALUES, current rows will have NULLs in the new column.

```
USE tempdb; SELECT ProductID, ProductNumber, ListPrice, Color INTO Product
FROM AdventureWorks2012.Production.Product WHERE Color IS NOT NULL;
ALTER TABLE Product ADD CONSTRAINT pkProd PRIMARY KEY (ProductID);
GO
ALTER TABLE Product ADD CreatedDate DATETIME CONSTRAINT dfDt DEFAULT(getdate()) WITH VALUES;
GO
SELECT TOP(3) * FROM Product ORDER BY NEWID();
```

ProductID	ProductNumber	ListPrice	Color	CreatedDate
977	BK-R19B-58	539.99	Black	2016-12-26 17:14:26.813
829	RW-T905	245.01	Black	2016-12-26 17:14:26.813
767	BK-R50B-62	782.99	Black	2016-12-26 17:14:26.813

Renaming Tables & Columns with sp_rename

The system stored procedure sp_rename can be used to rename tables, columns and other user-created database objects.

```
USE tempdb;                                          -- Create test table
SELECT * INTO Department FROM AdventureWorks2012.HumanResources.Department;
GO     -- (16 row(s) affected)
```

```
SELECT TOP 1 * FROM Department;
```

DepartmentID	Name	GroupName	ModifiedDate
1	Engineering	Research and Development	2002-06-01 00:00:00.000

```
EXEC sp_rename "Department.Name", "Department";              -- Rename table column
GO
```

```
SELECT TOP 1 * FROM Department;
```

DepartmentID	Department	GroupName	ModifiedDate
1	Engineering	Research and Development	2002-06-01 00:00:00.000

```
EXEC sp_rename "dbo.Department", "ProfitCenter";              -- Rename table
```

```
SELECT * FROM ProfitCenter;
```

DepartmentID	Department	GroupName	ModifiedDate
1	Engineering	Research and Development	2002-06-01 00:00:00.000

```
DROP TABLE tempdb.dbo.ProfitCenter;
```

DROP TABLE: A Dangerous Statement

The DROP TABLE statement is to delete a table, including content, for good. It is a very dangerous statement which we don't want to execute accidentally. Therefore, if appropriate we should comment it out in a T-SQL script to prevent unintentional execution.

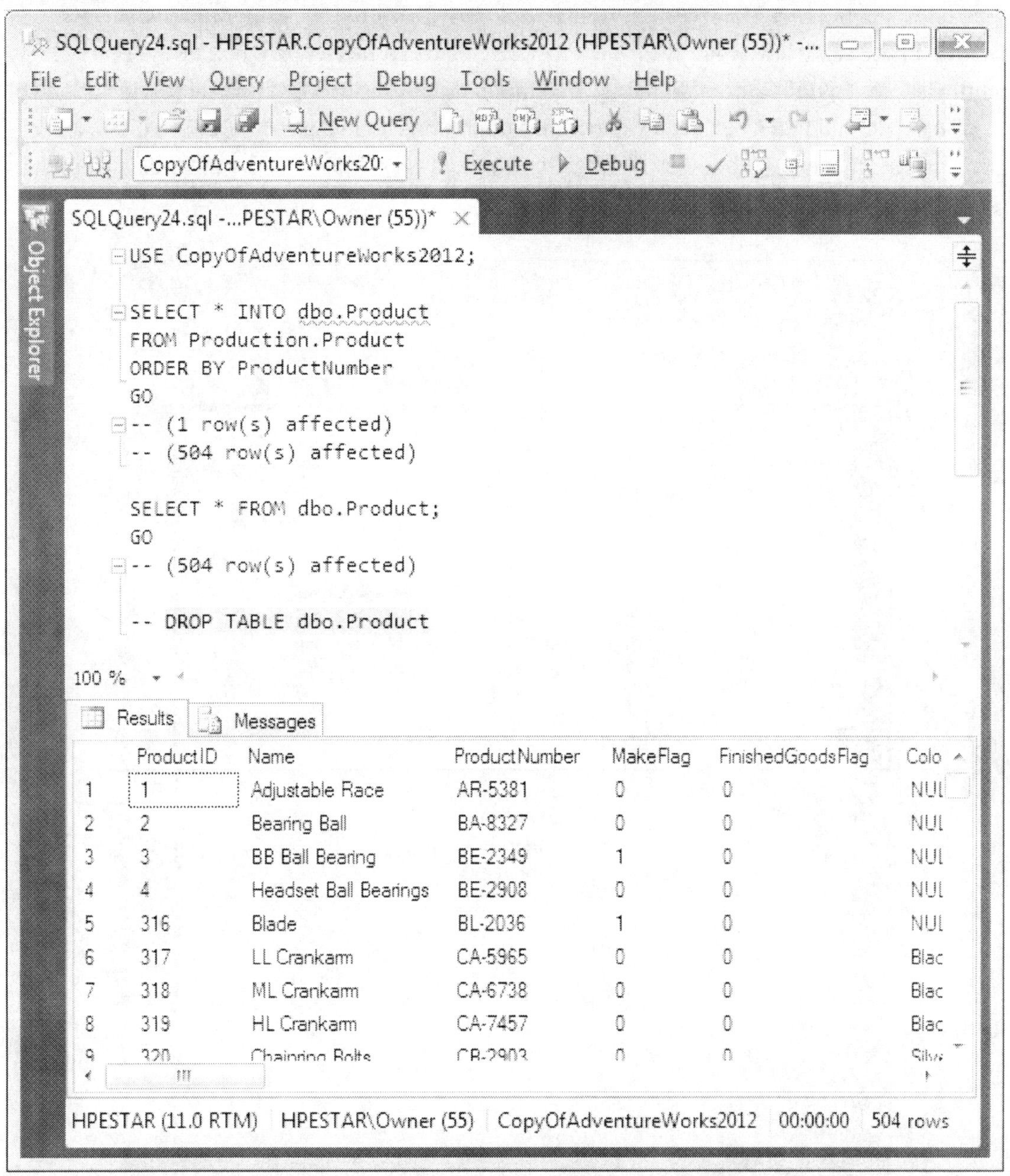

Table Constraints Inclusion in CREATE TABLE

Table constraints are user-defined database objects that restricts the behaviors of columns. PRIMARY KEY, UNIQUE KEY, FOREIGN KEY, or CHECK constraint, or a DEFAULT constraint can be included in the CREATE TABLE statement on the same line as the column or added as a separate line. In the definition of the Banking.Branch table UNIQUE and DEFAULT constraints are included in the same line while the PRIMARY KEY constraint has its own line at the end of column list. In the definition of Banking.Loan table, the PRIMARY KEY constraint is included with the column definition. FOREIGN KEY constraint definition can include ON DELETE CASCADE action option, meaning if the PRIMARY KEY is deleted all FOREIGN KEYs in the table referencing it should also be deleted.

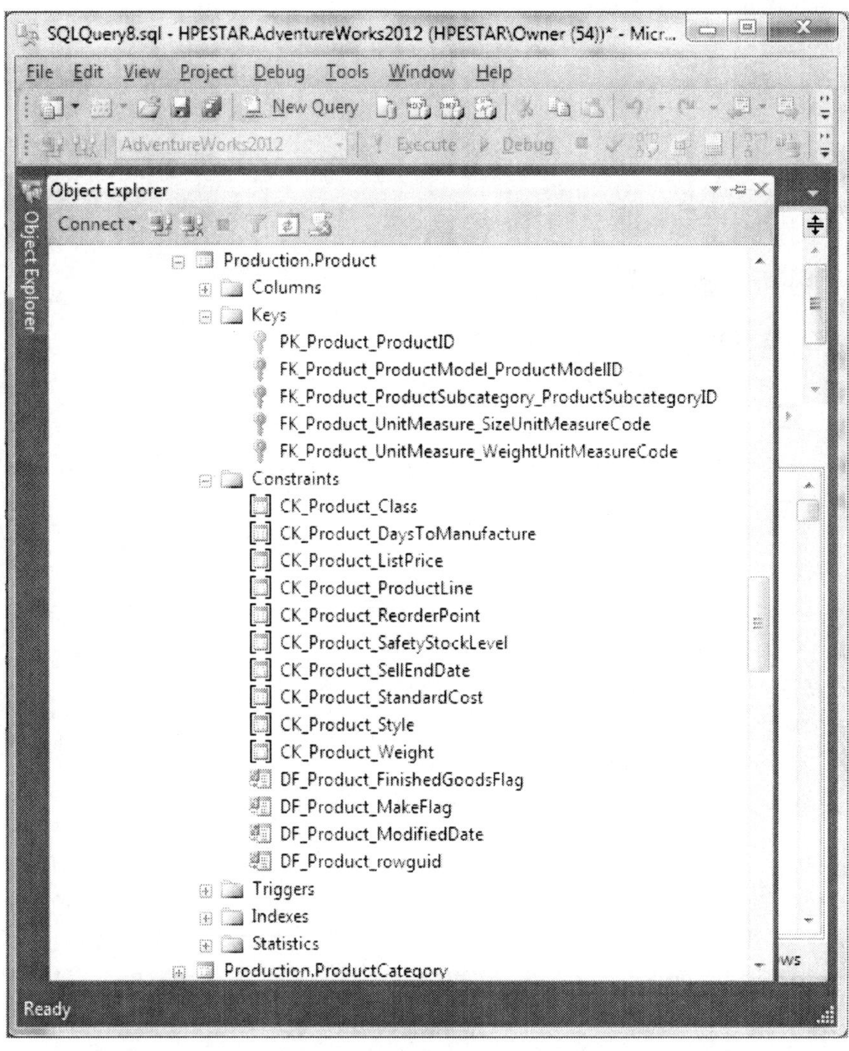

Nullability Column-Level Constraints in CREATE TABLE

The default is NULL, the column can contain NULL entries, the column is nullable. We have to specifically declare NOT NULL on the column line in CREATE TABLE if we want to add the cardinality constraint to the column. The NULL / NOT NULL constraint cannot be declared on a separate line. In the Production.Product table the Color column is nullable. The ListPrice column is not nullable instead has 0.0 price where there is no price.

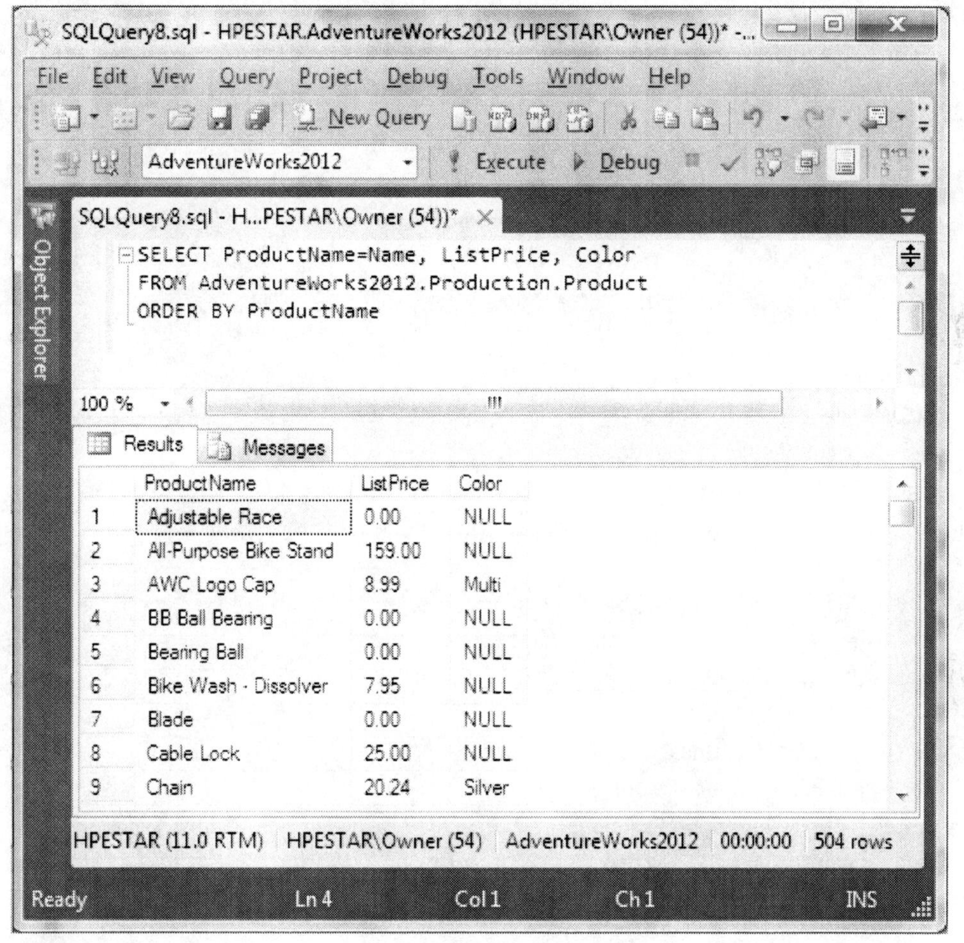

T-SQL Tidbits: Automatic Execution of Stored Procedure on Server Start

We have to compile the stored procedure in the master database prior to start configuration.

```
USE MASTER
GO
EXEC SP_PROCOPTION sprocAlpha, 'STARTUP', 'ON'
GO
```

PRIMARY KEY constraint on a column automatically implies NOT NULL

The UNIQUE KEY CONSTRAINT allows only one NULL entry in a column since two or more NULL entries would not be unique. Demonstration script:

```
USE tempdb;
CREATE TABLE Product    ( ProductID INT UNIQUE,
                          ProductName varchar(64) PRIMARY KEY
                        );
```

```
INSERT Product (ProductName) VALUES ('Mobile Phone xZing');
-- (1 row(s) affected)
```

```
-- One NULL is OK in ProductID column
-- Second NULL insert attempt errors out

INSERT Product (ProductName) VALUES ('Motor Bike');

/* Msg 2627, Level 14, State 1, Line 7
Violation of UNIQUE KEY constraint 'UQ__Product__B40CC6ECDF4DC6D3'.
Cannot insert duplicate key in object 'dbo.Product'.
The duplicate key value is (<NULL>).
The statement has been terminated. */
```

```
-- NULL value in PRIMARY KEY column not allowed

INSERT Product (ProductID) VALUES (2);

/* Msg 515, Level 16, State 2, Line 2
Cannot insert the value NULL into column
'ProductName', table 'tempdb.dbo.Product';
column does not allow nulls. INSERT fails.
The statement has been terminated. */
```

```
SELECT * FROM Product;
```

ProductID	ProductName
NULL	Mobile Phone xZing

The PRIMARY KEY constraint is a combination of UNIQUE and NOT NULL constraints.

PRIMARY KEY & FOREIGN KEY Constraints

The PRIMARY KEY constraint is to ensure a referenceable unique address for each row in a table. PK column value cannot be NULL. The underlying mechanism to carry out the enforcement action is a unique index which is clustered by default but in can be nonclustered. PRIMARY KEY constraint can be considered as a UNIQUE constraint with NOT NULL on the column. The typical PRIMARY KEY is the SURROGATE PRIMARY KEY INT IDENTITY(1,1) column. There can only be one PRIMARY KEY defined per table. A PRIMARY KEY can consist of multiple columns, a composite PRIMARY KEY. A PRIMARY KEY cannot be based on part of a column. Production.ProductSubcategory table PRIMARY KEY setup.

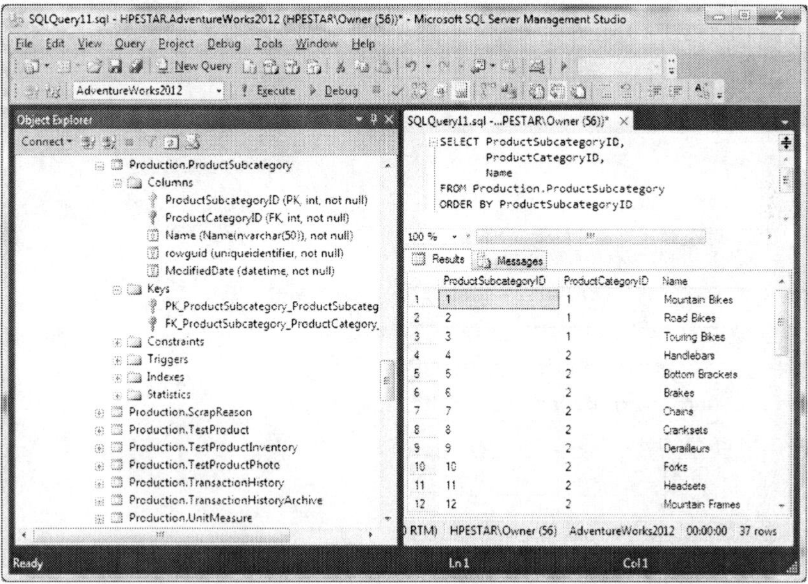

The ProductSubcategoryID is the PRIMARY KEY constraint. It is an INT IDENTITY(1,1) surrogate key. ProductCategoryID is a FOREIGN KEY referencing the Production.ProductCategory table ProductCategoryID column. "Name" is the NATURAL KEY. rowguid (used in replication) & ModifiedDate are row maintenance columns. The NATURAL KEY column Name has NOT NULL constraint and unique index defined. As such it can serve as PRIMARY KEY for the table, but we shall see why a meaningless integer number (INT IDENTITY) is better for PRIMARY KEY. Related to this topic: A heap is a table without a clustered index. The implication is if we choose nonclustered PRIMARY KEY, we have to define a clustered index on other column(s) so that the database engine can work with the table as normal. Clustered index speeds up range searches.

The SURROGATE PRIMARY KEY should not be exposed to end-users, it is for programming use only.

FOREIGN KEY constraint requires that the referenced PK value exists.

FOREIGN KEY column is nullable. FOREIGN KEY can be named differently from the referenced PRIMARY KEY, although for readability purposes usually the same. **Multiple FK columns can reference the same PK column**. In such a case only one FK column can have the same name as the PK column. Invalid FK reference results in error.

```
USE [AdventureWorks2012]
GO
```

```
INSERT INTO Production.ProductSubcategory
        (ProductCategoryID
        ,Name)
    VALUES
        (99
        ,'Inner Tube')
```

```
/*
Msg 547, Level 16, State 0, Line 2
The INSERT statement conflicted with the FOREIGN KEY constraint
"FK_ProductSubcategory_ProductCategory_ProductCategoryID".
The conflict occurred in database "AdventureWorks2012",
table "Production.ProductCategory", column 'ProductCategoryID'.
The statement has been terminated.
*/
```

DELETE attempt on a referenced PRIMARY KEY will give an error unless DELETE CASCADE is defined on the FK:

```
DELETE FROM Production.ProductSubcategory
WHERE ProductSubCategoryID = 4
GO
```

```
/* Msg 547, Level 16, State 0, Line 1
The DELETE statement conflicted with the REFERENCE constraint
"FK_Product_ProductSubcategory_ProductSubcategoryID".
The conflict occurred in database "AdventureWorks2012",
table "Production.Product", column 'ProductSubcategoryID'.
The statement has been terminated. */
```

Single Column & Composite PRIMARY KEY List with XML PATH

Query to form delimited list for composite PRIMARY KEY columns. STUFF function deletes the leading comma.

```
-- Show composite PRIMARY KEYs as a comma-delimited list
USE AdventureWorks2012;
SELECT  K.TABLE_SCHEMA,
        T.TABLE_NAME,
        PK_COLUMN_NAMES =
                STUFF(( SELECT
                                CONCAT(', ',    KK.COLUMN_NAME)             AS [text()]
                                FROM   INFORMATION_SCHEMA.KEY_COLUMN_USAGE kk
                        WHERE  K.CONSTRAINT_NAME = KK.CONSTRAINT_NAME
                                ORDER BY  KK.ORDINAL_POSITION
                                FOR XML Path ('')), 1, 1, '')
FROM    INFORMATION_SCHEMA.TABLE_CONSTRAINTS T
  INNER JOIN    INFORMATION_SCHEMA.KEY_COLUMN_USAGE K
        ON T.CONSTRAINT_NAME = K.CONSTRAINT_NAME
WHERE           T.CONSTRAINT_TYPE = 'PRIMARY KEY'
                AND K.ORDINAL_POSITION = 1
ORDER BY        K.TABLE_SCHEMA,
                T.TABLE_NAME;
-- (71 row(s) affected) - Partial results
```

TABLE_SCHEMA	TABLE_NAME	PK_COLUMN_NAMES
dbo	AWBuildVersion	SystemInformationID
dbo	DatabaseLog	DatabaseLogID
dbo	ErrorLog	ErrorLogID
HumanResources	Department	DepartmentID
HumanResources	Employee	BusinessEntityID
HumanResources	EmployeeDepartmentHistory	BusinessEntityID, StartDate, DepartmentID, ShiftID
HumanResources	EmployeePayHistory	BusinessEntityID, RateChangeDate
HumanResources	JobCandidate	JobCandidateID
HumanResources	Shift	ShiftID
Person	Address	AddressID
Person	AddressType	AddressTypeID
Person	BusinessEntity	BusinessEntityID
Person	BusinessEntityAddress	BusinessEntityID, AddressID, AddressTypeID
Person	BusinessEntityContact	BusinessEntityID, PersonID, ContactTypeID
Person	ContactType	ContactTypeID
Person	CountryRegion	CountryRegionCode
Person	EmailAddress	BusinessEntityID, EmailAddressID
Person	Password	BusinessEntityID
Person	Person	BusinessEntityID
Person	PersonPhone	BusinessEntityID, PhoneNumber, PhoneNumberTypeID

SSMS GUI Table Designer

SSMS Object Explorer includes a GUI Table Designer which can be launched the following ways for new or existing table from the right-click drop-down menus.

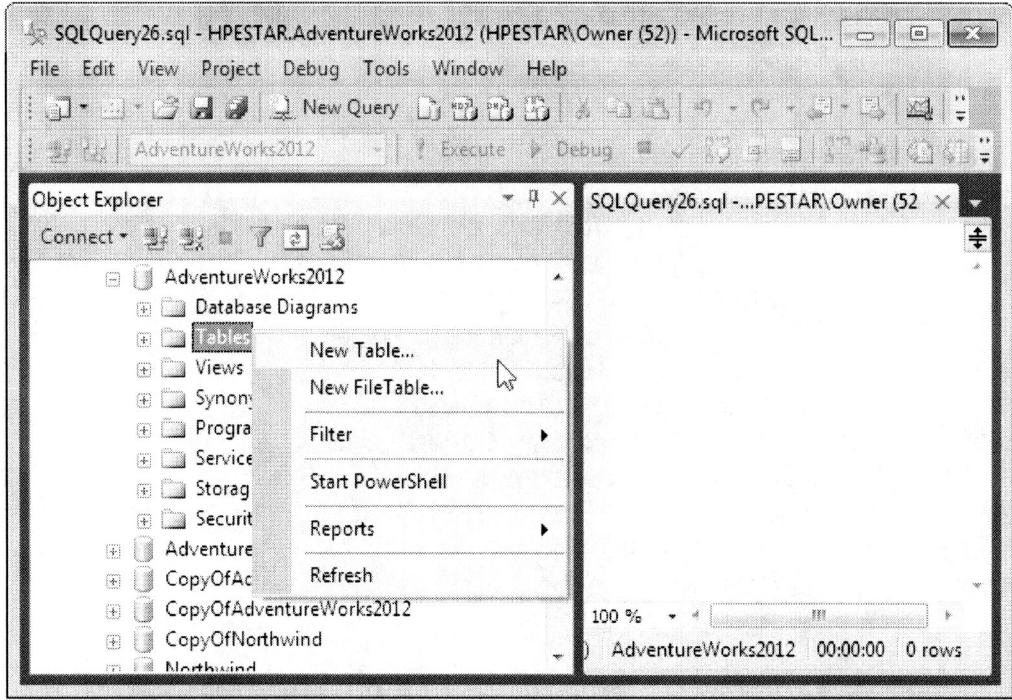

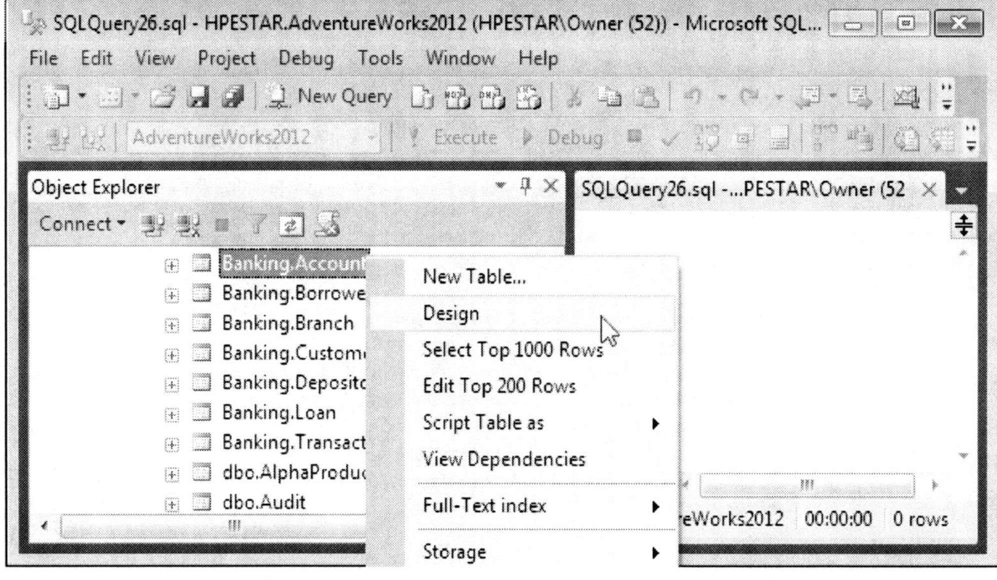

Basic GUI Table Design

The Table Designer provides line-by-line row design including all properties (bottom of dialog box) such as defaults, computed columns, identity and so on.

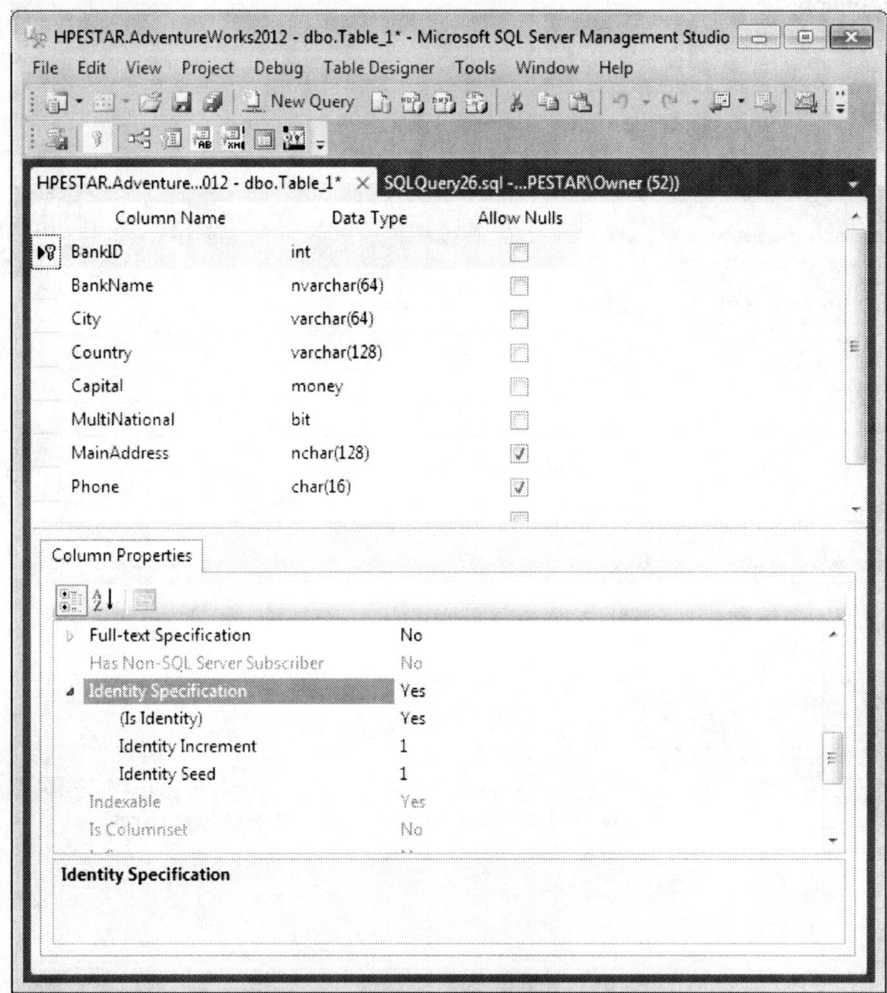

T-SQL Tidbits: Row-based(cursor) vs. Set-based Operations

The SQL language commands are designed for sets, therefore, that is our first choice: set-based operators. However, there are tasks which require row-based operations. One such task is index REBUILD on all tables in a database using metadata from INFORMATION_SCHEMA.TABLES view, cursor WHILE loop and dynamic SQL. We always have to be aware whether we are dealing with a single row or multiple rows in a table, subquery or virtual table. For example, when we program with the inserted table in a trigger or the OUTPUT clause, we have to assume that 1,000 rows may be in the inserted virtual table, therefore, set-based operations are required.

CHECK Constraint Definition

CHECK Constraint design window can be launched from toolbox icon: Manage Check Constraints or right-click drop-down menu. We create a constraint on Capital to be greater or equal to $5 billion.

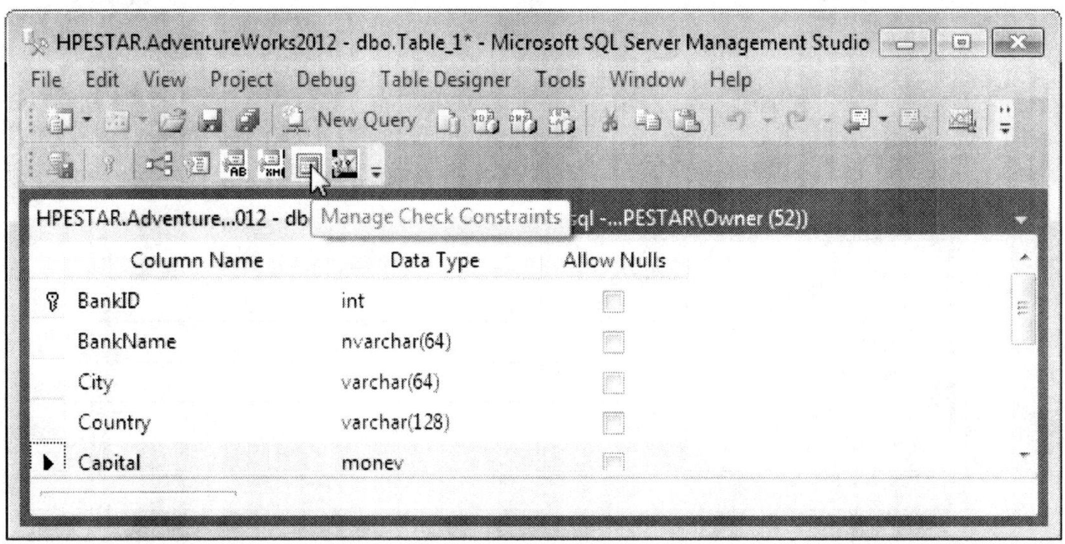

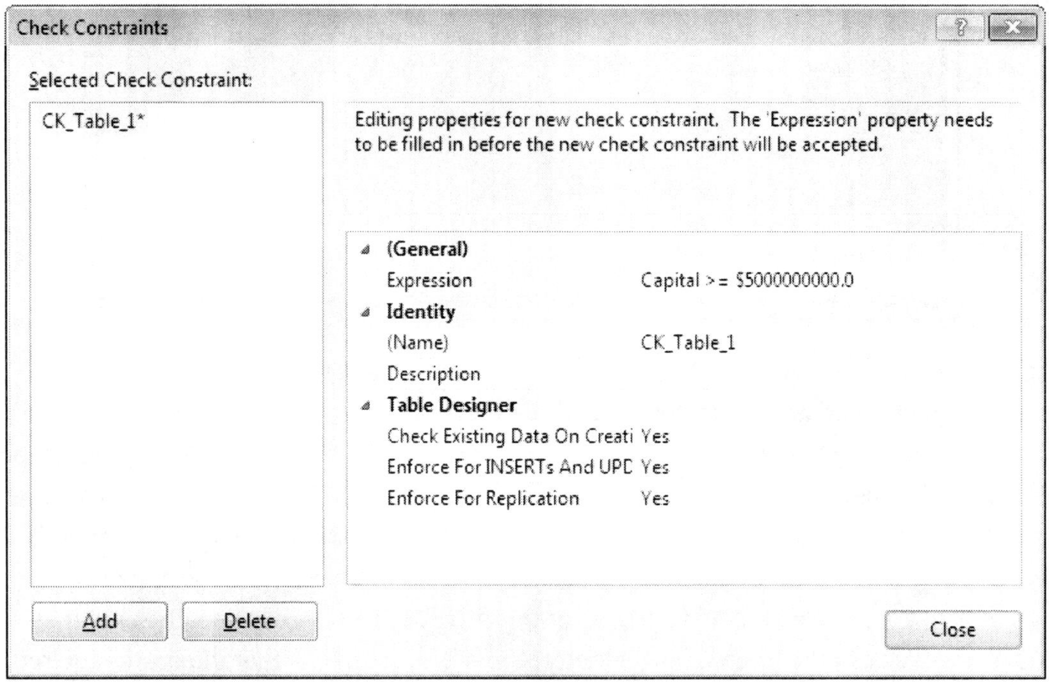

Managing Indexes and Keys

The Manage Indexes and Keys window can be launched by toolbox icon or right-click menu. We add UNIQUE KEY property to the BankName column.

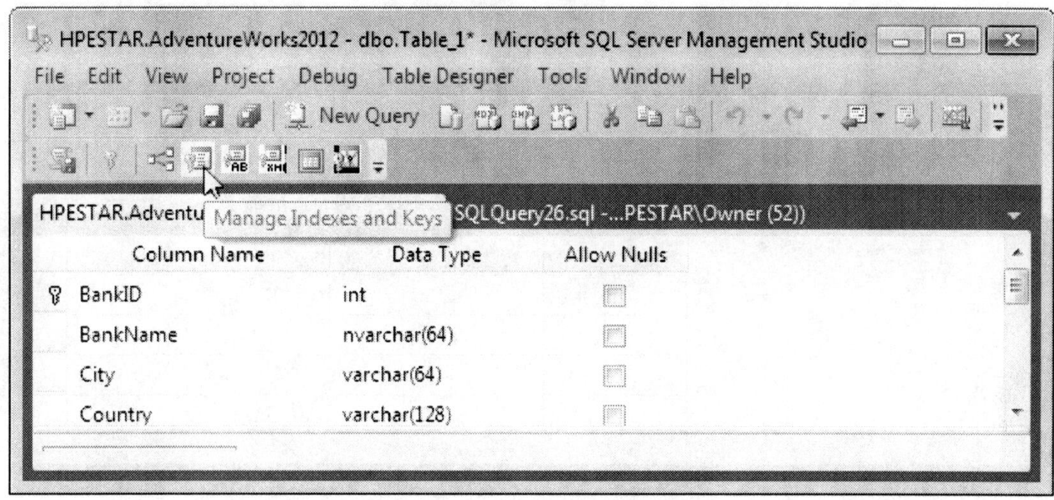

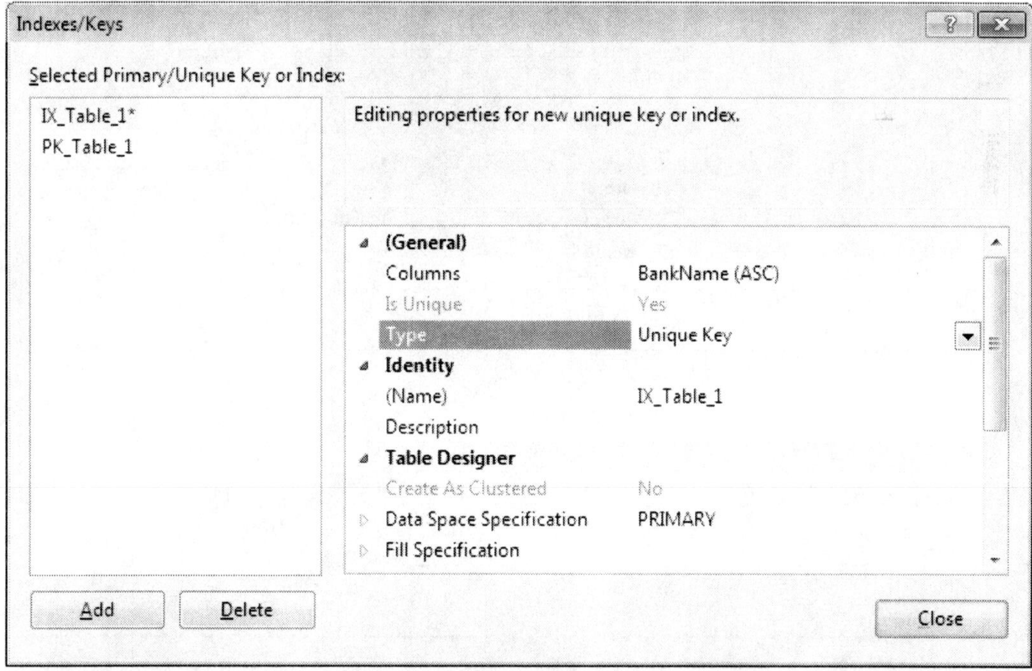

Setting PRIMARY KEY with a Single Click

PRIMARY KEY can simply be configured just by clicking on the gold key icon. A PRIMARY KEY constraint is created automatically.

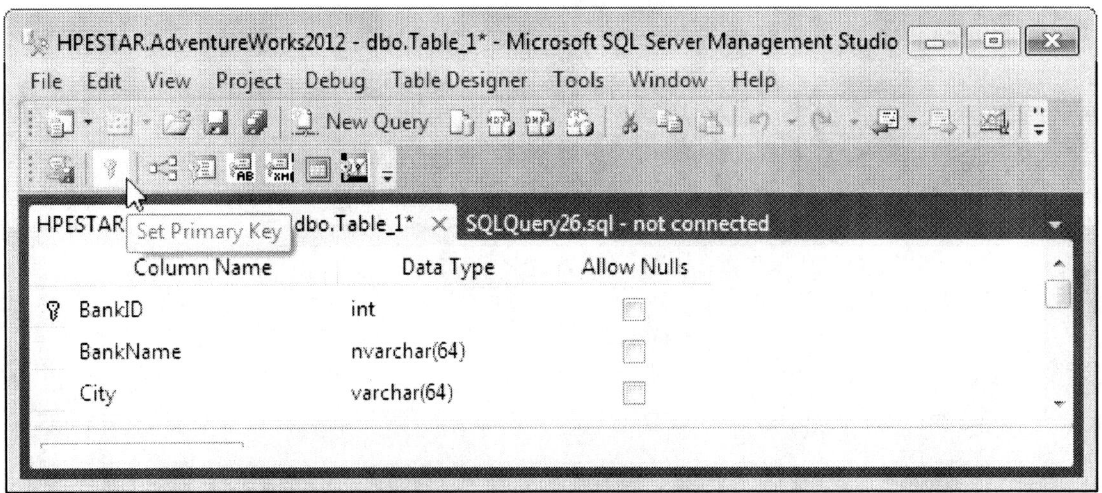

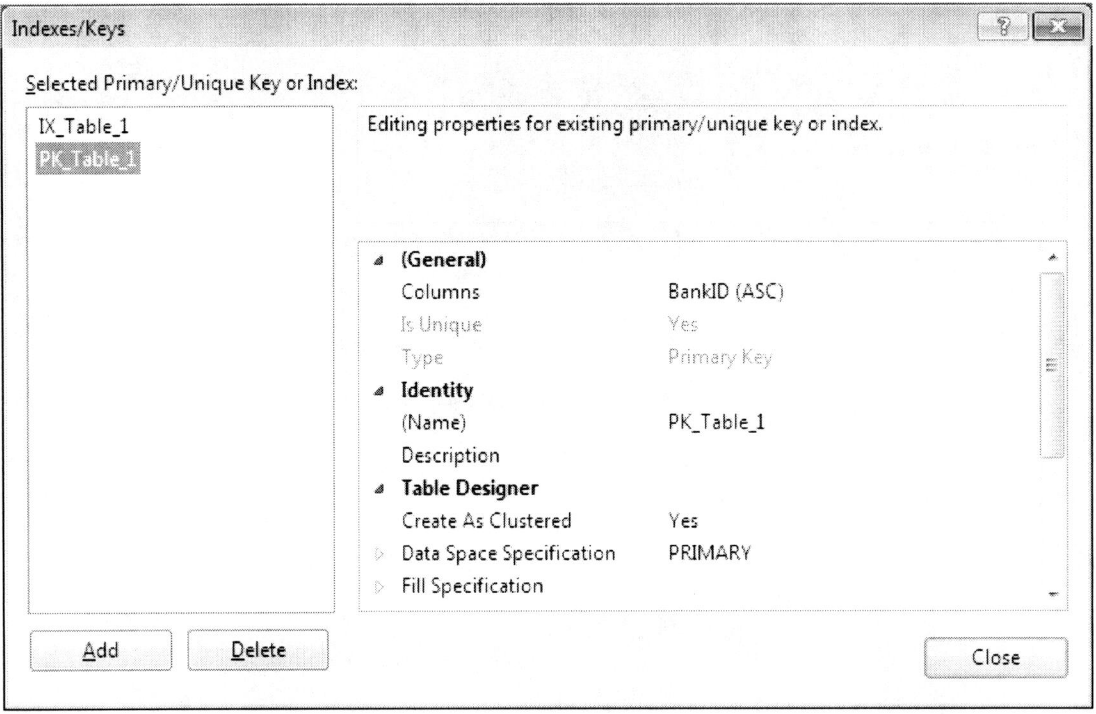

Configuring FOREIGN KEY: Declarative Referential Integrity

The Relationships facility can be used to create a FOREIGN KEY link (constraint). NOTE: demo only, BusinessEntityID column in the demo table has no relationship to AdventureWorks tables.

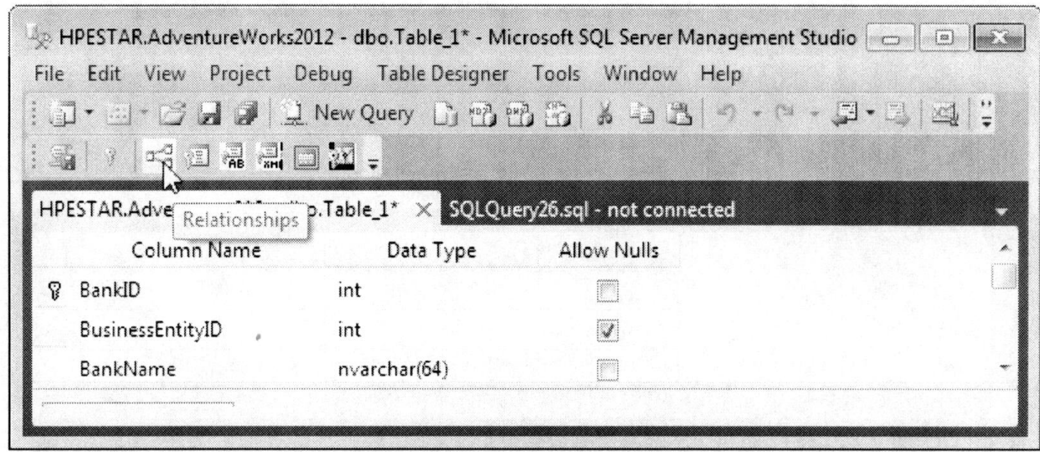

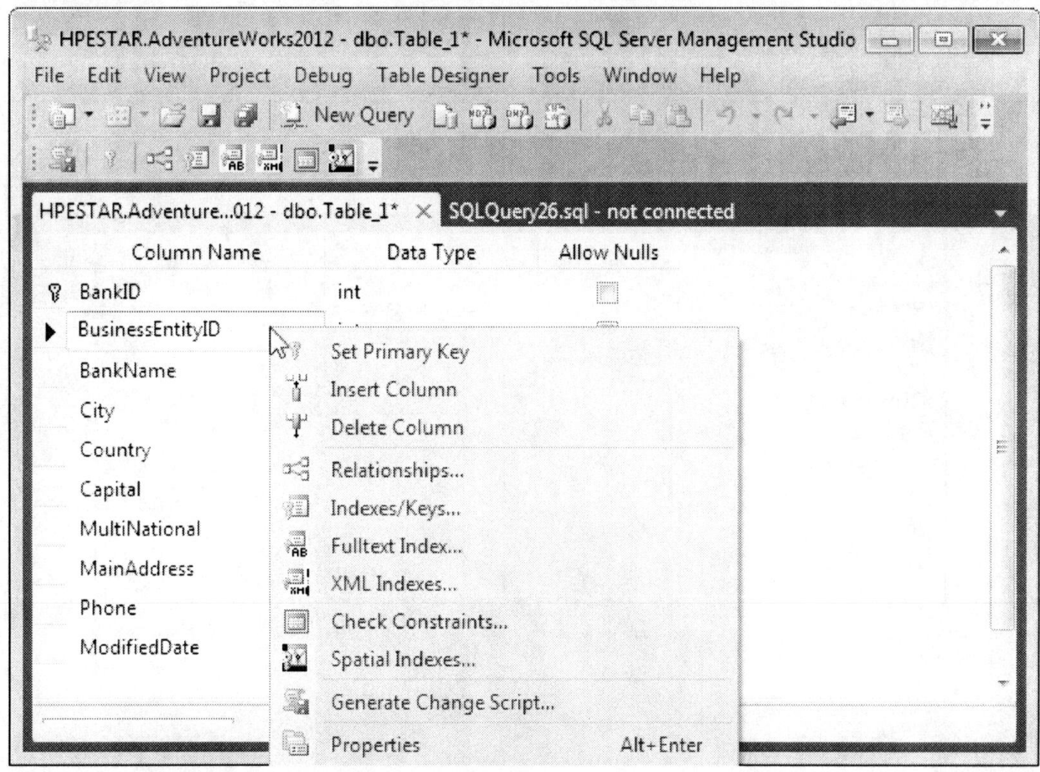

Tables And Columns Specific Tab Is To Define Mapping From FK To PK

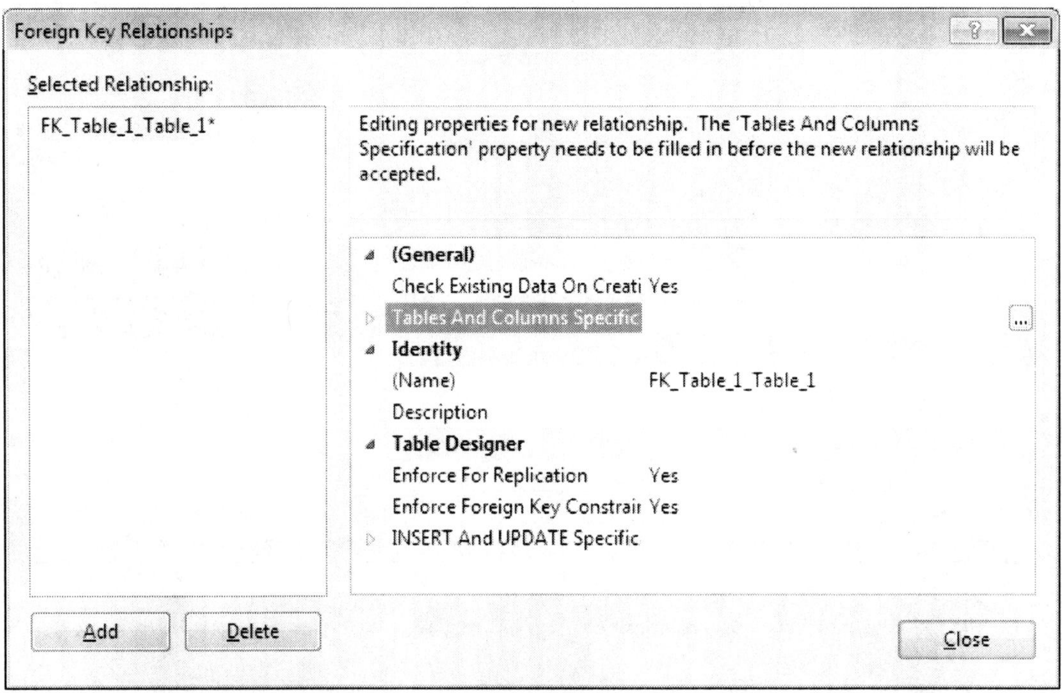

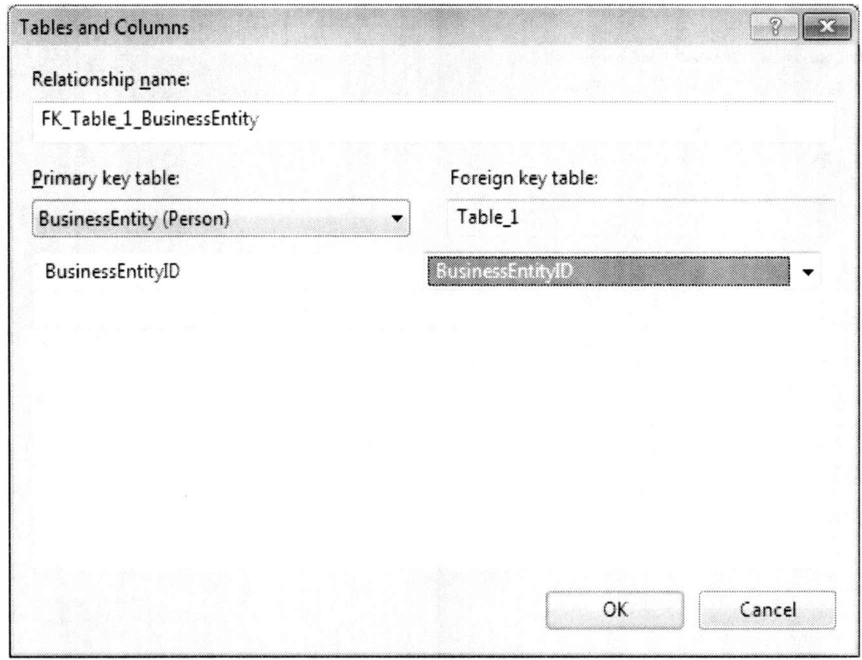

T-SQL Script Generation from GUI Table Designer

T-SQL code can be generated any time prior to saving the changes.

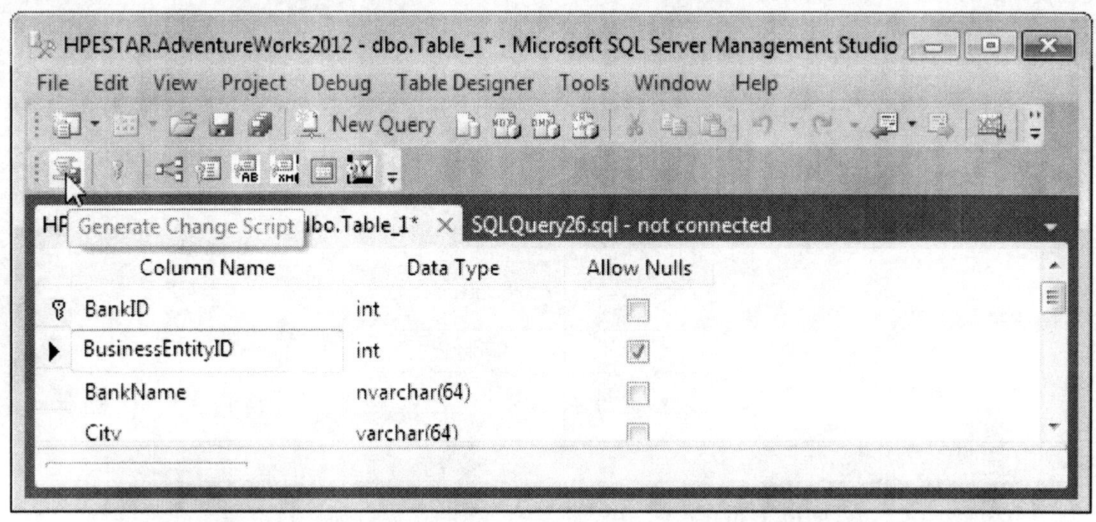

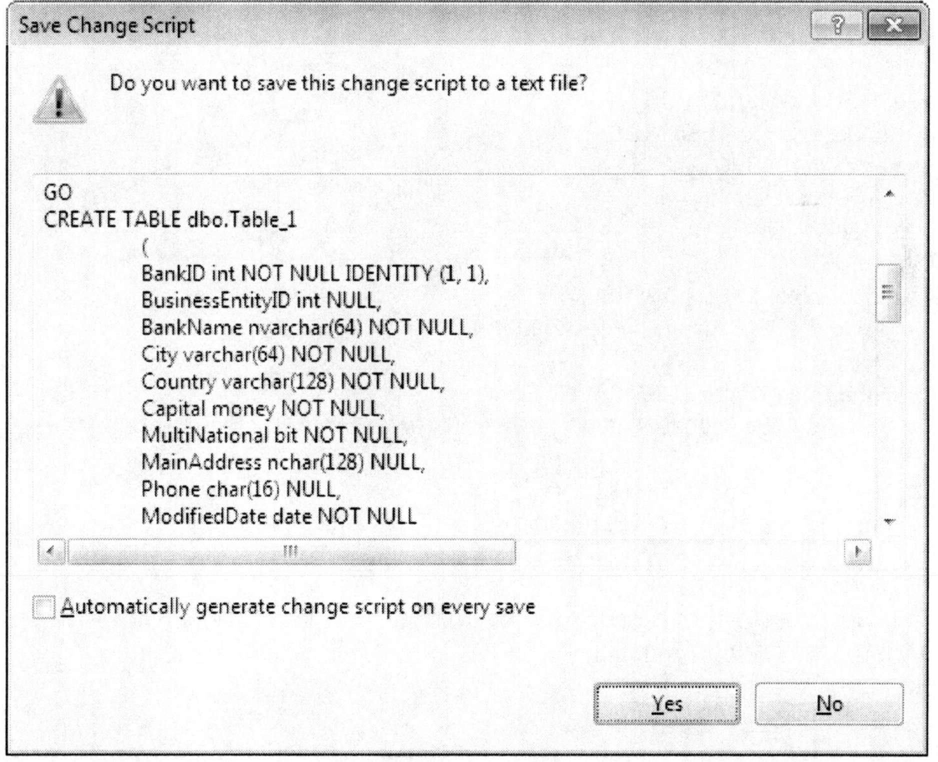

Generated CREATE TABLE & Related Objects Script

Code generated by the Table Designer.

```
/* To prevent any potential data loss issues, you should review this script in detail before running it
outside the context of the database designer.*/
BEGIN TRANSACTION
SET QUOTED_IDENTIFIER ON
SET ARITHABORT ON
SET NUMERIC_ROUNDABORT OFF
SET CONCAT_NULL_YIELDS_NULL ON
SET ANSI_NULLS ON
SET ANSI_PADDING ON
SET ANSI_WARNINGS ON
COMMIT
BEGIN TRANSACTION
GO
CREATE TABLE dbo.Table_1
	(
	BankID int NOT NULL IDENTITY (1, 1),
	BusinessEntityID int NULL,
	BankName nvarchar(64) NOT NULL,
	City varchar(64) NOT NULL,
	Country varchar(128) NOT NULL,
	Capital money NOT NULL,
	MultiNational bit NOT NULL,
	MainAddress nchar(128) NULL,
	Phone char(16) NULL,
	ModifiedDate date NOT NULL
	)  ON [PRIMARY]
GO
ALTER TABLE dbo.Table_1 ADD CONSTRAINT
	CK_Table_1 CHECK (Capital >= $5000000000.0)
GO
ALTER TABLE dbo.Table_1 ADD CONSTRAINT
	DF_Table_1_ModifiedDate DEFAULT CURRENT_TIMESTAMP FOR ModifiedDate
GO
ALTER TABLE dbo.Table_1 ADD CONSTRAINT
	PK_Table_1 PRIMARY KEY CLUSTERED
	(
	BankID
	) WITH( STATISTICS_NORECOMPUTE = OFF, IGNORE_DUP_KEY = OFF, ALLOW_ROW_LOCKS = ON,
ALLOW_PAGE_LOCKS = ON) ON [PRIMARY]

GO
```

```
-- T-SQL script continues

ALTER TABLE dbo.Table_1 ADD CONSTRAINT IX_Table_1 UNIQUE NONCLUSTERED (BankName)
        WITH( STATISTICS_NORECOMPUTE = OFF, IGNORE_DUP_KEY = OFF, ALLOW_ROW_LOCKS = ON,
ALLOW_PAGE_LOCKS = ON) ON [PRIMARY]
GO
ALTER TABLE dbo.Table_1 ADD CONSTRAINT FK_Table_1_Table_1 FOREIGN KEY (BankID)
        REFERENCES dbo.Table_1 (BankID) ON UPDATE  NO ACTION  ON DELETE  NO ACTION
GO
ALTER TABLE dbo.Table_1 SET (LOCK_ESCALATION = TABLE)
GO
COMMIT
```

Upon Exit or Save, a name can be assigned to the table. In this instance, the Table_1 is changed to MultiNationalBank. The Table Designer automatically replaces all the "Table_1" occurrences in the script with "MultiNationalBank".

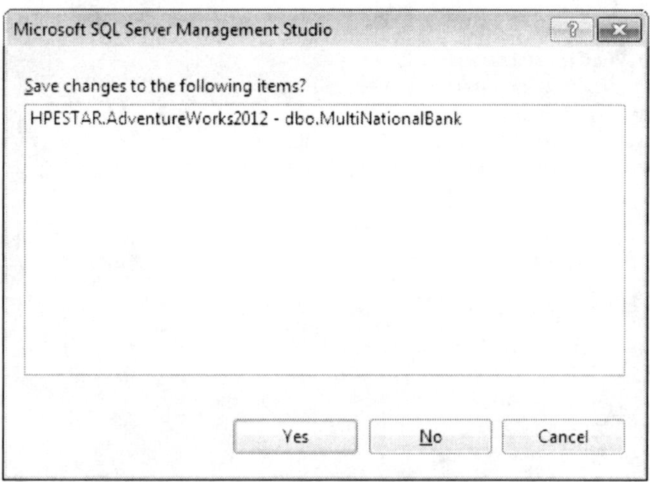

T-SQL Tidbits: Dynamic SQL Using Database Metadata

To write data-driven script or stored procedure, we have to combine dynamic SQL with metadata. The metadata query to get all the tables in the database.

```
SELECT CONCAT(QUOTENAME(TABLE_SCHEMA),'.',QUOTENAME(TABLE_NAME))
FROM INFORMATION_SCHEMA.TABLES WHERE TABLE_TYPE='BASE TABLE';
-- [Production].[ScrapReason], [HumanResources].[Shift], [Purchasing].[ShipMethod]...
```

We define a cursor with the query, a WHILE loop, build a dynamic SQL command, for example to REBUILD all indexes on the table, and execute it for each table When a new table is added to the database, the metadata query picks it up automatically.

One-to-Many Relationship Implementation

The cardinality of relationship implemented with PRIMARY KEY & FOREIGN KEY constraints is one-to-many. Many FKs can reference a single PK value. In the following demo, many products map to a single subcategory value 'Touring Bike'. The matching is not done on the name between tables, rather on the surrogate PK value 3.

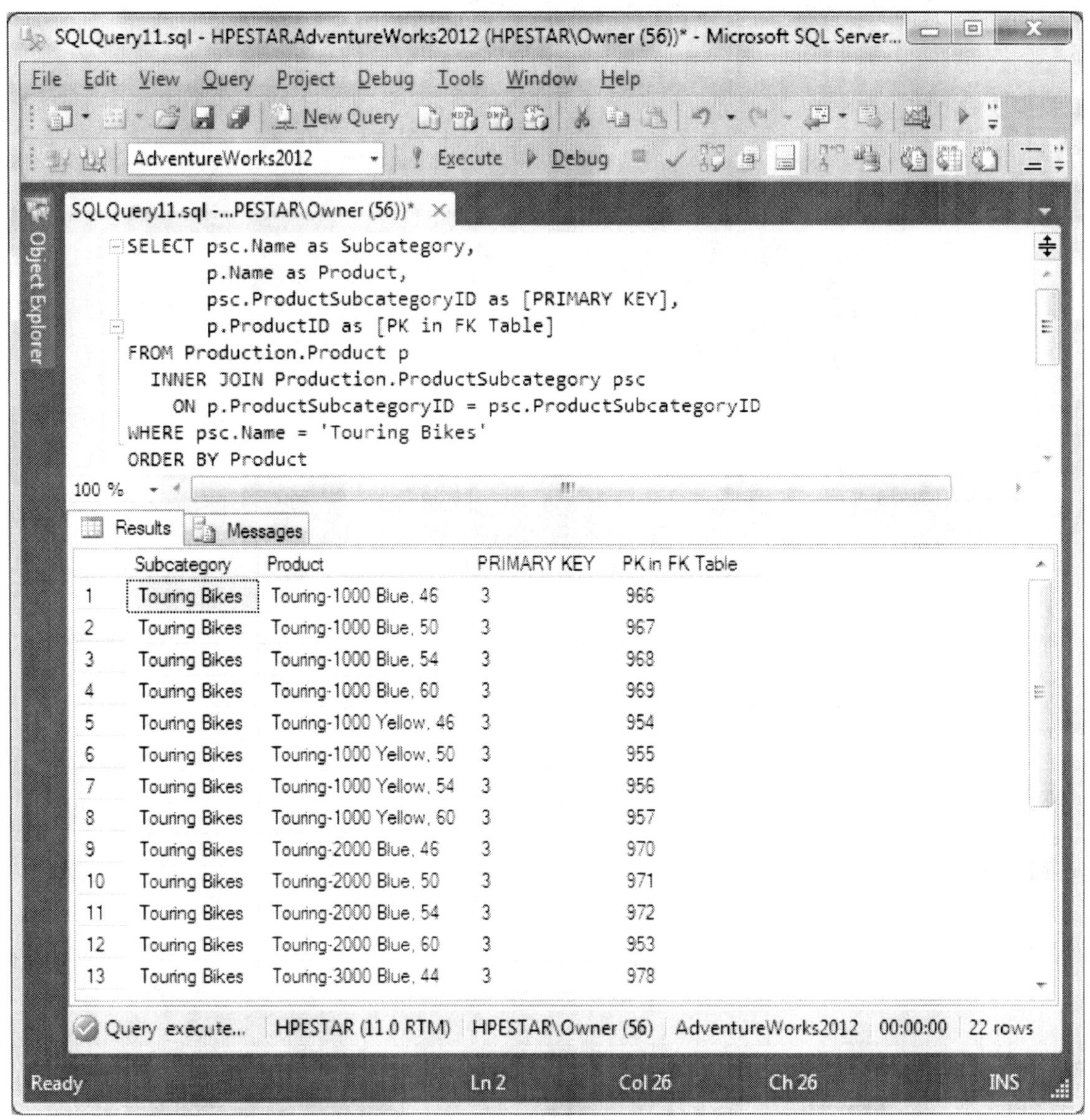

FOREIGN KEY Referencing A UNIQUE KEY

A FOREIGN KEY can reference a UNIQUE KEY or UNIQUE index column in another table in addition to the PRIMARY KEY. In the following demonstration a FOREIGN KEY is created from ProdNumber column pointing to Production.Product ProductNumber (UNIQUE index) column.

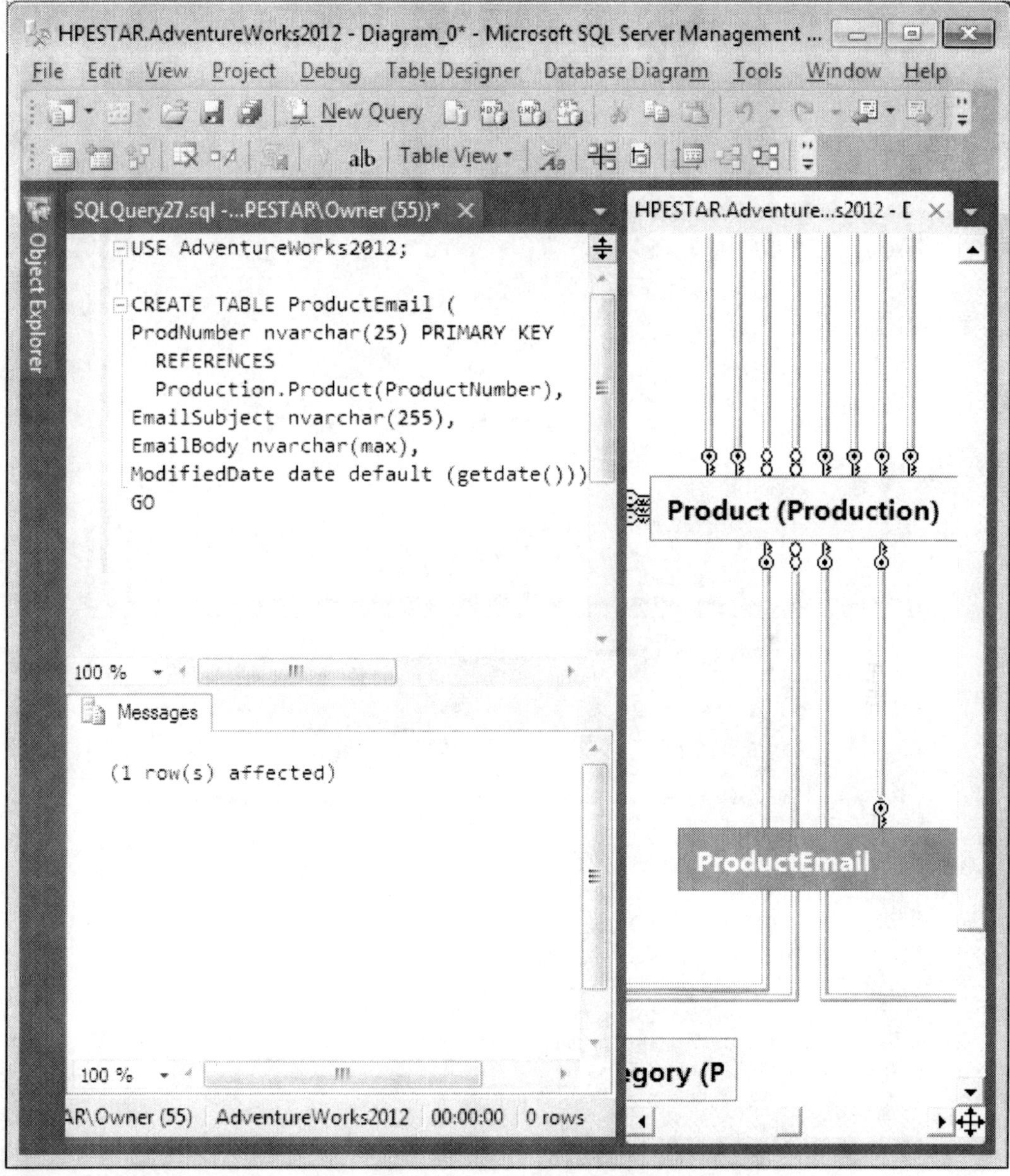

FOREIGN KEY Relationship Without Constraint

A table can have a FOREIGN KEY which is not supported by server-side constraint. In such instance the client-side application software has to ensure that the relationship is valid. Generally it is undesirable. **Whatever can be done on the server-side should be done there because it is more efficient development wise, maintenance wise and performance wise.** Demonstration to remove the FK constraint on the ProductID column in the [Order Details] table of the CopyOfNorthwind database.

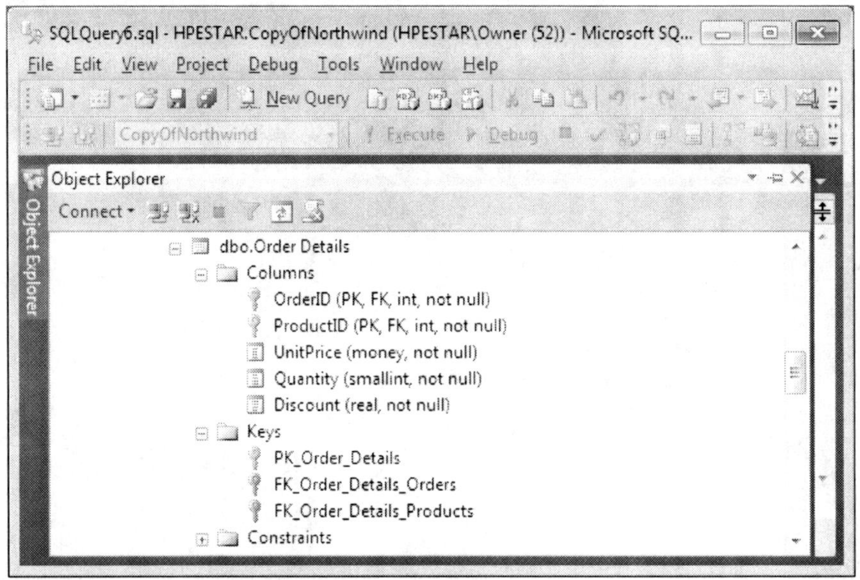

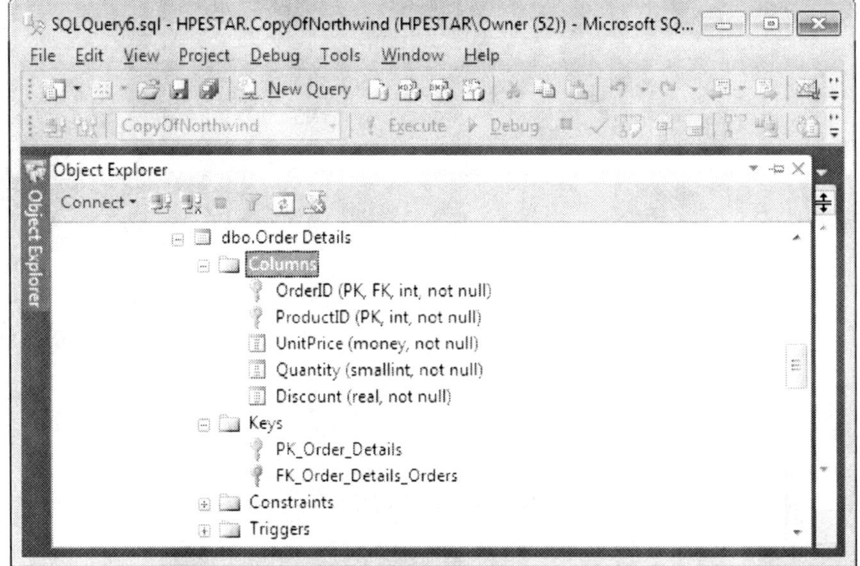

Database Diagram Design Tool in SSMS

Management Studio Object Explorer includes a diagramming tool for tables and their relationships with each other. While not as sophisticated as independent database design tools, it is excellent for working with a small number of tables.

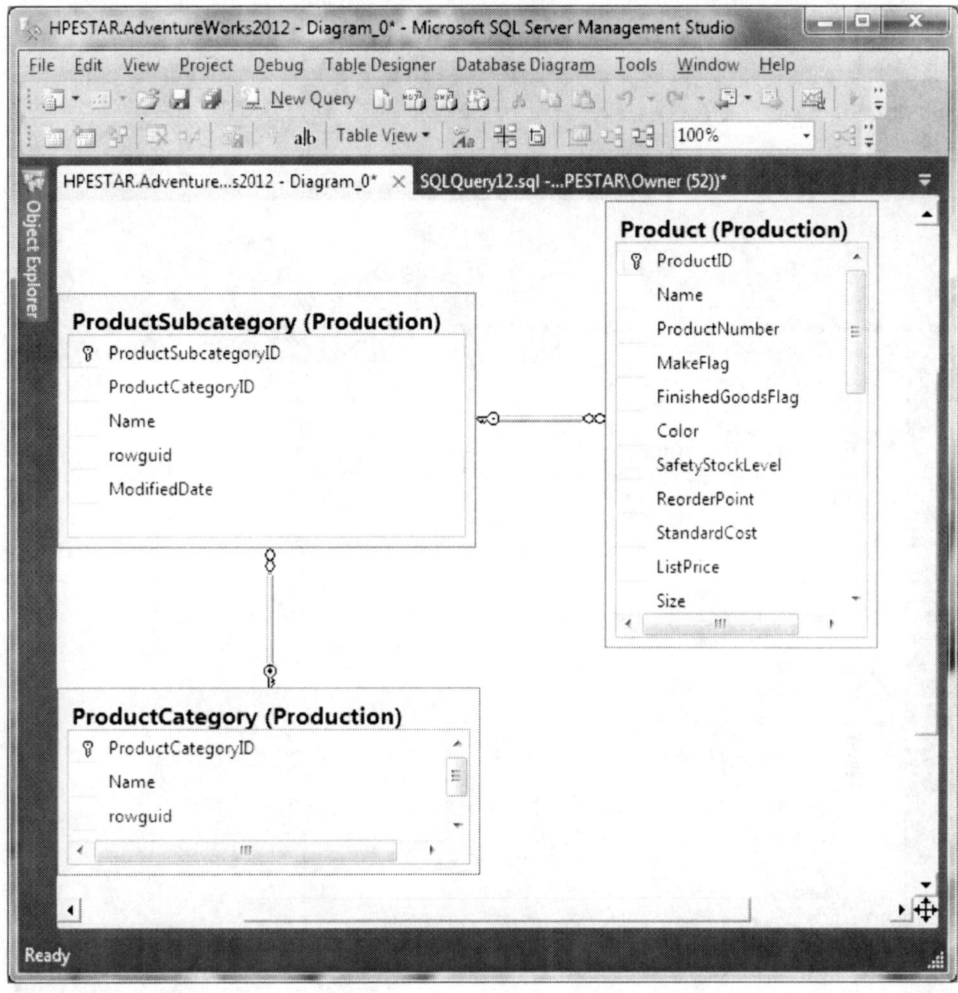

The diagramming tool has both reverse engineering and forward engineering features. **Reverse engineering**: it creates a diagram based on table and PK/FK constraints definitions. **Forward engineering**: it can change table and constraint setup in the database based on diagram changes. The Gold Key (PRIMARY KEY symbol) end of the connection line points to the PRIMARY KEY table, while the double "o" (infinite symbol in mathematics, here meaning many) end to the FOREIGN KEY table.

PRIMARY KEY & FOREIGN KEY as JOIN ON Keys

When we need data from two related tables we have to JOIN the tables. The typical JOIN keys are the PRIMARY KEY and FOREIGN KEY. In the following demonstration, we want to display the subcategory for each Touring Bike product from the Product table. Since the 'Touring Bike' subcategory value is in the ProductSubcategory table, we have to JOIN it to the Product table. The JOIN keys are: ProductSubcategoryID PRIMARY KEY in the ProductSubcategory table and ProductSubcategoryID FOREIGN KEY in the Product table. Naming the FK same as the PK is helpful with readability, therefore developer productivity.

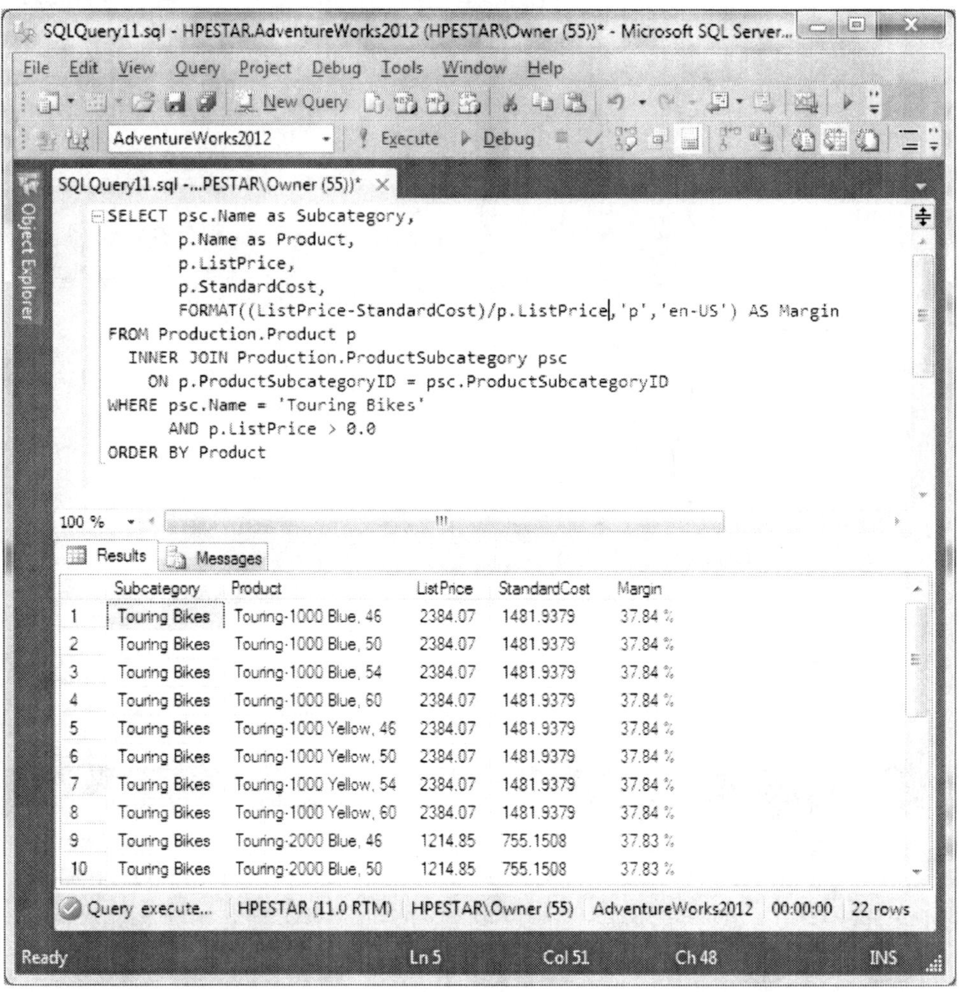

The Margin column is calculated with an expression. It is also formatted as percentage with US English culture.

Composite & Indirect FOREIGN KEY

A composite (more than one column) PRIMARY KEY requires matching composite FOREIGN KEY references. In the Sales.SalesOrderDetail table SpecialOfferID & ProductID constitute a composite FOREIGN KEY which references the SpecialOfferProduct table composite PRIMARY KEY. Thus ProductID indirectly references the Production.Product table.

NATURAL KEY is a Must in Every Table

NATURAL KEY is a unique key which can serve as PRIMARY KEY for identifying data. A product name is a natural key in a product table. A product number is also a NATURAL KEY in a product table. Note that product "number" should better be called product identification since it is frequently not a number rather it is alphanumeric like: AB342BL where BL stands for blue. The Name and ProductNumber columns are NATURAL KEYs in the Production.Product table. **Every table should have a NATURAL KEY**. If it does not, there is a definition problem. Naturally, test tables, work tables and staging tables are exceptions to this rule.

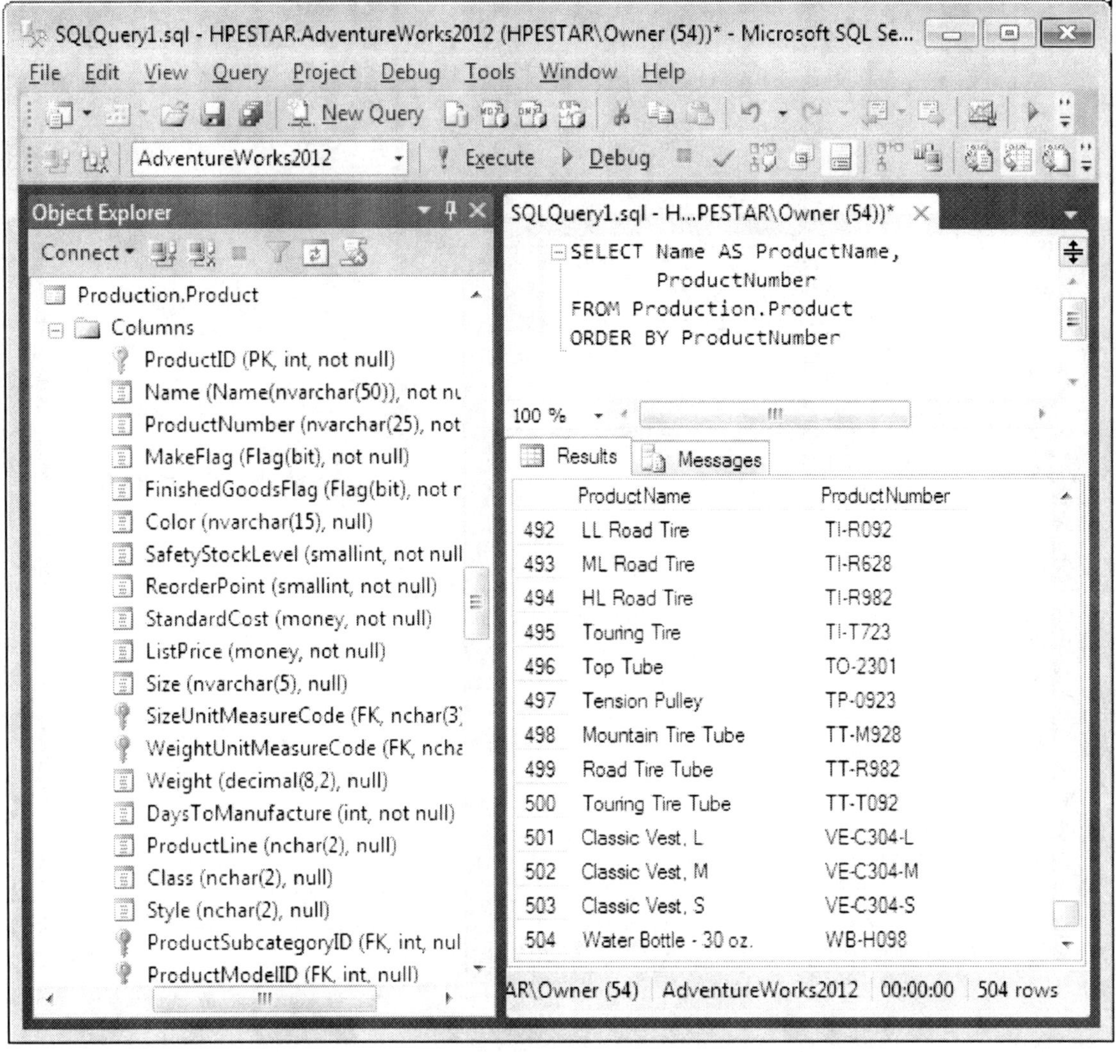

CANDIDATE KEY

A CANDIDATE KEY can be any column or a combination of columns that can qualify as UNIQUE KEY in a table with no NULL value. The ProductID, Name, ProductNumber, rowguid (16 byte random value like FA3C65CD-0A22-47E3-BDF6-53F1DC138C43, hyphens are for readability) are all CANDIDATE KEYs in the Production.Product table. Only one of them can be the PRIMARY KEY. In this instance the selected PRIMARY KEY is ProductID, a SURROGATE (to NATURAL KEY) INT IDENTITY (1,1) PRIMARY KEY.

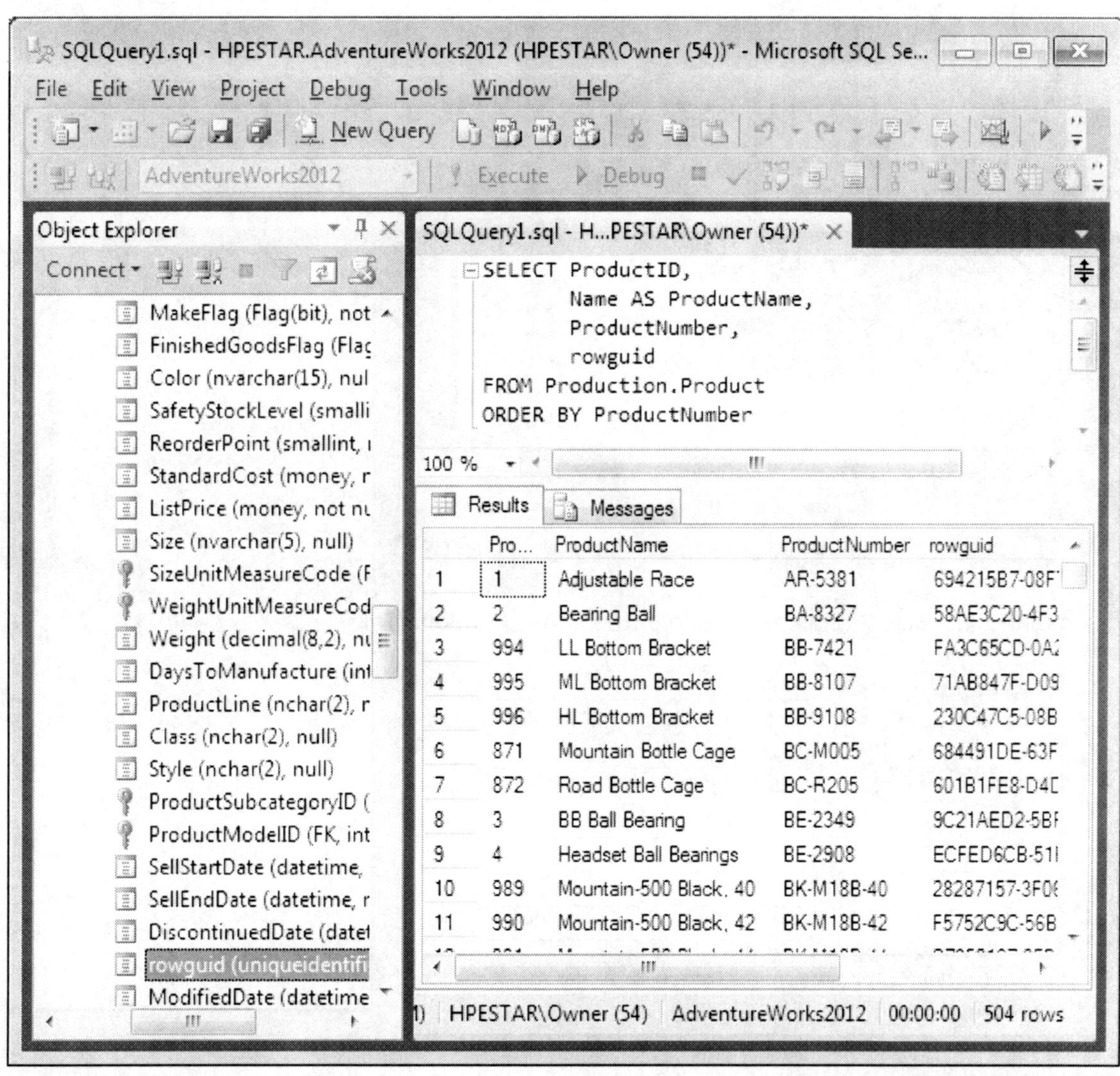

Logical Data Modeling in Visio

The following screenshots demonstrate logical / conceptual data modeling in Visio using the ORM diagram tool.

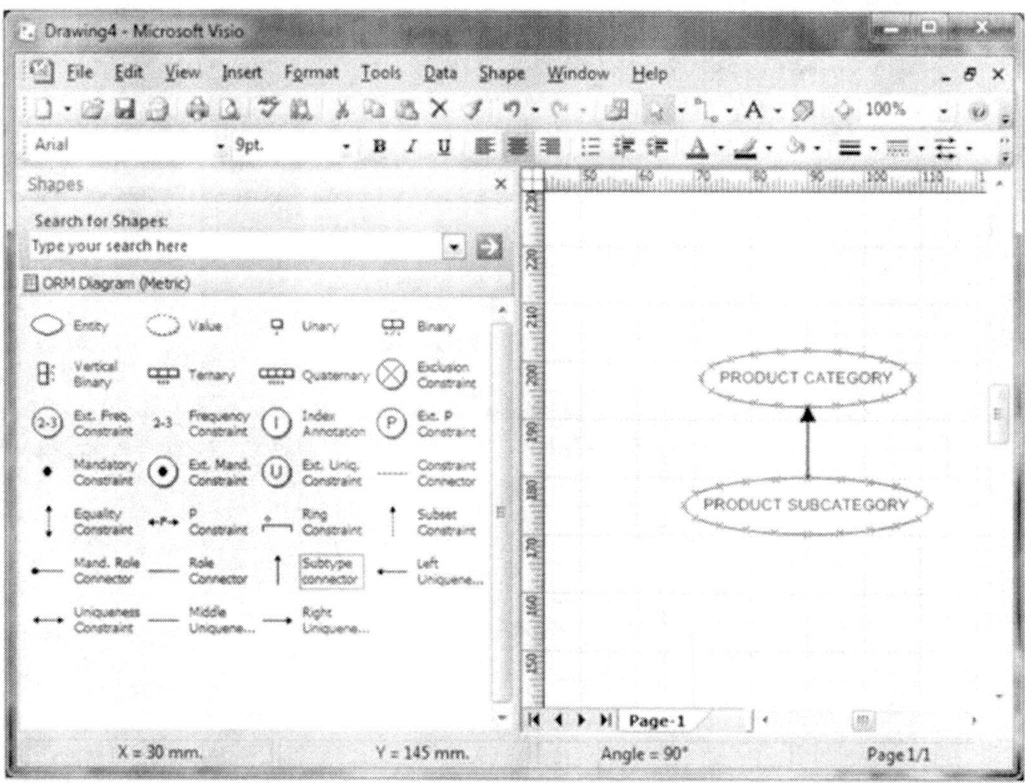

Following is the actual implementation of the above relationship.

```
CREATE TABLE [Production].[ProductCategory](
	[ProductCategoryID] [int] IDENTITY(1,1) PRIMARY KEY,
	[Name] [dbo].[Name] NOT NULL,
	[rowguid] [uniqueidentifier] ROWGUIDCOL  NOT NULL,
	[ModifiedDate] [datetime] NOT NULL	);

CREATE TABLE [Production].[ProductSubcategory](
	[ProductSubcategoryID] [int] IDENTITY(1,1) PRIMARY KEY,
	[ProductCategoryID] [int] NOT NULL REFERENCES
Production.ProductCategory(ProductCategoryID) ,
	[Name] [dbo].[Name] NOT NULL,
	[rowguid] [uniqueidentifier] ROWGUIDCOL  NOT NULL,
	[ModifiedDate] [datetime] NOT NULL	);
```

Branch Banking Conceptual Diagram Preparation In Visio ORM Diagram Tool

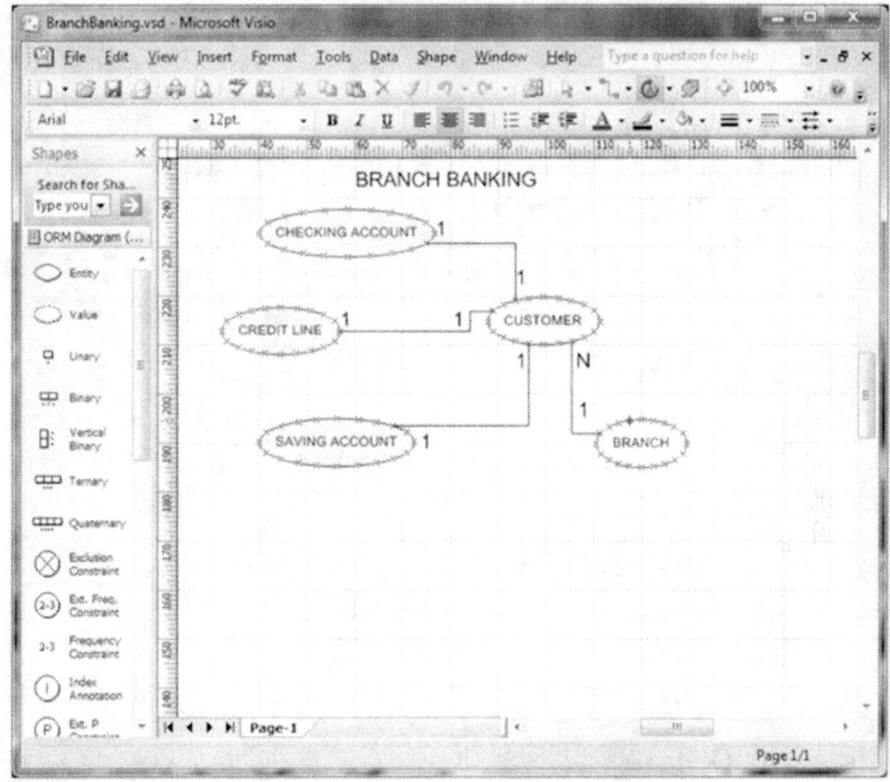

The actual implementation of Branch - Customer relationship.

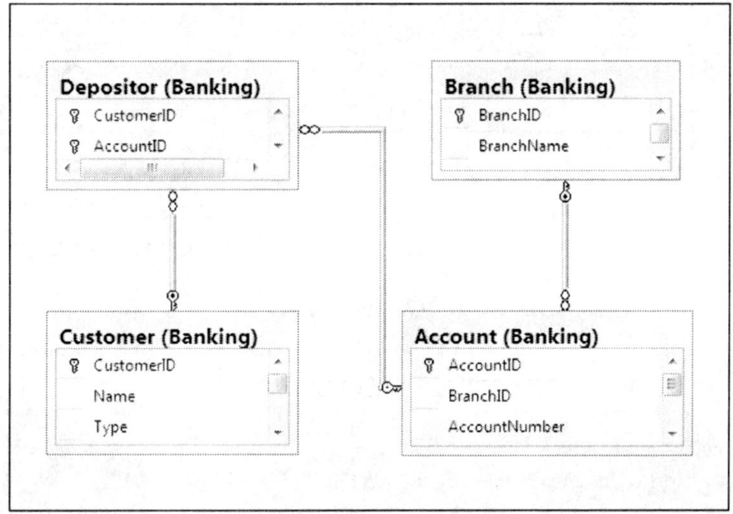

Relational Database Design with Visio

Office Visio can be used for physical database modeling and design. Another widely used database modeling tool is ERWIN (product of CA, Inc.). A sample database design diagram in Visio. Lines represent FOREIGN KEY constraints, arrowheads point to the referenced table.

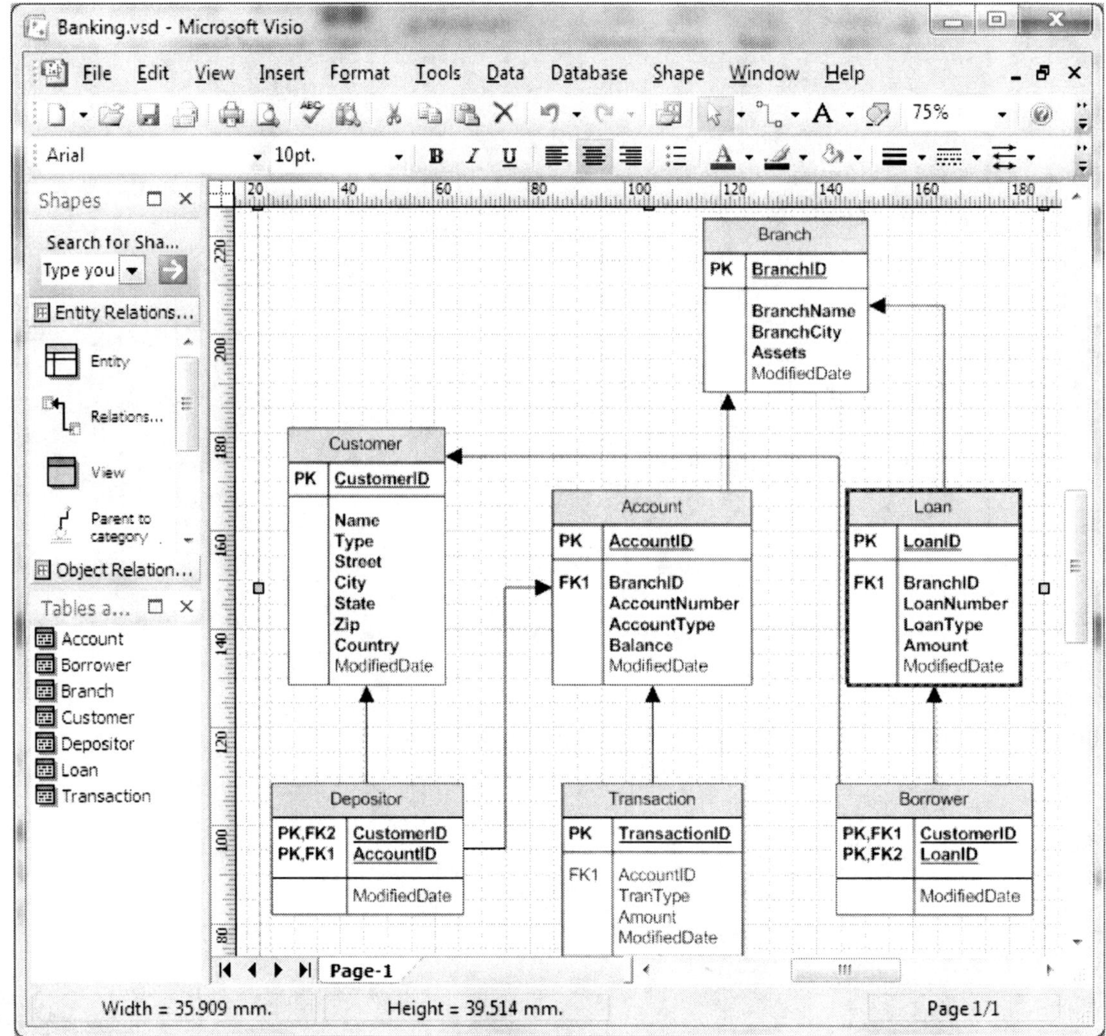

T-SQL Tidbits: Index REBUILD vs. DROP & CREATE

Index REBUILD will not disturb any table related objects. DROP & CREATE may require, for example, to DROP related keys like PRIMARY KEY or FOREIGN KEY constraints.

```
USE AdventureWorks2012;
ALTER INDEX ALL ON Production.Product REBUILD WITH (FILLFACTOR = 80, SORT_IN_TEMPDB = ON);
```

AdventureWorks Database Model in Visio

A segment of the AdventureWorks database design model in Visio. U indicates UNIQUE KEY or unique index.

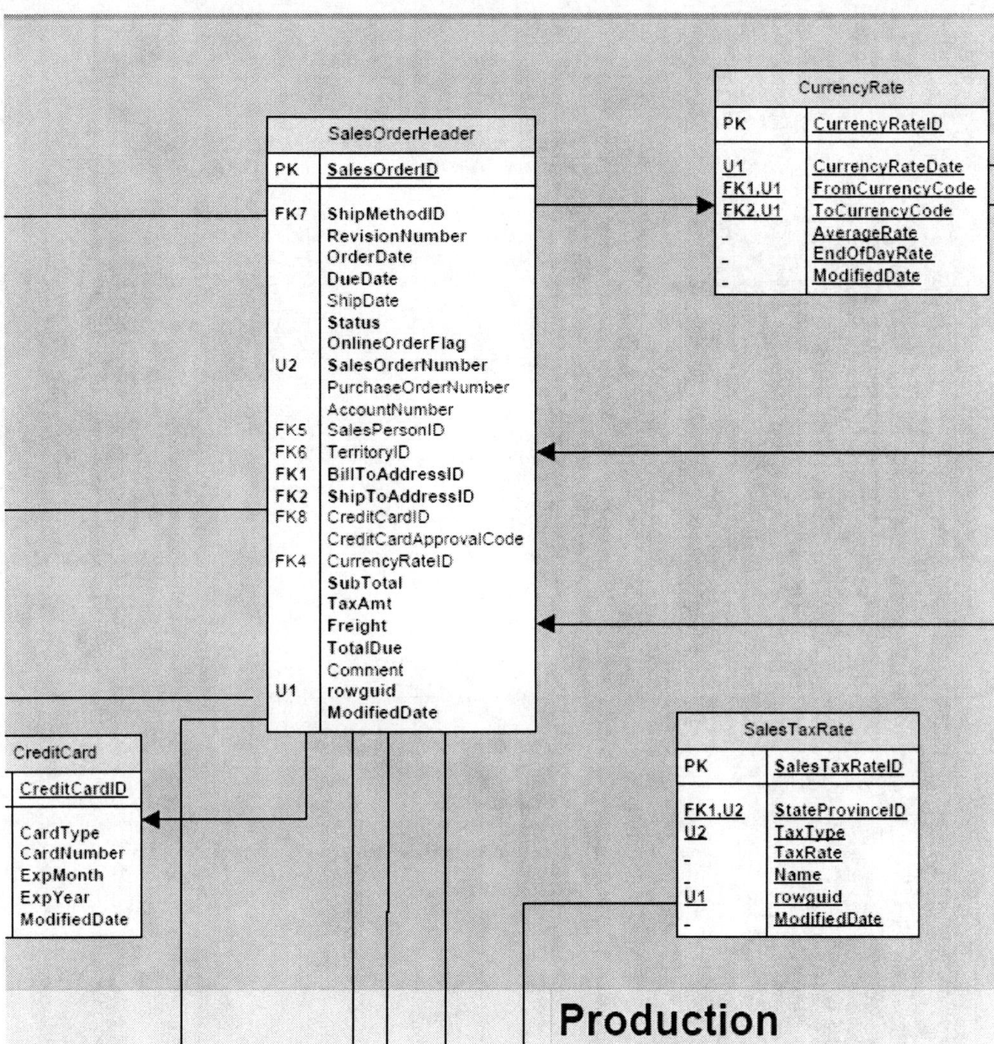

T-SQL Tidbits: Writing Data Directly to File From T-SQL

There is no direct T-SQL data export command. bcp, SSIS, ECHO/xp_cmdshell or SQLCMD (-i {.sql file input} -o {.txt file output} are the export methods.

```
DECLARE @cmd sysname, @var sysname = 'Hawaii Volcanoes';
SET @cmd = CONCAT('echo ', @var, ' > F:\temp\text_out.txt');
EXEC master..xp_cmdshell @cmd;
```

Reverse Engineering a Database with Visio

Visio can reverse engineer a database. Based on PRIMARY KEY & FOREIGN KEY constraints and table definitions, it can construct a database diagram automatically. Here are the first and an intermediate steps.

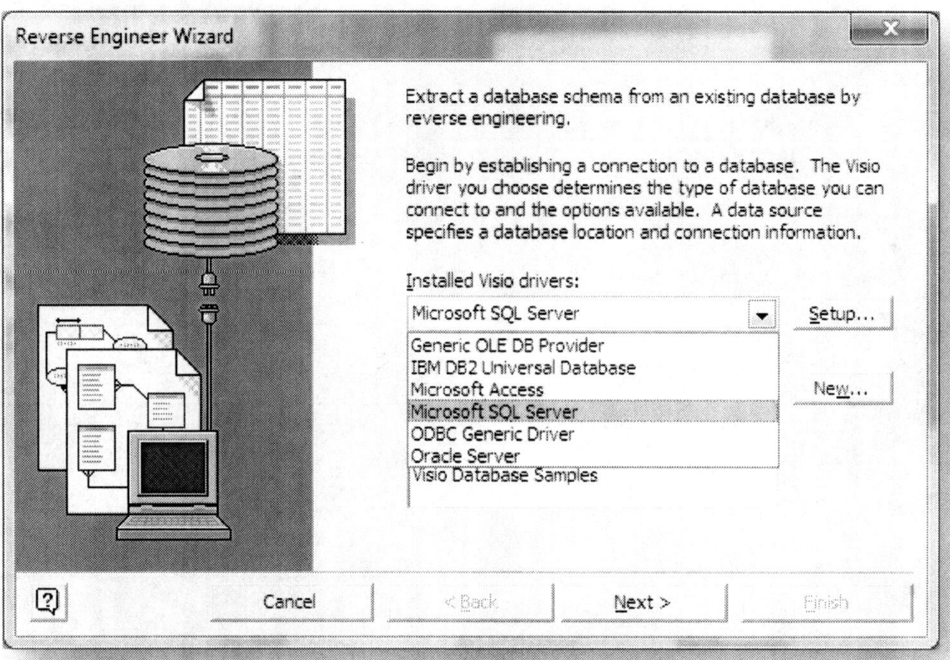

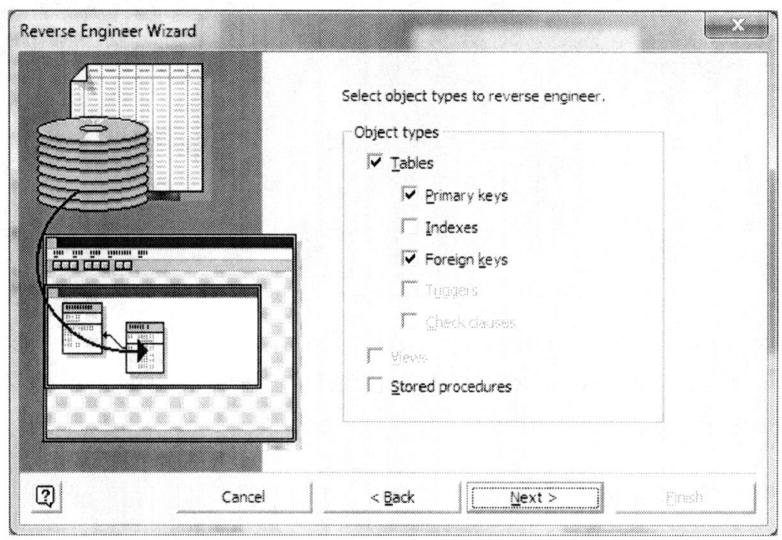

Reverse Engineered Diagram of Northwind

A section display from the reverse engineered diagram of Northwind sample database(not clear why "Discontinued" displays in bold):

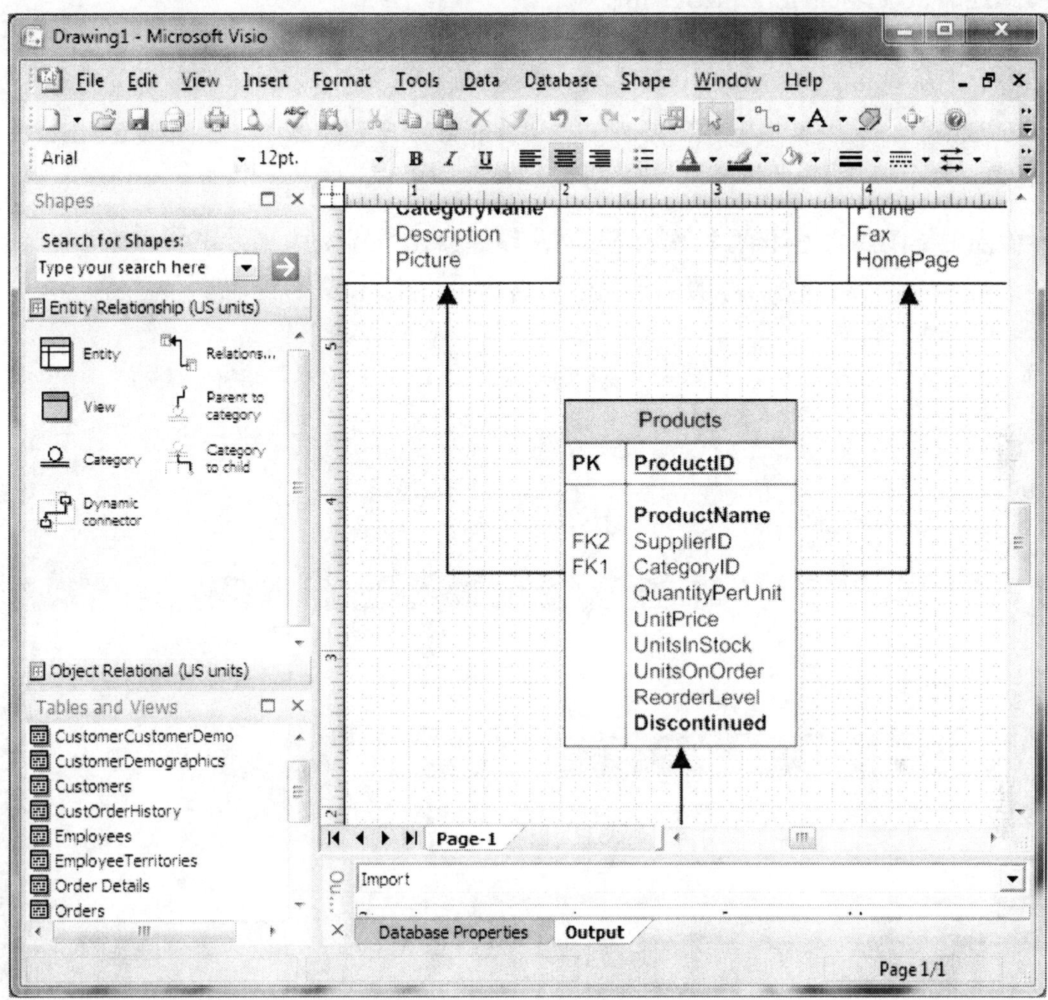

Modify (ALTER) Constraint

There is no ALTER command, rather a combination of DROP CONSTRAINT & ADD CONSTRAINT commands. FK dropped on CategoryID. FK created on SupplierID.

```
ALTER TABLE dbo.Products        DROP CONSTRAINT FK_Products_Categories;
ALTER TABLE dbo.Products WITH NOCHECK ADD CONSTRAINT
        FK_Products_Supplier FOREIGN KEY (SupplierID)
  REFERENCES dbo.Suppliers(SupplierID) ON UPDATE  NO ACTION  ON DELETE  NO ACTION ;
```

Forward Engineering a Database with Visio

Visio product itself does not have forward engineering feature. Alberto Ferrari developed an Office Addin for generating database scripts from a Visio database model diagram: Visio Forward Engineer Addin for Office 2010 (http://sqlblog.com/blogs/alberto_ferrari/archive/2010/04/16/visio-forward-engineer-addin-for-office-2010.aspx).

Codeplex blog post and free download for the same: Visio Forward Engineer Addin (http://forwardengineer.codeplex.com/).

Forward Engineering from SSMS Diagram Tool

The Database Diagram Tool in SSMS Object Explorer support graphical design and forward engineering.

Screenshot to show the creation of a new table "Automobile" in the Diagram Tool.

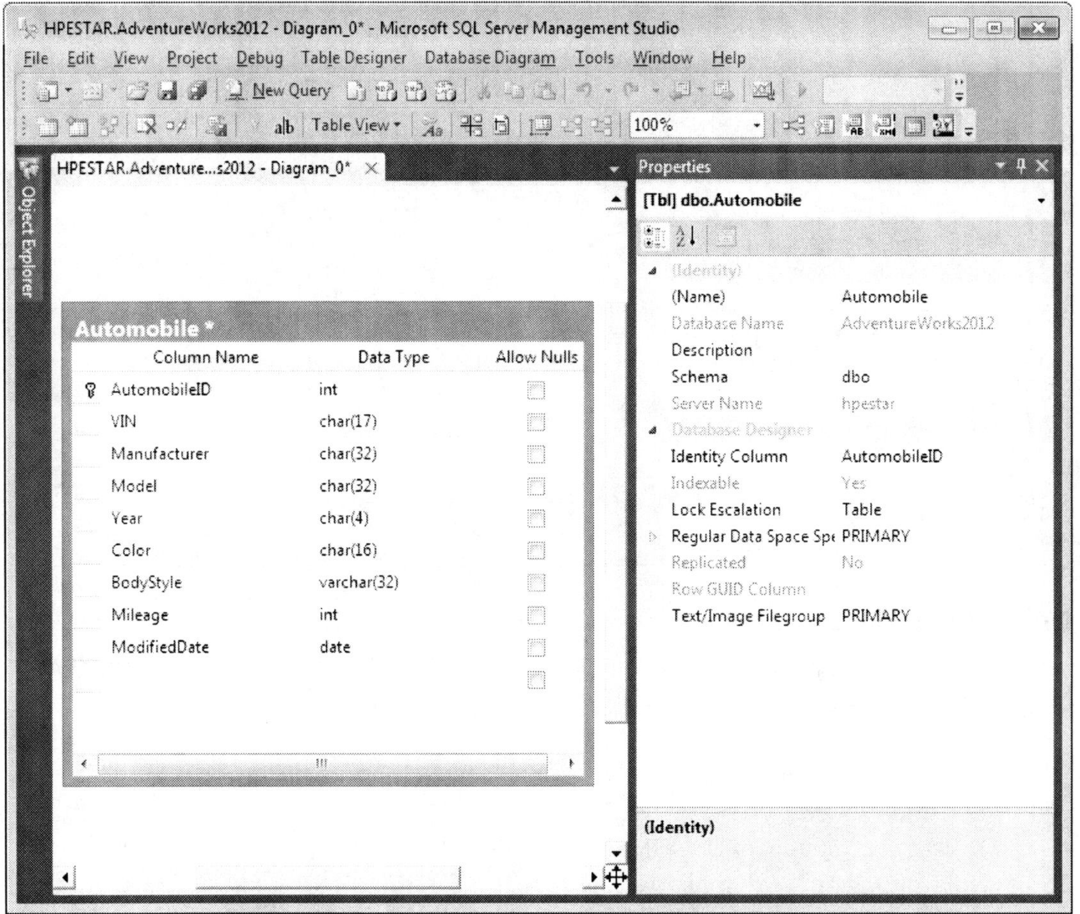

The Properties Dialog Box Allows The Individual Configuration Of Each Column

The Right Click drop-down menu has options to Add Indexes/Keys, Add XML Indexes, Add Spatial Indexes, Add Fulltext Indexes, Delete Tables from Database (DANGEROUS!), CHECK constraint and other table related database objects.

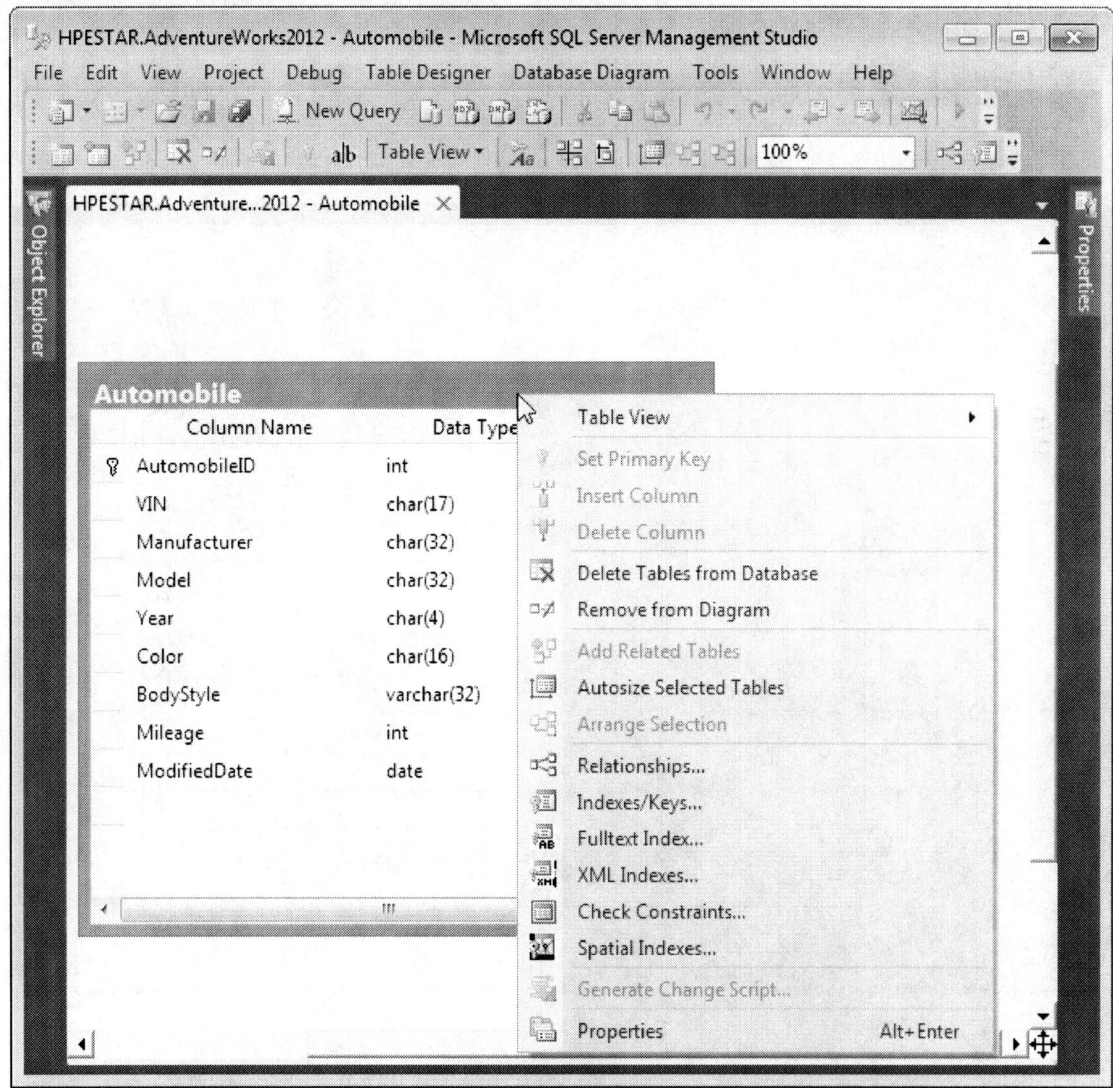

T-SQL Tidbits: SET Options For Execution Plans

SET XML_SHOWPLAN ON;	Produce plan in XML format
SET STATISTICS XML ON;	Produce XML plan and execute query
SET STATISTICS PROFILE ON;	Produce text plan and execute query

Forward Engineering Can Be Initiated By Exiting / Saving The Diagram

The save option dialog box activates automatically upon exit.

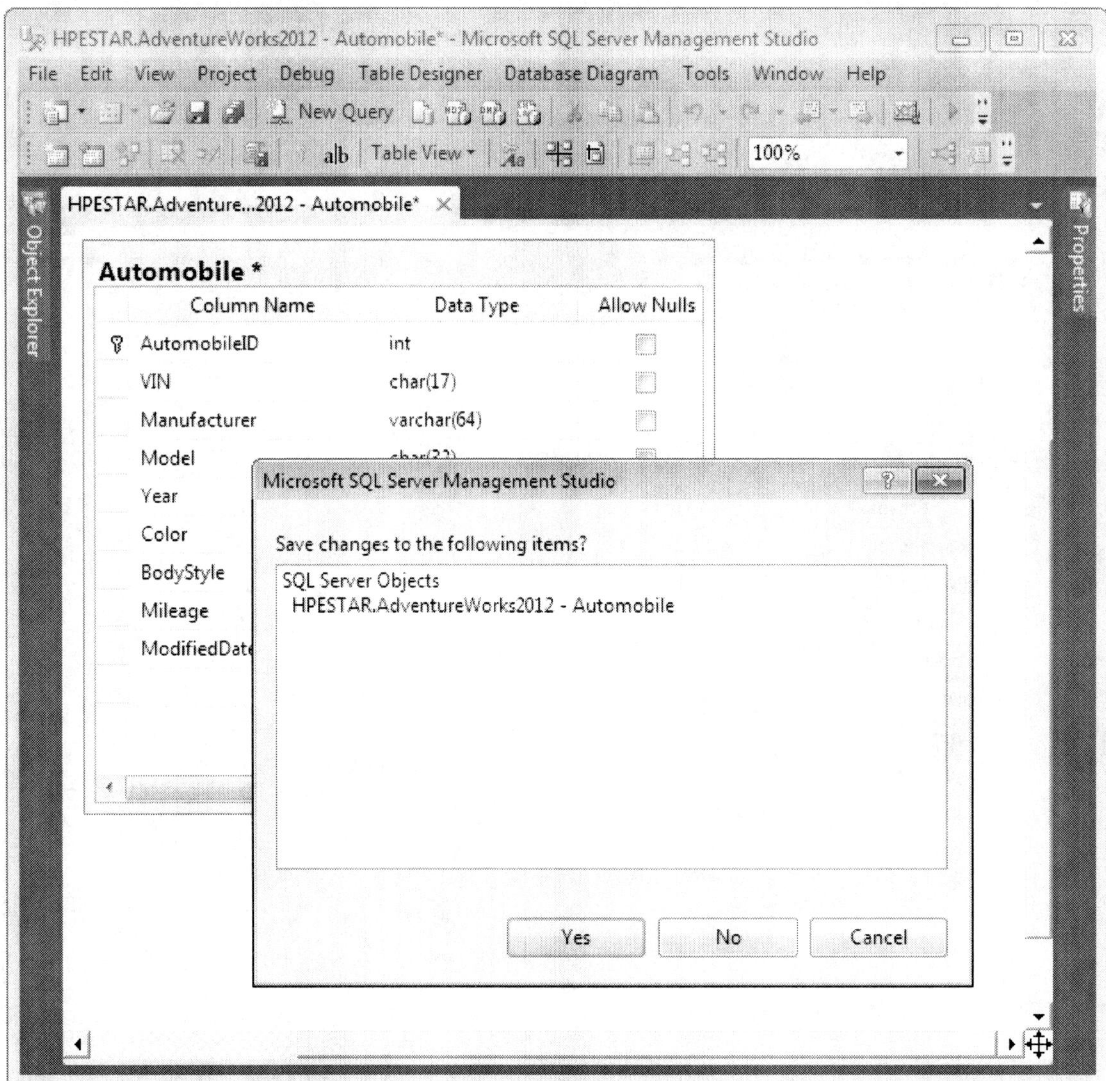

T-SQL Tidbits: PRIMARY KEY & Clustered Index

Generally each table should have a PRIMARY KEY. By default, SQL Server creates a unique clustered index for a PK unless NONCLUSTERED specified. Typical table has INT IDENTITY as surrogate primary key because that provides efficient (4 bytes) connection between tables in JOINs. The clustered index can be placed on a column which is searched for ranges of data. Since there can only be one clustered index on a table, it has to be applied to support business critical queries. The leaf level of a clustered index are the table data rows sorted on the clustered index key(s).

Save Change Script Panel Pops Up With The Generated T-SQL Change Script

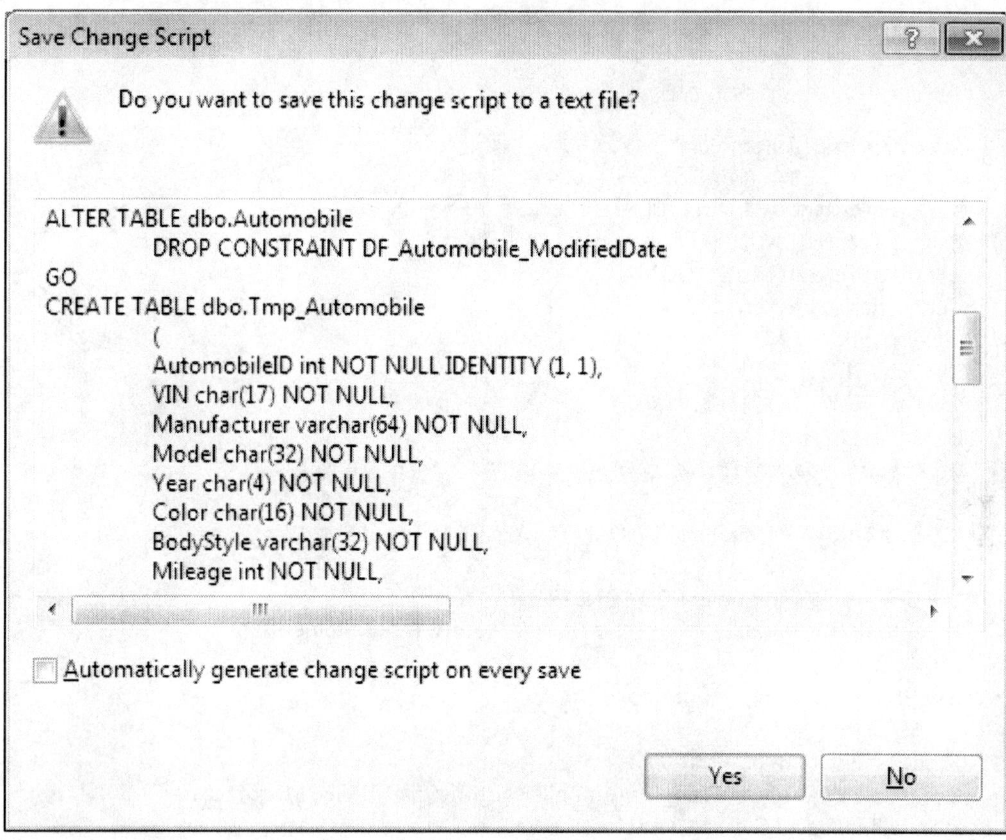

The generated T-SQL change script for changing Manufacturer data type to varchar(64).

```
/* To prevent any potential data loss issues, you should review this script in detail before running it
outside the context of the database designer.*/
BEGIN TRANSACTION
SET QUOTED_IDENTIFIER ON
SET ARITHABORT ON
SET NUMERIC_ROUNDABORT OFF
SET CONCAT_NULL_YIELDS_NULL ON
SET ANSI_NULLS ON
SET ANSI_PADDING ON
SET ANSI_WARNINGS ON
COMMIT
BEGIN TRANSACTION
GO
```

```
-- T-SQL script continued

ALTER TABLE dbo.Automobile
	DROP CONSTRAINT DF_Automobile_ModifiedDate
GO


CREATE TABLE dbo.Tmp_Automobile		(

	AutomobileID int NOT NULL IDENTITY (1, 1),
	VIN char(17) NOT NULL,
	Manufacturer varchar(64) NOT NULL,
	Model char(32) NOT NULL,
	Year char(4) NOT NULL,
	Color char(16) NOT NULL,
	BodyStyle varchar(32) NOT NULL,
	Mileage int NOT NULL,
	ModifiedDate date NOT NULL )  ON [PRIMARY]
GO
ALTER TABLE dbo.Tmp_Automobile SET (LOCK_ESCALATION = TABLE)
GO
ALTER TABLE dbo.Tmp_Automobile ADD CONSTRAINT
	DF_Automobile_ModifiedDate DEFAULT (getdate()) FOR ModifiedDate
GO
SET IDENTITY_INSERT dbo.Tmp_Automobile ON
GO
IF EXISTS(SELECT * FROM dbo.Automobile)
	 EXEC('INSERT INTO dbo.Tmp_Automobile (AutomobileID, VIN, Manufacturer, Model, Year,
Color, BodyStyle, Mileage, ModifiedDate)
		SELECT AutomobileID, VIN, CONVERT(varchar(64), Manufacturer), Model, Year, Color,
BodyStyle, Mileage, ModifiedDate FROM dbo.Automobile WITH (HOLDLOCK TABLOCKX)')
GO
SET IDENTITY_INSERT dbo.Tmp_Automobile OFF
GO
DROP TABLE dbo.Automobile
GO
EXECUTE sp_rename N'dbo.Tmp_Automobile', N'Automobile', 'OBJECT'
GO
ALTER TABLE dbo.Automobile ADD CONSTRAINT
	PK_Automobile PRIMARY KEY CLUSTERED
	(  AutomobileID
	) WITH( STATISTICS_NORECOMPUTE = OFF, IGNORE_DUP_KEY = OFF, ALLOW_ROW_LOCKS = ON,
ALLOW_PAGE_LOCKS = ON) ON [PRIMARY]
GO
COMMIT
```

Generate Change Script Option

Forward Engineering can also be initiated by the Generate Change Script option. The same option can be used when making any changes to the Diagram using the Diagram Tool.

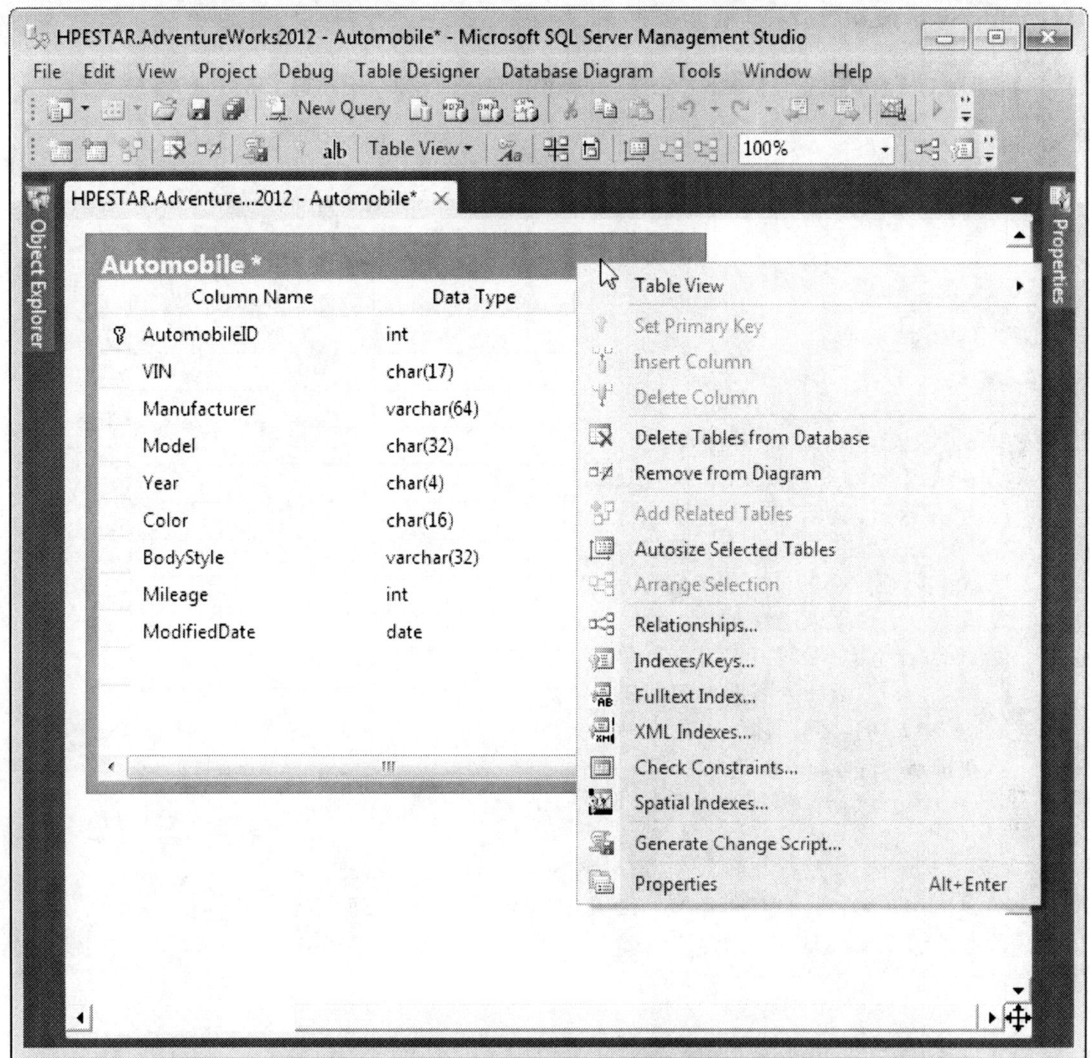

T-SQL Tidbits: String Concatenation Ye Olde Way & Using CONCAT()

Prior to SQL Server 2012 CONCAT() function, the "+" operator doubled as string concatenation operator.

```
DECLARE @text varchar(30) = 'Grand Canyon';
SELECT ConcatenatedString = @text + SPACE(1)+'State Park';              -- Grand Canyon State Park
SELECT ConcatenatedString = CONCAT (@text, SPACE(1), 'State Park');   -- Grand Canyon State Park
```

The Generated Script Of The Automobile Table By The Diagram Tool

```
USE [AdventureWorks2012]
GO

/****** Object:  Table [dbo].[Automobile]    Script Date: 7/22/2016 11:20:17 AM ******/
SET ANSI_NULLS ON
GO

SET QUOTED_IDENTIFIER ON
GO

SET ANSI_PADDING ON
GO

CREATE TABLE [dbo].[Automobile](
	[AutomobileID] [int] IDENTITY(1,1) NOT NULL,
	[VIN] [char](17) NOT NULL,
	[Manufacturer] [char](32) NOT NULL,
	[Model] [char](32) NOT NULL,
	[Year] [char](4) NOT NULL,
	[Color] [char](16) NOT NULL,
	[BodyStyle] [varchar](32) NOT NULL,
	[Mileage] [int] NOT NULL,
	[ModifiedDate] [date] NOT NULL,
 CONSTRAINT [PK_Automobile] PRIMARY KEY CLUSTERED
(
	[AutomobileID] ASC
)WITH (PAD_INDEX = OFF, STATISTICS_NORECOMPUTE = OFF, IGNORE_DUP_KEY = OFF,
ALLOW_ROW_LOCKS = ON, ALLOW_PAGE_LOCKS = ON) ON [PRIMARY]
) ON [PRIMARY]

GO

SET ANSI_PADDING ON
GO

ALTER TABLE [dbo].[Automobile] ADD  CONSTRAINT [DF_Automobile_ModifiedDate]
DEFAULT (getdate()) FOR [ModifiedDate]
GO
```

Scripting Single Database Object with Related Objects

The scripting feature works only through the graphical user interface (GUI) in SSMS Object Explorer. **There is no command to script a table.** Start with Right Click on the Banking.Account table.

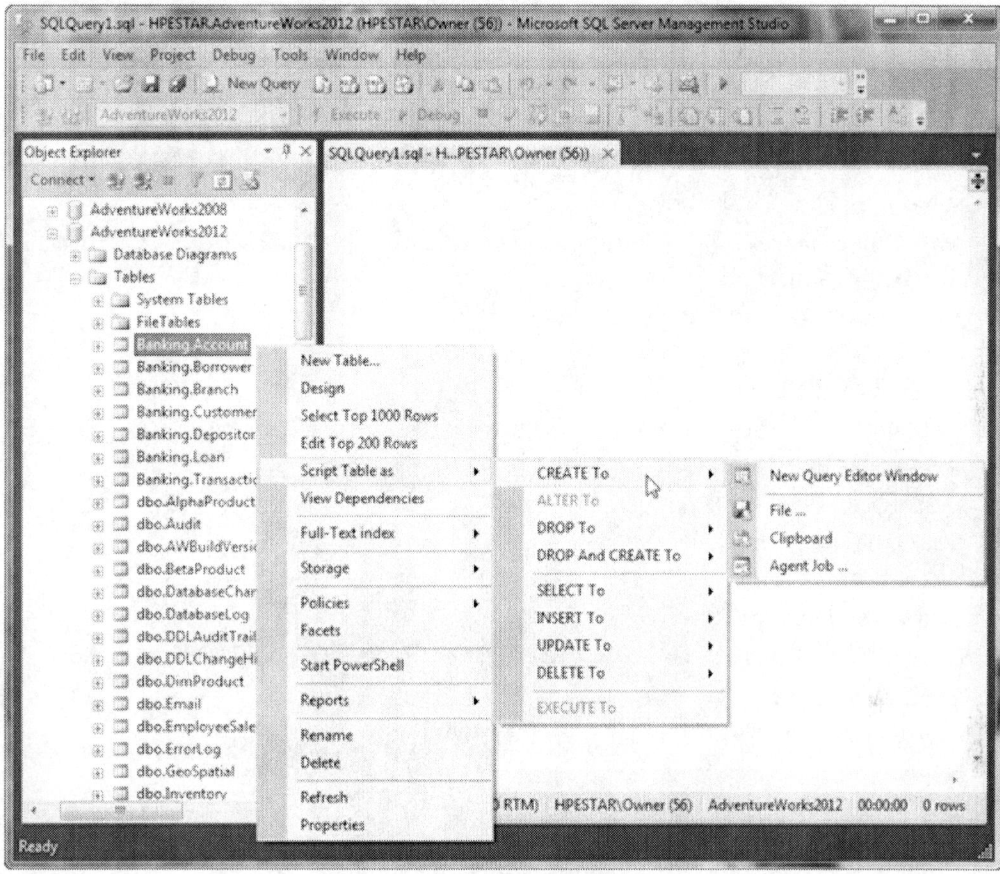

Generated script for the Banking.Account table and related objects.

```
USE [AdventureWorks2012]
GO
SET ANSI_NULLS ON
GO
SET QUOTED_IDENTIFIER ON
GO
SET ANSI_PADDING ON
GO
```

-- T-SQL script continued

```
CREATE TABLE [Banking].[Account](
	[AccountID] [int] IDENTITY(1,1) NOT NULL,
	[BranchID] [int] NOT NULL,
	[AccountNumber] [char](20) NOT NULL,
	[AccountType] [char](12) NOT NULL,
	[Balance] [money] NOT NULL,
	[ModifiedDate] [datetime] NULL,
PRIMARY KEY CLUSTERED
(
	[AccountID] ASC
)WITH (PAD_INDEX = OFF, STATISTICS_NORECOMPUTE = OFF, IGNORE_DUP_KEY = OFF,
ALLOW_ROW_LOCKS = ON,
ALLOW_PAGE_LOCKS = ON) ON [PRIMARY],
UNIQUE NONCLUSTERED
(	[AccountID] ASC
)WITH (PAD_INDEX = OFF, STATISTICS_NORECOMPUTE = OFF, IGNORE_DUP_KEY = OFF,
ALLOW_ROW_LOCKS = ON,
ALLOW_PAGE_LOCKS = ON) ON [PRIMARY],
UNIQUE NONCLUSTERED
(
	[AccountNumber] ASC
)WITH (PAD_INDEX = OFF, STATISTICS_NORECOMPUTE = OFF, IGNORE_DUP_KEY = OFF,
ALLOW_ROW_LOCKS = ON,
ALLOW_PAGE_LOCKS = ON) ON [PRIMARY]   ) ON [PRIMARY]
GO
SET ANSI_PADDING ON
GO
ALTER TABLE [Banking].[Account] ADD  DEFAULT (getdate()) FOR [ModifiedDate]
GO
```

```
ALTER TABLE [Banking].[Account]  WITH CHECK ADD FOREIGN KEY([BranchID])
REFERENCES [Banking].[Branch] ([BranchID])
ON DELETE CASCADE
GO

ALTER TABLE [Banking].[Account]  WITH CHECK ADD  CONSTRAINT [ATC]
CHECK  (([AccountType]='S' OR [AccountType]='C'))
GO
```

Scripting DB Objects With Script Wizard

The Script Wizard is a sophisticated tool for scripting out multiple objects, in fact all objects can be scripted in a single setup and execution. The generated script can be saved to single/multiple files, new query window or the Clipboard. The launching sequence of menus starts with Right Click on the database.

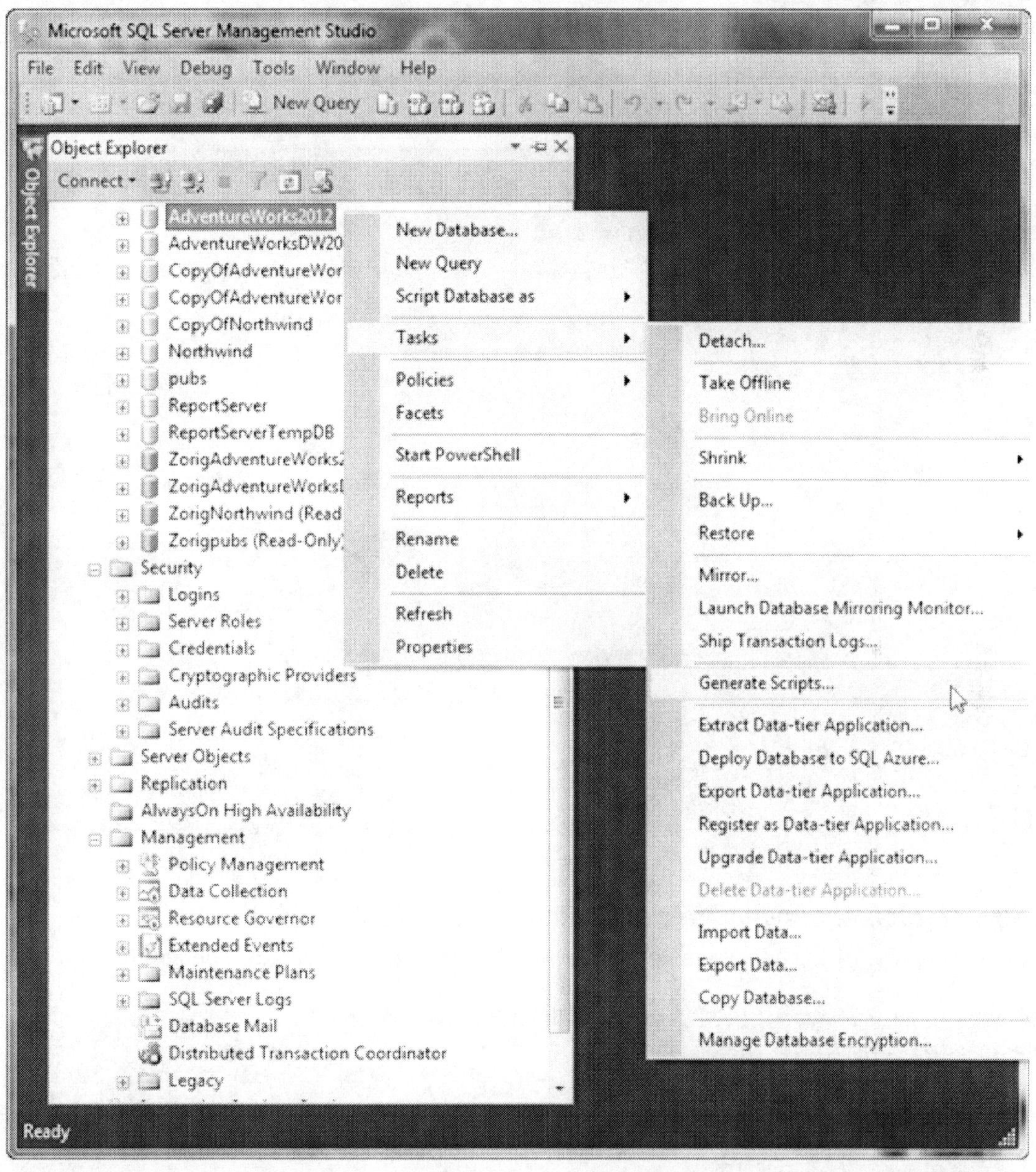

Script Wizard Optional Description Page

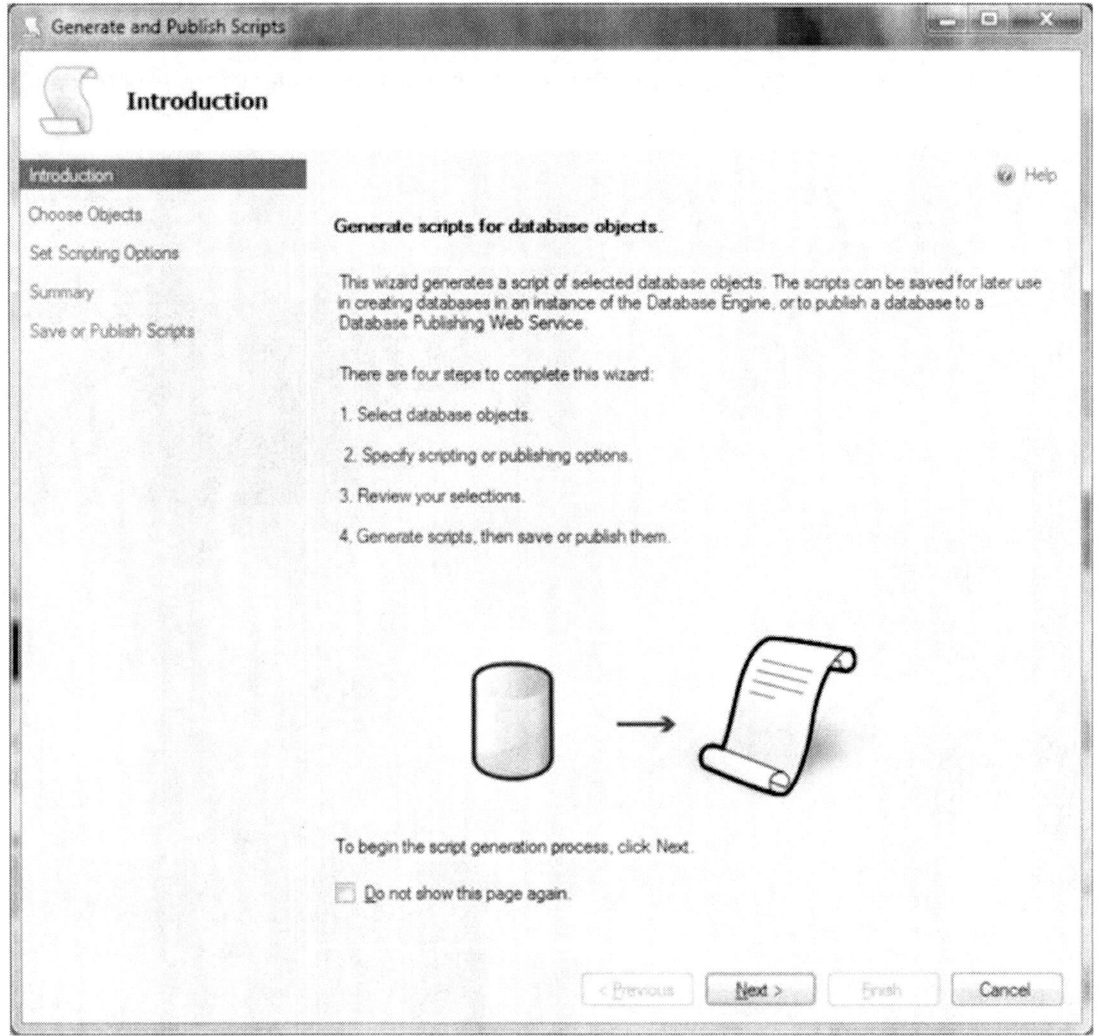

T-SQL Tidbits: Removing Special Characters from a String

We are using the [A-Z] style character range wildcard match to search for special characters.

```
DECLARE @string varchar(30) = CONCAT('Yellow',char(9),'Stone');
SELECT @string AS Input, IIF( PATINDEX(CONCAT('%[',char(9),'-',char(13),']%'), @string)> 0,
    REPLACE(REPLACE(REPLACE(REPLACE(REPLACE(@string,char(9),''),char(10),''),char(11),''),char(12),''),char(13),''),
          @string) AS Cleansed;
```

Input	Cleansed
Yellow Stone	YellowStone

Object Selection Panel For Scripting

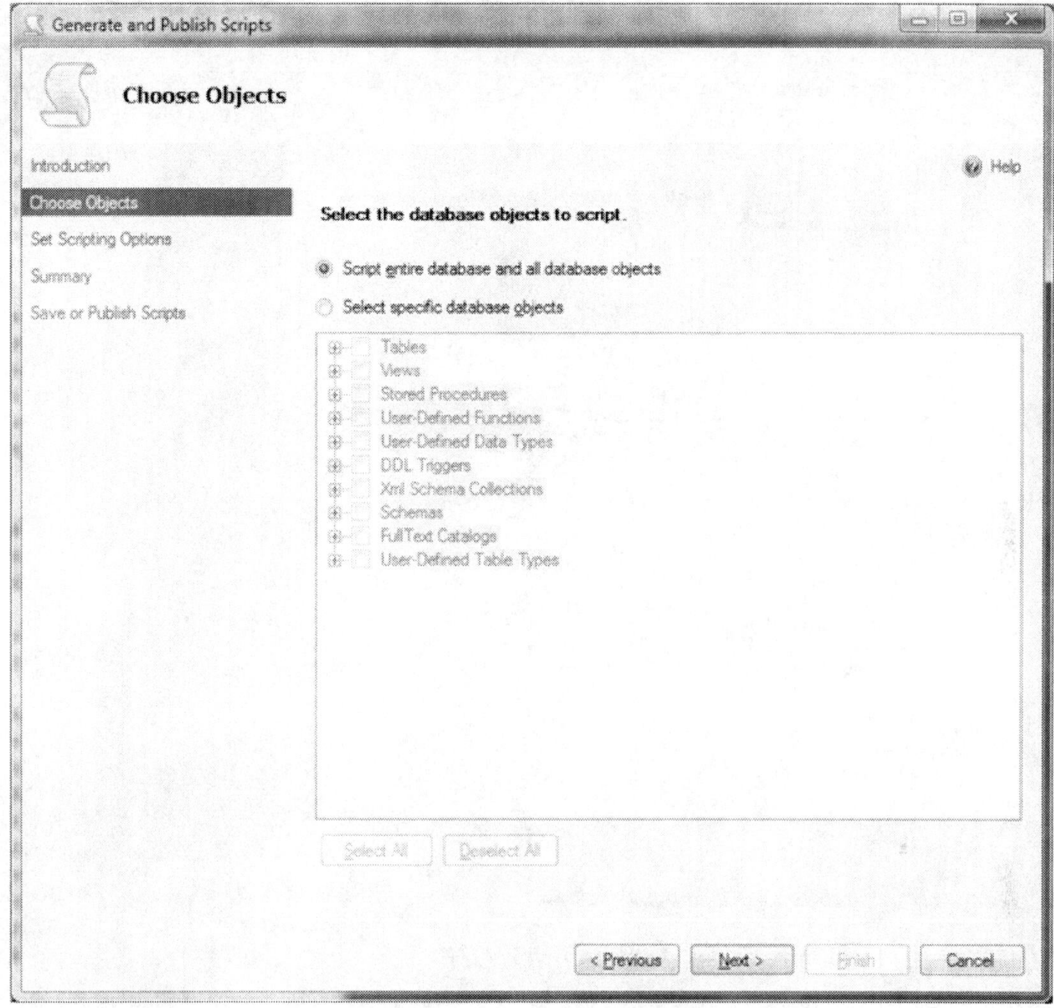

T-SQL Tidbits: Option RECOMPILE Maybe a Quick Fix for Parameter Sniffing

When a stored procedure executes in SSMS in 3 seconds, and 4 minutes when fetched by the application software, the likely culprit is parameter sniffing.

```
USE [AdventureWorks2012];                    -- Object delimiters used
DBCC DROPCLEANBUFFERS;                       -- Always use this command when testing in SSMS
EXECUTE  [dbo].[uspGetBillOfMaterials] 800, '20080205';
-- Change application code to:
EXECUTE  [dbo].[uspGetBillOfMaterials] 800, '20080205'  WITH RECOMPILE;
```

RECOMPILE option can also be included in sp definition.

Options can be set for generation, including scripting of related objects.

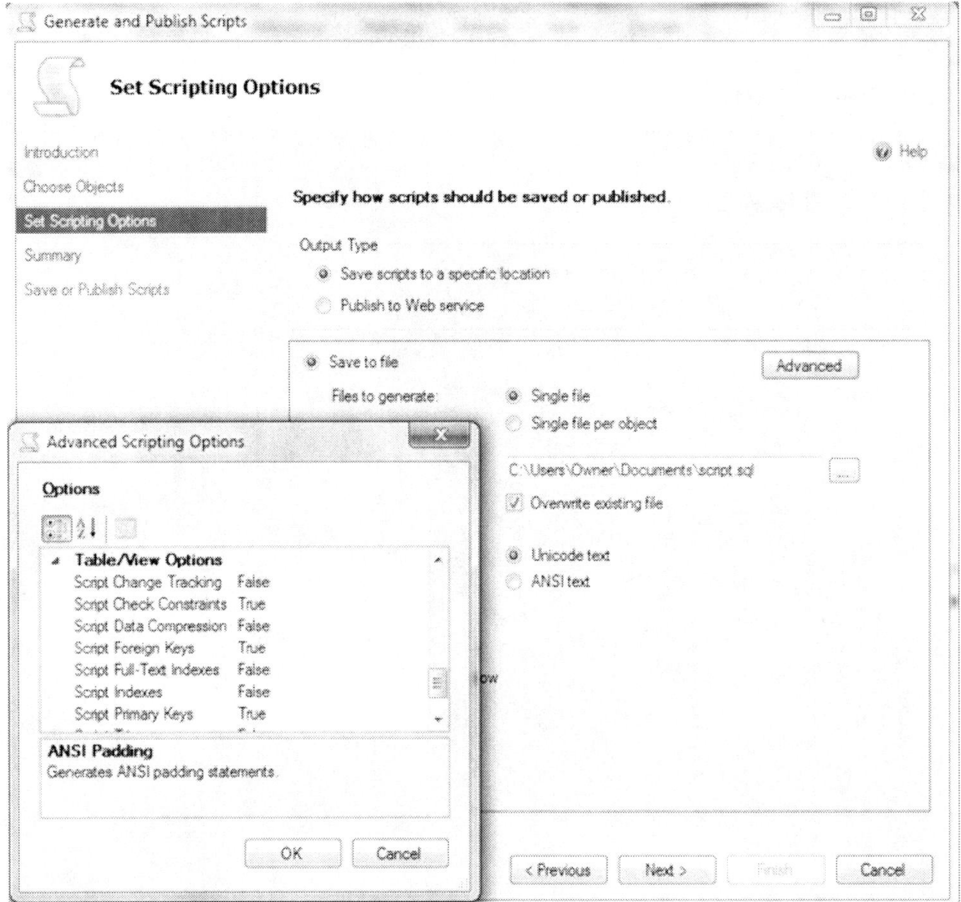

T-SQL Tidbits: Updating a Table through a CTE

Similarly to underlying table being updated through a view, a table can be updated through a CTE.

```
USE tempdb; SELECT ProductID, Name, ProductNumber, ListPrice, Color INTO Product
FROM AdventureWorks2012.Production.Product WHERE ProductSubcategoryID IS NOT NULL; -- (295 row(s) affected)
ALTER TABLE PRODUCT ADD CONSTRAINT pkProd PRIMARY KEY(ProductID);
```

```
WITH CTE AS (SELECT * FROM Product)  UPDATE CTE   SET Color = UPPER(Color)   WHERE Color = 'Blue';-- (26 row(s) affected)
```

```
SELECT * FROM Product ORDER BY Color;
```

ProductID	Name	ProductNumber	ListPrice	Color
978	Touring-3000 Blue, 44	BK-T18U-44	742.35	BLUE
979	Touring-3000 Blue, 50	BK-T18U-50	742.35	BLUE
842	Touring-Panniers, Large	PA-T100	125.00	Grey
855	Men's Bib-Shorts, S	SB-M891-S	89.99	Multi

The script generated by the Script Wizard for the Banking.Loan table and related objects

```
USE [AdventureWorks2012]
GO
SET ANSI_NULLS ON
GO
SET QUOTED_IDENTIFIER ON
GO
SET ANSI_PADDING ON
GO
CREATE TABLE [Banking].[Loan](
	[LoanID] [int] IDENTITY(1,1) NOT NULL,
	[BranchID] [int] NOT NULL,
	[LoanNumber] [char](20) NOT NULL,
	[LoanType] [varchar](30) NOT NULL,
	[Amount] [money] NOT NULL,
	[ModifiedDate] [datetime] NULL,
PRIMARY KEY CLUSTERED
(	[LoanID] ASC
)WITH (PAD_INDEX = OFF, STATISTICS_NORECOMPUTE = OFF, IGNORE_DUP_KEY = OFF,
ALLOW_ROW_LOCKS = ON, ALLOW_PAGE_LOCKS = ON) ON [PRIMARY],
UNIQUE NONCLUSTERED
(
	[LoanID] ASC
)WITH (PAD_INDEX = OFF, STATISTICS_NORECOMPUTE = OFF, IGNORE_DUP_KEY = OFF,
ALLOW_ROW_LOCKS = ON, ALLOW_PAGE_LOCKS = ON) ON [PRIMARY],
UNIQUE NONCLUSTERED
(
	[LoanNumber] ASC
)WITH (PAD_INDEX = OFF, STATISTICS_NORECOMPUTE = OFF, IGNORE_DUP_KEY = OFF,
ALLOW_ROW_LOCKS = ON, ALLOW_PAGE_LOCKS = ON) ON [PRIMARY]
) ON [PRIMARY]

GO
SET ANSI_PADDING ON
GO
ALTER TABLE [Banking].[Loan] ADD  DEFAULT (getdate()) FOR [ModifiedDate]
GO
ALTER TABLE [Banking].[Loan]  WITH CHECK ADD FOREIGN KEY([BranchID])
REFERENCES [Banking].[Branch] ([BranchID])
ON DELETE CASCADE
GO
```

SEQUENCE Objects

Sequence objects are new in SQL Server 2012. They are similar to the INT IDENTITY(1,1) sequence, however, there is a big difference: they don't "live" inside a table. They are table independent database objects. T-SQL demonstration script displays the flexibility of the new method for sequence number management.

```
-- Create a sequence object similar to INT IDENTITY(1,1)
CREATE SEQUENCE seqPurchaseOrder
AS INT
START WITH 1   INCREMENT BY 1;
GO
```

```
SELECT NEXT VALUE FOR seqPurchaseOrder;
GO 50
/* 1 2 3 .... 50 */
```

```
SELECT NEXT VALUE FOR seqPurchaseOrder;
GO
-- 51
```

```
SELECT NextOrderNo = NEXT VALUE FOR seqPurchaseOrder;
-- 52
```

```
SELECT NEXT VALUE FOR seqPurchaseOrder as NextOrderNo;
-- 54
```

```
EXEC sp_help seqPurchaseOrder;
```

Name	Owner	Type	Created_datetime
seqPurchaseOrder	dbo	sequence object	2016-06-27 09:14:32.940

```
DECLARE @List TABLE (id int identity(1,1) primary key, i int);
INSERT @List(i) SELECT NEXT VALUE FOR seqPurchaseOrder;
INSERT @List(i) SELECT NEXT VALUE FOR seqPurchaseOrder;
INSERT @List(i) SELECT NEXT VALUE FOR seqPurchaseOrder;
INSERT @List(i) SELECT NEXT VALUE FOR seqPurchaseOrder;
INSERT @List(i) VALUES (NEXT VALUE FOR seqPurchaseOrder);
SELECT * FROM @List
```

id	i
1	55
2	56
3	57
4	58
5	59

SEQUENCE Object Sharing

SEQUENCE is visible in other connections/session as well not only now but until it exists.

Create a new connection to test NEXT VALUE for seqPurchaseOrder.

```
-- Check current value
SELECT current_value
FROM sys.sequences
WHERE name = 'seqPurchaseOrder';
-- 58
```

```
-- Check metadata
SELECT name, object_id, schema_name(schema_id) as SchemaName, type
FROM sys.sequences;
```

name	object_id	SchemaName	type
seqPurchaseOrder	1338487847	dbo	SO

```
DECLARE @List TABLE (id int identity(1,1) primary key,
            i int default (NEXT VALUE FOR seqPurchaseOrder));
INSERT @List(i) DEFAULT VALUES;
INSERT @List(i) DEFAULT VALUES;
INSERT @List(i) DEFAULT VALUES;
INSERT @List(i) DEFAULT VALUES;
INSERT @List(i)DEFAULT VALUES;
SELECT * FROM @List
```

id	i
1	59
2	60
3	61
4	62
5	63

```
DROP SEQUENCE seqPurchaseOrder;
GO
```

```
SELECT NEXT VALUE FOR seqPurchaseOrder;
```

/* Error Message: Msg 208, Level 16, State 1, Line 2

Invalid object name 'seqPurchaseOrder'. */

Cyclical Sequence Objects

We can create cyclical sequence objects as well for enumerating cyclical temporal objects such as weekdays or months.

```
CREATE SEQUENCE seqCycleSeven
AS TINYINT
START WITH 1  INCREMENT BY 1  MINVALUE  1   MAXVALUE  7  CYCLE
GO
```

```
CREATE TABLE #Weekdays ( ID INT IDENTITY(1,1) PRIMARY KEY, Weekday nchar(20));
GO
```

```
-- Populate table with days progressing by addition of cycle number to current day
INSERT INTO #Weekdays
SELECT DATENAME(dw, dateadd(dd,NEXT VALUE for seqCycleSeven,CURRENT_TIMESTAMP));
GO 20
```

```
SELECT * FROM #Weekdays ORDER BY ID;
GO
```

ID	Weekday
1	Tuesday
2	Wednesday
3	Thursday
4	Friday
5	Saturday
6	Sunday
7	Monday
8	Tuesday
9	Wednesday
10	Thursday
11	Friday
12	Saturday
13	Sunday
14	Monday
15	Tuesday
16	Wednesday
17	Thursday
18	Friday
19	Saturday
20	Sunday

```
DROP SEQUENCE seqCycleSeven;  DROP TABLE #Weekdays;
```

Getting the Source Code with sp_helptext

The sp_helptext system procedure can be applied to get the source code for some objects, but not all. **Table source code can only be obtained with GUI scripting in Object Explorer.**

```
EXEC sp_helptext 'sp_who'
GO
-- Command(s) completed successfully. - 94 rows - Partial results.
```

```
CREATE PROCEDURE sys.Sp_who --- 1995/11/28 15:48
 @loginame SYSNAME = NULL --or 'active'
AS
  DECLARE @spidlow  INT,
      @spidhigh INT,
      @spid    INT,
      @sid     VARBINARY(85)

  SELECT @spidlow = 0,
     @spidhigh = 32767

  IF ( @loginame IS NOT NULL
     AND Upper(@loginame COLLATE latin1_general_ci_as) = 'ACTIVE' )
   BEGIN
     SELECT spid,
        ecid,
        status,
        loginame=Rtrim(loginame),
        hostname,
        blk=CONVERT(CHAR(5), blocked),
        dbname = CASE
              WHEN dbid = 0 THEN NULL
              WHEN dbid <> 0 THEN Db_name(dbid)
             END,
        cmd,
        request_id
     FROM   sys.sysprocesses_ex
     WHERE  spid >= @spidlow
        AND spid <= @spidhigh
        AND Upper(cmd) <> 'AWAITING COMMAND'

     RETURN ( 0 )
   END
```

CHAPTER 7: Normal Forms & Database Normalization

The Goals of Database Normalizaton

Database normalization is the design technique of logically organizing data in a database:

- Data should uniquely be addressable in a database by table, row and column identification - like x, y, z coordinates in 3D space.
- Data redundancy (storing the same data in more than one table) should be avoided.
- Data dependency (a property is fully dependent on the PRIMARY KEY) should ensure that a piece of data gets into the right table or if there is none, a new one is created.

The first goal is relatively easy to achieve yet data duplication in a table is a constant issue plaguing database installations. The second goal is simple as well yet it conflicts with deep-seated human insecurity of not seeing all the data together. The third goal on the other hand requires careful design considerations, it can be challenging for complex data relationships or if the database designer is not familiar with the application. If an OLTP database with many data access points is not normalized, the result is inefficiency in database application development and maintenance which can be quite costly to a company for years to come. Metadata query to list all FOREIGN KEYs in NorthWind followed by a high level database diagram.

```
select    fkschema = fk.constraint_schema,  fktable = fk.table_name, fkcolumn = fk.column_name,
          pkcolumn = pk.column_name,   pktable = pk.table_name, pkschema = pk.table_schema,
          fkname = rc.constraint_name
from  northwind.information_schema.referential_constraints rc
          inner join northwind.information_schema.key_column_usage fk
                    on fk.constraint_name = rc.constraint_name
          inner join northwind.information_schema.key_column_usage pk
                    on pk.constraint_name = rc.unique_constraint_name
where    fk.ordinal_position = pk.ordinal_position order by fkschema, fktable, fkcolumn;
```

fkschema	fktable	fkcolumn	pkcolumn	pktable	pkschema	fkname
dbo	CustomerCustomerDemo	CustomerID	CustomerID	Customers	dbo	FK_CustomerCustomerDemo_Customers
dbo	CustomerCustomerDemo	CustomerTypeID	CustomerTypeID	CustomerDemographics	dbo	FK_CustomerCustomerDemo
dbo	Employees	ReportsTo	EmployeeID	Employees	dbo	FK_Employees_Employees
dbo	EmployeeTerritories	EmployeeID	EmployeeID	Employees	dbo	FK_EmployeeTerritories_Employees
dbo	EmployeeTerritories	TerritoryID	TerritoryID	Territories	dbo	FK_EmployeeTerritories_Territories
dbo	Order Details	OrderID	OrderID	Orders	dbo	FK_Order_Details_Orders
dbo	Order Details	ProductID	ProductID	Products	dbo	FK_Order_Details_Products
dbo	Orders	CustomerID	CustomerID	Customers	dbo	FK_Orders_Customers
dbo	Orders	EmployeeID	EmployeeID	Employees	dbo	FK_Orders_Employees
dbo	Orders	ShipVia	ShipperID	Shippers	dbo	FK_Orders_Shippers

Orders & Related Tables Diagram in Northwind

The database diagram clearly shows the central role of the Orders table at a company which is a reseller not a manufacturer.

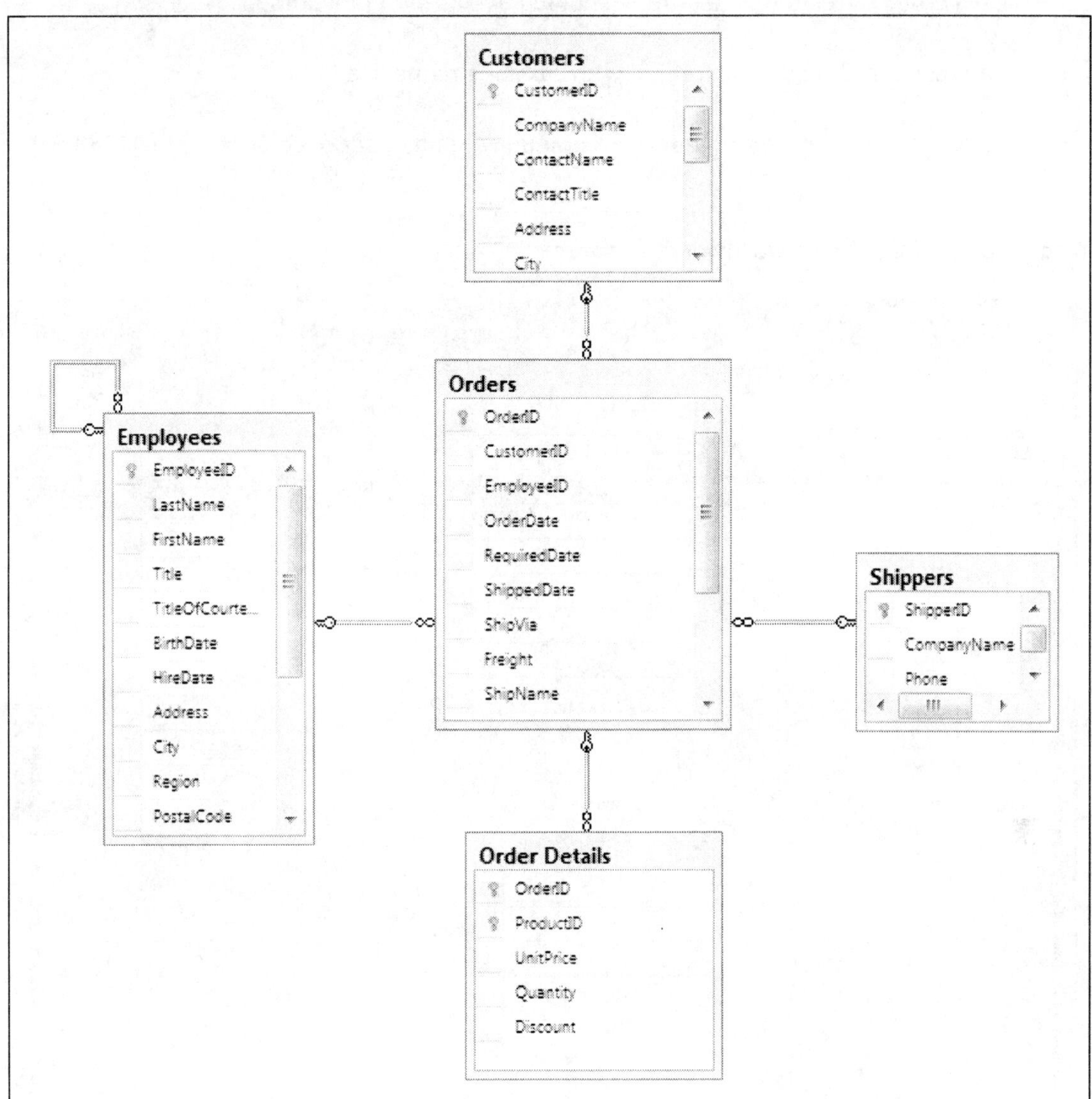

T-SQL Tidbits: What is Nondeterministic?

Nondeterministic functions may return different results each time they are called with the same input. Examples: @@ROWCOUNT, @@TRANCOUNT, getdate(), newid(), patindex() and more.

First Normal Form (1NF)

The first normal form establishes RDBMS basics. The rules make common sense.

- Each group of related data (entity) should have its own table (no piggybacking data).
- Each column should be identified with a unique name in a table.
- Each row should be identified with a unique column or set of columns (PRIMARY KEY).

Selected tables (entities) in Northwind database.

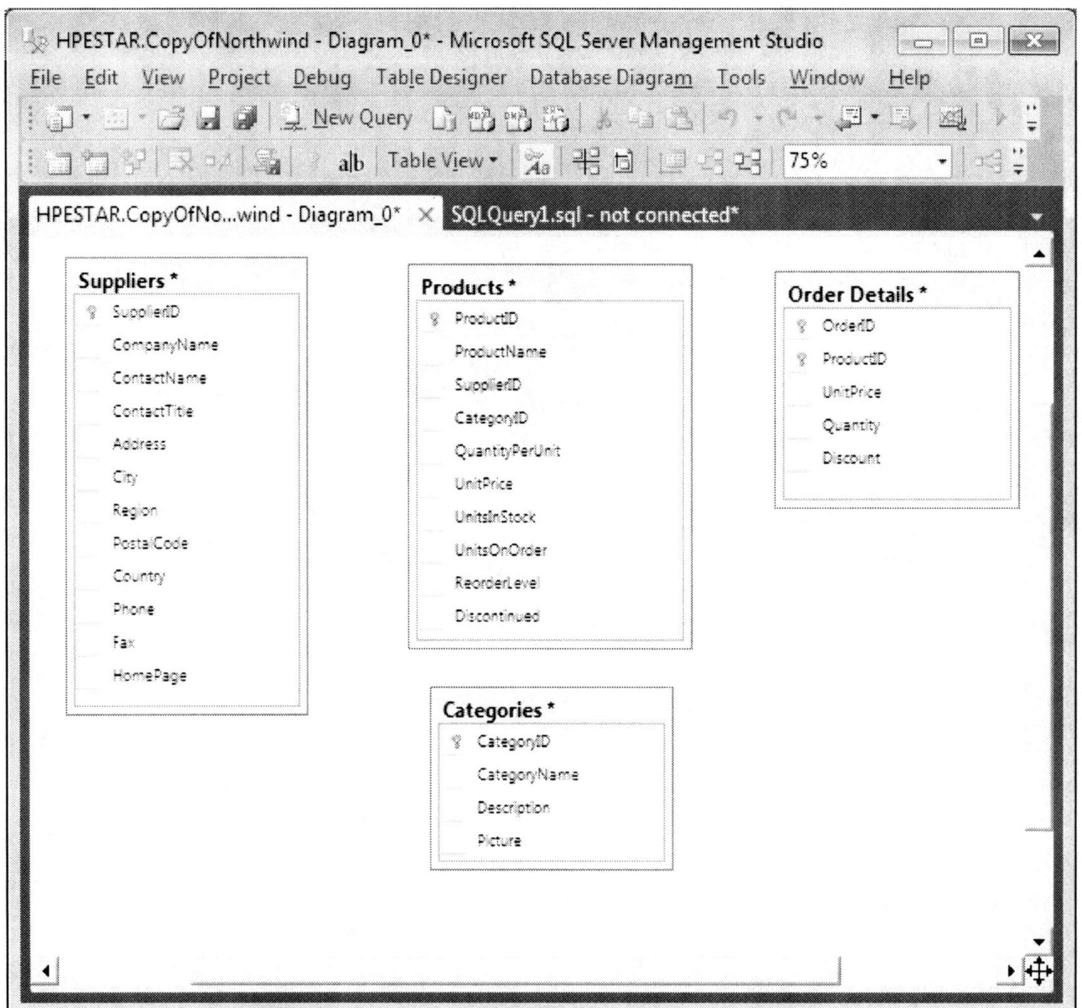

Second Normal Form (2NF)

The Second Normal Form addresses the issue of piggybacking data on a related table.

- Tables are in First Normal Form.
- Remove subsets of data that apply to multiple rows of a table and create a separate table for them.
- Create relationships between these new tables and their predecessors through the use of FOREIGN KEYs.

The tacit assumption here that there was no logical data modeling or that had a mistake. The database designer has created a set of tables and now taking a second look to see if all data belong to that table. Frequently the design starts with lead database developer preparing a first version of the design. Only big companies can afford the "luxury" of logical data modeling and professional database designer. That has to be qualified with a little known fact. Even a small company can hire a professional database designer for a month, surely money well spent. Categories table can easily piggyback on the Products table. Being a separate table increases the usefulness, flexibility and expandability of the design.

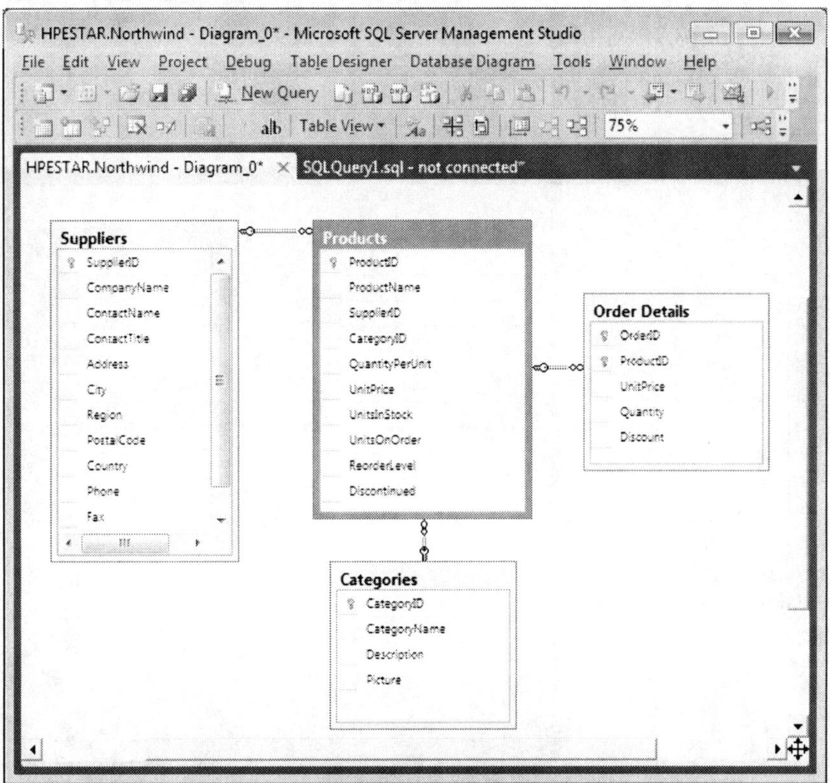

Third Normal Form (3NF)

The Third Normal Form addresses the issue of storing the data in the appropriate table.

- Tables are in Second Normal Form.
- Remove columns that are not dependent upon the PRIMARY KEY and move them to the correct table.

The royalty and ytd_sales columns are not fully dependent on the title_id PRIMARY KEY. In fact royalty schedule is specified in the roysched table and the dependency includes quantity sold. A view (virtual table) can be setup to return the current royalties based on books sold and the royalty schedule. A more appropriate table for ytd_sales would be saleshist (SalesHistory). The inclusion of the time dependent dynamic ytd_sales column is suspicious right off the bat since all the other columns are static.

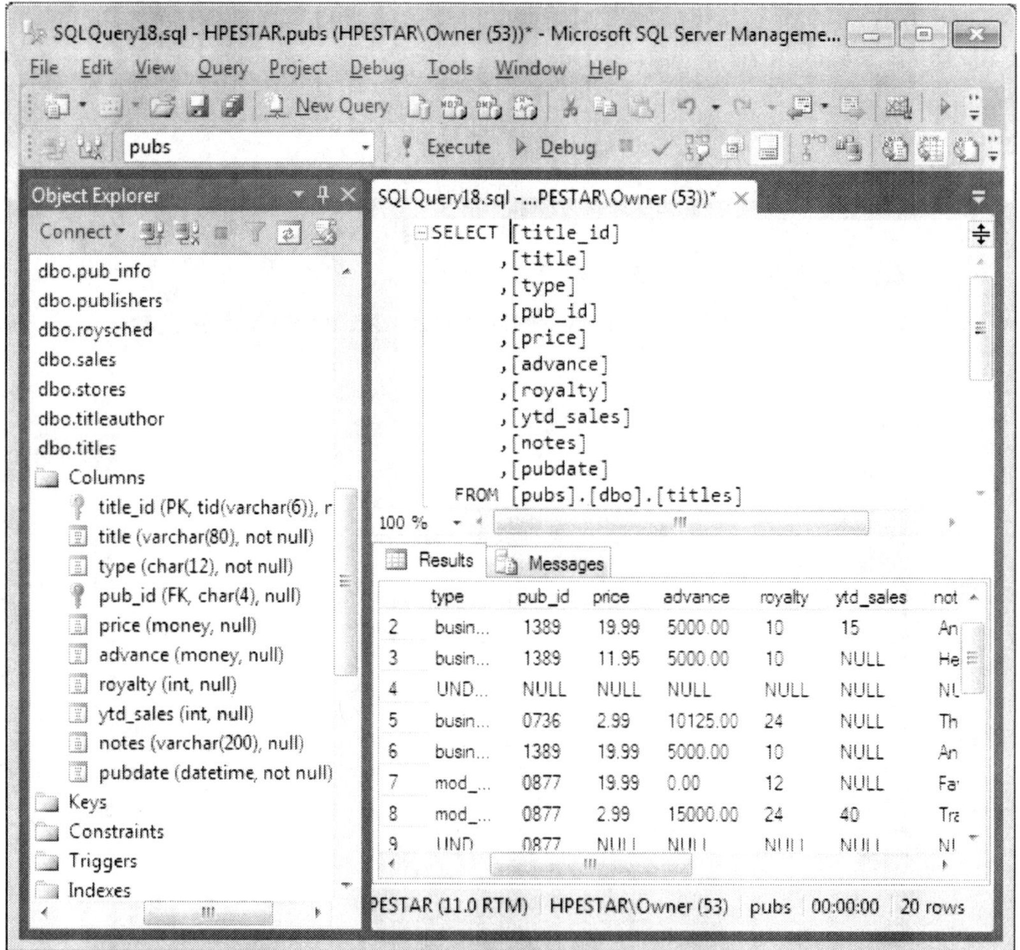

Fourth Normal Form (4NF)

The Fourth Normal Form addresses the issue of subtle data dependency:

- Tables are in Third Normal Form.
- A relation should not have multi-valued dependencies.

If we look at "Road-650 Black, 44" and "Road-650 Red, 44" bikes in Production.Product we see that they are the same bike with different color. So it would be sufficient to store only a single row "Road-650, 44" and setup a junction table between the Product table and the (new) Color table to indicate the color variations and other dependent information. We can see that the color occurs in 3 columns: Name, ProductNumber (first letter of color) and Color. By doing 4NF normalization we can remove the color reference from the Name and ProductNumber columns.

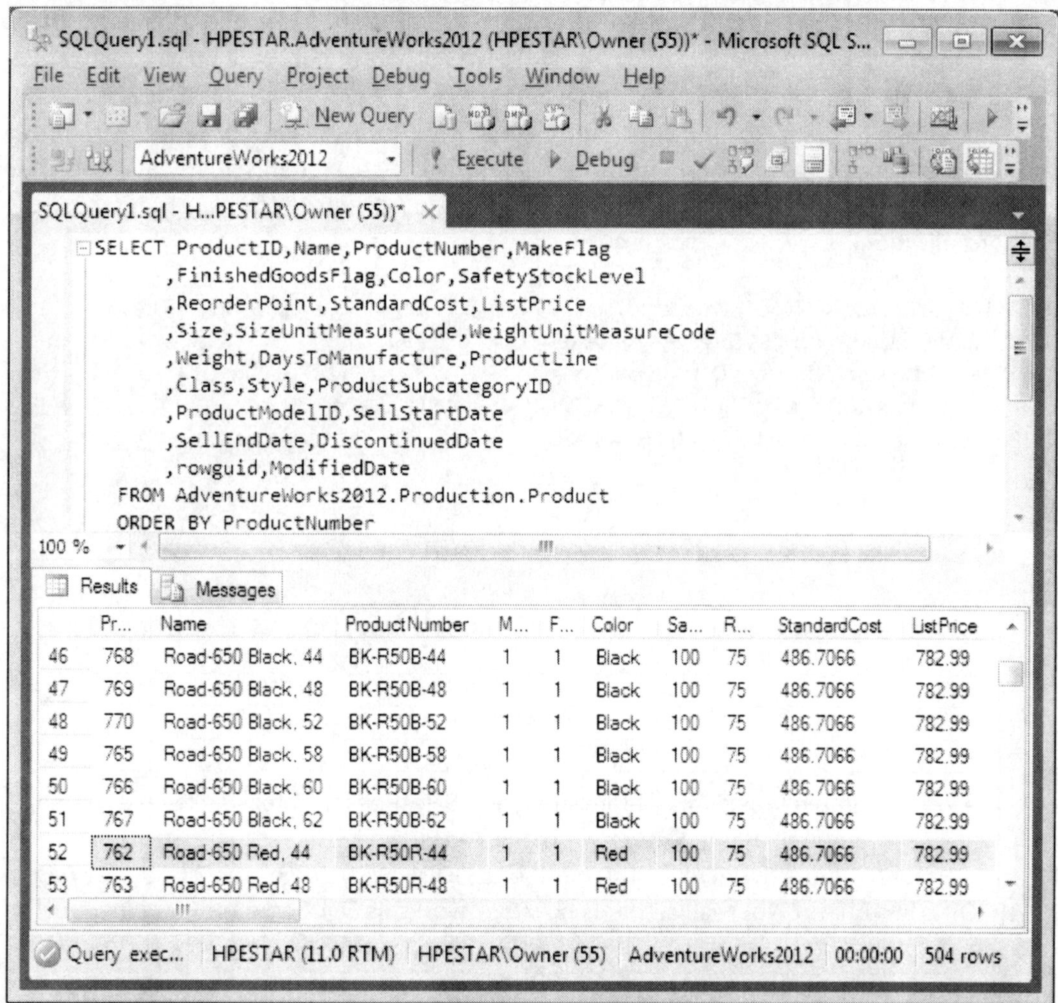

Database Denormalizaton

Database denormalization is a technique to reduce the number of tables in a normalized database. The author personally disagrees with this process: why would you go into the trouble and expense of creating a normalized database and then ruin it? Regardless of the author's opinion, denormalization is an accepted notion in the database industry. Too many tables require too many JOINs, that is the underlying justification. The trouble with this process is two-fold:

- There is no guideline when to stop with denormalization, 10% table reduction, 50%?
- Also, there are no guidelines as to which tables to eliminate when denormalizing.

If you eliminate too many tables you may just end up with a messy database instead of the original neat & efficient 3NF database thus creating a potential disaster for your employer. Typically you would look at the small static tables as candidates for elimination which are not FOREIGN KEY referenced from many tables. There are precise guidelines how to achieve a normalized database. It is a scientific process. Denormalization is not. Performance is another reason mentioned for denormalization, but that is generally not a valid claim. There are much better ways to achieve good performance than denormalizing a well-designed database system. Hypothetically, let's take a look at low population tables in AdventureWorks2012, as candidates for denormalization.

```
SELECT  TOP 10 SCHEMA_NAME(schema_id)+'.'+o.name AS TableName, max(i.rows) AS Rows
FROM    sys.sysobjects o INNER JOIN sys.sysindexes i   ON o.id = i.id
        INNER JOIN sys.objects oo     ON o.id = oo.object_id
WHERE   xtype = 'u' AND OBJECTPROPERTY(o.id,N'IsUserTable') = 1
GROUP BY schema_id, o.name ORDER BY Rows ASC;
```

TableName	Rows
dbo.ErrorLog	0
dbo.AWBuildVersion	1
Person.PhoneNumberType	3
HumanResources.Shift	3
Sales.ShoppingCartItem	3
Production.ProductCategory	4
Production.ProductReview	4
Production.Illustration	5
Purchasing.ShipMethod	5
Person.AddressType	6

Tables like PhoneNumberType, Shift, Shipmethod and SalesReason can likely be eliminated without dire consequences. However, why ruin a well-designed 3NF database such as AdventureWorks2012 just to decrease the number of JOINs with one or two? Is it annoying to have 10 JOINs in a query? Not really. That is how SQL works. Is SQL Server going to be much faster with 8 JOINs as opposed to 10 JOINs? No, there is no such a rule in query optimization.

Better Alternative to Denormalization

The best alternative is to use views for frequently used queries to avoid building JOINs again and again. The results of SELECT from a view must be sorted with ORDER BY just like the case for tables. There is no way around it. Demonstration of the powerful method.

```
USE AdventureWorks;
SELECT
                V.Name                                        AS Vendor,
                CONCAT(C.LastName, ', ', C.FirstName)         AS Contact,
                CT.Name                                       AS Title
FROM Person.Contact AS C
  INNER JOIN Purchasing.VendorContact VC
                ON C.ContactID = VC.ContactID
  INNER JOIN Person.ContactType CT
                ON CT.ContactTypeID = VC.ContactTypeID
  INNER JOIN Purchasing.Vendor V
                ON V.VendorID = VC.VendorID
ORDER BY Vendor, Contact;
-- (156 row(s) affected)
```

```
CREATE VIEW vVendorContact
AS
SELECT
                V.Name                                        AS Vendor,
                CONCAT(C.LastName, ', ', C.FirstName)         AS Contact,
                CT.Name                                       AS Title
FROM Person.Contact AS C
  INNER JOIN Purchasing.VendorContact VC     ON C.ContactID = VC.ContactID
  INNER JOIN Person.ContactType CT           ON CT.ContactTypeID = VC.ContactTypeID
  INNER JOIN Purchasing.Vendor V             ON V.VendorID = VC.VendorID
GO
```

```
SELECT TOP 5 * FROM vVendorContact ORDER BY Vendor, Contact;
```

Vendor	Contact	Title
A. Datum Corporation	Pellow, Frank	Assistant Sales Agent
A. Datum Corporation	Wilkie, Jay	Sales Agent
A. Datum Corporation	Yu, Wei	Sales Manager
Advanced Bicycles	Moeller, Jonathan	Sales Associate
Advanced Bicycles	Wilson, James	Sales Manager

We have created from the 4 tables JOIN, a very simple to use, very easy to remember view.

Ten Most Common Database Design Mistakes

Along his database career the author found the following list of common design issues:

- Not involving systems analysts and/or subject matter experts in conceptual design.
- Not employing accomplished database designer / lead developer to implement 3NF design standards.
- Denormalizing a well-designed database.
- Not having NATURAL KEY in addition to INT IDENTITY(1,1) SURROGATE PRIMARY KEY.
- Poor documentation & lack of naming convention for the project.
- Not using PRIMARY KEY, FOREIGN KEY, UNIQUE , CHECK & DEFAULT constraints to protect data integrity.
- Using client programs for data management instead of server side stored procedures, functions & views.
- Using triggers to fix design or client software problems.
- Not following the solution implementation hierarchy: constraints -> stored procedures -> triggers -> client SW.
- Lack of formal Quality Assurance process.

Working for a Company with Messy Database Design

In your career you may work for companies with proper 3NF design databases, companies with messy databases or somewhere in the middle. It is a joy to work in 3NF environment. On the other hand, if the database is badly designed, or more accurately lacks design, you have to be careful in criticizing it because you can pick up enemies quickly or even get fired. Badly designed database usually becomes an IT department political issue instead of remaining a technical issue. Most companies don't want to invest in redesigning the database properly. In such a situation you have to accept working with poorly designed databases, enjoy your nice paycheck and wait for an opportunity when new tables or database is needed to create proper 3NF design.

Query to List All Table Sizes in a Database

T-SQL script to list all table sizes in AdventureWorks2012 database. Note: the tables are uniquely named in AdventureWorks databases, so there are no duplicates if the schema name is not used. This assumption though not true generally. Objects can be named the same in different schemas.

```
declare @TableSpace table (TableName sysname, RowsK varchar(32), -- table variable
          ReservedMB varchar(32), DataMB varchar(32),
           IndexMB varchar(32), UnusedMB varchar(32));

insert @TableSpace
exec sp_MSforeachtable @command1="exec sp_spaceused '?';"  -- undocumented system procedure

update @TableSpace set RowsK = CONVERT(varchar,  1+convert(int, RowsK)/1024)
update @TableSpace set ReservedMB = CONVERT(varchar,
                  1+convert(int,LEFT(ReservedMB, charindex(' K', ReservedMB,-1)))/1024);
update @TableSpace set DataMB = CONVERT(varchar,
                  1+convert(int,LEFT(DataMB, charindex(' K', DataMB,-1)))/1024);
update @TableSpace set IndexMB = CONVERT(varchar,
                  convert(int,LEFT(IndexMB, charindex(' K', IndexMB,-1)))/1024);
update @TableSpace set UnusedMB = CONVERT(varchar,
                  convert(int,LEFT(UnusedMB, charindex(' K', UnusedMB,-1)))/1024);

select * from @TableSpace order by convert(int,DataMB) desc;
go
-- (71 row(s) affected) -- Partial results.
```

TableName	RowsK	ReservedMB	DataMB	IndexMB	UnusedMB
Person	20	84	30	51	2
SalesOrderDetail	119	18	10	6	1
DatabaseLog	2	7	7	0	0
TransactionHistory	111	11	7	3	0
WorkOrderRouting	66	8	6	1	0
SalesOrderHeader	31	9	6	2	0
WorkOrder	71	7	5	2	0
TransactionHistoryArchive	88	9	5	3	0
ProductPhoto	1	3	3	0	0
Address	20	6	3	2	0
CreditCard	19	3	2	0	0
EmailAddress	20	4	2	1	0
Password	20	2	2	0	0
PersonPhone	20	3	2	0	0
SalesTerritory	1	1	1	0	0
PhoneNumberType	1	1	1	0	0
Product	1	1	1	0	0
SalesTerritoryHistory	1	1	1	0	0
SalesPersonQuotaHistory	1	1	1	0	0
Employee	1	1	1	0	0

CHAPTER 8: Functional Database Design

Types of Table Relationships

The most frequent relationship is one-to-many (or many-to-one) indicating many FOREIGN KEY references to a single PRIMARY KEY table row. Example: Products & ProductCategories; A product category may have 50 different products. The next most popular one is many-to-many relationship indicating that a single row in Table Alpha can reference multiple rows in Table Beta. Example: Classes & Students at a college; A class may have 20 students and a student may take 5 different classes. In the following pubs table relationship diagram we can see:

- many-to-many relationship (oo - oo connectors): titleauthor table
- one-to-one relationship (2 gold keys): publishers & pub_info tables
- one-to-many: the remaining relationships

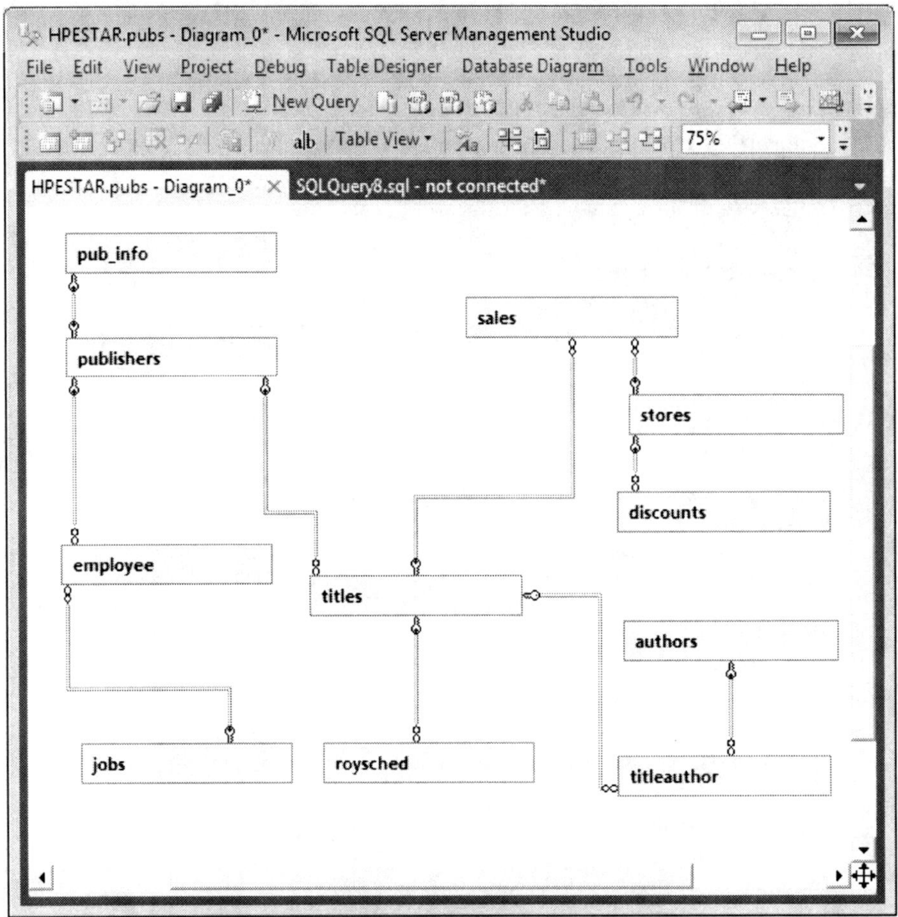

One-To-Many Relationship - FOREIGN KEY Reference

Northwind example shows that each product belongs to a category. CategoryID column in the Products table (FOREIGN KEY) references CategoryID in Categories table (PRIMARY KEY). One category can have 0 to many products. FK name can be different from PK name. However, if possible, PK name is the best choice for FK name. When multiple FK-s referencing the same PK, we have to choose different names for FK-s.

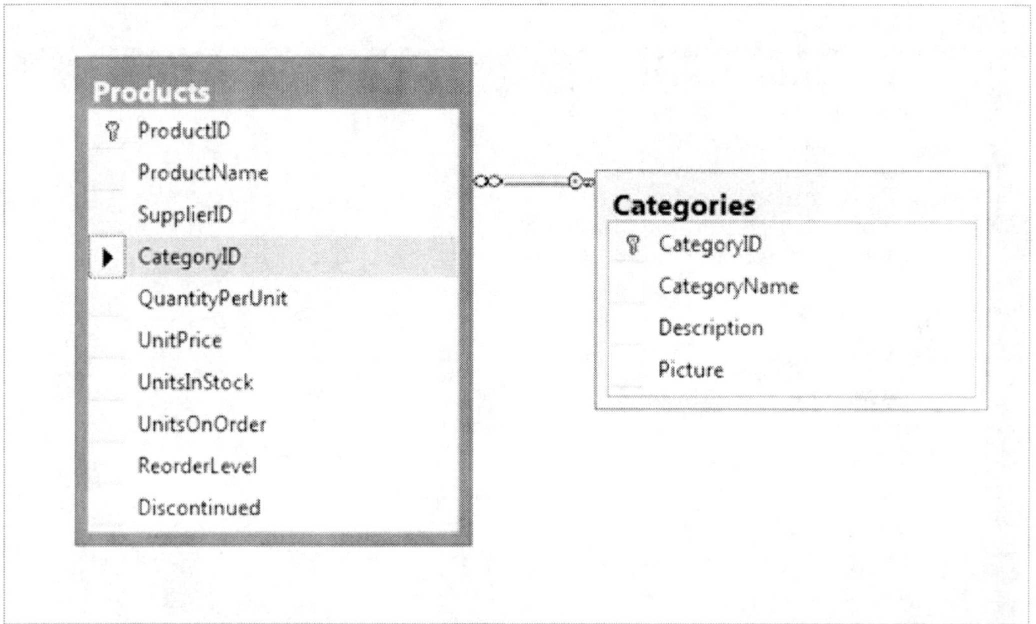

T-SQL-Tidbits: varchar(max), nvarchar(max), varbinary(max) & XML Data

They all can store up to 2GB (the varchar limit is 8,000 otherwise, nvarchar 4000) of text, binary objects or XML document. Since nvarchar is 2 bytes per letter, the maximum is 1GB of letters. Plain text can be stored in varchar(max). Chinese, Japanese, Korean and other UNICODE national text can be stored in nvarchar(max). Even in Hungarian the Ő & Ű letters are UNICODE, if varchar(max) is used, some underlying software translates them to O & U. XML data type is for XML document storage. **Varbinary(max) can be used for images, videos, Word documents, Excel documents, and so on.** Binary objects in varbinary(max) column are not displayed in readable format using SSMS. They have to be exported to the file system for display by the appropriate software. Full-text index can be created on varchar(max), nvarchar(max) & XML columns. **Word document in varbinary(max) column can also be full-text indexed using IFilter.**

BOL Article: **Querying varbinary(max) and xml Columns (Full-Text Search)**
http://msdn.microsoft.com/en-us/library/ms142531(v=sql.105).aspx

CategoryID in the Products table is a FOREIGN KEY (a pointer) to a PRIMARY KEY in the Categories table

Therefore, we can safely JOIN the two tables using the two ON KEYs.

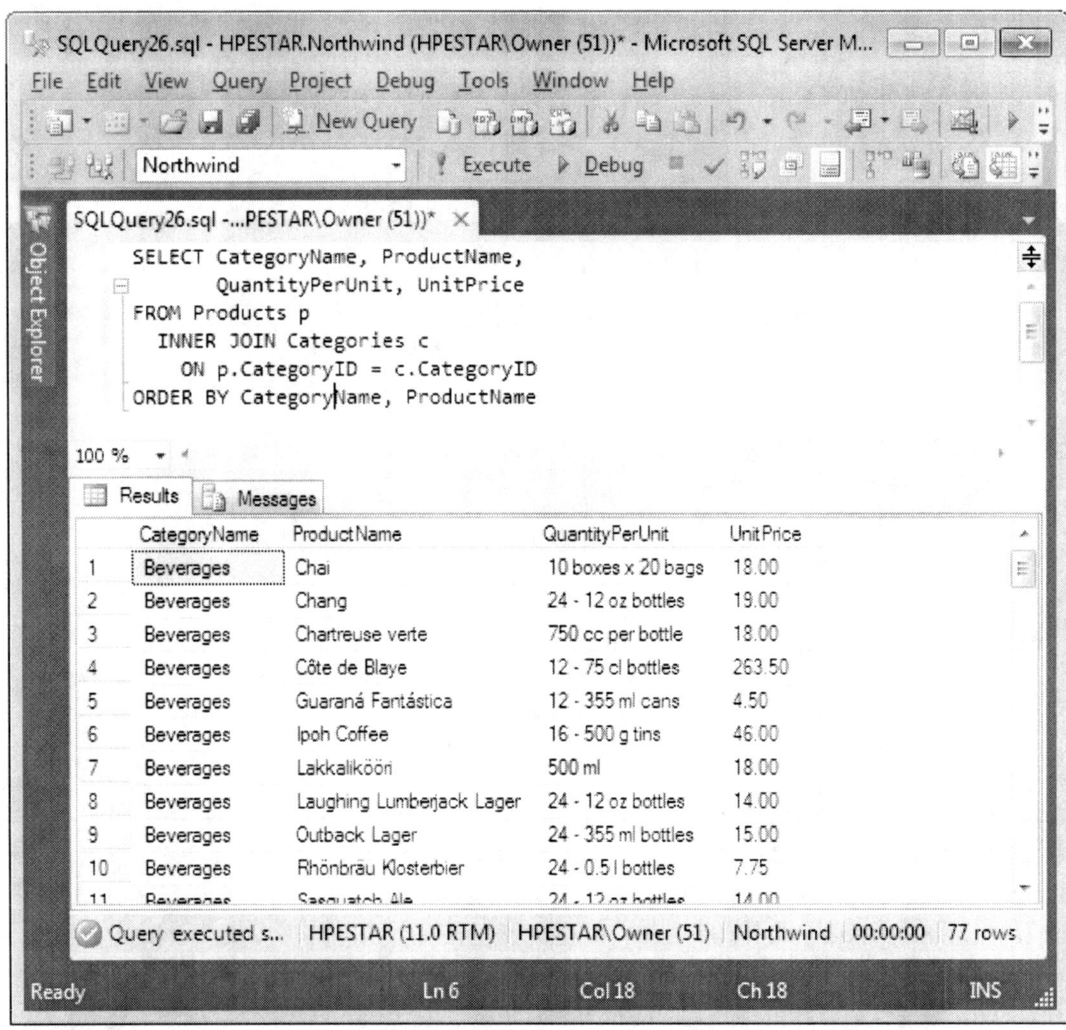

T-SQL Tidbits: UNION ALL with FOR XML Output

We have to use derived table with column alias to perform UNION ALL on XML output.

```
USE AdventureWorks2012;
SELECT * FROM (SELECT * FROM HumanResources.Shift WHERE ShiftID = 1  FOR XML RAW) X1 (XML_DATA)
UNION ALL
SELECT * FROM (SELECT * FROM HumanResources.Shift WHERE ShiftID = 1  FOR XML AUTO) X2 (XML_DATA)
UNION ALL
SELECT * FROM (SELECT * FROM HumanResources.Shift WHERE ShiftID = 1  FOR XML AUTO, ELEMENTS) X3 (XML_DATA)
UNION ALL
SELECT * FROM (SELECT * FROM HumanResources.Shift WHERE ShiftID = 1  FOR XML PATH('WorkShift')) X4 (XML_DATA);
```

The PRIMARY KEY and FOREIGN KEY should not be exposed to the database application user

The Business Intelligence consumer needs meaningful information not meaningless numbers. The software engineer can see the PK and FK values as part of his work.

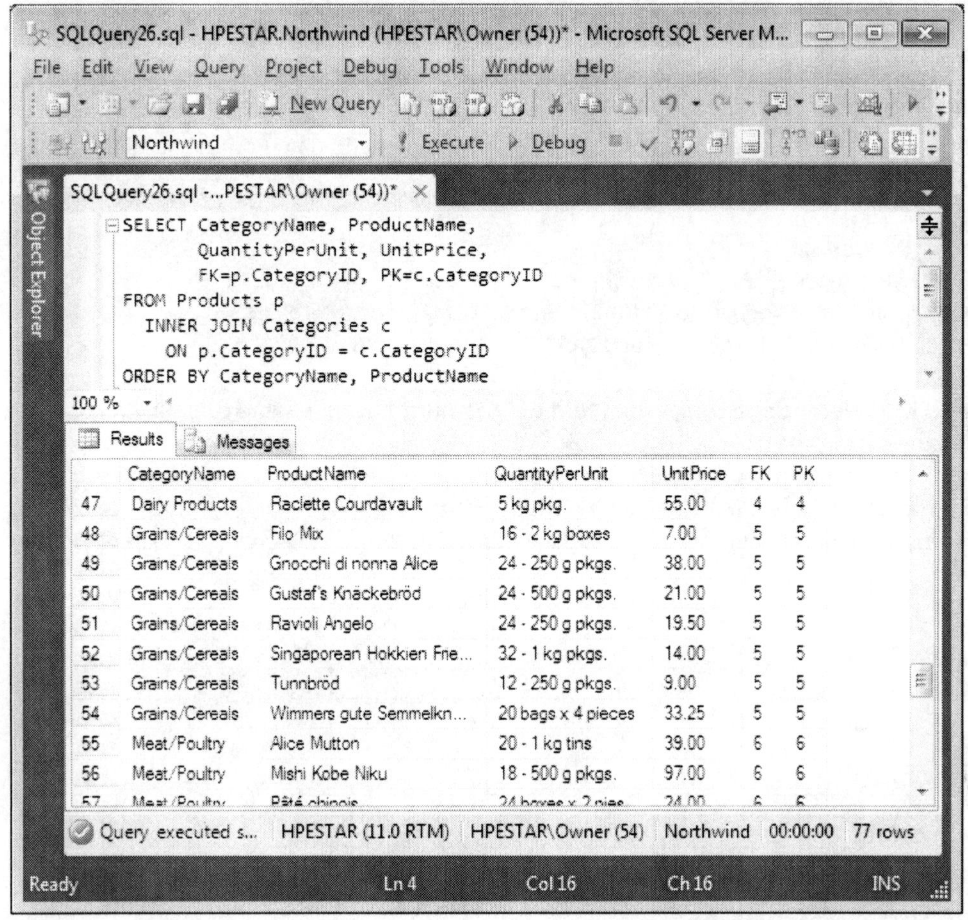

We could make the NATURAL KEY ProductName a PRIMARY KEY in the Products table. However, that is a string field (column) nvarchar(40) which can be 80 bytes in size (each UNICODE character is 2 bytes). That would present increased space use and decreased performance in JOINs. It would also present increased maintenance cost if we have to change a product name, for example, "Ravioli Angelo" to "Ravioli Los Angeles". The change would have to be performed in the PRIMARY KEY table and each FOREIGN KEY table. The 4-byte integer SURROGATE PRIMARY KEY ProductID solves all the problems above. Minimal space use, fast in JOINs and since a meaningless number (a database pointer), we never have to change it. If the ProductName changes, it is just a single UPDATE in the PRIMARY KEY table.

Composite PRIMARY KEY

A composite PRIMARY KEY consists of two or more columns. Junction tables typically apply composite PRIMARY KEYs. An example is the Production.ProductProductPhoto junction table.

ProductID (PK, FK, int, not null)
ProductPhotoID (PK, FK, int, not null)
Primary (Flag(bit), not null)
ModifiedDate (datetime, not null

The PRIMARY KEY is the composite of two FOREIGN KEYs: ProductID and ProductPhotoID. T-SQL script definition of the above composite PRIMARY KEY.

```
USE [AdventureWorks2012];
ALTER TABLE [Production].[ProductProductPhoto]
ADD  CONSTRAINT [PK_ProductProductPhoto_ProductID_ProductPhotoID]
PRIMARY KEY NONCLUSTERED (  [ProductID] ASC,      [ProductPhotoID] ASC  );
```

A FOREIGN KEY referencing a composite PRIMARY KEY must have the same column structure. Query to display all the data in the table.

```
SELECT   ProductID,ProductPhotoID,[Primary],ModifiedDate
FROM AdventureWorks2012.Production.ProductProductPhoto;      -- (504 row(s) affected) - Partial results.
```

ProductID	ProductPhotoID	Primary	ModifiedDate
813	1	1	2006-06-01 00:00:00.000
814	1	1	2006-06-01 00:00:00.000
815	160	1	2006-06-01 00:00:00.000
816	160	1	2006-06-01 00:00:00.000
817	160	1	2006-06-01 00:00:00.000
818	160	1	2006-06-01 00:00:00.000

NOTE: Use composite UNIQUE KEY and INT SURROGATE PRIMARY KEY in base tables.
Composite PRIMARY KEY requires composite FOREIGN KEY!

Composite NATURAL KEY

Assume we are merging data in a table from different external bank feeds. We have to use business commons sense to identify the NATURAL KEY. We know that the AccountNo must be unique in each bank, but may not be unique once we merge the data. Therefore we have to include the BankID in the NATURAL KEY as well.

```
CREATE TABLE BankCustomer( ID BIGINT IDENTITY(1,1) PRIMARY KEY NONCLUSTERED,
BankID INT NOT NULL,  AccountNo BIGINT NOT NULL,
UNIQUE CLUSTERED (BankID, AccountNo),                          -- COMPOSITE NATURAL KEY
Name varchar(60) NOT NULL,
CreatedDate datetime NOT NULL default( CURRENT_TIMESTAMP));
```

Parent-Child Hierarchy

When an employee's record includes the manager's ID, it is called self-reference since the manager is an employee also. A simple organizational chart (tree structure) can be established by self-referencing FOREIGN KEYs.

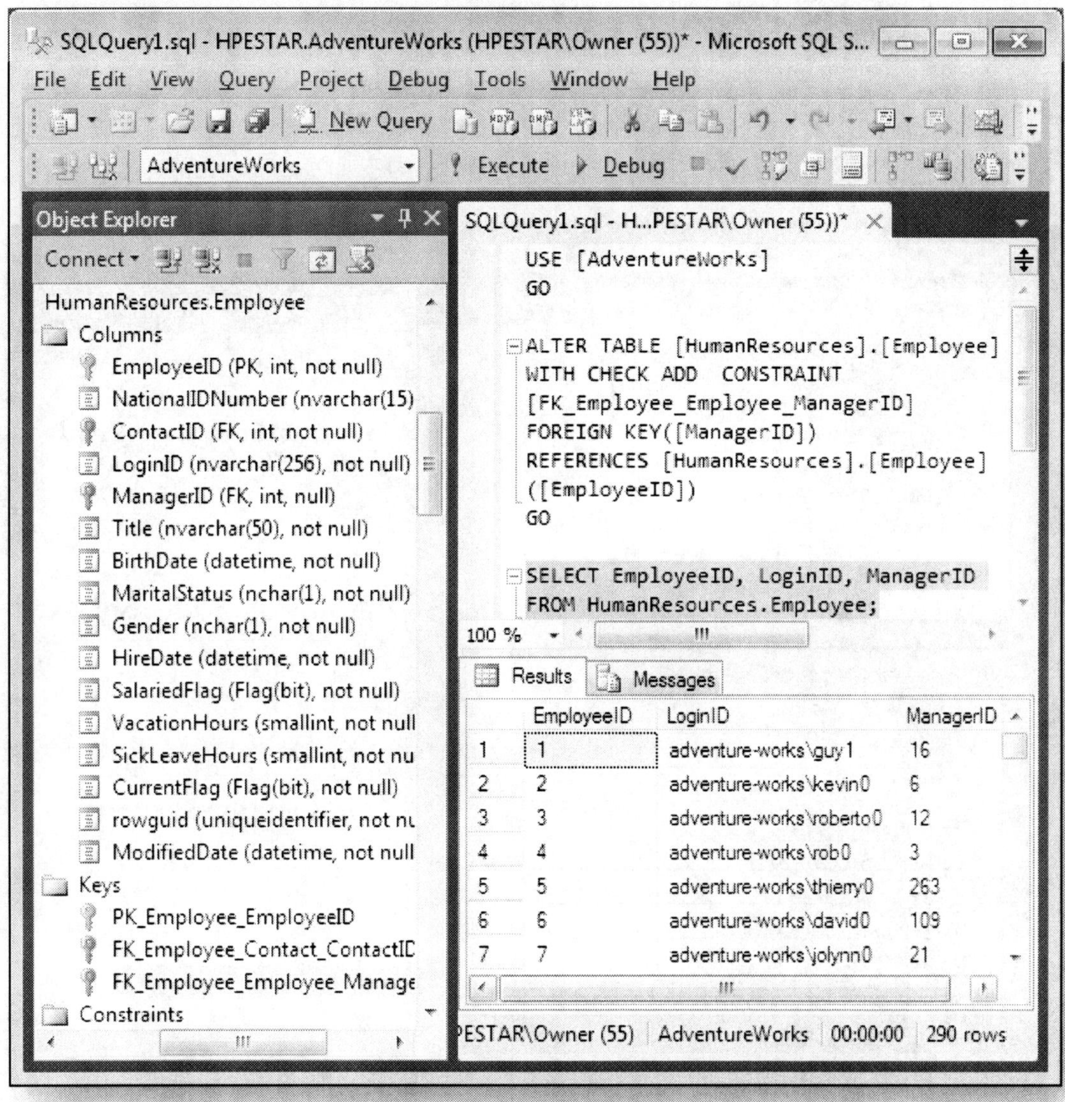

Reading the table: david0 is the supervisor of kevin0, and roberto0 is the supervisor of rob0.

Hierarchical Relationship - Multi-Level with FOREIGN KEYs

Product, ProductSubcategory and ProductCategory in AdventureWorks represent multi-level hierarchy which can be implemented with FOREIGN KEYs. To get the hierarchical information, we need to INNER JOIN the tables on the FOREIGN KEYS and PRIMARY KEYS. Column aliases are used to create meaningful column names from the 3 "Name"-s.

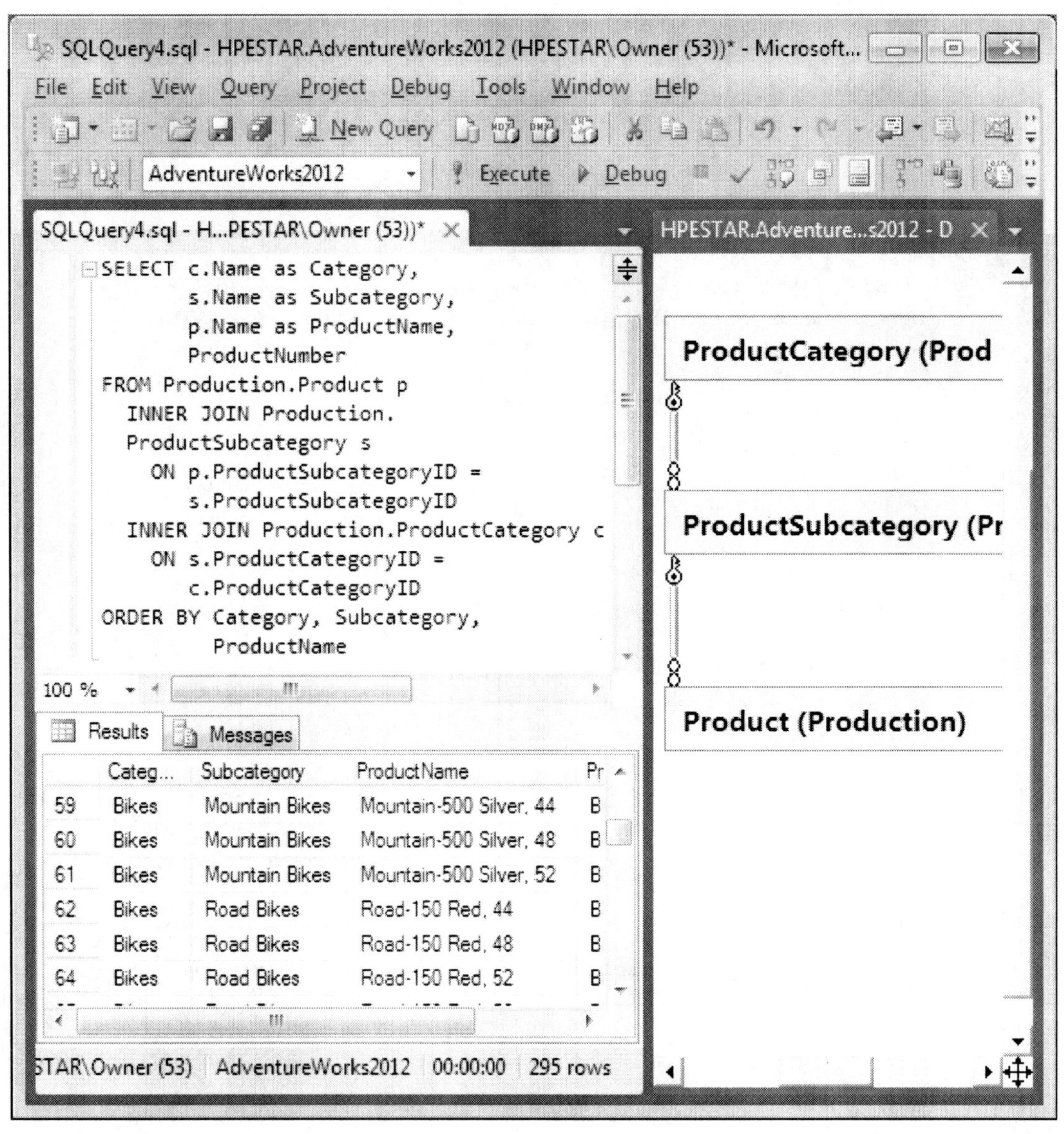

Tree Hierarchy Representation with hierarchyid

An alternate to using self-referencing FOREIGN KEY is the application of hierarchyid data type introduced with SQL Server 2008.

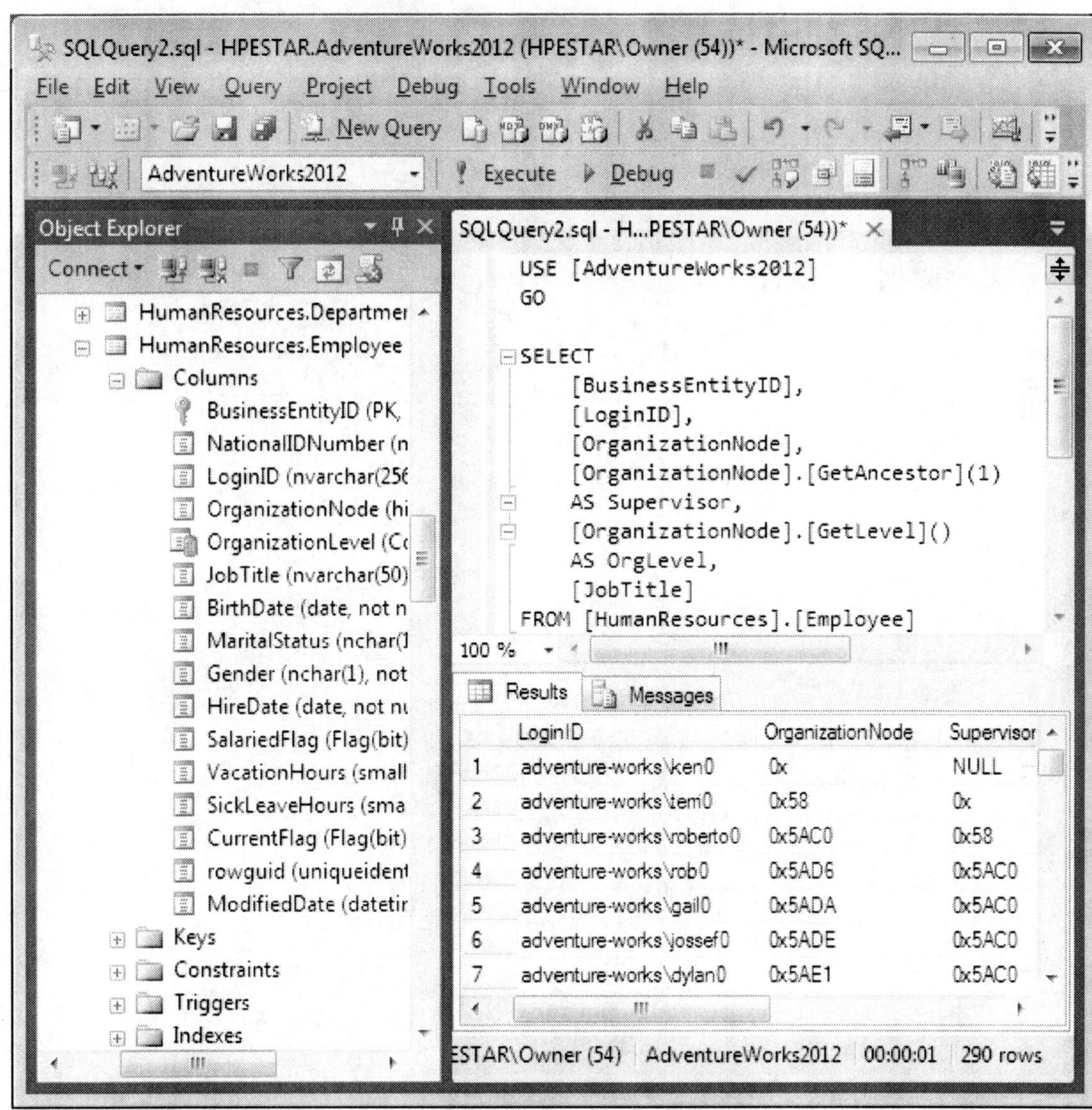

We can read from the table that ken0 (Ken Sanchez, CEO) is the supervisor of terri0 who in turn is the supervisor of roberto0 who is the supervisor of rob0.

Many-To-Many Relationship - Junction Table

Junction tables have many names, most popular among them are junction table, cross-reference table and bridge table. The titleauthor table in the pubs database is a junction table: a title (book) can have many authors and an author can write many titles. The PRIMARY KEY is a composite of two FOREIGN KEYs referencing the titles and authors tables.

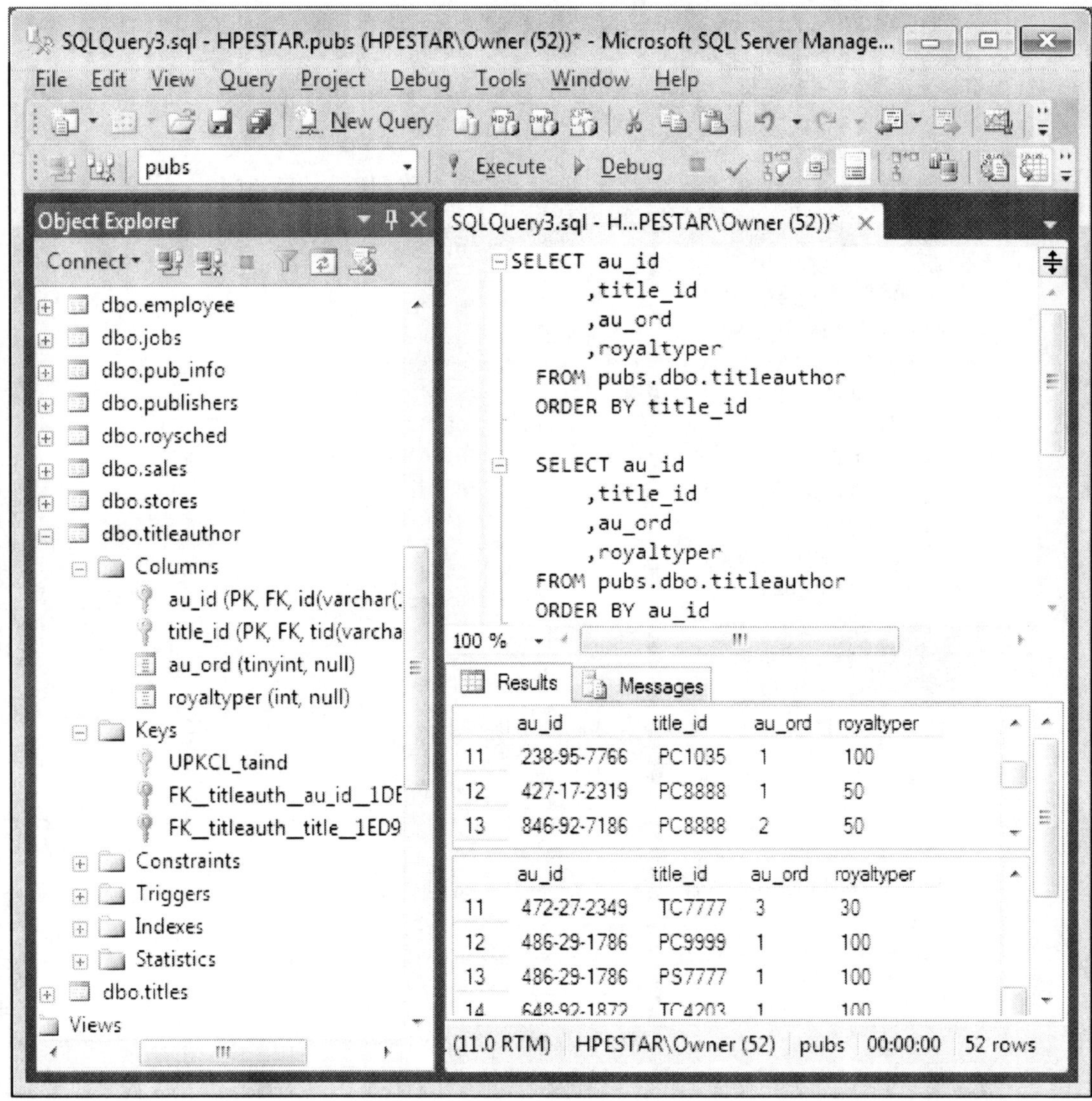

```
SELECT au_id
      ,title_id
      ,au_ord
      ,royaltyper
  FROM pubs.dbo.titleauthor
  ORDER BY title_id

  SELECT au_id
      ,title_id
      ,au_ord
      ,royaltyper
  FROM pubs.dbo.titleauthor
  ORDER BY au_id
```

	au_id	title_id	au_ord	royaltyper
11	238-95-7766	PC1035	1	100
12	427-17-2319	PC8888	1	50
13	846-92-7186	PC8888	2	50

	au_id	title_id	au_ord	royaltyper
11	472-27-2349	TC7777	3	30
12	486-29-1786	PC9999	1	100
13	486-29-1786	PS7777	1	100
14	648-92-1872	TC4203	1	100

Reading the author - title junction table: book title PC8888 has multiple (two) authors, while author 486-29-1786 wrote multiple (two) books.

Parent-Child or Master-Detail Tables Design

In the AdventureWorks series of sample databases, Sales.SalesOrderHeader and Sales.SalesOrderDetail tables are implemented as master-detail tables. Similarly for Purchasing.PurchaseOrderHeader and Purchasing.PurchaseOrderDetail. The PRIMARY KEY of SalesOrderHeader is SalesOrderID (INT IDENTITY(1,1)). The PRIMARY KEY of SalesOrderDetail is composite of SalesOrderID FOREIGN KEY and SalesOrderDetailID (INT IDENTITY(1,1)). The business meaning is that an order from a bicycle reseller can have many line items such mountain bikes, helmets, touring frames and jerseys.

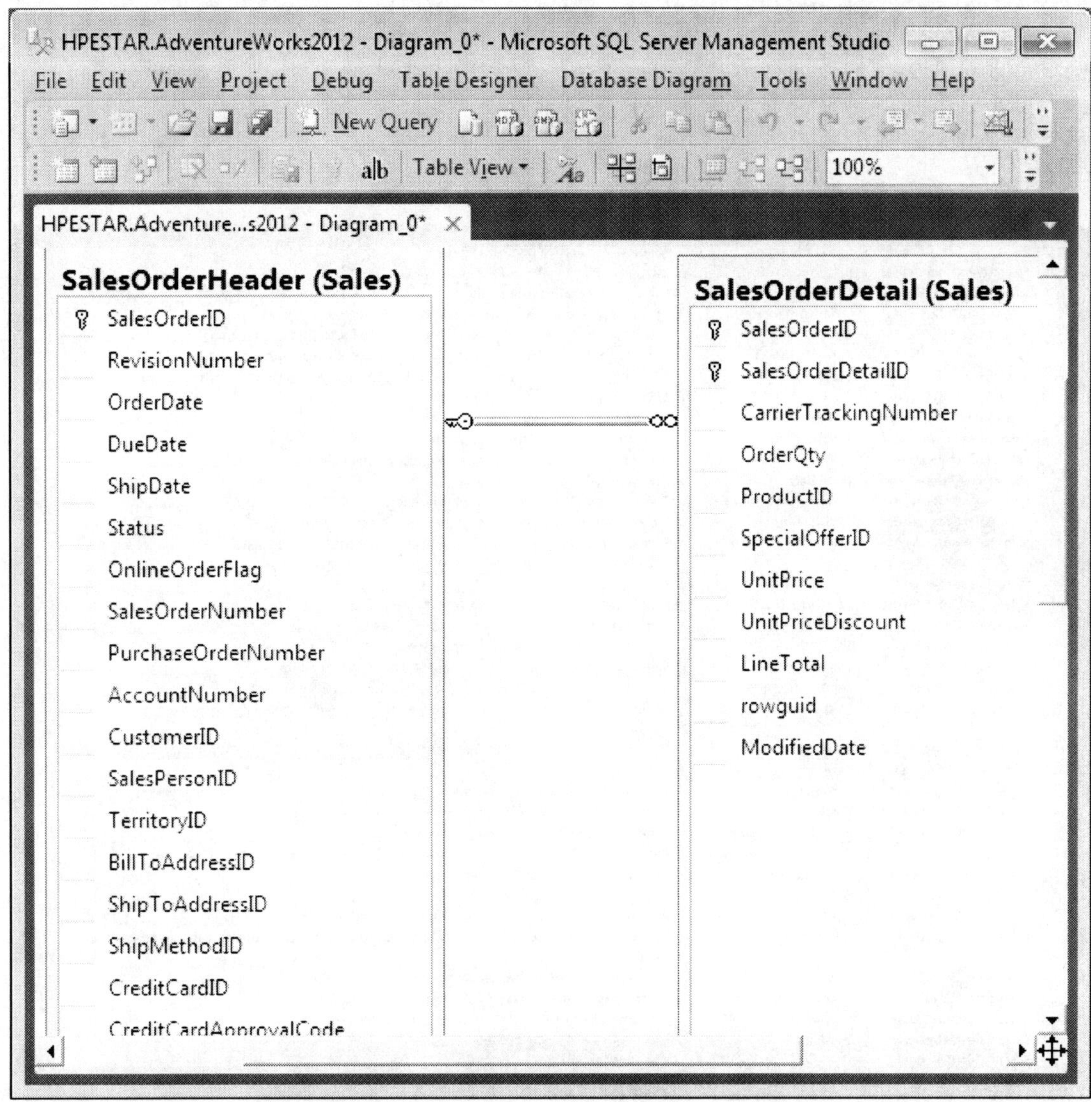

Column Descriptions of SalesOrderHeader & SalesOrderDetail Tables

UNION query to lists the column descriptions for the above master-detail tables from the data dictionary.

```
SELECT 'Sales.SalesOrderHeader' AS TableName, objname    AS ColumnName,
       value                                             AS [Description]
FROM fn_listextendedproperty (NULL, 'schema', 'Sales', 'table', 'SalesOrderHeader', 'Column', default)

UNION

SELECT 'Sales.SalesOrderDetail' AS TableName, objname    AS ColumnName,
       value                                             AS [Description]
FROM fn_listextendedproperty (NULL, 'schema', 'Sales', 'table', 'SalesOrderDetail', 'Column', default)

ORDER BY TableName DESC, ColumnName;
```

TableName	ColumnName	Description
Sales.SalesOrderHeader	AccountNumber	Financial accounting number reference.
Sales.SalesOrderHeader	BillToAddressID	Customer billing address. Foreign key to Address.AddressID.
Sales.SalesOrderHeader	Comment	Sales representative comments.
Sales.SalesOrderHeader	CreditCardApprovalCode	Approval code provided by the credit card company.
Sales.SalesOrderHeader	CreditCardID	Credit card identification number. Foreign key to CreditCard.CreditCardID.
Sales.SalesOrderHeader	CurrencyRateID	Currency exchange rate used. Foreign key to CurrencyRate.CurrencyRateID.
Sales.SalesOrderHeader	CustomerID	Customer identification number. Foreign key to Customer.BusinessEntityID.
Sales.SalesOrderHeader	DueDate	Date the order is due to the customer.
Sales.SalesOrderHeader	Freight	Shipping cost.
Sales.SalesOrderHeader	ModifiedDate	Date and time the record was last updated.
Sales.SalesOrderHeader	OnlineOrderFlag	0 = Order placed by sales person. 1 = Order placed online by customer.
Sales.SalesOrderHeader	OrderDate	Dates the sales order was created.
Sales.SalesOrderHeader	PurchaseOrderNumber	Customer purchase order number reference.
Sales.SalesOrderHeader	RevisionNumber	Incremental number to track changes to the sales order over time.
Sales.SalesOrderHeader	rowguid	ROWGUIDCOL number uniquely identifying the record. Used to support a merge replication sample.
Sales.SalesOrderHeader	SalesOrderID	Primary key.
Sales.SalesOrderHeader	SalesOrderNumber	Unique sales order identification number.
Sales.SalesOrderHeader	SalesPersonID	Sales person who created the sales order. Foreign key to SalesPerson.BusinessEntityID.
Sales.SalesOrderHeader	ShipDate	Date the order was shipped to the customer.
Sales.SalesOrderHeader	ShipMethodID	Shipping method. Foreign key to ShipMethod.ShipMethodID.
Sales.SalesOrderHeader	ShipToAddressID	Customer shipping address. Foreign key to Address.AddressID.
Sales.SalesOrderHeader	Status	Order current status. 1 = In process; 2 = Approved; 3 = Backordered; 4 = Rejected; 5 = Shipped; 6 = Cancelled
Sales.SalesOrderHeader	SubTotal	Sales subtotal. Computed as SUM(SalesOrderDetail.LineTotal)for the appropriate SalesOrderID.
Sales.SalesOrderHeader	TaxAmt	Tax amount.
Sales.SalesOrderHeader	TerritoryID	Territory in which the sale was made. Foreign key to SalesTerritory.SalesTerritoryID.
Sales.SalesOrderHeader	TotalDue	Total due from customer. Computed as Subtotal + TaxAmt + Freight.
Sales.SalesOrderDetail	CarrierTrackingNumber	Shipment tracking number supplied by the shipper.
Sales.SalesOrderDetail	LineTotal	Per product subtotal. Computed as UnitPrice * (1 - UnitPriceDiscount) * OrderQty.
Sales.SalesOrderDetail	ModifiedDate	Date and time the record was last updated.
Sales.SalesOrderDetail	OrderQty	Quantity ordered per product.
Sales.SalesOrderDetail	ProductID	Product sold to customer. Foreign key to Product.ProductID.
Sales.SalesOrderDetail	rowguid	ROWGUIDCOL number uniquely identifying the record. Used to support a merge replication sample.
Sales.SalesOrderDetail	SalesOrderDetailID	Primary key. One incremental unique number per product sold.
Sales.SalesOrderDetail	SalesOrderID	Primary key. Foreign key to SalesOrderHeader.SalesOrderID.
Sales.SalesOrderDetail	SpecialOfferID	Promotional code. Foreign key to SpecialOffer.SpecialOfferID.
Sales.SalesOrderDetail	UnitPrice	Selling price of a single product.
Sales.SalesOrderDetail	UnitPriceDiscount	Discount amount.

Diagram of PurchaseOrderHeader and Related Tables

Database diagram to display the special relationship to the child table PurchaseOrderDetail and PK-FK relationships to other tables.

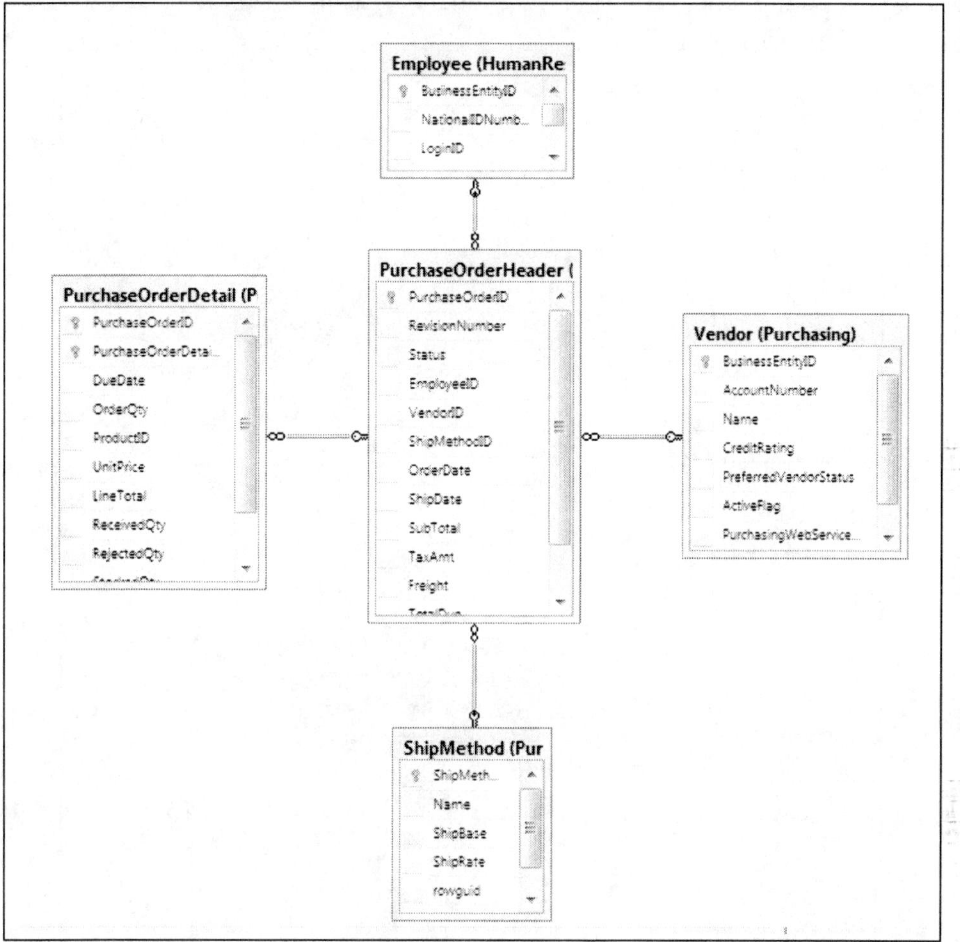

T-SQL-Tidbits: First Choice CONSTRAINTS To Enforce the Integrity of the Data

Since constraints handling is built into SQL Server engine, constraints are the first choice for data integrity enforcement over triggers, stored procedures and application software.

- PRIMARY KEY constraints: unique row id
- FOREIGN KEY constraints: connector between tables
- UNIQUE (KEY) constraints: unique column(s) values
- CHECK constraints: simple column level or table level; can use CASE expression
- UDF CHECK constraints complex with multi-table access
- DEFAULT definitions for column like 0, '', or getdate()
- Nullability (column is NULL or NOT NULL)

Multiple FOREIGN KEYs from One Table to Another

Database diagram to illustrate the double FOREIGN KEYs from BillOfMaterials table to the Product table. The FKs are named **ComponentID and ProductAssemblyID**. In the Product table **SizeUnitMeasureCode & WeightUnitMeasureCode** are double FKs to the UnitMeasure table.

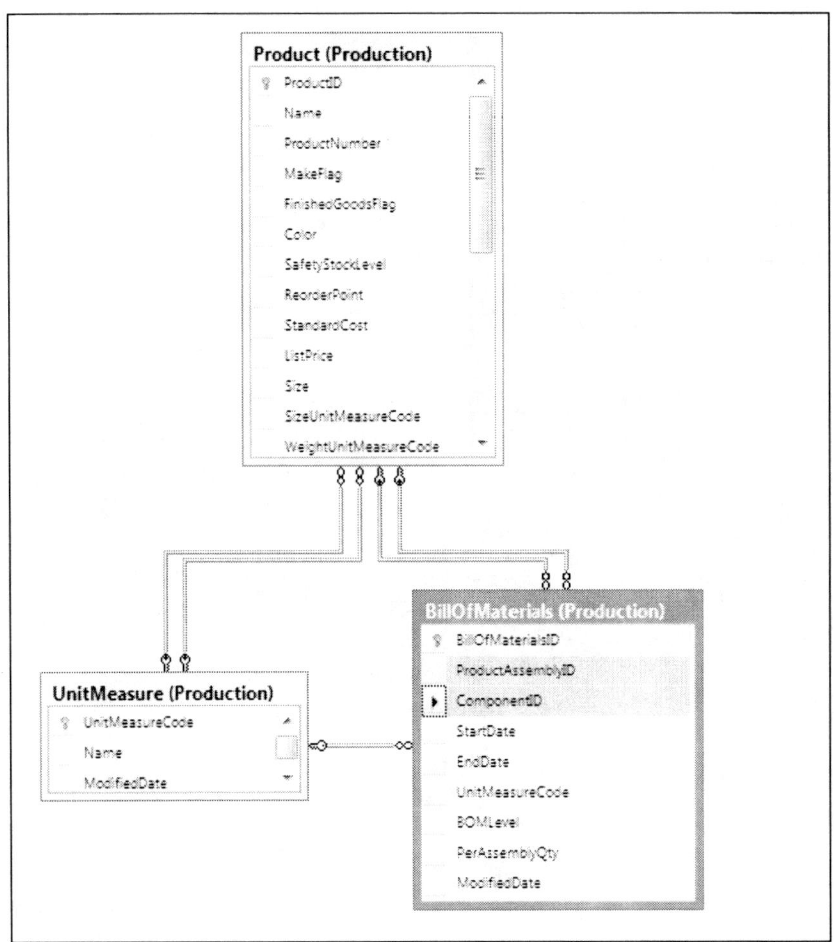

T-SQL Tidbits: Confusion about Single-column SELECT Query

An operator like "=" requires a single-value on both sides. The "IN" operator takes multiple values on the right hand side. **The cardinality of a single-column SELECT query must match the requirement of the operator when used as a subquery.**

```
SELECT ListPrice FROM Production.Product WHERE ListPrice > 0.0;                  -- multi value
SELECT MIN(ListPrice) FROM Production.Product WHERE ListPrice > 0.0;             -- single value
SELECT ListPrice FROM Production.Product WHERE ListPrice = 99.95;                -- not well-defined
SELECT DISTINCT ListPrice FROM Production.Product WHERE ListPrice = 99.95;  -- single or no value
```

Parent - Multiple Children Table Design

Database design & diagram to represent a parent table with two children table. Notice that in the children table the PRIMARY KEY is a FOREIGN KEY simultaneously.

```
CREATE TABLE Security   (
   Symbol              CHAR(7)  PRIMARY KEY,
   SecurityName        NVARCHAR(64),
   CUSIP               CHAR(9),
   ModifiedDate        DATETIME DEFAULT (CURRENT_TIMESTAMP)    );
```

```
CREATE TABLE Stock   (
   Symbol              CHAR(7)  PRIMARY KEY REFERENCES Security ON DELETE CASCADE,
   AuthShares          BIGINT,
   IssuedShares        BIGINT,
   ClosingPrice        DECIMAL(14, 2),
   ModifiedDate        DATETIME DEFAULT (CURRENT_TIMESTAMP)    );
```

```
CREATE TABLE Bond   (
   Symbol              CHAR(7)  PRIMARY KEY REFERENCES Security ON DELETE CASCADE,
   Rate                DECIMAL(14, 6),
   FaceValue           DECIMAL(14, 2),
   MaturityDate        DATE,
   ClosingPrice        DECIMAL(14, 2),
   ModifiedDate        DATETIME DEFAULT (CURRENT_TIMESTAMP)    );
```

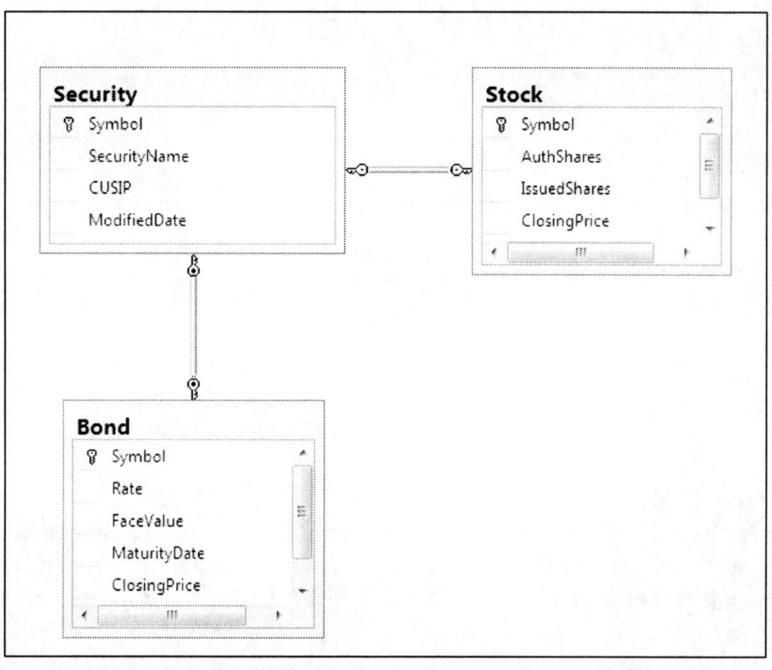

LookupHeader & Lookup Tables for Storing All Lookups

T-SQL script to demonstrate a simple implementation of LookupHeader & Lookup (detail) tables to prevent database "pollution" by many small lookup (code/translate) tables.

```
USE AdventureWorks2012;
```

```
CREATE TABLE LookupHeader
 (
        LookupHeaderID      INT IDENTITY(1, 1)      PRIMARY KEY,
        [Type]              VARCHAR(80)             UNIQUE,
        ModifiedDate        DATETIME                default ( CURRENT_TIMESTAMP)
 );
go
```

```
CREATE TABLE Lookup
 (
        LookupID            INT IDENTITY(1,1) PRIMARY KEY nonclustered,
        LookupHeaderID      INT NOT NULL REFERENCES LookupHeader(LookupHeaderID),
        Code                VARCHAR(6) NOT NULL,
        [Description]       VARCHAR(255),
        ModifiedDate        DATETIME default ( CURRENT_TIMESTAMP)
 );
go
```

```
-- composite PRIMARY KEY
ALTER TABLE dbo.Lookup
        ADD CONSTRAINT uq_lookup UNIQUE CLUSTERED ( LookupHeaderID, Code );
go
```

```
INSERT LookupHeader  ([Type]) VALUES ('Country');
INSERT LookupHeader  ([Type]) VALUES ('Department');
```

```
SELECT * FROM   LookupHeader ;
go
```

LookupHeaderID	Type	ModifiedDate
1	Country	2016-08-08 07:34:59.077
2	Department	2016-08-08 07:34:59.113

```
-- Populate department code
INSERT INTO LookUp (LookupHeaderID, Code, Description)  VALUES      (2, '1', 'Human Resources');
INSERT INTO LookUp (LookupHeaderID, Code, Description)  VALUES      (2, '2', 'Accounting');
INSERT INTO LookUp (LookupHeaderID, Code, Description)  VALUES      (2, '3', 'Engineering');
GO
```

-- T-SQL script continued

```
-- Populate country code lookup
INSERT INTO LookUp (LookupHeaderID, Code, Description)
SELECT 1, [CountryRegionCode],[Name]
 FROM [AdventureWorks2012].[Person].[CountryRegion]
ORDER BY CountryRegionCode;
go
```

```
-- Check lookup table content
SELECT * FROM   Lookup ORDER  BY LookupHeaderID, Code;
```

Partial display of the Lookup table content.

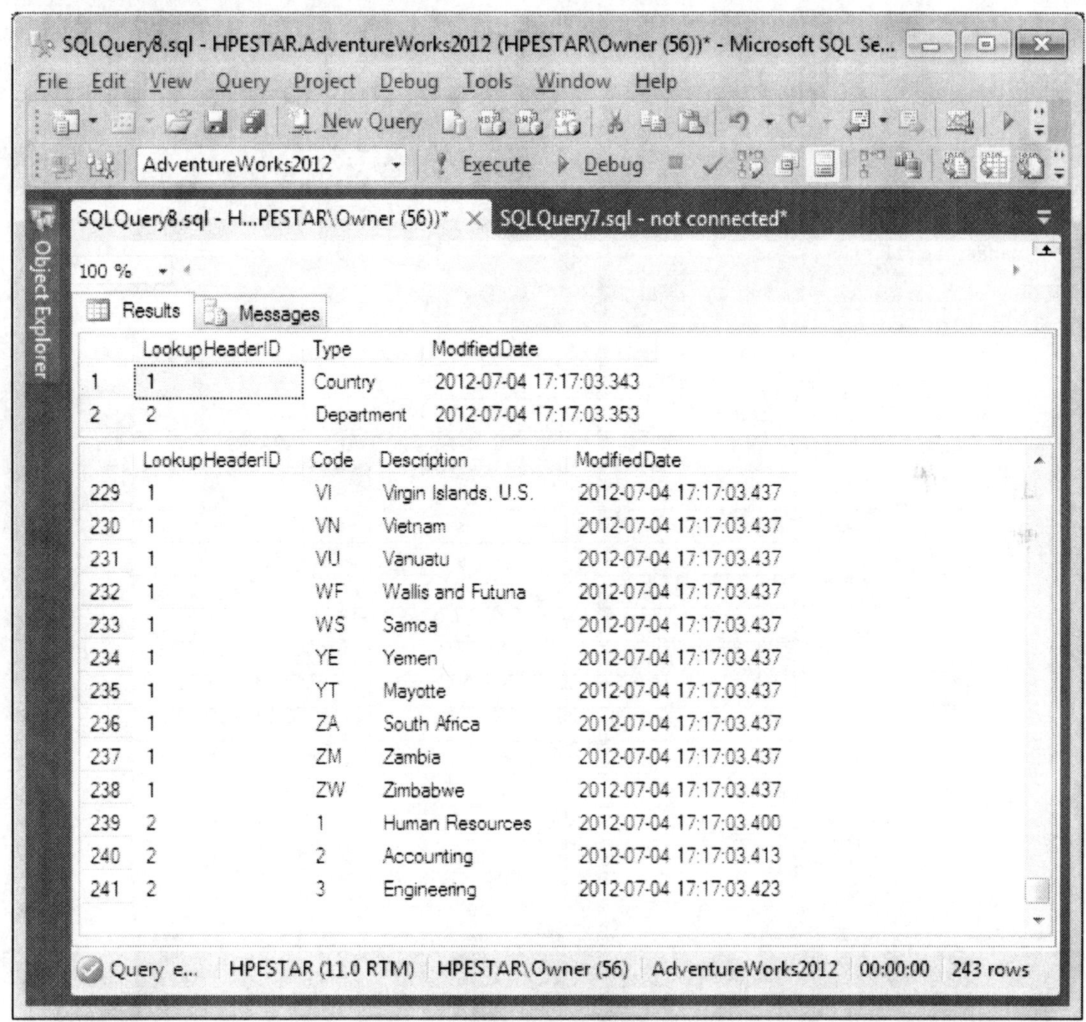

	LookupHeaderID	Type	ModifiedDate
1	1	Country	2012-07-04 17:17:03.343
2	2	Department	2012-07-04 17:17:03.353

	LookupHeaderID	Code	Description	ModifiedDate
229	1	VI	Virgin Islands, U.S.	2012-07-04 17:17:03.437
230	1	VN	Vietnam	2012-07-04 17:17:03.437
231	1	VU	Vanuatu	2012-07-04 17:17:03.437
232	1	WF	Wallis and Futuna	2012-07-04 17:17:03.437
233	1	WS	Samoa	2012-07-04 17:17:03.437
234	1	YE	Yemen	2012-07-04 17:17:03.437
235	1	YT	Mayotte	2012-07-04 17:17:03.437
236	1	ZA	South Africa	2012-07-04 17:17:03.437
237	1	ZM	Zambia	2012-07-04 17:17:03.437
238	1	ZW	Zimbabwe	2012-07-04 17:17:03.437
239	2	1	Human Resources	2012-07-04 17:17:03.400
240	2	2	Accounting	2012-07-04 17:17:03.413
241	2	3	Engineering	2012-07-04 17:17:03.423

History Table Design

AdventureWorks2012 EmployeeDepartmentHistory table follows the career of an employee from department to department each with StartDate and EndDate. If EndDate is NULL, that is the employee's current department. For employee ID 250 (BusinessEntityID) the current department is 5. The PRIMARY KEY is composite of BusinessEntityID (employee ID), DepartmentID, ShiftID and StartDate. The first 3 columns in the PRIMARY KEY are FOREIGN KEYs also. BusinessEntityID references (points to) the Employee table, DepartmentID the Department table and ShiftID the Shift table.

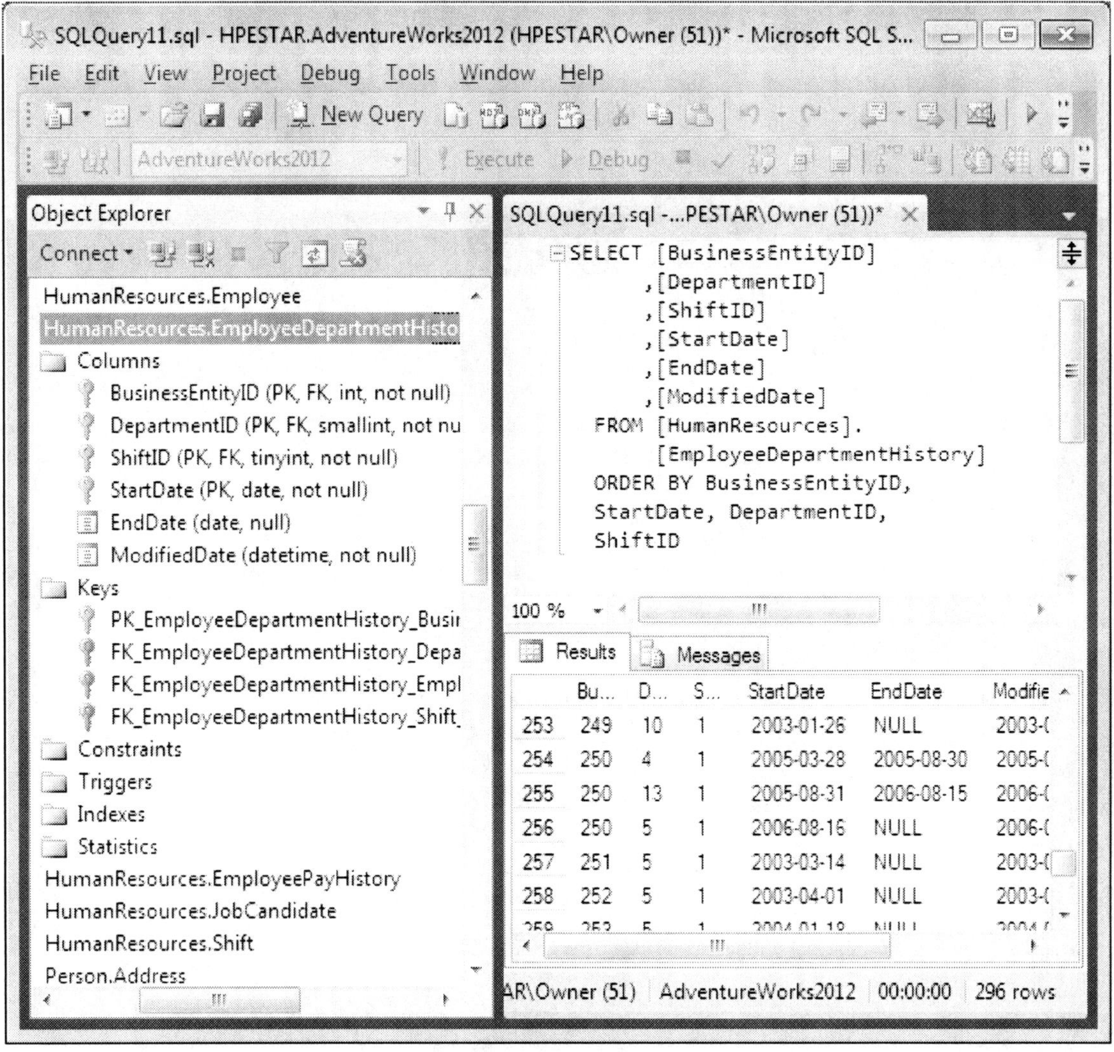

Implementing One-To-One Relationship

In a one-to-one relationship, a row in the main table can have no more than one matching row in the secondary table, and vice versa. **A one-to-one relationship requires that both of the related columns are primary keys.** One-to-one relationship tables are not very common because most of the time a single table is used. Nonetheless, we might use a one-to-one relationship tables to: Vertically partition a table with many columns; Vertically divide a table to a narrow and wide part for performance reasons - example: email header & email body; Isolate sensitive columns in a table for security reasons; Store information that applies only to a subset of the main table thus avoiding lots of NULLs in the rows. Demonstration to show the one-to-one relationship between Product and ProductInventory tables.

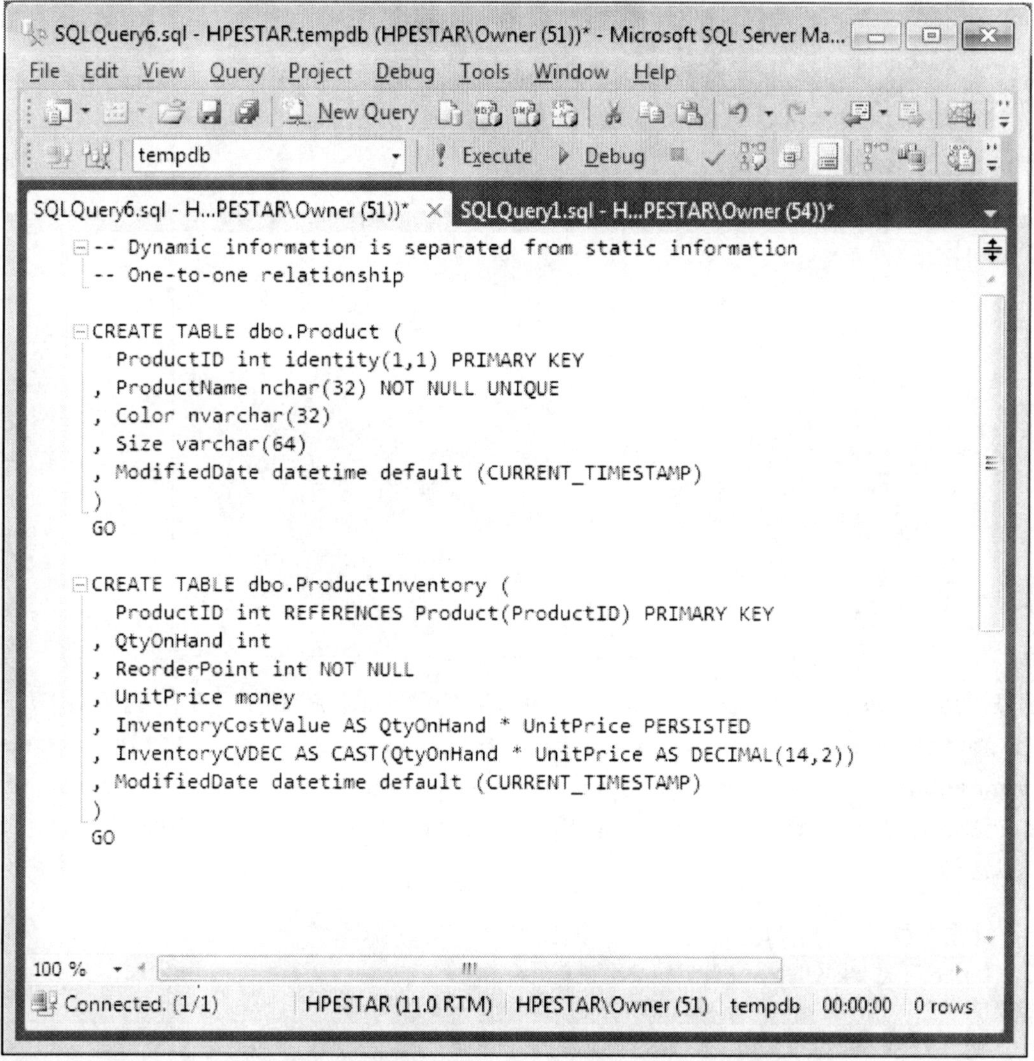

```
-- Dynamic information is separated from static information
-- One-to-one relationship

CREATE TABLE dbo.Product (
  ProductID int identity(1,1) PRIMARY KEY
, ProductName nchar(32) NOT NULL UNIQUE
, Color nvarchar(32)
, Size varchar(64)
, ModifiedDate datetime default (CURRENT_TIMESTAMP)
)
GO

CREATE TABLE dbo.ProductInventory (
  ProductID int REFERENCES Product(ProductID) PRIMARY KEY
, QtyOnHand int
, ReorderPoint int NOT NULL
, UnitPrice money
, InventoryCostValue AS QtyOnHand * UnitPrice PERSISTED
, InventoryCVDEC AS CAST(QtyOnHand * UnitPrice AS DECIMAL(14,2))
, ModifiedDate datetime default (CURRENT_TIMESTAMP)
)
GO
```

One-To-One Relationship between publisher & pub_info Tables

The intent of the database designer was to separate the bulk data (logo image, PR description) from the regular size columns which likely are more frequently used as well. The implementation: pub_id in pub_info table is PRIMARY KEY and FOREIGN KEY to publishers pub_id.

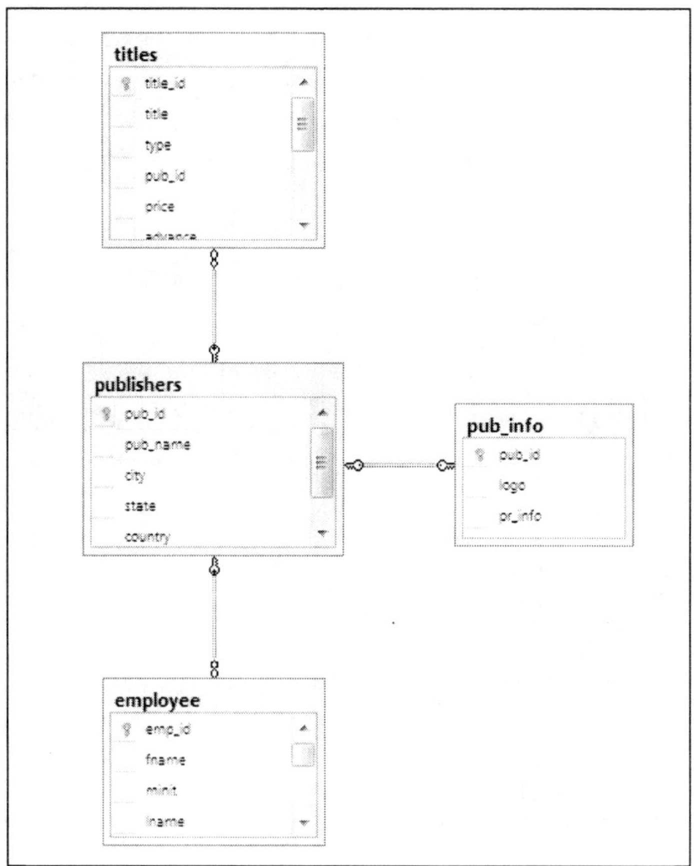

T-SQL Tidbits: Combining Datasets with UNION (ALL), EXCEPT & INTERSECT

These are the set operators. The most important: **the column lists of the SELECT queries must be compatible**. There are rules about the member SELECT queries. However, if we make the combination a derived table, we can do all the operations like GROUP BY, HAVING, we can do with a table.

```
SELECT ColA, ColB, Total=SUM(ColD)
FROM (SELECT ... UNION .... UNION .... SELECT) X                    -- derived table
GROUP BY ColA, ColB HAVING AVG(ColC) > 5.0 ORDER BY ColA;
```

Tables with Computed Columns

A column can be automatically generated by a formula/expression involving other columns. The generation is "on the fly" when needed. To persist the column the PERSISTED property must be used. **PERSISTED is a requirement for some use such as indexing to improve performance when column is queried**. All computed columns can be listed by a simple query.

```
SELECT object_name(object_id) as TableName, name AS ComputedColumn,
        definition AS Expression FROM sys.computed_columns ORDER BY name;
```

The demonstration introduces 2 computed columns into the ProductInventory table.

```
USE tempdb;
CREATE TABLE dbo.Product (
        ProductID int identity(1,1) PRIMARY KEY
        , ProductName nchar(32) NOT NULL UNIQUE
        , Color nvarchar(32)
        , Size varchar(64)
        , ModifiedDate datetime default (CURRENT_TIMESTAMP) );
```

```
-- Table with two computed columns
CREATE TABLE dbo.ProductInventory (
        ProductID int REFERENCES Product(ProductID) PRIMARY KEY
        , QtyOnHand int
        , ReorderPoint int NOT NULL
        , UnitPrice money
        , InventoryCostValue AS QtyOnHand * UnitPrice PERSISTED
        , InventoryCVDEC AS CAST(QtyOnHand * UnitPrice AS DECIMAL(14,0))
        , ModifiedDate datetime default (CURRENT_TIMESTAMP) );
GO
CREATE INDEX idxCostValue ON ProductInventory(InventoryCostValue);
GO
```

```
INSERT Product(ProductName, Color, Size) SELECT 'MusicMobile', 'White', '2" x 3"';
INSERT Product(ProductName, Color, Size) SELECT 'ReaderMobile',  'Black', '5" x 9"';
INSERT Product(ProductName, Color, Size) SELECT 'PhoneMobile',  'Blue', '2 1/2" x 4"';
INSERT Product(ProductName, Color, Size) SELECT 'DELTA laptop', 'Gray', '12" x 16" x 2"';
GO
```

```
SELECT * from dbo.Product;
```

ProductID	ProductName	Color	Size	ModifiedDate
1	MusicMobile	White	2" x 3"	2016-07-08 10:05:53.943
2	ReaderMobile	Black	5" x 9"	2016-07-08 10:05:53.947
3	PhoneMobile	Blue	2 1/2" x 4"	2016-07-08 10:05:53.947
4	DELTA laptop	Gray	12" x 16" x 2"	2016-07-08 10:05:53.947

```
-- T-SQL script continued

INSERT ProductInventory (ProductID, QtyOnHand, ReorderPoint, UnitPrice)  SELECT 1, 105, 30, $99.99;
INSERT ProductInventory (ProductID, QtyOnHand, ReorderPoint, UnitPrice)  SELECT 2, 105, 40, $299.99;
INSERT ProductInventory (ProductID, QtyOnHand, ReorderPoint, UnitPrice)  SELECT 3, 208, 30, $399.99;
INSERT ProductInventory (ProductID, QtyOnHand, ReorderPoint, UnitPrice)  SELECT 4, 103, 30, $599.99;
GO
```

```
SELECT * FROM ProductInventory;
GO
```

ProductID	QtyOnHand	ReorderPoint	UnitPrice	InventoryCostValue	InventoryCVDEC
1	105	30	99.99	10498.95	10499
2	105	40	299.99	31498.95	31499
3	208	30	399.99	83197.92	83198
4	103	30	599.99	61798.97	61799

Combination query with INNER JOIN and formatting.

```
SELECT          ProductName                                     AS [Product Name],
                QtyOnHand                                       AS [Quantity On Hand],
                ReorderPoint                                    AS [Reorder Point],
                FORMAT(UnitPrice,'c','en-US')                   AS [Unit Price],
                FORMAT(InventoryCostValue, 'c','en-US')         AS [ Inventory Cost Value],
                FORMAT(InventoryCVDEC, 'c','en-US')             AS [Inventory Cost Rounded]
FROM Product P
        INNER JOIN ProductInventory PI
                ON P.ProductID = PI.ProductID
ORDER BY ProductName;
GO
```

Product Name	Quantity On Hand	Reorder Point	Unit Price	Inventory Cost Value	Inventory Cost Rounded
DELTA laptop	103	30	$599.99	$61,798.97	$61,799.00
MusicMobile	105	30	$99.99	$10,498.95	$10,499.00
PhoneMobile	208	30	$399.99	$83,197.92	$83,198.00
ReaderMobile	105	40	$299.99	$31,498.95	$31,499.00

Since we created index on the PERSISTED computed column, search is fast.

```
SELECT * FROM ProductInventory WHERE InventoryCostValue = 31498.95;
```

```
-- Cleanup - FOREIGN KEY table must be dropped first
DROP TABLE tempdb.dbo.ProductInventory;
DROP TABLE tempdb.dbo.Product;
```

Building the Data Dictionary

The best way to build the data dictionary is the same time when the database objects are created. It can also be done in the final phases of the database development project when changes are rare to the object designs.

GUI Data Dictionary Maintenance

As an example, right click on a table column name and choose Properties.

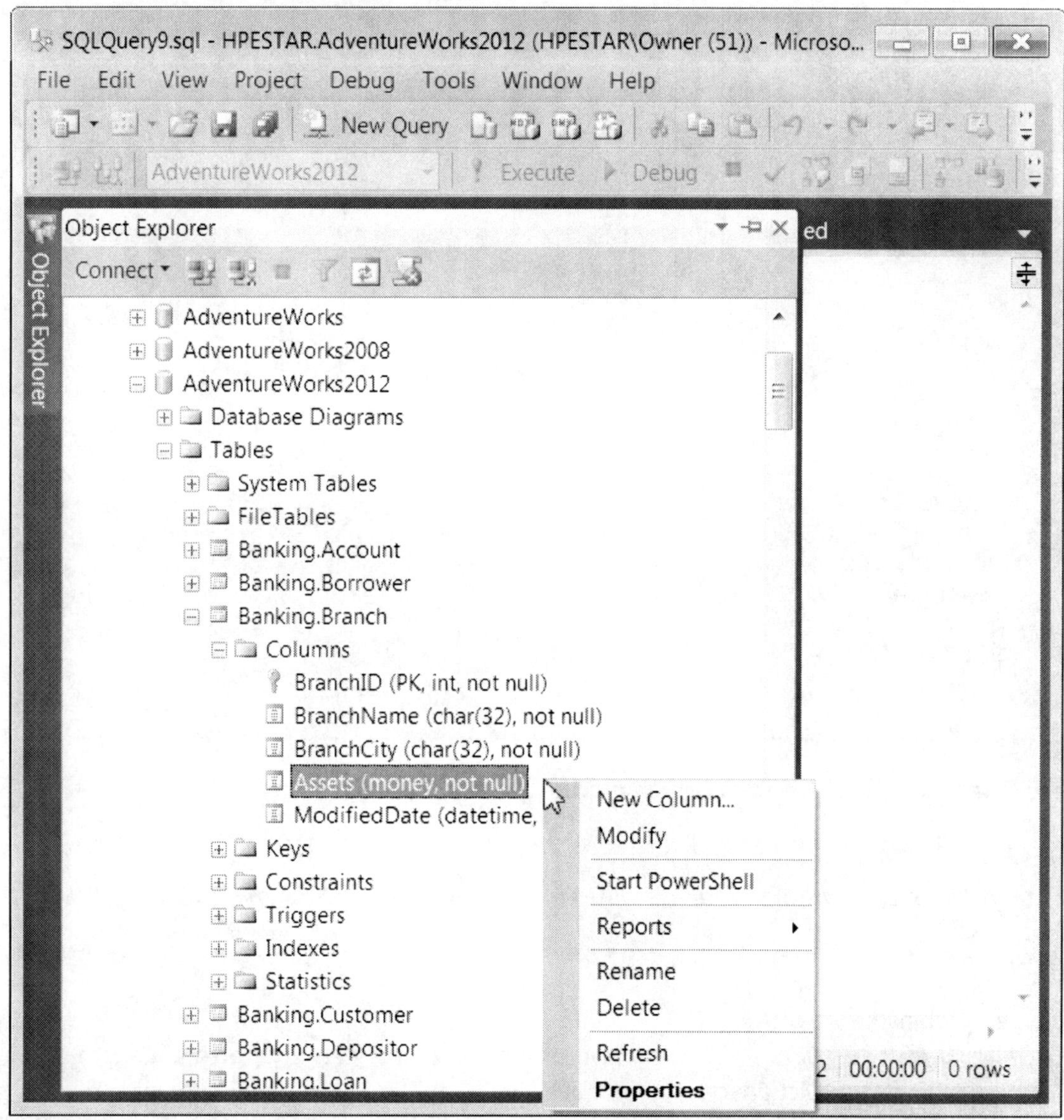

Extended Properties page can be used for Data Dictionary entry

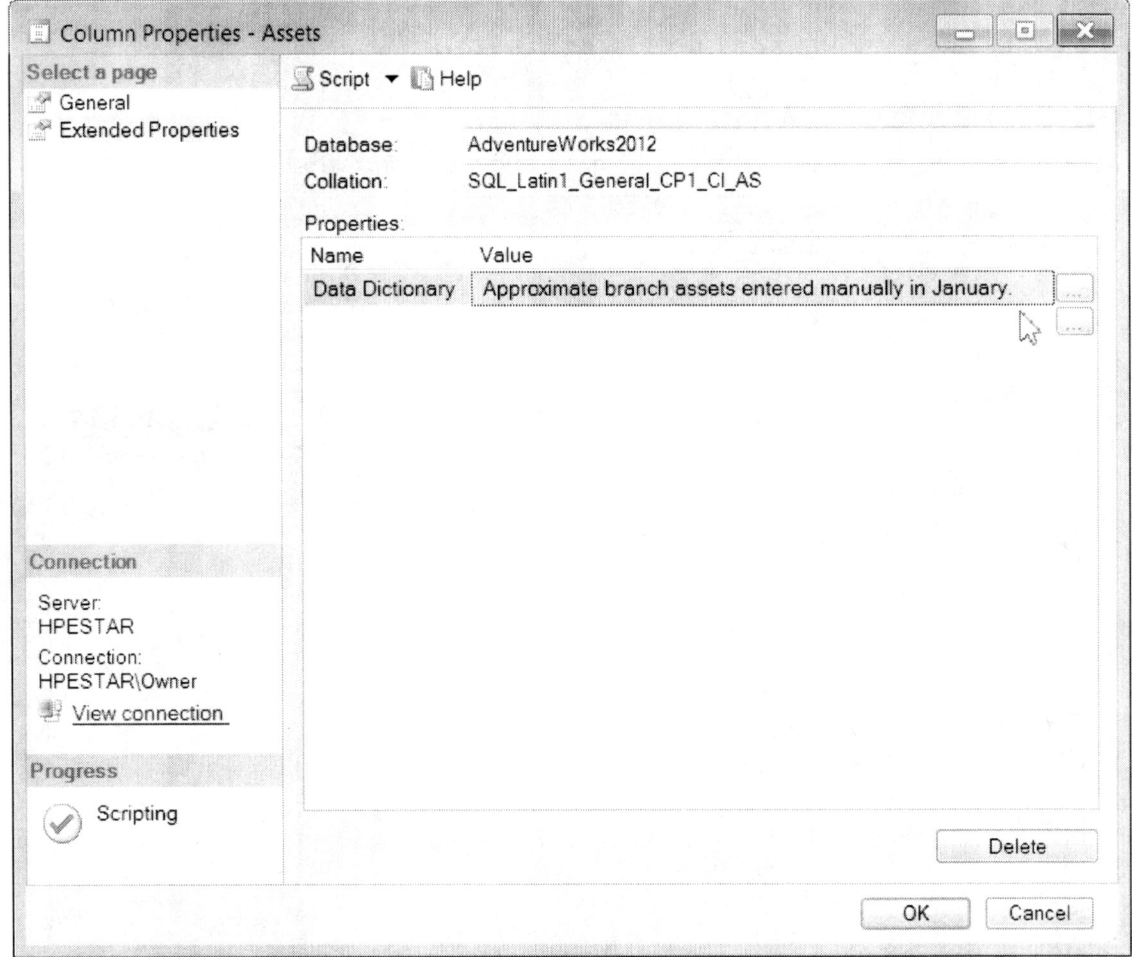

Check the new entry in the Data Dictionary with a query.

```
SELECT *
FROM fn_listextendedproperty (NULL, 'schema', 'Banking', 'table', 'Branch', 'Column', NULL);
GO
```

objtype	objname	name	value
COLUMN	Assets	Data Dictionary	Approximate branch assets entered manually in January.

Data Dictionary Maintenance with T-SQL Scripts

The advantage of using T-SQL scripts for Data Dictionary maintenance is that the script can be saved as a .sql file and rerun when necessary as is or after editing.

BOL: **AdventureWorks Data Dictionary**
http://msdn.microsoft.com/en-us/library/ms124438(v=sql.100).aspx

```
USE [AdventureWorks2012];
```

```
-- Delete Data Dictionary entry
EXEC sys.sp_dropextendedproperty @name=N'Data Dictionary' ,
        @level0type=N'SCHEMA',@level0name=N'Banking',
        @level1type=N'TABLE',@level1name=N'Branch',
        @level2type=N'COLUMN',@level2name=N'Assets';
GO
```

```
-- Add Data Dictionary entry
EXEC sys.sp_addextendedproperty @name=N'Data Dictionary',
        @value=N'Approximate branch assets entered manually in January each year.' ,
        @level0type=N'SCHEMA',@level0name=N'Banking', @level1type=N'TABLE',
        @level1name=N'Branch', @level2type=N'COLUMN',@level2name=N'Assets';
GO
```

```
-- Check new Data Dictionary entry
SELECT *
FROM fn_listextendedproperty (NULL, 'schema', 'Banking', 'table', 'Branch', 'Column', NULL);
```

objtype	objname	name	value
COLUMN	Assets	Data Dictionary	Approximate branch assets entered manually in January each year.

```
-- Data Dictionary entry for BranchName
EXEC sys.sp_addextendedproperty @name=N'Data Dictionary',
        @value=N'Name of the branch. Updated by supervisor only.' ,
        @level0type=N'SCHEMA',@level0name=N'Banking', @level1type=N'TABLE',
        @level1name=N'Branch', @level2type=N'COLUMN',@level2name=N'BranchName';
GO
```

Updating an Existing Data Dictionary Entry

```
-- Update Data Dictionary entry
EXEC sys.sp_updateextendedproperty @name=N'Data Dictionary',
@value=N'Approximate branch assets entered in January each year by an automated process.' ,
@level0type=N'SCHEMA',@level0name=N'Banking',
@level1type=N'TABLE',@level1name=N'Branch',
@level2type=N'COLUMN',@level2name=N'Assets'
GO
```

```
SELECT *
FROM fn_listextendedproperty (NULL, 'schema', 'Banking', 'table', 'Branch', 'Column', NULL);
GO
```

objtype	objname	name	value
COLUMN	Assets	Data Dictionary	Approximate branch assets entered in January each year by an automated process.

```
-- Data Dictionary entry for BranchCity
EXEC sys.sp_addextendedproperty @name=N'Data Dictionary',
	@value=N'City & State where branch is located.' ,
	@level0type=N'SCHEMA',@level0name=N'Banking', @level1type=N'TABLE',
	@level1name=N'Branch', @level2type=N'COLUMN',@level2name=N'BranchCity';
GO
```

```
-- Listing all Data Dictionary entries for table
SELECT *
FROM fn_listextendedproperty (NULL, 'schema', 'Banking', 'table', 'Branch', 'Column', NULL)
ORDER BY objname;
```

objtype	objname	name	value
COLUMN	Assets	Data Dictionary	Approximate branch assets entered in January each year by an automated process.
COLUMN	BranchCity	Data Dictionary	City & State where branch is located.
COLUMN	BranchName	Data Dictionary	Name of the branch. Updated by supervisor only.

Lead Developer as Database Designer

A senior database developer should be able to design a modest business application database. The reason is that he worked with a number of databases so well-familiar with the concept of 3NF relational database design. Naturally if the lead developer is not familiar with the business, then it is rather difficult, there is a steep learning curve. But then it is difficult also for a professional database designer. Getting a systems analyst on board is the best approach to work with the database designer.

Database Design Team at Big Budget Projects

Large companies for important projects may setup the following design team:

- 1-2 database designers
- 1-3 systems analysts
- 1-4 subject matter experts

Hiring Database Design Consultant where Resources Are Limited

Even a small company or a small project at large company should consider hiring a professional database designer on a consulting basis for a month or so to design the database. A well-designed 3NF database may reduce development from 50 man-months to 35 man-months, thus the payback may start before the project is completed. The payback continues after production deployment due to lower cost of future application software development and database maintenance. Once this author was consulting in stored procedure development at a small organization which was the fund raiser for a Connecticut seminary. Only one full-time manager/dba/developer, with consultants help. Quite shockingly, the database was excellent 3NF design. Only big-budget places can afford such a good 3NF design so goes the common wisdom. The manager explained that he hired a consultant expert database designer for a month. An excellent choice indeed.

Database System Solution Implementation Hierarchy

Frequently solutions can be implemented more than one way in a relational database system. For example, the constraint OrderQty > 0 can be implemented as CHECK constraint, stored procedure, trigger and as code in application software. There are great advantages to implement a solution at the lowest possible level of the following hierarchy.

- Table design
- Constraint
- Stored procedure
- Trigger
- Client software

List All Default Constraints with Definition

T-SQL metadata query to enumerate all column defaults with definition using a system view.

```
SELECT  SCHEMA_NAME(schema_id)                          AS SCHEMA_NAME,
        OBJECT_NAME(PARENT_OBJECT_ID)                   AS TABLE_NAME,
        COL_NAME (PARENT_OBJECT_ID, PARENT_COLUMN_ID)   AS COLUMN_NAME,
        Definition                                      AS DEFAULT_DEFINITION,
        NAME                                            AS DEFAULT_CONSTRAINT_NAME
FROM AdventureWorks2012.SYS.DEFAULT_CONSTRAINTS
ORDER BY 1, 2;  -- column numbers
-- (152 row(s) affected) - Partial results.
```

SCHEMA_NAME	TABLE_NAME	COLUMN_NAME	DEFAULT_DEFINITION	DEFAULT_CONSTRAINT_NAME
dbo	AWBuildVersion	ModifiedDate	(getdate())	DF_AWBuildVersion_ModifiedDate
dbo	ErrorLog	ErrorTime	(getdate())	DF_ErrorLog_ErrorTime
HumanResources	Department	ModifiedDate	(getdate())	DF_Department_ModifiedDate
HumanResources	Employee	SalariedFlag	((1))	DF_Employee_SalariedFlag
HumanResources	Employee	VacationHours	((0))	DF_Employee_VacationHours
HumanResources	Employee	SickLeaveHours	((0))	DF_Employee_SickLeaveHours
HumanResources	Employee	CurrentFlag	((1))	DF_Employee_CurrentFlag
HumanResources	Employee	rowguid	(newid())	DF_Employee_rowguid
HumanResources	Employee	ModifiedDate	(getdate())	DF_Employee_ModifiedDate
HumanResources	EmployeeDepartmentHistory	ModifiedDate	(getdate())	DF_EmployeeDepartmentHistory_ModifiedDate
HumanResources	EmployeePayHistory	ModifiedDate	(getdate())	DF_EmployeePayHistory_ModifiedDate
HumanResources	JobCandidate	ModifiedDate	(getdate())	DF_JobCandidate_ModifiedDate
HumanResources	Shift	ModifiedDate	(getdate())	DF_Shift_ModifiedDate
Person	Address	rowguid	(newid())	DF_Address_rowguid
Person	Address	ModifiedDate	(getdate())	DF_Address_ModifiedDate
Person	AddressType	rowguid	(newid())	DF_AddressType_rowguid
Person	AddressType	ModifiedDate	(getdate())	DF_AddressType_ModifiedDate
Person	BusinessEntity	rowguid	(newid())	DF_BusinessEntity_rowguid
Person	BusinessEntity	ModifiedDate	(getdate())	DF_BusinessEntity_ModifiedDate

The sp_helpconstraints system procedure to list all constraints (including default) on a table.

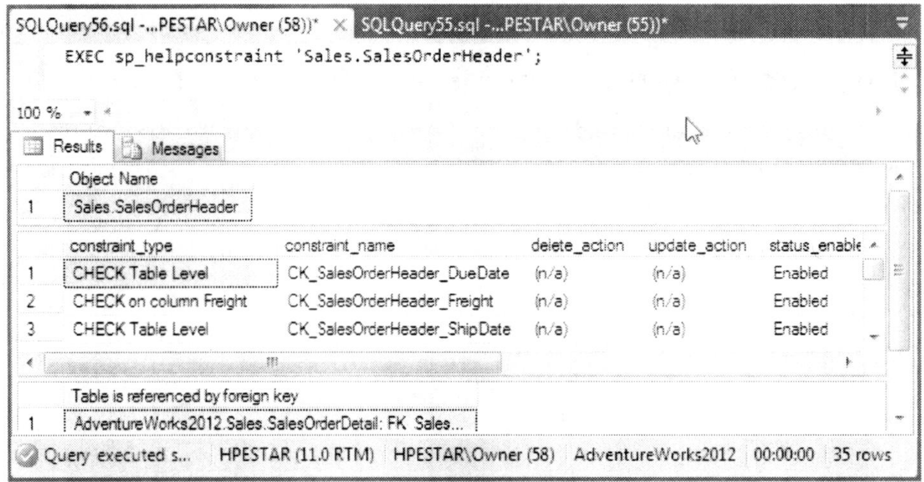

Partitioning Query via Pure SQL - Ye Olde Way

Add new sequence numbering column for subsets(partition by OrderID) with standard SQL only. The old way is not very efficient, the ROW_NUMBER() OVER PARTITION is better performing.

```
USE Northwind;
SELECT   OD.OrderID,
         SeqNo                                                                    AS LineItem,
         OD.ProductID,
         UnitPrice,
         Quantity                                                                 AS Qty,
         CONVERT(NUMERIC(3, 2), Discount)                                         AS Discount,
         CONVERT(NUMERIC(12, 2), UnitPrice * Quantity * ( 1.0 - Discount ))  AS LineTotal
FROM  [Order Details] OD
    INNER JOIN (SELECT count(*) SeqNo,   a.OrderID,   a.ProductID
         FROM   [Order Details] A
              INNER JOIN [Order Details] B ON A.ProductID >= B.ProductID   AND A.OrderID = B.OrderID
         GROUP  BY A.OrderID,   A.ProductID) a
       ON OD.OrderID = a.OrderID   AND OD.ProductID = a.ProductID
WHERE  OD.OrderID < 10300  ORDER  BY OD.OrderID,  OD.ProductID, SeqNo; -- (140 row(s) affected) - Partial results.
```

OrderID	LineItem	ProductID	UnitPrice	Qty	Discount	LineTotal
10255	1	2	15.20	20	0.00	304.00
10255	2	16	13.90	35	0.00	486.50
10255	3	36	15.20	25	0.00	380.00
10255	4	59	44.00	30	0.00	1320.00
10256	1	53	26.20	15	0.00	393.00
10256	2	77	10.40	12	0.00	124.80
10257	1	27	35.10	25	0.00	877.50

Partitioning Using the OVER Clause & RANK() Function

Find highest price products in each color using derived table x (subquery). CTE can also be used.

```
SELECT Color, ProductNumber, ListPrice FROM (
       (SELECT Color, ProductNumber, ListPrice, RANK() OVER( PARTITION BY Color
                 ORDER BY ListPrice DESC) AS [Rank]
       FROM AdventureWorks2012.Production.Product WHERE Color is not null) ) AS x
WHERE Rank=1 ORDER BY Color, ProductNumber; -- (30 row(s) affected) - Partial results.
```

Color	ProductNumber	ListPrice
Silver/Black	PD-R853	80.99
Silver/Black	PD-T852	80.99
White	SO-B909-L	9.50
White	SO-B909-M	9.50
Yellow	BK-T79Y-46	2384.07

CHAPTER 9: Advanced Database Design Concepts

FileTable - Integrating Folders with Database

Storing large number of binary files such as images, documents was a challenge until SQL Server 2012: FileTable integrates files in a folder into the database, yet keep them accessible at Windows file system level. In the past, there were two solutions:

- Keep only the filenames in the database table.
- Keep both the filenames and **binary file objects (varbinary(max))** in the table.

Using the first method, the files were not backed up with the database since they were not part of the database. Applying the second method, the binary objects were in the database, but as a deadweight, since not much can be done with them. FileTable is the best of both worlds: files are backed up / restored with the database, yet they remain visible at the file system level. So if a new file is dropped (copied) into the folder, it becomes visible to SQL Server instantaneously. FileTable requires the FILESTREAM feature as shown on the Server Properties dialog box.

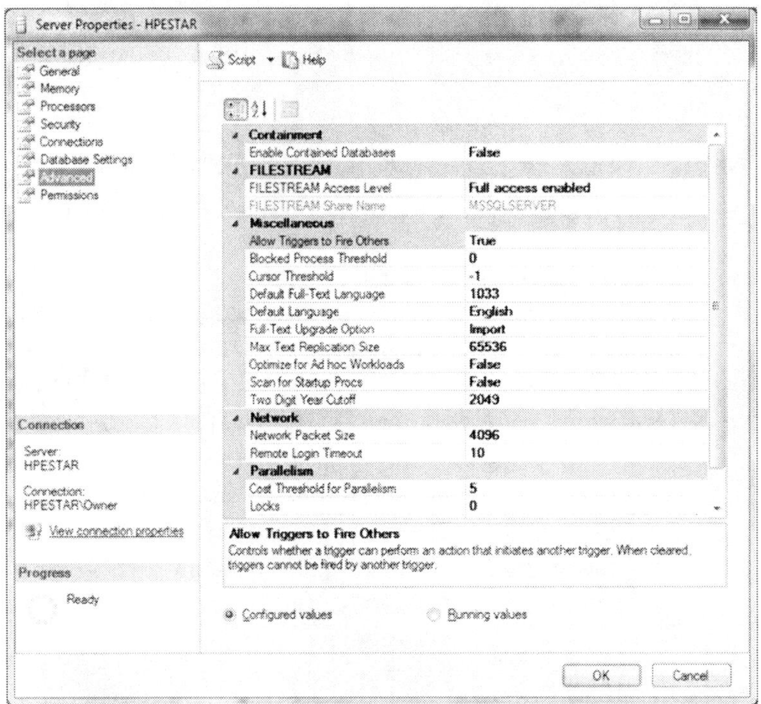

The CREATE TABLE statement for a FileTable

```
-- Create FileTable  -- new to SQL Server 2012
CREATE TABLE ImageStore
AS FileTable
  WITH (
      FileTable_Directory = 'ImageStore',
      FileTable_Collate_Filename = database_default
     );
GO
-- (1 row(s) affected)
```

We can determine the FileTable folder name which is visible at the file system level the following way.

```
SELECT DBName=DB_NAME ( database_id ), directory_name
  FROM sys.database_filestream_options
        WHERE directory_name is not null;
GO
```

DBName	directory_name
AdventureWorks2012	FSDIR

FileTable directory(path):

\\YOURSERVER\MSSQLSERVER\FSDIR\ImageStore

The dialog box for database options setup as related to FILESTREAM

"hpestar" is the name of the SQL Server instance (default instance, same name as the computer).

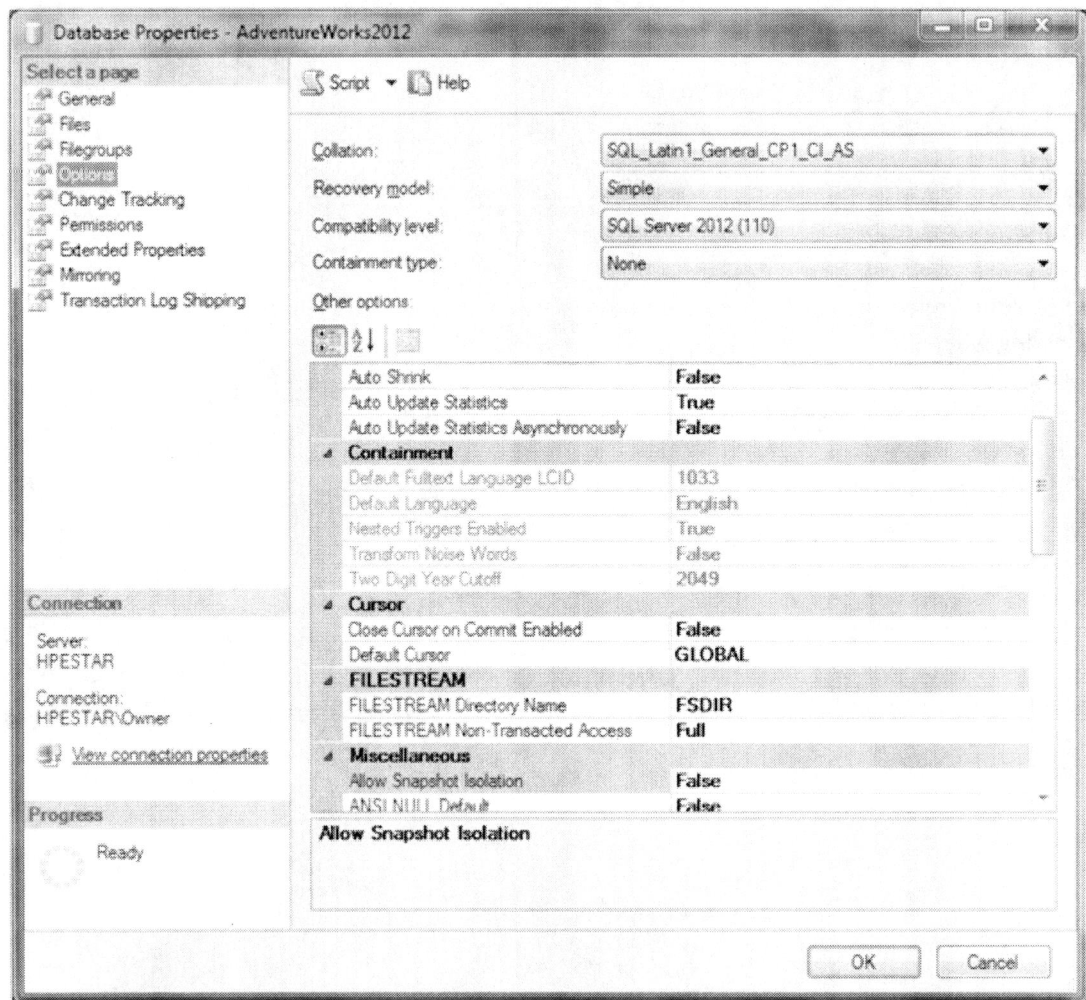

T-SQL Tidbits: UPDATE STATISTICS as Quick Fix for Performance Problems

Major discrepancy between estimated rows and actual rows in execution plans maybe a sign of out-of-date statistics. The quick solution is UPDATE STATISTICS.

Nonetheless, it is better not to get to the situation when emergency UPDATE STATISTICS is required. **Generally, indexes should be rebuilt every weekend , statistics updated every night & missing indexes created**. Index REBUILD updates statistics automatically. Lots of INSERTs, DELETEs & UPDATEs cause statistics to become outdated.

The FileTable folder is currently empty.

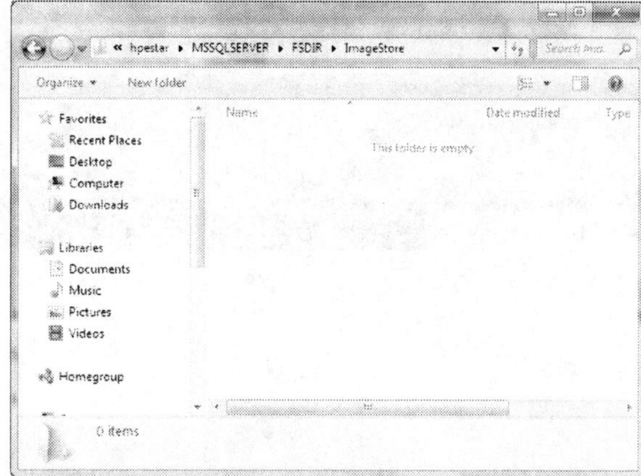

We shall now copy 3 photos in the ImageStore folder using Windows Copy & Paste operation.

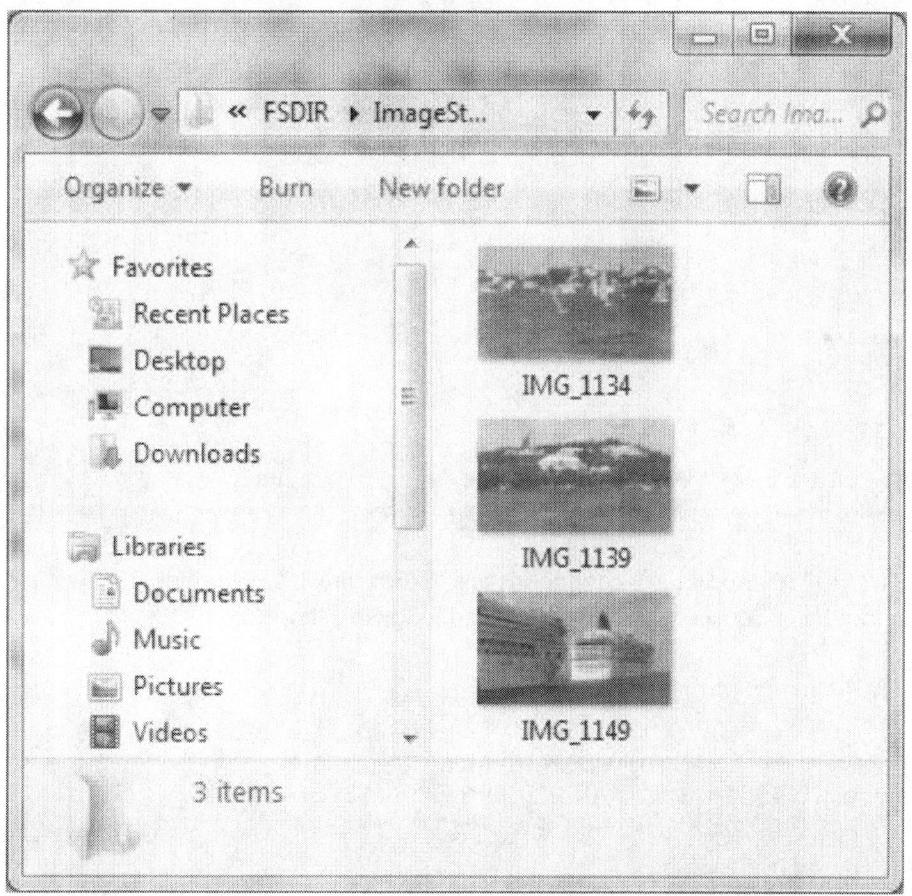

The photos are "visible" from the database side as well.

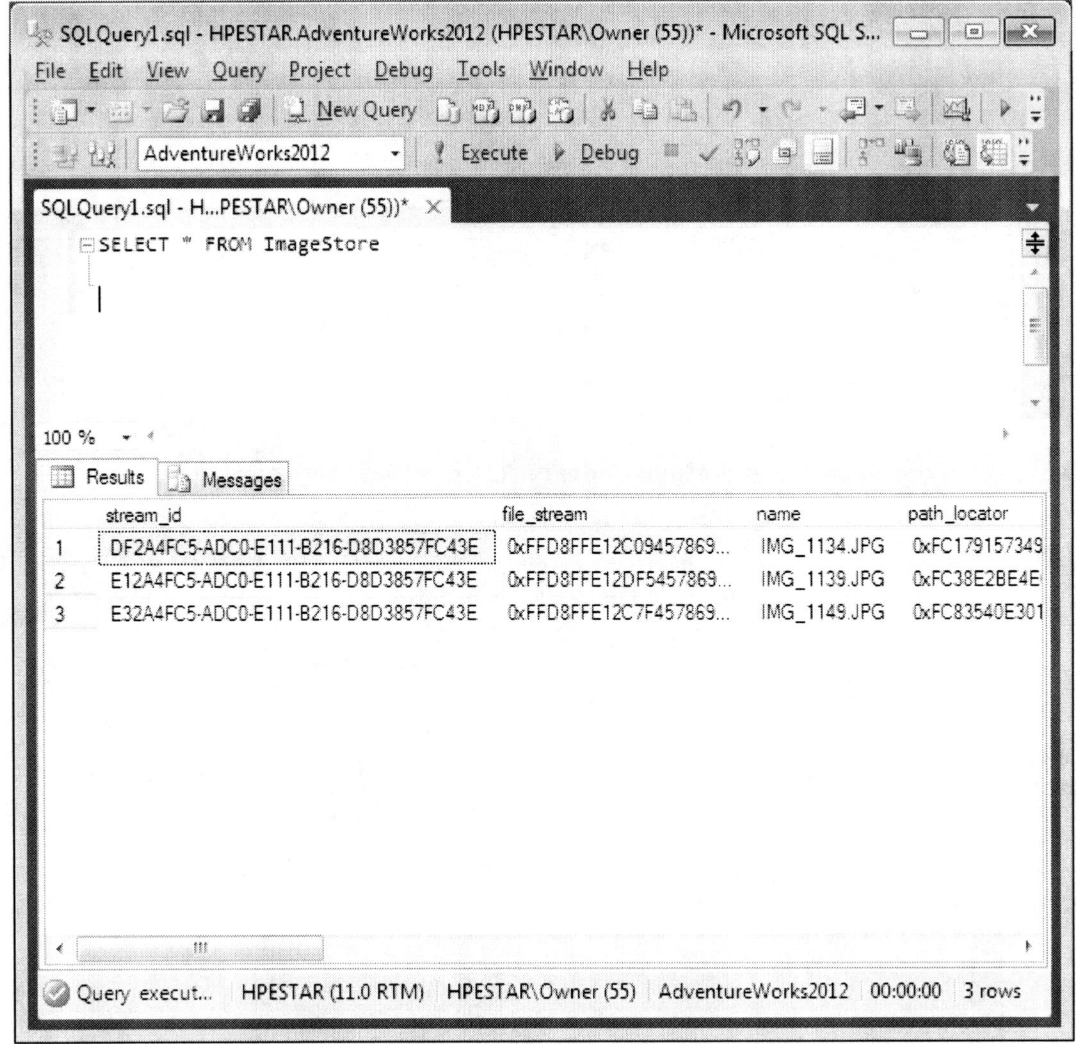

The INSERT, UPDATE and DELETE commands are operational on FileTable, however, a new column cannot be added as demonstrated in the following script:

```
SELECT * FROM ImageStore;
GO
UPDATE ImageStore SET name='RollerCoaster.jpg'
WHERE stream_id='E73EA731-AAAA-E111-9078-D8D3857FC43E';
GO
SELECT * FROM ImageStore;
```

Adding Files to FileTable Using T-SQL

There are two T-SQL methods available.

```
-- Adding files from T-SQL - method 1 xp_cmdshell copy
EXEC xp_cmdshell 'copy "C:\photo\000Test\xBermuda.jpg"
"\\HPESTAR\mssqlserver\FSDIR\ImageStore\xBermuda.jpg"'
GO
```

```
-- Adding files from T-SQL - method 2 OPENROWSET
INSERT INTO [dbo].[ImageStore] ([name],[file_stream])
SELECT 'Bermuda9.jpg', * FROM
    OPENROWSET(BULK N'C:\photo\2012\BERMUDA\BERMUDA\IMG_1154.jpg', SINGLE_BLOB)
                AS FileUpload
```

Deleting Files from FileTable Using T-SQL

```
SELECT * FROM ImageStore
GO
```

```
DELETE ImageStore
WHERE stream_id = '62F55342-ABAA-E111-9078-D8D3857FC43E'
GO
```

```
SELECT * FROM ImageStore
GO
```

```
-- Column(s) cannot be added to a FileTable
ALTER TABLE ImageStore
ADD AddDate smalldatetime NULL
CONSTRAINT AddDateDflt
DEFAULT CURRENT_TIMESTAMP WITH VALUES ;
GO
/* Msg 33422, Level 16, State 1, Line 2
The column 'AddDate' cannot be added to table 'ImageStore' as it is a FileTable.
Adding columns to the fixed schema of a FileTable object is not permitted.
*/
```

```
DROP TABLE ImageStore
GO
```

Data Compression: Compressed Table

The table compression option has been introduced with SQL Server 2008. Data is compressed inside a database table, and it reduces the size of the table. Performance benefit in addition to space saving: "reads" reduction; queries need to read fewer pages from the disk. Sufficient CPU resources are required for the SQL Server instance to compress and decompress table data, when data is read (SELECT) or written (INSERT, UPDATE, MERGE). Analysis is required to ensure that table compression has no adverse effect on business critical query performance. Data compression may not be available in all editions of SQL Server. In the demonstration, first we create a new table for testing.

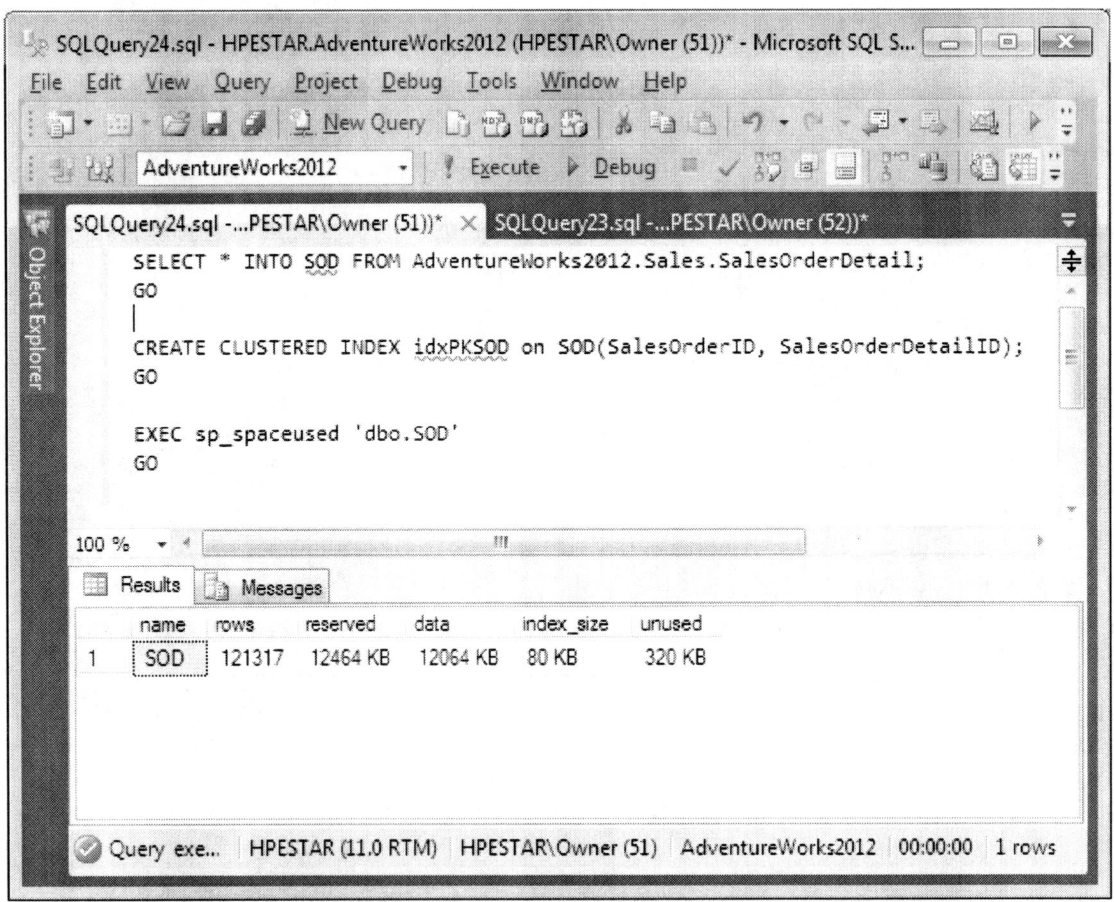

Switching to PAGE-LEVEL Compression

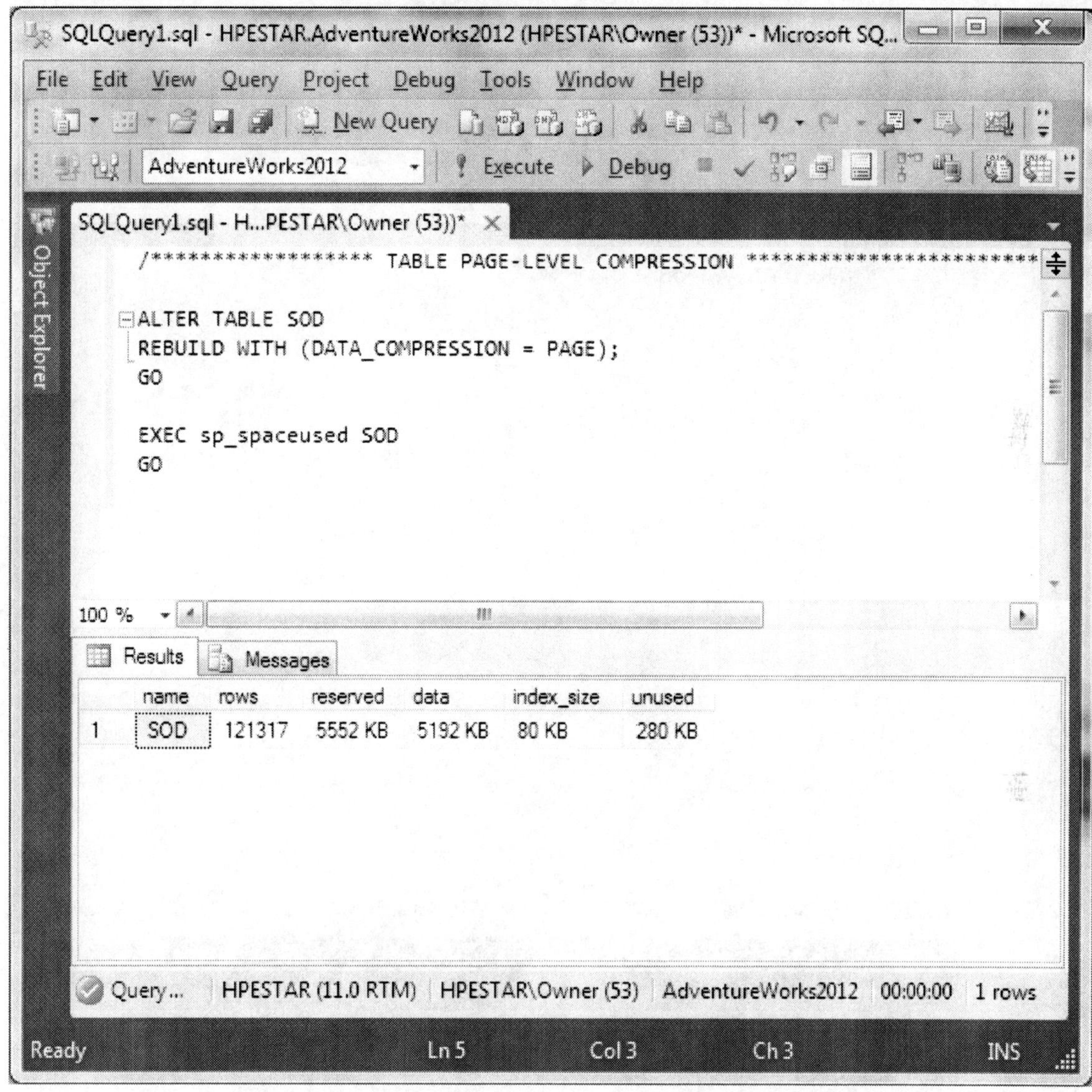

Data storage size decreased from around 12 MB to around 5 MB.

Testing ROW-LEVEL Compression

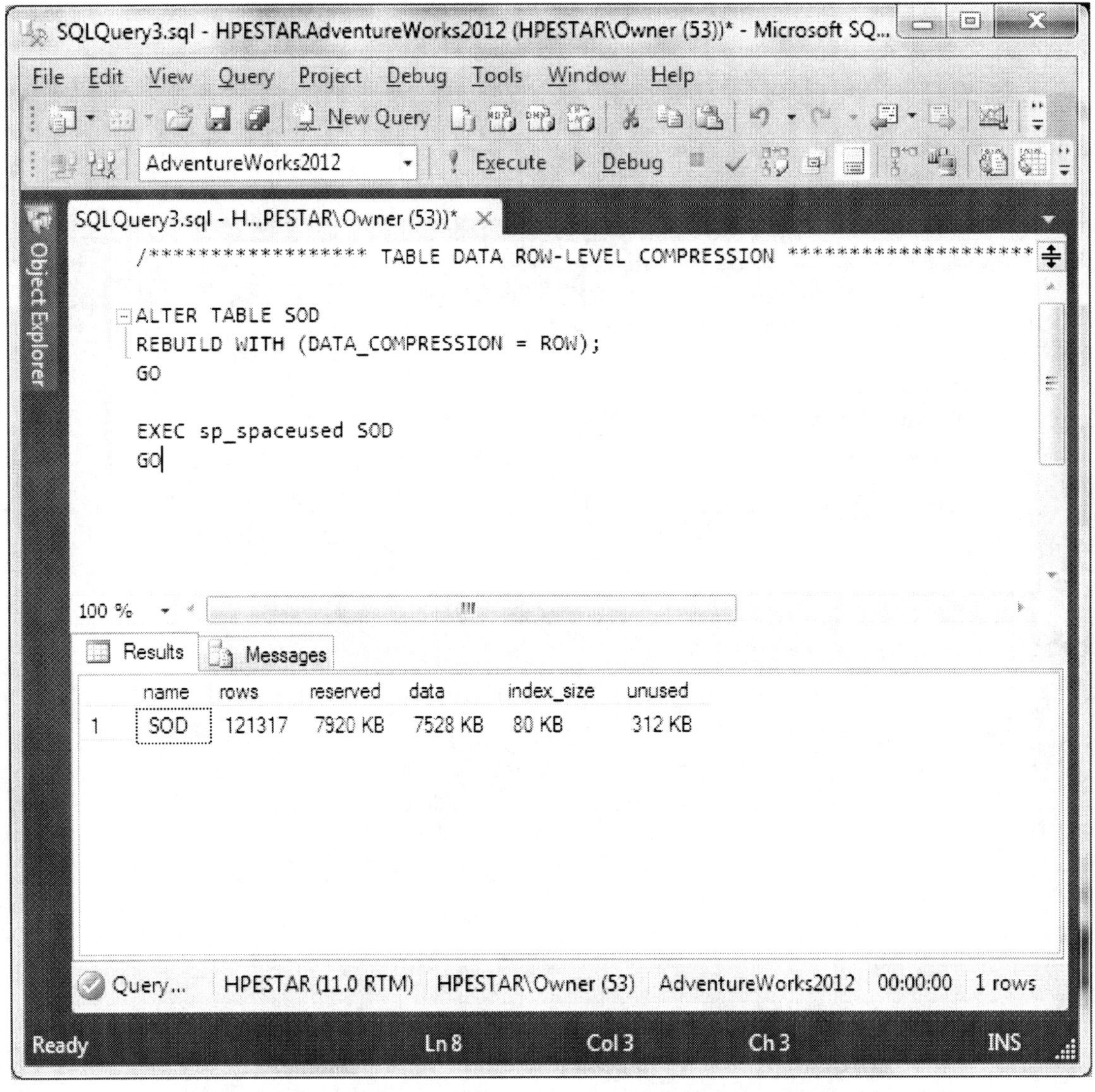

We can see the space reduction from 12MB to around 7.5MB.

Space reduction can be estimated with a system stored procedure.

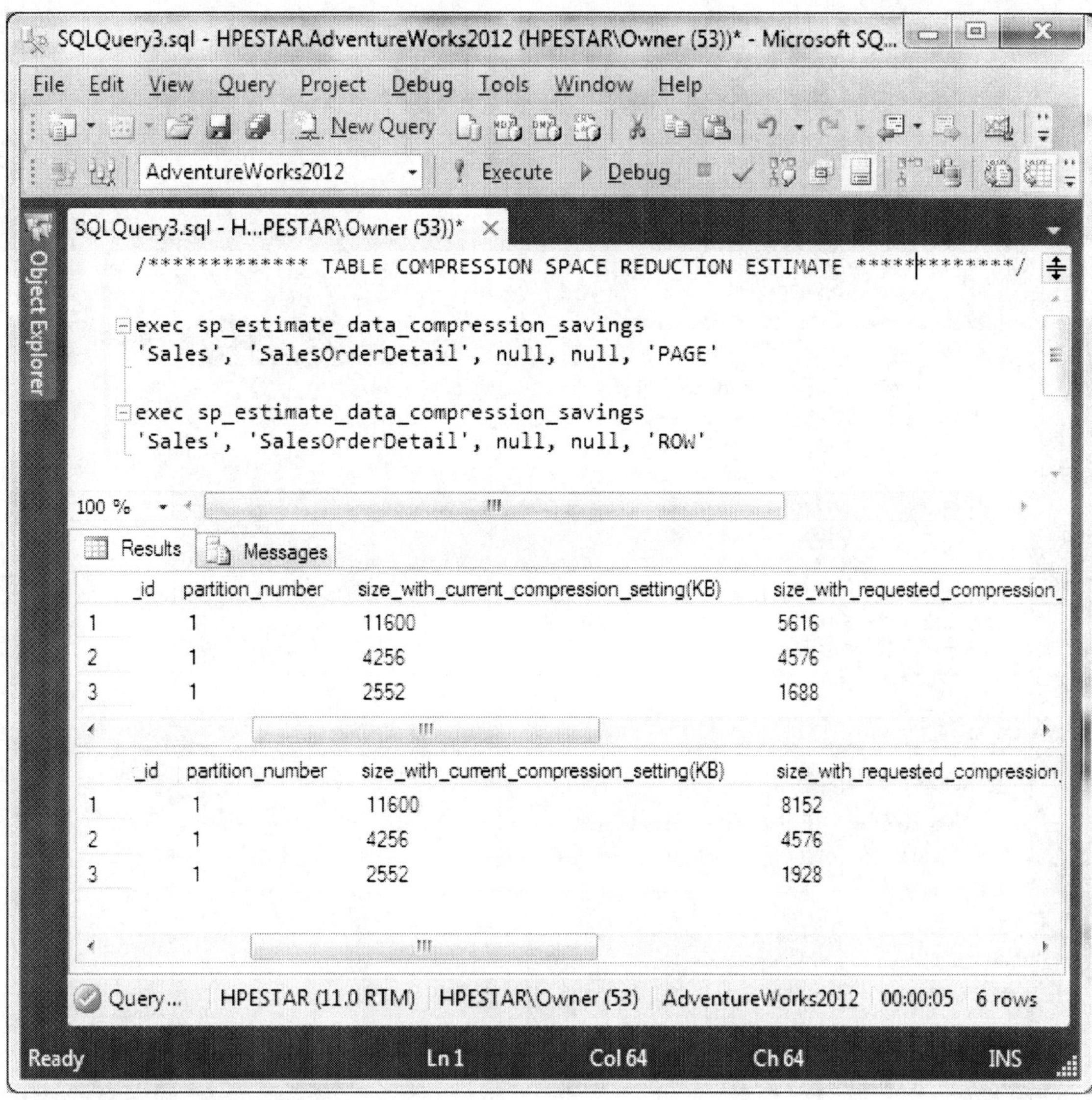

Careful and extensive considerations are required to decide to apply row, page or no compression to a table.

Query To Check How Many Rows Are Stored In An 8K Page In The Original Non-Compressed Table

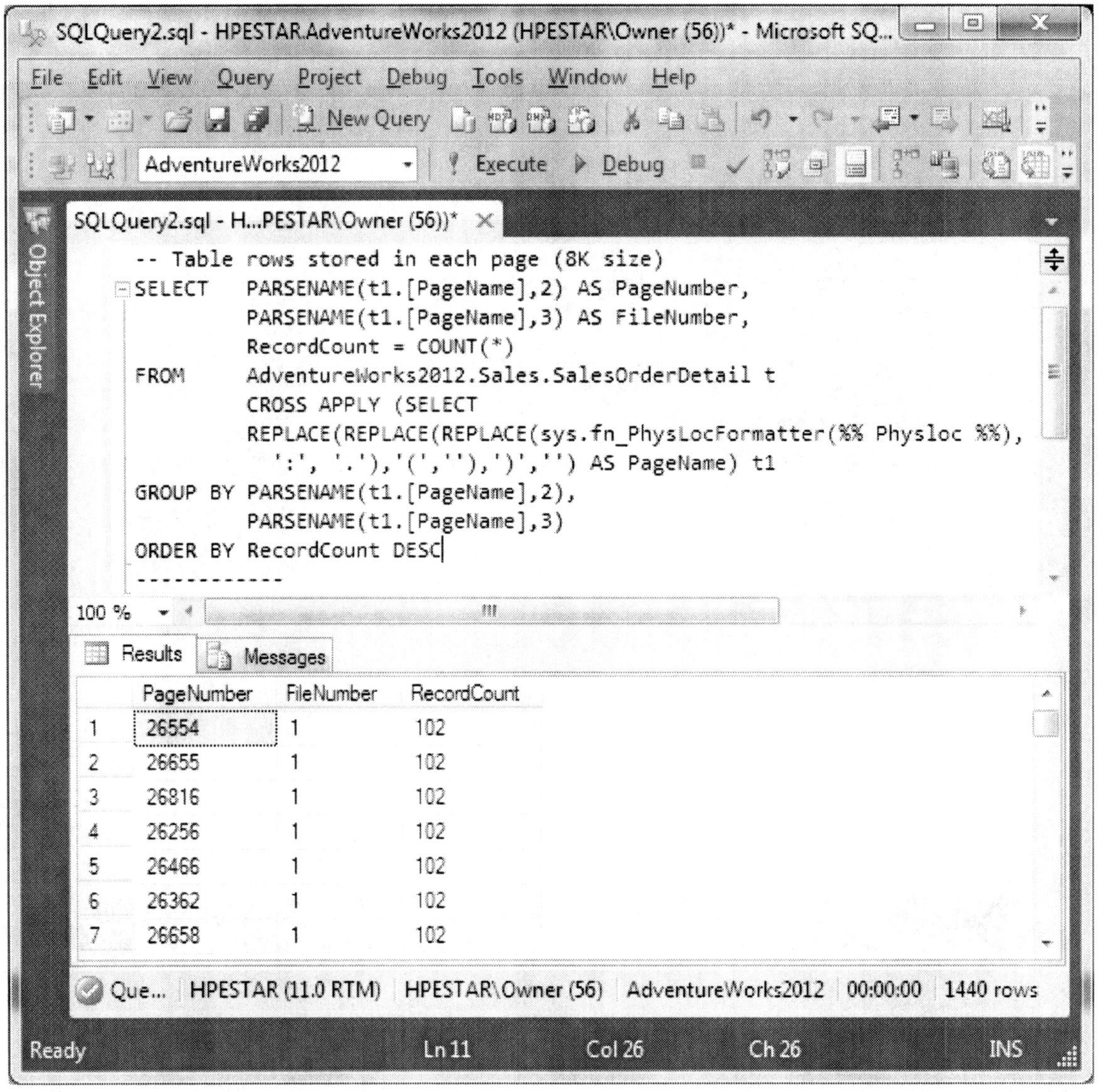


```
-- Table rows stored in each page (8K size)
SELECT   PARSENAME(t1.[PageName],2) AS PageNumber,
         PARSENAME(t1.[PageName],3) AS FileNumber,
         RecordCount = COUNT(*)
FROM     AdventureWorks2012.Sales.SalesOrderDetail t
         CROSS APPLY (SELECT
         REPLACE(REPLACE(REPLACE(sys.fn_PhysLocFormatter(%% Physloc %%),
           ':', '.'),'(',''),')','') AS PageName) t1
GROUP BY PARSENAME(t1.[PageName],2),
         PARSENAME(t1.[PageName],3)
ORDER BY RecordCount DESC
------------
```

	PageNumber	FileNumber	RecordCount
1	26554	1	102
2	26655	1	102
3	26816	1	102
4	26256	1	102
5	26466	1	102
6	26362	1	102
7	26658	1	102

Query to check the same for the compressed table SOD

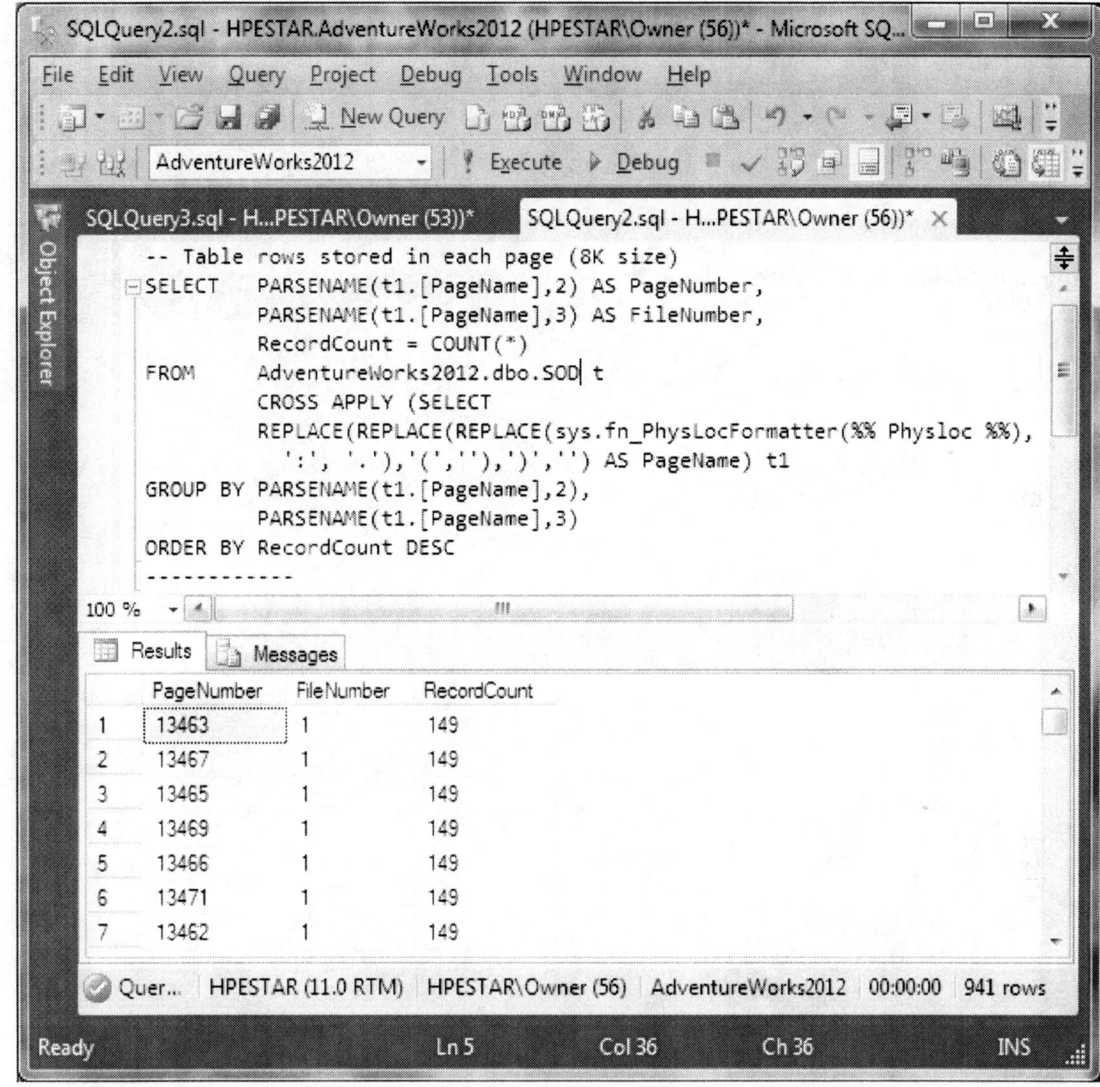

We can see that the best record (rows) count is 149 per page as opposed to 102 when the rows are not compressed. Since compression and decompression are processing intensive, we are trading CPU load vs. disk load. Which one to choose? PAGE compression is the true compression with maximum space saving. Choose PAGE compression for best disk IO reduction. As mentioned earlier careful preparation is required to make sure there are no undesirable side effects.

Data Compression: Compressed Index

Index can also be compressed. The following script creates and compresses an index with included columns.

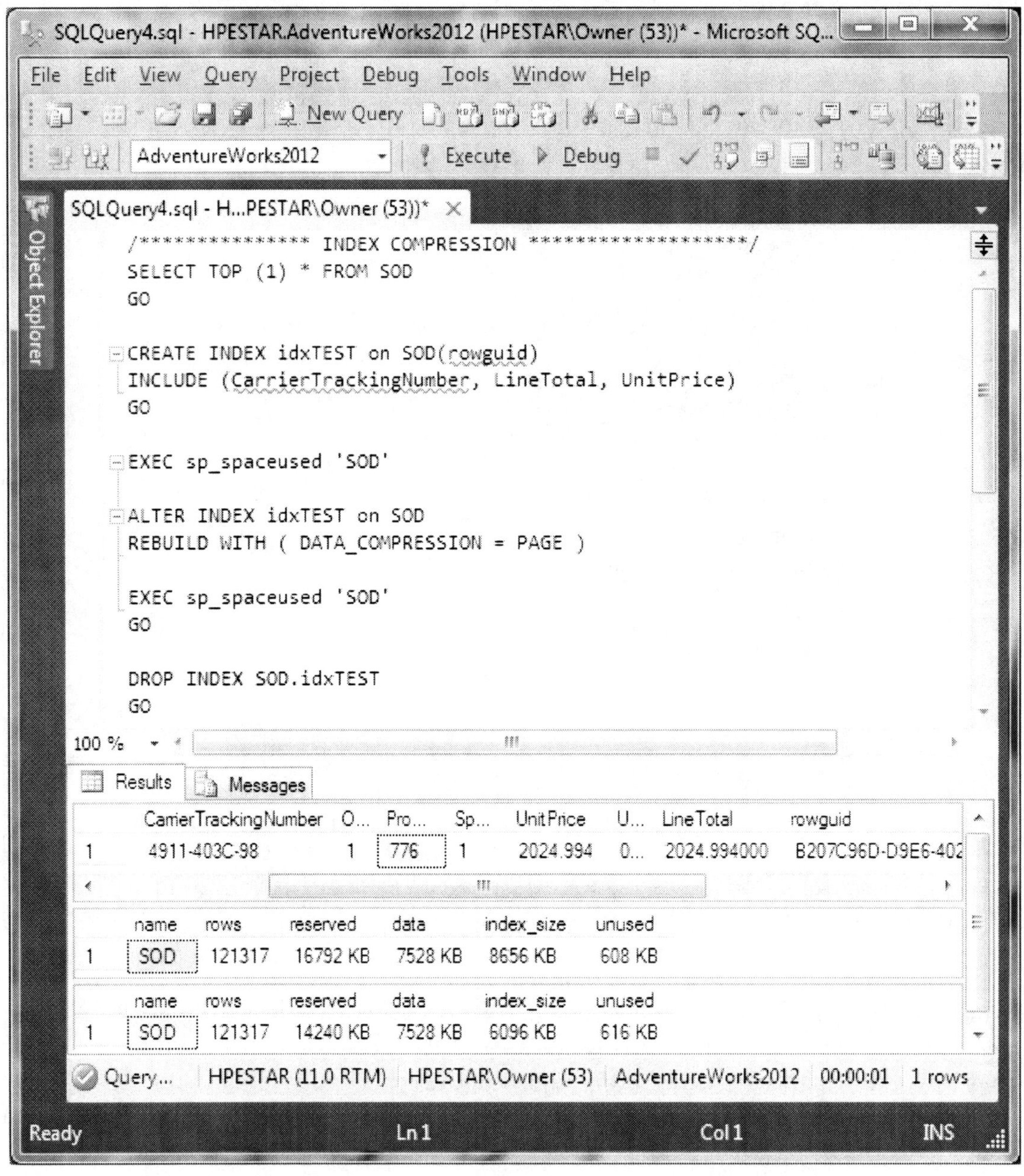
```
/*************** INDEX COMPRESSION *****************/
SELECT TOP (1) * FROM SOD
GO

CREATE INDEX idxTEST on SOD(rowguid)
INCLUDE (CarrierTrackingNumber, LineTotal, UnitPrice)
GO

EXEC sp_spaceused 'SOD'

ALTER INDEX idxTEST on SOD
REBUILD WITH ( DATA_COMPRESSION = PAGE )

EXEC sp_spaceused 'SOD'
GO

DROP INDEX SOD.idxTEST
GO
```

	CarrierTrackingNumber	O...	Pro...	Sp...	UnitPrice	U...	LineTotal	rowguid
1	4911-403C-98	1	776	1	2024.994	0...	2024.994000	B207C96D-D9E6-402

	name	rows	reserved	data	index_size	unused
1	SOD	121317	16792 KB	7528 KB	8656 KB	608 KB

	name	rows	reserved	data	index_size	unused
1	SOD	121317	14240 KB	7528 KB	6096 KB	616 KB

We can observe the index size reduction. Note that index_size includes all indexes.

The GUI Data Compression Wizard

The wizard can be started with Right Click on the table in SSMS Object Explorer.

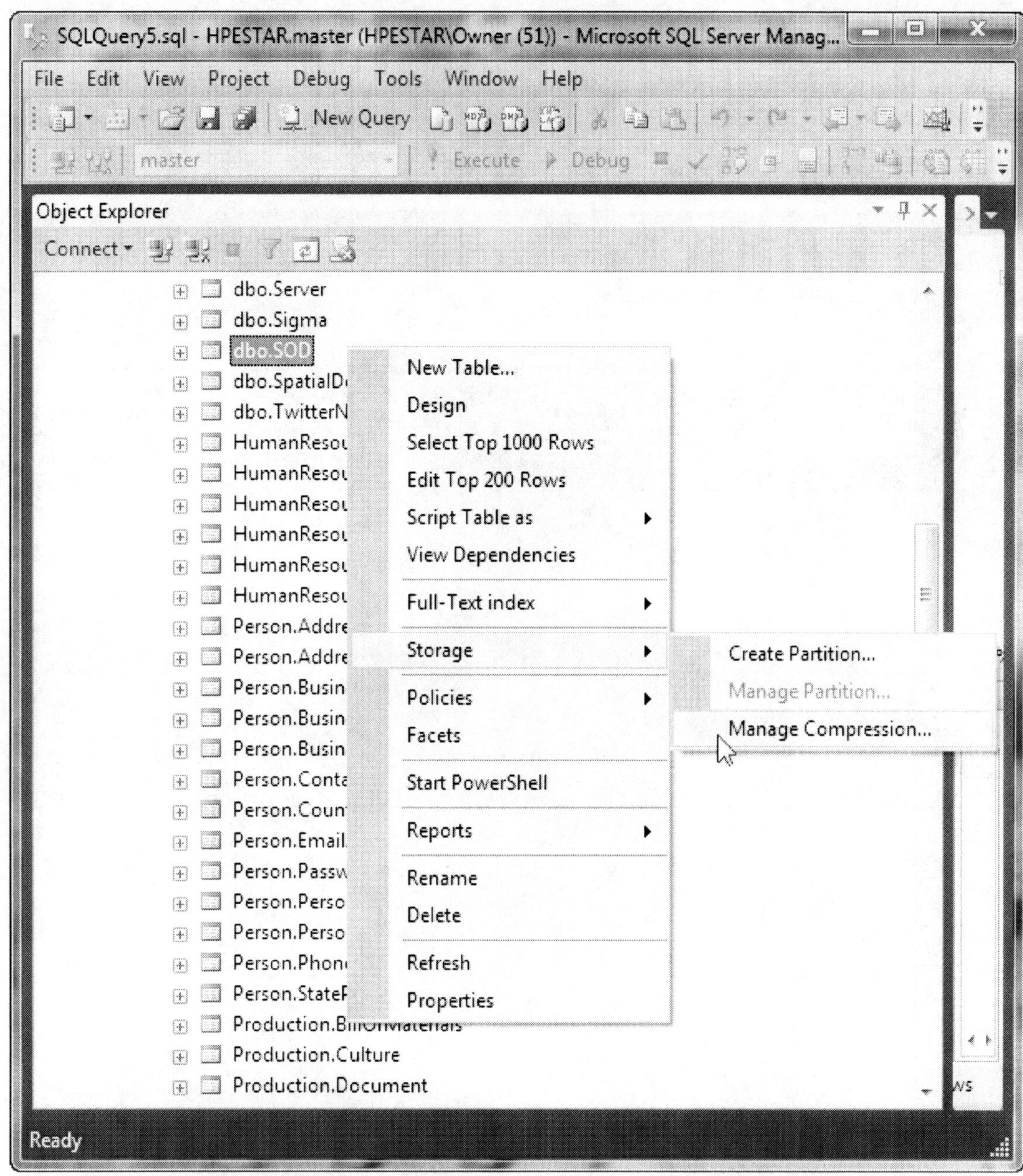

Space Saving Calculation Wizard Page

The figures include table & indexes total size.

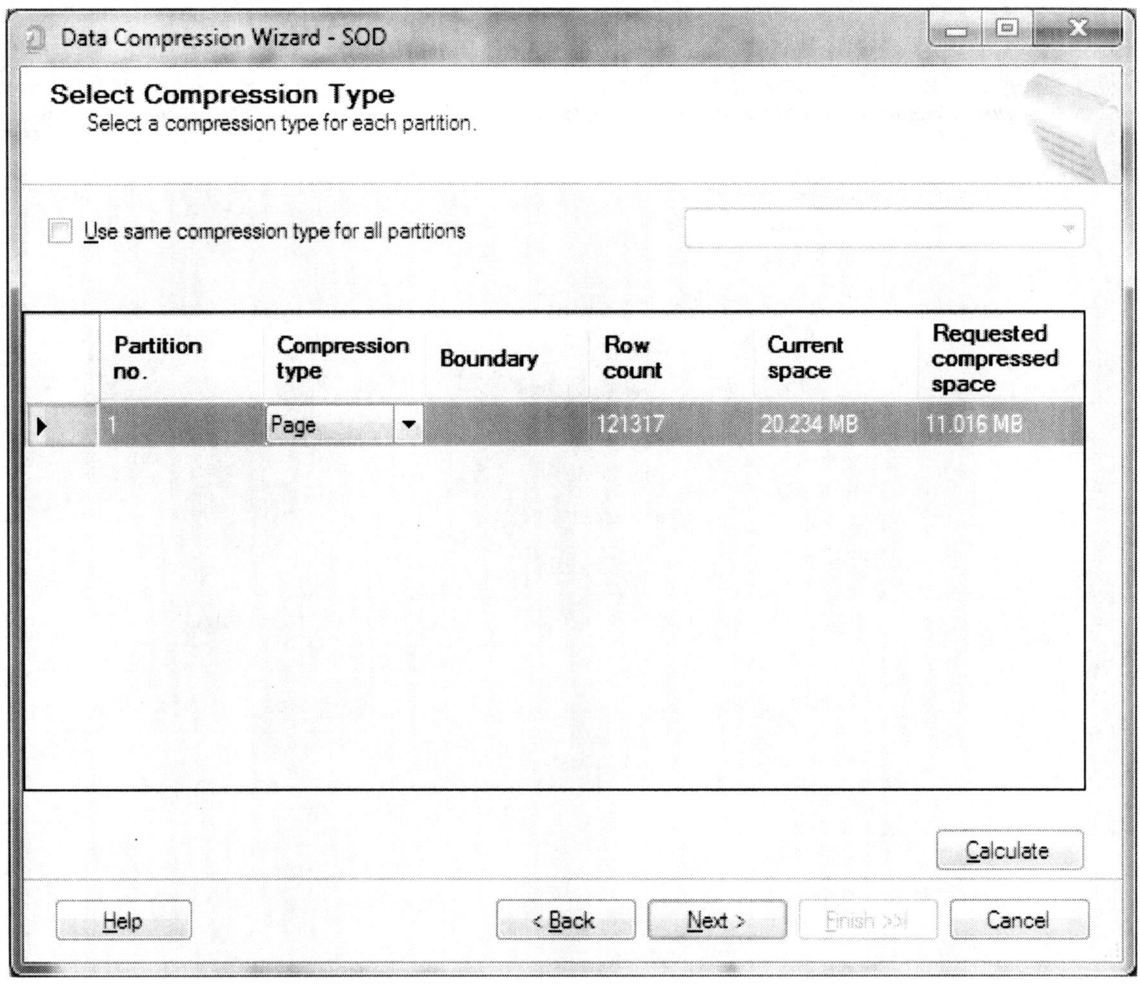

Output Panel Offers Scripting And Execution Options

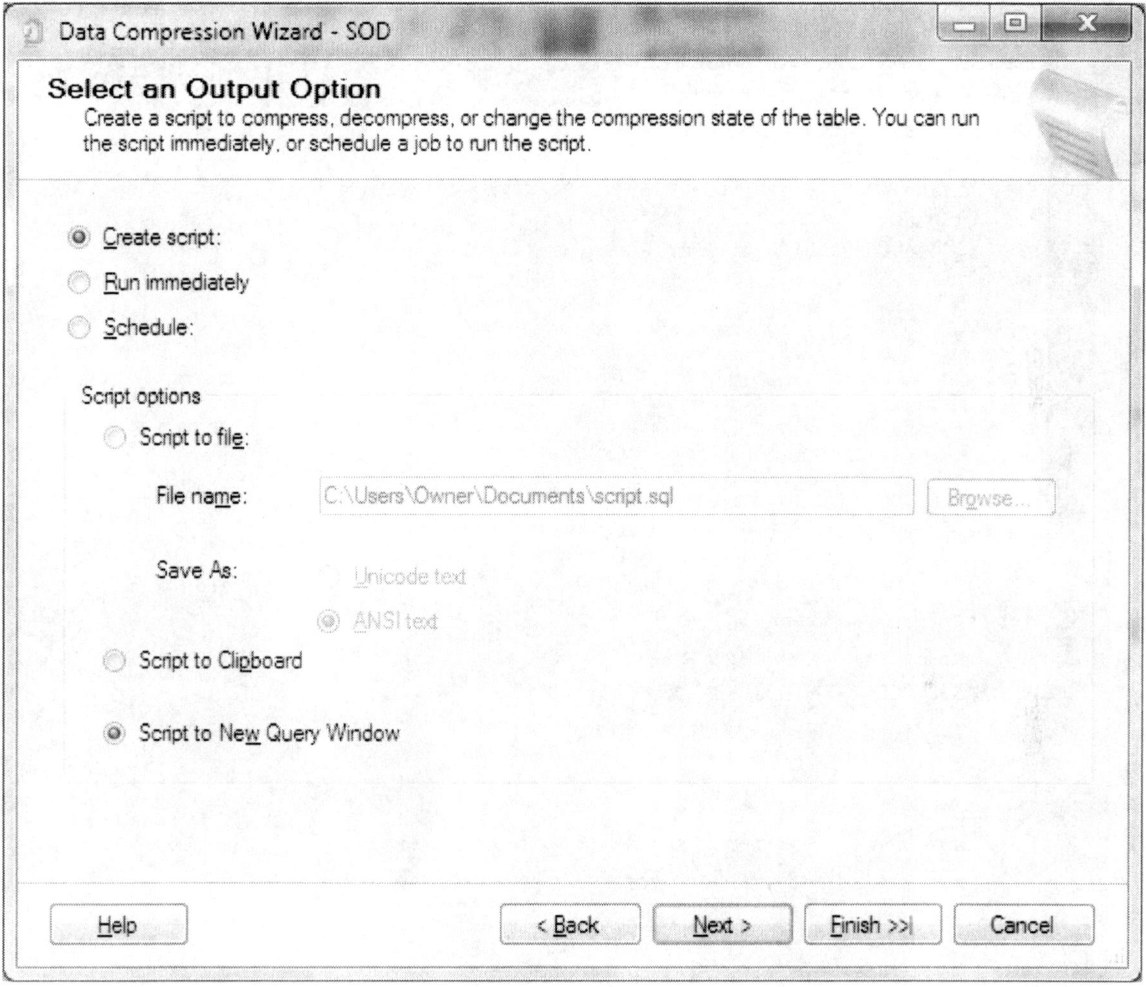

Testing the generated script with the sp_spaceused system stored procedure

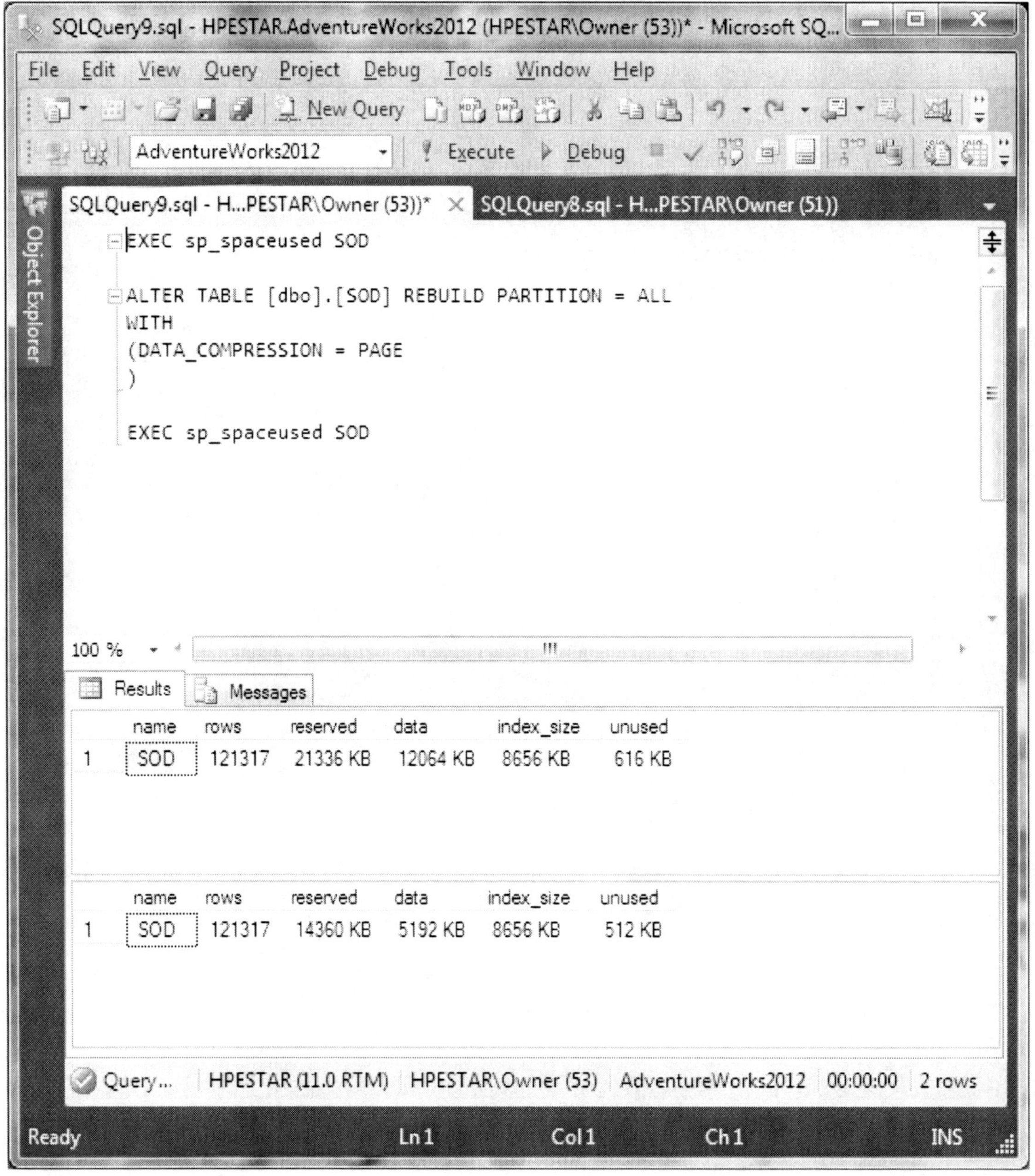

Indexes Can Be Compressed With The Wizard As Well

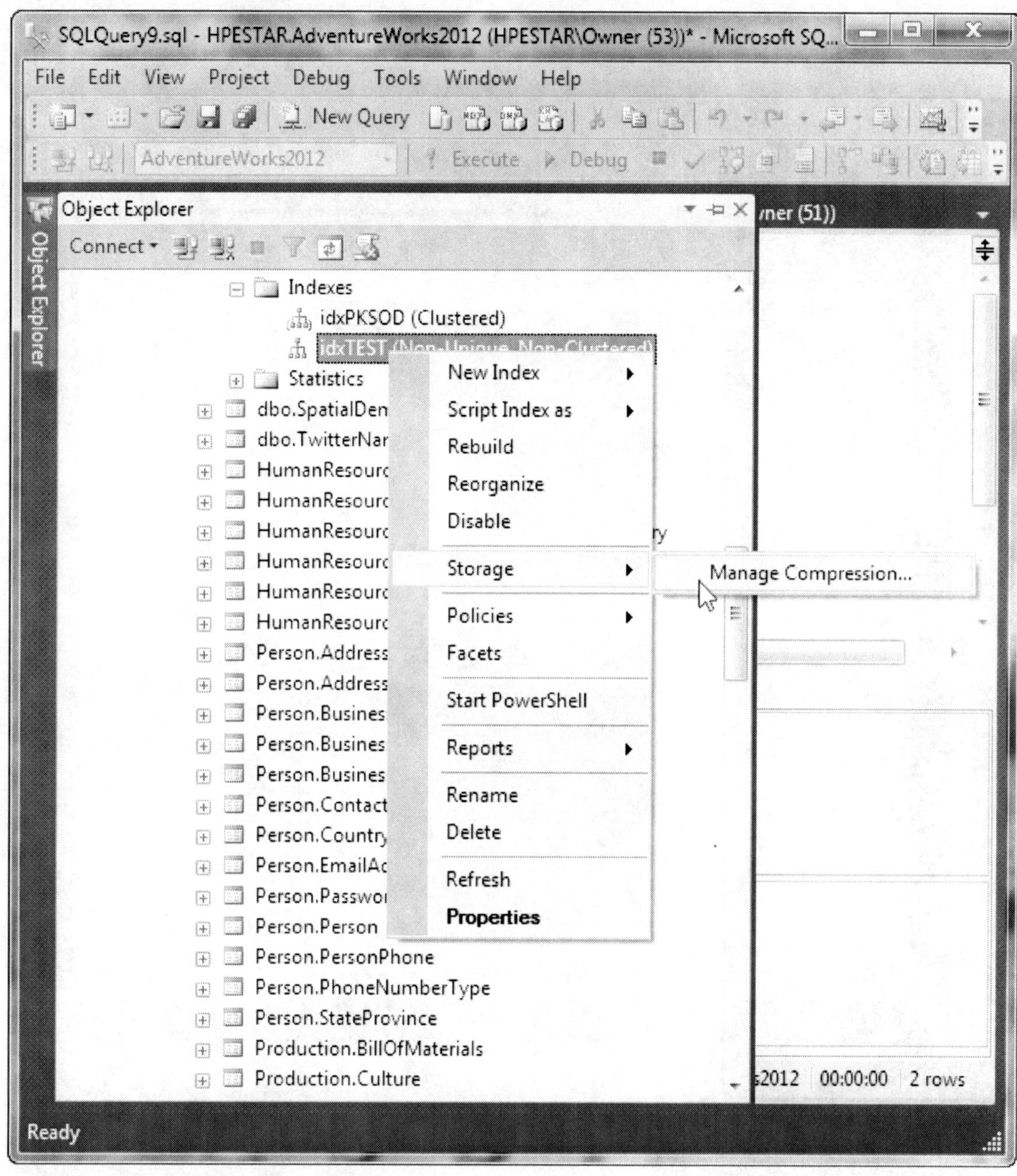

The generated script follows with measurement before and after index compression.

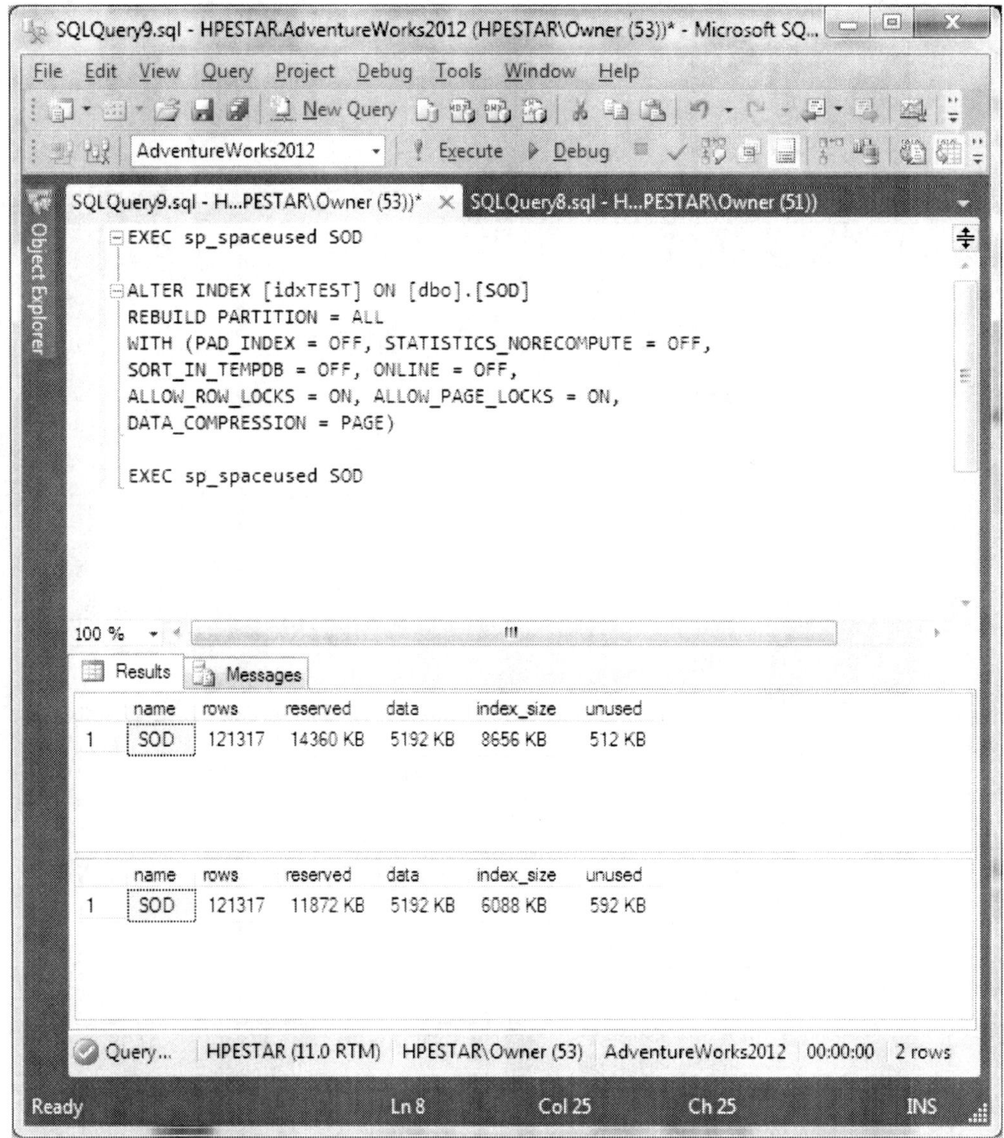

We can observe that the index size has been reduced from 8656KB to 6088 KB.

Articles
Data Compression: Strategy, Capacity Planning and Best Practices
http://msdn.microsoft.com/en-us/library/dd894051(v=sql.100).aspx
Data Compression http://msdn.microsoft.com/en-us/library/cc280449.aspx

Partitioned Table, Partition Function & Partition Scheme

When data is stored from New York, Chicago, Houston, London and Hong Kong operations in a table, it makes you wonder if the server trips over NYC data when looking for London information. Analogous, 95% of the time in a typical business the last 30 days data may be accessed in a table, yet the dominant storage is for the 5% access of the 5 years prior data. The solution is logical: partition the data according to a usage-based scheme. Partitioning can improve performance, the scalability and manageability of large tables and tables that have varying query access patterns. **Gains with partitioning is not automatic.** Careful design studies are necessary for a successful table partitioning implementation.

In order to carry out a demonstration, first we create a copy of AdventureWorks2012 database from a backup file.

```
/* RESTORE script to create a new copy of AdventureWorks2012
 * Folder  FS1 should exist; FSBeta should not exist; AW12 should exist
 * Folder Backup should exist */
USE [master]
GO
```

```
BACKUP DATABASE [AdventureWorks2012] TO
DISK = N'C:\Data\Backup\AW12.bak'
GO
```

```
RESTORE DATABASE [CopyOfAdventureWorks2012]
FROM  DISK = N'C:\Data\Backup\AW12.bak'
WITH  FILE = 1,  MOVE N'FSAlpha' TO N'F:\data\FS1\FSBeta',
MOVE N'AdventureWorks2012_Data' TO N'F:\AW12\xAdventureWorks2012_Data.mdf',
MOVE N'AdventureWorks2012_Log' TO N'F:\AW12\xAdventureWorks2012_log.ldf',
NOUNLOAD,  STATS = 5
GO
```

We will partition a table with SalesOrderDetail subset information. First a partition function is created.

```
USE CopyOfAdventureWorks2012;
GO

CREATE PARTITION FUNCTION pfSOD (int)
AS RANGE LEFT FOR VALUES (1, 20000, 40000, 60000, 80000, 150000) ;
GO
```

The next step is to test the partition function to make sure it works as intended.

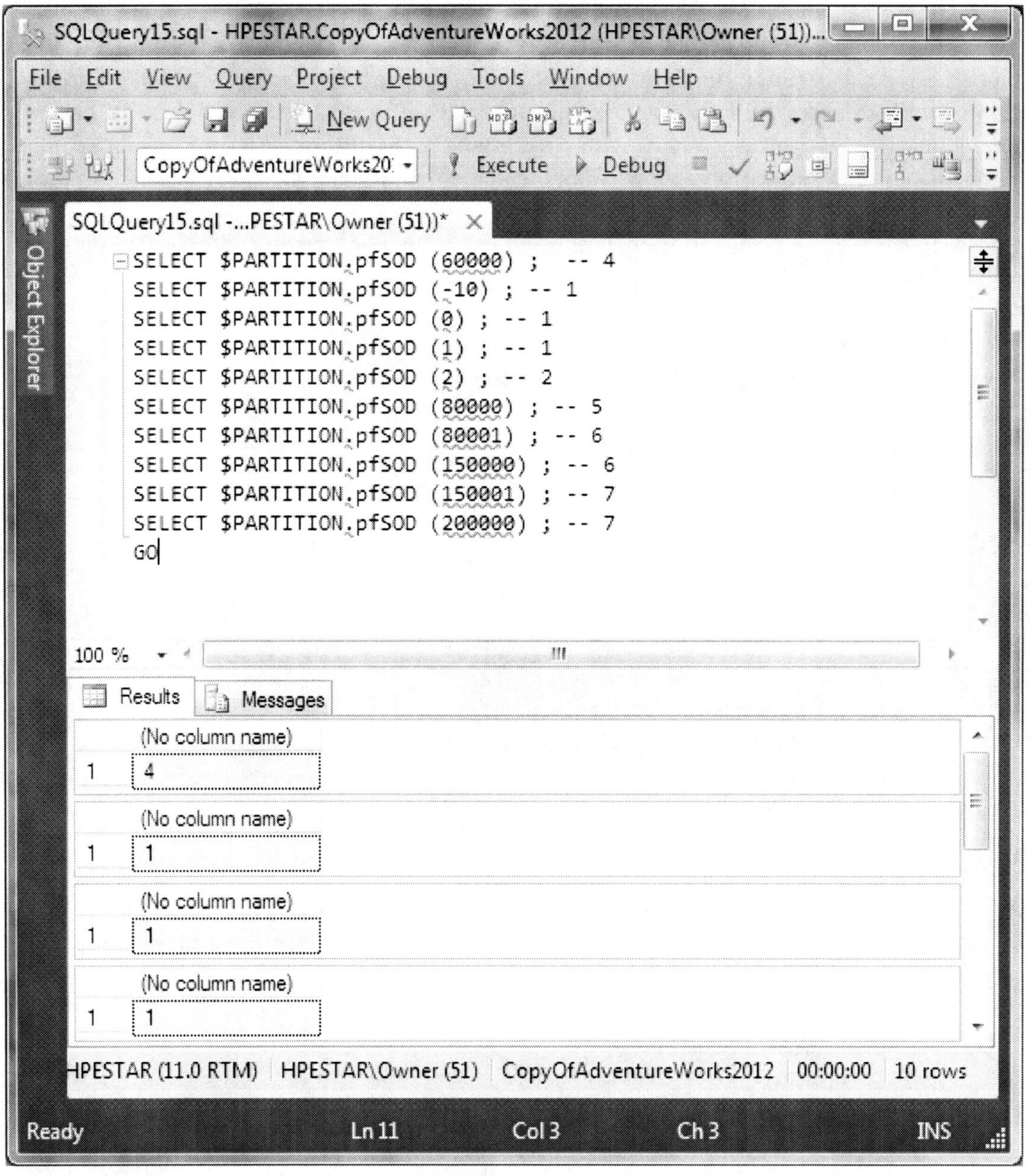

```
SELECT $PARTITION.pfSOD (60000) ;  -- 4
SELECT $PARTITION.pfSOD (-10) ; -- 1
SELECT $PARTITION.pfSOD (0) ; -- 1
SELECT $PARTITION.pfSOD (1) ; -- 1
SELECT $PARTITION.pfSOD (2) ; -- 2
SELECT $PARTITION.pfSOD (80000) ; -- 5
SELECT $PARTITION.pfSOD (80001) ; -- 6
SELECT $PARTITION.pfSOD (150000) ; -- 6
SELECT $PARTITION.pfSOD (150001) ; -- 7
SELECT $PARTITION.pfSOD (200000) ; -- 7
GO
```

T-SQL scripts to create FILEGROUPs for the partitions

```
USE [master]
GO
```

```
ALTER DATABASE [CopyOfAdventureWorks2012] ADD FILEGROUP [Test1FileGroup]
ALTER DATABASE [CopyOfAdventureWorks2012] ADD FILEGROUP [Test2FileGroup]
ALTER DATABASE [CopyOfAdventureWorks2012] ADD FILEGROUP [Test3FileGroup]
ALTER DATABASE [CopyOfAdventureWorks2012] ADD FILEGROUP [Test4FileGroup]
ALTER DATABASE [CopyOfAdventureWorks2012] ADD FILEGROUP [Test5FileGroup]
ALTER DATABASE [CopyOfAdventureWorks2012] ADD FILEGROUP [Test6FileGroup]
ALTER DATABASE [CopyOfAdventureWorks2012] ADD FILEGROUP [Test7FileGroup]
GO
```

```
ALTER DATABASE [CopyOfAdventureWorks2012]
ADD FILE ( NAME = N'Test1', FILENAME = N'F:\UTIL\Microsoft\sampledatabases\Test1.ndf' ,
SIZE = 3072KB , FILEGROWTH = 1024KB ) TO FILEGROUP [Test1FileGroup]
ALTER DATABASE [CopyOfAdventureWorks2012]
ADD FILE ( NAME = N'Test2', FILENAME = N'F:\UTIL\Microsoft\sampledatabases\Test2.ndf' ,
SIZE = 3072KB , FILEGROWTH = 1024KB ) TO FILEGROUP [Test2FileGroup]
ALTER DATABASE [CopyOfAdventureWorks2012]
ADD FILE ( NAME = N'Test3', FILENAME = N'F:\UTIL\Microsoft\sampledatabases\Test3.ndf' ,
SIZE = 3072KB , FILEGROWTH = 1024KB ) TO FILEGROUP [Test3FileGroup]
ALTER DATABASE [CopyOfAdventureWorks2012]
ADD FILE ( NAME = N'Test4', FILENAME = N'F:\UTIL\Microsoft\sampledatabases\Test4.ndf' ,
SIZE = 3072KB , FILEGROWTH = 1024KB ) TO FILEGROUP [Test4FileGroup]
ALTER DATABASE [CopyOfAdventureWorks2012]
ADD FILE ( NAME = N'Test5', FILENAME = N'F:\UTIL\Microsoft\sampledatabases\Test5.ndf' ,
SIZE = 3072KB , FILEGROWTH = 1024KB ) TO FILEGROUP [Test5FileGroup]
ALTER DATABASE [CopyOfAdventureWorks2012]
ADD FILE ( NAME = N'Test6', FILENAME = N'F:\UTIL\Microsoft\sampledatabases\Test6.ndf' ,
SIZE = 3072KB , FILEGROWTH = 1024KB ) TO FILEGROUP [Test6FileGroup]
ALTER DATABASE [CopyOfAdventureWorks2012]
ADD FILE ( NAME = N'Test7', FILENAME = N'F:\UTIL\Microsoft\sampledatabases\Test7.ndf' ,
SIZE = 3072KB , FILEGROWTH = 1024KB ) TO FILEGROUP [Test7FileGroup]
GO
```

T-SQL scripts to create a partition scheme, a partitioned table and populate the new table with INSERT SELECT

```
USE CopyOfAdventureWorks2012;
GO
```

```
CREATE PARTITION SCHEME psSOD
AS PARTITION pfSOD
TO (Test1FileGroup, Test2FileGroup, Test3FileGroup, Test4FileGroup,
Test5FileGroup, Test6FileGroup, Test7FileGroup) ;
GO
```

```
CREATE TABLE SODPartitioned   (col1 int, col2 char(30))  ON psSOD (col1) ;
GO
```

```
insert SODPartitioned
select     SalesOrderDetailID, 'Unit Price: '+convert(varchar,UnitPrice)
from AdventureWorks2012.Sales.SalesOrderDetail;
GO
```

```
insert SODPartitioned
select SalesOrderDetailID+1,  'Unit Price: '+convert(varchar,UnitPrice+1)
from AdventureWorks2012.Sales.SalesOrderDetail;
GO
```

```
insert SODPartitioned select SalesOrderDetailID+2,  'Unit Price: '+convert(varchar,UnitPrice+2)
from AdventureWorks2012.Sales.SalesOrderDetail;
```

Query To Check The Data Distribution Within The Partitions

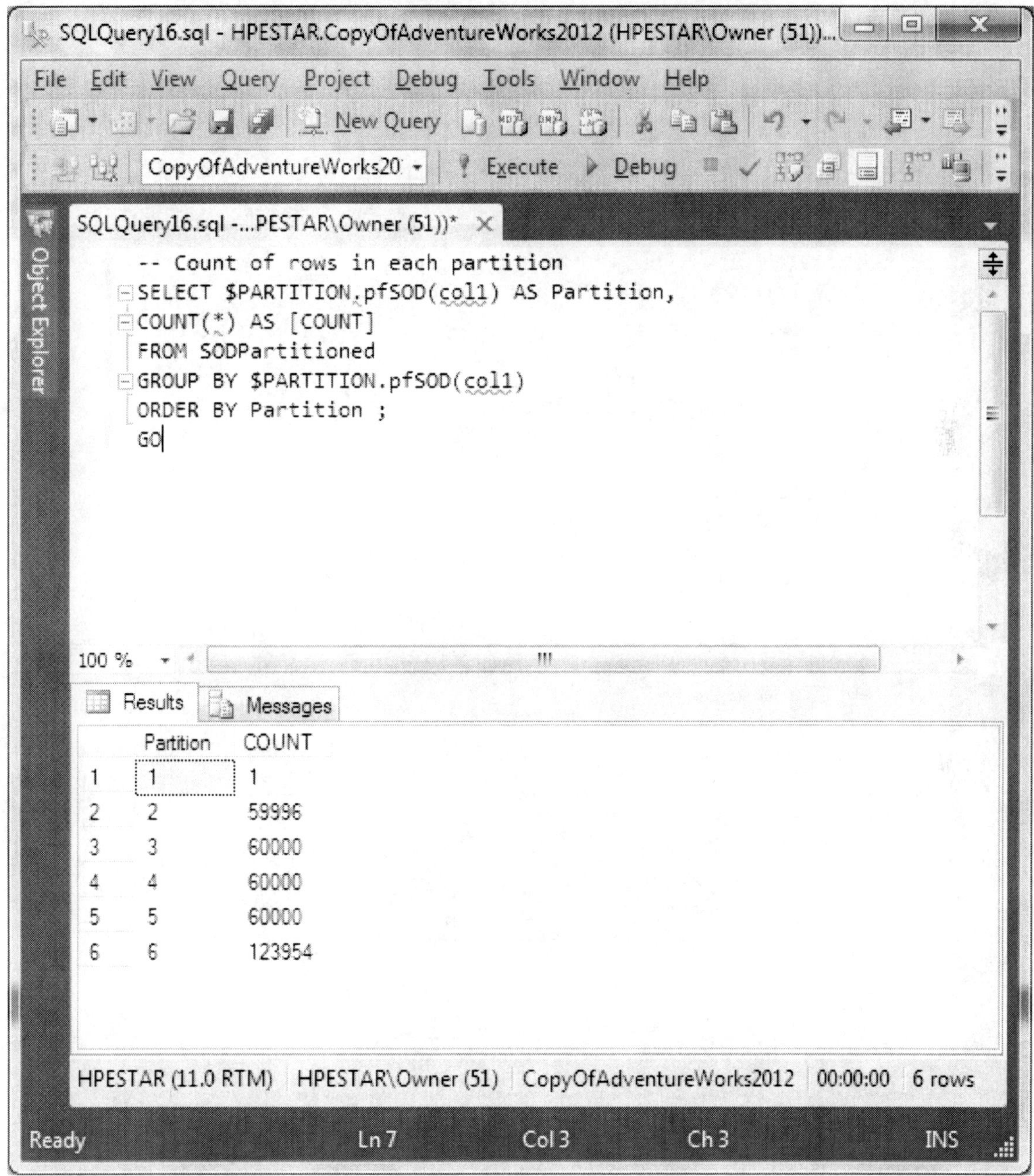

A few more counting queries to check entire table and a single partition population

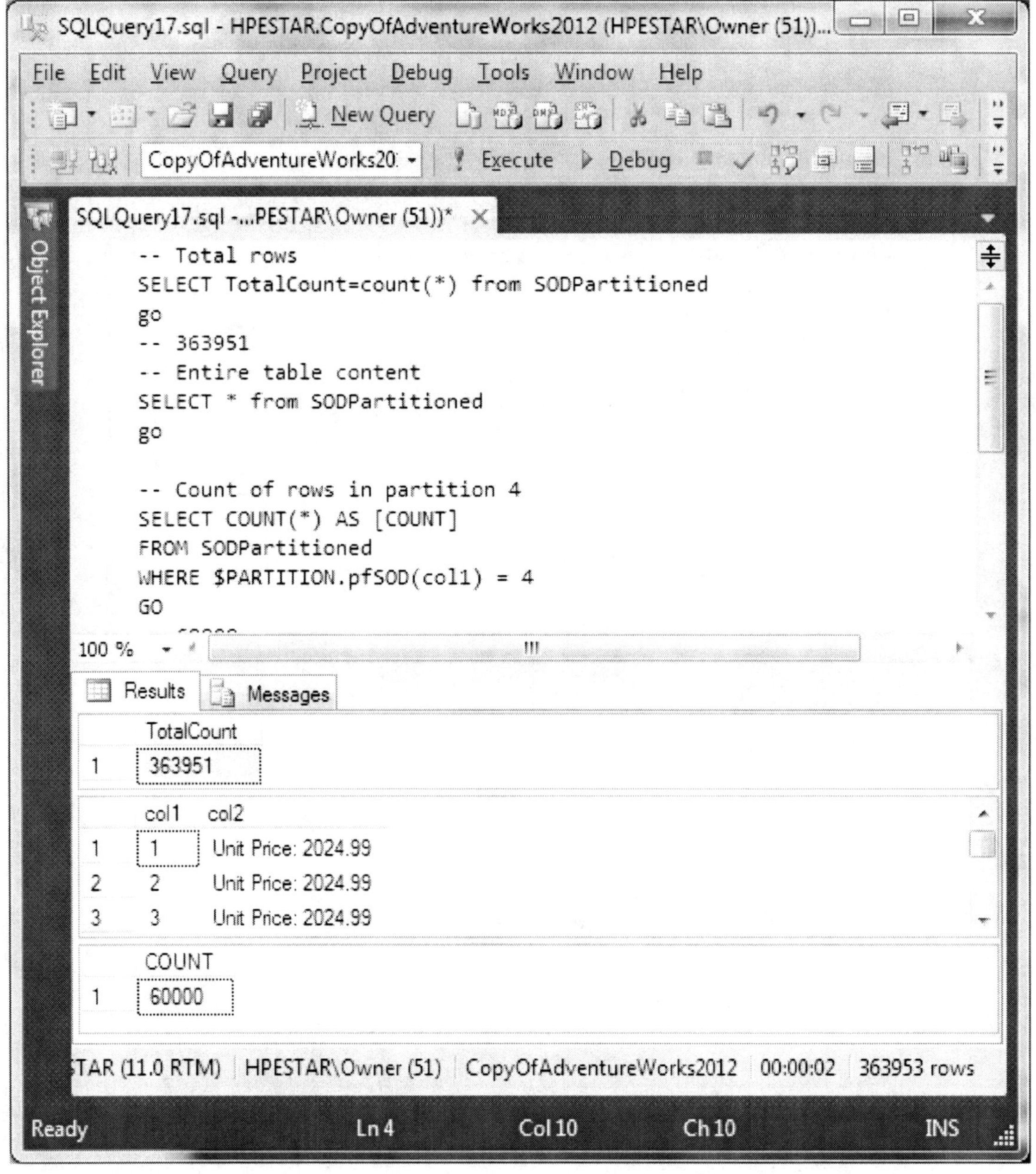

System views with "partition" prefix contain metadata on partitions.

In the following example, we partition for "UK", "US" and other countries.

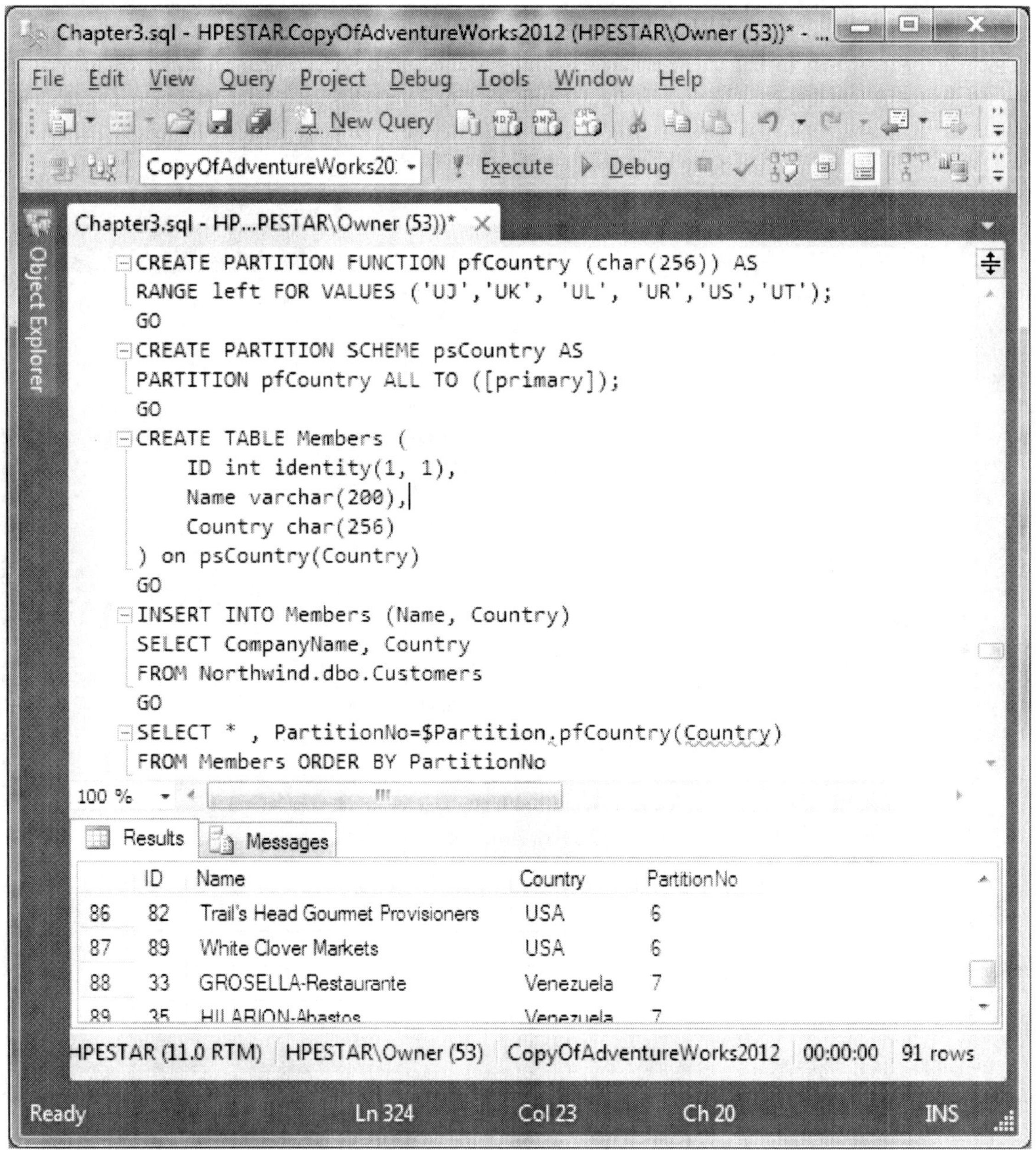

The GUI Create Partition Wizard

Object Explorer Create Partition Wizard provides GUI environment for partition design & setup.

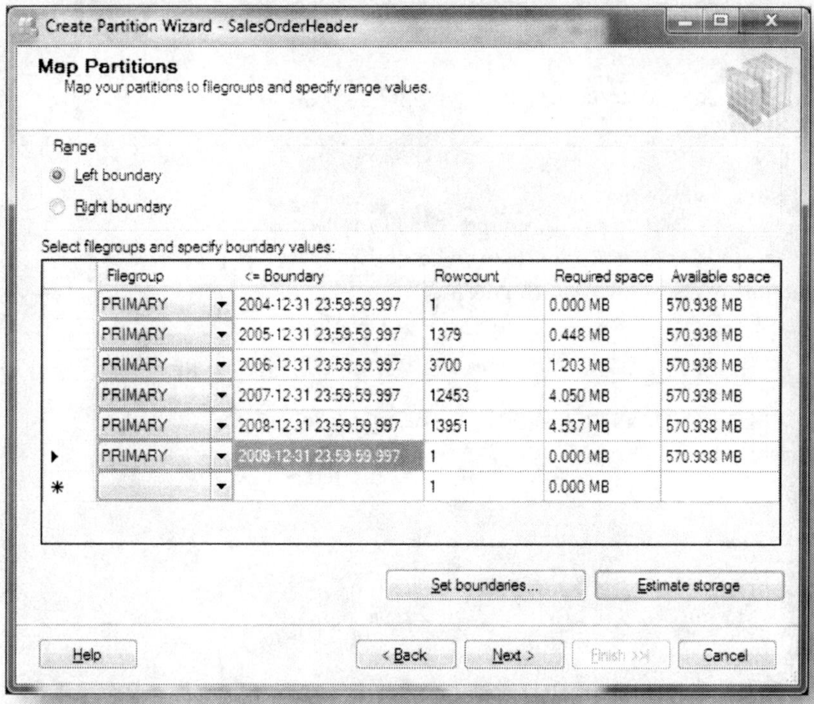

Rows Per Page Calculation

More rows per page (8K), better the performance. Narrower table & narrower indexes mean better performance due to the reduction of disk io.

```
SELECT    Schema_name(o.schema_id)            AS TableSchema,    Object_name(i.object_id)      AS TableName,
          LEFT(i.name, 20)                    AS IndexName,
          MIN(i.type_desc)                    AS IndexType,
          SUM(p.rows)                         AS Rows,           Sum(au.data_pages)            AS DataPages,
          SUM(p.rows) / Sum(au.data_pages)    AS RowsPerPage,
          MAX(p.partition_number)             AS Partitions
FROM   sys.objects o INNER JOIN sys.indexes AS i  ON i.object_id = o.object_id
   INNER JOIN sys.partitions AS p ON i.object_id = p.object_id AND i.index_id = p.index_id
   INNER JOIN sys.allocation_units AS au ON p.hobt_id = au.container_id
WHERE     Schema_name(o.schema_id) = 'Sales'
          AND Object_name(i.object_id) = 'SalesOrderDetail' AND au.type_desc = 'IN_ROW_DATA'
GROUP  BY o.schema_id, i.object_id, i.name  ORDER  BY IndexType, IndexName;
```

TableSchema	TableName	IndexName	IndexType	Rows	DataPages	RowsPerPage	Partitions
Sales	SalesOrderDetail	PK_SalesOrderDetail_	CLUSTERED	121317	1440	84	1
Sales	SalesOrderDetail	AK_SalesOrderDetail_	NONCLUSTERED	121317	528	229	1
Sales	SalesOrderDetail	idxSODPIDSID	NONCLUSTERED	121317	388	312	1
Sales	SalesOrderDetail	IX_SalesOrderDetail_	NONCLUSTERED	121317	317	382	1

Columnstore Index for Data Warehouse Performance

Columnstore index for static tables, new to SQL Server 2012, is designed for Data Warehouse performance enhancement. The first script is a timing script for a GROUP BY summary query, and the second script is the creation of the columnstore index.

```
-- Timing before creating Columnstore index (5th timing)
USE AdventureWorksDW2012;
dbcc dropcleanbuffers;
declare @start datetime = getdate()
SELECT SalesTerritoryKey, SUM(ExtendedAmount) AS SalesByTerritory
FROM FactResellerSales     GROUP BY SalesTerritoryKey;
select [Timing]=datediff(millisecond, @Start, getdate());
GO 5
-- 190 msec
```

```
CREATE NONCLUSTERED COLUMNSTORE INDEX [idxColStoreResellerSales]
ON [FactResellerSales]
(
   [ProductKey],
   [OrderDateKey],
   [ShipDateKey],
   [EmployeeKey],
   [PromotionKey],
   [CurrencyKey],
   [SalesTerritoryKey],
   [SalesOrderNumber],
   [SalesOrderLineNumber],
   [OrderQuantity],
   [UnitPrice],
   [ExtendedAmount],
   [UnitPriceDiscountPct],
   [DiscountAmount],
   [ProductStandardCost],
   [TotalProductCost],
   [SalesAmount],
   [TaxAmt],
   [Freight],
   [CarrierTrackingNumber],
   [CustomerPONumber],
   [OrderDate],
   [DueDate],
   [ShipDate]
);
```

Checking the same query after creating the index.

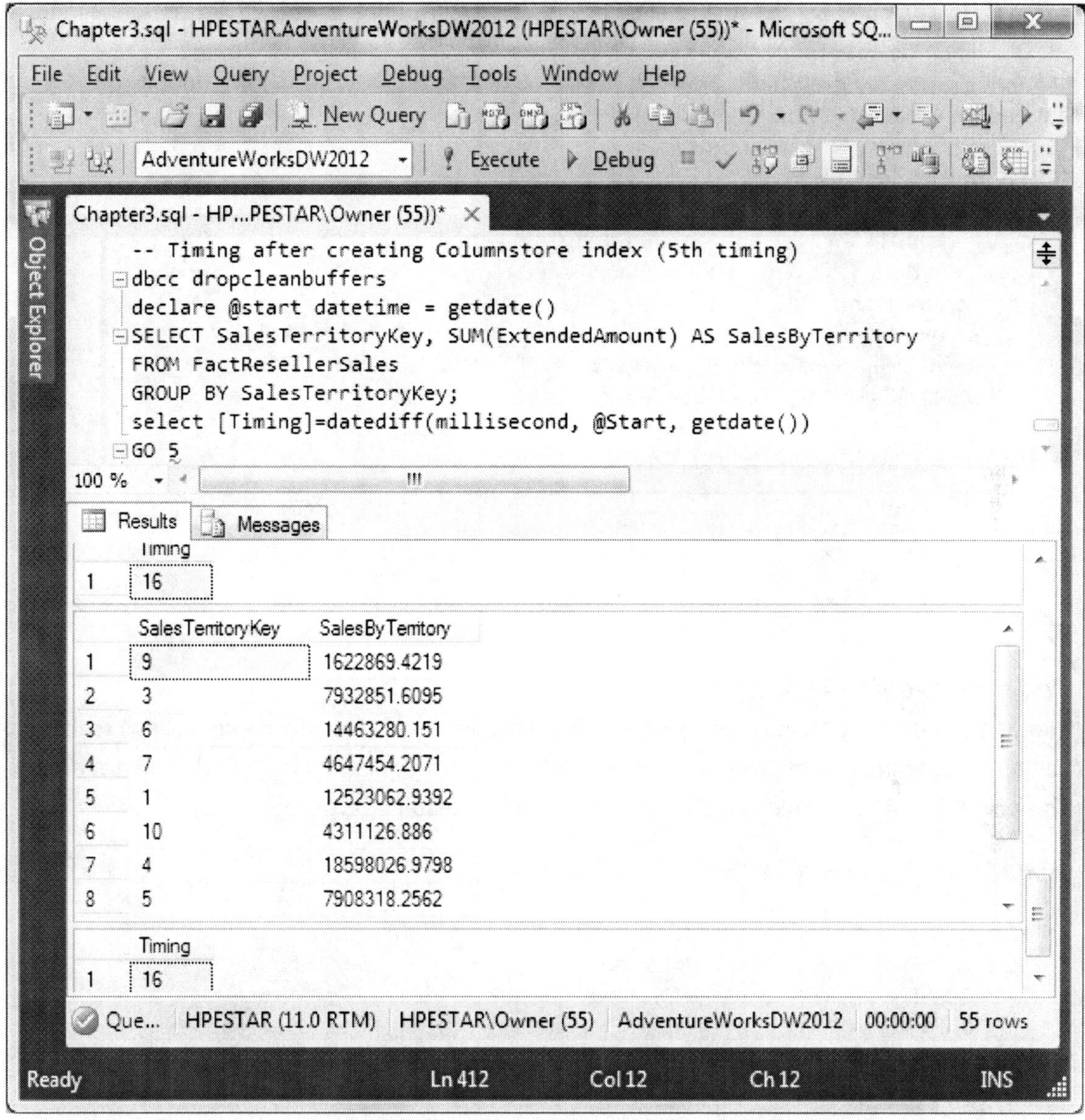

The performance gain on this particular query: from 190 msec to 16 msec. Generally columnstore index leads to significant query performance improvement in Data Warehouse environment.

DATE Data Type Solves Many Problems with DATETIME

DATE columns should be DATE type (3 bytes) not DATETIME type (8 bytes) with exception when time is needed for the record such as credit card or online banking transaction.

Example: Sales.Customer table create with one computed column which has unique index defined on AccountNumber(computed).

```
CREATE TABLE Sales.Customer(
	CustomerID int IDENTITY(1,1) PRIMARY KEY,
	PersonID int			REFERENCES Person.Person,
	StoreID int			REFERENCES Sales.Store,
	TerritoryID int			REFERENCES Sales.SalesTerritory,
	AccountNumber  AS (isnull('AW'+dbo.ufnLeadingZeros(CustomerID),'')) ,
	RowGuid uniqueidentifier ROWGUIDCOL  NOT NULL default (newid()),
	ModifiedDate DATE  NOT NULL default (CURRENT_TIMESTAMP));
```

```
SELECT TOP 2 * FROM Sales.Customer  ORDER BY AccountNumber;
```

CustomerID	PersonID	StoreID	TerritoryID	AccountNumber	rowguid	ModifiedDate
1	NULL	934	1	AW00000001	3F5AE95E-B87D-4AED-95B4-C3797AFCB74F	2008-10-13
2	NULL	1028	1	AW00000002	E552F657-A9AF-4A7D-A645-C429D6E02491	2008-10-13

Pad with Leading Zeros

Padding with leading zeros is a frequent business requirement. The ufnLeadingZeros() scalar-valued user-defined function converts the number into a string and pads it with leading zeros. The new **FORMAT command** can be utilized as well for leading zeros.

```
SELECT [dbo].[ufnLeadingZeros] (999);    -- 00000999
```

```
-- T-SQL script to pad with leading zeros
USE AdventureWorks2012;  DECLARE @Len tinyint=8;
SELECT   BusinessEntityID AS EmployeeID,    Rate,
         RIGHT(REPLICATE('0',@Len) + CAST(Rate AS VARCHAR(20)),@Len) AS PaddedRate
FROM   HumanResources.EmployeePayHistory;
```

EmployeeID	Rate	PaddedRate
1	125.50	00125.50
2	63.4615	00063.46
3	43.2692	00043.27

```
SELECT TOP(1) FORMAT(ProductID, '00000') FROM Production.Product;  -- 00980
SELECT FORMAT(999, '00000'); -- 00999
```

Database Design & Programming Standards

Standards have multiple purposes:

- Increase the productivity of the database developer.
- Increase the productivity of the project team.
- Decrease future maintenance cost of the RDBMS system.

Standards are about communications among project team members and among future software engineers who will come in contact with the work done presently by the software project team. Software standards are simple ordinary rules which should be followed. It is like when you turn on the left-turn signal in your car, the driver behind you anticipates you slowing down and making the next left turn. The situation is a little bit different though with software standards: there is no enforcing authority like the state authority in case of traffic rules. Many times argument can break out within the project team: "I like it this way", "it is really stupid to do it that way", "database expert Q says to do it this way in a blog" and so on. The following standards are pretty reasonable, and are based on industry acceptance, albeit not universal acceptance. The project manager has to enlist the support of all of the project team members for successful standards implementation. Database Design & Programming Standards to aid in optimal usability of SQL Server schema, scripts and stored procedures, user defined functions developed for applications by defining a reasonable, consistent and effective coding style. The identifier segment of the standard will formalize naming conventions. Without standards, database design, function, stored procedure and script development may become sloppy and unreadable, resulting in diminished productivity, usability, reusability, maintainability and extendibility.

Database Design Standards

Base design is normalized to 3NF or higher. History, log, Data Warehouse and reporting tables, containing second-hand data, need not be normalized. Similar considerations for staging and lookup tables. Each OLTP table has the following layout:

```
TableNameID (PRIMARY KEY) - commonly int identity(1,1) SURROGATE PRIMARY KEY
TableNameAlphaID (FOREIGN KEY if any)
TableNameBetaID (FOREIGN KEY if any)
natural-key column(s)
non-key columns
row maintenance columns
 RowGuid          uniqueidentifier
 IsActive         maintenance flag (bit 0 = not active, 1 = active)
 CreateDate       maintenance date (datetime if necessary)
 ModifiedDate     maintenance date (datetime if necessary)
 ModifiedByUser   last user who modified the record
```

Identifiers

CamelCase (Pascal case) naming convention: OrderDetail, ShippingCompany

With prefix example: vInvoiceHistory (view - Hungarian naming after Charles Simonyi)

Old-style naming example: sales_order_detail

Space usage is not a good idea in identifier: confusing & forces square brackets or double quotation marks use (delimited identifier).

Using spaces example: [sales order detail]

PREFIX ASSIGNMENT

Primary Key Clustered	pk
Primary Key Nonclustered	pknc
Index Clustered	idxc
Index Nonclustered	idxnc
Foreign Key	fk
Unique Constraint	uq
Check Constraint	chk
Column Default	dflt
Synonym	syn

Passed Parameter @p (input/output parameter) or @ - Example: @pStartDate, @StartDate

Local Variable @ - Example: @WeekOfTransaction

Table usually no prefix; exception large number of tables

Reporting table	rpt
Log table	log
History table	hist or arch
Date Warehouse table	dw, dim, fact
Common Table Expression	cte
View	v or view
User Defined Scalar Function	udf or fns or ufn or fn
User Defined Table Function	udf or fnt or ufn or fn
Stored Procedure	usp, sproc, or none

Principles of T-SQL Identifier Architecture

Each word in the naming must be functional. The first word must be the highest level category or action indicator. Examples for stored procedure names:

uspAccountPayableSummary
uspInsertAccountPayableTransaction
uspUpdateStockPrice
sprocInsertInventoryItem
sprocAccountReceivableSummary
AccountReceivableMonthly

Commonly accepted or easily understood abbreviations are allowed. Examples for business abbreviations usage in view naming:

vAPSummary
vAPDetail
vARSummary
vARMonthly
vGLTrialBalance

AdventureWorks2012 long stored procedure and view names.

```
SELECT name, type FROM sys.objects WHERE LEN(name) > 20 AND type in ('V', 'P') ORDER BY name;
```

name	type
uspGetBillOfMaterials	P
uspGetEmployeeManagers	P
uspGetManagerEmployees	P
uspGetWhereUsedProductID	P
uspSearchCandidateResumes	P
uspUpdateEmployeeHireInfo	P
uspUpdateEmployeeLogin	P
uspUpdateEmployeePersonalInfo	P
vAdditionalContactInfo	V
vEmployeeDepartmentHistory	V
vJobCandidateEducation	V
vJobCandidateEmployment	V
vProductAndDescription	V
vProductModelCatalogDescription	V
vProductModelInstructions	V
vSalesPersonSalesByFiscalYears	V
vStateProvinceCountryRegion	V
vStoreWithDemographics	V

Stored Procedure Outline

```
use {DatabaseName};
if (objectProperty(object_id('{schema}.{ProcedureName}'),
'IsProcedure') is not null)
    drop procedure {schema}.{ProcedureName}
go

create procedure {schema}.{ProcedureName}
  [{parameter}  {data type}]....
as
/*****************************************************************
* PROCEDURE: {ProcedureName}
* PURPOSE: {brief procedure description}
* NOTES: {special set up or requirements, etc.}
* CREATED:  {developer name} {date}
* LAST MODIFIED: {developer name} {date}

* DATE        AUTHOR          DESCRIPTION
-------------------------------------------------------------------
* {date}      {developer} {brief modification description}
*****************************************************************/
BEGIN
[declare {variable name} {data type}....
[{set session}] e.g. SET NOCOUNT ON
[{initialize variables}]

{body of procedure - comment only what is not obvious}

return (Value if any)

{error handler}
return (Value if any)
END
 go
```

User-Defined Function Outline

Similar to stored procedure outline

How to Create a Database with T-SQL Script

Database can be created by a script (CREATE DATABASE) or in SSMS Object Explorer using GUI. Here is a T-SQL script version.

```
-- SQL CREATE DATABASE
USE master;
GO
```

```
-- F:\DB\DATA\ folder should exist

CREATE DATABASE [Finance]
ON  PRIMARY
( NAME = N'Finance_Data',
FILENAME = N'F:\DB\DATA\Finance.mdf' , SIZE = 217152KB ,
MAXSIZE = UNLIMITED, FILEGROWTH = 16384KB )
LOG ON
( NAME = N'Finance_Log',
FILENAME = N'F:\DB\DATA\Finance_1.ldf' ,
SIZE = 67584KB , MAXSIZE = 2048GB , FILEGROWTH = 16384KB )
GO
```

```
-- SQL compatibility level 110 is SQL Server 2012
ALTER DATABASE [Finance] SET COMPATIBILITY_LEVEL = 110
GO
```

```
USE Finance;
-- SQL select into table create
SELECT * INTO POH
FROM AdventureWorks2012.Purchasing.PurchaseOrderHeader;
GO
```

```
 -- SQL select query for 3 random records
SELECT TOP (3) * FROM POH ORDER BY NEWID()
GO
```

PurchaseOrderID	RevisionNumber	Status	EmployeeID	VendorID
3506	1	4	261	1666
233	1	4	257	1578
84	1	3	261	1654

Adding New Column to a Table with ALTER TABLE

It happens quite often that a table in production for years needs a new column. While adding a new column to a populated table is relatively simple, there is a downside: application software needs to be retested to make sure it still works with the new table. One offending statement is "SELECT * FROM". The application software was programmed, let's say for example, 6 columns, after the addition SELECT * is sending 7 columns which causes error in the application. T-SQL scripts to demonstrate the addition of a new column to a table for sequencing or other purposes.

```
USE AdventureWorks2012;

SELECT NewProductID = ROW_NUMBER()    OVER (   ORDER BY ProductID),
      *
INTO   #Product
FROM   AdventureWorks.Production.Product
GO
-- (504 row(s) affected)
```

```
ALTER TABLE #Product ADD CountryOfOrigin nvarchar(32) not null DEFAULT ('USA');
GO
-- Command(s) completed successfully.
```

```
SELECT          ProductID,
                Name                          AS ProductName,
                ProductNumber,
                ListPrice,
                COALESCE(Color,'')            AS Color,
                CountryOfOrigin
FROM   #Product
ORDER BY ProductName;
GO
```

ProductID	ProductName	ProductNumber	ListPrice	Color	CountryOfOrigin
1	Adjustable Race	AR-5381	0.00		USA
879	All-Purpose Bike Stand	ST-1401	159.00		USA
712	AWC Logo Cap	CA-1098	8.99	Multi	USA
3	BB Ball Bearing	BE-2349	0.00		USA
2	Bearing Ball	BA-8327	0.00		USA
877	Bike Wash - Dissolver	CL-9009	7.95		USA
316	Blade	BL-2036	0.00		USA
843	Cable Lock	LO-C100	25.00		USA
952	Chain	CH-0234	20.24	Silver	USA
324	Chain Stays	CS-2812	0.00		USA
322	Chainring	CR-7833	0.00	Black	USA
320	Chainring Bolts	CB-2903	0.00	Silver	USA

```
-- Cleanup
DROP TABLE #Product
```

IDENTITY Column in a Table Variable

Using IDENTITY function for row numbering in new column with table variable. Statements must be in one batch, that is the scope of table variable.

```
DECLARE @Product TABLE
 (
   ID         INT IDENTITY(1, 1),     -- new column
   ProductID  int,
   ProductName varchar(64),
   ListPrice  money,
   Color      varchar(32)
 ) ;

INSERT @Product
    (ProductID,
     ProductName,
     ListPrice,
     Color)
SELECT ProductID,
    Name,
    ListPrice,
    Color
FROM  AdventureWorks2012.Production.Product
WHERE ListPrice > 0
    AND Color IS NOT NULL
ORDER BY Name;

SELECT TOP(7) *
FROM  @Product
ORDER BY ID;
GO
```

ID	ProductID	ProductName	ListPrice	Color
1	712	AWC Logo Cap	8.99	Multi
2	952	Chain	20.24	Silver
3	866	Classic Vest, L	63.50	Blue
4	865	Classic Vest, M	63.50	Blue
5	864	Classic Vest, S	63.50	Blue
6	948	Front Brakes	106.50	Silver
7	945	Front Derailleur	91.49	Silver

Note: the above "GO" (ending the batch) terminated the scope of @Product table variable.

```
SELECT TOP(7) *  FROM  @Product ;
/* Msg 1087, Level 15, State 2, Line 1     Must declare the table variable "@Product"  */
```

Partition Data By Country Query

Partition sales data by country and sequence sales staff from best to worst.

NOTE: ROW_NUMBER() only sequencing; to rank use the RANK() function.

```
SELECT CONCAT(LastName,', ', FirstName)                  AS SalesPerson,
       CountryRegionName                                 AS Country,
       ROW_NUMBER() OVER(
                    PARTITION BY CountryRegionName
                    ORDER BY SalesYTD DESC)              AS 'Row Number',
       FORMAT( SalesYTD, 'c', 'en-US')                   AS SalesYTD
INTO  #SalesPersonRank
FROM  AdventureWorks2012.Sales.vSalesPerson
WHERE  TerritoryName IS NOT NULL
       AND SalesYTD <> 0;
```

```
-- Add new column StarRank, which is 1 "*" for each $1,000,000 of sales
ALTER TABLE #SalesPersonRank ADD StarRank varchar(32) NOT NULL DEFAULT ('');
--Command(s) completed successfully.
```

```
-- New column empty so far, population follows with UPDATE
UPDATE #SalesPersonRank SET StarRank =
REPLICATE ('*', FLOOR(CONVERT(Money, REPLACE(SalesYTD,',',''))) / 1000000.0));
-- (14 row(s) affected)
```

```
SELECT * FROM #SalesPersonRank ORDER BY Country, [Row Number];
```

SalesPerson	Country	Row Number	SalesYTD	StarRank
Tsoflias, Lynn	Australia	1	$1,421,810.92	*
Saraiva, José	Canada	1	$2,604,540.72	**
Vargas, Garrett	Canada	2	$1,453,719.47	*
Varkey Chudukatil, Ranjit	France	1	$3,121,616.32	***
Valdez, Rachel	Germany	1	$1,827,066.71	*
Pak, Jae	United Kingdom	1	$4,116,871.23	****
Mitchell, Linda	United States	1	$4,251,368.55	****
Blythe, Michael	United States	2	$3,763,178.18	***
Carson, Jillian	United States	3	$3,189,418.37	***
Ito, Shu	United States	4	$2,458,535.62	**
Reiter, Tsvi	United States	5	$2,315,185.61	**
Mensa-Annan, Tete	United States	6	$1,576,562.20	*
Campbell, David	United States	7	$1,573,012.94	*
Ansman-Wolfe, Pamela	United States	8	$1,352,577.13	*

```
DROP TABLE #SalesPersonRank;
```

Diagram of Sales.SalesPerson & Related Tables

The sales staff is crucial in any business organization. It is reflected on the following diagram.

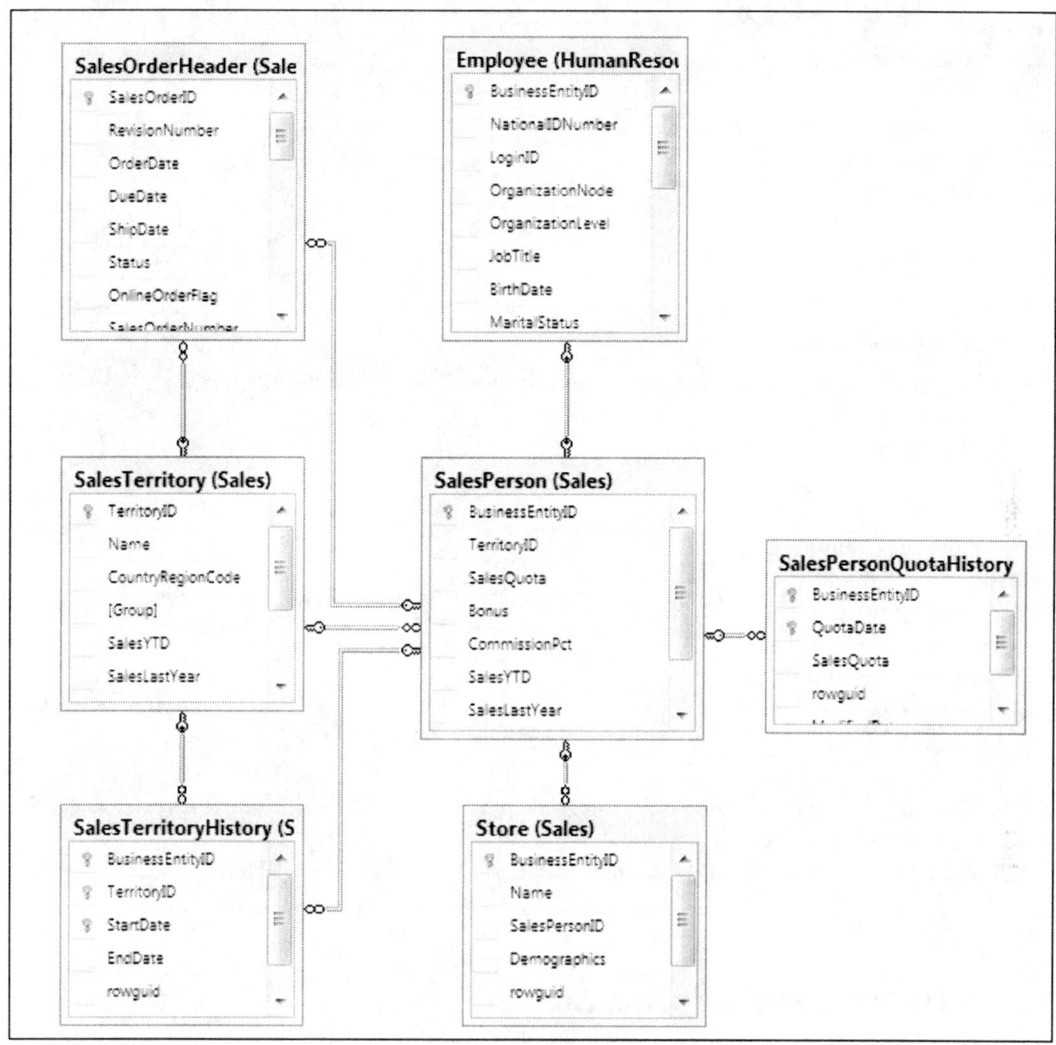

T-SQL Tidbits: Computed Column with IIF & TRY_PARSE Functions

```
USE tempdb; SELECT * INTO Address FROM AdventureWorks2012.Person.Address;  -- Create & populate test table
ALTER TABLE Address ADD CONSTRAINT pkAddress PRIMARY KEY (AddressID);       -- Add PRIMARY KEY
ALTER TABLE Address ADD PostalCodeType AS                                   -- Add computed column
   IIF (TRY_PARSE( PostalCode AS DECIMAL(10,0)) IS NULL, 'ALPHANUMERIC', 'NUMERIC');
SELECT TOP(3) AddressID, AddressLine1, City, PostalCode, PostalCodeType FROM Address ORDER BY NEWID();
```

AddressID	AddressLine1	City	PostalCode	PostalCodeType
24135	7437 Jason Ct	London	SW1P 2NU	ALPHANUMERIC
869	2583 Se 272nd St	Kent	98031	NUMERIC
21807	1026 Mt. Wilson Pl.	Lynnwood	98036	NUMERIC

Adding IDENTITY Column To Empty Table

Add IDENTITY column to a table for sequential unique numbering (autonumber).

```
USE tempdb;
CREATE TABLE Department
 (
   Name        varchar(32)  UNIQUE,
   GroupName    varchar(256),
   ModifiedDate date default (CURRENT_TIMESTAMP)
 );
GO -- Command(s) completed successfully.
```

```
-- Add new IDENTITY column
ALTER TABLE Department    ADD DepartmentID smallint IDENTITY(1, 1) PRIMARY KEY;
GO
-- Command(s) completed successfully.
```

```
-- Only one identity column per table
ALTER TABLE Department
  ADD SecondIdentity smallint IDENTITY(1, 1);
GO
/* Msg 2744, Level 16, State 2, Line 1
Multiple identity columns specified for table 'Department'. Only one identity  column per table is allowed.
*/
```

```
INSERT INTO Department ( DepartmentID, Name, Groupname) VALUES (17, 'Student Affairs', 'Executive');
/* Msg 544, Level 16, State 1, Line 1
Cannot insert explicit value for identity column in table 'Department'  when IDENTITY_INSERT is set to
OFF. */
```

SET IDENTITY INSERT tablename ON

```
-- SQL identity insert enabled
SET IDENTITY_INSERT Department ON;
```

```
INSERT INTO Department ( DepartmentID, Name, Groupname) VALUES (17, 'Student Affairs', 'Executive');
-- (1 row(s) affected)
```

```
-- SQL identity insert disabled (default)
SET IDENTITY_INSERT Department OFF;
GO
```

DBCC CHECKIDENT Command

DBCC CHECKIDENT can be used to check and reseed IDENTITY parameters.

```
DBCC CHECKIDENT('Production.Product');
/*Checking identity information: current identity value '999', current column value '999'.
DBCC execution completed. If DBCC printed error messages, contact your system administrator. */
```

```
-- SQL reseeding identity column;  reset identity column
DBCC CHECKIDENT ("dbo.Department", RESEED, 999);
/*Checking identity information: current identity value '17'.
DBCC execution completed. If DBCC printed error messages, contact your system administrator. */
```

```
INSERT INTO Department (Name, Groupname) VALUES ( 'Alumni Affairs', 'Executive');
```

```
SELECT * FROM Department;
```

Name	GroupName	ModifiedDate	DepartmentID
Student Affairs	Executive	2016-07-19	17
Alumni Affairs	Executive	2016-07-19	1000

```
-- Add more records to table with INSERT SELECT
INSERT INTO Department (Name, Groupname)
SELECT Name, GroupName  FROM AdventureWorks2012.HumanResources.Department;
```

```
SELECT * FROM Department ORDER BY DepartmentID;
```

Name	GroupName	ModifiedDate	DepartmentID
Student Affairs	Executive	2012-07-19	17
Alumni Affairs	Executive	2012-07-19	1000
Engineering	Research and Development	2012-07-19	1001
Tool Design	Research and Development	2012-07-19	1002
Sales	Sales and Marketing	2012-07-19	1003
Marketing	Sales and Marketing	2012-07-19	1004
Purchasing	Inventory Management	2012-07-19	1005
Research and Development	Research and Development	2012-07-19	1006
Production	Manufacturing	2012-07-19	1007
Production Control	Manufacturing	2012-07-19	1008
Human Resources	Executive General and Administration	2012-07-19	1009
Finance	Executive General and Administration	2012-07-19	1010
Information Services	Executive General and Administration	2012-07-19	1011
Document Control	Quality Assurance	2012-07-19	1012
Quality Assurance	Quality Assurance	2012-07-19	1013
Facilities and Maintenance	Executive General and Administration	2012-07-19	1014
Shipping and Receiving	Inventory Management	2012-07-19	1015
Executive	Executive General and Administration	2012-07-19	1016

```
DROP TABLE tempdb.dbo.Department;
```

ADD Partitioned Sequence Number to Table

Partition table by subcategory (ProductSubcategoryID) by applying ROW_NUMBER for sequencing within each partition.

```
SELECT ROW_NUMBER()    OVER ( PARTITION BY p.ProductSubcategoryID
                              ORDER BY ProductID)          AS RowID,
    ps.Name                                                AS SubCategory,
    p.Name                                                 AS ProductName,
    ProductNumber,
    Color,
    ListPrice
INTO  #ProductsByCategory
FROM  AdventureWorks.Production.Product p
    INNER JOIN AdventureWorks.Production.ProductSubcategory ps
        ON p.ProductSubcategoryID = ps.ProductSubcategoryID ;
GO
```

```
-- Add new column for display in currency format
ALTER TABLE #ProductsByCategory ADD Dollar varchar(32) not null DEFAULT ('');
GO
-- Command(s) completed successfully.
```

```
-- Populate new column with UPDATE
UPDATE #ProductsByCategory  SET Dollar = FORMAT(ListPrice, 'c', 'en-US');
GO
-- (295 row(s) affected)
```

```
SELECT *  FROM   #ProductsByCategory  ORDER BY Subcategory,  RowID;
```

RowID	SubCategory	ProductName	ProductNumber	Color	ListPrice	Dollar
1	Bib-Shorts	Men's Bib-Shorts, S	SB-M891-S	Multi	89.99	$89.99
2	Bib-Shorts	Men's Bib-Shorts, M	SB-M891-M	Multi	89.99	$89.99
3	Bib-Shorts	Men's Bib-Shorts, L	SB-M891-L	Multi	89.99	$89.99
1	Bike Racks	Hitch Rack - 4-Bike	RA-H123	NULL	120.00	$120.00
1	Bike Stands	All-Purpose Bike Stand	ST-1401	NULL	159.00	$159.00
1	Bottles and Cages	Water Bottle - 30 oz.	WB-H098	NULL	4.99	$4.99
2	Bottles and Cages	Mountain Bottle Cage	BC-M005	NULL	9.99	$9.99
3	Bottles and Cages	Road Bottle Cage	BC-R205	NULL	8.99	$8.99
1	Bottom Brackets	LL Bottom Bracket	BB-7421	NULL	53.99	$53.99
2	Bottom Brackets	ML Bottom Bracket	BB-8107	NULL	101.24	$101.24
3	Bottom Brackets	HL Bottom Bracket	BB-9108	NULL	121.49	$121.49
1	Brakes	Rear Brakes	RB-9231	Silver	106.50	$106.50
2	Brakes	Front Brakes	FB-9873	Silver	106.50	$106.50
1	Caps	AWC Logo Cap	CA-1098	Multi	8.99	$8.99
1	Chains	Chain	CH-0234	Silver	20.24	$20.24

```
-- Cleanup
DROP TABLE #ProductsByCategory
```

Add ROW_NUMBER & RANK Columns to Table

Add row number and rank number to SELECT INTO table create without partitioning and rank (dense ranking) high price items to low price items.

```
SELECT ROW_NUMBER()
     OVER(
      ORDER BY Name ASC)                                   AS ROWID,
    DENSE_RANK()
     OVER(
      ORDER BY ListPrice DESC)                             AS RANKID,
    ListPrice                                              AS Price,
    *
INTO   tempdb.dbo.RankedProduct
FROM   AdventureWorks2012.Production.Product
ORDER  BY       RANKID,
                ROWID;
GO
-- (504 row(s) affected)
```

```
SELECT * FROM   tempdb.dbo.RankedProduct;
GO
-- (504 row(s) affected) - Partial results.
```

ROWID	RANKID	Price	ProductID	Name	ProductNumber	MakeFlag	FinishedGoodsFlag	Color
376	1	3578.27	750	Road-150 Red, 44	BK-R93R-44	1	1	Red
377	1	3578.27	751	Road-150 Red, 48	BK-R93R-48	1	1	Red
378	1	3578.27	752	Road-150 Red, 52	BK-R93R-52	1	1	Red
379	1	3578.27	753	Road-150 Red, 56	BK-R93R-56	1	1	Red
380	1	3578.27	749	Road-150 Red, 62	BK-R93R-62	1	1	Red
332	2	3399.99	771	Mountain-100 Silver, 38	BK-M82S-38	1	1	Silver
333	2	3399.99	772	Mountain-100 Silver, 42	BK-M82S-42	1	1	Silver
334	2	3399.99	773	Mountain-100 Silver, 44	BK-M82S-44	1	1	Silver

```
DROP TABLE tempdb.dbo.RankedProduct;
GO
```

3-Part Name Table Reference

The above script can be executed from any database on this server instance since we are using three-part name as table reference. Referencing a table on a linked server requires 4-part name. Double dot in table reference means default value between dots. Example:

[LONDONPROD1].TranMaster..OnlineOrderDetail is equivalent to
[LONDONPROD1].TranMaster.dbo.OnlineOrderDetail .

CHAPTER 10: The Art of Database Design

The Nature of Connection Between Tables

There is only **one kind of connection between tables** which is defined as FOREIGN KEY **references** the PRIMARY KEY or UNIQUE KEY. Nonetheless, the application functional meaning of the connections can be many, for example, star schema in a data warehouse.

Categorical Relationship

```
USE AdventureWorks2012;
```

```
CREATE TABLE Production.ProductSubcategoryTest(
        ProductSubcategoryID int IDENTITY(1,1) PRIMARY KEY,
        ProductCategoryID int NOT NULL
                REFERENCES Production.ProductCategory(ProductCategoryID),
        Name dbo.Name NOT NULL,
        rowguid uniqueidentifier ROWGUIDCOL  NOT NULL DEFAULT( NEWID() ),
        ModifiedDate datetime NOT NULL DEFAULT( CURRENT_TIMESTAMP ));
-- (1 row(s) affected)
```

Based on the naming, with the help of our Human Intelligence, we conclude the connection is **categorization**, from subcategory to (super)category. The example clearly illustrates the importance of good naming in database design. SQL Server would work equally well with Table1 and Table2, but that would make the design practically unreadable.

The connection between Production.Product and Production.ProductSubcategory is also categorization at the bottom level of the Product --> Subcategory --> Category hierarchy.

```
ALTER TABLE Production.Product
        WITH CHECK
        ADD  CONSTRAINT FK_Product_ProductSubcategory_ProductSubcategoryID
        FOREIGN KEY(ProductSubcategoryID)
        REFERENCES Production.ProductSubcategory (ProductSubcategoryID)
GO
```

Information Object Belongs To Relationship

Since we are working with information in the data processing industry, it may not come as a big surprise that frequently we are dealing with information object rather than real world objects. The products in the AdventureWorks2012 database have information objects associated with them: photos, documents and reviews for example. The relationship is many information objects to one product.

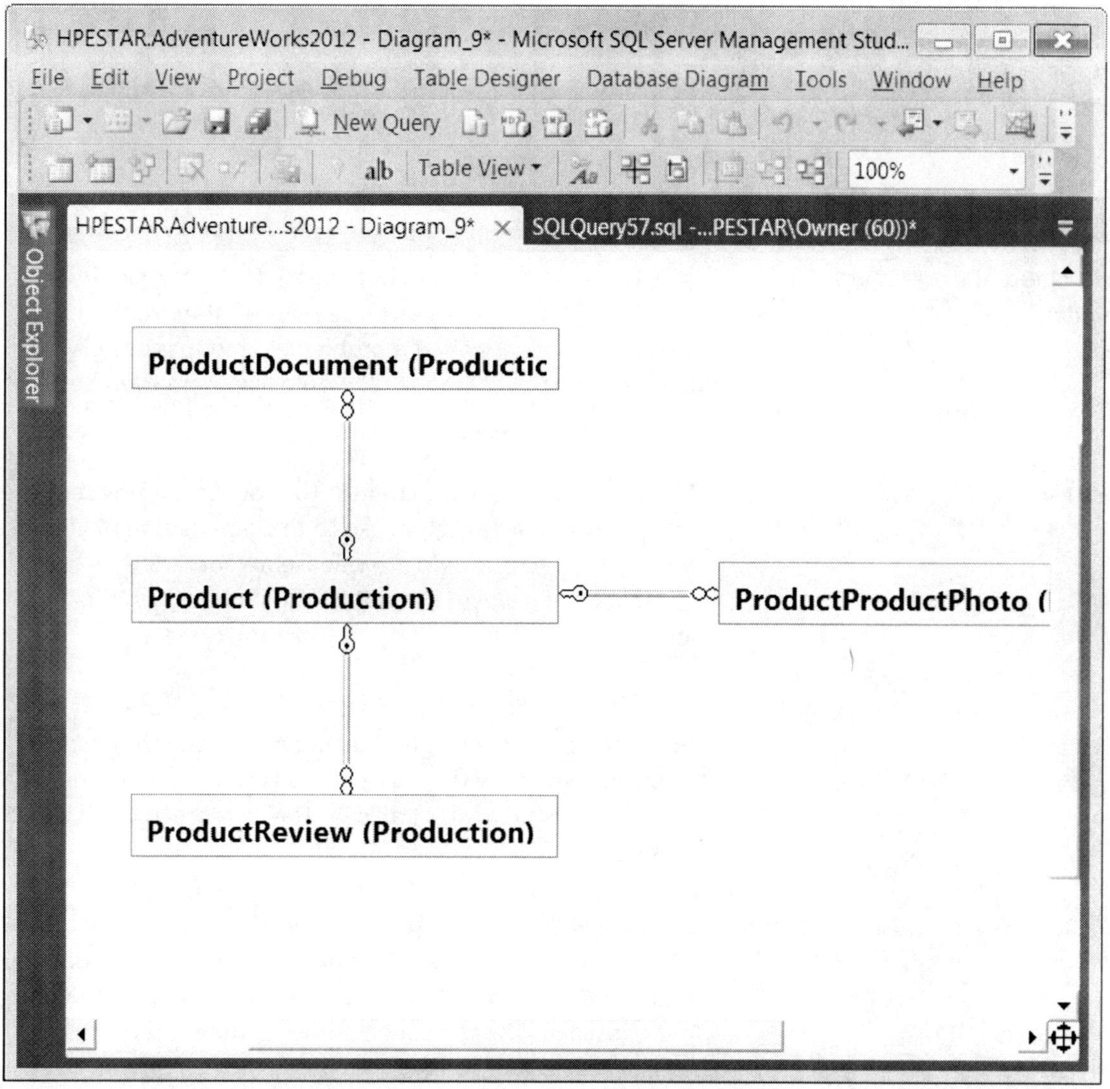

Checking Out Information Objects

Let's take a look at the ProductReview table. The information object is customer review about a product.

```
SELECT P.Name                          AS ProductName,
       R.ReviewerName,
        LEFT(R.Comments,256)           AS Comments
FROM Production.ProductReview R
       INNER JOIN Production.Product P
              ON P.ProductID = R.ProductID
ORDER BY      ProductName,
              ReviewerName;
GO
```

ProductName	ReviewerName	Comments
HL Mountain Pedal	David	A little on the heavy side, but overall the entry/exit is easy in all conditions. I've used these pedals for more than 3 years and I've never had a problem. Cleanup is easy. Mud and sand don't get trapped. I would like them even better if there was a w
HL Mountain Pedal	Jill	Maybe it's just because I'm new to mountain biking, but I had a terrible time getting use to these pedals. In my first outing, I wiped out trying to release my foot. Any suggestions on ways I can adjust the pedals, or is it just a learning curve thing?
Mountain Bike Socks, M	John Smith	I can't believe I'm singing the praises of a pair of socks, but I just came back from a grueling 3-day ride and these socks really helped make the trip a blast. They're lightweight yet really cushioned my feet all day. The reinforced toe is nearly bulle
Road-550-W Yellow, 40	Laura Norman	The Road-550-W from Adventure Works Cycles is everything it's advertised to be. Finally, a quality bike that is actually built for a woman and provides control and comfort in one neat package. The top tube is shorter, the suspension is weight-tuned and th

The Bike Photo Information Object

The digital bike photo is stored in binary format in the Production.ProductPhoto table using varbinary(max) data type. Visualization requires Reporting Services report or external graphics software. SSMS cannot display the image, only the binary content.

```
SELECT      P.Name                              AS ProductName,
            PP.ThumbnailPhotoFilename,
            PP.LargePhotoFilename
FROM Production.ProductProductPhoto PPP
      INNER JOIN Production.Product P
            ON P.ProductID = PPP.ProductID
      INNER JOIN Production.ProductPhoto PP
            ON PPP.ProductPhotoID = PP.ProductPhotoID
WHERE P.Name = 'Road-550-W Yellow, 40'
ORDER BY    ProductName;
GO
```

ProductName	ThumbnailPhotoFilename	LargePhotoFilename
Road-550-W Yellow, 40	racer02_yellow_f_small.gif	racer02_yellow_f_large.gif

The photo of the yellow road bike.

XML Diagram Object

The AdventureWorks2012 sample database includes a number of XML data type columns. These columns cannot be displayed in a formatted fashion using Management Studio, rather they require special software for formatting or visualization.

```
SELECT Diagram FROM AdventureWorks2012.Production.Illustration WHERE IllustrationID = 4;
-- Partial results
```


```
<Canvas>
  <!-- Layer 1/<Path> -->
  <Path StrokeThickness="0.500000" Stroke="#ff656565" StrokeMiterLimit="1.000000" Fill="#ff656565" Data="F1 M 111.049805,46.655762 L 114.526367,48.509766 L 112.671875,52.911621 L 109.694336,51.374512 L 111.049805,46.655762 Z" />
  <!-- Layer 1/<Path> -->
  <Path StrokeThickness="1.202600" Stroke="#ff989898" StrokeMiterLimit="1.000000" Data="F1 M 155.380859,314.981934" />
  <!-- Layer 1/<Path> -->
  <Path StrokeThickness="1.000000" Stroke="#ff000000" StrokeMiterLimit="1.000000" Data="F1 M 88.621094,132.691406 C 88.621094,132.691406 89.542969,135.905762 88.029785,130.630371 C 86.841797,126.486328 88.501953,126.418457 91.141113,125.661621 C 93.777832,124.904785 116.826172,118.705566 120.486328,117.249512 C 124.144531,115.791504 125.061523,117.566406 125.819336,120.205566 C 126.576172,122.842285 126.205078,121.554688 126.205078,121.554688 L 122.169922,123.121582 L 164.131836,264.715332 L 161.495117,268.324707 L 163.008789,273.599121 L 141.530273,279.757324 L 139.910156,274.105957 L 134.900391,272.280762 L 93.264160,131.816406 L 88.621094,132.691406 Z">
    <Path.Fill>
      <LinearGradientBrush MappingMode="Absolute" StartPoint="87.639160,198.240234" EndPoint="164.131836,198.240234">
        <LinearGradientBrush.GradientStops>
          <GradientStop Offset="0.000000" Color="#ffffffff" />
          <GradientStop Offset="0.258800" Color="#fffcfcfc" />
          <GradientStop Offset="0.396200" Color="#fff4f4f4" />
```


The diagram can be visualized by special XAML software.

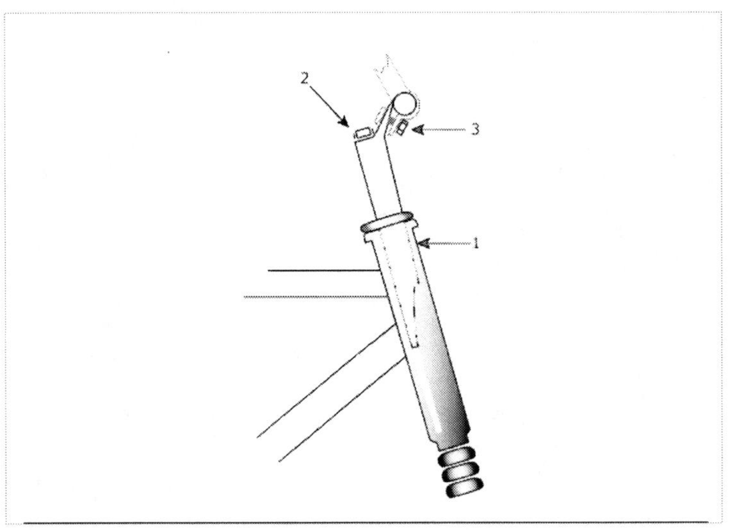

Exporting & Presenting XML Data from Production.ProductModel

XML columns contain semi-structured data. There is no general software which can make the XML data presentable. Each XML data requires specialized software for presentation. The Production.ProductModel table contains 2 XML columns. We export one cell from the first XML column, CatalogDescription, using bcp into an xhtml fil.

```
bcp "SELECT CatalogDescription FROM AdventureWorks2012.Production.ProductModel WHERE ProductModelID=19" queryout f:\data\xml\Product19.xhtml -c -t -S yourserver -T
```

```
Command Prompt
Microsoft Windows [Version 6.1.7601]
Copyright (c) 2009 Microsoft Corporation.  All rights reserved.

C:\Users\Owner>bcp "SELECT CatalogDescription FROM AdventureWorks2012.Production
.ProductModel WHERE ProductModelID=19" queryout f:\data\xml\Product19.xhtml -c -
t -S HPESTAR -T

Starting copy...

1 rows copied.
Network packet size (bytes): 4096
Clock Time (ms.) Total     : 32     Average : (31.25 rows per sec.)

C:\Users\Owner>_
```

When we double click on the new .xhtml file, the information appears in a presentable format without the XML tags.

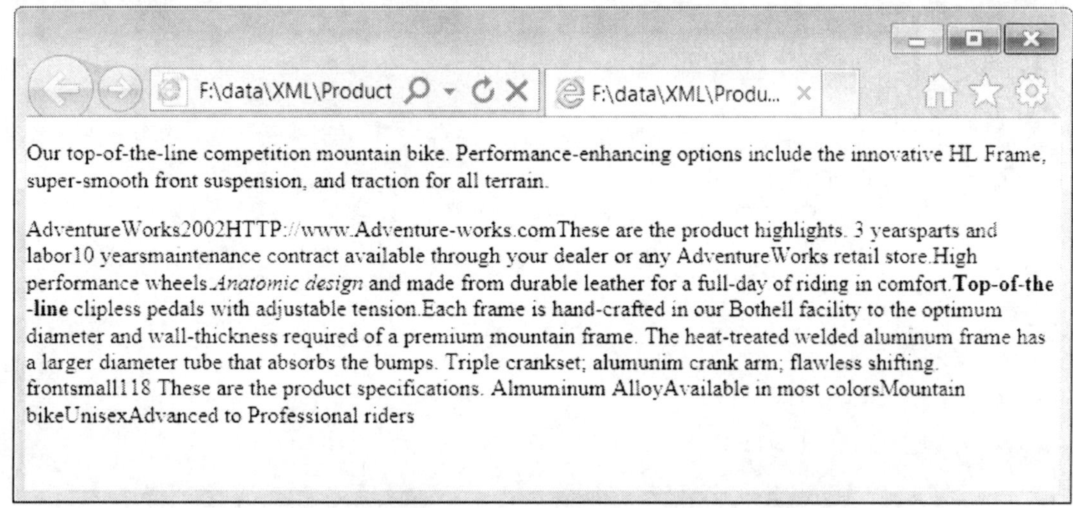

Product, ProductPhoto & ProductProductPhoto Tables Diagram

The ProductProductPhoto is a junction table representing many to many relationship between the Product and ProductPhoto. A product may have many photos and a photo may belong to many products.

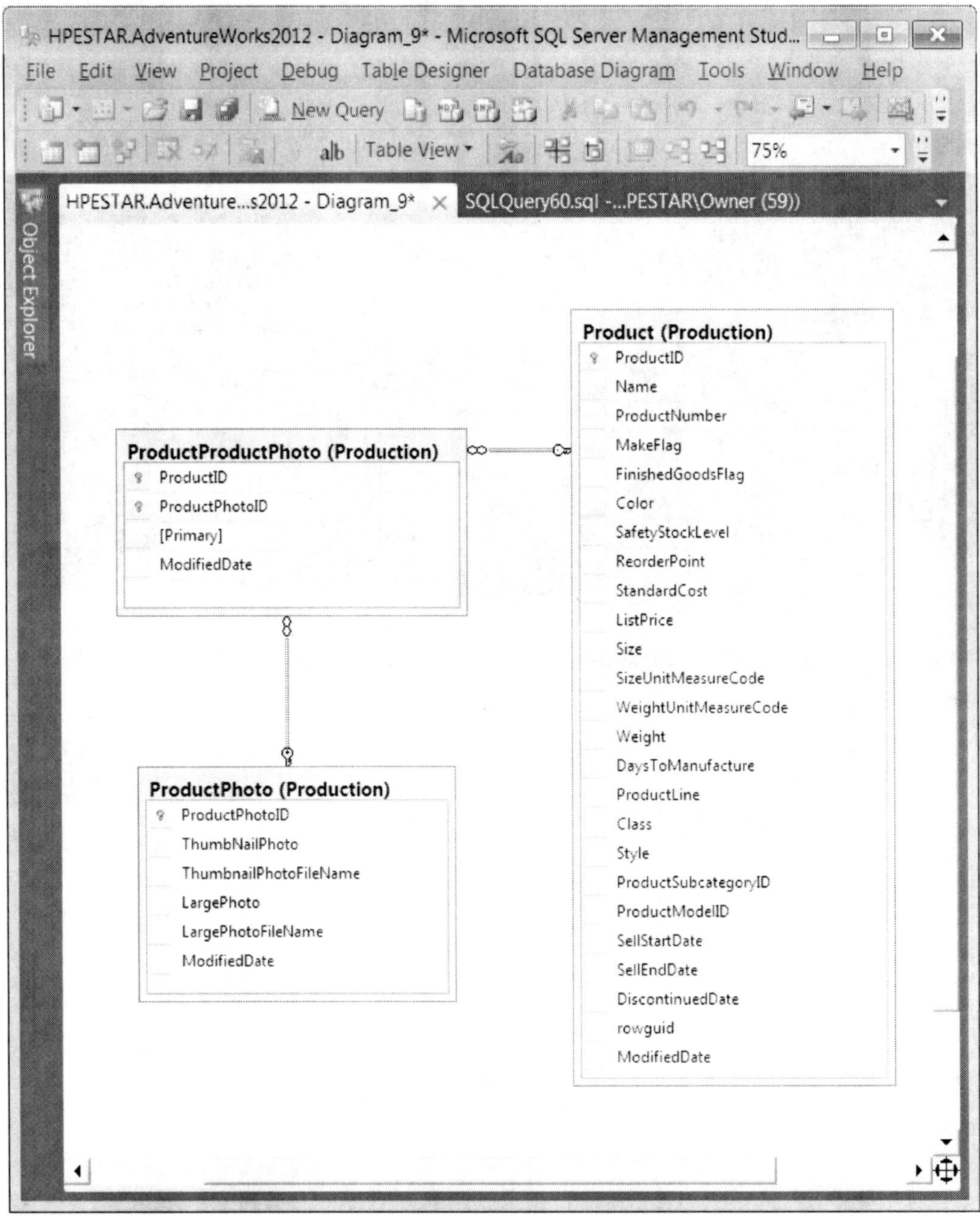

Graphical Query Design Using the Product & Photo Tables

The good database design lends itself to easy query building with Query Designer. To alias a table requires right click on the table and setting the Alias property.

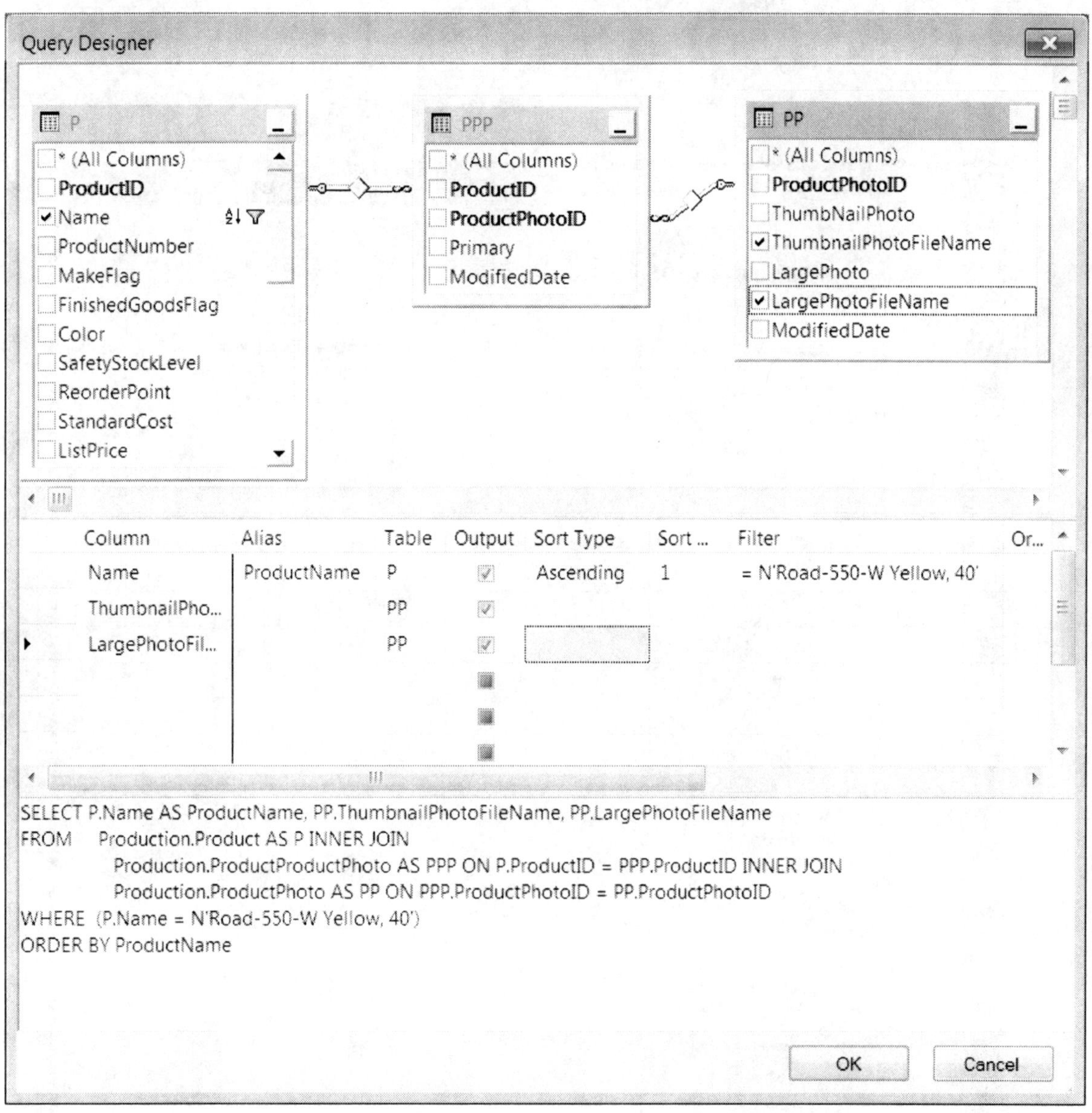

Company Received an Order Relationship

Vendor is a company supplying parts or finished product to AdventureWorks Cycles. Here is the relationship diagram. The purchase order to vendor FOREIGN KEY means a sale for the vendor. The detail to header FOREIGN KEY means the detail belongs to the header.

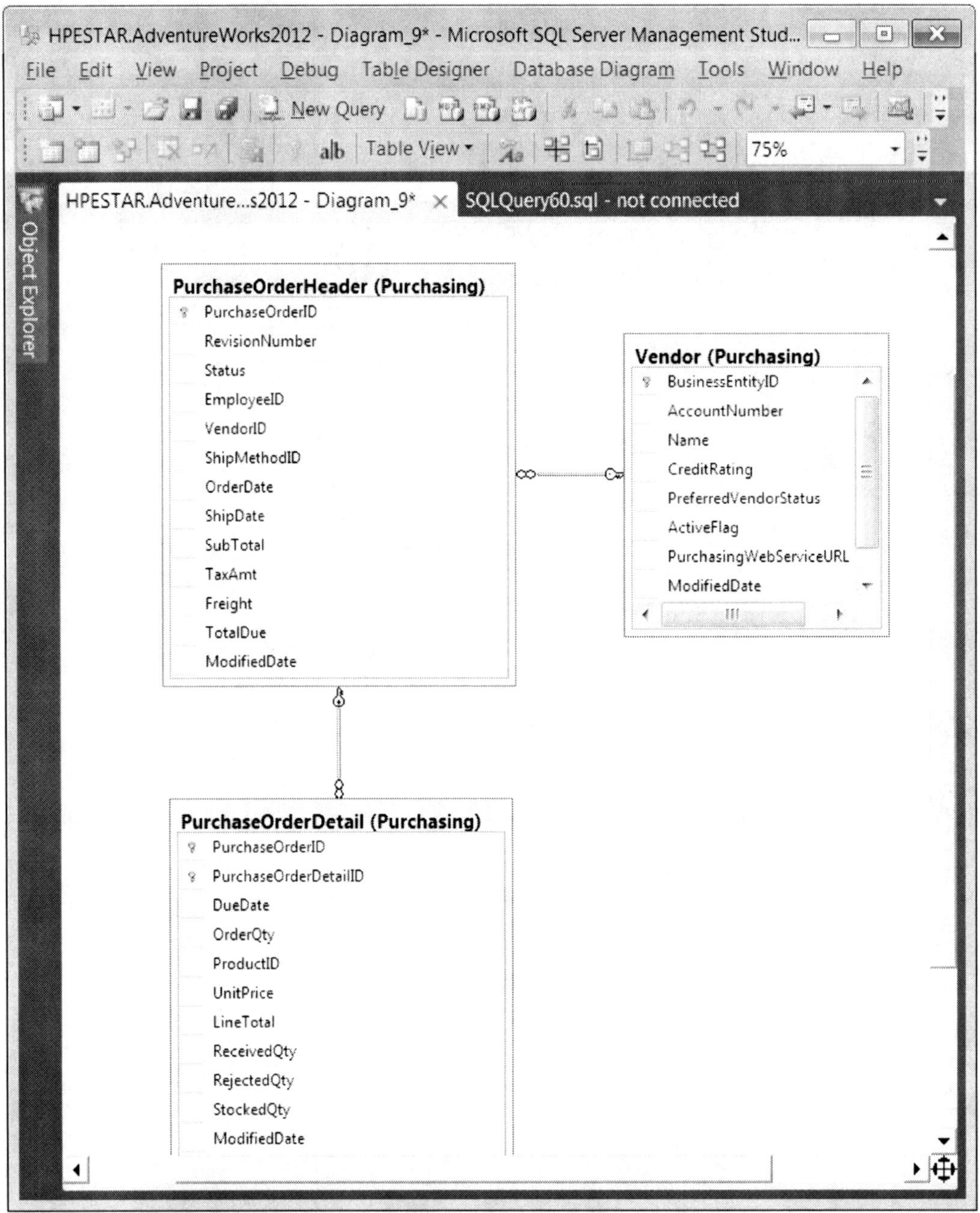

Querying the Vendor & Purchase Order Tables

The query list all purchase orders issued by AdventureWorks Cycles on a particular day.

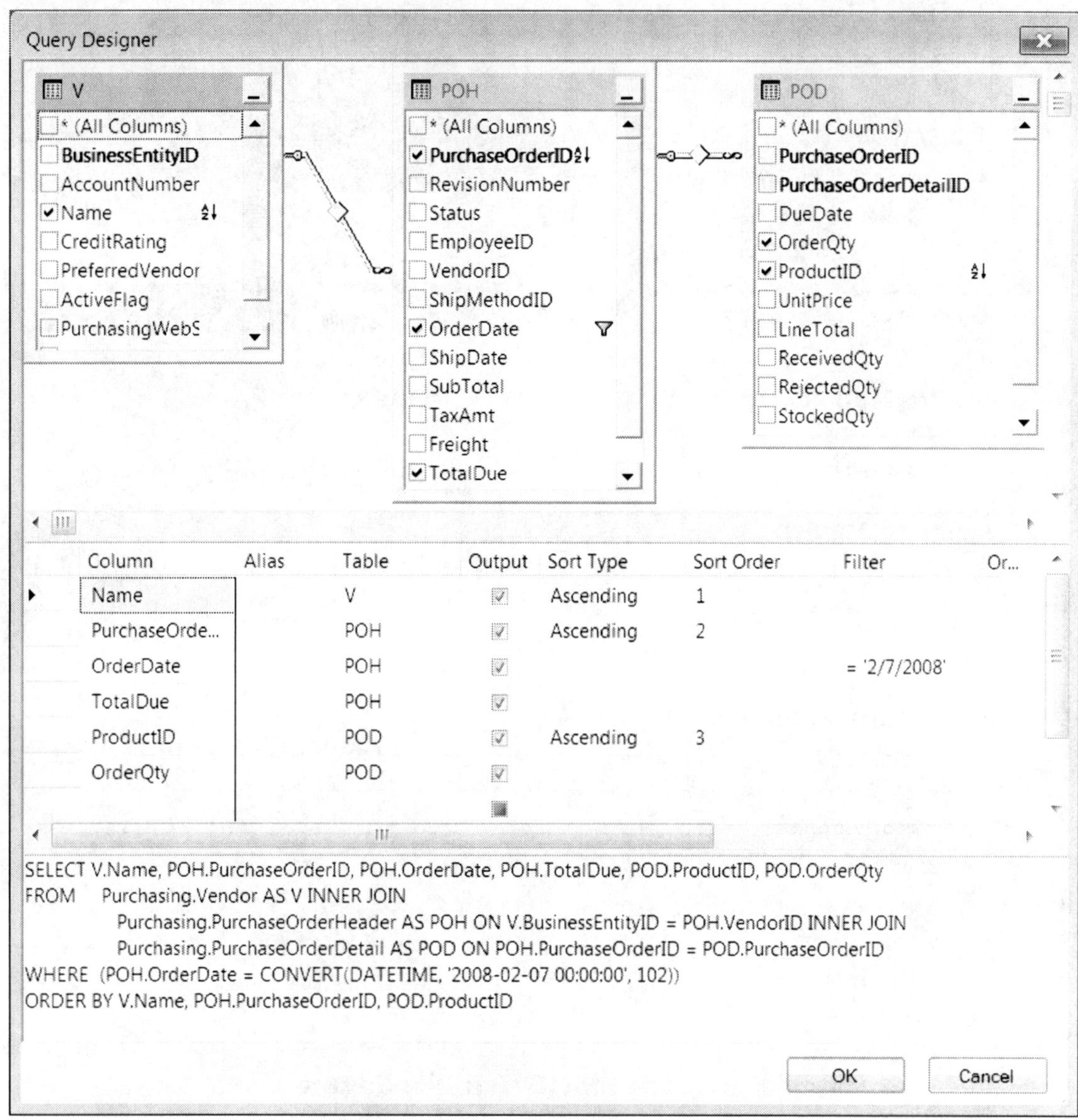

Upon execution the query returns 34 rows. Partial results.

Name	PurchaseOrderID	OrderDate	TotalDue	ProductID	OrderQty
Advanced Bicycles	1641	2008-02-07 00:00:00.000	555.9106	369	3
Allenson Cycles	1642	2008-02-07 00:00:00.000	9776.2665	530	550
American Bicycles and Wheels	1643	2008-02-07 00:00:00.000	189.0395	4	3

Type Relationship

A very frequent FOREIGN KEY representing an attribute of an object. For example a celebrity is a singer, actor, fashion model, writer, talk show host, sports figure and so on.

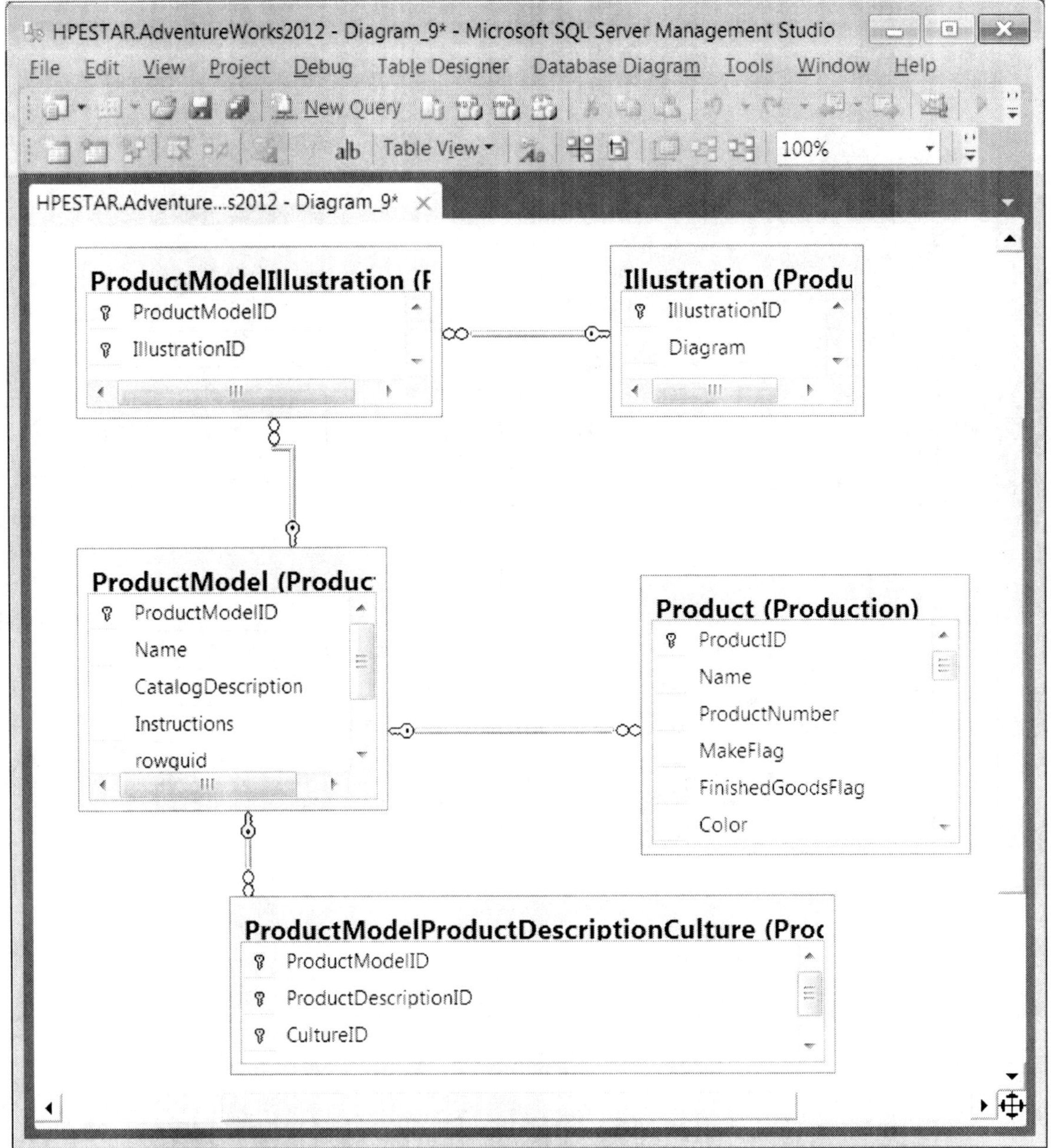

Obtaining Model Information for a Bike

We use the graphical query designer to see Model information for high-priced bikes.

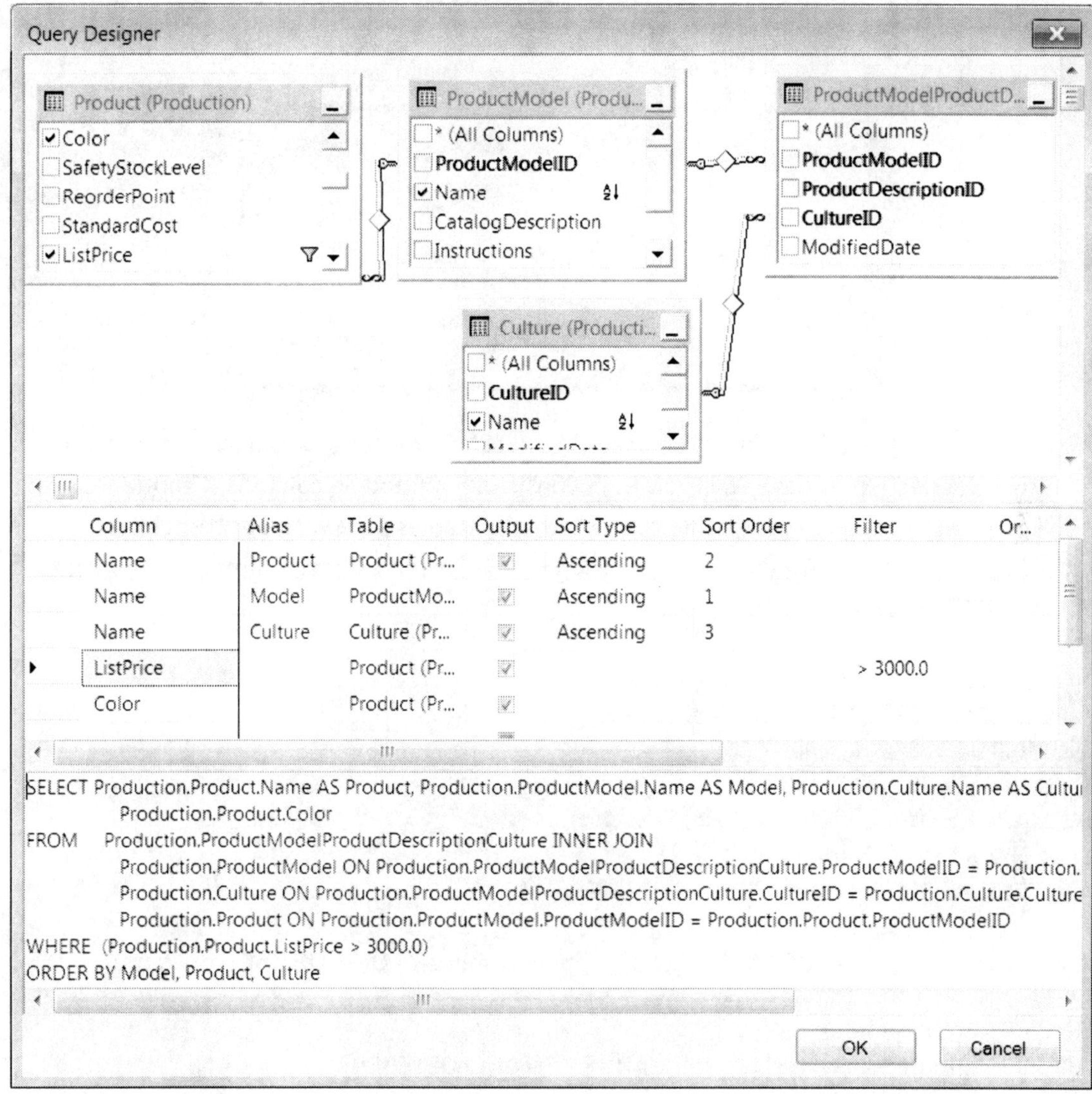

Partial results from the generated query.

Product	Model	Culture	ListPrice	Color
Mountain-100 Silver, 48	Mountain-100	English	3399.99	Silver
Mountain-100 Silver, 48	Mountain-100	French	3399.99	Silver
Mountain-100 Silver, 48	Mountain-100	Hebrew	3399.99	Silver
Mountain-100 Silver, 48	Mountain-100	Thai	3399.99	Silver
Road-150 Red, 44	Road-150	Arabic	3578.27	Red
Road-150 Red, 44	Road-150	Chinese	3578.27	Red

When to Use & Not to Use Composite PRIMARY KEYs

A composite PRIMARY KEY can be used in a junction table if it is unlikely that FOREIGN KEY reference needed from other tables. AdventureWorks2012 example of composite PRIMARY KEY with 4 columns in a junction table.

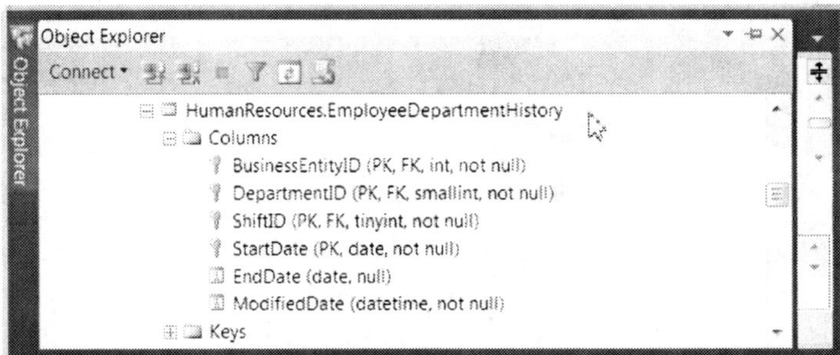

Composite PRIMARY KEY should not be used if FOREIGN KEY reference is necessary today or in the future: ineffective to have FOREIGN KEYs consisting of multiple columns & subtle violation of 3NF rules by duplication of PK table content in other tables as FKs. **The bottom line: COMPOSITE PRIMARY KEYs should not be used in regular tables.** Instead of the composite PRIMARY KEY design:

```
CREATE TABLE AlbumSong(
 AlbumTitle NVARCHAR(64) not null,
 DiskNo INTEGER  not null,
 TrackNo INTEGER  not null,
 PRIMARY KEY (AlbumTitle, DiskNo, TrackNo),
 Song NVARCHAR(128) not null,
 ModifiedDate DATE default(CURRENT_TIMESTAMP));
```

Design with **SURROGATE PRIMARY KEY** and apply composite **UNIQUE KEY** constraint:

```
CREATE TABLE AlbumSong(
 AlbumSongID INT IDENTITY(1,1) PRIMARY KEY NONCLUSTERED,
 AlbumTitle NVARCHAR(64) not null,
 DiskNo INTEGER  not null,
 TrackNo INTEGER  not null,
 UNIQUE CLUSTERED (AlbumTitle, DiskNo, TrackNo),
 Song NVARCHAR(128) not null,
 ModifiedDate DATE default(CURRENT_TIMESTAMP));
```

Where to place the clustered index should be based on performance considerations.

How To Design a Table

It is very important that we follow in order. Rules are with reference to the Celebrity table.

- Identify the NATURAL KEY column(s) (LastName, FirstName) & set it as UNIQUE (KEY)
- Design the non-key columns (BirthDate, BirthPlace, NameAtBirth)
- Design the row maintenance columns (CreatedDate)
- Configure the FOREIGN KEY(s) (CountryID)
- Configure the IDENTITY SURROGATE PRIMARY KEY (CelebrityID)

```
CREATE TABLE Profession (
	ProfessionID TINYINT IDENTITY(1,1) PRIMARY KEY,
	Name varchar(50) NOT NULL UNIQUE,
	CreatedDate DATETIME DEFAULT(CURRENT_TIMESTAMP) );
```

```
CREATE TABLE Country (
	ID TINYINT IDENTITY(1,1) PRIMARY KEY,
	Name varchar(128) NOT NULL UNIQUE,
	CreatedDate DATETIME DEFAULT(CURRENT_TIMESTAMP) );
```

```
CREATE TABLE Celebrity(
	CelebrityID SMALLINT IDENTITY(1,1) PRIMARY KEY nonclustered,
	CountryID TINYINT REFERENCES Country(ID),
	LastName nvarchar(40) NOT NULL CHECK( LEN(LastName) > 4),
	FirstName nvarchar(40),
	UNIQUE clustered (LastName, FirstName),
	BirthDate DATE NOT NULL,
	BirthPlace nvarchar(50),
	NameAtBirth nvarchar(60),
	CreatedDate DATETIME DEFAULT(CURRENT_TIMESTAMP) );
```

```
CREATE TABLE CelebrityProfessionXref(
	CelebrityID SMALLINT NOT NULL REFERENCES Celebrity(CelebrityID),
	ProfessionID TINYINT NOT NULL REFERENCES Profession(ProfessionID),
	PRIMARY KEY (CelebrityID, ProfessionID),
	CreatedDate DATETIME DEFAULT(CURRENT_TIMESTAMP) );
```

Without NATURAL KEY we don't have a table. The NATURAL KEY can be set as UNIQUE KEY or PRIMARY KEY. We can tentatively move the clustered index away from the PRIMARY KEY (default), however, final decision point is when we identify the business critical queries. Clustered index is helpful with range query performance.

Table-Related Database Objects

Table is the content object in a database. It has a number of supporting objects to keep the content accurate and accessible. The list of database object types in sys.objects system view.

```
SELECT SeqNo=ROW_NUMBER() OVER (ORDER BY type_desc),
    *
FROM ( SELECT DISTINCT type, type_desc
            FROM sys.objects ) x
ORDER BY SeqNo;
```

SeqNo	type	type_desc
1	C	CHECK_CONSTRAINT
2	D	DEFAULT_CONSTRAINT
3	F	FOREIGN_KEY_CONSTRAINT
4	IT	INTERNAL_TABLE
5	PK	PRIMARY_KEY_CONSTRAINT
6	SO	SEQUENCE_OBJECT
7	SQ	SERVICE_QUEUE
8	IF	SQL_INLINE_TABLE_VALUED_FUNCTION
9	FN	SQL_SCALAR_FUNCTION
10	P	SQL_STORED_PROCEDURE
11	TF	SQL_TABLE_VALUED_FUNCTION
12	TR	SQL_TRIGGER
13	S	SYSTEM_TABLE
14	TT	TYPE_TABLE
15	UQ	UNIQUE_CONSTRAINT
16	U	USER_TABLE
17	V	VIEW

Indexes have their own system view.

```
SELECT          OBJECT_NAME(object_ID)          AS TableName,
                name                            AS IndexName,
                 index_id,
                type_desc
FROM AdventureWorks2012.sys.indexes  ORDER BY TableName, index_id;
-- (333 row(s) affected) - Partial Results
```

TableName	IndexName	index_id	type_desc
Address	PK_Address_AddressID	1	CLUSTERED
Address	AK_Address_rowguid	2	NONCLUSTERED
Address	IX_Address_AddressLine1_AddressLine2_City_StateProvinceID_PostalCode	3	NONCLUSTERED
Address	IX_Address_StateProvinceID	4	NONCLUSTERED

Listing All PRIMARY KEYs

Getting database object information can start in sys.objects system view.

```
SELECT  SCHEMA_NAME(schema_id)                AS SchemaName,
        OBJECT_NAME(parent_object_id)         AS TableName,
        name                                  AS PKName
FROM AdventureWorks2012.sys.objects WHERE type = 'PK'
ORDER BY SchemaName, TableName;
GO
```

SchemaName	TableName	PKName
dbo	AWBuildVersion	PK_AWBuildVersion_SystemInformationID
dbo	DatabaseLog	PK_DatabaseLog_DatabaseLogID
dbo	ErrorLog	PK_ErrorLog_ErrorLogID
HumanResources	Department	PK_Department_DepartmentID
HumanResources	Employee	PK_Employee_BusinessEntityID
HumanResources	EmployeeDepartmentHistory	PK_EmployeeDepartmentHistory_BusinessEntityID_StartDate_DepartmentID
HumanResources	EmployeePayHistory	PK_EmployeePayHistory_BusinessEntityID_RateChangeDate
HumanResources	JobCandidate	PK_JobCandidate_JobCandidateID
HumanResources	Shift	PK_Shift_ShiftID
Person	Address	PK_Address_AddressID
Person	AddressType	PK_AddressType_AddressTypeID
Person	BusinessEntity	PK_BusinessEntity_BusinessEntityID
Person	BusinessEntityAddress	PK_BusinessEntityAddress_BusinessEntityID_AddressID_AddressTypeID
Person	BusinessEntityContact	PK_BusinessEntityContact_BusinessEntityID_PersonID_ContactTypeID
Person	ContactType	PK_ContactType_ContactTypeID
Person	CountryRegion	PK_CountryRegion_CountryRegionCode
Person	EmailAddress	PK_EmailAddress_BusinessEntityID_EmailAddressID
Person	Password	PK_Password_BusinessEntityID
Person	Person	PK_Person_BusinessEntityID
Person	PersonPhone	PK_PersonPhone_BusinessEntityID_PhoneNumber_PhoneNumberTypeID
Person	PhoneNumberType	PK_PhoneNumberType_PhoneNumberTypeID
Person	StateProvince	PK_StateProvince_StateProvinceID
Production	BillOfMaterials	PK_BillOfMaterials_BillOfMaterialsID
Production	Culture	PK_Culture_CultureID
Production	Document	PK_Document_DocumentNode
Production	Illustration	PK_Illustration_IllustrationID
Production	Location	PK_Location_LocationID
Production	Product	PK_Product_ProductID
Production	ProductCategory	PK_ProductCategory_ProductCategoryID
Production	ProductCostHistory	PK_ProductCostHistory_ProductID_StartDate
Production	ProductDescription	PK_ProductDescription_ProductDescriptionID
Production	ProductDocument	PK_ProductDocument_ProductID_DocumentNode
Production	ProductInventory	PK_ProductInventory_ProductID_LocationID
Production	ProductListPriceHistory	PK_ProductListPriceHistory_ProductID_StartDate
Production	ProductModel	PK_ProductModel_ProductModelID
Production	ProductModelIllustration	PK_ProductModelIllustration_ProductModelID_IllustrationID
Production	ProductModelProductDescriptionCulture	PK_ProductModelProductDescriptionCulture_ProductModelID_ProductDescriptionID_CultureID
Production	ProductPhoto	PK_ProductPhoto_ProductPhotoID
Production	ProductProductPhoto	PK_ProductProductPhoto_ProductID_ProductPhotoID
Production	ProductReview	PK_ProductReview_ProductReviewID
Production	ProductSubcategory	PK_ProductSubcategory_ProductSubcategoryID
Production	ScrapReason	PK_ScrapReason_ScrapReasonID
Production	TransactionHistory	PK_TransactionHistory_TransactionID
Production	TransactionHistoryArchive	PK_TransactionHistoryArchive_TransactionID
Production	UnitMeasure	PK_UnitMeasure_UnitMeasureCode
Production	WorkOrder	PK_WorkOrder_WorkOrderID
Production	WorkOrderRouting	PK_WorkOrderRouting_WorkOrderID_ProductID_OperationSequence
Purchasing	ProductVendor	PK_ProductVendor_ProductID_BusinessEntityID
Purchasing	PurchaseOrderDetail	PK_PurchaseOrderDetail_PurchaseOrderID_PurchaseOrderDetailID
Purchasing	PurchaseOrderHeader	PK_PurchaseOrderHeader_PurchaseOrderID
Purchasing	ShipMethod	PK_ShipMethod_ShipMethodID
Purchasing	Vendor	PK_Vendor_BusinessEntityID
Sales	CountryRegionCurrency	PK_CountryRegionCurrency_CountryRegionCode_CurrencyCode
Sales	CreditCard	PK_CreditCard_CreditCardID

Sales	Currency	PK_Currency_CurrencyCode
Sales	CurrencyRate	PK_CurrencyRate_CurrencyRateID
Sales	Customer	PK_Customer_CustomerID
Sales	PersonCreditCard	PK_PersonCreditCard_BusinessEntityID_CreditCardID
Sales	SalesOrderDetail	PK_SalesOrderDetail_SalesOrderID_SalesOrderDetailID
Sales	SalesOrderHeader	PK_SalesOrderHeader_SalesOrderID
Sales	SalesOrderHeaderSalesReason	PK_SalesOrderHeaderSalesReason_SalesOrderID_SalesReasonID
Sales	SalesPerson	PK_SalesPerson_BusinessEntityID
Sales	SalesPersonQuotaHistory	PK_SalesPersonQuotaHistory_BusinessEntityID_QuotaDate
Sales	SalesReason	PK_SalesReason_SalesReasonID
Sales	SalesTaxRate	PK_SalesTaxRate_SalesTaxRateID
Sales	SalesTerritory	PK_SalesTerritory_TerritoryID
Sales	SalesTerritoryHistory	PK_SalesTerritoryHistory_BusinessEntityID_StartDate_TerritoryID
Sales	ShoppingCartItem	PK_ShoppingCartItem_ShoppingCartItemID
Sales	SpecialOffer	PK_SpecialOffer_SpecialOfferID
Sales	SpecialOfferProduct	PK_SpecialOfferProduct_SpecialOfferID_ProductID
Sales	Store	PK_Store_BusinessEntityID

UNIQUEIDENTIFIER As PRIMARY KEY

For most applications INT IDENTITY(1,1) (SURROGATE) PRIMARY KEY is the perfect choice. However, some enterprise applications require the generation of a random rowid without any reference to a database. For those, UNIQUEIDENTIFIER can be used with NEWID() or NEWSEQUENTIALID() fill. **The latter is faster but not completely random therefore should not be used for secure applications.** INT IDENTITY() is fastest of the three (not in following test).

```
USE tempdb; SET NOCOUNT ON;
DECLARE @MaxCount Int = 100000,@START DATETIME,@END DATETIME, @i INT
CREATE TABLE TESTID ( ID UNIQUEIDENTIFIER DEFAULT NEWID() PRIMARY KEY,
-- CREATE TABLE TESTID ( ID UNIQUEIDENTIFIER DEFAULT NEWSEQUENTIALID() PRIMARY KEY,
COL1 CHAR(256) DEFAULT 'Everglades', COL2 CHAR(256) DEFAULT 'Everglades',
COL3 CHAR(256) DEFAULT 'Everglades', COL4 CHAR(256) DEFAULT 'Everglades',
COL5 CHAR(256) DEFAULT 'Everglades', COL6 CHAR(256) DEFAULT 'Everglades',
COL7 CHAR(256) DEFAULT 'Everglades', COL8 CHAR(256) DEFAULT 'Everglades',
COL9 CHAR(256) DEFAULT 'Everglades', COL10 CHAR(256) DEFAULT 'Everglades');
SELECT TOP(0) * INTO #Result FROM TESTID;
DBCC DROPCLEANBUFFERS;  SET @START = GETDATE(); SET @i = 1;
WHILE (@i < @MaxCount)
BEGIN INSERT TESTID DEFAULT VALUES; SET @i += 1; END
INSERT #Result SELECT t1.* FROM TESTID t1 INNER JOIN TESTID t2 ON t1.ID=t2.ID
SELECT  DATEDIFF(ms,@START,GETDATE());  DROP TABLE #Result; DROP TABLE TESTID;
```

```
-- Test with newid(): 22,436 msec
-- Test with newid(): 14,866 msec
-- Test with newid(): 14,576 msec
```

```
-- Test with newsequentialid(): 12,126 msec
-- Test with newsequentialid(): 11,290 msec
-- Test with newsequentialid(): 10,713 msec
```

List All PK & FK Columns in the Database

We can use INFORMATION_SCHEMA metadata system views for the task. The position indicates the placement of the column within a composite key.

```
USE AdventureWorks2012;
SELECT  k.table_schema                          AS SchemaName,
        k.table_name                            AS  TableName,
        k.column_name                           AS ColumnName,
        k.ordinal_position                      AS Position,
        c.constraint_type                       AS KeyConstraint
FROM   information_schema.table_constraints c
    INNER JOIN information_schema.key_column_usage k
      ON c.table_name = k.table_name
        AND c.constraint_name = k.constraint_name
ORDER BY SchemaName, TableName, KeyConstraint DESC, Position, ColumnName;
GO    -- (194 row(s) affected) - Partial results
```

SchemaName	TableName	ColumnName	Position	KeyConstraint
HumanResources	Department	DepartmentID	1	PRIMARY KEY
HumanResources	Employee	BusinessEntityID	1	PRIMARY KEY
HumanResources	Employee	BusinessEntityID	1	FOREIGN KEY
HumanResources	EmployeeDepartmentHistory	BusinessEntityID	1	PRIMARY KEY
HumanResources	EmployeeDepartmentHistory	StartDate	2	PRIMARY KEY
HumanResources	EmployeeDepartmentHistory	DepartmentID	3	PRIMARY KEY
HumanResources	EmployeeDepartmentHistory	ShiftID	4	PRIMARY KEY

Refreshing View Metadata

If any of the underlying tables changed, the view metadata is out of synch. The sp_refreshview system procedure updates the view metadata if WITH SCHEMABINDING is not specified. The first SELECT query generates all the refresh commands for views dependent on the Sales.SalesOrderHeader table.

```
USE AdventureWorks2012;
```

```
SELECT DISTINCT CONCAT('EXEC sp_refreshview ''', schema_name(schema_id),'.',name, ''';')
FROM sys.objects AS so
INNER JOIN sys.sql_expression_dependencies AS sed    ON so.object_id = sed.referencing_id
WHERE so.type = 'V' AND sed.referenced_id = OBJECT_ID('Sales.SalesOrderHeader');
```

The generated commands.

```
EXEC sp_refreshview 'dbo.vSalesOrder';
EXEC sp_refreshview 'Sales.vSalesByDateByProduct';
EXEC sp_refreshview 'Sales.vSalesPersonSalesByFiscalYears';
```

How to Get Database Object Definition Information

There are alternate ways of getting object definition metadata.

Scripting Object CREATE Definitions

This is the easiest and most reliable way. Start with a right click on the object in Object Explorer.

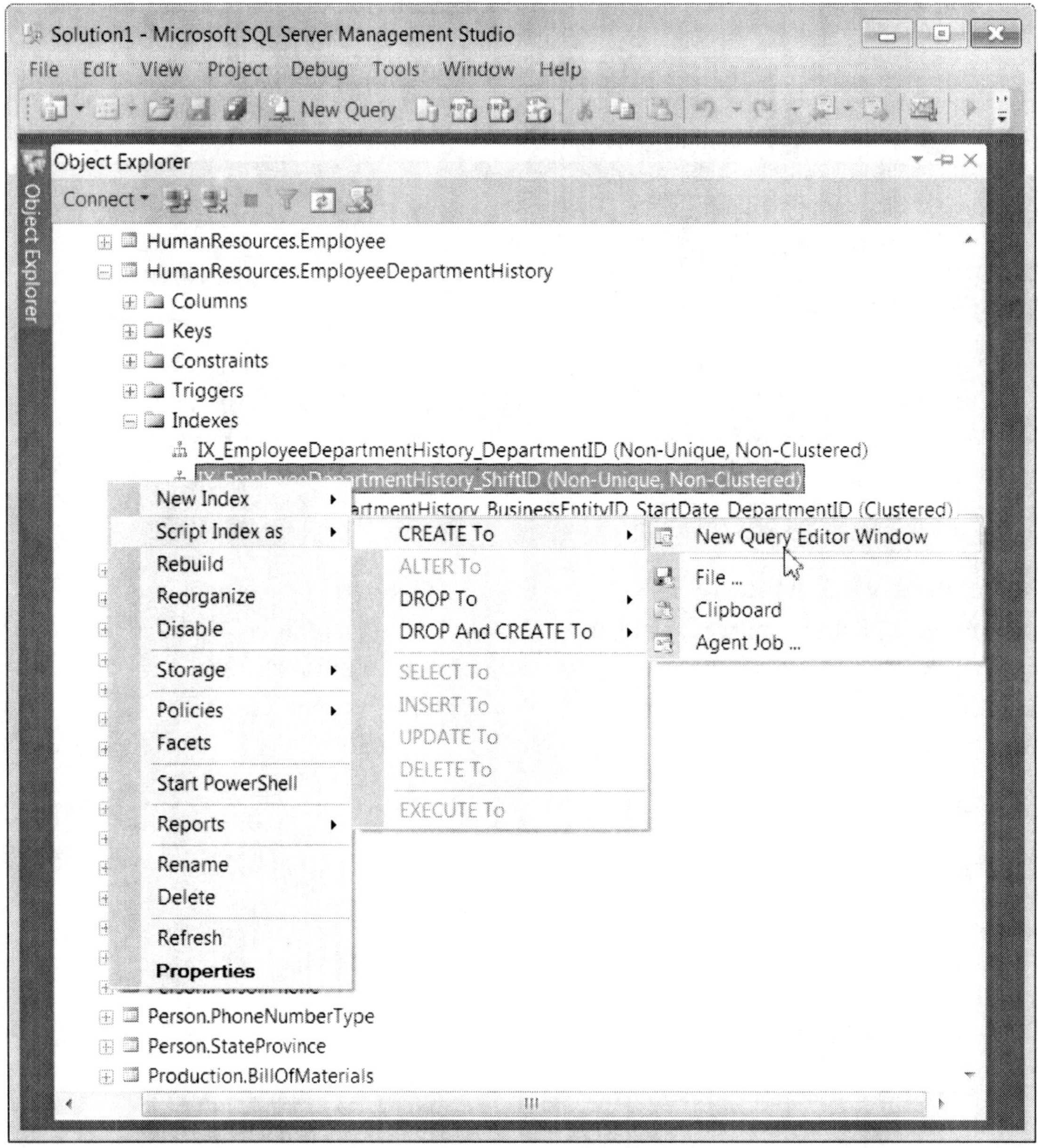

Single Object CREATE & Other Scripts from SSMS Object Explorer

Some of the scripts are generated complete. Others are just templates which require completion and testing.

Index CREATE Script

```
USE [AdventureWorks2012]
GO
```

```
/****** Object: Index [IX_EmployeeDepartmentHistory_ShiftID]    Script Date: .... ******/
CREATE NONCLUSTERED INDEX [IX_EmployeeDepartmentHistory_ShiftID]
ON [HumanResources].[EmployeeDepartmentHistory]
(
	[ShiftID] ASC
)
WITH (PAD_INDEX = OFF, STATISTICS_NORECOMPUTE = OFF, SORT_IN_TEMPDB = OFF,
DROP_EXISTING = OFF, ONLINE = OFF, ALLOW_ROW_LOCKS = ON, ALLOW_PAGE_LOCKS = ON,
FILLFACTOR = 85) ON [PRIMARY]
GO

EXEC sys.sp_addextendedproperty @name=N'MS_Description',
@value=N'Nonclustered index.' ,
@level0type=N'SCHEMA',@level0name=N'HumanResources',
@level1type=N'TABLE',@level1name=N'EmployeeDepartmentHistory',
@level2type=N'INDEX',@level2name=N'IX_EmployeeDepartmentHistory_ShiftID'
GO
```

Index DROP Script

```
/****** Object: Index [IX_EmployeeDepartmentHistory_ShiftID]    Script Date: ..... ******/
DROP INDEX [IX_EmployeeDepartmentHistory_ShiftID] ON
[HumanResources].[EmployeeDepartmentHistory]
GO
```

View DELETE Script

```
USE [AdventureWorks2012]
GO

DELETE FROM [Person].[vStateProvinceCountryRegion]
      WHERE <Search Conditions,,>
GO
```

View UPDATE Script

```
USE [AdventureWorks2012]
GO
UPDATE [Production].[vProductAndDescription]
  SET [ProductID] = <ProductID, int,>
    ,[Name] = <Name, Name,>
    ,[ProductModel] = <ProductModel, Name,>
    ,[CultureID] = <CultureID, nchar(6),>
    ,[Description] = <Description, nvarchar(400),>
 WHERE <Search Conditions,,>
GO
```

Inline Table-Valued Function ALTER Script

```
USE [AdventureWorks2012]
/****** Object:  UserDefinedFunction [Sales].[ufnStaffSalesByFiscalYear]    Script Date: ...... ******/
SET ANSI_NULLS ON
SET QUOTED_IDENTIFIER ON
GO
ALTER FUNCTION [Sales].[ufnStaffSalesByFiscalYear] (@OrderYear INT)
RETURNS TABLE  AS   RETURN
SELECT
      CONVERT(date, soh.OrderDate)                                              AS OrderDate
     ,CONCAT(p.FirstName, ' ', COALESCE(p.MiddleName, ''), ' ', p.LastName)     AS FullName
     ,e.JobTitle
     ,st.Name                                                                   AS SalesTerritory
     ,FORMAT(soh.SubTotal, 'c', 'en-US')                                        AS SalesAmount
     ,YEAR(DATEADD(mm, 6, soh.OrderDate))                                       AS FiscalYear
FROM Sales.SalesPerson sp
     INNER JOIN Sales.SalesOrderHeader soh          ON sp.BusinessEntityID = soh.SalesPersonID
     INNER JOIN Sales.SalesTerritory st             ON sp.TerritoryID = st.TerritoryID
     INNER JOIN HumanResources.Employee e           ON soh.SalesPersonID = e.BusinessEntityID
     INNER JOIN Person.Person p                     ON p.BusinessEntityID = sp.BusinessEntityID
WHERE            soh.OrderDate >= datefromparts(@OrderYear, 1, 1)
            AND soh.OrderDate < dateadd(yy,1, datefromparts(@OrderYear, 1, 1));
```

A view cannot be parameterized. We can however borrow the view query and parameterize it as an ITVF.

Article: **Inline Table-Valued Functions**
http://msdn.microsoft.com/en-us/library/aa175924(v=sql.80).aspx

Searching for Database Objects in Object Explorer Details

We start by positioning on AdventureWorks2012 in Object Explorer. We activate the Object Explorer Details window from the Views tab. Enter the keyword or wildcard in the search box and press the Enter key.

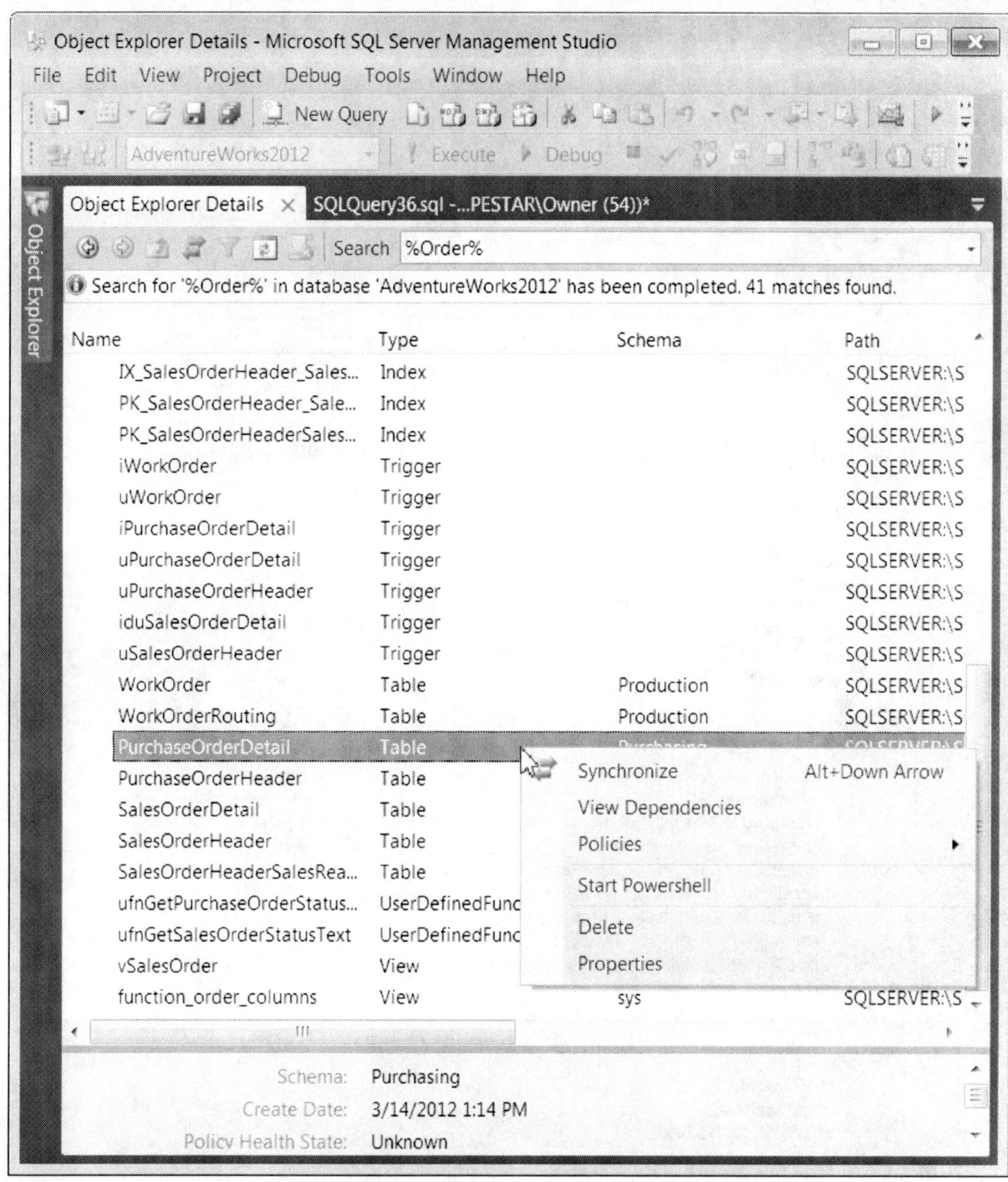

OBJECT_DEFINITION() Function for Getting Source Code

The OBJECT_DEFINITIION() function can be used to retrieve the database object definition source text for some objects such as view, stored procedure, trigger & function.

```
SELECT OBJECT_DEFINITION(object_id('INFORMATION_SCHEMA.TABLES'));
```

```
CREATE VIEW INFORMATION_SCHEMA.TABLES
AS
SELECT
        DB_NAME()                       AS TABLE_CATALOG,
        s.name                          AS TABLE_SCHEMA,
        o.name                          AS TABLE_NAME,
        CASE o.type
                WHEN 'U' THEN 'BASE TABLE'
                WHEN 'V' THEN 'VIEW'
        END                             AS TABLE_TYPE
FROM
        sys.objects o LEFT JOIN sys.schemas s
        ON s.schema_id = o.schema_id
WHERE
                o.type IN ('U', 'V')
```

```
SELECT OBJECT_DEFINITION(object_id('Sales.vSalesPersonSalesByFiscalYears'));
```

```
CREATE VIEW [Sales].[vSalesPersonSalesByFiscalYears] AS
SELECT   pvt.[SalesPersonID]
  ,pvt.[FullName]
  ,pvt.[JobTitle]
  ,pvt.[SalesTerritory]
  ,pvt.[2006]
  ,pvt.[2007]
  ,pvt.[2008]
FROM (SELECT    soh.[SalesPersonID]
     ,p.[FirstName] + ' ' + COALESCE(p.[MiddleName], '') + ' ' + p.[LastName] AS [FullName]
     ,e.[JobTitle]
     ,st.[Name] AS [SalesTerritory]
     ,soh.[SubTotal]
     ,YEAR(DATEADD(m, 6, soh.[OrderDate])) AS [FiscalYear]
  FROM [Sales].[SalesPerson] sp
     INNER JOIN [Sales].[SalesOrderHeader] soh
     ON sp.[BusinessEntityID] = soh.[SalesPersonID]
     INNER JOIN [Sales].[SalesTerritory] st
     ON sp.[TerritoryID] = st.[TerritoryID]
     INNER JOIN [HumanResources].[Employee] e
     ON soh.[SalesPersonID] = e.[BusinessEntityID]
                INNER JOIN [Person].[Person] p
                ON p.[BusinessEntityID] = sp.[BusinessEntityID]  ) AS soh
PIVOT (
  SUM([SubTotal])
  FOR [FiscalYear]
  IN ([2006], [2007], [2008])
) AS pvt;
```

Scripting Database Objects with PowerShell

PowerShell script can be used to script database object including tables. Scripting tables in the Purchasing schema of AdventureWorks2012 sample database. In all Command Prompt scripts the lines must be without carriage return or new line breaks (CR/NL).

```
sqlps
Set-Location SQLSERVER:\SQL\HPESTAR\DEFAULT\Databases\AdventureWorks2012\Tables;
ForEach ($item in Get-ChildItem  | Where-Object { $_.Schema -eq "Purchasing" })
{$item.Script()}
```

```
Command Prompt - sqlps
C:\Users\Owner>sqlps
Microsoft SQL Server PowerShell
Version 11.0.2100.60
Microsoft Corp. All rights reserved.

PS SQLSERVER:\> Set-Location SQLSERVER:\SQL\HPESTAR\DEFAULT\Databases\AdventureW
orks2012\Tables;
PS SQLSERVER:\SQL\HPESTAR\DEFAULT\Databases\AdventureWorks2012\Tables> ForEach (
$item in Get-ChildItem  | Where-Object { $_.Schema -eq "Purchasing" }) {$item.Sc
ript()}
SET ANSI_NULLS ON
SET QUOTED_IDENTIFIER ON
CREATE TABLE [Purchasing].[ProductVendor](
        [ProductID] [int] NOT NULL,
        [BusinessEntityID] [int] NOT NULL,
        [AverageLeadTime] [int] NOT NULL,
        [StandardPrice] [money] NOT NULL,
        [LastReceiptCost] [money] NULL,
        [LastReceiptDate] [datetime] NULL,
        [MinOrderQty] [int] NOT NULL,
        [MaxOrderQty] [int] NOT NULL,
        [OnOrderQty] [int] NULL,
        [UnitMeasureCode] [nchar](3) COLLATE SQL_Latin1_General_CP1_CI_AS NOT NU
LL,
        [ModifiedDate] [datetime] NOT NULL
```

Instead of the console the scripting output can be piped to a .sql file.

```
ForEach ($item in Get-ChildItem  | Where-Object { $_.Schema -eq "Purchasing" }) {$item.Script()
| Out-File "f:data\sql\PurchasingTables.sql" -Append }
```

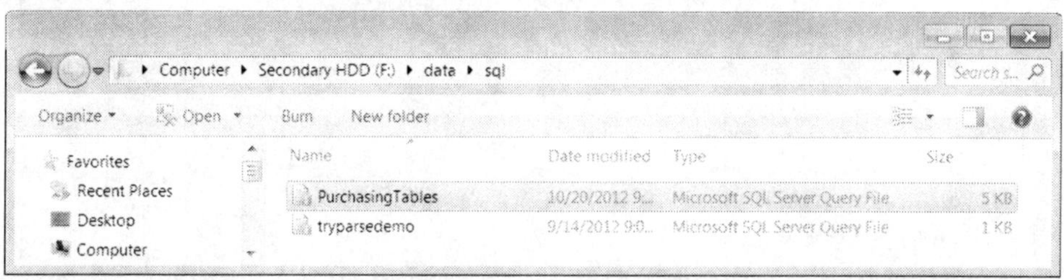

System Views since SQL Server 2005

SQL Server 2005 has introduced a large collection, 400 in SS 2012, of system views providing detail metadata and operational data which was not available before. As an example, the full-text index & full-text search functionalities have a number of supporting system views. The system tables are no longer accessible. System views cannot be altered or updated. **System views are read only**. The head of systems views list.

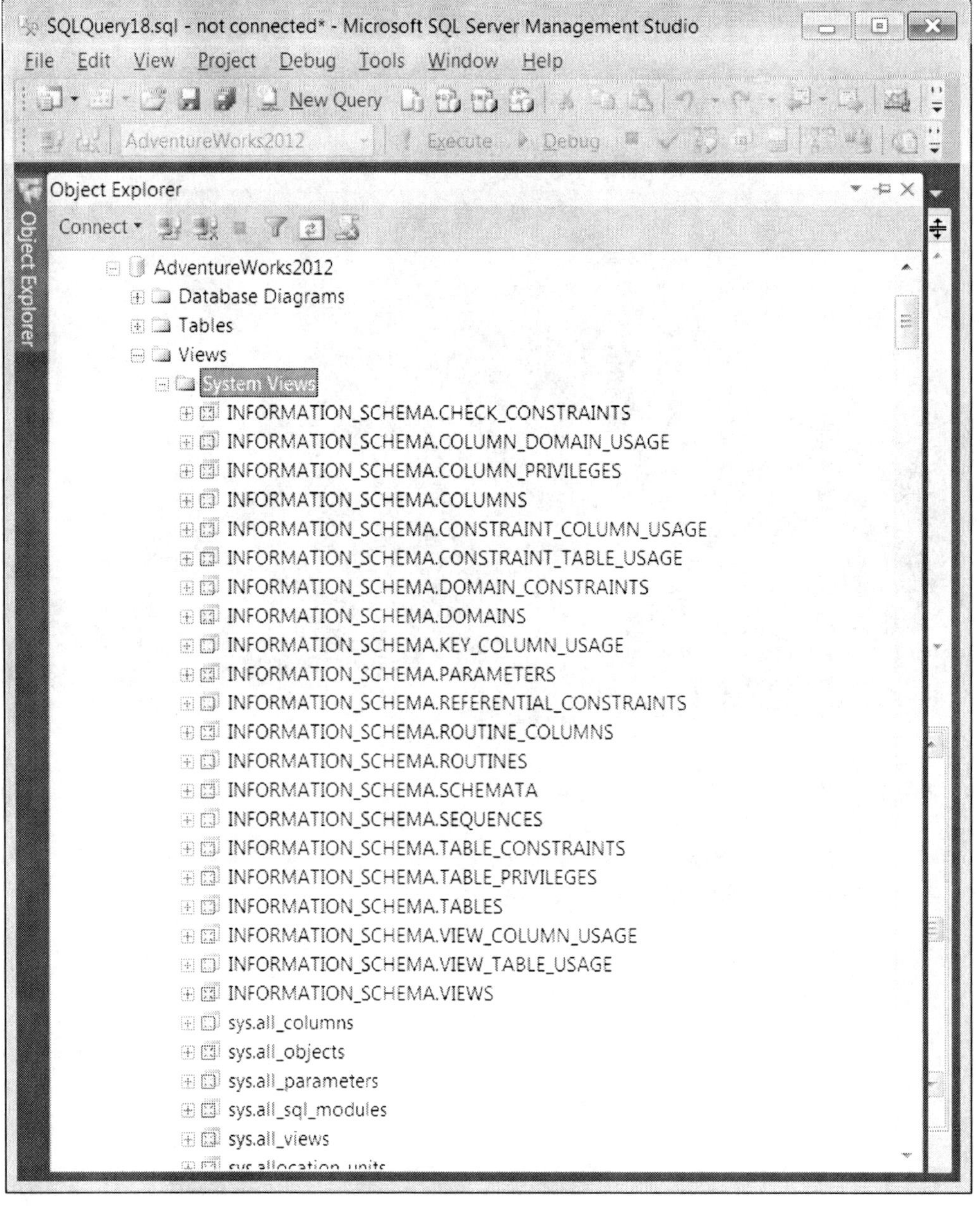

Querying Systems Views

Querying system views is not a trivial task. Frequently a group of tables involved and a Dynamic Management Function (DMF) CROSS APPLY may be necessary for useful results.

> Download site for SQL Server 2008 R2 System Views Map:
> *http://www.microsoft.com/en-us/download/details.aspx?id=722 .*

```
USE AdventureWorks2012;
SELECT ReferencedObject = CONCAT(SCHEMA_NAME(o2.schema_id), '.',
                                   ed.referenced_entity_name),
       ReferencedObjectType = o2.type,
       ReferencingObjectType = o1.type,
       ReferencingObject = CONCAT(SCHEMA_NAME(o1.schema_id), '.', o1.name)
FROM   sys.sql_expression_dependencies ed
    INNER JOIN sys.objects o1
        ON ed.referencing_id = o1.object_id
    INNER JOIN sys.objects o2
        ON ed.referenced_id = o2.object_id
WHERE  o1.type IN ( 'P', 'TR', 'V', 'TF' )
ORDER  BY        ReferencedObjectType, ReferencedObject, ReferencingObject;
-- (163 row(s) affected) - Partial results
```

ReferencedObject	ReferencedObjectType	ReferencingObjectType	ReferencingObject
HumanResources.Department	U	V	HumanResources.vEmployeeDepartment
HumanResources.Department	U	V	HumanResources.vEmployeeDepartmentHistory
HumanResources.Employee	U	TF	dbo.ufnGetContactInformation
HumanResources.Employee	U	P	dbo.uspGetEmployeeManagers
HumanResources.Employee	U	P	dbo.uspGetManagerEmployees
HumanResources.Employee	U	P	HumanResources.uspUpdateEmployeeHireInfo
HumanResources.Employee	U	P	HumanResources.uspUpdateEmployeeLogin
HumanResources.Employee	U	P	HumanResources.uspUpdateEmployeePersonalInfo
HumanResources.Employee	U	V	HumanResources.vEmployee
HumanResources.Employee	U	V	HumanResources.vEmployeeDepartment
HumanResources.Employee	U	V	HumanResources.vEmployeeDepartmentHistory
HumanResources.Employee	U	V	Sales.vSalesPerson
HumanResources.Employee	U	V	Sales.vSalesPersonSalesByFiscalYears
HumanResources.EmployeeDepartmentHistory	U	V	HumanResources.vEmployeeDepartment
HumanResources.EmployeeDepartmentHistory	U	V	HumanResources.vEmployeeDepartmentHistory
HumanResources.EmployeePayHistory	U	P	HumanResources.uspUpdateEmployeeHireInfo
HumanResources.JobCandidate	U	P	dbo.uspSearchCandidateResumes
HumanResources.JobCandidate	U	V	HumanResources.vJobCandidate
HumanResources.JobCandidate	U	V	HumanResources.vJobCandidateEducation
HumanResources.JobCandidate	U	V	HumanResources.vJobCandidateEmployment

Listing All System Views

Since SQL Server 2005 system tables are off limits, replaced by system views, 400 in SS 2012.

```
;WITH cteTableList AS (     SELECT CONCAT(SCHEMA_NAME(schema_id), '.', name)          AS TableName,
  (( ROW_NUMBER() OVER( ORDER BY CONCAT(SCHEMA_NAME(schema_id),'.', name)) ) % 3)      AS Remainder,
  (( ROW_NUMBER() OVER( ORDER BY CONCAT(SCHEMA_NAME(schema_id),'.', name)) - 1 )/ 3)   AS Quotient
                            FROM AdventureWorks2012.sys.system_views),
CTE AS (SELECT TableName, CASE WHEN Remainder=0 THEN 3 ELSE Remainder END AS Remainder, Quotient
        FROM cteTableList)
SELECT  MAX(CASE WHEN Remainder = 1 THEN TableName END),
        MAX(CASE WHEN Remainder = 2 THEN TableName END),
        MAX(CASE WHEN Remainder = 3 THEN TableName END)
FROM  CTE GROUP  BY Quotient ORDER  BY Quotient;
```

INFORMATION_SCHEMA.CHECK_CONSTRAINTS	INFORMATION_SCHEMA.COLUMN_DOMAIN_USAGE	INFORMATION_SCHEMA.COLUMN_PRIVILEGES
INFORMATION_SCHEMA.COLUMNS	INFORMATION_SCHEMA.CONSTRAINT_COLUMN_USAGE	INFORMATION_SCHEMA.CONSTRAINT_TABLE_USAGE
INFORMATION_SCHEMA.DOMAIN_CONSTRAINTS	INFORMATION_SCHEMA.DOMAINS	INFORMATION_SCHEMA.KEY_COLUMN_USAGE
INFORMATION_SCHEMA.PARAMETERS	INFORMATION_SCHEMA.REFERENTIAL_CONSTRAINTS	INFORMATION_SCHEMA.ROUTINE_COLUMNS
INFORMATION_SCHEMA.ROUTINES	INFORMATION_SCHEMA.SCHEMATA	INFORMATION_SCHEMA.SEQUENCES
INFORMATION_SCHEMA.TABLE_CONSTRAINTS	INFORMATION_SCHEMA.TABLE_PRIVILEGES	INFORMATION_SCHEMA.TABLES
INFORMATION_SCHEMA.VIEW_COLUMN_USAGE	INFORMATION_SCHEMA.VIEW_TABLE_USAGE	INFORMATION_SCHEMA.VIEWS
sys.all_columns	sys.all_objects	sys.all_parameters
sys.all_sql_modules	sys.all_views	sys.allocation_units
sys.assemblies	sys.assembly_files	sys.assembly_modules
sys.assembly_references	sys.assembly_types	sys.asymmetric_keys
sys.availability_databases_cluster	sys.availability_group_listener_ip_addresses	sys.availability_group_listeners
sys.availability_groups	sys.availability_groups_cluster	sys.availability_read_only_routing_lists
sys.availability_replicas	sys.backup_devices	sys.certificates
sys.change_tracking_databases	sys.change_tracking_tables	sys.check_constraints
sys.column_store_dictionaries	sys.column_store_segments	sys.column_type_usages
sys.column_xml_schema_collection_usages	sys.columns	sys.computed_columns
sys.configurations	sys.conversation_endpoints	sys.conversation_groups
sys.conversation_priorities	sys.credentials	sys.crypt_properties
sys.cryptographic_providers	sys.data_spaces	sys.database_audit_specification_details
sys.database_audit_specifications	sys.database_files	sys.database_filestream_options
sys.database_mirroring	sys.database_mirroring_endpoints	sys.database_mirroring_witnesses
sys.database_permissions	sys.database_principals	sys.database_recovery_status

sys.database_role_members	sys.databases	sys.default_constraints
sys.destination_data_spaces	sys.dm_audit_actions	sys.dm_audit_class_type_map
sys.dm_broker_activated_tasks	sys.dm_broker_connections	sys.dm_broker_forwarded_messages
sys.dm_broker_queue_monitors	sys.dm_cdc_errors	sys.dm_cdc_log_scan_sessions
sys.dm_clr_appdomains	sys.dm_clr_loaded_assemblies	sys.dm_clr_properties
sys.dm_clr_tasks	sys.dm_cryptographic_provider_properties	sys.dm_database_encryption_keys
sys.dm_db_file_space_usage	sys.dm_db_fts_index_physical_stats	sys.dm_db_index_usage_stats
sys.dm_db_log_space_usage	sys.dm_db_mirroring_auto_page_repair	sys.dm_db_mirroring_connections
sys.dm_db_mirroring_past_actions	sys.dm_db_missing_index_details	sys.dm_db_missing_index_group_stats
sys.dm_db_missing_index_groups	sys.dm_db_partition_stats	sys.dm_db_persisted_sku_features
sys.dm_db_script_level	sys.dm_db_session_space_usage	sys.dm_db_task_space_usage
sys.dm_db_uncontained_entities	sys.dm_exec_background_job_queue	sys.dm_exec_background_job_queue_stats
sys.dm_exec_cached_plans	sys.dm_exec_connections	sys.dm_exec_procedure_stats
sys.dm_exec_query_memory_grants	sys.dm_exec_query_optimizer_info	sys.dm_exec_query_resource_semaphores
sys.dm_exec_query_stats	sys.dm_exec_query_transformation_stats	sys.dm_exec_requests
sys.dm_exec_sessions	sys.dm_exec_trigger_stats	sys.dm_filestream_file_io_handles
sys.dm_filestream_file_io_requests	sys.dm_filestream_non_transacted_handles	sys.dm_fts_active_catalogs
sys.dm_fts_fdhosts	sys.dm_fts_index_population	sys.dm_fts_memory_buffers
sys.dm_fts_memory_pools	sys.dm_fts_outstanding_batches	sys.dm_fts_population_ranges
sys.dm_fts_semantic_similarity_population	sys.dm_hadr_auto_page_repair	sys.dm_hadr_availability_group_states
sys.dm_hadr_availability_replica_cluster_nodes	sys.dm_hadr_availability_replica_cluster_states	sys.dm_hadr_availability_replica_states
sys.dm_hadr_cluster	sys.dm_hadr_cluster_members	sys.dm_hadr_cluster_networks
sys.dm_hadr_database_replica_cluster_states	sys.dm_hadr_database_replica_states	sys.dm_hadr_instance_node_map
sys.dm_hadr_name_id_map	sys.dm_io_backup_tapes	sys.dm_io_cluster_shared_drives
sys.dm_io_pending_io_requests	sys.dm_logpool_hashentries	sys.dm_logpool_stats
sys.dm_os_buffer_descriptors	sys.dm_os_child_instances	sys.dm_os_cluster_nodes
sys.dm_os_cluster_properties	sys.dm_os_dispatcher_pools	sys.dm_os_dispatchers
sys.dm_os_hosts	sys.dm_os_latch_stats	sys.dm_os_loaded_modules
sys.dm_os_memory_allocations	sys.dm_os_memory_broker_clerks	sys.dm_os_memory_brokers
sys.dm_os_memory_cache_clock_hands	sys.dm_os_memory_cache_counters	sys.dm_os_memory_cache_entries
sys.dm_os_memory_cache_hash_tables	sys.dm_os_memory_clerks	sys.dm_os_memory_node_access_stats
sys.dm_os_memory_nodes	sys.dm_os_memory_objects	sys.dm_os_memory_pools
sys.dm_os_nodes	sys.dm_os_performance_counters	sys.dm_os_process_memory
sys.dm_os_ring_buffers	sys.dm_os_schedulers	sys.dm_os_server_diagnostics_log_configurations
sys.dm_os_spinlock_stats	sys.dm_os_stacks	sys.dm_os_sublatches
sys.dm_os_sys_info	sys.dm_os_sys_memory	sys.dm_os_tasks

sys.dm_os_threads	sys.dm_os_virtual_address_dump	sys.dm_os_wait_stats
sys.dm_os_waiting_tasks	sys.dm_os_windows_info	sys.dm_os_worker_local_storage
sys.dm_os_workers	sys.dm_qn_subscriptions	sys.dm_repl_articles
sys.dm_repl_schemas	sys.dm_repl_tranhash	sys.dm_repl_traninfo
sys.dm_resource_governor_configu ration	sys.dm_resource_governor_resource_ pool_affinity	sys.dm_resource_governor_resourc e_pools
sys.dm_resource_governor_worklo ad_groups	sys.dm_server_audit_status	sys.dm_server_memory_dumps
sys.dm_server_registry	sys.dm_server_services	sys.dm_tcp_listener_states
sys.dm_tran_active_snapshot_data base_transactions	sys.dm_tran_active_transactions	sys.dm_tran_commit_table
sys.dm_tran_current_snapshot	sys.dm_tran_current_transaction	sys.dm_tran_database_transactions
sys.dm_tran_locks	sys.dm_tran_session_transactions	sys.dm_tran_top_version_generator s
sys.dm_tran_transactions_snapshot	sys.dm_tran_version_store	sys.dm_xe_map_values
sys.dm_xe_object_columns	sys.dm_xe_objects	sys.dm_xe_packages
sys.dm_xe_session_event_actions	sys.dm_xe_session_events	sys.dm_xe_session_object_columns
sys.dm_xe_session_targets	sys.dm_xe_sessions	sys.endpoint_webmethods
sys.endpoints	sys.event_notification_event_types	sys.event_notifications
sys.events	sys.extended_procedures	sys.extended_properties
sys.filegroups	sys.filetable_system_defined_objects	sys.filetables
sys.foreign_key_columns	sys.foreign_keys	sys.fulltext_catalogs
sys.fulltext_document_types	sys.fulltext_index_catalog_usages	sys.fulltext_index_columns
sys.fulltext_index_fragments	sys.fulltext_indexes	sys.fulltext_languages
sys.fulltext_semantic_language_stat istics_database	sys.fulltext_semantic_languages	sys.fulltext_stoplists
sys.fulltext_stopwords	sys.fulltext_system_stopwords	sys.function_order_columns
sys.http_endpoints	sys.identity_columns	sys.index_columns
sys.indexes	sys.internal_tables	sys.key_constraints
sys.key_encryptions	sys.linked_logins	sys.login_token
sys.master_files	sys.master_key_passwords	sys.message_type_xml_schema_coll ection_usages
sys.messages	sys.module_assembly_usages	sys.numbered_procedure_paramete rs
sys.numbered_procedures	sys.objects	sys.openkeys
sys.parameter_type_usages	sys.parameter_xml_schema_collectio n_usages	sys.parameters
sys.partition_functions	sys.partition_parameters	sys.partition_range_values
sys.partition_schemes	sys.partitions	sys.plan_guides
sys.procedures	sys.registered_search_properties	sys.registered_search_property_list s
sys.remote_logins	sys.remote_service_bindings	sys.resource_governor_configuratio n
sys.resource_governor_resource_p ool_affinity	sys.resource_governor_resource_pool s	sys.resource_governor_workload_gr oups
sys.routes	sys.schemas	sys.securable_classes
sys.sequences	sys.server_assembly_modules	sys.server_audit_specification_detai ls
sys.server_audit_specifications	sys.server_audits	sys.server_event_notifications
sys.server_event_session_actions	sys.server_event_session_events	sys.server_event_session_fields

sys.server_event_session_targets	sys.server_event_sessions	sys.server_events
sys.server_file_audits	sys.server_permissions	sys.server_principal_credentials
sys.server_principals	sys.server_role_members	sys.server_sql_modules
sys.server_trigger_events	sys.server_triggers	sys.servers
sys.service_broker_endpoints	sys.service_contract_message_usages	sys.service_contract_usages
sys.service_contracts	sys.service_message_types	sys.service_queue_usages
sys.service_queues	sys.services	sys.soap_endpoints
sys.spatial_index_tessellations	sys.spatial_indexes	sys.spatial_reference_systems
sys.sql_dependencies	sys.sql_expression_dependencies	sys.sql_logins
sys.sql_modules	sys.stats	sys.stats_columns
sys.symmetric_keys	sys.synonyms	sys.sysaltfiles
sys.syscacheobjects	sys.syscharsets	sys.syscolumns
sys.syscomments	sys.sysconfigures	sys.sysconstraints
sys.syscurconfigs	sys.syscursorcolumns	sys.syscursorrefs
sys.syscursors	sys.syscursortables	sys.sysdatabases
sys.sysdepends	sys.sysdevices	sys.sysfilegroups
sys.sysfiles	sys.sysforeignkeys	sys.sysfulltextcatalogs
sys.sysindexes	sys.sysindexkeys	sys.syslanguages
sys.syslockinfo	sys.syslogins	sys.sysmembers
sys.sysmessages	sys.sysobjects	sys.sysoledbusers
sys.sysopentapes	sys.sysperfinfo	sys.syspermissions
sys.sysprocesses	sys.sysprotects	sys.sysreferences
sys.sysremotelogins	sys.sysservers	sys.system_columns
sys.system_components_surface_area_configuration	sys.system_internals_allocation_units	sys.system_internals_partition_columns
sys.system_internals_partitions	sys.system_objects	sys.system_parameters
sys.system_sql_modules	sys.system_views	sys.systypes
sys.sysusers	sys.table_types	sys.tables
sys.tcp_endpoints	sys.trace_categories	sys.trace_columns
sys.trace_event_bindings	sys.trace_events	sys.trace_subclass_values
sys.traces	sys.transmission_queue	sys.trigger_event_types
sys.trigger_events	sys.triggers	sys.type_assembly_usages
sys.types	sys.user_token	sys.via_endpoints
sys.views	sys.xml_indexes	sys.xml_schema_attributes
sys.xml_schema_collections	sys.xml_schema_component_placements	sys.xml_schema_components
sys.xml_schema_elements	sys.xml_schema_facets	sys.xml_schema_model_groups
sys.xml_schema_namespaces	sys.xml_schema_types	sys.xml_schema_wildcard_namespaces
sys.xml_schema_wildcards	NULL	NULL

FREE Downloads

SQL Server Dynamic Management Views Poster

http://www.quest.com/techbrief/sql-server-dynamic-management-views-poster813218.aspx

SQL Server 2008 System Views Map

http://www.microsoft.com/en-us/download/details.aspx?id=9301

List of master database System Functions

Some are internal and undocumented functions. Some are used for special tasks: fn_listextendedproperty, fn_trace_getinfo, fn_my_permissions & fn_varbintohexstr. The dm_prefix indicates **Dynamic Management Function** (DMF) such as dm_exec_sql_text.

```
SELECT * FROM sys.all_objects where is_ms_shipped=1
        AND     ( TYPE_DESC = 'SQL_TABLE_VALUED_FUNCTION'          OR
                  TYPE_DESC = 'SQL_SCALAR_FUNCTION'                OR
                  TYPE_DESC = 'SQL_INLINE_TABLE_VALUED_FUNCTION')
ORDER BY name; -- (96 row(s) affected)
```

List of System Tables Prior to SQL Server 2005

Some of the system tables were updatable in SQL Server 2000 and previous versions. SS 2005 introduced system views which are not updatable and barred access to system tables.

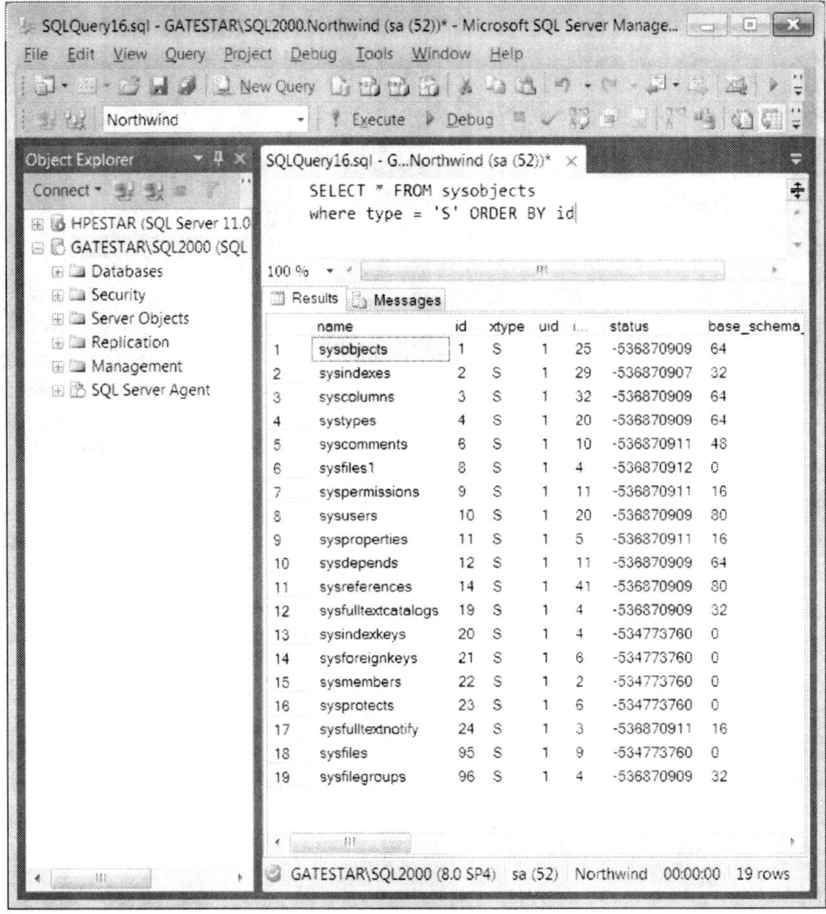

	name	id	xtype	uid	i...	status	base_schema_
1	sysobjects	1	S	1	25	-536870909	64
2	sysindexes	2	S	1	29	-536870907	32
3	syscolumns	3	S	1	32	-536870909	64
4	systypes	4	S	1	20	-536870909	64
5	syscomments	6	S	1	10	-536870911	48
6	sysfiles1	8	S	1	4	-536870912	0
7	syspermissions	9	S	1	11	-536870911	16
8	sysusers	10	S	1	20	-536870909	80
9	sysproperties	11	S	1	5	-536870911	16
10	sysdepends	12	S	1	11	-536870909	64
11	sysreferences	14	S	1	41	-536870909	80
12	sysfulltextcatalogs	19	S	1	4	-536870909	32
13	sysindexkeys	20	S	1	4	-534773760	0
14	sysforeignkeys	21	S	1	6	-534773760	0
15	sysmembers	22	S	1	2	-534773760	0
16	sysprotects	23	S	1	6	-534773760	0
17	sysfulltextnotify	24	S	1	3	-536870911	16
18	sysfiles	95	S	1	9	-534773760	0
19	sysfilegroups	96	S	1	4	-536870909	32

Other Methods of Metadata Access

Graphical Dependency Information

Object dependencies can be launched by a right click on the object.

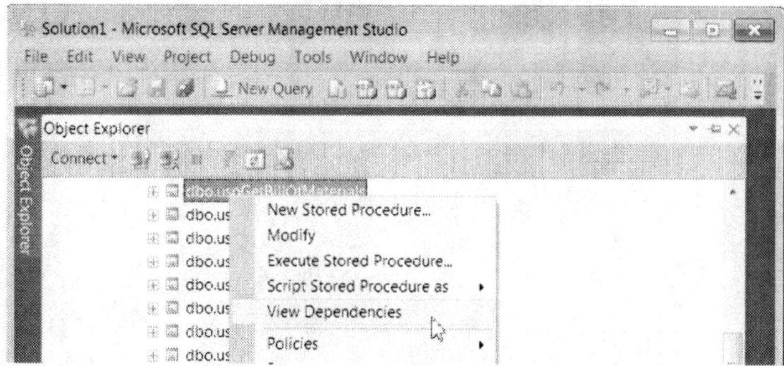

The dependency chart for the uspGetBillOfMaterials stored procedure.

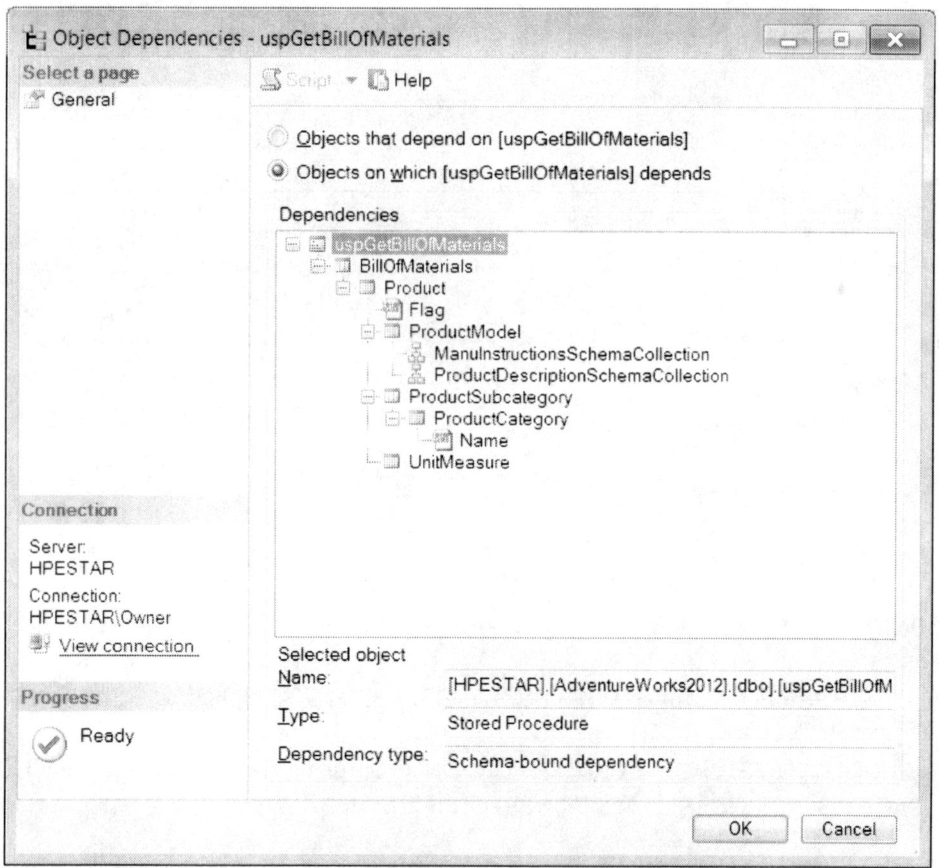

Scripting GUI Object Change

Most of the dialog panels have scripting options. In fact we don't even have to perform the action, we can just script it and execute the script in a (new) connection. The advantage of this approach that the generated script can be modified and saved for future use or reference. We start an index change with right click and properties.

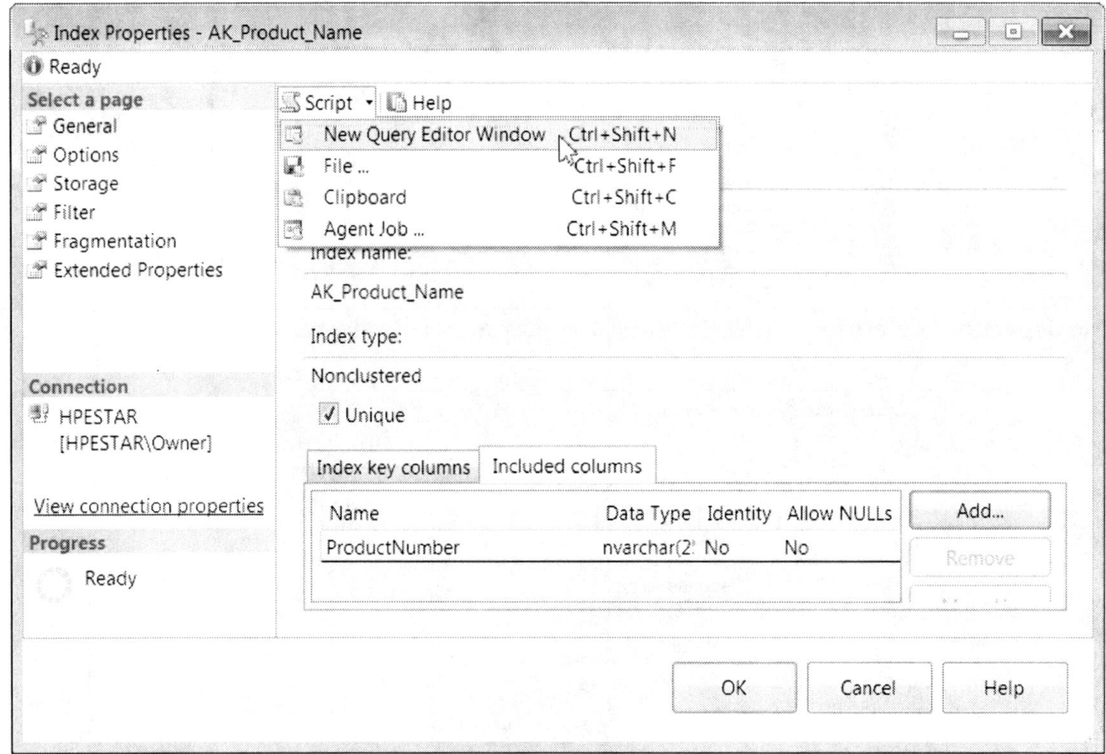

The generated script.

```
USE [AdventureWorks2012]
GO
SET ANSI_PADDING ON
GO
CREATE UNIQUE NONCLUSTERED INDEX [AK_Product_Name] ON [Production].[Product] (
[Name] ASC )
INCLUDE (       [ProductNumber]) WITH (PAD_INDEX = OFF, STATISTICS_NORECOMPUTE = OFF,
SORT_IN_TEMPDB = OFF,
IGNORE_DUP_KEY = OFF, DROP_EXISTING = ON, ONLINE = OFF, ALLOW_ROW_LOCKS = ON,
ALLOW_PAGE_LOCKS = ON, FILLFACTOR = 85) ON [PRIMARY]
GO
```

The sp_helpdb System Procedure

The sp_helpdb system procedure returns information on all or a specified database.

```
EXEC sp_helpdb;
-- Partial results
```

Accounting	3.88 MB	HPESTAR\Owner	17	May 24 2012	Status=ONLINE, Updateability=READ_WRITE, UserAccess=MULTI_USER, Recovery=FULL, Version=706, Collation=SQL_Latin1_General_CP1_CI_AS, SQLSortOrder=52, IsAutoCreateStatistics, IsAutoUpdateStatistics, IsFullTextEnabled	110
AdventureWorks	213.94 MB	HPESTAR\Owner	16	May 24 2012	Status=ONLINE, Updateability=READ_WRITE, UserAccess=MULTI_USER, Recovery=SIMPLE, Version=706, Collation=SQL_Latin1_General_CP1_CI_AS, SQLSortOrder=52, IsAnsiNullsEnabled, IsAnsiPaddingEnabled, IsAnsiWarningsEnabled, IsArithmeticAbortEnabled, IsAutoCreateStatistics, IsAutoUpdateStatistics, IsFullTextEnabled, IsNullConcat, IsQuotedIdentifiersEnabled, IsRecursiveTriggersEnabled	90

```
EXEC sp_helpdb AdventureWorks2012;
```

name	db_size	owner	dbid	created	status	compatibility_level
AdventureWorks2012	3118.38 MB	sa	7	May 19 2012	Status=ONLINE, Updateability=READ_WRITE, UserAccess=MULTI_USER, Recovery=SIMPLE, Version=706, Collation=SQL_Latin1_General_CP1_CI_AS, SQLSortOrder=52, IsAnsiNullsEnabled, IsAnsiPaddingEnabled, IsAnsiWarningsEnabled, IsArithmeticAbortEnabled, IsAutoCreateStatistics, IsAutoUpdateStatistics, IsFullTextEnabled, IsNullConcat, IsQuotedIdentifiersEnabled	110

The sp_help and sp_helptext System Procedures

The sp_help and sp_helptext provides database metadata in various formats including multiple result sets.

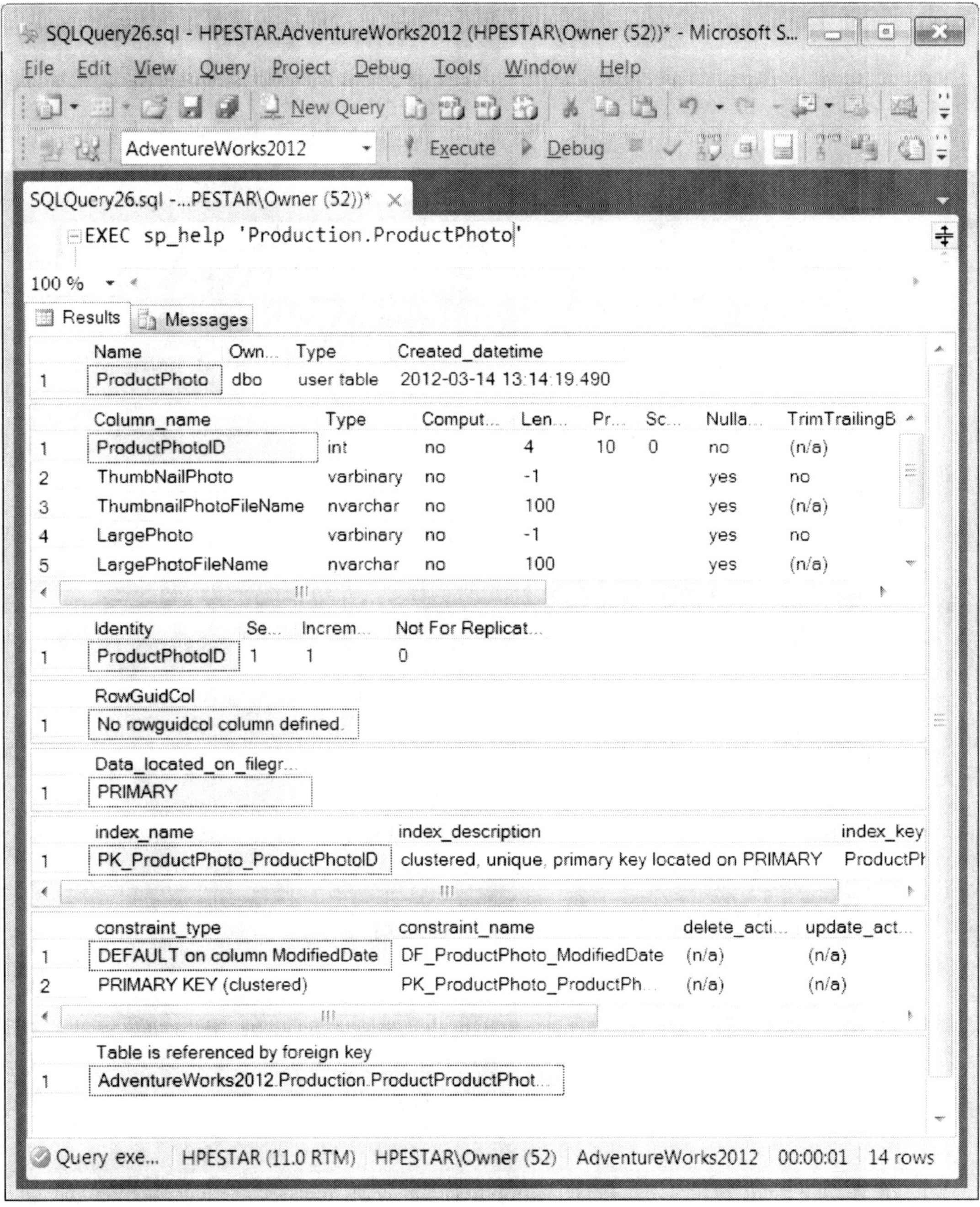

Using sp_helptext for Obtaining Definition

sp_helptext works only for some database objects. Table definition cannot be obtained by command, any command.

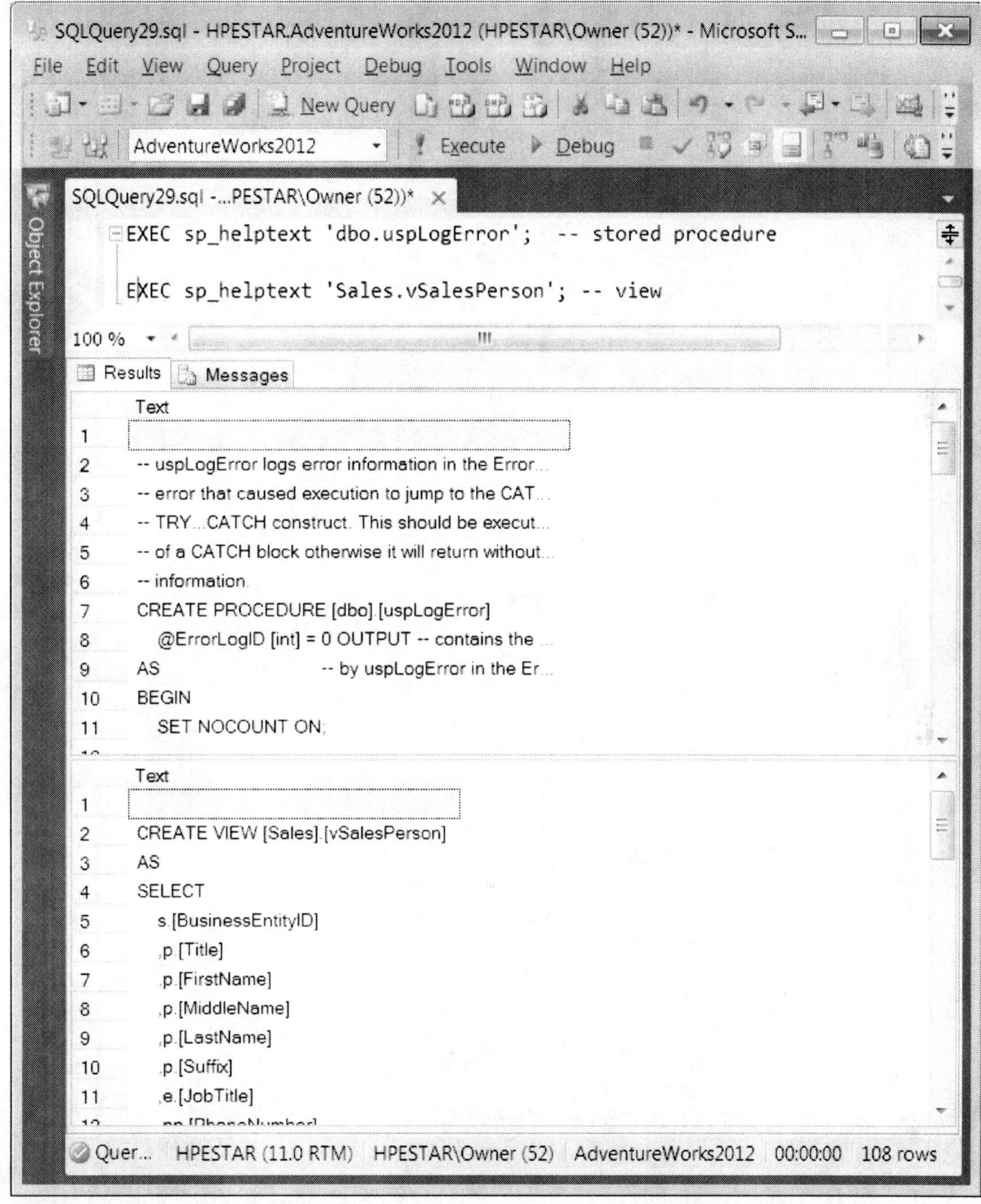

Partial List of sp_helpx System Procedures

The following list is from the master database System Stored Procedures.

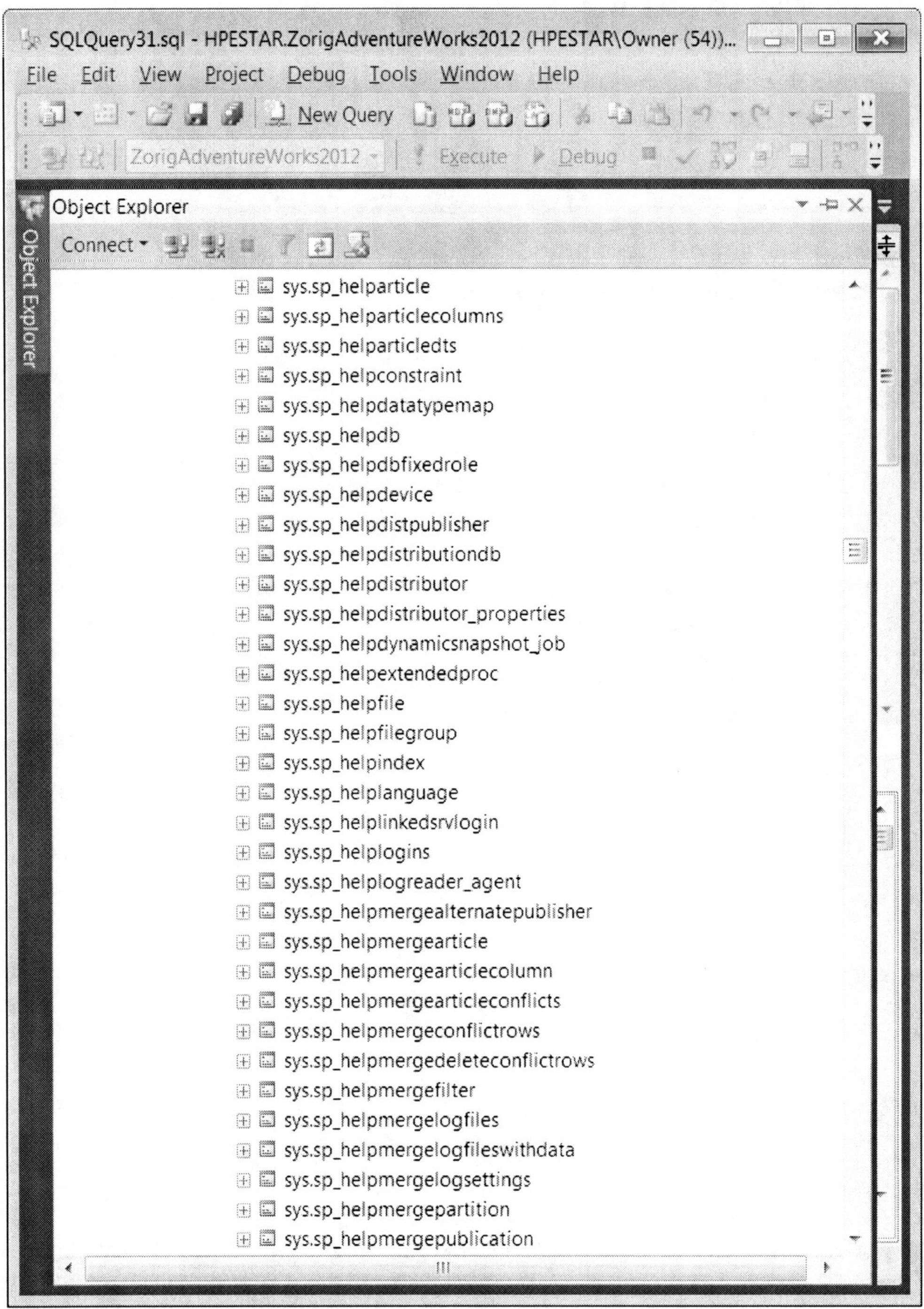

Listing All CHECK Constraints in a Database

We can use INFORMATION_SCHEMA views to perform this task.

```
USE AdventureWorks2012;
GO
```

```
SELECT      cc.CONSTRAINT_SCHEMA                    AS SCHEMA_NAME,
             TABLE_NAME,
            COLUMN_NAME,
            CHECK_CLAUSE,
            cc.CONSTRAINT_NAME
FROM    INFORMATION_SCHEMA.CHECK_CONSTRAINTS cc
            INNER JOIN INFORMATION_SCHEMA.CONSTRAINT_COLUMN_USAGE c
                    ON cc.CONSTRAINT_NAME = c.CONSTRAINT_NAME
ORDER BY    SCHEMA_NAME,
            TABLE_NAME,
            COLUMN_NAME;
-- (105 row(s) affected) - Partial results.
```

SCHEMA_NAME	TABLE_NAME	COLUMN_NAME	CHECK_CLAUSE	CONSTRAINT_NAME
HumanResources	Employee	BirthDate	([BirthDate]>='1930-01-01' AND [BirthDate]<=dateadd(year,(-18),getdate()))	CK_Employee_BirthDate
HumanResources	Employee	Gender	(upper([Gender])='F' OR upper([Gender])='M')	CK_Employee_Gender
HumanResources	Employee	HireDate	([HireDate]>='1996-07-01' AND [HireDate]<=dateadd(day,(1),getdate()))	CK_Employee_HireDate
HumanResources	Employee	MaritalStatus	(upper([MaritalStatus])='S' OR upper([MaritalStatus])='M')	CK_Employee_MaritalStatus
HumanResources	Employee	SickLeaveHours	([SickLeaveHours]>=(0) AND [SickLeaveHours]<=(120))	CK_Employee_SickLeaveHours
HumanResources	Employee	VacationHours	([VacationHours]>=(-40) AND [VacationHours]<=(240))	CK_Employee_VacationHours
HumanResources	EmployeeDepartmentHistory	EndDate	([EndDate]>=[StartDate] OR [EndDate] IS NULL)	CK_EmployeeDepartmentHistory_EndDate
HumanResources	EmployeeDepartmentHistory	StartDate	([EndDate]>=[StartDate] OR [EndDate] IS NULL)	CK_EmployeeDepartmentHistory_EndDate
HumanResources	EmployeePayHistory	PayFrequency	([PayFrequency]=(2) OR [PayFrequency]=(1))	CK_EmployeePayHistory_PayFrequency
HumanResources	EmployeePayHistory	Rate	([Rate]>=(6.50) AND [Rate]<=(200.00))	CK_EmployeePayHistory_Rate
Person	Person	EmailPromotion	([EmailPromotion]>=(0) AND [EmailPromotion]<=(2))	CK_Person_EmailPromotion

Creating a UDF CHECK Constraint

UDF CHECK constraint relies on a user-defined function for logic rather than the simple constraint expression. Demonstration script creates a test table with UDF check constraint.

```
USE tempdb;
SELECT TOP 10  P.BusinessEntityID, FirstName, LastName,          -- Create test table
               Email=convert(varchar(64),EmailAddress)
INTO Person FROM AdventureWorks2012.Person.Person P
               INNER JOIN AdventureWorks2012.Person.EmailAddress E
                    ON E.BusinessEntityID = P.BusinessEntityID;
GO
-- Create user-defined function (UDF) for checking
CREATE FUNCTION ufnEmailValidityCheck (@Email varchar(64))
RETURNS BIT  AS
BEGIN
IF EXISTS(SELECT 1 WHERE
   CHARINDEX('.',@Email,CHARINDEX('@',@Email))-CHARINDEX('@',@Email)>1
   AND CHARINDEX('.',REVERSE(LTRIM(RTRIM(@Email)))) > 2
   AND CHARINDEX('@',LTRIM(@Email)) > 2) RETURN(1)
RETURN (0)
END;
GO
 -- Create UDF check constraint
ALTER TABLE [dbo].[Person]  WITH CHECK
ADD CONSTRAINT [EmailCheck] CHECK (   dbo.ufnEmailValidityCheck (Email) = 1);
GO
 -- SQL check constraint violated missing . (period)
INSERT Person (BusinessEntityID, FirstName, LastName, Email)
VALUES (100000, 'Elvis', 'Presley', 'elvispresley@thekingcom');
/*  Msg 547, Level 16, State 0, Line 5
The INSERT statement conflicted with the CHECK constraint "EmailCheck". The conflict occurred
in database "tempdb", table "dbo.Person", column 'Email'.*/
 -- SQL check constraint met
INSERT Person (BusinessEntityID, FirstName, LastName, Email)
VALUES (100000, 'Elvis', 'Presley', 'elvispresley@theking.com');
GO   -- (1 row(s) affected)
 SELECT * FROM Person ORDER BY Email;  -- Partial results.
```

BusinessEntityID	FirstName	LastName	Email
8	Diane	Margheim	diane1@adventure-works.com
7	Dylan	Miller	dylan0@adventure-works.com
100000	Elvis	Presley	elvispresley@theking.com

List All DEFAULT Constraint Definitions

We can use system views to carry out the task.

```
USE AdventureWorks2012;
SELECT  SCHEMA_NAME(o.schema_id)  AS SchemaName,
        o.name                    AS TableName,
        c.name                    AS ColumnName,
        d.definition              AS DefaultDefinition,
        d.name                    AS ConstraintName
FROM sys.default_constraints d  INNER JOIN sys.columns c
            ON d.parent_object_id = c.object_id  AND d.parent_column_id = c.column_id
        INNER JOIN sys.objects o  ON o.object_id = c.object_id
ORDER BY SchemaName, TableName, ColumnName;  -- (152 row(s) affected) - Partial results.
```

SchemaName	TableName	ColumnName	DefaultDefinition	ConstraintName
dbo	AWBuildVersion	ModifiedDate	(getdate())	DF_AWBuildVersion_ModifiedDate
dbo	ErrorLog	ErrorTime	(getdate())	DF_ErrorLog_ErrorTime
HumanResources	Department	ModifiedDate	(getdate())	DF_Department_ModifiedDate
HumanResources	Employee	CurrentFlag	((1))	DF_Employee_CurrentFlag
HumanResources	Employee	ModifiedDate	(getdate())	DF_Employee_ModifiedDate
HumanResources	Employee	rowguid	(newid())	DF_Employee_rowguid
HumanResources	Employee	SalariedFlag	((1))	DF_Employee_SalariedFlag

All Tables Row Count without the COUNT() Function

Here is quick way to get a row count, not exact like COUNT(*) but really fast.

```
USE AdventureWorks2012;
SELECT  CONCAT(SCHEMA_NAME(schema_id),'.',o.name )   AS TableName,
        FORMAT(max(i.rows),'###,###,###')            AS Rows
FROM    sys.sysobjects o        INNER JOIN sys.sysindexes i        ON o.id = i.id
     INNER JOIN sys.objects oo      ON o.id = oo.object_id
WHERE   xtype = 'u'      AND    OBJECTPROPERTY(o.id,N'IsUserTable') = 1
GROUP BY schema_id, o.name   ORDER BY max(i.rows) DESC, TableName;
GO -- (71 row(s) affected)  - Partial results.
```

TableName	Rows
Sales.SalesOrderDetail	121,317
Production.TransactionHistory	113,443
Production.TransactionHistoryArchive	89,253
Production.WorkOrder	72,591
Production.WorkOrderRouting	67,131
Sales.SalesOrderHeader	31,465
Sales.SalesOrderHeaderSalesReason	27,647

Database Object-Definition from sys.sql_modules System View

The sys.sql_modules systems view contains definition for stored procedures, triggers, functions and views. Prior to SQL Server 2005 the sys.syscomments table was used to obtain object definition source code.

```
USE AdventureWorks2012;
GO
```

```
SELECT object_id, LEFT(definition,64) AS DefinitionPrefix
FROM sys.SQL_Modules ORDER BY object_id;
GO
-- (52 row(s) affected) - Partial results.
```

object_id	DefinitionPrefix
7671075	CREATE VIEW [Sales].[vStoreWithContacts] AS SELECT s.[
23671132	CREATE VIEW [Sales].[vStoreWithAddresses] AS SELECT s.
39671189	CREATE VIEW [Purchasing].[vVendorWithContacts] AS SELECT
55671246	CREATE VIEW [Purchasing].[vVendorWithAddresses] AS SELECT
71671303	CREATE FUNCTION [dbo].[ufnGetAccountingStartDate]() RETURNS [
87671360	CREATE FUNCTION [dbo].[ufnGetAccountingEndDate]() RETURNS [da
103671417	CREATE FUNCTION [dbo].[ufnGetContactInformation](@PersonID int
119671474	CREATE FUNCTION [dbo].[ufnGetProductDealerPrice](@ProductI
135671531	CREATE FUNCTION [dbo].[ufnGetProductListPrice](@ProductID [int
151671588	CREATE FUNCTION [dbo].[ufnGetProductStandardCost](@ProductID [

Retrieving the Full Definition of a Stored Procedure

```
SELECT          schema_name(schema_id)                  AS SchemaName,
                object_Name(m.object_ID)                AS ObjectName,
                definition                              AS ObjectDefinition
FROM   sys.SQL_Modules m
  INNER JOIN sys.objects o      ON m.object_id=o.object_id
WHERE  object_Name(m.object_ID) = 'uspGetBillOfMaterials'
GO
```

```
SchemaName          ObjectName                ObjectDefinition
dbo          uspGetBillOfMaterials            CREATE PROCEDURE [dbo].[uspGetBillOfMaterials]
   @StartProductID [int],
   @CheckDate [datetime]
AS
BEGIN
   SET NOCOUNT ON;

   -- Use recursive query to generate a multi-level Bill of Material (i.e. all level 1
   -- components of a level 0 assembly, all level 2 components of a level 1 assembly)
   -- The CheckDate eliminates any components that are no longer used in the product on this date.
   WITH [BOM_cte]([ProductAssemblyID], [ComponentID], [ComponentDesc], [PerAssemblyQty], [StandardCost], [ListPrice],
[BOMLevel], [RecursionLevel]) -- CTE name and columns
   AS (
      SELECT b.[ProductAssemblyID], b.[ComponentID], p.[Name], b.[PerAssemblyQty], p.[StandardCost], p.[ListPrice], b.[BOMLevel],
0 -- Get the initial list of components for the bike assembly
      FROM [Production].[BillOfMaterials] b
         INNER JOIN [Production].[Product] p
         ON b.[ComponentID] = p.[ProductID]
      WHERE b.[ProductAssemblyID] = @StartProductID
         AND @CheckDate >= b.[StartDate]
         AND @CheckDate <= ISNULL(b.[EndDate], @CheckDate)
      UNION ALL
      SELECT b.[ProductAssemblyID], b.[ComponentID], p.[Name], b.[PerAssemblyQty], p.[StandardCost], p.[ListPrice], b.[BOMLevel],
[RecursionLevel] + 1 -- Join recursive member to anchor
      FROM [BOM_cte] cte
         INNER JOIN [Production].[BillOfMaterials] b
         ON b.[ProductAssemblyID] = cte.[ComponentID]
         INNER JOIN [Production].[Product] p
         ON b.[ComponentID] = p.[ProductID]
      WHERE @CheckDate >= b.[StartDate]
         AND @CheckDate <= ISNULL(b.[EndDate], @CheckDate)
      )
   -- Outer select from the CTE
   SELECT b.[ProductAssemblyID], b.[ComponentID], b.[ComponentDesc], SUM(b.[PerAssemblyQty]) AS [TotalQuantity] ,
b.[StandardCost], b.[ListPrice], b.[BOMLevel], b.[RecursionLevel]
   FROM [BOM_cte] b
   GROUP BY b.[ComponentID], b.[ComponentDesc], b.[ProductAssemblyID], b.[BOMLevel], b.[RecursionLevel], b.[StandardCost],
b.[ListPrice]
   ORDER BY b.[BOMLevel], b.[ProductAssemblyID], b.[ComponentID]      OPTION (MAXRECURSION 25)
END;
```

Snowflake Schema Data Warehouse Design

If the following DW design were Star Schema, the DimProduct would be a flat dimension including DimProductSubcategory and DimProductCategory. In Snowflake Schema the dimension tables follow 3NF relational design.

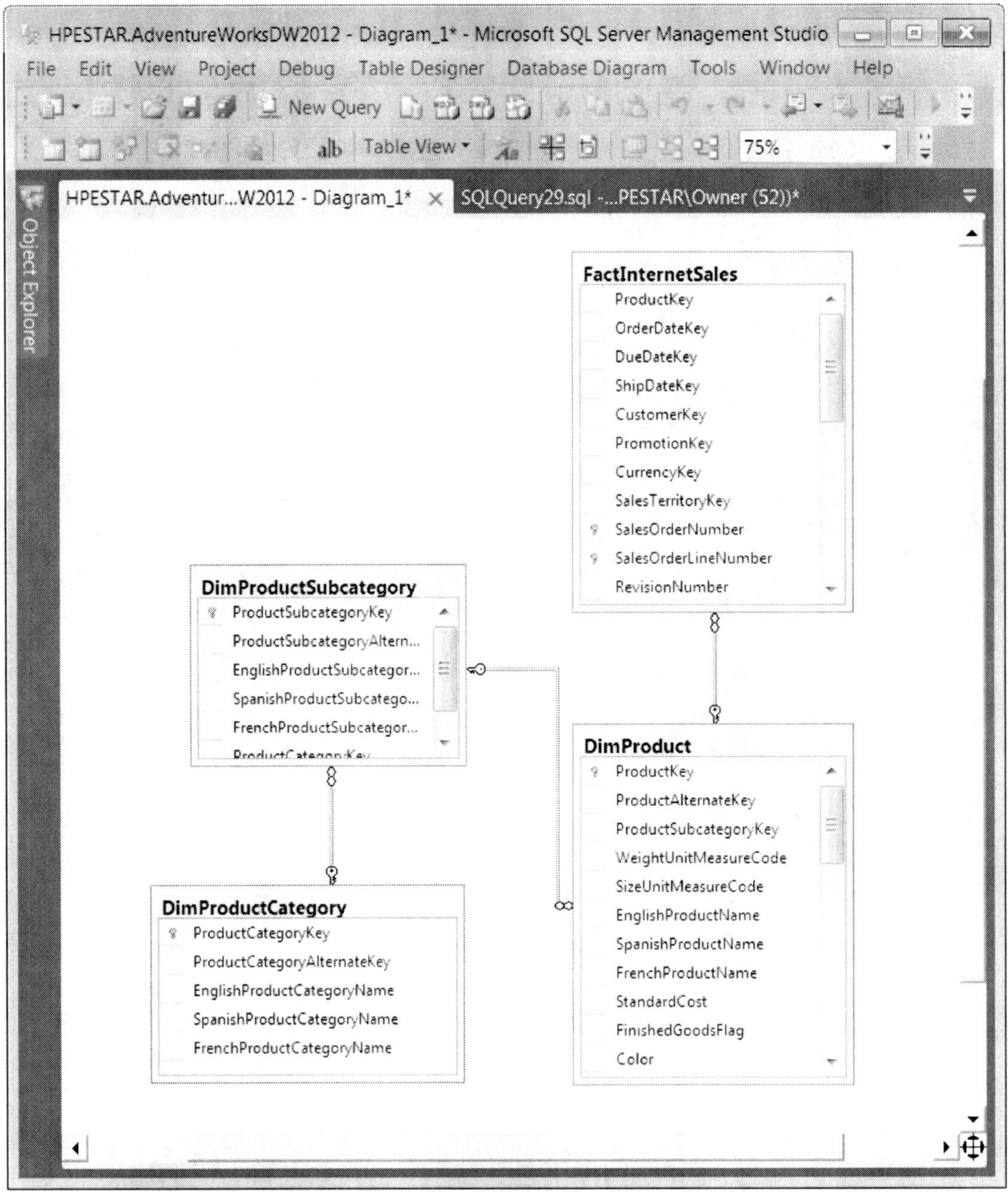

Object Explorer Table Editor

A table editor is available for directly editing data in a table. It is designed for limited use. First we create a test table, Department, then we launch the editor.

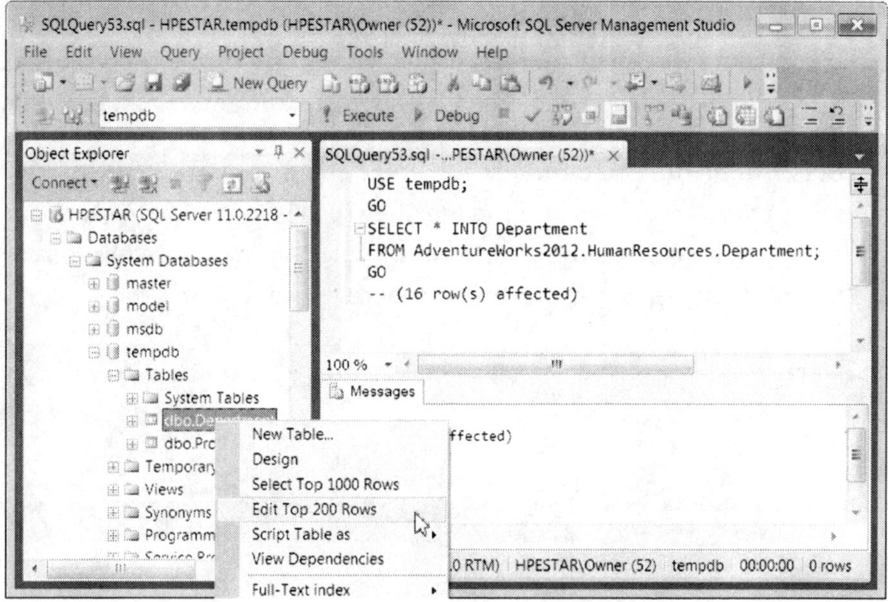

We added row 17 just by typing it in, then investigated the right click drop-down menu.

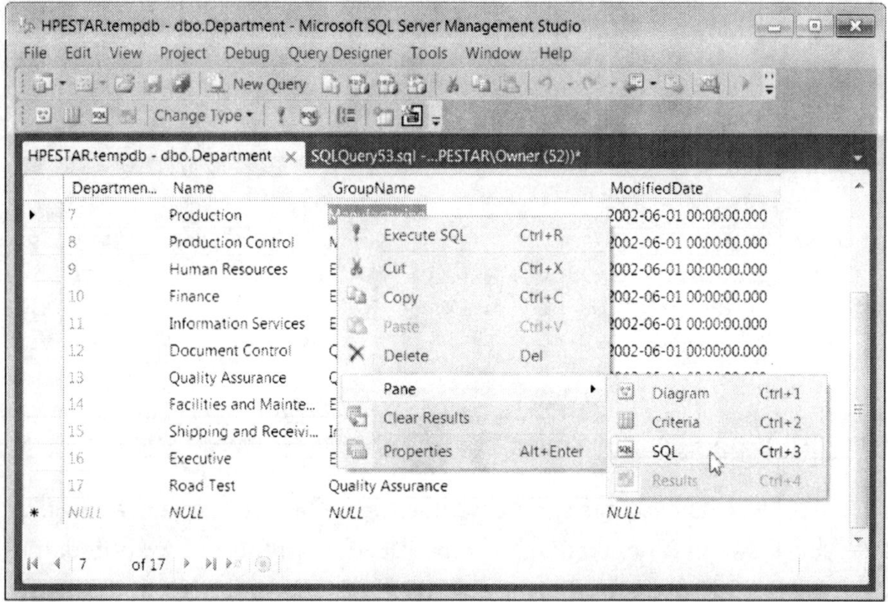

ALTER Object or DROP & CREATE

Important to remember: **DROP is a dangerous command.**

DROP object not only drops the target object, but all table data if a table, and all related objects such as indexes. So before we use DROP, we have to make sure we have backup of everything. Backup can be in the form of database backup, table data backup and/or .sql script files.

ALTER object is the preferred choice

As an example, if we drop a view and we have the CREATE VIEW script, we can recreate it. But DROP VIEW drops the view permissions also. If we do ALTER VIEW, the permissions remain untouched. We can use sp_helprotect system procedure to check permissions.

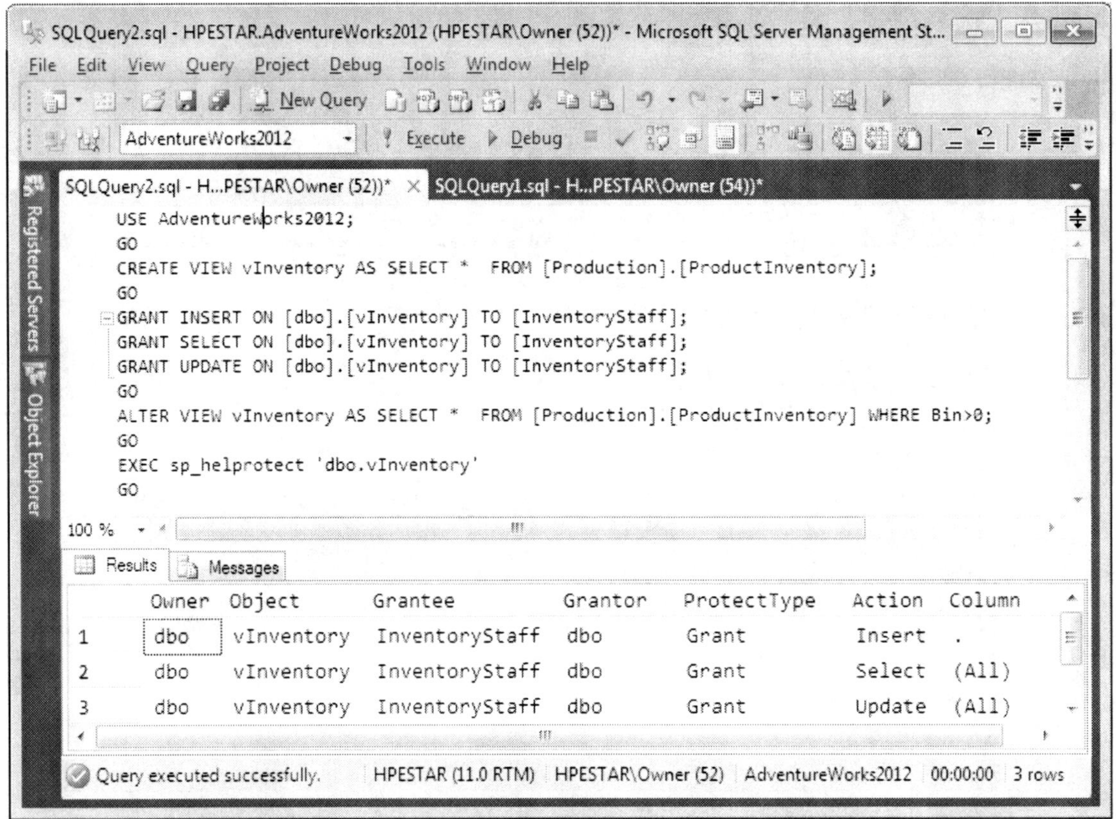

Saving the CREATE VIEW to a .sql file should include the GRANT statements as well. When we do SELECT INTO table creation & population, only the IDENTITY property is inherited. If needed, we would have to create all constraints and indexes.

Column Properties Page in Object Explorer

Object Explorer right click on a column launches the column properties page.

Production.Product table ProductNumber column properties. No changes can be performed on this page. To change the table, we have to launch the table designer.

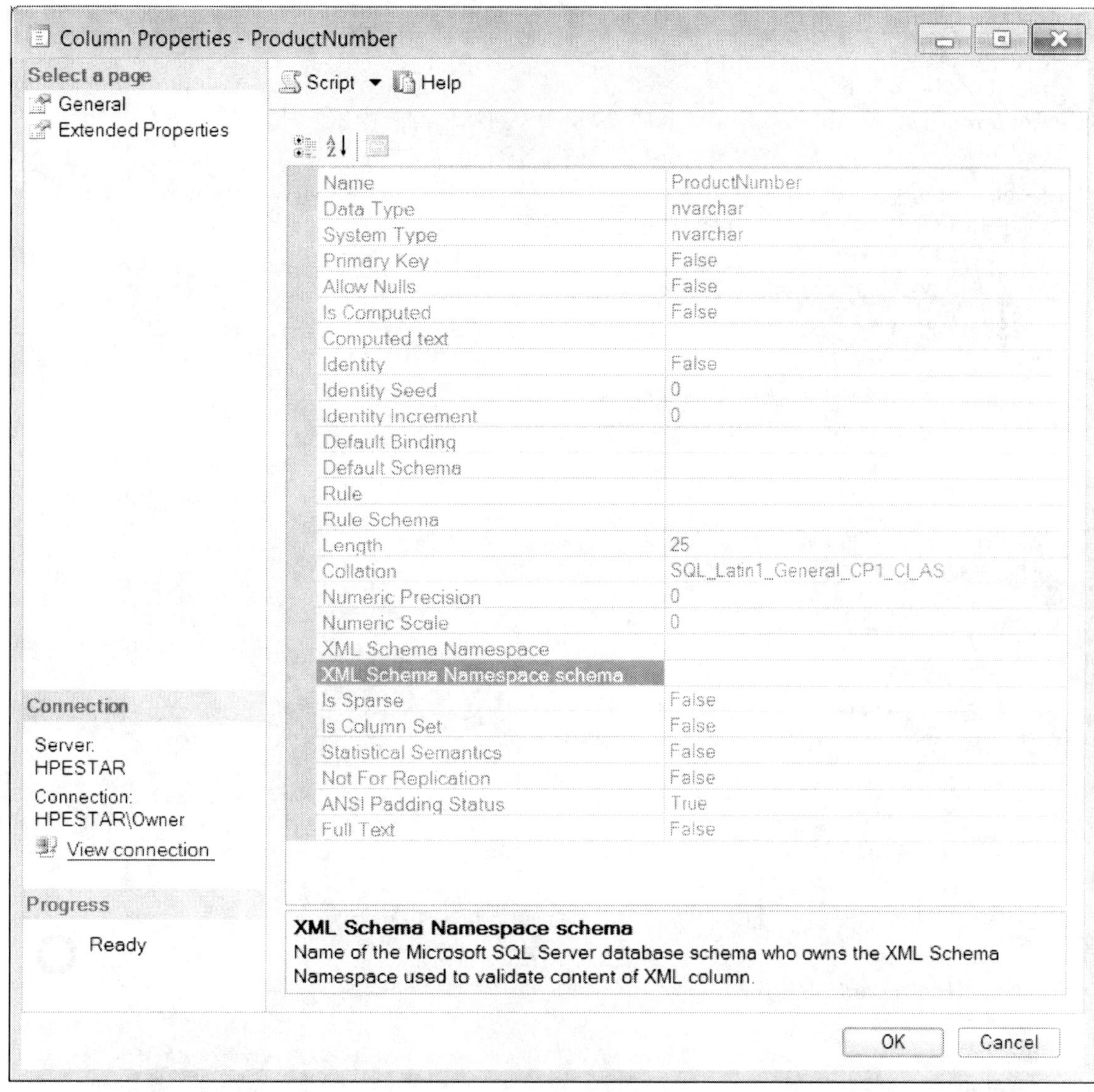

Listing All Columns with PK, FK & IDENTITY Properties

There are various ways for retrieving column properties including the COLUMNPROPERTY() function.

```
USE AdventureWorks2012;
```

```
SELECT c.TABLE_CATALOG                                          AS DatabaseName,
    c.TABLE_SCHEMA                                              AS SchemaName,
    c.TABLE_NAME                                                AS TableName,
    c.COLUMN_NAME                                               AS ColumnName,
    Columnproperty(Object_id(CONCAT(c.TABLE_SCHEMA,'.',c.TABLE_NAME)),
                    c.COLUMN_NAME, 'ISIDENTITY')                AS IsIdentity,
    CASE
     WHEN CONSTRAINT_NAME IN (SELECT NAME
                   FROM   sys.objects
                   WHERE  TYPE = 'PK') THEN 1
     ELSE 0    END                                              AS IsPrimaryKey,
    CASE
     WHEN CONSTRAINT_NAME IN (SELECT NAME
                   FROM   sys.objects
                   WHERE  TYPE = 'F') THEN 1
     ELSE 0    END                                              AS IsForeignKey
FROM   INFORMATION_SCHEMA.TABLES t
    INNER JOIN INFORMATION_SCHEMA.COLUMNS c
        ON c.TABLE_CATALOG = t.TABLE_CATALOG
         AND c.TABLE_SCHEMA = t.TABLE_SCHEMA
         AND c.TABLE_NAME = t.TABLE_NAME
    LEFT JOIN INFORMATION_SCHEMA.KEY_COLUMN_USAGE u
        ON c.TABLE_CATALOG = u.TABLE_CATALOG
         AND c.TABLE_SCHEMA = u.TABLE_SCHEMA
         AND c.TABLE_NAME = u.TABLE_NAME
         AND c.COLUMN_NAME = u.COLUMN_NAME
WHERE  TABLE_TYPE = 'BASE TABLE'
ORDER  BY SchemaName,    TableName,    c.ORDINAL_POSITION;
GO
-- (534 row(s) affected) - Partial results.
```

DatabaseName	SchemaName	TableName	ColumnName	IsIdentity	IsPrimaryKey	IsForeignKey
AdventureWorks2012	Person	EmailAddress	BusinessEntityID	0	0	1
AdventureWorks2012	Person	EmailAddress	BusinessEntityID	0	1	0
AdventureWorks2012	Person	EmailAddress	EmailAddressID	1	1	0
AdventureWorks2012	Person	EmailAddress	EmailAddress	0	0	0

The Collation Column Property & the COLLATE Clause

Each text column requires the collation property. The server & databases also have collation property as defaults only. When the database collation is changed, the actual column collations remain the same. New table columns will inherit the database default collation. New databases inherit the server collation. A column collation can be changed with ALTER TABLE. To change all text collations in a database may prove to be a big task.

```
USE tempdb;
```

```
SELECT * INTO Product FROM AdventureWorks2012.Production.Product;
-- (504 row(s) affected)
```

```
ALTER TABLE Product ALTER COLUMN Name nvarchar(50)
                COLLATE SQL_Latin1_General_CP1_CS_AS null;
-- Command(s) completed successfully.
```

Text operations with different collations result in error.

```
SELECT COUNT(*) FROM Product p
                    INNER JOIN AdventureWorks2012.Production.Product aw12
                        ON p.Name = aw12.Name;
GO
```

```
/*  Msg 468, Level 16, State 9, Line 3
Cannot resolve the collation conflict between "SQL_Latin1_General_CP1_CI_AS" and
"SQL_Latin1_General_CP1_CS_AS" in the equal to operation.   */
```

We can correct it in the query with the COLLATE clause. We can use a specific collation on one side of the expression, or the easy to remember DATABASE_DEFAULT.

```
SELECT COUNT(*) FROM Product p
                    INNER JOIN AdventureWorks2012.Production.Product aw12
                        ON p.Name = aw12.Name COLLATE DATABASE_DEFAULT;
-- 504
```

Restoring the original column collation.

```
ALTER TABLE Product alter column ProductName varchar(40)
                COLLATE SQL_Latin1_General_CP1_CI_AS null;
```

Listing All Database & Server Collations

Database collations can be enumerated by a query, while there is special function for server collations. QUOTENAME() function forms proper object names.

```
USE AdventureWorks2012;
GO
```

```
SELECT CONCAT(QUOTENAME(s.name), '.', QUOTENAME(t.name),
              '.', QUOTENAME(c.name))                         AS ColumnName,
              c.collation_name                                AS Collation
FROM sys.schemas s
  INNER JOIN sys.tables t
    ON t.schema_id = s.schema_id
  INNER JOIN sys.columns c
    ON c.object_id = t.object_id
WHERE collation_name is not null
ORDER BY ColumnName;
-- (104 row(s) affected) - Partial results.
```

ColumnName	Collation
[HumanResources].[Employee].[NationalIDNumber]	SQL_Latin1_General_CP1_CI_AS
[HumanResources].[Shift].[Name]	SQL_Latin1_General_CP1_CI_AS
[Person].[Address].[AddressLine1]	SQL_Latin1_General_CP1_CI_AS
[Person].[Address].[AddressLine2]	SQL_Latin1_General_CP1_CI_AS

All server collations can be obtained from a table-valued system function.

```
use master;
select   name                                        AS Name,
         COLLATIONPROPERTY(name, 'CodePage')          AS CodePage,
         LEFT(description,80)                        AS Description
from sys.fn_HelpCollations() order by Name;
-- (3885 row(s) affected) - Partial results;
```

Name	CodePage	Description
Modern_Spanish_CS_AS_KS_WS	1252	Modern-Spanish, case-sensitive, accent-sensitive, kanatype-sensitive, width-sens
Modern_Spanish_CS_AS_WS	1252	Modern-Spanish, case-sensitive, accent-sensitive, kanatype-insensitive, width-se
Mohawk_100_BIN	1252	Mohawk-100, binary sort
Mohawk_100_BIN2	1252	Mohawk-100, binary code point comparison sort
Mohawk_100_CI_AI	1252	Mohawk-100, case-insensitive, accent-insensitive, kanatype-insensitive, width-in

Designing Table for Multi-Language Support with UNICODE

Let's script the DimProductSubcategory table from AdventureWorks2012 to demonstrate multi-language support. nvarchar data type is for UNICODE data with each character 2 bytes. It has sufficient capacity to hold even Chinese, Japanese and Korean letters among others.

```
CREATE TABLE dbo.DimProductSubcategory(
	ProductSubcategoryKey int IDENTITY(1,1) NOT NULL,
	ProductSubcategoryAlternateKey int NULL,
	EnglishProductSubcategoryName nvarchar(50) NOT NULL,
	SpanishProductSubcategoryName nvarchar(50) NOT NULL,
	FrenchProductSubcategoryName nvarchar(50) NOT NULL,
	ProductCategoryKey int NULL,
	CONSTRAINT PK_DimProductSubcategory_ProductSubcategoryKey
		PRIMARY KEY CLUSTERED (ProductSubcategoryKey ASC),
	CONSTRAINT AK_DimProductSubcategory_ProductSubcategoryAlternateKey
		UNIQUE NONCLUSTERED (ProductSubcategoryAlternateKey ASC ) );
```

Since there are no COLLATE clauses for the English, Spanish & French names, the collation is the database default. The DATABASEPROPERTYEX() function can be used to retrieve it.

```
SELECT DATABASEPROPERTYEX('AdventureWorksDW2012', 'Collation');
-- SQL_Latin1_General_CP1_CI_AS
```

To get a Spanish language sort, we have to add the COLLATE clause to the ORDER BY clause.

```
SELECT * FROM DimProductSubcategory
ORDER BY SpanishProductSubcategoryName COLLATE Modern_Spanish_CI_AS_WS;
-- (37 row(s) affected) - Partial results.
```

ProductSubcategoryKey	ProductSubcategoryAlternateKey	EnglishProductSubcategoryName	SpanishProductSubcategoryName	FrenchProductSubcategoryName	ProductCategoryKey
4	4	Handlebars	Barra	Barre d'appui	2
2	2	Road Bikes	Bicicleta de carretera	Vélo de route	1
1	1	Mountain Bikes	Bicicleta de montaña	VTT	1
3	3	Touring Bikes	Bicicleta de paseo	Vélo de randonnée	1
8	8	Cranksets	Bielas	Pédalier	2
36	36	Pumps	Bomba	Pompe	4

Find all collations for a culture.

```
SELECT name, description = LEFT(description, 60) FROM   sys.fn_HelpCollations()
WHERE  name LIKE '%german%'  ORDER BY name;  -- (52 row(s) affected)
```

CHAPTER 11: New Programming Features in SS 2012

PARSE() Function

T-SQL script to demonstrate the use of the PARSE() function. The culture parameter provides support for languages & countries beyond the CONVERT() function available in past versions.

```
-- PARSE() returns the result of expression translated to requested data type - String to datetime
SELECT PARSE('SAT, 13 December 2014' AS datetime USING 'en-US') AS [Date&Time];
-- 2014-12-13 00:00:00.000
```

```
SELECT PARSE('Saturday, 13 December 2014' AS datetime USING 'en-US') AS [Date&Time];
-- 2014-12-13 00:00:00.000
```

```
SELECT PARSE('Saturday 13 December 2014' AS datetime USING 'en-US') AS [Date&Time];
-- 2014-12-13 00:00:00.000
```

```
SELECT PARSE('Saturday December 13 2014' AS datetime USING 'en-US') AS [Date&Time];
-- 2014-12-13 00:00:00.000
```

```
SELECT PARSE('Saturday December 13, 2014' AS datetime USING 'en-US') AS [Date&Time];
-- 2014-12-13 00:00:00.000
```

```
-- Inconsistent string date
SELECT PARSE('Monday, 13 December 2014' AS datetime USING 'en-US') AS [Date&Time];
/*Msg 9819, Level 16, State 1, Line 1
Error converting string value 'Monday, 13 December 2014' into data type datetime using culture 'en-US'*/
```

```
-- German culture
SELECT PARSE('Samstag December 13, 2014' AS datetime USING 'DE') AS [Date&Time];
-- 2014-12-13 00:00:00.000
```

```
-- Spanish
SELECT PARSE('Sábado December 13, 2014' AS datetime USING 'ES') AS [Date&Time];
-- 2014-12-13 00:00:00.000
```

```
-- Hungarian
SELECT PARSE('Szombat December 13, 2014' AS datetime USING 'HU') AS [Date&Time];
-- 2014-12-13 00:00:00.000
```

```
SELECT PARSE('Cumartesi December 13, 2014' AS datetime USING 'TR') AS [Date&Time]; -- Turkish
```

PARSE() Function Usage for Currency Conversion

```
-- German culture - Euro currency conversion
SELECT PARSE('€9999,95' AS money USING 'DE') AS Currency;
-- 9999.95
```

```
SELECT PARSE('€9999,95' AS money USING 'de-DE') AS Currency;
-- 9999.95
```

```
-- Italian culture - Euro currency conversion
SELECT PARSE('€9999,95' AS money USING 'IT') AS Currency;
-- 9999.95
```

```
-- Netherland culture - Euro currency conversion
SELECT PARSE('€9999,95' AS money USING 'NL') AS Currency;
-- 9999.95
```

```
-- Slovakian culture - Euro currency conversion
SELECT PARSE('€9999,95' AS money USING 'SK') AS Currency;
-- 9999.95
```

```
-- United States - Euro is not US currency
SELECT PARSE('€9999,95' AS money USING 'US') AS Currency;
/*
Msg 9818, Level 16, State 1, Line 1
The culture parameter 'US' provided in the function call is not supported.
*/
```

```
-- Italian
SELECT CONVERT(DECIMAL (12,0), PARSE('€99999,95' AS money USING 'IT')) AS DecimalValue;
-- 100000
```

```
-- PARSE with variable parameters
DECLARE @AMOUNT AS VARCHAR(12) = '$9999.00';   DECLARE @CULTURE AS CHAR(5) = 'EN-US';
SELECT DOLLAR = PARSE(@AMOUNT AS MONEY USING @CULTURE) ;
GO
-- 9999.00
```

```
-- PARSE invalid data
DECLARE @AMOUNT AS VARCHAR(12) = '$9999A.00';   DECLARE @CULTURE AS CHAR(5) = 'EN-US';
SELECT DOLLAR = PARSE(@AMOUNT AS MONEY USING @CULTURE);
GO
/*
Msg 9819, Level 16, State 1, Line 4
Error converting string value '$9999A.00' into data type money using culture 'EN-US'.
 */
```

TRY_CONVERT() Function

The TRY_CONVERT() function augments the CONVERT function to handle invalid data without giving an error. **It is a revolutionary new feature which makes invalid data handling significantly easier in T-SQL.**

```
-- CONVERT returns error on invalid data
SELECT [City]
          ,[PostalCode]
          ,CONVERT(INT, PostalCode)
 FROM AdventureWorks2012.Person.Address
 ORDER BY PostalCode;
/* Msg 245, Level 16, State 1, Line 1
Conversion failed when converting the nvarchar value '7L' to data type int.
*/
```

```
-- TRY_CONVERT() returns NULL for invalid data
SELECT DISTINCT [City]
          ,[PostalCode]
          ,TRY_CONVERT(INT, PostalCode) AS INTValue
 FROM AdventureWorks2012.Person.Address
 ORDER BY PostalCode;
```

City	PostalCode	INTValue
Union Gap	98903	98903
Ellensburg	98926	98926
Spokane	99202	99202
Kennewick	99337	99337
Walla Walla	99362	99362
Stoke-on-Trent	AS23	NULL
Birmingham	B29 6SL	NULL
Cambridge	BA5 3HX	NULL
W. York	BD1 4SJ	NULL
London	C2H 7AU	NULL
Cambridge	CB4 4BZ	NULL
Billericay	CM11	NULL

```
-- String date conversion to date data type
SET DATEFORMAT dmy; -- US date format
SELECT TRY_CONVERT(date, '31/12/2016') AS Result;
-- 2016-12-31
```

```
-- Invalid date
SELECT TRY_CONVERT(date, '12/31/2016') AS Result;
-- NULL
GO
```

TRY_CONVERT() Usage in Adding Column to Table

Add new column as sequential row number (rowid) to table using the identity(int,1,1) function.

> NOTE
>
> The IDENTITY values usually follow the ORDER BY specifications sequentially, but there is no guarantee. If ordering is important, create an empty table first with IDENTITY column and populate it with INSERT SELECT ORDER BY.

```
USE tempdb;

SELECT TRY_CONVERT(int, [SalesOrderID]) AS [NewSalesOrderID],   -- disable IDENTITY inheritance
      *
INTO   SOH
FROM   AdventureWorks.Sales.SalesOrderHeader   ORDER  BY OrderDate,   CustomerID;
GO
-- (31465 row(s) affected)
```

```
-- Take out duplicate SalesOrderID with the IDENTITY property
ALTER TABLE SOH DROP COLUMN SalesOrderID;
GO
```

```
-- Rename NewSalesOrderID to SalesOrderID
EXEC sp_rename 'dbo.SOH.NewSalesOrderID', 'SalesOrderID';
GO
```

```
-- Add IDENTITY function as new first column  for sequence generation - sequential ID
SELECT RowNumber = IDENTITY(INT, 1, 1),       *
INTO   #SOH   FROM   SOH  ORDER  BY OrderDate,  CustomerID;
GO
```

```
SELECT * INTO   SalesOrderHeader  FROM   #SOH ;   -- Create a permanent table
GO
SELECT TOP (5) *  FROM   SalesOrderHeader  ORDER  BY RowNumber ;
GO
```

RowNumber	SalesOrderID	RevisionNumber	OrderDate	DueDate	ShipDate
1	43676	1	2001-07-01 00:00:00.000	2001-07-13 00:00:00.000	2001-07-08 00:00:00.000
2	43695	1	2001-07-01 00:00:00.000	2001-07-13 00:00:00.000	2001-07-08 00:00:00.000
3	43674	1	2001-07-01 00:00:00.000	2001-07-13 00:00:00.000	2001-07-08 00:00:00.000
4	43660	1	2001-07-01 00:00:00.000	2001-07-13 00:00:00.000	2001-07-08 00:00:00.000
5	43672	1	2001-07-01 00:00:00.000	2001-07-13 00:00:00.000	2001-07-08 00:00:00.000

```
DROP TABLE SOH ;
DROP TABLE #SOH ;
DROP TABLE tempdb.dbo.SalesOrderHeader ;
```

TRY_PARSE() Function

The TRY_PARSE() function returns NULL instead of error in case of invalid data. T-SQL script to demonstrate the various uses of TRY_PARSE.

```
-- TRY_PARSE() parses or returns NULL if cast fails
SELECT TRY_PARSE('Monday, 13 December 2014' AS datetime USING 'en-US') AS [Date&Time];
-- NULL
```

```
SELECT TRY_PARSE('SAT, 13 December 2014' AS datetime USING 'en-US') AS [Date&Time];
-- 2014-12-13 00:00:00.000
```

```
-- Using the new feature with CASE Conditional.
SELECT CASE WHEN TRY_PARSE('Monday, 13 December 2014' AS datetime USING 'en-US') is NULL
        THEN (SELECT CONVERT(datetime, '19000101'))
    ELSE (SELECT PARSE('Monday, 13 December 2014' AS datetime USING 'en-US')) END;
-- 1900-01-01 00:00:00.000
```

```
-- TRY_PARSE with variable parameters and IIF conditional
DECLARE @AMOUNT AS VARCHAR(12) = '$9999.00', @CULTURE AS CHAR(5) = 'EN-US';

SELECT RESULT = IIF(TRY_PARSE(@AMOUNT AS MONEY USING @CULTURE) IS NOT NULL
                                        ,PARSE(@AMOUNT AS MONEY USING @CULTURE) ,-1.0);
-- 9999.0000
```

```
DECLARE @AMOUNT AS VARCHAR(12) = '$9999A.00'; DECLARE @CULTURE AS CHAR(5) = 'EN-US';

SELECT RESULT = IIF(TRY_PARSE(@AMOUNT AS MONEY USING @CULTURE) IS NOT NULL
                                        ,PARSE(@AMOUNT AS MONEY USING @CULTURE) ,-1.0);
-- -1.0000
```

```
DECLARE @AMOUNT AS VARCHAR(12) = '$9999A.00', @CULTURE AS CHAR(5) = 'EN-US';

SELECT RESULT = IIF(TRY_PARSE(@AMOUNT AS MONEY USING @CULTURE) IS NOT NULL
                                        ,PARSE(@AMOUNT AS MONEY USING @CULTURE) ,NULL);
GO
-- NULL
```

```
-- Note the multiplication by 100 using the German culture
DECLARE @AMOUNT AS VARCHAR(12) = '€77777.00'; DECLARE @CULTURE AS CHAR(5) = 'de-DE';

SELECT RESULT = IIF(TRY_PARSE(@AMOUNT AS MONEY USING @CULTURE) IS NOT NULL
                                        ,PARSE(@AMOUNT AS MONEY USING @CULTURE) ,NULL);
GO
-- 7777700.00
```

FORMAT() Function

FORMAT() function is borrowed from the .NET languages. It augments the CONVERT function. T-SQL scripts to demonstrate some of the functionalities.

SELECT FORMAT(1111.22,'c','en-us');	$1,111.22
SELECT FORMAT(1111.22,'c','en-gb');	£1,111.22
SELECT FORMAT(1111.22,'c','de');	1.111,22 €
SELECT FORMAT(1111.22,'c','it');	€ 1.111,22
SELECT FORMAT(1111.22,'c','hu');	1 111,22 Ft
SELECT FORMAT(1111.22,'c','tr');	1.111,22 TL
SELECT FORMAT(1111.22,'c','es');	1.111,22 €
SELECT FORMAT(1111.22,'c','nl');	1.111,22 €
SELECT FORMAT(1111.22,'c','pl');	1 111,22 zł
SELECT FORMAT(1111.22,'c','ru');	1 111,22p.
SELECT FORMAT(1111.22,'c','se');	kr 1 111,22

```
DECLARE @culture char(2)='fr' ;  SELECT FORMAT(1111.22, 'c', @culture); -- 1 111,22 €
```

```
SELECT FORMAT(1111.22,'c','gr');   /* Msg 9818, Level 16, State 1, Line 1
The culture parameter 'gr' provided in the function call is not supported.   */
```

```
SELECT FORMAT ( getdate(), 'yyyy/MM/dd hh:mm:ss tt', 'en-US' );       -- 2016/06/03 09:56:44 AM
SELECT FORMAT ( getdate(), 'MMM dd, yyyy hh:mm:ss tt', 'en-US' );    -- Jun 03, 2016 09:57:45 AM
```

```
SELECT FORMAT ( getdate(), 'y', 'en-US' ) ;           -- July, 2016
SELECT FORMAT ( getdate(), 'M', 'en-US' ) ;           -- July 10
SELECT FORMAT ( getdate(), 'd', 'en-US' ) ;           -- 7/10/2016
```

```
-- Percent formatting
SELECT TOP (4) ProductNumber, ListPrice, StandardCost, Markup = FORMAT(ListPrice / StandardCost, 'p', 'en-us')
FROM AdventureWorks2012.Production.Product  WHERE ListPrice > 0.0  ORDER BY ProductNumber;
```

ProductNumber	ListPrice	StandardCost	Markup
BB-7421	53.99	23.9716	225.22 %
BB-8107	101.24	44.9506	225.22 %
BB-9108	121.49	53.9416	225.22 %
BC-M005	9.99	3.7363	267.37 %

CONCAT() Function

The CONCAT() function concatenates two or more strings. Previously the + operator was the only available way to concatenate. **NOTE: CONCAT treats NULL as an empty string, this is different from the + operator concatenation.** T-SQL scripts to demonstrate usage.

```
-- Using + string concatenation operator
SELECT  'New'+SPACE(1)+'York'+SPACE(1)+'City' ;          -- New York City
```

```
-- Using the new CONCAT() function
SELECT  CONCAT('New', SPACE(1),'York', SPACE(1), 'City'); -- New York City
```

```
-- Concatenating string columns with CONCAT()
SELECT CONCAT(FirstName, ' ', LastName) AS FullName
FROM AdventureWorks2012.Person.Person
ORDER by FullName;
/* FullName
...
Blake Wright
Blake Young
Bob Alan
Bob Chapman
Bob Fernandez ... /
```

CHOOSE() Function

The CHOOSE() function returns an item from a list of values as specified by an index. T-SQL scripts to demonstrate usage.

```
SELECT CHOOSE ( 3, 'NYC', 'LA', 'Chicago', 'Houston' ) AS City;
-- Chicago
```

```
SELECT CHOOSE ( 3, 'one', 'two', 'three', 'four', 'five' ) AS Number;
-- three
```

```
DECLARE @weekday as tinyint=6;
SELECT CHOOSE(@weekday, 'Sunday', 'Monday', 'Tuesday', 'Wednesday', 'Thursday', 'Friday', 'Saturday');
-- Friday
```

```
-- Random weekday selection using newid() and rand() functions
DECLARE @weekday as tinyint=Round(Rand(Cast(Newid() AS VARBINARY)) * 6+1,0);
SELECT CHOOSE(@weekday, 'Sunday', 'Monday', 'Tuesday', 'Wednesday', 'Thursday', 'Friday', 'Saturday');
GO 10
-- Friday   Sunday  Tuesday .....
```

THROW Statement

The THROW statement passes the error incurred in TRY - CATCH to the application. Demonstration T-SQL script follows.

```
CREATE TABLE Alpha
(
	ID INT PRIMARY KEY
);
GO
```

```
BEGIN TRY
   INSERT Alpha(ID) VALUES(7);
   INSERT Alpha(ID) VALUES(7); -- Force error by attempting duplicate insert
END TRY
BEGIN CATCH
   PRINT 'In CATCH';
  -- The error message encountered will be passed down to the client software application
   THROW;
END CATCH;
/*
In CATCH

Msg 2627, Level 14, State 1, Line 7
Violation of PRIMARY KEY constraint 'PK__Alpha__3214EC272A076B44'. Cannot insert
duplicate key in object 'dbo.Alpha'. The duplicate key value is (1).
*/
```

```
-- No THROW catch  - Error message not materialized
BEGIN TRY
   INSERT Alpha(ID) VALUES(7);
END TRY
BEGIN CATCH
   PRINT 'In CATCH';
END CATCH;
/*
(0 row(s) affected)
In CATCH.
*/
```

```
-- Cleanup
DROP TABLE Alpha
GO
```

IIF() Function

The IIF() function returns one of two values based on a condition. Here is a T-SQL demonstration script.

```
SELECT TOP 10  ProductID, ListPrice,
               IIF ( Color is not null, Color, 'N/A' ) AS [Color]
FROM AdventureWorks2012.Production.Product
ORDER BY ProductID DESC;
GO
```

ProductID	ListPrice	Color
999	539.99	Black
998	539.99	Black
997	539.99	Black
996	121.49	N/A
995	101.24	N/A
994	53.99	N/A
993	539.99	Black
992	539.99	Black
991	539.99	Black
990	539.99	Black

DATEFROMPARTS() & DATETIMEFROMPARTS() Functions

The DATEFROMPARTS() & DATETIMEFROMPARTS() functions generate date / datetime value from date parts. Demonstration T-SQL script.

```
SELECT DATEFROMPARTS ( 2016, 10, 23 ) AS RealDate;
GO
-- 2016-10-23
```

```
SELECT DATETIMEFROMPARTS ( 2016, 10, 23, 10, 10, 10, 500 ) AS RealDateTime;
GO
-- 2016-10-23 10:10:10.500
```

```
DECLARE @Year smallint = 2016, @Month tinyint = 10, @Day tinyint = 23;
SELECT DATEFROMPARTS(@Year, @Month, @Day);
GO
-- 2016-10-23
```

EOMONTH() Function

The EOMONTH() function returns the last day of the month for the given input date parameter. T-SQL script to demonstrate usage.

```
SELECT EOMONTH('20140201') -- 2014-02-28
```

```
SELECT EOMONTH('20160201') -- 2016-02-29
GO
```

```
-- Future/past months optional parameter
DECLARE    @anydate DATE = '20161023';
SELECT
        CurrentMonthEnd        = EOMONTH(@anydate),
        NextMonthEnd           = EOMONTH(@anydate,  1),
        PrevMonthEnd           = EOMONTH(@anydate, -1);
GO
```

CurrentMonthEnd	NextMonthEnd	PrevMonthEnd
2016-10-31	2016-11-30	2016-09-30

```
-- Span 12 months of last day of month by using the sequence from spt_values
DECLARE    @anydate DATE = '20161023';
SELECT  TOP 12   LastDayOfMonth= EOMONTH(@anydate, number)
FROM master.dbo.spt_values WHERE type = 'P'  ORDER BY number;
GO
```

LastDayOfMonth
2016-10-31
2016-11-30
2016-12-31
2017-01-31
2017-02-28
2017-03-31
2017-04-30
2017-05-31
2017-06-30
2017-07-31
2017-08-31
2017-09-30

Result Set Paging with OFFSET & FETCH NEXT

Frequently a query produces a large results set. On the client side usually it has to be presented in small segments such as 20 lines at a time.

```
USE AdventureWorks2012;

SELECT ProductNumber, Name, ListPrice, Color
FROM Production.Product  ORDER BY ProductNumber
        OFFSET 0 ROWS    FETCH NEXT 10 ROWS ONLY;
-- (10 row(s) affected)
```

ProductNumber	Name	ListPrice	Color
AR-5381	Adjustable Race	0.00	NULL
BA-8327	Bearing Ball	0.00	NULL
BB-7421	LL Bottom Bracket	53.99	NULL
BB-8107	ML Bottom Bracket	101.24	NULL
BB-9108	HL Bottom Bracket	121.49	NULL
BC-M005	Mountain Bottle Cage	9.99	NULL
BC-R205	Road Bottle Cage	8.99	NULL
BE-2349	BB Ball Bearing	0.00	NULL
BE-2908	Headset Ball Bearings	0.00	NULL
BK-M18B-40	Mountain-500 Black, 40	539.99	Black

```
SELECT ProductNumber, Name, ListPrice, Color
FROM Production.Product  ORDER BY ProductNumber
        OFFSET 10 ROWS     FETCH NEXT 10 ROWS ONLY;
-- (10 row(s) affected)
```

ProductNumber	Name	ListPrice	Color
BK-M18B-42	Mountain-500 Black, 42	539.99	Black
BK-M18B-44	Mountain-500 Black, 44	539.99	Black
BK-M18B-48	Mountain-500 Black, 48	539.99	Black
BK-M18B-52	Mountain-500 Black, 52	539.99	Black
BK-M18S-40	Mountain-500 Silver, 40	564.99	Silver
BK-M18S-42	Mountain-500 Silver, 42	564.99	Silver
BK-M18S-44	Mountain-500 Silver, 44	564.99	Silver
BK-M18S-48	Mountain-500 Silver, 48	564.99	Silver
BK-M18S-52	Mountain-500 Silver, 52	564.99	Silver
BK-M38S-38	Mountain-400-W Silver, 38	769.49	Silver

```
SELECT ProductNumber, Name, ListPrice, Color
FROM Production.Product   ORDER BY ProductNumber OFFSET 500 ROWS    FETCH NEXT 10 ROWS ONLY;
-- (4 row(s) affected)
```

ProductNumber	Name	ListPrice	Color
VE-C304-L	Classic Vest, L	63.50	Blue
VE-C304-M	Classic Vest, M	63.50	Blue
VE-C304-S	Classic Vest, S	63.50	Blue
WB-H098	Water Bottle - 30 oz.	4.99	NULL

Result Paging Stored Procedure

The OFFSET FETCH functionality can be wrapped into a stored procedure protected by encryption.

```
USE AdventureWorks2012;
GO
```

```
CREATE PROCEDURE sprocProductPaging  (  @PageNumber int,   @RowsPerPage int  )
WITH ENCRYPTION                    -- Customers of your SW package cannot read the sp source code
AS
BEGIN
SELECT          ProductNumber,
                Name AS ProductName,
                ListPrice,
                Color
  FROM Production.Product p
  WHERE ProductSubcategoryID is not NULL
  ORDER BY ProductNumber
  OFFSET (@PageNumber-1) * @RowsPerPage ROWS
  FETCH NEXT @RowsPerPage ROWS ONLY;
END;
GO -- Command(s) completed successfully.
```

```
EXEC sprocProductPaging 10, 20
GO -- (20 row(s) affected)
```

ProductNumber	ProductName	ListPrice	Color
FR-T67Y-44	LL Touring Frame - Yellow, 44	333.42	Yellow
FR-T67Y-50	LL Touring Frame - Yellow, 50	333.42	Yellow
FR-T67Y-54	LL Touring Frame - Yellow, 54	333.42	Yellow
FR-T67Y-58	LL Touring Frame - Yellow, 58	333.42	Yellow
FR-T67Y-62	LL Touring Frame - Yellow, 62	333.42	Yellow
FR-T98U-46	HL Touring Frame - Blue, 46	1003.91	Blue
FR-T98U-50	HL Touring Frame - Blue, 50	1003.91	Blue
FR-T98U-54	HL Touring Frame - Blue, 54	1003.91	Blue
FR-T98U-60	HL Touring Frame - Blue, 60	1003.91	Blue
FR-T98Y-46	HL Touring Frame - Yellow, 46	1003.91	Yellow
FR-T98Y-50	HL Touring Frame - Yellow, 50	1003.91	Yellow
FR-T98Y-54	HL Touring Frame - Yellow, 54	1003.91	Yellow
FR-T98Y-60	HL Touring Frame - Yellow, 60	1003.91	Yellow
FW-M423	LL Mountain Front Wheel	60.745	Black
FW-M762	ML Mountain Front Wheel	209.025	Black
FW-M928	HL Mountain Front Wheel	300.215	Black
FW-R623	LL Road Front Wheel	85.565	Black
FW-R762	ML Road Front Wheel	248.385	Black
FW-R820	HL Road Front Wheel	330.06	Black
FW-T905	Touring Front Wheel	218.01	Black

LEAD() & LAG() Functions

THE LEAD() & LAG() analytical functions belong to the **OVER** family of functions.

```
USE AdventureWorks2012;
GO
 SELECT
        SalesOrderID,
        OrderQty,
        FORMAT(LineTotal, 'c', 'en-US')                                   AS LineTotal,
        LEAD(SalesOrderDetailID) OVER (ORDER BY SalesOrderDetailID )      AS [LEAD],
        SalesOrderDetailID                                                AS SODID,
        LAG(SalesOrderDetailID) OVER (ORDER BY SalesOrderDetailID  )      AS [LAG]
 FROM Sales.SalesOrderDetail sod
 WHERE SalesOrderID IN    (SELECT SalesOrderID FROM Sales.SalesOrderHeader
                           WHERE TotalDue >= 180000)
 ORDER BY SalesOrderDetailID;
--(111 row(s) affected) - Partial results.
```

SalesOrderID	OrderQty	LineTotal	LEAD	SODID	LAG
51131	11	$337.57	36817	36816	NULL
51131	12	$368.25	36818	36817	36816
51131	9	$5,421.11	36819	36818	36817
51131	2	$400.10	36820	36819	36818
51131	15	$200.76	36821	36820	36819
51131	2	$567.90	36822	36821	36820
51131	6	$8,582.65	36823	36822	36821
51131	4	$1,135.80	36824	36823	36822
51131	16	$12,206.44	36825	36824	36823
51131	8	$4,818.77	36826	36825	36824

.....

SalesOrderID	OrderQty	LineTotal	LEAD	SODID	LAG
55282	2	$76.20	55443	55442	55441
55282	4	$1,781.64	55444	55443	55442
55282	10	$146.94	55445	55444	55443
55282	3	$600.16	55446	55445	55444
55282	3	$1,807.04	55447	55446	55445
55282	28	$800.10	55448	55447	55446
55282	15	$18,685.15	55449	55448	55447
55282	8	$239.95	55450	55449	55448
55282	3	$1,336.23	55451	55450	55449
55282	7	$33.39	NULL	55451	55450

FIRST_VALUE() & LAST_VALUE() Analytic Functions

The FIRST_VALUE() and LAST_VALUE() analytic functions can be applied in conjunction with the OVER clause.

```
USE AdventureWorks2012;
GO
;WITH CTE AS
	(SELECT   PSC.Name AS Subcategory,
 FIRST_VALUE(P.Name) OVER (PARTITION BY PSC.Name ORDER BY ListPrice ASC) AS LeastExpensive,
	MIN(ListPrice) OVER (PARTITION BY PSC.Name ORDER BY ListPrice ASC)	AS LowPrice,
 LAST_VALUE(P.Name)  OVER (PARTITION BY PSC.Name ORDER BY ListPrice ASC) AS MostExpensive,
	MAX(ListPrice) OVER (PARTITION BY PSC.Name ORDER BY ListPrice ASC)	AS HighPrice,
	ROW_NUMBER() OVER (PARTITION BY PSC.Name ORDER BY ListPrice DESC)	AS RN
	FROM Production.Product P
	INNER JOIN Production.ProductSubcategory PSC
		ON P.ProductSubcategoryID = PSC.ProductSubcategoryID)
SELECT * FROM CTE WHERE RN = 1 ORDER BY Subcategory;
```

Subcategory	LeastExpensive	LowPrice	MostExpensive	HighPrice	RN
Bib-Shorts	Men's Bib-Shorts, S	89.99	Men's Bib-Shorts, L	89.99	1
Bike Racks	Hitch Rack - 4-Bike	120.00	Hitch Rack - 4-Bike	120.00	1
Bike Stands	All-Purpose Bike Stand	159.00	All-Purpose Bike Stand	159.00	1
Bottles and Cages	Water Bottle - 30 oz.	4.99	Mountain Bottle Cage	9.99	1
Bottom Brackets	LL Bottom Bracket	53.99	HL Bottom Bracket	121.49	1
Brakes	Rear Brakes	106.50	Front Brakes	106.50	1
Caps	AWC Logo Cap	8.99	AWC Logo Cap	8.99	1
Chains	Chain	20.24	Chain	20.24	1
Cleaners	Bike Wash - Dissolver	7.95	Bike Wash - Dissolver	7.95	1
Cranksets	LL Crankset	175.49	HL Crankset	404.99	1
Derailleurs	Front Derailleur	91.49	Rear Derailleur	121.46	1
Fenders	Fender Set - Mountain	21.98	Fender Set - Mountain	21.98	1
Forks	LL Fork	148.22	HL Fork	229.49	1
Gloves	Half-Finger Gloves, S	24.49	Full-Finger Gloves, L	37.99	1
Handlebars	LL Road Handlebars	44.54	HL Mountain Handlebars	120.27	1
Headsets	LL Headset	34.20	HL Headset	124.73	1
Helmets	Sport-100 Helmet, Blue	34.99	Sport-100 Helmet, Black	34.99	1
Hydration Packs	Hydration Pack - 70 oz.	54.99	Hydration Pack - 70 oz.	54.99	1
Jerseys	Long-Sleeve Logo Jersey, S	49.99	Short-Sleeve Classic Jersey, XL	53.99	1
Lights	Taillights - Battery-Powered	13.99	Headlights - Weatherproof	44.99	1
Locks	Cable Lock	25.00	Cable Lock	25.00	1
Mountain Bikes	Mountain-500 Black, 40	539.99	Mountain-100 Silver, 48	3399.99	1
Mountain Frames	LL Mountain Frame - Black, 40	249.79	HL Mountain Frame - Silver, 46	1364.50	1
Panniers	Touring-Panniers, Large	125.00	Touring-Panniers, Large	125.00	1
Pedals	LL Mountain Pedal	40.49	Touring Pedal	80.99	1
Pumps	Minipump	19.99	Mountain Pump	24.99	1
Road Bikes	Road-750 Black, 44	539.99	Road-150 Red, 56	3578.27	1
Road Frames	LL Road Frame - Black, 44	337.22	HL Road Frame - Red, 58	1431.50	1
Saddles	LL Mountain Seat/Saddle	27.12	HL Touring Seat/Saddle	52.64	1
Shorts	Men's Sports Shorts, S	59.99	Women's Mountain Shorts, L	69.99	1
Socks	Racing Socks, M	8.99	Mountain Bike Socks, L	9.50	1
Tights	Women's Tights, S	74.99	Women's Tights, L	74.99	1
Tires and Tubes	Patch Kit/8 Patches	2.29	HL Mountain Tire	35.00	1
Touring Bikes	Touring-3000 Blue, 44	742.35	Touring-1000 Blue, 60	2384.07	1
Touring Frames	LL Touring Frame - Blue, 50	333.42	HL Touring Frame - Yellow, 60	1003.91	1
Vests	Classic Vest, S	63.50	Classic Vest, L	63.50	1
Wheels	LL Mountain Front Wheel	60.745	HL Road Rear Wheel	357.06	1

CUME_DIST() & PERCENT_RANK() Analytic Functions

CUME_DIST() and PERCENT_RANK() analytic functions work in conjunction with the OVER clause.

```
SELECT  Department,
        CONCAT(LastName,', ', FirstName)                                    AS FullName,
        Rate,
        FORMAT(CUME_DIST () OVER (PARTITION BY Department ORDER BY Rate),'p')  AS CumuDist,
        FORMAT(PERCENT_RANK()  OVER (PARTITION BY Department ORDER BY Rate ),'p') AS PctRnk
FROM HumanResources.vEmployeeDepartmentHistory AS edh  -- view
   INNER JOIN HumanResources.EmployeePayHistory AS e
             ON e.BusinessEntityID = edh.BusinessEntityID
ORDER BY Department, Rate DESC;
-- (334 row(s) affected) - Partial results.
```

Department	FullName	Rate	CumuDist	PctRnk
Facilities and Maintenance	Altman, Gary	24.0385	100.00 %	100.00 %
Facilities and Maintenance	Kleinerman, Christian	20.4327	85.71 %	83.33 %
Facilities and Maintenance	Hedlund, Magnus	9.75	71.43 %	66.67 %
Facilities and Maintenance	Penor, Lori	9.25	57.14 %	0.00 %
Facilities and Maintenance	Macrae, Stuart	9.25	57.14 %	0.00 %
Facilities and Maintenance	Berry, Jo	9.25	57.14 %	0.00 %
Facilities and Maintenance	Coleman, Pat	9.25	57.14 %	0.00 %
Finance	Norman, Laura	60.0962	100.00 %	100.00 %
Finance	Norman, Laura	48.5577	92.31 %	91.67 %
Finance	Kahn, Wendy	43.2692	84.62 %	83.33 %
Finance	Norman, Laura	39.06	76.92 %	75.00 %
Finance	Liu, David	34.7356	69.23 %	66.67 %
Finance	Moreland, Barbara	26.4423	61.54 %	50.00 %
Finance	Seamans, Mike	26.4423	61.54 %	50.00 %
Finance	Tomic, Dragan	19.00	46.15 %	8.33 %
Finance	Sheperdigian, Janet	19.00	46.15 %	8.33 %
Finance	Poe, Deborah	19.00	46.15 %	8.33 %
Finance	Spoon, Candy	19.00	46.15 %	8.33 %
Finance	Walton, Bryan	19.00	46.15 %	8.33 %
Finance	Barber, David	13.4615	7.69 %	0.00 %
Human Resources	Barreto de Mattos, Paula	27.1394	100.00 %	100.00 %
Human Resources	Johnson, Willis	18.2692	83.33 %	60.00 %
Human Resources	Luthra, Vidur	18.2692	83.33 %	60.00 %
Human Resources	Martin, Mindy	16.5865	50.00 %	40.00 %
Human Resources	Culbertson, Grant	13.9423	33.33 %	0.00 %
Human Resources	Chen, Hao	13.9423	33.33 %	0.00 %

EXEC New Option: WITH RESULT SETS

The WITH RESULT SETS clause can be used to remap the result set of a stored procedure or system procedure execution.

```
EXEC sp_who;
GO
-- (145 row(s) affected) - Partial results.
```

spid	ecid	status	loginame	hostname	blk	dbname	cmd	request_id
1	0	background	sa		0	NULL	LOG WRITER	0
2	0	background	sa		0	NULL	RECOVERY WRITER	0
3	0	background	sa		0	NULL	LAZY WRITER	0
4	0	background	sa		0	master	SIGNAL HANDLER	0
5	0	background	sa		0	NULL	LOCK MONITOR	0

```
EXEC sp_who
 WITH RESULT SETS
 (
  (
  SPID INT,
  ECID INT,
  STATUS VARCHAR(32),
  LOGINAME SYSNAME,
  HOSTNAME SYSNAME,
  BLK TINYINT,
  DBNAME SYSNAME,
  CMD VARCHAR(64),
  REQUESTID INT
  )
);
-- (145 row(s) affected) - Partial results.
```

SPID	ECID	STATUS	LOGINAME	HOSTNAME	BLK	DBNAME	CMD	REQUESTID
47	0	background	sa		0	master	BRKR TASK	0
48	0	background	sa		0	master	BRKR TASK	0
51	0	sleeping	HPESTAR\Owner	HPESTAR	0	master	AWAITING COMMAND	0
52	0	sleeping	HPESTAR\Owner	HPESTAR	0	master	AWAITING COMMAND	0
53	0	sleeping	HPESTAR\Owner	HPESTAR	0	AdventureWorks2012	AWAITING COMMAND	0
54	0	sleeping	HPESTAR\Owner	HPESTAR	0	AdventureWorks2008	AWAITING COMMAND	0
55	0	sleeping	HPESTAR\Owner	HPESTAR	0	AdventureWorks2008	AWAITING COMMAND	0
56	0	sleeping	NT SERVICE\ReportServer	HPESTAR	0	ReportServer	AWAITING COMMAND	0
57	0	sleeping	HPESTAR\Owner	HPESTAR	0	AdventureWorks2008	AWAITING COMMAND	0
58	0	runnable	HPESTAR\Owner	HPESTAR	0	AdventureWorks2012	SELECT	0
59	0	sleeping	NT SERVICE\ReportServer	HPESTAR	0	ReportServer	AWAITING COMMAND	0
60	0	runnable	HPESTAR\Owner	HPESTAR	0	master	SELECT	0

CHAPTER 12: JOINing Tables with INNER & OUTER JOINs

SELECT with INNER JOIN

The SELECT statement is used to retrieve data from table(s). An INNER JOIN is a join in which the values in the columns being joined are compared using a comparison operator. Inner join also known as equi-join when equality condition is applied. Equi-join: PRIMARY KEY (table a) = FOREIGN KEY (table b).

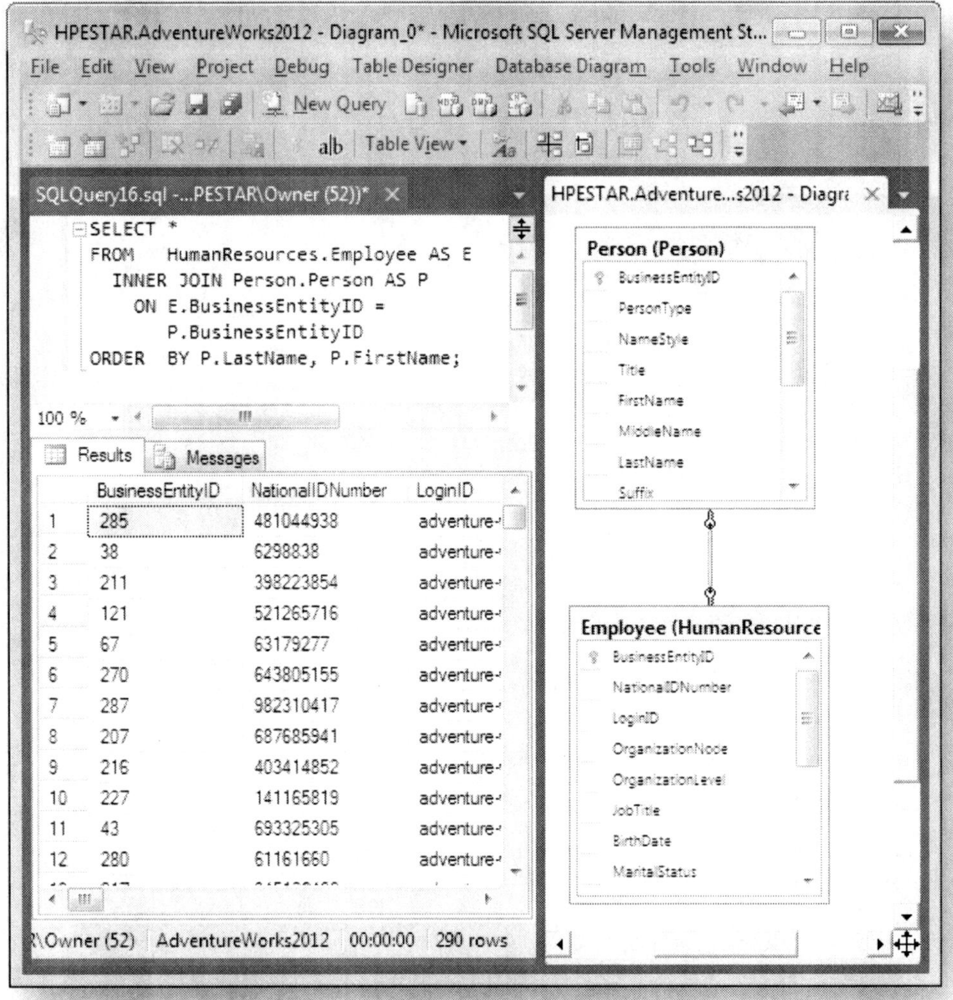

FOREIGN KEY Constraint as Base for INNER JOIN

The INNER JOIN is based on HumanResources.Employee.BusinessEntityID (PRIMARY KEY) is a FOREIGN KEY to Person.Person.BusinessEntityID. The Employee table is in one-to-one relationship with a subset of the Person table.

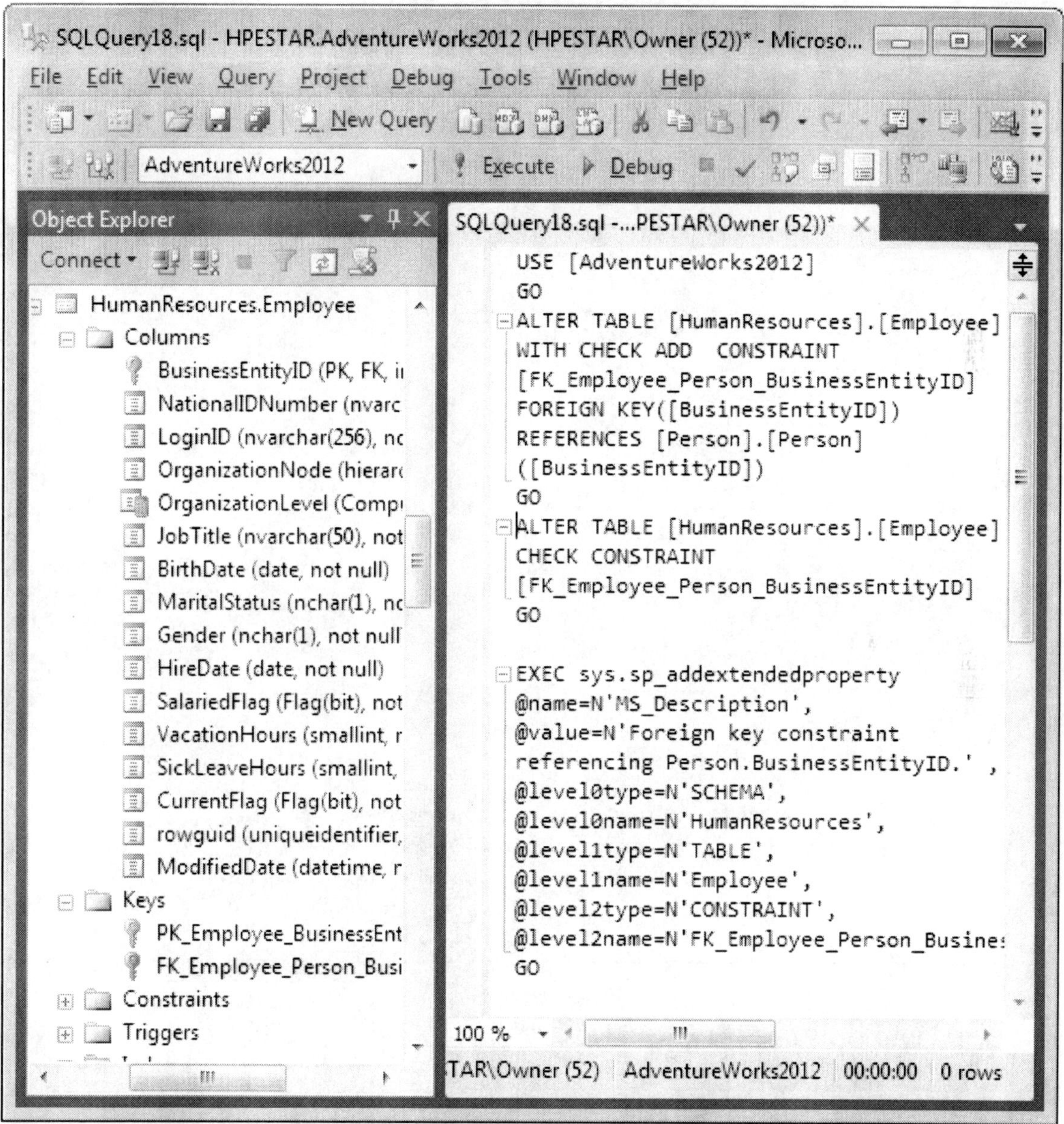

Diagram of Person.Person and Related Tables

The population of Person.Person includes all employees, contacts, and customers, therefore a key table in the database.

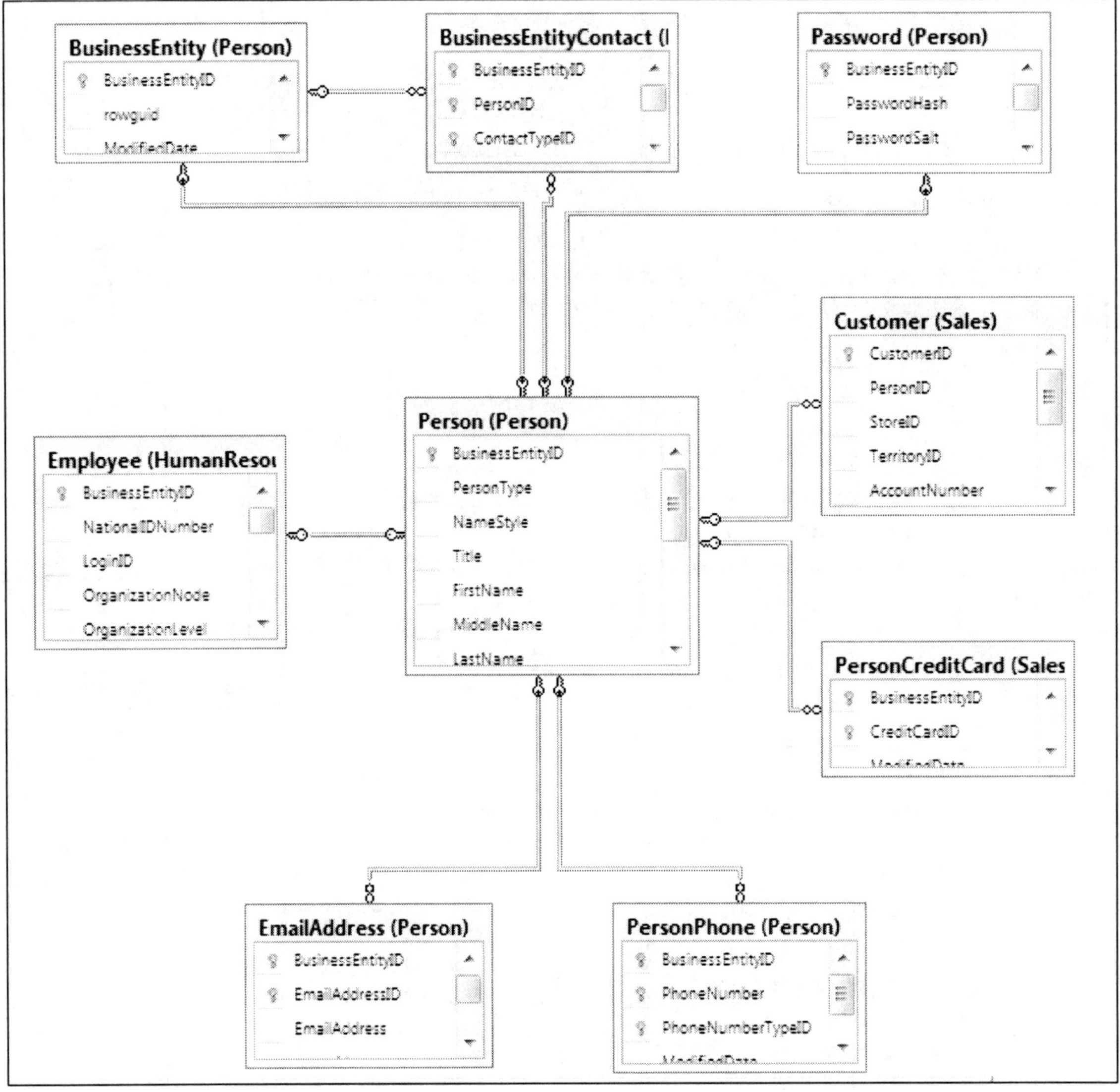


```
-- INNER JOIN ON PRIMARY KEY & FOREIGN KEY
SELECT * FROM Person.Person AS P
            INNER JOIN Person.PersonPhone AS PH
                  ON P.BusinessEntityID = PH.BusinessEntityID;
-- (19972 row(s) affected)
```

EQUI-JOIN BETWEEN FOREIGN KEY & PRIMARY KEY

EQUI JOIN means the equality operator is used to match the left and right keys. The reason for the popularity: the goal of most query is to gather information from related tables records (rows). Query to demonstrate why are 3 tables necessary to get a meaningful business report with just a few columns.

```
USE AdventureWorks;
GO
```

```
SELECT        CONCAT(LastName, ', ', FirstName)        AS Consumer,
              EmailAddress,
              Phone,
              CU.AccountNumber,
              C.ContactID,
              I.CustomerID
FROM Person.Contact AS C
  INNER JOIN Sales.Individual AS I
    ON C.ContactID = I.ContactID
  INNER JOIN Sales.Customer AS CU
    ON I.CustomerID = CU.CustomerID
WHERE CU.CustomerType = 'I'
ORDER BY LastName, FirstName ;
GO
-- (18484 row(s) affected) - Partial results.
```

Consumer	EmailAddress	Phone	AccountNumber	ContactID	CustomerID
Pal, Yolanda	yolanda11@adventure-works.com	1 (11) 500 555-0110	AW00023748	2837	23748
Palit, Punya	punya0@adventure-works.com	164-555-0118	AW00017574	14759	17574
Parker, Adam	adam29@adventure-works.com	808-555-0157	AW00018228	14771	18228
Parker, Alex	alex26@adventure-works.com	613-555-0123	AW00029252	14783	29252
Parker, Alexandra	alexandra50@adventure-works.com	974-555-0142	AW00016866	8977	16866
Parker, Allison	allison30@adventure-works.com	750-555-0124	AW00026501	9021	26501
Parker, Amanda	amanda51@adventure-works.com	978-555-0167	AW00018081	8985	18081
Parker, Amber	amber7@adventure-works.com	1 (11) 500 555-0198	AW00023959	8999	23959
Parker, Andrea	andrea23@adventure-works.com	612-555-0113	AW00020091	8461	20091
Parker, Angel	angel21@adventure-works.com	815-555-0120	AW00014273	14779	14273
Parker, Bailey	bailey28@adventure-works.com	604-555-0112	AW00019529	9007	19529
Parker, Blake	blake44@adventure-works.com	432-555-0151	AW00015008	3413	15008
Parker, Caleb	caleb28@adventure-works.com	593-555-0116	AW00026318	14760	26318
Parker, Carlos	carlos25@adventure-works.com	937-555-0143	AW00020676	14778	20676
Parker, Charles	charles43@adventure-works.com	266-555-0118	AW00021267	4105	21267
Parker, Chloe	chloe5@adventure-works.com	360-555-0121	AW00027480	8965	27480
Parker, Connor	connor28@adventure-works.com	936-555-0177	AW00028839	14763	28839
Parker, Courtney	courtney5@adventure-works.com	266-555-0176	AW00017612	9002	17612
Parker, Dalton	dalton42@adventure-works.com	535-555-0190	AW00013064	3722	13064
Parker, Devin	devin40@adventure-works.com	897-555-0155	AW00011684	4192	11684
Parker, Eduardo	eduardo41@adventure-works.com	131-555-0192	AW00012939	4269	12939

Diagram of Sales.Customer and Related Tables

Customer is the source of revenue for any business. Therefore, proper table design is paramount.

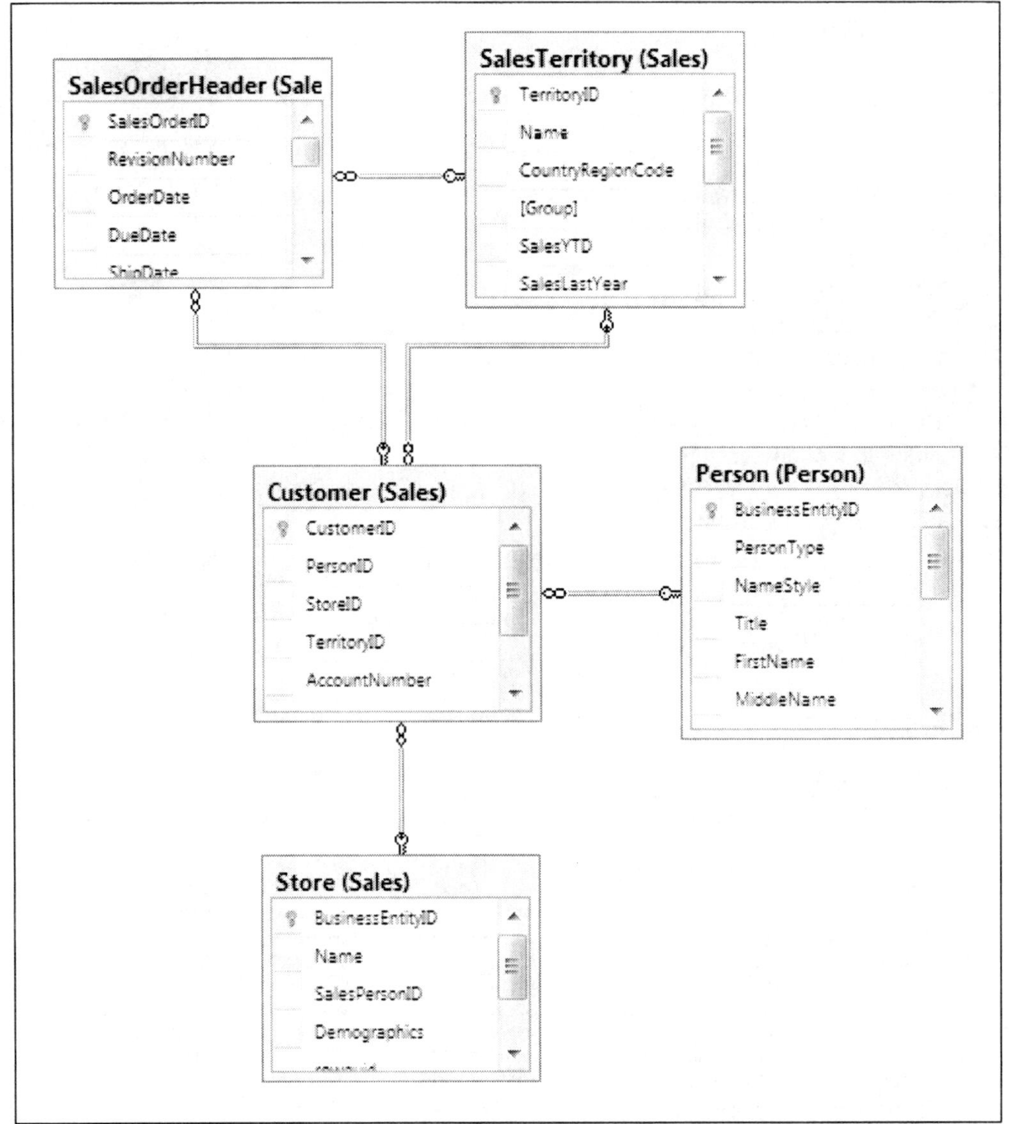


```
-- INNER JOIN ON PRIMARY KEY & FOREIGN KEY - NOTE: PK & FK named differently
SELECT * FROM Sales.Store AS S
                INNER JOIN Sales.Customer AS C   ON S.BusinessEntityID = C.StoreID;
-- (1336 row(s) affected)
```

Extracting All or Partial Data from JOINed Tables

T-SQL scripts to demonstrate how to JOIN two tables and extract all or subset of the information.

```
USE AdventureWorks2012;
```

```
-- SELECT all columns from the JOINed tables
SELECT *
FROM   HumanResources.Employee                  AS E      -- E is a table alias
    INNER JOIN Person.Person                    AS P      -- P is a table alias
        ON E.BusinessEntityID = P.BusinessEntityID
ORDER  BY P.LastName;
-- (290 row(s) affected)  - Partial results.
```

FirstName	MiddleName	LastName
Syed	E	Abbas
Kim	B	Abercrombie
Hazem	E	Abolrous
Pilar	G	Ackerman
Jay	G	Adams

```
SELECT E.*                              -- SELECT Employee columns from the JOINed tables
FROM   HumanResources.Employee AS E
    INNER JOIN Person.Person AS P    ON E.BusinessEntityID = P.BusinessEntityID
ORDER  BY P.LastName;
--  Partial results.
```

JobTitle	BirthDate	MaritalStatus	Gender
Pacific Sales Manager	1969-02-11	M	M
Production Technician - WC60	1961-01-14	M	F
Quality Assurance Manager	1971-11-27	S	M
Shipping and Receiving Supervisor	1966-10-11	S	M

```
-- SELECT Person columns from the JOINed tables
SELECT P.* FROM   HumanResources.Employee AS E
                INNER JOIN Person.Person AS P      ON E.BusinessEntityID = P.BusinessEntityID
ORDER  BY P.LastName;
-- Partial results.
```

BusinessEntityID	PersonType
285	SP
38	EM
211	EM

SELECT All Columns From The Joined Tables Using Table Alias And Wildcard

```
SELECT E.*, P.*
FROM   HumanResources.Employee                    AS E     -- E is a table alias
    INNER JOIN Person.Person                      AS P     -- P is a table alias
        ON E.BusinessEntityID = P.BusinessEntityID
ORDER  BY P.LastName;
-- Same results as SELECT * FROM
```

```
-- Count JOINed rows
SELECT count(*)
FROM   HumanResources.Employee AS E
    INNER JOIN Person.Person AS P
        ON E.BusinessEntityID = P.BusinessEntityID
-- 290
```

```
-- Vertically output reduction: eliminate columns from the available pool
SELECT   E.BusinessEntityID                 AS EmployeeID,   -- column alias
         E.JobTitle,
         P.FirstName,
         P.LastName
FROM   HumanResources.Employee AS E
    INNER JOIN Person.Person AS P    ON E.BusinessEntityID = P.BusinessEntityID
ORDER  BY P.LastName;
-- (290 row(s) affected) - Partial results.
```

EmployeeID	JobTitle	FirstName	LastName
285	Pacific Sales Manager	Syed	Abbas
38	Production Technician - WC60	Kim	Abercrombie
211	Quality Assurance Manager	Hazem	Abolrous
121	Shipping and Receiving Supervisor	Pilar	Ackerman

```
-- Create a new output column from the available pool of columns
SELECT   E.BusinessEntityID                          AS EmployeeID,
         E.JobTitle,
         CONCAT(P.FirstName, ' ', P.LastName)        AS NAME
FROM   HumanResources.Employee AS E
    INNER JOIN Person.Person AS P      ON E.BusinessEntityID = P.BusinessEntityID
ORDER  BY P.LastName;
-- (290 row(s) affected) - Partial results.
```

EmployeeID	JobTitle	NAME
285	Pacific Sales Manager	Syed Abbas
38	Production Technician - WC60	Kim Abercrombie
211	Quality Assurance Manager	Hazem Abolrous
121	Shipping and Receiving Supervisor	Pilar Ackerman

Table Aliases for Readability

The table alias serves as shorthand for table name to improve the **readability of queries**. It should be as short as possible and as meaningful as possible when we have to use a few letters. The next T-SQL query applies four table aliases: c, soh, sod, p.

```
USE AdventureWorks;
SELECT DISTINCT SalesPerson = CONCAT(c.FirstName,SPACE(1), c.LastName)
FROM   Person.Contact c
    INNER JOIN Sales.SalesOrderHeader soh
     ON soh.SalesPersonId = c.ContactID
    INNER JOIN Sales.SalesOrderDetail sod
     ON soh.SalesOrderId = sod.SalesOrderId
    INNER JOIN Production.Product p
     ON sod.ProductID = p.ProductID     AND p.Name LIKE ('%Touring Frame%');
GO /*    SalesPerson
         Carla Eldridge
         Carol Elliott
         Gail Erickson ....*/
```

Column Aliases for Readability & Presentation

The column alias serves as a meaningful column name either replacing a column name or filling in when there is no column name. In the previous example the = sign was used to establish the column alias. Alternate setting follows applying "AS" (it can be skipped) after the column. If the alias has spaces it has to be included in square brackets like [Bond Sales] or double quotes.

```
USE AdventureWorks;
SELECT DISTINCT  CONCAT(c.FirstName,' ', c.LastName)                    AS SalesPerson
FROM   Person.Contact c
    INNER JOIN Sales.SalesOrderHeader soh
     ON soh.SalesPersonId = c.ContactID
    INNER JOIN Sales.SalesOrderDetail sod
     ON soh.SalesOrderId = sod.SalesOrderId
    INNER JOIN Production.Product p
     ON sod.ProductID = p.ProductID   AND p.Name LIKE ('%Touring Frame%');
-- (17 row(s) affected) - Partial results.
```

SalesPerson
Carla Eldridge
Carol Elliott
Gail Erickson
Gary Drury
Janeth Esteves
Jauna Elson
John Emory

Derived Table Alias with a List of Column Aliases

Optionally column alias list can be specified for derived tables just like in CTE definition. T-SQL query demonstrates nested derived tables with table-column aliases (P & J).

```
SELECT DISTINCT ProdID, ProdName, ProdPrice, OrderQuantity
FROM     (
              SELECT   ID, ProductName, Price,                    -- Derived table columns
                       OrderQty                                   -- SOD column
              FROM AdventureWorks2012.Sales.SalesOrderDetail SOD
                INNER JOIN
                       (SELECT ProductID, Name, ListPrice
                        FROM AdventureWorks2012.Production.Product
                       ) P(ID, ProductName, Price)                -- inner derived table
                  ON SOD.ProductID = P.ID
         ) J (ProdID, ProdName, ProdPrice, OrderQuantity)         -- outer derived table
ORDER BY ProdPrice DESC, ProdName;
-- (2667 row(s) affected) - Partial results.
```

ProdID	ProdName	ProdPrice	OrderQuantity
750	Road-150 Red, 44	3578.27	3
750	Road-150 Red, 44	3578.27	6
750	Road-150 Red, 44	3578.27	1
750	Road-150 Red, 44	3578.27	4
750	Road-150 Red, 44	3578.27	2
750	Road-150 Red, 44	3578.27	5
751	Road-150 Red, 48	3578.27	6
751	Road-150 Red, 48	3578.27	3
751	Road-150 Red, 48	3578.27	2
751	Road-150 Red, 48	3578.27	5
751	Road-150 Red, 48	3578.27	4
751	Road-150 Red, 48	3578.27	1
752	Road-150 Red, 52	3578.27	5
752	Road-150 Red, 52	3578.27	3
752	Road-150 Red, 52	3578.27	6
752	Road-150 Red, 52	3578.27	1
752	Road-150 Red, 52	3578.27	4
752	Road-150 Red, 52	3578.27	2
753	Road-150 Red, 56	3578.27	6
753	Road-150 Red, 56	3578.27	3

INNER JOIN with Additional Conditions

The ON clause of a JOIN can include additional conditions as the following demonstration shows. The INNER JOIN is still based on FOREIGN KEY relationship, but only a subset of records (rows) returned due to the additional conditions, or JOIN predicates. The first query returns the distinct set of cases where the Selling Price was below the ListPrice for ProductID 800 which is a yellow road bike. The second query covers the remaining range where the Selling Price was equal or above the ListPrice.

```
USE AdventureWorks2012;
SELECT DISTINCT( P.ProductID ),
        ProductName = P.Name,              -- column alias
        P.ListPrice,
        SOD.UnitPrice AS 'Selling Price'   -- column alias
FROM   Sales.SalesOrderDetail AS SOD       -- table alias
    INNER JOIN  Production.Product AS P    -- table alias
     ON SOD.ProductID = P.ProductID
       AND SOD.UnitPrice < P.ListPrice               -- JOIN predicate
       AND  P.ProductID = 800;                       -- JOIN predicate
```

ProductID	ProductName	ListPrice	Selling Price
800	Road-550-W Yellow, 44	1120.49	600.2625
800	Road-550-W Yellow, 44	1120.49	672.294
800	Road-550-W Yellow, 44	1120.49	1000.4375

```
SELECT DISTINCT( P.ProductID ),
        ProductName = P.Name,
        P.ListPrice,
        SOD.UnitPrice AS 'Selling Price'
FROM   Sales.SalesOrderDetail AS SOD
    INNER JOIN  Production.Product AS P
     ON SOD.ProductID = P.ProductID
       AND SOD.UnitPrice >= P.ListPrice
       AND  P.ProductID BETWEEN 800 AND 900
ORDER BY ProductName;
-- (26 row(s) affected) - Partial results.
```

ProductID	ProductName	ListPrice	Selling Price
879	All-Purpose Bike Stand	159.00	159.00
877	Bike Wash - Dissolver	7.95	7.95
866	Classic Vest, L	63.50	63.50
865	Classic Vest, M	63.50	63.50
864	Classic Vest, S	63.50	63.50
878	Fender Set - Mountain	21.98	21.98
860	Half-Finger Gloves, L	24.49	24.49
859	Half-Finger Gloves, M	24.49	24.49
858	Half-Finger Gloves, S	24.49	24.49
876	Hitch Rack - 4-Bike	120.00	120.00

Counting Rows in JOINs

As the T-SQL script following shows, the basic FOREIGN KEY based JOIN returns 121,317 rows which is all the rows in Sales.SalesOrderDetail table. The additional condition P.ProductID = 800 selects a subset of 495 rows which is then divided between the < and >= conditions.

```
USE AdventureWorks2012;
SELECT Rows = count(*)
FROM   Sales.SalesOrderDetail AS SOD
    INNER JOIN  Production.Product AS P    ON SOD.ProductID = P.ProductID
-- 121317
```

```
SELECT Rows = count(*)
FROM   Sales.SalesOrderDetail AS SOD
    INNER JOIN  Production.Product AS P   ON SOD.ProductID = P.ProductID   AND P.ProductID = 800;
-- 495
```

```
SELECT Rows = count(*)
FROM   Sales.SalesOrderDetail AS SOD
    INNER JOIN  Production.Product AS P
     ON SOD.ProductID = P.ProductID
       AND SOD.UnitPrice < P.ListPrice
       AND P.ProductID = 800;
-- 285
```

```
SELECT Rows = count(*)
FROM   Sales.SalesOrderDetail AS SOD
    INNER JOIN  Production.Product AS P
     ON SOD.ProductID = P.ProductID
       AND SOD.UnitPrice >= P.ListPrice
       AND P.ProductID = 800;
-- 210
```

```
SELECT COUNT(P.ProductID)
FROM   Sales.SalesOrderDetail AS SOD
    INNER JOIN  Production.Product AS P
     ON SOD.ProductID = P.ProductID
       AND SOD.UnitPrice >= P.ListPrice
       AND  P.ProductID BETWEEN 800 AND 900;
-- 21085
```

```
SELECT COUNT(DISTINCT P.ProductID)
FROM   Sales.SalesOrderDetail AS SOD
    INNER JOIN  Production.Product AS P
     ON SOD.ProductID = P.ProductID   AND SOD.UnitPrice >= P.ListPrice
         AND  P.ProductID BETWEEN 800 AND 900;
```

INNER JOIN with 3 Tables

T-SQL query to demonstrate JOINing three tables. Due to the application of the FORMAT function, column name is lost. Therefore we have to alias the formatted column with the original column name or something else. Both INNER JOINs are based on FOREIGN KEY relationships. PV.ProductID is an FK to the Production.Product table, and the PV.VendorID is an FK to the Purchasing.Vendor table. The Purchasing.ProductVendor table is a junction table representing many-to-many relationships between products and vendors: a vendor may supply many products (see Beaumont Bikes in results) and a product may be supplied by many vendors (see Chainring in results).

```
USE AdventureWorks;
GO
SELECT          P.ProductNumber,
                P.Name                                          AS Product,
                V.Name                                          AS Vendor,
                FORMAT (PV.LastReceiptCost, 'c', 'en-US')       AS LastReceiptCost
FROM Production.Product AS P
 INNER JOIN Purchasing.ProductVendor AS PV
        ON P.ProductID = PV.ProductID
 INNER JOIN Purchasing.Vendor AS V
        ON V.VendorID = PV.VendorID
ORDER BY Product;
GO
-- (406 row(s) affected) - Partial results.
```

ProductNumber	Product	Vendor	LastReceiptCost
AR-5381	Adjustable Race	Litware, Inc.	$50.26
BA-8327	Bearing Ball	Wood Fitness	$41.92
CH-0234	Chain	Varsity Sport Co.	$15.74
CR-7833	Chainring	Beaumont Bikes	$25.42
CR-7833	Chainring	Bike Satellite Inc.	$26.37
CR-7833	Chainring	Training Systems	$28.70
CB-2903	Chainring Bolts	Beaumont Bikes	$47.47
CB-2903	Chainring Bolts	Bike Satellite Inc.	$45.37
CB-2903	Chainring Bolts	Training Systems	$49.64
CN-6137	Chainring Nut	Beaumont Bikes	$42.80
CN-6137	Chainring Nut	Bike Satellite Inc.	$40.49
CN-6137	Chainring Nut	Training Systems	$44.32
RA-7490	Cone-Shaped Race	Midwest Sport, Inc.	$44.22
CR-9981	Crown Race	Business Equipment Center	$50.26
RA-2345	Cup-Shaped Race	Bloomington Multisport	$48.76
DC-8732	Decal 1	SUPERSALES INC.	$0.21
DC-9824	Decal 2	SUPERSALES INC.	$0.21
LE-6000	External Lock Washer 1	Pro Sport Industries	$41.24
LE-6000	External Lock Washer 1	Aurora Bike Center	$43.27
LE-6000	External Lock Washer 1	Expert Bike Co	$41.17

T-SQL Query To Return All Road Frames Offered For Sale By AdventureWorks Cycles

```
USE AdventureWorks2012;
SELECT      UPPER(PC.Name)        AS Category,   PSC.Name              AS Subcategory,
            P.Name       AS Product,   FORMAT(ListPrice, 'c', 'en-US')   AS ListPrice,
            FORMAT(StandardCost, 'c', 'en-US')                        AS StandardCost
FROM Production.Product AS P
   INNER JOIN Production.ProductSubcategory AS PSC
            ON PSC.ProductSubcategoryID = P.ProductSubcategoryID
   INNER JOIN Production.ProductCategory AS PC
            ON PC.ProductCategoryID = PSC.ProductCategoryID
WHERE PSC.Name like 'Road Frames'  ORDER BY Category, Subcategory, Product;
```

Category	Subcategory	Product	ListPrice	StandardCost
COMPONENTS	Road Frames	HL Road Frame - Black, 44	$1,431.50	$868.63
COMPONENTS	Road Frames	HL Road Frame - Black, 48	$1,431.50	$868.63
COMPONENTS	Road Frames	HL Road Frame - Black, 52	$1,431.50	$868.63
COMPONENTS	Road Frames	HL Road Frame - Black, 58	$1,431.50	$1,059.31
COMPONENTS	Road Frames	HL Road Frame - Black, 62	$1,431.50	$868.63
COMPONENTS	Road Frames	HL Road Frame - Red, 44	$1,431.50	$868.63
COMPONENTS	Road Frames	HL Road Frame - Red, 48	$1,431.50	$868.63
COMPONENTS	Road Frames	HL Road Frame - Red, 52	$1,431.50	$868.63
COMPONENTS	Road Frames	HL Road Frame - Red, 56	$1,431.50	$868.63
COMPONENTS	Road Frames	HL Road Frame - Red, 58	$1,431.50	$1,059.31
COMPONENTS	Road Frames	HL Road Frame - Red, 62	$1,431.50	$868.63
COMPONENTS	Road Frames	LL Road Frame - Black, 44	$337.22	$204.63
COMPONENTS	Road Frames	LL Road Frame - Black, 48	$337.22	$204.63
COMPONENTS	Road Frames	LL Road Frame - Black, 52	$337.22	$204.63
COMPONENTS	Road Frames	LL Road Frame - Black, 58	$337.22	$204.63
COMPONENTS	Road Frames	LL Road Frame - Black, 60	$337.22	$204.63
COMPONENTS	Road Frames	LL Road Frame - Black, 62	$337.22	$204.63
COMPONENTS	Road Frames	LL Road Frame - Red, 44	$337.22	$187.16
COMPONENTS	Road Frames	LL Road Frame - Red, 48	$337.22	$187.16
COMPONENTS	Road Frames	LL Road Frame - Red, 52	$337.22	$187.16
COMPONENTS	Road Frames	LL Road Frame - Red, 58	$337.22	$187.16
COMPONENTS	Road Frames	LL Road Frame - Red, 60	$337.22	$187.16
COMPONENTS	Road Frames	LL Road Frame - Red, 62	$337.22	$187.16
COMPONENTS	Road Frames	ML Road Frame - Red, 44	$594.83	$352.14
COMPONENTS	Road Frames	ML Road Frame - Red, 48	$594.83	$352.14
COMPONENTS	Road Frames	ML Road Frame - Red, 52	$594.83	$352.14
COMPONENTS	Road Frames	ML Road Frame - Red, 58	$594.83	$352.14
COMPONENTS	Road Frames	ML Road Frame - Red, 60	$594.83	$352.14
COMPONENTS	Road Frames	ML Road Frame-W - Yellow, 38	$594.83	$360.94
COMPONENTS	Road Frames	ML Road Frame-W - Yellow, 40	$594.83	$360.94
COMPONENTS	Road Frames	ML Road Frame-W - Yellow, 42	$594.83	$360.94
COMPONENTS	Road Frames	ML Road Frame-W - Yellow, 44	$594.83	$360.94
COMPONENTS	Road Frames	ML Road Frame-W - Yellow, 48	$594.83	$360.94

INNER JOIN with Junction Table

Three tables INNER JOIN includes the titleauthor junction table which represent many-to-many relationship. All JOINs are EQUI-JOINs with FOREIGN KEYs and PRIMARY KEYs.

```
USE pubs;

SELECT          FORMAT(ytd_sales, 'c', 'en-US')                                  AS YTDSales,
                CONCAT(au.au_fname, ' ', au.au_lname)                            AS Author,
                FORMAT((ytd_sales * royalty) / 100,'c','en-US')                  AS AuthorRev,
                FORMAT((ytd_sales - (ytd_sales * royalty) / 100),'c','en-US')    AS PublisherRev
FROM titles t
        INNER JOIN titleauthor ta
                ON t.title_id = ta.title_id
        INNER JOIN authors au
                ON ta.au_id = au.au_id
ORDER BY        YTDSales DESC,          -- Major sort key
                Author ASC;             -- Minor sort key
GO    -- (25 row(s) affected) - Partial results.
```

YTDSales	Author	AuthorRev	PublisherRev
$8,780.00	Cheryl Carson	$1,404.00	$7,376.00
$4,095.00	Abraham Bennet	$409.00	$3,686.00
$4,095.00	Akiko Yokomoto	$409.00	$3,686.00

INNER JOIN with Table-Valued Function

Table-valued user-defined functions can be used in INNER JOIN (stored procedure results can only be used in JOINs with OPENQUERY).

```
USE AdventureWorks2012;
GO
```

```
-- Inline table-valued function - ITVF
CREATE FUNCTION ufnProduct (@ProductID int)
RETURNS TABLE AS
RETURN (SELECT * FROM Production.Product WHERE ProductID=@ProductID)
GO
```

```
DECLARE @PID INT = 800;
SELECT * FROM ufnProduct(@PID) u
                INNER JOIN Sales.SalesOrderDetail sod   ON u.ProductID = sod.ProductID;
GO    -- (495 row(s) affected)
```

NON-EQUI JOINs for Data Analytics

We can use not equal operators in JOIN predicates as demonstrated in the next query. The second predicate in the JOIN is less than JOIN.

```
USE AdventureWorks2012;
GO
-- List of "red" products sold at a discount
SELECT DISTINCT          p.ProductNumber,
                         p.Name                              AS ProductName,
                         FORMAT(p.ListPrice,'c','en-US')     AS ListPrice,
                         FORMAT(sod.UnitPrice,'c','en-US')   AS SellPrice
FROM Sales.SalesOrderDetail AS sod
   INNER JOIN Production.Product AS p
         ON sod.ProductID = p.ProductID
          AND sod.UnitPrice < p.ListPrice
WHERE Color = 'Red'
ORDER BY p.ProductNumber;
--(86 row(s) affected) - Partial results.
```

ProductNumber	ProductName	ListPrice	SellPrice
BK-R50R-44	Road-650 Red, 44	$782.99	$234.90
BK-R50R-44	Road-650 Red, 44	$782.99	$419.46
BK-R50R-44	Road-650 Red, 44	$782.99	$430.64
BK-R50R-44	Road-650 Red, 44	$782.99	$454.13
BK-R50R-44	Road-650 Red, 44	$782.99	$469.79
BK-R50R-44	Road-650 Red, 44	$782.99	$563.75
BK-R50R-44	Road-650 Red, 44	$782.99	$699.10
BK-R50R-48	Road-650 Red, 48	$782.99	$419.46
BK-R50R-48	Road-650 Red, 48	$782.99	$430.64
BK-R50R-48	Road-650 Red, 48	$782.99	$454.13
BK-R50R-48	Road-650 Red, 48	$782.99	$469.79
BK-R50R-48	Road-650 Red, 48	$782.99	$563.75

To resolve the duplicate issue which makes DISTINCT usage necessary, we have to include the SalesOrderID column.

```
SELECT                   p.ProductNumber,
                         p.Name                              AS ProductName,
                         FORMAT(p.ListPrice,'c','en-US')     AS ListPrice,
                         FORMAT(sod.UnitPrice,'c','en-US')   AS SellPrice,
                         sod.SalesOrderID
FROM Sales.SalesOrderDetail AS sod
   INNER JOIN Production.Product AS p
         ON sod.ProductID = p.ProductID
          AND sod.UnitPrice < p.ListPrice
WHERE Color = 'Red'   ORDER BY p.ProductNumber;
-- (8408 row(s) affected)
```

Interchangeability of ON & WHERE Predicates in INNER JOINs

We can freely place the predicates to either the ON clause or the WHERE clause in an INNER JOIN. This is not true for OUTER JOINs such as LEFT JOINs.

```
USE AdventureWorks2012;
-- List of "blue" products sold at a discount
SELECT DISTINCT p.ProductNumber, p.Name                    AS ProductName,
                FORMAT(p.ListPrice,'c','en-US')            AS ListPrice,
                FORMAT(sod.UnitPrice,'c','en-US')          AS SellPrice
FROM Sales.SalesOrderDetail AS sod
  INNER JOIN Production.Product AS p
       ON sod.ProductID = p.ProductID
       AND sod.UnitPrice < p.ListPrice
WHERE Color = 'Blue'  ORDER BY p.ProductNumber;
--(57 row(s) affected)
```

```
SELECT DISTINCT p.ProductNumber, p.Name                    AS ProductName,
                FORMAT(p.ListPrice,'c','en-US')            AS ListPrice,
                FORMAT(sod.UnitPrice,'c','en-US')          AS SellPrice
FROM Sales.SalesOrderDetail AS sod
  INNER JOIN Production.Product AS p
       ON sod.ProductID = p.ProductID
       AND sod.UnitPrice < p.ListPrice
       AND Color = 'Blue'
ORDER BY p.ProductNumber;
--(57 row(s) affected)
```

```
SELECT DISTINCT p.ProductNumber, p.Name                    AS ProductName,
                FORMAT(p.ListPrice,'c','en-US')            AS ListPrice,
                FORMAT(sod.UnitPrice,'c','en-US')          AS SellPrice
FROM Sales.SalesOrderDetail AS sod
  INNER JOIN Production.Product AS p
  ON sod.ProductID = p.ProductID
WHERE sod.UnitPrice < p.ListPrice   AND Color = 'Blue'  ORDER BY p.ProductNumber;
--(57 row(s) affected)
```

```
-- Old-style INNER JOIN with table list and WHERE clause
SELECT DISTINCT p.ProductNumber, p.Name                    AS ProductName,
                FORMAT(p.ListPrice,'c','en-US')            AS ListPrice,
                FORMAT(sod.UnitPrice,'c','en-US')          AS SellPrice
FROM Sales.SalesOrderDetail AS sod,  Production.Product AS p
WHERE sod.ProductID = p.ProductID
       AND sod.UnitPrice < p.ListPrice
      AND Color = 'Blue'
ORDER BY p.ProductNumber;         --(57 row(s) affected)
```

SELF-JOIN for Analytics Within a Table

When a table is JOINed to itself, it is a called a self-join. The purpose of such a JOIN is to examine data relations within the table. The Production.Product table is self-joined to itself on the ProductSubcategoryID FOREIGN KEY(not on a PRIMARY KEY), a many-to-many JOIN. Subsequently, we made the query "friendlier" by using subcategory names as opposed to ID-s.

```
SELECT DISTINCT  P1.ProductSubcategoryID,
                 P1.ListPrice                    AS ListPrice1,
                 P2.ListPrice                    AS ListPrice2
FROM   Production.Product P1
 INNER JOIN Production.Product P2
  ON P1.ProductSubcategoryID = P2.ProductSubcategoryID
  AND P1.ListPrice < P2.ListPrice
  AND P1.ListPrice < $15
  AND P2.ListPrice < $15;
```

ProductSubcategoryID	ListPrice1	ListPrice2
23	8.99	9.50
28	4.99	8.99
28	4.99	9.99
28	8.99	9.99
37	2.29	3.99
37	2.29	4.99
37	3.99	4.99

```
SELECT DISTINCT  PS.Name AS Subcategory,
                 P1.ListPrice      AS ListPrice1,
                 P2.ListPrice      AS ListPrice2
FROM   Production.ProductSubcategory PS
    INNER JOIN Production.Product P1
        ON PS.ProductSubcategoryID = P1.ProductSubcategoryID
    INNER JOIN Production.Product P2
        ON P1.ProductSubcategoryID = P2.ProductSubcategoryID
         AND P1.ListPrice < P2.ListPrice                  -- To prevent duplicate processing
         AND P1.ListPrice < $15
         AND P2.ListPrice < $15;
```

Subcategory	ListPrice1	ListPrice2
Bottles and Cages	4.99	8.99
Bottles and Cages	4.99	9.99
Bottles and Cages	8.99	9.99
Socks	8.99	9.50
Tires and Tubes	2.29	3.99
Tires and Tubes	2.29	4.99
Tires and Tubes	3.99	4.99

T-SQL SELF-JOIN Query Lists The Competing Suppliers For Each Product Purchased From Vendor

Since the ProductID in the ProductVendor table is part of a composite PRIMARY KEY, we can conclude that it is a many-to-many JOIN.

```
SELECT DISTINCT
                Vendor = V.[Name],
                P1.BusinessEntityID,
                Product = P.[Name],
                P1.ProductID
FROM   Production.Product P
    INNER JOIN Purchasing.ProductVendor P1
        ON P.ProductID = P1.ProductID
    INNER JOIN Purchasing.Vendor V
        ON P1.BusinessEntityID = V.BusinessEntityID
    INNER JOIN Purchasing.ProductVendor P2
        ON P1.ProductID = P2.ProductID
WHERE  P1.BusinessEntityID <> P2.BusinessEntityID
ORDER  BY Product, Vendor
-- (347 row(s) affected) - Partial results.
```

Vendor	BusinessEntityID	Product	ProductID
Beaumont Bikes	1602	Chainring	322
Bike Satellite Inc.	1604	Chainring	322
Training Systems	1514	Chainring	322
Beaumont Bikes	1602	Chainring Bolts	320
Bike Satellite Inc.	1604	Chainring Bolts	320
Training Systems	1514	Chainring Bolts	320
Beaumont Bikes	1602	Chainring Nut	321
Bike Satellite Inc.	1604	Chainring Nut	321
Training Systems	1514	Chainring Nut	321
Aurora Bike Center	1616	External Lock Washer 1	409
Expert Bike Co	1672	External Lock Washer 1	409
Pro Sport Industries	1686	External Lock Washer 1	409
Aurora Bike Center	1616	External Lock Washer 2	411
Pro Sport Industries	1686	External Lock Washer 2	411
Aurora Bike Center	1616	External Lock Washer 3	403
Expert Bike Co	1672	External Lock Washer 3	403
Pro Sport Industries	1686	External Lock Washer 3	403
Aurora Bike Center	1616	External Lock Washer 4	404
Expert Bike Co	1672	External Lock Washer 4	404
Pro Sport Industries	1686	External Lock Washer 4	404
Aurora Bike Center	1616	External Lock Washer 5	406
Expert Bike Co	1672	External Lock Washer 5	406
Pro Sport Industries	1686	External Lock Washer 5	406
Aurora Bike Center	1616	External Lock Washer 6	408
Expert Bike Co	1672	External Lock Washer 6	408

Applying SELF-JOIN for Numbering Result Lines

T-SQL script to demonstrate how SELF-JOIN can be used for numbering lines in query results. Note that in these days we would use **ROW_NUMBER()** function which has been introduced with SQL Server 2005.

```
USE Northwind ;
GO
```

```
SELECT  OD.OrderID,
            SeqNo                                       AS LineItem,
            OD.ProductID,
            FORMAT(UnitPrice,'c','en-US')               AS UnitPrice,
            Quantity,
            FORMAT(Discount, 'p')                       AS Discount
FROM    [Order Details] OD
  INNER JOIN (SELECT  count(* )  AS SeqNo,
          a.OrderID,
          a.ProductID
      FROM    [Order Details] A
          INNER JOIN [Order Details] B
           ON A.ProductID >= B.ProductID                        -- Prevent duplicates
             AND A.OrderID = B.OrderID
      GROUP BY A.OrderID,   A.ProductID) a
    ON OD.OrderID = a.OrderID
     AND OD.ProductID = a.ProductID
WHERE   OD.OrderID < 10400
ORDER BY        OD.OrderID,
                LineItem
-- (405 row(s) affected) - Partial results.
```

Vendor	AddressLine1	AddressLine2	City	State	Country
A. Datum Corporation	2596 Big Canyon Road		New York	New York	United States
Advanced Bicycles	7995 Edwards Ave.		Lynnwood	Washington	United States
Allenson Cycles	4659 Montoya		Altadena	California	United States
American Bicycles and Wheels	1667 Warren Street		West Covina	California	United States
American Bikes	7179 Montana		Torrance	California	United States
Anderson's Custom Bikes	9 Guadalupe Dr.		Burbank	California	United States
Aurora Bike Center	65 Park Glen Court		Port Orchard	Washington	United States
Australia Bike Retailer	28 San Marino Ct.		Bellingham	Washington	United States
Beaumont Bikes	2472 Alexander Place		West Covina	Idaho	United States
Bergeron Off-Roads	9830 May Way		Mill Valley	Montana	United States
Bicycle Specialists	1286 Cincerto Circle		Lake Oswego	Oregon	United States
Bike Satellite Inc.	2141 Delaware Ct.		Downey	Tennessee	United States
Bloomington Multisport	218 Fall Creek Road		West Covina	California	United States
Burnett Road Warriors	5807 Churchill Dr.		Corvallis	Oregon	United States
Business Equipment Center	6061 St. Paul Way		Everett	Montana	United States
Capital Road Cycles	628 Muir Road		Los Angeles	California	United States
Carlson Specialties	2313 B Southampton Rd		Missoula	Montana	United States
Chicago City Saddles	3 Gehringer Drive		Daly City	California	United States
Chicago Rent-All	15 Pear Dr.		Newport Beach	California	United States
Circuit Cycles	1 Mt. Dell Drive		Portland	Oregon	United States

INNER JOIN with 5 Tables

It takes accessing five tables to get the vendor name & address information in AdventureWorks. In fact this is the main complaint against 3NF relational database design: too many JOINs required to extract data. True, but the benefits of 3NF design are overwhelming. A way to overcome the "too many JOINs" issue is creating views which are pre-canned SELECT queries.

```
USE AdventureWorks;
GO
```

```
SELECT V.Name                       AS Vendor,
    A.AddressLine1,
    isnull(A.AddressLine2, '')      AS AddressLine2,
    A.City,
    SP.Name                         AS State,
    CR.Name               AS Country
FROM   Purchasing.Vendor AS V
    INNER JOIN Purchasing.VendorAddress AS VA
        ON VA.VendorID = V.VendorID
    INNER JOIN Person.Address AS A
        ON A.AddressID = VA.AddressID
    INNER JOIN Person.StateProvince AS SP
        ON SP.StateProvinceID = A.StateProvinceID
    INNER JOIN Person.CountryRegion AS CR
        ON CR.CountryRegionCode = SP.CountryRegionCode
ORDER  BY Vendor;
GO
-- (104 row(s) affected) - Partial results.
```

Vendor	AddressLine1	AddressLine2	City	State	Country
A. Datum Corporation	2596 Big Canyon Road		New York	New York	United States
Advanced Bicycles	7995 Edwards Ave.		Lynnwood	Washington	United States
Allenson Cycles	4659 Montoya		Altadena	California	United States
American Bicycles and Wheels	1667 Warren Street		West Covina	California	United States
American Bikes	7179 Montana		Torrance	California	United States
Anderson's Custom Bikes	9 Guadalupe Dr.		Burbank	California	United States
Aurora Bike Center	65 Park Glen Court		Port Orchard	Washington	United States
Australia Bike Retailer	28 San Marino Ct.		Bellingham	Washington	United States
Beaumont Bikes	2472 Alexander Place		West Covina	Idaho	United States
Bergeron Off-Roads	9830 May Way		Mill Valley	Montana	United States
Bicycle Specialists	1286 Cincerto Circle		Lake Oswego	Oregon	United States
Bike Satellite Inc.	2141 Delaware Ct.		Downey	Tennessee	United States
Bloomington Multisport	218 Fall Creek Road		West Covina	California	United States
Burnett Road Warriors	5807 Churchill Dr.		Corvallis	Oregon	United States
Business Equipment Center	6061 St. Paul Way		Everett	Montana	United States
Capital Road Cycles	628 Muir Road		Los Angeles	California	United States

Creating View as Workaround for "Too Many JOINs"

It is so simple to create a view, that counterproductive if not done for queries which are used again and again. Given that large database systems may have a great number of views, meaningful long names are paramount.

```
-- No implicit ORDER BY can be included in a view - no trick around it either
CREATE VIEW vProduct AS SELECT * FROM Production.Product ORDER  BY ProductNumber;
GO  /* Msg 1033, Level 15, State 1, Procedure vVendorAddress, Line 18
The ORDER BY clause is invalid in views, inline functions, derived tables, subqueries, and common table
expressions, unless TOP, OFFSET or FOR XML is also specified.  */
```

```
CREATE VIEW vVendorAddress  AS
SELECT V.Name                                          AS Vendor,
    A.AddressLine1,     isnull(A.AddressLine2, '')     AS AddressLine2,
    A.City,      SP.Name                               AS State,
    CR.Name                                            AS Country
FROM   Purchasing.Vendor AS V
    INNER JOIN Purchasing.VendorAddress AS VA      ON VA.VendorID = V.VendorID
    INNER JOIN Person.Address AS A                 ON A.AddressID = VA.AddressID
    INNER JOIN Person.StateProvince AS SP          ON SP.StateProvinceID = A.StateProvinceID
    INNER JOIN Person.CountryRegion AS CR          ON CR.CountryRegionCode = SP.CountryRegionCode
GO
SELECT TOP 5 * FROM vVendorAddress ORDER BY Vendor;
```

Vendor	AddressLine1	AddressLine2	City	State	Country
A. Datum Corporation	2596 Big Canyon Road		New York	New York	United States
Advanced Bicycles	7995 Edwards Ave.		Lynnwood	Washington	United States
Allenson Cycles	4659 Montoya		Altadena	California	United States
American Bicycles and Wheels	1667 Warren Street		West Covina	California	United States
American Bikes	7179 Montana		Torrance	California	United States

Create Indexed View for Performance

We can turn frequently used (complex) queries into indexed views and gain in performance.

```
USE AdventureWorks2012;
GO
CREATE VIEW Sales.ivSalesOrders WITH SCHEMABINDING AS
        SELECT OrderDate, OrderCount=COUNT_BIG(*), OrderTotal=SUM(SubTotal) FROM
        Sales.SalesOrderHeader GROUP BY OrderDate;
GO
CREATE UNIQUE CLUSTERED INDEX idxIVOrderDate on Sales.ivSalesOrders(OrderDate);
```

MSDN Article: **Improving Performance with SQL Server 2008 Indexed Views**
http://msdn.microsoft.com/en-us/library/dd171921(v=sql.100).aspx

How to Design Views

The beauty of view that it is very simple to create: just prefix almost any SELECT query with "create view vname as", and a new server-side object type 'V', a view is created. A view turns a SELECT statement into a virtual table which can be used in JOINs for example. Data is not stored in view, it is evaluated "on the fly". However, the ease of creation and the benefits of views may lead to an uncontrolled "view jungle". Salient view design points:

- Systematic, goal-oriented & logical approach required for view creation; View should only be created if increases productivity on ongoing basis.

- Good naming is important for a number of reasons among them to prevent proliferation of views; As an example, vLaptopSalesLast12Months is a self-documenting name.

- Views can include data from tables, JOINs and other views (views can be nested); Including complex views in JOINs can create problem for the optimizer, a workaround is: SELECT * INTO #table FROM vViewName and use the temporary table in the query instead of the view.

- GROUP BY clause, CTE and OPENQUERY can be used in view definition; UNION operator cannot be used in a view; Trigger cannot be created on a view.

- Data in the underlying table(s) can be UPDATE-d (INSERT, DELETE) through a view; In some installation a view (vTableName) is created for each table, and applications access the view not the table; WITH ENCRYPTION can be specified when creating a view; usually not a good idea due to maintenance problems.

- View definition can be obtained a few ways. First method is using a system procedure. Second method is building a view on system views JOIN and querying the view.

```
exec sp_helptext 'dbo.vAuthorsInSameCity';
```

```
CREATE VIEW vModuleDefinition AS SELECT SchemaName=schema_name(schema_id),
    ObjectName=object_Name(m.object_ID), ObjectDefinition=definition
FROM sys.SQL_Modules m INNER JOIN sys.objects o ON m.object_id=o.object_id ;
GO --Command(s) completed successfully.
```

```
SELECT SchemaName, ObjectName, DefinitionPrefix = LEFT(ObjectDefinition, 30)
FROM vModuleDefinition WHERE SchemaName='dbo' AND ObjectName='vAuthorsInSameCity';
```

SchemaName	ObjectName	DefinitionPrefix
dbo	vAuthorsInSameCity	CREATE VIEW vAuthorsInSameCity

Non-Key INNER JOIN for Analytics

So far we have seen INNER JOINs based on FOREIGN KEY to PRIMARY equality relationships. The next INNER JOIN is based on the equality of the first 5 letters of last names. It is also a SELF-JOIN. In addition to the last name part equality, two more conditions are reducing the result set. The < condition is intended to reduce duplicates and the first letter of last name is 'S' limits the query results further. This is a many-to-many JOIN.

```
USE AdventureWorks2012;

SELECT DISTINCT
   CONCAT( A.FirstName, space(1), A.LastName)       AS Person,
   CONCAT( B.FirstName, space(1), B.LastName)       AS LastNameNeighbor
FROM  Person.Person A
    INNER JOIN  Person.Person B
      ON LEFT(A.LastName, 5) = LEFT(B.LastName, 5)
        AND A.LastName < B.LastName
        AND LEFT(A.LastName, 1) = 'S'
ORDER  BY          Person,
                   LastNameNeighbor;
-- (169 row(s) affected) - Partial results.
```

Person	LastNameNeighbor
Abigail Smith	Lorrin Smith-Bates
Adriana Smith	Lorrin Smith-Bates
Alexander Smith	Lorrin Smith-Bates
Alexandra Smith	Lorrin Smith-Bates
Alexis Smith	Lorrin Smith-Bates
Allen Smith	Lorrin Smith-Bates
Alyssa Smith	Lorrin Smith-Bates
Andre Smith	Lorrin Smith-Bates
Andrew Smith	Lorrin Smith-Bates
Arthur Smith	Lorrin Smith-Bates
Ashley Smith	Lorrin Smith-Bates
Austin Smith	Lorrin Smith-Bates
Barry Srini	Sethu Srinivasan
Ben Smith	Lorrin Smith-Bates
Benjamin Smith	Lorrin Smith-Bates
Beth Srini	Sethu Srinivasan
Brandon Smith	Lorrin Smith-Bates
Brandy Srini	Sethu Srinivasan
Brett Srini	Sethu Srinivasan
Brianna Smith	Lorrin Smith-Bates

JOINing Tables without Relationship for Combinatorics

SQL Server will execute such a JOIN on any pair of compatible columns as demonstrated by the next T-SQL query. Note this is only a demo, there is no business meaning to it unless the combinatorial results are useful for some application. A more practical example in the pubs database matching author city with publisher city using a JOIN.

```
USE Northwind;   -- Cross database JOIN query
SELECT  P.ProductID,
        P.ProductName             AS NorthwindProduct,
        PP.Name                   AS AWProduct
FROM dbo.Products P
         INNER JOIN AdventureWorks2008.Production.Product PP     ON P.ProductID = PP.ProductID
ORDER BY P.ProductID;
```

ProductID	NorthwindProduct	AWProduct
1	Chai	Adjustable Race
2	Chang	Bearing Ball
3	Aniseed Syrup	BB Ball Bearing
4	Chef Anton's Cajun Seasoning	Headset Ball Bearings

Cartesian Product

When all rows in one table combined with all rows of another table it is called a Cartesian product. The cardinality of such a JOIN is (Table 1 Rows) x (Table 2 Rows).

```
-- Old-fashioned no JOIN predicate 2-table query - Cardinality 4x4 = 16
SELECT Category1 = A.Name, Category2 = B.Name
FROM Production.ProductCategory A, Production.ProductCategory B ORDER BY Category1, Category2;
```

```
-- Equivalent CROSS JOIN
SELECT Category1 = A.Name, Category2 = B.Name
FROM Production.ProductCategory A  CROSS JOIN Production.ProductCategory B
ORDER BY Category1, Category2;
```

Category1	Category2
Accessories	Accessories
Accessories	Bikes
Accessories	Clothing
Accessories	Components
Bikes	Accessories
Bikes	Bikes
Bikes	Clothing
Bikes	Components
Clothing	Accessories
Clothing	Bikes
Clothing	Clothing
Clothing	Components
Components	Accessories
Components	Bikes
Components	Clothing
Components	Components

SQL OUTER JOIN for Inclusion of Unmatched Rows

We have seen that INNER JOINs return rows only when there is at least one row from both tables that satisfies the join condition or conditions such as FOREIGN KEY matching the referenced PRIMARY KEY. Inner join queries do not return the rows that do not meet the ON condition with a row from the other table.

OUTER JOINs, however, return all rows from one or both tables in the JOIN. All rows are returned from the left table in a LEFT OUTER JOIN (including non-matching rows), and all rows are returned from the right table in a RIGHT OUTER JOIN. All rows from both tables are returned in a FULL OUTER JOIN. LEFT OUTER JOIN is totally equivalent to RIGHT OUTER JOIN. LEFT OUTER JOIN is mostly used by programmers in countries where the writing is left to right. **RIGHT OUTER JOIN is typically used by developers in countries where the writing is right to left. The non-matching rows in an OUTER JOIN are returned with NULL value fields**, therefore, they can be distinquished from the matching rows with a null test.

The following are synonyms:

LEFT JOIN - LEFT OUTER JOIN

RIGHT JOIN - RIGHT OUTER JOIN

FULL JOIN - FULL OUTER JOIN

The legacy syntax for outer joins *= (left join) or =* (right join) is not supported anymore. T-SQL example script lists products (left table) even if they are not being sold such as assembly parts.

```
USE AdventureWorks2012;
SELECT          P.Name,         SOD.SalesOrderID,
                CASE    WHEN SalesOrderID is null THEN 'Non-matching'
                        ELSE 'Matching' END              AS JoinInfo
FROM   Production.Product P
    LEFT OUTER JOIN Sales.SalesOrderDetail SOD     ON P.ProductID = SOD.ProductID
ORDER BY P.Name;  -- (121555 row(s) affected)  - Partial results.
```

Name	SalesOrderID	JoinInfo
Adjustable Race	NULL	Non-matching
All-Purpose Bike Stand	51179	Matching
All-Purpose Bike Stand	51488	Matching
All-Purpose Bike Stand	51520	Matching
All-Purpose Bike Stand	51558	Matching
All-Purpose Bike Stand	51882	Matching
All-Purpose Bike Stand	51903	Matching
All-Purpose Bike Stand	51970	Matching
All-Purpose Bike Stand	52010	Matching
All-Purpose Bike Stand	52032	Matching

LEFT JOIN: Include Unmatched Rows from Left Table

In the LEFT JOIN example, the Vendor table is LEFT JOINed to the PurchaseOrderHeader table to find out which vendors did not supply anything. The LEFT JOIN is based on FOREIGN KEY relationship.

```
USE AdventureWorks2012;

SELECT Vendor = V.Name
FROM   Purchasing.Vendor V
     LEFT JOIN Purchasing.PurchaseOrderHeader POH
          ON V.BusinessEntityID = POH.VendorID
WHERE  POH.VendorID IS NULL                    -- Test if POH columns are null
ORDER by Vendor;   -- (18 row(s) affected) - Partial results.
```

Vendor
A. Datum Corporation
Cycling Master
Electronic Bike Co.
GMA Ski & Bike
Holiday Skate & Cycle
Illinois Trek & Clothing

T-SQL query to check which pedal products for sale were reviewed and which ones not.

```
SELECT   p.Name              AS ProductName,
         ProductNumber,
         pr.ProductReviewID,
         pr.ReviewerName,
         pr.Rating
FROM Production.Product p
   LEFT JOIN Production.ProductReview pr
          ON p.ProductID = pr.ProductID
WHERE p.ProductSubcategoryID is not null    AND p.Name like '%pedal%'  ORDER BY ProductNumber;
-- (8 row(s) affected)
```

ProductName	ProductNumber	ProductReviewID	ReviewerName	Rating
LL Mountain Pedal	PD-M282	NULL	NULL	NULL
ML Mountain Pedal	PD-M340	NULL	NULL	NULL
HL Mountain Pedal	PD-M562	2	David	4
HL Mountain Pedal	PD-M562	3	Jill	2
LL Road Pedal	PD-R347	NULL	NULL	NULL
ML Road Pedal	PD-R563	NULL	NULL	NULL
HL Road Pedal	PD-R853	NULL	NULL	NULL
Touring Pedal	PD-T852	NULL	NULL	NULL

RIGHT JOIN - Same as LEFT with Tables Switched

The RIGHT JOIN is totally equivalent, including performance, to the corresponding LEFT JOIN. RIGHT JOIN is more frequently used in countries where they write right to left.

```
USE AdventureWorks2012;

SELECT Vendor = V.Name
FROM   Purchasing.PurchaseOrderHeader POH
    RIGHT JOIN Purchasing.Vendor V
      ON V.BusinessEntityID = POH.VendorID
WHERE  POH.VendorID IS NULL
ORDER by Vendor;
-- (18 row(s) affected) - Partial results.
```

Vendor
A. Datum Corporation
Cycling Master
Electronic Bike Co.
GMA Ski & Bike
Holiday Skate & Cycle

T-SQL RIGHT JOIN examples progress toward a query to provide users with a good report.

```
USE AdventureWorks2012;

SELECT ST.Name AS  Territory,
    SP.BusinessEntityID
FROM   Sales.SalesTerritory ST
    RIGHT OUTER JOIN Sales.SalesPerson SP
      ON ST.TerritoryID = SP.TerritoryID;
-- (17 row(s) affected)
```

```
SELECT   isnull(ST.Name, ' ')                         AS Territory,
         SP.BusinessEntityID,
         CONCAT (C.FirstName, ' ', C.LastName)        AS Name
FROM   Sales.SalesTerritory ST
    RIGHT OUTER JOIN Sales.SalesPerson SP
      ON ST.TerritoryID = SP.TerritoryID
    INNER JOIN Person.Person C
      ON SP.BusinessEntityID = C.BusinessEntityID;
-- (17 row(s) affected)
```

Add a WHERE condition filter on Sales.SalesPerson SalesYTD column

The NULLs indicate the no match rows in the RIGHT OUTER JOIN.

```
SELECT  ST.CountryRegionCode,
        ST.Name                                         AS Territory,
        SP.BusinessEntityID                             AS EmployeeID,
        CONCAT(C.FirstName, ' ', C.LastName )           AS Name
FROM  Sales.SalesTerritory ST
    RIGHT OUTER JOIN Sales.SalesPerson SP
     ON ST.TerritoryID = SP.TerritoryID
    INNER JOIN Person.Person C
     ON SP.BusinessEntityID = C.BusinessEntityID
WHERE SP.SalesYTD > 1000.0
ORDER BY        CountryRegionCode,
                Territory;
GO
-- (17 row(s) affected)
```

CountryRegionCode	Territory	EmployeeID	Name
NULL	NULL	274	Stephen Jiang
NULL	NULL	285	Syed Abbas
NULL	NULL	287	Amy Alberts
AU	Australia	286	Lynn Tsoflias
CA	Canada	278	Garrett Vargas
CA	Canada	282	José Saraiva
DE	Germany	288	Rachel Valdez
FR	France	290	Ranjit Varkey Chudukatil
GB	United Kingdom	289	Jae Pak
US	Central	277	Jillian Carson
US	Northeast	275	Michael Blythe
US	Northwest	283	David Campbell
US	Northwest	284	Tete Mensa-Annan
US	Northwest	280	Pamela Ansman-Wolfe
US	Southeast	279	Tsvi Reiter
US	Southwest	276	Linda Mitchell
US	Southwest	281	Shu Ito

```
-- Counting the RIGHT JOIN  match rows using a ProductSubcategory column
SELECT COUNT( S.Name)
FROM Production.ProductSubcategory S RIGHT JOIN Production.Product P
  ON S.ProductSubcategoryID = P.ProductSubcategoryID;
-- 295
```

Cardinality of OUTER JOINs

The number of rows returned in an OUTER JOIN is equal to the matching rows plus the non-matching rows from either or both tables. **To identify the non-matching rows (the ones with the NULLs) in an outer join we have to choose a not-nullable column like the PRIMARY KEY column.** T-SQL script demonstrates the cardinality involved with a LEFT JOIN.

```
USE AdventureWorks2012;

-- Rows in LEFT JOIN
SELECT Rows = count(*)
FROM   Production.Product P
    LEFT OUTER JOIN Sales.SalesOrderDetail SOD
            ON P.ProductID = SOD.ProductID
-- 121555

-- Rows in right table
SELECT Rows = count(*)
FROM Sales.SalesOrderDetail
-- 121317

-- Non-matching rows in left table
SELECT Rows = count(*)
FROM   Production.Product P
    LEFT OUTER JOIN Sales.SalesOrderDetail SOD
            ON P.ProductID = SOD.ProductID
WHERE SalesOrderID is NULL
-- 238

-- Right table rows + non-matching left table rows = rows returned by left join
SELECT 121317 + 238
-- 121555
```

Since the count queries are single valued, we can do the following summation.

```
SELECT (SELECT Rows = count(*)  FROM Sales.SalesOrderDetail )
+
(SELECT Rows = count(*)
FROM   Production.Product P
    LEFT OUTER JOIN Sales.SalesOrderDetail SOD
            ON P.ProductID = SOD.ProductID
WHERE SalesOrderID is NULL);
GO -- 121555
```

LEFT JOIN & RIGHT JOIN on the Same Table

LEFT JOIN & RIGHT JOIN can be combined on the same table to keep all rows from that table even if they don't match the other two tables. The Production.Product table has a FOREIGN KEY referencing the ProductSubcategory table and another FOREIGN KEY referencing the UnitMeasure table.

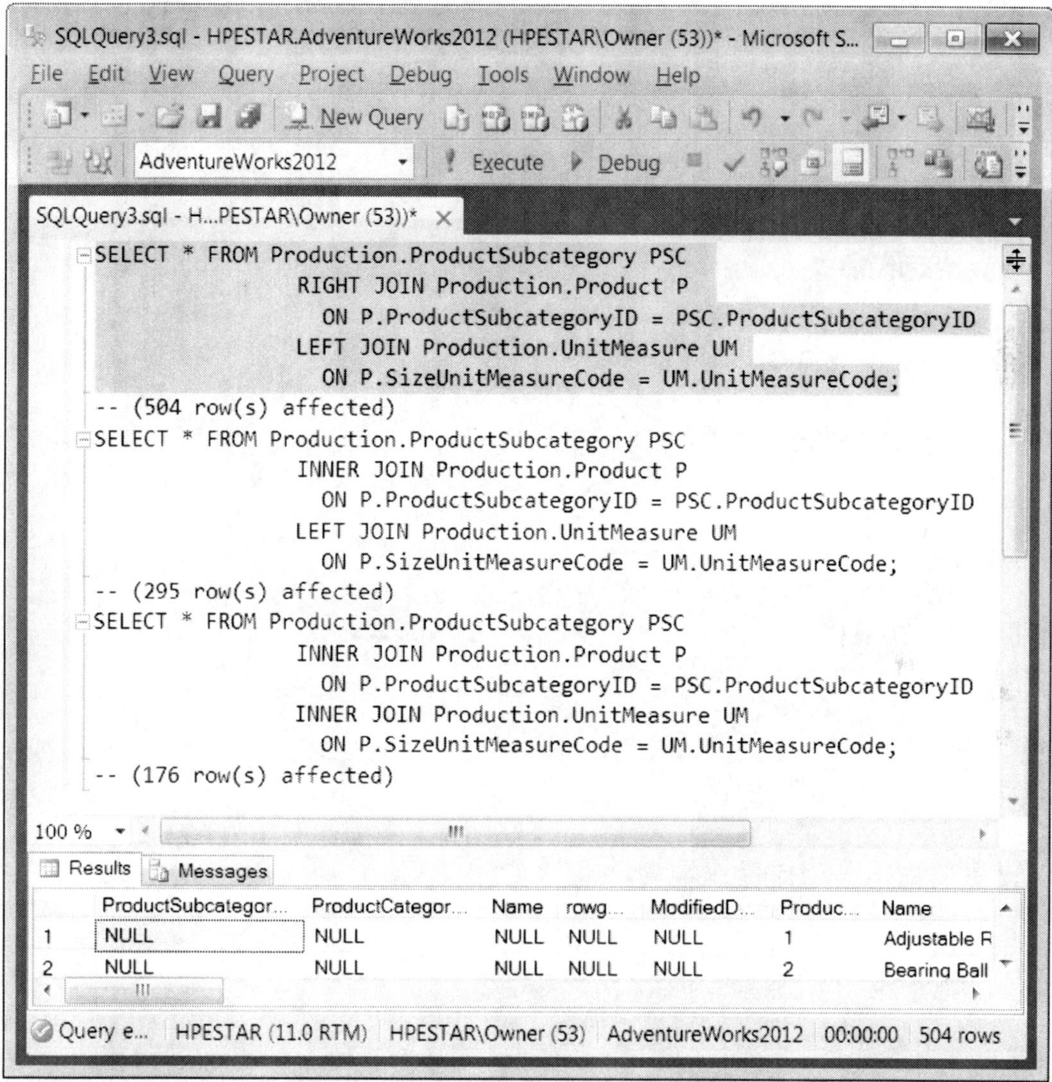

T-SQL Tidbits: The inserted & deleted Virtual Tables

The inserted & deleted tables are available only in triggers and the OUTPUT clause. UPDATE is a combination of deleted & inserted rows. This is similar to transaction logging.

FULL JOIN to Include All Unmatched Rows

The operation FULL JOIN combines LEFT JOIN and RIGHT JOIN, therefore it does not matter which is the left table or right table, it is a fully symmetrical set operation. T-SQL script demonstrates FULL OUTER JOIN.

```
USE tempdb;
-- Create tables for demo
SELECT distinct Color INTO Color
FROM AdventureWorks2012.Production.Product
WHERE Color is not null;
GO
```

```
SELECT ID=IDENTITY(int, 1, 1), * INTO NormalColor
FROM Color;
SELECT ID=IDENTITY(int, 1, 1), Color=CONCAT('Light', Color)  INTO LightColor
FROM Color;
```

```
DELETE NormalColor WHERE Color = 'Red';
```

```
DELETE LightColor WHERE Color = 'LightBlue';
```

```
-- Demo tables ready - full join query
SELECT   NormalColor      = n.Color,
         LightColor       = l.Color
FROM   NormalColor n      FULL OUTER JOIN LightColor l    ON n.ID = l.ID
ORDER BY NormalColor;
```

NormalColor	LightColor
NULL	LightRed
Black	LightBlack
Blue	NULL
Grey	LightGrey
Multi	LightMulti
Silver	LightSilver
Silver/Black	LightSilver/Black
White	LightWhite
Yellow	LightYellow

```
DROP TABLE  tempdb.dbo.Color;  DROP TABLE tempdb.dbo.NormalColor;
DROP TABLE tempdb.dbo.LightColor;
GO
```

CROSS JOIN for Cartesian Product

A CROSS JOIN with no connecting columns for joining produces a Cartesian product: combines all rows of the left table with all rows of the right tables. If the left table has x rows and the right table y rows, the CROSS JOIN is going to have x*y rows. That is called Cartesian explosion as it happens sometimes unintentionally in database development. In fact, a huge CROSS JOIN can bring SQL Server "to its knees", overwhelming CPU and disk resources. On the same note, no matter how powerful is the hardware platform, a bad runaway query can make SQL Server unresponsive to normal queries from other connections. T-SQL script to demonstrate CROSS JOIN.

```
USE AdventureWorks2012;
```

```
-- Cardinality of CROSS JOIN
SELECT count(*) from HumanResources.Employee;          -- 290
SELECT count(*) from HumanResources.Department;        -- 16
SELECT 16 * 290;                                        -- 4640
```

```
SELECT          E.BusinessEntityID                AS EMPLOYEEID,
                D.Name                            AS DEPARTMENT
FROM   HumanResources.Employee E   CROSS JOIN HumanResources.Department D
ORDER  BY       EMPLOYEEID,        DEPARTMENT;
-- (4640 row(s) affected) - Partial results.
```

EMPLOYEEID	DEPARTMENT
1	Production Control
1	Purchasing
1	Quality Assurance
1	Research and Development
1	Sales
1	Shipping and Receiving
1	Tool Design
2	Document Control
2	Engineering
2	Executive
2	Facilities and Maintenance
2	Finance
2	Human Resources
2	Information Services
2	Marketing
2	Production

CTE Use for Sequence Generation & Duplicate Removal

A CROSS JOIN can be used to create combinatorical results. In the next example, a multiplication table is created using a CROSS JOIN which is also a SELF-JOIN. CTE stands for Common Table Expression, which can be used as a table in SELECT and other queries. The master database spt_values table is used to get a sequence of numbers. The ".." in the table reference means: use the default schema which is "dbo".

```
; WITH cteNumber                                   -- cte for numbers 1 to 10
   AS (SELECT NUMBER   FROM   master..spt_values  WHERE  TYPE = 'P'
         AND NUMBER BETWEEN 1 AND 10)
SELECT MULTIPLICATION=CONCAT( ltrim(str(B.NUMBER)) , ' * '
             , ltrim(str(A.NUMBER)) , ' = ' ,  ltrim(str(A.NUMBER * B.NUMBER)) )
FROM   cteNumber A   CROSS JOIN cteNumber B;  -- (100 row(s) affected) - Partial results.
```

MULTIPLICATION
3 * 3 = 9
3 * 4 = 12
3 * 5 = 15

Two ways of removing duplicates with CTE-s.

```
USE tempdb;     SELECT ProductNumber, Name AS ProductName, ListPrice
INTO Product FROM AdventureWorks2012.Production.Product  WHERE ListPrice > 0.0;
GO -- (304 row(s) affected)
INSERT Product                            -- Insert duplicates
SELECT TOP (50) ProductNumber, Name AS ProductName, ListPrice * 1.1
FROM AdventureWorks2012.Production.Product  WHERE ListPrice > 0.0 ORDER BY NEWID();
GO -- (50 row(s) affected)
```

```
WITH cteDups AS ( SELECT ProductNumber, MIN(ListPrice) AS LowPrice  FROM Product
GROUP BY ProductNumber HAVING COUNT(*) > 1)
DELETE P  FROM Product P INNER JOIN cteDups cte on P.ProductNumber = cte.ProductNumber
                  AND P.ListPrice > cte.LowPrice;
GO -- (50 row(s) affected)
```

```
-- Insert duplicates
INSERT Product SELECT TOP (70) ProductNumber, Name AS ProductName, ListPrice * 1.1
FROM AdventureWorks2012.Production.Product WHERE ListPrice > 0.0 ORDER BY NEWID();
GO -- (70 row(s) affected)
```

```
WITH cteDups AS ( SELECT *, ROW_NUMBER() OVER (PARTITION BY ProductNumber ORDER BY ListPrice)
AS RN  FROM Product )     DELETE cteDups WHERE RN > 1;
GO  -- (70 row(s) affected)
```

INNER JOIN with 7 Tables

T-SQL query lists AdventureWorks Cycles retail (web) customers with total purchase amount and order dates. The name & address displays multiple times if a customer did multiple purchases. Generally, that is undesirable, and requires end-user report design considerations how to resolve it. The sorting uses Sales.SalesOrderHeader OrderDate which is datetime data type, instead of the mdy format string report date. mdy string format dates do not sort in chronological order.

```
USE AdventureWorks;
GO
```

```
SELECT CONCAT(C.LastName, ', ', C.FirstName)              AS CustomerName,
        A.City,
        SP.Name                                            AS State,
        CR.Name                                            AS Country,
        A.PostalCode,
        FORMAT(SOH.TotalDue, 'c','en-US')                  AS SalesAmount,
        FORMAT(SOH.OrderDate,'d')                          AS OrderDate
FROM Person.Contact AS C
  INNER JOIN Sales.Individual AS I
        ON C.ContactID = I.ContactID
  INNER JOIN Sales.CustomerAddress AS CA
        ON CA.CustomerID = I.CustomerID
  INNER JOIN Person.Address AS A
        ON A.AddressID = CA.AddressID
  INNER JOIN Person.StateProvince SP
        ON SP.StateProvinceID = A.StateProvinceID
  INNER JOIN Person.CountryRegion CR
        ON CR.CountryRegionCode = SP.CountryRegionCode
  INNER JOIN Sales.SalesOrderHeader SOH
        ON C.ContactID = SOH.CustomerID
ORDER BY CustomerName, soh.OrderDate ;
-- (16493 row(s) affected)  - Partial results.
```

CustomerName	City	State	Country	PostalCode	SalesAmount	OrderDate
Adams, Aaron	Downey	California	United States	90241	$734.70	3/4/2004
Adams, Adam	Newport Beach	California	United States	92625	$2,566.12	4/16/2004
Adams, Alex	Lake Oswego	Oregon	United States	97034	$2,410.63	3/18/2003
Adams, Alex	Lake Oswego	Oregon	United States	97034	$1,293.38	12/9/2003
Adams, Alex	Lake Oswego	Oregon	United States	97034	$2,643.12	2/1/2004
Adams, Angel	Burlingame	California	United States	94010	$865.20	5/24/2003
Adams, Angel	Burlingame	California	United States	94010	$2,597.81	3/1/2004
Adams, Carlos	Langford	British Columbia	Canada	V9	$44.18	6/28/2004
Adams, Connor	Westminster	British Columbia	Canada	V3L 1H4	$183.74	4/14/2004
Adams, Elijah	Seattle	Washington	United States	98104	$8.04	11/2/2003

INNER JOIN with GROUP BY Subquery

We have to make the GROUP BY subquery into a derived table first. Subsequently, we can apply it just like any other table in a query.

```
USE AdventureWorks2012;
GO
```

```
SELECT  Subcategory = Name,
        Color,
        ColorCount,
        AvgListPrice
FROM    (
        SELECT ProductSubcategoryID,                    -- grouping column
         Color = COALESCE(Color, 'N/A'),                -- grouping column with transformation
         ColorCount = COUNT(*),                         -- aggregate function
         AvgListPrice = AVG(COALESCE(ListPrice, 0.0))   -- aggregate function
        FROM   AdventureWorks2008.Production.Product
        GROUP  BY       ProductSubcategoryID,
                        Color) x                        -- derived table (subquery)
    INNER JOIN Production.ProductSubcategory psc
         ON psc.ProductSubcategoryID = x.ProductSubcategoryID
ORDER  BY Subcategory,
        Color;
GO
-- (48 row(s) affected) - Partial results.
```

Subcategory	Color	ColorCount	AvgListPrice
Bib-Shorts	Multi	3	89.990000
Bike Racks	N/A	1	120.000000
Bike Stands	N/A	1	159.000000
Bottles and Cages	N/A	3	7.990000
Bottom Brackets	N/A	3	92.240000
Brakes	Silver	2	106.500000
Caps	Multi	1	8.990000
Chains	Silver	1	20.240000
Cleaners	N/A	1	7.950000
Cranksets	Black	3	278.990000
Derailleurs	Silver	2	106.475000
Fenders	N/A	1	21.980000

Handling Non-additive Columns in GROUP BY Summary Queries

Frequently occurs that it would be nice if there is a "SUM" function for a non-additive column such as color. There is none. The MIN function can be used on a string column like color, the MAX function, and even a range can be presented like: CONCAT(MIN(Color), ' - ', MAX(Color)) XML PATH to the rescue! With XML PATH the group of non-additive members can be turned into a delimited string list. Naturally, the list must be modest size, otherwise we have a results presentation issue.

```
SELECT  Subcategory         = ps.[Name],        ColorList= Stuff((SELECT DISTINCT  ', ' + Color AS [text()]
                                                FROM AdventureWorks2012.Production.Product p
                                                WHERE p.ProductSubcategoryID = ps.ProductSubcategoryID
                                                FOR XML PATH ('')),1,1,''),
        AvgPrice= AVG(ListPrice),  ItemCount          = COUNT(ProductID)
FROM    AdventureWorks2012.Production.ProductSubcategory ps
                INNER JOIN   AdventureWorks2012.Production.Product p
 ON ps.ProductSubcategoryID = p.ProductSubcategoryID  WHERE Color is not NULL AND ListPrice > 0.0
GROUP BY ps.ProductSubcategoryID,  ps.[Name]  ORDER BY Subcategory;
GO -- (23 row(s) affected) - Partial results.
```

Subcategory	ColorList	AvgPrice	ItemCount
Helmets	Black, Blue, Red	34.99	3
Hydration Packs	Silver	54.99	1
Jerseys	Multi, Yellow	51.99	8
Mountain Bikes	Black, Silver	1683.365	32
Mountain Frames	Black, Silver	678.2535	28

Adding UDF Computed Column to Table

In addition to expressions, a computed column can be defined by a scalar-valued function which can even have complex INNER JOINs. Demonstration uses a simple query in UDF.

```
USE tempdb;
GO
CREATE FUNCTION dbo.ufnLatestProductPrice (@ProductID INT)       -- Price lookup scalar-valued UDF
RETURNS MONEY  AS BEGIN RETURN (SELECT ListPrice FROM AdventureWorks2012.Production.Product
     WHERE ProductID = @ProductID); END
GO
SELECT ProductID, ProductNumber, Name, Color   INTO Product        -- Test table
FROM AdventureWorks.Production.Product  WHERE ListPrice > 0.0 ORDER BY ProductID;
GO  -- (304 row(s) affected)
ALTER TABLE Product ADD Price AS (dbo.ufnLatestProductPrice (ProductID));
GO
SELECT TOP (2) * FROM Product ORDER BY Price DESC;
```

ProductID	ProductNumber	Name	Color	Price
749	BK-R93R-62	Road-150 Red, 62	Red	3578.27
750	BK-R93R-44	Road-150 Red, 44	Red	3578.27

Making Queries Readable & Results Presentable

A database developer has to make a query readable for productivity gain in development and ease of maintenance. At the same time the results must be readable to the user. The next query with results demonstrates how to achieve both objectives.

```
USE AdventureWorks2012;
GO
```

```
SELECT PC.Name                                    AS Category,
       PSC.Name                                   AS Subcategory,
       PM.Name                                    AS Model,
       P.Name                                     AS ProductName,
       FORMAT(ListPrice,'c','en-US')              AS Price
FROM Production.Product AS P
   INNER JOIN Production.ProductModel AS PM
        ON PM.ProductModelID = P.ProductModelID
   INNER JOIN Production.ProductSubcategory AS PSC
        ON PSC.ProductSubcategoryID = P.ProductSubcategoryID
   INNER JOIN Production.ProductCategory AS PC
        ON PC.ProductCategoryID = PSC.ProductCategoryID
ORDER BY Category, Subcategory, ProductName;
GO
-- (295 row(s) affected) - Partial results.
```

The confusing 4 "Name" columns are clarified by well-chosen column aliases. The meaningful column aliases are used in the ORDER BY clause even though not required. To help the user, the list price is currency formatted.

Category	Subcategory	Model	ProductName	Price
Accessories	Bike Racks	Hitch Rack - 4-Bike	Hitch Rack - 4-Bike	$120.00
Accessories	Bike Stands	All-Purpose Bike Stand	All-Purpose Bike Stand	$159.00
Accessories	Bottles and Cages	Mountain Bottle Cage	Mountain Bottle Cage	$9.99
Accessories	Bottles and Cages	Road Bottle Cage	Road Bottle Cage	$8.99
Accessories	Bottles and Cages	Water Bottle	Water Bottle - 30 oz.	$4.99
Accessories	Cleaners	Bike Wash	Bike Wash - Dissolver	$7.95
Accessories	Fenders	Fender Set - Mountain	Fender Set - Mountain	$21.98
Accessories	Helmets	Sport-100	Sport-100 Helmet, Black	$34.99
Accessories	Helmets	Sport-100	Sport-100 Helmet, Blue	$34.99
Accessories	Helmets	Sport-100	Sport-100 Helmet, Red	$34.99

A 12 Tables JOIN Query

The next query JOINs 11 tables, some of the tables occur more than once in the query.

```
USE AdventureWorks;
```

```
DECLARE        @Year int,
               @Month int

SET @Year      = 2004;
SET @Month     = 1;

SELECT SOH.SalesOrderNumber                          AS SON,
    SOH.PurchaseOrderNumber                          AS PO,
    S.Name                                           AS Store,
    CONVERT(VARCHAR, SOH.OrderDate, 110)             AS OrderDate,
    CONVERT(VARCHAR, SOH.ShipDate, 110)              AS ShipDate,
    FORMAT(TotalDue,'c','en-US')                     AS [Total Due],
    CONCAT(C.FirstName,' ',C.LastName)               AS SalesStaff,
    SM.Name                                          AS ShpngMethod,
    BA.AddressLine1                                  AS BlngAddress1,
    Isnull(BA.AddressLine2, '')                      AS BlngAddress2,
    BA.City                                          AS BlngCity,
    BSP.Name                                         AS BlngStateProvince,
    BA.PostalCode                                    AS BlngPostalCode,
    BCR.Name                                         AS BlngCountryRegion,
    SA.AddressLine1                                  AS ShpngAddress1,
    Isnull(SA.AddressLine2, '')                      AS ShpngAddress2,
    SA.City                                          AS ShpngCity,
    SSP.Name                                         AS ShpngStateProvince,
    SA.PostalCode                                    AS ShpngPostalCode,
    SCR.Name                                         AS ShpngCountryRegion,
    CONCAT(CC.FirstName,' ',CC.LastName)             AS CustomerContact,
    CC.Phone                                         AS CustomerPhone,
    SOH.AccountNumber
FROM   Person.Address SA
    INNER JOIN Person.StateProvince SSP
        ON SA.StateProvinceID = SSP.StateProvinceID
    INNER JOIN Person.CountryRegion SCR
        ON SSP.CountryRegionCode = SCR.CountryRegionCode
    INNER JOIN Sales.SalesOrderHeader SOH
        INNER JOIN Person.Contact CC
            ON SOH.ContactID = CC.ContactID
        INNER JOIN Person.Address BA
            INNER JOIN Person.StateProvince BSP
                ON BA.StateProvinceID = BSP.StateProvinceID
            INNER JOIN Person.CountryRegion BCR
```

```
-- T-SQL query continued

                    ON BSP.CountryRegionCode =
                       BCR.CountryRegionCode
                 ON SOH.BillToAddressID = BA.AddressID
          ON SA.AddressID = SOH.ShipToAddressID
     INNER JOIN Person.Contact C
            INNER JOIN HumanResources.Employee E
                 ON C.ContactID = E.ContactID
          ON SOH.SalesPersonID = E.EmployeeID
     INNER JOIN Purchasing.ShipMethod SM
          ON SOH.ShipMethodID = SM.ShipMethodID
     INNER JOIN Sales.Store S
          ON SOH.CustomerID = S.CustomerID
WHERE  SOH.OrderDate >= datefromparts(@Year, @month, 1)
     AND  SOH.OrderDate < dateadd(mm,1,datefromparts(@Year, @month, 1))
ORDER  BY Store,   OrderDate DESC;
GO
-- (96 row(s) affected) - Partial results.
```

SON	PO	Store	OrderDate	ShipDate	Total Due	SalesStaff	ShpngMethod	BlngAddress1
SO61257	PO3741176337	Activity Center	01-01-2004	01-08-2004	$12,764.08	Tsvi Reiter	CARGO TRANSPORT 5	Factory Stores Of America
SO61256	PO1421187796	All Cycle Shop	01-01-2004	01-08-2004	$201.08	Tete Mensa-Annan	CARGO TRANSPORT 5	25111 228th St Sw
SO61251	PO6380165323	All Seasons Sports Supply	01-01-2004	01-08-2004	$2,863.30	Michael Blythe	CARGO TRANSPORT 5	Ohms Road
SO61263	PO5452121402	Amalgamated Parts Shop	01-01-2004	01-08-2004	$39,103.04	Rachel Valdez	CARGO TRANSPORT 5	Brunnenstr 422
SO61227	PO10730172247	Area Bike Accessories	01-01-2004	01-08-2004	$75,916.89	Shu Ito	CARGO TRANSPORT 5	6900 Sisk Road
SO61187	PO13978135025	Basic Bike Company	01-01-2004	01-08-2004	$72.92	David Campbell	CARGO TRANSPORT 5	15 East Main
SO61190	PO12441157171	Best Cycle Store	01-01-2004	01-08-2004	$49,337.61	Rachel Valdez	CARGO TRANSPORT 5	Berliner Platz 45
SO61221	PO15399128383	Best o' Bikes	01-01-2004	01-08-2004	$5,872.73	Michael Blythe	CARGO TRANSPORT 5	250880 Baur Blvd
SO61173	PO522171689	Better Bike Shop	01-01-2004	01-08-2004	$38,511.29	Tsvi Reiter	CARGO TRANSPORT 5	42525 Austell Road
SO61254	PO4872176154	Bicycle Exporters	01-01-2004	01-08-2004	$10,665.06	Rachel Valdez	CARGO TRANSPORT 5	Hellweg 4934
SO61243	PO7859152962	Bike Dealers Association	01-01-2004	01-08-2004	$18,976.48	Shu Ito	CARGO TRANSPORT 5	9952 E. Lohman Ave.
SO61250	PO4930183869	Bikes for Kids and Adults	01-01-2004	01-08-2004	$3,852.87	Jae Pak	CARGO TRANSPORT 5	9900 Ronson Drive
SO61209	PO11484136165	Casual Bicycle Store	01-01-2004	01-08-2004	$37,314.33	Jillian Carson	CARGO TRANSPORT 5	Westside Plaza
SO61204	PO15312134209	Citywide Service and Repair	01-01-2004	01-08-2004	$29,797.18	Jae Pak	CARGO TRANSPORT 5	Box 99354 300 Union Street
SO61192	PO10092119585	Classic Cycle Store	01-01-2004	01-08-2004	$3,691.57	Jillian Carson	CARGO TRANSPORT 5	630 Oldgate Lane

Order of Tables or Predicates Does Not Matter

Frequent question: does the order of tables matter in a JOIN? Should I put BETWEEN predicate before LIKE predicate? Valid syntax variations do not matter. The database engine translates the query to an internal form prior to creating an execution plan. Thus the different variations get translated to the same internal form. The only way we have some control over the database engine if we rewrite a single statement complex query to a multi-statements script.

Nondeterministic CTE

CTE is evaluated for every reference, therefore it may return different results if certain functions are used such as newid(), thus yielding a nondeterministic CTE.

```
;WITH CTE AS (SELECT Random = NEWID()),
CTE1 AS (SELECT * FROM CTE),
CTE2 AS (SELECT * FROM CTE),
CTE3 AS (SELECT * FROM CTE),
CTE4 AS (SELECT * FROM CTE),
CTE5 AS (SELECT * FROM CTE)
SELECT * FROM CTE1
UNION ALL
SELECT * FROM CTE2
UNION ALL
SELECT * FROM CTE3
UNION ALL
SELECT * FROM CTE4
UNION ALL
SELECT * FROM CTE5
UNION ALL
SELECT * FROM CTE
UNION ALL
SELECT * FROM CTE
UNION ALL
SELECT * FROM CTE;
```

Random
08D45FE2-52C6-4E15-83A3-0B2F27837887
D6A094E6-0C8A-43E4-B6C4-8821F6EE8E73
281A5852-3D9A-4F2A-99FA-F60EE28FD2E0
C327ED19-5C03-4D9B-A8E8-6ACABAA08F1C
80DDE508-A6AA-4F2B-AB2F-CEEF7EC5E163
5F611B03-46F4-4EED-A8E0-76020527899D
FF8DAE17-65F6-4D80-8AF5-29EBAEBD2FEB
CF342DC9-4CF9-46FD-87F0-3213106C447D

The CROSS APPLY Operator

The APPLY (CROSS APPLY & OUTER APPLY) operators were introduced with SQL Server 2005. The CROSS APPLY operator merges rows from tables (or views) with rows from table-valued function, a form of JOIN.

```
USE AdventureWorks2012;
SELECT
        q.last_execution_time                    AS LastRun,
        t.TEXT                                   AS QueryText,
        q.sql_handle                             AS SQLHandle
FROM    sys.dm_exec_query_stats AS q                         -- system view
                CROSS APPLY
                sys.dm_exec_sql_text(q.sql_handle) AS t      -- table-valued system function
WHERE LEFT(t.TEXT,8)='SELECT *'  ORDER BY LastRun DESC;
```

LastRun	QueryText
2016-08-01 14:46:12.537	SELECT * FROM Sales.SalesOrderHeader
2016-08-01 14:44:54.257	SELECT * FROM Production.Product
2016-08-01 13:29:25.213	SELECT * FROM sys.dm_os_wait_stats
2016-08-01 09:36:57.980	select * from sys.sysforeignkeys s
2016-08-01 09:36:39.077	select * from sysforeignkeys s

```
-- Return the top N purchase order by amount - inline table-valued function
CREATE FUNCTION dbo.ufnGetTopNPurchases(@VendorID AS INT, @N AS INT)
RETURNS TABLE  AS
RETURN
  SELECT TOP ( @N ) *    FROM Purchasing.PurchaseOrderHeader
  WHERE VendorID = @VendorID    ORDER BY TotalDue DESC;
GO   -- Command(s) completed successfully.
```

```
-- List the top 5 highest purchases from vendors
SELECT  V.VendorID,
        P.PurchaseOrderID,
        FORMAT(P.TotalDue, 'c','en-US')      AS TotalDue
FROM    Purchasing.Vendor AS V  CROSS APPLY  dbo.ufnGetTopNPurchases(V.VendorID, 5) AS P
ORDER BY  V.VendorID, TotalDue DESC
-- (395 row(s) affected) - Partial results.
```

VendorID	PurchaseOrderID	TotalDue
74	325	$1,654.75
74	1727	$855.22
74	2517	$855.22
74	3307	$855.22
74	167	$785.61

Using CROSS APPLY with Columns Specified Table Alias

A regular table alias would result in error in the following delimited string list query. Table alias with column(s) specifications "o(list)" works, the table alias is "o", it has one column "list".

CROSS APPLY: Most Popular Sales Products Info

```
CREATE FUNCTION ufnProductDetails (@ProductID INT) RETURNS TABLE  AS RETURN
(          SELECT ProductNumber, ListPrice, Color
           FROM Production.Product WHERE ProductID = @ProductID  );
GO
;WITH CTE AS (     SELECT ProductID FROM Sales.SalesOrderDetail
                                        GROUP BY ProductID HAVING COUNT(*) > 1000)
SELECT ProductNumber, ListPrice, Color
FROM CTE CROSS APPLY ufnProductDetails (ProductID)
WHERE Color is not null ORDER BY ProductNumber;  -- (15 row(s) affected);
```

CHAPTER 13: Basic SELECT Statement Syntax & Examples

Simple SELECT Statement Variations

SELECT is the most famous statement in the SQL language. It is used to query tables, and generate reports for users. Although SQL Server Reporting Services and other 3rd party packages available for reporting purposes, frequently reports are generated straight from the database with SELECT queries. The next query returns all rows, all columns sorted on DepartmentID.

```
USE AdventureWorks2012;
```

```
SELECT * FROM   HumanResources.Department  ORDER BY DepartmentID;
-- (16 row(s) affected)
```

DepartmentID	Name	GroupName	ModifiedDate
1	Engineering	Research and Development	1998-06-01 00:00:00.000
2	Tool Design	Research and Development	1998-06-01 00:00:00.000
3	Sales	Sales and Marketing	1998-06-01 00:00:00.000
4	Marketing	Sales and Marketing	1998-06-01 00:00:00.000
5	Purchasing	Inventory Management	1998-06-01 00:00:00.000
6	Research and Development	Research and Development	1998-06-01 00:00:00.000
7	Production	Manufacturing	1998-06-01 00:00:00.000
8	Production Control	Manufacturing	1998-06-01 00:00:00.000
9	Human Resources	Executive General and Administration	1998-06-01 00:00:00.000
10	Finance	Executive General and Administration	1998-06-01 00:00:00.000
11	Information Services	Executive General and Administration	1998-06-01 00:00:00.000
12	Document Control	Quality Assurance	1998-06-01 00:00:00.000
13	Quality Assurance	Quality Assurance	1998-06-01 00:00:00.000
14	Facilities and Maintenance	Executive General and Administration	1998-06-01 00:00:00.000
15	Shipping and Receiving	Inventory Management	1998-06-01 00:00:00.000
16	Executive	Executive General and Administration	1998-06-01 00:00:00.000

Since the time part of ModifiedDate is not being used, and that makes business sense, we can format it just as date.

```
SELECT TOP (3) DepartmentID, Name, GroupName, CONVERT(DATE, ModifiedDate) AS ModifiedDate
FROM   HumanResources.Department  ORDER BY DepartmentID;
-- (16 row(s) affected)
```

DepartmentID	Name	GroupName	ModifiedDate
1	Engineering	Research and Development	1998-06-01
2	Tool Design	Research and Development	1998-06-01
3	Sales	Sales and Marketing	1998-06-01

SELECT query with sort on EnglishProductName in DESCending order

ASCending sort is the default.

```
USE AdventureWorksDW2012
GO
```

```
SELECT *
FROM DimProduct
ORDER BY EnglishProductName DESC
GO
-- (606 row(s) affected) - Partial results.
```

EnglishProductName	SpanishProductName	FrenchProductName	StandardCost
Women's Tights, S	Mallas para mujer, P	Collants pour femmes, taille S	30.9334
Women's Tights, M	Mallas para mujer, M	Collants pour femmes, taille M	30.9334
Women's Tights, L	Mallas para mujer, G	Collants pour femmes, taille L	30.9334
Women's Mountain Shorts, S			26.1763
Women's Mountain Shorts, M			26.1763
Women's Mountain Shorts, L			26.1763
Water Bottle - 30 oz.			1.8663
Touring-Panniers, Large	Cesta de paseo, grande	Sacoches de vélo de randonnée, grande capacité	51.5625
Touring-3000 Yellow, 62	Paseo: 3000, amarilla, 62	Vélo de randonnée 3000 jaune, 62	461.4448
Touring-3000 Yellow, 58	Paseo: 3000, amarilla, 58	Vélo de randonnée 3000 jaune, 58	461.4448

The next query sorts on the SpanishProductName column in ascending order.

```
SELECT *
FROM DimProduct
ORDER BY SpanishProductName ASC
GO
-- (606 row(s) affected) - Partial results.
```

EnglishProductName	SpanishProductName
HL Crankset	Bielas GA
LL Crankset	Bielas GB
ML Crankset	Bielas GM
Mountain Pump	Bomba de montaña
Cable Lock	Cable antirrobo
Chain	Cadena
Mountain Bike Socks,	Calcetines para bicicleta de montaña, G

Sorting on FrenchProductName, if empty, use EnglishProductName.

```
SELECT * FROM DimProduct ORDER BY FrenchProductName, EnglishProductName;
GO
```

Using the TOP Clause in SELECT Queries

The TOP clause limits the number of rows returned as specified in the TOP expression according the sorted order if any. In the following query, the sorting is based on a major key (LastName) and a minor key (FirstName).

```
USE AdventureWorks2012
GO
```

```
SELECT   TOP 100 *
FROM     Person.Person ORDER BY LastName, FirstName
-- (100 row(s) affected) - Partial results.
```

BusinessEntityID	PersonType	Title	FirstName	LastName	EmailPromotion
285	SP	Mr.	Syed	Abbas	0
293	SC	Ms.	Catherine	Abel	1
295	SC	Ms.	Kim	Abercrombie	0
2170	GC	NULL	Kim	Abercrombie	2
38	EM	NULL	Kim	Abercrombie	2
211	EM	NULL	Hazem	Abolrous	0
2357	GC	NULL	Sam	Abolrous	1
297	SC	Sr.	Humberto	Acevedo	2
291	SC	Mr.	Gustavo	Achong	2
299	SC	Sra.	Pilar	Ackerman	0

The total population of the Person.Person table is 19,972 rows.

```
SELECT   * FROM     Person.Person ORDER BY LastName, FirstName
-- (19972 row(s) affected)
```

We can also count the rows applying the COUNT function.

```
SELECT   RowsCount = count(*)  FROM     Person.Person
-- 19972
```

When counting, it is safe to count the PRIMARY KEY (ProductID) values.

```
SELECT   RowsCount = count(ProductID)    FROM     Production.Product;
-- 504
```

```
SELECT   RowsCount = count(Color)    FROM     Production.Product;        -- 256
```

Using the WHERE Clause in SELECT Queries

The WHERE clause filters the rows to be returned according the one or more predicates. The next T-SQL scripts demonstrate simple WHERE clause predicates, including multiple WHERE conditions.

```
-- Last name starts with S
SELECT *
FROM    Person.Person
WHERE   LEFT(LastName,1) = 'S'
ORDER BY LastName;
-- (2130 row(s) affected)
```

```
-- First name is Shelly
SELECT  *
FROM    Person.Person
WHERE   FirstName = 'Shelly'
ORDER BY LastName;
-- (1 row(s) affected)
```

```
-- First name is John
SELECT  *
FROM    Person.Person
WHERE   FirstName = 'John'
ORDER BY LastName;
-- (58 row(s) affected)
```

```
-- First name John, last name starts with S - Multiple WHERE conditions
SELECT  *
FROM    Person.Person
WHERE   FirstName = 'John'
        AND LEFT(LastName,1) = 'S'
ORDER BY LastName ;
-- (2 row(s) affected)
```

```
-- Last name starts with S OR first name starts with J
SELECT  *
FROM    Person.Person
WHERE   LEFT(FirstName,1) = 'J'   OR LEFT(LastName,1) = 'S'
ORDER BY LastName;
-- (4371 row(s) affected)
```

```
-- Last name starts with S AND first name starts with J
SELECT  *
FROM    Person.Person  WHERE   LEFT(FirstName,1) = 'J'    AND LEFT(LastName,1) = 'S'
ORDER BY LastName;    -- (221 row(s) affected)
```

Using Literals in SELECT Queries

Literals or constants are used commonly in T-SQL queries, also as defaults for columns, local variables, and parameters. The format of a literal depends on the data type of the value it represents. The database engine may perform implicit conversion to match data types. Explicit conversion of literals can be achieved with the CONVERT or CAST functions. T-SQL scripts demonstrate literal use in WHERE clause predicates.

```
USE AdventureWorks2012;
-- Integer literal  in WHERE clause predicate
SELECT * FROM Production.Product
WHERE ProductID = 800;
-- (1 row(s) affected)
```

```
-- String literal in WHERE clause predicate
SELECT * FROM Production.Product WHERE Color = 'Blue';
-- (26 row(s) affected)
```

```
USE AdventureWorksDW2012;
-- UNICODE (2 bytes per character) string literal
SELECT * FROM DimProduct
WHERE SpanishProductName = N'Jersey clásico de manga corta, G';
-- (1 row(s) affected)
```

```
-- UNICODE string literal
SELECT * FROM DimProduct
WHERE FrenchProductName = N'Roue arrière de vélo de randonnée';
-- (1 row(s) affected)
```

```
USE AdventureWorks2012;
-- Money literal in WHERE clause predicate
SELECT * FROM Production.Product
WHERE ListPrice > = $2000.0;
-- (35 row(s) affected)
```

```
-- Floating point literal with implicit conversion to MONEY
SELECT * FROM Production.Product  WHERE ListPrice > = 2.000E+3;
-- (35 row(s) affected)
```

```
-- Hex (binary) literal
SELECT * FROM Production.Product  WHERE rowguid >= 0x23D89CEE9F444F3EB28963DE6BA2B737
-- (302 row(s) affected)
```

```
-- The rest of the 504 products
SELECT * FROM Production.Product  WHERE rowguid < 0x23D89CEE9F444F3EB28963DE6BA2B737
-- (202 row(s) affected)
```

Date & Time Literals in SELECT Queries

Date and time literals appear to come from an infinite pool. Every country has tens of string date & time variations. Despite the many external string representation, **date, datetime, datetime, time, smalldatetime** and other temporal data types have unique, well-defined representation within the database engine.

ymd date literal format is the cleanest. There is eternal confusion about the North American mdy string date format and the European dmy string date format. The date and time format with "T" separator (last one) is the ISO date time format literal. ANSI Date literal - YYYYMMDD - the best choice since it work in any country.

CONVERT or CAST Date Time Literal	Result
SELECT [Date] = CAST('20160228' AS date)	2016-02-28
SELECT [Datetime] = CAST('20160228' AS datetime)	2016-02-28 00:00:00.000
SELECT [SmallDatetime] = CAST('20160228' AS smalldatetime)	2016-02-28 00:00:00
SELECT [Datetime] = CONVERT(datetime,'2016-02-28')	2016-02-28 00:00:00.000
SELECT [Datetime2] = CONVERT(datetime2,'2016-02-28')	2016-02-28 00:00:00.0000000
SELECT [Datetime] = CONVERT(datetime, '20160228')	2016-02-28 00:00:00.000
SELECT [Datetime2] = CONVERT(datetime2,'20160228')	2016-02-28 00:00:00.0000000
SELECT [Datetime] = CAST('Mar 15, 2016' AS datetime)	2016-03-15 00:00:00.000
SELECT [Datetime2] = CAST('Mar 15, 2016' AS datetime2)	2016-03-15 00:00:00.0000000
SELECT [Date] = CAST('Mar 15, 2016' AS date)	2016-03-15
SELECT CAST('16:40:31' AS datetime)	1900-01-01 16:40:31.000
SELECT CAST('16:40:31' AS time)	16:40:31.0000000
SELECT [Datetime] = CAST('Mar 15, 2016 12:07:34.444' AS datetime)	2016-03-15 12:07:34.443
SELECT [Datetime2] = CAST('Mar 15, 2016 12:07:34.4445555' AS datetime2)	2016-03-15 12:07:34.4445555
SELECT [Datetime] = CAST('2016-03-15T12:07:34.513' AS datetime)	2016-03-15 12:07:34.513

ymd, dmy & mdy String Date Format Literals

Date and time string literals are the least understood part of the T-SQL language by database developers. It is a constant source of confusion and frustration, in addition huge economic cost of lost programmer's productivity. ymd, dmy & mdy are the main string date formats. Some countries use ydm format. Setting dateformat overrides the implicit setting by language.

The basic principles:

- **There is only one DATETIME data type internal format**, independent where SQL Server is operated: New York, London, Amsterdam, Berlin, Moscow, Hong Kong, Singapore, Tokyo, Melbourne or Rio de Janeiro.
- There are hundreds of national string date & time formats which have nothing to do with SQL Server.
- String date must be properly converted to DATETIME format.

```
SET DATEFORMAT ymd
SELECT convert(datetime,'16/05/08')                -- 2016-05-08 00:00:00.000
```

```
-- Setting DATEFORMAT to UK-Style (European)
SET DATEFORMAT dmy
SELECT convert(datetime,'20/05/16')                -- 2016-05-20 00:00:00.000
```

```
-- Setting DATEFORMAT to US-Style
SET DATEFORMAT mdy
SELECT convert(datetime,'05/20/16')                -- 2016-05-20 00:00:00.000
SELECT convert(datetime,'05/20/2016')              -- 2016-05-20 00:00:00.000
```

Interestingly we can achieve the same implicit conversion action by setting language.

```
-- Setting DATEFORMAT ymd  via language
SET LANGUAGE Japanese;  SELECT convert(datetime,'16/05/08') ;        -- 2016-05-08 00:00:00.000
```

```
-- Setting DATEFORMAT to UK-Style (European) via language
SET LANGUAGE British;  SELECT convert(datetime,'20/05/16');          -- 2016-05-20 00:00:00.000
SELECT convert(datetime,'05/20/16');
/* Msg 242, Level 16, State 3, Line 3
The conversion of a varchar data type to a datetime data type resulted in an out-of-range value.  */
```

```
-- Setting DATEFORMAT to US-Style via language
SET LANGUAGE English;  SELECT convert(datetime,'05/20/16');          -- 2016-05-20 00:00:00.000
SELECT convert(datetime,'05/20/2016');             -- 2016-05-20 00:00:00.000
SELECT convert(datetime,'20/05/2016');
/* Msg 242, Level 16, State 3, Line 4
The conversion of a varchar data type to a datetime data type resulted in an out-of-range value.  */
```

Setting DATEFIRST with Literal

DATEFIRST indicates the first day of the week which may vary by country, culture or business. The next T-SQL script demonstrates how it can be set by integer literal 1-7. It overrides the implicit setting by language. @@DATEFIRST is a system (SQL Server database engine) variable.

```
SET DATEFIRST 7 -- Sunday as first day of the week
SELECT DATEPART(dw, '20160315');                          -- 3
SELECT DATENAME(dw, '20160315');      SELECT @@DATEFIRST                    -- Tuesday 7
```

```
SET DATEFIRST 1 -- Monday as first day of the week
SELECT DATEPART(dw, '20160315');                          -- 2
SELECT DATENAME(dw, '20160315');      SELECT @@DATEFIRST                    -- Tuesday 1
```

Language Setting - SET LANGUAGE

DATEFIRST is tied to the language setting, just the like the date format (ymd, dmy, or mdy).

```
SET LANGUAGE us_english;              SELECT DATEPART(dw, '20160315');      -- 3
SELECT DATENAME(dw, '20160315');      SELECT @@DATEFIRST                    -- Tuesday 7
```

```
SET LANGUAGE german;                  SELECT DATEPART(dw, '20160315');      -- 2
SELECT DATENAME(dw, '20160315');      SELECT @@DATEFIRST                    -- Dienstag 1
```

```
SET LANGUAGE british;                 SELECT DATEPART(dw, '20160315');      -- 2
SELECT DATENAME(dw, '20160315');      SELECT @@DATEFIRST                    -- Tuesday 1
```

```
SET LANGUAGE hungarian;               SELECT DATEPART(dw, '20160315');      -- 2
SELECT DATENAME(dw, '20160315');      SELECT @@DATEFIRST                    -- kedd 1
```

```
SET LANGUAGE spanish;                 SELECT DATEPART(dw, '20160315');      -- 2
SELECT DATENAME(dw, '20160315');      SELECT @@DATEFIRST                    -- Martes 1
```

DATETIMEOFFSET Data Type with Zone Awareness

DATETIMEOFFSET data type can be used to store time zone information in addition to datetime. The offset is from UTC (Coordinated Universal Time).

```
DECLARE @datetimeoffset datetimeoffset(3) = '2016-10-23 12:24:10 +03:00';
DECLARE @date date= @datetimeoffset, @datetime datetime = @datetimeoffset;
SELECT @datetimeoffset AS [@datetimeoffset], @date AS [date], @datetime AS [datetime];
```

@datetimeoffset	date	datetime
2016-10-23 12:24:10.000 +03:00	2016-10-23	2016-10-23 12:24:10.000

The sys.syslanguages System View

The syslanguages table contains not only language related information, but date related settings as well.

```
SELECT
	langid,
	dateformat,
	datefirst,
	name					AS native_language,
	alias					AS english,
	left(shortmonths, 15)			AS shortmonths,
	left(days,15)				AS days
FROM AdventureWorks2012.sys.syslanguages
ORDER BY langid;
GO
-- (34 row(s) affected)  -  Partial results.
```

langid	dateformat	datefirst	native_language	english	shortmonths	days
0	mdy	7	us_english	English	Jan,Feb,Mar,Apr	Monday,Tuesday,
1	dmy	1	Deutsch	German	Jan,Feb,Mär,Apr	Montag,Dienstag
2	dmy	1	Français	French	janv,févr,mars,	lundi,mardi,mer
3	ymd	7	日本語	Japanese	01,02,03,04,05,	月曜日,火曜日,水曜日,木曜日
4	dmy	1	Dansk	Danish	jan,feb,mar,apr	mandag,tirsdag,
5	dmy	1	Español	Spanish	Ene,Feb,Mar,Abr	Lunes,Martes,Mi
6	dmy	1	Italiano	Italian	gen,feb,mar,apr	lunedì,martedì,
7	dmy	1	Nederlands	Dutch	jan,feb,mrt,apr	maandag,dinsdag
8	dmy	1	Norsk	Norwegian	jan,feb,mar,apr	mandag,tirsdag,
9	dmy	7	Português	Portuguese	jan,fev,mar,abr	segunda-feira,t
10	dmy	1	Suomi	Finnish	tammi,helmi,maa	maanantai,tiist
11	ymd	1	Svenska	Swedish	jan,feb,mar,apr	måndag,tisdag,o
12	dmy	1	čeština	Czech	I,II,III,IV,V,V	pondělí,úterý,s
13	ymd	1	magyar	Hungarian	jan,febr,márc,á	hétfő,kedd,szer
14	dmy	1	polski	Polish	I,II,III,IV,V,V	poniedziałek,wt
15	dmy	1	română	Romanian	Ian,Feb,Mar,Apr	luni,marţi,mier
16	ymd	1	hrvatski	Croatian	sij,vel,ožu,tra	ponedjeljak,uto
17	dmy	1	slovenčina	Slovak	I,II,III,IV,V,V	pondelok,utorok
18	dmy	1	slovenski	Slovenian	jan,feb,mar,apr	ponedeljek,tore
19	dmy	1	ελληνικά	Greek	Ιαν,Φεβ,Μαρ,Απρ	Δευτέρα,Τρίτη,Τ
20	dmy	1	български	Bulgarian	януари,февруари	понеделник,втор
21	dmy	1	русский	Russian	янв,фев,мар,апр	понедельник,вто
22	dmy	1	Türkçe	Turkish	Oca,Şub,Mar,Nis	Pazartesi,Salı,
23	dmy	1	British	British English	Jan,Feb,Mar,Apr	Monday,Tuesday,
24	dmy	1	eesti	Estonian	jaan,veebr,märt	esmaspäev,teisi
25	ymd	1	latviešu	Latvian	jan,feb,mar,apr	pirmdiena,otrdi
26	ymd	1	lietuvių	Lithuanian	sau,vas,kov,bal	pirmadienis,ant
27	dmy	7	Português (Brasil)	Brazilian	Jan,Fev,Mar,Abr	Segunda-Feira,T
28	ymd	7	繁體中文	Traditional Chinese	01,02,03,04,05,	星期一,星期二,星期三,星期四
29	ymd	7	한국어	Korean	01,02,03,04,05,	월요일,화요일,수요일,목요일
30	ymd	7	简体中文	Simplified Chinese	01,02,03,04,05,	星期一,星期二,星期三,星期四
31	dmy	1	Arabic	Arabic	Jan,Feb,Mar,Apr	Monday,Tuesday,
32	dmy	7	ไทย	Thai	ม.ค.,ก.พ.,มี.ค.	จันทร์,อังคาร,พ
33	dmy	1	norsk (bokmål)	Bokmål	jan,feb,mar,apr	mandag,tirsdag,

DBCC USEROPTIONS & @@options

The DBCC USEROPTIONS command displays some of the connection (session) settings. As we have seen these settings play an important part on how date literals are interpreted by the system such as dateformat. We can also query the @@options system variable.

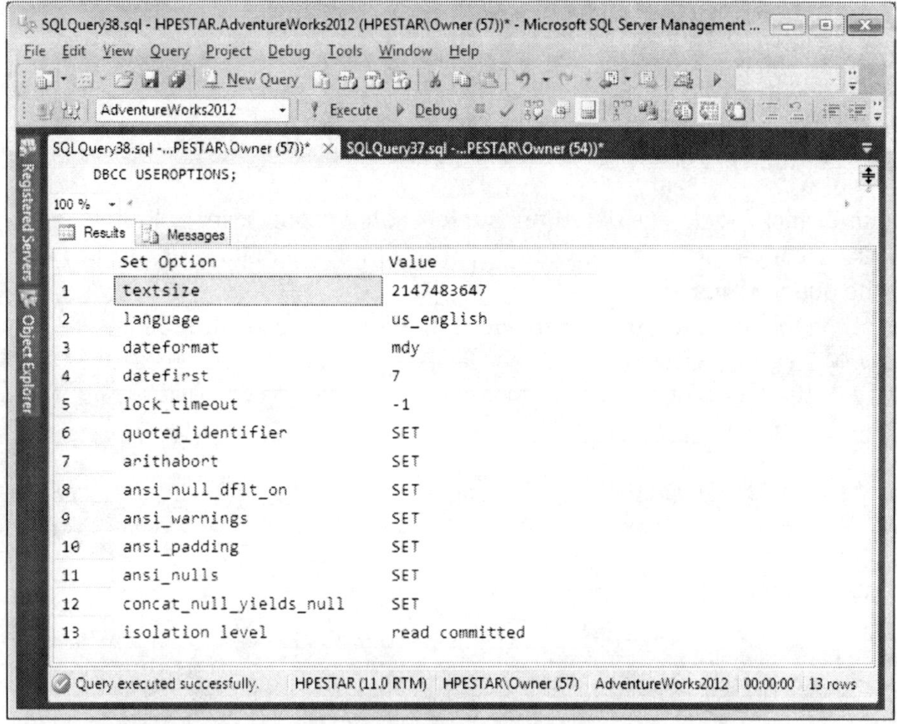

```
DECLARE @options int = @@options; PRINT @options;
IF ( (1 & @options) = 1 ) PRINT 'DISABLE_DEF_CNST_CHK';
IF ( (2 & @options) = 2 ) PRINT 'IMPLICIT_TRANSACTIONS';
IF ( (4 & @options) = 4 ) PRINT 'CURSOR_CLOSE_ON_COMMIT';
IF ( (8 & @options) = 8 ) PRINT 'ANSI_WARNINGS';
IF ( (16 & @options) = 16 ) PRINT 'ANSI_PADDING';
IF ( (32 & @options) = 32 ) PRINT 'ANSI_NULLS';
IF ( (64 & @options) = 64 ) PRINT 'ARITHABORT';
IF ( (128 & @options) = 128 ) PRINT 'ARITHIGNORE';
IF ( (256 & @options) = 256 ) PRINT 'QUOTED_IDENTIFIER';
IF ( (512 & @options) = 512 ) PRINT 'NOCOUNT';
IF ( (1024 & @options) = 1024 ) PRINT 'ANSI_NULL_DFLT_ON';
IF ( (2048 & @options) = 2048 ) PRINT 'ANSI_NULL_DFLT_OFF';
IF ( (4096 & @options) = 4096 ) PRINT 'CONCAT_NULL_YIELDS_NULL' ;
IF ( (8192 & @options) = 8192 ) PRINT 'NUMERIC_ROUNDABORT';
IF ( (16384 & @options) = 16384 ) PRINT 'XACT_ABORT';
```

Easy SELECT Queries for Fun & Learning

T-SQL scripts to demonstrate simple, easy-to-read SELECT query variations. Important note: alias column names cannot be reused in successive computed columns by expressions or anywhere else in the query except the ORDER BY clause.

```
-- Datetime range with string literal date
SELECT  * FROM   Person.Person
WHERE   ModifiedDate <= '2002-08-09 00:00:00.000'  ORDER BY LastName;
-- (38 row(s) affected)
```

NOTE

The string literal above looks like datetime, but it is not. It is only a string literal. The database engine will try to convert it to datetime data type at runtime (implicit conversion), and if successful the query will be executed.

The syntax of the following query is OK, however, it will fail at execution time.

```
SELECT  * FROM   Person.Person  WHERE   ModifiedDate <= 'New York City'  ORDER BY LastName;
/* Msg 241, Level 16, State 1, Line 1 Conversion failed when converting date and/or time from character
string. */
```

```
-- Complimentary (remaining) datetime range specified again with string literal
SELECT * FROM   Person.Person  WHERE   ModifiedDate > '2002-08-09 00:00:00.000'  ORDER BY
LastName;
-- (19934 row(s) affected)
```

```
-- Total rows in Person.Person
SELECT ( 38 + 19934 ) AS TotalRows;   -- 19972
```

```
SELECT count(* ) FROM   Person.Person -- 19972
```

```
SELECT TableRows = count(* ),  Calc = 38 + 19934  FROM   Person.Person;  -- 19972     19972
```

```
-- Get prefix left of comma or entire string if there is no comma present
SELECT TOP 4                                                                    ProductNumber,
        LEFT(Name, COALESCE(NULLIF(CHARINDEX(',',Name)-1,-1),LEN(Name)))        AS NamePrefix,
        Name                                                                    AS ProductName
FROM AdventureWorks2012.Production.Product   WHERE CHARINDEX(',',Name) > 0
ORDER BY ProductName;
```

ProductNumber	NamePrefix	ProductName
VE-C304-L	Classic Vest	Classic Vest, L
VE-C304-M	Classic Vest	Classic Vest, M
VE-C304-S	Classic Vest	Classic Vest, S
GL-F110-L	Full-Finger Gloves	Full-Finger Gloves, L

NULL refers to no information available. Note: "=" and "!=" operators are not used with NULL; "IS" or "IS NOT" operators are applicable.

```
SELECT *
FROM    Person.Person
WHERE   AdditionalContactInfo IS NOT NULL
ORDER BY LastName;
-- (10 row(s) affected)
```

```
SELECT *
FROM    Person.Person
WHERE   AdditionalContactInfo IS NULL
ORDER BY LastName;
-- (19962 row(s) affected)
```

```
SELECT   DISTINCT FirstName
FROM    Person.Person
ORDER BY FirstName;      -- (1018 row(s) affected)
```

```
-- Summary revenue by product, interesting sort
USE AdventureWorks2012;
GO
SELECT  TOP 10 p.Name                                          AS ProductName,
  FORMAT(SUM(((OrderQty * UnitPrice) * (1.0 - UnitPriceDiscount))),'c','en-US') AS SubTotal
FROM Production.Product AS p
INNER JOIN Sales.SalesOrderDetail AS sod
ON p.ProductID = sod.ProductID
GROUP BY p.Name
ORDER BY REVERSE(p.Name);
```

ProductName	SubTotal
Water Bottle - 30 oz.	$28,654.16
Hydration Pack - 70 oz.	$105,826.42
LL Mountain Frame - Black, 40	$1,198.99
ML Mountain Frame - Black, 40	$14,229.41
Mountain-300 Black, 40	$501,648.88
Mountain-500 Black, 40	$101,734.12
LL Mountain Frame - Silver, 40	$69,934.28
ML Mountain Frame-W - Silver, 40	$195,826.39
Mountain-500 Silver, 40	$145,089.43
Mountain-400-W Silver, 40	$323,703.82

DISTINCT & GROUP BY operations are generally "expensive".

```
SELECT   DISTINCT LastName FROM     Person.Person ORDER BY LastName;  -- (1206 row(s) affected)
```

```
-- LastName popularity descending
SELECT LastName,     Frequency = count(* )
FROM     Person.Person
GROUP BY LastName
ORDER BY Frequency DESC;
GO
```

LastName	Frequency
Diaz	211
Hernandez	188
Sanchez	175
Martinez	173
Torres	172
Martin	171
Perez	170
Gonzalez	169
Lopez	168
Rodriguez	166

```
-- Sort on column not in SELECT list - Note: demo only, confusing to end user
SELECT   LastName
FROM     Person.Person
ORDER BY FirstName;
-- (19972 row(s) affected)
```

```
-- Sort on column not in SELECT list
SELECT   Name = CONCAT(LastName, ', ', FirstName )
FROM     Person.Person
ORDER BY LastName;
-- (19972 row(s) affected)
```

```
-- Sort on column alias
SELECT   Name = CONCAT(LastName, ', ', FirstName )
FROM     Person.Person
ORDER BY Name;
-- (19972 row(s) affected)
```

```
SELECT   CONCAT(LastName, ', ', FirstName ) AS FullName
FROM     Person.Person
WHERE    LastName >= 'K'  ORDER BY LastName;
-- (12057 row(s) affected)
```

The NULLIF Function Actually Creates A NULL

```
SELECT   CONCAT(LastName, ', ', FirstName )  AS FullName
FROM     Person.Person  WHERE   LastName < 'K'  ORDER BY LastName;
-- (7915 row(s) affected)
```

```
-- Cardinality check
SELECT Difference= ((count(*)) - (12057 + 7915)) FROM  Person.Person; -- 0
```

```
-- Using the NULLIF function in counting
-- Count of all list prices - no NULLs in column
SELECT COUNT(ListPrice) FROM   AdventureWorks2012.Production.Product
-- 504
```

```
-- Counts only when ListPrice != 0 - does not count NULLs (ListPrice = 0.0)
SELECT COUNT(NULLIF(ListPrice,0.0)) FROM   AdventureWorks2012.Production.Product
-- 304
```

```
SELECT COUNT(ListPrice)   FROM   AdventureWorks2012.Production.Product   WHERE ListPrice = 0;
-- 200
```

Cardinality of DISTINCT & GROUP BY Clauses

The cardinality of DISTINCT and the cardinality of GROUP BY are the same with the same column(s).

```
-- FirstName by popularity descending
SELECT FirstName,
           Freq = count(* )
FROM     Person.Person
GROUP BY FirstName
ORDER BY Freq DESC;
-- (1018 row(s) affected)
```

FirstName	Freq
Richard	103
Katherine	99
Marcus	97
James	97
Jennifer	96
Dalton	93
Lucas	93
Alexandra	93
Morgan	92
Seth	92

```
SELECT   DISTINCT FirstName  FROM     Person.Person  ORDER BY FirstName;  -- (1018 row(s) affected)
```

Column Alias Can only Be Used in ORDER BY

Column aliases cannot be used in other computed columns (expressions), neither in the WHERE clause or GROUP BY clause.

```
SELECT   TableRows = count(* ),
         Calculated = 38 + 19934,
         Difference = (count(*) - 38 - 19934)
FROM  Person.Person;
```

TableRows	Calculated	Difference
19972	19972	0

Workarounds for Column Alias Use Restriction

There is a simple workaround for recycling column aliases in other clauses than just the ORDER BY: make the query into a derived table (x) and include it in an outer query. Similarly, CTEs can be used instead of derived tables.

```
-- Derived table workaround
SELECT TableRows, Calculated, Difference = TableRows - Calculated
FROM (
         SELECT   TableRows = count(* ),      Calculated = 38 + 19934,
         FROM  Person.Person
         ) x ;  -- Derived table
GO
```

TableRows	Calculated	Difference
19972	19972	0

```
-- CTE workaround
;WITH CTE AS (
         SELECT   TableRows = count(* ),      Calculated = 38 + 19934
         FROM  Person.Person)
-- Outer query
SELECT TableRows, Calculated, Difference = TableRows - Calculated
FROM CTE;
```

TableRows	Calculated	Difference
19972	19972	0

When the Clock Strikes Midnight: datetime Behaviour

This is one of the most troublesome issues in T-SQL programming (midnight bug, Cinderella syndrome): the predicate YYYYMMDD (date string literal) = DatetimeColumn does not include the entire day, only records with time at midnight: 00:00:00.000 .

```
USE AdventureWorks2012;
-- Note: only midnight 2003-08-09 included
-- Even a second after midnight is not included like 2003-08-09 00:00:01.000
SELECT  * FROM   Person.Person
WHERE      ModifiedDate BETWEEN '2002-08-09 00:00:00.000'   AND '2003-08-09 00:00:00.000'
ORDER BY LastName;
GO -- (396 row(s) affected)
```

```
-- Entire day of 2003-08-09 included
-- The count same as before because no records after midnight 2003-08-09
SELECT  * FROM   Person.Person
WHERE     ModifiedDate >= '2002-08-09 00:00:00.000'  AND ModifiedDate <  '2003-08-10 00:00:00.000'
ORDER BY LastName;
GO  -- (396 row(s) affected)
```

To get the orders for the entire day today, **we have to use the >= and < operators with the datetime OrderDate**. The >= **predicate** will get it from last midnight and on. The **< predicate** will get it up to next midnight. (Note: demo only, there is no current data in Sales.SalesOrderHeader.)

```
SELECT * FROM Sales.SalesOrderHeader
WHERE OrderDate >=   CONVERT(DATE, getdate())                        -- Today's date
   AND OrderDate <    DATEADD(dd,1,CONVERT(DATE, getdate()));        -- Tomorrow's date
```

LEFT(), RIGHT() & SUBSTRING() String Functions

```
SELECT   FirstCharOfFirstName = LEFT(FirstName,1),                  -- column alias
         FirstCharOfLastName  = LEFT(LastName,1),                   -- column alias
         LastCharOfLastName  = RIGHT(LastName,1),                   -- column alias
         FullName = CONCAT(FirstName, SPACE(1), LastName) ,         -- column alias
         *                                                          -- wild card, all columns
FROM     Person.Person
WHERE    SUBSTRING(FirstName,1,1) = 'J'
      AND SUBSTRING (LastName,1,1) = 'S'
      AND (RIGHT(LastName,1) = 'H' OR RIGHT(LastName,1) = 'Z')
ORDER BY LastName;
-- (59 row(s) affected) - Partial result.
```

FirstCharOfFirstName	FirstCharOfLastName	LastCharOfLastName	FullName	BusinessEntityID
J	S	z	Jacqueline Sanchez	8975
J	S	z	Jada Sanchez	9499
J	S	z	Jade Sanchez	9528
J	S	z	Janelle Sanchez	18590
J	S	z	Jared Sanchez	15266
J	S	z	Jarrod Sanchez	2948
J	S	z	Jay Sanchez	10298
J	S	z	Jennifer Sanchez	20440
J	S	z	Jeremiah Sanchez	15292
J	S	z	Jermaine Sanchez	8040

```
-- Sort on first column
SELECT BusinessEntityID, JobTitle, SUBSTRING(JobTitle, 5, 7)  AS MiddleOfJobTitle
FROM   HumanResources.Employee
WHERE  BirthDate <= '1960/12/31'    -- date literal (constant)
ORDER BY 1;
-- (27 row(s) affected) - Partial results.
```

BusinessEntityID	JobTitle	MiddleOfJobTitle
5	Design Engineer	gn Engi
6	Design Engineer	gn Engi
12	Tool Designer	Design
15	Design Engineer	gn Engi
23	Marketing Specialist	eting S
27	Production Supervisor - WC60	uction

```
-- String functions usage in formatting
DECLARE @SSN char(9) = '123456789';
SELECT SSN=CONCAT(LEFT(@SSN,3),'-', SUBSTRING(@SSN,4,2),'-', RIGHT(@SSN,4));
-- 123-45-6789
```

ASCII value range is 0-127. Extended ASCII: 128-255. Size is 8-bit, one byte.

```
SELECT TOP 5    ProductNumber,
                SUBSTRING(ProductNumber,9,1)            AS MiddleSubstring,
                ASCII(SUBSTRING(ProductNumber,9,1))     AS ASCIIValue
FROM AdventureWorks2008.Production.Product
WHERE LEN(ProductNumber) > 8
ORDER BY Name;                      - OK syntax, but does not make sense
```

ProductNumber	MiddleSubstring	ASCIIValue
VE-C304-L	L	76
VE-C304-M	M	77
VE-C304-S	S	83
GL-F110-L	L	76
GL-F110-M	M	77

> **NOTE**
> Table columns and columns by expressions (computed) can be mixed in a query at will.

```
-- Computed (expressions) & table columns
SELECT FirstCharOfFirstName = LEFT(FirstName,1),        -- string expression
       FirstCharOfLastName  = LEFT(LastName,1),         -- string expression
       FullName = CONCAT(LastName, ', ', FirstName ),   -- string expression
       SquareOfID = SQUARE(BusinessEntityID),           -- math expression
       *                                                -- wild card, all table columns
FROM   Person.Person
WHERE  LEFT(FirstName,1) = 'J'
   AND LEFT(LastName,2) = 'Sm'
ORDER BY FullName;
-- (14 row(s) affected)  - Partial results.
```

FirstCharOfFirstName	FirstCharOfLastName	FullName	SquareOfID	BusinessEntityID
J	S	Smith, Jacob	348680929	18673
J	S	Smith, James	308986084	17578
J	S	Smith, Jasmine	129572689	11383
J	S	Smith, Jeff	3139984	1772
J	S	Smith, Jennifer	122699929	11077
J	S	Smith, Jeremiah	20511841	4529
J	S	Smith, Jessica	145829776	12076
J	S	Smith, John	332041284	18222
J	S	Smith, Jonathan	312228900	17670
J	S	Smith, Jose	300710281	17341
J	S	Smith, Joseph	357474649	18907
J	S	Smith, Joshua	351825049	18757
J	S	Smith, Julia	121616784	11028
J	S	Smith, Justin	324900625	18025

Transact-SQL Reserved Keywords

List of reserved keywords in SQL Server 2012 Transact-SQL. Keywords can only be used as delimited identifiers such as [Inner] or "Order".

ADD	EXTERNAL	PROCEDURE
ALL	FETCH	PUBLIC
ALTER	FILE	RAISERROR
AND	FILLFACTOR	READ
ANY	FOR	READTEXT
AS	FOREIGN	RECONFIGURE
ASC	FREETEXT	REFERENCES
AUTHORIZATION	FREETEXTTABLE	REPLICATION
BACKUP	FROM	RESTORE
BEGIN	FULL	RESTRICT
BETWEEN	FUNCTION	RETURN
BREAK	GOTO	REVERT
BROWSE	GRANT	REVOKE
BULK	GROUP	RIGHT
BY	HAVING	ROLLBACK
CASCADE	HOLDLOCK	ROWCOUNT
CASE	IDENTITY	ROWGUIDCOL
CHECK	IDENTITY_INSERT	RULE
CHECKPOINT	IDENTITYCOL	SAVE
CLOSE	IF	SCHEMA
CLUSTERED	IN	SECURITYAUDIT
COALESCE	INDEX	SELECT
COLLATE	INNER	SEMANTICKEYPHRASETABLE
COLUMN	INSERT	SEMANTICSIMILARITYDETAILSTABLE
COMMIT	INTERSECT	SEMANTICSIMILARITYTABLE
COMPUTE	INTO	SESSION_USER
CONSTRAINT	IS	SET
CONTAINS	JOIN	SETUSER
CONTAINSTABLE	KEY	SHUTDOWN
CONTINUE	KILL	SOME
CONVERT	LEFT	STATISTICS
CREATE	LIKE	SYSTEM_USER
CROSS	LINENO	TABLE
CURRENT	LOAD	TABLESAMPLE
CURRENT_DATE	MERGE	TEXTSIZE
CURRENT_TIME	NATIONAL	THEN
CURRENT_TIMESTAMP	NOCHECK	TO
CURRENT_USER	NONCLUSTERED	TOP
CURSOR	NOT	TRAN
DATABASE	NULL	TRANSACTION
DBCC	NULLIF	TRIGGER
DEALLOCATE	OF	TRUNCATE
DECLARE	OFF	TRY_CONVERT
DEFAULT	OFFSETS	TSEQUAL
DELETE	ON	UNION
DENY	OPEN	UNIQUE
DESC	OPENDATASOURCE	UNPIVOT
DISK	OPENQUERY	UPDATE
DISTINCT	OPENROWSET	UPDATETEXT
DISTRIBUTED	OPENXML	USE
DOUBLE	OPTION	USER
DROP	OR	VALUES
DUMP	ORDER	VARYING
ELSE	OUTER	VIEW
END	OVER	WAITFOR
ERRLVL	PERCENT	WHEN
ESCAPE	PIVOT	WHERE
EXCEPT	PLAN	WHILE
EXEC	PRECISION	WITH
EXECUTE	PRIMARY	WITHIN GROUP
EXISTS	PRINT	WRITETEXT
EXIT	PROC	

Case Sensitive Sort with Latin1_General_CS_AI

For case sensitive sort on a column with case insensitive collation, we have use a case sensitive (CS) collation such as Latin1_General_CS_AI.

```
-- CASE INSENSITIVE sort using default collation
SELECT lname FROM
        (SELECT TOP 5 UPPER (LastName) AS lname FROM Person.Person ORDER BY FirstName) x
UNION ALL   SELECT lname FROM
        (SELECT TOP 5 LOWER (LastName) AS lname FROM Person.Person ORDER BY FirstName) y
ORDER BY lname;
-- ADAMS, adams, alexander, ALEXANDER, leonetti, LEONETTI, WRIGHT, WRIGHT, wright, wright
```

```
-- CASE SENSITIVE sort using %CS% collation
SELECT lname FROM ( SELECT lname FROM
  (SELECT TOP 5 UPPER (LastName) AS lname FROM Person.Person ORDER BY FirstName) x
  UNION ALL  SELECT lname FROM
  (SELECT TOP 5 LOWER (LastName) AS lname FROM Person.Person ORDER BY FirstName) y  ) z
ORDER BY lname COLLATE Latin1_General_CS_AI;
-- adams,ADAMS,alexander,ALEXANDER,leonetti,LEONETTI,wright,wright,WRIGHT,WRIGHT
```

The ORDER BY Clause for Sorting Query Results

The ORDER BY clause is located at the very end of the query. In fact the sorting itself takes place after the query executed and generated **an unordered result set**. Although frequently, especially for small sets, the results appear to be sorted, **only an ORDER BY clause can guarantee proper sorting**. INSERT, UPDATE, DELETE & MERGE statement do not support sorting, **the database engine performs all set operations unordered**. T-SQL scripts demonstrate the many variations of the ORDER BY clause.

```
USE AdventureWorks2012;
GO
```

```
-- A column can be used for sorting even though not explicitly used in the SELECT list
SELECT *
FROM   Production.Product
ORDER  BY Name ASC;
GO
```

```
-- Sort on the second column, whatever it may be
SELECT *
FROM   Production.Product
ORDER  BY 2 DESC;
GO
```

```
-- ASCending is the default sort order, it is not necessary to use
SELECT  Name AS ProductName,
        *
FROM   Production.Product
ORDER  BY ProductName ASC;
GO
```

```
SELECT  TOP (10) Name AS ProductName,          *
FROM   Production.Product   ORDER  BY 1 ASC;
```

ProductName	ProductID	Name	ProductNumber	MakeFlag	FinishedGoodsFlag	Color	SafetyStockLevel
Adjustable Race	1	Adjustable Race	AR-5381	0	0	NULL	1000
All-Purpose Bike Stand	879	All-Purpose Bike Stand	ST-1401	0	1	NULL	4
AWC Logo Cap	712	AWC Logo Cap	CA-1098	0	1	Multi	4
BB Ball Bearing	3	BB Ball Bearing	BE-2349	1	0	NULL	800
Bearing Ball	2	Bearing Ball	BA-8327	0	0	NULL	1000
Bike Wash - Dissolver	877	Bike Wash - Dissolver	CL-9009	0	1	NULL	4
Blade	316	Blade	BL-2036	1	0	NULL	800
Cable Lock	843	Cable Lock	LO-C100	0	1	NULL	4
Chain	952	Chain	CH-0234	0	1	Silver	500
Chain Stays	324	Chain Stays	CS-2812	1	0	NULL	1000

Using Column Alias in the ORDER BY Clause

Column alias can be used in an ORDER BY clause. In fact, it should be used to make the query more readable.

```
-- ProductName is a column alias, it can only be used in the ORDER BY clause, not anywhere before
SELECT ProductName = Name, *
FROM Production.Product
WHERE ProductName like '%glove%'
ORDER BY ProductName ASC ;
GO
/* ERROR
Msg 207, Level 16, State 1, Line 3
Invalid column name 'ProductName'.
*/
```

```
-- The TOP clause uses the ORDER BY sorting to select the 5 rows
SELECT TOP (5) ProductName = Name, *
FROM Production.Product
WHERE Name like '%glove%'
ORDER BY ProductName ASC ;
```

ProductName	ProductID	Name	ProductNumber	MakeFlag	FinishedGoodsFlag	Color	SafetyStockLevel
Full-Finger Gloves, L	863	Full-Finger Gloves, L	GL-F110-L	0	1	Black	4
Full-Finger Gloves, M	862	Full-Finger Gloves, M	GL-F110-M	0	1	Black	4
Full-Finger Gloves, S	861	Full-Finger Gloves, S	GL-F110-S	0	1	Black	4
Half-Finger Gloves, L	860	Half-Finger Gloves, L	GL-H102-L	0	1	Black	4
Half-Finger Gloves, M	859	Half-Finger Gloves, M	GL-H102-M	0	1	Black	4

```
-- Descending sort on name which is string data type
SELECT TOP (10) ProductName = Name, *
FROM Production.Product
WHERE Name like '%road%'
ORDER BY ProductName DESC ;
```

.

ProductName	ProductID	Name	ProductNumber	MakeFlag	FinishedGoodsFlag	Color	SafetyStockLevel
Road-750 Black, 58	977	Road-750 Black, 58	BK-R19B-58	1	1	Black	100
Road-750 Black, 52	999	Road-750 Black, 52	BK-R19B-52	1	1	Black	100
Road-750 Black, 48	998	Road-750 Black, 48	BK-R19B-48	1	1	Black	100
Road-750 Black, 44	997	Road-750 Black, 44	BK-R19B-44	1	1	Black	100
Road-650 Red, 62	761	Road-650 Red, 62	BK-R50R-62	1	1	Red	100
Road-650 Red, 60	760	Road-650 Red, 60	BK-R50R-60	1	1	Red	100
Road-650 Red, 58	759	Road-650 Red, 58	BK-R50R-58	1	1	Red	100
Road-650 Red, 52	764	Road-650 Red, 52	BK-R50R-52	1	1	Red	100
Road-650 Red, 48	763	Road-650 Red, 48	BK-R50R-48	1	1	Red	100
Road-650 Red, 44	762	Road-650 Red, 44	BK-R50R-44	1	1	Red	100

Using Table Alias in the ORDER BY Clause

Unlike the column alias, table alias can be used anywhere in the query within the scope of the alias.

```
-- Using table alias in ORDER BY
SELECT P.*
FROM   Production.Product P
ORDER  BY P.Name ASC;
GO
```

ProductID	Name	ProductNumber	MakeFlag	FinishedGoodsFlag	Color	SafetyStockLevel
958	Touring-3000 Blue, 54	BK-T18U-54	1	1	Blue	100
959	Touring-3000 Blue, 58	BK-T18U-58	1	1	Blue	100
960	Touring-3000 Blue, 62	BK-T18U-62	1	1	Blue	100
961	Touring-3000 Yellow, 44	BK-T18Y-44	1	1	Yellow	100
962	Touring-3000 Yellow, 50	BK-T18Y-50	1	1	Yellow	100
963	Touring-3000 Yellow, 54	BK-T18Y-54	1	1	Yellow	100
964	Touring-3000 Yellow, 58	BK-T18Y-58	1	1	Yellow	100
965	Touring-3000 Yellow, 62	BK-T18Y-62	1	1	Yellow	100
842	Touring-Panniers, Large	PA-T100	0	1	Grey	4
870	Water Bottle - 30 oz.	WB-H098	0	1	NULL	4
869	Women's Mountain Shorts, L	SH-W890-L	0	1	Black	4
868	Women's Mountain Shorts, M	SH-W890-M	0	1	Black	4
867	Women's Mountain Shorts, S	SH-W890-S	0	1	Black	4
854	Women's Tights, L	TG-W091-L	0	1	Black	4
853	Women's Tights, M	TG-W091-M	0	1	Black	4
852	Women's Tights, S	TG-W091-S	0	1	Black	4

```
-- Specific column list instead of all (*)
SELECT  Name,
        ProductNumber,
        ListPrice AS PRICE
FROM  Production.Product  P
ORDER  BY P.Name ASC;
GO
```

```
SELECT          Name,
                ProductNumber,
                ListPrice AS PRICE
FROM  Production.Product  P
ORDER  BY P.ListPrice DESC;
```

```
-- Equivalent to above with column alias usage
SELECT          Name,
                ProductNumber,
                ListPrice AS PRICE
FROM  Production.Product  P ORDER  BY PRICE DESC;
```

Easy ORDER BY Queries for Exercises

T-SQL scripts demonstrate easily readable queries with sorted result sets.

```
USE pubs ;
```

```
SELECT TYPE,   AvgPrice=FORMAT(AVG(price) , 'c', 'en-US')
FROM   titles WHERE  royalty = 10 GROUP  BY TYPE ORDER  BY TYPE ;
```

TYPE	AvgPrice
business	$17.31
popular_comp	$20.00
psychology	$14.14
trad_cook	$17.97

```
SELECT              type = type,
                    AvgPrice = FORMAT(AVG(price),'c', 'en-US')
FROM   titles  WHERE  royalty = 10  GROUP  BY type  ORDER  BY AvgPrice;
```

type	AvgPrice
psychology	$14.14
business	$17.31
trad_cook	$17.97
popular_comp	$20.00

```
SELECT   type                                  AS [type],
         FORMAT(AVG(price),'c', 'en-US')       AS AvgPrice
FROM   titles   GROUP  BY [type]  ORDER  BY [type] desc;
```

type	AvgPrice
UNDECIDED	NULL
trad_cook	$15.96
psychology	$13.50
popular_comp	$21.48
mod_cook	$11.49
business	$13.73

An Aggregate Function Can Be Used in an ORDER BY Clause

The NULL related warning message can be turned off: SET ANSI_WARNINGS OFF; alternately ISNULL function can be used in the query.

```
SELECT TYPE, AVG(price) Avg FROM titles  GROUP  BY TYPE ORDER  BY AVG(price);
/* Warning: Null value is eliminated by an aggregate or other SET operation.
(6 row(s) affected) */
```

Eliminate NULL in result with COALESCE or ISNULL functions

```
SELECT [type] = type,
       AvgPrice = COALESCE(FORMAT(AVG(price),'c', 'en-US') ,'')
FROM  titles  GROUP  BY [type]  ORDER  BY [type] desc;
```

type	AvgPrice
UNDECIDED	
trad_cook	$15.96
psychology	$13.50
popular_comp	$21.48
mod_cook	$11.49
business	$13.73

```
SELECT          pub_name                          Publisher,
                FORMAT(AVG(price),'c', 'en-US')   AvgPrice
FROM  titles
    INNER JOIN publishers
     ON  titles.pub_id = publishers.pub_id
GROUP  BY pub_name
ORDER  BY pub_name;
```

Publisher	AvgPrice
Algodata Infosystems	$18.98
Binnet & Hardley	$15.41
New Moon Books	$9.78

```
SELECT TOP(3) * FROM  titles ORDER  BY title;
```

title_id	title	type	pub_id	price	advance	royalty	ytd_sales	notes	pubdate
PC1035	But Is It User Friendly?	popular_comp	1389	22.95	7000.00	16	8780	A survey of software for the naive user, focusing on the 'friendliness' of each.	1991-06-30 00:00:00.000
PS1372	Computer Phobic AND Non-Phobic Individuals: Behavior Variations	psychology	0877	21.59	7000.00	10	375	A must for the specialist, this book examines the difference between those who hate and fear computers and those who don't.	1991-10-21 00:00:00.000
BU1111	Cooking with Computers: Surreptitious Balance Sheets	business	1389	11.95	5000.00	10	3876	Helpful hints on how to use your electronic resources to the best advantage.	1991-06-09 00:00:00.000

```
SELECT TOP(3) *  FROM  publishers  ORDER  BY pub_name;
```

pub_id	pub_name	city	state	country
1389	Algodata Infosystems	Berkeley	CA	USA
0877	Binnet & Hardley	Washington	DC	USA
1622	Five Lakes Publishing	Chicago	IL	USA

Sorting Products by Attributes

```
USE Northwind;
```

```
SELECT          UnitsInStock,
                ProductID,
                ProductName,
                QuantityPerUnit,
                FORMAT( UnitPrice, 'c', 'en-US') AS UnitPrice  -- Column alias is same as column
FROM   Northwind.dbo.Products WHERE  UnitsInStock BETWEEN 15 AND 25  ORDER  BY
UnitsInStock;
```

UnitsInStock	ProductID	ProductName	QuantityPerUnit	UnitPrice
15	7	Uncle Bob's Organic Dried Pears	12 - 1 lb pkgs.	$30.00
15	26	Gumbär Gummibärchen	100 - 250 g bags	$31.23
15	48	Chocolade	10 pkgs.	$12.75
15	70	Outback Lager	24 - 355 ml bottles	$15.00
17	38	Côte de Blaye	12 - 75 cl bottles	$263.50
17	43	Ipoh Coffee	16 - 500 g tins	$46.00
17	62	Tarte au sucre	48 pies	$49.30
17	2	Chang	24 - 12 oz bottles	$19.00
19	60	Camembert Pierrot	15 - 300 g rounds	$34.00
20	24	Guaraná Fantástica	12 - 355 ml cans	$4.50
20	35	Steeleye Stout	24 - 12 oz bottles	$18.00
20	51	Manjimup Dried Apples	50 - 300 g pkgs.	$53.00
21	54	Tourtière	16 pies	$7.45
21	56	Gnocchi di nonna Alice	24 - 250 g pkgs.	$38.00
22	11	Queso Cabrales	1 kg pkg.	$21.00
22	64	Wimmers gute Semmelknödel	20 bags x 4 pieces	$33.25
24	13	Konbu	2 kg box	$6.00
24	63	Vegie-spread	15 - 625 g jars	$43.90
25	19	Teatime Chocolate Biscuits	10 boxes x 12 pieces	$9.20

```
-- A second key is necessary for unique ordering
SELECT  TOP(8)  UnitsInStock,
                ProductID,
                ProductName,
                QuantityPerUnit,
                FORMAT( UnitPrice, 'c', 'en-US') AS UnitPrice
FROM   Northwind.dbo.Products
WHERE  UnitsInStock BETWEEN 15 AND 25 ORDER  BY UnitsInStock, ProductName;
```

UnitsInStock	ProductID	ProductName	QuantityPerUnit	UnitPrice
15	48	Chocolade	10 pkgs.	$12.75
15	26	Gumbär Gummibärchen	100 - 250 g bags	$31.23
15	70	Outback Lager	24 - 355 ml bottles	$15.00
15	7	Uncle Bob's Organic Dried Pears	12 - 1 lb pkgs.	$30.00
17	2	Chang	24 - 12 oz bottles	$19.00
17	38	Côte de Blaye	12 - 75 cl bottles	$263.50
17	43	Ipoh Coffee	16 - 500 g tins	$46.00
17	62	Tarte au sucre	48 pies	$49.30

Changing WHERE condition changes the cardinality of result set

```
SELECT          UnitsInStock,
                ProductID,
                ProductName,
                QuantityPerUnit,
                FORMAT( UnitPrice, 'c', 'en-US')          AS UnitPrice
FROM   Northwind.dbo.Products
WHERE  UnitsInStock = 15 or UnitsInStock =  25  -- same as UnitsInStock IN (15, 25)
ORDER  BY UnitsInStock, ProductName;
```

UnitsInStock	ProductID	ProductName	QuantityPerUnit	UnitPrice
15	48	Chocolade	10 pkgs.	$12.75
15	26	Gumbär Gummibärchen	100 - 250 g bags	$31.23
15	70	Outback Lager	24 - 355 ml bottles	$15.00
15	7	Uncle Bob's Organic Dried Pears	12 - 1 lb pkgs.	$30.00
25	19	Teatime Chocolate Biscuits	10 boxes x 12 pieces	$9.20

```
SELECT   TOP(7)   UnitsInStock,
                  ProductID,
                  ProductName,
                  QuantityPerUnit,
                  FORMAT( UnitPrice, 'c', 'en-US')          AS UnitPrice
FROM   Northwind.dbo.Products  ORDER  BY UnitsInStock DESC, ProductName ASC;
```

UnitsInStock	ProductID	ProductName	QuantityPerUnit	UnitPrice
125	75	Rhönbräu Klosterbier	24 - 0.5 l bottles	$7.75
123	40	Boston Crab Meat	24 - 4 oz tins	$18.40
120	6	Grandma's Boysenberry Spread	12 - 8 oz jars	$25.00
115	55	Pâté chinois	24 boxes x 2 pies	$24.00
113	61	Sirop d'érable	24 - 500 ml bottles	$28.50
112	33	Geitost	500 g	$2.50
112	36	Inlagd Sill	24 - 250 g jars	$19.00

```
SELECT   TOP(5)   UnitsInStock, ProductID, ProductName,        QuantityPerUnit,
                  FORMAT( UnitPrice, 'c', 'en-US') AS UnitPrice
FROM   Northwind.dbo.Products
WHERE  UnitsInStock > 15   AND UnitsInStock < 25  ORDER  BY UnitsInStock DESC, ProductName ASC;
```

UnitsInStock	ProductID	ProductName	QuantityPerUnit	UnitPrice
24	13	Konbu	2 kg box	$6.00
24	63	Vegie-spread	15 - 625 g jars	$43.90
22	11	Queso Cabrales	1 kg pkg.	$21.00
22	64	Wimmers gute Semmelknödel	20 bags x 4 pieces	$33.25
21	56	Gnocchi di nonna Alice	24 - 250 g pkgs.	$38.00

The "Tricky" BETWEEN & NOT BETWEEN Operators

They are very English-like, but results should be verified to make sure they work as intended.

```
SELECT  TOP(5)  UnitsInStock, ProductID, ProductName,       QuantityPerUnit,
                FORMAT( UnitPrice, 'c', 'en-US') AS UnitPrice
FROM   Northwind.dbo.Products
WHERE  UnitsInStock BETWEEN 15 AND 25
ORDER  BY UnitsInStock DESC, ProductName ASC;
GO
```

UnitsInStock	ProductID	ProductName	QuantityPerUnit	UnitPrice
25	19	Teatime Chocolate Biscuits	10 boxes x 12 pieces	$9.20
24	13	Konbu	2 kg box	$6.00
24	63	Vegie-spread	15 - 625 g jars	$43.90
22	11	Queso Cabrales	1 kg pkg.	$21.00
22	64	Wimmers gute Semmelknödel	20 bags x 4 pieces	$33.25

```
SELECT  TOP(5)  UnitsInStock, ProductID, ProductName,       QuantityPerUnit,
                FORMAT( UnitPrice, 'c', 'en-US') AS UnitPrice
FROM   Northwind.dbo.Products
WHERE  UnitsInStock NOT BETWEEN 15 AND 25
ORDER  BY UnitsInStock DESC, ProductName ASC;
```

UnitsInStock	ProductID	ProductName	QuantityPerUnit	UnitPrice
125	75	Rhönbräu Klosterbier	24 - 0.5 l bottles	$7.75
123	40	Boston Crab Meat	24 - 4 oz tins	$18.40
120	6	Grandma's Boysenberry Spread	12 - 8 oz jars	$25.00
115	55	Pâté chinois	24 boxes x 2 pies	$24.00
113	61	Sirop d'érable	24 - 500 ml bottles	$28.50

```
SELECT          Orders.OrderID,
                Shippers.*
FROM   Shippers
    INNER JOIN Orders
      ON ( Shippers.ShipperID = Orders.ShipVia )
ORDER  BY Orders.OrderID;
GO
-- (830 row(s) affected) - Partial results.
```

OrderID	ShipperID	CompanyName	Phone
10248	3	Federal Shipping	(503) 555-9931
10249	1	Speedy Express	(503) 555-9831
10250	2	United Package	(503) 555-3199
10251	1	Speedy Express	(503) 555-9831
10252	2	United Package	(503) 555-3199
10253	2	United Package	(503) 555-3199

A second key is frequently required in sorting exception is PRIMARY KEY column.

```
SELECT   OrderID,
         ProductID,
         FORMAT( UnitPrice, 'c', 'en-US')              AS UnitPrice,
         Quantity,
         Discount
FROM  [Order Details]  ORDER  BY OrderID ASC, ProductID ASC;
GO
-- (2155 row(s) affected) - Partial results.
```

OrderID	ProductID	UnitPrice	Quantity	Discount
10248	11	$14.00	12	0
10248	42	$9.80	10	0
10248	72	$34.80	5	0
10249	14	$18.60	9	0
10249	51	$42.40	40	0
10250	41	$7.70	10	0
10250	51	$42.40	35	0.15
10250	65	$16.80	15	0.15

```
-- Sort keys are different from expression column EmployeeName
SELECT   CONCAT(LastName,', ', FirstName)  AS EmployeeName ,
         Title, City, Country
FROM   Northwind.dbo.Employees ORDER  BY LastName,  FirstName ASC;
```

EmployeeName	Title	City	Country
Buchanan, Steven	Sales Manager	London	UK
Callahan, Laura	Inside Sales Coordinator	Seattle	USA
Davolio, Nancy	Sales Representative	Seattle	USA
Dodsworth, Anne	Sales Representative	London	UK
Fuller, Andrew	Vice President, Sales	Tacoma	USA
King, Robert	Sales Representative	London	UK
Leverling, Janet	Sales Representative	Kirkland	USA
Peacock, Margaret	Sales Representative	Redmond	USA
Suyama, Michael	Sales Representative	London	UK

```
-- Equivalent sort
SELECT TOP(3)    CONCAT(LastName,', ', FirstName) AS EmployeeName ,    Title, City, Country
FROM   Northwind.dbo.Employees  ORDER  BY EmployeeName ASC;
```

EmployeeName	Title	City	Country
Buchanan, Steven	Sales Manager	London	UK
Callahan, Laura	Inside Sales Coordinator	Seattle	USA
Davolio, Nancy	Sales Representative	Seattle	USA

Using Multiple Keys in the ORDER BY Clause

If a single sort key does not result in unique ordering, multiple keys can be used. In the next example the Price (major) key is based on a column which is not unique. If we add Name as a second (minor) key, unique ordering will be guaranteed since Name is a unique column, it has a unique index and not null. It's worth noting if Name would allow nulls, we would need a third key for unique ordering.

```
-- Single key sort
SELECT   P.Name,
         P.ProductNumber,
         P.ListPrice                AS PRICE
FROM   Production.Product  P
WHERE  P.ProductLine = 'R'   AND P.DaysToManufacture < 4    ORDER  BY  P. ListPrice DESC;
```

Name	ProductNumber	PRICE
HL Road Frame - Black, 58	FR-R92B-58	1431.50
HL Road Frame - Red, 58	FR-R92R-58	1431.50
HL Road Frame - Red, 62	FR-R92R-62	1431.50
HL Road Frame - Red, 44	FR-R92R-44	1431.50
HL Road Frame - Red, 48	FR-R92R-48	1431.50
HL Road Frame - Red, 52	FR-R92R-52	1431.50
HL Road Frame - Red, 56	FR-R92R-56	1431.50
HL Road Frame - Black, 62	FR-R92B-62	1431.50
HL Road Frame - Black, 44	FR-R92B-44	1431.50
HL Road Frame - Black, 48	FR-R92B-48	1431.50
HL Road Frame - Black, 52	FR-R92B-52	1431.50
ML Road Frame-W - Yellow, 40	FR-R72Y-40	594.83

```
-- Double key sort - PRICE is the major key, Name is the minor key
SELECT   P.Name,
         P.ProductNumber,
         P.ListPrice                AS PRICE
FROM   Production.Product  P
WHERE  P.ProductLine = 'R'   AND P.DaysToManufacture < 4   ORDER  BY  PRICE DESC, Name;
```

Name	ProductNumber	PRICE
HL Road Frame - Black, 44	FR-R92B-44	1431.50
HL Road Frame - Black, 48	FR-R92B-48	1431.50
HL Road Frame - Black, 52	FR-R92B-52	1431.50
HL Road Frame - Black, 58	FR-R92B-58	1431.50
HL Road Frame - Black, 62	FR-R92B-62	1431.50
HL Road Frame - Red, 44	FR-R92R-44	1431.50
HL Road Frame - Red, 48	FR-R92R-48	1431.50
HL Road Frame - Red, 52	FR-R92R-52	1431.50
HL Road Frame - Red, 56	FR-R92R-56	1431.50
HL Road Frame - Red, 58	FR-R92R-58	1431.50
HL Road Frame - Red, 62	FR-R92R-62	1431.50
ML Road Frame - Red, 44	FR-R72R-44	594.83

ORDER BY in Complex Queries

An ORDER BY can be in a complex query and/or ORDER BY can be complex itself. T-SQL scripts demonstrate complex ORDER BY usage.

```
-- We cannot tell just by query inspection if the second key is sufficient for unique ordering or not
-- If we inspect the result set it becomes obvious that we need a third key at least (SalesOrderID unsorted)
SELECT  ProductName              = P.Name,
        NonDiscountSales         = ( OrderQty * UnitPrice ),
        Discounts                = ( ( OrderQty * UnitPrice ) * UnitPriceDiscount ),
        SalesOrderID
FROM   Production.Product P
    INNER JOIN Sales.SalesOrderDetail SOD
        ON P.ProductID = SOD.ProductID
ORDER  BY       ProductName DESC,
                NonDiscountSales DESC;
GO
```

ProductName	NonDiscountSales	Discounts	SalesOrderID
Women's Tights, S	1049.86	104.986	47355
Women's Tights, S	824.89	41.2445	46987
Women's Tights, S	783.6455	39.1823	47400
Women's Tights, S	742.401	37.1201	50206
Women's Tights, S	701.1565	35.0578	46993
Women's Tights, S	701.1565	35.0578	46671
Women's Tights, S	701.1565	35.0578	50688
Women's Tights, S	701.1565	35.0578	49481
Women's Tights, S	659.912	32.9956	48295
Women's Tights, S	659.912	32.9956	46967
Women's Tights, S	618.6675	30.9334	46652
Women's Tights, S	608.9188	12.1784	46672
Women's Tights, S	608.9188	12.1784	47365
Women's Tights, S	565.4246	11.3085	47004
Women's Tights, S	565.4246	11.3085	50663

NOTE

Even though SELECT DISTINCT results may appear to be sorted, **only ORDER BY clause can guarantee sort**. This holds true for any kind of SELECT statement, simple or complex.

```
SELECT DISTINCT JobTitle   FROM   HumanResources.Employee ;
```

```
SELECT DISTINCT JobTitle   FROM   HumanResources.Employee ORDER  BY JobTitle;
```

ORDER BY with ROW_NUMBER()

T-SQL queries demonstrate sorting with not matching and matching ROW_NUMBER() sequence number.

```
SELECT
  ROW_NUMBER()  OVER(  PARTITION BY CountryRegionName   ORDER BY SalesYTD ASC) AS SeqNo,
  CountryRegionName AS Country,   FirstName,  LastName,   JobTitle,
  FORMAT(SalesYTD, 'c', 'en-US') AS SalesYTD,
  FORMAT(SalesLastYear, 'c', 'en-US') AS SalesLastYear
FROM   Sales.vSalesPerson               ORDER  BY JobTitle,    SalesYTD DESC;
```

SeqNo	Country	FirstName	LastName	JobTitle	SalesYTD	SalesLastYear
2	United States	Amy	Alberts	European Sales Manager	$519,905.93	$0.00
3	United States	Stephen	Jiang	North American Sales Manager	$559,697.56	$0.00
1	United States	Syed	Abbas	Pacific Sales Manager	$172,524.45	$0.00
11	United States	Linda	Mitchell	Sales Representative	$4,251,368.55	$1,439,156.03
1	United Kingdom	Jae	Pak	Sales Representative	$4,116,871.23	$1,635,823.40
10	United States	Michael	Blythe	Sales Representative	$3,763,178.18	$1,750,406.48
9	United States	Jillian	Carson	Sales Representative	$3,189,418.37	$1,997,186.20
1	France	Ranjit	Varkey Chudukatil	Sales Representative	$3,121,616.32	$2,396,539.76
2	Canada	José	Saraiva	Sales Representative	$2,604,540.72	$2,038,234.65
8	United States	Shu	Ito	Sales Representative	$2,458,535.62	$2,073,506.00
7	United States	Tsvi	Reiter	Sales Representative	$2,315,185.61	$1,849,640.94
1	Germany	Rachel	Valdez	Sales Representative	$1,827,066.71	$1,307,949.79
6	United States	Tete	Mensa-Annan	Sales Representative	$1,576,562.20	$0.00
5	United States	David	Campbell	Sales Representative	$1,573,012.94	$1,371,635.32
1	Canada	Garrett	Vargas	Sales Representative	$1,453,719.47	$1,620,276.90
1	Australia	Lynn	Tsoflias	Sales Representative	$1,421,810.92	$2,278,548.98
4	United States	Pamela	Ansman-Wolfe	Sales Representative	$1,352,577.13	$1,927,059.18

```
-- ROW_NUMBER() ORDER BY in synch with sort ORDER BY
SELECT   ROW_NUMBER()  OVER(  ORDER BY JobTitle, SalesYTD DESC) AS SeqNo,
    CountryRegionName AS Country,   FirstName,  LastName,   JobTitle,
    FORMAT(SalesYTD, 'c', 'en-US') AS SalesYTD,  FORMAT(SalesLastYear, 'c', 'en-US') AS SalesLastYear
FROM   Sales.vSalesPerson  ORDER  BY          SeqNo;
```

SeqNo	Country	FirstName	LastName	JobTitle	SalesYTD	SalesLastYear
1	United States	Amy	Alberts	European Sales Manager	$519,905.93	$0.00
2	United States	Stephen	Jiang	North American Sales Manager	$559,697.56	$0.00
3	United States	Syed	Abbas	Pacific Sales Manager	$172,524.45	$0.00
4	United States	Linda	Mitchell	Sales Representative	$4,251,368.55	$1,439,156.03
5	United Kingdom	Jae	Pak	Sales Representative	$4,116,871.23	$1,635,823.40
6	United States	Michael	Blythe	Sales Representative	$3,763,178.18	$1,750,406.48
7	United States	Jillian	Carson	Sales Representative	$3,189,418.37	$1,997,186.20
8	France	Ranjit	Varkey Chudukatil	Sales Representative	$3,121,616.32	$2,396,539.76
9	Canada	José	Saraiva	Sales Representative	$2,604,540.72	$2,038,234.65
10	United States	Shu	Ito	Sales Representative	$2,458,535.62	$2,073,506.00
11	United States	Tsvi	Reiter	Sales Representative	$2,315,185.61	$1,849,640.94
12	Germany	Rachel	Valdez	Sales Representative	$1,827,066.71	$1,307,949.79
13	United States	Tete	Mensa-Annan	Sales Representative	$1,576,562.20	$0.00
14	United States	David	Campbell	Sales Representative	$1,573,012.94	$1,371,635.32
15	Canada	Garrett	Vargas	Sales Representative	$1,453,719.47	$1,620,276.90
16	Australia	Lynn	Tsoflias	Sales Representative	$1,421,810.92	$2,278,548.98
17	United States	Pamela	Ansman-Wolfe	Sales Representative	$1,352,577.13	$1,927,059.18

ORDER BY Clause with CASE Conditional Expression

Sort by LastName, MiddleName if exists else FirstName, and FirstName in case MiddleName is used.

```
USE AdventureWorks;

SELECT          FirstName,
                COALESCE(MiddleName, '')        AS MName,  -- ISNULL can also be used
                LastName,
                AddressLine1,
                COALESCE(AddressLine2, '')      AS Addr2,
                City,
                SP.Name                         AS [State],
                CR.Name                         AS Country,
                I.CustomerID
FROM  Person.Contact AS C
   INNER JOIN Sales.Individual AS I
       ON C.ContactID = I.ContactID
   INNER JOIN Sales.CustomerAddress AS CA
       ON CA.CustomerID = I.CustomerID
   INNER JOIN Person.[Address] AS A
       ON A.AddressID = CA.AddressID
   INNER JOIN Person.StateProvince SP
       ON SP.StateProvinceID = A.StateProvinceID
   INNER JOIN Person.CountryRegion CR
       ON CR.CountryRegionCode = SP.CountryRegionCode
ORDER  BY LastName,
     CASE
      WHEN MiddleName != '' THEN MiddleName
      ELSE FirstName
     END,
     FirstName;
-- (18508 row(s) affected) -Partial results.
```

FirstName	MName	LastName	AddressLine1	Addr2	City	State	Country	CustomerID
Chloe	A	Adams	3001 N. 48th Street		Marysville	Washington	United States	19410
Eduardo	A	Adams	4283 Meaham Drive		San Diego	California	United States	25292
Kaitlyn	A	Adams	3815 Berry Dr.		Westminster	British Columbia	Canada	11869
Mackenzie	A	Adams	9639 Ida Drive		Langford	British Columbia	Canada	14640
Sara	A	Adams	7503 Hill Drive		Milwaukie	Oregon	United States	16986
Adam		Adams	9381 Bayside Way		Newport Beach	California	United States	13323
Amber		Adams	9720 Morning Glory Dr.		Brisbane	Queensland	Australia	26746
Angel		Adams	9556 Lyman Rd.		Burlingame	California	United States	18504
Aaron	B	Adams	4116 Stanbridge Ct.		Downey	California	United States	28866
Noah	B	Adams	6738 Wallace Dr.		El Cajon	California	United States	16977
Bailey		Adams	1817 Adobe Drive		Kirkland	Washington	United States	13280
Ben		Adams	1534 Land Ave		Bremerton	Washington	United States	28678
Alex	C	Adams	237 Bellwood Dr.		Lake Oswego	Oregon	United States	21139
Courtney	C	Adams	6089 Santa Fe Dr.		Torrance	California	United States	18075
Ian	C	Adams	7963 Elk Dr	#4	Versailles	Yveline	France	29422

Special Sorting, Like United States On Top Of The Country Pop-Up List

It requires CASE or IIF conditional expression.

```
-- Major sort key is Color if not null, else product name
-- Minor sort on ProductNumber
SELECT ProductID,
    ProductNumber,
    Name AS ProductName,
    FORMAT(ListPrice, 'c', 'en-US')  AS ListPrice,
    Color
FROM   Production.Product
WHERE  Name LIKE ( '%Road%' )
ORDER  BY        CASE
                          WHEN Color IS NULL THEN Name
                          ELSE Color
                 END,
                 ProductNumber DESC;
-- (103 row(s) affected) - Partial results.
```

ProductID	ProductNumber	ProductName	ListPrice	Color
768	BK-R50B-44	Road-650 Black, 44	$782.99	Black
977	BK-R19B-58	Road-750 Black, 58	$539.99	Black
999	BK-R19B-52	Road-750 Black, 52	$539.99	Black
998	BK-R19B-48	Road-750 Black, 48	$539.99	Black
997	BK-R19B-44	Road-750 Black, 44	$539.99	Black
813	HB-R956	HL Road Handlebars	$120.27	NULL
512	RM-R800	HL Road Rim	$0.00	NULL
519	SA-R522	HL Road Seat Assembly	$196.92	NULL
913	SE-R995	HL Road Seat/Saddle	$52.64	NULL
933	TI-R982	HL Road Tire	$32.60	NULL
811	HB-R504	LL Road Handlebars	$44.54	NULL
510	RM-R436	LL Road Rim	$0.00	NULL
517	SA-R127	LL Road Seat Assembly	$133.34	NULL
911	SE-R581	LL Road Seat/Saddle	$27.12	NULL
931	TI-R092	LL Road Tire	$21.49	NULL
812	HB-R720	ML Road Handlebars	$61.92	NULL
511	RM-R600	ML Road Rim	$0.00	NULL
518	SA-R430	ML Road Seat Assembly	$147.14	NULL
912	SE-R908	ML Road Seat/Saddle	$39.14	NULL
932	TI-R628	ML Road Tire	$24.99	NULL
717	FR-R92R-62	HL Road Frame - Red, 62	$1,431.50	Red
706	FR-R92R-58	HL Road Frame - Red, 58	$1,431.50	Red
721	FR-R92R-56	HL Road Frame - Red, 56	$1,431.50	Red

T-SQL queries demonstrate complex sorting with the CASE expression usage.

CASE expression returns a SINGLE SCALAR VALUE of the same data type.

```
SELECT  SellStartDate,
        SellEndDate,
        *
FROM  Production.Product
WHERE  Name LIKE ( '%mountain%' )
ORDER  BY CASE
             WHEN SellEndDate IS NULL THEN SellStartDate
             ELSE SellEndDate
        END DESC, Name;
GO
-- (94 row(s) affected) -Partial results.
```

SellStartDate	SellEndDate	ProductID	Name	ProductNumber
2007-07-01 00:00:00.000	NULL	986	Mountain-500 Silver, 44	BK-M18S-44
2007-07-01 00:00:00.000	NULL	987	Mountain-500 Silver, 48	BK-M18S-48
2007-07-01 00:00:00.000	NULL	988	Mountain-500 Silver, 52	BK-M18S-52
2007-07-01 00:00:00.000	NULL	869	Women's Mountain Shorts, L	SH-W890-L
2007-07-01 00:00:00.000	NULL	868	Women's Mountain Shorts, M	SH-W890-M
2007-07-01 00:00:00.000	NULL	867	Women's Mountain Shorts, S	SH-W890-S
2006-07-01 00:00:00.000	2007-06-30 00:00:00.000	817	HL Mountain Front Wheel	FW-M928
2006-07-01 00:00:00.000	2007-06-30 00:00:00.000	825	HL Mountain Rear Wheel	RW-M928
2006-07-01 00:00:00.000	2007-06-30 00:00:00.000	815	LL Mountain Front Wheel	FW-M423
2006-07-01 00:00:00.000	2007-06-30 00:00:00.000	823	LL Mountain Rear Wheel	RW-M423
2006-07-01 00:00:00.000	2007-06-30 00:00:00.000	814	ML Mountain Frame - Black, 38	FR-M63B-38
2006-07-01 00:00:00.000	2007-06-30 00:00:00.000	830	ML Mountain Frame - Black, 40	FR-M63B-40

```
-- 2 keys descending sort
SELECT          PRODUCTNAME  = P.Name,
                SALETOTAL    = ( OrderQty * UnitPrice ),
                NETSALETOTAL = ( ( OrderQty - RejectedQty ) * UnitPrice )
FROM  Production.Product P
   INNER JOIN Purchasing.PurchaseOrderDetail SOD
       ON P.ProductID = SOD.ProductID
ORDER  BY PRODUCTNAME  DESC,  SALETOTAL DESC;

-- Column alias sorting of GROUP BY aggregation results
SELECT [YEAR]=YEAR(OrderDate), Orders = COUNT(*)
FROM AdventureWorks2012.Sales.SalesOrderHeader
GROUP BY YEAR(OrderDate)  ORDER BY [YEAR];
```

YEAR	Orders
2005	1379
2006	3692
2007	12443
2008	13951

ORDER BY Clause with IIF Conditional Function

Sort by LastName, MiddleName if exists else FirstName, and FirstName in case MiddleName is used.

```
USE AdventureWorks;

SELECT          FirstName,
                COALESCE(MiddleName, '')        AS MName,  -- ISNULL can also be used
                LastName,
                AddressLine1,
                COALESCE(AddressLine2, '')      AS Addr2,
                City,
                SP.Name                         AS [State],
                CR.Name                         AS Country,
                I.CustomerID
FROM   Person.Contact AS C
    INNER JOIN Sales.Individual AS I
        ON C.ContactID = I.ContactID
    INNER JOIN Sales.CustomerAddress AS CA
        ON CA.CustomerID = I.CustomerID
    INNER JOIN Person.[Address] AS A
        ON A.AddressID = CA.AddressID
    INNER JOIN Person.StateProvince SP
        ON SP.StateProvinceID = A.StateProvinceID
    INNER JOIN Person.CountryRegion CR
        ON CR.CountryRegionCode = SP.CountryRegionCode
ORDER  BY       LastName,
                IIF( MiddleName != '',
                        MiddleName,             -- TRUE condition return value
                        FirstName),             -- FALSE condition return value
                FirstName;
GO
-- (18508 row(s) affected) -Partial results.
```

FirstName	MName	LastName	AddressLine1	Addr2	City	State	Country	CustomerID
Chloe	A	Adams	3001 N. 48th Street		Marysville	Washington	United States	19410
Eduardo	A	Adams	4283 Meaham Drive		San Diego	California	United States	25292
Kaitlyn	A	Adams	3815 Berry Dr.		Westminster	British Columbia	Canada	11869
Mackenzie	A	Adams	9639 Ida Drive		Langford	British Columbia	Canada	14640
Sara	A	Adams	7503 Hill Drive		Milwaukie	Oregon	United States	16986
Adam		Adams	9381 Bayside Way		Newport Beach	California	United States	13323
Amber		Adams	9720 Morning Glory Dr.		Brisbane	Queensland	Australia	26746
Angel		Adams	9556 Lyman Rd.		Burlingame	California	United States	18504
Aaron	B	Adams	4116 Stanbridge Ct.		Downey	California	United States	28866
Noah	B	Adams	6738 Wallace Dr.		El Cajon	California	United States	16977
Bailey		Adams	1817 Adobe Drive		Kirkland	Washington	United States	13280
Ben		Adams	1534 Land Ave		Bremerton	Washington	United States	28678
Alex	C	Adams	237 Bellwood Dr.		Lake Oswego	Oregon	United States	21139
Courtney	C	Adams	6089 Santa Fe Dr.		Torrance	California	United States	18075
Ian	C	Adams	7963 Elk Dr	#4	Versailles	Yveline	France	29422

ORDER BY Clause with the RANK() Function

T-SQL query demonstrates the combination of CASE expression and RANK() function in an ORDER BY clause. Note that while such a complex sort is technically impressive, ultimately it has to make sense to the user, the Business Intelligence consumer.

```
-- SQL complex sorting
USE AdventureWorks;

SELECT      ContactID,
            FirstName,
            LastName,
            COALESCE(Title, '') AS Title
FROM   Person.Contact
WHERE  LEFT(FirstName, 1) = 'M'
ORDER  BY CASE
            WHEN LEFT(LastName, 1) = 'A' THEN RANK()
                        OVER( ORDER BY CONCAT(FirstName, SPACE(1), LastName))
            WHEN LEFT(LastName, 1) = 'M' THEN RANK()
                        OVER( ORDER BY CONCAT(LastName,', ', FirstName), Title)
            WHEN LEFT(LastName, 1) = 'U' THEN RANK()
                        OVER(  ORDER BY CONCAT(LastName,', ', FirstName)   DESC)
            ELSE RANK()
                        OVER( ORDER BY LastName ASC, FirstName DESC)
    END;
```

ContactID	FirstName	LastName	Title
9500	Mackenzie	Adams	
10144	Mackenzie	Allen	
10128	Madeline	Allen	
11708	Madison	Alexander	
11527	Madison	Anderson	
19872	Morgan	Bailey	
8059	Michelle	Bailey	
8080	Melissa	Bailey	
18291	Megan	Bailey	
8070	Mariah	Bailey	
2432	Maria	Bailey	
14378	Marcus	Bailey	
8063	Makayla	Bailey	
8032	Mackenzie	Bailey	
9521	Morgan	Baker	
3320	Miguel	Baker	
15437	Mason	Baker	
9546	Mary	Baker	
1082	Mary	Baker	
9539	Maria	Baker	

ORDER BY Clause with Custom Mapped Sort Sequence

Typically we rely on alphabets or numbers for sorting. What if, for example, we don't want United States way down on a website drop-down menu, rather than on the top with Canada and United Kingdom just above "lucky" Australia? We have to do custom mapping for such a sort in the ORDER BY clause.

```
USE AdventureWorks;
SELECT          AddressLine1,
                City,
                SP.StateProvinceCode                AS State,
                PostalCode,
                CR.Name                             AS  Country
FROM   Person.[Address] A
    INNER JOIN Person.StateProvince SP              ON A.StateProvinceID = SP.StateProvinceID
    INNER JOIN Person.CountryRegion CR              ON SP.CountryRegionCode = CR.CountryRegionCode
ORDER  BY (      CASE     WHEN CR.Name = 'United States' THEN 0
                          WHEN CR.Name = 'Canada' THEN 1
                          WHEN CR.Name = 'United Kingdom' THEN 2   ELSE 3  END ),
                Country,
                City
                AddressLine1;
-- (19614 row(s) affected) - Partial results.
```

AddressLine1	City	State	PostalCode	Country
9355 Armstrong Road	York	ENG	YO15	United Kingdom
939 Vista Del Diablo	York	ENG	YO15	United Kingdom
9458 Flame Drive	York	ENG	YO15	United Kingdom
9557 Steven Circle	York	ENG	Y03 4TN	United Kingdom

Sorting on the Last Word of a String

```
USE tempdb;  SELECT BusinessEntityID, FULLNAME = CONCAT(FirstName , SPACE(1), LastName )
INTO   People FROM   AdventureWorks2012.Person.Person ORDER  BY BusinessEntityID ;
ALTER TABLE People ADD CONSTRAINT pkBEID PRIMARY KEY (BusinessEntityID);
```

```
SELECT *   FROM   People
ORDER  BY REVERSE(LEFT(REVERSE(FullName), charindex(' ', REVERSE(FullName) + ' '  ) - 1)),
         FullName ;
GO -- (19972 row(s) affected) - Partial results.
```

BusinessEntityID	FULLNAME
285	Syed Abbas
293	Catherine Abel
295	Kim Abercrombie

ORDER BY Clause with Custom Alphanumeric Sort Sequence

A frequent requirement is custom sorting on alphanumeric field (column). The next T-SQL query demonstrates special alphanumeric sorting.

```
USE AdventureWorks;

SELECT AddressLine1,
                isnull(AddressLine2, '')      AS Addressline2,
                City,
                SP.StateProvinceCode          AS State,
                PostalCode,
                CR.Name                       AS Country
FROM   Person.[Address] A
    INNER JOIN Person.StateProvince SP
     ON A.StateProvinceID = SP.StateProvinceID
    INNER JOIN Person.CountryRegion CR
     ON SP.CountryRegionCode = CR.CountryRegionCode
ORDER BY (      CASE
                        WHEN Ascii([AddressLine1]) BETWEEN 65 AND 90 THEN 0 -- Upper case alpha
                        WHEN Ascii([AddressLine1]) BETWEEN 48 AND 57 THEN 1 -- Digits
                        ELSE 2
                END ),
                AddressLine1,
                City;
GO
-- (19614 row(s) affected) - Partial results.
```

AddressLine1	Addressline2	City	State	PostalCode	Country
Zur Lindung 46		Leipzig	NW	04139	Germany
Zur Lindung 6		Saarlouis	SL	66740	Germany
Zur Lindung 6		Solingen	NW	42651	Germany
Zur Lindung 609		Sulzbach Taunus	SL	66272	Germany
Zur Lindung 7		Berlin	HE	14129	Germany
Zur Lindung 7		Neunkirchen	SL	66578	Germany
Zur Lindung 764		Paderborn	HH	33041	Germany
Zur Lindung 78		Berlin	HH	10791	Germany
Zur Lindung 787		München	NW	80074	Germany
00, rue Saint-Lazare		Dunkerque	59	59140	France
02, place de Fontenoy		Verrieres Le Buisson	91	91370	France
035, boulevard du Montparnasse		Verrieres Le Buisson	91	91370	France
081, boulevard du Montparnasse		Saint-Denis	93	93400	France
081, boulevard du Montparnasse		Seattle	WA	98104	United States
084, boulevard du Montparnasse		Les Ulis	91	91940	France
1 Corporate Center Drive		Miami	FL	33127	United States
1 Mt. Dell Drive		Portland	OR	97205	United States
1 Smiling Tree Court	Space 55	Los Angeles	CA	90012	United States
1, allée des Princes		Courbevoie	92	92400	France

Working with Synonyms

A synonym is a shorthand name for a longer name including multi-part names. **While prefix like "sn" or "syn" is not required, it is a good practice since otherwise a synonym can be confused with a (real) table for example, leading to loss of DBA or developer productivity.**

```
USE tempdb;
GO
```

```
-- Create synonyms for a 3-part names
CREATE SYNONYM snCustomerAW  FOR AdventureWorks.Sales.Customer;
CREATE SYNONYM snCustomerAW12  FOR AdventureWorks2012.Sales.Customer;
```

```
-- Create a synonym for 4-part name linked server
CREATE SYNONYM snCustomerLDNAW12  FOR
        [LONDONPROD8].AdventureWorks2012.Sales.Customer;
GO -- Command(s) completed successfully.
```

```
-- Query the Customer tables by using the synonyms
SELECT * FROM snCustomerAW ORDER BY AccountNumber;     -- (19185 row(s) affected)
SELECT * FROM snCustomerAW12 ORDER BY AccountNumber;  -- (19820 row(s) affected)
GO
```

```
-- Delete a synonym
DROP SYNONYM snCustomerAW;  -- Command(s) completed successfully.
GO
```

```
-- Enumerating all synonyms in database
SELECT  name                                    AS "Name"
        ,base_object_name                       AS "Definition"
        ,PARSENAME(base_object_name, 4)         AS "Server"
        ,PARSENAME(base_object_name, 3)         AS "Database"
        ,PARSENAME(base_object_name, 2)         AS "Schema"
        ,PARSENAME(base_object_name, 1)         AS "Object"
 FROM sys.synonyms ORDER BY Definition;
```

Name	Definition	Server	Database	Schema	Object
CustomerAW12	[AdventureWorks2012].[Sales].[Customer]	NULL	AdventureWorks2012	Sales	Customer
CustomerLNDAW12	[LONDONPROD8].[AdventureWorks2012].[Sales].[Customer]	LONDONPROD8	AdventureWorks2012	Sales	Customer

Date & Time Conversion To / From String

While there are only a few internal representation of date and time, string representations are many, even not deterministic since they may change from one country to another such as weekday and month names. T-SQL scripts demonstrate the myriad of date and time conversion possibilities.

The CONVERT() Function with Style Number Parameter

```
-- String source  format: mon dd yyyy hh:mmAM (or PM)
-- 100 is the style number parameter for CONVERT
SELECT [Date&Time] = convert(datetime, 'Oct 23 2020 11:01AM', 100)
```

Date&Time
2020-10-23 11:01:00.000

```
-- Default without style number
SELECT convert(datetime, 'Oct 23 2020 11:01AM')                    -- 2020-10-23 11:01:00.000
```

```
-- Without century (yy) string date conversion with style number 0
-- Input format: mon dd yy hh:mmAM (or PM)
SELECT [Date&Time] = convert(datetime, 'Oct 23 20 11:01AM', 0)
```

Date&Time
2020-10-23 11:01:00.000

```
-- Default without style number
SELECT convert(datetime, 'Oct 23 20 11:01AM')                      -- 2020-10-23 11:01:00.000
```

Convert string date & time to datetime (8-bytes internal representation) data type.

```
SELECT convert(datetime, '10/23/2016', 101)          -- mm/dd/yyyy

SELECT convert(datetime, '2016.10.23', 102)          -- yyyy.mm.dd ANSI date with century

SELECT convert(datetime, '23/10/2016', 103)          -- dd/mm/yyyy

SELECT convert(datetime, '23.10.2016', 104)-- dd.mm.yyyy

SELECT convert(datetime, '23-10-2016', 105)          -- dd-mm-yyyy

-- mon (month) types are nondeterministic conversions, dependent on language setting.
SELECT convert(datetime, '23 OCT 2016', 106)         -- dd mon yyyy
```

String Datetime Formats With "Mon" Are Nondeterministic, Language Dependent

```
SELECT [Date&Time] = convert(datetime, 'Oct 23, 2016', 107) -- mon dd, yyyy
```

Date&Time
2016-10-23 00:00:00.000

```
SELECT [Date&Time ]=convert(datetime, '20:10:44', 108)        -- hh:mm:ss
```

Date&Time
1900-01-01 20:10:44.000

```
SELECT [Date&Time ]=convert(datetime, 'Oct 23 2016 11:02:44:013AM', 109) -- mon dd yyyy hh:mm:ss:mmmAM (or PM)
```

Date&Time
2016-10-23 11:02:44.013

```
SELECT convert(datetime, '10-23-2016', 110)                    -- mm-dd-yyyy
SELECT convert(datetime, '2016/10/23', 111)                    -- yyyy/mm/dd
```

```
-- YYYYMMDD ISO date format works at any language setting - international standard
SELECT [Date&Time ]=convert(datetime, '20161023')
```

Date&Time
2016-10-23 00:00:00.000

```
SELECT [Date&Time ]=convert(datetime, '20161023', 112)        -- ISO yyyymmdd
```

Date&Time
2016-10-23 00:00:00.000

```
SELECT [Date&Time ]=convert(datetime, '23 Oct 2016 11:02:07:577', 113) -- dd mon yyyy hh:mm:ss:mmm
```

Date&Time
2016-10-23 11:02:07.577

```
SELECT [Date&Time ]=convert(datetime, '20:10:25:300', 114)            -- hh:mm:ss:mmm(24h)
```

Date&Time
1900-01-01 20:10:25.300

```
SELECT [Date&Time ]=convert(datetime, '2016-10-23 20:44:11', 120)   -- yyyy-mm-dd hh:mm:ss(24h)
```

Date&Time
2016-10-23 20:44:11.000

Style 126 Is ISO 8601 Format: International Standard; Works With Any Language Setting

```
SELECT [Date&Time ]=convert(datetime, '2018-10-23T18:52:47.513', 126) -- yyyy-mm-ddThh:mm:ss(.mmm)
```

Date&Time
2018-10-23 18:52:47.513

```
SELECT [Date&Time ]=convert(datetime, '2016-10-23 20:44:11.500', 121)          -- yyyy-mm-dd hh:mm:ss.mmm
```

Date&Time
2016-10-23 20:44:11.500

```
-- Islamic / Hijri date conversion

SELECT CONVERT(nvarchar(32), convert(datetime,'2016-10-23'), 130);
-- 22 محرم 1438 12:00:00:000AM

SELECT [Date&Time ]=convert(datetime, N'23 شوال 1441  6:52:47:513PM', 130)
```

Date&Time
2020-06-14 18:52:47.513

```
SELECT [Date&Time ]=convert(datetime, '23/10/1441  6:52:47:513PM',    131)
```

Date&Time
2020-06-14 18:52:47.513

```
-- Convert DDMMYYYY format to datetime with intermediate conversion using STUFF().

SELECT STUFF(STUFF('31012016',3,0,'-'),6,0,'-');
-- 31-01-2016

SELECT [Date&Time ]=convert(datetime, STUFF(STUFF('31012016',3,0,'-'),6,0,'-'), 105)
```

Date&Time
2016-01-31 00:00:00.000

```
-- Equivalent
SELECT STUFF(STUFF('31012016',3,0,'/'),6,0,'/');   -- 31/01/2016
SELECT [Date&Time ]=convert(datetime, STUFF(STUFF('31012016',3,0,'/'),6,0,'/'), 103)
```

String to Datetime Conversion Without Century

String to datetime conversion without century - some exceptions. Nondeterministic means language setting (also regional setting) dependent such as Mar/Mär/mars/márc .

```
SELECT [Date&Time ]=convert(datetime, 'Oct 23 16 11:02:44AM')          -- Default
```

Date&Time
2016-10-23 11:02:44.000

SELECT convert(datetime, '10/23/16', 1)	mm/dd/yy	U.S.
SELECT convert(datetime, '16.10.23', 2)	yy.mm.dd	ANSI
SELECT convert(datetime, '23/10/16', 3)	dd/mm/yy	UK/FR
SELECT convert(datetime, '23.10.16', 4)	dd.mm.yy	German
SELECT convert(datetime, '23-10-16', 5)	dd-mm-yy	Italian
SELECT convert(datetime, '23 OCT 16', 6)	dd mon yy	non-det.
SELECT convert(datetime, 'Oct 23, 16', 7)	mon dd, yy	non-det.
SELECT convert(datetime, '20:10:44', 8)	hh:mm:ss	
SELECT convert(datetime, 'Oct 23 16 11:02:44:013AM', 9)	Default with msec	
SELECT convert(datetime, '10-23-16', 10)	mm-dd-yy	U.S.
SELECT convert(datetime, '16/10/23', 11)	yy/mm/dd	Japan
SELECT convert(datetime, '161023', 12)	yymmdd	ISO
SELECT convert(datetime, '23 Oct 16 11:02:07:577', 13)	dd mon yy hh:mm:ss:mmm EU dflt	
SELECT convert(datetime, '20:10:25:300', 14)	hh:mm:ss:mmm(24h)	
SELECT convert(datetime, '2016-10-23 20:44:11',20)	yyyy-mm-dd hh:mm:ss(24h) ODBC can.	
SELECT convert(datetime, '2016-10-23 20:44:11.500', 21)	yyyy-mm-dd hh:mm:ss.mmm ODBC	

Combine Date & Time String into Datetime

```
DECLARE @DateTimeValue varchar(32), @DateValue char(8), @TimeValue char(6)
 SELECT @DateValue = '20200718',            @TimeValue = '211920'
SELECT              @DateTimeValue =
                    CONCAT(
                    convert(varchar, convert(datetime, @DateValue), 111),
                    ' ', substring(@TimeValue, 1, 2) , ':', substring(@TimeValue, 3, 2) , ':',
substring(@TimeValue, 5, 2)  )

SELECT   DateInput = @DateValue, TimeInput = @TimeValue,  DateTimeOutput = @DateTimeValue;
GO
```

DateInput	TimeInput	DateTimeOutput
20200718	211920	2020/07/18 21:19:20

```
SELECT DATETIMEFROMPARTS (2020, 07, 1, 21, 01, 20, 700)          -- New in SQL Server 2012
```

Date and Time Internal Storage Format

DATETIME 8 bytes internal storage structure:

- 1st 4 bytes: number of days after the base date 1900-01-01
- 2nd 4 bytes: number of clock-ticks (3.33 milliseconds) since midnight

```
SELECT CONVERT(binary(8), CURRENT_TIMESTAMP);
```

Hex
0x0000A09C00F23CE1

DATE 3 bytes internal storage structure:

- 3 bytes integer: number of days after the first date 0001-01-01
- Note: hex byte order reversed

SMALLDATETIME 4 bytes internal storage structure

- 1st 2 bytes: number of days after the base date 1900-01-01
- 2nd 2 bytes: number of minutes since midnight

```
SELECT Hex=CONVERT(binary(4), convert(smalldatetime, getdate()));
```

Hex
0xA09C0375

Date & Time Operations Using System Operators & Functions

```
-- Conversion from hex (binary) to datetime value
DECLARE @dtHex binary(8)= 0x00009966002d3344;  DECLARE @dt datetime = @dtHex;
SELECT @dt;  -- 2007-07-09 02:44:34.147
```

```
-- SQL convert seconds to HH:MM:SS -
DECLARE  @Seconds INT;  SET @Seconds = 20000 ;
SELECT HH = @Seconds / 3600, MM = (@Seconds%3600) / 60, SS = (@Seconds%60) ;
```

HH	MM	SS
5	33	20

Extract Date Only from DATETIME Data Type

```
DECLARE @Now datetime = CURRENT_TIMESTAMP -- getdate()

SELECT  DateAndTime        = @Now      -- Date portion and Time portion
        ,DateString                    = REPLACE(LEFT(CONVERT (varchar, @Now, 112),10),' ','-')
        ,[Date]                        = CONVERT(DATE, @Now)  -- SQL Server 2008 and on - date part
        ,Midnight1                     = dateadd(day, datediff(day,0, @Now), 0)
        ,Midnight2                     = CONVERT(DATETIME,CONVERT(int, @Now))
        ,Midnight3                     = CONVERT(DATETIME,CONVERT(BIGINT,@Now) &
(POWER(Convert(bigint,2),32)-1));
```

DateAndTime	DateString	Date	Midnight1	Midnight2	Midnight3
2020-07-28 15:01:51.960	20200728	2020-07-28	2020-07-28 00:00:00.000	2020-07-29 00:00:00.000	2020-07-29 00:00:00.000

```
-- Compare today with database dates
SELECT          TOP (10)  OrderDate = CONVERT(date, OrderDate),
                Today = CONVERT(date, getdate()),
                DeltaDays = DATEDIFF(DD, OrderDate, getdate())
FROM AdventureWorks2012.Sales.SalesOrderHeader  ORDER BY NEWID();  -- random sort
```

OrderDate	Today	DeltaDays
2008-01-15	2012-08-10	1669
2006-07-14	2012-08-10	2219
2008-07-05	2012-08-10	1497
2008-03-01	2012-08-10	1623
2007-10-01	2012-08-10	1775
2007-01-15	2012-08-10	2034
2008-05-27	2012-08-10	1536
2008-04-18	2012-08-10	1575
2008-04-25	2012-08-10	1568
2006-12-17	2012-08-10	2063

String Date Formats Without Time

```
-- String date format yyyy/mm/dd from datetime
SELECT CONVERT(VARCHAR(10), GETDATE(), 111) AS [YYYY/MM/DD] ;
```

YYYY/MM/DD
2012/07/28

```
SELECT CONVERT(VARCHAR(10), GETDATE(), 112) AS [YYYYMMDD];
```

YYYYMMDD
20120728

```
SELECT REPLACE(CONVERT(VARCHAR(10), GETDATE(), 111),'/',' ') AS [YYYY MM DD];
```

YYYY MM DD
2020 07 28

```
-- Converting to special (non-standard) date formats: DD-MMM-YY
SELECT UPPER(REPLACE(CONVERT(VARCHAR,GETDATE(),6),' ','-')) AS CustomDate;
```

CustomDate
28-JUL-20

```
-- SQL convert date string to datetime - time set to 00:00:00.000 or 12:00AM

PRINT CONVERT(datetime,'07-10-2020',110) ;          -- Jul 10 2020 12:00AM
PRINT CONVERT(datetime,'2020/07/10',111) ;          -- Jul 10 2020 12:00AM
PRINT CONVERT(datetime,'20200710',  112);           -- Jul 10 2020 12:00AM
GO
```

```
-- SQL Server cast string to date / datetime
DECLARE @DateValue char(8) = '20200718'

SELECT [Date] = CAST (@DateValue AS datetime);
GO
```

Date
2020-07-18 00:00:00.000

String date to string date conversion with nested CONVERT

```
SELECT CONVERT(varchar, CONVERT(datetime, '20140508'), 100) AS StringDate;
```

StringDate
May 8 2014 12:00AM

```
-- T-SQL convert date to integer
DECLARE @Date datetime;  SET @Date = getdate();
SELECT DateAsInteger = CAST (CONVERT(varchar,@Date,112) as INT);
GO
```

DateAsInteger
20120728

```
-- SQL Server convert integer to datetime
DECLARE @iDate int = 20151225;
SELECT IntegerToDatetime = CAST(convert(varchar,@iDate) as datetime)
GO
```

IntegerToDatetime
2015-12-25 00:00:00.000

```
-- Alternates: date-only datetime values

SELECT [DATE-ONLY]=CONVERT(DATETIME, FLOOR(CONVERT(FLOAT, GETDATE())));

SELECT [DATE-ONLY]=CONVERT(DATETIME, FLOOR(CONVERT(MONEY, GETDATE())));

SELECT [DATE-ONLY]=CONVERT(DATETIME, CONVERT(DATE, GETDATE()));
```

```
-- CAST string to datetime
-- String date preparation, length is 10 characters
SELECT CONVERT(varchar, GETDATE(), 101), LEN (CONVERT(varchar, GETDATE(), 101))
--        07/28/2018      10
```

```
SELECT [DATE-ONLY]=CAST(CONVERT(varchar, GETDATE(), 101) AS DATETIME);
```

DATE-ONLY
2018-07-28 00:00:00.000

DATEADD() and DATEDIFF() Functions

```
-- T-SQL strip time from date
SELECT getdate() AS [DateTime], dateadd(dd, datediff(dd, 0, getdate()), 0) [DateOnly];
```

DateTime	DateOnly
2012-07-28 17:24:07.300	2012-07-28 00:00:00.000

```
-- First day of current month
SELECT dateadd(month, datediff(month, 0, getdate()), 0)  AS FirstDayOfCurrentMonth;
SELECT dateadd(dd,1, EOMONTH(getdate(),-1));  -- New to SQL Server 2012
```

FirstDayOfCurrentMonth
2020-07-01 00:00:00.000

```
 -- 15th day of current month
SELECT dateadd(day,14,dateadd(month, datediff(month,0,getdate()),0))
                                                        AS MiddleOfCurrentMonth;
SELECT dateadd(dd,15, EOMONTH(getdate(),-1));  -- New to SQL Server 2012
```

MiddleOfCurrentMonth
2012-07-15 00:00:00.000

```
-- First Monday of current month
SELECT   dateadd(day, (9-datepart(weekday,
         dateadd(month, datediff(month, 0, getdate()), 0)))%7,
         dateadd(month, datediff(month, 0, getdate()), 0))  AS [First Monday Of Current Month];
GO
```

First Monday Of Current Month
2012-07-02 00:00:00.000

```
-- Next Monday calculation from the reference date which was a Monday
DECLARE @Now datetime = GETDATE();
DECLARE @NextMonday datetime = dateadd(dd, ((datediff(dd, '19000101', @Now)
                 / 7) * 7) + 7, '19000101');
SELECT [Now]=@Now, [Next Monday]=@NextMonday;
GO
```

Now	Next Monday
2012-07-28 17:35:29.657	2012-07-30 00:00:00.000

Last Date & First Date Calculations

```
-- Last Friday of current month

SELECT   dateadd(day, -7+(6-datepart(weekday,

          dateadd(month, datediff(month, 0, getdate())+1, 0)))%7,

          dateadd(month, datediff(month, 0, getdate())+1, 0)) ;
```

```
-- First day of next month

SELECT dateadd(month, datediff(month, 0, getdate())+1, 0) ;
```

```
-- 15th of next month

SELECT dateadd(day,14, dateadd(month, datediff(month, 0, getdate())+1, 0));
```

```
-- First Monday of next month

SELECT   dateadd(day, (9-datepart(weekday,
         dateadd(month, datediff(month, 0, getdate())+1, 0)))%7,
         dateadd(month, datediff(month, 0, getdate())+1, 0));
```

```
-- Next 12 months start & end - EOMONTH is new to SQL Server 2012
SELECT TOP 12
         DATEADD(DD,1, EOMONTH(getdate(),number-1))      AS Start,
         EOMONTH(getdate(),number)                       AS [End]
FROM master.dbo.spt_values   -- get integer sequence
WHERE type='P'  ORDER BY number;
GO
```

Start	End
2016-08-01	2016-08-31
2016-09-01	2016-09-30
2016-10-01	2016-10-31
2016-11-01	2016-11-30
2016-12-01	2016-12-31
2017-01-01	2017-01-31
2017-02-01	2017-02-28
2017-03-01	2017-03-31
2017-04-01	2017-04-30
2017-05-01	2017-05-31
2017-06-01	2017-06-30
2017-07-01	2017-07-31

BETWEEN Operator for Date Range

Date time range SELECT using the using >= and < operators. Count Sales Orders for date range 2007 OCT-NOV.

```
DECLARE  @StartDate DATETIME,  @EndDate DATETIME
SET @StartDate = convert(DATETIME,'10/01/2007',101)
SET @EndDate   = convert(DATETIME,'11/30/2007',101)
SELECT @StartDate, @EndDate
-- 2007-10-01 00:00:00.000  2007-11-30 00:00:00.000
SELECT dateadd(DAY,1,@EndDate),     dateadd(ms,-3,dateadd(DAY,1,@EndDate))
-- 2007-12-01 00:00:00.000  2007-11-30 23:59:59.997

SELECT [Sales Orders for 2007 OCT-NOV] = COUNT(* )
FROM   AdventureWorks2012.Sales.SalesOrderHeader
WHERE  OrderDate >= @StartDate
       AND OrderDate < dateadd(DAY,1,@EndDate)
```

Sales Orders for 2007 OCT-NOV
3668

Equivalent date range query using BETWEEN comparison. It requires a bit of trick programming. 23.59.59.997 is the last available time in a day.

```
SELECT [Sales Orders for 2007 OCT-NOV] = COUNT(* )
FROM   AdventureWorks2012.Sales.SalesOrderHeader
WHERE   OrderDate BETWEEN @StartDate
        AND dateadd(ms,-3, dateadd(DAY, 1, @EndDate))
GO
```

Sales Orders for 2007 OCT-NOV
3668

The BETWEEN operator can be used with string dates as well. Note: anything after midnight on 2004-02-10 is not included.

```
USE AdventureWorks;
DECLARE @sdate char(8)= '20040201', @edate char(8) = '20040210';
SELECT POs=COUNT(*) FROM Purchasing.PurchaseOrderHeader
WHERE OrderDate BETWEEN @sdate AND @edate;
GO
```

POs
108

BETWEEN Dates Without Time: Entire 2004-02-10 Day Included This Fashion

```
SELECT POs=COUNT(*) FROM Purchasing.PurchaseOrderHeader
WHERE datediff(dd,0,OrderDate)
        BETWEEN datediff(dd,0,'20040201 12:11:39') AND datediff(dd,0,'20040210 14:33:19')
```

POs
108

The datetime range BETWEEN is equivalent to >=...AND....<= operators.

```
SELECT POs=COUNT(*) FROM Purchasing.PurchaseOrderHeader
WHERE OrderDate  BETWEEN '2004-02-01 00:00:00.000' AND '2004-02-10  00:00:00.000'
```

POs
108

Orders with datetime OrderDate-s of

'2004-02-10 00:00:01.000'	1 second after midnight (start of day at 12:00AM)
'2004-02-10 00:01:00.000'	1 minute after midnight
'2004-02-10 01:00:00.000'	1 hour after midnight
'2004-02-10 23:00:00.000'	23 hours after midnight

would not included in the preceding two queries. Only datetime OrderDate of '2004-02-10 00:00:00.000' would be included. That would be OK if the time part is not used. But even in that case and order can be entered accidentally with a time part, that would throw off the count.

To include the entire day of 2004-02-10, move the day up by one and use the < operator:

```
SELECT POs=COUNT(*) FROM Purchasing.PurchaseOrderHeader
WHERE OrderDate >= '20040201' AND OrderDate < '20040211';
```

POs
108

The reason we cannot detect a difference is due to lack of data passed midnight on 2004-02-11.

```
SELECT  [PurchaseOrderID], [RevisionNumber], [Status],
        [EmployeeID], [VendorID], [ShipMethodID], [OrderDate]
FROM [AdventureWorks].[Purchasing].[PurchaseOrderHeader] WHERE PurchaseOrderID = 1665;
```

PurchaseOrderID	RevisionNumber	Status	EmployeeID	VendorID	ShipMethodID	OrderDate
1665	0	4	261	43	5	2004-02-10 00:00:00.000

Advance the datetime one second from midnight, the BETWEEN datetime query is not going to count it

```
UPDATE [AdventureWorks].[Purchasing].[PurchaseOrderHeader]
	SET OrderDate = '2004-02-10 00:00:01.000'
WHERE PurchaseOrderID = 1665;  -- (1 row(s) affected)
```

This is the current value for OrderDate datetime.

PurchaseOrderID	RevisionNumber	Status	EmployeeID	VendorID	ShipMethodID	OrderDate
1665	0	4	261	43	5	2004-02-10 00:00:01.000

The following queries are not going to count this passed midnight record any more.

```
SELECT POs=COUNT(*) FROM Purchasing.PurchaseOrderHeader
WHERE OrderDate BETWEEN '2004-02-01 00:00:00.000' AND '2004-02-10  00:00:00.000'
```

POs
107

```
USE AdventureWorks; SELECT POs=COUNT(*) FROM Purchasing.PurchaseOrderHeader
WHERE OrderDate BETWEEN '20040201' AND '20040210'
```

POs
107

While the query we designed specifically for a case like this will count it correctly.

```
SELECT POs=COUNT(*) FROM Purchasing.PurchaseOrderHeader
WHERE OrderDate >= '20040201' AND OrderDate < '20040211'
```

POs
108

We restore the data to its original value.

```
UPDATE [AdventureWorks].[Purchasing].[PurchaseOrderHeader]
	SET OrderDate = '2004-02-10 00:00:00.000'
WHERE PurchaseOrderID = 1665;     -- (1 row(s) affected)
```

Date Validation Function ISDATE()

```
DECLARE @StringDate varchar(32);
SET @StringDate = '2011-03-15 18:50';
IF EXISTS( SELECT * WHERE ISDATE(@StringDate) = 1)
   PRINT 'VALID DATE: ' + @StringDate
ELSE
   PRINT 'INVALID DATE: ' + @StringDate;
```

```
VALID DATE: 2011-03-15 18:50
```

```
DECLARE @StringDate varchar(32) ;
SET @StringDate = '20112-03-15 18:50';
IF EXISTS( SELECT * WHERE ISDATE(@StringDate) = 1)
   PRINT 'VALID DATE: ' + @StringDate
ELSE  PRINT 'INVALID DATE: ' + @StringDate;
GO
```

```
INVALID DATE: 20112-03-15 18:50
```

First and Last Day of Date Periods

Calculating date periods markers is a very important task in T-SQL programming, especially related to reporting queries.

```
DECLARE @Date DATE = '20161023';  SELECT ReferenceDate   = @Date;

SELECT FirstDayOfYear  = CONVERT(DATE, dateadd(yy, datediff(yy,0, @Date),0));

SELECT LastDayOfYear   = CONVERT(DATE, dateadd(yy, datediff(yy,0, @Date)+1,-1));

SELECT FDofSemester = CONVERT(DATE, dateadd(qq,((datediff(qq,0,@Date)/2)*2),0));

SELECT LastDayOfSemester  = CONVERT(DATE, dateadd(qq,((datediff(qq,0,@Date)/2)*2)+2,-1));

SELECT FirstDayOfQuarter  = CONVERT(DATE, dateadd(qq, datediff(qq,0, @Date),0));

SELECT LastDayOfQuarter = CONVERT(DATE, dateadd(qq, datediff(qq,0,@Date)+1,-1));
```

LastDayOfQuarter
2016-12-31

The brand-new EOMonth() function simplifies month start/end formulas

```
SELECT LastDayOfMonth = EOMonth (@Date);  -- New in SQL Server 2012

SELECT FirstDayOfMonth = CONVERT(DATE, dateadd(mm, datediff(mm,0, @Date),0));

SELECT LastDayOfMonth  = CONVERT(DATE, dateadd(mm, datediff(mm,0, @Date)+1,-1));

SELECT FirstDayOfWeek  = CONVERT(DATE, dateadd(wk, datediff(wk,0, @Date),0));

SELECT LastDayOfWeek   = CONVERT(DATE, dateadd(wk, datediff(wk,0, @Date)+1,-1));
GO
```

Month Sequence Generator

Sometimes date based data may have gaps missing months. For reporting purposes we may want to include all months from start date to end date. To do that we have to generate a continuous sequence of months, and use it to fill in the gaps. Calendar table can also be used for such a task.

```
DECLARE @Date date = '2000-01-01'
SELECT MonthStart=dateadd(MM, number, @Date)
FROM  master.dbo.spt_values
WHERE type='P' AND  dateadd(MM, number, @Date) <= CURRENT_TIMESTAMP
ORDER BY MonthStart;    -- (151 row(s) affected) - Partial results.
```

MonthStart
2000-01-01
2000-02-01
2000-03-01
2000-04-01
2000-05-01
2000-06-01
2000-07-01
2000-08-01
2000-09-01
2000-10-01
2000-11-01
2000-12-01
2001-01-01
2001-02-01
2001-03-01
2001-04-01

Selected U.S. & International Date Styles

The U.S. date style is m/d/y.

```
DECLARE @DateTimeValue varchar(32) = '10/23/2016';

SELECT StringDate=@DateTimeValue,   [SSMS-Style] = CONVERT(datetime, @DatetimeValue);

SELECT @DateTimeValue = '10/23/2016 23:01:05';

SELECT StringDate = @DateTimeValue,  [SSMS-Style] = CONVERT(datetime, @DatetimeValue);
GO
```

StringDate	SSMS-Style
10/23/2016	2016-10-23 00:00:00.000

StringDate	SSMS-Style
10/23/2016 23:01:05	2016-10-23 23:01:05.000

The UK or British/French style is dmy.

```
DECLARE @DateTimeValue varchar(32) = '23/10/16 23:01:05';

SELECT StringDate = @DateTimeValue,  [SSMS-Style] = CONVERT(datetime, @DatetimeValue, 3);

 SELECT @DateTimeValue = '23/10/2016 04:01 PM';

SELECT StringDate = @DateTimeValue,  [SSMS-Style] = CONVERT(datetime, @DatetimeValue, 103);
GO
```

The German style is dmy as well with a new twist to it: period instead of slash.

```
DECLARE @DateTimeValue varchar(32)  = '23.10.16 23:01:05';
SELECT StringDate = @DateTimeValue,  [SSMS -Style] = CONVERT(datetime, @DatetimeValue, 4);
 SELECT @DateTimeValue = '23.10.2016 04:01 PM';
SELECT StringDate = @DateTimeValue,  [SSMS -Style] = CONVERT(datetime, @DatetimeValue, 104);
GO
```

```
-- Nondeterministic month name (mon)
SET LANGUAGE Spanish; SELECT CONVERT(varchar, getdate(), 100);          -- Ago 10 2018  4:43PM
SET LANGUAGE Turkish; SELECT CONVERT(varchar, getdate(), 100);          -- Agu 10 2018  4:44PM
SET LANGUAGE Polish; SELECT CONVERT(varchar, getdate(), 100);           -- VIII 10 2018  4:46PM
SET LANGUAGE Hungarian; SELECT CONVERT(varchar, getdate(), 100);        -- aug 10 2018  4:46PM
SET LANGUAGE Russian; SELECT CONVERT(nvarchar, getdate(), 100);         -- авг 10 2018  4:47PM
```

The DATEPART() Function to Decompose a Date

The DATEPART() function returns a part of a date.

```
DECLARE @dt datetime = getdate();
SELECT DATEPART(YEAR, @dt)              AS YYYY,
       DATEPART(MONTH, @dt)             AS MM,
       DATEPART(DAY, @dt)               AS DD;
```

YYYY	MM	DD
2016	7	29

```
SELECT * FROM Northwind.dbo.Orders
WHERE DATEPART(YEAR, OrderDate)                  = '1996'  AND
      DATEPART(MONTH,OrderDate)                  = '07'    AND
      DATEPART(DAY, OrderDate)                   = '10'
```

```
/*OrderID    CustomerID    EmployeeID    OrderDate    RequiredDate    ShippedDate
      ShipVia  Freight  ShipName    Shipaddress    ShipCity ShipRegion    ShipPostalCode
      ShipCountry
10253   HANAR  3     1996-07-10 00:00:00.000  1996-07-24 00:00:00.000  1996-07-16 00:00:00.000
      2      58.17   Hanari Carnes    Rua do Paço, 67   Rio de Janeiro   RJ    05454-876
      Brazil  */
```

Alternate syntax for DATEPART.

```
SELECT * FROM Northwind.dbo.Orders
WHERE       YEAR(OrderDate)      = 1996      AND
            MONTH(OrderDate)     = 07        AND
            DAY(OrderDate)       = 10
GO
```

```
-- Additional datepart parameters including Julian date
DECLARE @dt datetime = getdate();
SELECT DATEPART(DAY, @dt)                 AS DD,
       DATEPART(WEEKDAY, @dt)             AS WD,
       DATEPART(DAYOFYEAR, @dt)           AS JulianDate,
       DATEPART(WEEK, @dt)                AS Week,
       DATEPART(ISO_WEEK, @dt)            AS ISOWeek,
       DATEPART(HOUR, @dt)                AS HH;
```

DD	WD	JulianDate	Week	ISOWeek	HH
10	5	223	33	32	17

The DATENAME() Function to Get Date Part Names

The DATENAME() function can be used to find out the words for months and weekdays.

```
SELECT DayName=DATENAME(weekday, OrderDate), SalesPerWeekDay = COUNT(*)
FROM AdventureWorks2008.Sales.SalesOrderHeader
GROUP BY DATENAME(weekday, OrderDate), DATEPART(weekday,OrderDate)
ORDER BY DATEPART(weekday,OrderDate);
```

DayName	SalesPerWeekDay
Sunday	4482
Monday	4591
Tuesday	4346
Wednesday	4244
Thursday	4483
Friday	4444
Saturday	4875

DATENAME application for month names

```
SELECT MonthName=DATENAME(month, OrderDate), SalesPerMonth = COUNT(*)
FROM AdventureWorks2008.Sales.SalesOrderHeader
GROUP BY DATENAME(month, OrderDate), MONTH(OrderDate) ORDER BY MONTH(OrderDate);
```

MonthName	SalesPerMonth
January	2483
February	2686
March	2750
April	2740
May	3154
June	3079
July	2094
August	2411
September	2298
October	2282
November	2474
December	3014

```
SELECT DATENAME(MM,dateadd(MM,7,-1))  -- July  - Month name from month number
```

Extract Date from Text with PATINDEX Pattern Matching

```
USE tempdb;
go
```

```
CREATE TABLE InsiderTransaction (
    InsiderTransactionID int identity primary key,
    TradeDate datetime,
    TradeMsg varchar(256),
    ModifiedDate datetime default (getdate())  );
```

```
-- Populate table with dummy data
INSERT InsiderTransaction (TradeMsg)
VALUES ('INSIDER TRAN QABC Hammer, Bruce D. CSO 09-02-08 Buy 2,000 6.10');
INSERT InsiderTransaction (TradeMsg)
VALUES ('INSIDER TRAN QABC Schmidt, Steven CFO 08-25-08 Buy 2,500 6.70') ;
INSERT InsiderTransaction (TradeMsg)
VALUES ('INSIDER TRAN QABC  Hammer, Bruce D. CSO  08-20-08 Buy 3,000 8.59');
INSERT InsiderTransaction (TradeMsg)
VALUES ('INSIDER TRAN QABC Walters,  Jeff CTO 08-15-08  Sell 5,648 8.49');
INSERT InsiderTransaction (TradeMsg)
VALUES  ('INSIDER TRAN  QABC  Walters, Jeff CTO   08-15-08 Option Exercise 5,648 2.15');
INSERT InsiderTransaction (TradeMsg)
VALUES('INSIDER TRAN QABC Hammer, Bruce D. CSO 07-31-08  Buy 5,000 8.05');
INSERT InsiderTransaction (TradeMsg)
VALUES('INSIDER TRAN QABC Lennot, Mark  Director  08-31-07 Buy 1,500 9.97');
INSERT InsiderTransaction (TradeMsg)
VALUES('INSIDER TRAN QABC  O''Neal, Linda COO  08-01-08 Sell 5,000 6.50');
```

Pattern match for MM-DD-YY using the PATINDEX string function to extract dates from stock trade message text.

```
SELECT   InsiderTransactionID ,        substring(TradeMsg,
         patindex('%[01][0-9]-[0123][0-9]-[0-9][0-9]%', TradeMsg),8) AS TradeDate
FROM InsiderTransaction  WHERE  patindex('%[01][0-9]-[0123][0-9]-[0-9][0-9]%', TradeMsg) > 0;
```

InsiderTransactionID	TradeDate
1	09-02-08
2	08-25-08
3	08-20-08
4	08-15-08
5	08-15-08
6	07-31-08
7	08-31-07
8	08-01-08

Valid Ranges for Date & Time Data Types

- DATE (3 bytes) date range:
- January 1, 1 through December 31, 9999 A.D.

- SMALLDATETIME (4 bytes) date range:
- January 1, 1900 through June 6, 2079

- DATETIME (8 bytes) date range:
- January 1, 1753 through December 31, 9999

- DATETIME2 (6-8 bytes) date range:
- January 1, 1 A.D. through December 31, 9999 A.D.

Smalldatetime has limited range. The statement below will give a date range error.

```
SELECT CONVERT(smalldatetime, '2110-01-01')
/* Msg 242, Level 16, State 3, Line 1
The conversion of a varchar data type to a smalldatetime data type
resulted in an out-of-range value. */
```

```
-- Date Columbus discovers America
SELECT CONVERT(datetime, '14921012');
/* Msg 242, Level 16, State 3, Line 2
The conversion of a varchar data type to a datetime data type resulted in an out-of-range value. */
```

```
SELECT CONVERT(datetime2, '14921012');    -- 1492-10-10 00:00:00.0000000
```

```
SELECT CONVERT(date, '14921012');                    -- 1492-10-12
```

Last Week Calculations

```
-- SQL last Friday - Implied string to datetime conversions in dateadd & datediff
DECLARE @BaseFriday CHAR(8), @LastFriday datetime, @LastMonday datetime;
SET @BaseFriday = '19000105';
SELECT   @LastFriday = dateadd(dd,
         (datediff (dd, @BaseFriday, CURRENT_TIMESTAMP) / 7) * 7, @BaseFriday) ;
SELECT [Last Friday] = @LastFriday ;
```

Last Friday
2012-07-27 00:00:00.000

```
-- Last Monday (last week's Monday)
SELECT   @LastMonday=dateadd(dd,  (datediff (dd, @BaseFriday,
          CURRENT_TIMESTAMP) / 7) * 7 - 4, @BaseFriday)
SELECT [Last Monday]= @LastMonday;
```

Last Monday
2012-07-23 00:00:00.000

```
-- Last week - SUN - SAT
SELECT          [Last Week] = CONCAT(CONVERT(varchar,dateadd(day, -1, @LastMonday), 101), ' - ',
                CONVERT(varchar, dateadd(day, 1,  @LastFriday), 101))
```

Last Week
07/22/2012 - 07/28/2012

```
-- Next 10 weeks including this one; SUN - SAT
SELECT   TOP 10   [ Week] = CONCAT(CONVERT(varchar,dateadd(day, -1+number*7, @LastMonday), 101),
         ' - ',    CONVERT(varchar, dateadd(day, 1+number*7,  @LastFriday), 101))
FROM master.dbo.spt_values  WHERE type = 'P';
```

Week
08/05/2012 - 08/11/2012
08/12/2012 - 08/18/2012
08/19/2012 - 08/25/2012
08/26/2012 - 09/01/2012
09/02/2012 - 09/08/2012
09/09/2012 - 09/15/2012
09/16/2012 - 09/22/2012
09/23/2012 - 09/29/2012
09/30/2012 - 10/06/2012
10/07/2012 - 10/13/2012

Specific Day Calculations

```
-- First day of current month
SELECT dateadd(month, datediff(month, 0, getdate()), 0);
```

```
-- 15th day of current month
SELECT dateadd(day,14,dateadd(month,datediff(month,0,getdate()),0));
```

```
-- First Monday of current month
SELECT    dateadd(day, (9-datepart(weekday,
          dateadd(month, datediff(month, 0, getdate()), 0)))%7,
          dateadd(month, datediff(month, 0, getdate()), 0)) ;
```

```
-- Next Monday calculation from the reference date which was a Monday
DECLARE @Now datetime = GETDATE();
DECLARE @NextMonday datetime = dateadd(dd, ((datediff(dd, '19000101', @Now)  / 7) * 7) + 7,
'19000101');
SELECT [Now]=@Now, [Next Monday]=@NextMonday;
```

```
-- Last Friday of current month
SELECT    dateadd(day, -7+(6-datepart(weekday,
          dateadd(month, datediff(month, 0, getdate())+1, 0)))%7,
          dateadd(month, datediff(month, 0, getdate())+1, 0)) ;
```

```
-- First day of next month
SELECT dateadd(month, datediff(month, 0, getdate())+1, 0);
```

```
-- 15th of next month
SELECT dateadd(day,14, dateadd(month, datediff(month, 0, getdate())+1, 0));
```

```
-- First Monday of next month
SELECT    dateadd(day, (9-datepart(weekday,
          dateadd(month, datediff(month, 0, getdate())+1, 0)))%7,
           dateadd(month, datediff(month, 0, getdate())+1, 0))  AS NextMonthMonday;
```

NextMonthMonday
2012-08-06 00:00:00.000

CHAPTER 14: Subqueries in SELECT Statements

Subqueries

Subquery ("inner query") is query within a query which is called the "outer query".

When a subquery involves columns form the outer query, it is called correlated subquery.

When a subquery has a table alias, it is called a derived table.

With SQL Server 2005 a new kind of subquery was introduced: Common Table Expression (CTE). A query can have one or more CTEs. If they are related, they are called nested CTEs. CTEs support recursion.

Correlated subquery is used to retrieve the last freight cost for the customer.

```
-- Correlated subquery - it has reference to an outer query column: A.CustomerID
USE Northwind;

SELECT   A.CustomerID,
     FORMAT(MIN(A.OrderDate), 'd')                              AS FirstOrder,
     FORMAT(MAX(A.OrderDate), 'd')                              AS LastOrder,
     FORMAT( (SELECT   TOP 1 B.Freight
               FROM     Orders B
               WHERE    B.CustomerID = A.CustomerID
               ORDER BY OrderDate DESC),'c','en-US')             AS LastFreight
FROM     Orders A
GROUP BY A.CustomerID ORDER BY A.CustomerID; -- (89 row(s) affected) - Partial results.
```

CustomerID	FirstOrder	LastOrder	LastFreight
ALFKI	8/25/1997	4/9/1998	$1.21
ANATR	9/18/1996	3/4/1998	$39.92
ANTON	11/27/1996	1/28/1998	$58.43
AROUT	11/15/1996	4/10/1998	$33.80
BERGS	8/12/1996	3/4/1998	$151.52
BLAUS	4/9/1997	4/29/1998	$31.14
BLONP	7/25/1996	1/12/1998	$7.09
BOLID	10/10/1996	3/24/1998	$16.16
BONAP	10/16/1996	5/6/1998	$38.28
BOTTM	12/20/1996	4/24/1998	$24.12
BSBEV	8/26/1996	4/14/1998	$123.83
CACTU	4/29/1997	4/28/1998	$0.33

Non-Correlated Subqueries

In the next query, the inner query is not linked to the outer query at all (no outer column is used in the inner query). The implication is that the inner query can be executed by itself. The inner query needs to return a single value in this instance due to the ">=" operator. If it were to return multiple values, error would result.

```
SELECT          Name,
                FORMAT(ListPrice, 'c','en-US')          AS ListPrice,
                ProductNumber,
                FORMAT(StandardCost, 'c','en-US')       AS StandardCost
FROM AdventureWorks2012.Production.Product
WHERE ListPrice >= (SELECT ListPrice  FROM AdventureWorks.Production.Product
                                      WHERE Name = 'Road-250 Black, 48' )
ORDER BY ListPrice DESC, Name;
GO -- -- (21 row(s) affected) - Partial results.
```

Name	ListPrice	ProductNumber	StandardCost
Road-150 Red, 44	$3,578.27	BK-R93R-44	$2,171.29
Road-150 Red, 48	$3,578.27	BK-R93R-48	$2,171.29
Road-150 Red, 52	$3,578.27	BK-R93R-52	$2,171.29
Road-150 Red, 56	$3,578.27	BK-R93R-56	$2,171.29
Road-150 Red, 62	$3,578.27	BK-R93R-62	$2,171.29
Mountain-100 Silver, 38	$3,399.99	BK-M82S-38	$1,912.15

The IN Set Operator & ANY, SOME & ALL Comparison Modifiers

ANY & SOME are the same. Some results with ANY & ALL are the same as with IN & NOT IN.

```
SELECT COUNT(*) FROM Person.Address;    -- 19614
SELECT COUNT(*) FROM Person.Address
        WHERE City NOT IN (SELECT City FROM Person.Address WHERE AddressLine1 like '%court%');
-- 3184
SELECT COUNT(*) FROM Person.Address
        WHERE City IN (SELECT City FROM Person.Address WHERE AddressLine1 like '%court%');
-- 16430
SELECT COUNT(*) FROM Person.Address
        WHERE City <> ALL (SELECT City FROM Person.Address WHERE AddressLine1 like '%court%');
-- 3184
SELECT COUNT(*) FROM Person.Address
        WHERE City < ALL (SELECT City FROM Person.Address WHERE AddressLine1 like '%court%');
-- 12
SELECT COUNT(*) FROM Person.Address
        WHERE City < ANY (SELECT City FROM Person.Address WHERE AddressLine1 like '%court%');
-- 19496
```

MSDN Article: **Comparison Operators Modified by ANY, SOME, or ALL**
http://msdn.microsoft.com/en-us/library/ms187074(v=SQL.105).aspx

Subquery returned more than 1 value Error

The following query fails. The reason: the ">=" requires a single value on the right side. The subquery returns 46 values.

```
-- Non-correlated subquery
SELECT          Name,
                FORMAT(ListPrice, 'c','en-US')          AS ListPrice,
                ProductNumber,
                FORMAT(StandardCost, 'c','en-US')       AS StandardCost
FROM AdventureWorks2012.Production.Product
WHERE ListPrice >=
  (SELECT ListPrice
   FROM AdventureWorks.Production.Product
   WHERE Name LIKE 'Road%' )
ORDER BY ListPrice DESC, Name;
GO
/* Msg 512, Level 16, State 1, Line 3
Subquery returned more than 1 value. This is not permitted when the subquery follows =, !=, <, <= , >, >=
or when the subquery is used as an expression. */
```

If we change the WHERE clause predicate operator from ">=" to "IN" then the query will execute correctly since the IN operator works with a set of values on the right side.

```
-- Non-correlated subquery
SELECT  Name,
        FORMAT(ListPrice, 'c','en-US')          AS ListPrice,
        ProductNumber,
        FORMAT(StandardCost, 'c','en-US')       AS StandardCost
FROM AdventureWorks2012.Production.Product
WHERE ListPrice IN
        (SELECT ListPrice
         FROM AdventureWorks.Production.Product  WHERE Name LIKE 'Road%' )
ORDER BY ListPrice DESC, Name;
-- (253 row(s) affected)  -- Partial results.
```

Name	ListPrice	ProductNumber	StandardCost
AWC Logo Cap	$8.99	CA-1098	$6.92
Racing Socks, L	$8.99	SO-R809-L	$3.36
Racing Socks, M	$8.99	SO-R809-M	$3.36
Road Bottle Cage	$8.99	BC-R205	$3.36
Road-650 Black, 44	$782.99	BK-R50B-44	$486.71
Road-650 Black, 48	$782.99	BK-R50B-48	$486.71
Road-650 Black, 52	$782.99	BK-R50B-52	$486.71

Correlated Subqueries

In a correlated subquery there is a reference to an outer query column. In other words, the subquery by itself cannot be executed due to the correlation. In the next query, the inner query references soh.SalesOrderID column from the outer query in the WHERE clause predicate which is like an EQUI-JOIN.

```
SELECT          soh.SalesOrderID,
                FORMAT (soh.OrderDate, 'yyyy-MM-dd')                    AS OrderDate,

                ( SELECT FORMAT(MAX(sod.UnitPrice),'c','en-US')
                  FROM   AdventureWorks2012.Sales.SalesOrderDetail AS sod
                  WHERE  soh.SalesOrderID = sod.SalesOrderID )          AS MaxUnitPrice,

                FORMAT(TotalDue, 'c', 'en-US')                          AS TotalDue
FROM    AdventureWorks2012.Sales.SalesOrderHeader AS soh
ORDER BY MaxUnitPrice DESC, SalesOrderID;    -- (31465 row(s) affected) - Partial results.
```

SalesOrderID	OrderDate	MaxUnitPrice	TotalDue
51087	2007-07-01	$953.63	$2,721.27
51099	2007-07-01	$953.63	$5,276.64
51119	2007-07-01	$953.63	$2,040.14
51173	2007-07-01	$953.63	$1,457.54
51701	2007-08-01	$953.63	$2,634.93
51798	2007-08-01	$953.63	$907.09
51805	2007-08-01	$953.63	$907.09
51808	2007-08-01	$953.63	$1,827.45
51861	2007-08-01	$953.63	$11,762.43
53489	2007-09-01	$953.63	$1,814.18

The next query with correlated subquery list sales staff with 0.015 commission rate.

```
SELECT CONCAT(p.LastName,', ', p.FirstName) AS SalesPerson, e.BusinessEntityID AS EmployeeID
FROM AdventureWorks2012.Person.Person AS p
                INNER JOIN AdventureWorks2012.HumanResources.Employee AS e
                            ON e.BusinessEntityID = p.BusinessEntityID
WHERE 0.015 IN  (SELECT CommissionPct   FROM AdventureWorks2012.Sales.SalesPerson sp
                            WHERE e.BusinessEntityID = sp.BusinessEntityID)  ORDER BY SalesPerson;
```

SalesPerson	EmployeeID
Carson, Jillian	277
Mitchell, Linda	276
Saraiva, José	282

Single-Valued Correlated Subqueries

The query syntax determines if we can use a single-valued subquery or multiple-valued. A subquery can be the argument of a function.

```
USE AdventureWorks2012;
```

```
-- Single value subquery in SELECT list
SELECT  SOH.SalesOrderID                                AS SOID,
        CONVERT(DATE,SOH.OrderDate)                     AS OrderDate,
        FORMAT(SOH.Subtotal,'c0','en-US')               AS Subtotal,
        (SELECT MAX(SOD.UnitPrice)
         FROM Sales.SalesOrderDetail AS SOD
         WHERE SOH.SalesOrderID=SOD.SalesOrderID)       AS MaxUnitPrice
FROM Sales.SalesOrderHeader SOH    ORDER BY SOID;
--(31467 row(s) affected) - Partial results.
```

SOID	OrderDate	Subtotal	MaxUnitPrice
43659	2005-07-01	$20,566	2039.994
43660	2005-07-01	$1,294	874.794

```
-- Make the subquery the argument of the FORMAT function
SELECT  TOP (10)        SOH.SalesOrderID                        AS SOID,
                        CONVERT(DATE,SOH.OrderDate)             AS OrderDate,
                        FORMAT(SOH.Subtotal,'c0','en-US')       AS Subtotal,
                        FORMAT(
    (SELECT MAX(SOD.UnitPrice)
    FROM Sales.SalesOrderDetail AS SOD
    WHERE SOH.SalesOrderID=SOD.SalesOrderID)
                        ,'c2','en-US')                          AS MaxUnitPrice
FROM Sales.SalesOrderHeader SOH   ORDER BY SOID;
```

SOID	OrderDate	Subtotal	MaxUnitPrice
43659	2005-07-01	$20,566	$2,039.99
43660	2005-07-01	$1,294	$874.79
43661	2005-07-01	$32,726	$2,039.99
43662	2005-07-01	$28,833	$2,146.96
43663	2005-07-01	$419	$419.46
43664	2005-07-01	$24,433	$2,039.99
43665	2005-07-01	$14,353	$2,039.99
43666	2005-07-01	$5,056	$2,146.96
43667	2005-07-01	$6,107	$2,039.99
43668	2005-07-01	$35,944	$2,146.96

Correlated Subqueries with Same Table

In a correlated subquery, we can use a table from the outer query. In such a case table alias usage is required. In the next query with correlated subquery which lists same part suppliers, the ProductVendor table is referenced by both the outer query and inner query, therefore table alias is required.

```
SELECT          p.Name                          AS ProductName,
                v.Name                          AS Vendor,
                pv1.BusinessEntityID            AS VendorID
FROM AdventureWorks2012.Purchasing.ProductVendor pv1
  INNER JOIN AdventureWorks2012.Production.Product p ON p.ProductID = pv1.ProductID
  INNER JOIN AdventureWorks2012.Purchasing.Vendor v  ON v.BusinessEntityID = pv1.BusinessEntityID
WHERE pv1.ProductID IN    (     SELECT pv2.ProductID
                                FROM AdventureWorks2012.Purchasing.ProductVendor pv2
                                WHERE pv1.BusinessEntityID <> pv2.BusinessEntityID)
ORDER  BY ProductName, Vendor;          -- (347 row(s) affected) - Partial results.
```

ProductName	Vendor	VendorID
Internal Lock Washer 7	Aurora Bike Center	1616
Internal Lock Washer 7	Pro Sport Industries	1686
Internal Lock Washer 8	Aurora Bike Center	1616
Internal Lock Washer 8	Pro Sport Industries	1686
Internal Lock Washer 9	Aurora Bike Center	1616
Internal Lock Washer 9	Pro Sport Industries	1686
LL Crankarm	Proseware, Inc.	1678

CROSS APPLY with Correlated Subquery

The CROSS APPLY operator can connect tables with correlated subqueries as demonstrated following, INNER JOIN would not work in this case. OUTER APPLY includes non matching rows.

```
USE AdventureWorks;     DECLARE  @Year  INT = 2003, @Month INT = 2;
SELECT   s.Name                                                 AS Customer,
         FORMAT(SalesAmount.OrderTotal,'c','en-US')             AS [Total Sales]
FROM     Sales.Customer AS c   INNER JOIN Sales.Store AS s   ON s.CustomerID = c.CustomerID
    CROSS APPLY  (      SELECT   soh.CustomerId,   Sum(sod.LineTotal)  AS OrderTotal
                        FROM     Sales.SalesOrderHeader AS soh
                INNER JOIN Sales.SalesOrderDetail AS sod    ON sod.SalesOrderId = soh.SalesOrderId
                        WHERE soh.CustomerId = c.CustomerId
                AND OrderDate > = DATEFROMPARTS(@Year, @Month, 1)
                AND OrderDate <   DATEADD(mm, 1, DATEFROMPARTS(@Year, @Month, 1))
                        GROUP BY soh.CustomerId)                AS SalesAmount
ORDER BY Customer;      -- (132 row(s) affected) - Partial results.
```

Customer	Total Sales
Ace Bicycle Supply	$647.99
Affordable Sports Equipment	$50,953.32
Alpine Ski House	$939.59
Basic Sports Equipment	$159.56

Derived Tables: SELECT from SELECT

A non-correlated subquery can be made into a derived table by enclosing it in parenthesis and assigning a table alias, such as "CAT" in the following example. It can then be used like a regular table for example in JOINs.

```
USE Northwind;

SELECT  c.CategoryName  AS Category,
        p.ProductName,    p.UnitPrice,    CAT.NoOfProducts
FROM    Categories c
     INNER JOIN Products p
       ON c.CategoryID = p.CategoryID
     INNER JOIN
                         (SELECT  c.CategoryID,
                                  NoOfProducts = count(* )
                          FROM    Categories c
                            INNER JOIN Products p1
                                  ON c.CategoryID = p1.CategoryID
                          GROUP BY c.CategoryID)                    AS CAT

       ON c.CategoryID = CAT.CategoryID
ORDER BY Category;
-- (77 row(s) affected)  - Partial results.
```

Category	ProductName	UnitPrice
Dairy Products	Raclette Courdavault	55.00
Dairy Products	Camembert Pierrot	34.00
Dairy Products	Gudbrandsdalsost	36.00
Dairy Products	Flotemysost	21.50
Dairy Products	Mozzarella di Giovanni	34.80
Grains/Cereals	Gustaf's Knäckebröd	21.00
Grains/Cereals	Tunnbröd	9.00
Grains/Cereals	Singaporean Hokkien Fried Mee	14.00
Grains/Cereals	Filo Mix	7.00
Grains/Cereals	Gnocchi di nonna Alice	38.00
Grains/Cereals	Ravioli Angelo	19.50

Results from the subquery (derived table).

CategoryID	NoOfProducts
1	12
2	12
3	13
4	10
5	7
6	6
7	5
8	12

The UNION & UNION ALL Set Operators

UNION (distinct, duplicates eliminated) and UNION ALL (duplicates allowed) merge two or more sets of data into one set. Important points to remember about UNION:

- First SELECT column list establishes column names and data types; if INTO used it goes here
- Subsequent SELECTs must match the column structure; column names can be any; NULL if no data
- ORDER BY goes at the very end with the last SELECT

T-SQL UNION query merges data from different countries into a single result set.

```
USE NorthWind;
SELECT   ContactName, CompanyName, City, Country, Phone
FROM   Customers WHERE  Country IN ( 'USA', 'Canada' )                    -- (16 row(s) affected)
UNION
SELECT   ContactName, CompanyName                AS Company,
         City,  Country, Phone                   AS Telephone
FROM   Customers WHERE  Country IN ( 'Germany', 'France' )                -- (22 row(s) affected)
UNION
SELECT   ContactName              AS Contact,
         CompanyName,     City,   Country,
         Phone                    AS Telephone
FROM   Customers WHERE  Country IN ( 'Brazil', 'Spain' )                  -- (14 row(s) affected)
ORDER  BY CompanyName,    ContactName ASC;  -- (52 row(s) affected)  - Partial results.
```

ContactName	CompanyName	City	Country	Phone
Maria Anders	Alfreds Futterkiste	Berlin	Germany	030-0074321
Hanna Moos	Blauer See Delikatessen	Mannheim	Germany	0621-08460
Frédérique Citeaux	Blondesddsl père et fils	Strasbourg	France	88.60.15.31
Martín Sommer	Bólido Comidas preparadas	Madrid	Spain	(91) 555 22 82

Applying Aggregates on Different Datasets & Merging with UNION ALL

Quick summary of sales orders (money in) and purchase orders (money out) for AdventureWorks Cycles.

```
SELECT COUNT(*) AS OrderCount, SUM(Subtotal) AS NetTotalValue,
                 SUM(TotalDue) AS TotalDueValue  FROM Sales.SalesOrderHeader
UNION ALL
SELECT COUNT(*), -SUM(Subtotal), -SUM(TotalDue)  FROM Purchasing.PurchaseOrderHeader;
```

OrderCount	NetTotalValue	TotalDueValue
31467	109847935.9843	123218533.5677
4012	-63791994.838	-70479332.6383

CTE: Common Table Expression for Structured Coding

Common Table Expression is new in SQL Server 2005. It is similar to derived tables in one aspect with a difference: it is defined at the very beginning of a the query, above the main(outer) query. In addition, CTEs can be nested and defined as recursive.

```
USE AdventureWorks;

WITH CTE(ManagerID, StaffCount)
AS
(
    SELECT ManagerID, COUNT(*)
    FROM HumanResources.Employee AS e
    GROUP BY ManagerID
)

SELECT      CONCAT(LEFT(FirstName,1), '. ', LastName)       AS Manager,
            e.Title, StaffCount
FROM CTE s
        INNER JOIN HumanResources.Employee e
    ON s.ManagerID = e.EmployeeID
        INNER JOIN Person.Contact c
    ON c.ContactID = e.ContactID
ORDER BY Manager;
-- (47 row(s) affected) - Partial results.
```

Manager	Title	StaffCount
A. Alberts	European Sales Manager	3
A. Hill	Production Supervisor - WC10	7
A. Wright	Master Scheduler	4
B. Diaz	Production Supervisor - WC40	12
B. Welcker	Vice President of Sales	3
C. Kleinerman	Maintenance Supervisor	4
C. Petculescu	Production Supervisor - WC10	5
C. Randall	Production Supervisor - WC30	6
D. Bradley	Marketing Manager	8
D. Hamilton	Production Supervisor - WC40	6
D. Liu	Accounts Manager	7
D. Miller	Research and Development Manager	3
E. Gubbels	Production Supervisor - WC20	10
G. Altman	Facilities Manager	2
H. Abolrous	Quality Assurance Manager	2

Multiple CTEs Query

A query can have multiple CTEs, they can even be nested (CTE has reference to previous CTE). The two CTEs in the following query are first name and last name frequencies.

```
USE AdventureWorks2012;

WITH cteLastNameFreq

   AS (SELECT      LastName            AS [LastNames],
                   count(* )           AS [LNFrequency]
      FROM    Person.Person
      GROUP BY LastName),

   cteFirstNameFreq
   AS (SELECT      FirstName           AS [FirstNames],
                   count(* )           AS [FNFrequency]
     FROM    Person.Person
     GROUP BY FirstName)

SELECT   CONCAT(rtrim(FirstName), ' ', rtrim(LastName))         AS [Name],
                   isnull(Title,'')                             AS [Title] ,
                   f.FNFrequency,
                   l.LNFrequency
FROM    Person.Person c
     INNER JOIN cteFirstNameFreq AS f
      ON c.FirstName = f.FirstNames
     INNER JOIN cteLastNameFreq AS l
      ON c.LastName = l.LastNames
WHERE   LastName LIKE 'P%' ORDER BY [Name];
-- (1187 row(s) affected) - Partial results;
```

Name	Title	FNFrequency	LNFrequency
Aaron Patterson		56	117
Aaron Perez		56	170
Aaron Perry		56	122
Aaron Phillips		56	80
Aaron Powell		56	116
Abby Patel		19	86
Abby Perez		19	170
Abigail Patterson		76	117
Abigail Patterson		76	117
Abigail Perry		76	122
Abigail Peterson		76	92
Abigail Powell		76	116

Testing Common Table Expressions

A CTE can be tested independently of the main query if it does not have nesting (reference to a previous CTE). The following screen snapshot displays the execution of the first CTE SELECT query.

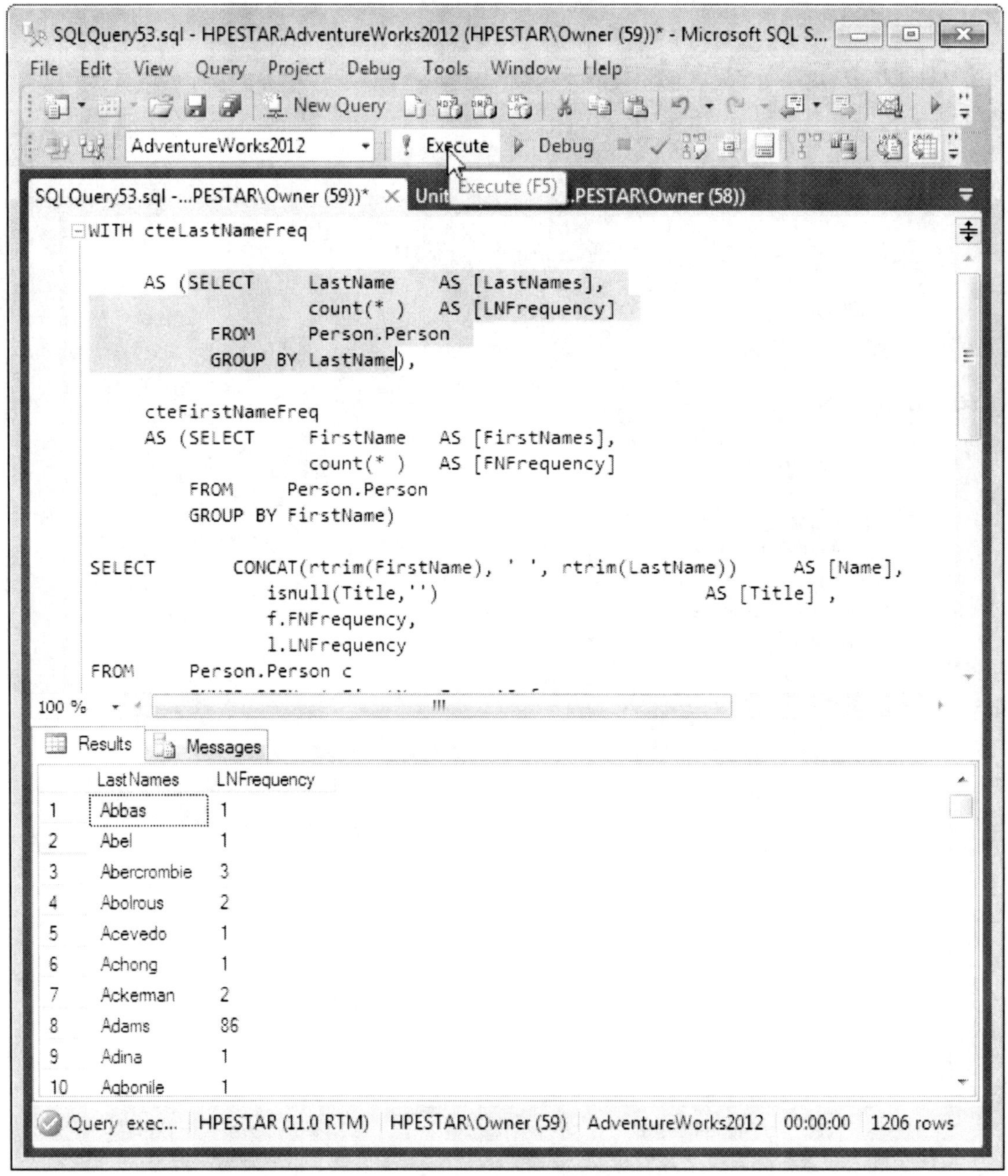

Nested CTEs Queries

CTEs can be nested by reference to a previous CTE like a table.

```
;WITH CTE1
   AS (SELECT 1 AS NUMBER
      UNION ALL
      SELECT 1),
   CTE2
   AS (SELECT 1 AS NUMBER
      FROM   CTE1 x,
             CTE1 y),
   CTE3
   AS (SELECT 1 AS NUMBER
      FROM   CTE2 x,
             CTE2 y),
   CTE4
   AS (SELECT 1 AS NUMBER
      FROM   CTE3 x,
             CTE3 y),
   CTE8BIT
   AS (SELECT ROW_NUMBER()
              OVER(ORDER BY NUMBER) AS INTSequence
      FROM   CTE4)
SELECT *
FROM   CTE8BIT
ORDER BY INTSequence;
-- (256 row(s) affected) - Partial results.
```

INTSequence
241
242
243
244
245
246
247
248
249
250
251
252
253
254
255
256

CTE nesting: cteLastSalary has a nested reference to cteLastSalaryChange

```
USE AdventureWorks2012;

WITH cteLastSalaryChange
   AS (SELECT      BusinessEntityID              AS EmployeeID,
                   Max(RateChangeDate)                AS ChangeDate
      FROM    HumanResources.EmployeePayHistory     GROUP BY BusinessEntityID),

   cteLastSalary
   AS (SELECT      eph.BusinessEntityID                   AS EmployeeID,      Rate
      FROM   HumanResources.EmployeePayHistory eph
          INNER JOIN cteLastSalaryChange lsc
           ON lsc.EmployeeID = eph.BusinessEntityID
             AND lsc.ChangeDate = eph.RateChangeDate)

-- SELECT * FROM cteLastSalary  -- for testing & debugging

SELECT TOP 1 FORMAT( Rate, 'c', 'en-US') AS SecondHighestPayRate
FROM     (SELECT   TOP 2 Rate      FROM     cteLastSalary      ORDER BY Rate DESC) a    -- Derived table
ORDER BY Rate ASC;
```

SecondHighestPayRate
$84.13

Testing Nested CTEs

Nested CTEs can be tested independently of the main query the following way.

```
USE AdventureWorks2012;
WITH cteLastSalaryChange
   AS (SELECT      BusinessEntityID              AS EmployeeID,
                   Max(RateChangeDate)                AS ChangeDate
      FROM    HumanResources.EmployeePayHistory
      GROUP BY BusinessEntityID),
   cteLastSalary
   AS (SELECT      eph.BusinessEntityID                   AS EmployeeID,
                   Rate
      FROM   HumanResources.EmployeePayHistory eph
          INNER JOIN cteLastSalaryChange lsc
           ON lsc.EmployeeID = eph.BusinessEntityID
             AND lsc.ChangeDate = eph.RateChangeDate)
SELECT * FROM cteLastSalary  -- for testing & debugging
```

In Query Editor, uncomment the testing line, select (highlight) the top part of the query and execute it

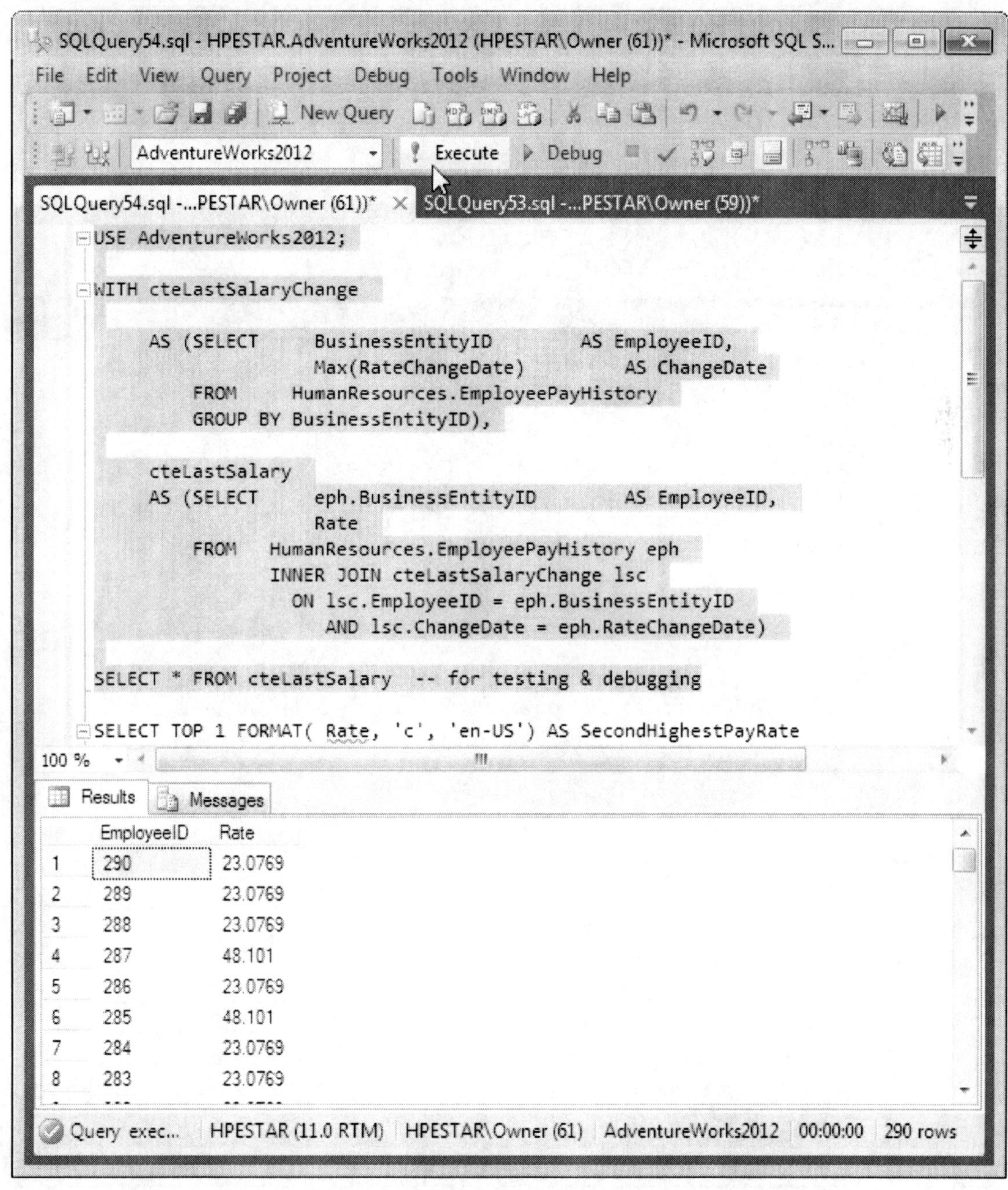

Recursive CTEs for Tree Hierarchy Processing

Recursive CTEs are one of the most exciting new features introduced with SQL Server 2005. They allow tree processing, such as organizational charts or bill of materials parts assembly, as well as generating sets of data without tables. The following recursive CTE generates 1 million integers all by itself. The query execution time is 10 seconds as it can be seen in the lower right.

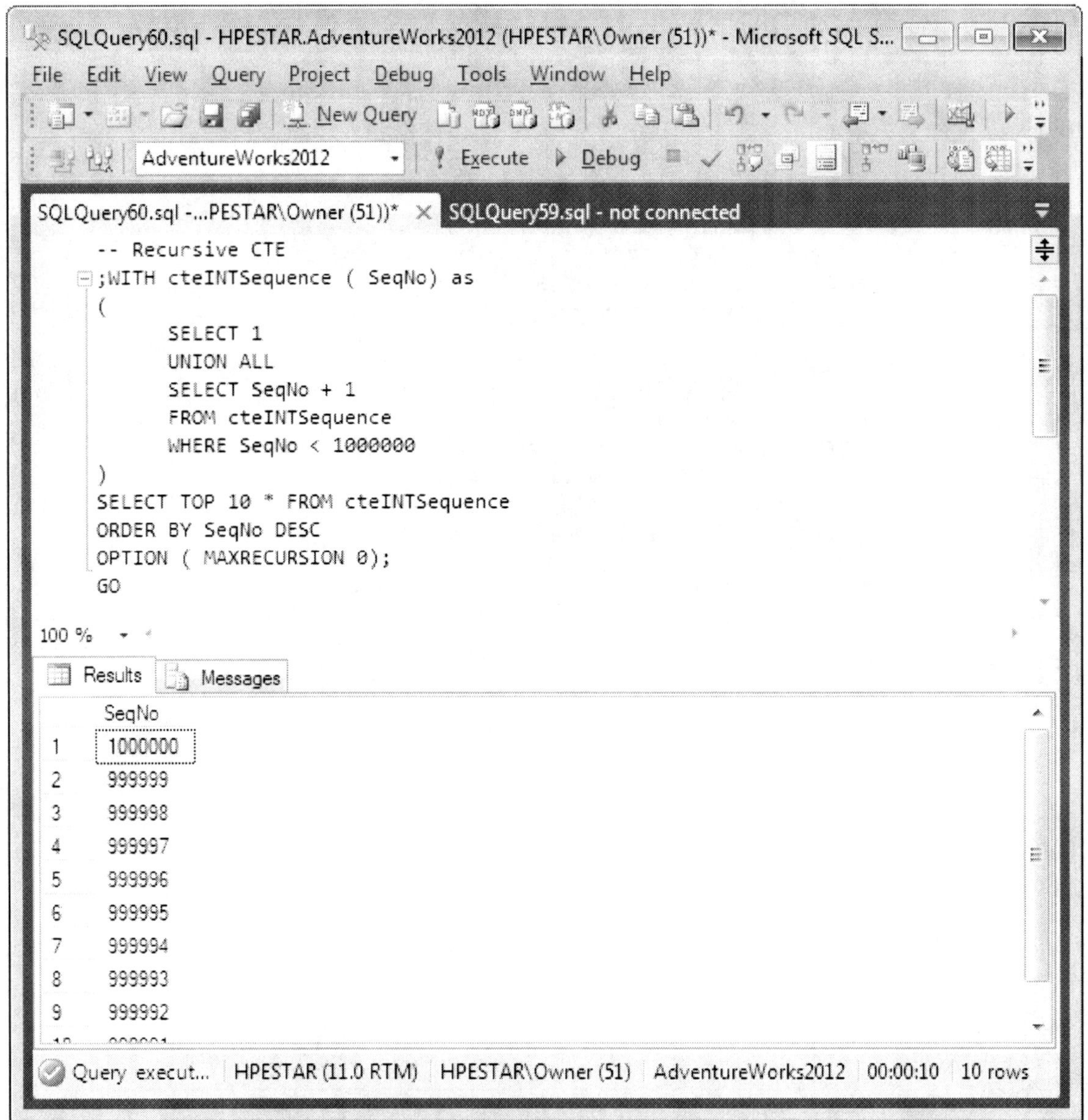

Recursive CTE Generation of Date & Month Sequences

Date sequence can be generated without a calendar table (Note: generally it is helpful to have a calendar table in the database) using recursive CTE.

```
DECLARE @StartDate date = '20160701', @Range smallint = 1000;

WITH cteSEQ ( SeqNo) as
(
    SELECT 0                                    -- Anchor member
    UNION ALL                                   -- Assemble set
    SELECT SeqNo + 1                            -- Recursive member
    FROM cteSEQ
    WHERE SeqNo < @Range
)
SELECT TOP 10 [DATE]=DATEADD(day, SeqNo, @StartDate)
FROM cteSEQ
OPTION ( MAXRECURSION 0);
GO
```

DATE
2016-07-01
2016-07-02
2016-07-03
2016-07-04
2016-07-05
2016-07-06
2016-07-07
2016-07-08
2016-07-09
2016-07-10

```
-- Month sequence generation
DECLARE @StartDate date = '20160701', @Range smallint = 100;
WITH cteSEQ ( SeqNo) as
(
    SELECT 0                                    -- Anchor member
    UNION ALL                                   -- Assemble set
    SELECT SeqNo + 1                            -- Recursive member
    FROM cteSEQ
    WHERE SeqNo < @Range
)
SELECT TOP 3 [DATE]=DATEADD(month, SeqNo, @StartDate)
FROM cteSEQ  OPTION ( MAXRECURSION 0);
```

Recursive CTE Parsing of Characters in a String

The difference between a WHILE loop parsing and recursive CTE is that the latter can be the part of a single statement. WHILE loop requires multiple statements. The following example inserts a "_" (underscore) after each alphabet letter except "Z".

```
DECLARE @alpha varchar( max)  = 'ABCDEFGHIJKLMNOPQRSTUVWXYZ';
```

```
;With CTE (Pointer, Output) AS
(SELECT 2, STUFF(@alpha, 2, 0, '_')
UNION ALL
SELECT Pointer + 2, STUFF(Output, Pointer+2 , 0, '_')
FROM CTE Where Pointer < 2 * (LEN(@alpha) - 1))
SELECT * FROM CTE ORDER BY Pointer;
```

Pointer	Output
2	A_BCDEFGHIJKLMNOPQRSTUVWXYZ
4	A_B_CDEFGHIJKLMNOPQRSTUVWXYZ
6	A_B_C_DEFGHIJKLMNOPQRSTUVWXYZ
8	A_B_C_D_EFGHIJKLMNOPQRSTUVWXYZ
10	A_B_C_D_E_FGHIJKLMNOPQRSTUVWXYZ
12	A_B_C_D_E_F_GHIJKLMNOPQRSTUVWXYZ
14	A_B_C_D_E_F_G_HIJKLMNOPQRSTUVWXYZ
16	A_B_C_D_E_F_G_H_IJKLMNOPQRSTUVWXYZ
18	A_B_C_D_E_F_G_H_I_JKLMNOPQRSTUVWXYZ
20	A_B_C_D_E_F_G_H_I_J_KLMNOPQRSTUVWXYZ
22	A_B_C_D_E_F_G_H_I_J_K_LMNOPQRSTUVWXYZ
24	A_B_C_D_E_F_G_H_I_J_K_L_MNOPQRSTUVWXYZ
26	A_B_C_D_E_F_G_H_I_J_K_L_M_NOPQRSTUVWXYZ
28	A_B_C_D_E_F_G_H_I_J_K_L_M_N_OPQRSTUVWXYZ
30	A_B_C_D_E_F_G_H_I_J_K_L_M_N_O_PQRSTUVWXYZ
32	A_B_C_D_E_F_G_H_I_J_K_L_M_N_O_P_QRSTUVWXYZ
34	A_B_C_D_E_F_G_H_I_J_K_L_M_N_O_P_Q_RSTUVWXYZ
36	A_B_C_D_E_F_G_H_I_J_K_L_M_N_O_P_Q_R_STUVWXYZ
38	A_B_C_D_E_F_G_H_I_J_K_L_M_N_O_P_Q_R_S_TUVWXYZ
40	A_B_C_D_E_F_G_H_I_J_K_L_M_N_O_P_Q_R_S_T_UVWXYZ
42	A_B_C_D_E_F_G_H_I_J_K_L_M_N_O_P_Q_R_S_T_U_VWXYZ
44	A_B_C_D_E_F_G_H_I_J_K_L_M_N_O_P_Q_R_S_T_U_V_WXYZ
46	A_B_C_D_E_F_G_H_I_J_K_L_M_N_O_P_Q_R_S_T_U_V_W_XYZ
48	A_B_C_D_E_F_G_H_I_J_K_L_M_N_O_P_Q_R_S_T_U_V_W_X_YZ
50	A_B_C_D_E_F_G_H_I_J_K_L_M_N_O_P_Q_R_S_T_U_V_W_X_Y_Z

Generate Month Names in Different Languages

The following query can be used to generate month names in any of the SQL Server 2012 supported languages.

```
SET language Spanish;  -- Se cambió la configuración de idioma a Español.
;WITH CTE AS
(   SELECT    1 MonthNo, CONVERT(DATE, '19000101') MonthFirst
    UNION ALL
    SELECT    MonthNo+1, DATEADD(Month, 1, MonthFirst)
    FROM  CTE
    WHERE Month(MonthFirst) < 12    )
SELECT  MonthNo AS MonthNumber,  DATENAME(MONTH, MonthFirst) AS MonthName
FROM  CTE
ORDER BY MonthNo;
SET language English; -- Changed language setting to us_english.
```

```
SET language Hungarian;  -- Nyelvi beállítás átállítva a következőre: magyar.
;WITH CTE AS
(   SELECT    1 MonthNo, CONVERT(DATE, '19000101') MonthFirst
    UNION ALL
    SELECT    MonthNo+1, DATEADD(Month, 1, MonthFirst)
    FROM  CTE
    WHERE Month(MonthFirst) < 12    )
SELECT  MonthNo AS MonthNumber,  DATENAME(MONTH, MonthFirst) AS MonthName
FROM  CTE
ORDER BY MonthNo;
SET language English; -- Changed language setting to us_english.
```

MonthNumber	MonthName
1	Enero
2	Febrero
3	Marzo
4	Abril
5	Mayo
6	Junio
7	Julio
8	Agosto
9	Septiembre
10	Octubre
11	Noviembre
12	Diciembre

MonthNumber	MonthName
1	január
2	február
3	március
4	április
5	május
6	június
7	július
8	augusztus
9	szeptember
10	október
11	november
12	december

Graphical Organizational Chart of AdventureWorks Cycles

T-SQL recursive CTE query generates the entire company chart of AdventureWorks Cycles. The anchor term is Ken Sanchez CEO with ManagerID as NULL. Everybody else in the company has a ManagerID which is not NULL.

```
USE AdventureWorks;

WITH cteEmployeeTree
  AS (SELECT      Root.EmployeeName,  Root.ManagerName,
                  Root.EmployeeId, Root.ManagerId,
                  CONVERT(VARCHAR(MAX),Root.PathSequence) AS PathLabel
    FROM   (SELECT EmployeeName = CONCAT(c.FirstName, SPACE(1), c.LastName),
            ManagerName = convert(VARCHAR(128),''),
            e.EmployeeId,
            e.ManagerId,
            char(64 + ROW_NUMBER()  OVER(ORDER BY e.EmployeeId)) AS PathSequence
        FROM   HumanResources.Employee e
            INNER JOIN Person.Contact c
             ON e.ContactID = c.ContactID
        WHERE  e.ManagerId IS NULL) Root                    -- Anchor/root term (above)
    UNION ALL                                               -- Build a set
    SELECT        Branch.EmployeeName,                      -- Recursive term (below)
                  Branch.ManagerName,
                  Branch.EmployeeId, Branch.ManagerId,
                  PathLabel = Branch.PathLabel + CONVERT(VARCHAR(MAX),  Branch.PathSequence)
    FROM   (SELECT EmployeeName = CONCAT(c.FirstName, SPACE(1), c.LastName),
           ManagerName = CONVERT(VARCHAR(128),CONCAT(cm.FirstName, SPACE(1), cm.LastName)),
            e.EmployeeId,
            e.ManagerId,
            cte.PathLabel,
            PathSequence = char(64 + ROW_NUMBER()  OVER(ORDER BY e.EmployeeId))
        FROM   cteEmployeeTree cte
            INNER JOIN HumanResources.Employee e
             ON e.ManagerId = cte.EmployeeId
            INNER JOIN Person.Contact c
             ON e.ContactID = c.ContactID
            INNER JOIN HumanResources.Employee em
             ON em.EmployeeID = e.ManagerID
            INNER JOIN Person.Contact cm
             ON em.ContactID = cm.ContactID) Branch)
-- Outer / main query
SELECT   CONCAT(REPLICATE(CHAR(9), LEN(PathLabel)-1),   -- tabs for indenting
                  EmployeeName) AS EmployeeName
FROM     cteEmployeeTree  ORDER BY PathLabel;
```

The resulting organizational chart was generated by Word as tabs (CHAR(9)) were converted to table columns (partial results).

EmployeeName				
Ken Sánchez				
	David Bradley			
		Kevin Brown		
		Sariya Harnpadoungsataya		
		Mary Gibson		
		Jill Williams		
		Terry Eminhizer		
		Wanida Benshoof		
		John Wood		
		Mary Dempsey		
	Terri Duffy			
		Roberto Tamburello		
			Rob Walters	
			Gail Erickson	
			Jossef Goldberg	
			Dylan Miller	
				Diane Margheim
				Gigi Matthew
				Michael Raheem
			Ovidiu Cracium	
				Thierry D'Hers
				Janice Galvin
			Michael Sullivan	
			Sharon Salavaria	
	Jean Trenary			
		Janaina Bueno		
		Dan Bacon		
		François Ajenstat		
		Dan Wilson		
		Ramesh Meyyappan		
		Stephanie Conroy		
			Ashvini Sharma	
			Peter Connelly	
		Karen Berg		
	Laura Norman			
		Paula Barreto de Mattos		
			Willis Johnson	
			Mindy Martin	
			Vidur Luthra	
			Hao Chen	
			Grant Culbertson	
		Wendy Kahn		
			Sheela Word	
				Mikael Sandberg
				Arvind Rao
				Linda Meisner
				Fukiko Ogisu
				Gordon Hee
				Frank Pellow
				Eric Kurjan
				Erin Hagens
				Ben Miller
				Annette Hill
				Reinout Hillmann
		David Barber		
		David Liu		
			Deborah Poe	
			Candy Spoon	
			Bryan Walton	
			Dragan Tomic	
			Barbara Moreland	
			Janet Sheperdigian	
			Mike Seamans	
	James Hamilton			
		Peter Krebs		
			JoLynn Dobney	
				Simon Rapier
				James Kramer
				Nancy Anderson
				Bryan Baker
				Eugene Kogan
				Thomas Michaels
			Taylor Maxwell	
				Kendall Keil
				Bob Hohman
				Pete Male
				Diane Tibbott
				Denise Smith

Graphical Bill of Materials for Mountain-100 Silver, 44 Bike

T-SQL query will generate bill of materials (assembly) listing for Mountain-100 Silver, 44 mountain bike. The AdventureWorks2012 database image for Mountain-100 Silver, 44 in Production.ProductPhoto table **varbinary(max) data type column**.

```
USE AdventureWorks2012;
DECLARE         @StartProductID int          = 773,          -- Mountain-100 Silver, 44
                @CheckDate datetime          = '20080201';

  WITH cteBOM(ProductAssemblyID, ComponentID, ComponentName,   RecursionLevel)    AS (
    SELECT b.ProductAssemblyID, b.ComponentID, p.Name,   0
         FROM Production.BillOfMaterials b
          INNER JOIN Production.Product p
            ON b.ComponentID = p.ProductID
    WHERE       b.ProductAssemblyID = @StartProductID
                AND @CheckDate >= b.StartDate
                AND @CheckDate <= ISNULL(b.EndDate, @CheckDate)       -- Anchor/root member (above)
    UNION ALL                                                         -- Build a set
    SELECT      b.ProductAssemblyID, b.ComponentID, p.Name,           -- Recursive member (below)
                RecursionLevel + 1
    FROM cteBOM c
      INNER JOIN Production.BillOfMaterials b
        ON b.ProductAssemblyID = c.ComponentID
      INNER JOIN Production.Product p
        ON b.ComponentID = p.ProductID
    WHERE       @CheckDate >= b.StartDate           AND @CheckDate <= ISNULL(b.EndDate, @CheckDate)   )
-- Outer/main query
  SELECT CONCAT(REPLICATE(CHAR(9), RecursionLevel),  -- Generate indents with tab character
                (SELECT Name FROM Production.Product WHERE ProductID=ProductAssemblyID)) AS PartName,
                ComponentName
         FROM cteBOM    GROUP BY  RecursionLevel,ProductAssemblyID,ComponentName
  ORDER BY      RecursionLevel, ProductAssemblyID,ComponentName     OPTION (MAXRECURSION 10);
-- (87 row(s) affected)
```

The resulting graphical bill of materials for the mountain bike.

PartName	ComponentName			
Mountain-100 Silver, 44	Chain			
Mountain-100 Silver, 44	Front Brakes			
Mountain-100 Silver, 44	Front Derailleur			
Mountain-100 Silver, 44	HL Bottom Bracket			
Mountain-100 Silver, 44	HL Crankset			
Mountain-100 Silver, 44	HL Headset			
Mountain-100 Silver, 44	HL Mountain Frame - Silver, 44			
Mountain-100 Silver, 44	HL Mountain Front Wheel			
Mountain-100 Silver, 44	HL Mountain Handlebars			
Mountain-100 Silver, 44	HL Mountain Pedal			
Mountain-100 Silver, 44	HL Mountain Rear Wheel			
Mountain-100 Silver, 44	HL Mountain Seat Assembly			
Mountain-100 Silver, 44	Rear Brakes			
Mountain-100 Silver, 44	Rear Derailleur			
	HL Mountain Seat Assembly	HL Mountain Seat/Saddle		
	HL Mountain Seat Assembly	Pinch Bolt		
	HL Mountain Seat Assembly	Seat Lug		
	HL Mountain Seat Assembly	Seat Post		
	HL Mountain Frame - Silver, 44	Chain Stays		
	HL Mountain Frame - Silver, 44	Decal 1		
	HL Mountain Frame - Silver, 44	Decal 2		
	HL Mountain Frame - Silver, 44	Down Tube		
	HL Mountain Frame - Silver, 44	Head Tube		
	HL Mountain Frame - Silver, 44	HL Fork		
	HL Mountain Frame - Silver, 44	Paint - Silver		
	HL Mountain Frame - Silver, 44	Seat Stays		
	HL Mountain Frame - Silver, 44	Seat Tube		
	HL Mountain Frame - Silver, 44	Top Tube		
	HL Headset	Adjustable Race		
	HL Headset	Crown Race		
	HL Headset	Headset Ball Bearings		
	HL Headset	Keyed Washer		
	HL Headset	Lock Nut 19		
	HL Headset	Lower Head Race		
	HL Mountain Handlebars	Handlebar Tube		
	HL Mountain Handlebars	HL Grip Tape		
	HL Mountain Handlebars	Mountain End Caps		
	HL Mountain Handlebars	Stem		
	HL Mountain Front Wheel	HL Hub		
	HL Mountain Front Wheel	HL Mountain Rim		
	HL Mountain Front Wheel	HL Mountain Tire		
	HL Mountain Front Wheel	HL Nipple		
	HL Mountain Front Wheel	Mountain Tire Tube		
	HL Mountain Front Wheel	Reflector		
	HL Mountain Front Wheel	Spokes		
	HL Mountain Rear Wheel	HL Hub		
	HL Mountain Rear Wheel	HL Mountain Rim		
	HL Mountain Rear Wheel	HL Mountain Tire		
	HL Mountain Rear Wheel	HL Nipple		
	HL Mountain Rear Wheel	Mountain Tire Tube		
	HL Mountain Rear Wheel	Reflector		
	HL Mountain Rear Wheel	Spokes		
	Rear Derailleur	Guide Pulley		
	Rear Derailleur	Rear Derailleur Cage		
	Rear Derailleur	Tension Pulley		
	Front Derailleur	Front Derailleur Cage		
	Front Derailleur	Front Derailleur Linkage		
	HL Crankset	Chainring		
	HL Crankset	Chainring Bolts		

	HL Crankset	Chainring Nut		
	HL Crankset	Freewheel		
	HL Crankset	HL Crankarm		
	HL Bottom Bracket	BB Ball Bearing		
	HL Bottom Bracket	HL Shell		
		BB Ball Bearing	Bearing Ball	
		BB Ball Bearing	Cone-Shaped Race	
		BB Ball Bearing	Cup-Shaped Race	
		BB Ball Bearing	Lock Ring	
		Chain Stays	Metal Sheet 5	
		Down Tube	Metal Sheet 3	
		Mountain End Caps	Metal Sheet 2	
		Handlebar Tube	Metal Sheet 6	
		Head Tube	Metal Sheet 4	
		HL Hub	HL Shell	
		HL Hub	HL Spindle/Axle	
		Stem	Metal Bar 1	
		Seat Stays	Metal Sheet 7	
		Seat Tube	Metal Bar 2	
		Top Tube	Metal Sheet 2	
		HL Fork	Blade	
		HL Fork	Fork Crown	
		HL Fork	Fork End	
		HL Fork	Steerer	
			Blade	Metal Sheet 5
			Fork End	Metal Sheet 2
			Fork Crown	Metal Sheet 5
			Steerer	Metal Sheet 6

PIVOT Operator to Transform Rows Into Columns

The PIVOT operator, new to SQL Server 2005, can be used to create pivot table also called cross tabulation (crosstab). The data to be PIVOTed is generated by a CTE.

```
USE AdventureWorks2012;
;WITH CTE      AS (SELECT   YEAR             = YEAR(orderDate),
                            QUARTER          = DatePart(qq,OrderDate),
                            Sales            = Sum(TotalDue)
     FROM     Sales.SalesOrderHeader    GROUP BY YEAR(OrderDate), DatePart(qq,OrderDate))
SELECT * FROM CTE;
```

YEAR	QUARTER	Sales
2007	4	14886562.6775
2006	3	11555907.1472
2007	1	7492396.3224
2007	2	9379298.7027
2006	1	6562121.6796
2006	4	9397824.1785
2008	3	56178.9223
2007	3	15413231.8434
2005	3	5203127.8807
2008	1	12744940.3554
2005	4	7490122.7457
2008	2	16087078.2305
2006	2	6947995.43

PIVOT operator takes the data from the CTE source, aggregates it and transforms it to columns.

```
;WITH CTE     AS (SELECT    YEAR             = YEAR(orderDate),
                            QUARTER          = DatePart(qq,OrderDate),
                            Sales            = Sum(TotalDue)
     FROM     Sales.SalesOrderHeader     GROUP BY YEAR(OrderDate), DatePart(qq,OrderDate)      )
SELECT     YEAR
                  ,FORMAT ([1], 'c','en-US') AS Q1
                  ,FORMAT ([2], 'c','en-US') AS Q2
                  ,FORMAT ([3], 'c','en-US') AS Q3
                  ,FORMAT ([4], 'c','en-US') AS Q4
FROM     (SELECT * FROM CTE) AS PivotInput
     PIVOT       (SUM(Sales)   FOR QUARTER IN ( [1],[2],[3],[4] ) ) AS PivotOutput  ORDER BY YEAR;
```

YEAR	Q1	Q2	Q3	Q4
2005	NULL	NULL	$5,203,127.88	$7,490,122.75
2006	$6,562,121.68	$6,947,995.43	$11,555,907.15	$9,397,824.18
2007	$7,492,396.32	$9,379,298.70	$15,413,231.84	$14,886,562.68
2008	$12,744,940.36	$16,087,078.23	$56,178.92	NULL

UNPIVOT Crosstab View Results

The vSalesPersonSalesByFiscalYears view is a crosstab listing of sales person (rows) and sales by year (columns). The UNPIVOT operation transforms the year columns into rows.

Using Subquery in Column List of SELECT

A subquery can be used in the column list of a SELECT statement.

```
USE Northwind;
GO
```

```
;WITH CTE AS
(
 SELECT ShipCity,
        CONVERT(DATE, OrderDate)                                       AS OrderDate,
        (SELECT CONVERT(DATE, MAX(OrderDate))   FROM dbo.Orders)       AS CurrentOrderDate,
        DATEDIFF(dd,OrderDate,(SELECT MAX(OrderDate) FROM dbo.Orders)) AS DeltaDays,
        ROW_NUMBER() OVER (PARTITION BY ShipCity
                              ORDER BY OrderDate DESC)                 AS RN
 FROM dbo.Orders
)

SELECT TOP 20 ShipCity, OrderDate, CurrentOrderDate, DeltaDays
FROM CTE
WHERE RN=1     ORDER BY DeltaDays DESC;
GO
```

ShipCity	OrderDate	CurrentOrderDate	DeltaDays
Walla Walla	1997-05-22	1998-05-06	349
Elgin	1997-09-08	1998-05-06	240
Montréal	1997-10-30	1998-05-06	188
Reims	1997-11-12	1998-05-06	175
Caracas	1997-12-18	1998-05-06	139
Lille	1997-12-22	1998-05-06	135
Vancouver	1998-01-01	1998-05-06	125
Kirkland	1998-01-08	1998-05-06	118
Strasbourg	1998-01-12	1998-05-06	114
Lyon	1998-01-23	1998-05-06	103
San Francisco	1998-02-12	1998-05-06	83
Luleå	1998-03-04	1998-05-06	63
Barcelona	1998-03-05	1998-05-06	62
Cowes	1998-03-06	1998-05-06	61
Resende	1998-03-09	1998-05-06	58
Leipzig	1998-03-12	1998-05-06	55
Bergamo	1998-03-16	1998-05-06	51
Münster	1998-03-23	1998-05-06	44
Nantes	1998-03-24	1998-05-06	43
Versailles	1998-03-24	1998-05-06	43

CHAPTER 15: SELECT INTO Table Creation & Population

Simple SELECT INTO Statement Variations

SELECT INTO is an easy way to create a table for ad-hoc purposes in database development and administration. **An added benefit is minimal logging, therefore good performance**. INSERT SELECT is logged, although with special setup minimal logging can be achieved in some cases.

```
-- Create and populate copy of the product table in tempdb
USE tempdb;
SELECT ProductID, ProductNumber, ProductName=Name, StandardCost, ListPrice, Color
INTO Product FROM AdventureWorks2012.Production.Product; -- (504 row(s) affected)
```

```
-- ALTER TABLE: add PERSISTED computed column - NULLIF to prevent zero divide error
ALTER TABLE Product ADD ProfitMargin
                        AS 100 * (ListPrice-StandardCost)/(NULLIF(ListPrice,0.0)) PERSISTED;
```

```
CREATE INDEX idxProfit on Product(ProfitMargin); -- index to support frequent searches on this column
```

```
SELECT * FROM Product ORDER BY ProductName;  -- (504 row(s) affected) - Partial results.
```

ProductID	ProductNumber	ProductName	StandardCost	ListPrice	Color	ProfitMargin
872	BC-R205	Road Bottle Cage	3.3623	8.99	NULL	62.5995
329	EC-R098	Road End Caps	0.00	0.00	NULL	NULL
922	TT-R982	Road Tire Tube	1.4923	3.99	NULL	62.5989
750	BK-R93R-44	Road-150 Red, 44	2171.2942	3578.27	Red	39.32
751	BK-R93R-48	Road-150 Red, 48	2171.2942	3578.27	Red	39.32

```
DROP TABLE tempdb.dbo.Product;
```

```
-- Copy all persons into new table with last name starting with 'A'
SELECT   BusinessEntityID                    AS ID,
         CONCAT(FirstName, ' ', LastName)  AS FullName,      PersonType
INTO   ListA FROM   AdventureWorks2012.Person.Person
WHERE  LEFT(LastName, 1) = 'A' ORDER BY LastName, FirstName;  -- (911 row(s) affected)
SELECT TOP (3) ID, FullName, PersonType FROM ListA ORDER BY ID;
```

ID	FullName	PersonType
38	Kim Abercrombie	EM
43	Nancy Anderson	EM
67	Jay Adams	EM

SELECT TOP(0) Creates an Empty Table

```
USE AdventureWorks2012;
```

```
-- Create a copy of table in a different schema, same name
-- The WHERE clause predicate with >=, < comparison is better performing than the YEAR function
SELECT * INTO dbo.SalesOrderHeader FROM Sales.SalesOrderHeader
WHERE OrderDate >= '20080101' AND OrderDate < '20090101'; -- YEAR(OrderDate)=2008
-- (13951 row(s) affected)

-- Remove a column with ALTER TABLE
ALTER TABLE dbo.SalesOrderHeader DROP COLUMN ModifiedDate;
-- Command(s) completed successfully.
```

```
-- Create a table without population
SELECT TOP (0)    SalesOrderID,      OrderDate
INTO  SOH  FROM  Sales.SalesOrderHeader;  -- (0 row(s) affected)
ALTER TABLE SOH ADD CONSTRAINT pkSOH PRIMARY KEY (SalesOrderID);  -- Add PRIMARY KEY
```

```
-- SELECT INTO cannot be used to target an existing table
SELECT * INTO  SOH FROM  Sales.SalesOrderHeader;
/* Msg 2714, Level 16, State 6, Line 1 There is already an object named 'SOH' in the database. */
```

> NOTE
> IDENTITY column is automatically populated.
> Direct insert into IDENTITY column requires using of SET IDENTITY_INSERT.

```
INSERT SOH (SalesOrderID, OrderDate)
SELECT SalesOrderID, OrderDate
FROM  Sales.SalesOrderHeader ORDER BY SalesOrderID;
GO
/* ERROR due to SalesOrderID in SOH inherited the IDENTITY property.
Msg 544, Level 16, State 1, Line 1
Cannot insert explicit value for identity column in table 'SOH' when IDENTITY_INSERT is set to OFF. */
```

```
-- Turn on forced IDENTITY insert
SET IDENTITY_INSERT dbo.SOH ON;
GO
```

```
INSERT SOH(SalesOrderID, OrderDate)
SELECT SalesOrderID, OrderDate  FROM  Sales.SalesOrderHeader ORDER BY SalesOrderID;
GO
-- (31465 row(s) affected)
```

```
SET IDENTITY_INSERT dbo.SOH OFF;
```

Any Kind of SELECT Result Set Can Be Turned into a Table

```
-- Filter on date
SELECT *
INTO   SOH1
FROM   Sales.SalesOrderHeader WHERE  OrderDate >= '20080101' AND OrderDate < '20090101';
-- (13951 row(s) affected)
```

```
-- Descending sort for population
SELECT * INTO   SOH2 FROM   Sales.SalesOrderHeader  ORDER  BY SalesOrderID DESC ;
-- (31465 row(s) affected)

-- Create a clustered index on the new table to help with range searches on OrderDate
CREATE CLUSTERED INDEX idxSOH2CI ON SOH2( OrderDate DESC);
```

```
-- 3 columns only
SELECT  SalesOrderID,
        OrderDate,
        SubTotal
INTO   SOH3
FROM   Sales.SalesOrderHeader;
-- (31465 row(s) affected)
```

```
-- SELECT INTO with GROUP BY query source
SELECT  [Year]=YEAR(OrderDate),
        Orders=COUNT(*)
INTO   SOH4
FROM   Sales.SalesOrderHeader
GROUP  BY YEAR(OrderDate)
-- (4 row(s) affected)
```

```
SELECT * FROM SOH4 ORDER BY Year DESC;
```

Year	Orders
2008	13951
2007	12443
2006	3692
2005	1379

```
-- All source columns, and a new populated datetime column
SELECT   *,          [CreateDate]=getdate()
INTO   SOH5
FROM   Sales.SalesOrderHeader ;
-- (31465 row(s) affected)
```

SELECT INTO Can Create Temporary Tables or Tables in tempdb

```
-- SELECT INTO temporary table
SELECT TotalOrders = COUNT(*)
INTO   #TotalOrders
FROM   Sales.SalesOrderHeader ;
-- (1 row(s) affected)
```

```
SELECT * FROM #TotalOrders;
```

TotalOrders
31465

```
-- Empty table create with one NULL row
SELECT   Name=CONVERT(VARCHAR(45), NULL),
         Age=CONVERT(INT, NULL)
INTO   tempdb.dbo.Person;
```

```
INSERT tempdb.dbo.Person (Name, Age)
SELECT 'Roger Bond', 45;
-- (1 row(s) affected)
```

```
SELECT * FROM tempdb.dbo.Person;
```

Name	Age
NULL	NULL
Roger Bond	45

```
DELETE tempdb.dbo.Person WHERE Name is NULL;
-- (1 row(s) affected)
```

```
SELECT * FROM tempdb.dbo.Person;
```

Name	Age
Roger Bond	45

```
-- Create gaps in ID sequence; increment by 2:  2, 4, 6, 8 instead of 1, 2, 3, 4
SELECT   2 * [BusinessEntityID]                    AS BusinessEntityID
         ,[PhoneNumber]
         ,[PhoneNumberTypeID]
          ,[ModifiedDate]
 INTO dbo.Phone
 FROM [AdventureWorks2012].[Person].[PersonPhone] pp    ORDER BY pp.BusinessEntityID;
-- (19972 row(s) affected)
```

The SELECT INTO Created Table is a "Regular" Table

```
-- Populate with 100 random rows
SELECT TOP (100) *
INTO   POH
FROM   Purchasing.PurchaseOrderHeader ORDER  BY NEWID(); -- (100 row(s) affected)
```

```
SELECT          PurchaseOrderID,
                CONVERT(date, OrderDate)          AS OrderDate,
                FORMAT(SubTotal, 'c', 'en-US')    AS SubTotal
FROM POH;
```

PurchaseOrderID	OrderDate	SubTotal
3553	2008-08-03	$9,948.33
1637	2008-02-07	$25,531.28
2796	2008-05-31	$97.97
684	2007-09-26	$270.81
3478	2008-07-28	$28,072.28
1904	2008-03-09	$43,878.45
755	2007-10-01	$50,860.43
2660	2008-05-19	$944.37
2787	2008-05-31	$34,644.23
601	2007-09-19	$146.29

```
-- SELECT INTO with data transformation
SELECT    CultureID
         ,UPPER(Name)                          AS Name
         ,CONVERT(date,ModifiedDate)           AS ModifiedDate
INTO dbo.Culture
FROM [AdventureWorks2012].[Production].[Culture]
ORDER BY CultureID;
-- (8 row(s) affected)
```

```
SELECT * FROM dbo.Culture WHERE CultureID != '' ORDER BY CultureID;  -- exclude empty ID
```

CultureID	Name	ModifiedDate
ar	ARABIC	2002-06-01
en	ENGLISH	2002-06-01
es	SPANISH	2002-06-01
fr	FRENCH	2002-06-01
he	HEBREW	2002-06-01
th	THAI	2002-06-01
zh-cht	CHINESE	2002-06-01

SELECT INTO with IDENTITY Column

The column data types are inherited in SELECT INTO table create. The IDENTITY property is also inherited in a SELECT INTO unless it is prevented with special coding. No other constraint is inherited.

```
-- IDENTITY property of ProductID is inherited
SELECT TOP (0) ProductID, ProductNumber, ListPrice, Color
INTO tempdb.dbo.Product
FROM AdventureWorks2012.Production.Product;  -- (0 row(s) affected)
```

```
INSERT tempdb.dbo.Product (ProductID, ProductNumber, ListPrice, Color)
SELECT 20001, 'FERRARI007RED', $400000, 'Red';
GO
/* Msg 544, Level 16, State 1, Line 1
Cannot insert explicit value for identity column in table 'Product'
when IDENTITY_INSERT is set to OFF. */
```

```
-- The following is one way to check for IDENTITY property
USE tempdb;
EXEC sp_help 'dbo.Product';
```

Identity	Seed	Increment	Not For Replication
ProductID	1	1	0

```
USE AdventureWorks2012;
DROP TABLE tempdb.dbo.Product;
GO
```

```
-- The following construct will prevent IDENTITY inheritance
SELECT TOP (0)    CAST(ProductID AS INT) AS ProductID,  -- Cast/Convert the identity column
                  ProductNumber,
                  ListPrice,
                  Color
INTO tempdb.dbo.Product  FROM AdventureWorks2012.Production.Product;
-- (0 row(s) affected)
```

```
INSERT tempdb.dbo.Product (ProductID, ProductNumber, ListPrice, Color)
SELECT 20001, 'FERRARI007RED', $400000, 'Firehouse Red';
GO
```

```
SELECT * FROM tempdb.dbo.Product;
```

ProductID	ProductNumber	ListPrice	Color
20001	FERRARI007RED	400000.00	Firehouse Red

SELECT INTO From Multiple-Table Queries

SELECT INTO works with any query with some restrictions such as XML data type columns cannot be included.

```
SELECT  JobCandidateID
        ,BusinessEntityID
        ,Resume
        ,ModifiedDate
 INTO dbo.Resume
 FROM AdventureWorks2012.HumanResources.JobCandidate;
/* ERROR MESSAGE
Msg 458, Level 16, State 0, Line 2
Cannot create the SELECT INTO target table "dbo.Resume" because the xml column "Resume"
is typed with a schema collection "HRResumeSchemaCollection" from database "AdventureWorks2012".
Xml columns cannot refer to schemata across databases.
*/
```

```
-- SELECT INTO from joined tables
 SELECT         soh.SalesOrderID,
                OrderDate,
                OrderQty,
                ProductID
INTO  SalesOrder
FROM  Sales.SalesOrderHeader soh
    INNER JOIN Sales.SalesOrderDetail sod
        ON soh.SalesOrderID = sod.SalesOrderID ;
-- (121317 row(s) affected)
```

```
SELECT TOP(5) * FROM SalesOrder ORDER BY SalesOrderID DESC;
```

SalesOrderID	OrderDate	OrderQty	ProductID
75123	2008-07-31 00:00:00.000	1	878
75123	2008-07-31 00:00:00.000	1	879
75123	2008-07-31 00:00:00.000	1	712
75122	2008-07-31 00:00:00.000	1	878
75122	2008-07-31 00:00:00.000	1	712

```
-- Check column types - partial results
EXEC sp_help SalesOrder;
```

Column_name	Type	Computed	Length	Prec	Scale
SalesOrderID	int	no	4	10	0
OrderDate	datetime	no	8		
OrderQty	smallint	no	2	5	0
ProductID	int	no	4	10	0

SELECT INTO with Sorted Table Population

We can create ordering in a new temporary table by using the IDENTITY function. **There is no guarantee though that the IDENTITY sequence will be the same as the ORDER BY clause specifications.** Unique identity values on the other hand are guaranteed.

```
SELECT   ID=IDENTITY(int, 1, 1),
         ProductNumber,
         ProductID=CAST(ProductID AS INT),
         ListPrice,
         COALESCE(Color, 'N/A') AS Color
INTO  #Product
FROM  Production.Product WHERE ListPrice > 0.0 ORDER BY ProductNumber;
GO -- (304 row(s) affected)
```

```
SELECT TOP 10 * FROM #Product  ORDER BY ID;
```

ID	ProductNumber	ProductID	ListPrice	Color
1	BB-7421	994	53.99	N/A
2	BB-8107	995	101.24	N/A
3	BB-9108	996	121.49	N/A
4	BC-M005	871	9.99	N/A
5	BC-R205	872	8.99	N/A
6	BK-M18B-40	989	539.99	Black
7	BK-M18B-42	990	539.99	Black
8	BK-M18B-44	991	539.99	Black
9	BK-M18B-48	992	539.99	Black
10	BK-M18B-52	993	539.99	Black

```
-- Permanent table create
SELECT * INTO ProductByProdNo FROM #Product ORDER BY ID;
GO -- (304 row(s) affected)
```

```
SELECT TOP (6) * FROM ProductByProdNo ORDER BY ID;
```

ID	ProductNumber	ProductID	ListPrice	Color
1	BB-7421	994	53.99	N/A
2	BB-8107	995	101.24	N/A
3	BB-9108	996	121.49	N/A
4	BC-M005	871	9.99	N/A
5	BC-R205	872	8.99	N/A
6	BK-M18B-40	989	539.99	Black

SELECT INTO with Random Population

We can create a random population by sorting with the NEWID() function.

```
USE tempdb;

SELECT TOP(5)   ID          = ContactID,
                FullName    = CONCAT(FirstName, ' ', LastName),
                Email       = EmailAddress
INTO   dbo.Person
FROM   AdventureWorks.Person.Contact
WHERE  EmailPromotion = 2
ORDER  BY NEWID();
-- (5 row(s) affected)
```

```
SELECT *  FROM   dbo.Person;
GO
```

ID	FullName	Email
1075	Diane Glimp	diane0@adventure-works.com
15739	Jesse Mitchell	jesse36@adventure-works.com
5405	Jose Patterson	jose33@adventure-works.com
1029	Wanida Benshoof	wanida0@adventure-works.com
8634	Andrea Collins	andrea26@adventure-works.com

```
-- Rerun the script again after dropping the table
DROP TABLE tempdb.dbo.Person;
GO
-- Command(s) completed successfully.
```

```
SELECT TOP(5) ID          = ContactID,
       FullName           = CONCAT(FirstName, ' ', LastName),
       Email              = EmailAddress
INTO   dbo.Person
FROM   AdventureWorks.Person.Contact
WHERE  EmailPromotion = 2 ORDER  BY NEWID();
```

```
SELECT * FROM   dbo.Person;
```

ID	FullName	Email
9984	Sydney Clark	sydney81@adventure-works.com
15448	Denise Raman	denise13@adventure-works.com
12442	Carson Jenkins	carson5@adventure-works.com
1082	Mary Baker	mary1@adventure-works.com
18728	Emma Kelly	emma46@adventure-works.com

Combining SELECT INTO with INSERT SELECT

First we create an empty table with identity property using SELECT INTO, then we populate it with INSERT SELECT.

```
-- Following will fail - only one IDENTITY column per table
SELECT TOP (0)   IDENTITY(int, 1, 1)                    AS ID,
         ProductID,
         Name                                           AS ProductName,
         ListPrice,
         COALESCE(Color, 'N/A')                         AS Color
INTO  #Product  FROM  Production.Product;
GO
/* ERROR Msg 8108, Level 16, State 1, Line 1
Cannot add identity column, using the SELECT INTO statement, to table '#Product',
which already has column 'ProductID' that inherits the identity property.  */
```

```
SELECT TOP (0)   IDENTITY(int, 1, 1)          AS ID,
         CAST(ProductID AS INT)               AS ProductID, -- IDENTITY will not be inherited
         Name                                 AS ProductName,
         ListPrice,
         COALESCE(Color, 'N/A')               AS Color
INTO  #Product  FROM  Production.Product;
GO
-- (0 row(s) affected)
```

```
DECLARE @Rows tinyint = 5;
INSERT INTO #Product   (ProductID, ProductName,  ListPrice,  Color)
SELECT TOP (@Rows)       ProductID,
                 Name,
                 ListPrice,
                 Color
FROM  Production.Product
WHERE  ListPrice > 0.0    AND Color IS NOT NULL  ORDER BY ListPrice DESC;
-- (5 row(s) affected)
```

```
SELECT *  FROM  #Product;
```

ID	ProductID	ProductName	ListPrice	Color
1	749	Road-150 Red, 62	3578.27	Red
2	750	Road-150 Red, 44	3578.27	Red
3	751	Road-150 Red, 48	3578.27	Red
4	752	Road-150 Red, 52	3578.27	Red
5	753	Road-150 Red, 56	3578.27	Red

Copy Table into Different Database with SELECT INTO

It requires 3-part name referencing to operate between databases (cross database). The current database requires only 2-part object name referencing.

```
USE tempdb;
SELECT *, CopyDate = CONVERT(DATE,GETDATE())
INTO Department
FROM AdventureWorks.HumanResources.Department  ORDER BY DepartmentID;
GO
```

```
SELECT TOP (5) DepartmentID, Department=Name, CopyDate  FROM Department ORDER BY DepartmentID;
```

DepartmentID	Department	CopyDate
1	Engineering	2016-07-19
2	Tool Design	2016-07-19
3	Sales	2016-07-19
4	Marketing	2016-07-19
5	Purchasing	2016-07-19

```
-- SQL drop table - full referencing of table for mistake reduction
DROP TABLE tempdb.dbo.Department;
```

Combining SELECT INTO with UPDATE

After creating a populated table with SELECT INTO, we perform UPDATE to change a column.

```
USE tempdb;
SELECT TOP 100 * INTO   PurchaseOrderHeader
FROM   AdventureWorks.Purchasing.PurchaseOrderHeader  ORDER  BY NEWID();
GO
```

```
-- The following logic updates dates to different values - multiple value assignment operator
DECLARE @OrderDate DATETIME = CURRENT_TIMESTAMP;
UPDATE PurchaseOrderHeader  SET    @OrderDate = OrderDate = dateadd(day, -1, @OrderDate);
GO
```

```
SELECT TOP (5)  PurchaseOrderID,    VendorID,  OrderDate  FROM   PurchaseOrderHeader;
```

PurchaseOrderID	VendorID	OrderDate
631	39	2016-07-18 09:03:18.193
759	32	2016-07-17 09:03:18.193
2652	33	2016-07-16 09:03:18.193
769	80	2016-07-15 09:03:18.193
949	30	2016-07-14 09:03:18.193

```
DROP TABLE tempdb.dbo.PurchaseOrderHeader;
```

SELECT INTO Table Create from Complex Query

SELECT INTO table create works from simple to very complex queries.

```
USE AdventureWorks;

SELECT          SalesStaff          = CONCAT(C.LastName, ', ', C.FirstName),
                ZipCode             = A.PostalCode,
                TotalSales          = FORMAT(SUM(SOD.LineTotal),'c', 'en-US'),
                PercentOfTotal      = FORMAT( SUM(SOD.LineTotal) /
                                      SUM(SUM(SOD.LineTotal))  OVER (PARTITION BY 1, 2 ),'p')
INTO   tempdb.dbo.SalesSummary
FROM   Person.Contact C
    INNER JOIN Person.[Address] A
        ON A.AddressID = C.ContactID
    INNER JOIN Sales.SalesOrderHeader SOH
        ON SOH.SalesPersonID = C.ContactID
    INNER JOIN Sales.SalesOrderDetail SOD
        ON SOD.SalesOrderID = SOH.SalesOrderID
WHERE  TerritoryID IS NOT NULL
GROUP  BY C.FirstName,    C.LastName,    A.PostalCode,    C.ContactID
ORDER  BY SalesStaff,    ZipCode;
-- (17 row(s) affected)

-- SELECT 10 rows random, then sort them by name (SalesStaff) - derived table construct
SELECT * FROM
(
        SELECT TOP (10) *
        FROM   tempdb.dbo.SalesSummary ORDER  BY NEWID()
) x             -- x is called a derived table; also dubbed SELECT FROM SELECT
ORDER BY SalesStaff;
```

SalesStaff	ZipCode	TotalSales	PercentOfTotal
Dusza, Maciej	98027	$9,293,903.00	11.55 %
Dyck, Shelley	98027	$10,367,007.43	12.88 %
Ecoffey, Linda	98027	$10,065,803.54	12.51 %
Eldridge, Carla	98027	$3,609,447.21	4.48 %
Elliott, Carol	98027	$7,171,012.75	8.91 %
Emanuel, Michael	98055	$5,926,418.36	7.36 %
Erickson, Gail	98055	$8,503,338.65	10.56 %
Estes, Julie	98055	$172,524.45	0.21 %
Esteves, Janeth	98055	$1,827,066.71	2.27 %
Evans, Twanna	98055	$1,421,810.92	1.77 %

```
DROP TABLE tempdb.dbo.SalesSummary ;
```

SELECT INTO Table Create from System Procedure Execution

Using OPENROWSET and OPENQUERY, we can make the result sets of system procedures and user stored procedures table-like.

```
SELECT * INTO  #spwho
FROM  OPENROWSET ( 'SQLOLEDB',
           'SERVER=.;Trusted_Connection=yes',
           'SET FMTONLY OFF EXEC sp_who');
GO  -- (64 row(s) affected) - it varies, depends on the number server connections
```

```
SELECT TOP (5) *  FROM  #spwho  ORDER BY spid;
```

spid	ecid	status	loginame	hostname	blk	dbname	cmd	request_id
1	0	background	sa		0	NULL	LOG WRITER	0
2	0	background	sa		0	NULL	RECOVERY WRITER	0
3	0	background	sa		0	NULL	LAZY WRITER	0
4	0	background	sa		0	NULL	LOCK MONITOR	0
5	0	background	sa		0	master	SIGNAL HANDLER	0

```
/* Requirement for OPENQUERY operation on current instance.

DATA ACCESS to current SQL Server named instance can be setup the following way:

exec sp_serveroption @server = 'PRODSVR\SQL2008'   -- computer name for default instance
    ,@optname = 'DATA ACCESS'
    ,@optvalue = 'TRUE' ;

This way, OPENQUERY can be used against current instance. Usually OPENQUERY is used to access linked servers.   */
```

```
SELECT   DB_NAME(dbid) AS DB,  *
INTO   #splock FROM   OPENQUERY(HPESTAR, 'EXEC sp_lock');
GO
-- (156 row(s) affected)  - it varies, depends how busy is the system with OLTP activities
```

```
SELECT TOP(2) * FROM   #splock ;
```

DB	spid	dbid	ObjId	IndId	Type	Resource	Mode	Status
ReportServer	52	5	0	0	DB		S	GRANT
msdb	54	4	0	0	DB		S	GRANT

System procedure to list all tables in a database. Corresponding procedure for linked server: sp_tables_ex.

```
EXEC pubs..sp_tables @table_type = "'TABLE'";
```

SELECT INTO from OPENQUERY Stored Procedure Execution

The following is the only way to make stored procedure results table-like. The bill-of-materials stored procedure is recursive.

```
USE AdventureWorks2012;
GO
SELECT Name FROM Production.Product
WHERE ProductID = 900;   -- LL Touring Frame - Yellow, 50
```

```
-- First we test the query execution
DECLARE @RC int;  DECLARE @StartProductID int; DECLARE @CheckDate datetime;

EXECUTE @RC = [dbo].[uspGetBillOfMaterials]     @StartProductID = 900 , @CheckDate = '20080216';
GO
-- 24 rows returned
```

```
-- Transform query into SELECT INTO table create  - Single quotes (around date literal) must be doubled
SELECT * INTO BOM900
FROM OPENQUERY(HPESTAR, 'EXECUTE [AdventureWorks2012].[dbo].[uspGetBillOfMaterials]
900,''20080216''');
GO
-- (1 row(s) affected)                    -- create table
-- (24 row(s) affected)                   -- inserts
```

```
SELECT * FROM BOM900;
```

ProductAssemblyID	ComponentID	ComponentDesc	TotalQuantity	StandardCost	ListPrice	BOMLevel	RecursionLevel
900	324	Chain Stays	2.00	0.00	0.00	2	0
900	325	Decal 1	2.00	0.00	0.00	2	0
900	326	Decal 2	1.00	0.00	0.00	2	0
900	327	Down Tube	1.00	0.00	0.00	2	0
900	399	Head Tube	1.00	0.00	0.00	2	0
900	496	Paint - Yellow	8.00	0.00	0.00	2	0
900	532	Seat Stays	4.00	0.00	0.00	2	0
900	533	Seat Tube	1.00	0.00	0.00	2	0
900	534	Top Tube	1.00	0.00	0.00	2	0
900	802	LL Fork	1.00	65.8097	148.22	2	0
324	486	Metal Sheet 5	1.00	0.00	0.00	3	1
327	483	Metal Sheet 3	1.00	0.00	0.00	3	1
399	485	Metal Sheet 4	1.00	0.00	0.00	3	1
532	484	Metal Sheet 7	1.00	0.00	0.00	3	1
533	478	Metal Bar 2	1.00	0.00	0.00	3	1
534	482	Metal Sheet 2	1.00	0.00	0.00	3	1
802	316	Blade	2.00	0.00	0.00	3	1
802	331	Fork End	2.00	0.00	0.00	3	1
802	350	Fork Crown	1.00	0.00	0.00	3	1
802	531	Steerer	1.00	0.00	0.00	3	1
316	486	Metal Sheet 5	1.00	0.00	0.00	4	2
331	482	Metal Sheet 2	1.00	0.00	0.00	4	2
350	486	Metal Sheet 5	1.00	0.00	0.00	4	2
531	487	Metal Sheet 6	1.00	0.00	0.00	4	2

Execution of SELECT INTO from Dynamic SQL

T-SQL script demonstrates SELECT INTO execution within a dynamic SQL. Biggest challenge is to get the single quotes right. CHAR(39) use is an option.

```
-- SQL Server 2008 new feature: instant assignment to a localvariable
DECLARE @DynamicQuery nvarchar(max) =
    'SELECT *
    INTO BOM400
    FROM OPENQUERY(' + QUOTENAME(CONVERT(sysname, @@SERVERNAME))+ ',
    ''EXECUTE [AdventureWorks2012].[dbo].[uspGetWhereUsedProductID] 400,
    ''''2007-11-21'''''')' ;
```

```
PRINT @DynamicQuery;      -- test query;  this is the static query which will be executed
/*
SELECT *
    INTO BOM400
    FROM OPENQUERY([HPESTAR],
    'EXECUTE [AdventureWorks2012].[dbo].[uspGetWhereUsedProductID] 400,
    ''2007-11-21''')
*/
```

```
EXEC sp_executeSQL @DynamicQuery;
GO -- (64 row(s) affected)
```

```
SELECT TOP ( 5 ) * FROM BOM400 ORDER BY NEWID() ;
GO
```

ProductAssemblyID	ComponentID	ComponentDesc	TotalQuantity	StandardCost	ListPrice	BOMLevel	RecursionLevel
761	818	Road-650 Red, 62	1.00	486.7066	782.99	1	1
987	823	Mountain-500 Silver, 48	1.00	308.2179	564.99	1	1
990	823	Mountain-500 Black, 42	1.00	294.5797	539.99	1	1
765	826	Road-650 Black, 58	1.00	486.7066	782.99	1	1
770	818	Road-650 Black, 52	1.00	486.7066	782.99	1	1

```
-- Cleanup
DROP TABLE BOM400;
```

SELECT INTO Table Create from View

Transact-SQL script demonstrates how to import view query results into a table.

```
SELECT [FullName],
    [SalesPersonID]                                     AS StaffID,
    [SalesTerritory],
    COALESCE(FORMAT([2006], 'c','en-US'), '')           AS [2006],
    COALESCE(FORMAT([2007], 'c','en-US'), '')           AS [2007],
    COALESCE(FORMAT([2008], 'c','en-US'), '')           AS [2008]
INTO #Sales
FROM [AdventureWorks2012].[Sales].[vSalesPersonSalesByFiscalYears]
ORDER BY SalesTerritory, FullName;
GO
```

```
SELECT *
FROM #Sales
ORDER BY SalesTerritory, FullName;
GO
```

FullName	StaffID	SalesTerritory	2006	2007	2008
Lynn N Tsoflias	286	Australia			$1,421,810.92
Garrett R Vargas	278	Canada	$930,259.47	$1,225,468.28	$1,453,719.47
José Edvaldo Saraiva	282	Canada	$2,088,491.17	$1,233,386.47	$2,604,540.72
Jillian Carson	277	Central	$2,737,537.88	$4,138,847.30	$3,189,418.37
Ranjit R Varkey Chudukatil	290	France		$1,388,272.61	$3,121,616.32
Rachel B Valdez	288	Germany			$1,827,066.71
Michael G Blythe	275	Northeast	$1,602,472.39	$3,928,252.44	$3,763,178.18
David R Campbell	283	Northwest	$1,017,402.86	$1,139,529.55	$1,573,012.94
Pamela O Ansman-Wolfe	280	Northwest	$1,226,461.83	$746,063.63	$1,352,577.13
Tete A Mensa-Annan	284	Northwest		$735,983.49	$1,576,562.20
Tsvi Michael Reiter	279	Southeast	$2,645,436.95	$2,210,390.19	$2,315,185.61
Linda C Mitchell	276	Southwest	$2,260,118.45	$3,855,520.42	$4,251,368.55
Shu K Ito	281	Southwest	$1,593,742.92	$2,374,727.02	$2,458,535.62
Jae B Pak	289	United Kingdom		$4,386,467.42	$4,116,871.23

SELECT INTO Data Import from Excel

T-SQL OPENROWSET query imports data into a temporary table from Excel. Your Excel library maybe different than the one in the example. SQL Server Import and Export Wizard is the best way to exchange date between SS database and Excel.

```
SELECT * INTO ContactList FROM OPENROWSET('Microsoft.Jet.OLEDB.4.0',
        'Excel 8.0;Database=D:\data\excel\Contact.xls', 'SELECT * FROM [Contact$]')
-- (19972 row(s) affected)
```

CHAPTER 16: Modify Data - INSERT, UPDATE, DELETE & MERGE

INSERT VALUES - Table Value Constructor

T-SQL scripts illustrate the use of INSERT VALUES with Table Value Constructor (a list of values). Because the text columns are defined as nvarchar the string literals are prefixed with "N" indicating UNICODE literal. Since only Latin letters used, the "N" can be omitted.

```
USE tempdb;
SELECT TOP 0 * INTO dbo.Department FROM AdventureWorks2012.HumanResources.Department;
-- This is necessary because IDENTITY property was inherited in the SELECT INTO
SET IDENTITY_INSERT dbo.Department ON;
GO
INSERT dbo.Department (DepartmentID, Name, GroupName, ModifiedDate) VALUES
(1, N'Engineering', N'Research and Development', getdate()),
(2, N'Tool Design', N'Research and Development', getdate()),
(3, N'Sales', N'Sales and Marketing', getdate()),
(4, N'Marketing', N'Sales and Marketing', getdate()),
(5, N'Purchasing', N'Inventory Management', getdate()),
(6, N'Research and Development', N'Research and Development', getdate()),
(7, N'Production', N'Manufacturing', getdate()),
(8, N'Production Control', N'Manufacturing', getdate()),
(9, N'Human Resources', N'Executive General and Administration', getdate()),
(10, N'Finance', N'Executive General and Administration', getdate()),
(11, N'Information Services', N'Executive General and Administration', getdate()),
(12, N'Document Control', N'Quality Assurance', getdate()),
(13, N'Quality Assurance', N'Quality Assurance', getdate()),
(14, N'Facilities and Maintenance', N'Executive General and Administration', getdate()),
(15, N'Shipping and Receiving', N'Inventory Management', getdate()),
(16, N'Executive', N'Executive General and Administration',getdate());
GO
SET IDENTITY_INSERT dbo.Department OFF;
GO
SELECT TOP 4 * FROM dbo.Department ORDER BY DepartmentID;
```

DepartmentID	Name	GroupName	ModifiedDate
1	Engineering	Research and Development	2016-08-02 06:35:44.623
2	Tool Design	Research and Development	2016-08-02 06:35:44.623
3	Sales	Sales and Marketing	2016-08-02 06:35:44.623
4	Marketing	Sales and Marketing	2016-08-02 06:35:44.623

INSERT VALUES - Ye Olde Way

T-SQL scripts illustrate the INSERT VALUES for single row insert, the only available method prior to SQL Server 2008.

```
USE AdventureWorks2012;
GO
```

```
CREATE TABLE Shift(
	ShiftID tinyint IDENTITY(1,1) NOT NULL,
	Name dbo.Name NOT NULL,
	StartTime time(7) NOT NULL,
	EndTime time(7) NOT NULL,
	ModifiedDate datetime NOT NULL,
	CONSTRAINT PK_Shift_ShiftID PRIMARY KEY CLUSTERED (ShiftID ASC) );
GO
```

```
SET IDENTITY_INSERT Shift ON;			-- To force insert into ShiftID
```

```
INSERT Shift (ShiftID, Name, StartTime, EndTime, ModifiedDate)
VALUES (1, N'Day', CAST(0x0700D85EAC3A0000 AS Time), CAST(0x07001882BA7D0000 AS Time),
CAST(0x0000921E00000000 AS DateTime))
INSERT Shift (ShiftID, Name, StartTime, EndTime, ModifiedDate)
VALUES (2, N'Evening', CAST(0x07001882BA7D0000 AS Time), CAST(0x070058A5C8C00000 AS Time),
getdate());
INSERT Shift (ShiftID, Name, StartTime, EndTime, ModifiedDate)
VALUES (3, N'Night', CAST(0x070058A5C8C00000 AS Time), CAST(0x0700D85EAC3A0000 AS Time),
CURRENT_TIMESTAMP);
GO
```

```
SET IDENTITY_INSERT Shift OFF;
```

```
ALTER TABLE Shift ADD  CONSTRAINT DF_Shift_ModifiedDate  DEFAULT (getdate()) FOR ModifiedDate
GO
```

```
SELECT * FROM Shift ORDER BY ShiftID;
GO
```

ShiftID	Name	StartTime	EndTime	ModifiedDate
1	Day	07:00:00.0000000	15:00:00.0000000	2002-06-01 00:00:00.000
2	Evening	15:00:00.0000000	23:00:00.0000000	2018-08-20 19:31:02.293
3	Night	23:00:00.0000000	07:00:00.0000000	2018-08-20 19:31:02.293

```
DROP TABLE Shift;
GO
```

INSERT SELECT

INSERT SELECT Literal List

T-SQL scripts demonstrate the insertion of literal records (rows) using INSERT SELECT.

```
USE tempdb;
GO
SELECT TOP 0 * INTO dbo.Department FROM AdventureWorks2012.HumanResources.Department;
GO
-- This is necessary because IDENTITY property was inherited in the SELECT INTO
SET IDENTITY_INSERT dbo.Department ON;
GO
INSERT dbo.Department (DepartmentID, Name, GroupName, ModifiedDate)
SELECT 1, N'Engineering', N'Research and Development', CURRENT_TIMESTAMP  UNION
SELECT 2, N'Tool Design', N'Research and Development', CURRENT_TIMESTAMP  UNION
SELECT 3, N'Sales', N'Sales and Marketing', CURRENT_TIMESTAMP  UNION
SELECT 4, N'Marketing', N'Sales and Marketing', CURRENT_TIMESTAMP  UNION
SELECT 5, N'Purchasing', N'Inventory Management', CURRENT_TIMESTAMP  UNION
SELECT 6, N'Research and Development', N'Research and Development', CURRENT_TIMESTAMP  UNION
SELECT 7, N'Production', N'Manufacturing', CURRENT_TIMESTAMP  UNION
SELECT 8, N'Production Control', N'Manufacturing', CURRENT_TIMESTAMP  UNION
SELECT 9, N'Human Resources', N'Executive General and Administration', CURRENT_TIMESTAMP  UNION
SELECT 10, N'Finance', N'Executive General and Administration', CURRENT_TIMESTAMP  UNION
SELECT 11, N'Information Services', N'Executive General and Administration', CURRENT_TIMESTAMP
UNION
SELECT 12, N'Document Control', N'Quality Assurance', CURRENT_TIMESTAMP  UNION
SELECT 13, N'Quality Assurance', N'Quality Assurance', CURRENT_TIMESTAMP  UNION
SELECT 14, N'Facilities and Maintenance', N'Executive General and Administration',
CURRENT_TIMESTAMP  UNION
SELECT 15, N'Shipping and Receiving', N'Inventory Management', CURRENT_TIMESTAMP  UNION
SELECT 16, N'Executive', N'Executive General and Administration', CURRENT_TIMESTAMP;
GO
SET IDENTITY_INSERT dbo.Department OFF;
GO
SELECT TOP 4 * FROM dbo.Department ORDER BY DepartmentID;
GO
```

DepartmentID	Name	GroupName	ModifiedDate
1	Engineering	Research and Development	2016-08-02 06:35:44.623
2	Tool Design	Research and Development	2016-08-02 06:35:44.623
3	Sales	Sales and Marketing	2016-08-02 06:35:44.623
4	Marketing	Sales and Marketing	2016-08-02 06:35:44.623

```
-- Cleanup
DROP TABLE tempdb.dbo.Department;
```

INSERT SELECT from Table

T-SQL script demonstrates table population with table SELECT.

```
USE tempdb;
SELECT TOP 0 * INTO dbo.Department FROM AdventureWorks2012.HumanResources.Department;
GO
-- This is necessary because IDENTITY property was inherited in the SELECT INTO
SET IDENTITY_INSERT dbo.Department ON;
GO
INSERT dbo.Department (DepartmentID, Name, GroupName, ModifiedDate)
SELECT TOP 15 DepartmentID, Name, GroupName, ModifiedDate
FROM AdventureWorks2012.HumanResources.Department  ORDER BY DepartmentID;
GO
-- (15 row(s) affected)
SELECT TOP 4 * FROM dbo.Department ORDER BY DepartmentID;
```

DepartmentID	Name	GroupName	ModifiedDate
1	Engineering	Research and Development	2016-08-02 06:35:44.623
2	Tool Design	Research and Development	2016-08-02 06:35:44.623
3	Sales	Sales and Marketing	2016-08-02 06:35:44.623
4	Marketing	Sales and Marketing	2016-08-02 06:35:44.623

SCOPE_IDENTITY() for Last-Inserted IDENTITY Value

The last inserted IDENTITY value can be returned with the SCOPE_IDENTITY() or @@IDENTITY system function (variable). SCOPE_IDENTITY() is better choice since it is within the current connection scope. @@IDENTITY is at server level. The best choice though is the OUTPUT clause.

```
INSERT dbo.Department (DepartmentID, Name, GroupName, ModifiedDate)
SELECT TOP 1 DepartmentID, Name, GroupName, ModifiedDate
FROM AdventureWorks2012.HumanResources.Department  ORDER BY DepartmentID DESC;
GO
-- (1 row(s) affected)
```

Alternate is SELECT @@IDENTITY; @@ variables are system variables.

```
DECLARE @LastID INT = SCOPE_IDENTITY();
SELECT @LastID;   -- 16
```

```
SET IDENTITY_INSERT dbo.Department OFF;
GO
```

```
-- Cleanup
DROP TABLE tempdb.dbo.Department;
```

INSERT with Subset of Columns

Only the required columns must be present in the INSERT column list. A column with default or NULL property can be omitted. In the next T-SQL script, ModifiedDate is filled by default with getdate().

```
USE tempdb;
SELECT TOP 0 * INTO dbo.Department FROM AdventureWorks2012.HumanResources.Department;
GO
ALTER TABLE dbo.Department ADD CONSTRAINT DF_Dept_ModDate
DEFAULT getdate() FOR ModifiedDate;
GO
SET IDENTITY_INSERT dbo.Department ON;
GO
INSERT dbo.Department (DepartmentID, Name, GroupName)
SELECT DepartmentID, Name, GroupName  FROM AdventureWorks2012.HumanResources.Department;
GO  -- (16 row(s) affected)
SELECT TOP 4 * FROM dbo.Department ORDER BY DepartmentID;
```

DepartmentID	Name	GroupName	ModifiedDate
1	Engineering	Research and Development	2016-08-02 06:35:44.623
2	Tool Design	Research and Development	2016-08-02 06:35:44.623
3	Sales	Sales and Marketing	2016-08-02 06:35:44.623
4	Marketing	Sales and Marketing	2016-08-02 06:35:44.623

Capturing Last-Inserted IDENTITY Set Values with OUTPUT

When more than one row is inserted with one statement, the OUTPUT clause can be used to capture the list of just inserted IDENTITY values.

```
DECLARE @LastInserted TABLE (ID INT);
INSERT dbo.Department (DepartmentID, Name, GroupName)
        OUTPUT inserted.DepartmentID INTO @LastInserted
SELECT DepartmentID+1000, Name, GroupName  FROM
AdventureWorks2012.HumanResources.Department;
SELECT TOP 5 * FROM @LastInserted ORDER BY ID;
GO
```

ID
1001
1002
1003
1004
1005

```
SET IDENTITY_INSERT dbo.Department OFF;
DROP TABLE tempdb.dbo.Department;
```

INSERT EXEC Stored Procedure

Data can be directly inserted from the execution of a user-defined stored procedure or system procedure. We create a table and a stored procedure, then perform INSERT EXEC.

```
USE AdventureWorks2012;
IF OBJECT_ID ('dbo.EmployeeSales', 'U') IS NOT NULL    DROP TABLE dbo.EmployeeSales;
IF OBJECT_ID ('dbo.uspGetEmployeeSales', 'P') IS NOT NULL    DROP PROCEDURE uspGetEmployeeSales;
CREATE TABLE dbo.EmployeeSales
 (
   BusinessEntityID          VARCHAR(11) NOT NULL PRIMARY KEY,
   LastName                  VARCHAR(40) NOT NULL,
   SalesDollars              MONEY NOT NULL,
   DataSource                VARCHAR(20) NOT NULL
 );
GO

CREATE PROCEDURE dbo.uspGetEmployeeSales AS
 BEGIN
   SELECT          e.BusinessEntityID, c.LastName, sp.SalesYTD, 'PROCEDURE'
   FROM   HumanResources.Employee AS e
       INNER JOIN Sales.SalesPerson AS sp
           ON e.BusinessEntityID = sp.BusinessEntityID
       INNER JOIN Person.Person AS c
           ON e.BusinessEntityID = c.BusinessEntityID
   WHERE  e.BusinessEntityID > 280      ORDER  BY    e.BusinessEntityID,   c.LastName;
 END;
GO

--INSERT...EXECUTE user-defined stored procedure
INSERT EmployeeSales EXECUTE uspGetEmployeeSales;

SELECT * FROM   EmployeeSales;
```

BusinessEntityID	LastName	SalesDollars	DataSource
281	Ito	2458535.6169	PROCEDURE
282	Saraiva	2604540.7172	PROCEDURE
283	Campbell	1573012.9383	PROCEDURE
284	Mensa-Annan	1576562.1966	PROCEDURE
285	Abbas	172524.4512	PROCEDURE
286	Tsoflias	1421810.9242	PROCEDURE
287	Alberts	519905.932	PROCEDURE
288	Valdez	1827066.7118	PROCEDURE
289	Pak	4116871.2277	PROCEDURE
290	Varkey Chudukatil	3121616.3202	PROCEDURE

Insert Into A Table Via The Direct Execution Of An SQL Query With The EXEC Command

```
SELECT Population = count(*)  FROM   dbo.EmployeeSales;
```

Population
10

```
--INSERT...EXECUTE('string') example
INSERT EmployeeSales
EXECUTE ('          SELECT e.BusinessEntityID, c.LastName,      sp.SalesYTD, ''EXEC SQL STRING''
                    FROM HumanResources.Employee AS e        INNER JOIN Sales.SalesPerson AS sp
                    ON e.BusinessEntityID = sp.BusinessEntityID        INNER JOIN Person.Person AS c
                    ON e.BusinessEntityID = c.BusinessEntityID
                    WHERE e.BusinessEntityID BETWEEN 270 and 280
                    ORDER BY e.BusinessEntityID, c.LastName ');
GO
-- (7 row(s) affected)
```

Inserted number of rows can be captured for later use. **Capture must be done immediately after the monitored statement.** Any following statement will change @@ROWCOUNT value.

```
DECLARE @InsertCount int = @@ROWCOUNT;
SELECT @InsertCount;  -- 7
GO
```

```
SELECT * FROM   dbo.EmployeeSales ORDER BY BusinessEntityID ;
```

BusinessEntityID	LastName	SalesDollars	DataSource
274	Jiang	559697.5639	EXEC SQL STRING
275	Blythe	3763178.1787	EXEC SQL STRING
276	Mitchell	4251368.5497	EXEC SQL STRING
277	Carson	3189418.3662	EXEC SQL STRING
278	Vargas	1453719.4653	EXEC SQL STRING
279	Reiter	2315185.611	EXEC SQL STRING
280	Ansman-Wolfe	1352577.1325	EXEC SQL STRING
281	Ito	2458535.6169	PROCEDURE
282	Saraiva	2604540.7172	PROCEDURE
283	Campbell	1573012.9383	PROCEDURE
284	Mensa-Annan	1576562.1966	PROCEDURE
285	Abbas	172524.4512	PROCEDURE
286	Tsoflias	1421810.9242	PROCEDURE
287	Alberts	519905.932	PROCEDURE
288	Valdez	1827066.7118	PROCEDURE
289	Pak	4116871.2277	PROCEDURE
290	Varkey Chudukatil	3121616.3202	PROCEDURE

INSERT EXEC System Procedure

Data can be inserted into a table by the execution of a system procedure. We create a test table with SELECT INTO FROM OPENQUERY. We can also create the table manually if we know the data type of columns.

```
-- DATA ACCESS must be turned on at YOURSERVER SQL Server instance
SELECT TOP(0) * INTO #SPWHO
FROM OPENQUERY(YOURSERVER, 'exec sp_who');          -- will not work with sp_who2 due to duplicate
column name
```

```
/* Table created
CREATE TABLE [dbo].[#SPWHO](
        [spid] [smallint] NOT NULL,
        [ecid] [smallint] NOT NULL,
        [status] [nchar](30) NOT NULL,
        [loginame] [nvarchar](128) NULL,
        [hostname] [nchar](128) NOT NULL,
        [blk] [char](5) NULL,
        [dbname] [nvarchar](128) NULL,
        [cmd] [nchar](16) NOT NULL,
        [request_id] [int] NOT NULL
); */
```

```
INSERT #SPWHO   EXEC sp_who
```

The blk column contains blocking spid if any. A large update for example may block other queries until it completes. The spid of the current session is @@SPID.

```
SELECT * FROM  #SPWHO
GO -- (42 row(s) affected) - Partial results.
```

spid	ecid	status	loginame	hostname	blk	dbname	cmd	request_id
21	0	background	sa		0	master	TASK MANAGER	0
22	0	background	sa		0	master	CHECKPOINT	0
23	0	sleeping	sa		0	master	TASK MANAGER	0
24	0	background	sa		0	master	BRKR TASK	0
25	0	sleeping	sa		0	master	TASK MANAGER	0
26	0	sleeping	sa		0	master	TASK MANAGER	0
27	0	sleeping	sa		0	master	TASK MANAGER	0
28	0	sleeping	sa		0	master	TASK MANAGER	0
29	0	sleeping	sa		0	master	TASK MANAGER	0
30	0	sleeping	sa		0	master	TASK MANAGER	0
40	0	background	sa		0	master	BRKR TASK	0
42	0	background	sa		0	master	BRKR TASK	0
43	0	background	sa		0	master	BRKR TASK	0
51	0	sleeping	YOURSERVER \Owner	YOURSERVER	0	AdventureWorks2012	AWAITING COMMAND	0
52	0	sleeping	NT SERVICE\SQLSERVERAGENT	YOURSERVER	0	msdb	AWAITING COMMAND	0

```
DROP TABLE #SPWHO
GO
```

INSERT Only New Rows Omit the Rest

INSERT only new records. If record exists, do nothing. Note: DELETE will not rollback IDENTITY current value. Therefore with repeated testing, the IDENTITY current value will roll ahead.

```
USE AdventureWorks2012;
SELECT COUNT(*) FROM HumanResources.Department;                    -- 16
```

```
-- All rows exists, no new row insertion
INSERT HumanResources.Department (Name, GroupName)
SELECT Name, GroupName
FROM AdventureWorks2008.HumanResources.Department D
WHERE NOT EXISTS (      SELECT * FROM HumanResources.Department DD  -- Correlated subquery
                        WHERE D.Name = DD.Name
                          AND D.GroupName = DD.GroupName);
GO -- (0 row(s) affected)
```

```
-- Prefix Name with "ZZZ", 16 successful new inserted rows
INSERT HumanResources.Department (Name, GroupName)
SELECT CONCAT('ZZZ', Name), GroupName
FROM AdventureWorks2008.HumanResources.Department D
WHERE NOT EXISTS (      SELECT * FROM HumanResources.Department DD
        WHERE DD.Name = CONCAT('ZZZ', D.Name)    AND DD.GroupName = D.GroupName);
GO -- (16 row(s) affected)
```

```
DELETE TOP ( 7 ) HumanResources.Department WHERE Name LIKE ('ZZZ%');      -- (7 row(s) affected)
```

Only 7 rows will be inserted since the rest are duplicates.

```
INSERT HumanResources.Department (Name, GroupName)
SELECT CONCAT('ZZZ', Name), GroupName
FROM AdventureWorks2008.HumanResources.Department D
WHERE NOT EXISTS (      SELECT * FROM HumanResources.Department DD
              WHERE DD.Name = CONCAT('ZZZ', D.Name)    AND DD.GroupName = DD.GroupName);
GO
-- (7  row(s) affected)
```

```
SELECT * FROM HumanResources.Department;    -- (32 row(s) affected)  -- Partial results;
```

DepartmentID	Name	GroupName	ModifiedDate
16	Executive	Executive General and Administration	2002-06-01 00:00:00.000
65	ZZZEngineering	Research and Development	2018-08-13 08:32:43.133

```
DELETE HumanResources.Department
WHERE Name LIKE ('ZZZ%');           -- (16 row(s) affected)
SELECT COUNT(*) FROM HumanResources.Department;                    -- 16
```

DELETE - A Dangerous Operation

DELETE is a logged operation. DELETE may be slow from large table with indexes due to index reorganization. Warning: **DELETE is a dangerous operation since it removes data. Protection: regular database backup and/or creating a copy of the table prior to DELETE with SELECT INTO.**

```
USE [AdventureWorks2012]
GO
-- Create test table with SELECT INTO
SELECT [SalesOrderID]
    ,CONVERT(INT,[SalesOrderDetailID]) AS SalesOrderDetailID
    ,[CarrierTrackingNumber]
    ,[OrderQty]
    ,[ProductID]
    ,[SpecialOfferID]
    ,[UnitPrice]
    ,[UnitPriceDiscount]
    ,[LineTotal]
    ,[rowguid]
    ,[ModifiedDate]
INTO tempdb.dbo.SOD
FROM [Sales].[SalesOrderDetail];
GO -- (121317 row(s) affected)
```

```
-- Increase table population 64 fold
INSERT  tempdb.dbo.SOD  SELECT * FROM tempdb.dbo.SOD;
GO 6
/* Beginning execution loop
(121317 row(s) affected)
(242634 row(s) affected)
(485268 row(s) affected)
(970536 row(s) affected)
(1941072 row(s) affected)
(3882144 row(s) affected)
Batch execution completed 6 times.     Execution time - 00:01.27  */
```

```
CREATE INDEX idxSOD on tempdb.dbo.SOD (SalesOrderID, ProductID);
-- Command(s) completed successfully. Time: 00:00:06
```

```
SELECT COUNT(*) FROM tempdb.dbo.SOD;  -- 7764288
```

```
-- Delete even SalesOrderID records
DELETE FROM tempdb.dbo.SOD WHERE SalesOrderID % 2 = 0;
-- (3925184 row(s) affected)  - Execution time - 00:01:30
```

TRUNCATE TABLE & DBCC CHECKIDENT

TRUNCATE TABLE command is very fast since it is minimally logged. It also resets IDENTITY column to (1,1). Warning: **TRUNCATE is a dangerous operation since it removes all the data in a table**. Protection: regular database backup and/or creating a copy of the table prior to TRUNCATE with SELECT INTO. Creating PRIMARY KEY & FOREIGN KEY constraints is also demonstrated.

```
SELECT COUNT(*) FROM tempdb.dbo.SOD;  -- 3839104
```

```
TRUNCATE TABLE tempdb.dbo.SOD;
-- Command(s) completed successfully.  Execution time: 00:00:00
```

```
SELECT COUNT(*) FROM tempdb.dbo.SOD;   -- 0
GO
```

```
DROP TABLE tempdb.dbo.SOD;
GO -- Command(s) completed successfully
```

```
-- Create & populate new test parent-child tables with SELECT INTO
USE tempdb;  SELECT * INTO SOH FROM AdventureWorks2012.Sales.SalesOrderHeader;
SELECT * INTO SOD FROM AdventureWorks2012.Sales.SalesOrderDetail;
ALTER TABLE SOH ADD CONSTRAINT pkSOHa PRIMARY KEY (SalesOrderID);
ALTER TABLE SOD ADD CONSTRAINT pkSODa PRIMARY KEY (SalesOrderDetailID);
ALTER TABLE SOD ADD CONSTRAINT fkSODa
        FOREIGN KEY (SalesOrderID) REFERENCES SOH(SalesOrderID);
GO -- (31467 row(s) affected) -- (121317 row(s) affected)
```

```
DBCC CHECKIDENT ("dbo.SOD");                    -- Next IDENTITY value will be 121318.
/* Checking identity information: current identity value '121317', current column value '121317'.
DBCC execution completed. If DBCC printed error messages, contact your system administrator.  */
DBCC CHECKIDENT ("dbo.SOH");     -- ... current identity value '75128' ...
```

```
TRUNCATE TABLE SOD;
GO  -- Command(s) completed successfully.
```

```
DBCC CHECKIDENT ("dbo.SOD");              -- IDENTITY is reset
/* Checking identity information: current identity value 'NULL', current column value 'NULL'.
DBCC execution completed. If DBCC printed error messages, contact your system administrator. */
```

```
EXEC sp_help SOD;
GO -- Partial results.
```

Identity	Seed	Increment	Not For Replication
SalesOrderDetailID	1	1	0

Reseeding IDENTITY

```
-- Without this command, it may not start at 1
DBCC CHECKIDENT ("SOD", RESEED, 1);
```

```
-- Populate the table with 5 rows
INSERT INTO SOD
	([SalesOrderID],[CarrierTrackingNumber],[OrderQty],[ProductID],[SpecialOfferID],[UnitPrice]
	,[UnitPriceDiscount] ,[LineTotal],[rowguid],[ModifiedDate])
 SELECT   TOP (5) [SalesOrderID],[CarrierTrackingNumber],[OrderQty],[ProductID],[SpecialOfferID]
	,[UnitPrice] ,[UnitPriceDiscount],[LineTotal],[rowguid],[ModifiedDate]
FROM AdventureWorks2012.Sales.SalesOrderDetail;
GO -- (5 row(s) affected)
```

```
-- Next value assigned is 6
DBCC CHECKIDENT ("dbo.SOD");
/*Checking identity information: current identity value '5', current column value '5'.
DBCC execution completed. If DBCC printed error messages, contact your system administrator. */
```

```
SELECT * FROM SOD;  -- (5 row(s) affected) - Partial results.
```

SalesOrderID	SalesOrderDetailID	CarrierTrackingNumber	OrderQty	ProductID	SpecialOfferID	UnitPrice	UnitPriceDiscount	LineTotal
43659	1	4911-403C-98	1	776	1	2024.994	0.00	2024.994000
43659	2	4911-403C-98	3	777	1	2024.994	0.00	6074.982000
43659	3	4911-403C-98	1	778	1	2024.994	0.00	2024.994000
43659	4	4911-403C-98	1	771	1	2039.994	0.00	2039.994000
43659	5	4911-403C-98	1	772	1	2039.994	0.00	2039.994000

Checking @@ERROR - Ye Olde Way

The following method has a much improved implementation with TRY...CATCH and THROW.

```
DECLARE @ErrorLcl INT,  @RowCountLcl INT;
-- Execute the UPDATE statement with error (INT date)
UPDATE Purchasing.PurchaseOrderHeader   SET ModifiedDate = 19010101
   WHERE PurchaseOrderID = 1000;
```

```
-- Save the @@ERROR & @@ROWCOUNT values in local  variables before they are reset.
SELECT @ErrorLcl = @@ERROR, @RowCountLcl = @@ROWCOUNT;
```

```
IF @ErrorLcl <> 0
		PRINT CONCAT('Error: ', @ErrorLcl, ' Rows: ', @RowCountLcl);
ELSE
		PRINT CONCAT('Execution OK. Rows: ', @RowCountLcl);
```

/* Msg 8115, Level 16, State 2, Line 4 Arithmetic overflow error converting expression to data type datetime. The statement has been terminated.
Error: 8115 Rows: 0 */

UPDATE - A Complex Operation

UPDATE changes data content at a row and column level (cell). It is a logged operation: deleted row contains previous data, inserted row contains new data. Warning: UPDATE is a dangerous operation since it changes the data in a table. Protection: regular database backup and/or creating a copy of the table prior to UPDATE with SELECT INTO.

Some UPDATEs are reversible, such as some calculated UPDATE, others may be irreversible.

Checking Cardinality & Changes by UPDATE Prior to Execution

Since UPDATE is replaces previous data, it is very important to check prior to execution that is works correctly. It is quite simple to convert UPDATE into a checking SELECT. We intend to UPDATE the SalesYTD column with the last day sales for each salesperson.

```
USE AdventureWorks2012;
SELECT   sp.BusinessEntityID, SalesYTD,
                   [NewSalesYTD]=SalesYTD
         + (SELECT SUM(SODa.SubTotal)
          FROM   Sales.SalesOrderHeader AS SODa
          WHERE  CONVERT(date,SODa.OrderDate) = CONVERT(date,(SELECT MAX(OrderDate)
           FROM   Sales.SalesOrderHeader AS SODb
           WHERE
              SODb.SalesPersonID = SODa.SalesPersonID))
              AND sp.BusinessEntityID =  SODa.SalesPersonID
          GROUP  BY SODa.SalesPersonID)
FROM Sales.SalesPerson sp  ORDER BY sp.BusinessEntityID;
GO
```

BusinessEntityID	SalesYTD	NewSalesYTD
274	559697.5639	597350.4859
275	3763178.1787	4133185.161
276	4251368.5497	4534079.5941
277	3189418.3662	3527404.588
278	1453719.4653	1599132.4735
279	2315185.611	2548077.4756
280	1352577.1325	1503691.0098
281	2458535.6169	2678660.7921
282	2604540.7172	3030519.8258
283	1573012.9383	1714964.9067
284	1576562.1966	1719945.1917
285	172524.4512	176721.5652
286	1421810.9242	1649155.9058
287	519905.932	520578.226
288	1827066.7118	1962768.1658
289	4116871.2277	4556655.2802
290	3121616.3202	3240852.6195

ANSI Style UPDATE

T-SQL supports ANSI UPDATE, in addition T-SQL supports the FROM clause in UPDATE.

```
USE AdventureWorks2012;
UPDATE Sales.SalesPerson
SET    SalesYTD = SalesYTD
            + (SELECT SUM(SODa.SubTotal)
              FROM   Sales.SalesOrderHeader AS SODa
              WHERE  CONVERT(date,SODa.OrderDate) =
                      CONVERT(date,(SELECT MAX(OrderDate)
               FROM   Sales.SalesOrderHeader AS SODb
               WHERE
                   SODb.SalesPersonID = SODa.SalesPersonID))
                   AND Sales.SalesPerson.BusinessEntityID =   SODa.SalesPersonID
              GROUP  BY SODa.SalesPersonID);
GO
-- (17 row(s) affected)
```

```
SELECT BusinessEntityID, SalesQuota, SalesYTD, SalesLastYear
FROM Sales.SalesPerson
ORDER BY BusinessEntityID;
GO
```

BusinessEntityID	SalesQuota	SalesYTD	SalesLastYear
274	NULL	597350.4859	0.00
275	300000.00	4133185.161	1750406.4785
276	250000.00	4534079.5941	1439156.0291
277	250000.00	3527404.588	1997186.2037
278	250000.00	1599132.4735	1620276.8966
279	300000.00	2548077.4756	1849640.9418
280	250000.00	1503691.0098	1927059.178
281	250000.00	2678660.7921	2073505.9999
282	250000.00	3030519.8258	2038234.6549
283	250000.00	1714964.9067	1371635.3158
284	300000.00	1719945.1917	0.00
285	NULL	176721.5652	0.00
286	250000.00	1649155.9058	2278548.9776
287	NULL	520578.226	0.00
288	250000.00	1962768.1658	1307949.7917
289	250000.00	4556655.2802	1635823.3967
290	250000.00	3240852.6195	2396539.7601

UPDATE from Table in Another Database

UPDATE can be performed with data from a second database. ZorigAdventureWorks2012 is an original read-only copy of the AdventureWorks2012 database. The "Z" prefix is to force it to the end of alphabetical database list in SSMS Object Explorer.

```
UPDATE Sales.SalesPerson
        SET SalesYTD = (
                                SELECT SalesYTD
                                FROM ZorigAdventureWorks2012.Sales.SalesPerson sp
                                WHERE sp.BusinessEntityID =
Sales.SalesPerson.BusinessEntityID
                        );
GO
```

```
SELECT  BusinessEntityID,
        SalesQuota,
        SalesYTD,
        SalesLastYear
FROM Sales.SalesPerson
ORDER BY BusinessEntityID;
GO
```

BusinessEntityID	SalesQuota	SalesYTD	SalesLastYear
274	NULL	559697.5639	0.00
275	300000.00	3763178.1787	1750406.4785
276	250000.00	4251368.5497	1439156.0291
277	250000.00	3189418.3662	1997186.2037
278	250000.00	1453719.4653	1620276.8966
279	300000.00	2315185.611	1849640.9418
280	250000.00	1352577.1325	1927059.178
281	250000.00	2458535.6169	2073505.9999
282	250000.00	2604540.7172	2038234.6549
283	250000.00	1573012.9383	1371635.3158
284	300000.00	1576562.1966	0.00
285	NULL	172524.4512	0.00
286	250000.00	1421810.9242	2278548.9776
287	NULL	519905.932	0.00
288	250000.00	1827066.7118	1307949.7917
289	250000.00	4116871.2277	1635823.3967
290	250000.00	3121616.3202	2396539.7601

UPDATE Syntax Challenges

The UPDATE statement in SQL has perplexing and potentially confusing syntax. Typically mastered by expert DBA-s and SQL developers, and the rest of the database community uses it in an insecure manner: never sure if it works as intended. Simple T-SQL examples demonstrate some of the issues with the UPDATE syntax and offer solutions.

First we create a new table for experimentation from the AdventureWorks2012 database and perform a demo inner join UPDATE on the new table.

```
USE tempdb;

SELECT ProductID,
    ProductName = Name,
    StandardCost AS Cost,
    ListPrice,
    Color,
    CONVERT(date, ModifiedDate) AS ModifiedDate
INTO   Product
FROM   AdventureWorks2012.Production.Product
WHERE  ListPrice > 0.0
        AND Color IS NOT NULL;
GO
-- (245 row(s) affected)
```

```
SELECT TOP 5 * FROM Product
ORDER BY ProductID DESC;
GO
```

ProductID	ProductName	Cost	ListPrice	Color	ModifiedDate
999	Road-750 Black, 52	343.6496	539.99	Black	2008-03-11
998	Road-750 Black, 48	343.6496	539.99	Black	2008-03-11
997	Road-750 Black, 44	343.6496	539.99	Black	2008-03-11
993	Mountain-500 Black, 52	294.5797	539.99	Black	2008-03-11
992	Mountain-500 Black, 48	294.5797	539.99	Black	2008-03-11

We shall proceed and update ALL (no WHERE clause) the rows in the Product table. We increase the ListPrice by 5%.

```
UPDATE Product     SET ListPrice = ListPrice * 1.05;  -- (245 row(s) affected)
```

In this instance a reversible UPDATE. But not always.

```
UPDATE Product     SET ListPrice = ListPrice / 1.05;
-- (245 row(s) affected)
```

UPDATE with INNER JOIN

The UPDATE uses a table alias from the FROM clause.

```
SELECT TOP 2 * FROM Product  WHERE Color = 'Yellow' ORDER BY ProductID DESC;
```

ProductID	ProductName	Cost	ListPrice	Color	ModifiedDate
976	Road-350-W Yellow, 48	1082.51	1700.99	Yellow	2008-03-11
975	Road-350-W Yellow, 44	1082.51	1700.99	Yellow	2008-03-11

```
UPDATE p  SET   p.ModifiedDate = DATEADD(HH,1,awp.ModifiedDate)
FROM   Product p    INNER JOIN AdventureWorks2012.Production.Product awp
                         ON p.ProductID = awp.ProductID  AND  p.Size LIKE '4%' ;
-- (91 row(s) affected)
```

Capturing Affected Rows with @@ROWCOUNT

When we have to know the number of updated rows, it is best to capture it into local variable and use it from there in the program logic.

```
DECLARE @UpdatedRows  int;   -- capture @@ROWCOUNT for subsequent  use in the program

UPDATE p  SET   p.ModifiedDate = DATEADD(mm,1,awp.ModifiedDate)
FROM   Product p
    INNER JOIN AdventureWorks2012.Production.Product awp    ON p.ProductID = awp.ProductID
WHERE  p.Color = 'Yellow' ;
-- (36 row(s) affected)

SET @UpdatedRows = @@ROWCOUNT;

SELECT @@ROWCOUNT;                  -- @@ROWCOUNT already changed
-- 1
SELECT TOP 5 * FROM Product  WHERE Color = 'Yellow' ORDER BY ProductID DESC;

SELECT @@ROWCOUNT;                  -- @@ROWCOUNT changed again
-- 5
SELECT @UpdatedRows;                -- local variable kept the UPDATE count
-- 36
```

ProductID	ProductName	Cost	ListPrice	Color	ModifiedDate
976	Road-350-W Yellow, 48	1082.51	1700.99	Yellow	2008-04-11
975	Road-350-W Yellow, 44	1082.51	1700.99	Yellow	2008-04-11
974	Road-350-W Yellow, 42	1082.51	1700.99	Yellow	2008-04-11
973	Road-350-W Yellow, 40	1082.51	1700.99	Yellow	2008-04-11
965	Touring-3000 Yellow, 62	461.4448	742.35	Yellow	2008-04-11

UPDATE with Common Table Expression

UPDATE can be issued through a CTE to UPDATE the underlying table, Product in this case. Prices are increased 5% for products with over $1,000.00 list price.

```
SELECT TOP 5 * FROM Product  WHERE ListPrice > 1000.0 ORDER BY ProductID DESC;
GO
```

ProductID	ProductName	Cost	ListPrice	Color	ModifiedDate
976	Road-350-W Yellow, 48	1082.51	1700.99	Yellow	2008-04-11
975	Road-350-W Yellow, 44	1082.51	1700.99	Yellow	2008-04-11
974	Road-350-W Yellow, 42	1082.51	1700.99	Yellow	2008-04-11
973	Road-350-W Yellow, 40	1082.51	1700.99	Yellow	2008-04-11
972	Touring-2000 Blue, 54	755.1508	1214.85	Blue	2008-03-11

```
;WITH CTE
   AS (SELECT Price = ListPrice
      FROM   Product
      WHERE  ListPrice > 1000.0)
UPDATE CTE
SET   Price = Price * 1.05
GO
-- (86 row(s) affected)
```

```
SELECT TOP 5 * FROM Product  WHERE ListPrice > 1000.0 ORDER BY ProductID DESC;
```

ProductID	ProductName	Cost	ListPrice	Color	ModifiedDate
976	Road-350-W Yellow, 48	1082.51	1786.0395	Yellow	2008-04-11
975	Road-350-W Yellow, 44	1082.51	1786.0395	Yellow	2008-04-11
974	Road-350-W Yellow, 42	1082.51	1786.0395	Yellow	2008-04-11
973	Road-350-W Yellow, 40	1082.51	1786.0395	Yellow	2008-04-11
972	Touring-2000 Blue, 54	755.1508	1275.5925	Blue	2008-03-11

Similar data modification with ANSI SQL UPDATE.

```
UPDATE Product
SET   ListPrice = (SELECT p8.ListPrice * 1.05
            FROM   AdventureWorks2012.Production.Product p8    WHERE  Product.ProductID =
p8.ProductID)
WHERE  EXISTS (SELECT *  FROM   AdventureWorks2012.Production.Product p8
         WHERE  Product.ProductID = p8.ProductID    AND Product.ListPrice > 1000.0);
```

Four Methods of UPDATE with GROUP BY Query

UPDATE can be done a few ways with GROUP BY aggregates.

```
USE tempdb;
SELECT Color=ISNULL(Color,'N/A'), ItemCount=0 INTO ProductColor
FROM AdventureWorks2008.Production.Product
GROUP BY Color
GO
-- (10 row(s) affected)
```

```
SELECT * FROM ProductColor
GO
```

Color	ItemCount
N/A	0
Black	0
Blue	0
Grey	0
Multi	0
Red	0
Silver	0
Silver/Black	0
White	0
Yellow	0

ANSI UPDATE

```
UPDATE ProductColor
SET ItemCount = (SELECT ProductColorCount FROM  (SELECT Color=ISNULL(Color, 'N/A'),
                    ProductColorCount=COUNT(*)
                     FROM AdventureWorks2008.Production.Product
                     GROUP BY Color) cg WHERE  ProductColor.Color = cg.Color)
GO -- (10 row(s) affected)
```

FROM Clause UPDATE with Derived Table

```
UPDATE pc   SET pc.ItemCount = cg.ProductColorCount
FROM ProductColor pc
INNER JOIN (SELECT Color=ISNULL(Color, 'N/A'), ProductColorCount=COUNT(*)
        FROM AdventureWorks2008.Production.Product GROUP BY Color) cg
ON pc.Color = cg.Color;
-- (10 row(s) affected)
```

FROM Clause UPDATE with CTE

```
;WITH CTE AS (SELECT Color=ISNULL(Color, 'N/A'), ProductColorCount=COUNT(*)
        FROM AdventureWorks2008.Production.Product
        GROUP BY Color)
UPDATE pc
SET pc.ItemCount = CTE.ProductColorCount
FROM ProductColor pc
INNER JOIN CTE
ON pc.Color = CTE.Color;
GO
-- (10 row(s) affected)
```

CTE UPDATE

```
;WITH CTE AS (SELECT * FROM ProductColor pc
        INNER JOIN (SELECT ColorPrd=ISNULL(Color, 'N/A'), ProductColorCount=COUNT(*)
        FROM AdventureWorks2008.Production.Product
        GROUP BY Color) cg
                        ON pc.Color = cg.ColorPrd)
UPDATE CTE SET CTE.ItemCount = CTE.ProductColorCount;
GO-- (10 row(s) affected)
```

```
SELECT * FROM ProductColor;  -- Partial results.
```

Color	ItemCount
N/A	248
Black	93
Blue	26
Grey	1

```
DROP TABLE tempdb.dbo.ProductColor;
```

UPDATE with the .WRITE Clause

The .WRITE (expression, @Offset,@Length) clause can be applied for a partial / full update of varchar(max), nvarchar(max), & varbinary(max) columns.

Article: **SQL Server 2005 UPDATE statement with new .WRITE Clause**
http://beyondrelational.com/modules/1/justlearned/0/tips/8862/sql-server-2005-update-statement-with-new-write-clause.aspx

MERGE for Combination INSERT, UPDATE or DELETE

The MERGE statement can be used to INSERT, UPDATE and/or DELETE all in one statement.

```
USE tempdb;
go
```

```
-- Setup 2 test tables
SELECT TOP (5000) ResellerKey,
            OrderDateKey,
            ProductKey,
            OrderQuantity,
            SalesAmount
INTO   FactResellerSales
FROM   AdventureWorksDW2012.dbo.FactResellerSales
ORDER BY OrderDateKey ;
go
-- (5000 row(s) affected)
```

```
SELECT TOP (8000) ResellerKey,
            OrderDateKey,
            ProductKey,
            OrderQuantity,
            SalesAmount
INTO   ResellerSalesTransaction
FROM   AdventureWorksDW2012.dbo.FactResellerSales ;
go
-- (8000 row(s) affected)
```

```
DELETE rsc
FROM   ResellerSalesTransaction rsc
    JOIN (SELECT TOP 1000 *
        FROM   ResellerSalesTransaction
        ORDER  BY ResellerKey DESC) x
      ON x.ResellerKey = rsc.ResellerKey ;
go
-- (1010 row(s) affected)
```

```
UPDATE TOP (6000) ResellerSalesTransaction
SET    SalesAmount = SalesAmount * 1.1 ;
go
-- (6000 row(s) affected)
```

MERGE is a very powerful statement

```
SELECT TOP (10) *
FROM   FactResellerSales
ORDER  BY ResellerKey,        OrderDateKey,        ProductKey ;
go
```

ResellerKey	OrderDateKey	ProductKey	OrderQuantity	SalesAmount
1	20050801	270	1	183.9382
1	20050801	275	1	356.898
1	20050801	285	1	178.5808
1	20050801	314	2	4293.924
1	20050801	317	1	874.794
1	20050801	319	2	1749.588
1	20050801	324	2	838.9178
1	20050801	326	1	419.4589
1	20050801	328	1	419.4589
1	20050801	332	2	838.9178

```
SELECT BeforeFactCount=COUNT(*)
FROM   FactResellerSales ;
-- 5000
```

```
-- Ready for the MERGE (update if exists,  insert otherwise)
MERGE FactResellerSales AS fact                                    -- TARGET
USING (SELECT *
    FROM   ResellerSalesTransaction) AS feed                      -- SOURCE
ON ( fact.ProductKey = feed.ProductKey
   AND fact.ResellerKey = feed.ResellerKey  AND fact.OrderDateKey = feed.OrderDateKey )
WHEN MATCHED THEN
  UPDATE SET fact.OrderQuantity +=  feed.OrderQuantity,
         fact.SalesAmount +=  feed.SalesAmount
WHEN NOT MATCHED THEN
  INSERT (ResellerKey,
       OrderDateKey,
       ProductKey,
       OrderQuantity,
       SalesAmount)
  VALUES (feed.ResellerKey,
       feed.OrderDateKey,
       feed.ProductKey,
       feed.OrderQuantity,
       feed.SalesAmount)
OUTPUT deleted.*, $action, inserted.*   /* INTO table, #temptable or @tablevariable */;
go  -- (6990 row(s) affected)
```

Checking results after MERGE

```
SELECT TOP (10) *
FROM   FactResellerSales  ORDER  BY          ResellerKey,    OrderDateKey,    ProductKey;
```

ResellerKey	OrderDateKey	ProductKey	OrderQuantity	SalesAmount
1	20050801	270	2	386.2702
1	20050801	275	2	749.4858
1	20050801	285	2	375.0197
1	20050801	314	4	9017.2404
1	20050801	317	2	1837.0674
1	20050801	319	4	3674.1348
1	20050801	324	4	1761.7274
1	20050801	326	2	880.8637
1	20050801	328	2	880.8637
1	20050801	332	4	1761.7274

```
SELECT AfterFactCount=COUNT(*)   FROM   FactResellerSales ;
go
-- 7658

DROP TABLE ResellerSalesTransaction;  DROP TABLE FactResellerSales;
go
```

Using MERGE Instead of UPDATE

MERGE statement can be used in the UPDATE only mode to replace UPDATE.

```
-- Prepare 2 test tables
USE tempdb;
SELECT TOP (5000) ResellerKey,  OrderDateKey, ProductKey, OrderQuantity, SalesAmount
INTO   FactResellerSales FROM   AdventureWorksDW2012.dbo.FactResellerSales;
GO -- (5000 row(s) affected)
SELECT TOP (8000) ResellerKey,  OrderDateKey, ProductKey, OrderQuantity, SalesAmount
INTO   ResellerSalesTransaction FROM   AdventureWorksDW2012.dbo.FactResellerSales;
GO -- (8000 row(s) affected)
```

```
-- Alter the test data
DELETE rsc
FROM   ResellerSalesTransaction rsc
     INNER JOIN (SELECT TOP 1000 * FROM   ResellerSalesTransaction
         ORDER  BY ResellerKey DESC) x   -- subquery inner join
       ON x.ResellerKey = rsc.ResellerKey;
GO --(1010 row(s) affected)
UPDATE TOP (6000) ResellerSalesTransaction SET SalesAmount = SalesAmount * 1.1;
GO -- (6000 row(s) affected)
```

```
SELECT BeforeFactCount=COUNT(*) FROM   FactResellerSales;
GO -- 5000
```

```
-- Ready for the MERGE UPDATE only mode
MERGE FactResellerSales AS fact                                    -- TARGET
USING (SELECT * FROM   ResellerSalesTransaction) AS feed           -- SOURCE
ON ( fact.ProductKey = feed.ProductKey
   AND fact.ResellerKey = feed.ResellerKey
   AND fact.OrderDateKey = feed.OrderDateKey )
WHEN MATCHED THEN
  UPDATE SET fact.OrderQuantity = fact.OrderQuantity + feed.OrderQuantity,
        fact.SalesAmount = fact.SalesAmount + feed.SalesAmount
OUTPUT deleted.*, $action, inserted.*   /* INTO table, #temptable or @tablevariable */;
GO -- 4332 row(s) affected)
```

```
SELECT AfterFactCount=COUNT(*) FROM   FactResellerSales;
GO -- 5000
```

```
DROP TABLE ResellerSalesTransaction;  DROP TABLE FactResellerSales;
```

CHAPTER 17: The Magic of Transact-SQL Programming

IF...ELSE Conditional

IF... ELSE is a step toward a bona fide programming language.

```
DECLARE @StringNumber varchar(32) ;
SET @StringNumber = '12,000,000';
IF EXISTS( SELECT * WHERE ISNUMERIC(@StringNumber) = 1)
	PRINT 'VALID NUMBER: ' + @StringNumber
ELSE	PRINT 'INVALID NUMBER: ' + @StringNumber;
GO
-- VALID NUMBER: 12,000,000
```

```
DECLARE @StringNumber varchar(32) = '12,000:000';

IF EXISTS( SELECT * WHERE ISNUMERIC(@StringNumber) = 1)
	PRINT CONCAT('VALID NUMBER: ' , @StringNumber)
ELSE	PRINT CONCAT('INVALID NUMBER: ', @StringNumber);
GO
-- INVALID NUMBER: 12,000:000
```

```
DECLARE @StringDate varchar(32);

SET @StringDate = '2017-03-15 18:50';

IF EXISTS( SELECT * WHERE ISDATE(@StringDate) = 1)
	PRINT 'VALID DATE: ' + @StringDate
ELSE	PRINT 'INVALID DATE: ' + @StringDate;
GO
-- Result: VALID DATE: 2017-03-15 18:50
```

```
DECLARE @StringDate varchar(32) = '20116-03-15 18:50';
IF EXISTS( SELECT * WHERE ISDATE(@StringDate) = 1)
	PRINT CONCAT('VALID DATE: ', @StringDate)
ELSE	PRINT CONCAT('INVALID DATE: ', @StringDate);
-- Result: INVALID DATE: 20116-03-15 18:50
```

WHILE Looping - UPDATE in Batches

WHILE looping can be used to break down large transaction to small batches. Executing in small batches is safer and does not block other OLTP transactions for a long time. Blocking can be seen by running sp_who system stored procedure

```
EXEC sp_who;
```

UPDATE of 121,317 rows is batched to 13 batches of 10,000 or less.

```
USE tempdb;
SELECT * INTO SOD
FROM AdventureWorks2012.Sales.SalesOrderDetail ORDER BY SalesOrderDetailID;
GO
--(121317 row(s) affected)
```

```
WHILE (2 > 1)   -- Infinite loop until BREAK is issued
 BEGIN
  UPDATE TOP ( 10000 ) SOD
  SET    UnitPriceDiscount = 0.08,  ModifiedDate = CONVERT(DATE, getdate())
  WHERE  ModifiedDate < CONVERT(DATE, getdate());

  IF @@ROWCOUNT = 0
   BEGIN
    BREAK;
   END
  -- 1 second delay - Very important for other OLTP transactions execution
  WAITFOR DELAY '00:00:01'
 END; -- WHILE
GO
```

(10000 row(s) affected)
(10000 row(s) affected)
(10000 row(s) affected)
(10000 row(s) affected)
(10000 row(s) affected)
(10000 row(s) affected)
(10000 row(s) affected)
(10000 row(s) affected)
(10000 row(s) affected)
(10000 row(s) affected)
(10000 row(s) affected)
(10000 row(s) affected)
(1317 row(s) affected)
(0 row(s) affected)

```
DROP TABLE tempdb.dbo.SOD
```

WHILE Loop Usage in Cursors

Transact-SQL logic will visit all databases on the current SQL Server instance using a cursor.
NOTE: **cursor solutions do not scale well, first choice is set-based logic if appropriate.**

```
DECLARE @CurrentDB sysname;
DECLARE AllDBCursor CURSOR  STATIC LOCAL FOR
	SELECT   name FROM    MASTER.dbo.sysdatabases
	WHERE    name NOT IN ('master','tempdb','model','msdb') ORDER BY name;
OPEN AllDBCursor;
FETCH  AllDBCursor INTO @CurrentDB;
WHILE (@@FETCH_STATUS = 0) -- loop through all db-s
 BEGIN
/***** PROCESSING (like BACKUP database)   *****/
	PRINT @CurrentDB;
	FETCH  AllDBCursor   INTO @CurrentDB;
 END; -- while
CLOSE AllDBCursor; DEALLOCATE AllDBCursor;
```

```
/*.... AdventureWorks  AdventureWorks2008 AdventureWorks2012 AdventureWorksDW2012 .... */
```

Transact-SQL script demonstrates a subcategory cursor.

```
USE AdventureWorks2012;
DECLARE curSubcategory CURSOR STATIC LOCAL  FOR            -- declare cursor
	SELECT ProductSubcategoryID, Subcategory=Name
	FROM Production.ProductSubcategory ORDER BY Subcategory;
DECLARE @Subcategory varchar(40), @PSID int
OPEN curSubcategory
FETCH NEXT FROM curSubcategory INTO @PSID, @Subcategory  -- fetch cursor
WHILE (@@fetch_status = 0)                  -- cursor fetch_status
BEGIN -- begin cursor loop
/***** USER DEFINED PROCESSING CODE HERE  *****/
	DECLARE @Msg varchar(128);
  SELECT @Msg = CONCAT('ProductSubcategory info: ', @Subcategory,' ',CONVERT(varchar, @PSID));
	PRINT @Msg;
FETCH NEXT FROM curSubcategory INTO @PSID, @Subcategory;   -- fetch cursor
END; -- end cursor loop
CLOSE curSubcategory;  DEALLOCATE curSubcategory;
```

```
/* ... ProductSubcategory info: Bike Stands 27       ProductSubcategory info: Bottles and Cages 28
ProductSubcategory info: Bottom Brackets 5  ... */
```

BOL Article: **DECLARE CURSOR (Transact-SQL)**
http://msdn.microsoft.com/en-us/library/ms180169(v=sql.110).aspx

T-SQL Transaction

Transact-SQL language has been extended with features beyond ANSI SQL such as variables, IF... ELSE and WHILE. **"Transact" refers to the capability to execute business transactions which require the synchronized update of tables as one or none at all.**

DELETE from 2 Tables with TRANSACTION Control

DELETE PRIMARY KEY rows from PK table and related FOREIGN KEY rows from FK table in a single transaction. NOTE: Deleting lots of rows may interfere with online access in an ecommerce database.

Alternate method: define tables with CASCADE ON DELETE action.

```
BEGIN TRANSACTION
```

```
-- First delete from FOREIGN KEY table
DELETE OmegaFK
FROM Omega AS OmegaFK
 INNER JOIN Delta AS DeltaPK
  ON DeltaPK.ColApk = OmegaFK.ColBfk
WHERE DeltaPK.ColApk = {single value A} ;
```

```
IF @@ERROR <> 0
BEGIN
	ROLLBACK TRANSACTION;
	RAISERROR('FK delete failed.', 10, 1);
END
-- if no error, delete from PRIMARY KEY table
ELSE
	DELETE
	FROM Delta
	WHERE ColApk = = {single value A};
```

```
-- Commit transaction only if both DELETE-s succeeded
IF @@ERROR <> 0
BEGIN
	ROLLBACK TRANSACTION;
	RAISERROR('PK delete failed.', 10, 1);
ELSE
	COMMIT TRANSACTION;
```

Stored Procedure with Input & Output Parameters

A stored procedure usually returns a table-like result set from the SELECT(s) in the stored procedure. Scalar value can also be returned with the OUTPUT option.

```
USE AdventureWorks2012;
GO
CREATE PROCEDURE uspQuarterSales     @StartYear INT,     @TotalSales MONEY OUTPUT
AS
 BEGIN -- sproc definition
  SET NOCOUNT ON -- turn off rows affected messages
  SELECT @TotalSales = SUM(SubTotal)
  FROM  Sales.SalesOrderHeader   WHERE OrderDate >= DATEADD(YY,@StartYear-1900,'19000101')

  SELECT  YEAR = YEAR(OrderDate),
       COALESCE(FORMAT(SUM(CASE
           WHEN DATEPART(QQ,OrderDate) = 1 THEN SubTotal
                   END),'c','en-US'),'') AS 'Q1',
       COALESCE(FORMAT(SUM(CASE
           WHEN DATEPART(QQ,OrderDate) = 2 THEN SubTotal
                   END),'c','en-US'),'') AS 'Q2',
       COALESCE(FORMAT(SUM(CASE
           WHEN DATEPART(QQ,OrderDate) = 3 THEN SubTotal
                   END),'c','en-US'),'') AS 'Q3',
       COALESCE(FORMAT(SUM(CASE
           WHEN DATEPART(QQ,OrderDate) = 4 THEN SubTotal
                   END),'c','en-US'),'') AS 'Q4'
  FROM   Sales.SalesOrderHeader soh
  WHERE  OrderDate >= DATEADD(YY,@StartYear-1900,'19000101')
  GROUP BY YEAR(OrderDate)    ORDER BY YEAR(OrderDate);
 END; -- sproc definition
GO
```

```
-- Execute stored procedure with INPUT/OUTPUT parameters
DECLARE @TotSales money
EXEC uspQuarterSales 2007, @TotSales OUTPUT;
SELECT TotalSales = @TotSales;
```

YEAR	Q1	Q2	Q3	Q4
2007	$6,679,873.80	$8,357,874.88	$13,681,907.05	$13,291,381.43
2008	$11,398,376.28	$14,379,545.19	$50,840.63	

TotalSales
67839799.2669

Dynamic SQL Stored Procedure to REBUILD Indexes

The following dynamic SQL stored procedure uses database metadata to loop through all tables in the database, assemble and execute the index REBUILD command.

```
USE AdventureWorks2012;
GO
```

```
CREATE PROC sprocAllTablesIndexREBUILD @FILLFACTOR INT = 90
AS
 BEGIN
   DECLARE @DatabaseName SYSNAME = DB_NAME(),
       @TableName    VARCHAR(256);
   DECLARE @DynamicSQL NVARCHAR(max) = CONCAT('DECLARE cursorForAllTables CURSOR     STATIC
         FOR    SELECT CONCAT(TABLE_SCHEMA,''.'', TABLE_NAME) AS TABLENAME    FROM ',
         @DatabaseName,  '.INFORMATION_SCHEMA.TABLES WHERE   TABLE_TYPE = ''BASE TABLE''');
    BEGIN
      EXEC sp_executeSQL
       @DynamicSQL; -- create tables cursor
      OPEN cursorForAllTables;

      FETCH NEXT FROM cursorForAllTables INTO @TableName;
      WHILE ( @@FETCH_STATUS = 0 )
       BEGIN
         SET @DynamicSQL = CONCAT('ALTER INDEX ALL ON ', @TableName,
                  ' REBUILD WITH ( FILLFACTOR = ',
                          CONVERT(VARCHAR, @FILLFACTOR),  ')'   );
         PRINT @DynamicSQL;  -- test & debug
         EXEC sp_executeSQL
          @DynamicSQL;
         FETCH NEXT FROM cursorForAllTables INTO @TableName;
       END; -- cursor WHILE
      CLOSE cursorForAllTables;    DEALLOCATE cursorForAllTables;
   END;
 END; -- sproc
GO
-- Command(s) completed successfully.
```

```
-- Reindex tables with 85% fill factor leaving 15% free space for growth
EXEC sprocAllTablesIndexREBUILD 85;
/*
ALTER INDEX ALL ON Production.ScrapReason REBUILD WITH ( FILLFACTOR = 85)
ALTER INDEX ALL ON HumanResources.Shift REBUILD WITH ( FILLFACTOR = 85)
 ....  */
```

EXECUTE AS Clause

The WITH EXECUTE AS clause can be optionally specified in the CREATE PROC statement. Stored procedures just like views can be used to implement secutiry access to a database.

```
USE AdventureWorks2012;
GO
CREATE PROC sprocProduct WITH EXECUTE AS OWNER AS  BEGIN
   SELECT * FROM Production.Product ORDER BY ProductNumber;    RETURN @@ROWCOUNT;
END;
GO
-- InventoryStaff is a user-defined database role
GRANT EXEC ON TruncTest TO InventoryStaff;
```

```
DECLARE @rows int;    EXEC @Rows = sprocProduct;;   -- Partial result.
```

ProductID	Name	ProductNumber	MakeFlag	FinishedGoodsFlag
1	Adjustable Race	AR-5381	0	0
2	Bearing Ball	BA-8327	0	0
994	LL Bottom Bracket	BB-7421	1	1

```
SELECT @Rows;   -- 504
```

Blog: **SQL Server Security with EXECUTE AS OWNER**
http://clay.lenharts.net/blog/2008/01/24/sql-server-security-with-execute-as-owner/

The EXECUTE AS clause can be used with UDF-s, triggers & queues also.

Functions (excluding inline TVF), Stored Procedures, & DML Triggers
{ EXEC | EXECUTE } AS { CALLER | SELF | OWNER | 'database_user' }
DDL Triggers with Database Scope
{ EXEC | EXECUTE } AS { CALLER | SELF | 'database_user' }
DDL Triggers with Server Scope & logon triggers
{ EXEC | EXECUTE } AS { CALLER | SELF | 'server_login' }
Queues
{ EXEC | EXECUTE } AS { SELF | OWNER | 'database_user' }

SELF - specified user is the person creating the module
CALLER - will take on the permissions of the current user
OWNER - will take on the permissions of the owner of the module being called
'database_user' - a specific database user
'server_login' - a specific server login

User-Defined Functions

Table-Valued Functions

A table-valued function returns a table variable, therefore, it has to be invoked like it were a table in a query. T-SQL table-valued function creates a table from a delimited string of values.

```
CREATE FUNCTION dbo.ufnSplitDelimitedString (  @StringList VARCHAR(MAX),     @Delimiter CHAR(1))
RETURNS @TableList TABLE(ID int identity(1,1), StringLiteral VARCHAR(128))
BEGIN
    IF @StringList = '' RETURN;
    IF @Delimiter = ''
    BEGIN
      WITH Split AS                                    -- Recursive CTE
          ( SELECT CharOne=LEFT(@StringList,1),R=RIGHT(@StringList,len(@StringList)-1)
            UNION ALL
            SELECT LEFT(R,1), R=RIGHT(R, len(R)-1)
            FROM Split    WHERE LEN(R)>0  )               -- End of CTE
     INSERT @TableList
     SELECT CharOne FROM Split    OPTION ( MAXRECURSION 0);
     RETURN;
    END; -- IF
   DECLARE @XML xml=CONCAT('<root><csv>',replace(@StringList,@Delimiter,'</csv><csv>'),
                                  '</csv></root>');
    INSERT @TableList
    SELECT rtrim(ltrim(replace(Word.value('.','nvarchar(128)'),char(10),'')))     AS ListMember
    FROM @XML.nodes('/root/csv') AS WordList(Word);
RETURN;
END; -- FUNCTION
GO
```

```
SELECT * FROM dbo.ufnSplitDelimitedString ('New York, California, Arizona, Texas, Toronto, Grand
Canyon, Yosemite,   Yellowstone, Niagara Falls, Belgium, Denmark, South Africa, Sweden', ',');
```

ID	StringLiteral
1	New York
2	California
3	Arizona
4	Texas
5	Toronto
6	Grand Canyon
7	Yosemite
8	Yellowstone
9	Niagara Falls
10	Belgium
11	Denmark
12	South Africa
13	Sweden

Table-Valued Function for PRIME Numbers Generation

Transact-SQL table-valued function generates prime numbers up to the input parameter limit.

```
USE AdventureWorks2012;
GO

CREATE FUNCTION ufnPrimeNumbers ( @Stop INT)
RETURNS @Result TABLE  (Prime INT)
BEGIN
WITH CTE ( SeqNo)
   AS (SELECT 0
      UNION ALL
      SELECT SeqNo + 1
      FROM   CTE
      WHERE  SeqNo < @Stop)
INSERT @Result
SELECT PrimeNo = N2.SeqNo
FROM   CTE N1
     INNER JOIN CTE N2
   ON  N2.SeqNo % N1.SeqNo > 0
     AND N2.SeqNo % 2 > 0
     AND N1.SeqNo < N2.SeqNo
     AND N2.SeqNo > 1
     AND N1.SeqNo >= 1
GROUP  BY N2.SeqNo
HAVING ( N2.SeqNo - COUNT(*) ) = 2
OPTION ( MAXRECURSION 0);
RETURN ;
END;
GO
```

```
SELECT * FROM dbo.ufnPrimeNumbers (1000);
GO
-- (167 row(s) affected) - Partial results.
```

Prime
3
5
7
11
13
17
19
23
29
31

Inline Functions

An inline user-defined function, returns table, can be used as a parameterized view.

```
USE AdventureWorks2012
GO
```

```
CREATE FUNCTION Sales.ufnStaffSalesByFiscalYear (@OrderYear INT)
RETURNS TABLE  AS
RETURN
SELECT
     CONVERT(date, soh.OrderDate)                                                    AS OrderDate
    ,CONCAT(p.FirstName, ' ', COALESCE(p.MiddleName, ''), ' ', p.LastName)      AS FullName
    ,e.JobTitle
    ,st.Name                                                                          AS SalesTerritory
    ,FORMAT(soh.SubTotal, 'c', 'en-US')                                          AS SalesAmount
    ,YEAR(DATEADD(mm, 6, soh.OrderDate))                                            AS FiscalYear
FROM Sales.SalesPerson sp
    INNER JOIN Sales.SalesOrderHeader soh
        ON sp.BusinessEntityID = soh.SalesPersonID
    INNER JOIN Sales.SalesTerritory st
        ON sp.TerritoryID = st.TerritoryID
    INNER JOIN HumanResources.Employee e
        ON soh.SalesPersonID = e.BusinessEntityID
    INNER JOIN Person.Person p
        ON p.BusinessEntityID = sp.BusinessEntityID
WHERE           soh.OrderDate >= datefromparts(@OrderYear, 1, 1)
          AND soh.OrderDate < dateadd(yy,1, datefromparts(@OrderYear, 1, 1));
GO
-- Command(s) completed successfully.
```

```
SELECT * FROM Sales.ufnStaffSalesByFiscalYear (2007)
ORDER BY FullName, CONVERT(money, SalesAmount) DESC;   --  SalesAmount (string) does not sort correctly
--( 1476  row(s) affected)  -- Partial results.
```

OrderDate	FullName	JobTitle	SalesTerritory	SalesAmount	FiscalYear
2007-08-01	David R Campbell	Sales Representative	Northwest	$101,609.29	2008
2007-07-01	David R Campbell	Sales Representative	Northwest	$93,397.64	2008
2007-04-01	David R Campbell	Sales Representative	Northwest	$75,104.65	2007
2007-07-01	David R Campbell	Sales Representative	Northwest	$74,149.95	2008
2007-04-01	David R Campbell	Sales Representative	Northwest	$73,963.26	2007
2007-08-01	David R Campbell	Sales Representative	Northwest	$71,283.24	2008
2007-09-01	David R Campbell	Sales Representative	Northwest	$66,871.84	2008
2007-01-01	David R Campbell	Sales Representative	Northwest	$63,864.71	2007
2007-11-01	David R Campbell	Sales Representative	Northwest	$63,339.26	2008
2007-10-01	David R Campbell	Sales Representative	Northwest	$60,519.95	2008

Scalar Functions

A scalar user-defined function returns a scalar value. It can be used in a query wherever a single value is required.

```
USE AdventureWorks2012;
GO
CREATE FUNCTION dbo.ufnNumberToEnglish (@Number INT)
RETURNS VARCHAR(1024)   AS
 BEGIN
    DECLARE @Below20 TABLE      ( ID   INT IDENTITY ( 0, 1 ),    Word VARCHAR(32) );
    DECLARE @Tens TABLE   (  ID   INT IDENTITY ( 2, 1 ),     Word VARCHAR(32) );
    INSERT @Below20  (Word)
    VALUES('Zero'), ('One'),('Two'),  ('Three'), ('Four'), ('Five'), ('Six'), ('Seven'), ('Eight'),
         ('Nine'), ('Ten'),  ('Eleven'),  ('Twelve'), ('Thirteen'),  ('Fourteen'),  ('Fifteen'),
         ('Sixteen'), ('Seventeen'), ('Eighteen'), ('Nineteen');
    INSERT @Tens
    VALUES('Twenty'),   ('Thirty'),  ('Forty'),   ('Fifty'),   ('Sixty'),   ('Seventy'),   ('Eighty'),  ('Ninety');
    DECLARE @English VARCHAR(1024) = (SELECT CASE
            WHEN @Number = 0 THEN ''
            WHEN @Number BETWEEN 1 AND 19
                    THEN (SELECT Word FROM   @Below20 WHERE  ID = @Number)
            WHEN @Number BETWEEN 20 AND 99 THEN
      CONCAT((SELECT Word FROM   @Tens
WHERE  ID = @Number / 10), '-', dbo.ufnNumberToEnglish(@Number%10))
       WHEN @Number BETWEEN 100 AND 999 THEN CONCAT((
           dbo.ufnNumberToEnglish(@Number / 100) ), ' Hundred ',
dbo.ufnNumberToEnglish(@Number%100))
      WHEN @Number BETWEEN 1000 AND 999999 THEN CONCAT((
          dbo.ufnNumberToEnglish(@Number / 1000) ), ' Thousand ',
dbo.ufnNumberToEnglish(@Number%1000))
     WHEN @Number BETWEEN 1000000 AND 999999999 THEN CONCAT((
         dbo.ufnNumberToEnglish(@Number / 1000000) ), ' Million ',
dbo.ufnNumberToEnglish(@Number%1000000))
      ELSE ' INVALID INPUT'   END);
    SELECT @English = RTRIM(@English);
    SELECT @English = RTRIM(LEFT(@English, len(@English) - 1))     WHERE  RIGHT(@English, 1) = '-';
    RETURN ( @English );                                        END;
GO  -- Command(s) completed successfully.
```

```
SELECT dbo.ufnNumberToEnglish (9999);  -- Nine Thousand Nine Hundred Ninety-Nine
```

```
SELECT dbo.ufnNumberToEnglish (1000001);  -- One Million One
```

```
SELECT dbo.ufnNumberToEnglish (7777777);
-- Seven Million Seven Hundred Seventy-Seven Thousand Seven Hundred Seventy-Seven
```

Dynamic PIVOT Script

Static PIVOT has pretty limited role since it has to be changed when data changes effects the PIVOT range. Dynamic SQL makes PIVOT data driven. Instead of hard-wired columns, dynamic PIVOT builds the columns from the data dynamically.

```
USE AdventureWorks;
GO
```

```
DECLARE @OrderYear AS TABLE
 (
   YYYY INT NOT NULL PRIMARY KEY
 );
DECLARE @DynamicSQL AS NVARCHAR(4000) ;

INSERT INTO @OrderYear
SELECT DISTINCT YEAR(OrderDate)
FROM   Sales.SalesOrderHeader;

DECLARE @ReportColumnNames AS NVARCHAR(MAX),  @IterationYear    AS INT;

SET @IterationYear = (SELECT MIN(YYYY)      FROM   @OrderYear);
SET @ReportColumnNames = N'';

-- Assemble pivot list dynamically
WHILE ( @IterationYear IS NOT NULL )
 BEGIN
    SET @ReportColumnNames = @ReportColumnNames + N','
                   + QUOTENAME(CAST(@IterationYear AS NVARCHAR(10)));
    SET @IterationYear = (SELECT MIN(YYYY)
                 FROM   @OrderYear
                 WHERE  YYYY > @IterationYear);
 END;

SET @ReportColumnNames = SUBSTRING(@ReportColumnNames, 2,
               LEN(@ReportColumnNames));

PRINT @ReportColumnNames; -- [2001],[2002],[2003],[2004]

SET @DynamicSQL = CONCAT(N'SELECT * FROM (SELECT [Store (Freight Summary)]=s.Name,
         YEAR(OrderDate) AS OrderYear,  Freight = convert(money, convert(varchar, Freight))
         FROM Sales.SalesOrderHeader soh
         INNER JOIN Sales.Store s
         ON soh.CustomerID = s.CustomerID) as Header
         PIVOT (SUM(Freight)    FOR OrderYear IN(', @ReportColumnNames,N'))  AS Pvt ORDER BY 1;');
-- T-SQL script continued
```

```
PRINT @DynamicSQL; -- Testing & debugging
/* SELECT * FROM (SELECT [Store (Freight Summary)]=s.Name,
        YEAR(OrderDate) AS OrderYear,  Freight = convert(money, convert(varchar, Freight))
        FROM Sales.SalesOrderHeader soh
        INNER JOIN Sales.Store s    ON soh.CustomerID = s.CustomerID) as Header
        PIVOT (SUM(Freight)   FOR OrderYear IN([2001],[2002],[2003],[2004])) AS Pvt ORDER BY 1;*/

-- Execute dynamic sql
EXEC sp_executesql  @DynamicSQL;
GO  -- (633 row(s) affected) - Partial results.
```

Store (Freight Summary)	2001	2002	2003	2004
A Bike Store	921.55	1637.24	NULL	NULL
A Great Bicycle Company	142.08	114.34	15.24	NULL
A Typical Bike Shop	976.61	1529.08	NULL	NULL
Acceptable Sales & Service	12.58	25.17	NULL	NULL

INSERT, UPDATE & DELETE through a View

Underlying table can be modified through a view, thus adding flexibility to security access since a view can be permissioned independently of the table.

```
USE tempdb;
SELECT CONVERT(INT, ProductID) AS ID, Name AS ProductName, ListPrice, ModifiedDate INTO
Product
FROM AdventureWorks2012.Production.Product;
GO -- (504 row(s) affected)
CREATE VIEW vProduct AS SELECT * FROM Product;
GO
UPDATE vProduct SET ModifiedDate = '2018-01-01';
GO -- (504 row(s) affected)
INSERT vProduct VALUES (2000, 'Three-Wheeler Bike', $999.99, getdate());
GO -- (1 row(s) affected)
DELETE TOP (10) FROM vProduct;
GO -- (1 row(s) affected)
SELECT TOP (1) * FROM Product; -- 322 Chainring        0.00      2018-01-01 00:00:00.000
GO
DROP VIEW dbo.vProduct;
DROP TABLE tempdb.dbo.Product;
GO
```

CREATE VIEW WITH CHECK OPTION

The WITH CHECK OPTION checks that data is not INSERTed or UPDATEd through a view which would make the data not visible, like a yellow bike in the vBlueProduct view.

```
USE tempdb; SELECT ProductID, ProductNumber, ListPrice, Color INTO Product
FROM AdventureWorks2012.Production.Product WHERE Color IS NOT NULL;
ALTER TABLE Product ADD CONSTRAINT pkProd PRIMARY KEY (ProductID);
GO
CREATE VIEW vBlueProduct AS SELECT * FROM Product WHERE Color = 'Blue' WITH CHECK OPTION;
GO
INSERT vBlueProduct (ProductNumber, ListPrice, Color) VALUES( 'COMPETEBK38YL',1999.95, 'Yellow');
GO /* Msg 550, Level 16, State 1, Line 1
The attempted insert or update failed because the target view either specifies WITH CHECK OPTION ...*/
```

Using Views for Security

Views can be permissioned just like tables. That provides flexibility in configuring security. A user can view the content of a table just through a SELECT permission on a view over the table.

```
USE [AdventureWorks2012];
GRANT DELETE ON [HumanResources].[vJobCandidate] TO [MaryS];
GRANT INSERT ON [HumanResources].[vJobCandidate] TO [MaryS];
GRANT SELECT ON [HumanResources].[vJobCandidate] TO [MaryS];
GRANT UPDATE ON [HumanResources].[vJobCandidate] TO [MaryS];
```

MSDN Article: **Using Views as Security Mechanisms**
http://msdn.microsoft.com/en-us/library/aa905180(v=sql.80).aspx

Sensitive Data Audit Trigger

Triggers can be used to track sensitive data changes into an audit table. The OUTPUT clause is an alternative, but not exactly equivalent.

```
USE Payroll;
GO
CREATE TRIGGER uTrgEmployeeUpdate   ON Employee  AFTER UPDATE  AS
  IF ( Update(Salary)   OR Update(SSN) )     BEGIN
      INSERT INTO CorpSecurityEmployeeAudit   (       auditlogtype, auditEmployeeDeptID,
          auditEmployeeID, auditEmployeeSalary, auditEmployeeSSN, auditUpdatedBy)
      SELECT       'PREVIOUSDATA', DeptID, EmployeeID, Salary, SSN, User_name()
      FROM   DELETED
      INSERT INTO CorpSecurityEmployeeAudit        (auditlogtype, auditEmployeeDeptID,
          auditEmployeeID, auditEmployeeSalary, uditEmployeeSSN, auditUpdatedBy)
      SELECT'NEWDATA', DeptID, EmployeeID, Salary, SSN, User_name()    FROM   INSERTED
  END;
```

Automatic Timestamp Trigger

Whenever the Person.Contact is updated, the ModifiedDate will be updated to current time by the update after trigger. NOTE: disable/drop other update triggers on this table, if any, for the test. Triggers can be nested. We use the TRIGGER_NESTLEVEL() function to avoid an infinite loop. **Note that the trigger is designed to handle multiple rows UPDATE. We always have to assume the underlying operation is multiple rows rather than a single row.**

AFTER trigger is only for table. INSTEAD OF trigger is both for table & view.

```
USE AdventureWorks;
GO
```

```
CREATE TRIGGER uTrgContactTimestamp ON Person.Contact  FOR UPDATE
AS
 BEGIN
  IF TRIGGER_NESTLEVEL() > 1      RETURN;
   UPDATE Person.Contact  SET    Person.Contact.ModifiedDate = CURRENT_TIMESTAMP
   FROM   Person.Contact c
        INNER JOIN INSERTED i
          ON c.ContactID = i.ContactID
 END
GO
-- (1 row(s) affected)
```

```
SELECT * FROM   Person.Contact
WHERE  FirstName = 'Kim'   AND MiddleName = 'B'      AND LastName = 'Abercrombie'
GO
-- ModifiedDate: 2000-02-10 00:00:00.000
```

```
-- Updating a column will automatically update the ModifiedDate
UPDATE Person.Contact            SET    Phone = '299 484-3924'
WHERE  FirstName = 'Kim'    AND MiddleName = 'B'     AND LastName = 'Abercrombie'
GO
```

```
SELECT *  FROM   Person.Contact WHERE  FirstName = 'Kim'
AND MiddleName = 'B'    AND LastName = 'Abercrombie'
GO -- ModifiedDate: 2018-08-11 07:22:01.157
```

```
-- Cleanup
DROP TRIGGER Person.uTrgContactTimestamp
```

INSTEAD OF Trigger

Triggers can be: AFTER trigger (DML), INSTEAD OF trigger (DML) and DDL trigger. When we don't specify INSTEAD in trigger create, it is an AFTER trigger by default. INSTEAD of trigger does some other processing instead of carrying out the programmed action such as DELETE below. **INSTEAD OF TRIGGER can be defined on views as well.** Example: an INSERT into a view is not allowed if the view is the JOIN of two tables. **An INSTEAD of trigger on the view can perform the insertion into the underlying table(s).**

MSDN Article: **SQL Server 2000's INSTEAD OF Triggers**
http://msdn.microsoft.com/en-us/library/aa224818(v=sql.80).aspx

```
USE tempdb;
GO
-- Create and populate test table
SELECT EmployeeID = BusinessEntityID, FirstName, LastName, IsDeleted = convert(char(1), 'N')
INTO Employee FROM AdventureWorks2012.Person.Person;
GO -- (19972 row(s) affected)
```

```
ALTER TABLE Employee ADD CONSTRAINT pkEmp PRIMARY KEY ( EmployeeID);
GO  -- Command(s) completed successfully.
```

```
CREATE TRIGGER trgInsteadEmpDelete ON Employee
INSTEAD OF DELETE AS  BEGIN
UPDATE Employee SET IsDeleted = 'Y' WHERE EmployeeID in (SELECT EmployeeID from deleted);
END
GO
```

```
-- Test instead of trigger
SELECT * FROM Employee WHERE EmployeeID = 10;
```

EmployeeID	FirstName	LastName	IsDeleted
10	Michael	Raheem	N

```
DELETE Employee WHERE EmployeeID = 10;
SELECT * FROM Employee WHERE EmployeeID = 10;
```

EmployeeID	FirstName	LastName	IsDeleted
10	Michael	Raheem	Y

Security implications of instead of UPDATE triggers on views: limit updatable columns.

Recursive Product Assembly

Recursive Common Table Expression (CTE) is used to assemble a bike frame based on the BillOfMaterials table.

```
USE AdventureWorks2012; DECLARE @ProductID int = 831;
WITH CTE(AssemblyID, ComponentID, PerAssemblyQty, AssemblyLevel) AS
(       SELECT bom0.ProductAssemblyID, bom0.ComponentID, bom0.PerAssemblyQty,
                0 AS AssemblyLevel
        FROM Production.BillOfMaterials AS bom0
        WHERE bom0.ProductAssemblyID = @ProductID AND bom0.EndDate is null
        UNION ALL
        SELECT bom.ProductAssemblyID, bom.ComponentID, p.PerAssemblyQty, AssemblyLevel + 1
        FROM Production.BillOfMaterials AS bom    INNER JOIN CTE AS p
                        ON bom.ProductAssemblyID = p.ComponentID   AND bom.EndDate is null   )
SELECT  pp.Name AS ProductName, AssemblyID, ComponentID,
        p.Name AS AssemblyName, PerAssemblyQty, AssemblyLevel
FROM CTE        INNER JOIN Production.Product AS p        ON CTE.ComponentID = p.ProductID
                INNER JOIN Production.Product AS pp       ON CTE.AssemblyID = pp.ProductID
ORDER BY AssemblyLevel, AssemblyID, ComponentID; -- (24 row(s) affected) - Partial results.
```

ProductName	AssemblyID	ComponentID	AssemblyName	PerAssemblyQty	AssemblyLevel
ML Mountain Frame - Black, 44	831	324	Chain Stays	2.00	0
ML Mountain Frame - Black, 44	831	325	Decal 1	2.00	0
ML Mountain Frame - Black, 44	831	326	Decal 2	1.00	0
ML Mountain Frame - Black, 44	831	327	Down Tube	1.00	0

The XACT_STATE() Function for Transaction Rescue

The XACT_STATE() function can be used to rescue part of a transaction if returns 1.

```
USE tempdb; SELECT * INTO Product FROM AdventureWorks2012.Production.Product;
SET XACT_ABORT OFF;
BEGIN TRY    BEGIN TRANSACTION
      DELETE FROM Product  WHERE ProductID = 800;
      INSERT INTO Product (ProductID)  VALUES (2000);                -- Inherited identity INSERT conflict
  COMMIT TRANSACTION;    PRINT 'TRY finished OK without error';  END TRY
BEGIN CATCH    IF (XACT_STATE()) = 1    BEGIN
     PRINT 'First part of transaction is committable.' + ' Committing transaction.'
     COMMIT TRANSACTION;       END;
   ELSE  IF (XACT_STATE()) = -1  BEGIN ROLLBACK; PRINT 'Uncommittable transaction'; END
END CATCH;
GO  -- First part of transaction is committable. Committing transaction.
```

Article: **Try/Catch Block in SQL Server 2005**
http://www.databasejournal.com/features/mssql/article.php/3587891/TryCatch-Block-in-SQL-Server-2005.htm

Percent on Base Calculation

When deriving percent on base, we need to calculate the overall total in a single value subquery to use it as denominator in the percentile calculation.

```
USE AdventureWorks2012;
```

```
SELECT YEAR(OrderDate) AS [Year],
    FORMAT(SUM(TotalDue),'c0','en-US') AS YearTotal,
    FORMAT(SUM(TotalDue) /
        (SELECT SUM(TotalDue) FROM Sales.SalesOrderHeader),'p0') AS Percentile
FROM Sales.SalesOrderHeader
GROUP BY YEAR(OrderDate)
ORDER BY YEAR ASC;
```

Year	YearTotal	Percentage
2005	$12,693,251	10 %
2006	$34,463,848	28 %
2007	$47,171,490	38 %
2008	$28,888,198	23 %

Adding a Grand Total line with ROLLUP.

```
SELECT COALESCE(CONVERT(varchar,YEAR(OrderDate)), 'Grand Total') AS [Year],
    FORMAT(SUM(TotalDue),'c0','en-US') AS [SalesTotal],
    FORMAT(SUM(TotalDue) /
        (SELECT SUM(TotalDue) FROM Sales.SalesOrderHeader),'p0') AS Percentage
FROM Sales.SalesOrderHeader
GROUP BY YEAR(OrderDate)
    WITH ROLLUP
ORDER BY YEAR ASC;
```

Year	SalesTotal	Percentage
2005	$12,693,251	10 %
2006	$34,463,848	28 %
2007	$47,171,490	38 %
2008	$28,888,198	23 %
Grand Total	$123,216,786	100 %

CHAPTER 18: Exporting & Importing Data

Saving a T-SQL Script as .sql File

Any T-SQL script can be saved as .sql file. One easy way is saving from Management Studio Query Editor. Here is the script we will save.

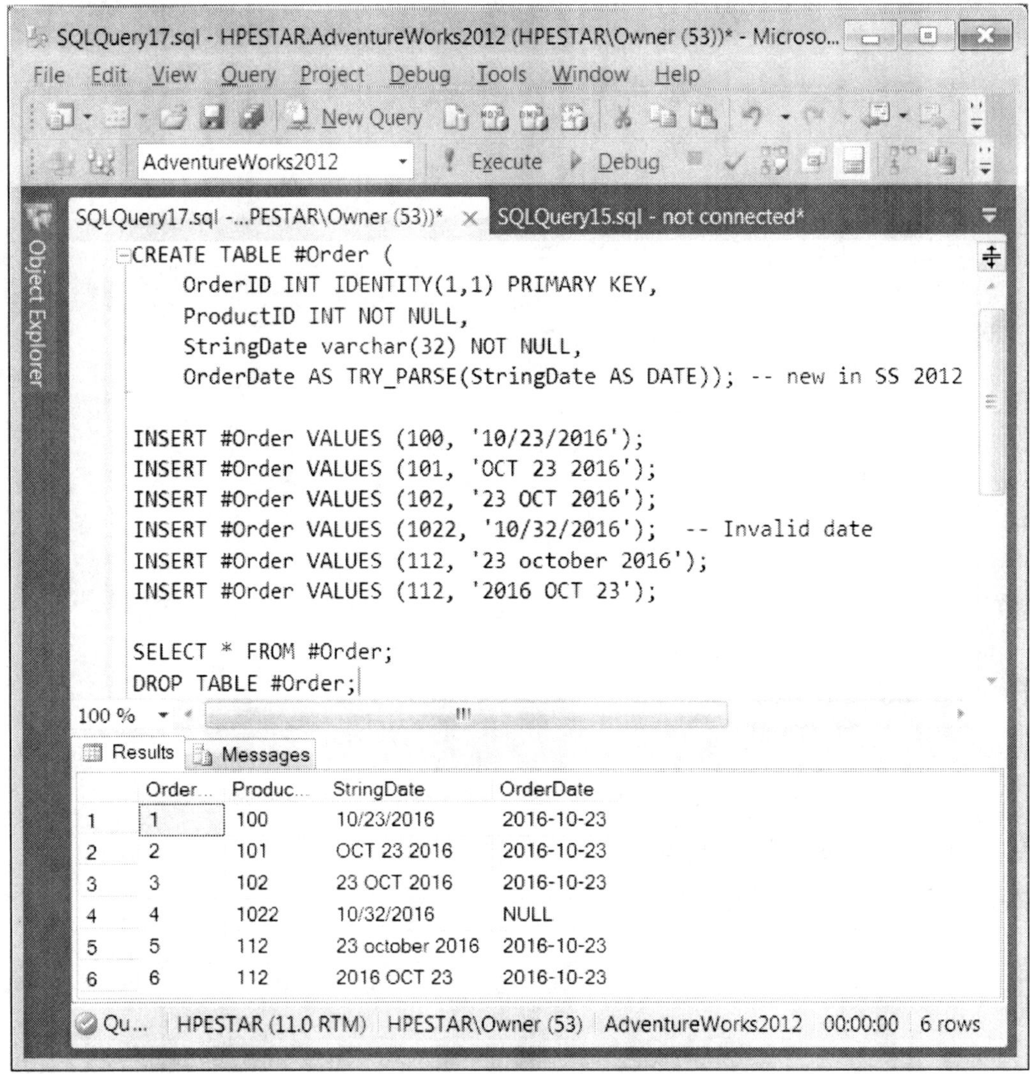

Click on File, click on Save .. As, choose a path and enter the file name for the script.

To load it back: click on File, click on Open File, locate file in Open File dialog pop-up.

Executing a .sql Script File Using SQLCMD

The SQLCMD command line utility can be used to execute a .sql script file typically with the -i (input) and -o (output) options. **Note: with any of the Command Prompt utilities the command line should not be broken with carriage return or line feed (CR/LF), it has to be one long line.**

```
SQLCMD -S"HPESTAR" -Uyourlogin -Psecret007 -i "f:\data\sql\tryparsedemo.sql" -
o"f:\data\result\tryparsedemo.txt"
```

"HPESTAR" is the name of the SQL Server. With Windows authentication:

```
SQLCMD -S"HPESTAR"  -i "f:\data\sql\tryparsedemo.sql" -o"f:\data\result\tryparsedemo.txt"
```

```
Command Prompt
Microsoft Windows [Version 6.1.7601]
Copyright (c) 2009 Microsoft Corporation.  All rights reserved.

C:\Users\Owner>SQLCMD -S"HPESTAR"  -i "f:\data\sql\tryparsedemo.sql" -o"f:\data\
result\tryparsedemo.txt"

C:\Users\Owner>_
```

The output file collects warnings, messages, errors and results.

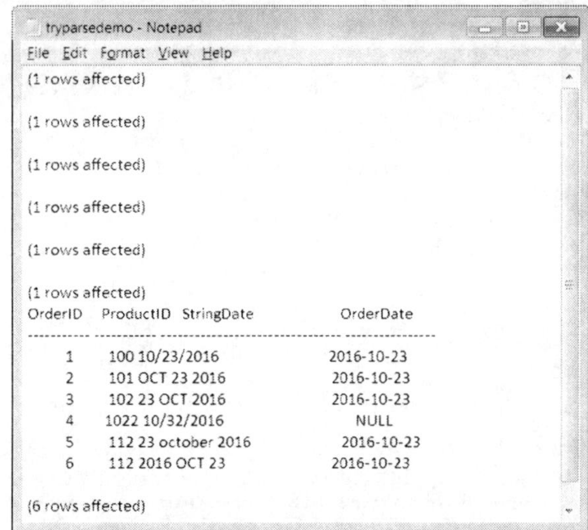

```
tryparsedemo - Notepad
File Edit Format View Help
(1 rows affected)

(1 rows affected)

(1 rows affected)

(1 rows affected)

(1 rows affected)

(1 rows affected)
OrderID  ProductID StringDate                 OrderDate
----------- ----------- -------------------------------- ---------------
      1     100 10/23/2016                 2016-10-23
      2     101 OCT 23 2016                2016-10-23
      3     102 23 OCT 2016                2016-10-23
      4    1022 10/32/2016                 NULL
      5     112 23 october 2016            2016-10-23
      6     112 2016 OCT 23                2016-10-23

(6 rows affected)
```

Making a T-SQL Script Rerunnable

It takes special attention to make a T-SQL script re-executable as many times as desired. A CREATE VIEW script can only be executed once.

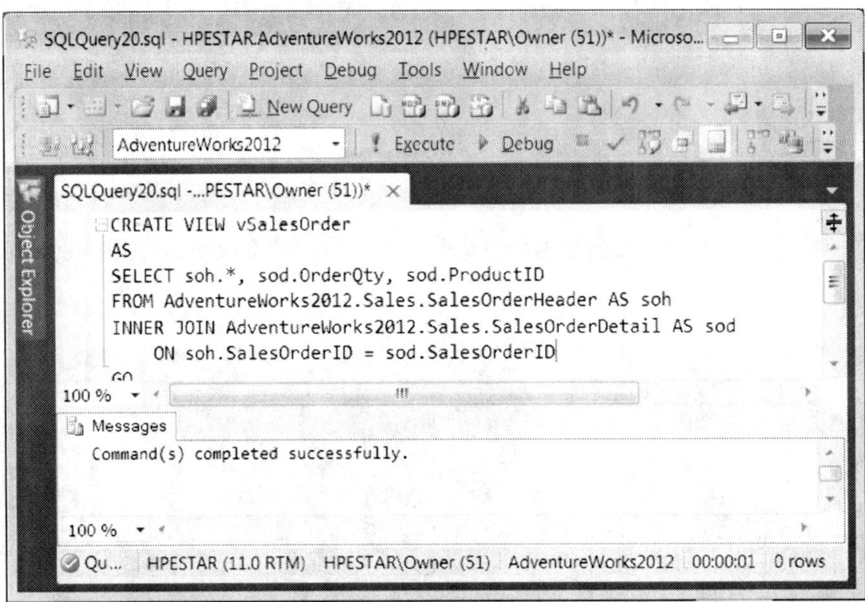

Repeat execution gives an error.

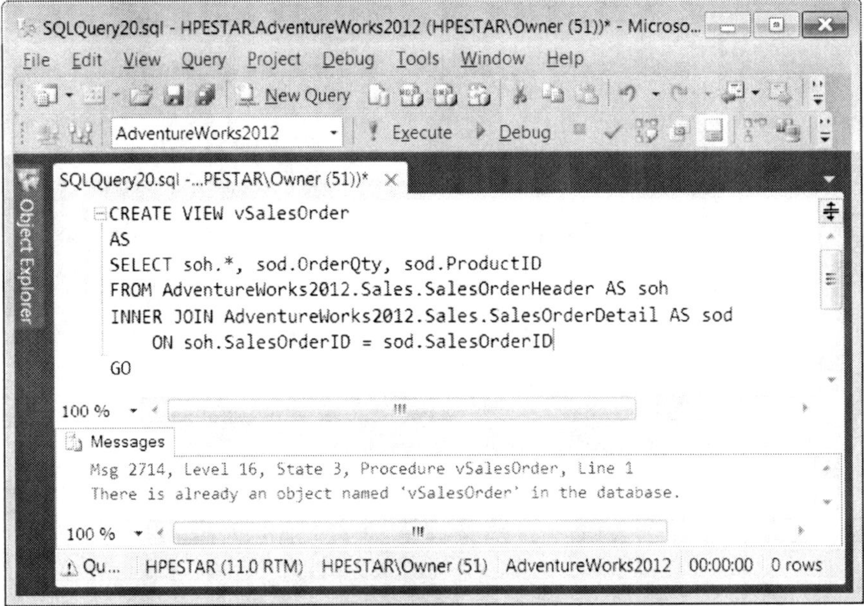

IF...ELSE Conditional Way to Make a Script Rerunnable

IF...ELSE is frequently the solution to prepare a rerunnable script. In this instance, first we check if the view exists. If it doesn't exist, we just go ahead and create it. If indeed it exists, we drop it first, then create it again.

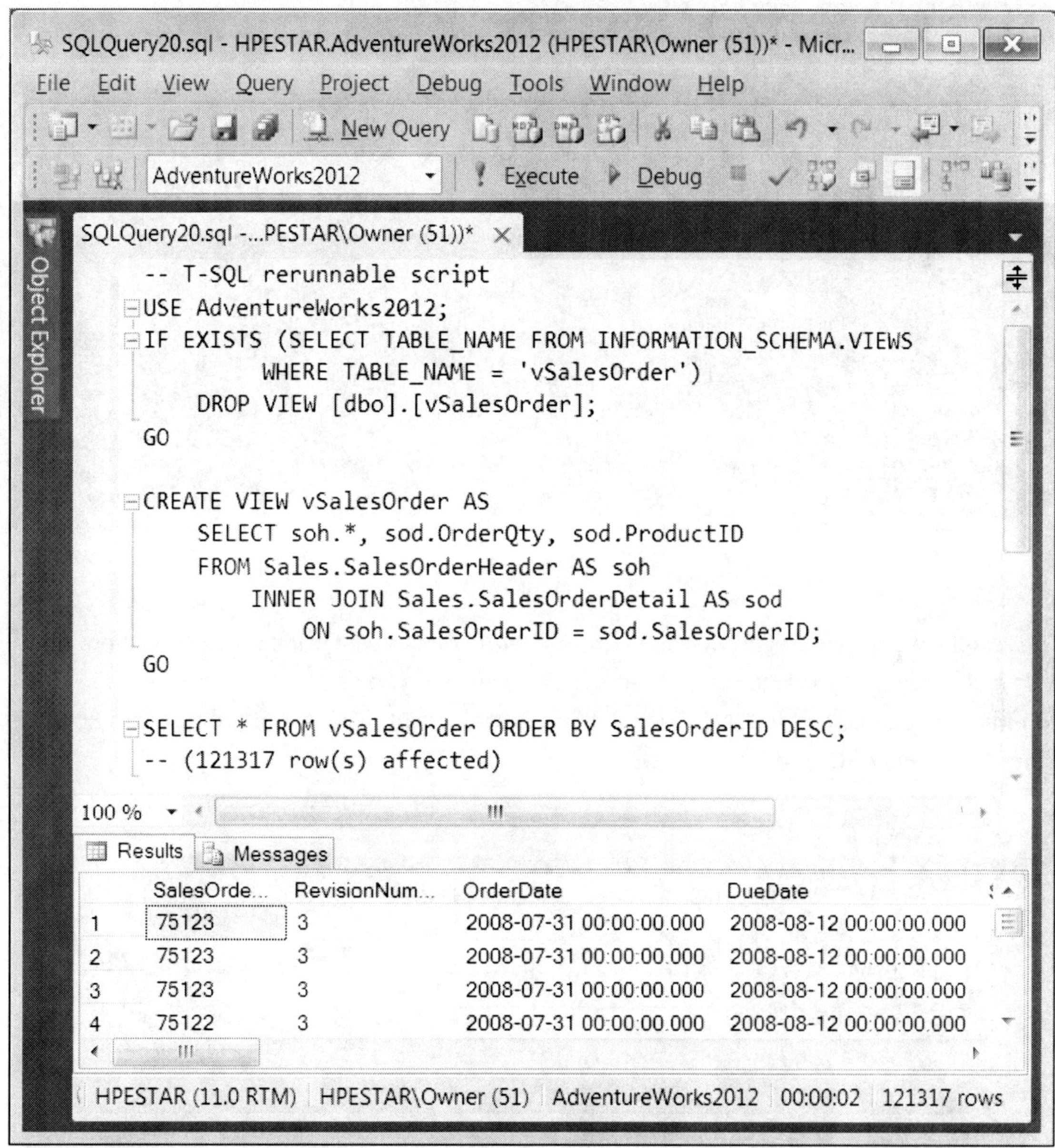

```
-- T-SQL rerunnable script
USE AdventureWorks2012;
IF EXISTS (SELECT TABLE_NAME FROM INFORMATION_SCHEMA.VIEWS
        WHERE TABLE_NAME = 'vSalesOrder')
    DROP VIEW [dbo].[vSalesOrder];
GO

CREATE VIEW vSalesOrder AS
    SELECT soh.*, sod.OrderQty, sod.ProductID
    FROM Sales.SalesOrderHeader AS soh
        INNER JOIN Sales.SalesOrderDetail AS sod
            ON soh.SalesOrderID = sod.SalesOrderID;
GO

SELECT * FROM vSalesOrder ORDER BY SalesOrderID DESC;
-- (121317 row(s) affected)
```

	SalesOrde...	RevisionNum...	OrderDate	DueDate
1	75123	3	2008-07-31 00:00:00.000	2008-08-12 00:00:00.000
2	75123	3	2008-07-31 00:00:00.000	2008-08-12 00:00:00.000
3	75123	3	2008-07-31 00:00:00.000	2008-08-12 00:00:00.000
4	75122	3	2008-07-31 00:00:00.000	2008-08-12 00:00:00.000

bcp Usage for Exporting & Importing Data

bcp (Bulk Copy Program) is a command line utility for moving data. The Production.Product table is exported to a flat file with bcp using Windows authentication.

For SQL Server authentication, add the "-Uyourlogin -Pyourpasswrd" parameters. **Note: the command must be one long line without breaks.**

```
Command Prompt
Microsoft Windows [Version 6.1.7601]
Copyright (c) 2009 Microsoft Corporation.  All rights reserved.

C:\Users\Owner>bcp AdventureWorks2012.Production.Product out F:\data\export\prod
uctz.txt -w -T -S"HPESTAR"

Starting copy...
SQLState = S1000, NativeError = 0
Error = [Microsoft][SQL Server Native Client 11.0]Warning: BCP import with a for
mat file will convert empty strings in delimited columns to NULL.

504 rows copied.
Network packet size (bytes): 4096
Clock Time (ms.) Total     : 125    Average : (4032.00 rows per sec.)

C:\Users\Owner>_
```

The **results of a query execution** can be exported with bcp as well using the queryout option. Rule is the same, no carriage return or line feed in the command no matter how long is it. The command can be edited in SSMS Query Editor and pasted into Command Prompt with Right Mouse Click Paste. CTRL-V does not work.

```
Command Prompt

C:\Users\Owner>bcp "SELECT * from AdventureWorks2012.HumanResources.Department"
queryout F:\data\export\departmentz.txt -w -T -S"HPESTAR"

Starting copy...

16 rows copied.
Network packet size (bytes): 4096
Clock Time (ms.) Total     : 453    Average : (35.32 rows per sec.)

C:\Users\Owner>_
```

Importing Data with the bcp Utility

Importing is very similar to exporting. For better control though it is necessary to use a format file. First we create an empty table for the data.

```
use tempdb;
select TOP 0 * into product1 from AdventureWorks2012.Production.Product;
go
```

We are ready to execute the bcp import command.

```
Command Prompt

C:\Users\Owner>bcp tempdb.dbo.product1 in F:\data\export\productz.txt -w -T -S"H
PESTAR"

Starting copy...

504 rows copied.
Network packet size (bytes): 4096
Clock Time (ms.) Total     : 312    Average : (1615.38 rows per sec.)

C:\Users\Owner>
```

Checking the results.

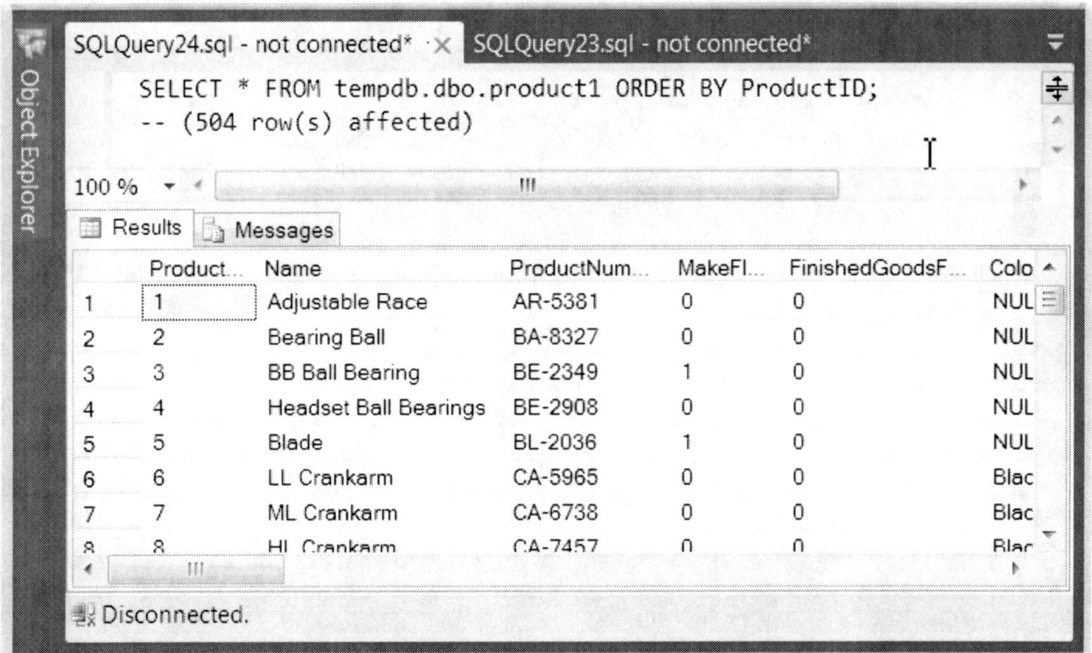

Exporting Data with SQL Server Import and Export Wizard

We will export a view query results to a new Excel worksheet. The SELECT query returns 8,914 rows from the vPersonDemographics view.

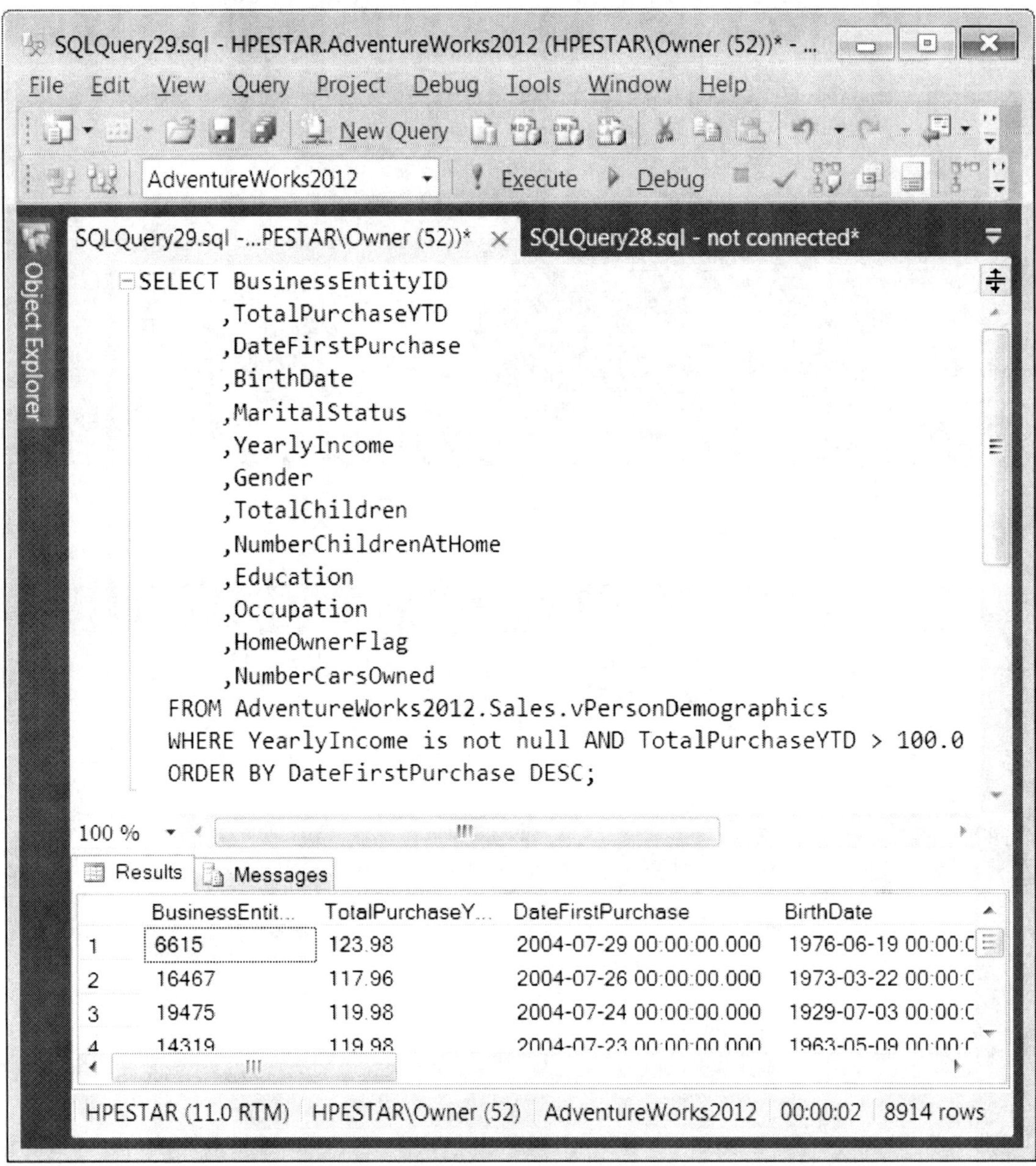

Starting the SSIS Import and Export Wizard

We start the SSIS Import/Export Wizard by a Right Click on the database in Object Explorer. It does not matter much if we choose Import Data or Export data since it only presets the destination or source pages respectively.

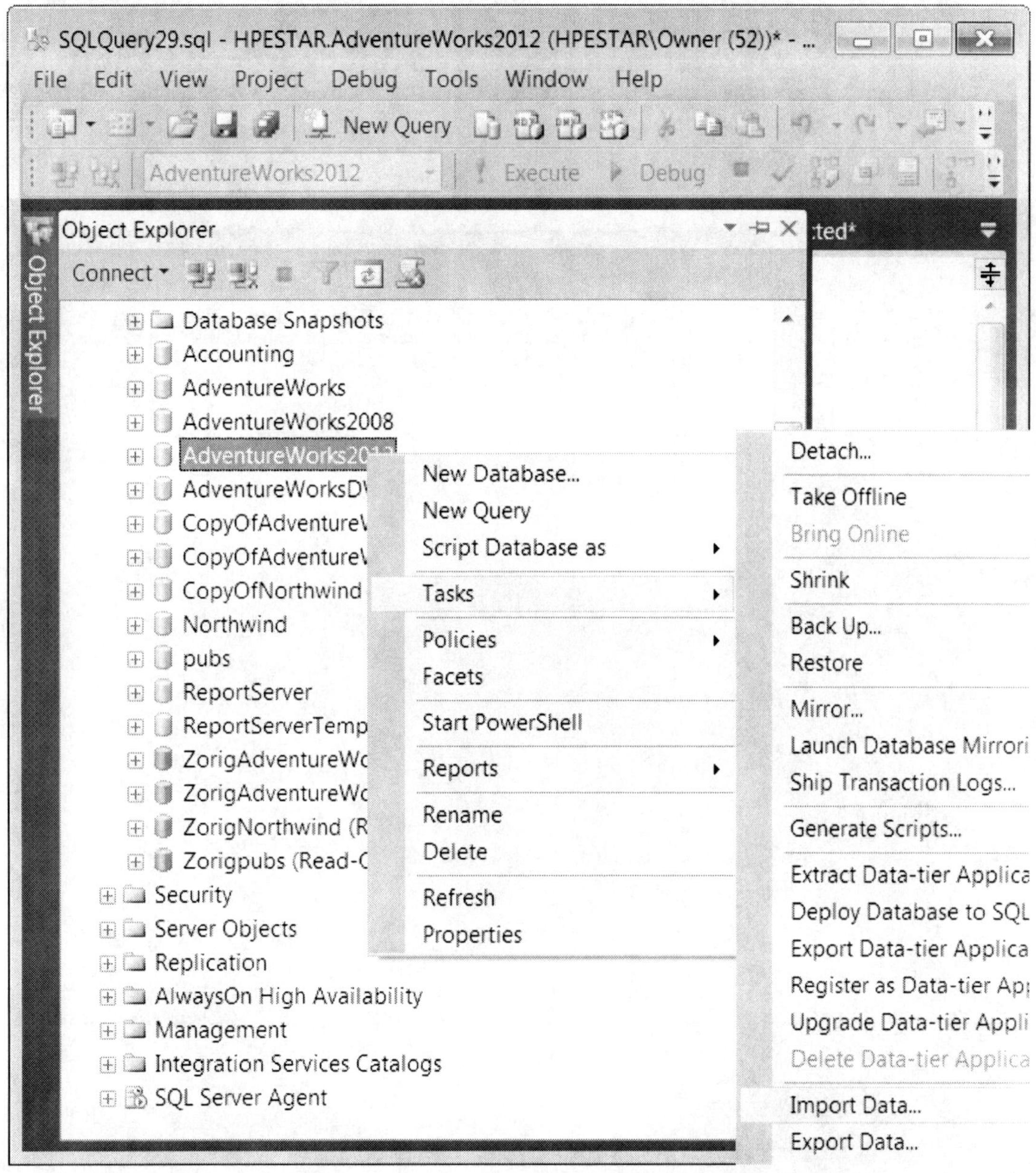

Optional Wizard Starting Welcome Screen

There is a checkmark option on the bottom to turn it off.

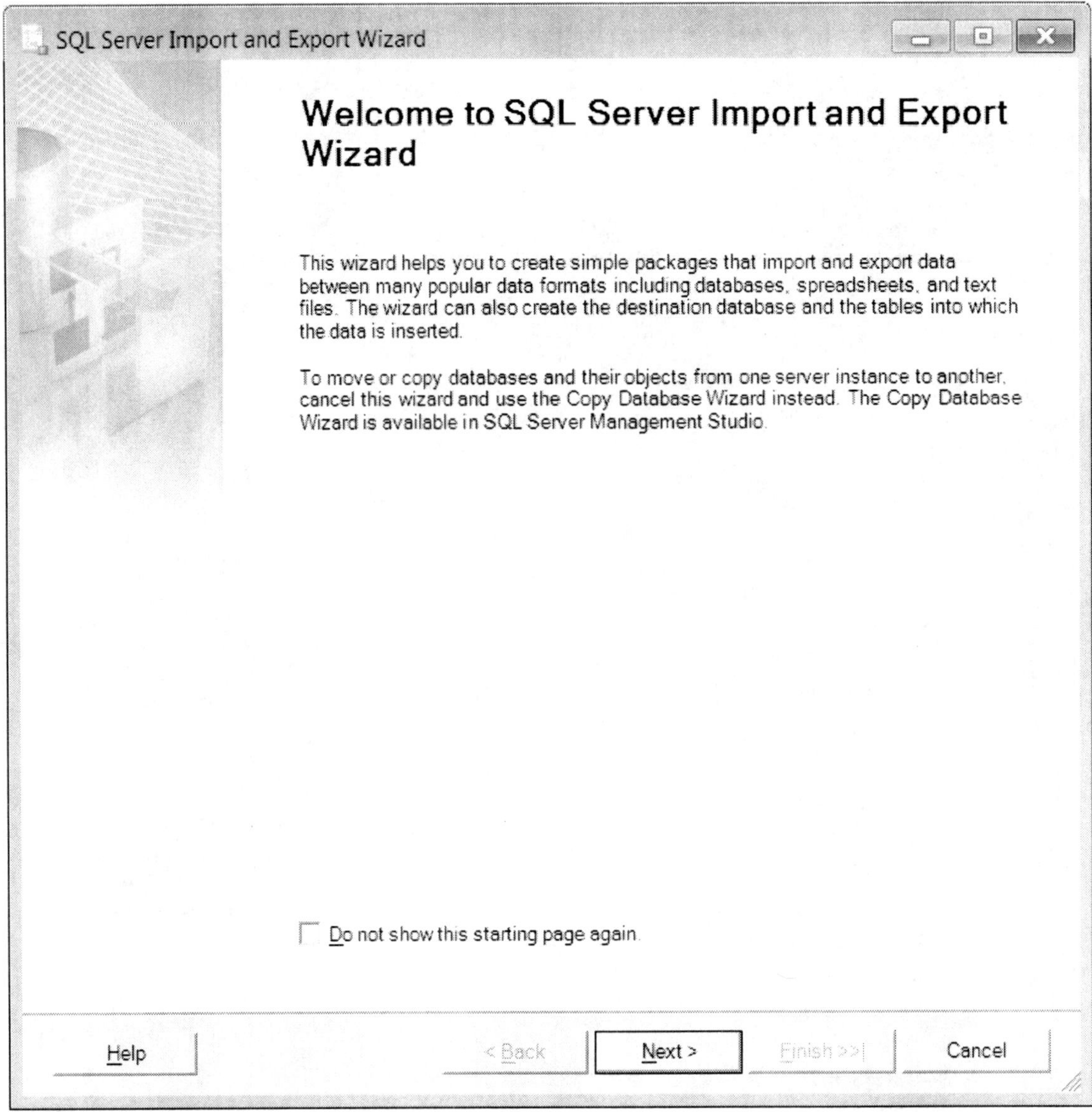

Configuring the Data Source Page

The data source is a database, therefore the server and database must be set up on this page.

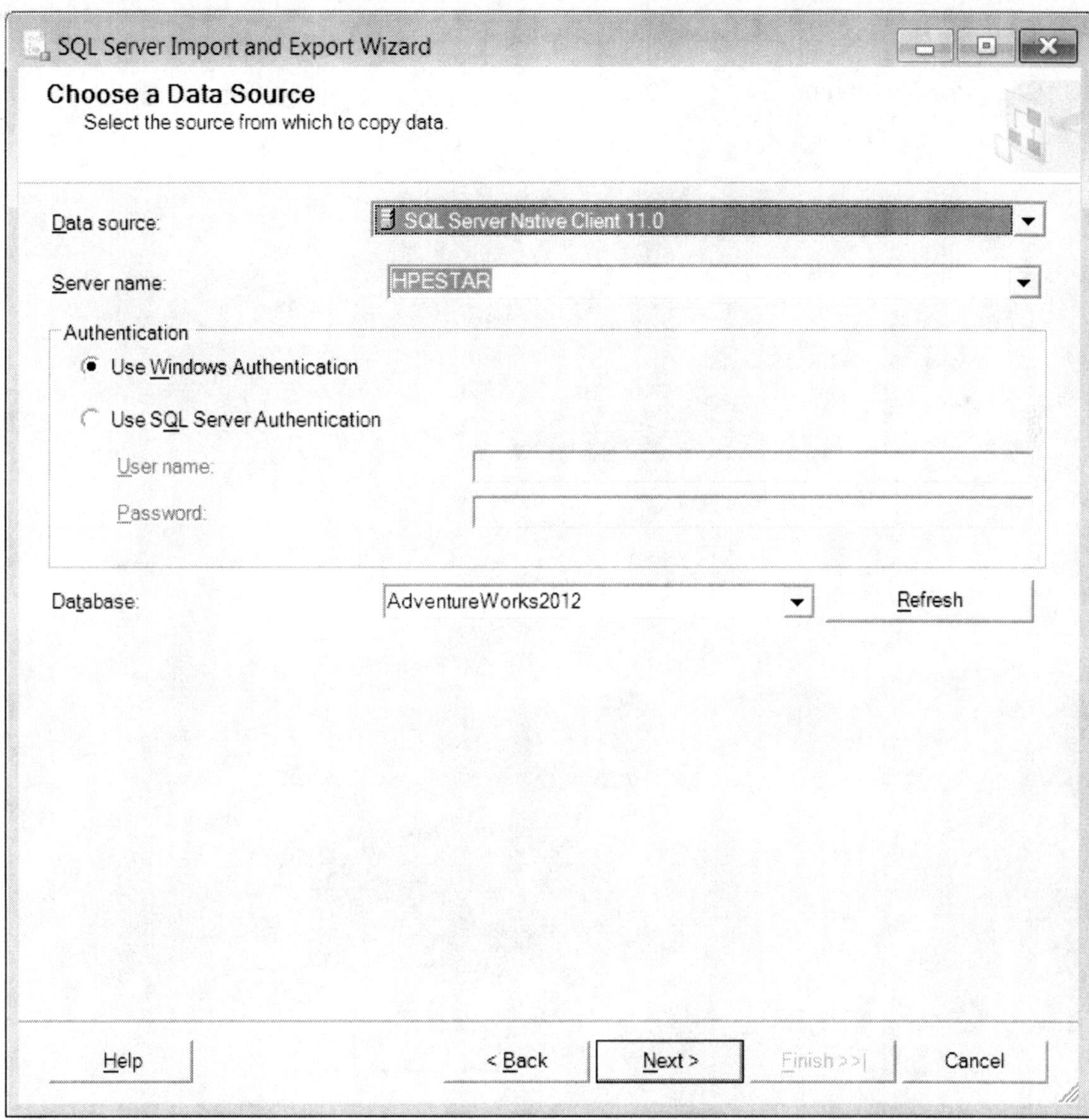

Configuring the Destination Page

The destination is a new Excel worksheet. Path & name must be given.

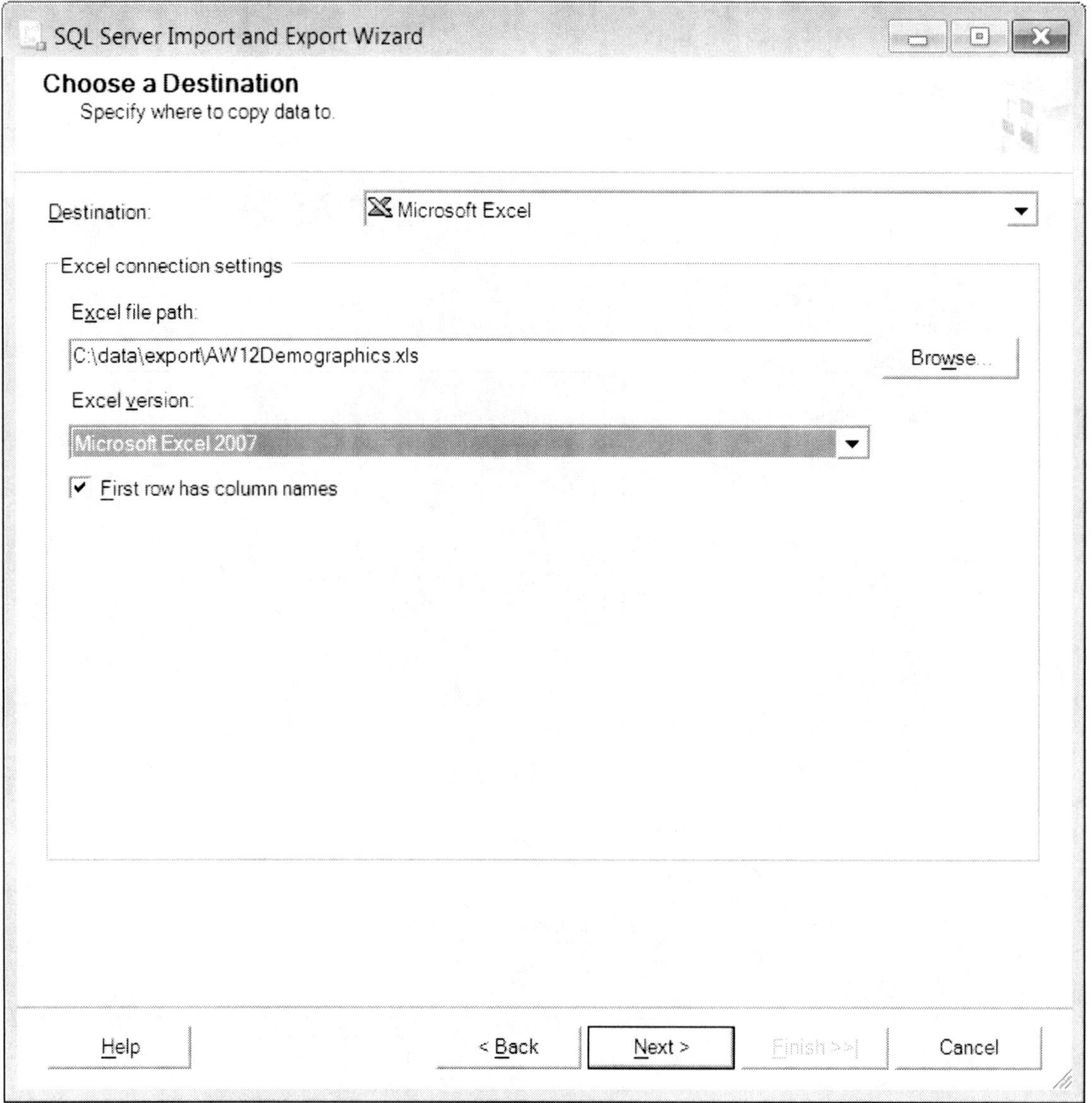

Specifying Table/View or Query Source

The Wizard logic branches based on what radio button we choose. If the choose table/view source, the next dialog box offers the entire list of tables/views in the database for checkmark selection.

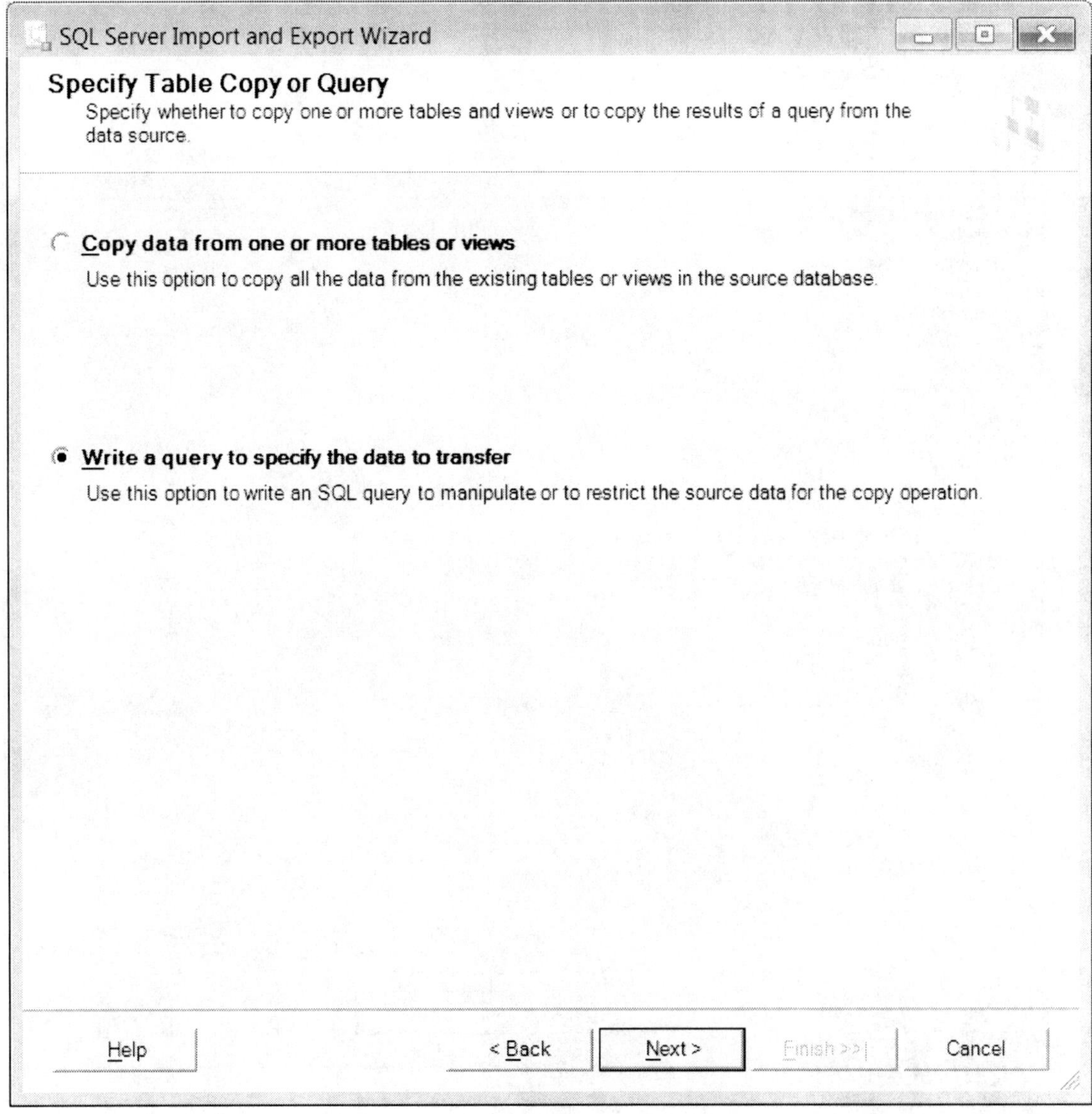

Entering the Query Source

We should use a tested query in order to avoid a failure in the execution of the generated SSIS package. Parse option is available for syntax checking.

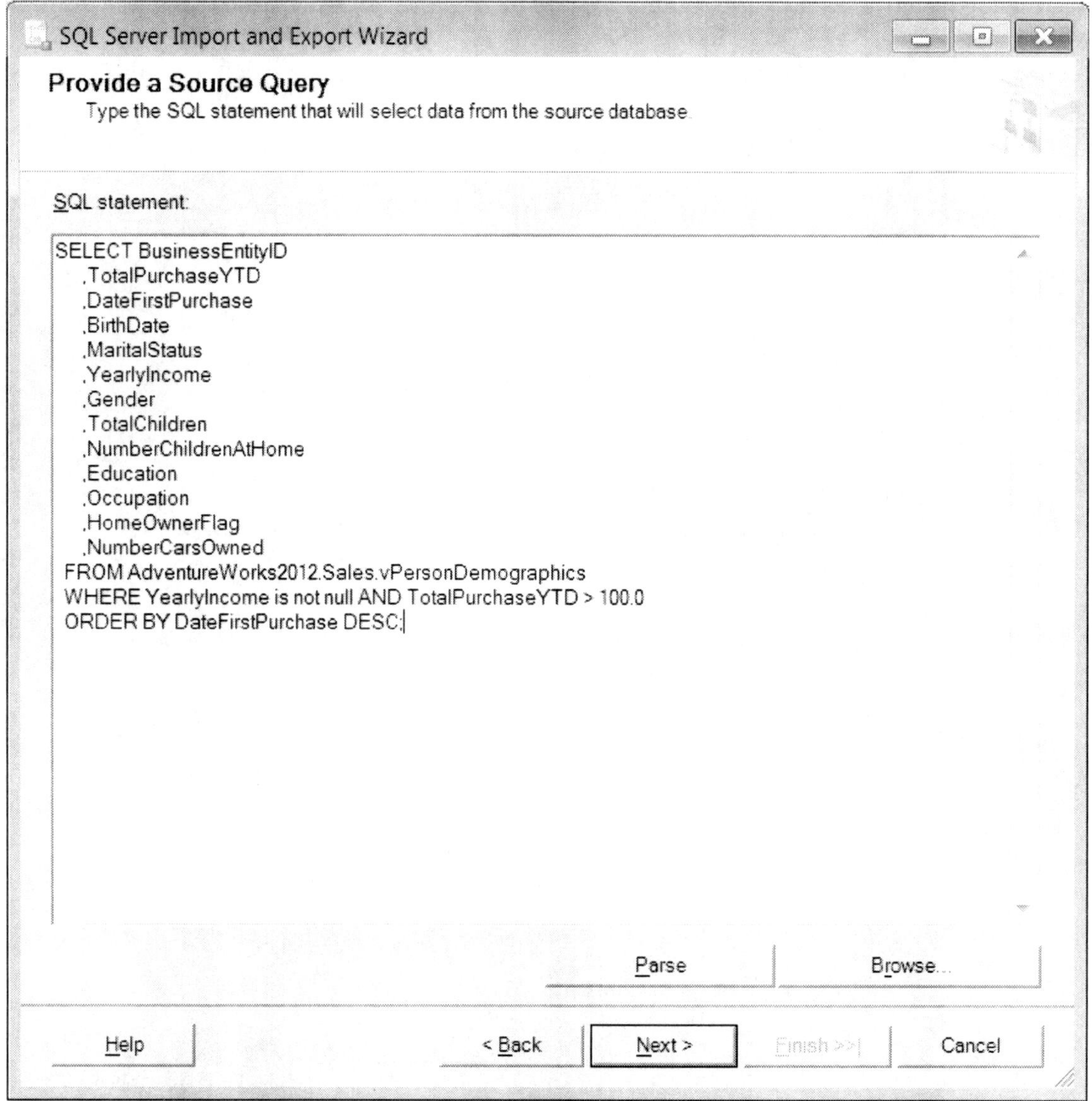

Option to Edit Mappings & Review Data

If you trust the Wizard, you can just click "Next". Otherwise, you can edit column mappings and review the data.

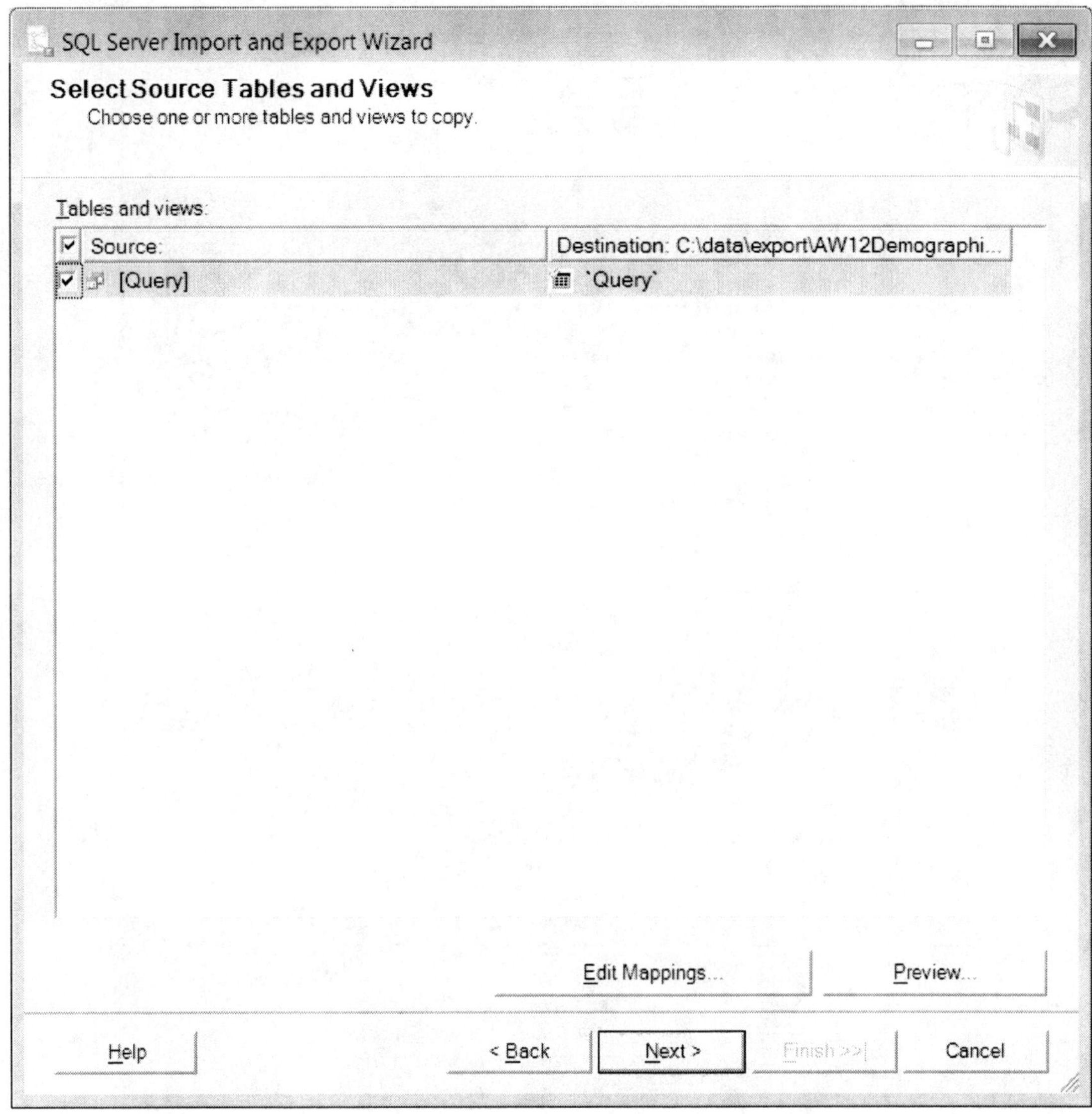

Edit Mappings & Preview

The next Wizard screen offers popup windows for editing the column mappings, changing the CREATE TABLE SQL and preview the data. We don't perform any change.

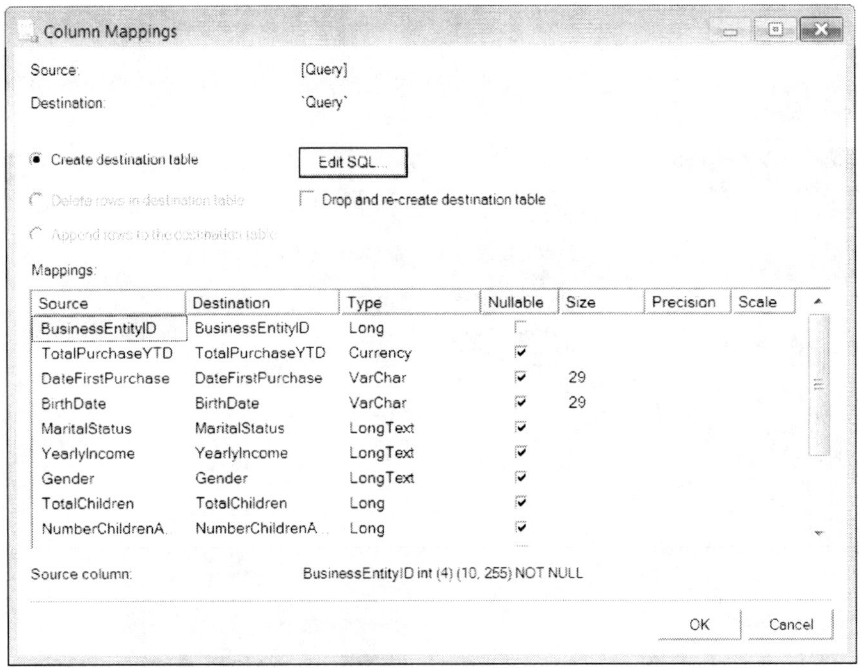

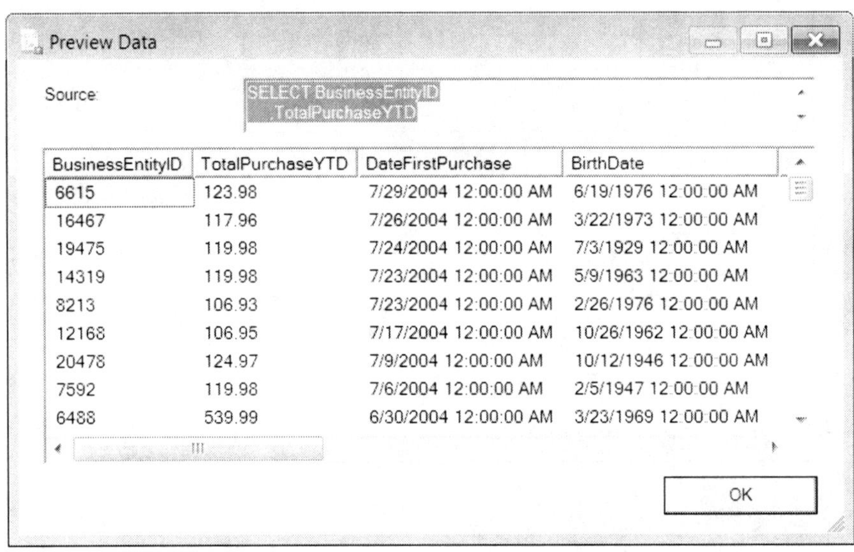

Review Data Type Mappings

Column data mappings can be reviewed in detail on this dialog box.

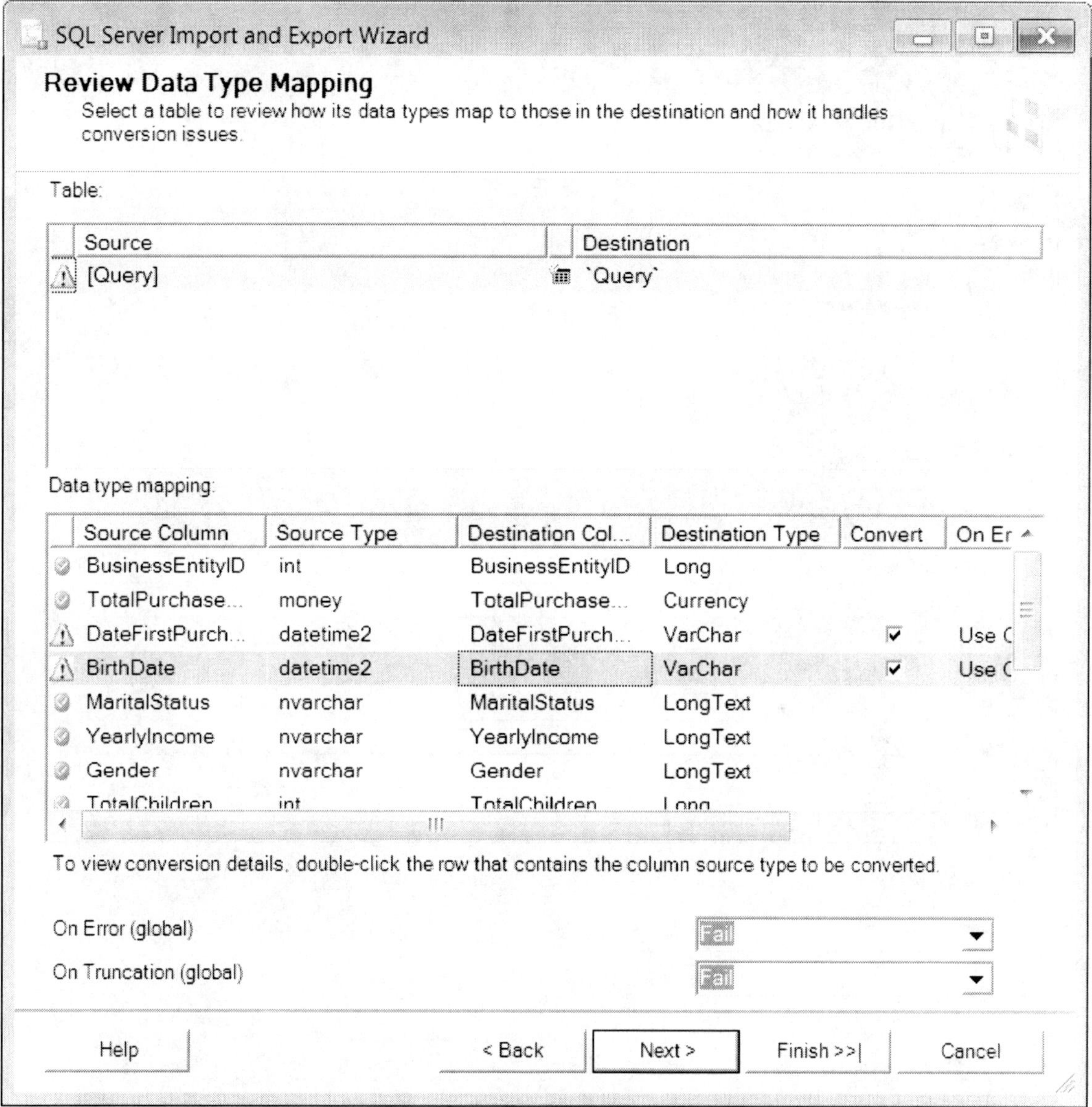

Save and/or Run Package

The Wizard generated SSIS package can be saved for future use or enhancements. If we run it immediately without saving, it will just go away after execution.

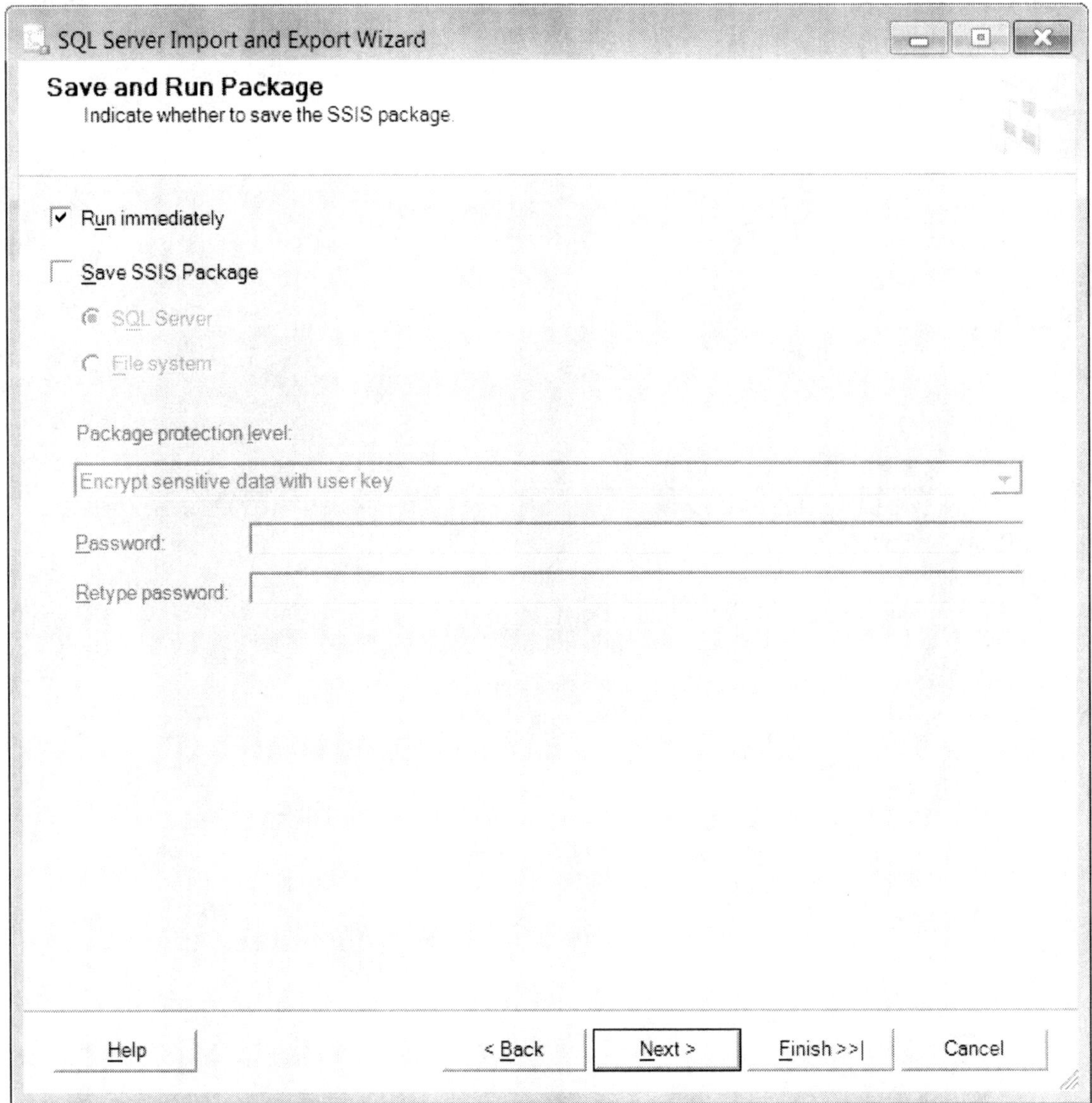

Verification Screen before Execution

At this point we still can go back and make changes should it be necessary. Once we click on Finish and we did not checkmark Save, the package will execute and goes away on success or failure.

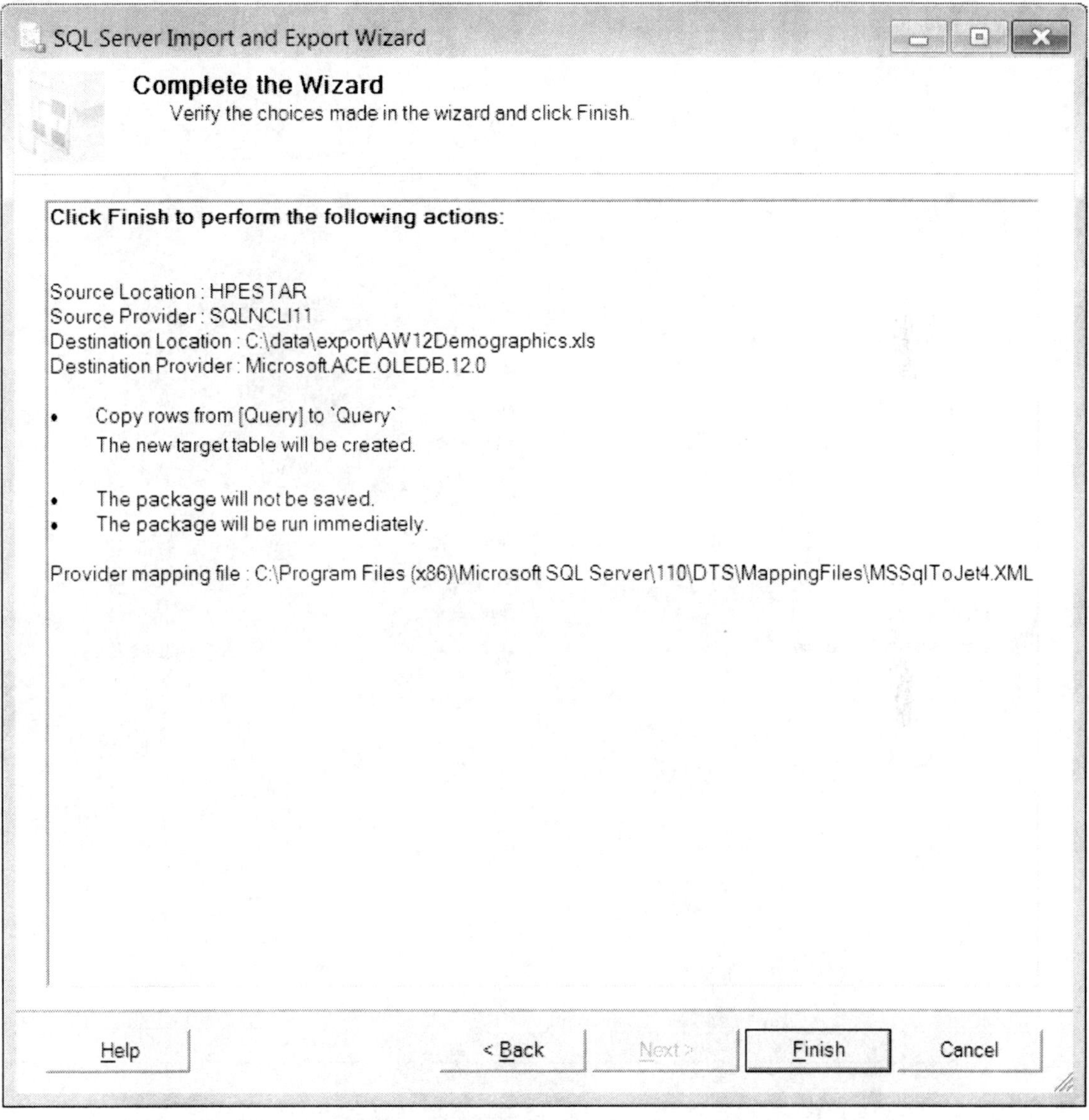

Execution Results Screen

If there are errors in the execution of the package, they will show in this window. The current Wizard generated SSIS package executed successfully.

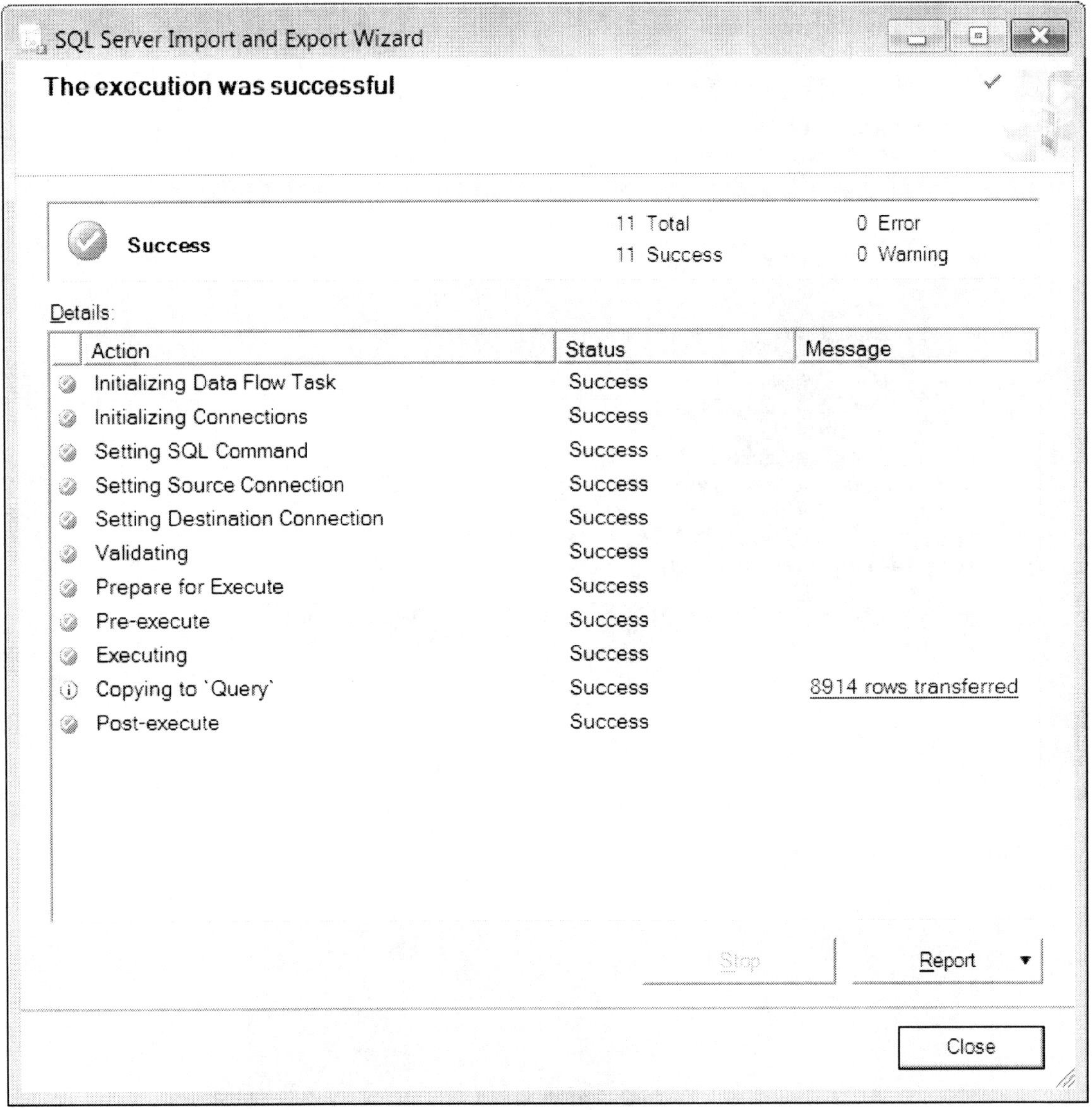

Checking Results in Excel

If the double click on the destination filename, the transferred data is displayed by Excel.

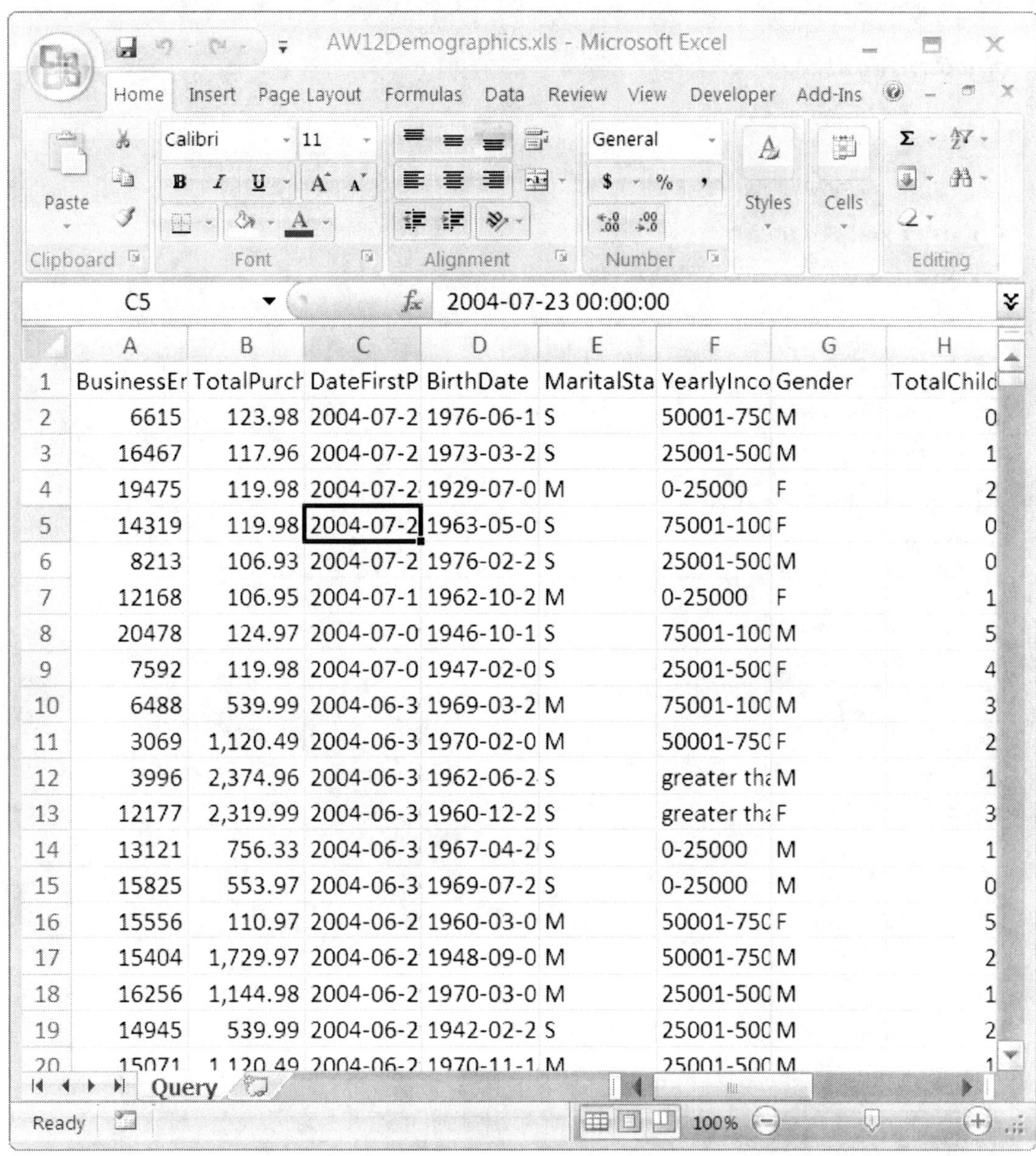

	A	B	C	D	E	F	G	H
1	BusinessEr	TotalPurch	DateFirstP	BirthDate	MaritalSta	YearlyInco	Gender	TotalChild
2	6615	123.98	2004-07-2	1976-06-1	S	50001-750	M	0
3	16467	117.96	2004-07-2	1973-03-2	S	25001-500	M	1
4	19475	119.98	2004-07-2	1929-07-0	M	0-25000	F	2
5	14319	119.98	2004-07-2	1963-05-0	S	75001-100	F	0
6	8213	106.93	2004-07-2	1976-02-2	S	25001-500	M	0
7	12168	106.95	2004-07-1	1962-10-2	M	0-25000	F	1
8	20478	124.97	2004-07-0	1946-10-1	S	75001-100	M	5
9	7592	119.98	2004-07-0	1947-02-0	S	25001-500	F	4
10	6488	539.99	2004-06-3	1969-03-2	M	75001-100	M	3
11	3069	1,120.49	2004-06-3	1970-02-0	M	50001-750	F	2
12	3996	2,374.96	2004-06-3	1962-06-2	S	greater th	M	1
13	12177	2,319.99	2004-06-3	1960-12-2	S	greater th	F	3
14	13121	756.33	2004-06-3	1967-04-2	S	0-25000	M	1
15	15825	553.97	2004-06-3	1969-07-2	S	0-25000	M	0
16	15556	110.97	2004-06-2	1960-03-0	M	50001-750	F	5
17	15404	1,729.97	2004-06-2	1948-09-0	M	50001-750	M	2
18	16256	1,144.98	2004-06-2	1970-03-0	M	25001-500	M	1
19	14945	539.99	2004-06-2	1942-02-2	S	25001-500	M	2
20	15071	1,120.49	2004-06-2	1970-11-1	M	25001-500	M	1

Importing Data with SQL Server Import and Export Wizard

Importing with the Wizard is very similar to the exporting process. We are going to import the just created AW12Demographics.xls Excel worksheet into a new database table. We start the Wizard the same as for export. First we configure the source as Excel worksheet.

Specify Data Source

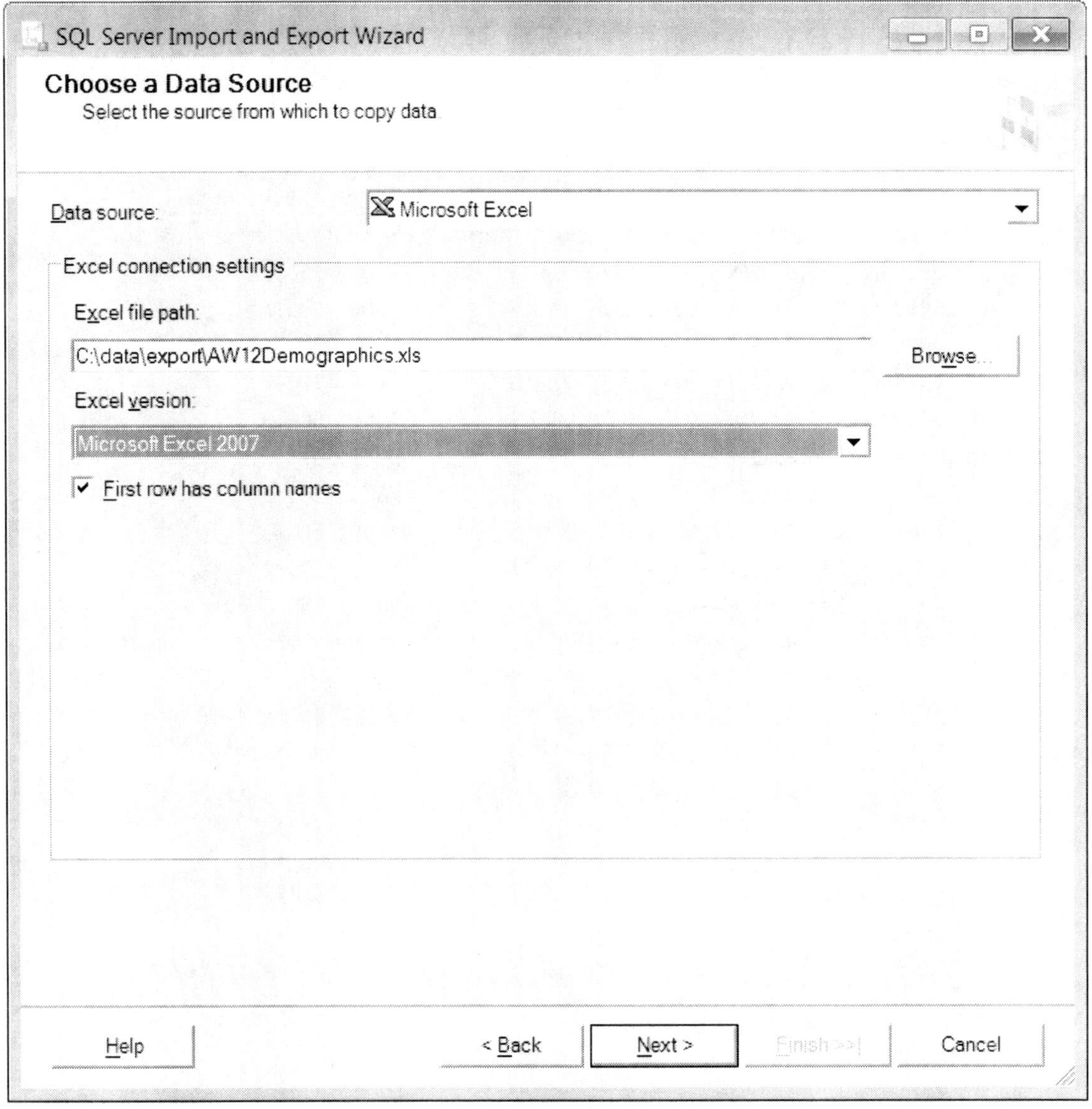

Specify Data Destination as Database

AdventureWorks2012 is the destination for the data movement.

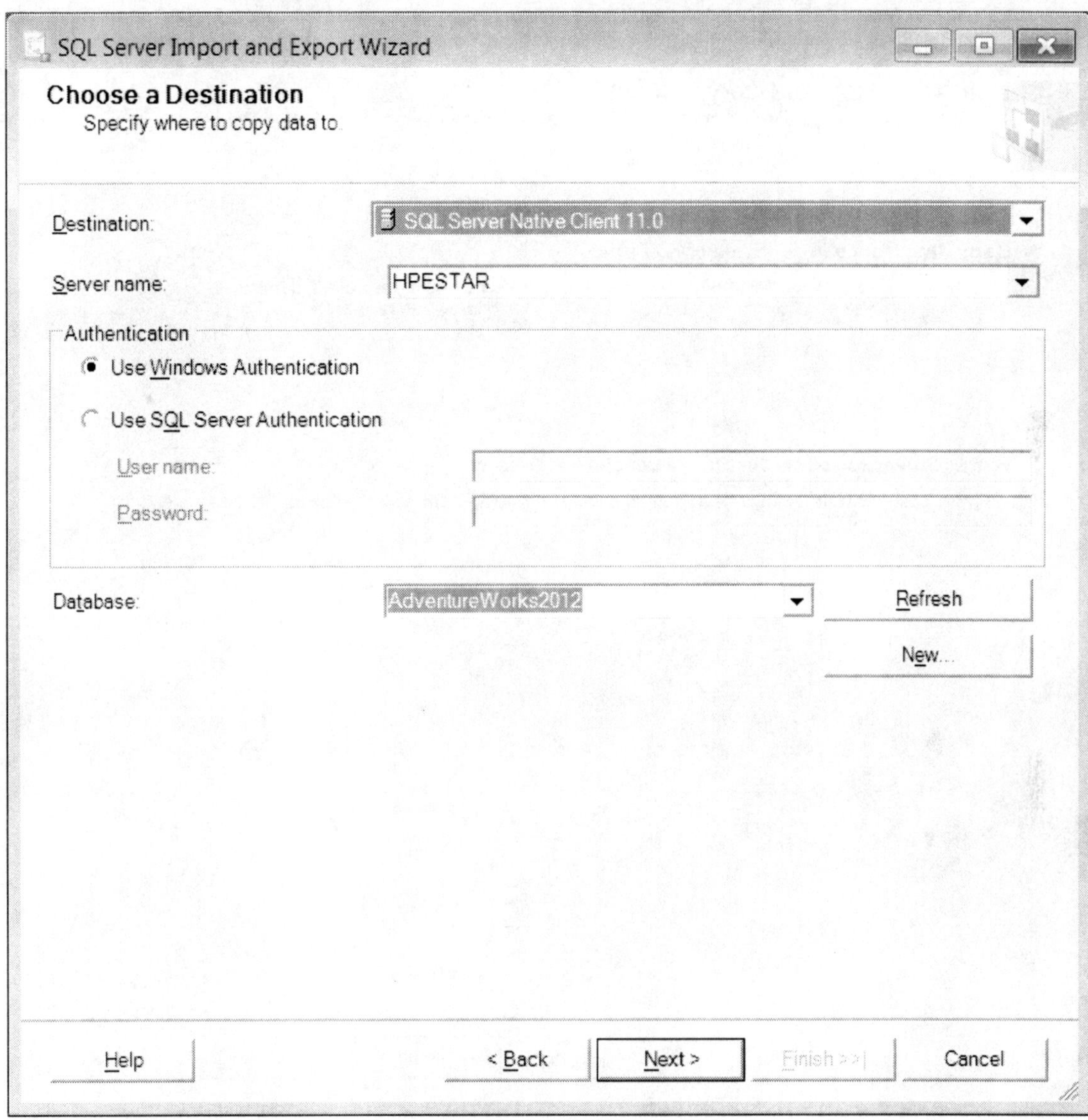

Excel Worksheet Source Is Considered a Table

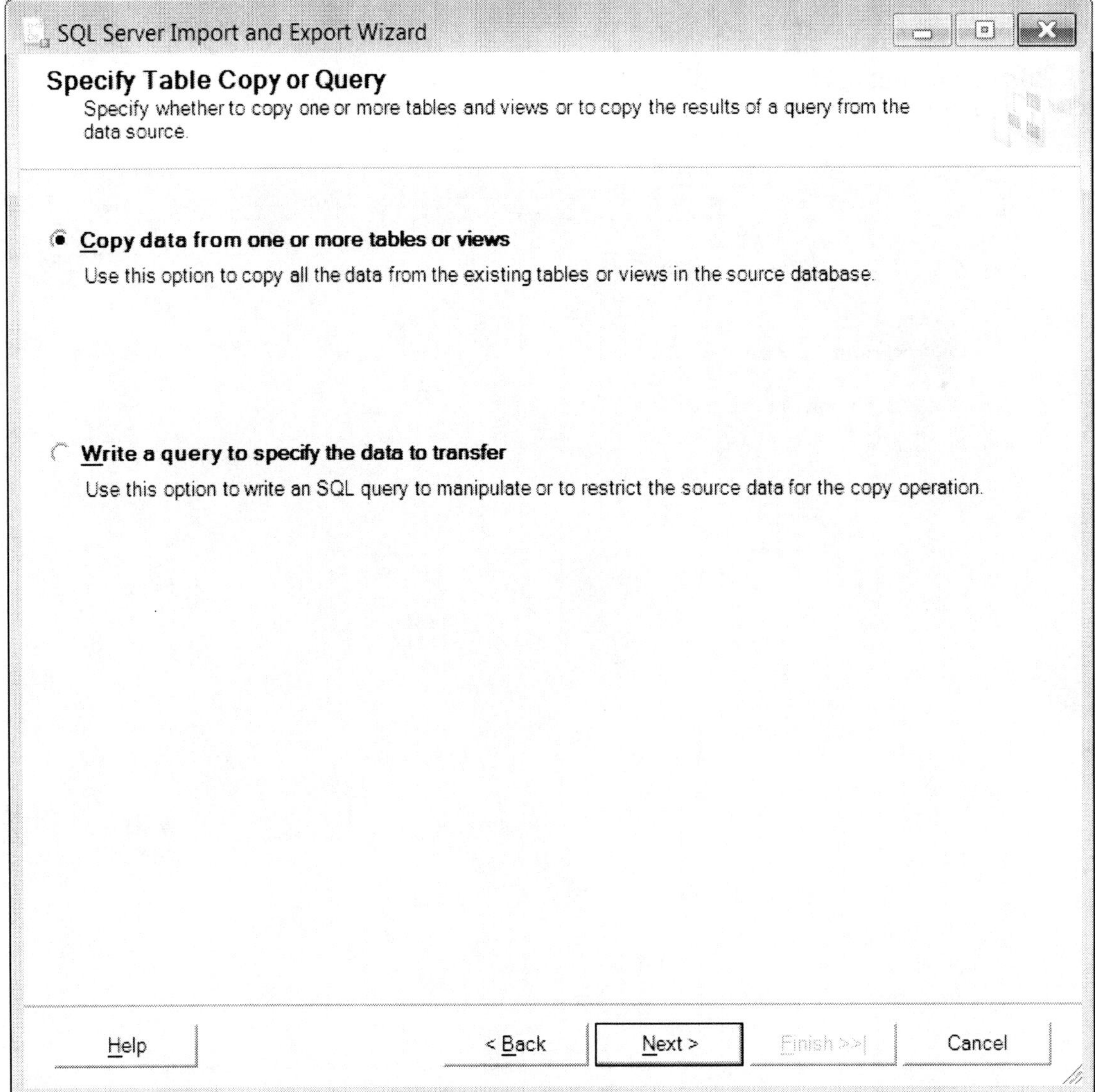

Select Excel Sheet and Assign Database Table Name

All the data is on the 'Query' sheet.

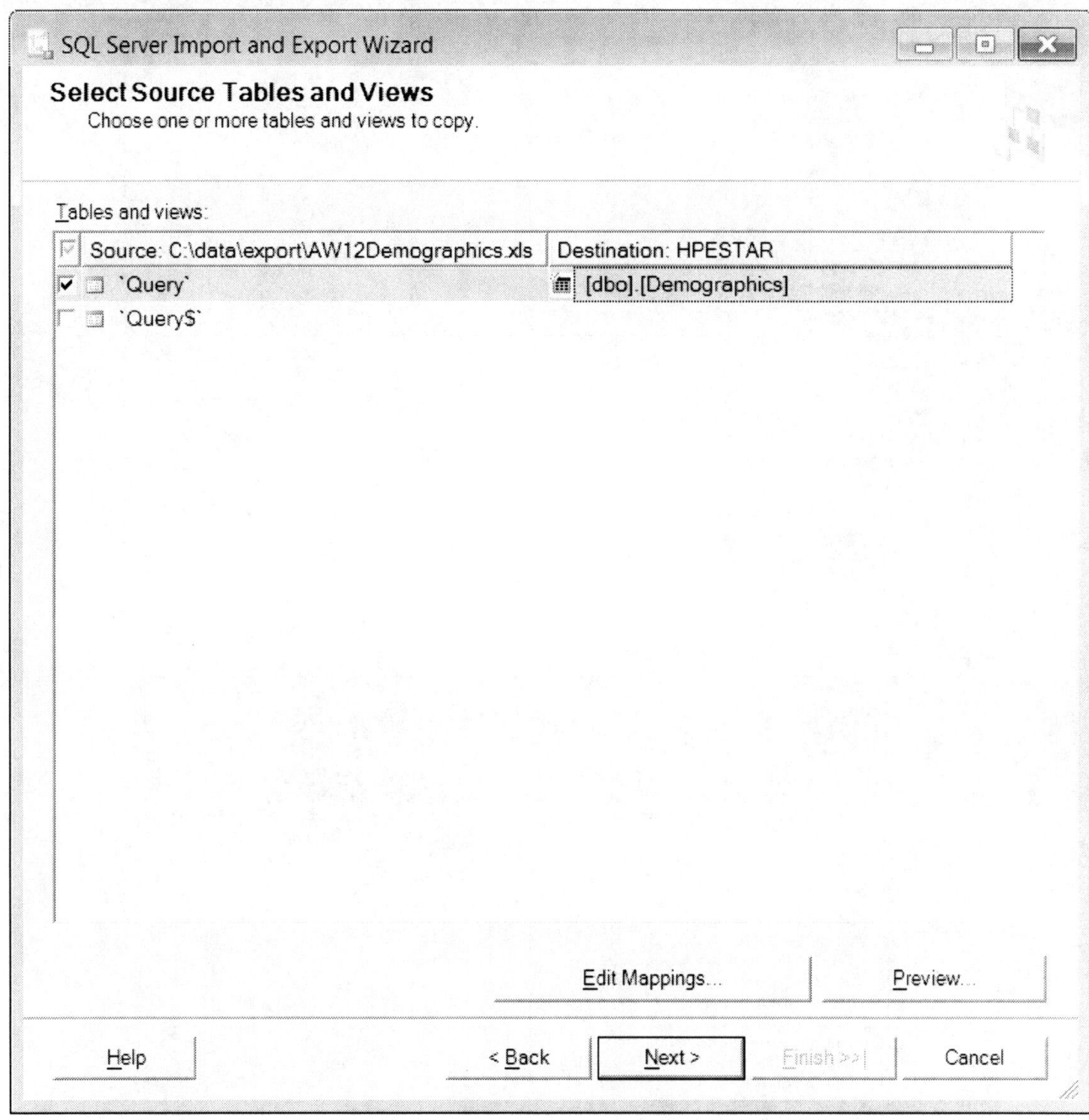

Column Mappings & CREATE TABLE Edit Panels

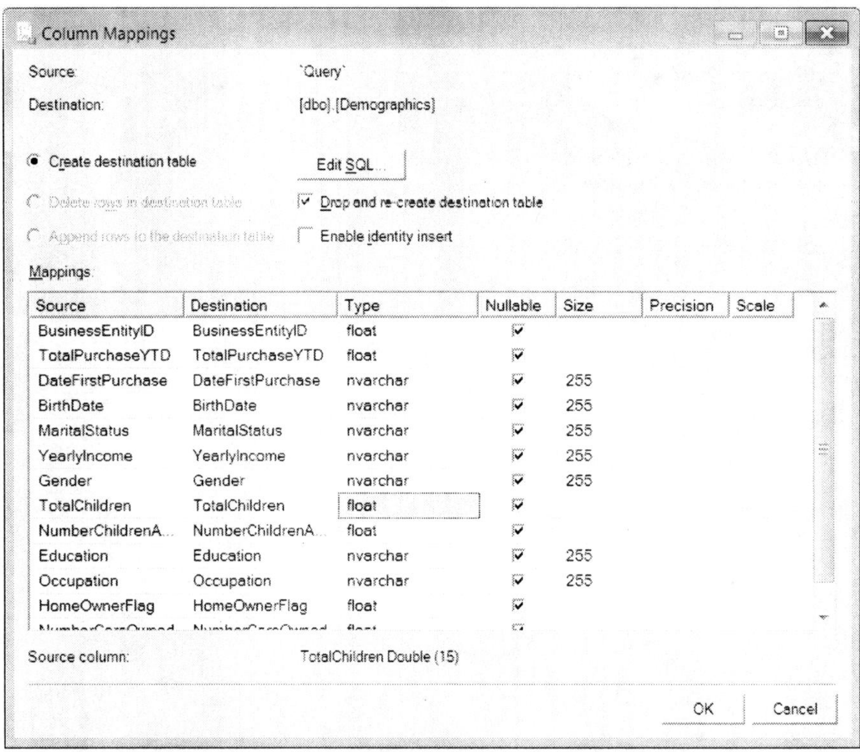

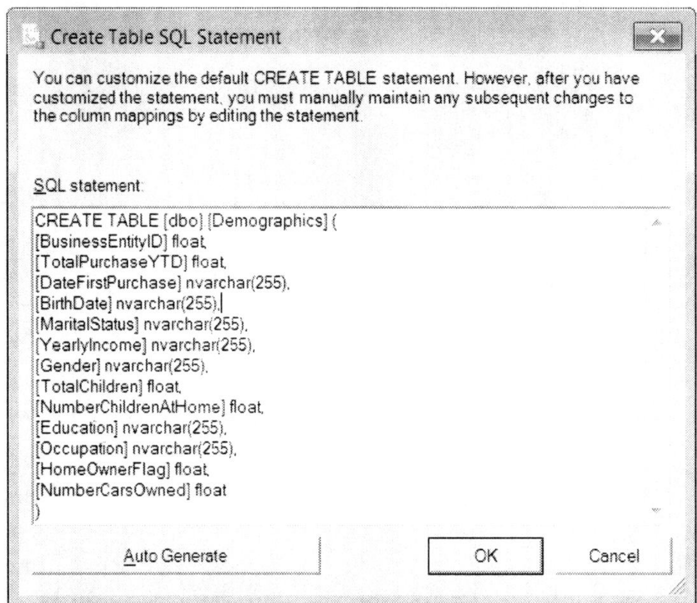

Source Data Inspection with Preview Data

This is a very important step. If the data does not look correct here, it will not be correct in the database table either.

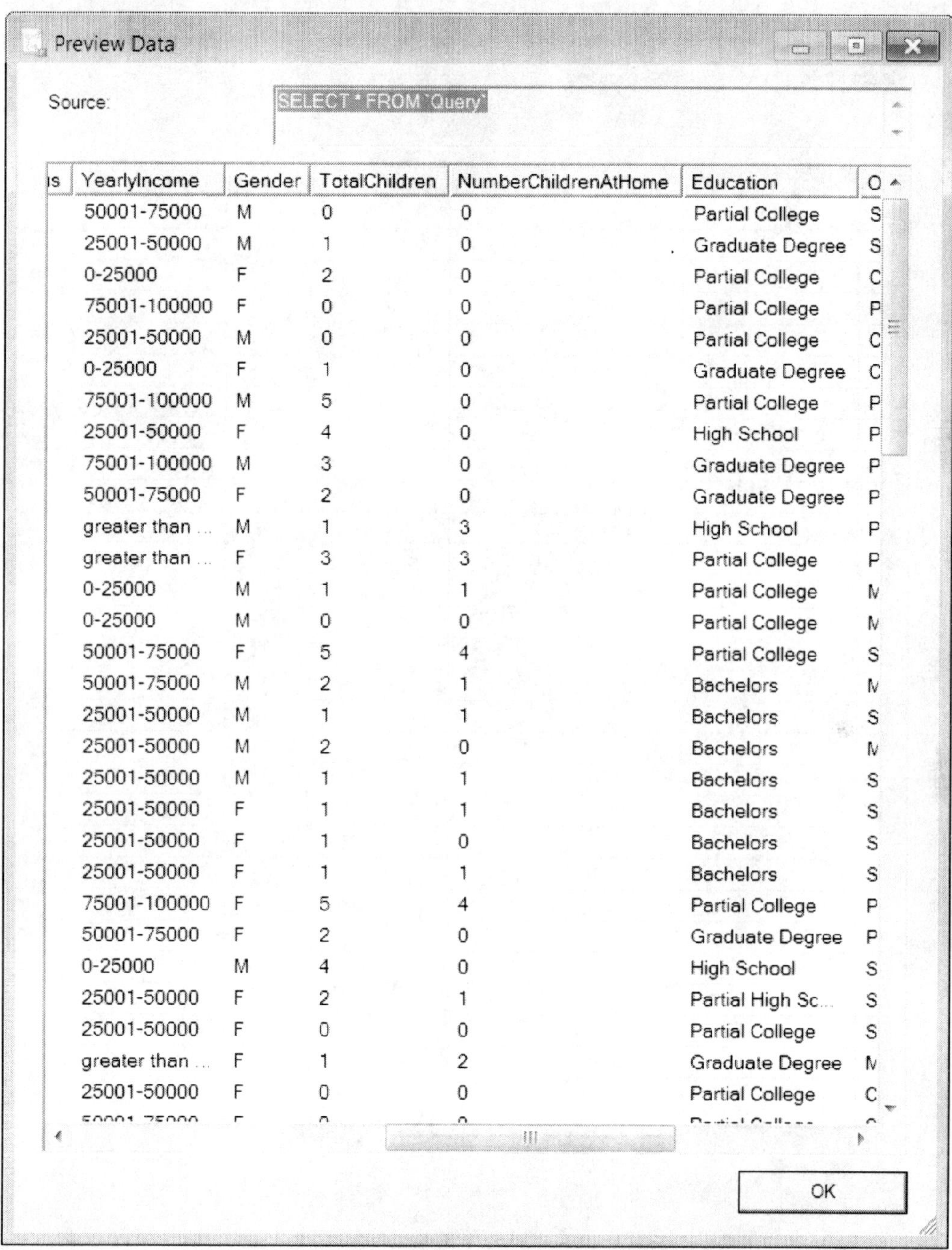

YearlyIncome	Gender	TotalChildren	NumberChildrenAtHome	Education	O
50001-75000	M	0	0	Partial College	S
25001-50000	M	1	0	Graduate Degree	S
0-25000	F	2	0	Partial College	C
75001-100000	F	0	0	Partial College	P
25001-50000	M	0	0	Partial College	C
0-25000	F	1	0	Graduate Degree	C
75001-100000	M	5	0	Partial College	P
25001-50000	F	4	0	High School	P
75001-100000	M	3	0	Graduate Degree	P
50001-75000	F	2	0	Graduate Degree	P
greater than ...	M	1	3	High School	P
greater than ...	F	3	3	Partial College	P
0-25000	M	1	1	Partial College	M
0-25000	M	0	0	Partial College	M
50001-75000	F	5	4	Partial College	S
50001-75000	M	2	1	Bachelors	M
25001-50000	M	1	1	Bachelors	S
25001-50000	M	2	0	Bachelors	M
25001-50000	M	1	1	Bachelors	S
25001-50000	F	1	1	Bachelors	S
25001-50000	F	1	0	Bachelors	S
25001-50000	F	1	1	Bachelors	S
75001-100000	F	5	4	Partial College	P
50001-75000	F	2	0	Graduate Degree	P
0-25000	M	4	0	High School	S
25001-50000	F	2	1	Partial High Sc...	S
25001-50000	F	0	0	Partial College	S
greater than ...	F	1	2	Graduate Degree	M
25001-50000	F	0	0	Partial College	C

Indicate Saving and/or Run the SSIS Package

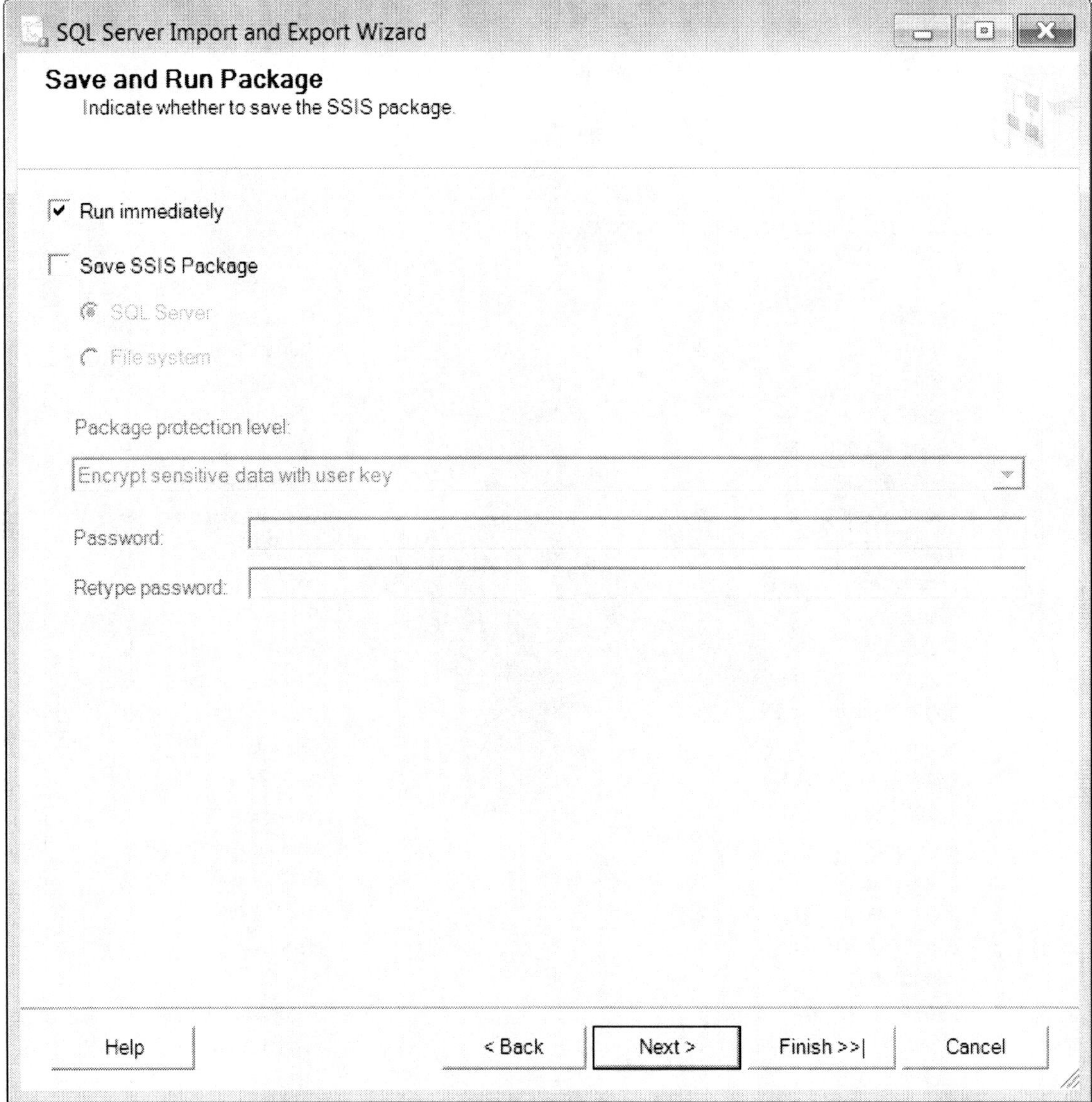

The Final Release Screen for Execution

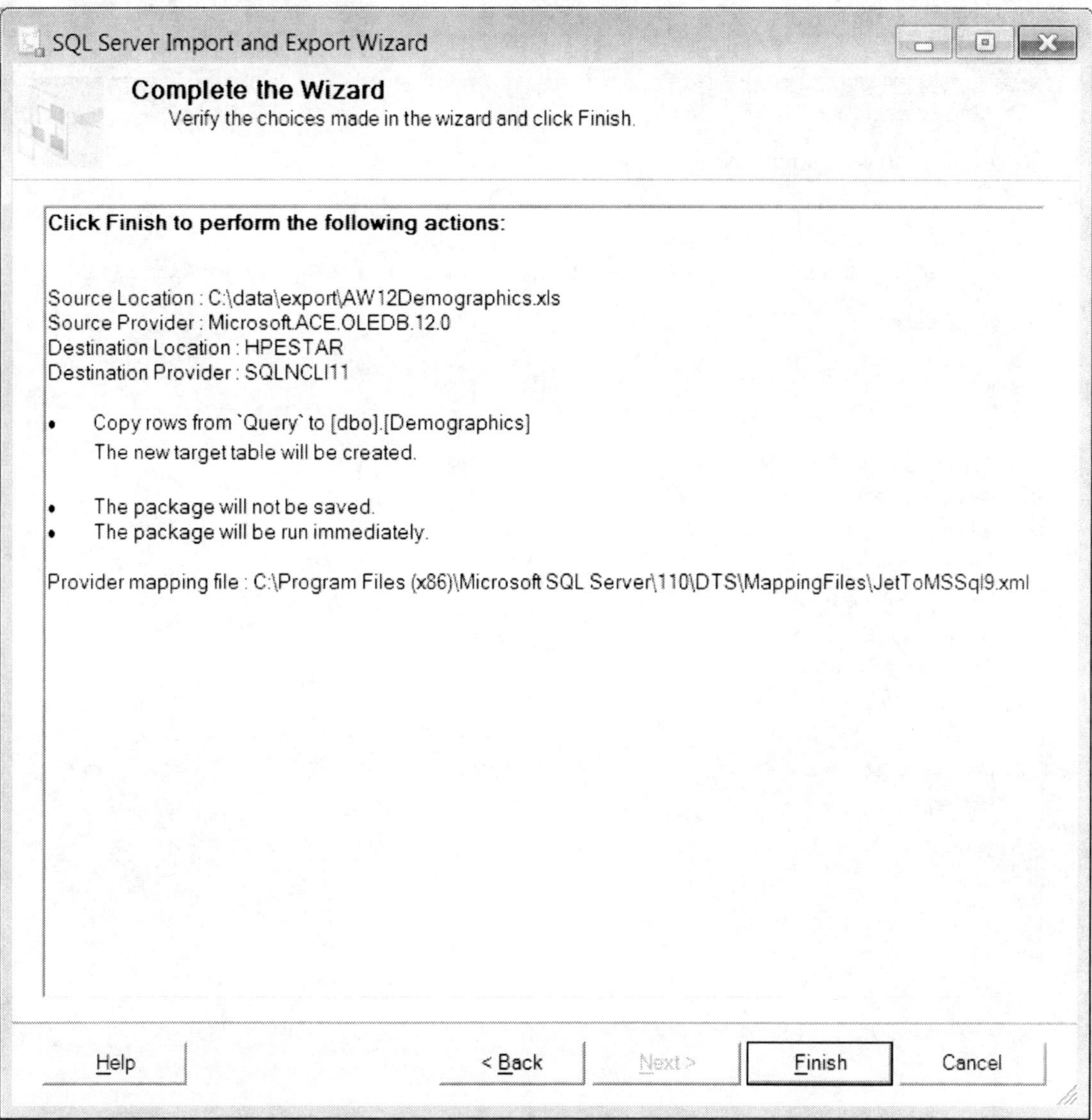

Successful Execution Screen

In case of errors, hyperlink to errors will display.

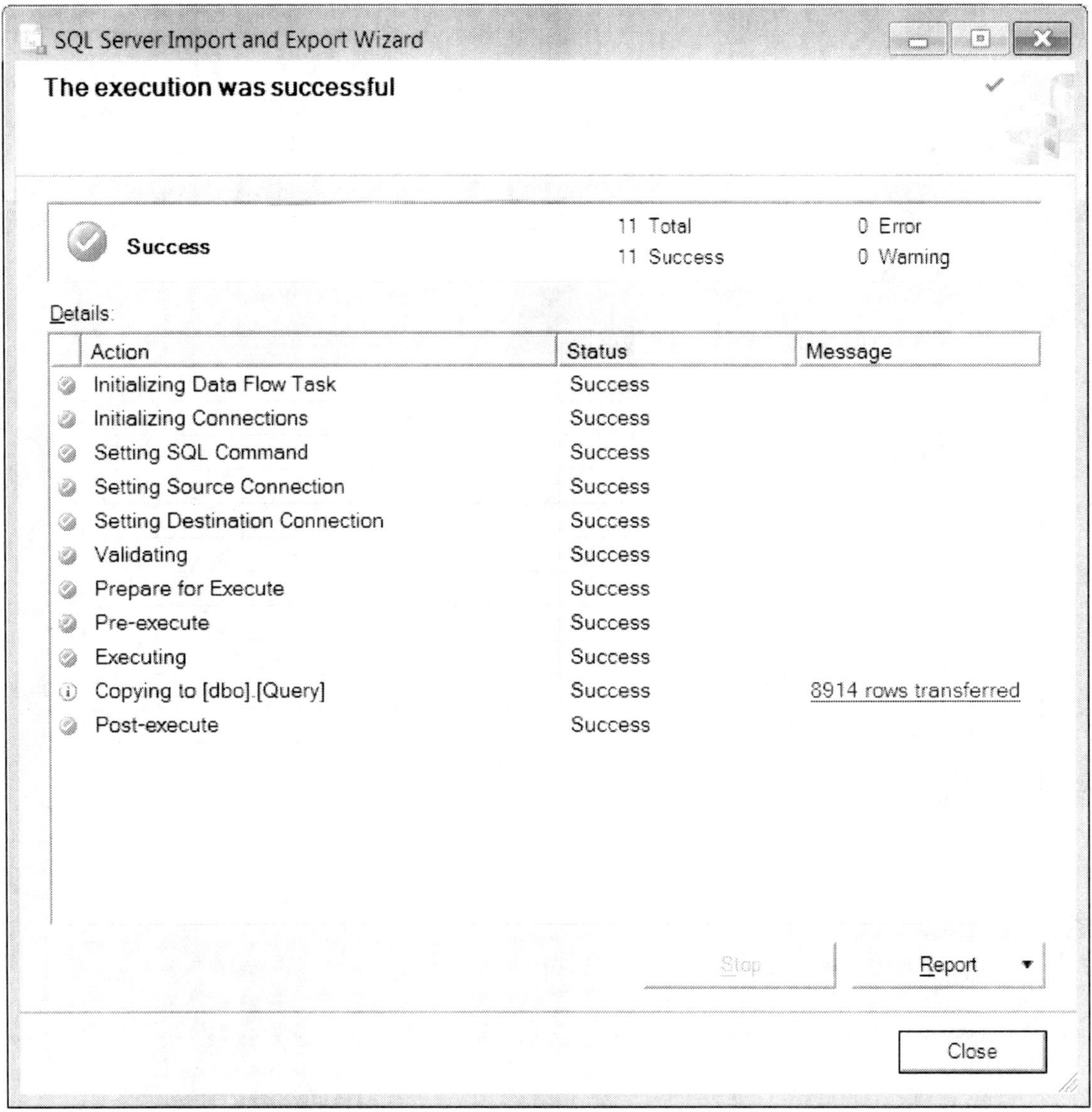

Check New Table in Database

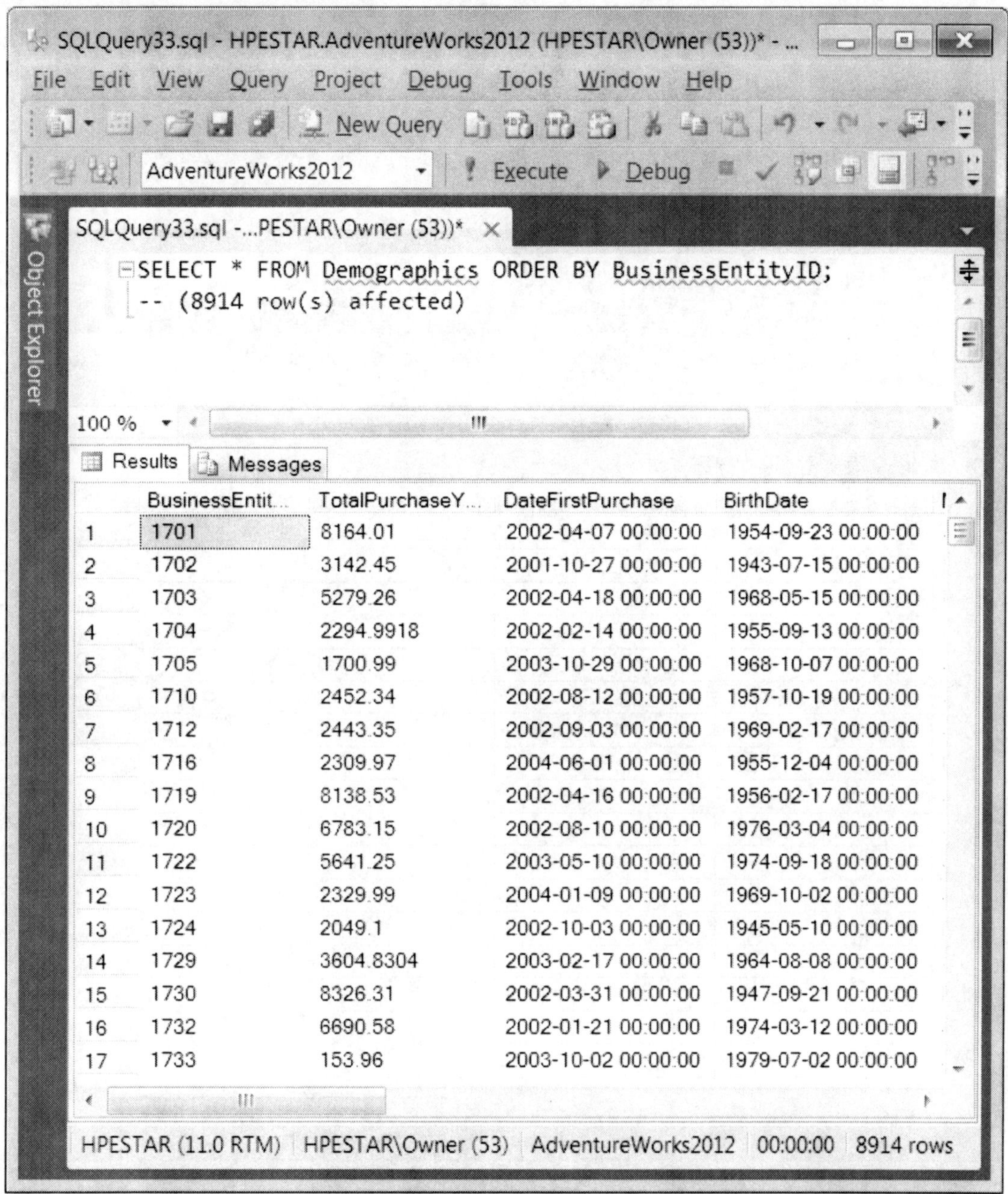

Exporting Database Table to Excel

The Wizard sequence is very similar to exporting query results. We shall export Sales.SalesOrderHeader table.

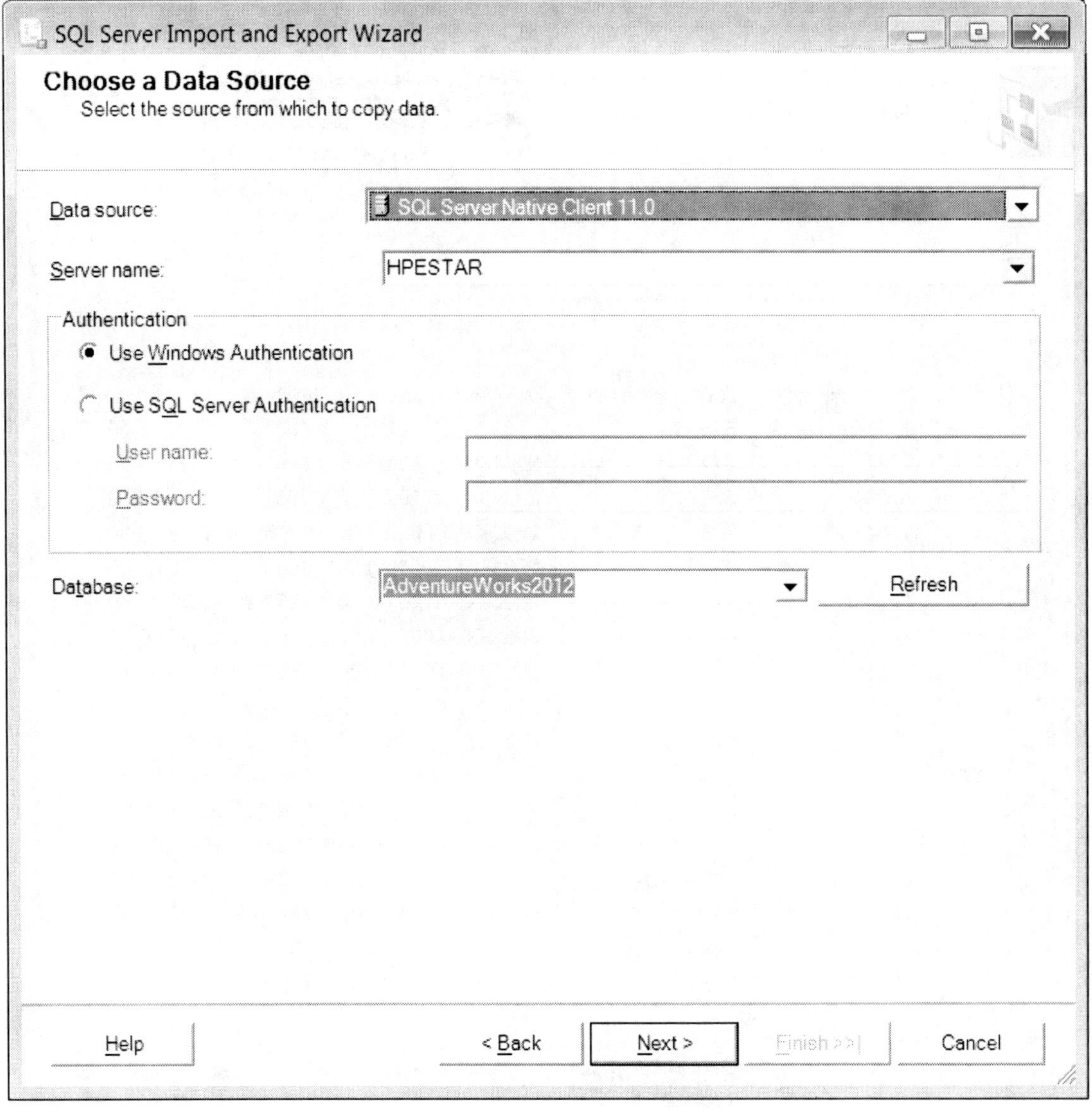

Specify Destination

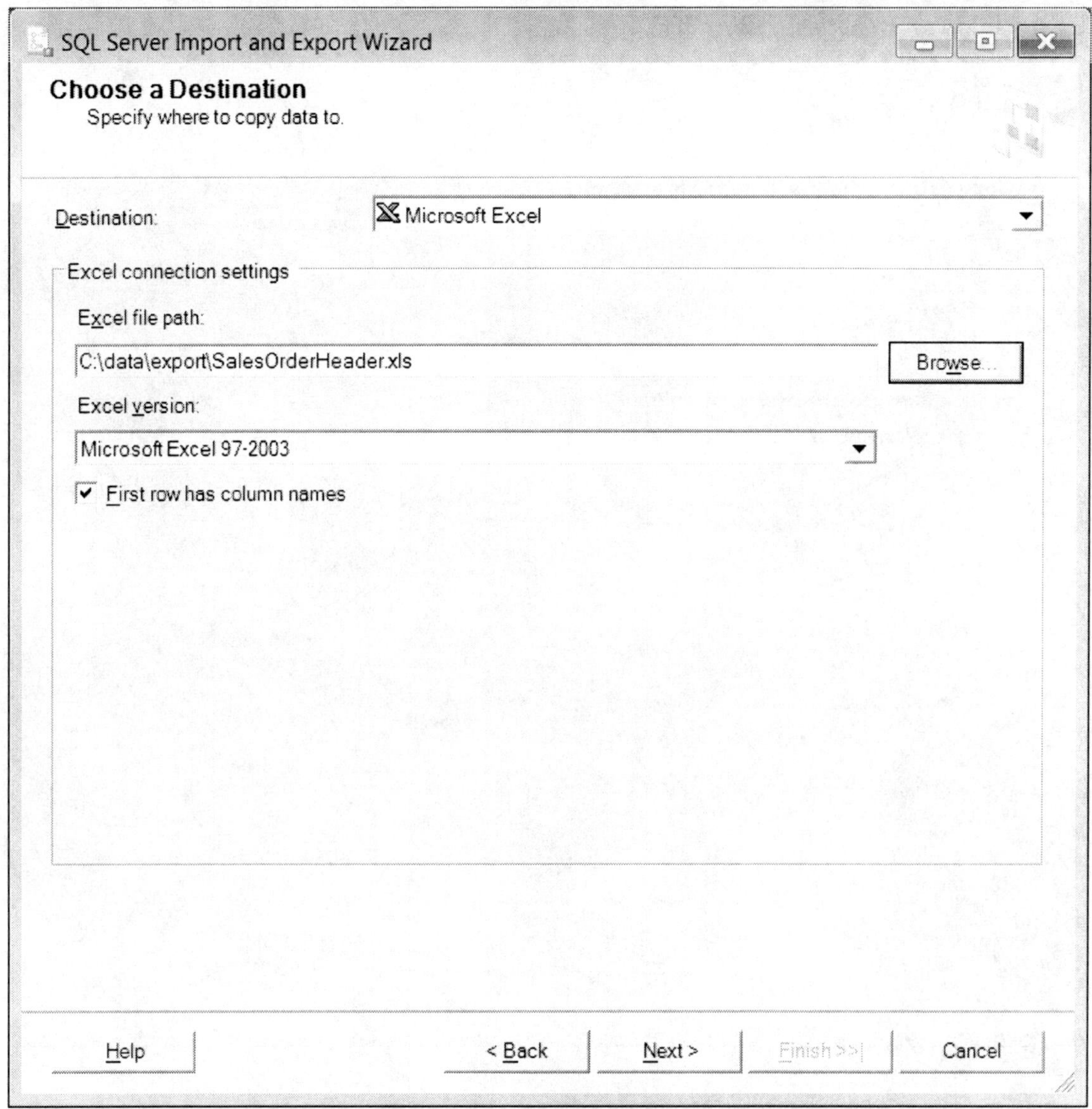

Choose Table Copy or Query

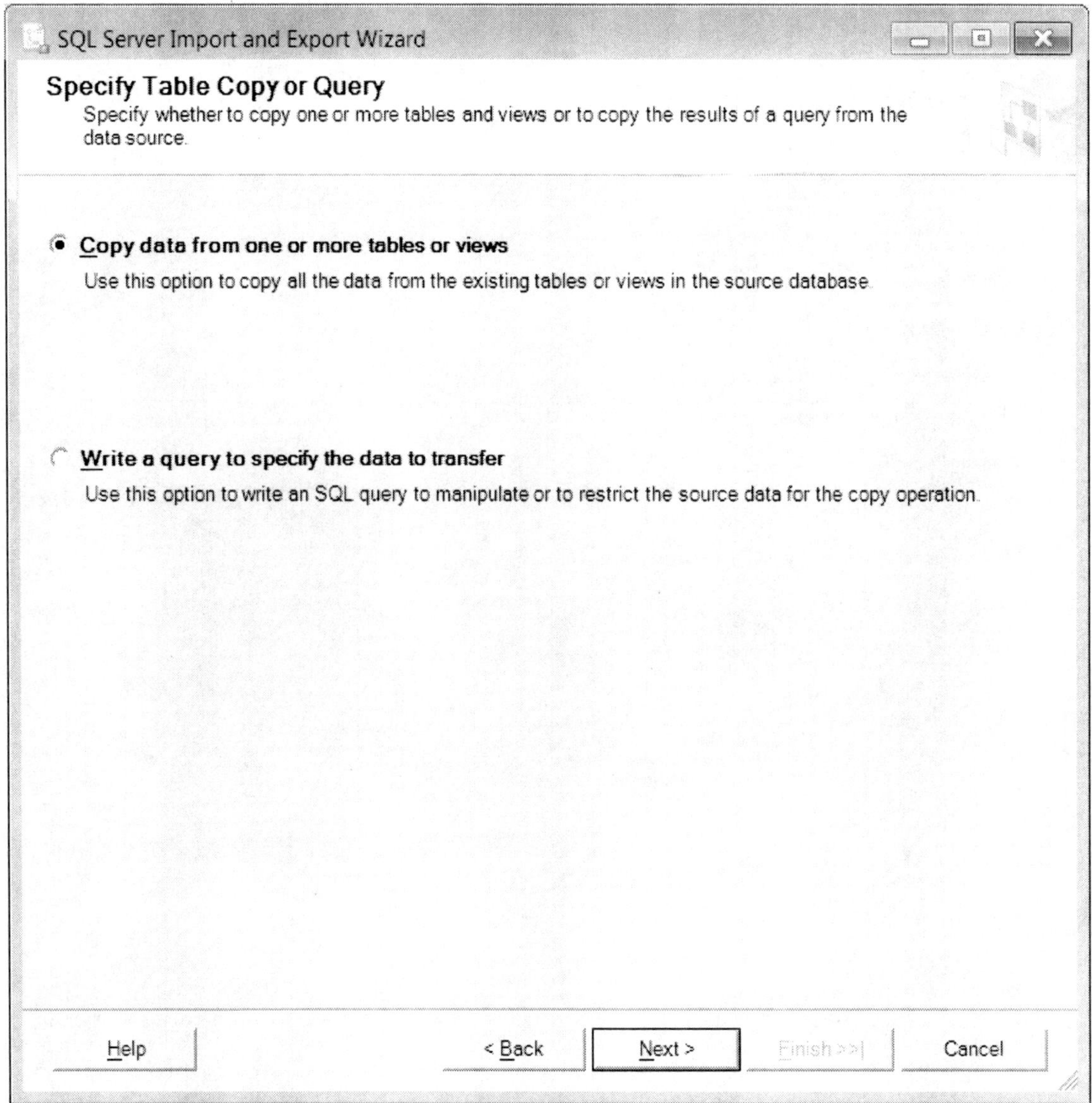

Checkmark Source Table

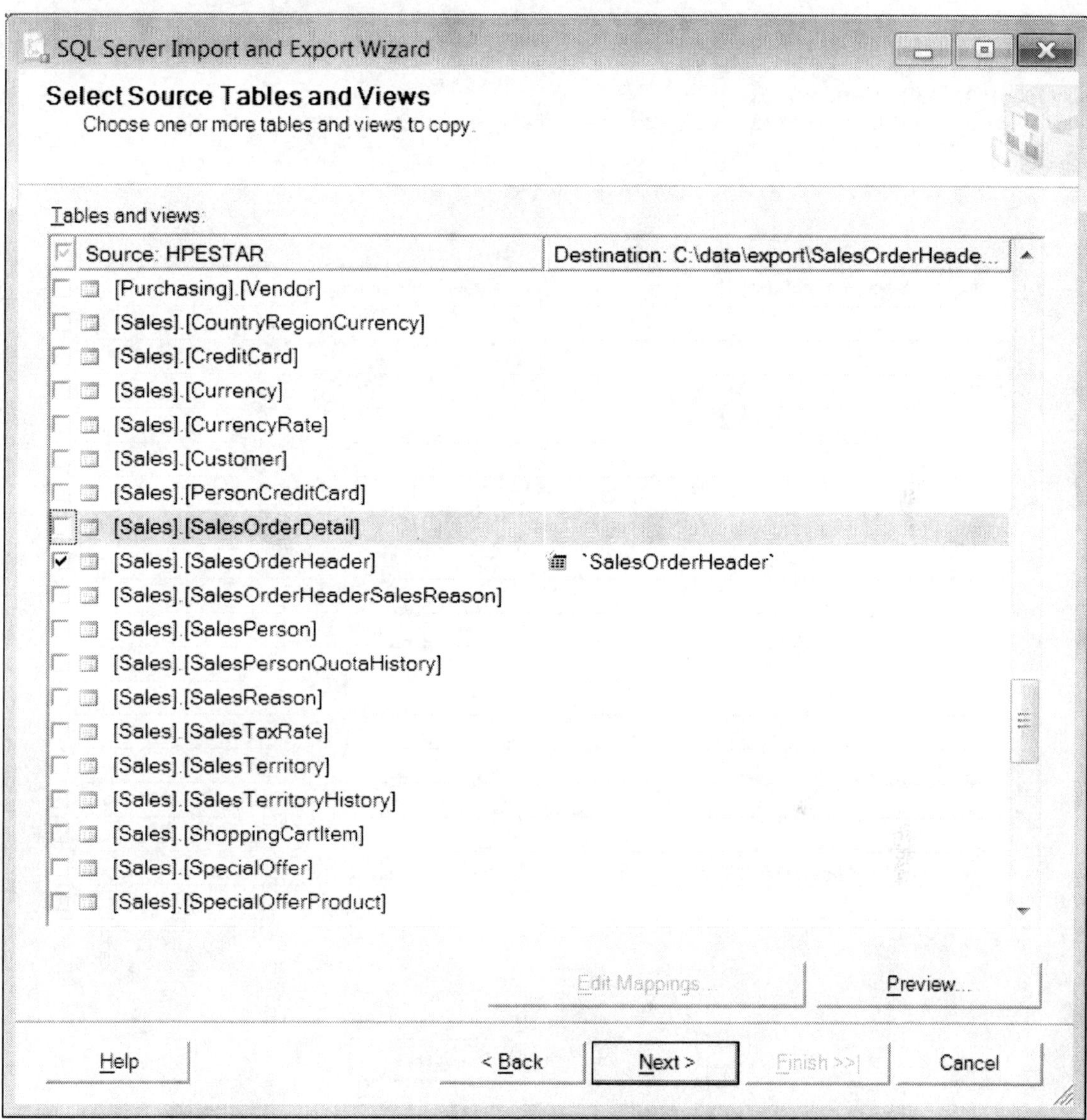

Check Data Type Mapping

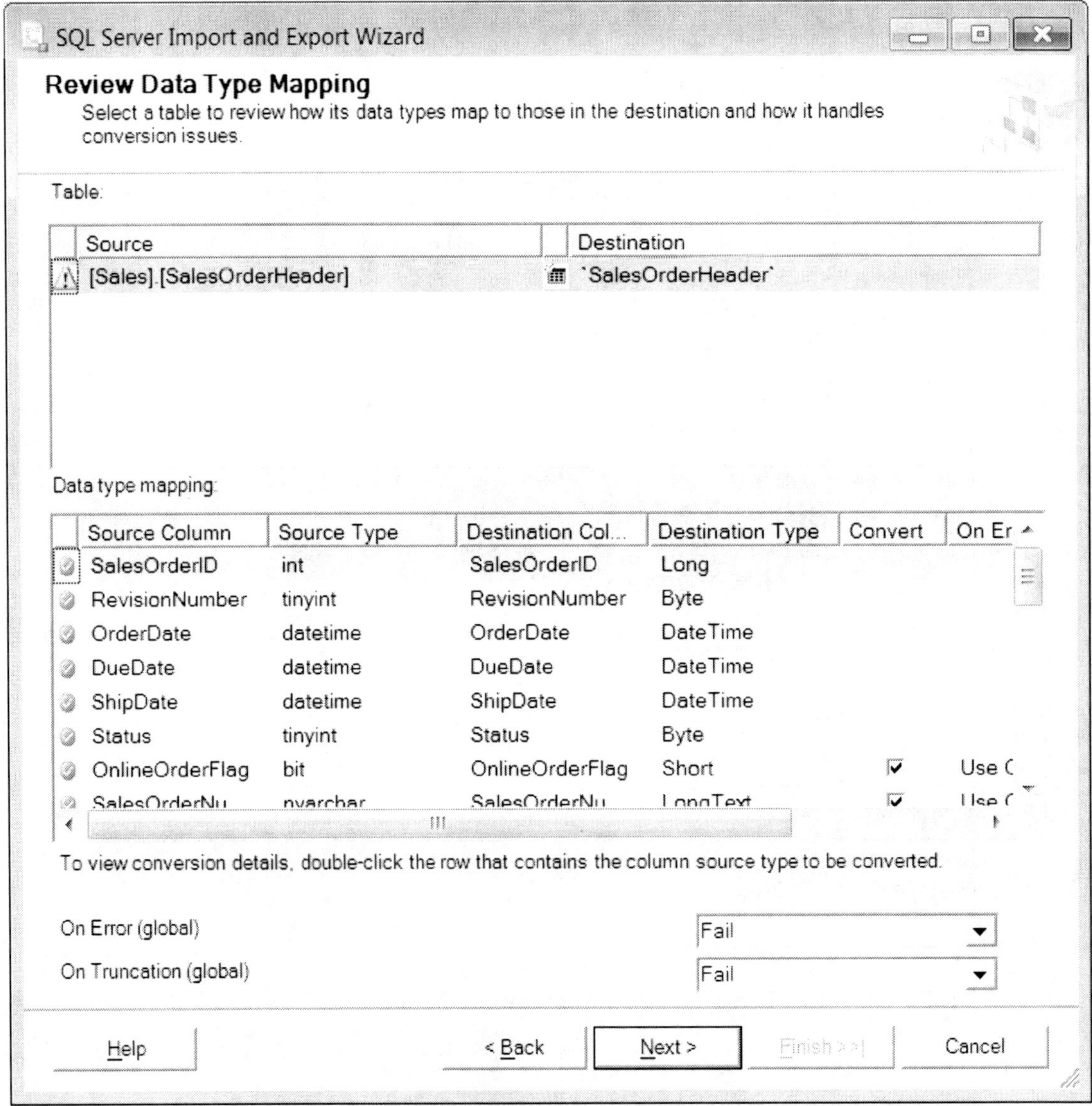

Save and/or Run Package

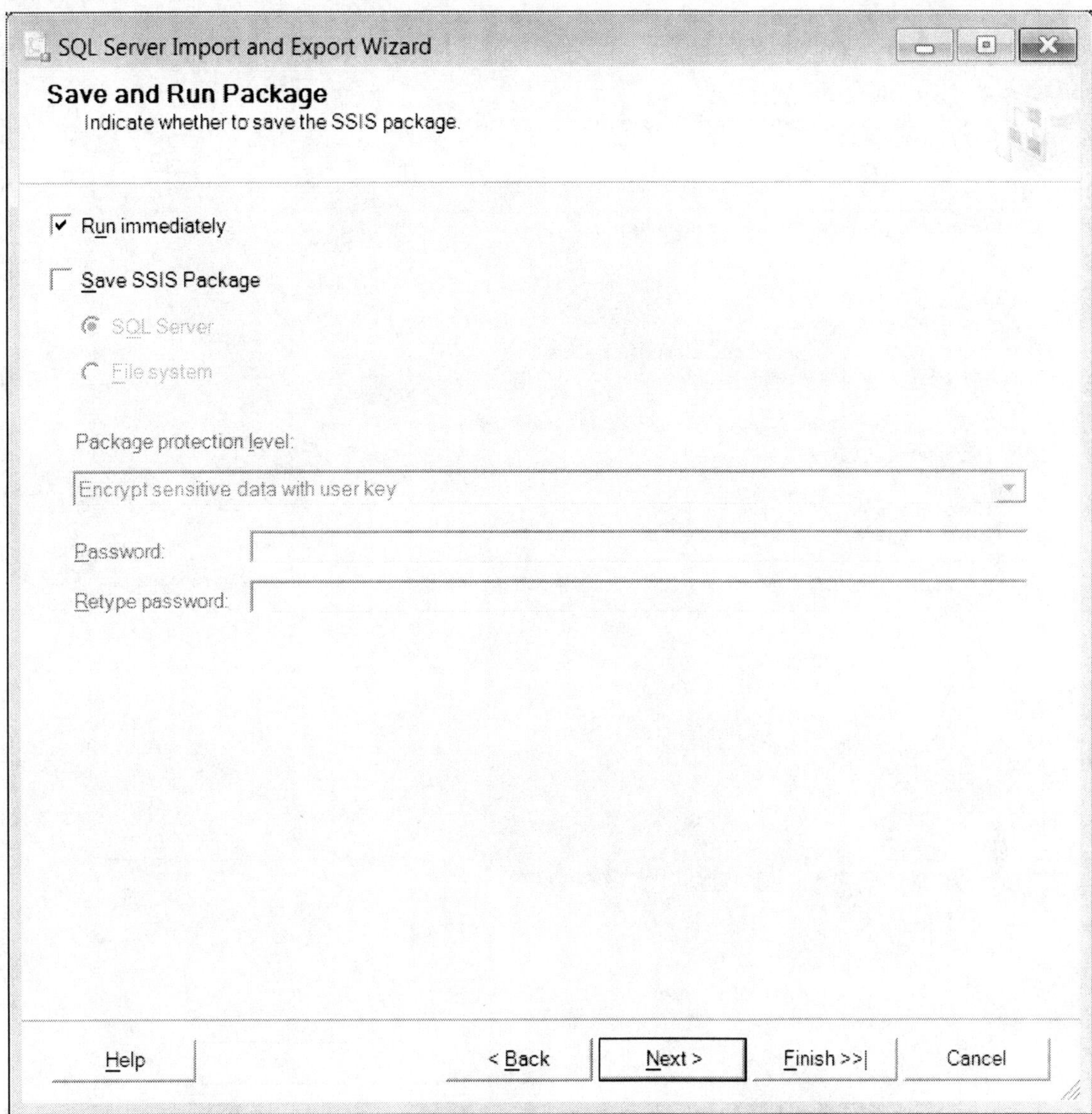

Complete the Wizard

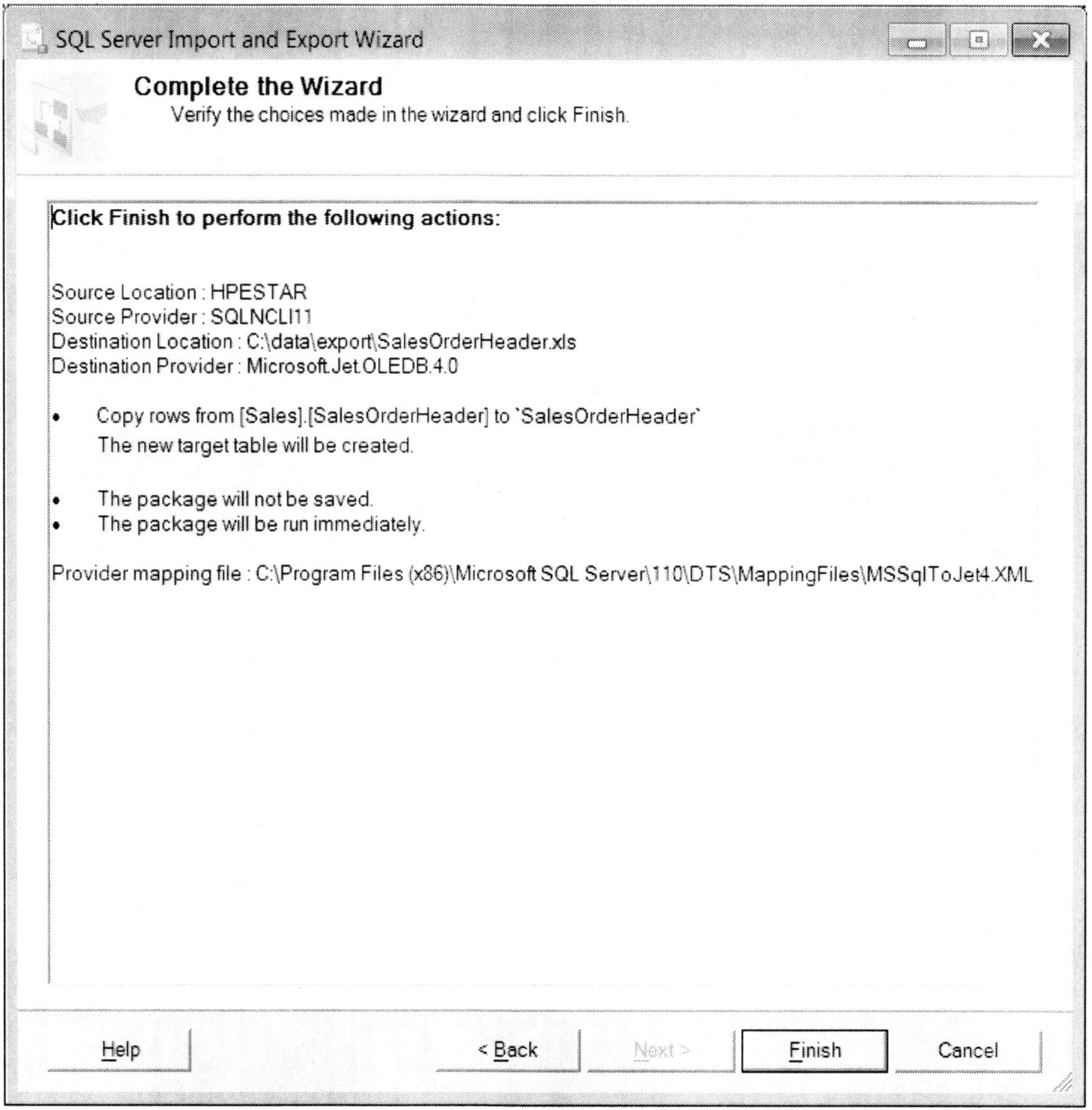

Successful Execution Screen

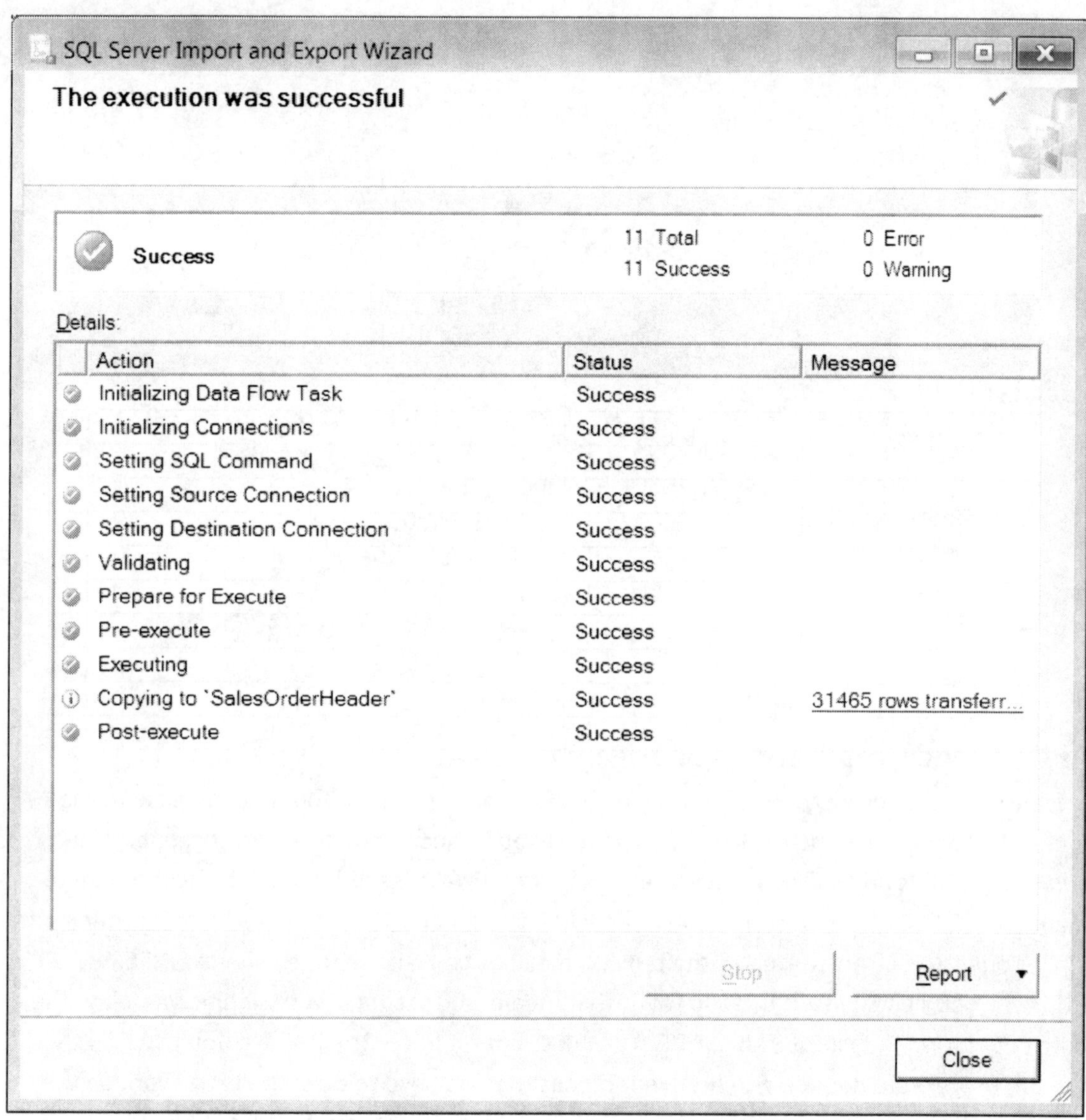

Check Data in Excel

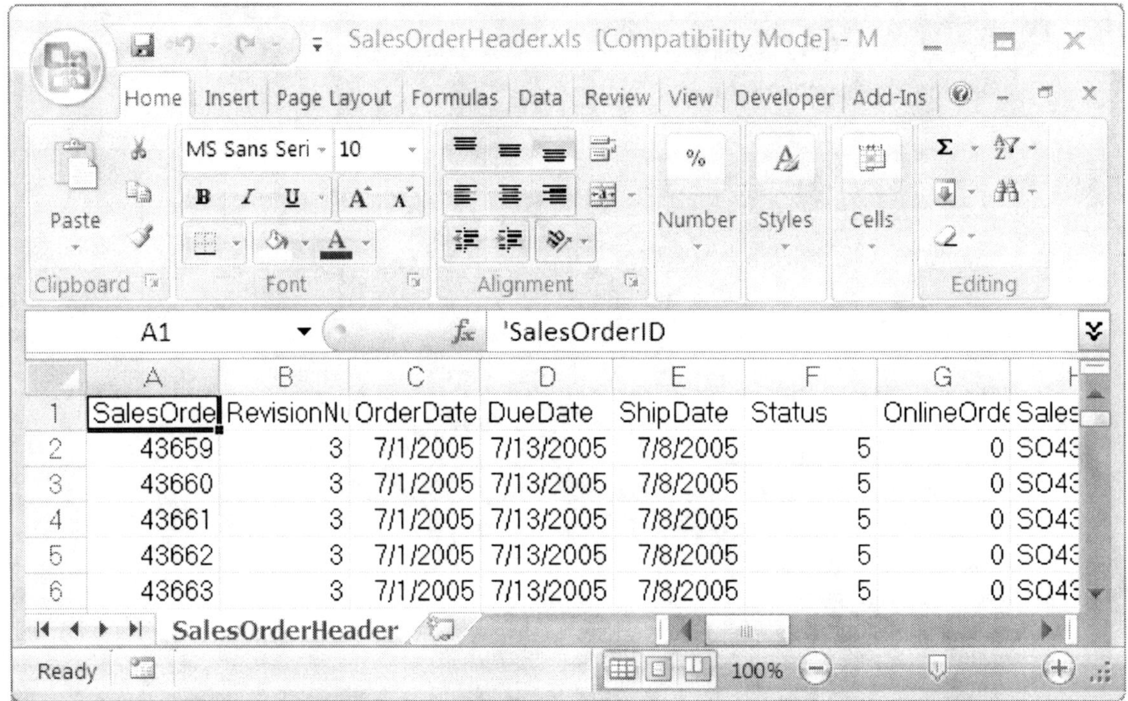

Performance Implications of Triggers

Since triggers can be very complex, they may add significant execution time increase to the underlying operations such as INSERT. Therefore, our objective **to keep the trigger code as small as possible and efficient.** However, that is not always feasible: once this author had to maintain a 2,000 lines enterprise trigger at Swiss bank. If an INSERT takes 300 milliseconds longer due to an insert trigger on the table, it may not be an issue for single row INSERTs. However, for a batch insert of 1000 rows, that means 300 seconds, very significant delay. The batch operation BULK INSERT has FIRE_TRIGGERS option to control it. If we don't specify the option, triggers are not going to fire. That means that we have to do some extra work on the imported data: we have to write a script to do the same processing the trigger would be doing. Similar consideration for bcp and SSIS.

MSDN Article: **Controlling Trigger Execution When Bulk Importing Data** http://msdn.microsoft.com/en-us/library/ms187640(v=sql.105).aspx
Article: **Designing and implementing triggers in Microsoft SQL Server** http://searchsqlserver.techtarget.com/feature/Designing-and-implementing-triggers-in-Microsoft-SQL-Server

Exporting Data Directly into a Flat File

There is no equivalent of BULK INSERT, however, with xp_cmdshell & ECHO commands we can export data directly into a flat file.

> Security blog on xp_cmdshell (usually disabled on production servers):
> http://blogs.msdn.com/b/sqlsecurity/archive/2008/01/10/xp-cmdshell.aspx .

```
USE AdventureWorks;
GO
CREATE PROC uspWeeklySupplierSummary  @FilePath VARCHAR(100) AS  BEGIN SET NOCOUNT ON;
  DECLARE  @Line NVARCHAR(1000), @Command NVARCHAR(2000) ,@Return INT;
  DECLARE  @VendorID  INT,  @VendorName NVARCHAR(50), @ProductName NVARCHAR(50);
  SET @Line = '******** SUPPLIERS PRODUCTS REPORT ********';
  SET @Command = CONCAT('echo ', @Line , ' >>', @FilePath);
  EXEC @Return = master..xp_cmdshell  @Command, no_output;
  DECLARE curVendor CURSOR LOCAL  FAST_FORWARD FOR
  SELECT  VendorID, Name  FROM  Purchasing.Vendor  WHERE   CreditRating = 1   ORDER BY VendorID;
  OPEN curVendor  FETCH NEXT FROM curVendor  INTO @VendorID,  @VendorName;
  WHILE @@FETCH_STATUS = 0       BEGIN
    SET @Line = '. '; SET @Command = CONCAT('echo ', @Line,' >>', @FilePath);
    EXEC @Return = master..xp_cmdshell  @Command, no_output;
    SET @Line = '***** Products From Supplier: ' + @VendorName;
    SET @Command = CONCAT('echo ', @Line, ' >>', @FilePath);
    EXEC @Return = master..xp_cmdshell  @Command, no_output
    DECLARE curProduct CURSOR FAST_FORWARD FOR
    SELECT v.Name  FROM   Purchasing.ProductVendor pv INNER JOIN Production.Product v
    ON  pv.ProductID = v.ProductID   AND pv.VendorID = @VendorID;
    OPEN curProduct; FETCH NEXT FROM curProduct INTO @ProductName;
    IF @@FETCH_STATUS <> 0    BEGIN
      SET @Line = '*** NO PRODUCTS AVAILABLE AT THIS TIME *** ';
      SET @Command = CONCAT('echo ', @Line,' >>', @FilePath);
      EXEC @Return = master..xp_cmdshell  @Command,  no_output;
     END;
    WHILE @@FETCH_STATUS = 0   BEGIN
      SET @Line = CONCAT( SPACE(1), @ProductName );
      SET @Command = CONCAT('echo ', @Line,' >>',@FilePath);
      EXEC @Return = master..xp_cmdshell  @Command,  no_output;
      FETCH NEXT FROM curProduct   INTO @ProductName;
     END;    CLOSE curProduct;  DEALLOCATE curProduct;
    FETCH NEXT FROM curVendor  INTO @VendorID, @VendorName;
   END ;    CLOSE curVendor;    DEALLOCATE curVendor;
 END
GO
```

```
EXEC uspWeeklySupplierSummary   'F:\data\export\SUPPWeek31.txt' ;
```

Command Prompt Commands List by HELP

Command Prompt commands can be used for data transport as well including COPY & XCOPY. We can get the entire command list by typing the "HELP" command. It is like a time machine back to the programming style of 1960-s.

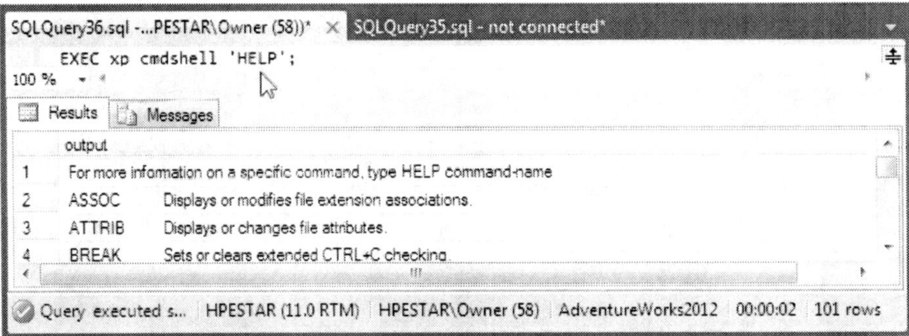

Command List

ASSOC	Displays or modifies file extension associations.
ATTRIB	Displays or changes file attributes.
BREAK	Sets or clears extended CTRL+C checking.
BCDEDIT	Sets properties in boot database to control boot loading.
CACLS	Displays or modifies access control lists (ACLs) of files.
CALL	Calls one batch program from another.
CD	Displays the name of or changes the current directory.
CHCP	Displays or sets the active code page number.
CHDIR	Displays the name of or changes the current directory.
CHKDSK	Checks a disk and displays a status report.
CHKNTFS	Displays or modifies the checking of disk at boot time.
CLS	Clears the screen.
CMD	Starts a new instance of the Windows command interpreter.
COLOR	Sets the default console foreground and background colors.
COMP	Compares the contents of two files or sets of files.
COMPACT	Displays or alters the compression of files on NTFS partitions.
CONVERT	Converts FAT volumes to NTFS. You cannot convert the current drive.
COPY	Copies one or more files to another location.
DATE	Displays or sets the date.
DEL	Deletes one or more files.
DIR	Displays a list of files and subdirectories in a directory.
DISKCOMP	Compares the contents of two floppy disks.
DISKCOPY	Copies the contents of one floppy disk to another.
DISKPART	Displays or configures Disk Partition properties.
DOSKEY	Edits command lines, recalls Windows commands, and creates macros.
DRIVERQUERY	Displays current device driver status and properties.
ECHO	Displays messages, or turns command echoing on or off.
ENDLOCAL	Ends localization of environment changes in a batch file.
ERASE	Deletes one or more files.
EXIT	Quits the CMD.EXE program (command interpreter).
FC	Compares two files or sets of files, and displays the differences between them.
FIND	Searches for a text string in a file or files.

FINDSTR	Searches for strings in files.
FOR	Runs a specified command for each file in a set of files.
FORMAT	Formats a disk for use with Windows.
FSUTIL	Displays or configures the file system properties.
FTYPE	Displays or modifies file types used in file extension associations.
GOTO	Directs the Windows command interpreter to a labeled line in a batch program.
GPRESULT	Displays Group Policy information for machine or user.
GRAFTABL	Enables Windows to display an extended character set in graphics mode.
HELP	Provides Help information for Windows commands.
ICACLS	Display, modify, backup, or restore ACLs for files and directories.
IF	Performs conditional processing in batch programs.
LABEL	Creates, changes, or deletes the volume label of a disk.
MD	Creates a directory.
MKDIR	Creates a directory.
MKLINK	Creates Symbolic Links and Hard Links
MODE	Configures a system device.
MORE	Displays output one screen at a time.
MOVE	Moves one or more files from one directory to another directory.
OPENFILES	Displays files opened by remote users for a file share.
PATH	Displays or sets a search path for executable files.
PAUSE	Suspends processing of a batch file and displays a message.
POPD	Restores the previous value of the current directory saved by PUSHD.
PRINT	Prints a text file.
PROMPT	Changes the Windows command prompt.
PUSHD	Saves the current directory then changes it.
RD	Removes a directory.
RECOVER	Recovers readable information from a bad or defective disk.
REM	Records comments (remarks) in batch files or CONFIG.SYS.
REN	Renames a file or files.
RENAME	Renames a file or files.
REPLACE	Replaces files.
RMDIR	Removes a directory.
ROBOCOPY	Advanced utility to copy files and directory trees
SET	Displays, sets, or removes Windows environment variables.
SETLOCAL	Begins localization of environment changes in a batch file.
SC	Displays or configures services (background processes).
SCHTASKS	Schedules commands and programs to run on a computer.
SHIFT	Shifts the position of replaceable parameters in batch files.
SHUTDOWN	Allows proper local or remote shutdown of machine.
SORT	Sorts input.
START	Starts a separate window to run a specified program or command.
SUBST	Associates a path with a drive letter.
SYSTEMINFO	Displays machine specific properties and configuration.
TASKLIST	Displays all currently running tasks including services.
TASKKILL	Kill or stop a running process or application.
TIME	Displays or sets the system time.
TITLE	Sets the window title for a CMD.EXE session.
TREE	Graphically displays the directory structure of a drive or path.
TYPE	Displays the contents of a text file.
VER	Displays the Windows version.
VERIFY	Tells Windows whether to verify that your files are written correctly to a disk.
VOL	Displays a disk volume label and serial number.
XCOPY	Copies files and directory trees.
WMIC	Displays WMI information inside interactive command shell.

BULK INSERT Command

BULK INSERT is a T-SQL command which corresponds to bcp "in" action for uploading a file into a database table. The command includes an optional format file. Generally it is a good idea to use format file with BULK INSERT and bcp for more reliable and successful data transfer.

Format File Generation with bcp

Format file can be created manually by an editor or automatically by bcp. Execute at Command Prompt as one line with no breaks to create a non-XML format file:

```
bcp AdventureWorks2012.HumanResources.Department format nul -T -n -f
f:\data\bcpdemo\hrdept.fmt
```

The generated format file:

```
11.0
4
1    SQLSMALLINT    0    2     ""   1    DepartmentID      ""
2    SQLNCHAR       2    100   ""   2    Name              SQL_Latin1_General_CP1_CI_AS
3    SQLNCHAR       2    100   ""   3    GroupName         SQL_Latin1_General_CP1_CI_AS
4    SQLDATETIME    0    8     ""   4    ModifiedDate      ""
```

11.0 refers to SQL Server 2012 internal version number.

Export Data with bcp Format File Option

We use the format file for exporting the data at Command Prompt.

```
bcp AdventureWorks2012.HumanResources.Department out  f:\data\bcpdemo\hrdept.txt  -f
f:\data\bcpdemo\hrdept.fmt  -T
```

This is how the exported data looks in Notepad:

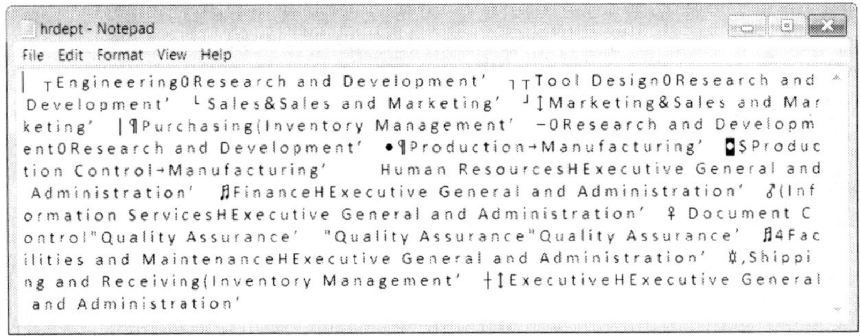

Import Data with BULK INSERT Format File Option

The same format file can be used to import the data into the database with BULK INSERT. First we create an empty table for the data import.

```
USE tempdb;
SELECT TOP(0)
         [DepartmentID] = CONVERT(INT, DepartmentID) --prevent IDENTITY inheritance
        ,[Name]
        ,[GroupName]
        ,[ModifiedDate]
INTO Department
FROM [AdventureWorks2012].[HumanResources].[Department];
GO
-- (0 row(s) affected)
```

```
BULK INSERT Department
        FROM 'f:\data\bcpdemo\hrdept.txt'
        WITH (FORMATFILE = 'f:\data\bcpdemo\hrdept.fmt');
GO
-- (16 row(s) affected)
```

```
SELECT TOP (3) * FROM Department ORDER BY NEWID();
GO
```

DepartmentID	Name	GroupName	ModifiedDate
14	Facilities and Maintenance	Executive General and Administration	2002-06-01 00:00:00.000
15	Shipping and Receiving	Inventory Management	2002-06-01 00:00:00.000
3	Sales	Sales and Marketing	2002-06-01 00:00:00.000

We can use the -n native mode for exporting data and DATAFILETYPE for importing.

```
bcp AdventureWorks2012.HumanResources.Shift out f:\temp\shift.txt -n -T
```

```
CREATE TABLE [Shift](
        [ShiftID] [tinyint]  NOT NULL,
        [Name] [dbo].[Name] NOT NULL,
        [StartTime] [time](7) NOT NULL,
        [EndTime] [time](7) NOT NULL,
        [ModifiedDate] [datetime] NOT NULL,
);
```

```
BULK INSERT Shift    FROM 'f:\temp\shift.txt'    WITH (DATAFILETYPE='native');
```

Importing & Exporting Images

Importing & exporting images and other binary large objects (BLOB) like documents require special techniques. We use OPENROWSET BULK method to import an image. **Typically varbinary(max) data type is used to store binary objects in the database.**

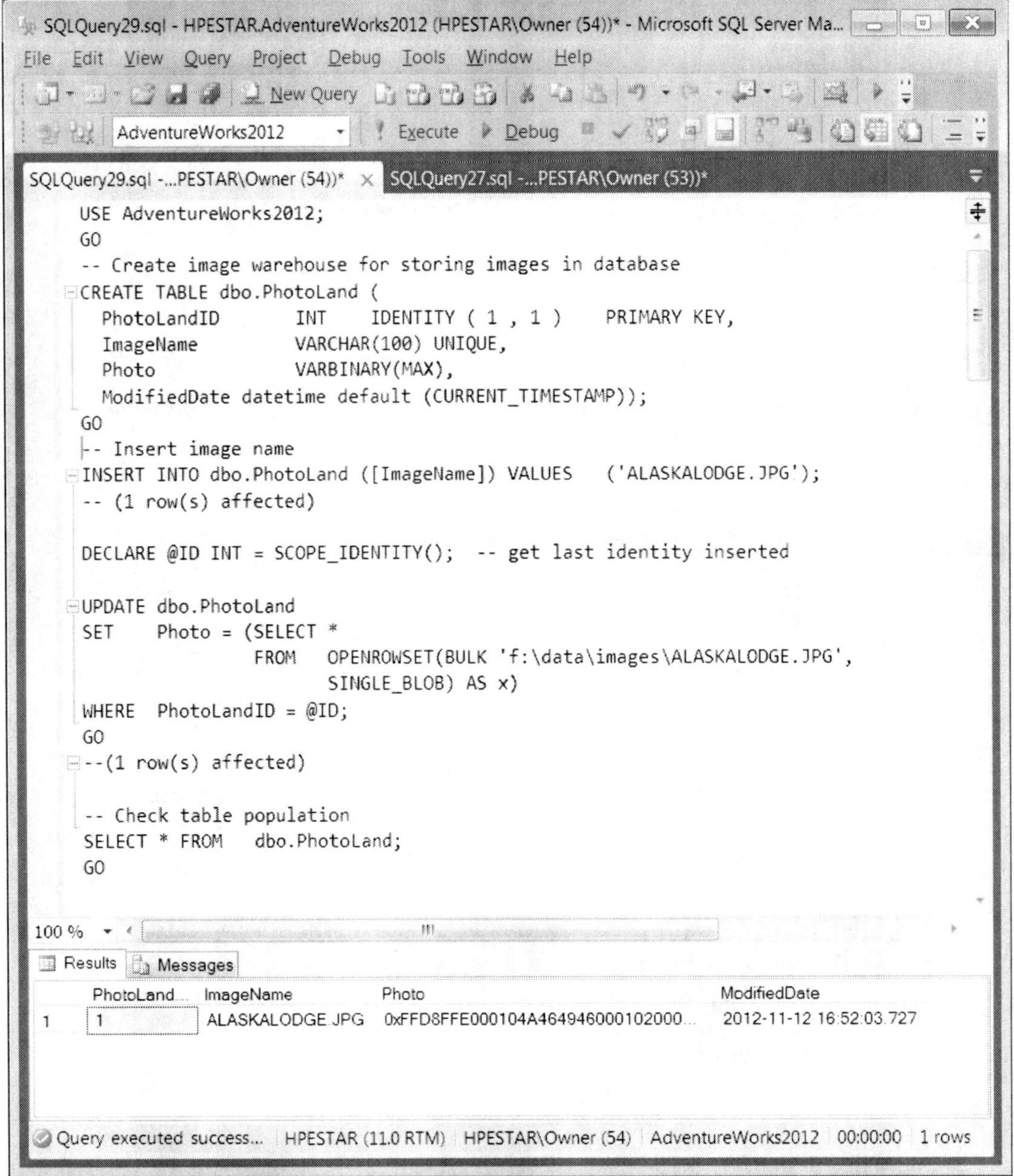

Exporting Image with bcp

The bcp command can be used to export an image. In the following demo, it is executed from xp_cmdshell. **NOTE: on most production servers the xp_cmdshell option is disabled due to security concerns.**

```
DECLARE  @Command NVARCHAR(4000);

-- Keep the command on ONE LINE - here it wraps around
SET @Command = 'bcp "SELECT Photo FROM AdventureWorks2012.dbo.PhotoLand WHERE
PhotoLandID=1"  queryout "F:\temp\ALASKALODGE.jpg" -T -n' ;

PRINT @Command -- debugging

EXEC xp_cmdshell   @Command;
GO
/*NULL
Starting copy...
NULL
1 rows copied.
Network packet size (bytes): 4096
Clock Time (ms.) Total     : 203    Average : (4.93 rows per sec.)
NULL  */
```

Building a bcp Format File Interactively for Image Export

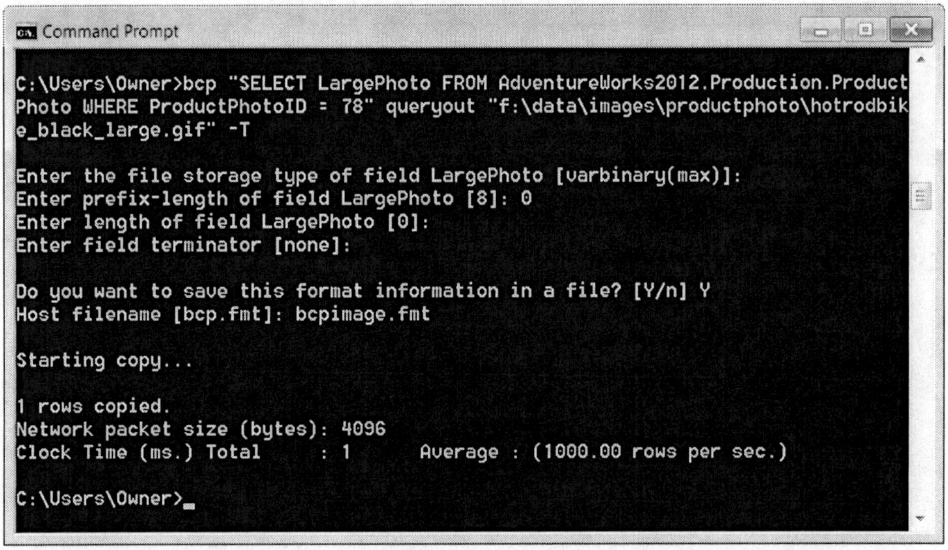

```
Command Prompt

C:\Users\Owner>bcp "SELECT LargePhoto FROM AdventureWorks2012.Production.Product
Photo WHERE ProductPhotoID = 78" queryout "f:\data\images\productphoto\hotrodbik
e_black_large.gif" -T

Enter the file storage type of field LargePhoto [varbinary(max)]:
Enter prefix-length of field LargePhoto [8]: 0
Enter length of field LargePhoto [0]:
Enter field terminator [none]:

Do you want to save this format information in a file? [Y/n] Y
Host filename [bcp.fmt]: bcpimage.fmt

Starting copy...

1 rows copied.
Network packet size (bytes): 4096
Clock Time (ms.) Total     : 1      Average : (1000.00 rows per sec.)

C:\Users\Owner>_
```

Exporting All Images from Table

The content of the previously created bcp format file.

```
11.0
1
1    SQLBINARY    0    0    ""  1    LargePhoto        ""
```

T-SQL script for exporting all images to the file system from Production.ProductPhoto table LargePhoto column, which is varbinary(max) data type.

```
USE AdventureWorks2012;
GO
```

```
DECLARE  @Command   VARCHAR(4000),  @PhotoID  INT,  @ImageFileName VARCHAR(128) ;
DECLARE PHOTOcursor CURSOR  FOR
        SELECT ProductPhotoID,  LargePhotoFileName  FROM  Production.ProductPhoto
        WHERE  LargePhotoFileName != 'no_image_available_large.gif';

OPEN PHOTOcursor FETCH NEXT FROM PHOTOcursor INTO @PhotoID,  @ImageFileName;

WHILE (@@FETCH_STATUS = 0) -- Cursor loop
 BEGIN
-- No carriage return or new line in bcp command string!
  SET @Command = CONCAT('bcp "SELECT LargePhoto FROM
AdventureWorks2012.Production.ProductPhoto WHERE ProductPhotoID = ',
  convert(VARCHAR,@PhotoID) + '" queryout "f:\data\images\productphoto\',
  @ImageFileName,'" -T -f "f:\data\images\bcpimage.fmt" ');

  PRINT @Command -- debugging
  EXEC xp_cmdshell @Command, no_output;

  FETCH NEXT FROM PHOTOcursor  INTO @PhotoID,    @ImageFileName;
 END;  -- cursor loop

CLOSE PHOTOcursor; DEALLOCATE PHOTOcursor;
GO
```

Product Photo Icons in the ProductPhoto Folder

The folder contains 100 exported product photos. The photos cannot be visualized in SSMS. but in the file system or SSRS reports. The following is a partial list of image icons.

In SSIS the Export Column & Import Column Transformations can be used for exporting and importing a set of images to and from folders.

CHAPTER 19: Maintaining Data Integrity in the Enterprise

Why is Data Integrity Paramount

A business or organization can only operate efficiently with good quality data. Computers were the real engine of economic progress since the 1950-s. Without computers, we would pretty much be at post Second World War level. Computers work with data and produce data. As the saying goes: garbage in, garbage out. Therefore it is our job as database designers, database developers and database administrators to ensure the data integrity in a database. What are the sources of the bad data? They can be data feeds received from various sources, data entry by people, and bugs in database or application programming. The best way to minimize bugs is putting each piece of new software through rigorous quality assurance (QA) process. To prevent bad data getting into the database there are a number of possibilities: table design, constraints, stored procedures, triggers and application software.

At the lowest level, constraints make up the guarding force over data integrity. The default constraint is different from the rest: it provides predefined default value if no value is provided for a cell (a column in a row), it does not give an error message.

```
USE AdventureWorks2012;
SELECT          ConstraintType = type_desc,   [Count] = COUNT(*)
FROM sys.objects
WHERE type_desc in      (
                        'CHECK_CONSTRAINT',
                        'DEFAULT_CONSTRAINT',
                        'FOREIGN_KEY_CONSTRAINT',
                        'PRIMARY_KEY_CONSTRAINT',
                        'UNIQUE_CONSTRAINT'
                        )
GROUP BY type_desc  ORDER BY type_desc;
```

ConstraintType	Count
CHECK_CONSTRAINT	89
DEFAULT_CONSTRAINT	152
FOREIGN_KEY_CONSTRAINT	90
PRIMARY_KEY_CONSTRAINT	71
UNIQUE_CONSTRAINT	1

Entity Integrity

Entity Integrity defines a row as a unique entity for a particular table. The main enforcing mechanisms are: NOT NULL constraint and unique index. PRIMARY KEY implies not null, and unique index automatically created. In the Production.Product table ProductID is the INT IDENTITY PRIMARY KEY, Name & ProductNumber are NATURAL KEYs and rowguid is a system generated unique key. All four keys are not null and all have unique index defined. The implication is that we can use any of 4 columns for row identification. However, ProductID INT (4 bytes) column is the most efficient row (record) identifier.

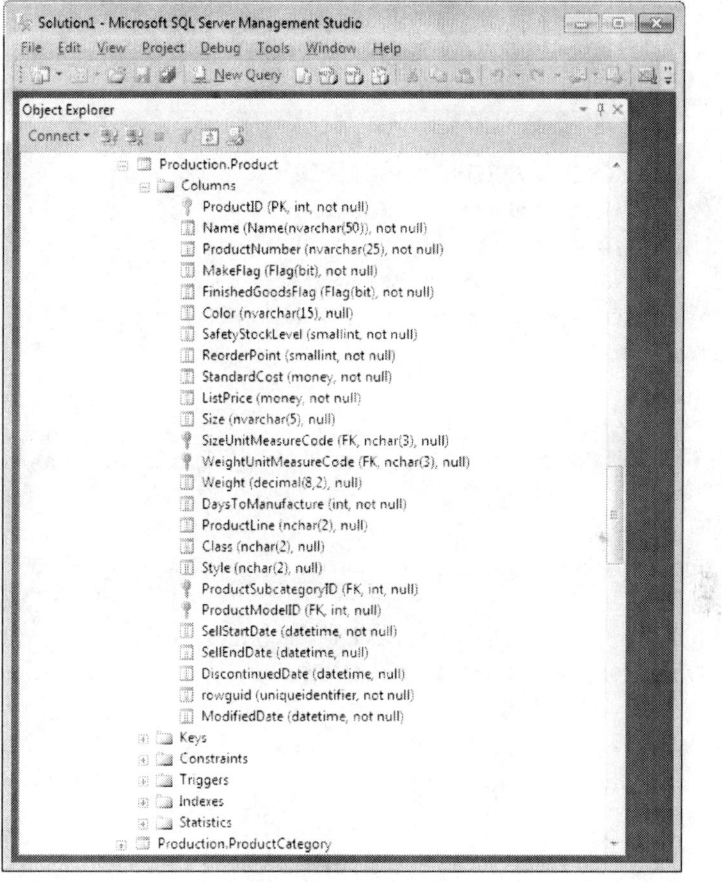

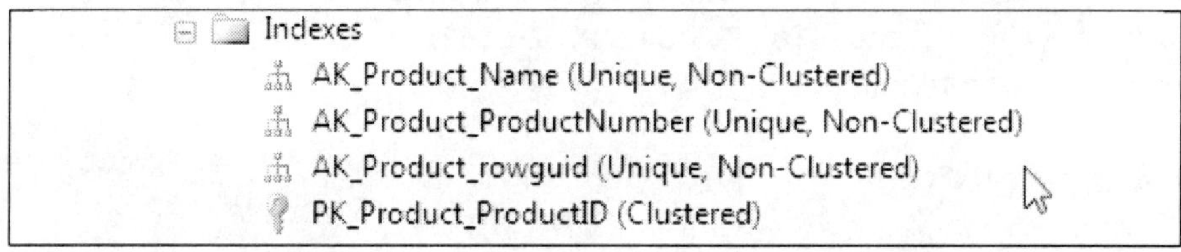

How to Remove Duplicates in a Table

The best way to prevent duplicates is by placing a UNIQUE KEY or unique index on the unique column(s). PRIMARY KEY & UNIQUE KEY constraints automatically create a unique index on the key column(s). If the entire row is a duplicate, removal is real simple with the DISTINCT clause.

```
SELECT DISTINCT * INTO T2 FROM T1;
GO
```

If duplicates are only in one or more columns, then duplicates removal is fairly easy with the ROW_NUMBER method, it is more involved with the GROUP BY method (prior to SQL Server 2005).

```
-- Create test table
USE tempdb;
SELECT          ProductID=CONVERT(int, ProductID),
                ProductName = Name,   ProductNumber,
                ListPrice = ListPrice + 1.00
INTO Product
FROM AdventureWorks2012.Production.Product    WHERE ListPrice > 0.0;
GO  -- (304 row(s) affected)
```

```
-- Unique index prevents duplicates
CREATE UNIQUE INDEX idxProd ON Product(ProductName, ProductNumber);
GO
```

```
-- Try to insert  duplicates on ProductName & ProductNumber
INSERT INTO Product
SELECT          TOP (100) ProductID=CONVERT(int, ProductID) + 1000,
                ProductName = Name, ProductNumber,
                ListPrice = ListPrice + 2.00
FROM AdventureWorks2008.Production.Product
WHERE ListPrice > 0.0 ORDER BY NEWID();
GO
/*  Msg 2601, Level 14, State 1, Line 2
Cannot insert duplicate key row in object 'dbo.Product' with unique index 'idxProd'.
The duplicate key value is (Fender Set - Mountain, FE-6654).
The statement has been terminated.  */
```

```
DROP INDEX Product.idxProd;
GO
```

Rows with Duplicates Can Be Numbered in Ordered or Random Manner

```
-- Insert 100 duplicates on ProductName & ProductNumber
INSERT INTO Product
SELECT        TOP (100) ProductID=CONVERT(int, ProductID) + 1000,
              ProductName = Name, ProductNumber,   ListPrice = ListPrice + 2.00
FROM AdventureWorks2008.Production.Product
WHERE ListPrice > 0.0
ORDER BY NEWID();
GO
```

```
-- Quantify duplicates with GROUP BY query
SELECT ProductName, ProductNumber, [Count] = count(*)
FROM Product
GROUP BY ProductName, ProductNumber
        HAVING count(*) > 1
ORDER BY ProductName, ProductNumber;
GO -- (100 row(s) affected) - Partial results.
```

ProductName	ProductNumber	Count
Bike Wash - Dissolver	CL-9009	2
Classic Vest, L	VE-C304-L	2
Classic Vest, S	VE-C304-S	2
Front Brakes	FB-9873	2
Full-Finger Gloves, M	GL-F110-M	2

```
-- Quantify duplicates with ROW_NUMBER OVER - we don't care about duplicates ordering
;WITH CTE AS (
   SELECT RN=ROW_NUMBER() OVER (PARTITION BY ProductName, ProductNumber
   ORDER BY NEWID() ),  ProductName, ProductNumber
   FROM Product)
SELECT * FROM CTE WHERE RN > 1
ORDER BY ProductName, ProductNumber;
GO -- (100 row(s) affected) - Partial results.
```

RN	ProductName	ProductNumber
2	Bike Wash - Dissolver	CL-9009
2	Classic Vest, L	VE-C304-L
2	Classic Vest, S	VE-C304-S
2	Front Brakes	FB-9873
2	Full-Finger Gloves, M	GL-F110-M

Remove Duplicates with CTE & ROW_NUMBER OVER PARTITION BY

```
-- To removal of duplicates is real easy with CTE & ROW_NUMBER
;WITH CTE AS (
   SELECT RN=ROW_NUMBER() OVER (PARTITION BY ProductName, ProductNumber
   ORDER BY NEWID()),  ProductName, ProductNumber    FROM Product)
DELETE CTE  WHERE RN > 1;
GO -- (100 row(s) affected)
```

```
-- Test for duplicates again
SELECT ProductName, ProductNumber, [Count] = count(*)
FROM Product  GROUP BY ProductName, ProductNumber  HAVING count(*) > 1
ORDER BY ProductName, ProductNumber;
GO -- (0 row(s) affected)
```

```
SELECT COUNT(*) FROM Product;  -- 304
GO
```

Remove Duplicates with GROUP BY

```
-- Insert  duplicates on ProductName & ProductNumber
INSERT INTO Product     SELECT      TOP (100) ProductID=CONVERT(int, ProductID) + 1000,
                        ProductName = Name, ProductNumber,     ListPrice = ListPrice + 2.00
FROM AdventureWorks2008.Production.Product  WHERE ListPrice > 0.0  ORDER BY NEWID();
GO
```

```
-- Sample of conflicting data - It is a business decision what to keep
SELECT TOP (4) * FROM Product WHERE ProductNumber IN
   ( SELECT ProductNumber FROM Product   GROUP BY ProductNumber HAVING count(*) > 1    )
ORDER BY ProductNumber;
```

ProductID	ProductName	ProductNumber	ListPrice
992	Mountain-500 Black, 48	BK-M18B-48	540.9900
1992	Mountain-500 Black, 48	BK-M18B-48	541.9900
993	Mountain-500 Black, 52	BK-M18B-52	540.9900
1993	Mountain-500 Black, 52	BK-M18B-52	541.9900

```
-- Assume it does not matter which duplicate to keep: any ProductID and any ListPrice OK
SELECT ProductID=MIN(ProductID), ProductName, ProductNumber, ListPrice=MIN(ListPrice)
INTO Product1 FROM Product GROUP BY ProductName, ProductNumber ORDER BY ProductID;
GO  -- (304 row(s) affected)
```

Domain Integrity

A domain defines the possible values for a column. Domain Integrity rules enforce the validity data in a column:

Data type	table design
Data length	table design
Nullability	table design
Collation	table design
Allowable values	check constraints - table design
Default value	default constraints - table design

CHECK constraint is used for simple rules such as OrderQty > 0. UDF CHECK constraints can be used for complex rules. In addition, at the development phase, triggers, stored procedures and client-side application software can be developed to enforce Domain Integrity.

Server-side CHECK constraints are the most desirable. Client-side Domain Integrity enforcement is the least desirable. However, it may happen that there is no database expert on the project and developers feel more confident programming data validity rules in the application software. Ultimately what counts is valid data in the database. Usually big-budget projects can do everything the right way due to the availability of expert-level resources in all areas of the software development project. Basic table definition data from INFORMATION_SCHEMA views.

```
SELECT          COLUMN_NAME, ORDINAL_POSITION, DATA_TYPE, IS_NULLABLE,
                CHARACTER_MAXIMUM_LENGTH, COLLATION_NAME, COLUMN_DEFAULT
FROM INFORMATION_SCHEMA.COLUMNS WHERE TABLE_NAME = 'SalesOrderHeader';
```

COLUMN_NAME	ORDINAL_POSITION	DATA_TYPE	IS_NULLABLE	CHARACTER_MAXIMUM_LENGTH	COLLATION_NAME	COLUMN_DEFAULT
SalesOrderID	1	int	NO	NULL	NULL	NULL
RevisionNumber	2	tinyint	NO	NULL	NULL	((0))
OrderDate	3	datetime	NO	NULL	NULL	(getdate())
DueDate	4	datetime	NO	NULL	NULL	NULL
ShipDate	5	datetime	YES	NULL	NULL	NULL
tatus	6	tinyint	NO	NULL	NULL	((1))
OnlineOrderFlag	7	bit	NO	NULL	NULL	((1))
SalesOrderNumber	8	nvarchar	NO	25	SQL_Latin1_General_CP1_CI_AS	NULL
PurchaseOrderNumber	9	nvarchar	YES	25	SQL_Latin1_General_CP1_CI_AS	NULL
AccountNumber	10	nvarchar	YES	15	SQL_Latin1_General_CP1_CI_AS	NULL
CustomerID	11	int	NO	NULL	NULL	NULL
SalesPersonID	12	int	YES	NULL	NULL	NULL
TerritoryID	13	int	YES	NULL	NULL	NULL
BillToAddressID	14	int	NO	NULL	NULL	NULL
ShipToAddressID	15	int	NO	NULL	NULL	NULL
ShipMethodID	16	int	NO	NULL	NULL	NULL
CreditCardID	17	int	YES	NULL	NULL	NULL
CreditCardApprovalCode	18	varchar	YES	15	SQL_Latin1_General_CP1_CI_AS	NULL
CurrencyRateID	19	int	YES	NULL	NULL	NULL
SubTotal	20	money	NO	NULL	NULL	((0.00))
TaxAmt	21	money	NO	NULL	NULL	((0.00))
Freight	22	money	NO	NULL	NULL	((0.00))
TotalDue	23	money	NO	NULL	NULL	NULL
Comment	24	nvarchar	YES	128	SQL_Latin1_General_CP1_CI_AS	NULL
rowguid	25	uniqueidentifier	NO	NULL	NULL	(newid())
ModifiedDate	26	datetime	NO	NULL	NULL	(getdate())

Domain Integrity Summary Display with sp_help

The sp_help system procedure provides a convenient way to display a summary of Domain Integrity definitions for a table.

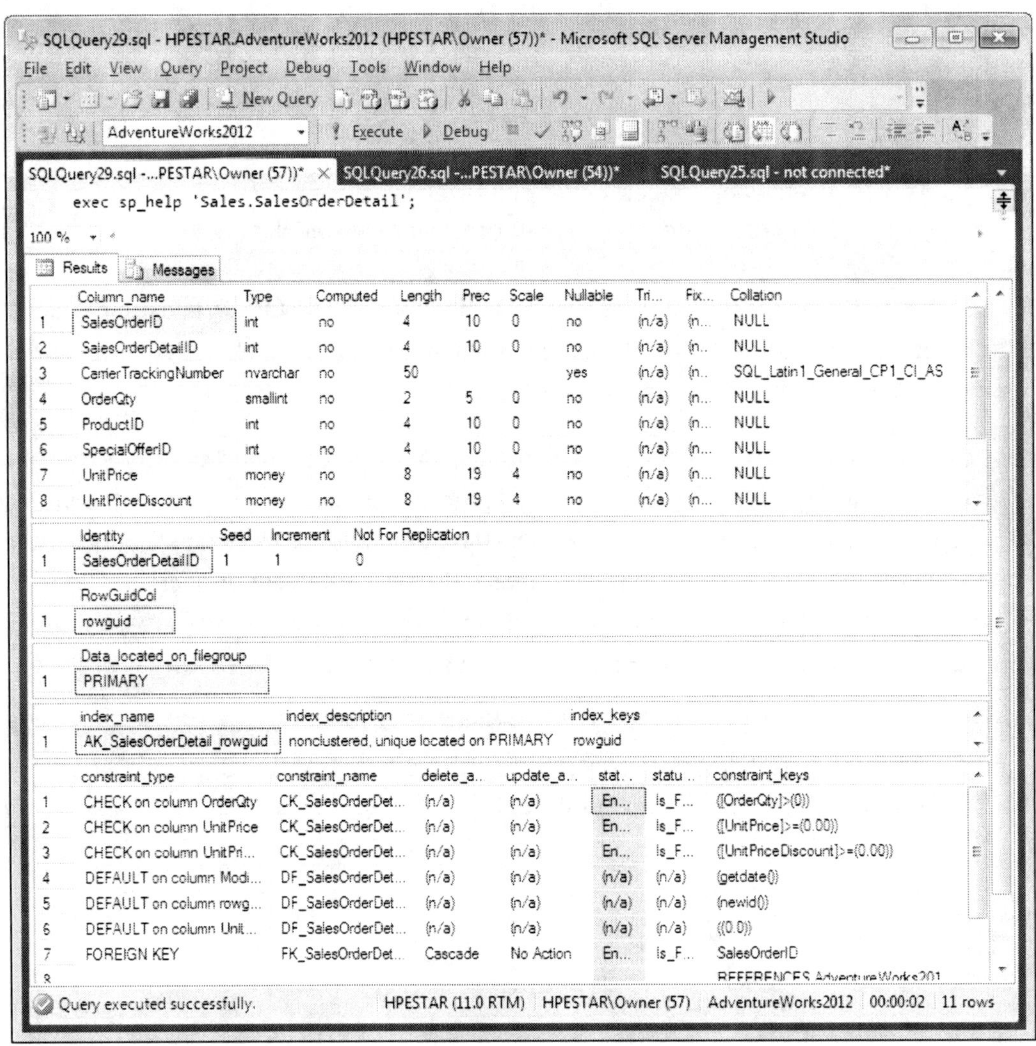

We can query "sys" system views metadata for column definition as well.

```
SELECT * FROM sys.columns
WHERE object_name(object_id) = 'PurchaseOrderHeader'  ORDER BY column_id;
-- (13 row(s) affected) - Partial results.
```

object_id	name	column_id	system_type_id	user_type_id	max_length	precision	scale	collation_name
946102411	PurchaseOrderID	1	56	56	4	10	0	NULL

THE COLUMNPROPERTY() Function

The COLUMNPROPERTY() function can be used for programmatic discovery of column properties. Script to generate SELECT queries for all properties.

```
USE AdventureWorks2012;
GO
```

```
DECLARE @Parms TABLE (Property varchar(32))
INSERT  @Parms VALUES
('AllowsNull'), ('ColumnId'),
('FullTextTypeColumn'), ('IsComputed'),
('IsCursorType'), ('IsDeterministic'),
('IsFulltextIndexed'), ('IsIdentity'),
('IsIdNotForRepl'), ('IsIndexable'),
('IsOutParam'), ('IsPrecise'),
('IsRowGuidCol'), ('IsSystemVerified'),
('IsXmlIndexable'), ('Precision'),
('Scale'), ('StatisticalSemantics'),
('SystemDataAccess'), ('UserDataAccess'),
('UsesAnsiTrim'), ('IsSparse'),
('IsColumnSet')
SELECT CONCAT('SELECT COLUMNPROPERTY( OBJECT_ID(''Person.Person''), ''LastName'', ''',
                    Property, ''') AS [', Property, '];')
FROM @Parms
GO  -- Partial results.
```

```
SELECT COLUMNPROPERTY( OBJECT_ID('Person.Person'), 'LastName', 'AllowsNull') AS [AllowsNull];
SELECT COLUMNPROPERTY( OBJECT_ID('Person.Person'), 'LastName', 'ColumnId') AS [ColumnId];
SELECT COLUMNPROPERTY( OBJECT_ID('Person.Person'), 'LastName', 'FullTextTypeColumn') AS [FullTextTypeColumn];
SELECT COLUMNPROPERTY( OBJECT_ID('Person.Person'), 'LastName', 'IsComputed') AS [IsComputed];
SELECT COLUMNPROPERTY( OBJECT_ID('Person.Person'), 'LastName', 'IsCursorType') AS [IsCursorType];
```

Executing the queries, the column properties are returned one by one.

Column List Using System Views & Data Dictionary

We can combine sys. system views with data dictionary description to get a valuable list when working with domain integrity.

```
USE AdventureWorks2012;
SELECT SCHEMA_NAME(T.schema_id)     AS SchemaName,
    T.name                          AS TableName,
    C.name                          AS ColumnName,
    TP.name                         AS ColumnType,
    C.max_length                    AS ColumnLength,
    COALESCE(EP.value, Space(1))    AS ColumnDesc
FROM   sys.tables AS T
    INNER JOIN sys.columns AS C
        ON T.object_id = C.object_id
    INNER JOIN sys.types AS TP
        ON  C.system_type_id = TP.user_type_id
    LEFT JOIN sys.extended_properties AS EP
        ON EP.major_id = T.object_id
            AND EP.minor_id = C.column_id
ORDER  BY SchemaName,   TableName,  ColumnName;
GO  -- (643 row(s) affected) - Partial Results.
```

Purchasing	PurchaseOrderHeader	EmployeeID	int	4	Employee who created the purchase order. Foreign key to Employee.BusinessEntityID.
Purchasing	PurchaseOrderHeader	Freight	money	8	Shipping cost.
Purchasing	PurchaseOrderHeader	ModifiedDate	datetime	8	Date and time the record was last updated.
Purchasing	PurchaseOrderHeader	OrderDate	datetime	8	Purchase order creation date.
Purchasing	PurchaseOrderHeader	PurchaseOrderID	int	4	Primary key.
Purchasing	PurchaseOrderHeader	PurchaseOrderID	int	4	Clustered index created by a primary key constraint.
Purchasing	PurchaseOrderHeader	RevisionNumber	tinyint	1	Incremental number to track changes to the purchase order over time.
Purchasing	PurchaseOrderHeader	RevisionNumber	tinyint	1	Nonclustered index.
Purchasing	PurchaseOrderHeader	ShipDate	datetime	8	Estimated shipment date from the vendor.
Purchasing	PurchaseOrderHeader	ShipMethodID	int	4	Shipping method. Foreign key to ShipMethod.ShipMethodID.
Purchasing	PurchaseOrderHeader	Status	tinyint	1	Order current status. 1 = Pending; 2 = Approved; 3 = Rejected; 4 = Complete
Purchasing	PurchaseOrderHeader	Status	tinyint	1	Nonclustered index.
Purchasing	PurchaseOrderHeader	SubTotal	money	8	Purchase order subtotal. Computed as SUM(PurchaseOrderDetail.LineTotal)for the appropriate PurchaseOrderID.
Purchasing	PurchaseOrderHeader	TaxAmt	money	8	Tax amount.
Purchasing	PurchaseOrderHeader	TotalDue	money	8	Total due to vendor. Computed as Subtotal + TaxAmt + Freight.
Purchasing	PurchaseOrderHeader	VendorID	int	4	Vendor with whom the purchase order is placed. Foreign key to Vendor.BusinessEntityID.

Declarative Referential Integrity

Referential Integrity refers to ensuring that relationships between tables remain consistent. Declarative means it is part of table setup, not in programming objects like stored procedure. When one table attempts to create a FOREIGN KEY to another (PK) table, Referential Integrity requires that the primary key value exists in the referenced (PK) table. The optional cascading update & cascading delete ensure that changes made to the primary table are reflected in the linked referencing (FK) table. For example, if a row is deleted in the primary table, then all referencing rows are automatically deleted in the linked (FK) table when ON DELETE CASCADE is set. All three Referential Integrity constraint actions are demonstrated by the following script.

```
USE tempdb;

-- Create 2 test tables with PK-FK relationship
CREATE TABLE Product (
	ProductID INT PRIMARY KEY,
	ProductName varchar(50) UNIQUE,
	ProductNumber varchar(20) UNIQUE,
	ListPrice MONEY);
GO
```

```
-- First we test without the DELETE CASCADE action
CREATE TABLE OrderDetail (
	SalesOrderID INT,
	SalesOrderDetailID INT,
	PRIMARY KEY (SalesOrderID, SalesOrderDetailID),
	OrderQty INT ,
	ProductID INT REFERENCES Product(ProductID)  -- ON DELETE CASCADE  );
GO
```

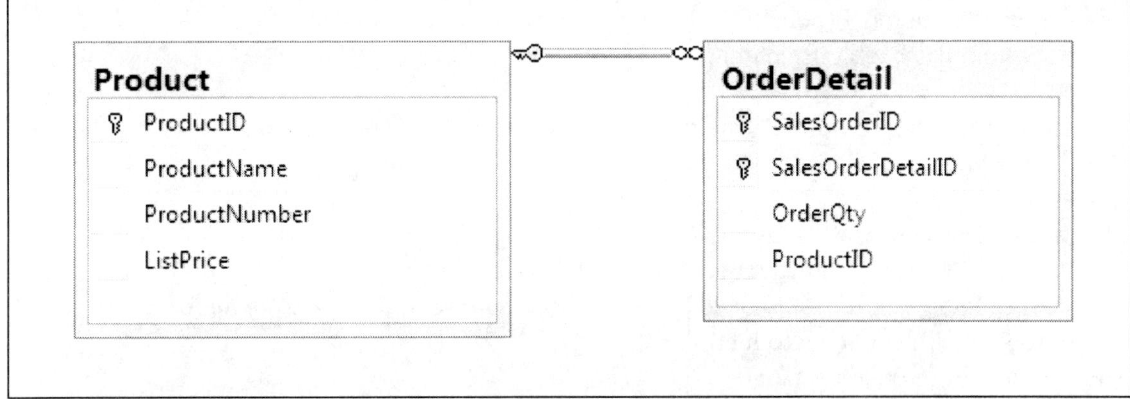

FOREIGN KEY Constraint Protects Two Ways

```
-- Populate test tables
INSERT Product
SELECT ProductID, Name, ProductNumber, ListPrice
FROM AdventureWorks2012.Production.Product
ORDER BY ProductID;
GO
--(504 row(s) affected)
```

```
INSERT OrderDetail
SELECT          SalesOrderID,
                SalesOrderDetailID,
                OrderQty,
                ProductID
FROM AdventureWorks2012.Sales.SalesOrderDetail
ORDER BY SalesOrderID, SalesOrderDetailID;
GO
-- (121317 row(s) affected)
```

```
-- Attempting to insert into FK table a reference to a non-existing (PK) ProductID
INSERT OrderDetail
SELECT          SalesOrderID = 100000,
                SalesOrderDetailID = 1000000,
                OrderQty = 5,
                ProductID = 2000
GO
/* Msg 547, Level 16, State 0, Line 1
The INSERT statement conflicted with the FOREIGN KEY constraint
"FK__OrderDeta__Produ__59FA5E80". The conflict occurred in database "tempdb", table
"dbo.Product", column 'ProductID'.
The statement has been terminated.   */
```

```
-- Attempting to delete from  PK table a ProductID which is referenced from the FK table
DELETE Product WHERE ProductID = 800;
GO
/* Msg 547, Level 16, State 0, Line 1
The DELETE statement conflicted with the REFERENCE constraint
"FK__OrderDeta__Produ__59FA5E80". The conflict occurred in database "tempdb", table
"dbo.OrderDetail", column 'ProductID'.
The statement has been terminated.  */
```

ON DELETE CASCADE Action Causes DELETE Chain Reaction

```
-- Change FOREIGN KEY:  specify ON DELETE  CASCADE  option
-- Lookup FK constraints name
SELECT * FROM INFORMATION_SCHEMA.REFERENTIAL_CONSTRAINTS;
```

CONSTRAINT_CATALOG	CONSTRAINT_SCHEMA	CONSTRAINT_NAME	UNIQUE_CONSTRAINT_CATALOG	UNIQUE_CONSTRAINT_SCHEMA	UNIQUE_CONSTRAINT_NAME	MATCH_OPTION	UPDATE_RULE	DELETE_RULE
tempdb	dbo	FK__OrderDeta__Produ__0A9D95DB	tempdb	dbo	PK__Product__B40CC6ED66641298	SIMPLE	NO ACTION	NO ACTION

```
BEGIN TRANSACTION
GO
ALTER TABLE dbo.OrderDetail  DROP CONSTRAINT FK__OrderDeta__Produ__0A9D95DB;
GO
ALTER TABLE dbo.Product SET (LOCK_ESCALATION = TABLE)
GO
COMMIT TRANSACTION -- Command(s) completed successfully.
```

```
BEGIN TRANSACTION;
GO
ALTER TABLE dbo.OrderDetail  ADD CONSTRAINT FK__OrderDeta__Produ__0A9D95DB
FOREIGN KEY (ProductID)  REFERENCES dbo.Product (ProductID) ON DELETE  CASCADE;
GO
ALTER TABLE dbo.OrderDetail SET (LOCK_ESCALATION = TABLE);
GO
COMMIT TRANSACTION;  -- Command(s) completed successfully.
```

```
SELECT * FROM INFORMATION_SCHEMA.REFERENTIAL_CONSTRAINTS;
```

CONSTRAINT_CATALOG	CONSTRAINT_SCHEMA	CONSTRAINT_NAME	UNIQUE_CONSTRAINT_CATALOG	UNIQUE_CONSTRAINT_SCHEMA	UNIQUE_CONSTRAINT_NAME	MATCH_OPTION	UPDATE_RULE	DELETE_RULE
tempdb	dbo	FK__OrderDeta__Produ__0A9D95DB	tempdb	dbo	PK__Product__B40CC6ED66641298	SIMPLE	NO ACTION	CASCADE

```
SELECT COUNT(*) FROM OrderDetail;
GO   -- 121317
```

```
-- Cascading DELETE: first DELETE all referencing FK records, then DELETE PK record
DELETE Product WHERE ProductID = 800;
GO
-- (1 row(s) affected)
```

```
SELECT COUNT(*) FROM OrderDetail;
GO  -- 120822
```

FOREIGN KEY Constraints Represent the Only Connections Among Tables

While we talk about linked tables in functional terms such as master/header-detail, parent-child, dimension-fact, junction, etc., **there is only a single way to connect tables: FOREIGN KEY references PRIMARY KEY in another table**. We are going to demonstrate it in a grand manner: we will create 290 tables with the names of all the employees of AdventureWorks Cycles (fictional) company in a new test database. We shall connect all of them with FOREIGN KEY constraints: employee (FK table) references manager (PK table).

```
USE master;
GO
CREATE DATABASE AWOrgChart;
GO
USE AWOrgChart;
GO
```

```
DECLARE @SQL NVARCHAR(max) = '';

WITH CTE (ID, Emp, Mgr, MgrNode) -- CTE with column names
  AS
(    SELECT E.BusinessEntityID,
          Emp=CONCAT(P.FirstName, SPACE(1), P.LastName),
          NULL,
          NULL
     FROM   AdventureWorks2012.HumanResources.Employee E
          INNER JOIN AdventureWorks2012.Person.Person P
               ON E.BusinessEntityID = P.BusinessEntityID
     WHERE  E.OrganizationNode = 0x                          -- Root node
     UNION
     SELECT E.BusinessEntityID,
         CONCAT(P.FirstName, SPACE(1), P.LastName)                AS Emp,
         CONCAT(PP.FirstName, SPACE(1), PP.LastName)              AS Mgr,
         E.OrganizationNode.GetAncestor(1)                        AS SuperNode
     FROM   AdventureWorks2012.HumanResources.Employee E
          INNER JOIN AdventureWorks2012.Person.Person P
               ON E.BusinessEntityID = P.BusinessEntityID
          INNER JOIN AdventureWorks2012.HumanResources.Employee EE
               ON ( EE.OrganizationNode =  E.OrganizationNode.GetAncestor(1) )
          INNER JOIN AdventureWorks2012.Person.Person PP
               ON EE.BusinessEntityID = PP.BusinessEntityID)
```

```
SELECT @SQL = CONCAT(@SQL, CONCAT('CREATE TABLE ', QUOTENAME(Emp),
                    '( ID INT PRIMARY KEY ,',
                         ' MgrID INT ',
                                   CASE
               WHEN Mgr IS NOT NULL THEN CONCAT(' REFERENCES ',
                                   QUOTENAME(Mgr),   '(ID)')
               ELSE ''   END, '); '))
FROM   CTE;

PRINT @SQL;  -- Partial text.
```

CREATE TABLE [Ken Sánchez](ID INT PRIMARY KEY , MgrID INT);
CREATE TABLE [Terri Duffy](ID INT PRIMARY KEY , MgrID INT REFERENCES [Ken Sánchez](ID));
CREATE TABLE [Roberto Tamburello](ID INT PRIMARY KEY , MgrID INT REFERENCES [Terri Duffy](ID));
CREATE TABLE [Rob Walters](ID INT PRIMARY KEY , MgrID INT REFERENCES [Roberto Tamburello](ID));
CREATE TABLE [Gail Erickson](ID INT PRIMARY KEY , MgrID INT REFERENCES [Roberto Tamburello](ID));
CREATE TABLE [Jossef Goldberg](ID INT PRIMARY KEY , MgrID INT REFERENCES [Roberto Tamburello](ID));
CREATE TABLE [Dylan Miller](ID INT PRIMARY KEY , MgrID INT REFERENCES [Roberto Tamburello](ID));
CREATE TABLE [Diane Margheim](ID INT PRIMARY KEY , MgrID INT REFERENCES [Dylan Miller](ID));
CREATE TABLE [Gigi Matthew](ID INT PRIMARY KEY , MgrID INT REFERENCES [Dylan Miller](ID));
CREATE TABLE [Michael Raheem](ID INT PRIMARY KEY , MgrID INT REFERENCES [Dylan Miller](ID));
CREATE TABLE [Ovidiu Cracium](ID INT PRIMARY KEY , MgrID INT REFERENCES [Roberto Tamburello](ID));
CREATE TABLE [Thierry D'Hers](ID INT PRIMARY KEY , MgrID INT REFERENCES [Ovidiu Cracium](ID));

The functional meaning of Terry Duffy "references" Ken Sanchez: Duffy reports to Sanchez.

```
EXEC sp_executeSQL @SQL;  -- Dynamic SQL execution: create 290 linked tables
GO
```

```
-- USE master;
DROP DATABASE AWOrgChart;
```

Diagram Tool Can Be Used for Organizational Charts

We can use the diagram tool in the AWOrgChart database as an orgchart tool. We add a chosen table to the diagram, for example, [Ken Sanchez]. With the right click menu, we add related tables, set view to table name only & arrange selection. The result is orgchart with the CEO and executive managers.

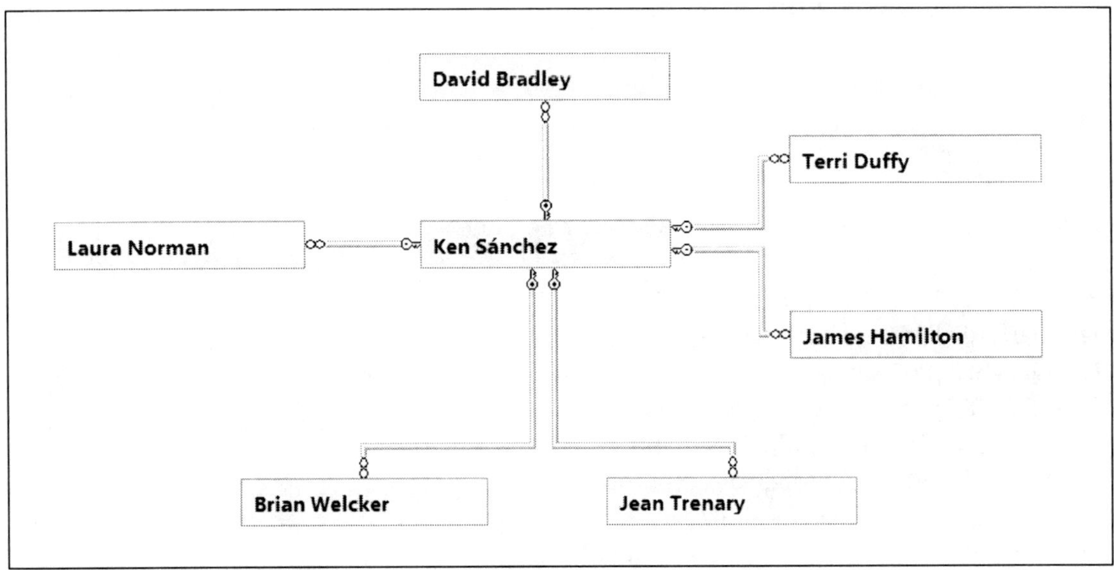

Orgchart starting with [David Hamilton]. Hamilton reports to Krebs (Gold Key).

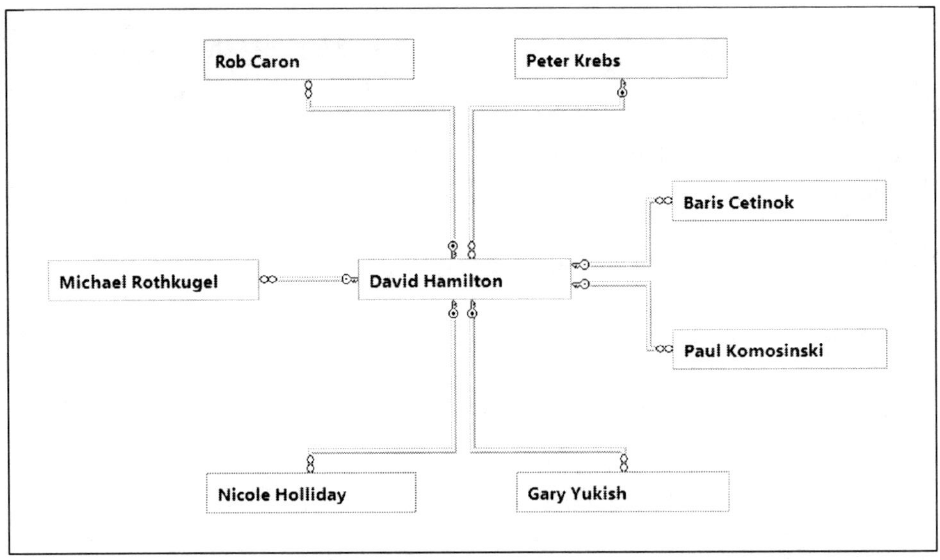

Chain of Command Recursive Query

Find all ancestors (superiors) of a tree node(employee), all the up to the root of the tree (CEO in this instance).

```
USE AdventureWorks; DECLARE @EmployeeID INT = 100;
WITH CTE(Name, EmployeeID, ManagerID, Level)
   AS (SELECT      CONCAT(FirstName,' ', LastName),
                   EmployeeID,    ManagerID,  0 AS Level
      FROM   HumanResources.Employee AS E
         INNER JOIN Person.Contact AS C
             ON C.ContactID = E.ContactID
      WHERE  EmployeeID = @EmployeeID
      UNION ALL
      SELECT       CONCAT(C.FirstName,' ',C.LastName),
                   HRE.EmployeeID,  HRE.ManagerID,  Level + 1
      FROM   HumanResources.Employee AS HRE
         INNER JOIN Person.Contact AS C
             ON C.ContactID = HRE.ContactID
         INNER JOIN CTE AS E
             ON E.ManagerID = HRE.EmployeeID)
SELECT STUFF((SELECT CONCAT(', ', Name)
        FROM   CTE      ORDER  BY Level
        FOR XML path('')), 1, 2, '') AS [Chain of Command];
```

Chain of Command
Lane Sacksteder, Yuhong Li, Peter Krebs, James Hamilton, Ken Sánchez

Enterprise-Level Business Rules Enforcement

Enterprise-Level Business Rules can be enforced by stored procedures & triggers on the server-side and application programs on the client-side. While stored procedures & application programs can be used to implement a complex set of business rules, they can only effect the current application. Stored procedure or application cannot catch an UPDATE transaction, for example, coming from a legacy application nobody dares to touch at the IT department. In a way stored procedure can be configured to perform after-the-fact near-real-time updates for recently posted data: configure the stored procedure as SQL Server Agent job and schedule it to run each minute.

Special Role of Triggers

Triggers, on the other hand, can catch, for example, an INSERT to the ProductPrice table, wherever it is coming from; current in-house application software, old in-house application, another profit-center of the enterprise application or 3rd party software package. An example for an enterprise business rule: convert foreign currency pricing to USD in the INSERT record to ProductPrice using the latest conversion rates from the ForeignExchange table. A constraint cannot be used to implement such a rule, a trigger can. Trigger code almost as flexible as stored procedure code. Triggers can also be used for cross-database referential integrity enforcement. While triggers are compiled into one database, they can access tables in another database. Because of their omnipotent nature, triggers are frequently misapplied as fix-it-all tools.

WARNING
Triggers are high maintenance database objects. Triggers are not for junior staff. Dropped/disabled triggers do not "COMPLAIN": stealth behavior.

Triggers are just like silent workhorses. They can be forgotten after months of operation since they don't have to be called explicitly from the client-side application programs, they are event launched on the server-side. DDL trigger can be applied to guard DML triggers, but then someone or something has to guard the DDL trigger as well. On the other hand, a dropped stored procedure causes user error ("complains"). Dropped trigger can cause user error also, but the error cannot easily be traced back the trigger.

The following update trigger will prevent last name update from new software, old software, other department's software or even 3rd party software package.

```
CREATE TRIGGER trgEmployee  ON Employee FOR UPDATE AS
  IF (UPDATE(LastName))                    BEGIN
    RAISERROR ('Last name cannot be changed', 16, 1);   ROLLBACK TRAN;    RETURN;      END
GO
```

Product Reorder Trigger

The UPDATE trigger is attached to the Products table. It fires whenever there is an UPDATE for the table, no matter what kind of software application from what part of the world executed the UPDATE statement. **A trigger should never return a result set**. However, there is no error if we try to return a result set with a SELECT statement just like in a stored procedure. For testing & debugging purposes we can return results.

```
USE Northwind
GO
```

```
-- Logging table for product reorder notices
CREATE TABLE Reorder (
        ID INT IDENTITY(1,1) PRIMARY KEY,
        Message varchar(256),
        CreateDate datetime default (CURRENT_TIMESTAMP));
GO
```

```
IF EXISTS (select * from sys.objects where type='TR' and name = 'trgProductReorder')
        DROP TRIGGER trgProductReorder
GO
```

```
CREATE TRIGGER trgProductReorder
ON Products FOR UPDATE
AS
 BEGIN
   SET NOCOUNT ON;
   DECLARE @MsgText     varchar(128),    @QtyOnHand    int,   @ReorderLevel int;
   SELECT @MsgText = CONCAT('Please place a reorder  for ',  Rtrim(ProductName))
   FROM   inserted;

   SELECT @QtyOnHand = UnitsInStock,   @ReorderLevel = ReorderLevel   FROM   inserted;

   IF @QtyOnHand < @ReorderLevel
        INSERT Reorder  (Message)        SELECT @MsgText;

 --select * from deleted -- for testing &debugging only
 --select * from inserted
 --select @MsgText
 END
GO
```

A Trigger Should Never Return A Result Set Like A Stored Procedure

Check Data Manipulation Language (DML) trigger existence with sp_helptrigger system procedure.

```
EXEC sp_helptrigger Products ;
GO
```

trigger_name	trigger_owner	isupdate	isdelete	isinsert	isafter	isinsteadof	trigger_schema
trgProductReorder	dbo	1	0	0	1	0	dbo

```
-- Test trigger
/* For demonstration purposes, the debugging statements in trigger were uncommented */
UPDATE Products
        SET    UnitsInStock = 10
        WHERE  ProductID = 77;
GO
```

SQL Server UPDATE is implemented as complete deleted (old) and inserted (new) rows. Even if 1 byte updated, a complete row deleted and complete row inserted generated for logging.

deleted table row:

ProductID	ProductName	SupplierID	CategoryID	QuantityPerUnit	UnitPrice	**UnitsInStock**	UnitsOnOrder	ReorderLevel	Discontinued
77	Original Frankfurter grüne Soße	12	2	12 boxes	13.00	**50**	0	15	0

inserted table row:

ProductID	ProductName	SupplierID	CategoryID	QuantityPerUnit	UnitPrice	**UnitsInStock**	UnitsOnOrder	ReorderLevel	Discontinued
77	Original Frankfurter grüne Soße	12	2	12 boxes	13.00	**10**	0	15	0

```
SELECT * FROM   Reorder;
GO
```

ID	Message	CreateDate
1	Please place a reorder for Original Frankfurter grüne Soße	2016-11-25 06:06:45.043

```
DROP TRIGGER trgProductReorder;
DROP TABLE Reorder;
```

Trigger Examples In AdventureWorks2012

List of triggers in the sample database. parent_object_id is the object_id of the trigger parent table. SELF-JOIN is required to get the parent information.

```
USE AdventureWorks2012;
SELECT
   o.name                                                    AS TriggerName,
   SCHEMA_NAME(po.schema_id)                                 AS TableSchema,
   OBJECT_NAME(o.parent_object_id)                           AS TableName,
   OBJECTPROPERTY( o.object_id, 'ExecIsUpdateTrigger')       AS [isupdate],
   OBJECTPROPERTY( o.object_id, 'ExecIsDeleteTrigger')       AS [isdelete],
   OBJECTPROPERTY( o.object_id, 'ExecIsInsertTrigger')       AS [isinsert],
   OBJECTPROPERTY( o.object_id, 'ExecIsAfterTrigger')        AS [isafter],
   OBJECTPROPERTY( o.object_id, 'ExecIsInsteadOfTrigger')    AS [isinsteadof],
   OBJECTPROPERTY( o.object_id, 'ExecIsTriggerDisabled')     AS [disabled]
FROM sys.objects AS o
        INNER JOIN sys.objects AS po    ON o.parent_object_id = po.object_id
WHERE o.[type] = 'TR'  ORDER BY TableSchema, TableName, TriggerName;
```

TriggerName	TableSchema	TableName	isupdate	isdelete	isinsert	isafter	isinsteadof	disabled
dEmployee	HumanResources	Employee	0	1	0	0	1	0
iuPerson	Person	Person	1	0	1	1	0	0
iWorkOrder	Production	WorkOrder	0	0	1	1	0	0
uWorkOrder	Production	WorkOrder	1	0	0	1	0	0
iPurchaseOrderDetail	Purchasing	PurchaseOrderDetail	0	0	1	1	0	0
uPurchaseOrderDetail	Purchasing	PurchaseOrderDetail	1	0	0	1	0	0
uPurchaseOrderHeader	Purchasing	PurchaseOrderHeader	1	0	0	1	0	0
dVendor	Purchasing	Vendor	0	1	0	0	1	0
iduSalesOrderDetail	Sales	SalesOrderDetail	1	1	1	1	0	0
uSalesOrderHeader	Sales	SalesOrderHeader	1	0	0	1	0	0

Alternate method of obtaining all triggers information.

```
SELECT * FROM sys.triggers ORDER BY name; -- Partial results.
```

name	object_id	parent_class	parent_class_desc	parent_id	type	type_desc
ddlDatabaseTriggerLog	261575970	0	DATABASE	0	TR	SQL_TRIGGER
dEmployee	1739153241	1	OBJECT_OR_COLUMN	1237579447	TR	SQL_TRIGGER
dVendor	1851153640	1	OBJECT_OR_COLUMN	766625774	TR	SQL_TRIGGER
iduSalesOrderDetail	1819153526	1	OBJECT_OR_COLUMN	1154103152	TR	SQL_TRIGGER
iPurchaseOrderDetail	1771153355	1	OBJECT_OR_COLUMN	850102069	TR	SQL_TRIGGER
iuPerson	1755153298	1	OBJECT_OR_COLUMN	1765581328	TR	SQL_TRIGGER
iWorkOrder	1867153697	1	OBJECT_OR_COLUMN	846626059	TR	SQL_TRIGGER
uPurchaseOrderDetail	1787153412	1	OBJECT_OR_COLUMN	850102069	TR	SQL_TRIGGER
uPurchaseOrderHeader	1803153469	1	OBJECT_OR_COLUMN	946102411	TR	SQL_TRIGGER
uSalesOrderHeader	1835153583	1	OBJECT_OR_COLUMN	1266103551	TR	SQL_TRIGGER
uWorkOrder	1883153754	1	OBJECT_OR_COLUMN	846626059	TR	SQL_TRIGGER

Trigger Can Be Modified in Object Explorer

When the Modify Trigger option is picked, Object Explorer loads it as ALTER TRIGGER script.

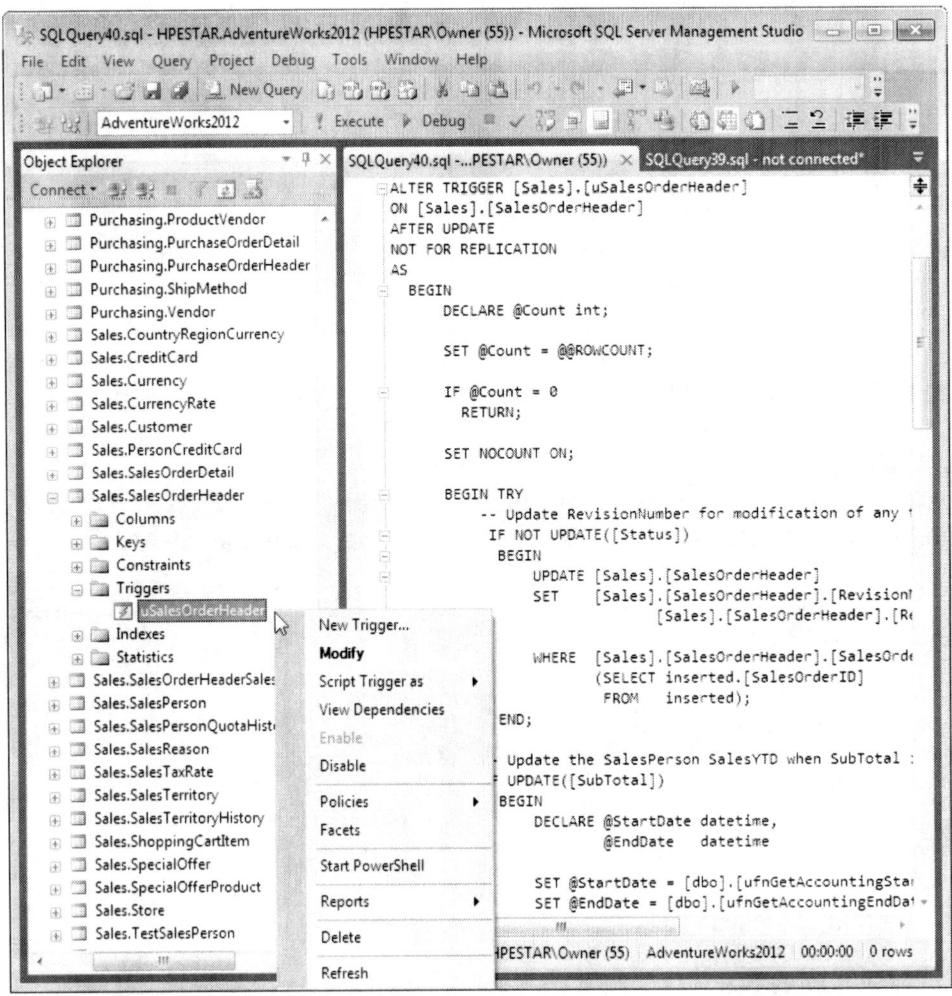

Programmatic way to get trigger definition.

```
SELECT OBJECT_DEFINITION( object_id('Person.iuPerson'));
```

CREATE TRIGGER [Person].[iuPerson] ON [Person].[Person]
AFTER INSERT, UPDATE NOT FOR REPLICATION AS
BEGIN
DECLARE @Count int;
SET @Count = @@ROWCOUNT;
IF @Count = 0 RETURN;
SET NOCOUNT ON;
IF UPDATE([BusinessEntityID]) OR UPDATE([Demographics])

Full-Text Index & Full-Text Search

Full-Text Search in SQL Server 2012 allows users and application programs, such as C#, to execute Full-Text Search queries against text-based data in SQL Server 2012 tables. Prior to running full-text search queries on a table, full-text catalog and full-text indexes on table text column(s) must be created.

MSDN Article: **Full-Text Search**
http://msdn.microsoft.com/en-us/library/ms142571.aspx

```
USE AdventureWorks2012;
SELECT * INTO dbo.JobCandidate FROM HumanResources.JobCandidate; ; -- (13 row(s) affected)
GO
CREATE UNIQUE INDEX idxHRJC ON JobCandidate(JobCandidateID);
CREATE FULLTEXT CATALOG HRFullText AS DEFAULT;
CREATE FULLTEXT INDEX ON JobCandidate(Resume) KEY INDEX idxHRJC WITH STOPLIST = SYSTEM;
GO
```

```
SELECT JobCandidateID FROM JobCandidate WHERE CONTAINS(Resume, ' "production line" ');      -- 2
SELECT JobCandidateID FROM JobCandidate WHERE CONTAINS(Resume, ' "C#" ');                   -- 3
SELECT JobCandidateID FROM JobCandidate WHERE CONTAINS (Resume, ' "machin*" ' );            -- 1, 7
SELECT * FROM CONTAINSTABLE(JobCandidate, Resume, 'ISABOUT ("mach*",
      tool WEIGHT(0.9), automatic WEIGHT(0.1)   ) ' );
```

KEY	RANK
1	51
7	22

```
SELECT jc.JobCandidateID, x.* FROM JobCandidate jc
        INNER JOIN CONTAINSTABLE(JobCandidate, Resume, 'ISABOUT ("mach*",
                tool WEIGHT(0.9), automatic WEIGHT(0.1) ) ' ) x ON x.[KEY] = jc.JobCandidateID;
```

JobCandidateID	KEY	RANK
1	1	51
7	7	22

```
SELECT JobCandidateID FROM JobCandidate WHERE CONTAINS(Resume, '(ingénierie NEAR expérimenté)'); -- 7
SELECT JobCandidateID FROM JobCandidate WHERE CONTAINS(Resume, '(visual and basic)'); -- 3
SELECT JobCandidateID FROM JobCandidate WHERE CONTAINS(Resume, '(visual or basic)'); -- 2, 3
SELECT JobCandidateID FROM JobCandidate WHERE CONTAINS (Resume,'FORMSOF(INFLECTIONAL,"computer")'); -- 1
GO
```

```
DROP TABLE dbo.JobCandidate; DROP FULLTEXT CATALOG HRFullText;
```

MSDN Article: **Query with Full-Text Search**
http://msdn.microsoft.com/en-us/library/ms142583.aspx

Article: **Full Text Index Queries using CONTAINS and CONTAINSTABLE**
http://www.databasejournal.com/features/mssql/article.php/3857056/Full-Text-Index-Queries-using-CONTAINS-and-CONTAINSTABLE.htm

CHAPTER 20: Query & Stored Procedure Optimization

Optimization Basics

Optimization revolves around techniques for the reduction of the resource requirements to carry out an operation such as a SELECT query. There are four ways to do optimization:

- Configure the hardware platform for overall best performance (HW - DBA)
- Configure SQL Server for best performance (SW - DBA)
- Engineering the query / script the optimal way (SW - Developer)
- Creating indexes on the tables (SW - Developer/DBA)

The HW solution aims for fast "reads" and fast CPU processing. In the last two software solution instances the usual objective is "reads" (logical 8K page reads) reduction. While the final objective is the "duration" reduction, that measure involves blocking as well so it is not as reliable as the "reads" measure. Using the first software engineering technique, we aim to eliminate unneeded operations or find a replacement which is less resource intensive. The second indexing technique is purely "reads" reduction in focus, we are not changing the query or the script. T-SQL has 2 statistics commands for taking basic performance measures. For even tests, we don't want to use cache memory (fast), but only disk (slow). A "cold" execute of a query may take 8 seconds, while the next (using cache) 1 second only.

```
USE AdventureWorks2012;
DBCC DROPCLEANBUFFERS; -- Forces reload of data pages (forces disk io) in cache buffer memory
SET STATISTICS IO ON; SET STATISTICS TIME ON;
        EXEC uspGetBillOfMaterials 801, '2008-01-05';
SET STATISTICS TIME OFF; SET STATISTICS IO OFF; -- Messages
```

```
DBCC execution completed. If DBCC printed error messages, contact your system administrator.
SQL Server parse and compile time:
  CPU time = 0 ms, elapsed time = 0 ms.
 SQL Server Execution Times:
  CPU time = 0 ms,  elapsed time = 0 ms.
Table 'Product'. Scan count 0, logical reads 178, physical reads 3, read-ahead reads 0, lob logical reads 0, lob physical reads 0, lob read-ahead reads 0.
Table 'BillOfMaterials'. Scan count 90, logical reads 181, physical reads 4, read-ahead reads 0, lob logical reads 0, lob physical reads 0, lob read-ahead reads 0.
Table 'Worktable'. Scan count 2, logical reads 510, physical reads 0, read-ahead reads 0, lob logical reads 0, lob physical reads 0, lob read-ahead reads 0.
 SQL Server Execution Times:     CPU time = 16 ms,  elapsed time = 6 ms.
 SQL Server Execution Times:  CPU time = 16 ms,  elapsed time = 6 ms.
```

No Disk IO Needed When All Pages for a Query Are in Buffer Cache

When we execute a query shortly after the previous execution, most pages may still be on cache memory, thus reduction in the need for (slow) disk io.

```
USE AdventureWorks2012;  SET STATISTICS IO ON;   SET STATISTICS TIME ON;
        EXEC uspGetBillOfMaterials 801, '2008-01-05';
SET STATISTICS TIME OFF;  SET STATISTICS IO OFF;            -- Messages
```

SQL Server parse and compile time: CPU time = 0 ms, elapsed time = 0 ms.
SQL Server Execution Times: CPU time = 0 ms, elapsed time = 0 ms.
Table 'Product'. Scan count 0, logical reads 178, **physical reads 0**, read-ahead reads 0, lob logical reads 0, lob physical reads 0, lob read-ahead reads 0.
Table 'BillOfMaterials'. Scan count 90, logical reads 181, **physical reads 0,** read-ahead reads 0, lob logical reads 0, lob physical reads 0, lob read-ahead reads 0.
Table 'Worktable'. Scan count 2, logical reads 510, physical reads 0, read-ahead reads 0, lob logical reads 0, lob physical reads 0, lob read-ahead reads 0.
SQL Server Execution Times: CPU time = 0 ms, elapsed time = 2 ms.

We can see that physical reads have been eliminated, hence the faster execution. Note, however, timing will vary due to server activities. Therefore, to obtain good measurements we should average over multiple executions, for example 3, 11 or 31. When we monitor a similar execution sequence in SQL Server Profiler, we can see that the logical reads (Reads) were the same but the execution was faster (2 milliseconds) the second time due to the lack of disk io (physical reads). Note: STATISTICS IO and Profiler are 2 different piece of software, hence the difference in figures.

CPU	Reads	Writes	Duration
0	1096	0	7
0	1096	0	2

Database Engine Internal JOINs

Execution plan has various internal operations such as JOINing, merging and sorting.

MSDN Article: **Understanding Nested Loops Joins** http://msdn.microsoft.com/en-us/library/aa178178(v=sql.80).aspx
MSDN Article: **Understanding Merge Joins** http://msdn.microsoft.com/en-us/library/aa178419(v=sql.80).aspx
MSDN Article: **Understanding Hash Joins** http://msdn.microsoft.com/en-us/library/aa178403(v=sql.80).aspx

Optimizing a Query by Reengineering

Less fancy way of saying is rewriting the query. Consider an INNER JOIN query with a view which may look simple until we look at the view underlying code. The database engine has to expand the view definition "on the fly" and develop a plan for the more complex query.

```
USE [AdventureWorks2012];
DBCC DROPCLEANBUFFERS;  SET STATISTICS IO ON;  SET STATISTICS TIME ON;
SELECT    LTRIM(CONCAT(ISNULL(Title,''),SPACE(1), FullName))                    AS SalesPerson,
          JobTitle, SalesTerritory, FORMAT([2008],'c0','en-US')                  AS [2008]
FROM [Sales].[vSalesPersonSalesByFiscalYears] VSP
  INNER JOIN Person.Person P     ON CONCAT(FirstName, ' ', MiddleName, ' ', LastName) = VSP.FullName
ORDER BY [2008] DESC; SET STATISTICS TIME OFF;  SET STATISTICS IO OFF;
```

SalesPerson	JobTitle	SalesTerritory	2008
Linda C Mitchell	Sales Representative	Southwest	$4,251,369
Jae B Pak	Sales Representative	United Kingdom	$4,116,871
Michael G Blythe	Sales Representative	Northeast	$3,763,178

```
DBCC execution completed. If DBCC printed error messages, contact your system administrator.
(14 row(s) affected)
Table 'Worktable'. Scan count 0, logical reads 0, physical reads 0, read-ahead reads 0, lob logical reads 0, lob physical reads 0, lob read-ahead reads 0.
Table 'SalesOrderHeader'. Scan count 5, logical reads 865, physical reads 2, read-ahead reads 784, lob logical reads 0, lob physical reads 0, lob read-ahead reads 0.
Table 'Employee'. Scan count 0, logical reads 28, physical reads 1, read-ahead reads 0, lob logical reads 0, lob physical reads 0, lob read-ahead reads 0.
Table 'Person'. Scan count 5, logical reads 4240, physical reads 2, read-ahead reads 3817, lob logical reads 0, lob physical reads 0, lob read-ahead reads 0.
Table 'SalesTerritory'. Scan count 0, logical reads 28, physical reads 1, read-ahead reads 0, lob logical reads 0, lob physical reads 0, lob read-ahead reads 0.
Table 'SalesPerson'. Scan count 0, logical reads 34, physical reads 1, read-ahead reads 0, lob logical reads 0, lob physical reads 0, lob read-ahead reads 0.
Table 'Worktable'. Scan count 0, logical reads 0, physical reads 0, read-ahead reads 0, lob logical reads 0, lob physical reads 0, lob read-ahead reads 0.
 SQL Server Execution Times: CPU time = 172 ms,  elapsed time = 1162 ms.
```

Performance Optimization by Disk Configuration

The following disk configuration aims to achieve good performance by assigning dedicated disks to various OS, SS and file system operations.

- Drive C 60 GB RAID 1 mirrored hard drive: operating system / SQL Server software
- Drive D 60 GB RAID 1 mirrored hard drive: temporary database (tempdb) data file
- Drive E 300 GB RAID 5 hard drive array: application database data files
- Drive F 60 GB RAID 1 mirrored hard drive: transaction logs
- Drive G 60 GB RAID 1 mirrored hard drive: temporary database (tempdb) log file
- Drive H 120 GB RAID 0 hard drive: staging files, feeds, disk-to-disk-to-tape backups

JOIN on INT Columns Faster Than on nvarchar Strings

Our suspicion is that JOINing on nvarchar fields may be improved if we replace it with JOIN on INT columns (4 bytes). Actually, we are in luck, it is just an easy rewrite of the query.

```
USE [AdventureWorks2012]
GO
DBCC DROPCLEANBUFFERS;
SET STATISTICS IO ON;
SET STATISTICS TIME ON;
SELECT  LTRIM(CONCAT(ISNULL(Title,''),SPACE(1), FullName))              AS SalesPerson,
        JobTitle, SalesTerritory, FORMAT([2008],'c0','en-US')           AS [2008]
FROM [Sales].[vSalesPersonSalesByFiscalYears] VSP
 INNER JOIN Person.Person P
  ON P.BusinessEntityID = VSP.SalesPersonID  ORDER BY [2008] DESC;
SET STATISTICS TIME OFF;  SET STATISTICS IO OFF;
GO
```

```
DBCC execution completed. If DBCC printed error messages, contact your system administrator.

(14 row(s) affected)
Table 'Person'. Scan count 0, logical reads 90, physical reads 2, read-ahead reads 0, lob logical reads 0, lob physical reads 0, lob read-ahead reads 0.
Table 'SalesOrderHeader'. Scan count 14, logical reads 12333, physical reads 9, read-ahead reads 352, lob logical reads 0, lob physical reads 0, lob read-ahead reads 0.
Table 'Employee'. Scan count 0, logical reads 28, physical reads 2, read-ahead reads 0, lob logical reads 0, lob physical reads 0, lob read-ahead reads 0.
Table 'SalesTerritory'. Scan count 0, logical reads 28, physical reads 1, read-ahead reads 0, lob logical reads 0, lob physical reads 0, lob read-ahead reads 0.
Table 'SalesPerson'. Scan count 1, logical reads 2, physical reads 1, read-ahead reads 0, lob logical reads 0, lob physical reads 0, lob read-ahead reads 0.

 SQL Server Execution Times:
   CPU time = 16 ms,  elapsed time = 68 ms.
```

When we compare the statistics we observe the elimination of 2 worktables and we reduced the "reads" on the Person table by the more efficient JOIN. The low CPU in the Profiler comparison screenshot indicative of the simpler JOIN. Even though the total "reads" are higher, the indexed INT JOIN proves to be quite advantageous over varchar JOIN as reflected in the lower CPU figure.

CPU	Reads	Writes	Duration
0	0	0	0
236	5314	0	1144
0	0	0	0
78	14194	0	302

Examining the Actual Execution Plan

There are two execution plan which can be turned by clicking on the corresponding icons: estimated and actual. The execution plan can be helpful with missing indexes and improvement considerations. Understanding a complex execution plan requires extensive studying and experience.

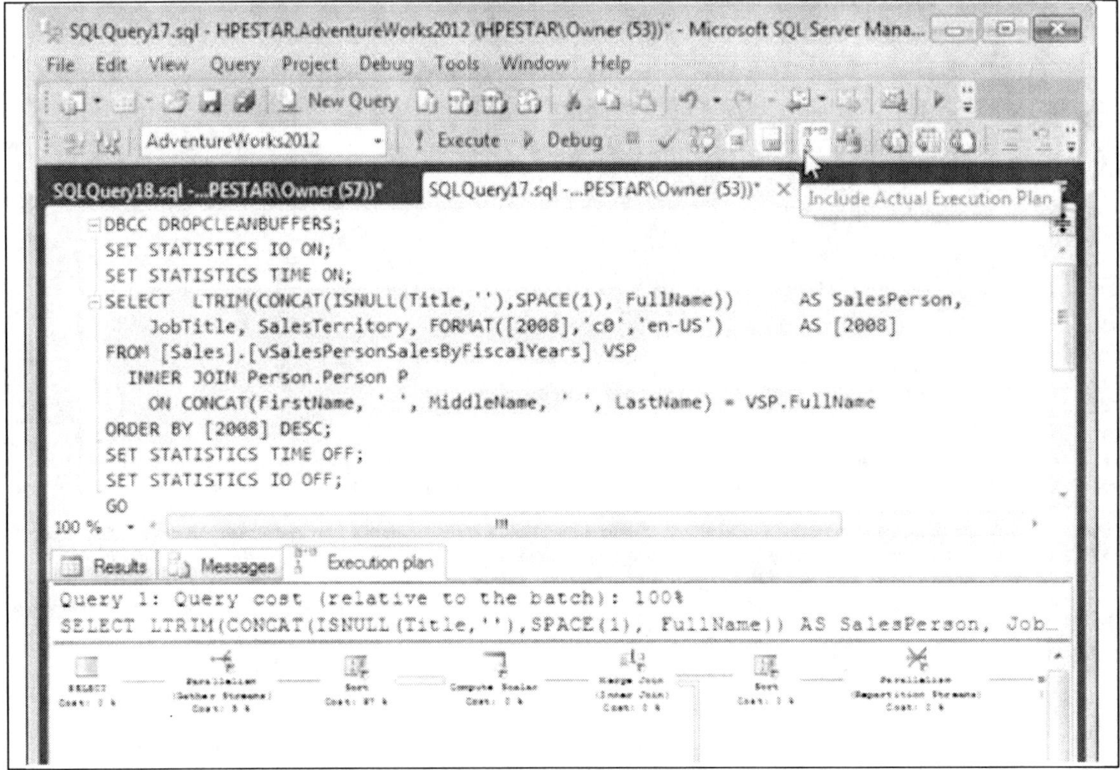

Optimizing with Query JOIN Hints

JOIN hints (LOOP, MERGE, HASH, REMOTE) specify an internal JOIN strategy for the database engine.

Warning: Query hints should be used only as a last resort by experienced database developers and database administrators (DBAs). First choice is proper query design, indexing, index & statistics maintenance.

BOL Article: **Join Hints**
http://msdn.microsoft.com/en-us/library/ms173815.aspx

Comparing Execution Plan Cost Summary Pop-ups

When hovering with the mouse over the SELECT on the left side of the execution plan, a cost summary panel pops up.

SELECT		SELECT	
Cached plan size	120 KB	Cached plan size	96 KB
Degree of Parallelism	4	Degree of Parallelism	1
Estimated Operator Cost	0 (0%)	Estimated Operator Cost	0 (0%)
Memory Grant	1018816	Estimated Subtree Cost	1.60204
Estimated Subtree Cost	15132.9	Memory Grant	7352
Estimated Number of Rows	2608890	Estimated Number of Rows	1306.27

Statement (left)

```
SELECT LTRIM(CONCAT(ISNULL
(Title,''),SPACE(1), FullName)) AS
SalesPerson,
JobTitle, SalesTerritory, FORMAT
([2008],'c0','en-US') AS [2008]
FROM [Sales].
[vSalesPersonSalesByFiscalYears] VSP
  INNER JOIN Person.Person P
    ON CONCAT(FirstName, ' ',
MiddleName, ' ', LastName) =
VSP.FullName
ORDER BY [2008] DESC;
```

Statement (right)

```
SELECT LTRIM(CONCAT(ISNULL
(Title,''),SPACE(1), FullName)) AS
SalesPerson,
JobTitle, SalesTerritory, FORMAT
([2008],'c0','en-US') AS [2008]
FROM [Sales].
[vSalesPersonSalesByFiscalYears] VSP
  INNER JOIN Person.Person P
    ON P.BusinessEntityID =
VSP.SalesPersonID
ORDER BY [2008] DESC;
```

Side by side comparison of the cost panels shows dramatic differences. Cost of 15,132 versus 1.6 are simply shocking. The example powerfully illustrates the challenges in query optimization whereby relatively simple rewrite may result in huge performance improvement. We cannot say much about the optimization state of a query just by looking at cost. Only when we compare it to a different version of the query we can say if worsened, improved or much improved. We can also notice the huge difference in rows: 2.6 million vs. 1,300. Memory requirement for the nvarchar JOIN is over a million grants, while only 7 thousands for the INT JOIN.

Poorly written query not only slow in execution but very resource intensive as well, therefore it slows down other queries executing simultaneously. Hence the need to optimize queries especially frequently executed ones.

An extreme bad query can bring down the mightiest server to its "knees". We can see why just by looking at this very simple example with bad and good INNER JOINs.

Optimizing with Setting Server Max Memory

If server max memory is not set, it may lead to operational problems. A rule of thumb: max memory should be 80% of physical memory. That is easy for 64-bit system, it is a challenge for 32-bit. Setting max memory to 64GB.

```
EXEC sys.sp_configure N'max server memory (MB)', N'65536';
GO
RECONFIGURE WITH OVERRIDE;
GO
```

Article: **Suggested Max Memory Settings for SQL Server 2005/2008**
http://sqlserverperformance.wordpress.com/2009/10/29/suggested-max-memory-settings-for-sql-server-20052008/

Optimizing with Multi Statements Query Using Temporary Tables

Assume that the fast INT JOIN is not available. Another technique: instead of a single statement query multi statements since we have more control over the execution plan. In the current example we are forcing the optimizer to evaluate the view query first and store the results into a temporary table. Note: messages shows the long (real) name of #VSP temporary table, personalized to this connection.

```
DBCC DROPCLEANBUFFERS;  SET STATISTICS IO ON;  SET STATISTICS TIME ON;
SELECT * INTO #VSP FROM [Sales].[vSalesPersonSalesByFiscalYears];
```

```
SELECT  LTRIM(CONCAT(ISNULL(Title,''),SPACE(1), FullName))           AS SalesPerson,
        JobTitle, SalesTerritory, FORMAT([2008],'c0','en-US')        AS [2008]
FROM #VSP    INNER JOIN Person.Person P
   ON CONCAT(FirstName, ' ', MiddleName, ' ', LastName) = #VSP.FullName
ORDER BY [2008] DESC;   SET STATISTICS TIME OFF;  SET STATISTICS IO OFF;
GO
DROP TABLE #VSP;  -- Messages
```

```
DBCC execution completed. If DBCC printed error messages, contact your system administrator.
Table 'SalesOrderHeader'. Scan count 14, logical reads 12452, physical reads 9, read-ahead reads 352, lob logical reads 0, lob physical reads 0, lob read-ahead reads 0.
Table 'Person'. Scan count 0, logical reads 42, physical reads 2, read-ahead reads 0, lob logical reads 0, lob physical reads 0, lob read-ahead reads 0.
Table 'Employee'. Scan count 0, logical reads 28, physical reads 2, read-ahead reads 0, lob logical reads 0, lob physical reads 0, lob read-ahead reads 0.
Table 'SalesTerritory'. Scan count 0, logical reads 28, physical reads 1, read-ahead reads 0, lob logical reads 0, lob physical reads 0, lob read-ahead reads 0.
Table 'SalesPerson'. Scan count 1, logical reads 2, physical reads 1, read-ahead reads 0, lob logical reads 0, lob physical reads 0, lob read-ahead reads 0.
(14 row(s) affected)
(1 row(s) affected)
 SQL Server Execution Times:  CPU time = 94 ms,  elapsed time = 362 ms.
SQL Server parse and compile time:   CPU time = 0 ms, elapsed time = 70 ms.
SQL Server parse and compile time:      CPU time = 0 ms, elapsed time = 236 ms.
(14 row(s) affected)
Table 'Person'. Scan count 1, logical reads 3826, physical reads 0, read-ahead reads 3817, lob logical reads 0, lob physical reads 0, lob read-ahead reads 0.
Table 'Worktable'. Scan count 1, logical reads 42166, physical reads 0, read-ahead reads 0, lob logical reads 0, lob physical reads 0, lob read-ahead reads 0.
Table '#VSP_____________________________________________________________________________________________________________000000000074'. Scan count
1, logical reads 1, physical reads 0, read-ahead reads 0, lob logical reads 0, lob physical reads 0, lob read-ahead reads 0.
(1 row(s) affected)
 SQL Server Execution Times:   CPU time = 266 ms,  elapsed time = 832 ms
```

Obstacle: Worktable 42K "reads" Cannot Be Decreased

This course of action is not as good as the JOIN on the INT (integer) keys. Yet the combination of costs came down to 6, a reasonable figure relatively speaking. The Estimated Number of Rows are "reasonable" as well, just like the Memory Grants.

CPU	Reads	Writes	Duration
125	15849	3	1155
203	42536	123	356

SELECT INTO

Cached plan size	120 KB
Degree of Parallelism	1
Estimated Operator Cost	0 (0%)
Estimated Subtree Cost	1.6378
Estimated Number of Rows	1306.27

Statement

SELECT * INTO #VSP FROM [Sales].[vSalesPersonSalesByFiscalYears];

SELECT

Cached plan size	32 KB
Degree of Parallelism	1
Estimated Operator Cost	0 (0%)
Memory Grant	1024
Estimated Subtree Cost	4.18429
Estimated Number of Rows	19972

Statement

```
SELECT LTRIM(CONCAT(ISNULL
(Title,''),SPACE(1), FullName)) AS
SalesPerson,
JobTitle, SalesTerritory, FORMAT
([2008],'c0','en-US') AS [2008]
FROM #VSP
  INNER JOIN Person.Person P
    ON #VSP.FullName = CONCAT
(FirstName, ' ', MiddleName, ' ',
LastName)
ORDER BY [2008] DESC;
```

The 42K "reads" is huge, in this case on an internal work table which is outside our direct control, however, indirectly we may be able to influence it. The common goal of optimization is "reads" reduction usually with indexing if the query is engineered correctly. With indexing we may be able to bring down the reads to 500 or even 50.

Optimizing with Covering Index

We can achieve miracles in query optimization with indexing but at a cost: index represents an overhead since it slows down some operations such as INSERT or DELETE and it has to be maintained. First we add a computed column to the Person.Person table, them create a "covering" index on it which includes the Title used in the SELECT clause. Note: computed column and covering index are "luxury" items which are used to support **business critical queries** only. In a covering index all columns are present in the index for the query as keys or included column. **Note: there is no "free lunch" with indexing only tradeoff**. Covering index tends to be wide and may slow down other than the target queries.

```
ALTER TABLE Person.Person ADD FullName
        AS CONCAT(FirstName, ' ', MiddleName, ' ', LastName)        PERSISTED;
GO  --Command(s) completed successfully.
```

```
CREATE INDEX idxFullName on Person.Person(FullName) INCLUDE (Title);
GO  -- Command(s) completed successfully.
```

```
-- DROP INDEX Person.Person.idxFullName;
```

The new query using the new column in the INNER JOIN:

```
SELECT  LTRIM(CONCAT(ISNULL(Title,''),SPACE(1), #VSP.FullName))        AS SalesPerson,
        JobTitle, SalesTerritory, FORMAT([2008],'c0','en-US')          AS [2008]
FROM #VSP   INNER JOIN Person.Person P     ON P.FullName = #VSP.FullName
```

The result is simply amazing: the 42K "reads" on the work table is gone. The 123 "writes" are gone as well. Duration is not a stable measure because it includes blocking as well. If there is no blocking duration is proportionally higher with higher CPU, Reads & Writes.

CPU	Reads	Writes	Duration
140	15802	1	551
16	81	0	117

PERSISTED computed column can be indexed and also used in an indexed view.

TechNet Article: **Top 10 Hidden Gems in SQL Server 2005**
http://technet.microsoft.com/en-us/library/cc917696.aspx

Optimizing with Indexed View

Consider implementing frequent business critical queries as indexed views. Following is a simple demonstration how to create an index view on a single table GROUP BY summary query.

```
USE AdventureWorks2012;
GO
CREATE VIEW Sales.ivPO WITH SCHEMABINDING AS
        SELECT OrderDate, OrderCount=COUNT_BIG(*), OrderTotal=SUM(SubTotal)
        FROM Purchasing.PurchaseOrderHeader GROUP BY OrderDate;
GO
CREATE UNIQUE CLUSTERED INDEX idxIVPO on Sales.ivPO (OrderDate);
GO
SELECT TOP(3) * FROM Sales.ivPO ORDER BY OrderDate DESC;
```

OrderDate	OrderCount	OrderTotal
2008-10-23 00:00:00.000	1	1020.00
2008-09-03 00:00:00.000	16	266248.6785
2008-09-02 00:00:00.000	16	255574.2315

Optimizing with Indexing

The general rule is that all JOIN keys and WHERE condition columns should be indexed. Since PRIMARY KEY is automatically indexed, the rule means that all FOREIGN KEYs should be indexed since that is not automatic.

```
USE tempdb;   SELECT [SalesOrderID]
    ,CONVERT(INT,[SalesOrderDetailID]) AS [SalesOrderDetailID] -- inhibit identity inheritence
    ,[CarrierTrackingNumber]  ,[OrderQty], [ProductID], [SpecialOfferID], [UnitPrice]
    ,[UnitPriceDiscount], [LineTotal], [rowguid],[ModifiedDate]
INTO SOD  FROM [AdventureWorks2012].[Sales].[SalesOrderDetail];
GO  -- (121317 row(s) affected)
INSERT SOD SELECT * FROM SOD;   -- increase size of table by duplicating itself
GO 5
/* Beginning execution loop
(121317 row(s) affected) (242634 row(s) affected) (485268 row(s) affected)
(970536 row(s) affected) (1941072 row(s) affected) Batch execution completed 5 times. */
SELECT FORMAT(COUNT(*), '###,###,###') FROM SOD;  -- 3,882,144
SELECT * INTO Product FROM AdventureWorks2012.Production.Product;
```

MSDN Article: **Clustered and Nonclustered Indexes Described**
http://msdn.microsoft.com/en-us/library/ms190457.aspx

The Larger the Table the More Benefits of Indexing

```
DBCC DROPCLEANBUFFERS; SET STATISTICS IO ON; SET STATISTICS TIME ON;
        SELECT * FROM SOD INNER JOIN Product P  ON SOD.ProductID = P.ProductID     WHERE P.ProductID = 800;
SET STATISTICS TIME OFF;  SET STATISTICS IO OFF;
```

DBCC execution completed. If DBCC printed error messages, contact your system administrator. (15840 row(s) affected)
Table 'SOD'. Scan count 5, logical reads 54796, physical reads 0, read-ahead reads 1719, lob logical reads 0, lob physical reads 0, lob read-ahead reads 0.
Table 'Product'. Scan count 1, logical reads 14, physical reads 0, read-ahead reads 0, lob logical reads 0, lob physical reads 0, lob read-ahead reads 0.
Table 'Worktable'. Scan count 0, logical reads 0, physical reads 0, read-ahead reads 0, lob logical reads 0, lob physical reads 0, lob read-ahead reads 0. SQL Server Execution Times: CPU time = 483 ms, elapsed time = 845 ms.

```
CREATE CLUSTERED INDEX idxPrd ON SOD(ProductID); CREATE UNIQUE INDEX idxPrd ON Product(ProductID);
DBCC DROPCLEANBUFFERS; SET STATISTICS IO ON; SET STATISTICS TIME ON;
        SELECT * FROM SOD INNER JOIN Product P  ON SOD.ProductID = P.ProductID   WHERE P.ProductID = 800;
SET STATISTICS TIME OFF;  SET STATISTICS IO OFF;
```

DBCC execution completed. If DBCC printed error messages, contact your system administrator.
SQL Server parse and compile time: CPU time = 0 ms, elapsed time = 2 ms. (15840 row(s) affected)
Table 'SOD'. Scan count 1, logical reads 210, physical reads 0, read-ahead reads 206, lob logical reads 0, lob physical reads 0, lob read-ahead reads 0.
Table 'Product'. Scan count 0, logical reads 3, physical reads 0, read-ahead reads 0, lob logical reads 0, lob physical reads 0, lob read-ahead reads 0. (1 row(s) affected) SQL Server Execution Times: CPU time = 47 ms, elapsed time = 517 ms.

Check Data & Indexes Fragmentation on a Table

The sys.dm_db_index_physical_stats Dynamic Management Function (DMF) can be used to obtain index fragmentation information(Ye Olde Way: DBCC SHOWCONTIG). The clustered index line represents the data fragmentation. 20% fragmentation is considered low, 80% considered high.

```
SELECT object_NAME(object_id) AS TableName, i ndex_id,
        index_type_desc, FORMAT(avg_fragmentation_in_percent, 'p0') AS PcntFrag
        FROM sys.dm_db_index_physical_stats(DB_ID(N'AdventureWorks2012'),
          OBJECT_ID(N'AdventureWorks2012.Sales.SalesOrderDetail'), NULL, NULL , 'LIMITED');
```

TableName	index_id	index_type_desc	PcntFrag
SalesOrderDetail	1	CLUSTERED INDEX	21 %
SalesOrderDetail	2	NONCLUSTERED INDEX	0 %
SalesOrderDetail	3	NONCLUSTERED INDEX	11 %
SalesOrderDetail	10	NONCLUSTERED INDEX	0 %
SalesOrderDetail	13	NONCLUSTERED INDEX	90 %

MSDN Article: **Reorganize and Rebuild Indexes**
http://msdn.microsoft.com/en-us/library/ms189858.aspx

Clustered Index for Business Critical Query Support

Clustered index is another "luxury" item in optimization since there can only be one on a table and 0 to many nonclustered indexes. In this example nonclustered index does some improvement, but not significant. Cleanup commands for the indexing example script.

```
-- DROP INDEX SOD.idxPrd; DROP INDEX Product.idxPrd;
DROP TABLE SOD;  DROP TABLE Product;
```

SQL Profiler statistics on the sequence of batches we sent to the server from SSMS Query Editor.

SQL Server Profiler - [Untitled - 1 (HPESTAR)]

File Edit View Replay Tools Window Help

TextData	CPU	Reads	Writes	Duration	SPID	EventClass
USE tempdb;	0	0	0	0	53	SQL:BatchCompleted
SELECT [SalesOrderID] ,CONVE...	218	3327	672	782	53	SQL:BatchCompleted
INSERT SOD SELECT * FROM SOD; -...	796	496577	2968	832	53	SQL:BatchCompleted
INSERT SOD SELECT * FROM SOD; -...	1685	1026720	3103	1700	53	SQL:BatchCompleted
INSERT SOD SELECT * FROM SOD; -...	3354	2086787	6433	3505	53	SQL:BatchCompleted
INSERT SOD SELECT * FROM SOD; -...	6645	4207017	12832	6709	53	SQL:BatchCompleted
INSERT SOD SELECT * FROM SOD; -...	13229	8447507	25504	13339	53	SQL:BatchCompleted
/* Beginning execution loop (121...	719	55189	9	249	53	SQL:BatchCompleted
DBCC DROPCLEANBUFFERS; SET STATI...	732	57035	1	1182	53	SQL:BatchCompleted
CREATE CLUSTERED INDEX idxPrd ON ...	15398	133236	51211	13607	53	SQL:BatchCompleted
DBCC DROPCLEANBUFFERS; SET STATI...	109	225	0	497	53	SQL:BatchCompleted
-- DROP INDEX SOD.idxPrd -- DROP...	16	480	0	147	53	SQL:BatchCompleted

We can see the reads of 57,035 decreased to 225 after creating the indexes. Not only we speeded up this query but other queries as well by decreasing the load on the server. The execution plan displays **table scan** prior to index creation.

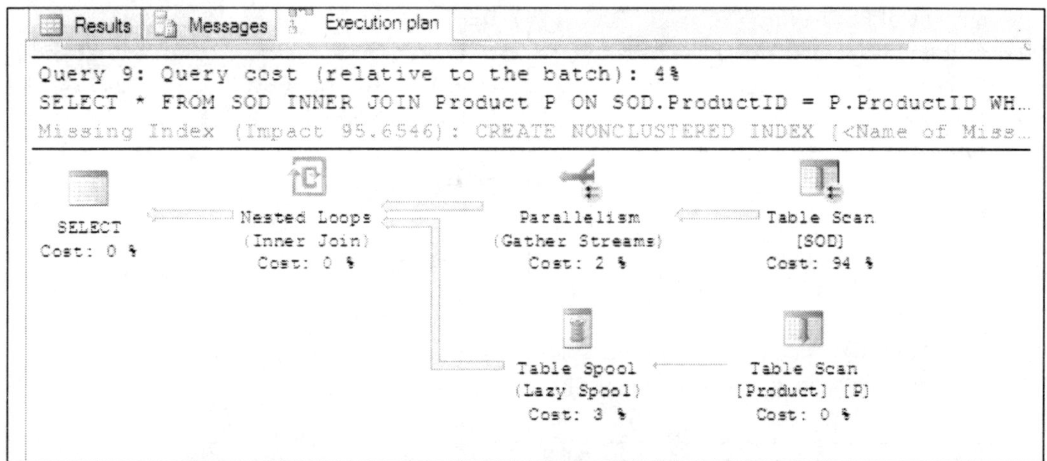

Execution Plan after Index Creation & Cost Comparison

The execution plan shows clustered index seek instead of table scan after index creation. Generally our aim with indexing is to replace table scan or index scan with index seek.

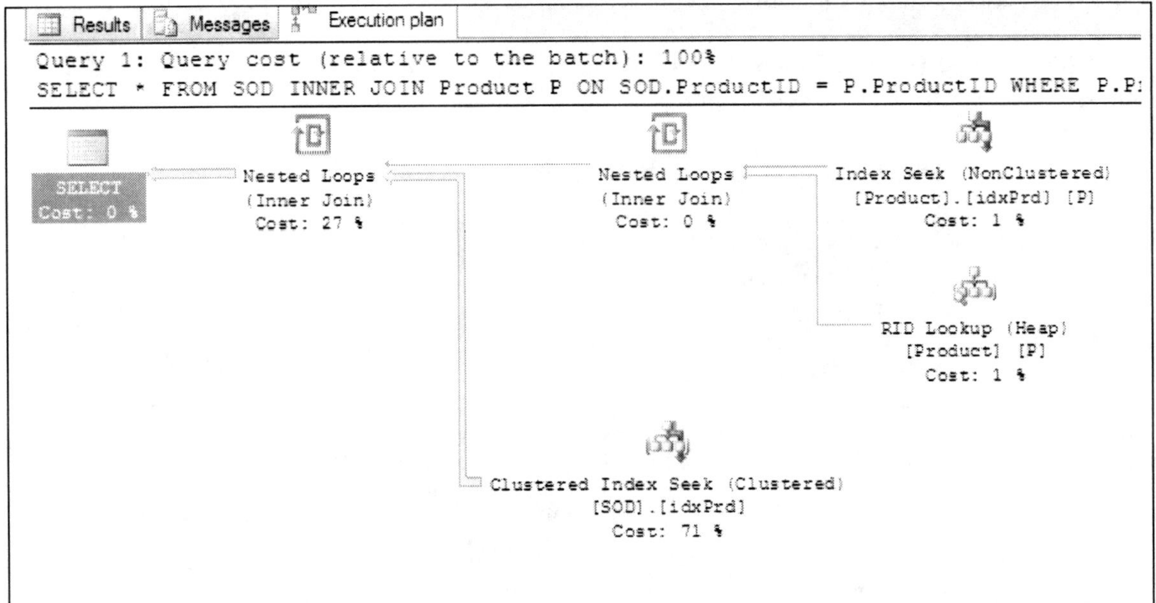

Cost comparison before and after index create reflects a very significant improvement in cost, roughly 200 fold.

SELECT (before)

Cached plan size	56 KB
Degree of Parallelism	4
Estimated Operator Cost	0 (0%)
Estimated Subtree Cost	45.4362
Memory Grant	72
Estimated Number of Rows	15513.1

Statement

```
SELECT * FROM SOD INNER JOIN
Product P
        ON SOD.ProductID = P.ProductID
    WHERE P.ProductID = 800;
```

SELECT (after)

Cached plan size	56 KB
Degree of Parallelism	1
Estimated Operator Cost	0 (0%)
Estimated Subtree Cost	0.247049
Estimated Number of Rows	15840

Statement

```
SELECT * FROM SOD INNER JOIN Product
P
        ON SOD.ProductID = P.ProductID
    WHERE P.ProductID = 800;
```

SHOWPLAN_XML Option to Find Missing Indexes

The SHOWPLAN_XML option produces the execution plan in XML format which can be turned into graphical plan also. At the beginning the XML execution plan, missing index information is included. A covering index is recommended for the target query below which reduces the logical reads from 1713 (clustered index scan) to 8 (NC index seek).

NOTE. We can't cover every query with covering index(as often suggested by automatic software), only BUSINESS CRITICAL queries. Other queries may slow down due to **wide** covering index. First choice is a regular index (no INCLUDE) even for BUSINESS CRITICAL queries.

```
USE tempdb;
SELECT * INTO SOD FROM AdventureWorks2012.Sales.SalesOrderDetail;
ALTER TABLE SOD ADD CONSTRAINT pkSOD PRIMARY KEY nonclustered (SalesOrderDetailID);
GO --(121329 row(s) affected)
```

```
DBCC DROPCLEANBUFFERS;   SET STATISTICS IO ON;
SELECT SalesOrderDetailID, ProductID, OrderQty, LineTotal FROM SOD
WHERE LineTotal BETWEEN 5000.0 AND 5999.99;  SET STATISTICS IO OFF
GO  -- (852 row(s) affected)
-- Table 'SOD'. Scan count 1, logical reads 1713, physical reads 0,...
```

```
SET SHOWPLAN_XML ON;
GO
SELECT SalesOrderDetailID, ProductID, OrderQty, LineTotal FROM SOD
WHERE LineTotal BETWEEN 5000.0 AND 5999.99;
GO
SET SHOWPLAN_XML OFF;
GO
```

```
<MissingIndexes>
        <MissingIndexGroup Impact="89.8949">
         <MissingIndex Database="[tempdb]" Schema="[dbo]" Table="[SOD]">
          <ColumnGroup Usage="INEQUALITY">
           <Column Name="[LineTotal]" ColumnId="9" />
          </ColumnGroup>
          <ColumnGroup Usage="INCLUDE">
           <Column Name="[SalesOrderDetailID]" ColumnId="2" />
           <Column Name="[OrderQty]" ColumnId="4" />
           <Column Name="[ProductID]" ColumnId="5" />
          </ColumnGroup>
         </MissingIndex>
        </MissingIndexGroup>
       </MissingIndexes>
```

```
CREATE INDEX idxLineTotal on SOD (LineTotal) INCLUDE (SalesOrderDetailID, OrderQty, ProductID);
```

```
DBCC DROPCLEANBUFFERS;   SET STATISTICS IO ON;
SELECT SalesOrderDetailID, ProductID, OrderQty, LineTotal FROM SOD
WHERE LineTotal BETWEEN 5000.0 AND 5999.99;   SET STATISTICS IO OFF;
GO -- Table 'SOD'. Scan count 1, logical reads 8, physical reads 0, ...
```

Non-SARGable Predicates Force Index Scan

The term SARGable stands for Search ARGument ABLE. It means the WHERE clause OR join ON clause predicate written such a way that the database engine can use the index on the column. Basically means if we form an expression with the indexed column, index scan will be performed instead of index seek, in other words, index will not be used to speed up the query. The (SOD.ProductID +1 - 1) expression in the ON clause causes clustered index scan. The relative query costs are 1% (SARGable) and 99% (non-SARGable) in the batch of 2 queries.

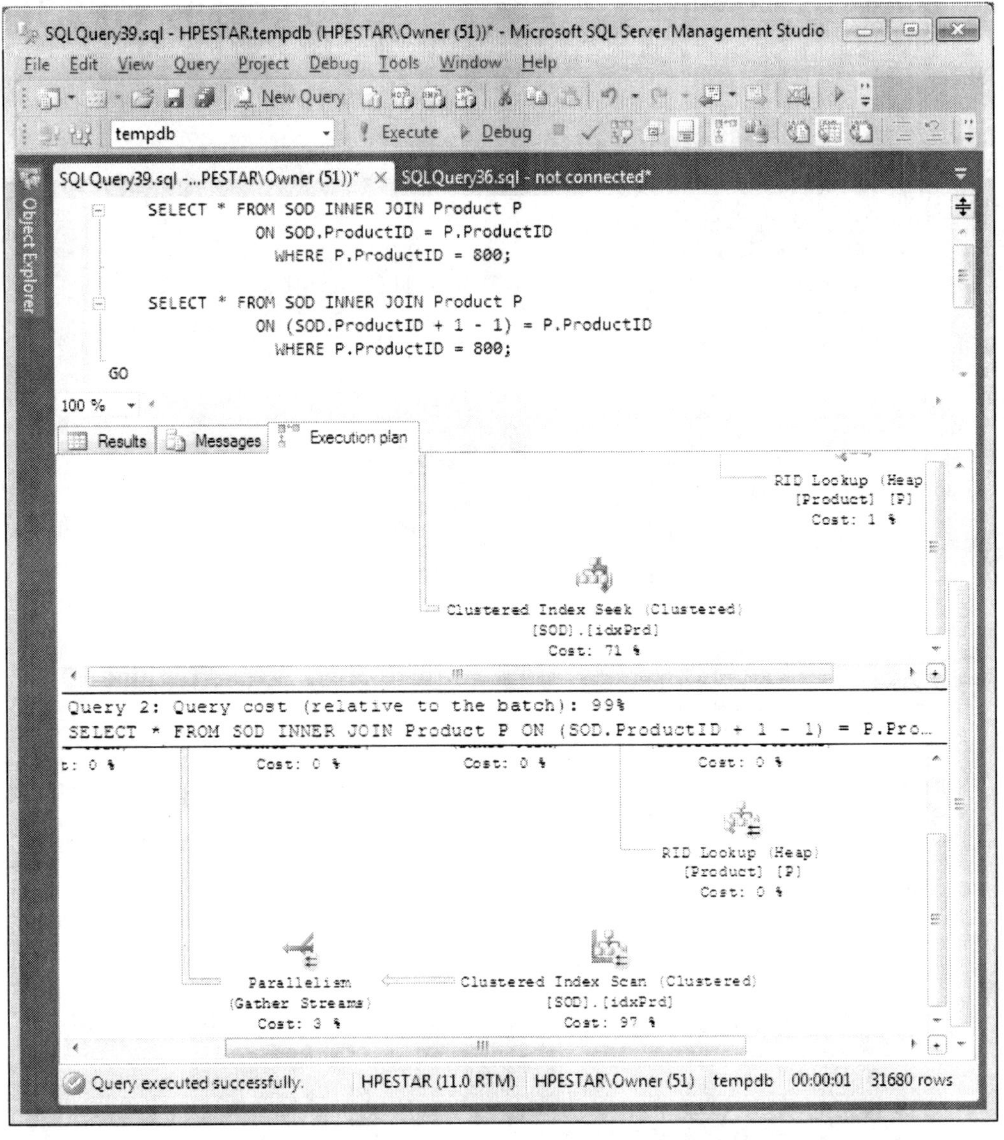

SARGable Predicate Construction

It is a challenge to remember all the time to make the predicate SARGable. Frequently, so much easier to make it non-SARGable.

```
YEAR(OrderDate) = 2016 AND MONTH(OrderDate) = 10                    -- non-SARGable
OrderDate >= '2016-10-01' AND OrderDate < DATEADD(MM,1, '2016-10-01') -- SARGable
```

The payoff can be great as shown by the previous SARGable & non-SARGable examples, duration in msec.

CPU	Reads	Writes	Duration
125	223	0	668
1527	51451	0	11497

Clustered Index Seek (Clustered)	
Scanning a particular range of rows from a clustered index.	
Physical Operation	Clustered Index Seek
Logical Operation	Clustered Index Seek
Actual Execution Mode	Row
Estimated Execution Mode	Row
Storage	RowStore
Actual Number of Rows	15840
Actual Number of Batches	0
Estimated Operator Cost	0.174279 (71%)
Estimated I/O Cost	0.156698
Estimated CPU Cost	0.017581
Estimated Subtree Cost	0.174279
Number of Executions	1
Estimated Number of Executions	1
Estimated Number of Rows	15840
Estimated Row Size	112 B
Actual Rebinds	0
Actual Rewinds	0
Ordered	True
Node ID	54

Object
[tempdb].[dbo].[SOD].[idxPrd]
Output List
[tempdb].[dbo].[SOD].SalesOrderID, [tempdb].[dbo].[SOD].SalesOrderDetailID, [tempdb].[dbo].[SOD].CarrierTrackingNumber, [tempdb].[dbo].[SOD].OrderQty, [tempdb].[dbo].[SOD].ProductID, [tempdb].[dbo].[SOD].SpecialOfferID, [tempdb].[dbo].[SOD].UnitPrice, [tempdb].[dbo].[SOD].UnitPriceDiscount, [tempdb].[dbo].[SOD].LineTotal, [tempdb].[dbo].[SOD].rowguid, [tempdb].[dbo].[SOD].ModifiedDate
Seek Predicates
Seek Keys[1]: Prefix: [tempdb].[dbo].[SOD].ProductID = Scalar Operator((800))

Clustered Index Scan (Clustered)	
Scanning a clustered index, entirely or only a range.	
Physical Operation	Clustered Index Scan
Logical Operation	Clustered Index Scan
Actual Execution Mode	Row
Estimated Execution Mode	Row
Actual Number of Rows	15840
Actual Number of Batches	0
Estimated I/O Cost	37.8224
Estimated Operator Cost	39.9576 (97%)
Estimated CPU Cost	2.13526
Estimated Subtree Cost	39.9576
Number of Executions	4
Estimated Number of Executions	1
Estimated Number of Rows	15840
Estimated Row Size	112 B
Actual Rebinds	0
Actual Rewinds	0
Ordered	False
Node ID	58

Predicate
([tempdb].[dbo].[SOD].[ProductID]+(1)-(1))=(800)
Object
[tempdb].[dbo].[SOD].[idxPrd]
Output List
[tempdb].[dbo].[SOD].SalesOrderID, [tempdb].[dbo].[SOD].SalesOrderDetailID, [tempdb].[dbo].[SOD].CarrierTrackingNumber, [tempdb].[dbo].[SOD].OrderQty, [tempdb].[dbo].[SOD].ProductID, [tempdb].[dbo].[SOD].SpecialOfferID, [tempdb].[dbo].[SOD].UnitPrice, [tempdb].[dbo].[SOD].UnitPriceDiscount, [tempdb].[dbo].[SOD].LineTotal, [tempdb].[dbo].[SOD].rowguid, [tempdb].[dbo].[SOD].ModifiedDate

Stored Procedure Parameter Sniffing & Prevention

When SQL Server database engine compiles a stored procedure, it may use the actual parameters supplied to prepare an execution plan. If the parameters are atypical, the plan may be slow for typical parameters. For consistent stored procedure performance parameter sniffing should be eliminated. A telltale sign of parameter sniffing when suddenly a stored procedure executes in 2 minutes, as an example, instead of the usual 10 seconds. *This is different when the first (cold from disk) execution of a stored procedure is much longer than the second & on (warm since pages in buffer memory) execution.* Parameter sniffing may show up also as 5 minutes execution in one environment (like application) & 2 seconds in SSMS.

Article: **Batch Compilation, Recompilation, and Plan Caching Issues in SQL Server 2005**
http://technet.microsoft.com/en-us/library/cc966425.aspx

Here are the most popular two ways of preventing parameter sniffing

First prevention method: remap parameters to local variables and use those only.

```
USE AdventureWorks2012;
GO
CREATE PROCEDURE uspProductByColor @pcolor varchar(20)   AS BEGIN
        DECLARE @color varchar(20) = @pcolor;            -- remapping
        SET NOCOUNT ON;
        SELECT * FROM Production.Product WHERE Color = @color  ORDER BY name;    END
GO
EXEC uspProductByColor 'Red';  -- 38 rows returned
```

Second prevention method: RECOMPILE stored procedure at each execution (for large procedure compilation time may be significant).

```
CREATE PROCEDURE uspProductByColor @pcolor varchar(20)
WITH RECOMPILE AS BEGIN  SET NOCOUNT ON;
   SELECT * FROM Production.Product WHERE Color = @pcolor   ORDER BY name; END
```

Optimizing with MERGE

Single statement MERGE can perform better than multi statements INSERT/UPDATE/DELETE.

Technet Article: **Optimizing MERGE Statement Performance**
http://technet.microsoft.com/en-us/library/cc879317(v=sql.105).aspx

Stress Testing a View with Include Client Statistics Feature

Client Statistics feature can be turned by icon or right click drop-down menu option. It calculates averages for up to 10 trials. DBCC DROPCLEANBUFFERS equalizes the tests by purging the cached data pages from buffer memory. Note: server load will influence timings. Query drop-down has option to Reset Client Statistics.

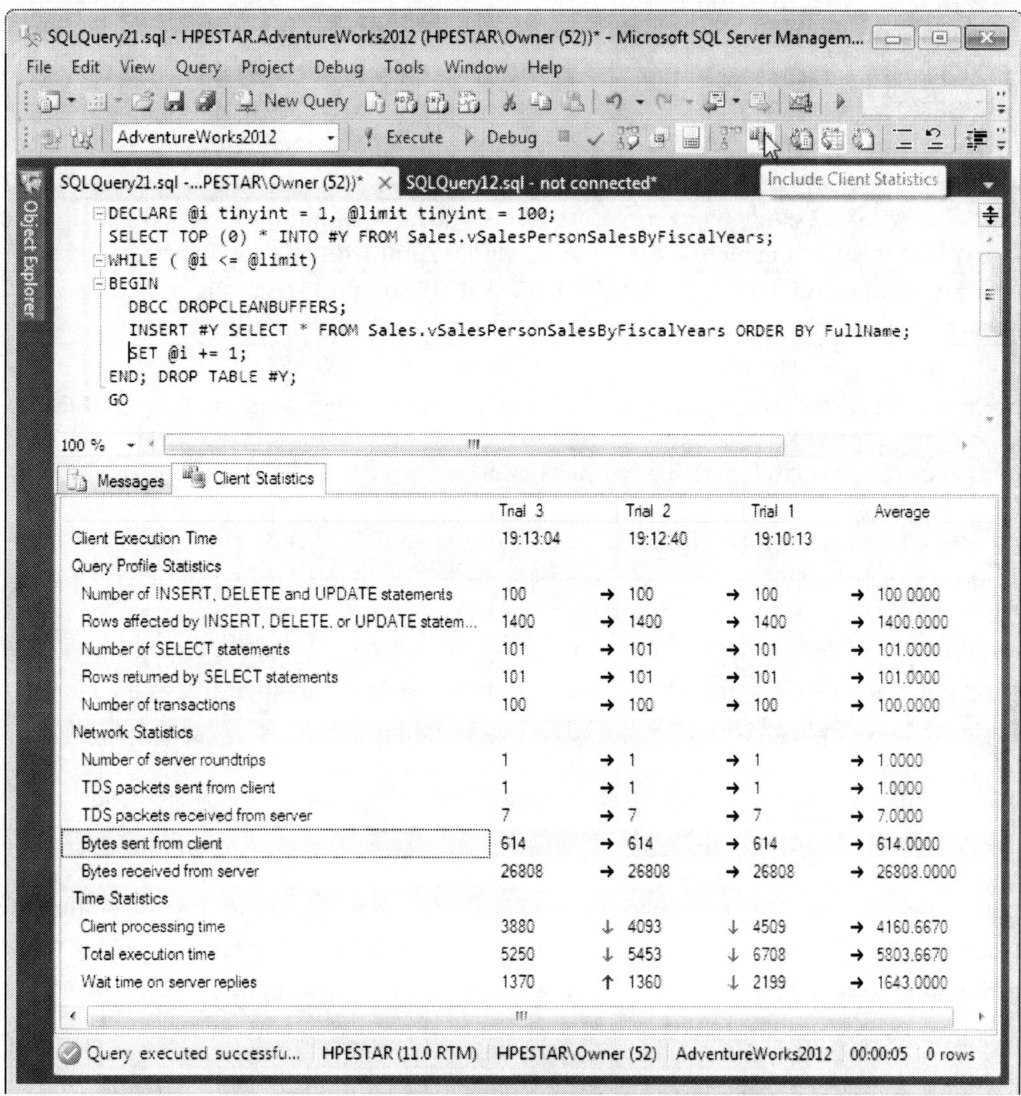

Maximum Capacity Specifications for SQL Server
http://msdn.microsoft.com/en-us/library/ms143432.aspx

10 Point Optimization Guide

Performance tuning and optimization are a huge topic. We only touch the tip of the iceberg. Nonetheless, the important elements of optimization can be summarized quite easily. It starts with prioritizing what is business critical, what is not. If 500 users are unhappy with a stored procedure, that is business critical. If one user is unhappy with a slow report, that is not business critical, unless that user is the CEO.

1. **REBUILD indexes every weekend**. Use FILLFACTOR for dynamic tables with lots of INSERTs. FILLFACTOR 70 means 70% data and 30% empty space. Free database maintenance scripts at http://ola.hallengren.com/ - SQL Server Backup, Integrity Check, and Index and Statistics Maintenance.
2. **UPDATE STATISTICS every night**. The database engine query optimizer uses the statistics to prepare efficient execution plans. Turn on Auto Update Statistics / Asynchronously options.
3. **Eliminate missing indexes**. All FOREIGN KEY & WHERE condition columns should be considered for indexing.

4. Optimize all business critical queries. WHERE & ON clause predicates should be SARGable.

5. Examine execution plan for business critical queries to make sure they are efficient.

6. Optimize all business critical stored procedures. In a sproc all queries should be optimized and looping should be kept at an absolute minimum. Non-scalable cursors should be avoided.

7. Server memory max should be set in server properties. That is quite a challenge with 32-bit OS. For 64 bit OS with 65GB of memory, max memory should be set to 55GB, as a general guideline, to leave enough room for SS and other program operations.

8. Disk configuration should be optimized. Article: http://technet.microsoft.com/en-us/library/cc966412.aspx .

9. Operational solutions for performance problems which cannot be readily resolved due to lack of resources. For example, external feed arrives 11AM every day and promptly uploaded in 1/2 hour thus slowing down the system and annoying users. Instead schedule uploading with SQL Server Agent to low use time like 11pm.

10. Database design should be efficient. Narrow and fixed row size tables are the best performant. Note: frequently database design is frozen, "as is" , for budget reasons or a 3rd party package. Even in a such a case, index & statistics maintenance can improve performance.

Object Explorer GUI REBUILD Indexes

The indexes can be rebuilt in SSMS Object Explorer using Graphical User Interface. REBUILD indexes updates statistics as well. T-SQL command syntax example:

```
ALTER INDEX ALL ON [Sales].[SalesOrderDetail] REBUILD WITH ( FILLFACTOR = 90);
```

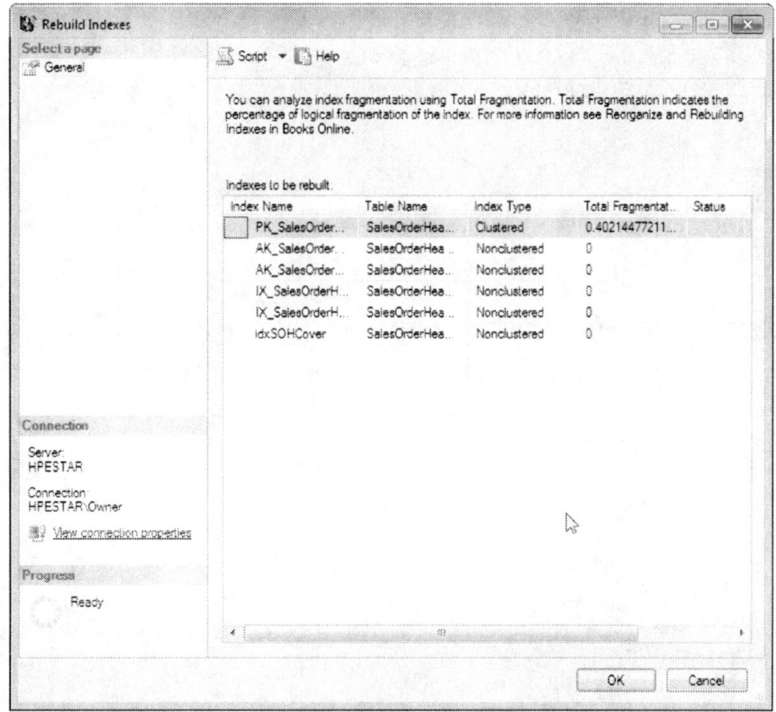

UPDATE STATISTICS on All Tables Stored Procedure

The UPDATE STATISTICS on all tables stored procedure has one parameter: the sample percent for scanning. Lower the number, faster the update. WITH FULLSCAN option does 100% sampling, it may be slow for large tables. Create & execute stored procedure script.

```
CREATE PROCEDURE sprocUpdateAllStats (@Sample int)  AS
BEGIN   DECLARE @SQL AS NVARCHAR(1024), @Table sysname, @Schema sysname;
DECLARE curAllTables CURSOR LOCAL STATIC FOR
            SELECT TABLE_SCHEMA, TABLE_NAME
            FROM INFORMATION_SCHEMA.TABLES
            WHERE TABLE_TYPE='BASE TABLE'
            ORDER BY TABLE_SCHEMA, TABLE_NAME;
OPEN curAllTables;   FETCH NEXT FROM curAllTables  INTO @Schema, @Table;

WHILE (@@FETCH_STATUS = 0) BEGIN
 SET @SQL =          CONCAT('UPDATE STATISTICS ',
                     QUOTENAME( @Schema),'.', QUOTENAME( @Table),
                     ' WITH SAMPLE ', CONVERT(char(3), @sample), ' PERCENT;');
--                   ' WITH FULLSCAN; ');
 PRINT @SQL;
 -- UPDATE STATISTICS [Sales].[Store] WITH SAMPLE 10 PERCENT;

 EXEC sp_executesql @SQL;
  FETCH NEXT FROM curAllTables          INTO @Schema, @Table;   END -- while
 CLOSE curAllTables;  DEALLOCATE curAllTables;
END
GO
```

```
EXEC sprocUpdateAllStats 10;
```

Optimizing with Server Options: optimize for ad hoc workloads

There are optimization related server options. This one for workloads that contain many single use ad hoc batches such as dynamic SQL queries. This helps to ease memory pressure by preventing the plan cache to be filled with compiled plans that are single use.

```
USE master;
GO
EXEC sys.sp_configure N'optimize for ad hoc workloads', N'1';
GO
RECONFIGURE WITH OVERRIDE;
GO
```

Blocking of a Query by Another Query

SQL Server applies locks at the row, page and table level in order to maintain data integrity. If another query tries to operate on the locked part, it may get blocked. It is easy to see how blocking can degrade the performance of the server. We can simulate blocking. In connection 1 we execute and leave open a transaction. In connection 2 we execute a query which intends to operate on the locked table. The result is blocking of connection 2 query by connection 1 query.

```
BEGIN TRAN;                                    -- Connection 1
UPDATE HumanResources.Shift SET ModifiedDate = convert(datetime, ModifiedDate);
-- ROLLBACK TRAN;
```

```
BEGIN TRAN;                                    -- Connection 2
UPDATE HumanResources.Shift SET ModifiedDate = convert(datetime, ModifiedDate);
COMMIT TRAN;
```

Checking blocking by **sp_who** system procedure (exec sp_who in a 3rd connection) and **Activity Monitor** (right click on server menu). The Activity Monitor chart even shows the Head Blocker which is very helpful to trace the source of a blocking chain. A quick resolution is killing the head blocker (kill 55). Long term fix is making the blocking query efficient.

	spid	ecid	status	loginame	hostname	blk	dbname	cmd
36	52	0	runnable	HPES...	HPEST...	0	master	SELECT
37	53	0	sleeping	NT SE...	HPEST...	0	ReportServer	AWAITING COMMAND
38	54	0	sleeping	HPES...	HPEST...	0	master	AWAITING COMMAND
39	55	0	sleeping	HPES...	HPEST...	0	AdventureWorks2012	AWAITING COMMAND
40	56	0	sleeping	NT SE...	HPEST...	0	ReportServer	AWAITING COMMAND
41	57	0	suspended	HPES...	HPEST...	55	AdventureWorks2012	UPDATE

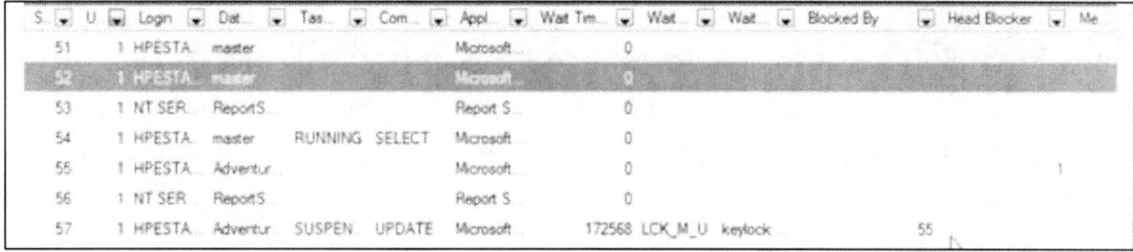

S...	U...	Login	Dat...	Tas...	Com...	Appl...	Wait Tim...	Wait...	Wait...	Blocked By	Head Blocker	Me
51	1	HPESTA...	master			Microsoft...	0					
52	1	HPESTA...	master			Microsoft...	0					
53	1	NT SER...	ReportS...			Report S...	0					
54	1	HPESTA...	master	RUNNING	SELECT	Microsoft...	0					
55	1	HPESTA...	Adventur...			Microsoft...	0				1	
56	1	NT SER...	ReportS...			Report S...	0					
57	1	HPESTA...	Adventur...	SUSPEN...	UPDATE	Microsoft...	172568	LCK_M_U	keylock...	55		

HOLDLOCK, ROWLOCK, TABLOCK & Other Table Hints

Table hints can be applied to carry out critical operations in multi-user environment.

BOL Article: **Table Hints** http://msdn.microsoft.com/en-us/library/ms187373.aspx

Activity Monitor

The Activity Monitor provides real time operational information in list and graphical chart formats based on operational DMV-s.

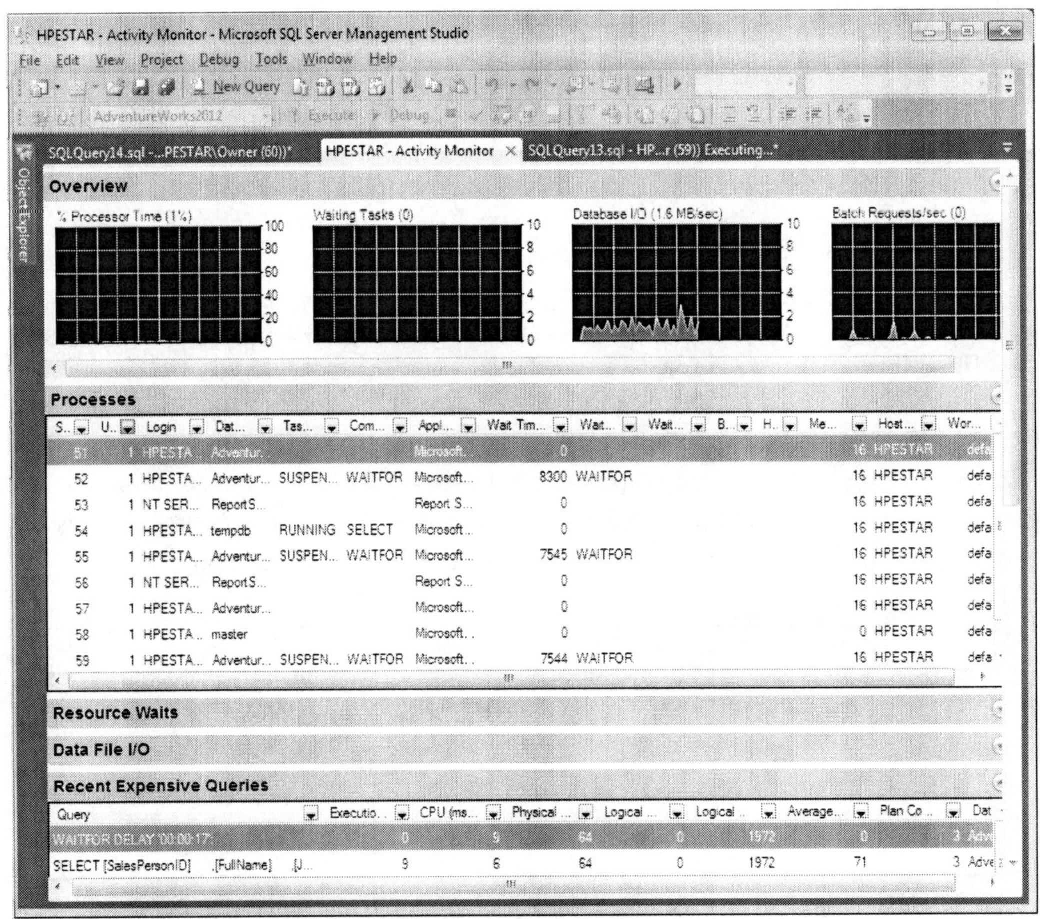

Operational Solutions for Performance Problems

Frequently real fix cannot be carried out quickly or at all for a performance issue due to software complexities and limited expert-level resources. In such a case we have to think about implementing operational solutions:

- Users complain about slow online reports. Setup reports as night jobs with automatic email distribution.
- Reports slow OLTP activities. Restore last night DB backup under new name as reporting DB. Usually, only a small fraction of reports need to be real-time.

Server & Database Standard Reports

The Server Standard Reports can be accessed via the right click on server drop-down menu in SSMS Object Explorer (top left). The Database Standard Reports can be accessed via the right click on database drop down menu (top right). The reports are based on Dynamic Management Views (DMV-s). They represent operational data since the last restart of the server. At the bottom, partial display of the Index Usage Statistics report.

Server Standard Reports	Database Standard Reports
Server Dashboard	Disk Usage
Configuration Changes History	Disk Usage by Top Tables
Schema Changes History	Disk Usage by Table
Scheduler Health	Disk Usage by Partition
Memory Consumption	Backup and Restore Events
Activity - All Blocking Transactions	All Transactions
Activity - All Cursors	All Blocking Transactions
Activity - Top Cursors	Top Transactions by Age
Activity - All Sessions	Top Transactions by Blocked Transactions Count
Activity - Top Sessions	Top Transactions by Locks Count
Activity - Dormant Sessions	Resource Locking Statistics by Objects
Activity - Top Connections	Object Execution Statistics
Top Transactions by Age	Database Consistency History
Top Transactions by Blocked Transactions Count	Index Usage Statistics
Top Transactions by Locks Count	Index Physical Statistics
Performance - Batch Execution Statistics	Schema Changes History
Performance - Object Execution Statistics	User Statistics
Performance - Top Queries by Average CPU Time	
Performance - Top Queries by Average IO	
Performance - Top Queries by Total CPU Time	
Performance - Top Queries by Total IO	
Service Broker Statistics	
Transaction Log Shipping Status	

⊟ HumanResources.Employee

Index Name	Index Type	# User Seeks	# User Scans	# User Updates
PK_Employee_BusinessEntityID	CLUSTERED	697	0	0

⊟ HumanResources.Shift

Index Name	Index Type	# User Seeks	# User Scans	# User Updates
PK_Shift_ShiftID	CLUSTERED	0	5	5

⊟ Person.Person

Batching Large INSERT, UPDATE & DELETE

Batch processing jobs best executed at low use time like night or weekend. Frequently, however, we may not have a choice, we have to run them during transactional activities. We can minimize conflict by breaking down a large job to small batches and providing 1 second or so wait time for other queries to execute. During that 1 second hundreds of short transactions may execute. DELETE from large tables may prove to be very slow due to restructuring of the index pages.

```
USE tempdb;   SELECT      ProductID=CONVERT(int, ProductID), ProductName=Name,
                          ProductNumber, ListPrice, Color, Size
INTO Product FROM AdventureWorks2008.Production.Product;
```

```
INSERT Product SELECT * FROM Product; -- Double table rows at each execution
GO 16 /* .....   (16515072 row(s) affected)      Batch execution completed 16 times.   */
SELECT FORMAT(COUNT(*),'###,###,###') FROM Product;   -- 33,030,144
CREATE CLUSTERED INDEX idxProductID  on Product(ProductID);
GO -- 12 minutes 44 seconds
```

```
DECLARE @BatchSize int = 10000;
WHILE (@@ROWCOUNT > 0)   BEGIN          WAITFOR DELAY '00:00:01';
        DELETE TOP (@BatchSize) FROM Product   WHERE ProductNumber = 'CA-5965';  END
GO   -- 3 minutes 8 seconds
/*(10000 row(s) affected) (10000 row(s) affected) (10000 row(s) affected) (10000 row(s) affected) (10000 row(s) affected)
(10000 row(s) affected) (5536 row(s) affected) (0 row(s) affected)*/
```

```
SELECT FORMAT(COUNT(*),'###,###,###') FROM Product;   -- 32,964,608  -- 5 seconds
DROP TABLE tempdb.dbo.Product;
```

Updating STATISTICS with sp_updatestats

The sp_updatestats system procedure can be used to UPDATE STATISTICS all tables in a database. It is usually faster than running UPDATE STATISTICS on each table.

```
USE AdventureWorks2012;    EXEC sp_updatestats;
```

MSDN Article: **sp_updatestats**
http://msdn.microsoft.com/en-us/library/aa260337(v=sql.80).aspx

Database option is available for automatic update of STATISTICS (time decided by server):

```
USE [master]; ALTER DATABASE [AdventureWorks2012] SET AUTO_UPDATE_STATISTICS ON WITH NO_WAIT;
```

Database Engine Tuning Advisor

The Database Engine Tuning Advisor (DETA or DTA) provides indexing & statistics recommendations based on the supplied workload. A single query can be analyzed as well, right click Query drop-down menu.

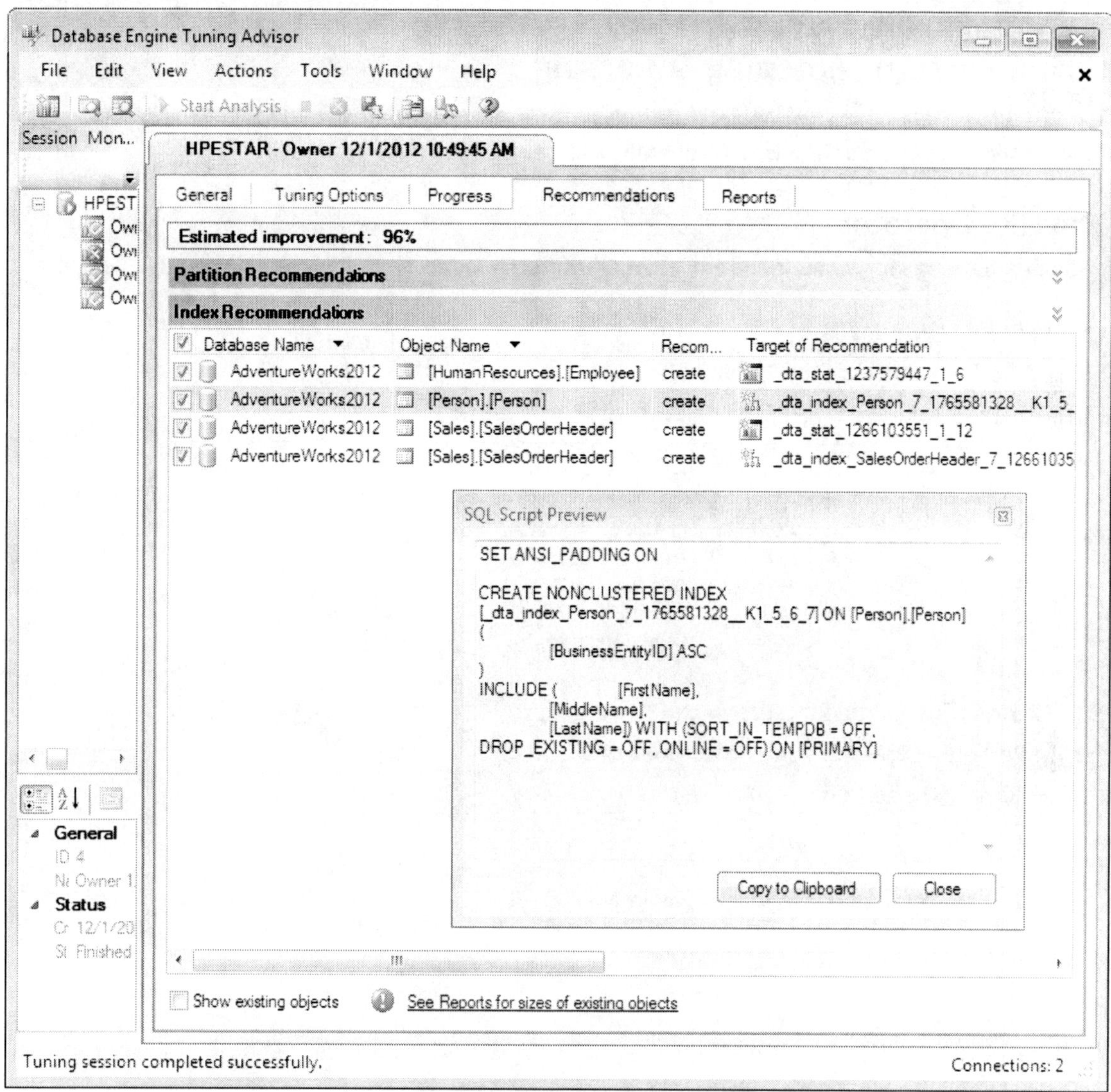

DBCC HELP Command

With the DBCC HELP command you can get syntax assistance with any of the DBCC commands.

```
DBCC HELP (checkdb);
```

CHAPTER 21: Advanced T-SQL Programming Topics

String Pattern Matching & Parsing

The CHARINDEX() function, PATINDEX() function and LIKE operator offer substring search in string functionality with some differences. Frequently, all 3 can be used for the same result.

The LIKE Operator

LIKE operator usage for numeric and alphanumeric differentiation.

```
USE AdventureWorks2012;
SELECT AddressID, City, StateProvinceID, PostalCode
FROM Person.Address WHERE PostalCode LIKE '%[^0-9]%';
-- (3644 row(s) affected) - Partial results.
```

AddressID	City	StateProvinceID	PostalCode
532	Ottawa	57	K4B 1S2
497	Burnaby	7	V5A 4X1
15272	Haney	7	V2W 1W2
14068	Cambridge	14	CB4 4BZ

```
SELECT AddressID, City, StateProvinceID, PostalCode
FROM Person.Address WHERE PostalCode NOT LIKE '%[^0-9]%';
-- (15970 row(s) affected) - Partial results.
```

AddressID	City	StateProvinceID	PostalCode
26916	Dunkerque	145	59140
28885	Lille	145	59000
708	Paris	161	75017
23902	Lieusaint	163	77127

Elaborate patterns can be formed from regular characters and wildcard characters. Underscore (_) matches any character.

```
DECLARE @Pattern varchar(20) = '[CFPS]___[eo]n'
SELECT DISTINCT LastName FROM Person.Person WHERE LastName  LIKE @Pattern;
-- Campen, Cannon, Carson,  Fulton, Patten, Slaven, Sutton
```

The CHARINDEX() Function

The CHARINDEX() function locates a substring within a string. A string with 2 hyphens (-) is split into 3 parts.

```
SELECT        ProductNumber,
              [Part1] = LEFT(ProductNumber,CHARINDEX('-',ProductNumber) - 1),
              [Part2] = SUBSTRING(ProductNumber,CHARINDEX('-',ProductNumber) + 1,
                        CHARINDEX('-',ProductNumber,CHARINDEX('-',
                        ProductNumber) + 1) - (CHARINDEX('-',ProductNumber) + 1)),
              [Part3] = RIGHT(ProductNumber,CHARINDEX('-',REVERSE(ProductNumber)) - 1)
FROM AdventureWorks2012.Production.Product
WHERE LEN(ProductNumber) - LEN(REPLACE(ProductNumber, '-','')) = 2;   -- 2 hyphens in string
-- (213 row(s) affected) - Partial results.
```

ProductNumber	Part1	Part2	Part3
BK-M18B-40	BK	M18B	40
BK-M18B-42	BK	M18B	42
BK-M18B-44	BK	M18B	44
BK-M18B-48	BK	M18B	48
BK-M18B-52	BK	M18B	52

Find the left part of a string before the comma. We get an error without the NULLIF function due to subtracting 1 from the LEN() result which may be 0 (zero).

```
SELECT Name, LEFT(Name,CHARINDEX(',',Name)-1) AS NamePrefix
FROM AdventureWorks2012.Production.Product ORDER BY Name;
/* Msg 537, Level 16, State 3, Line 1
Invalid length parameter passed to the LEFT or SUBSTRING function. */
```

```
SELECT  ProductNumber,
        NamePrefix=LEFT(Name,COALESCE(NULLIF(CHARINDEX(',',Name)-1,-1),LEN(Name))),
        ProductName=Name
FROM AdventureWorks2012.Production.Product ORDER BY ProductName;
-- (504 row(s) affected) - Partial results;
```

ProductNumber	NamePrefix	ProductName
FR-T67Y-58	LL Touring Frame - Yellow	LL Touring Frame - Yellow, 58
FR-T67Y-62	LL Touring Frame - Yellow	LL Touring Frame - Yellow, 62
HB-T721	LL Touring Handlebars	LL Touring Handlebars
SA-T467	LL Touring Seat Assembly	LL Touring Seat Assembly

The PATINDEX() Function

The PATINDEX() function can be used for complex pattern searches.

```
use AdventureWorks2012;
```

```
select          [Name]                    AS ProductName,
                ProductNumber,
                [Description],
                ListPrice
from [Production].[Product] p
  inner join [Production].[ProductModelProductDescriptionCulture] pmpdc
      on p.ProductModelID = pmpdc.ProductModelID
  inner join  [Production].[ProductDescription] pd
      on pmpdc.ProductDescriptionID = pd.ProductDescriptionID
where patindex( '%mountain%innovative%', pd.[Description]) > 0
order by ProductNumber DESC;
-- (8 row(s) affected) - Partial results.
```

ProductName	ProductNumber	Description	ListPrice
Mountain-100 Silver, 48	BK-M82S-48	Top-of-the-line competition mountain bike. Performance-enhancing options include the innovative HL Frame, super-smooth front suspension, and traction for all terrain.	3399.99

Searching UNICODE Chinese text.

```
select [Name] AS ProductName, ProductNumber, [Description], ListPrice
from [Production].[Product] p
  inner join [Production].[ProductModelProductDescriptionCulture] pmpdc
      on p.ProductModelID = pmpdc.ProductModelID
  inner join  [Production].[ProductDescription] pd
      on pmpdc.ProductDescriptionID = pd.ProductDescriptionID
where patindex( N'%量的%快速%', pd.[Description]) > 0
order by ProductNumber DESC;
```

ProductName	ProductNumber	Description	ListPrice
HL Headset	HS-3479	高质量的一英寸无螺纹车头碗组具有油口，可确保快速润滑。	124.73

Complex pattern match with wildcards.

```
SELECT PATINDEX('%[A-T,0-9]%[Q,0-9]%[0-9]%','ZQZQXYZABC123');  --2
```

Composable DML - INSERT into 2 Tables with One Statement

Composable DML is new to SQL Server 2012. It expands the concept of SELECT subquery to INSERT/UPDATE/DELETE/MERGE operation using the OUTPUT clause with some restrictions.

```
USE tempdb;
CREATE TABLE PurchaseOrderDetail(                    -- Create 2 empty tables for testing
        PurchaseOrderID int NOT NULL,
        PurchaseOrderDetailID int NOT NULL,
        DueDate datetime NOT NULL,
        OrderQty smallint NOT NULL,
        ProductID int NOT NULL,
        UnitPrice money NOT NULL,
        LineTotal  money,
        ReceivedQty decimal(8, 2) NOT NULL,
        RejectedQty decimal(8, 2) NOT NULL,
        StockedQty  int,
        ModifiedDate datetime NOT NULL);
```

```
SELECT * INTO POD FROM PurchaseOrderDetail;
```

```
INSERT PurchaseOrderDetail  OUTPUT inserted.*            -- Test query with OUTPUT
SELECT * FROM AdventureWorks2012.Purchasing.PurchaseOrderDetail
GO
-- (8845 row(s) affected)
```

```
TRUNCATE TABLE PurchaseOrderDetail;
GO
-- Command(s) completed successfully.
```

```
INSERT POD                                               -- Composable DML
SELECT *  FROM (
        INSERT PurchaseOrderDetail      OUTPUT inserted.*
        SELECT * FROM AdventureWorks2012.Purchasing.PurchaseOrderDetail ) X ;
GO
```

```
SELECT COUNT(*) FROM POD;                                -- 8845
SELECT COUNT(*) FROM PurchaseOrderDetail;                -- 8845
GO
```

```
DROP TABLE POD;  DROP TABLE PurchaseOrderDetail;
```

Double Assignment Operator

The multiple value assignment operator allows more than one assignment for the same value.

```
USE tempdb;
SELECT          CONVERT(int, SalesOrderID)                    AS ID,
                CONVERT(date, ModifiedDate)                   AS TestDate
INTO  DateSequence  FROM  AdventureWorks2012.Sales.SalesOrderHeader ;
go --(31465 row(s) affected)
SELECT TOP 2 * FROM  DateSequence ;
```

ID	TestDate
43659	2005-07-08
43660	2005-07-08

```
-- Multiple assignment UPDATE
DECLARE @Date date = dateadd(day, 1, CURRENT_TIMESTAMP),   @id  int = 0 ;
UPDATE DateSequence SET @id = ID = @id + 1,  @Date = TestDate = dateadd (Day, -1, @Date);
SELECT TOP 2 * FROM  DateSequence ORDER BY TestDate DESC;
```

ID	TestDate
1	2012-10-21
2	2012-10-20

When to Use OUTER JOIN

INNER JOIN returns only the matching rows as specified in the ON clause. **OUTER JOIN returns the matching and non matching rows.** If we want to see the products not sold (QtySold NULL) in the given period also, we have to use RIGHT OUTER JOIN (or RIGHT JOIN) directed toward the Product table.

```
SELECT P.Name AS ProductName, SUM(SOD.OrderQty) AS QtySold FROM Sales.SalesOrderHeader AS SOH
        INNER JOIN Sales.SalesOrderDetail AS SOD ON SOH.SalesOrderID = SOD.SalesOrderID
            AND SOH.OrderDate >= '20080101' AND SOH.OrderDate < '20080201'
        INNER JOIN Production.Product AS P ON SOD.ProductID = P.ProductID
WHERE P.ListPrice > 0.0 GROUP BY P.Name  ORDER BY ProductName; -- (145 row(s) affected)
```

```
SELECT P.Name AS ProductName, SUM(SOD.OrderQty) AS QtySold FROM Sales.SalesOrderHeader AS SOH
        INNER JOIN Sales.SalesOrderDetail AS SOD ON SOH.SalesOrderID = SOD.SalesOrderID
            AND SOH.OrderDate >= '20080101' AND SOH.OrderDate < '20080201'
        RIGHT OUTER JOIN Production.Product AS P ON SOD.ProductID = P.ProductID
WHERE  P.ListPrice > 0.0 GROUP BY P.Name  ORDER BY ProductName; -- (304 row(s) affected) - Partial results.
```

ProductName	QtySold
Bike Wash - Dissolver	208
Cable Lock	NULL
Chain	24

Running Total & Average Calculation with the OVER Clause

Running total support is a new feature of SQL Server 2012. OVER clause makes the RT calculation a breeze.

```
USE AdventureWorks2012;
GO
```

```
SELECT SalesOrderID,
  FORMAT(TotalDue,'c0','en-US')                                          AS TotalDue,
  FORMAT(COUNT(TotalDue) OVER( ORDER BY SalesOrderID), '###,###') AS RunningCount,
  FORMAT(SUM(TotalDue) OVER( ORDER BY SalesOrderID), 'c0','en-US')  AS RunningTotal,
  FORMAT(AVG(TotalDue) OVER( ORDER BY SalesOrderID), 'c0','en-US')  AS RunningAvg
FROM Sales.SalesOrderHeader
WHERE OrderDate >='20080201'  AND OrderDate < DATEADD(mm,1,'20080201')
ORDER BY SalesOrderID;
GO -- (2032 row(s) affected) - Partial results.
```

SalesOrderID	TotalDue	RunningCount	RunningTotal	RunningAvg
63119	$247	1	$247	$247
63120	$234	2	$481	$240
63121	$187	3	$668	$223
63122	$213	4	$881	$220
63123	$16,320	5	$17,201	$3,440
63124	$36,462	6	$53,663	$8,944
63125	$9,603	7	$63,266	$9,038

Running Total with Subquery - Ye Olde Way

Calculating cumulative totals with subquery is quite inefficient, but it works.

```
USE AdventureWorks2012;
GO
```

```
DECLARE @Year INT = 2005, @Month INT = 7;
SELECT   RN = ROW_NUMBER()
              OVER(ORDER BY SalesOrderID),
      OrderDate = convert(CHAR(10),OrderDate,111), -- date formatting
      SalesOrderId,
      TotalDue = '$' + convert(VARCHAR,TotalDue,1), -- Currency formatting
      [Running Total] = '$' + convert(VARCHAR,
      (SELECT sum(TotalDue)
       FROM   Sales.SalesOrderHeader
       WHERE  SalesOrderID <= soh.SalesOrderID     -- Key predicate in the process
```

```
        AND year(OrderDate) = @Year
        AND month(OrderDate) = @Month),
                    1)
FROM    Sales.SalesOrderHeader soh
WHERE   year(OrderDate) = @Year
    AND month(OrderDate) = @Month
ORDER BY RN;
GO
-- (184 row(s) affected) - Partial results.
```

RN	OrderDate	SalesOrderId	TotalDue	Running Total
1	2005/07/01	43659	$23,153.23	$23,153.23
2	2005/07/01	43660	$1,457.33	$24,610.56
3	2005/07/01	43661	$36,865.80	$61,476.36
4	2005/07/01	43662	$32,474.93	$93,951.30
5	2005/07/01	43663	$472.31	$94,423.61
6	2005/07/01	43664	$27,510.41	$121,934.02
7	2005/07/01	43665	$16,158.70	$138,092.71
8	2005/07/01	43666	$5,694.86	$143,787.57
9	2005/07/01	43667	$6,876.36	$150,663.94
10	2005/07/01	43668	$40,487.72	$191,151.66
11	2005/07/01	43669	$807.26	$191,958.92
12	2005/07/01	43670	$6,893.25	$198,852.17
13	2005/07/01	43671	$9,153.61	$208,005.78
14	2005/07/01	43672	$6,895.41	$214,901.19
15	2005/07/01	43673	$4,216.03	$219,117.21

Running Total with Multiple Assignment UPDATE

Cumulative total can be generated a fast way using double assignment SET in UPDATE command. There are some restrictions such as no table partitioning. It should not be used in production unless there is a serious performance problem.

```
USE AdventureWorks2012;
```

```
DECLARE @RunningTotal MONEY;
DECLARE @Result TABLE(
            SalesOrderID INT    NOT NULL    PRIMARY KEY,
            TotalDue    MONEY,
            RunningTotal MONEY
            );
SET @RunningTotal = 0.0;
INSERT INTO @Result
      (SalesOrderID,        TotalDue)
```

```
SELECT   SalesOrderID,       TotalDue
FROM     Sales.SalesOrderHeader
ORDER BY SalesOrderID
-- (31465 row(s) affected)

UPDATE @Result
SET   @RunningTotal = RunningTotal = @RunningTotal + TotalDue;
-- (31465 row(s) affected)

SELECT   SalesOrderId,
         FORMAT(TotalDue,'c0','en-US')          AS TotalDue,
         FORMAT(RunningTotal, 'c0','en-US')     AS RunningTotal
FROM     @Result ORDER BY SalesOrderID;
GO
-- (31465 row(s) affected) -- Partial results.
```

SalesOrderId	TotalDue	RunningTotal
43659	$23,153	$23,153
43660	$1,457	$24,611
43661	$36,866	$61,476
43662	$32,475	$93,951
43663	$472	$94,424
43664	$27,510	$121,934
43665	$16,159	$138,093

Defining Custom User-Defined Data Type

For consistency across the database, custom user-defined data types can be configured. Once defined, the custom data types can be used in any table or for any variable.

```
USE [AdventureWorks2012];
GO
CREATE TYPE dbo.AccountNo FROM char(11) NOT NULL;
GO
CREATE TABLE Customer (
         CustomerID INT IDENTITY(1,1) PRIMARY KEY,                -- Identity & PK constraint
         AccountNumber AccountNo UNIQUE,                          -- Unique constraint
         Balance MONEY CHECK ( Balance >= 0.0),                   -- CHECK constraint
         ModifiedDate datetime default (CURRENT_TIMESTAMP));      -- Default constraint
GO

DECLARE @Account dbo.AccountNo = '12345678901';
```

Subtotal, Total & Grand Total GROUPING Function

It is a challenge to generate multi-level totals in T-SQL. The GROUPING() function tells us what level we are on in the GROUP BY summary.

```
USE AdventureWorks2012;
```

```
SELECT *
FROM   (SELECT COALESCE(CONVERT(VARCHAR, YEAR(OrderDate)), '')                  AS YYYY,
        COALESCE(LEFT(CONVERT(VARCHAR, OrderDate, 111), 7), '')                 AS MM,
        FORMAT(COUNT(*), '###,###')                                             AS ORDERS,
        FORMAT(SUM(TotalDue), 'c0', 'en-US')                                    AS SALES,
        CASE    WHEN GROUPING(LEFT(CONVERT(VARCHAR, OrderDate, 111), 7)) = 0
            AND GROUPING(YEAR(OrderDate)) = 1 THEN 'SUBTOTAL'
          ELSE ''
        END                                                                     AS GRPMM,
         CASE   WHEN GROUPING(YEAR(OrderDate)) = 0
            AND GROUPING(LEFT(CONVERT(VARCHAR, OrderDate, 111), 7)) =  1 THEN  'TOTAL'
          ELSE ''
        END                                                                     AS GRPYY,
         CASE   WHEN GROUPING(LEFT(CONVERT(VARCHAR, OrderDate, 111), 7)) = 1
            AND GROUPING(YEAR(OrderDate)) = 1 THEN 'GRAND TOTAL'
          ELSE ''
        END                                                                     AS GRPALL
     FROM  Sales.SalesOrderHeader
   GROUP  BY YEAR(OrderDate),  LEFT(CONVERT(VARCHAR, OrderDate, 111), 7) WITH CUBE) rpt
WHERE  GRPMM != ''  OR GRPYY != ''   OR GRPALL != ''
ORDER  BY CASE  WHEN GRPALL != '' THEN 3   WHEN GRPYY != '' THEN 2    ELSE 1  END,
      YYYY,  MM ;
```

YYYY	MM	ORDERS	SALES	GRPMM	GRPYY	GRPALL
	2008/01	1,946	$3,359,927	SUBTOTAL		
	2008/02	2,032	$4,662,656	SUBTOTAL		
	2008/03	2,109	$4,722,358	SUBTOTAL		
	2008/04	2,128	$4,269,365	SUBTOTAL		
	2008/05	2,386	$5,813,557	SUBTOTAL		
	2008/06	2,374	$6,004,156	SUBTOTAL		
	2008/07	976	$56,179	SUBTOTAL		
2005		1,379	$12,693,251		TOTAL	
2006		3,692	$34,463,848		TOTAL	
2007		12,443	$47,171,490		TOTAL	
2008		13,951	$28,888,198		TOTAL	
		31,465	$123,216,786			GRAND TOTAL

The GROUP BY Clause with GROUPING SETS

A GROUP BY clause that uses GROUPING SETS is equivalent to multiple GROUP BY queries combined with UNION ALL operator.

```
USE AdventureWorks2012;

SELECT T."Group"                                AS N'Continent',
    T.CountryRegionCode                         AS N'Country',
    S.Name                                      AS N'Dealer',
    CN.LastName                                 AS N'SalesStaff',
    FORMAT(SUM(TotalDue), 'c0','en-US')         AS N'TotalSales'
FROM   AdventureWorks.Sales.Customer C
    INNER JOIN AdventureWorks.Sales.Store S
        ON C.CustomerID = S.CustomerID
    INNER JOIN AdventureWorks.Sales.SalesTerritory T
        ON C.TerritoryID = T.TerritoryID
    INNER JOIN AdventureWorks.Sales.SalesOrderHeader H
        ON S.CustomerID = H.CustomerID
    INNER JOIN AdventureWorks.Person.Contact CN
        ON H.SalesPersonID = CN.ContactID
GROUP  BY GROUPING SETS( CUBE(T."Group", T.CountryRegionCode), S.Name, CN.LastName  )
ORDER  BY Continent, Country, Dealer, SalesStaff;
-- (664 row(s) affected) - Partial results.
```

Continent	Country	Dealer	SalesStaff	TotalSales
NULL	NULL	Year-Round Sports	NULL	$197,777
NULL	NULL	Yellow Bicycle Company	NULL	$102,699
NULL	AU	NULL	NULL	$2,185,110
NULL	CA	NULL	NULL	$19,316,294
NULL	DE	NULL	NULL	$2,741,548
NULL	FR	NULL	NULL	$6,215,065
NULL	GB	NULL	NULL	$5,758,606
NULL	US	NULL	NULL	$72,049,624
Europe	NULL	NULL	NULL	$14,715,219
Europe	DE	NULL	NULL	$2,741,548
Europe	FR	NULL	NULL	$6,215,065
Europe	GB	NULL	NULL	$5,758,606
North America	NULL	NULL	NULL	$91,365,917
North America	CA	NULL	NULL	$19,316,294
North America	US	NULL	NULL	$72,049,624
Pacific	NULL	NULL	NULL	$2,185,110
Pacific	AU	NULL	NULL	$2,185,110

SELECT Top N from Each Group

Top 3 in each group is a very popular interview question.

```
USE AdventureWorks2012;
```

```
DECLARE @TopN tinyint = 3;
WITH cteBestSalesByProduct
  AS (SELECT ROW_NUMBER() OVER( PARTITION BY sod.ProductID
             ORDER BY Sum(sod.LineTotal) DESC)                    AS  SeqNo,
      CONCAT(FirstName, SPACE(1), LastName)                       AS  [Name],
       p.Name                                                     AS  ProductName,
      FORMAT(CONVERT(MONEY, Sum(sod.LineTotal)), 'c', 'en-US')    AS  TotalBySalesPerson,
      p.ProductNumber,
      sod.ProductID
    FROM   Sales.SalesOrderDetail AS sod
      INNER JOIN Production.Product AS p
        ON sod.ProductID = p.ProductID
      INNER JOIN Sales.SalesOrderHeader AS soh
        ON sod.SalesOrderID = soh.SalesOrderID
      INNER JOIN Person.Person AS pe
        ON soh.SalesPersonID = pe.BusinessEntityID
    WHERE  soh.SalesPersonID IS NOT NULL
    GROUP  BY       CONCAT(FirstName, SPACE(1), LastName),
                    sod.ProductID,
                    p.ProductNumber,
                    p.Name )
SELECT *
FROM   cteBestSalesByProduct cte
WHERE  SeqNo <= @TopN
ORDER  BY      ProductID,
               SeqNo;
-- (749 row(s) affected) - Partial results.
```

SeqNo	Name	ProductName	TotalBySalesPerson	ProductNumber	ProductID
1	Jae Pak	Women's Mountain Shorts, L	$19,385.51	SH-W890-L	869
2	Linda Mitchell	Women's Mountain Shorts, L	$15,371.85	SH-W890-L	869
3	Michael Blythe	Women's Mountain Shorts, L	$11,411.44	SH-W890-L	869
1	Jillian Carson	Water Bottle - 30 oz.	$936.04	WB-H098	870
2	Linda Mitchell	Water Bottle - 30 oz.	$833.59	WB-H098	870
3	Rachel Valdez	Water Bottle - 30 oz.	$758.01	WB-H098	870
1	Jillian Carson	Patch Kit/8 Patches	$163.51	PK-7098	873
2	Jae Pak	Patch Kit/8 Patches	$120.91	PK-7098	873
3	Ranjit Varkey Chudukatil	Patch Kit/8 Patches	$104.42	PK-7098	873

SELECT Top N from Each Group Ye Olde Way

SQL Server 2005 has introduced revolutionary enhancements including the OVER clause and recursive CTE-s. It was a bit cumbersome to program certain tasks prior to SS 2005.

```
USE AdventureWorks2012; DECLARE @Top TINYINT = 3;                -- TOP N products in each subcategory
SELECT Subcategory,     ProductName,   ProductID
FROM  ( SELECT PSC.Name                                          AS SubCategory,
         P1.Name                                                 AS ProductName,    P1.ProductID,
        (SELECT COUNT(*)
        FROM   Production.ProductSubcategory PSC     LEFT JOIN Production.Product P2
        ON P2.ProductSubcategoryID =        PSC.ProductSubcategoryID
        WHERE  P2.ProductSubcategoryID = P1.ProductSubcategoryID AND P2.ProductID <= P1.ProductID) AS RN
  FROM   Production.ProductSubcategory PSC    LEFT JOIN Production.Product P1
         ON P1.ProductSubcategoryID = PSC.ProductSubcategoryID  ) AS    X -- derived table
WHERE  RN <= @Top  ORDER  BY Subcategory,  ProductID;  -- (90 row(s) affected) - Partial results.
```

UPDATE PRIMARY KEY & Connecting FK in a Transaction

Disable & Enable FOREIGN KEY Constraint

The update PRIMARY KEY task (with disable constraint & enable constraint) demonstrates the importance of transaction to protect the integrity of the database: it prevents the database left in a disarray if something goes wrong. Demo only! No reason to change surrogate PK ever!

```
USE tempdb;
SELECT CONVERT(INT,ProductSubcategoryID) AS ProductSubcategoryID, ProductCategoryID, Name
INTO Subcategory FROM AdventureWorks2012.Production.ProductSubcategory; -- (37 row(s) affected)
SELECT * INTO Product FROM AdventureWorks2012.Production.Product;          --(504 row(s) affected)
ALTER TABLE Subcategory ALTER COLUMN ProductSubcategoryID INT NOT NULL;
ALTER TABLE Subcategory ADD CONSTRAINT pkSubcat PRIMARY KEY(ProductSubcategoryID);
ALTER TABLE Product ADD CONSTRAINT pkProd PRIMARY KEY(ProductID);
ALTER TABLE Product ADD CONSTRAINT fkSubcat FOREIGN KEY (ProductSubcategoryID)
REFERENCES Subcategory(ProductSubcategoryID);
GO
```

```
SET XACT_ABORT ON;                -- Automatic rollback in case of error
GO
BEGIN TRAN
ALTER TABLE Product NOCHECK CONSTRAINT fkSubcat;          -- Disable constraint
UPDATE Subcategory SET ProductSubcategoryID = 999 WHERE ProductSubcategoryID = 8; --(1 row(s) affected)
UPDATE Product SET ProductSubcategoryID = 999 WHERE ProductSubcategoryID = 8;     -- (3 row(s) affected)
ALTER TABLE Product CHECK CONSTRAINT fkSubcat;            -- Enable constraint
COMMIT TRAN
GO
```

```
DROP TABLE tempdb.dbo.Product; DROP TABLE tempdb.dbo.Subcategory;
```

Transaction Control with XACT_ABORT Setting

The set option XACT_ABORT rolls back the uncommitted part of the transaction if anything goes wrong. The 3rd INSERT in the stored procedure transaction when @i equals 3 referenced ProductID 5 PK which does not exist. XACT_ABORT rolled back the transaction automatically.

```
USE tempdb; SELECT * INTO Product FROM AdventureWorks2012.Production.Product;
ALTER TABLE Product ADD CONSTRAINT pkProd PRIMARY KEY (ProductID);
SELECT SalesOrderDetailID, ProductID, OrderQty, ModifiedDate
        INTO OrderDetail FROM AdventureWorks2012.Sales.SalesOrderDetail;
ALTER TABLE OrderDetail ADD CONSTRAINT pkOrderDet PRIMARY KEY (SalesOrderDetailID);
ALTER TABLE OrderDetail ADD CONSTRAINT fkProdID
                FOREIGN KEY (ProductID) REFERENCES Product(ProductID);
GO
CREATE PROCEDURE dbo.sprocInsertOrderDetail AS
 BEGIN
    SET NOCOUNT ON ;      SET XACT_ABORT ON ;      DECLARE @i INT = 1;
    WHILE (@i < 5)      BEGIN;   BEGIN TRAN ;  PRINT CONCAT(CONVERT(varchar, @i), ' TRAN STARTS');
        INSERT OrderDetail( ProductID, OrderQty, ModifiedDate) VALUES (@i, 1, getdate());
        INSERT OrderDetail( ProductID, OrderQty, ModifiedDate) VALUES (@i+1, 5, getdate());
        INSERT OrderDetail( ProductID, OrderQty, ModifiedDate) VALUES (@i+2, 10, getdate());
        COMMIT ;  PRINT 'TRAN COMPLETES'; SET @i = @i + 1 ;
    END; -- End WHILE
END ;
GO
EXEC dbo.sprocInsertOrderDetail;
GO -- Messages
```

```
/* 1 TRAN STARTS  TRAN COMPLETES
2 TRAN STARTS   TRAN COMPLETES
3 TRAN STARTS    Msg 547, Level 16, State 0, Procedure sprocInsertOrderDetail, Line 7
The INSERT statement conflicted with the FOREIGN KEY constraint "fkProdID". The conflict occurred in database "tempdb", table "dbo.Product", column 'ProductID'.  */
```

```
SELECT * FROM OrderDetail WHERE ModifiedDate > '20120101' ORDER BY SalesOrderDetailID;
GO
```

SalesOrderDetailID	ProductID	OrderQty	ModifiedDate
121318	1	1	2016-12-26 12:00:05.467
121319	2	5	2016-12-26 12:00:05.467
121320	3	10	2016-12-26 12:00:05.467
121321	2	1	2016-12-26 12:00:05.467
121322	3	5	2016-12-26 12:00:05.467
121323	4	10	2016-12-26 12:00:05.467

```
DROP TABLE tempdb.dbo.OrderDetail;
DROP TABLE tempdb.dbo.Product;
```

Table-Valued Parameters

Table-valued parameters were introduced with SQL Server 2008. They can be used to send parameters to SQL statement, stored procedure or function as next demonstrated. The parameter has to be defined as user-defined table data type. User-defined data type is to define custom column data types.

```
USE AdventureWorks2012;
GO
```

```
-- Create new user-defined table data type
CREATE TYPE dbo.utpProdInfo AS TABLE(
        ProdID          int,
        ProdNbr         char(12),
        StandardCost    money,
        ListPrice       money,
        Color   char(16));
GO
```

```
-- Create user- defined table-valued function(UDF) with table-valued parameter
CREATE FUNCTION ufnColorGrouping (@Input dbo.utpProdInfo READONLY)
        RETURNS @Result TABLE (Color char(16), AvgListPrice money)   AS
BEGIN
 INSERT @Result
 SELECT Color, avg(ListPrice) FROM @Input
 GROUP BY Color
 RETURN
END;
GO
```

```
-- Create stored procedure with table-valued parameter
CREATE PROCEDURE uspPriceRange
                        @Input dbo.utpProdInfo READONLY
AS
BEGIN
 SELECT Color,  MinPrice=format(min(ListPrice), 'c0','en-US'),
                MaxPrice=format(max(ListPrice), 'c0','en-US')
  FROM @Input
  GROUP BY Color
  ORDER BY MAX(ListPrice)  DESC
END;
GO
```

Among the TVP's Benefits: Simple but Powerful Modular Programming

```
-- Test TVF with table-valued parameter
DECLARE @PriceDetail dbo.utpProdInfo
INSERT @PriceDetail SELECT ProductID, ProductNumber, StandardCost, ListPrice, Color
          FROM Production.Product WHERE Color is not null;
```

```
SELECT * FROM ufnColorGrouping (@PriceDetail)
ORDER BY AvgListPrice DESC
```

Color	AvgListPrice
Red	1401.95
Yellow	959.0913
Blue	923.6792
Silver	850.3053
Black	725.121
Grey	125.00
Silver/Black	64.0185
Multi	59.865
White	9.245

```
-- Test stored procedure with table-valued parameter
DECLARE @PriceDetail dbo.utpProdInfo;
INSERT @PriceDetail SELECT ProductID, ProductNumber, StandardCost, ListPrice, Color
          FROM Production.Product WHERE Color is not null;
```

```
EXEC uspPriceRange @PriceDetail;
GO
```

Color	MinPrice	MaxPrice
Red	$35	$3,578
Silver	$0	$3,400
Black	$0	$3,375
Blue	$35	$2,384
Yellow	$54	$2,384
Grey	$125	$125
Multi	$9	$90
Silver/Black	$40	$81
White	$9	$10

```
-- Cleanup
DROP FUNCTION ufnColorGrouping;
DROP PROC uspPriceRange;
DROP TYPE dbo.utpProdInfo;
```

Creating Comma Delimited String from a Column

XML PATH is the most popular way of accomplishing it, but other methods available as well.

```
;WITH CTE AS (
SELECT   ps.[Name]                                          AS Subcategory,
        Stuff((SELECT ', ' + Color AS [text()]
                FROM AdventureWorks2012.Production.Product p
                WHERE p.ProductSubcategoryID = ps.ProductSubcategoryID
                            AND Color is not null
                GROUP BY Color ORDER BY Color
                FOR XML PATH ('')),1,1,'')                  AS ColorList,
        Stuff((SELECT ', ' + Size AS [text()]
                FROM AdventureWorks2012.Production.Product p
                WHERE p.ProductSubcategoryID = ps.ProductSubcategoryID
                            AND Size is not null
                GROUP BY Size ORDER BY Size
                FOR XML PATH ('')),1,1,'')                  AS SizeList
FROM    AdventureWorks2012.Production.ProductSubcategory ps )
SELECT * FROM CTE WHERE ColorList is not null AND SizeList is not null  ORDER BY Subcategory;
```

Subcategory	ColorList	SizeList
Bib-Shorts	Multi	L, M, S
Gloves	Black	L, M, S
Hydration Packs	Silver	70
Jerseys	Multi, Yellow	L, M, S, XL
Mountain Bikes	Black, Silver	38, 40, 42, 44, 46, 48, 52
Mountain Frames	Black, Silver	38, 40, 42, 44, 46, 48, 52
Road Bikes	Black, Red, Yellow	38, 40, 42, 44, 48, 52, 56, 58, 60, 62
Road Frames	Black, Red, Yellow	38, 40, 42, 44, 48, 52, 56, 58, 60, 62
Shorts	Black	L, M, S, XL
Socks	White	L, M
Tights	Black	L, M, S
Touring Bikes	Blue, Yellow	44, 46, 50, 54, 58, 60, 62
Touring Frames	Blue, Yellow	44, 46, 50, 54, 58, 60, 62
Vests	Blue	L, M, S

```
DECLARE @CSVList VARCHAR(MAX) = '';   -- Multiple variable assignment method
SELECT @CSVList = CONCAT(Color, ', ', @CSVList)
FROM (SELECT DISTINCT Color FROM AdventureWorks2012.Production.Product
                            WHERE Color is not null) x;
SELECT CommaDelimitedList=@CSVList;
-- Yellow, White, Silver/Black, Silver, Red, Multi, Grey, Blue, Black,
```

Configuring Comma Delimited Result Sets in SSMS

It requires special setup for CSV result sets when using Management Studio. This feature is applicable for the Results to Text mode.

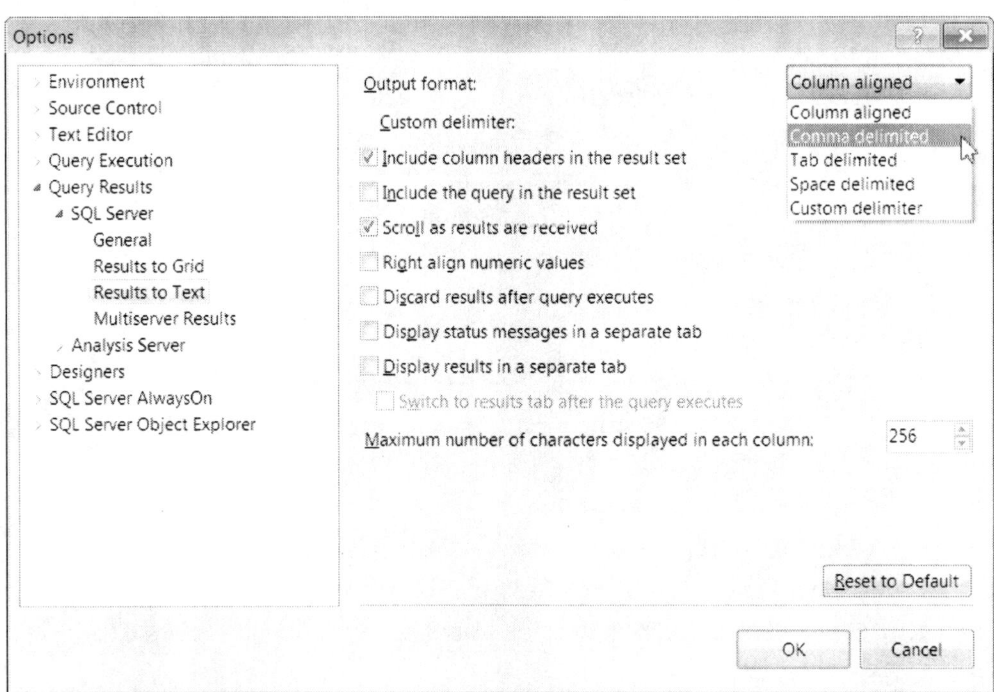

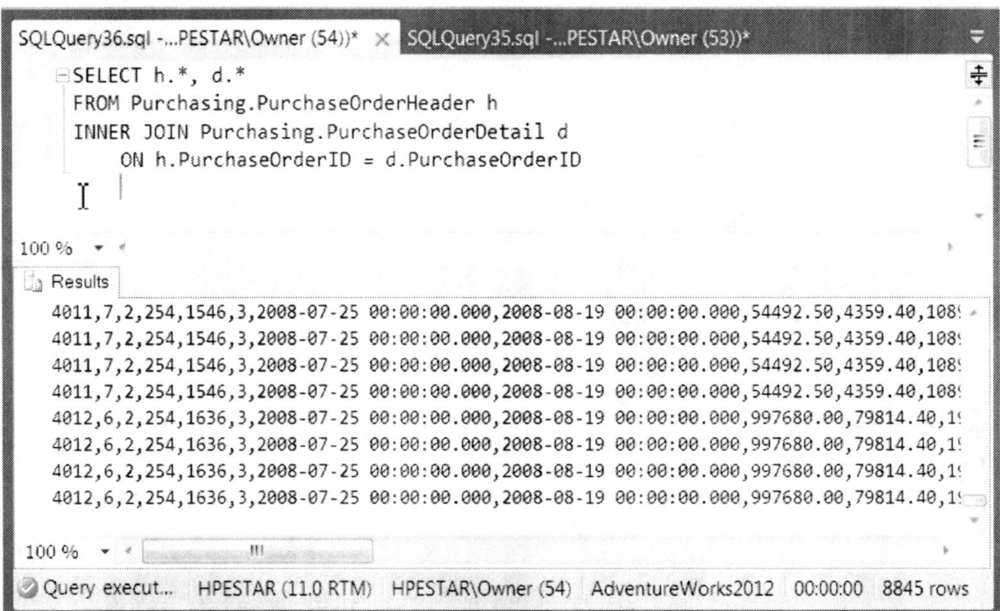

Nesting Cursors

Cursors should be avoided with a few exceptions: better performance (rare but happens) or cannot be done by set-based statements. Being new to set-based logic is not a good excuse for using cursors because they do not scale well. Single-level cursor example.

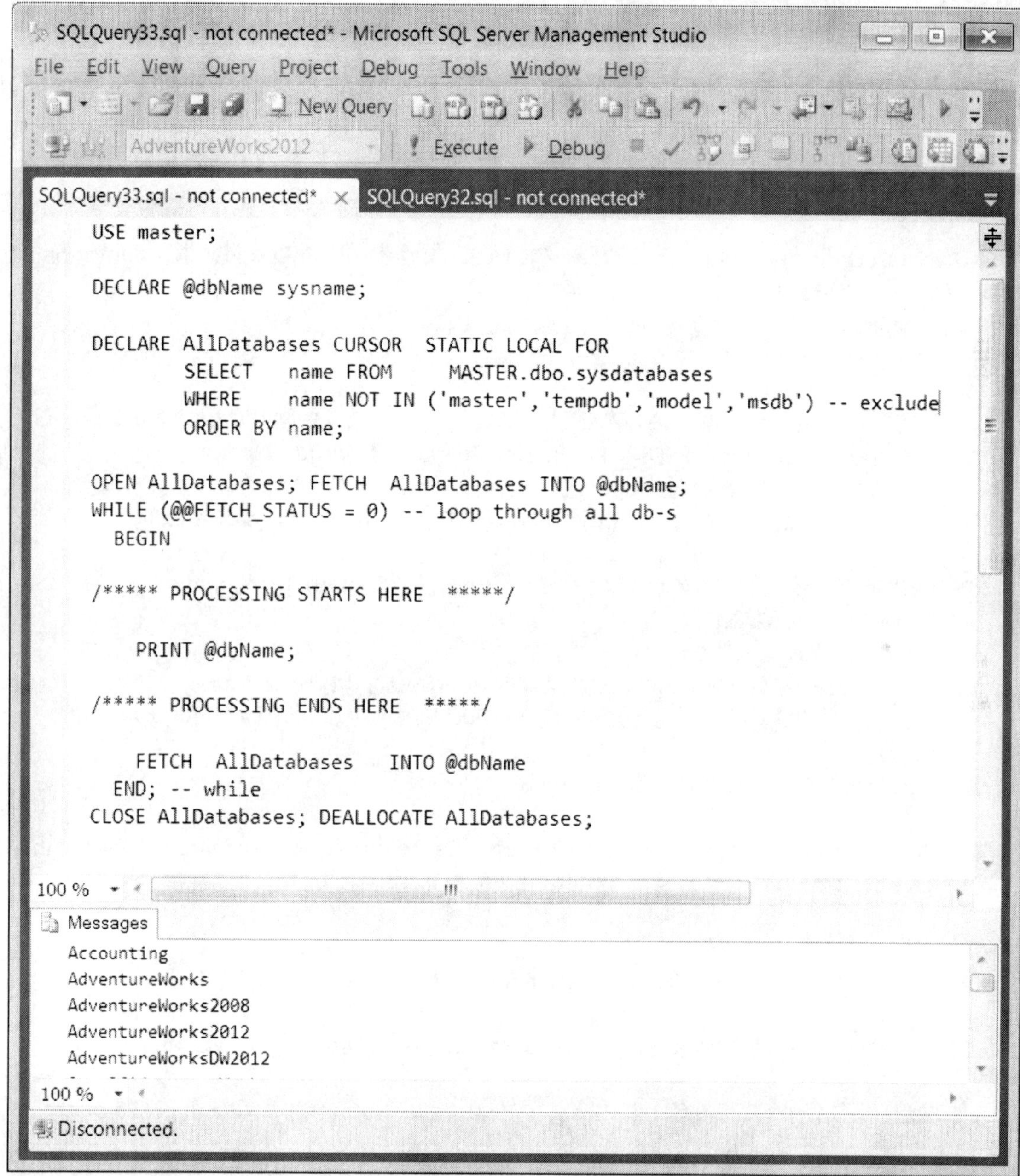
```
USE master;

DECLARE @dbName sysname;

DECLARE AllDatabases CURSOR  STATIC LOCAL FOR
        SELECT   name FROM     MASTER.dbo.sysdatabases
        WHERE    name NOT IN ('master','tempdb','model','msdb') -- exclude
        ORDER BY name;

OPEN AllDatabases; FETCH  AllDatabases INTO @dbName;
WHILE (@@FETCH_STATUS = 0) -- loop through all db-s
  BEGIN

/***** PROCESSING STARTS HERE  *****/

    PRINT @dbName;

/***** PROCESSING ENDS HERE  *****/

    FETCH  AllDatabases   INTO @dbName
  END; -- while
CLOSE AllDatabases; DEALLOCATE AllDatabases;
```

Nested Cursors

Outer cursor over period Purchase Orders. Inner cursor over products ordered for each PO.

```
USE AdventureWorks2012;
DBCC DROPCLEANBUFFERS; -- Preparation for performance timing - empty memory buffers
DECLARE @StartTime datetime = Getdate();
DECLARE @IterationID INT,  @OrderDetail VARCHAR(max),  @ProductName VARCHAR(10);
DECLARE @Result TABLE ( PurchaseOrderID INT, ProductList VARCHAR(max) ) ;

DECLARE PurchaseOrdersInPeriod CURSOR STATIC LOCAL FOR   -- OUTER CURSOR declaration
 SELECT PurchaseOrderID  FROM  Purchasing.PurchaseOrderHeader
 WHERE Year(OrderDate) = 2008 AND Month(OrderDate) = 2 ORDER BY PurchaseOrderID;

OPEN PurchaseOrdersInPeriod; FETCH NEXT FROM PurchaseOrdersInPeriod INTO @IterationID;
PRINT 'OUTER LOOP START';
WHILE ( @@FETCH_STATUS = 0 ) -- sql cursor fetch_status
 BEGIN    SET @OrderDetail = SPACE(0);

   DECLARE POLineItems CURSOR STATIC LOCAL FOR          -- INNER CURSOR declaration
    SELECT p.productNumber  FROM  Purchasing.PurchaseOrderDetail pd
        INNER JOIN Production.Product p ON pd.ProductID = p.ProductID
    WHERE pd.PurchaseOrderID = @IterationID ORDER BY PurchaseOrderDetailID;

   OPEN POLineItems; FETCH NEXT FROM POLineItems INTO @ProductName;
   PRINT 'INNER LOOP START';
   WHILE ( @@FETCH_STATUS = 0 )
    BEGIN      SET @OrderDetail = CONCAT(@OrderDetail, @ProductName,', ');
      FETCH NEXT FROM POLineItems INTO @ProductName;    PRINT 'INNER LOOP' ;
    END -- inner while
   CLOSE POLineItems;  DEALLOCATE POLineItems;

   SET @OrderDetail = LEFT(@OrderDetail, Len(@OrderDetail) - 1); -- Truncate trailing comma
   INSERT INTO @Result  VALUES   (@IterationID,@OrderDetail);
   FETCH NEXT FROM PurchaseOrdersInPeriod INTO @IterationID ;  PRINT 'OUTER LOOP';
 END -- outer while
CLOSE PurchaseOrdersInPeriod; DEALLOCATE PurchaseOrdersInPeriod;

SELECT * FROM  @Result ORDER BY PurchaseOrderID; -- Results (268 row(s) affected)

SELECT ExecutionMsec = Datediff(millisecond, @StartTime, Getdate()); -- Timing 653 msec
GO
```

Nested Cursor Loops Processing Partial Results

PurchaseOrderID	ProductList
1573	CR-7833
1574	RA-2345
1575	PB-6109
1576	CR-9981
1577	SD-2342, SD-9872
1578	PA-187B, PA-361R, PA-529S, PA-632U, PA-823Y
1579	SE-R581, SE-R908, SE-R995, SE-T312, SE-T762
1580	RF-9198
1581	RC-0291
1582	RM-M464, RM-M692
1583	TP-0923
1584	FC-3982, FL-2301
1585	RM-M464, RM-M692
1586	NI-9522
1587	FW-5160, FW-5800, FW-7160, FW-9160
1588	PD-M282, PD-M340
1589	HN-5400, HN-5811, HN-5818, HN-6320, HN-7161
1590	MS-2348, MS-6061, MT-1000
1591	KW-4091
1592	RM-R436, RM-R600

Set-Based Operations Equivalent Code

```
DBCC DROPCLEANBUFFERS;
DECLARE @StartTime datetime = CURRENT_TIMESTAMP;
SELECT poh.PurchaseOrderID,OrderDetail = Stuff((
                          -- correlated subquery
                          SELECT CONCAT(', ', ProductNumber) AS [text()]
                          FROM  Purchasing.PurchaseOrderDetail pod
                                INNER JOIN Production.Product p
                                ON pod.ProductID = p.ProductID
                          WHERE  pod.PurchaseOrderID =  poh.PurchaseOrderID
                          ORDER  BY PurchaseOrderDetailID
                          FOR XML PATH ('')), 1, 1, '')
FROM   Purchasing.PurchaseOrderHeader poh
WHERE  Year(OrderDate) = 2004 AND Month(OrderDate) = 2
ORDER  BY PurchaseOrderID;
SELECT ExecutionMsec = Datediff(millisecond, @StartTime, Getdate())
-- Timing: 33 msec
```

Advanced Graphical Query Designer

While SSMS GUI query / view designer cannot handle very complex queries, it does a pretty good job with "normal" relational database queries.

Aliasing Tables in the Diagram Pane

We start with right click on the top table frame in the Diagram Pane.

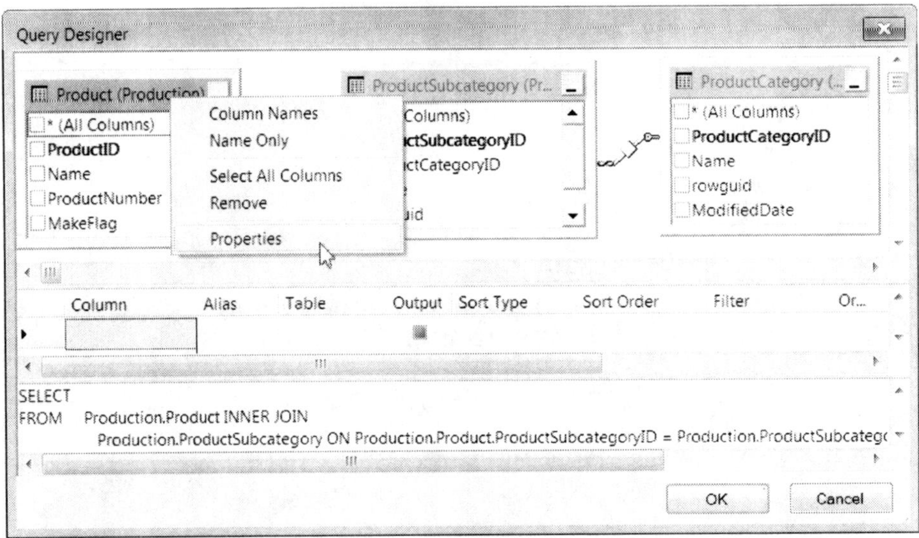

In the pop-up dialog box we enter the alias for the table.

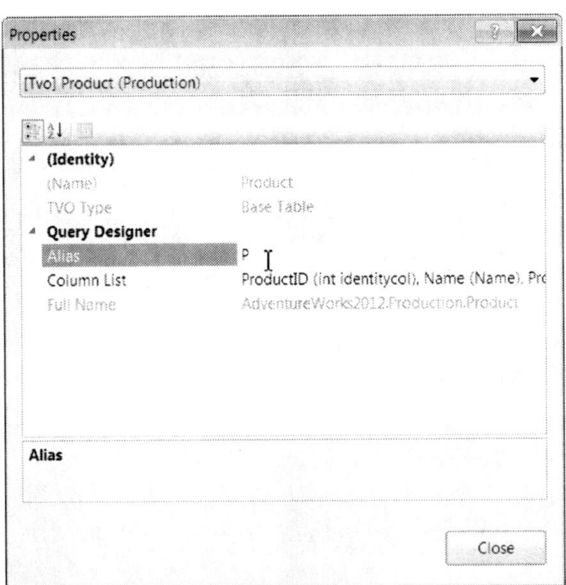

Specifying OUTER JOIN in Diagram Pane

To change the INNER JOIN to RIGHT JOIN, right click on the connection square in the middle and click on Properties.

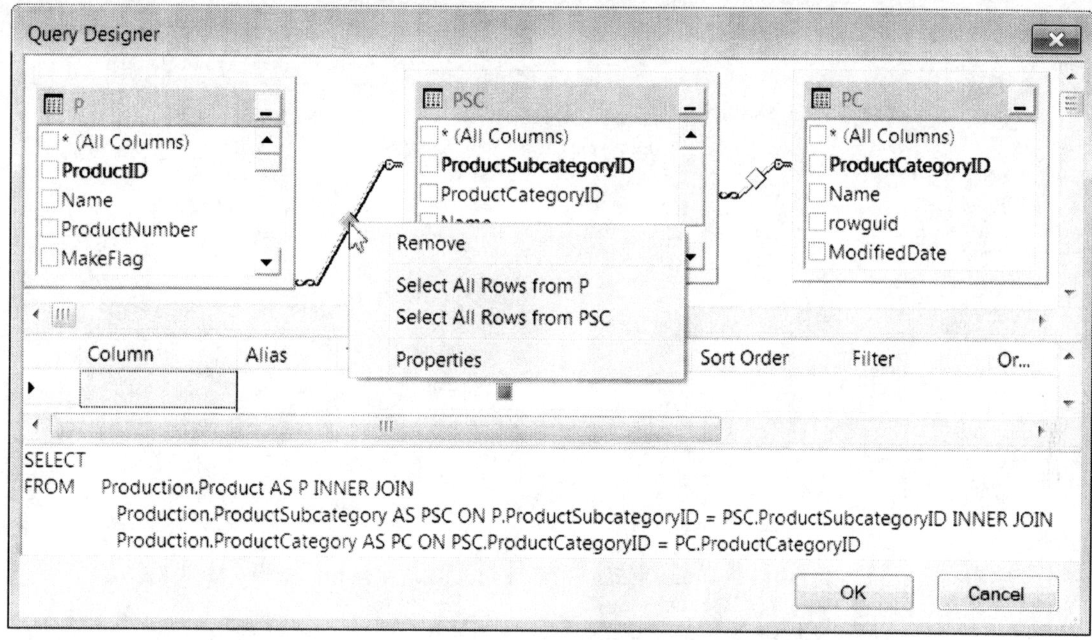

With checkmark selection we can specify LEFT JOIN, RIGHT JOIN or FULL JOIN.

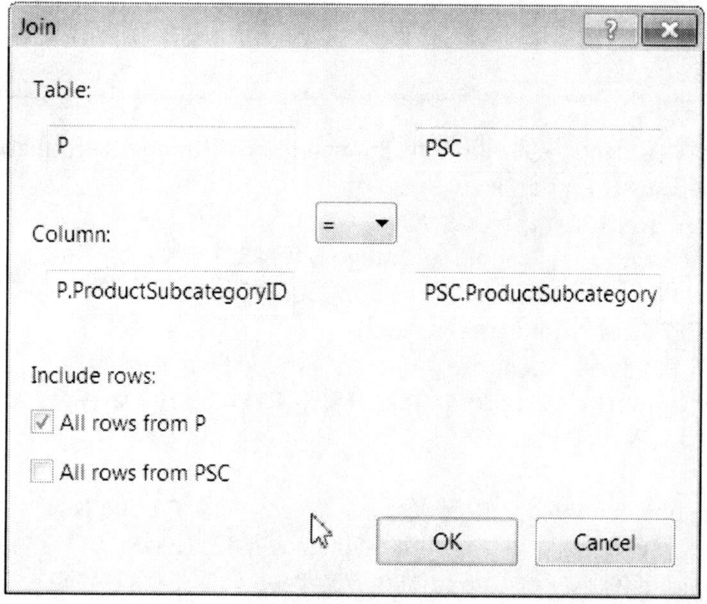

Query Designer Generated Query

This is the final graphical image in Query Designer prior to the exiting to Query Editor.

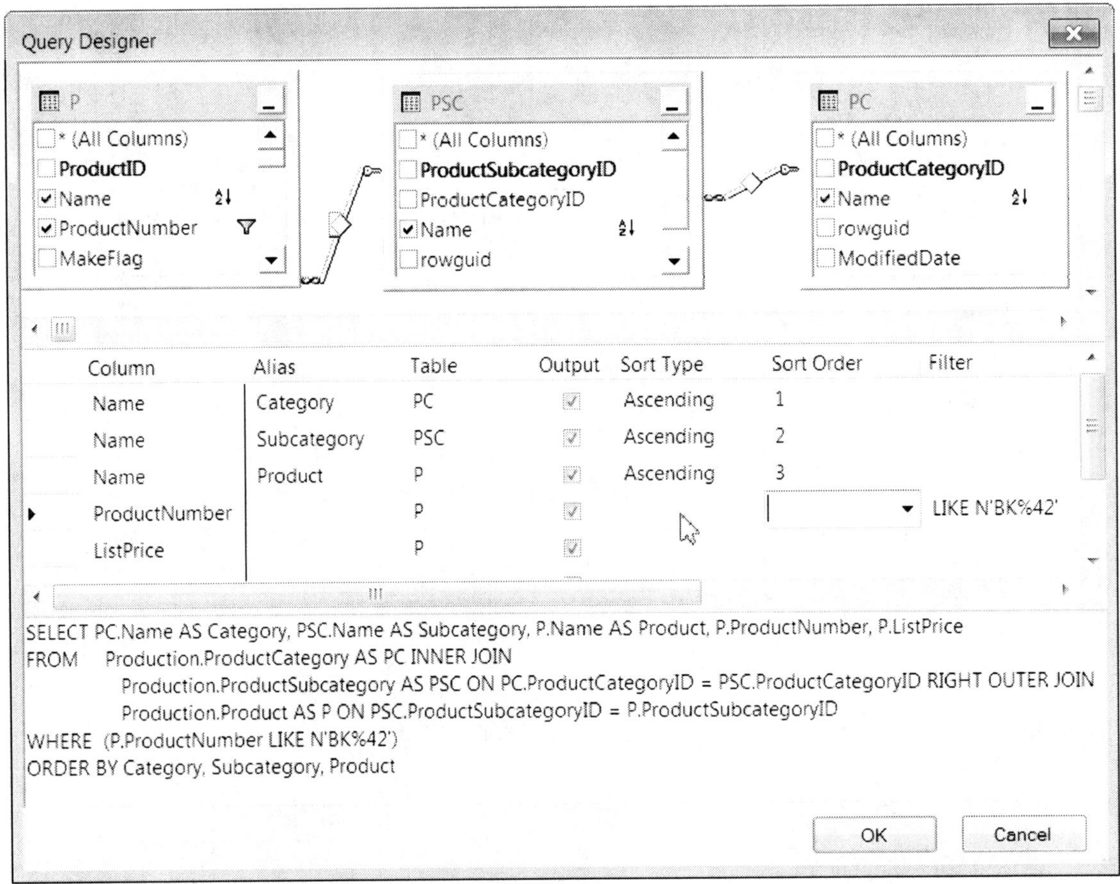

```
SELECT  PC.Name AS Category, PSC.Name AS Subcategory, P.Name AS Product,
              P.ProductNumber, P.ListPrice
FROM     Production.ProductCategory AS PC
        INNER JOIN Production.ProductSubcategory AS PSC
              ON PC.ProductCategoryID = PSC.ProductCategoryID
        RIGHT OUTER JOIN Production.Product AS P
              ON PSC.ProductSubcategoryID = P.ProductSubcategoryID
WHERE  (P.ProductNumber LIKE N'BK%42') ORDER BY Product, Subcategory, Category;
-- (9 row(s) affected) - Partial results.
```

Category	Subcategory	Product	ProductNumber	ListPrice
Bikes	Mountain Bikes	Mountain-500 Silver, 42	BK-M18S-42	564.99
Bikes	Road Bikes	Road-350-W Yellow, 42	BK-R79Y-42	1700.99

Template Explorer & Browser

The Template Explorer & Browser helps to start coding by providing a framework code with optional parameter replacements.

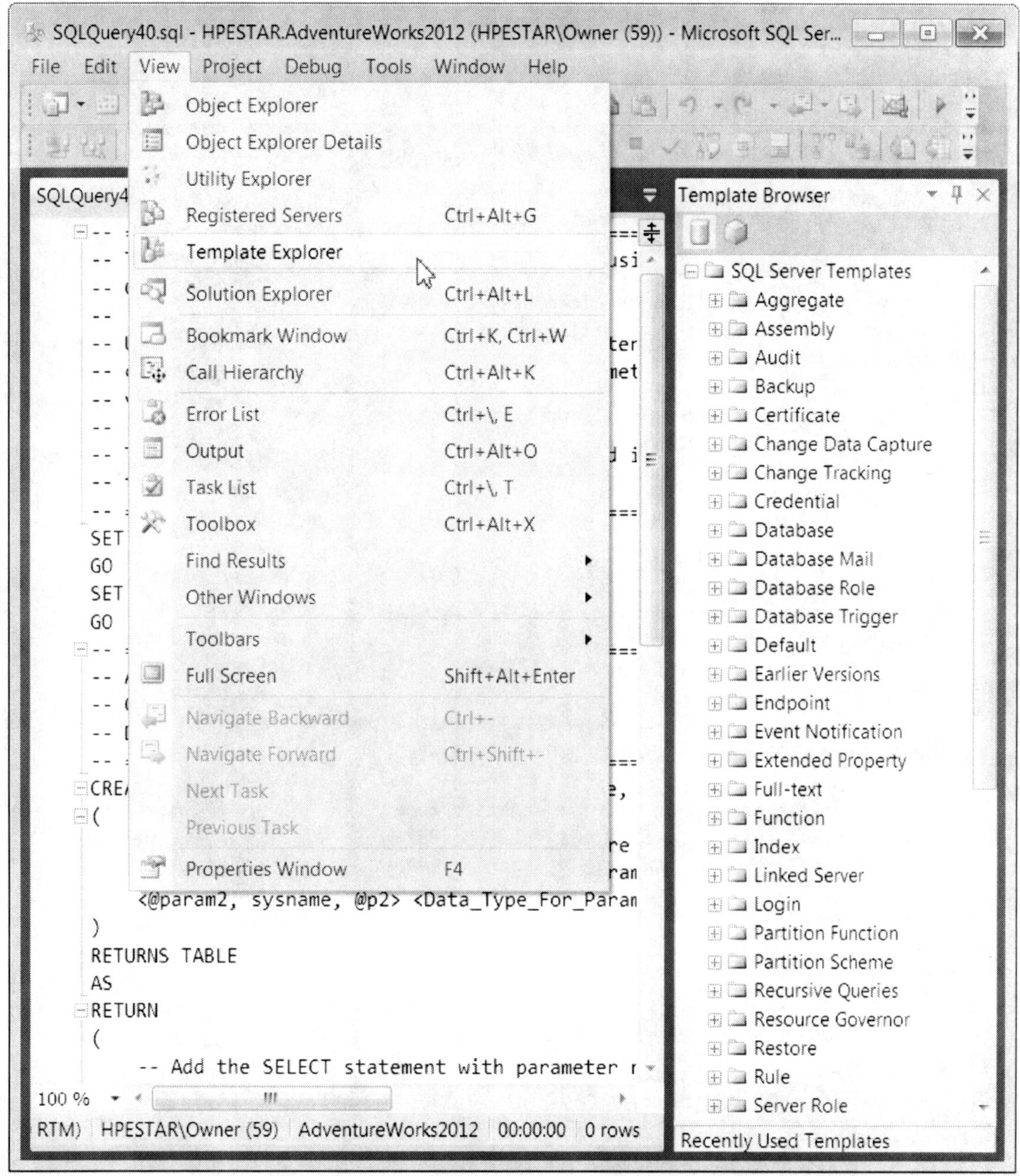

Create Inline Function Template

Double on the template name to get the starter code in a new Query Editor window.

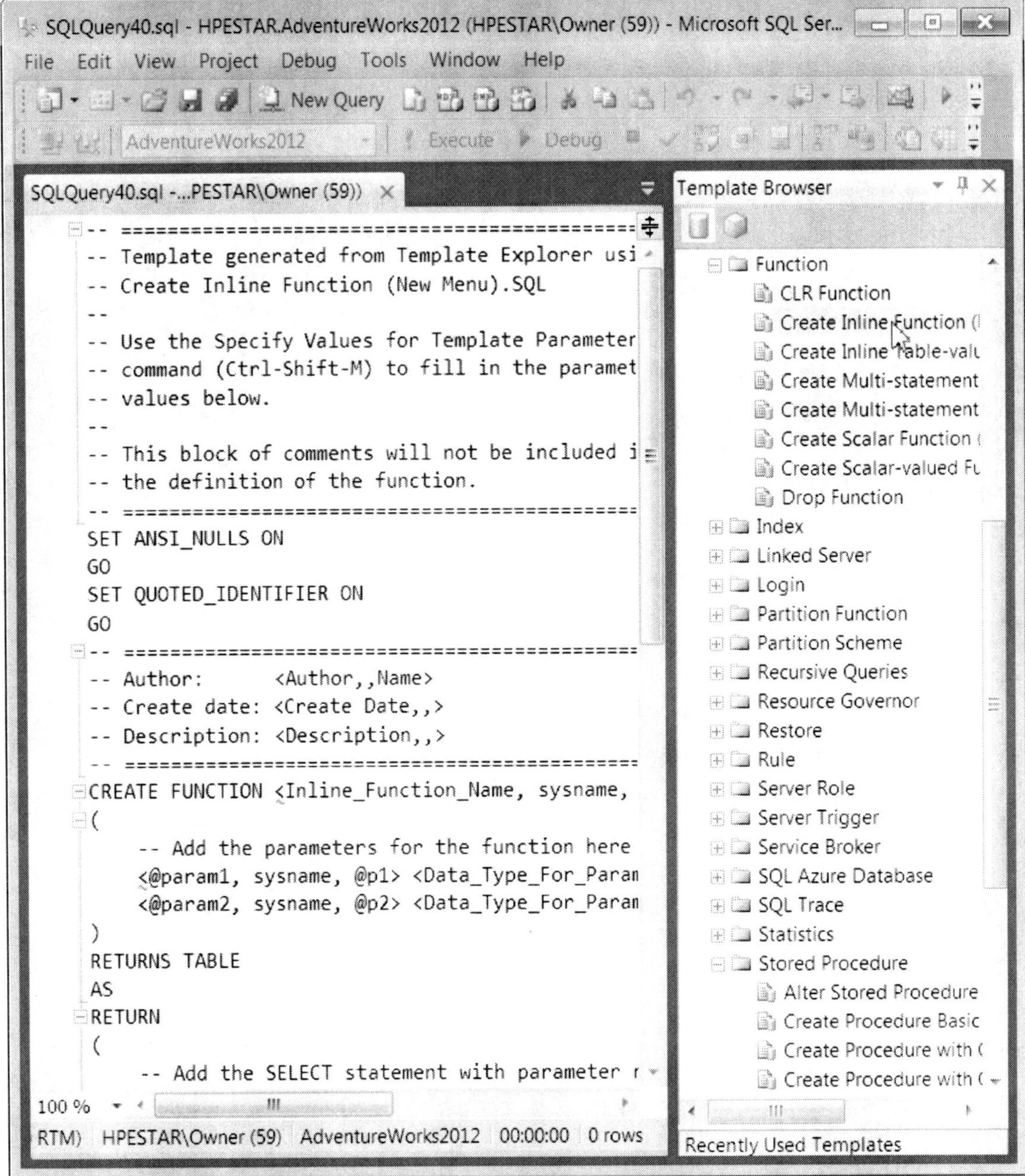

Template Parameters Specifications

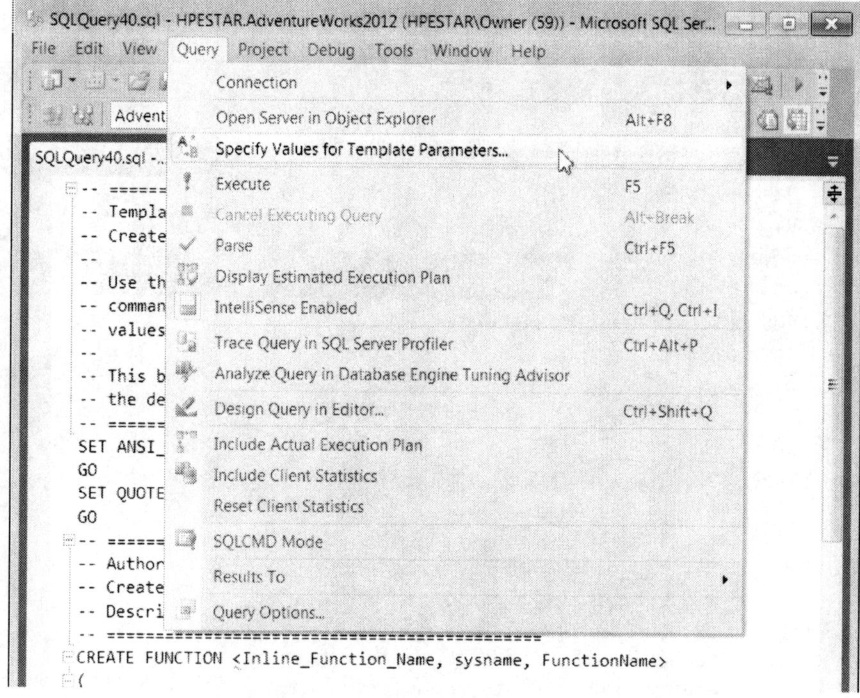

The values must be filled in for the parameter in the dialog box.

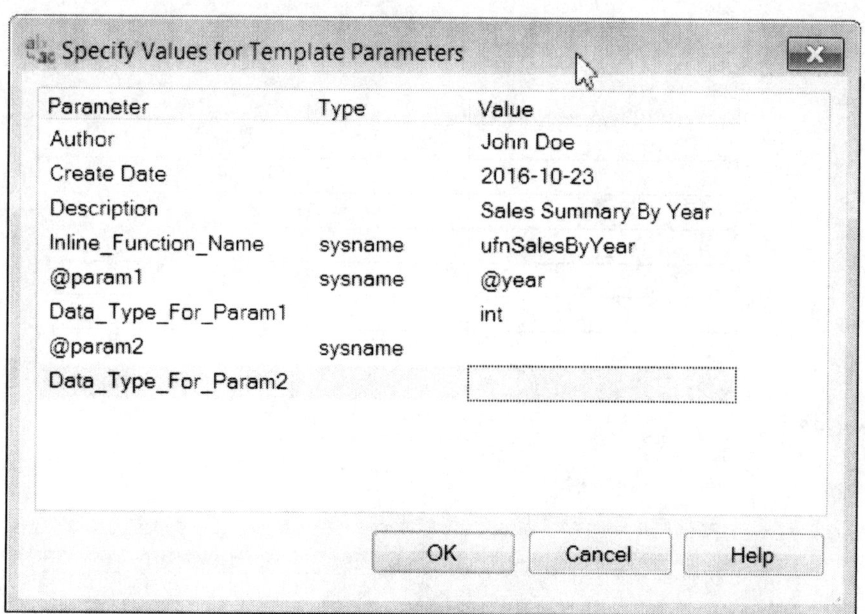

Completion of the Function by Entering the SELECT Query with Parameter

Inline user-defined function can be used as a makeover for a view with accepting parameters feature.

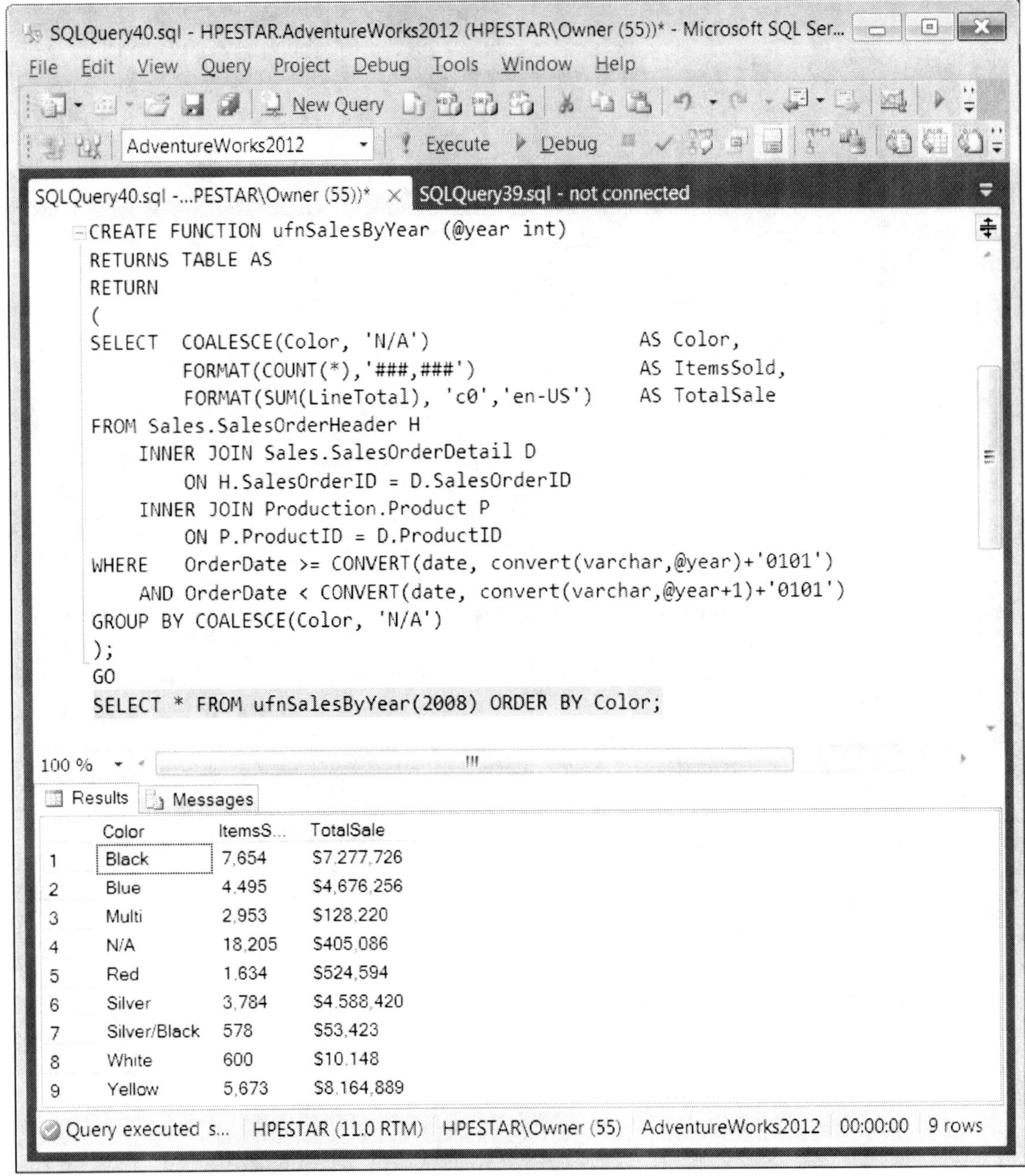

	Color	ItemsS...	TotalSale
1	Black	7,654	$7,277,726
2	Blue	4,495	$4,676,256
3	Multi	2,953	$128,220
4	N/A	18,205	$405,086
5	Red	1,634	$524,594
6	Silver	3,784	$4,588,420
7	Silver/Black	578	$53,423
8	White	600	$10,148
9	Yellow	5,673	$8,164,889

Entering PowerShell from Object Explorer

In addition to executing sqlps in Command Prompt, we can enter PowerShell from SSMS Object Explorer via the right click drop-down menu. Entering the get-childitem command will list all the views in the path (directory).

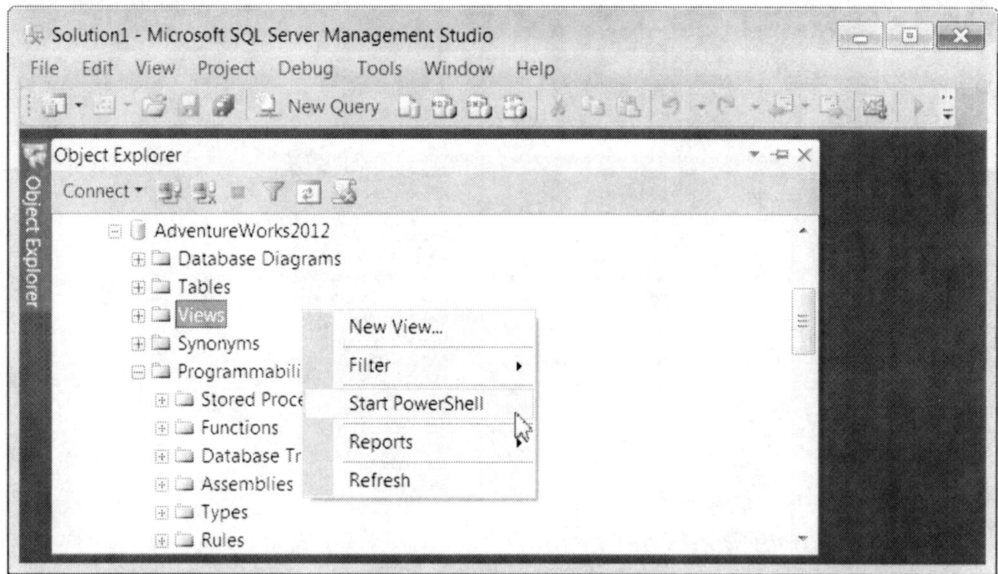

PowerShell Command List

The following command will list all the PowerShell commands.

```
get-command | out-file 'f:\temp\command.txt'
```

CommandType	Name	Definition
-----------	----	----------
Alias	%	ForEach-Object
Alias	?	Where-Object
Function	A:	Set-Location A:
Alias	ac	Add-Content
Cmdlet	Add-Computer	Add-Computer [-DomainName] <...
Cmdlet	Add-Content	Add-Content [-Path] <String[...
Cmdlet	Add-History	Add-History [[-InputObject] ...
Cmdlet	Add-Member	Add-Member [-MemberType] <PS...
Cmdlet	Add-PSSnapin	Add-PSSnapin [-Name] <String...
Cmdlet	Add-RoleMember	Add-RoleMember [-MemberName]...
Cmdlet	Add-SqlAvailabilityDatabase	Add-SqlAvailabilityDatabase ...
Cmdlet	Add-SqlAvailabilityGroupList...	Add-SqlAvailabilityGroupList...
Cmdlet	Add-Type	Add-Type [-TypeDefinition] <...
Alias	asnp	Add-PSSnapIn
Function	B:	Set-Location B:
Cmdlet	Backup-ASDatabase	Backup-ASDatabase [-BackupFi...
Cmdlet	Backup-SqlDatabase	Backup-SqlDatabase [-Databas...
Function	C:	Set-Location C:
Alias	cat	Get-Content
Alias	cd	Set-Location
Function	cd..	Set-Location ..
Function	cd\	Set-Location \

Getting Help on PowerShell Commands

We can access help for a command just by typing "help" and the command name. "help" example for format-list.

```
help format-list
```

```
SQL Server Powershell
PS SQLSERVER:\SQL\HPESTAR\DEFAULT\Databases\AdventureWorks2012\Views> help forma
t-list

NAME
    Format-List

SYNOPSIS
    Formats the output as a list of properties in which each property appears o
    n a new line.


SYNTAX
    Format-List [[-Property] <Object[]>] [-DisplayError] [-Expand <string>] [-F
    orce] [-GroupBy <Object>] [-InputObject <psobject>] [-ShowError] [-View <st
    ring>] [<CommonParameters>]


DESCRIPTION
    The Format-List cmdlet formats the output of a command as a list of propert
    ies in which each property is displayed on a separate line. You can use For
    mat-List to format and display all or selected properties of an object as a
     list (format-list *).

    Because more space is available for each item in a list than in a table, Wi
    ndows PowerShell displays more properties of the object in the list, and th
```

Using the OUTPUT Clause with UPDATE for Audit Trail

The EmpSalaryHist table is used to track salary changes in the Employee table.

```
-- Table with important data requiring audit trail (history)
CREATE TABLE Employee( EmployeeID INT IDENTITY(1,1) PRIMARY KEY,   SSno char(9) not null UNIQUE,
FirstName varchar(30) not null, LastName varchar(30) not null, Salary smallmoney,
ModifiedDate datetime default(getdate()));
```

```
-- Audit trail table
CREATE TABLE EmpSalaryHist (ID INT IDENTITY(1,1) PRIMARY KEY, EmployeeID INT NOT NULL ,
ChangeDate DATE NOT NULL default(getdate()),
UNIQUE (EmployeeID, ChangeDate), PrevSalary smallmoney not null, NewSalary smallmoney not null,
ModifiedDate datetime default(getdate()));
```

```
-- 5% raise to all "Smith"-s
UPDATE Employee SET Salary *= 1.05
OUTPUT inserted.EmployeeID, deleted.Salary, inserted.Salary
INTO EmpSalaryHist(EmployeeID, PrevSalary, NewSalary)
WHERE LastName = 'Smith';
```

Adding Cyclical SEQUENCE Number Column to Table

Rows in the test table will be updated with a cycling sequence number from 101 to 150 where ListPrice > 200.0.

```
USE tempdb;
GO
SELECT ProductID, ProductNumber, Color, ListPrice
INTO Product FROM AdventureWorks2012.Production.Product WHERE ListPrice > 100.0;
GO  -- (214 row(s) affected)
```

```
CREATE SEQUENCE Seq101To150
  AS INT START WITH 101  INCREMENT BY 1  MINVALUE 101  MAXVALUE 150   CYCLE;
```

```
ALTER TABLE Product ADD SeqNo INT;
GO
```

```
UPDATE Product SET SeqNo = NEXT VALUE FOR Seq101To150   WHERE ListPrice > 200.0;
GO  -- (189 row(s) affected)
```

```
SELECT TOP(2) * FROM Product ORDER BY SeqNo DESC;
```

ProductID	ProductNumber	Color	ListPrice	SeqNo
764	BK-R50R-52	Red	782.99	150
829	RW-T905	Black	245.01	150

Limiting UPDATE-s with INSTEAD OF Trigger on View

View by itself is considered a security mechanism by limiting access to the underlying tables. We can go one step further with INSTEAD OF UPDATE trigger: limit what column can be updated. We only permit UPDATE to the Title & Promo columns in the following INSTEAD of trigger implementation.

```
USE AdventureWorks2012;
SELECT   P.BusinessEntityID AS ID, P.Title, CONCAT(P.LastName,', ', P.FirstName) AS FullName,
                    P.EmailPromotion, CC.CardType, CC.CardNumber, CC.ExpMonth, CC.ExpYear
INTO Person  FROM   Person.Person AS P INNER JOIN
     Sales.PersonCreditCard AS PCC ON P.BusinessEntityID = PCC.BusinessEntityID INNER JOIN
     Sales.CreditCard AS CC ON PCC.CreditCardID = CC.CreditCardID  ORDER BY ID;
GO
```

```
CREATE VIEW vPerson ( PersonID, Title, Name, Promo, CCType, CCNo, CCExpMo, CCExpYr)
AS SELECT ID, Title, FullName, EmailPromotion, CardType, CardNumber, ExpMonth, ExpYear FROM
dbo.Person;
GO
```

```
GRANT SELECT ON [dbo].[vPerson] TO [HRStaff];
GRANT DELETE ON [dbo].[vPerson] TO [HRStaff];
GRANT INSERT ON [dbo].[vPerson] TO [HRStaff];
GRANT UPDATE ON [dbo].[vPerson] TO [HRStaff];
GO
```

```
CREATE TRIGGER trgVPerson ON vPerson INSTEAD OF UPDATE  AS
IF @@ROWCOUNT = 0  RETURN;
UPDATE P          SET P.Title = I.Title,  P.EmailPromotion = I.Promo
FROM Person P     INNER JOIN inserted I       ON P.ID = I.PersonID;
GO
```

```
SELECT * FROM vPerson WHERE PersonID = 10124;
```

PersonID	Title	Name	Promo	CCType	CCNo	CCExpMo	CCExpYr
10124	NULL	Carlson, Marie	1	Distinguish	55554832637693	1	2005

```
UPDATE vPerson SET Title = 'Ms' WHERE PersonID = 10124;                          -- will take
```

```
UPDATE vPerson SET CCNo = '1234567890123456' WHERE PersonID = 10124;     -- will NOT take
```

```
SELECT * FROM vPerson WHERE PersonID = 10124;
```

PersonID	Title	Name	Promo	CCType	CCNo	CCExpMo	CCExpYr
10124	Ms	Carlson, Marie	1	Distinguish	55554832637693	1	2005

TRY...CATCH Block With TRANSACTION

If the TRY is successful the transaction is committed, otherwise the transaction (previous statements if any) is rolled back and the error is logged into an errorlog table.

```
USE tempdb; -- Create & configure table for testing
IF OBJECT_ID ('dbo.Product', 'U') IS NOT NULL DROP TABLE dbo.Product ;
SELECT ID=CONVERT(INT,ProductID), ProductName=Name, ListPrice, ModifiedDate
INTO Product FROM AdventureWorks2012.Production.Product WHERE ListPrice > 0;  -- (304 row(s) affected)
ALTER TABLE PRODUCT ADD CONSTRAINT uqProd UNIQUE (ProductName);
ALTER TABLE PRODUCT ADD CONSTRAINT dfProd DEFAULT (CURRENT_TIMESTAMP) FOR ModifiedDate;
ALTER TABLE PRODUCT ADD rowguid UNIQUEIDENTIFIER default(newsequentialid());
GO -- Command(s) completed successfully.
```

```
IF OBJECT_ID ('dbo.ErrorLogForTransactions', 'U') IS NOT NULL  DROP TABLE dbo.ErrorLogForTransactions ;
CREATE TABLE ErrorLogForTransactions(  ID INT IDENTITY(1,1) PRIMARY KEY,
      UserName sysname, TableName sysname, ErrorNumber sysname,  ErrorSeverity sysname,
      ErrorState sysname, ErrorMessage nvarchar(1024),  rowguid UNIQUEIDENTIFIER default(newid()),
      ModifiedDate datetime default (getdate()));
GO -- Command(s) completed successfully.
```

```
IF OBJECT_ID ('dbo.uspInsertNewProduct', 'P') IS NOT NULL DROP PROC dbo.uspInsertNewProduct ;
GO
CREATE PROCEDURE uspInsertNewProduct ( @NewProduct NVARCHAR(64),  @Price  SMALLMONEY) AS
BEGIN    DECLARE  @TableName    SYSNAME,  @ErrorMessage NVARCHAR(1024);
  BEGIN TRY;    BEGIN TRANSACTION;
   SELECT @ErrorMessage = 'Duplicate insert failed',  @TableName = 'Product';
   INSERT dbo.Product (ID, ProductName,  ListPrice)
          SELECT max(ID)+1, @NewProduct,   @Price FROM Product;     COMMIT TRANSACTION;
 END TRY
 BEGIN CATCH    ROLLBACK TRANSACTION;     INSERT dbo.ErrorLogForTransactions
        (UserName,  TableName,  ErrorNumber,  errorSeverity,  errorState, ErrorMessage)
        VALUES(suser_sname(),@TableName,ERROR_NUMBER(),ERROR_SEVERITY(),
         ERROR_STATE(),ERROR_MESSAGE());     RAISERROR (@ErrorMessage,16,1);   END CATCH
END
GO
```

```
EXEC uspInsertNewProduct  'xDelta SmartPhone', 999.99;                    -- Valid INSERT
DECLARE @NewProduct varchar(64) = (SELECT TOP(1) ProductName FROM Product), @Price SMALLMONEY = 999.99;
EXEC uspInsertNewProduct  @NewProduct, @Price;                            -- Invalid INSERT - duplicate name
GO
```

```
SELECT * FROM ErrorLogForTransactions;
```

ID	UserName	TableName	ErrorNumber	ErrorSeverity	ErrorState	ErrorMessage	ModifiedDate
1	HPESTAR\Owner	Product	2627	14	1	Violation of UNIQUE KEY constraint 'uqProd'. Cannot insert duplicate key in object 'dbo.Product'. The duplicate key value is (All-Purpose Bike Stand).	2016-12-09 13:35:23.687

SET TRANSACTION ISOLATION LEVEL Command

The syntax for the command:

```
SET TRANSACTION ISOLATION LEVEL

  { READ UNCOMMITTED

  | READ COMMITTED

  | REPEATABLE READ

  | SNAPSHOT

  | SERIALIZABLE

  } [ ; ]
```

Preparation for demonstrating levels. We have to use 2 connections to represent 2 users of the database. First we create a test table.

```
USE tempdb;
SELECT * INTO Product FROM AdventureWorks2012.Production.Product;
-- (504 row(s) affected)
```

In connection 1 we simulate a large (slow) transaction on the Product table.

```
BEGIN TRAN;
SELECT StartTime = CURRENT_TIMESTAMP;
UPDATE Product SET ListPrice=ListPrice * 1.05;
WAITFOR DELAY '00:00:20'; -- 20 sec delay to keep transaction pending
ROLLBACK TRAN;
SELECT FinishTime = CURRENT_TIMESTAMP;
```

In connection 2 we test the isolation levels. We start execution after connection 1 started. Code for the first test.

```
SET TRANSACTION ISOLATION LEVEL READ UNCOMMITTED
SELECT StartTime = CURRENT_TIMESTAMP;
SELECT TOP (2) * FROM Product ORDER BY ListPrice DESC;
SELECT FinishTime = CURRENT_TIMESTAMP;
```

READ UNCOMMITTED Isolation Level - Dirty Reads

The SELECT with TOP started 4 seconds later after the UPDATE, yet it finished immediately without waiting for the UPDATE transaction to come to a conclusion (ROLLBACK or COMMIT).

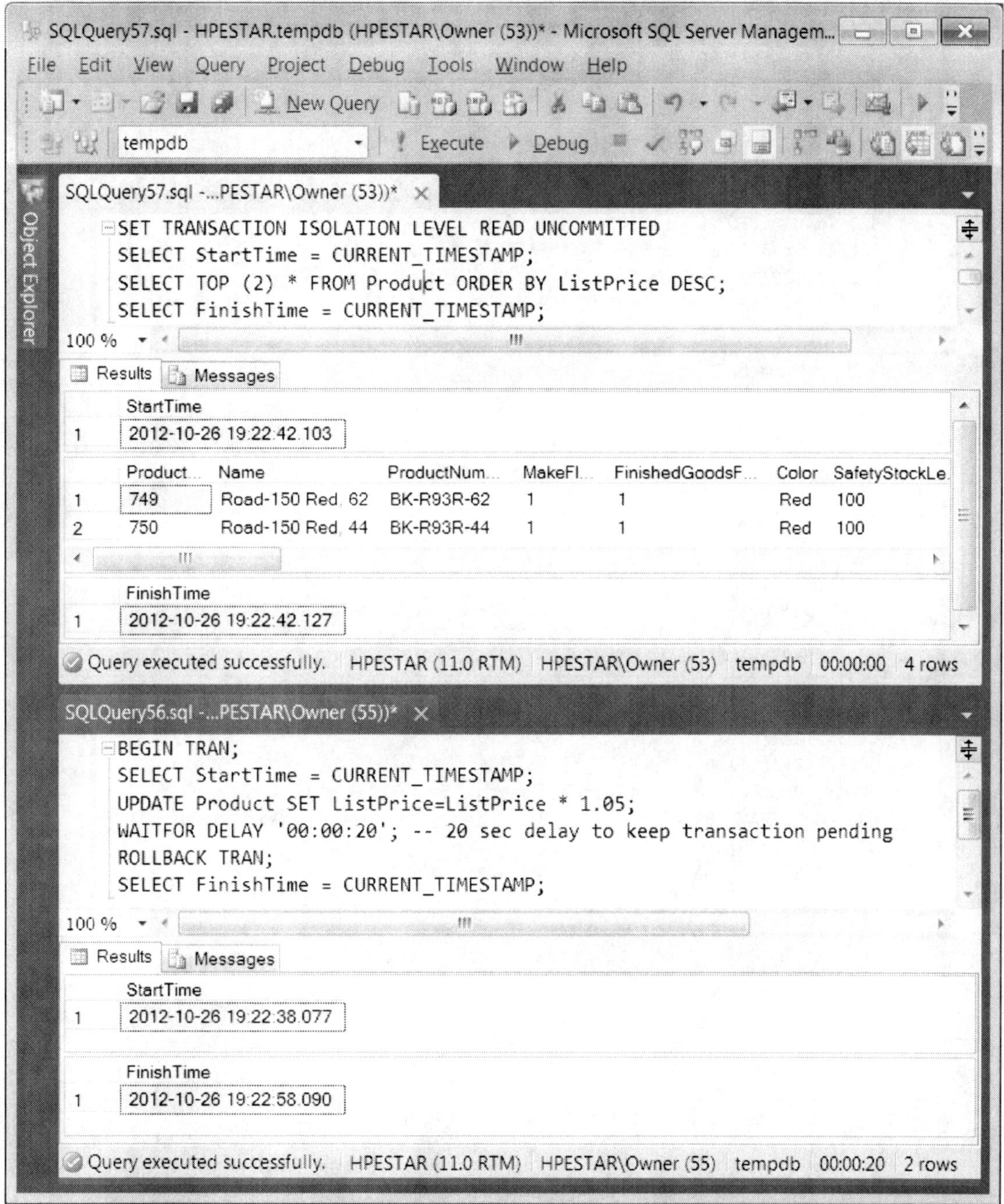

READ COMMITTED Isolation Level - Default for SQL Server

The SELECT query waits until the exclusive lock is removed by the UPDATE transaction. To prevent such a wait, frequently the NOLOCK hint (dirty reads) is used.

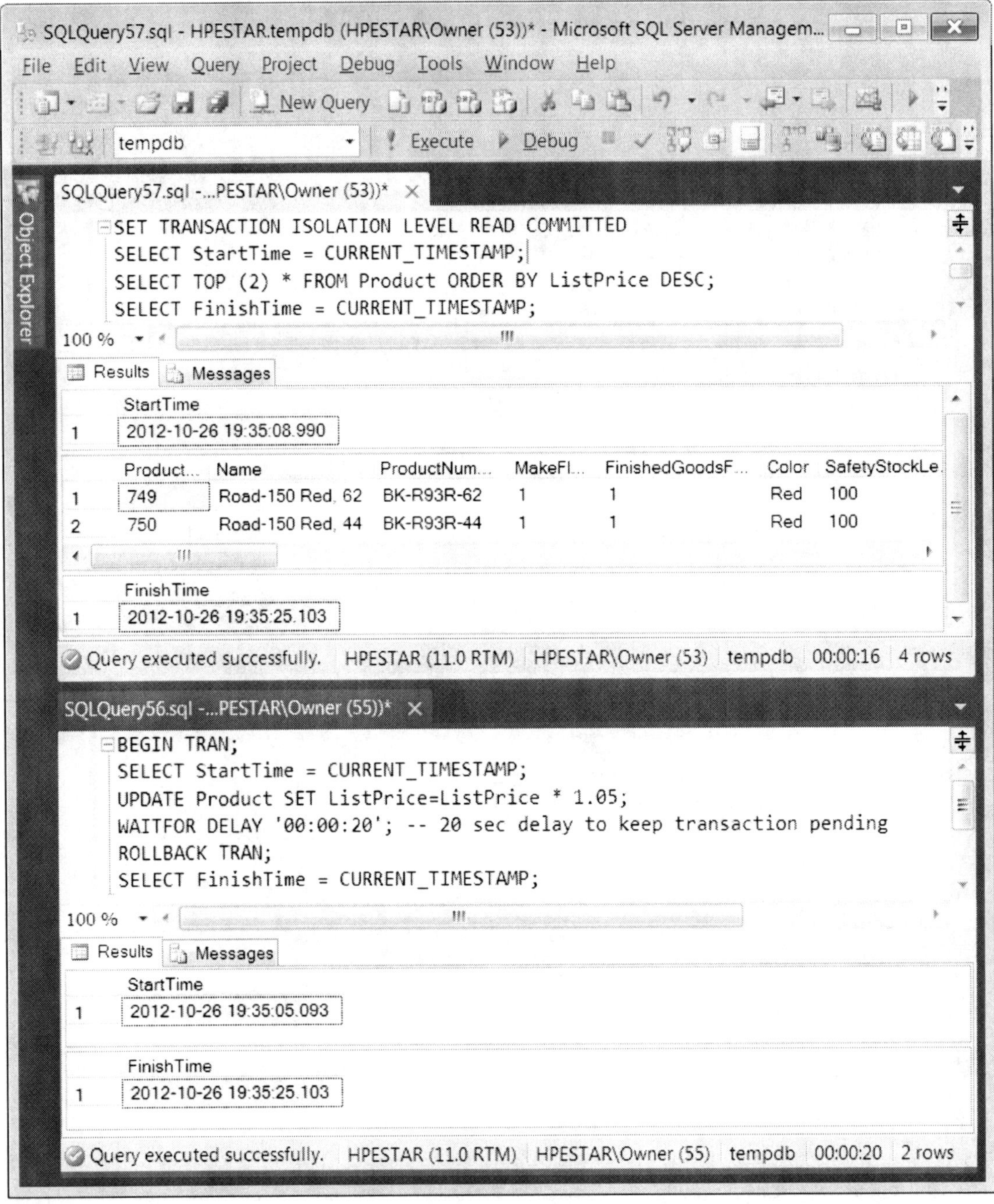

```
SET TRANSACTION ISOLATION LEVEL READ COMMITTED
SELECT StartTime = CURRENT_TIMESTAMP;
SELECT TOP (2) * FROM Product ORDER BY ListPrice DESC;
SELECT FinishTime = CURRENT_TIMESTAMP;
```

	StartTime
1	2012-10-26 19:35:08.990

	Product...	Name	ProductNum...	MakeFl...	FinishedGoodsF...	Color	SafetyStockLe
1	749	Road-150 Red, 62	BK-R93R-62	1	1	Red	100
2	750	Road-150 Red, 44	BK-R93R-44	1	1	Red	100

	FinishTime
1	2012-10-26 19:35:25.103

Query executed successfully. | HPESTAR (11.0 RTM) | HPESTAR\Owner (53) | tempdb | 00:00:16 | 4 rows

```
BEGIN TRAN;
SELECT StartTime = CURRENT_TIMESTAMP;
UPDATE Product SET ListPrice=ListPrice * 1.05;
WAITFOR DELAY '00:00:20'; -- 20 sec delay to keep transaction pending
ROLLBACK TRAN;
SELECT FinishTime = CURRENT_TIMESTAMP;
```

	StartTime
1	2012-10-26 19:35:05.093

	FinishTime
1	2012-10-26 19:35:25.103

Query executed successfully. | HPESTAR (11.0 RTM) | HPESTAR\Owner (55) | tempdb | 00:00:20 | 2 rows

REPEATABLE READ Isolation Level

The UPDATE (transaction by itself) must wait until the exclusive lock is released by the 2 SELECT statements transaction. The ListPrice changed after the COMMIT transaction.

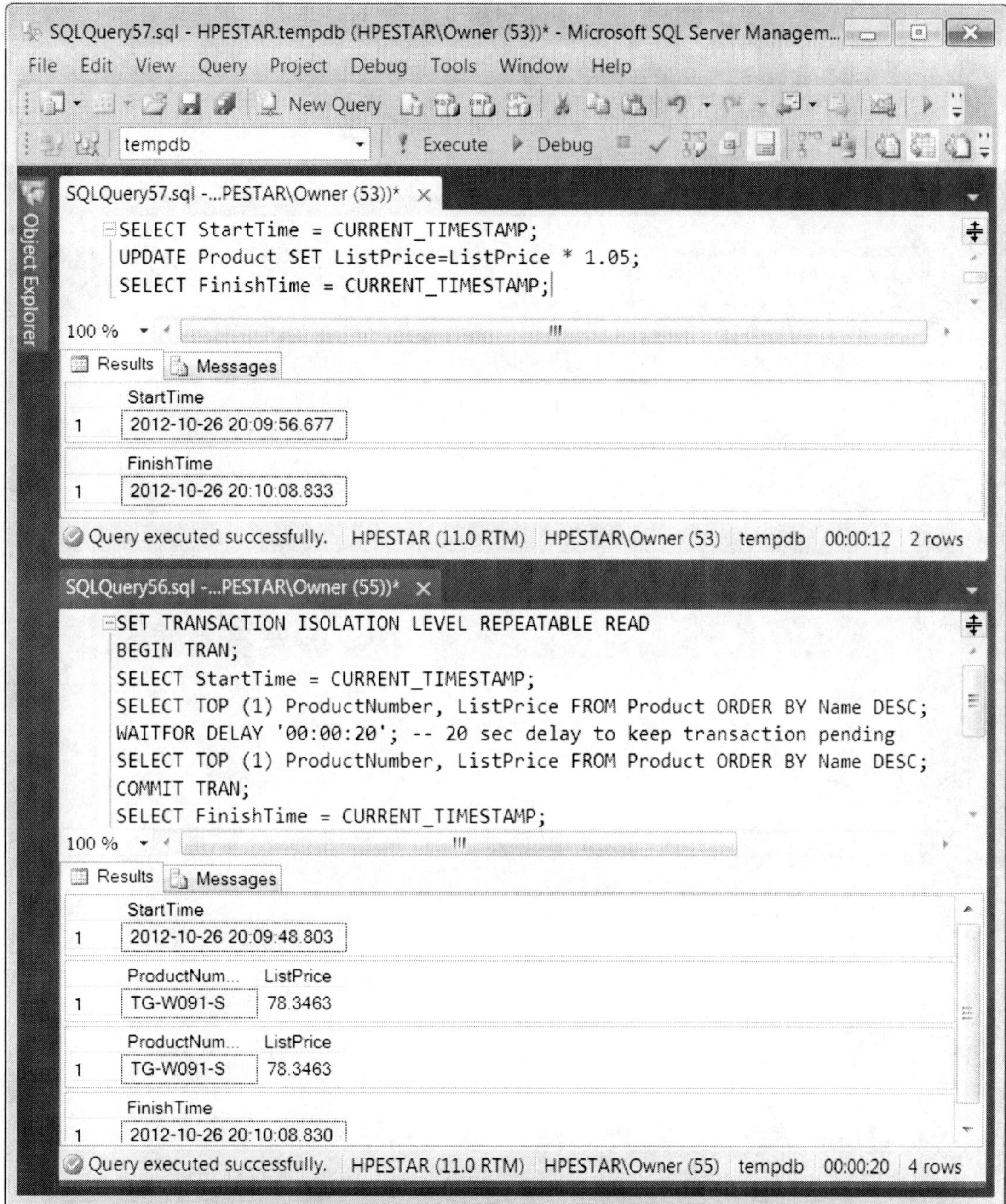

Redefining the Product table without IDENTITIY & testing it

```
DROP TABLE tempdb.dbo.Product;
SELECT ID = CONVERT(INT, ProductID), Name, ProductNumber, ListPrice, Color
INTO tempdb.dbo.Product FROM AdventureWorks2012.Production.Product;
```

REPEATABLE READ blocks UPDATE & DELETE, but not INSERT. The row counts differ.

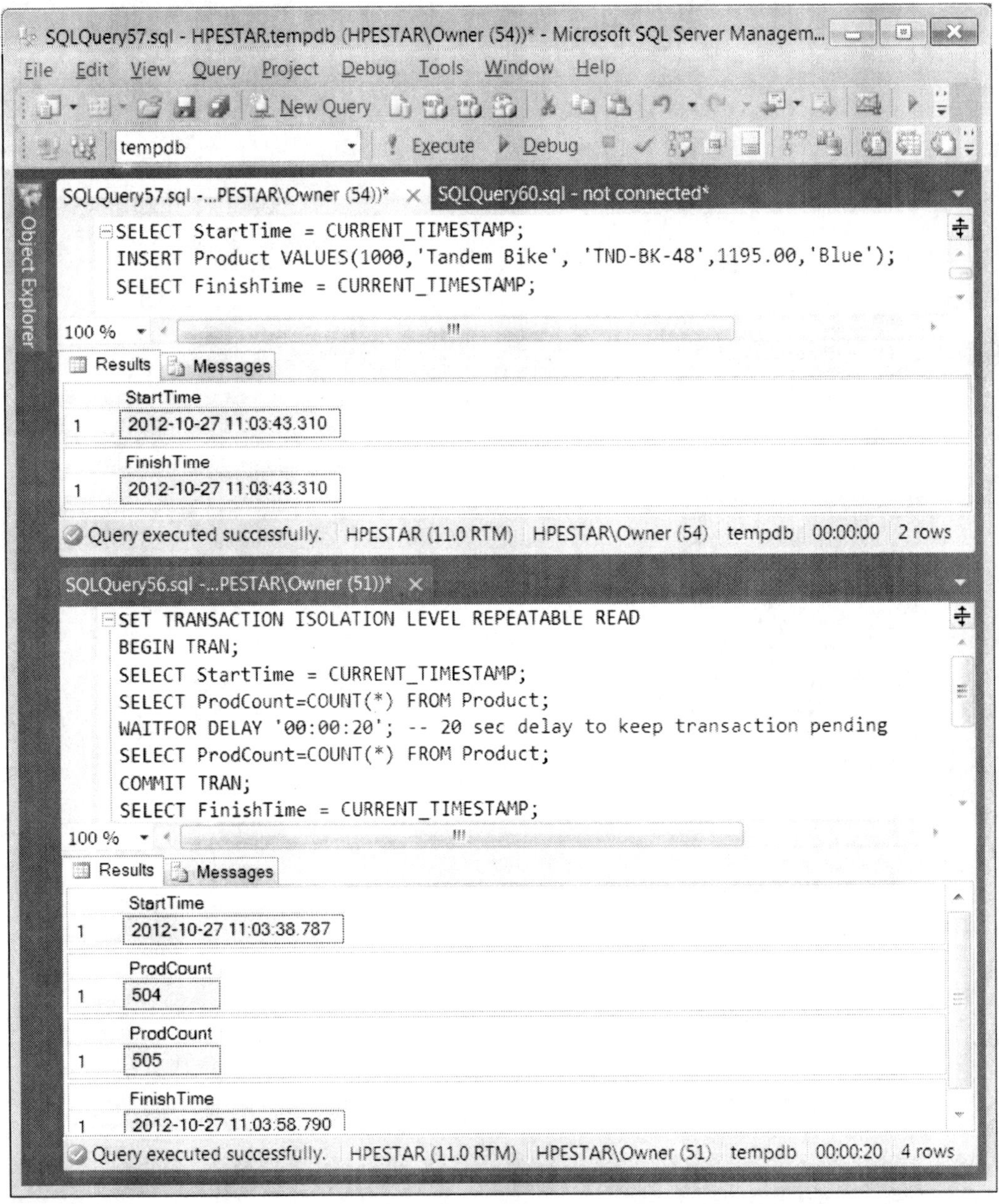

SERIALIZABLE Isolation Level

SERIALIZABLE isolation level blocks INSERT as well in addition to blocking UPDATE & DELETE. The row counts are the same. Use this restrictive pessimistic isolation level carefully, it can cause deadlocks and performance problems. It is like placing HOLDLOCK on all tables in the query.

Article: **Deadlock heaven: Serializable IsolationLevel**
http://nexussharp.wordpress.com/2012/01/30/deadlock-heaven-serializable-isolationlevel/

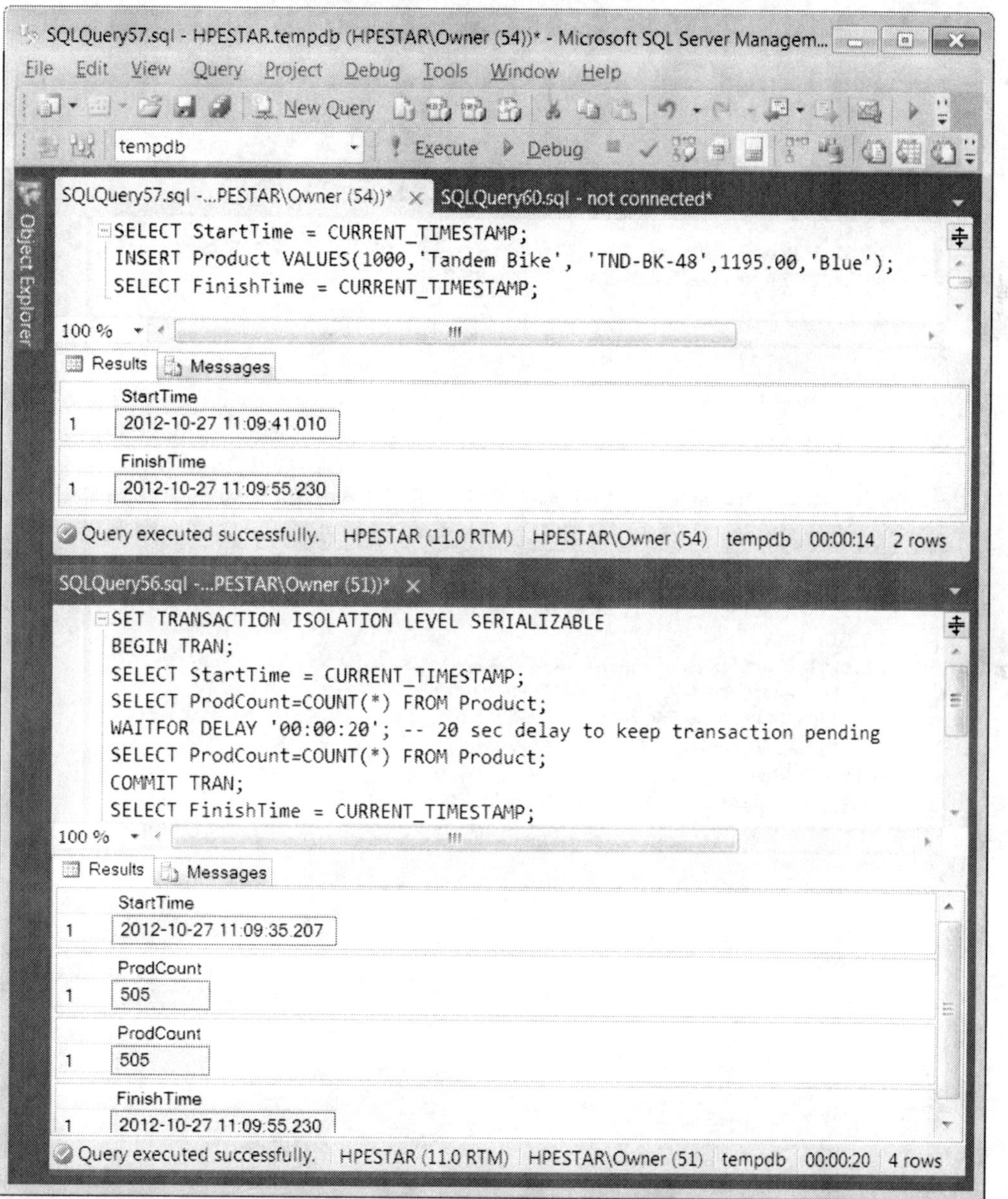

SNAPSHOT Isolation Level

The optimistic SNAPSHOT isolation produces the same results as SERIALIZABLE without blocking INSERT, UPDATE & DELETE. Use snapshot isolation, for example, to isolate concurrent UPDATEs on the same table causing blocks.

Article: **Snapshot Isolation Level in SQL Server - What, Why and How - Part 1**
http://www.databasejournal.com/features/mssql/snapshot-isolation-level-in-sql-server-what-why-and-how-part-1.html

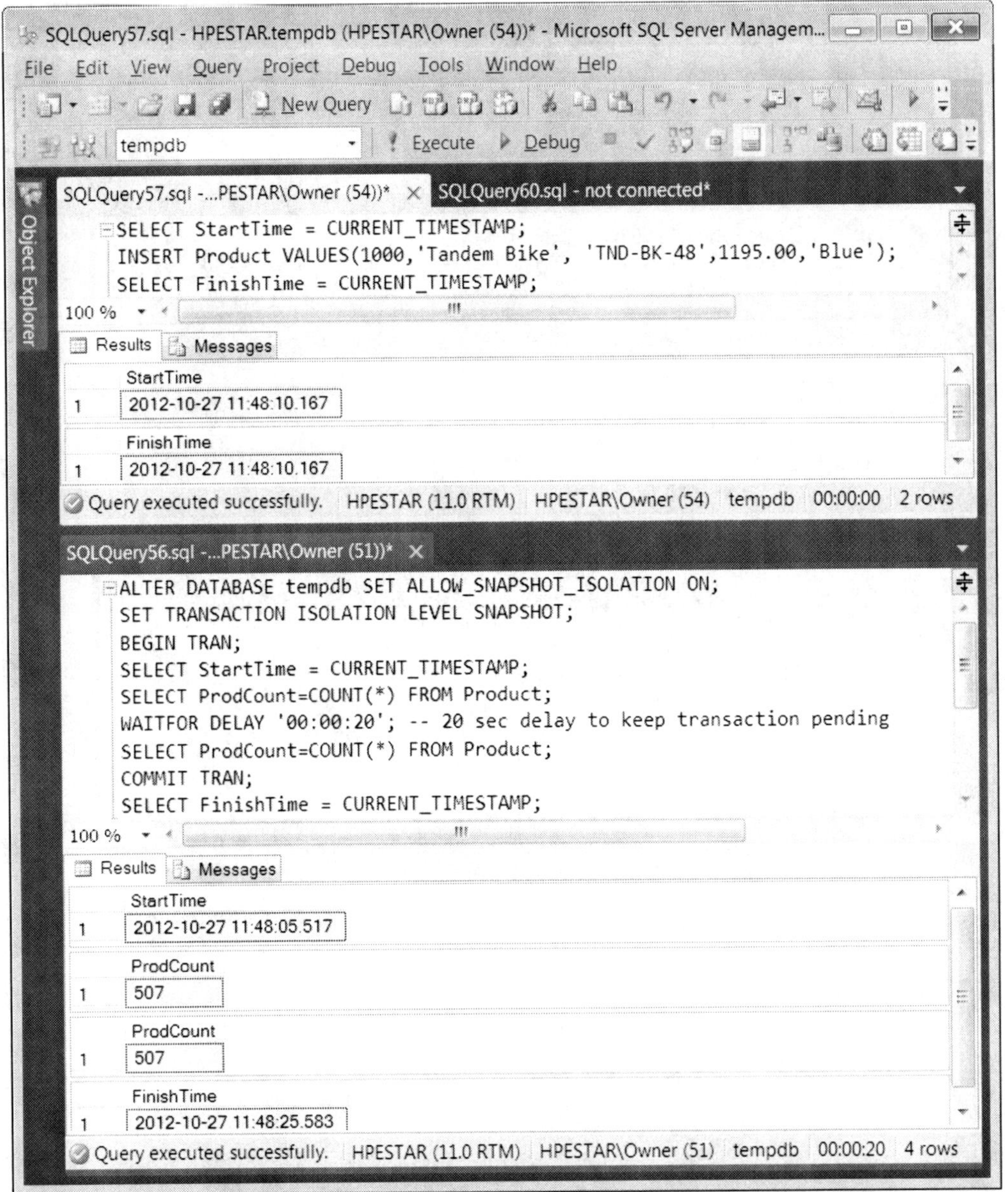

Tabular Summary of Isolation Levels

DBCC command returns the isolation level property for the database among other database options.

```
USE tempdb;
DBCC USEROPTIONS;
/* (13 row(s) affected)
DBCC execution completed. If DBCC printed error messages,
contact your system administrator. */
```

Set Option	Value
textsize	2147483647
language	us_english
dateformat	mdy
datefirst	7
lock_timeout	-1
quoted_identifier	SET
arithabort	SET
ansi_null_dflt_on	SET
ansi_warnings	SET
ansi_padding	SET
ansi_nulls	SET
concat_null_yields_null	SET
isolation level	**read committed**

Dirty Reads & Phantom Reads

Dirty Reads: reading uncommitted data; there is no guarantee that data read will ever be committed.

Phantom Reads: data working with in the first connection changed by another transaction in the second connection since first read. Subsequent reads of the data in the first connection same transaction could be different.

Isolation level	Dirty read	Nonrepeatable read	Phantom read
Read uncommitted	Yes	Yes	Yes
Read committed	No	Yes	Yes
Repeatable read	No	No	Yes
Serializable	No	No	No
Snapshot	No	No	No

INSERT Data Into Parent-Child Tables in One Transaction

The business meaning of transaction: either insert successfully to both tables or do nothing, return an error. First we prepare the test data to be inserted in two temporary tables by SELECT INTO table create and populate.

```
USE AdventureWorks2012
GO
```

```
DECLARE @SourceSOID int = 50701;
SELECT OrderDate
        ,DueDate ,ShipDate,Status,OnlineOrderFlag,PurchaseOrderNumber
        ,AccountNumber,CustomerID,SalesPersonID,TerritoryID,BillToAddressID
        ,ShipToAddressID,ShipMethodID,CreditCardID,CreditCardApprovalCode
        ,CurrencyRateID,SubTotal,TaxAmt,Freight,Comment
 INTO #SOH
 FROM Sales.SalesOrderHeader
 WHERE SalesOrderID = @SourceSOID;   -- (1 row(s) affected)
```

```
SELECT SalesOrderID,
        CarrierTrackingNumber,OrderQty,ProductID,SpecialOfferID,UnitPrice,UnitPriceDiscount
INTO #SOD
FROM Sales.SalesOrderDetail
WHERE SalesOrderID = @SourceSOID;
GO  -- (6 row(s) affected)
```

```
SELECT * FROM #SOH;
```

OrderDate	DueDate	ShipDate	Status	OnlineOrderFlag	PurchaseOrderNumber	AccountNumber	CustomerID	SalesPersonID	TerritoryID	BillToAddressID	ShipToAddressID	ShipMethodID	CreditCardID	CreditCardApprovalCode	CurrencyRateID	SubTotal	TaxAmt	Freight	Comment
2007-06-01 00:00:00.000	2007-06-13 00:00:00.000	2007-06-08 00:00:00.000	5	0	PO2407199018	10-4020-000225	29882	279	5	933	933	5	12808	56789Vi66226	NULL	777.2902	73.4748	22.9609	NULL

```
SELECT * FROM #SOD;
GO
```

CarrierTrackingNumber	OrderQty	ProductID	SpecialOfferID	UnitPrice	UnitPriceDiscount
B67A-4C0A-B3	1	843	1	15.00	0.00
B67A-4C0A-B3	1	726	1	202.332	0.00
B67A-4C0A-B3	1	722	1	183.9382	0.00
B67A-4C0A-B3	4	855	1	53.994	0.00
B67A-4C0A-B3	2	813	1	65.6018	0.00
B67A-4C0A-B3	1	716	1	28.8404	0.00

ROLLBACK Does Not Roll Back Everything

ROLLBACK has no effect on IDENTITY seed, table variable or writing to a flat file. The implication is that IDENTITY column will have gaps where ROLLBACKs happened. With RAISERROR we return an error flag to the calling application program.

```
BEGIN TRANSACTION DECLARE @Insert TABLE(ID INT); DECLARE @Error INT; DECLARE @ID INT;
INSERT INTO Sales.SalesOrderHeader(OrderDate
        ,DueDate ,ShipDate,Status,OnlineOrderFlag,PurchaseOrderNumber
        ,AccountNumber,CustomerID,SalesPersonID,TerritoryID,BillToAddressID
        ,ShipToAddressID,ShipMethodID,CreditCardID,CreditCardApprovalCode
        ,CurrencyRateID,SubTotal,TaxAmt,Freight,Comment )
OUTPUT inserted.SalesOrderID INTO @Insert(ID)  -- This is the PRIMARY KEY value
SELECT * FROM #SOH; -- (1 row(s) affected)
SET @Error = @@ERROR;  IF @Error <>0 BEGIN          ROLLBACK TRANSACTION;
        RAISERROR ('An error occurred inserting Sales.SalesOrderHeader',12,1);   END
ELSE BEGIN  SELECT * FROM @Insert; -- debugging   -- 75124
SELECT @ID = ID FROM @Insert;  -- FOREIGN KEY value
INSERT Sales.SalesOrderDetail ( SalesOrderID,    CarrierTrackingNumber, OrderQty, ProductID,
                SpecialOfferID,  UnitPrice, UnitPriceDiscount)
SELECT @ID, * FROM #SOD;  -- (6 row(s) affected)
SET @Error = @@ERROR;  IF @Error <>0 BEGIN    ROLLBACK TRANSACTION;
        RAISERROR ('An error occurred inserting Sales.SalesOrderDetail',16,1);    END
ELSE    COMMIT TRAN;  END
```

XACT_ABORT & Automatic ROLLBACK TRANSACTION

XACT_ABORT is SET option. When ON (other option is OFF) the current transaction automatically rolls back if a T-SQL statement raises a run-time error. @@TRANCOUNT system variable indicates the number of active transactions for the current connection.

```
SET XACT_ABORT ON;
DBCC USEROPTIONS;  -- Check if option is set or not. - Partial results
IF ( (16384 & @@options) = 16384 ) PRINT 'XACT_ABORT';  -- Alternate way of checking
```

Set Option	Value
xact_abort	SET

MSDN Articles: **SET XACT_ABORT**
http://msdn.microsoft.com/en-us/library/aa259192(v=SQL.80).aspx
@@TRANCOUNT
http://msdn.microsoft.com/en-us/library/aa933178(v=sql.80).aspx

Optimistic Concurrency Control

A table can have only one rowversion(formerly timestamp) column which is used for version-stamping rows. The value in the rowversion column is updated automatically every time a row in the table inserted or updated. Of course this means we cannot use it as a PRIMARY KEY, because we may get many FK orphans quickly if updates are performed on other columns. When a row is modified in a table, the timestamp is updated with the current database timestamp value obtained from the @@DBTS function.

Rowversion is the synonym for timestamp starting with SQL Server 2005. It is an 8 bytes unique binary key within the database. A quick demo of rowversion data type follows. **Rowversion values may not be consecutive.** Since all the columns in the demo table have default values, we can use the DEFAULT VALUES clause for INSERT.

```
USE tempdb;
GO
```

```
CREATE TABLE Alpha ( ID int IDENTITY(1,1) PRIMARY KEY,
        Number int default(datepart(ss,CURRENT_TIMESTAMP)),
        String varchar(16) default(datename(dw, CURRENT_TIMESTAMP)),
        ModifiedDate date default(CURRENT_TIMESTAMP),
        RowStamp rowversion);
GO
```

```
INSERT Alpha DEFAULT VALUES;
GO 100
```

```
SELECT TOP(5) * FROM Alpha ORDER BY ID;
GO
```

ID	Number	String	ModifiedDate	RowStamp
1	43	Sunday	2012-10-28	0x0000000000000840
2	43	Sunday	2012-10-28	0x0000000000000841
3	43	Sunday	2012-10-28	0x0000000000000842
4	43	Sunday	2012-10-28	0x0000000000000843
5	43	Sunday	2012-10-28	0x0000000000000844

The rowversion (timestamp) starts changing as soon as the transaction begins. If the transaction is rolled back, it returns to the original value.

The main purpose is row versioning in multi user environment, in other words concurrency checking. The users may be humans or computer programs.

Pessimistic Concurrency Control vs. Optimistic

Pessimistic concurrency means locking the data at the row, page, or table level and don't allow anyone to modify it until the target user is done modifying the data and saving it back into the database. Trouble with this method: it may take a few minutes for the target user to update a record during which period other users may be prevented from doing their work (locked out from the table by blocking). If the target user called away for a meeting for example in the middle of data entry, you need to unlock the table by a timeout mechanism in order to prevent damaging disruption to data access by other users.

Optimistic concurrency means reading a record in a table and displaying it for the target user, but not locking it. Other users can read and modify the record at anytime while the target user is performing the manual update on the computer screen. When the target user releases the record for database update you need to check if someone changed it in between the initial read and the release (like 1-5 minutes). Usually this is not a problem due to the work distribution among staff (business process organization), nevertheless you have to program for it to avoid conflicting updates and damage to database integrity.

Assume you are a developer and developing a program in Visual Basic to update the name and address table of customers. There will be 100 staff member who can perform this application function. How can you be sure that while target staff Alpha typing in the change, staff Beta is not changing the same row?

Here is what you can do:

- Read the name and address table including the rowversion. You display the info to the user for update and save the rowversion.
- Certain amount of time later, like 2 minutes, the user presses the submit button after changes were typed in.
- You open a transaction with Begin Transaction.
- You read the rowversion of the name and address row.
- You compare the current rowversion to the saved rowversion.
- If the rowversions are same, you update the row and commit the transaction.
- If rowversions are different, you roll back the transaction and notify the user about the fact that the data was changed by someone else. You can let then the user decide what to do or follow the appropriate company business rule for data entry conflict resolution.

This is pretty common practice in multi-user environment. The alternate would be to examine a datetime column, or the entire row which is more processing intensive and less reliable as well due to potential blocking.

Example Showing rowversion (formerly timestamp) in Action

```
USE tempdb;
```

```
CREATE TABLE Star
 (
        StarID                  INT IDENTITY PRIMARY KEY,              -- SURROGATE PK
        FirstName               VARCHAR(25),
        LastName                VARCHAR(30),
        UNIQUE (LastName, FirstName),                                   -- NATURAL KEY
        ModifiedDate            DATE default( CURRENT_TIMESTAMP),
        VERSIONSTAMP            ROWVERSION
 );
go
```

```
-- Populate table
INSERT Star     (FirstName, LastName)
VALUES          ('Tom', 'Jones'),
                ('Jessica', 'Simpson'),
                ('Luciano', 'Pavarotti'),
                ('Stevie',  'Brock'),
                ('Christina', 'Aguilera'),
                ('Frank', 'Sinatra'),
                ('Doris', 'Day'),
                ('Elvis', 'Presley');
go
```

```
SELECT * FROM   Star ORDER BY StarID;
go
```

StarID	FirstName	LastName	ModifiedDate	VERSIONSTAMP
1	Tom	Jones	2018-11-07	0x00000000000007E0
2	Jessica	Simpson	2018-11-07	0x00000000000007E1
3	Luciano	Pavarotti	2018-11-07	0x00000000000007E2
4	Stevie	Brock	2018-11-07	0x00000000000007E3
5	Christina	Aguilera	2018-11-07	0x00000000000007E4
6	Frank	Sinatra	2018-11-07	0x00000000000007E5
7	Doris	Day	2018-11-07	0x00000000000007E6
8	Elvis	Presley	2018-11-07	0x00000000000007E7

Simulation of Conflicting Updates of the Same Record

```
-- Temporary table to store current record version
CREATE TABLE #semaphore
 (
   ID                    INT IDENTITY(1, 1) PRIMARY KEY,
   StartVersion          BIGINT,
   PK                    INT
 );
```

```
INSERT INTO #semaphore (StartVersion, PK)
SELECT VERSIONSTAMP, StarID
FROM   Star
WHERE  StarID = 1;
```

```
SELECT * FROM #semaphore;
```

ID	StartVersion	PK
1	2016	1

```
-- We send the info to "our" application user;  user is making changes on the app form;
SELECT StarID, FirstName, LastName
FROM Star
WHERE StarID = 1;
```

```
-- SIMULATION: somebody else updating the same record meanwhile
-- Execute the following UPDATE statement in a different SSMS connection
/*********************************************************
UPDATE Star
SET     FirstName = 'Celine',
        LastName = 'Dion'
WHERE  StarID = 1
*********************************************************/
```

```
SELECT StarID, FirstName, LastName FROM Star WHERE StarID = 1;
```

StarID	FirstName	LastName
1	Celine	Dion

We Envelope the UPDATE Attempt into a Transaction

```
-- We are attempting to update, but cannot because current version is different
BEGIN TRANSACTION
```

```
IF (SELECT StartVersion
    FROM   #semaphore
    WHERE PK=1 )
       =
   (SELECT VERSIONSTAMP
    FROM   Star
    WHERE  StarID = 1)
  BEGIN
      UPDATE Star
      SET    FirstName = 'Julia',
             LastName = 'Roberts'
      WHERE  StarID = 1
      COMMIT TRANSACTION
  END
ELSE
  BEGIN
      ROLLBACK TRANSACTION
      PRINT 'ROLLBACK - UPDATE CONFLICT'
      RAISERROR ('Star update conflict.',10,0)
  END;
```

```
/* Messages
ROLLBACK - UPDATE CONFLICT
Star update conflict.   */
```

RAISERROR returns error flag to application. The application will follow a business rule to handle the exception.

LAG() & LEAD() Function Usage with OVER PARTITION BY

The LAG() and LEAD() functions provide backward and forward reference to items in a sequence, new feature of SS 2012.

```
USE AdventureWorks2012;
```

```
-- Create populated test table
SELECT TerritoryID, MONTH(OrderDate) AS Month, SUM(SubTotal) AS MonthlySales
INTO  SalesByMonth2007
FROM Sales.SalesOrderHeader AS SOH
WHERE YEAR(OrderDate) = 2007
GROUP BY TerritoryID, MONTH(OrderDate)
GO  -- (120 row(s) affected)
```

```
SELECT TOP (3) * FROM SalesByMonth2007 ORDER BY newid();
GO
```

TerritoryID	Month	MonthlySales
7	3	126171.9109
3	8	378577.9115
8	9	236069.3624

```
SELECT TerritoryID, Month,
LAG(MonthlySales, 1, 0) OVER (PARTITION BY TerritoryID ORDER BY Month) AS PrevMonthSales,
MonthlySales                                                           AS CurrentMonthSales,
LEAD(MonthlySales,1, 0) OVER (PARTITION BY TerritoryID ORDER BY Month) AS NextMonthSales
FROM SalesByMonth2007
ORDER BY TerritoryID, Month;    -- (120 row(s) affected) - Partial results.
```

TerritoryID	Month	PrevMonthSales	CurrentMonthSales	NextMonthSales
1	1	0.00	240562.5086	440116.2746
1	2	240562.5086	440116.2746	120849.7791
1	3	440116.2746	120849.7791	285641.6387
1	4	120849.7791	285641.6387	533190.1173
1	5	285641.6387	533190.1173	143297.7549
1	6	533190.1173	143297.7549	475272.0915
1	7	143297.7549	475272.0915	829531.9575
1	8	475272.0915	829531.9575	691839.5031
1	9	829531.9575	691839.5031	447548.4438
1	10	691839.5031	447548.4438	745956.6587
1	11	447548.4438	745956.6587	781557.8013
1	12	745956.6587	781557.8013	0.00
2	1	0.00	239629.7733	277660.0743
2	2	239629.7733	277660.0743	152395.7408
2	3	277660.0743	152395.7408	335168.9164

Xquery Examples

The XML data type has the following methods for exposing the data: Query, Value, Exist, Modify, and Nodes.

The query() Method

The query() method takes an XQuery expression that evaluates to a list of XML nodes and allows the extraction of fragments of an XML document. The result is an instance of untyped XML. First we create xml data with the FOR XML AUTO clause, then query it.

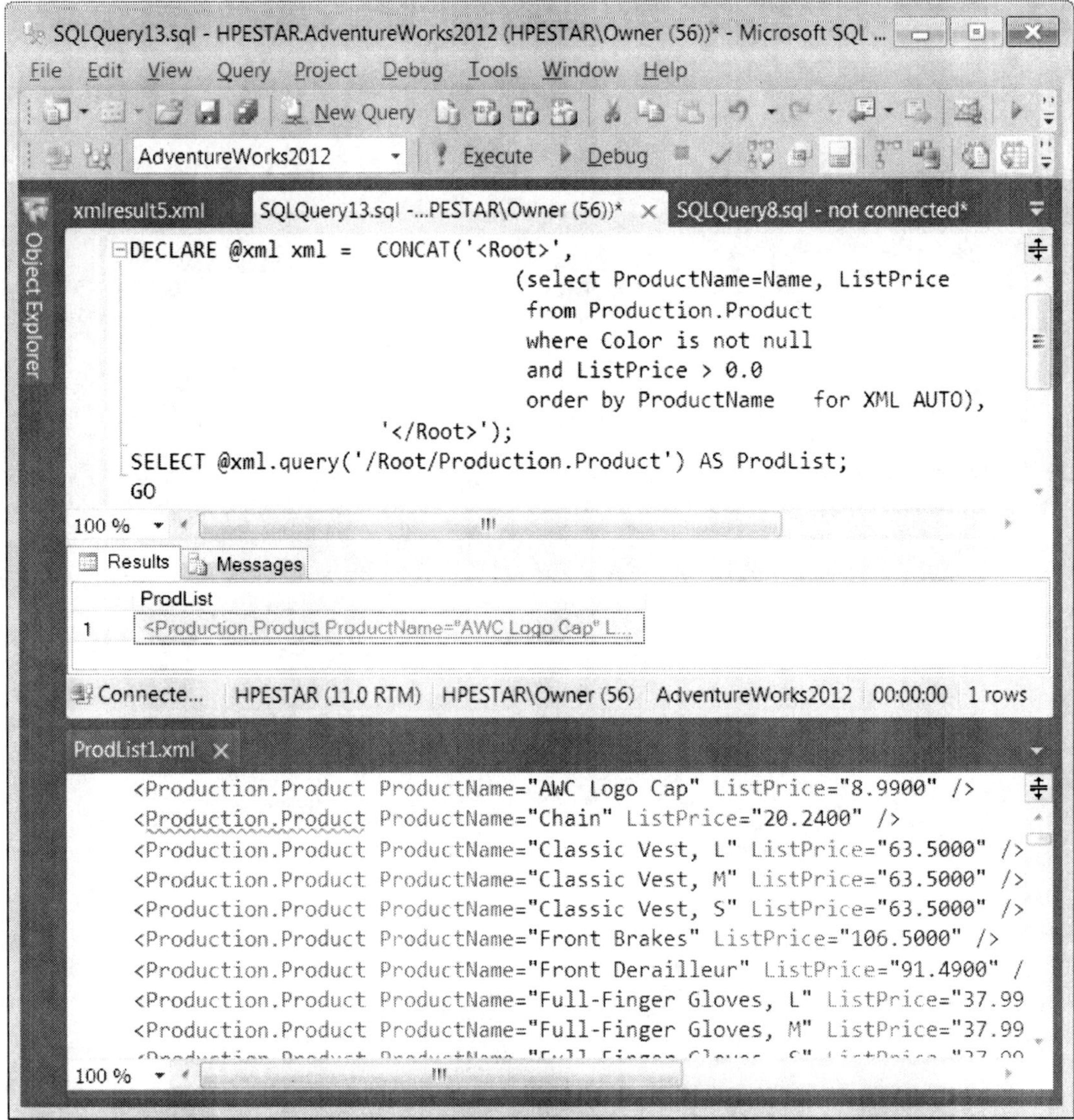
```
DECLARE @xml xml =  CONCAT('<Root>',
                        (select ProductName=Name, ListPrice
                         from Production.Product
                         where Color is not null
                         and ListPrice > 0.0
                         order by ProductName   for XML AUTO),
                    '</Root>');
SELECT @xml.query('/Root/Production.Product') AS ProdList;
GO
```

	ProdList
1	<Production.Product ProductName="AWC Logo Cap" L...

```
<Production.Product ProductName="AWC Logo Cap" ListPrice="8.9900" />
<Production.Product ProductName="Chain" ListPrice="20.2400" />
<Production.Product ProductName="Classic Vest, L" ListPrice="63.5000" />
<Production.Product ProductName="Classic Vest, M" ListPrice="63.5000" />
<Production.Product ProductName="Classic Vest, S" ListPrice="63.5000" />
<Production.Product ProductName="Front Brakes" ListPrice="106.5000" />
<Production.Product ProductName="Front Derailleur" ListPrice="91.4900" /
<Production.Product ProductName="Full-Finger Gloves, L" ListPrice="37.99
<Production.Product ProductName="Full-Finger Gloves, M" ListPrice="37.99
```

The query() Method Retrieves Assembly Instructions from XML Column

inst is a derived table representing the inner query which retrieves information from the ProductModel table XML column. The outer query formats and filters the data to return the final result set.

```
USE AdventureWorks2012;
SELECT  ProductModelID,
        rtrim(ltrim(convert(nvarchar(max),[Procedure])))  AS  [Procedure]
FROM
(SELECT ProductModelID,Instructions.query(
' declare namespace AWPMMI="http://schemas.microsoft.com/sqlserver/2004/07/adventure-works/ProductModelManuInstructions";
  for $Step in /AWPMMI:root/AWPMMI:Location[1]/AWPMMI:step
    return string($Step)'
) AS  [Procedure]
FROM Production.ProductModel WHERE Instructions is not null) inst
WHERE ProductModelID = 53;
GO
```

ProductModelID	Procedure
53	
Visually examine the pedal spindles to determine left and right pedals. The left and right pedals have different threading directions. It is important you identify them correctly.	
Apply a small amount of grease to the left pedal and thread the pedal onto the left crank arm by hand.	
If the threads do not turn easily, back the spindle out and re-start.	
Securely tighten the spindle against the crank arm using a small wrench.	
Apply a small amount of grease to the right pedal and thread the pedal onto the right crank arm by hand. If the threads do not turn easily, back the spindle out and re-start. Securely tighten the spindle against the crank arm using a small wrench.	
Inspect per specification FI-520.	

When we examine the Procedure string with convert(varbinary(max), ...), we can see that it has next line (hex 0A) an leading spaces (hex 20) imbedded for formatting purposes. We can check the size of XML data with the DATALENGTH() function:

```
select   MinLen = min(datalength(resume)),  MaxLen = max(datalength(resume)),
         AvgLen = avg(datalength(resume))
from AdventureWorks2012.HumanResources.JobCandidate;
-- 3931          9080          6241
```

value() Method

The value() method performs an XQuery against the XML and returns a scalar value.

```
DECLARE @xmlDoc xml =' <root><MP3List><MP3ListID>99</MP3ListID></MP3List> </root>';
SELECT @xmlDoc.value('(/root//MP3List/MP3ListID/text())[1]','nvarchar(32)' );   -- 99
```

nodes() Method

The nodes() method shreds an XML data type instance into relational data. It returns a rowset. In the XML resume example, each column returned as scalar value.

exist() Method

The exist() method returns bit 1 (true) if the XQuery expression returns at least one XML node.

Bike models are listed if <Summary> element is included in XML ProductDescription.

```
SELECT          Name                                              AS ModelName,
                CatalogDescription.query('
declare namespace pd="http://schemas.microsoft.com/sqlserver/2004/07/adventure-
works/ProductModelDescription";
  <Product
    ProductModelID= "{ sql:column("ProductModelID") }"
    />
')                                                                AS ProductModelID
FROM AdventureWorks2012.Production.ProductModel
WHERE CatalogDescription.exist('
  declare namespace  pd="http://schemas.microsoft.com/sqlserver/2004/07/adventure-
works/ProductModelDescription";
   /pd:ProductDescription[(pd:Summary)]'
  ) = 1
ORDER BY ModelName;
GO
```

ModelName	ProductModelID
Mountain-100	<Product ProductModelID="19" />
Mountain-500	<Product ProductModelID="23" />
Road-150	<Product ProductModelID="25" />
Road-450	<Product ProductModelID="28" />
Touring-1000	<Product ProductModelID="34" />
Touring-2000	<Product ProductModelID="35" />

The CatalogDescription XML data for ProductModelID 23


```
<?xml-stylesheet href="ProductDescription.xsl" type="text/xsl"?>
<p1:ProductDescription
xmlns:p1="http://schemas.microsoft.com/sqlserver/2004/07/adventure-
works/ProductModelDescription"
xmlns:wm="http://schemas.microsoft.com/sqlserver/2004/07/adventure-
works/ProductModelWarrAndMain" xmlns:wf="http://www.adventure-
```

```
works.com/schemas/OtherFeatures" xmlns:html="http://www.w3.org/1999/xhtml"
ProductModelID="23" ProductModelName="Mountain-500">
 <p1:Summary>
  <html:p>Suitable for any type of riding, on or off-road.
                        Fits any budget. Smooth-shifting with a comfortable ride.
          </html:p>
 </p1:Summary>
 <p1:Manufacturer>
  <p1:Name>AdventureWorks</p1:Name>
  <p1:Copyright>2002</p1:Copyright>
  <p1:ProductURL>HTTP://www.Adventure-works.com</p1:ProductURL>
 </p1:Manufacturer>
 <p1:Features>Product highlights include:
        <wm:Warranty><wm:WarrantyPeriod>1
year</wm:WarrantyPeriod><wm:Description>parts and
labor</wm:Description></wm:Warranty><wm:Maintenance><wm:NoOfYears>3
years</wm:NoOfYears><wm:Description>maintenance contact available through
dealer</wm:Description></wm:Maintenance><wf:wheel>Stable, durable wheels suitable for
novice riders.</wf:wheel><wf:saddle>Made from synthetic leather and features gel padding for
increased comfort.</wf:saddle><wf:pedal><html:b>Expanded platform</html:b> so you can
ride in any shoes; great for all-around riding.</wf:pedal><wf:crankset> Super rigid spindle.
</wf:crankset><wf:BikeFrame>Our best value frame utilizing the same, ground-breaking
technology as the ML aluminum frame.</wf:BikeFrame></p1:Features>
 <!-- add one or more of these elements... one for each specific product in this product model --
>
 <p1:Picture>
  <p1:Angle>front</p1:Angle>
  <p1:Size>small</p1:Size>
  <p1:ProductPhotoID>1</p1:ProductPhotoID>
 </p1:Picture>
 <!-- add any tags in <specifications> -->
 <p1:Specifications> These are the product specifications.
        <Height>Varies</Height> Centimeters.
        <Material>Aluminum Alloy</Material><Color>Available in all
colors.</Color><ProductLine>Mountain
bike</ProductLine><Style>Unisex</Style><RiderExperience>Novice to Intermediate
riders</RiderExperience></p1:Specifications>
</p1:ProductDescription>
```

modify() Method

The modify() method modifies the contents of an XML document. It can only be used in the SET statement or the SET clause of an UPDATE statement for tables with XML columns.

```
DECLARE @XML xml = '<Root>
 <Picture>
  <Angle>front</Angle>
  <Size>small</Size>
  <ProductPhotoID>1</ProductPhotoID>
 </Picture>     </Root>';          SELECT @XML;
```

```
<Root><Picture><Angle>front</Angle><Size>small</Size><ProductPhotoID>1</ProductPhotoID
></Picture></Root>
```

```
-- update angle
SET @XML.modify('
 replace value of (/Root/Picture/Angle[1]/text())[1]
 with    "side" ');          SELECT @XML;
```

```
<Root><Picture><Angle>side</Angle><Size>small</Size><ProductPhotoID>1</ProductPhotoID>
</Picture></Root>
```

```
-- update size
SET @XML.modify('
 replace value of (/Root/Picture/Size[1]/text())[1]
 with    "medium" ');    SELECT @XML;
```

```
<Root><Picture><Angle>side</Angle><Size>medium</Size><ProductPhotoID>1</ProductPhotoI
D></Picture></Root>
```

```
-- update productphotoid
SET @XML.modify('
 replace value of (/Root/Picture/ProductPhotoID[1]/text())[1]
 with    "99" ');          SELECT @XML;
```

```
<Root><Picture><Angle>side</Angle><Size>medium</Size><ProductPhotoID>99</ProductPhot
oID></Picture></Root>
```

Insert (XML DML)

Insert(XML DML) inserts one or more nodes as child nodes or siblings of the target node.

```
DECLARE @XML xml = '<Root>
 <Picture ID = "4">
  <Angle>front</Angle>
  <Size>small</Size>
  <ProductPhotoID>1</ProductPhotoID>
 </Picture>      </Root>';
SELECT @XML;
```

```
<Root>
  <Picture ID="4">
    <Angle>front</Angle>
    <Size>small</Size>
    <ProductPhotoID>1</ProductPhotoID>
  </Picture>
</Root>
```

```
SET @XML.modify('insert  <Picture ID = "1">
   <Angle>front</Angle>
   <Size>large</Size>
   <ProductPhotoID>45</ProductPhotoID>
 </Picture> as first    into   (/Root)[1] ');
SELECT @XML;
```

```
<Root>
  <Picture ID="1">
    <Angle>front</Angle>
    <Size>large</Size>
    <ProductPhotoID>45</ProductPhotoID>
  </Picture>
  <Picture ID="4">
    <Angle>front</Angle>
    <Size>small</Size>
    <ProductPhotoID>1</ProductPhotoID>
  </Picture>
</Root>
```

Delete (XML DML)

The delete(XML DML) deletes nodes from an XML instance.

```
DECLARE @XML xml = '<Root>
<Picture ID = "1">
  <Angle>front</Angle>
  <Size>large</Size>
  <ProductPhotoID>45</ProductPhotoID>
 </Picture>
 <Picture ID = "4">
  <Angle>front</Angle>
  <Size>small</Size>
  <ProductPhotoID>1</ProductPhotoID>
 </Picture>
 <Picture ID = "8">
  <Angle>above</Angle>
  <Size>small</Size>
  <ProductPhotoID>12</ProductPhotoID>
 </Picture>       </Root>';
```

```
SET @XML.modify('
 delete /Root/Picture[@ID=4]  ');
```

```
SELECT @XML;
```

```
<Root>
  <Picture ID="1">
    <Angle>front</Angle>
    <Size>large</Size>
    <ProductPhotoID>45</ProductPhotoID>
  </Picture>
  <Picture ID="8">
    <Angle>above</Angle>
    <Size>small</Size>
    <ProductPhotoID>12</ProductPhotoID>
  </Picture>
</Root>
```

Calculate Percent Ratios by Groups

Ratio calculation is important in Business Intelligence. It can be done in various or all levels of a hierarchical relationship, in this example Product --> Subcategory hierarchy.

```
USE AdventureWorks2012;
SELECT  S.Name                                                              AS Subcategory,
   FORMAT(1.0 * SUM(CASE WHEN Color in ( 'Black', 'Yellow', 'Silver')
   THEN 1 ELSE 0 END) / COUNT(*), 'p')                                      AS RatioOfBlkYlwSlv
FROM Production.Product P
          INNER JOIN Production.ProductSubcategory S
                    ON P.ProductSubcategoryID= S.ProductSubcategoryID
WHERE Color is not null and P.ProductSubcategoryID is not null
GROUP BY S.Name  ORDER BY S.Name;   -- (23 row(s) affected) - Partial results.
```

Subcategory	RatioOfBlkYlwSlv
Pedals	0.00 %
Road Bikes	53.49 %
Road Frames	48.48 %
Shorts	100.00 %
Socks	0.00 %

Working with hierarchyid Data Type

Orgchart Based on AdventureWorks2012

Let's take a look at the hierarchyid and related data in the Employee table first.

```
USE AdventureWorks2012;
SELECT TOP(20) BusinessEntityID, NationalIdNumber, OrganizationNode, OrganizationLevel,
          OrgNodeText=CONVERT(varchar, OrganizationNode),  JobTitle
FROM HumanResources.Employee  ORDER BY OrganizationNode;
```

BusinessEntityID	NationalIdNumber	OrganizationNode	OrganizationLevel	OrgNodeText	JobTitle
1	295847284	0x	0	/	Chief Executive Officer
2	245797967	0x58	1	/1/	Vice President of Engineering
3	509647174	0x5AC0	2	/1/1/	Engineering Manager
4	112457891	0x5AD6	3	/1/1/1/	Senior Tool Designer
5	695256908	0x5ADA	3	/1/1/2/	Design Engineer
6	998320692	0x5ADE	3	/1/1/3/	Design Engineer

```
-- Convert text node to hierarchyid
SELECT CONVERT(hierarchyid, '/3/1/22/4/');   -- 0x7AF07610
```

hierarchyid Based Organizational Chart with Recursive CTE

TAB (CHAR(9)) is used to create the indentation using OrganizationLevel.

```
;WITH cteOrgChart(ManagerID, EmployeeID, EmployeeLevel)
   AS (SELECT    OrganizationNode,                              -- anchor member
                 OrganizationNode,  OrganizationLevel
      FROM   HumanResources.Employee
      WHERE  OrganizationLevel = 0
      UNION ALL
      SELECT     e.OrganizationNode.GetAncestor(1),              -- recursive member
                 e.OrganizationNode, OrganizationLevel
      FROM   HumanResources.Employee e
          INNER JOIN cteOrgChart d
           ON e.OrganizationNode.GetAncestor(1) = d.EmployeeID)

-- SELECT * FROM     cteOrgChart  -- for testing & debugging

SELECT   Employee = CONCAT(replicate(CHAR(9),(EmployeeLevel)), P.LastName, ', ',
P.FirstName)
FROM     cteOrgChart OC
      INNER JOIN HumanResources.Employee E
        ON OC.EmployeeID = E.OrganizationNode
      INNER JOIN Person.Person P
        ON E.BusinessEntityID = P.BusinessEntityID
ORDER BY E.OrganizationNode;
-- (290 row(s) affected)  - Partial Results.
```

Employee				
Sánchez, Ken				
	Duffy, Terri			
		Tamburello, Roberto		
			Walters, Rob	
			Erickson, Gail	
			Goldberg, Jossef	
			Miller, Dylan	
				Margheim, Diane
				Matthew, Gigi
				Raheem, Michael
			Cracium, Ovidiu	
				D'Hers, Thierry
				Galvin, Janice
			Sullivan, Michael	
			Salavaria, Sharon	
	Bradley, David			

Inline User-Defined Function OrgChart at Any Level

We can easily wrap the company orgchart logic into a parameterized function to get the orgchart for any executive or manager in the company.

```
CREATE FUNCTION ufnOrgChart ( @OrganizationNode hierarchyid )
RETURNS TABLE AS RETURN
(WITH cteOrgChart(ManagerID, EmployeeID, EmployeeLevel)
   AS (SELECT OrganizationNode,
         OrganizationNode,
         0
      FROM   HumanResources.Employee
      WHERE  OrganizationNode = @OrganizationNode
      UNION ALL
      SELECT e.OrganizationNode.GetAncestor(1),
         e.OrganizationNode,
         EmployeeLevel+1
      FROM   HumanResources.Employee e
         INNER JOIN cteOrgChart d
          ON e.OrganizationNode.GetAncestor(1) = d.EmployeeID)
SELECT   Employee = CONCAT(replicate(CHAR(9),(EmployeeLevel)), P.LastName, ', ',
                           P.FirstName)
FROM     cteOrgChart OC
      INNER JOIN HumanResources.Employee E
       ON OC.EmployeeID = E.OrganizationNode
      INNER JOIN Person.Person P
       ON E.BusinessEntityID = P.BusinessEntityID  );
GO
```

```
SELECT * FROM ufnOrgChart (0x84);  -- (29 row(s) affected) - Partial Results.
```

Employee			
Norman, Laura			
	Barreto de Mattos, Paula		
	Liu, David		
	Kahn, Wendy		
	Barber, David		
		Word, Sheela	
			Sandberg, Mikael
			Rao, Arvind
			Meisner, Linda
			Ogisu, Fukiko

hierarchyid System Functions

Specialized system hierarchyid functions available to deal with hierarchyid data.

```
SELECT          BusinessEntityID, JobTitle, OrganizationNode, OrganizationLevel,
                OrganizationNode.ToString()                AS TextOrgNode,
                OrganizationNode.GetLevel()                AS NodeLevel,
                OrganizationNode.GetAncestor(1)            AS Ancestor,
                OrganizationNode.IsDescendantOf(0x58)      AS [0x58 Descendant]
FROM HumanResources.Employee  ORDER BY TextOrgNode;
 -- (290 row(s) affected) - Partial results.
```

BusinessEntityID	JobTitle	OrganizationNode	OrganizationLevel	TextOrgNode	NodeLevel	Ancestor	0x58 Descendant
1	Chief Executive Officer	0x	0	/	0	NULL	0
2	Vice President of Engineering	0x58	1	/1/	1	0x	1
3	Engineering Manager	0x5AC0	2	/1/1/	2	0x58	1
4	Senior Tool Designer	0x5AD6	3	/1/1/1/	3	0x5AC0	1
5	Design Engineer	0x5ADA	3	/1/1/2/	3	0x5AC0	1
6	Design Engineer	0x5ADE	3	/1/1/3/	3	0x5AC0	1

Sort Outline Numbering with hierarchyid

Certain sorts which are obvious to us, due to our Human Intelligence, are a challenge in traditional SQL programming due to lack of tree/hierarchy structure processing. Such a case is outline numbers which are easily convertible to hierarchyid, hence the simple solution.

```
CREATE TABLE #OutlineNumber   (Nbr Varchar(64));
INSERT #OutlineNumber Values
 ('1'), ('1.1'), ('1.1.1'), ('1.1.9'), ('1.1.10'), ('1.1.11'), ('2'), ('2.1'), ('2.1.1'), ('10.1.2'), ('11.1.9');
SELECT * FROM #OutlineNumber ORDER BY Nbr;
```

Nbr	
1	
1.1	
1.1.1	
1.1.10	
1.1.11	
1.1.9	out of order
10.1.2	out of order
11.1.9	out of order
2	
2.1	
2.1.1	

Sort Outline Numbering with hierarchyid continued

```
-- Sorting on hierarchyid by converting outline string with "/" replaces "." & "/" prefix, suffix
SELECT *, [HierarchyID].ToString() AS TextHierarchyID FROM
  (SELECT *, CONVERT(hierarchyid, CONCAT('/',REPLACE(Nbr, '.', '/') ,'/')) AS [HierarchyID]
   FROM #OutlineNumber) x /* derived table */ ORDER BY HierarchyID;
```

Nbr	HierarchyID	TextHierarchyID
1	0x58	/1/
1.1	0x5AC0	/1/1/
1.1.1	0x5AD6	/1/1/1/
1.1.9	0x5AE980	/1/1/9/
1.1.10	0x5AEA80	/1/1/10/
1.1.11	0x5AEB80	/1/1/11/
2	0x68	/2/
2.1	0x6AC0	/2/1/
2.1.1	0x6AD6	/2/1/1/
10.1.2	0xAAB680	/10/1/2/
11.1.9	0xAEBA60	/11/1/9/

WHERE Clause Predicate with datetime Issues

When we use the equal operator on datetime OrderDate & string date, we only get the "midnight" records (time part 00:00:00.000). **This approach works as long as all records are midnight records.** It is better to use the >= and < operators because that always works.

```
USE tempdb; SELECT * INTO SOD FROM AdventureWorks2012.Sales.SalesOrderHeader
                                        WHERE OrderDate='2008-02-01';
GO -- (244 row(s) affected)
DECLARE @date int = 20080201;
SELECT cast(cast(@date as char(8)) as datetime);   -- 2008-02-01 00:00:00.000
SELECT COUNT(*) FROM SOD WHERE OrderDate = cast(@date as char(8)); -- 244
SELECT COUNT(*) FROM SOD WHERE OrderDate = @date; -- Implicit conversion fails
/* Msg 8115, Level 16, State 2, Line 4 Arithmetic overflow error converting expression to data type datetime.*/
GO
DECLARE @date char(8) = '20080201';
SELECT cast(@date  as datetime);   -- 2008-02-01 00:00:00.000
-- Implicit conversion succeeds if all records are midnight records
SELECT COUNT(*) FROM SOD WHERE OrderDate = @date; -- 244
-- Totally accurate way of doing it
SELECT COUNT(*) FROM SOD WHERE OrderDate >= @date AND OrderDate < DATEADD(dd,1,@date); -- 244
UPDATE top(100) SOD SET OrderDate = DATEADD(ss,1,OrderDate); -- Advance datetime 1 sec after midnight
-- Equal operator returns wrong count (midnight records only)
SELECT COUNT(*) FROM SOD WHERE OrderDate = @date; -- 144  - counted only the midnight records
SELECT COUNT(*) FROM SOD WHERE OrderDate >= @date AND OrderDate < DATEADD(dd,1,@date); -- 244
GO
```

Dynamic SQL PIVOT

Dynamic SQL PIVOT transposes rows into columns based on dynamic data. Dynamic PIVOT contrasts hard-wired PIVOT. Prior to coding the dynamic SQL, write out & test the static query.

Database security article: **Dynamic SQL & SQL Injection**
http://blogs.msdn.com/b/raulga/archive/2007/01/04/dynamic-sql-sql-injection.aspx

We need the following data-driven column header list of years:

[2005], [2006], [2007], [2008]

We need the following static PIVOT query to be generated dynamically:

```
SELECT * FROM (SELECT [Store (Freight Summary)] = S.Name,
              YEAR(OrderDate) AS OrderYear, Freight
FROM    Sales.SalesOrderHeader SOH
INNER JOIN Sales.Customer C ON SOH.CustomerID = C.CustomerID
INNER JOIN Sales.Store S ON C.StoreID = S.BusinessEntityID) as Header
PIVOT (SUM(Freight) FOR OrderYear IN( [2005], [2006], [2007], [2008])) AS Pvt ORDER BY 1;
-- (633 row(s) affected) - Partial results.
```

Store (Freight Summary)	2005	2006	2007	2008
Sensible Sports	NULL	NULL	364.2076	472.8672
Separate Parts Corporation	1243.1035	4883.5698	2493.3725	NULL
Serious Cycles	4868.9888	3511.0184	354.9403	NULL
Seventh Bike Store	831.2495	4329.8166	4866.4755	2024.7107
Sharp Bikes	912.9061	549.7834	NULL	NULL
Sheet Metal Manufacturing	NULL	6050.2523	9169.2709	3328.5167
Shipping Specialists	NULL	NULL	NULL	12.9692
Showcase for Cycles	NULL	NULL	35.2509	6.2386
Simple Bike Parts	87.9217	100.5808	31.1732	29.8886
Sixth Bike Store	426.1619	1346.1144	79.9409	NULL
Sleek Bikes	NULL	NULL	3407.692	2364.0185
Small Bike Accessories Shop	NULL	NULL	1116.6658	992.0197
Small Bike Shop	2359.1319	5277.5806	3681.3405	2216.5242
Small Cycle Store	152.3481	989.9408	801.0264	553.2965
Social Activities Club	177.3895	52.9214	9.7198	29.8886
Solid Bike Parts	1134.6482	1535.374	372.4571	NULL
Some Discount Store	2499.3443	733.0964	38.0211	1.1373
South Bike Company	NULL	NULL	1043.9713	837.2011
Spa and Exercise Outfitters	NULL	94.3411	3777.5336	2441.4004

Dynamic SQL PIVOT: Dealer Freight Cost by Year

```
USE AdventureWorks2012;

DECLARE  @OrderYear  AS  TABLE( YYYY INT    NOT NULL    PRIMARY KEY  )
DECLARE  @DynamicSQL  AS NVARCHAR(MAX)

INSERT INTO @OrderYear
SELECT DISTINCT YEAR(OrderDate)  FROM   Sales.SalesOrderHeader

DECLARE  @ReportColumnNames  AS NVARCHAR(MAX),     @IterationYear      AS INT
SET @IterationYear = (SELECT MIN(YYYY) FROM   @OrderYear)
SET @ReportColumnNames = N''

-- Assemble pivot list dynamically
WHILE (@IterationYear IS NOT NULL)
 BEGIN
  SET @ReportColumnNames = CONCAT(@ReportColumnNames, N', ',
   QUOTENAME(CAST(@IterationYear AS NVARCHAR(10))))
  SET @IterationYear = (SELECT MIN(YYYY)
             FROM   @OrderYear    WHERE  YYYY > @IterationYear)
 END

SET @ReportColumnNames =
SUBSTRING(@ReportColumnNames,2,LEN(@ReportColumnNames))

PRINT @ReportColumnNames

-- Assemble final code
SET @DynamicSQL = CONCAT(N'SELECT * FROM (SELECT [Store (Freight Summary)]=S.Name,
                            YEAR(OrderDate) AS OrderYear,  Freight
FROM    Sales.SalesOrderHeader SOH
INNER JOIN Sales.Customer C ON SOH.CustomerID = C.CustomerID
INNER JOIN Sales.Store S ON C.StoreID = S.BusinessEntityID) as Header
PIVOT (SUM(Freight)
FOR OrderYear IN(', @ReportColumnNames, N'))  AS Pvt ORDER BY 1;')

PRINT @DynamicSQL; -- Testing & debugging

EXEC sp_executesql @DynamicSQL;
GO
```

RANK() OVER PARTITION BY with GROUP BY Query

Find the highest sale for each sales person with amount, sales count, total sales amount and territory. The basic query is to rank, with the RANK() window function, the highest sale for each sales person in each territory. The second step is selecting rank = 1 sales two ways: derived table (subquery x) & CTE. We can easily change the query for the entire company by removing TerritoryID from the queries.

NOTE. Same rule applies when using OVER clause window functions with GROUP BY: the column must be in the GROUP BY clause or the argument of an aggregate function such as SUM, AVG or MAX.

```
SELECT   TerritoryID, SalesPersonID, Count(*)                                AS Sales,
         FORMAT(SUM(Subtotal), 'c0', 'en-US')                                AS TotalSalesAmount,
         FORMAT(MAX(Subtotal), 'c0', 'en-US')                                AS MaxSalesAmount,
         RANK() OVER( PARTITION BY (SalesPersonID) ORDER BY MAX(Subtotal) DESC) AS Rank
FROM AdventureWorks2012.Sales.SalesOrderHeader WHERE SalesPersonID IS NOT NULL
GROUP BY TerritoryID, SalesPersonID   ORDER BY SalesPersonID, Rank;   -- (35 row(s) affected) - Partial results.
```

TerritoryID	SalesPersonID	Sales	TotalSalesAmount	MaxSalesAmount	Rank
1	274	10	$233,066	$112,612	1
6	274	10	$176,649	$84,714	2
5	274	9	$149,972	$79,994	3
4	274	14	$413,889	$74,205	4
2	274	4	$83,216	$48,694	5
3	274	1	$35,332	$35,332	6
2	275	136	$2,929,231	$146,155	1
4	275	135	$3,505,268	$106,930	2

```
SELECT TerritoryID, SalesPersonID, Sales, TotalSalesAmount, MaxSalesAmount FROM (
    SELECT    TerritoryID, SalesPersonID, Count(*)                                AS Sales,
              FORMAT(SUM(Subtotal), 'c0', 'en-US')                                AS TotalSalesAmount,
              FORMAT(MAX(Subtotal), 'c0', 'en-US')                                AS MaxSalesAmount,
              RANK() OVER( PARTITION BY (SalesPersonID) ORDER BY MAX(Subtotal) DESC) AS Rank
    FROM AdventureWorks2012.Sales.SalesOrderHeader WHERE SalesPersonID IS NOT NULL
    GROUP BY TerritoryID, SalesPersonID
) x WHERE Rank = 1 ORDER BY TerritoryID, SalesPersonID;          -- (17 row(s) affected) - Partial results.
```

TerritoryID	SalesPersonID	Sales	TotalSalesAmount	MaxSalesAmount
1	274	10	$233,066	$112,612
1	280	95	$3,325,103	$93,592
1	283	189	$3,729,945	$109,253

```
;WITH CTE AS ( ...BASIC RANKING QUERY... )
SELECT TerritoryID, SalesPersonID, Sales, TotalSalesAmount, MaxSalesAmount
FROM CTE WHERE Rank = 1 ORDER BY TerritoryID, SalesPersonID;
```

Date Range Programming with Datetime Column

The time portion of a datetime column presents a big problem ("midnight bug") when looking for a time range of records (rows). The equal operator picks up only the midnight records, nothing beyond as demonstrated. Similar issue for the BETWEEN operator. Best solution is to use DATE (SQL Server2008) if time portion is of no interest. With datetime we cannot assume that the time portion is 00:00:00.000 since it may have been changed unintentionally.

```
USE tempdb;
SELECT * INTO SOH FROM AdventureWorks2012.Sales.SalesOrderHeader; -- Create test table
GO
-- (31465 row(s) affected)
SELECT COUNT(SalesOrderID), MAX(OrderDate) FROM SOH WHERE OrderDate = '2008-02-01';
-- 244    2008-02-01 00:00:00.000
SELECT COUNT(SalesOrderID), MAX(OrderDate) FROM SOH
WHERE OrderDate BETWEEN '2008-02-01' AND '2008-02-01';
-- 244    2008-02-01 00:00:00.000
-- Advance order date 1 second passed midnight
UPDATE SOH SET OrderDate = dateadd(ss, 1, OrderDate) WHERE OrderDate = '2008-02-01';
-- (244 row(s) affected)
-- Due to the non-zero time portion, no equal match
SELECT COUNT(SalesOrderID), MAX(OrderDate) FROM SOH WHERE OrderDate = '2008-02-01';
-- 0      NULL
-- The BETWEEN operator also fails
SELECT COUNT(SalesOrderID), MAX(OrderDate) FROM SOH
WHERE OrderDate BETWEEN '2008-02-01' AND '2008-02-01';
-- 0      NULL
-- A safe way to get all the sales - not the best performant if there is index on OrderDate
SELECT COUNT(SalesOrderID), MAX(OrderDate) FROM SOH
WHERE YEAR(OrderDate)=2008 AND MONTH(OrderDate) = 2 AND DAY(OrderDate) = 1;
--244    2008-02-01 00:00:01.000
-- Another way to get all sales - no performance issue in case of index on OrderDate
SELECT COUNT(SalesOrderID), MAX(OrderDate) FROM SOH
WHERE OrderDate >= '2008-02-01' AND OrderDate < DATEADD(dd,1,'2008-02-01');
-- 244    2008-02-01 00:00:01.000
-- Using the BETWEEN operator - performance issue in case of index on OrderDate
SELECT COUNT(SalesOrderID), MAX(OrderDate) FROM SOH
WHERE CONVERT(DATE, OrderDate) BETWEEN '2008-02-01' AND '2008-02-01';
-- 244    2008-02-01 00:00:01.000
GO
DROP TABLE tempdb.dbo.SOH;
```

The BETWEEN Operator for DATE & DATETIME Ranges

```
-- BETWEEN dates implementation for datetime OrderDate
DECLARE @StartDate datetime ='20080201', @EndDate datetime = '20080205';
SELECT OrderCount=COUNT(*) FROM AdventureWorks2012.Sales.SalesOrderHeader
WHERE OrderDate >= @StartDate and OrderDate < DATEADD(DD,1,@EndDate);
GO
-- 502
```

```
-- BETWEEN dates implementation for datetime OrderDate using DATE data type
DECLARE @StartDate date ='20080201', @EndDate date = '20080205';
SELECT OrderCount=COUNT(*) FROM AdventureWorks2012.Sales.SalesOrderHeader
WHERE OrderDate >= @StartDate and OrderDate < DATEADD(DD,1,@EndDate);
GO
-- 502
```

```
-- Past midnight and next midnight
SELECT  dateadd(dd, datediff(dd, 0, CURRENT_TIMESTAMP)+0, 0),
        dateadd(dd, 1+datediff(dd, 0, CURRENT_TIMESTAMP)+0, 0)
-- 2016-10-23 00:00:00.000    2016-10-24 00:00:00.000
```

```
-- Orders for today (date range 1 day)
SELECT * FROM AdventureWorks2012.Sales.SalesOrderHeader
WHERE OrderDate >= dateadd(dd, datediff(dd, 0, CURRENT_TIMESTAMP)+0, 0)
  AND OrderDate <  dateadd(dd, 1+datediff(dd, 0, CURRENT_TIMESTAMP)+0, 0)
GO
```

```
-- Create a copy of the PurchaseOrderHeader (similar to SalesOrderHeader) table
USE tempdb;
SELECT * INTO POH FROM AdventureWorks2012.Purchasing.PurchaseOrderHeader
GO
-- (4012 row(s) affected)
```

```
-- Purchase order count for the entire month of MARCH 2008
SELECT COUNT(*) FROM POH WHERE OrderDate >='2008-03-01  00:00:00.000'
                 AND OrderDate < '2008-04-01  00:00:00.000'
-- 313
```

```
-- Equivalent datetime or date comparison queries
SELECT COUNT(*) FROM POH WHERE OrderDate >='2008-03-01' AND OrderDate < '2008-04-01'
-- 313
```

BETWEEN for Date Ranges cont.

```
-- SQL date between - performance issue due to CAST if OrderDate is indexed
SELECT COUNT(*) FROM POH WHERE
        CAST(OrderDate AS DATE) BETWEEN '2008-03-01' AND '2008-03-31';
-- 313
```

```
-- SQL datetime between with explicit inclusive lower and upper limits
/***** WORKS BUT NOT BEST PRACTICES *****/
SELECT COUNT(*) FROM POH WHERE OrderDate
BETWEEN '2008-03-01 00:00:00.000' AND '2008-03-31 23:59:59.997'; -- 313
```

```
/***** NOT BEST PRACTICES - WRONG RESULT IF TIME PART IS NOT 12:00AM *****/
SELECT COUNT(*) FROM POH WHERE OrderDate
        BETWEEN '2008-03-01 00:00:00.000' AND '2008-03-31 00:00:00.000' ; --313
SELECT COUNT(*) FROM POH WHERE OrderDate BETWEEN '2008-03-01' AND '2008-03-31';
-- 313
/******************************************************************/
```

```
-- TIME PART assumed to be 12:00AM = 00:00:00.000 if not specified
SELECT COUNT(*) FROM POH WHERE OrderDate BETWEEN '2008-01-02' AND '2008-01-07';
-- 60
UPDATE TOP(1) POH SET OrderDate = DATEADD (second, 1, OrderDate)
        WHERE  OrderDate='2008-01-07';          -- (1 row(s) affected)
-- The 1 second passed midnight record is no longer included in the BETWEEN range
SELECT COUNT(*) FROM POH WHERE OrderDate BETWEEN '2008-01-02' AND '2008-01-07';
-- 59
```

```
-- BETWEEN is inclusive operator - it includes the limits
SELECT COUNT(*) FROM POH WHERE OrderDate
        BETWEEN '2008-01-02 00:00:00.000' AND '2008-01-07 00:00:00.000';  -- 59
```

```
-- Include midnight and midnight+1 sec records for 2008-01-07
SELECT COUNT(*) FROM POH WHERE OrderDate
        BETWEEN '2008-01-02 00:00:00.000' AND '2008-01-07 00:00:01.000'; -- 60
```

```
-- Date range query - good performance if OrderDate indexed ( SARGABLE)
SELECT [Sales]=COUNT(*) FROM Purchasing.PurchaseOrderHeader
WHERE OrderDate >= CONVERT(DATE,'20080301')
        AND OrderDate < CONVERT(DATE,'20080316');
-- 137
```

4-Week 13 Month Calendar

The Christian (Gregorian, Western) calendar, used in most parts of the World, has been introduced by Pope Gregory in 1582. It appears to be irregular due to using 12 months instead of 13 months. While 13 month calendars were proposed in the past, its urgency rapidly increasing due to the expansion of Business Intelligence. 4 weeks 13 months calendar totals to 364 days, almost on the mark!

```
SELECT 4 * 7 * 13 -- 364
```

To include the remaining 1 or 2 (leap year) days, we have to make the last week of the year longer with 1 or 2 days, tentatively named **Earthday** and **Starday**. Each month starts with Monday. Therefore, each year starts with Monday. The new month is tentatively called **Undecimber** after undecim, Latin for 11. This naming follows the Latin number sequence starting with September (septem Latin for 7). The year ends two ways:

- Friday, Saturday, Sunday, Earthday (Undecimber 29)
- Friday, Saturday, Sunday, Earthday, Starday (Undecimber 30) - leap year
- January 1 is Monday in each year
- Each month calendar identical with Undecimber having an extra day or two

```
DECLARE @4week13month TABLE( ID INT IDENTITY(1,1),
 Mon char(3), Tue char(3), Wed char(3), Thu char(3), Fri char(3), Sat char(3), Sun char(3));
INSERT @4week13month VALUES ('MON', 'TUE', 'WED', 'THU', 'FRI', 'SAT', 'SUN'),
('1','2','3','4','5','6','7'), ('8','9','10','11','12','13','14'),
('15','16','17','18','19','20','21'),('22','23','24','25','26','27','28');
SELECT * FROM @4week13month ORDER BY ID;
```

MON	TUE	WED	THU	FRI	SAT	SUN
1	2	3	4	5	6	7
8	9	10	11	12	13	14
15	16	17	18	19	20	21
22	23	24	25	26	27	28

The SQL significance of such a calendar is immense: week can be used in GROUP BY summaries just like month. Currently week-based analysis is misaligned with month-based analysis. Some businesses do use 13-month calendars for business analysis and reporting.

The **benefits of 13 month calendar** are presented at:
http://en.wikipedia.org/wiki/International_Fixed_Calendar

DDL Trigger on DATABASE CREATE

DDL trigger carries out action, in this instance just sending a message, when a new database is created. The screenshot segment shows the DDL trigger listing in SSMS Object Explorer.

```
USE master;
GO
CREATE TRIGGER trgNewDatabase
ON ALL SERVER  FOR CREATE_DATABASE  AS
BEGIN
DECLARE @database sysname, @event_data XML = EVENTDATA()
 SET @database = @event_data.value('(/EVENT_INSTANCE/DatabaseName)[1]', 'sysname')
 RAISERROR( 'trgNewDatabase DDL trigger message: %s DB has been created', 16,1, @database)
END
GO -- Command(s) completed successfully.
```

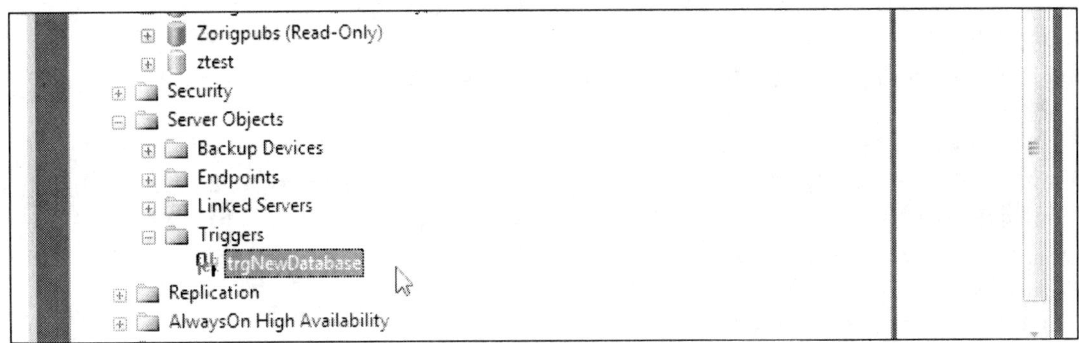


```
CREATE DATABASE zTest1;
GO  /* Messages
Msg 50000, Level 16, State 1, Procedure trgNewDatabase, Line 10
trgNewDatabase DDL trigger message: zTest1 DB has been created */
```

```
DROP DATABASE zTest1;
GO -- Command(s) completed successfully.
```

```
DROP TRIGGER [trgNewDatabase] ON ALL SERVER
GO -- Command(s) completed successfully.
```

Spatial Data Types: Geometry & Geography

The POLYGON & STLength() Functions

The geometry data type and geography data type are used for spatial and mapping applications. The geometry data type can store polygons. The perimeter of a polygon can be calculated by the STLength() spatial function and the polygon itself can be visualized in Management Studio Spatial results.

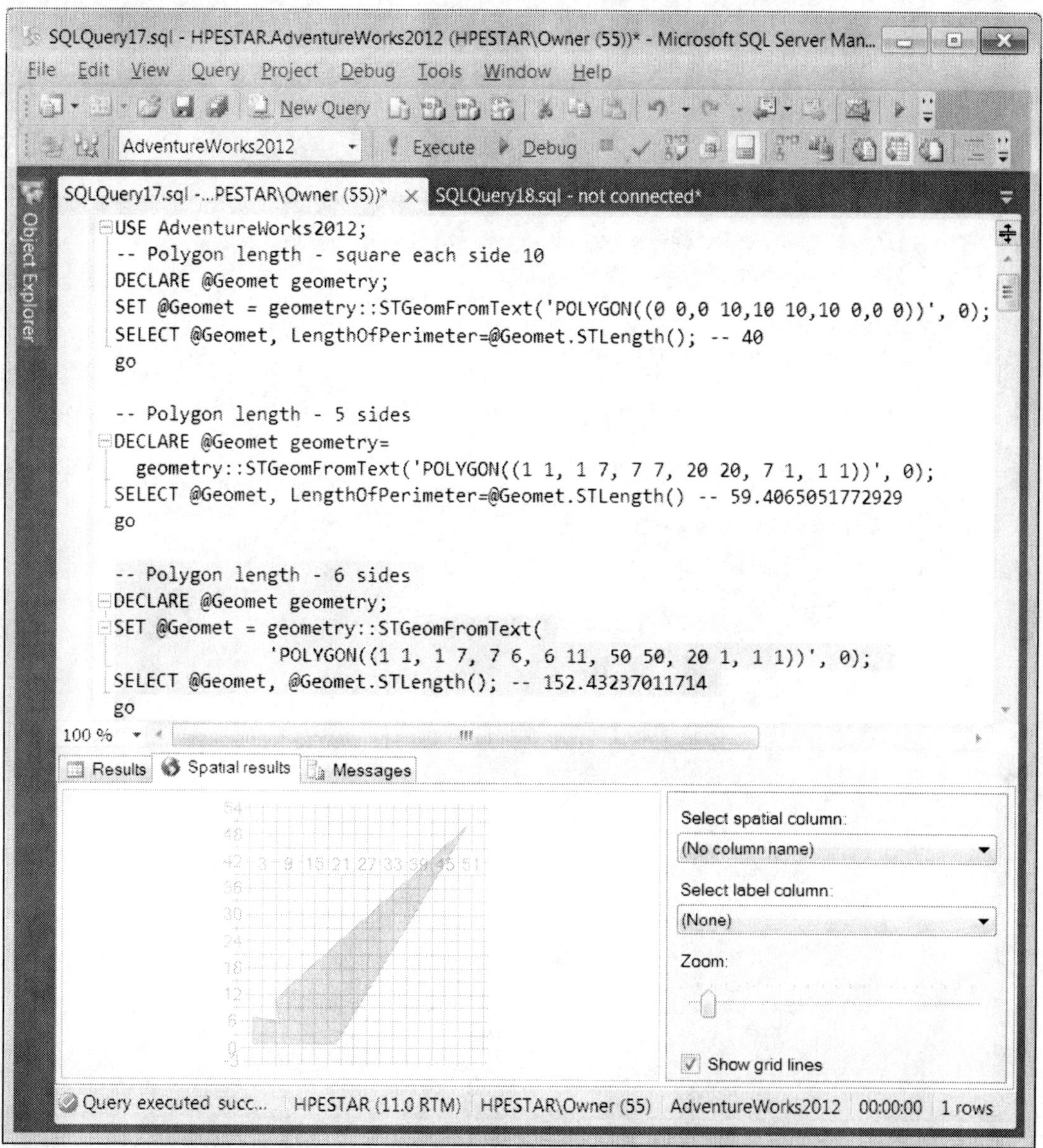

Polygon Difference & Intersection

The STDifference() and STIntersection functions will calculate the difference and intersection of two polygons. The example is for a small square inside a bigger square. The difference is displayed in Spatial results which is the dark area. The intersection coincidentally is the white small square.

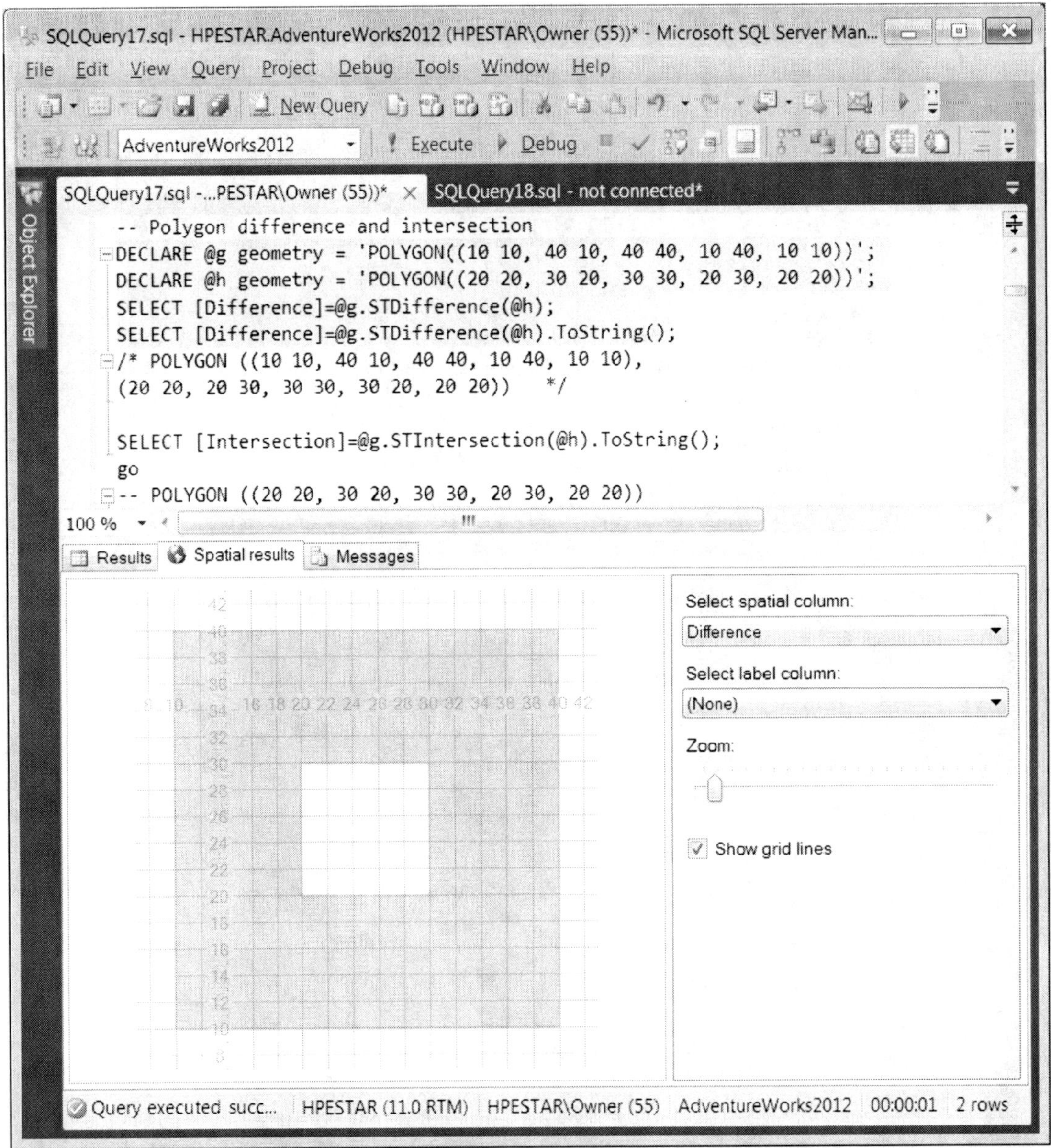

Geometry Area & CIRCULARSTRING Functions

```
-- Area of a polygon - triangle
DECLARE @Geomet geometry;
SET @Geomet = geometry::STGeomFromText('POLYGON((3 3,40 40, 80 3, 3 3))', 0);
SELECT @Geomet, AreaOfPolygon=@Geomet.STArea();
GO
-- 1424.5
```

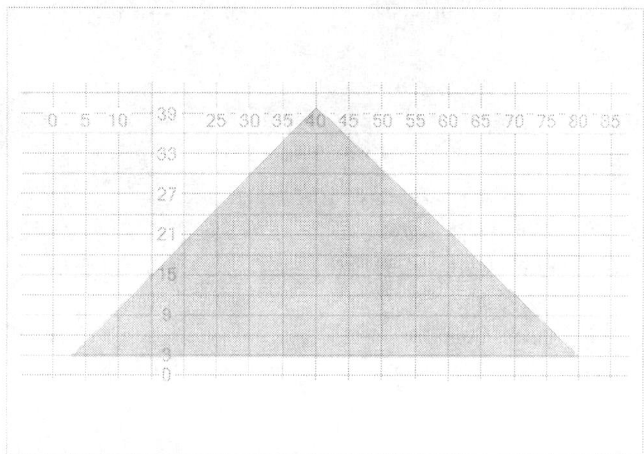

The STBuffer() function "draws" the thick border.

```
SELECT geometry::Parse('CIRCULARSTRING(-2 2, 2 -2, 4 2, 2 4, -2 2)').STBuffer(.3);
```

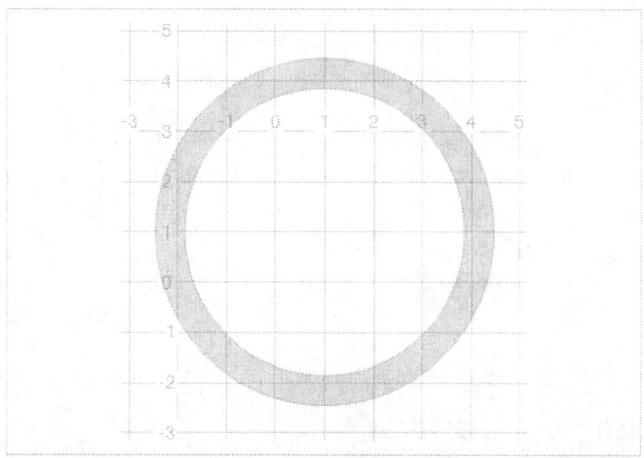

Working with geometry Data in Tables

```
IF OBJECT_ID ( 'dbo.GeometryTest', 'U' ) IS NOT NULL     DROP TABLE dbo.GeometryTest;
go
```

```
create table GeometryTest
(
        GeometryTestID int identity(1,1) primary key,
        Geom geometry ,
        GeomText as Geom.STAsText(),                    -- computed column
        GeomDim as Geom.STDimension());                 -- computed column
go
```

```
insert GeometryTest (Geom) values
        (geometry::STPointFromText ( 'POINT (85 115)',0)),
        (geometry::STPointFromText ( 'POINT (100 100)',0)),
        (geometry::STGeomFromText ('LINESTRING (70 70, 30 150,  150 150)', 0)),
        (geometry::STGeomFromText ('POLYGON ((0 0, 300 0, 300 300, 0 300, 0 0))', 0));
```

```
select * from GeometryTest
go
```

GeometryTestID	Geom	GeomText	GeomDim
1	0x00000000010C0000000000405540000000000000C05C40	POINT (85 115)	0
2	0x00000000010C00000000000059400000000000005940	POINT (100 100)	0
3	0x000000000104030000000000000000805140000000000000805140000000000003E400000000000C0624000000000000C062400000000000C06240010000000100000000010000000FFFFFFFF0000000002	LINESTRING (70 70, 30 150, 150 150)	1
4	0x0000000001040500000000000000000000000000000000000000000000000C0724000000000000000000000000000000C072400000000000C0724000000000000000000000000000000C072400000000000000000000000000000000000100000002000000000100000 0FFFFFFFF0000000003	POLYGON ((0 0, 300 0, 300 300, 0 300, 0 0))	2

```
declare @gmtry1 geometry,  @gmtry2 geometry, @combo geometry;
select @gmtry1 = Geom from GeometryTest where GeometryTestID=3
select @gmtry2 = Geom from GeometryTest where GeometryTestID=4
select @combo = @gmtry1.STIntersection(@gmtry2)
select Intersection = @Combo.STAsText();
go
```

Intersection
LINESTRING (150 150, 30 150, 70 70)

Surveying Spatial Locations in Person.Address with TABLESAMPLE

Since the limit is 5000 for Spatial results graphics, we use TABLESAMPLE random sampling. The outline of the Unites States is clearly visible in the spatial graphics. 4810 dots and partial results.

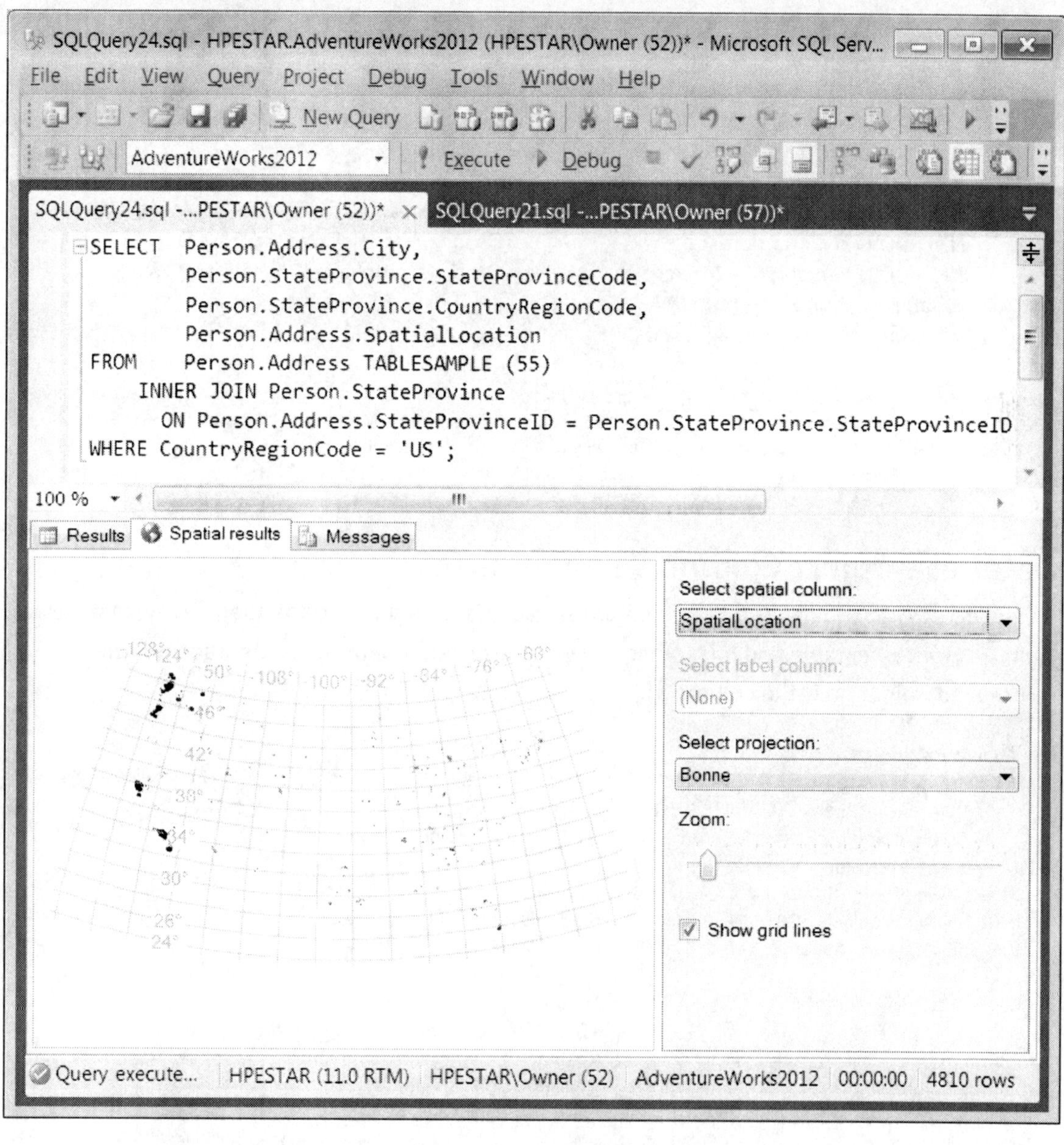

City	StateProvinceCode	CountryRegionCode	SpatialLocation
Concord	CA	US	0xE6100000010CA18642EB19FF4240E84C0794157B5EC0
Seattle	WA	US	0xE6100000010CCC2A6CCDCBCA474094427543D1995EC0
Torrance	CA	US	0xE6100000010C943F7FEBB1E440402956F3FF52A05DC0
Woodburn	OR	US	0xE6100000010CBF692502648C4640839FE7AD54AB5EC0
Puyallup	WA	US	0xE6100000010C827BF9CD1598474096246A5843935EC0

The geography Data Type in Map Application

Locating address in a rectangular Earth region based on the Person.Address table geo SpatialLocation column data.

```
USE AdventureWorks2012;   DECLARE @Rectangle geography;
SET @Rectangle = geography::STGeomFromText(
        'POLYGON((-50.0 50.0, -90.0 50.0, -90.0 25.0, -50.0 25.0, -50.0 50.0))', 4326);
SELECT          s.BusinessEntityID   ,s.Name                          AS Dealer
                ,a.AddressLine1 ,a.City ,sp.StateProvinceCode  ,a.PostalCode
 FROM Sales.Store s
        INNER JOIN Person.BusinessEntityAddress bea ON s.BusinessEntityID =bea.BusinessEntityID
        INNER JOIN Person.Address a                 ON bea.AddressID = a.AddressID
        INNER JOIN Person.StateProvince sp          ON a.StateProvinceID = sp.StateProvinceID
WHERE  a.SpatialLocation.STIntersects(@Rectangle) = 1     ORDER BY Dealer;
GO  -- (240 row(s) affected) - Partial results.
```

BusinessEntityID	Dealer	AddressLine1	City	StateProvinceCode	PostalCode
2051	A Bicycle Association	6405 Erie Blvd. Hills Plaza	De Witt	NY	13214
354	Acclaimed Bicycle Company	830 Highway 499 So	Mcdonough	GA	30253
836	Active Cycling	Indian Mound Mall	Heath	OH	43056
1916	Active Life Toys	55 Standish Court	Mississauga	ON	L5B 3V4

Database Object Column Dependencies

A view object dependencies on table columns query is based on 2 dependencies system views. Type U is for (user) table and V is for view. The referenced_major_id is the table id, the referenced_minor_id is the column id.

```
USE AdventureWorks2012;
SELECT    ReferencingObject = CONCAT(SCHEMA_NAME(o1.schema_id),'.',o1.name),
          ReferencedObject = CONCAT(SCHEMA_NAME(o2.schema_id), '.', ed.referenced_entity_name),
          ColumnName = c.name, ReferencedType = o2.type,  ReferencingType = o1.type
FROM   sys.sql_expression_dependencies ed
    INNER JOIN sys.objects o1              ON ed.referencing_id = o1.object_id
    INNER JOIN sys.objects o2              ON ed.referenced_id = o2.object_id
    INNER JOIN sys.sql_dependencies d      ON ed.referencing_id = d.object_id
                                           AND d.referenced_major_id = ed.referenced_id
    INNER JOIN sys.columns c               ON c.object_id = ed.referenced_id
                                           AND d.referenced_minor_id = c.column_id
WHERE  CONCAT(SCHEMA_NAME(o1.schema_id),'.',o1.name) = 'Sales.vSalesPersonSalesByFiscalYears'
ORDER  BY ReferencedObject,  c.column_id;    -- (13 row(s) affected) - Partial results.
```

ReferencingObject	ReferencedObject	ColumnName	ReferencedType	ReferencingType
Sales.vSalesPersonSalesByFiscalYears	HumanResources.Employee	BusinessEntityID	U	V
Sales.vSalesPersonSalesByFiscalYears	HumanResources.Employee	JobTitle	U	V
Sales.vSalesPersonSalesByFiscalYears	Person.Person	BusinessEntityID	U	V
Sales.vSalesPersonSalesByFiscalYears	Person.Person	FirstName	U	V

Data Encryption & Decryption

Data encryption is an important part of keeping sensitive data, such as credit card numbers, safe. When we encrypt successively, the encrypted string varies.

```
USE AdventureWorks2012;
CREATE CERTIFICATE CertQ  ENCRYPTION BY PASSWORD = '007SkyFall$'
WITH SUBJECT ='CertQ',  START_DATE = '2012/01/01', EXPIRY_DATE = '2016/01/01';
```

```
DECLARE  @CypherText VARBINARY(MAX);
SET @CypherText = EncryptByCert(Cert_ID('CertQ'),'United States of America');
SELECT  @CypherText;
/*
0xDFAD2CABDDD07E75A74722CECF799B4AADBFE704D29F366DBF6F22C229E7EB6D94BC082BB2DFC7795C1AA92F7452D0AE2EF91
A2356B22F8508E37F7BC440CF926BC89C0FFCBBB04DF75206F2C6282FE87756D2003F40D738F92499674749BA8C9204A3BCAC9A7
8366939786A8D4E421DC71289E9D9D8140678EFD329BB5D7822
*/
SELECT Decyphered = CONVERT(VARCHAR(256),DecryptByCert(Cert_ID('CertQ'),
@CypherText,N'007SkyFall$'));
GO  -- United States of America
```

```
DECLARE  @CypherText VARBINARY(MAX);
SET @CypherText = EncryptByCert(Cert_ID('CertQ'),'United States of America');
SELECT  @CypherText;
/*
0x77E17C2A7B30E68B3AA5792400842FBDA19E121F8BEFCF787F3C6F68D720CC6B992BBF1C27168CC7B5592359437494BF1F719FF
67A1B5131C5AA69EEEA539DC5AA261BBAEDC12201BDC2EC1E31280FD0B76E8773CDB57582BE857F24FD86997582ACFAE07028A9
0A0FA9D29A69FB53FC24261828F53884636A4452597A18A908
*/
SELECT Decyphered = CONVERT(VARCHAR(256), DecryptByCert(Cert_ID('CertQ'),
@CypherText,N'007SkyFall$'));
GO  -- United States of America
```

```
 DECLARE  @CypherText VARBINARY(MAX), @cleartext varchar(256)='Yellowstone National Park
ID, MT ,WY';
SET @CypherText = EncryptByCert(Cert_ID('CertQ'), @cleartext);   SELECT  @CypherText;
/*
0x386D15B848B3200CA2F0FD1341550AD16C61A19B71D2A14256B8C281249B5F9471EEB9C81DE9FA21CBE4602E099E1F7F363923
B8E0BF2960CAF13824D5EE0E852BA0B156532D50B336377648C6580BDFEB85453F34D722038FF6F7BD695343617E39E68259B05D
65F686CE63A68CFC795D86F94ADC75D0974882721A5083842C
*/
SELECT Decyphered = CONVERT(VARCHAR(256),DecryptByCert(Cert_ID('CertQ'),
@CypherText,N'007SkyFall$'));
GO  -- Yellowstone National Park ID, MT ,WY
```

Database Backup

Full Database Backup with Verification

Full database backup and verify script for the AdventureWorks2012 database.

```
USE master;
GO
-- Backup database
BACKUP DATABASE [AdventureWorks2012] TO  DISK = N'F:\data\backup\AW2012.bak' WITH
NAME = N'AdventureWorks2012-Full DB Backup', STATS = 5;
GO
-- Verify database backup
DECLARE @backupSetId as int;
SELECT @backupSetId = position from msdb..backupset where
database_name=N'AdventureWorks2012' and backup_set_id=(select max(backup_set_id) from
msdb..backupset where database_name=N'AdventureWorks2012' );

IF @backupSetId is null begin raiserror(N'Verify failed. Backup info for DB
"AdventureWorks2012" not found.', 16, 1) end;

RESTORE VERIFYONLY FROM  DISK = N'F:\data\backup\AW2012.bak' WITH  FILE =
@backupSetId,  NOUNLOAD,  NOREWIND;
GO
```

```
/* Messages
5 percent processed.
10 percent processed.
15 percent processed.
.......
95 percent processed.
Processed 27920 pages for database 'AdventureWorks2012', file 'AdventureWorks2012_Data' on file 1.
Processed 80 pages for database 'AdventureWorks2012', file 'FSAlpha' on file 1.
Processed 2 pages for database 'AdventureWorks2012', file 'AdventureWorks2012_Log' on file 1.
100 percent processed.
BACKUP DATABASE successfully processed 28002 pages in 7.931 seconds (27.582 MB/sec).

The backup set on file 1 is valid.   */
```

Full Database Backup with Datestamp in Filename

```
DECLARE @BackupPathFile nvarchar(256)
 = N'f:\data\backup\AW2012_' + CONVERT(varchar, CURRENT_TIMESTAMP, 112) + '.BAK'
PRINT @BackupPathFile  -- f:\data\backup\AW2012_20121114.BAK
BACKUP DATABASE [AdventureWorks2012] TO  DISK = @BackupPathFile
```

Backup of a Single Table

Here is the list of options available.

- SELECT * INTO table2 FROM table1
- SSMS Script Wizard generates script with INSERTs
- SSMS execute SELECT query & the save the output to a file
- bcp table to a file
- SS Import/Export Wizard - export table to a table or file

The first one is the easiest, the last one is the most flexible. We have to pay attention that the export is reversible. For example, if we use CSV format then the strings should be enclosed in double quotes for example in order not to conflict with commas used for column separation. Execute the query.

```
SELECT * FROM Production.Product ORDER BY ProductNumber;
```

On upper left corner in results, right click, save results as, .csv (comma delimited). Sounds safe. But it is not because the some product names contain commas. That makes the data export irreversible, and probably useless for any application.

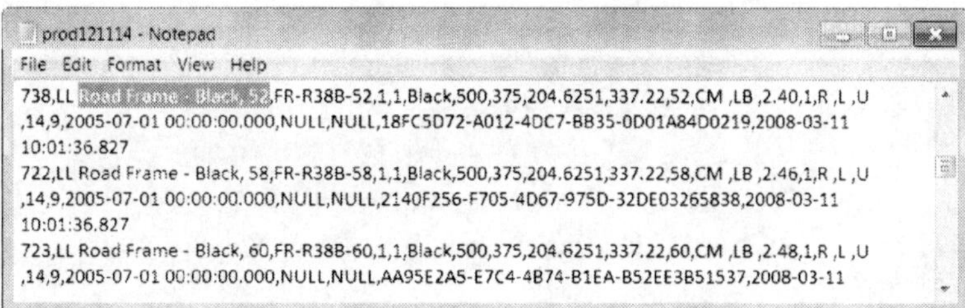

The SS Import & Export Wizard has option to specify Text qualifier for flat file destination.

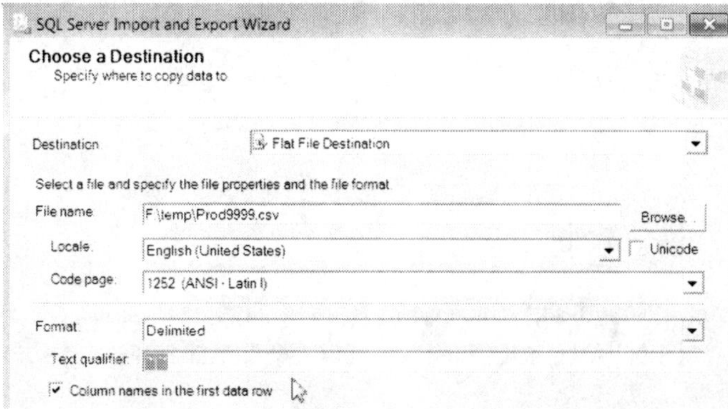

Setting SSMS Query Options to Include Double Quotes with Strings

There is a query option in SSMS setting to set double quote as text qualifier when saving in csv format. Click on Query, click on Query Options. Configure as shown.

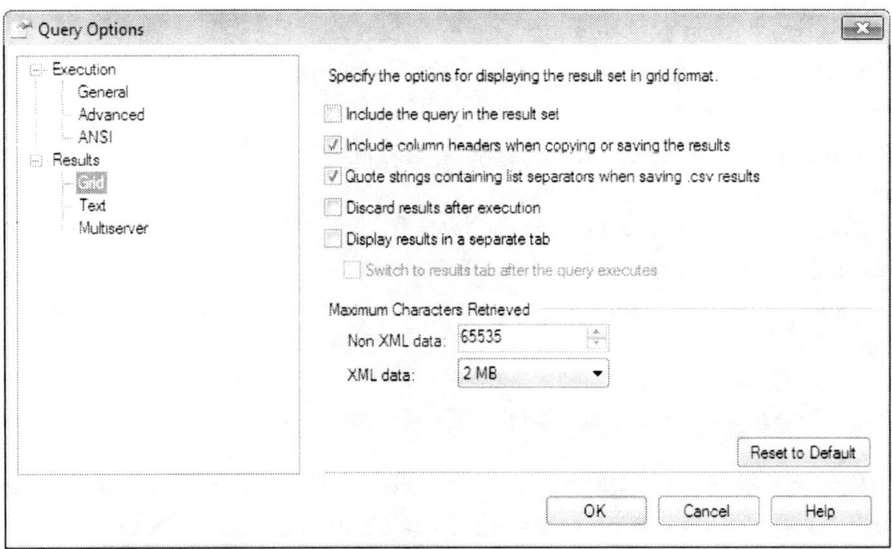

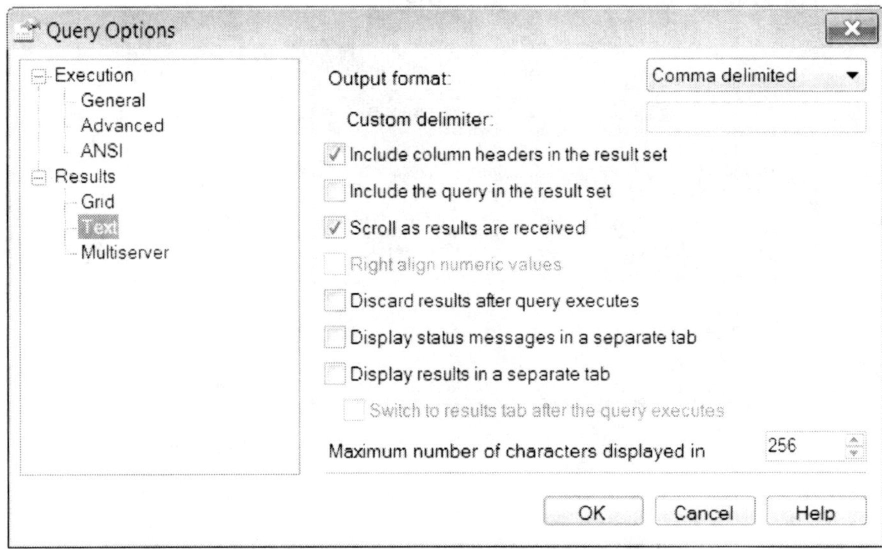

The output will be proper csv file.

793,"Road-250 Black, 44",BK-R89B-44,1,1,Black,100,75,1554.9479,2443.35,44,CM ,LB ,14.77,4,R ,H ,U ,2,26,2006-07-01 00:00:00.000,NULL,NULL,1FF419B5-52AF-4F7E-AEAE-4FEC5E99DE35,2008-03-11 10:01:36.827

Database Restore

To restore a database backup to a new database we have to indicate the location (path & name) of the database files. FILE=1 refers to the first backup set in AW2012.BAK. A backup file can contain more than one backup.

```
USE [master]
RESTORE DATABASE [rptAdventureWorks2012] FROM  DISK = N'f:\data\backup\AW2012.BAK'
WITH  FILE = 1,
MOVE N'FSAlpha' TO N'F:\data\db\data\FSAlpha',
MOVE N'AdventureWorks2012_Data' TO N'F:\data\db\data\AdventureWorks2012_Data.mdf',
MOVE N'AdventureWorks2012_Log' TO N'F:\data\db\log\AdventureWorks2012_log.ldf',
NOUNLOAD,  STATS = 5
GO
```

```
/* Messages
5 percent processed.
10 percent processed.
15 percent processed.
.....
55 percent processed.
60 percent processed.
65 percent processed.
70 percent processed.
75 percent processed.
80 percent processed.
85 percent processed.
90 percent processed.
95 percent processed.
100 percent processed.
Processed 27920 pages for database 'rptAdventureWorks2012', file
'AdventureWorks2012_Data' on file 1.
Processed 2 pages for database 'rptAdventureWorks2012', file 'AdventureWorks2012_Log' on
file 1.
Processed 81 pages for database 'rptAdventureWorks2012', file 'FSAlpha' on file 1.

RESTORE DATABASE successfully processed 28002 pages in 25.375 seconds (8.621 MB/sec). */
```

Restore of a Single Table

Restoring a table can be tricky. When exporting a table, basically the data content goes, and some metadata such as column names. SELECT INTO copies the data, column names, data types, sizes and the IDENTITY property if any. Constraints and indexes are not exported. Before restoring, the current table should be emptied. DELETE and TRUNCATE are not exactly the same. TRUNCATE is faster due to minimal logging. TRUNCATE also resets the IDENTITY SEED.

```
SELECT * INTO tempdb.dbo.Product
FROM Adventureworks2012.Production.Product;
GO  - (504 row(s) affected)
```

```
use tempdb;
CREATE UNIQUE INDEX idxProd on Product(Name);
GO
```

```
DELETE Product; -- (504 row(s) affected)
DBCC CHECKIDENT(Product);
/*Checking identity information: current identity value '999', current column value 'NULL'.
DBCC execution completed. If DBCC printed error messages, contact your system
administrator.*/
```

```
TRUNCATE TABLE Product;
GO
DBCC CHECKIDENT(Product);
GO
/*Checking identity information: current identity value 'NULL', current column value 'NULL'.
DBCC execution completed. If DBCC printed error messages, contact your system
administrator.*/
```

```
-- Restore the content of table
INSERT Product
SELECT *
FROM Adventureworks2012.Production.Product;
/*Msg 8101, Level 16, State 1, Line 1
An explicit value for the identity column in table 'Product' can only be specified when a column
list is used and IDENTITY_INSERT is ON.*/
```

Repopulating Table with IDENTITY Column

IDENTITY is an obstacle in moving back the original data. We have to set the IDENTITY_INSERT flag and we have to specify all the columns in the INSERT statement. After repopulating we have to check if IDENTITY is seeded at the right value and rebuild the out-of-shape index.

```
SET IDENTITY_INSERT Product ON;
GO
INSERT INTO [dbo].[Product]
        ([ProductID],[Name]
        ,[ProductNumber],[MakeFlag]
        ,[FinishedGoodsFlag],[Color]
        ,[SafetyStockLevel],[ReorderPoint]
        ,[StandardCost],[ListPrice]
        ,[Size],[SizeUnitMeasureCode]
        ,[WeightUnitMeasureCode],[Weight]
        ,[DaysToManufacture],[ProductLine]
        ,[Class] ,[Style]
        ,[ProductSubcategoryID],[ProductModelID]
        ,[SellStartDate],[SellEndDate]
        ,[DiscontinuedDate],[rowguid],[ModifiedDate])
SELECT *
FROM Adventureworks2012.Production.Product;
GO
-- (504 row(s) affected)
SET IDENTITY_INSERT Product OFF;
```

```
DBCC CHECKIDENT(Product) ;
GO
/*Checking identity information: current identity value '999', current column value '999'.
DBCC execution completed. If DBCC printed error messages, contact your system
administrator.*/
```

```
ALTER INDEX [idxProd] ON [dbo].[Product] REBUILD;
```

A good strategy is to save the table script with all related item scripts onto a disk .sql file.

That way we isolate table definition with constraints, defaults and indexes from table content.

The Database Maintenance Plan Wizard

The SQL Server Maintenance Plan Wizard is an SSMS Object Explorer GUI tool to prepare a partial or complete maintenance plan for a database(s).

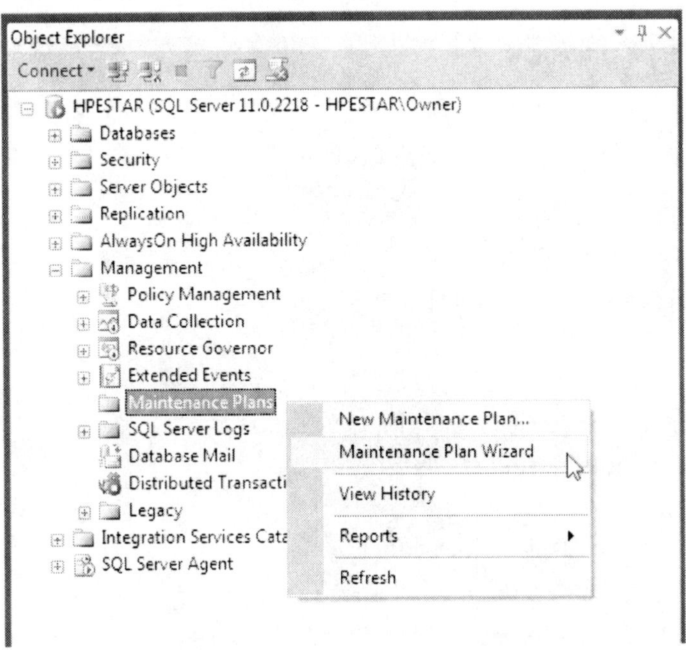

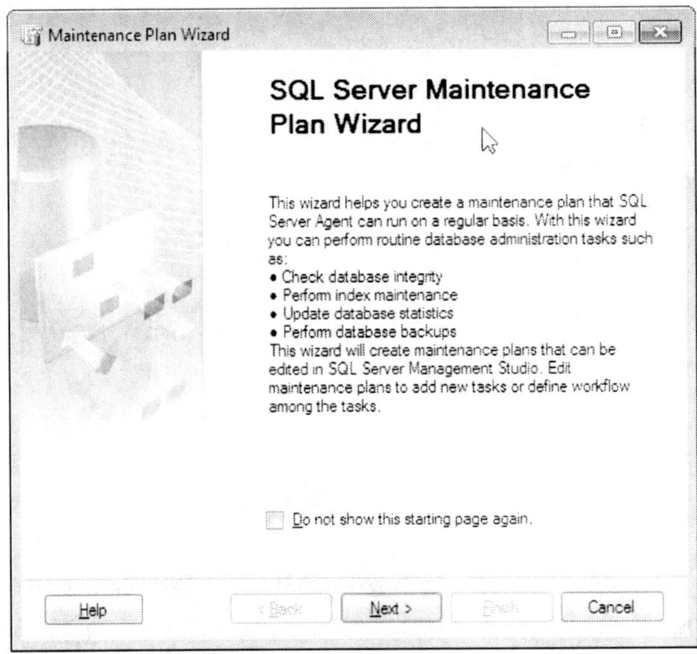

Follow the Plan Wizard Step by Step

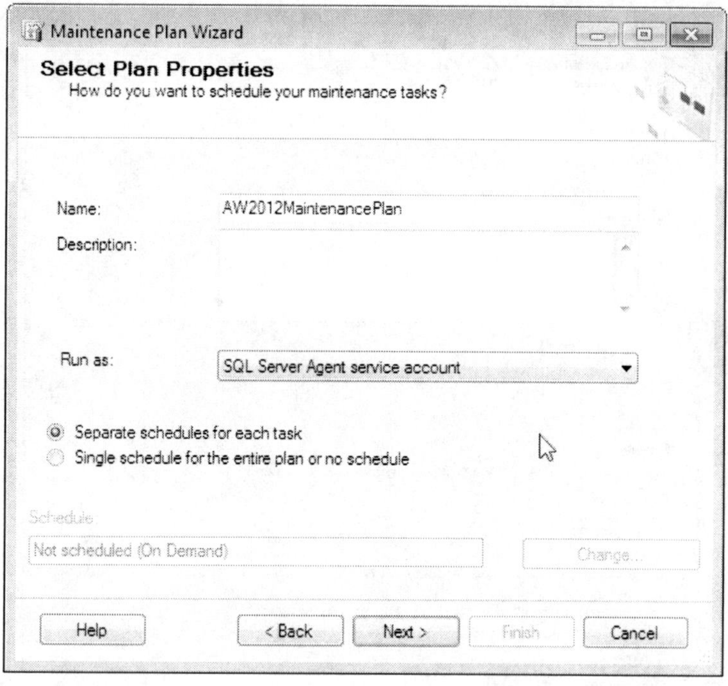

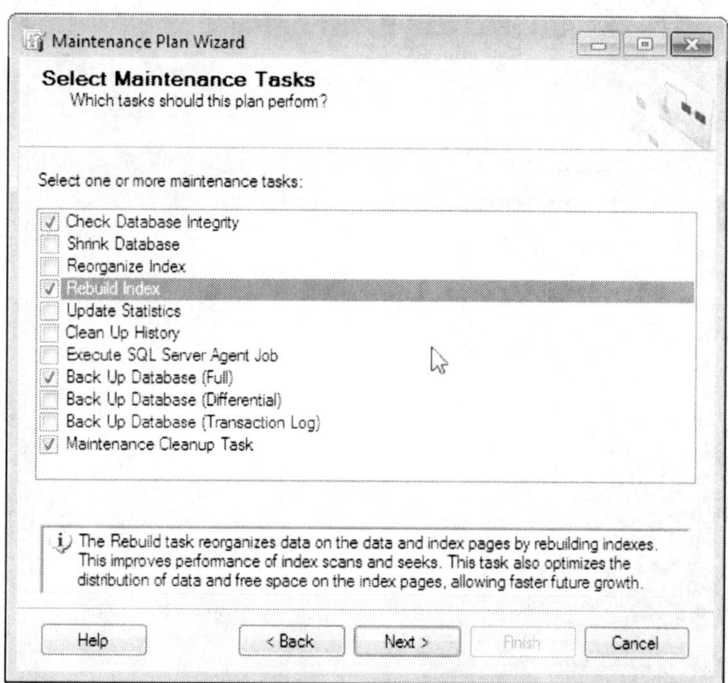

One or More Databases Can Be Specified, Schedule Setup

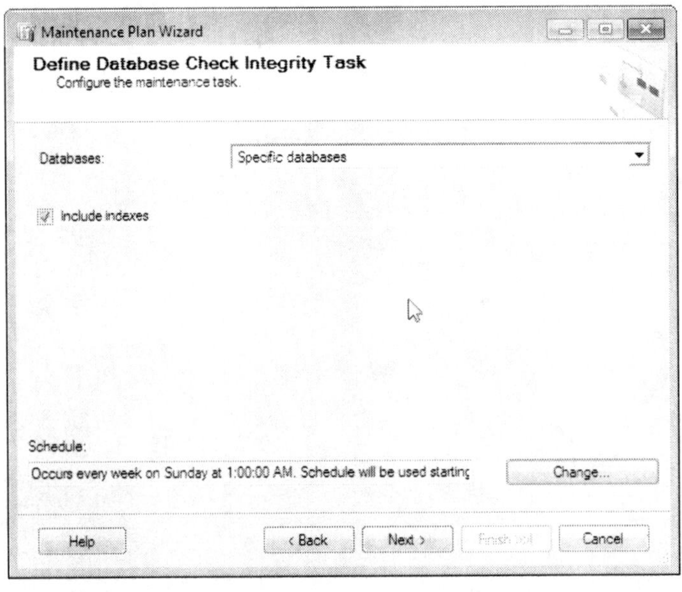

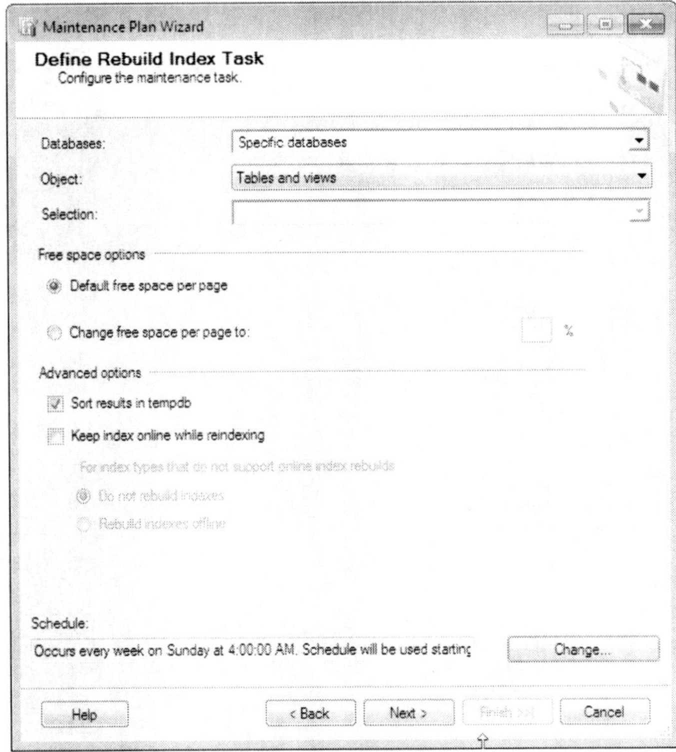

Full Database Backup Specifications

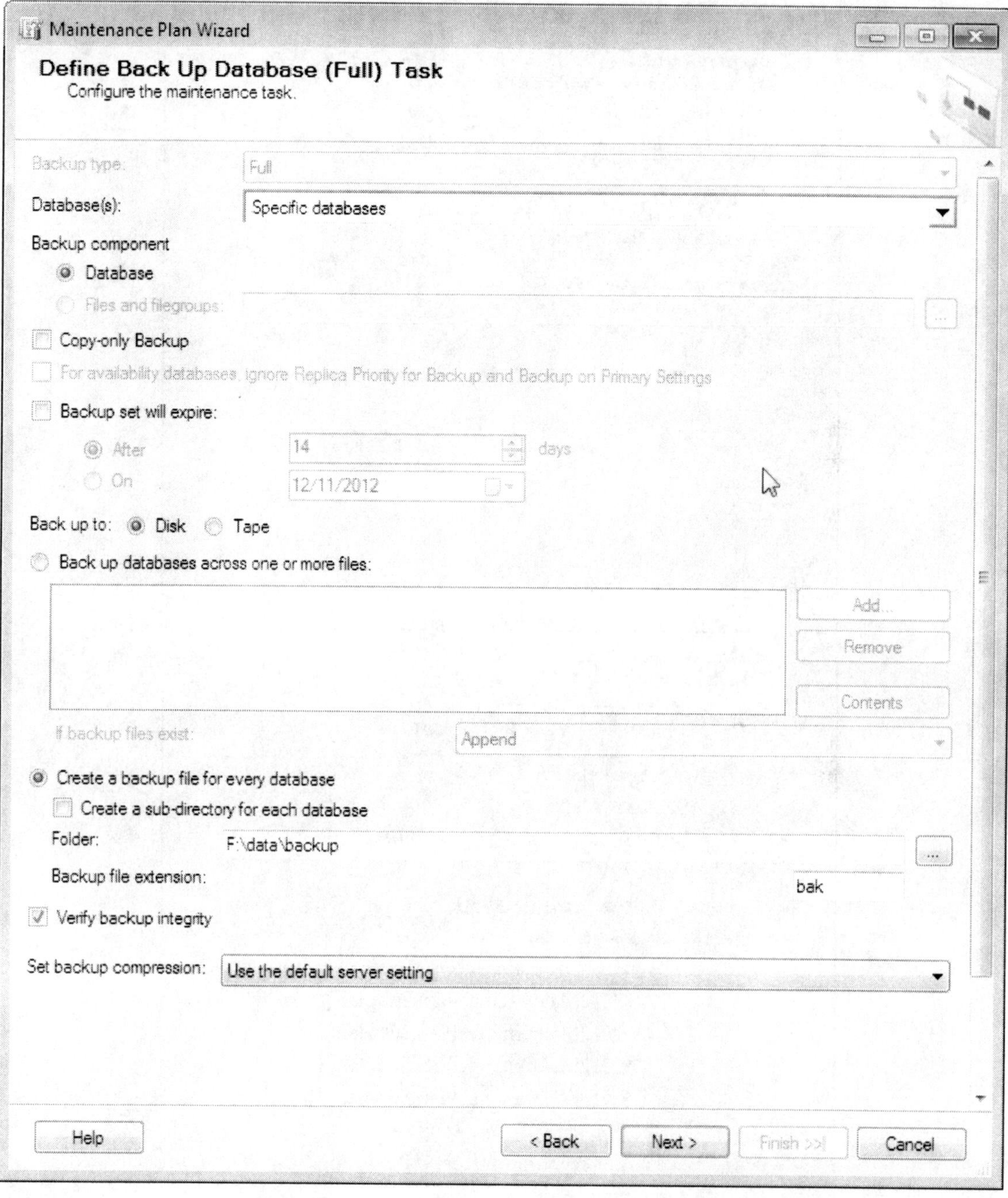

Create the Maintenance Plan & Schedule the Jobs

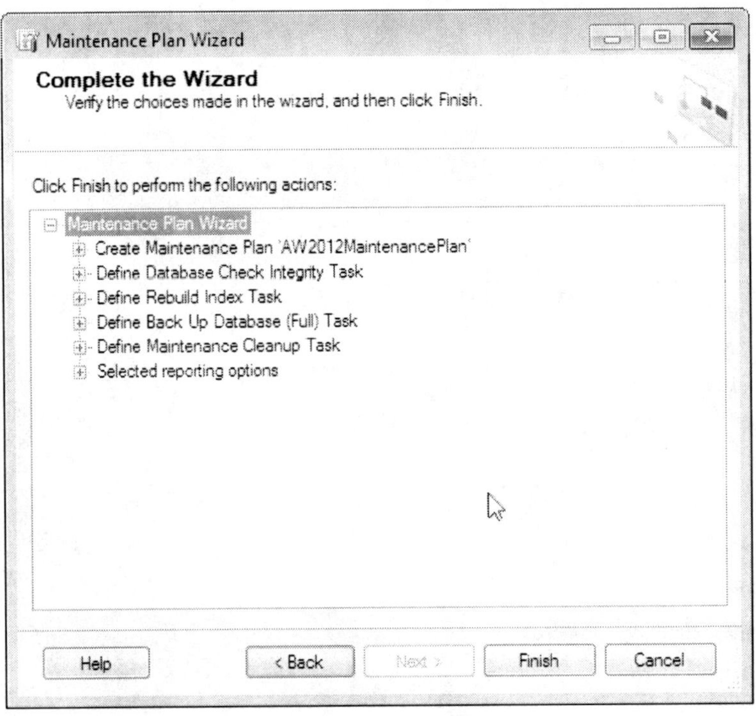

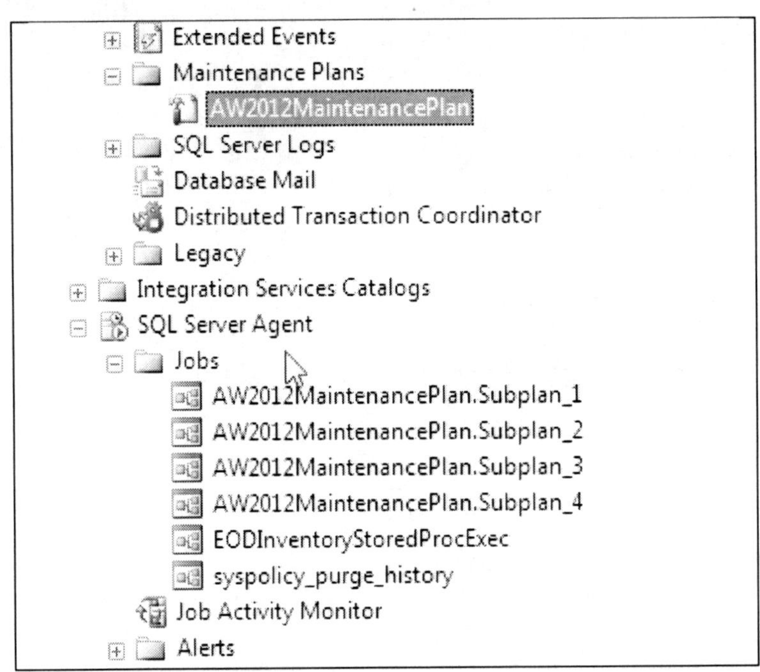

Configure Stored Procedure As SS Agent Job & Schedule

SSMS Object Explorer GUI editor can be used to setup a new job with schedule. It can also be done programmatically. The EOWBatchProcessing job scripted.

```
USE [msdb]; BEGIN TRANSACTION
DECLARE @ReturnCode INT; SELECT @ReturnCode = 0;
IF NOT EXISTS (SELECT name FROM msdb.dbo.syscategories WHERE name=N'Database Maintenance' AND category_class=1)
BEGIN
EXEC @ReturnCode = msdb.dbo.sp_add_category @class=N'JOB', @type=N'LOCAL', @name=N'Database Maintenance'
IF (@@ERROR <> 0 OR @ReturnCode <> 0) GOTO QuitWithRollback;   END
DECLARE @jobId BINARY(16)
EXEC @ReturnCode = msdb.dbo.sp_add_job @job_name=N'EOWBatchProcessing',
                  @enabled=1,                    @notify_level_eventlog=0,
                  @notify_level_email=0, @notify_level_netsend=0,
                  @notify_level_page=0,  @delete_level=0,
                  @description=N'Process all end of week jobs.',     @category_name=N'Database Maintenance',
                  @owner_login_name=N'HPESTAR\Owner',                @job_id = @jobId OUTPUT
IF (@@ERROR <> 0 OR @ReturnCode <> 0) GOTO QuitWithRollback
EXEC @ReturnCode = msdb.dbo.sp_add_jobstep @job_id=@jobId, @step_name=N'EOWInventory',
                  @step_id=1,                    @cmdexec_success_code=0,
                  @on_success_action=1, @on_success_step_id=0,
                  @on_fail_action=2,             @on_fail_step_id=0,
                  @retry_attempts=0,             @retry_interval=0,
                  @os_run_priority=0, @subsystem=N'TSQL',        @command=N'exec uspInventoryEOW;',
                  @database_name=N'AdventureWorks2018',          @flags=0
IF (@@ERROR <> 0 OR @ReturnCode <> 0) GOTO QuitWithRollback
EXEC @ReturnCode = msdb.dbo.sp_update_job @job_id = @jobId, @start_step_id = 1
IF (@@ERROR <> 0 OR @ReturnCode <> 0) GOTO QuitWithRollback
EXEC @ReturnCode = msdb.dbo.sp_add_jobschedule @job_id=@jobId, @name=N'EOWProcessingSATAM',
                  @enabled=1,                    @freq_type=8,
                  @freq_interval=65,             @freq_subday_type=1,
                  @freq_subday_interval=0,       @freq_relative_interval=0,
                  @freq_recurrence_factor=1,     @active_start_date=20181127,
                  @active_end_date=99991231,     @active_start_time=40000,
                  @active_end_time=235959,       @schedule_uid=N'0610654b-da58-46ff-9a96-39d69a0686a1'
IF (@@ERROR <> 0 OR @ReturnCode <> 0) GOTO QuitWithRollback
EXEC @ReturnCode = msdb.dbo.sp_add_jobserver @job_id = @jobId, @server_name = N'(local)'
IF (@@ERROR <> 0 OR @ReturnCode <> 0) GOTO QuitWithRollback
COMMIT TRANSACTION
GOTO EndSave
QuitWithRollback:    IF (@@TRANCOUNT > 0) ROLLBACK TRANSACTION
EndSave:
```

How to Read varbinary(max) Columns

Usually the binary objects such as images or Word documents in varbinary(max) columns have to be exported to the file system and the appropriate software is used to "read" them. Clean plain text is readable after conversion to varchar(max) or nvarchar(max).

```
SELECT Title AS DocTitle, LEN(Document) AS Length,
       CONVERT(varchar(max), substring(Document,1806, 60)) AS DocumentSegment
FROM Production.Document WHERE DocumentNode = 0x6B40;
```

DocTitle	Length	DocumentSegment
Lubrication Maintenance	22528	NG: Do not over lubricate parts. If oil gets on the wheel ri

FOR XML Clause

A SELECT query returns results as a table-like rowset. With a FOR XML clause the results are returned in XML format.

FOR XML RAW

The FOR XML RAW mode generates a single <row> element per row in the rowset that is returned by the SELECT statement. Tree structure can be generated by nesting queries.

```
SELECT * FROM HumanResources.Shift ORDER BY ShiftID FOR XML RAW;
```

```
<row ShiftID="1" Name="Day" StartTime="07:00:00" EndTime="15:00:00" ModifiedDate="2002-06-01T00:00:00" />
<row ShiftID="2" Name="Evening" StartTime="15:00:00" EndTime="23:00:00" ModifiedDate="2002-06-01T00:00:00"
/>
<row ShiftID="3" Name="Night" StartTime="23:00:00" EndTime="07:00:00" ModifiedDate="2002-06-01T00:00:00" />
```

FOR XML AUTO

The **FOR XML AUTO mode generates nesting** in the resulting XML by using heuristics based on the way the SELECT statement is specified. Tree structure can be generated by nesting queries. **Note: no table alias use** in the following query. Products are nested within Subcategory(s).

```
SELECT Subcategory.Name AS [SubcategoryName], Product.Name AS [ProductName],
Product.ProductNumber
FROM Production.Product AS Product  INNER JOIN Production.ProductSubcategory AS
Subcategory
 ON Product.ProductSubcategoryID = Subcategory.ProductSubcategoryID
WHERE Subcategory.ProductSubcategoryID = 23 FOR XML AUTO;
```

```
<Subcategory SubcategoryName="Socks">
  <Product ProductName="Mountain Bike Socks, M" ProductNumber="SO-B909-M" />
  <Product ProductName="Mountain Bike Socks, L" ProductNumber="SO-B909-L" />
  <Product ProductName="Racing Socks, M" ProductNumber="SO-R809-M" />
  <Product ProductName="Racing Socks, L" ProductNumber="SO-R809-L" />
</Subcategory>
```

Compare FOR XML RAW and XML FOR AUTO on a single table SELECT query.

```
SELECT TOP(1) ProductID AS ID, Name AS ProductName, ListPrice as Price FROM Production.Product FOR XML RAW;
SELECT TOP(1) ProductID AS ID, Name AS ProductName, ListPrice as Price FROM Production.Product FOR XML AUTO;
```

```
<row ID="1" ProductName="Adjustable Race" Price="0.0000" />
<Production.Product ID="1" ProductName="Adjustable Race" Price="0.0000" />
```

FOR XML AUTO, ELEMENTS

With the ELEMENTS directive, data will be listed on its own line.

```
SELECT Subcategory.Name AS [SubcategoryName], Product.Name AS [ProductName], Product.ProductNumber
FROM Production.Product AS Product  INNER JOIN Production.ProductSubcategory AS Subcategory
        ON Product.ProductSubcategoryID = Subcategory.ProductSubcategoryID
WHERE Subcategory.ProductSubcategoryID = 23 FOR XML AUTO, ELEMENTS;
```

```
/* <Subcategory>
 <SubcategoryName>Socks</SubcategoryName>
 <Product>
  <ProductName>Mountain Bike Socks, M</ProductName>
  <ProductNumber>SO-B909-M</ProductNumber>
 </Product>
 <Product>
  ......
 </Product>
</Subcategory> */
```

FOR XML EXPLICIT

FOR XML EXPLICIT mode allows wide control over the shape of XML document. Attributes & elements can be freely combined in deciding the shape of the XML document. One of the options with XML EXPLICIT is the ELEMENT directive. The UNION ALL operator is used to assemble tag & data information.

```
SELECT          1                   AS Tag,
                NULL                AS Parent,
                ProductNumber       AS [ProductHeader!1!ProdNo],
                NULL                AS [ProductDetail!2!ProductName!ELEMENT],
                NULL                AS [ProductDetail!2!ListPrice!ELEMENT],
                NULL                AS [ProductDetail!2!Color!ELEMENT],
                NULL                AS [ProductDetail!2!Size!ELEMENT]
FROM   AdventureWorks2012.Production.Product P WHERE ProductSubcategoryID is not NULL      UNION ALL
SELECT          2, 1, ProductNumber, Name, ListPrice, Color, Size
FROM   AdventureWorks2012.Production.Product P  WHERE ProductSubcategoryID is not NULL
ORDER BY [ProductHeader!1!ProdNo], Tag   FOR XML EXPLICIT;   -- (590 row(s) affected) - Partial results.
```

```
<ProductHeader ProdNo="BK-M68B-46">
 <ProductDetail>
  <ProductName>Mountain-200 Black, 46</ProductName>
  <ListPrice>2294.9900</ListPrice>
  <Color>Black</Color>
  <Size>46</Size>
 </ProductDetail>
</ProductHeader>
<ProductHeader ProdNo="BK-M68S-38">
 <ProductDetail>
  <ProductName>Mountain-200 Silver, 38</ProductName>
  <ListPrice>2319.9900</ListPrice>
  <Color>Silver</Color>
  <Size>38</Size>
 </ProductDetail>
</ProductHeader>
```

FOR XML PATH

The FOR XML PATH mode together with the nested FOR XML query capability provides the flexibility of the EXPLICIT mode in a simpler manner. The example lists sales orders with detail line and header information.

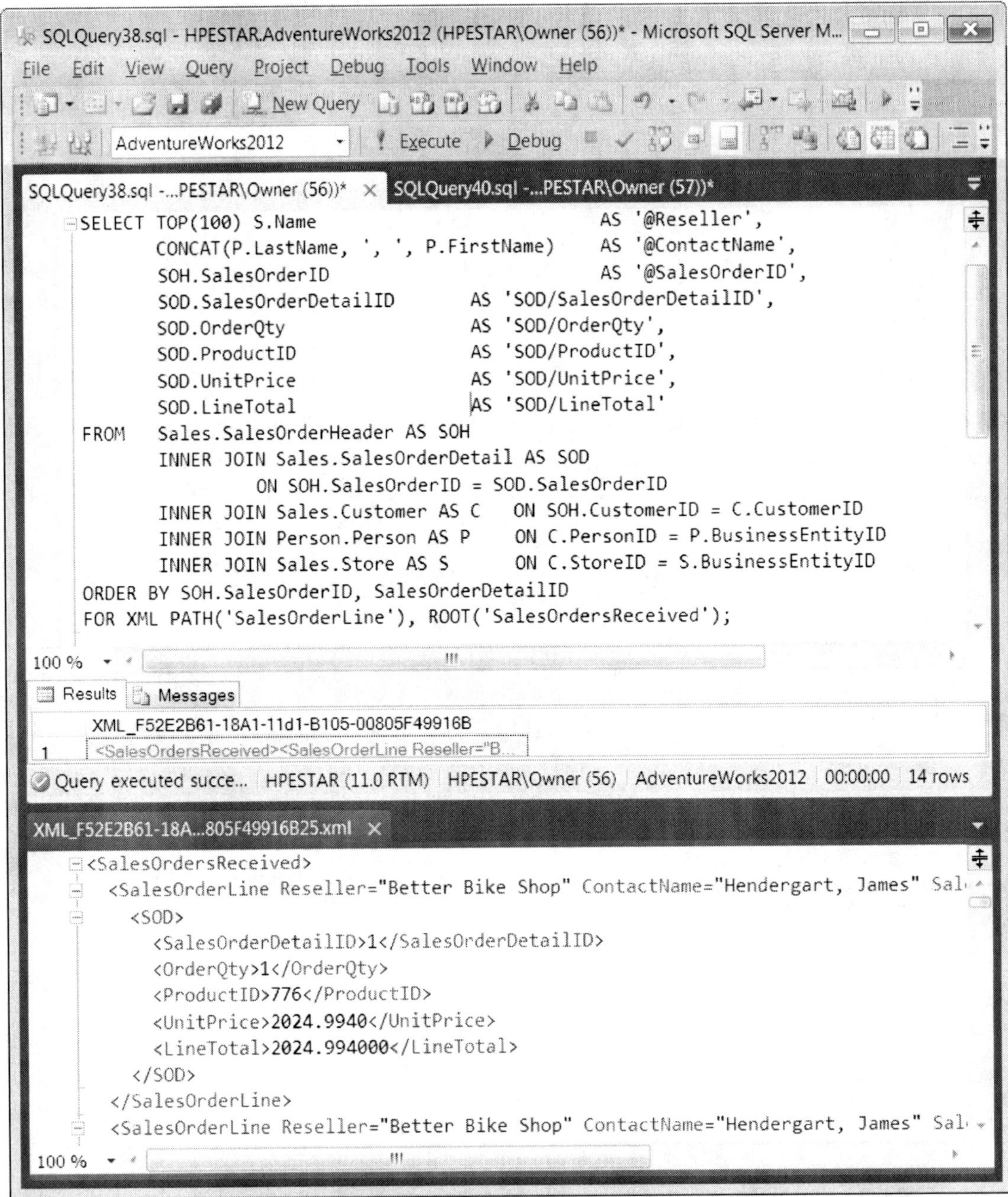

Concatenation Loop With XML PATH

The FOR XML PATH clause makes it possible to do program looping within a query without requiring multiple statements. One way is to implement it as a correlated subquery.

```
Use AdventureWorks2012;
Go
```

```
SELECT   PM.Name AS Model
         ,(SELECT CONCAT(P.Name, ', ')
          FROM Production.Product AS P   WHERE P.ProductModelID = PM.ProductModelID
          ORDER BY P.Name FOR XML PATH('') ) AS ProductLineup
FROM Production.ProductModel AS PM ORDER BY Model;
-- (128 row(s) affected) - Partial result.
```

Model	ProductLineup
All-Purpose Bike Stand	All-Purpose Bike Stand,
Bike Wash	Bike Wash - Dissolver,
Cable Lock	Cable Lock,
Chain	Chain,
Classic Vest	Classic Vest, L, Classic Vest, M, Classic Vest, S,

A popular solution for the trailing comma issue is making it leading comma and taking it out from the first position with the STUFF function. Since the product name may contain commas, we use "|" as string list delimiter.

```
SELECT  PM.Name AS Model
         ,LTRIM(RTRIM(STUFF((SELECT CONCAT('| ', P.Name)
         FROM Production.Product AS P   WHERE P.ProductModelID = PM.ProductModelID
         ORDER BY P.Name FOR XML PATH('') ), 1, 1, ''))) AS ProductLineup
FROM Production.ProductModel AS PM ORDER BY Model; -- (128 row(s) affected) - Partial result.
```

Model	ProductLineup
ML Mountain Frame	ML Mountain Frame - Black, 40| ML Mountain Frame - Black, 44| ML Mountain Frame - Black, 48

BOL Article: **CREATE XML SCHEMA COLLECTION** http://msdn.microsoft.com/en-us/library/ms176009.aspx
BOL Article: **Examples of Bulk Import and Export of XML Documents** http://msdn.microsoft.com/en-us/library/ms191184.aspx

Top Salaried Employees By Department Using RANK()

First we create a view with columns we need, so we can concentrate on the actual task: ranking employees by salary in each department with the RANK() function. Note: ROW_NUMBER() would omit ties, we need RANK(). Interestingly we have to use the ROW_NUMBER() window function & nested CTE-s to get the most recent salary from the history table.

```
USE AdventureWorks2012;
GO
CREATE VIEW vEmployeeDepartment   AS  WITH cteEPHAll AS
        (SELECT BusinessEntityID AS EmployeeID, Rate as Salary,
        ROW_NUMBER() OVER (PARTITION BY BusinessEntityID ORDER BY RateChangeDate DESC) AS RN
        FROM HumanResources.EmployeePayHistory )
, cteEPH AS (SELECT EmployeeID, Salary FROM cteEPHAll WHERE RN = 1)
SELECT  E.BusinessEntityID AS EmployeeID,CONCAT(LastName, ', ', FirstName) as FullName,
        D.Name AS Department, EPH.Salary
FROM HumanResources.Employee E  INNER JOIN Person.Person P  ON E.BusinessEntityID = P.BusinessEntityID
INNER JOIN HumanResources.Department D
INNER JOIN HumanResources.EmployeeDepartmentHistory EDH     ON EDH.DepartmentID = D.DepartmentID
                                                            ON EDH.BusinessEntityID = E.BusinessEntityID
INNER JOIN cteEPH EPH ON EPH.EmployeeID = E.BusinessEntityID WHERE EDH.EndDate IS NULL;
GO  -- Command(s) completed successfully.
```

```
SELECT TOP (4) * FROM vEmployeeDepartment ORDER BY FullName;
```

EmployeeID	FullName	Department	Salary
285	Abbas, Syed	Sales	48.101
38	Abercrombie, Kim	Production	12.45
211	Abolrous, Hazem	Quality Assurance	28.8462
121	Ackerman, Pilar	Shipping and Receiving	19.2308

```
SELECT Department, FullName, Salary FROM  (SELECT Department, FullName, Salary,
        RANK() OVER (PARTITION BY Department ORDER BY Salary DESC) AS Rnk
FROM vEmployeeDepartment ) x
WHERE Rnk=1 ORDER BY Department, Fullname;  -- (16 row(s) affected) - Partial results.
```

Department	FullName	Salary
Document Control	Arifin, Zainal	17.7885
Engineering	Duffy, Terri	63.4615
Executive	Sánchez, Ken	125.50

There are no ties. However if we use Rnk=2 for second highest pay, we will see ties.

Department	FullName	Salary
Document Control	Kharatishvili, Tengiz	16.8269
Document Control	Norred, Chris	16.8269

Interesting T-SQL Scripts

Challenging String Manipulations

```
-- Displaying hidden characters (whitespace) in a string; TAB character appears as space;
DECLARE @text varchar(64) = 'New'+char(9)+'York'+char(9)+'City'+char(9);
SELECT @text, CONVERT(varbinary(64), @text);
-- New York City 0x4E65770959 6F726B0943697479 09
```

```
-- Working with SUBSTRING & ASCII functions
SELECT      TOP (5)
            ProductNumber,
            MiddleOfString     =     SUBSTRING(ProductNumber,4,5),
            SecondChar         =     SUBSTRING(ProductNumber,2,1),
            ASCIIValue         =     ASCII(SUBSTRING(ProductNumber,2,1))
FROM AdventureWorks2012.Production.Product  ORDER BY NEWID();
```

ProductNumber	MiddleOfString	SecondChar	ASCIIValue
FR-R72R-44	R72R-	R	82
BK-R89B-48	R89B-	K	75
HN-4402	4402	N	78
LJ-1220	1220	J	74
BA-8327	8327	A	65

```
-- Compare empty string and NULL string
DECLARE @NullString varchar(32) = NULL, @EmptyString varchar(32)= '';
```

```
SELECT LEN(@EmptyString); SELECT LEN(@NullString);   -- 0  NULL
```

```
SELECT DATALENGTH(@EmptyString); SELECT DATALENGTH(@NullString);  -- 0  NULL
```

```
-- Testing for empty string and null string
SELECT 'Miami' WHERE @EmptyString = '';  SELECT 'Miami' WHERE @NullString is null;
-- Miami Miami
```

```
SELECT 'Miami' WHERE LEN(@EmptyString)=0;  SELECT 'Miami' WHERE LEN(@NullString) = 0;
-- Miami  (0 row(s) affected)
```

```
SELECT @EmptyString + @NullString+'Vegas';                    -- NULL
```

```
SELECT CONCAT(@EmptyString,@NullString, 'Vegas');             -- Vegas
```

String & Powershell Scripts

```
-- Parsing for filename in path-file string
-- Find last \ (first \ in reverse), remove prefix; Find first .(dot), remove suffix.
DECLARE @path varchar(128) = 'F:\data\excel\SAMPLEFILENAME10.xls.txt';

SELECT @path = REVERSE(COALESCE(LEFT(REVERSE(@path),
NULLIF(CHARINDEX('\',REVERSE(@path),1)-1,-1)),REVERSE(@path)));

SELECT COALESCE(LEFT(@path, NULLIF(CHARINDEX('.',@path,1)-1,-1)),@path);
-- SAMPLEFILENAME10

-- PowerShell compare files in a folder (1 more file in one of the folders)
EXEC xp_cmdshell 'sqlps Compare-Object (Get-Childitem f:\temp\mass) (Get-ChildItem
f:\temp\mass1)'
/* output
InputObject                 SideIndicator
-----------                 -------------
title - Copy.xls            =>            */
```

Combining RANK() with GROUP BY Aggregates

The RANK() function can be used on GROUP BY aggregate functions. Ranking is one on average sales order amounts (Subtotal).

```
SELECT  TerritoryID, SalesPersonID, Count(*)          AS Sales,
        FORMAT(SUM(Subtotal), 'c0', 'en-US')          AS SalesAmount,
        FORMAT(AVG(Subtotal), 'c0', 'en-US')          AS AvgSalesAmount,
        RANK() OVER( ORDER BY AVG(Subtotal) DESC)     AS Rank
FROM AdventureWorks2012.Sales.SalesOrderHeader
GROUP BY TerritoryID, SalesPersonID ORDER BY Rank;
GO -- (45 row(s) affected) - Partial results.
```

TerritoryID	SalesPersonID	Sales	SalesAmount	AvgSalesAmount	Rank
3	276	44	$1,843,442	$41,896	1
3	274	1	$35,332	$35,332	2
1	280	95	$3,325,103	$35,001	3
4	274	14	$413,889	$29,564	4
1	276	72	$2,084,593	$28,953	5
4	277	107	$2,948,287	$27,554	6
3	281	19	$517,140	$27,218	7

Date & Datetime Manipulations

```
-- Count business days for a date range
CREATE FUNCTION ufnWeekDaysCount (  @DateStart DATETIME,  @DateEnd   DATETIME)
RETURNS INT AS   BEGIN
   IF ( @DateStart IS NULL OR @DateEnd IS NULL )
    RETURN ( 0 )
   DECLARE @i INT = 0;
   WHILE ( @DateStart <= @DateEnd )   BEGIN
      SET @i = @i + CASE
               WHEN datename(dw, @DateStart) IN ( 'Saturday', 'Sunday' )
               THEN 0    ELSE 1     END
      SET @DateStart = @DateStart + 1
    END -- while
   RETURN ( @i )
 END -- function
GO
```

```
SELECT dbo.ufnWeekDaysCount('2016-01-01', '2016-12-31');      -- 261
```

```
-- YEAR(), MONTH(), DATENAME() functions in aggregate query
SELECT  YEAR              = YEAR(OrderDate),
        MONTH             = MONTH(OrderDate),
        MMM               = UPPER(left(DATENAME(MONTH,OrderDate),3)),
         Sales            = FORMAT(sum(TotalDue),'c0','en-US'),
        OrderCount        = COUNT(* )
FROM    AdventureWorks2012.Sales.SalesOrderHeader
GROUP BY        YEAR(OrderDate),  MONTH(OrderDate),  DATENAME(MONTH,OrderDate)
ORDER BY        YEAR, MONTH;
GO -- (37 row(s) affected) - Partial results.
```

YEAR	MONTH	MMM	Sales	OrderCount
2008	5	MAY	$5,813,557	2386
2008	6	JUN	$6,004,156	2374

```
-- Month start/end is easy with EOMONTH() - Find month ending weekday
SELECT  DATEADD(DD,1,EOMONTH(GETDATE(),-2) )        AS FirstDayOfPreviousMonth,
        EOMONTH(GETDATE(),-1)                       AS LastDayOfPreviousMonth
-- 2016-11-01    2016-11-30
```

```
SELECT DATENAME(DW, EOMONTH(CURRENT_TIMESTAMP)) -- Monday
```

Find Sprocs, Triggers, Functions & Views Where Column is Used

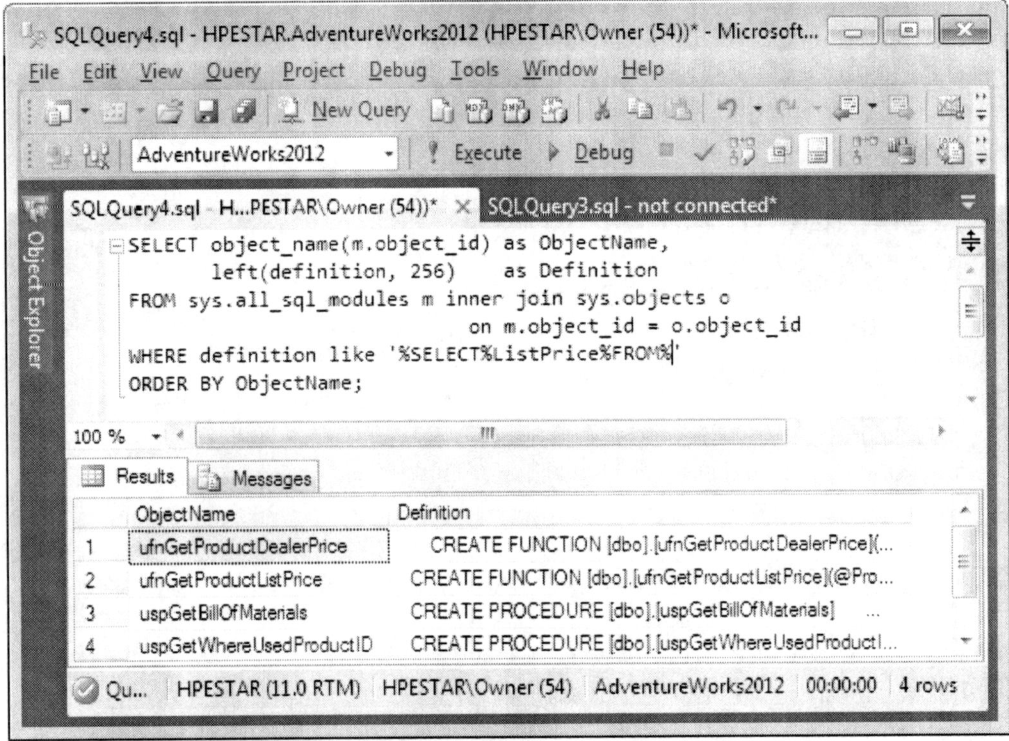

```
SELECT object_name(m.object_id) as ObjectName,
       left(definition, 256)    as Definition
FROM sys.all_sql_modules m inner join sys.objects o
                          on m.object_id = o.object_id
WHERE definition like '%SELECT%ListPrice%FROM%'
ORDER BY ObjectName;
```

	ObjectName	Definition
1	ufnGetProductDealerPrice	CREATE FUNCTION [dbo].[ufnGetProductDealerPrice](...
2	ufnGetProductListPrice	CREATE FUNCTION [dbo].[ufnGetProductListPrice](@Pro...
3	uspGetBillOfMaterials	CREATE PROCEDURE [dbo].[uspGetBillOfMaterials] ...
4	uspGetWhereUsedProductID	CREATE PROCEDURE [dbo].[uspGetWhereUsedProductI...

Designing the Query in GUI Query Designer

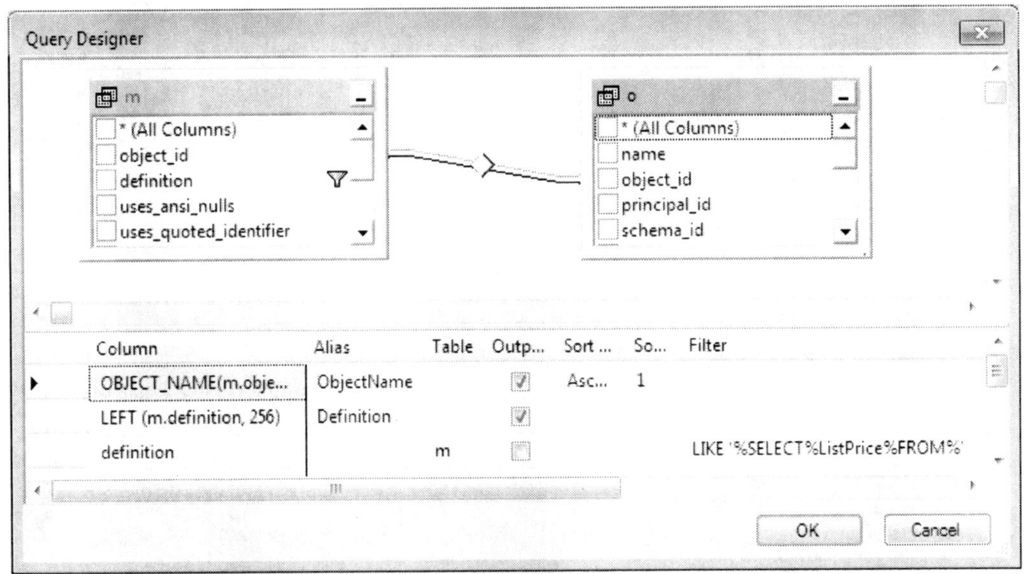

Transforming Dynamic SQL Result Set into a View

A view is "clean", a dynamic SQL script can be pretty "messy". By wrapping dynamic SQL into a view, we get the best of both worlds: the power of dynamic SQL and the table-like access to a view.

```
USE AdventureWorks2012;
GO
CREATE PROC sprocListDepartment AS   BEGIN
DECLARE @SQL nvarchar(max) =
 'SELECT DepartmentID, Name, GroupName FROM HumanResources.Department ORDER BY
DepartmentID DESC';
EXEC sp_executeSQL @SQL;
END
GO
```

```
CREATE VIEW vDepartment AS
SELECT * FROM OPENQUERY( HPESTAR, 'exec AdventureWorks2012.dbo.sprocListDepartment
WITH RESULT SETS  ((ID int, Department varchar(50), GroupName varchar(50)))');
GO
```

```
SELECT * FROM vDepartment;    -- (16 row(s) affected)
```

Accessing a View from Excel

A view can be accessed from Excel by logging in to SQL Server, choosing a database and picking the view.

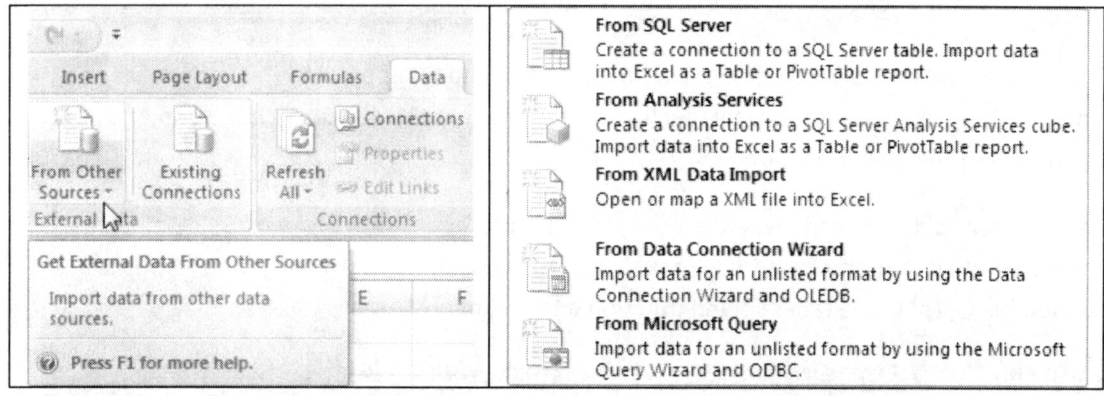

Simple PIVOT to Transpose Rows into Columns

The following PIVOT transposes the Gender column into [M] & [F] columns using the COUNT() aggregate function for cell values in the pivot table.

```
USE AdventureWorks2012;

WITH CTE (Gender, City, State, Country)
AS (SELECT   E.Gender, A.City, SP.StateProvinceCode, SP.CountryRegionCode
FROM  Person.BusinessEntityAddress AS PA
        INNER JOIN  Person.Address AS A ON PA.AddressID = A.AddressID
        INNER JOIN  HumanResources.Employee AS E
        INNER JOIN  Person.Person AS P ON E.BusinessEntityID = P.BusinessEntityID
                                        ON PA.BusinessEntityID = P.BusinessEntityID
        INNER JOIN Person.StateProvince AS SP  ON A.StateProvinceID = SP.StateProvinceID)

SELECT * FROM CTE
        PIVOT ( COUNT(Gender)  FOR Gender IN ([M], [F])) AS PivotTable
ORDER BY [M] DESC;  -- (32 row(s) affected) - Partial results.
```

City	State	Country	M	F
Seattle	WA	US	32	12
Bellevue	WA	US	25	11
Edmonds	WA	US	20	5
Redmond	WA	US	15	6
Renton	WA	US	12	5
Monroe	WA	US	12	2
Issaquah	WA	US	12	3
Everett	WA	US	11	7
Sammamish	WA	US	10	7
Bothell	WA	US	9	4

On the **client-side**, this PIVOT query can be imbedded in a C# application program for example. It can also be stored (save) in a .sql file. It can just remain in SSMS query editor and disappear when we exit the editor or SSMS.

On the **server-side**, we can make the query into 3 database objects: view, table-valued function (TVF) or stored procedure. For view & TVF, ORDER BY clause has to be removed. Here is the headblock for inline table-valued function definition.

```
CREATE FUNCTION ufnPivotGender() RETURNS TABLE AS RETURN ( WITH CTE (Gender, City, State, Country) .....);
```

UPDATE varchar(max) with .WRITE

The .WRITE feature of UPDATE has been introduced with SQL Server 2005 for varchar(max).

```
USE tempdb;
CREATE TABLE Document ( DocumentID INT IDENTITY(1,1) PRIMARY KEY,
        Name varchar(128) NOT NULL UNIQUE,
        Content varchar(max),  CreatedDate datetime default (CURRENT_TIMESTAMP));
GO
```

```
INSERT Document (Name, Content) VALUES ('Installation instruction', SPACE(0));
PRINT ''; PRINT CONCAT ('DocumentID: ',SCOPE_IDENTITY());   -- DocumentID: 1
GO
```

```
UPDATE dbo.Document SET Content .WRITE((SELECT DocumentSummary
    FROM AdventureWorks2012.Production.Document WHERE DocumentNode = 0x5B40), 0, 0)
WHERE DocumentID = 1;
GO
```

```
SELECT DocumentID, Name, LEFT(Content, 40) AS ContentPrefix, CreatedDate FROM Document;
```

DocumentID	Name	ContentPrefix	CreatedDate
1	Installation instruction	It is important that you maintain your b	2012-12-25 19:48:17.457

Querying the Database from a Client C# Program

The general program logic for SQL Server database access is very similar for other languages such as C++, VB or Java. First connection has to be established to SQL Server and the database, then a SQL query or stored procedure execution command is sent to the server, and finally the server returns a result set which has to be processed in a C# loop.

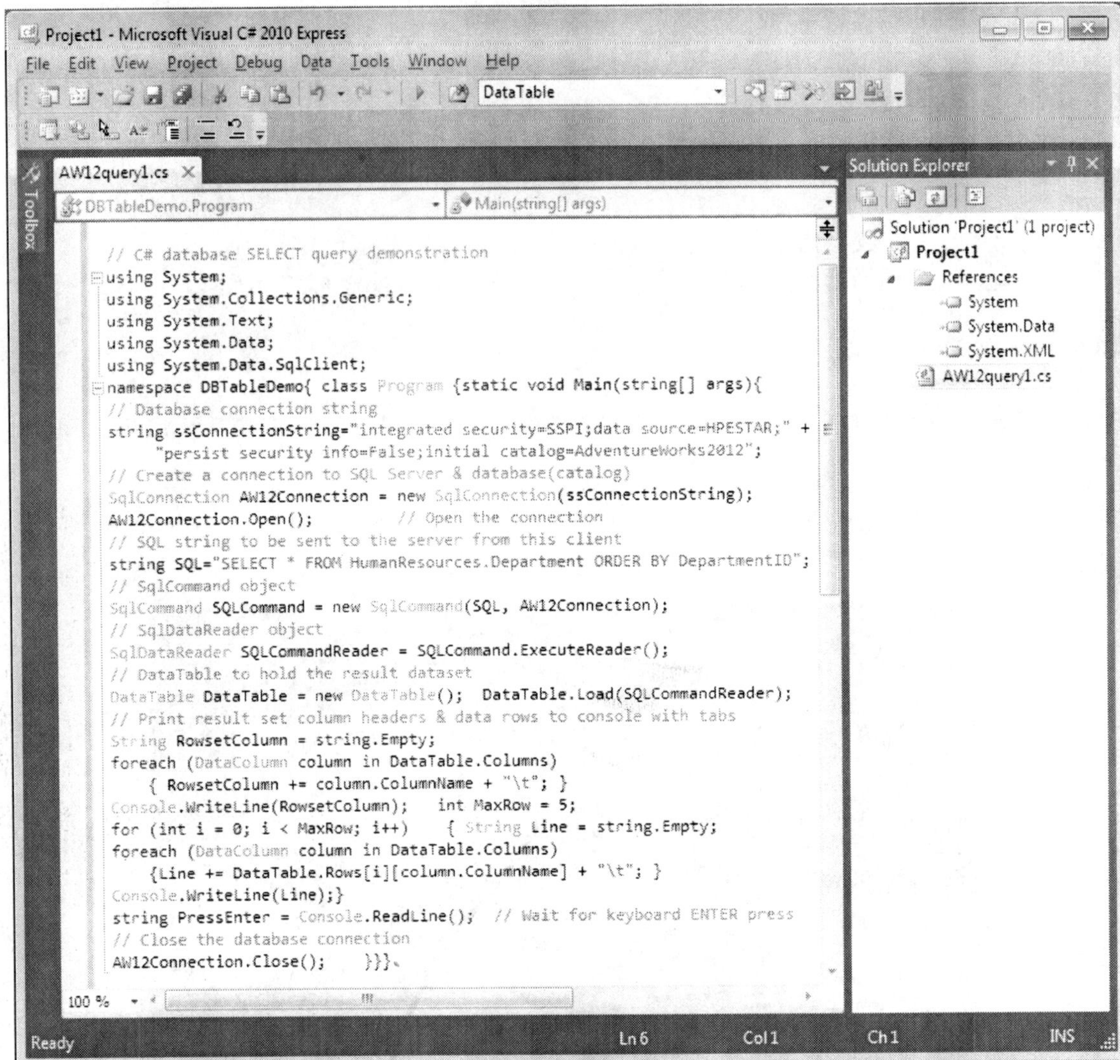

C# Code Listing

```
// C# database SELECT query demonstration
using System;
using System.Collections.Generic;
```

```
using System.Text;
using System.Data;
using System.Data.SqlClient;
namespace DBTableDemo{ class Program {static void Main(string[] args){
// Database connection string
string ssConnectionString="integrated security=SSPI;data source=HPESTAR;" +
    "persist security info=False;initial catalog=AdventureWorks2012";
// Create a connection to SQL Server & database(catalog)
SqlConnection AW12Connection = new SqlConnection(ssConnectionString);
AW12Connection.Open();        // Open the connection
// SQL string to be sent to the server from this client
string SQL="SELECT * FROM HumanResources.Department ORDER BY DepartmentID";
// SqlCommand object
SqlCommand SQLCommand = new SqlCommand(SQL, AW12Connection);
// SqlDataReader object
SqlDataReader SQLCommandReader = SQLCommand.ExecuteReader();
// DataTable to hold the result dataset
DataTable DataTable = new DataTable();  DataTable.Load(SQLCommandReader);
// Print result set column headers & data rows to console with tabs
String RowsetColumn = string.Empty;
foreach (DataColumn column in DataTable.Columns)
   { RowsetColumn += column.ColumnName + "\t"; }
Console.WriteLine(RowsetColumn);   int MaxRow = 5;
for (int i = 0; i < MaxRow; i++)    { String Line = string.Empty;
foreach (DataColumn column in DataTable.Columns)
   {Line += DataTable.Rows[i][column.ColumnName] + "\t"; }
Console.WriteLine(Line);}
string PressEnter = Console.ReadLine();  // Wait for keyboard ENTER press
// Close the database connection
AW12Connection.Close();    }}}
```

Console Image with Data Display from HumanResources.Department

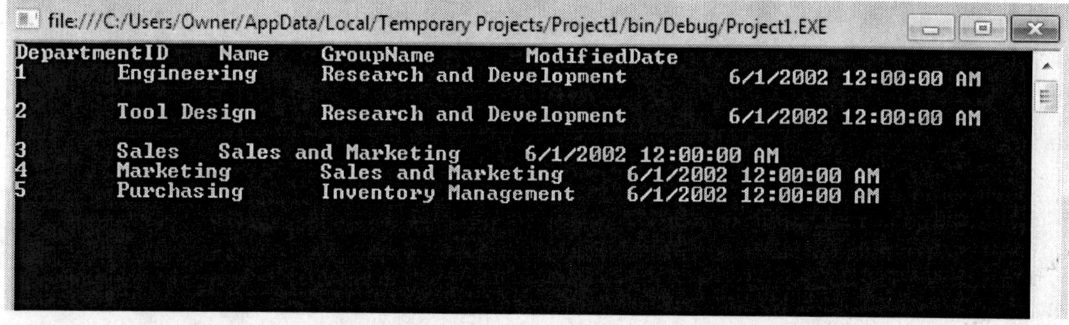

How to Prepare for the Exam & Job Interview

Exam 70-461: Querying Microsoft SQL Server 2012

Best Preparation: Practice, Practice & Practice

On your own copy of SQL Server practice all T-SQL scripts in the book. SQL Server 2012 Express Edition is available free. A better choice is **SQL Server 2012 Developer Edition** (same as Enterprise Edition, not for production) is available for around $50.

Carnegie Hall (music theatre) Joke: A pedestrian on 57St., NYC, stopped a man and inquired, "Could you tell me how to get to Carnegie Hall?" "Yes," said the man. "**Practice!**"

Eliminate Invalid Syntax Choices

As quickly as possible you want to narrow down the possible choices on a multi-choice question. The easiest way is to identify bad syntax. This again requires practice! Different kind of practice: you have to experiment with invalid syntax variations. Example question:

Which statement will create a new calculated column with alias "Alpha" in a SELECT list?
A. SUM (col1, col2) AS Alpha
B. col1+col2 AS Alpha
C. Alpha = SUM(col1, col2)
D. col1+col2

Answers A & C can be eliminated due to invalid syntax. D is valid, but missing column alias.

```
SELECT SUM(StandardCost, ListPrice ) AS Alpha FROM AdventureWorks2012.Production.Product;
/* Msg 174, Level 15, State 1, Line 1 The SUM function requires 1 argument(s). */
```

Eliminate Unrelated Functionality Choices

This is another essential exam method to success: you don't want to waste time considering unrelated answers. As an example FORMAT & IDENTITY RESET are unrelated to the question.

How would you rollback a transaction?
A. IDENTITY RESET B. FORMAT C. ROLLBACK TRANSACTION D. COMMIT TRANSACTION

Exam Related Questions & Answers

Is this book a fast way to pass the exam?

Definitely not. It is the slow, learning way of passing the exam, passing the interview and become a successful database professional on the job.

How long does it take to master the book?

That depends on you. At 10 pages a day, it will take 77 days. You need to practice each query, script, stored procedure, view, function, trigger and so on your own copy of SQL Server to gain hands-on experience. "SQL must become part of your DNA". You have to vary the scripts, "play with them", try out syntax variations, even try invalid syntax.

What topics are on the exam?

The following web references deal with the exam topics.

Exam 70-461: Querying Microsoft SQL Server 2012 http://www.microsoft.com/learning/en/us/exam.aspx?id=70-461
70-461 Exam Guide Querying Microsoft SQL Server 2012 http://www.katieandemil.com/exam-70-461-querying-microsoft-sql-server-2012-pdf-vce-ebook-free
SQL 70-461 - Query SQL Server 2012 Study guide http://advancedmaster.blogspot.com/2012/04/sql-70-461-query-sql-server-2012-study.html

How about practice tests?

At the time of the writing of this book, no practice test information is listed at the Microsoft exam website. However, practice test information is listed for the SS 2008 developer exam.

Exam 70-433: TS: Microsoft SQL Server 2008, Database Development http://www.microsoft.com/learning/en/us/exam.aspx?id=70-433

What kind of questions?

According to web search information about past developer tests, around 50 questions may be:

- Multiple choices
- Drag & drop to assemble valid script such as to create a stored procedure or view from valid & invalid parts
- Typing a simple query in whole such as a GROUP BY query

Is Learning This Book Guarantee for Passing?

Nobody can give you such a guarantee except yourself by diligent preparation. Learning this book will give you a fair chance of passing the exam, passing job interview and starting a career as a database administrator (DBA), database designer or database developer. You have to practice each T-SQL script, try out variations, and even try out invalid syntax.

Do I have to Practice the Small Scripts at the Bottom of Pages?

It does not matter if the T-SQL query is on the top or bottom of the page, it can be on the exam. Even if it's not on the exam, it may help you answer related question correctly.

Can I Just Half Learn the Book & Pass the Exam?

The likelihood of passing the exam is very low without full preparation.

Should I Learn the Reference Articles as well?

Yes. However, some of the references cover complex database subjects, you should concentrate on the easy parts and practice the simple queries (if any) in the reference article.

What If I Don't Pass?

The passing score may be 700 out of 1000. As soon as you leave the exam area, write down all the subject areas where you were weak and where you were strong. Restudy the weak areas and take the test within a few weeks again.

Exam policies and FAQ
http://www.microsoft.com/learning/en/us/certification-exam-policies.aspx

Can I Chew Gum During the Exam?

You have to check with the testing center before the exam about gum, coffee and bottled water. You may not be allowed, for example, to reach into your pocket for gum, but you may carry it in on a napkin. Most exam places have observation cameras.

How long is the exam?

The exam may be in parts like 4 sections 45 minutes each. Not likely that you can carry time over from one section to another. At the very beginning of the exam, instructions are given on the screen, pay lots of attention to them and pay attention to time usage during the exam.

Should I Guess the Answer?

Tips for Taking Microsoft Exams
http://www.pearsonitcertification.com/articles/article.aspx?p=1713588

What is the best way to learn JOINs?

JOINs are an essential knowledge for a database developer. SSMS has the wonderful GUI Query Designer tool for learning JOINs. Why the graphical Query Designer may not support complex queries, with CTE-s for example, it does a wonderful job in visual representation of INNER JOINs, LEFT JOINs and RIGHT JOINs. The query in the SQL pane builds automatically as you are designing the JOINs in the diagram pane. Upon exit, the SQL query is transferred into SSMS Query Editor window.

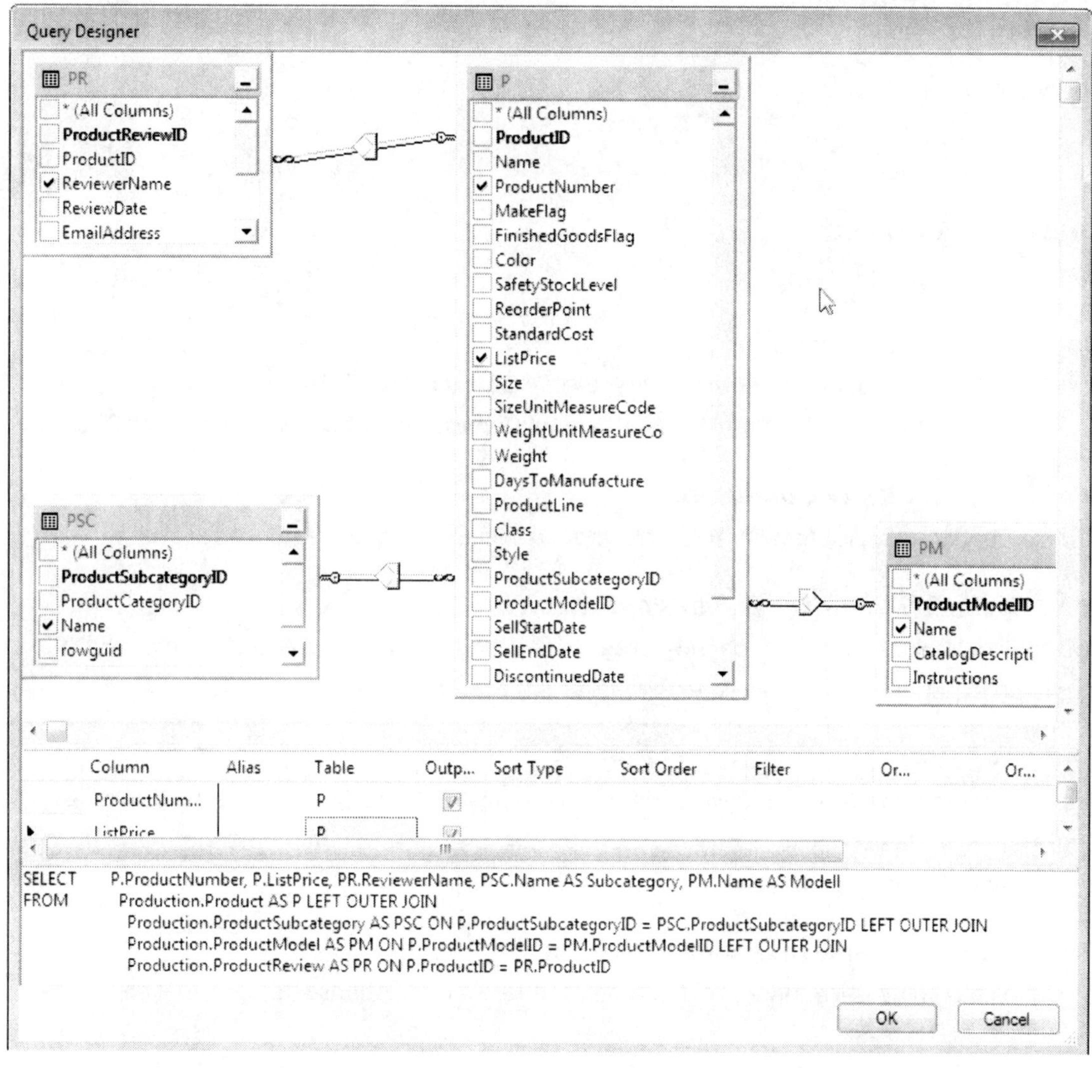

Job Interview

Database Developer Interview

Formal written test may be given. After passing 70-461, interview test should be easy for a few months.

Telephone Interview

You want to take it within 2 months of passing 40-461, else prepare thoroughly before the interview.

Question & Answers

Do I Have to Say Queries Verbally?

Yes. Practice simple query types by reading the T-SQL loud: SELECT Department, EmpCount=COUNT(*) FROM Employee GROUP BY Department ORDER BY EmpCount DESC;

What if I Don't Know Something?

Just say that you are not familiar with that area. If there is a close area, talk about that.

What if the Job Requires 2 Years of Experience?

You can just make a claim that passing exam 40-461 and learning this book inside out with hands-on experience is equivalent to 2 years of job experience.

Do I Have to Know Database Design?

Yes. As a competent database developer you are expected to design simple tables with KEY (PRIMARY KEY, UNIQUE KEY) constraints, CHECK constraints & default constraints. You have to also be able to connect tables with FOREIGN KEY constraints.

How about Database Interview Questions?

This book has some. Also there are a number of interview questions sites on the web. Here is one.

SQL Server database developer interview questions and answers
http://www.techrepublic.com/blog/programming-and-development/sql-server-database-developer-interview-questions-and-answers/5745

This page is intentionally left blank.

APPENDIX A: Job Interview Questions

Selected Database Design Questions

D1. What is your approach to database design?
D2. Some of our legacy databases are far from 3NF. Can you work in such an environment?
D3. Can UNIQUE KEY be used instead of PRIMARY KEY?
D4. Can a FOREIGN KEY be NULL?
D5. Can a PRIMARY KEY be NULL?
D6. Can a PRIMARY KEY be based on non-clustered unique index?
D7. Do you implement OrderQty > 0 condition as a CHECK constraint or in the application software?
D8. What is a heap?
D9. Can a table have 2 IDENTITY columns, 2 FOREIGN KEYs, 2 PRIMARY KEYs and 2 clustered indexes?
D10. Should each table have a NATURAL KEY or is INT IDENTITY PK sufficient?
D11. How can you prevent entry of "U.S", "USA", etc. instead of "United States" into Country column?
D12. How would you implement ManagerID in an Employee table with EmployeeID as PRIMARY KEY?
D13. How would you implement the relationship between OrderMaster and OrderDetail tables?
D14. Product table has the Color column. Would you create a Color table & change column to ColorID FK?
D15. Can you insert directly into an IDENTITY column?
D16. Which one is better? Composite PRIMARY KEY on NATURAL KEY, or INT IDENTITY PRIMARY KEY & UNIQUE KEY on NATURAL KEY?
D17. What is the lifetime of a regular table created in tempdb?
D18. How many different ways can you connect tables in a database?
D19. How would you connect the Vehicle and Owner tables?
D20. Can you have the same table names in different schemas?
D21. How do you implement: only some values in PRIMARY KEY column can have FK reference?

Selected Database Programming Questions

P1. Write a query to list all departments with employee count based on the Department column of Employee table.
P2. Same as above but the Employee table has the DepartmentID column.
P3. Write an INSERT statement for a new "Social Technology" department with GroupName "Sales & Marketing".
P4. Same query es in P2, but the new department should be included even though no employees yet.
P5. Write a query to generate 1000 sequential numbers without a table.
P6. Write a query with SARGable predicate to list all orders from OrderMaster received on 2016-10-23. OrderDate is datetime.
P7. Write a query to add a header record DEPARTMENTNAME to the departments listing from the Department table. If there are 20 departments, the result set should have 21 records.
P8. Make the previous query a derived table in an outer SELECT * query
P9. Write an ORDER BY clause for the previous query with CASE expression to sort DEPARTMENTNAME as first record and alphabetically descending from there on.
P10. Same as above with the IIF conditional.
P11. The table-valued dbo.ufnSplitCSV splits a comma delimited string (input parameter). The Product table has some ProductName-s with comma(s). Write a CROSS APPLY query to return ProductName-s with comma and each split string value from the UDF as separate line. ProductName should repeat for each split part.

ProductName	SplitPart
Full-Finger Gloves, L	Full-Finger Gloves
Full-Finger Gloves, L	L

P12. You need the inserted lines count 10 lines down following the INSERT statement. What should be the statement immediately following the INSERT statement?
P13. What is the result of the second query? What is it called?
SELECT COUNT_BIG(*) FROM Sales.SalesOrderDetail; -- 121317
SELECT COUNT_BIG(*) FROM Sales.SalesOrderDetail x, Sales.SalesOrderDetail y;
P14. Declare & Assign the string variable @Text varchar(32) the literal '2016/10/23 10:20:12' without the "/" and ":".
P15. You want to add a parameter to a frequently used view. What is the workaround?
P16. When converting up to 40 characters string, can you use varchar instead of varchar(40)?
P17. Can you roll back IDENTITY seeds and table variables with ROLLBACK TRANSACTION?
P18. How do you decide where to place the clustered index?
P19. What is the simplest solution for the collation error: "Cannot resolve collation conflict..."?
P20. Which system table can be used for integer sequence up to 2^12 values?
P21. You get a complex query assignment on an unfamiliar database. What do you do?

APPENDIX B: Job Interview Answers

Selected Database Design Answers

D1. I prefer 3NF design due to high database developer productivity and low maintenance cost.
D2. I did have such projects in the past. I can handle them. Hopefully, introduce some improvements.
D3. Partially yes since UNIQUE KEYs can be FK referenced, fully no. Every table should a PRIMARY KEY.
D4. Yes.
D5. No.
D6. Yes. The default is clustered unique index. Only unique index is required.
D7. CHECK constraint. A server-side object solution is more reliable than code in application software.
D8. A table without clustered index. Database engine generally works better if a table has clustered index.
D9. No, yes, no, no.
D10. A table should be designed with NATURAL KEY(s). INT IDENTITY PK is not a replacement for NK.
D11. Lookup table with UDF CHECK Constraint. UDF checks the Lookup table for valid entries.
D12. ManagerID as a FOREIGN KEY referencing the PRIMARY KEY of the same table; self-referencing.
D13. OrderID PRIMARY KEY of OrderMaster. OrderID & LineItemID composition PK of OrderDetail. OrderID of OrderDetail FK to OrderID of OderMaster.
D14. Yes. It makes sense for color to be in its own table.
D15. No. Only if you SET IDENTITY_INSERT tablename ON.
D16. Meaningless INT IDENTITY PRIMARY KEY with UNIQUE KEY ON NATURAL KEY is better.
D17. Until SQL Server restarted. tempdb starts empty as copy of model database.
D18. There is only one way: FOREIGN KEY constraint.
D19. With the OwnerVehicleXref junction table reflecting many-to-many relationship.
D20. Yes. A table is identified by SchemaName.TableName . dbo is the default schema.
D21. Add a flag column to the PK table. Create a UDF CHECK constraint for the FK column.

Selected Database Programming Answers

P1. SELECT Department, Employees=COUNT(*) FROM Employee GROUP BY Department ORDER BY Department;
P2. SELECT d.Department, Employees = COUNT(EmployeeID) FROM Employee e INNER JOIN Department d ON e.DepartmentID = d.DepartmentID GROUP BY d.Department ORDER BY Department;
P3. INSERT Department (Name, GroupName) VALUES ('Social Technology', 'Sales & Marketing');
P4. SELECT d.Department, Employees = COUNT(EmployeeID) FROM Employee e RIGHT JOIN Department d ON e.DepartmentID = d.DepartmentID GROUP BY d.Department ORDER BY Department;
P5. ;WITH Seq AS (SELECT SeqNo = 1 UNION ALL SELECT SeqNo+1 FROM Seq WHERE SeqNo < 100) SELECT * FROM Seq;
P6. SELECT * FROM OrderMaster WHERE OrderDate >='20161023' AND OrderDate < DATEADD(DD,1,'20161023');
P7. SELECT AllDepartments = 'DEPARTMENTNAME' UNION SELECT Department FROM Department;
P8. SELECT * FROM (SELECT AllDepartments = 'DEPARTMENTNAME' UNION SELECT Name FROM HumanResources.Department) x
P9. ORDER BY CASE WHEN AllDepartments = 'DEPARTMENTNAME' THEN 1 ELSE 2 END, AllDepartments DESC;
P10. ORDER BY IIF(AllDepartments = 'DEPARTMENTNAME', 1 , 2), AllDepartments DESC;
P11. SELECT ProductName, S.SplitPart FROM Product P CROSS APPLY dbo.ufnSplitCSV (Name) S WHERE ProductName like '%,%';
P12. DECLARE @InsertedCount INT = @@ROWCOUNT;
P13. 121317*121317; Cartesian product.
P14. DECLARE @Text varchar(32) = REPLACE(REPLACE ('2016/10/23 10:20:12', '/', SPACE(0)), ':', SPACE(0));
P15. Table-valued INLINE user-defined function.
P16. varchar(40). It is a good idea to specify the length always. The default is 30.
P17. No. ROLLBACK has no effect on IDENTITY seeds or table variables. If an INSERT advanced the IDENTITY seed by 5 during the rollbacked transaction, it will stay that way after the ROLLBACK. It means a gap in the IDENTITY sequence.
P18. Business critical queries are the determining factor in placing the clustered index. Clustered index speeds up range queries.
P19. Place "COLLATE DATABASE_DEFAULT" on the right side of the expression.
P20. spt_values table. `SELECT N = number FROM master.dbo.spt_values WHERE type='P' ORDER BY N;`
P21. You study the database diagram and start building the query with SSMS Graphical Query Designer.

INDEX of Pass SQL Exam 70-461 & Job Interview: Programming SQL Server 2012

Index of the Most Important Topics

D

E

F

G

O

P

S

T

U

V

W

X

Y

CPSIA information can be obtained at www.ICGtesting.com
Printed in the USA
BVOW01s0157151214

379435BV00007B/74/P